GOWER AND DAVIES'

PRINCIPLES OF

MODERN COMPANY LAW

AUSTRALIA

Law Book Co.
Sydney

CANADA and USA

Carswell
Toronto

HONG KONG

Sweet & Maxwell Asia

NEW ZEALAND

Brookers
Wellington

SINGAPORE AND MALAYSIA

Sweet & Maxwell Asia
Singapore and Kuala Lumpur

GOWER AND DAVIES'
PRINCIPLES OF
MODERN COMPANY LAW

EIGHTH EDITION

By

PAUL L. DAVIES, Q.C. (hon), F.B.A.

Cassel Professor of
Commercial Law
London School of Economics
and Political Science
Honorary Bencher of Gray's Inn

with contributions from

SARAH WORTHINGTON
Barrister
Professor of Law at the
London School of Economics and
Political Science

and

EVA MICHELER
Senior Lecturer in Law
London School of Economics and
Political Science
Ao Universitätsprofessor
Wirtschaftsuniversität Wien

First Edition 1954
Second Edition 1957
   Second impression 1959
   Third impression 1961
   Fourth impression 1963
   Fifth impression 1965
   Sixth impression 1967
   Seventh impression 1968
Third Edition 1969
Fourth Edition 1979
   First Supplement 1980
   Second Supplement 1988
Fifth Edition 1992
   Second Impression 1994
Sixth Edition 1997
Seventh Edition 2003
   Second Impression 2005
Third impression 2007
Eighth Edition 2008

Published in 2008 by
Sweet & Maxwell Ltd, 100 Avenue Road,
Swiss Cottage, London NW3 3PF
Typeset by
YHT Ltd, London
Printed in the UK by CPI William Clowes
Beccles NR34 7TL

No natural forests were destroyed to make this product:
only farmed timber was used and replanted

A CIP catalogue record for this book is available from the
British Library.

978–0421–94900–3 (P/b)

PREFACE

It hardly needs saying that the major part of the preparation of the eighth edition of this work has consisted in the analysis and incorporation of the Companies Act 2006. However, in terms of changes to the organisation of the work, as compared with the previous edition, recent reform of financial services law has had a greater impact. The prior domestic rules on disclosure of directors' interests in shares and of substantial holdings of voting shares (whether on the part of directors or others) were substantially reformed under the impact of the Market Abuse and Transparency Directives. Although neither Directive required this step, the domestic transposition took the form of moving the relevant rules largely out of the Companies Act and into the Financial Services and Markets Act and rules made thereunder by the Financial Services Authority, thus also restricting the range of companies subject to the rules. Hence, the chapter on disclosure and market transparency—chapter 23 in the previous edition—has become chapter 26 of the new edition and has been moved from Part Five to Part Six of the work.

Even where no organisational change was required, the five new EU Directives relevant to this work—the Prospectus, Market Abuse, Transparency, Takeover and (to a lesser extent) Cross-Border Merger Directives—brought about significant changes to the substantive law, as compared with the account given in the previous edition. These changes are reflected in particular in chapters 25, 26, and 28-30 of the book. Thus, whilst it may be true to say that the Commission has become rather timid in making proposals for reform in the area of 'core' company law, the impact of its single financial market proposals on company law has been highly significant.

The Companies Act reforms, by contrast, proceeded at a more leisurely pace—sometimes a glacial one—than the Community reforms (other than the Takeover Directive), and with much greater transparency in the policy-making process. Consequently, most of the changes actually made by the 2006 Act were foreshadowed in the previous edition, so that the purely domestic elements of the Act required no organisational reworking of the book. Of course, not everything which the Company Law Review recommended was enacted and the Act added some new twists of its own, whilst the Operating and Financial Review was cast in the role of the Cheshire Cat, as discussed in chapter 21.

The 2006 Act has been criticised for its length. Undoubtedly, it is long, but some of the criticism is misplaced, because it fails to appreciate that length is not necessarily the enemy of good law. A law which permitted private companies to reduce their capital only on the basis of court approval would be shorter than one which provided the alternative of an out-of-court reduction based on a solvency statement, but not necessarily a more attractive one. Equally, separating clearly the rules applying to private companies from those applying to public companies may lead to more sections and to repetition, but nevertheless provide an Act which users can handle more easily. The 2006 Act will stand or fall by its substance and, on that, one can only refer the reader to the following text.

In preparing this edition I have had the support of my LSE colleagues, Professor Sarah Worthington and Dr Eva Micheler, who took sole responsibility for, respectively, chapters 31 and 27. I am extremely grateful to them.

I am grateful, as well, to the publishers, who responded flexibly to my changing commitments and shepherded the book through the production process with great care.

The usual concluding statement about the date on which the law is stated is difficult to give in relation to the 2006 Act, which was implemented over a period of time, beginning with Royal Assent (November 8, 2006) and scheduled to end with (probably) a seventh Commencement Order coming into effect on October 1, 2009. In general, the approach has been to assume that the whole of the Act is in force, though in cases where substantial portions of the Act will not be in force in the first year of the life of this edition, that fact has been noted (but without giving an account of the law the Act will replace). This has meant that in some cases the statutory instruments necessary to give full effect to the Act have not been available at the time of writing and in other cases the text has had to proceed on the basis of draft instruments. The draft instruments are available on the web-site of the Department of Business, Enterprise and Regulatory Reform. References to sections, unless otherwise indicated, are to those of the Companies Act 2006.

Paul Davies
No Ruz, March, 2008.

CONTENTS

Part One

INTRODUCTORY

Part Two

SEPARATE LEGAL PERSONALITY AND LIMITED LIABILITY

Part Three

CORPORATE GOVERNANCE: THE BOARD AND SHAREHOLDERS

Part Four

CORPORATE GOVERNANCE: MAJORITY AND MINORITY SHAREHOLDERS

Part Five

ACCOUNT AND AUDIT

Part Six

EQUITY FINANCE

Part Seven

DEBT FINANCE

APPENDIX

TABLE OF CASES

TABLE OF STATUTES

TABLE OF STATUTORY INSTRUMENTS

TABLE OF EUROPEAN MATERIAL

TABLE OF TAKEOVER CODE

ABBREVIATIONS

AADB	Accountancy and Actuarial Discipline Board
ADR	American Depositary Receipt
AGM	Annual General Meeting
AIM	Alternative Investment Market
APB	Auditing Practices Board
ARC	Accounting Regulatory Committee
ARD	Accounting Reference Date
ARP	Accounting Reference Period
ASB	Accounting Standards Board
BERR	Department for Business, Enterprise & Regulatory Reform
BoT	Board of Trade
BR	Business Review
CA	Companies Act
CARD	Consolidated Admissions Requirements Directive
CC	Combined Code on Corporate Governance
CEO	Chief Executive Officer
CESR	Committee of European Securities Regulators
CfD	Contract for Differences
CFO	Chief Financial Officer
CIB	Companies Investigation Branch (of BERR)
CIC	Community Interest Company
CIO	Charitable Incorporated Organisation
CJA	Criminal Justice Act 1993
CLR	Company Law Review
CPR	Civil Procedure Rules
CRR	Capital Redemption Reserve
DB	Defined Benefit (pension scheme)
DC	Defined Contribution (pension scheme)

DEPP	Decision Procedure and Penalties Manual (of FSA)
DTI	Department of Trade and Industry
DTR	Disclosure and Transparency Rule (of FSA)
DR	Directors' Report
DRR	Directors' Remuneration Report
EBLR	European Business Law Review
EBOR	European Business Organization Law Review
ECJ	European Court of Justice
ECtHR	European Court of Human Rights
EEA	European Economic Area
EEIG	European Economic Interest Grouping
EG	Enforcement Guide (of FSA)
ESV	Enlightened Shareholder Value
FRC	Financial Reporting Council
FRRP	Financial Reporting Review Panel
FRS	Financial Reporting Standard
FRSEE	Financial Reporting Standard for Smaller Entities
FSA	Financial Services Authority
FSAP	Financial Services Action Plan (of the EC Commission)
FSMA	Financial Services and Markets Act 2000
FSMT	Financial Services and Markets Tribunal
GAAP	Generally Accepted Accounting Principles
GP.	General Principle (of the City Code on Takeovers and Mergers)
HKCFAR	Hong Kong Court of Final Appeal Reports
HLG	High Level Group of Company Law Experts
IA	Insolvency Act
IAASB	International Auditing and Assurance Standards Board
IAS	International Accounting Standards
IASB	International Accounting Standards Board
IFRS	International Financial Reporting Standards
IPO	Initial Public Offering
ISA	International Standard on Auditing
JCLS	Journal of Corporate Law Studies
KPI	Key Performance Indicators
LLP	Limited Liability Partnership
LR	Listing Rules (of FSA)
LSE	London Stock Exchange
Ltd	Limited
Ltip	Long-term incentive plan
MAD	Market Abuse Directive (Directive 2003/6/EC)
MAR	Code of Market Conduct (of FSA)
MIFID	Directive on Markets in Financial Instruments
MTF	Multilateral Trading Facility
MO	Management Organ (of an SE)

Nasdaq	National Association of Securities Dealers Automated Quotation System (a U S stock exchange)
NED	Non-Executive Director
OEIC	Open-ended Investment Company
OFR	Operating and Financial Review
OR	Official Receiver
OSOV	One Share One Vote
OTC	Over the counter
PCP	Permissible Capital Payment
PD	Prospectus Directive (Directive 2003/71/EC)
PIE	Public Interest Entity
PLC	Public Limited Company
POB	Public Oversight Board
PR	Prospectus Rules (of FSA)
RIE	Recognised Investment Exchange
RINGA	Relevant Information not Generally Available
RIS	Regulated Information Service
RS	Reporting Standard or Statement
SCE	European Cooperative Society
SE	Societas Europaea or European Company
SNB	Special Negotiating Body (of employee representatives)
SO	Supervisory Organ (of an SE)
SPV	Special Purpose Vehicle
SSAP	Statement of Standard Accounting Practice
TD	Transparency Directive (Directive 2004/109/EC)
UCITS	Undertakings for Collective Investment in Transferable Securities
USR	Uncertificated Securities Regulations
UKLA	United Kingdom Listing Authority

DOCUMENTS FROM THE COMPANY LAW REVIEW AND THE GOVERNMENT RESPONSE TO IT

Completing	CLR, *Completing the Structure*, URN 00/1335, November 2000
Developing	CLR, *Developing the Framework*, URN 00/656, March 2000
Final Report	CLR, *Final Report*, 2 vols, URN 01/943, July, 2001
Formation	CLR, *Company Formation and Capital Maintenance*, URN 99/1145, October 1999
Maintenance	CLR, *Capital Maintenance: Other Issues*, URN 00/880, June 2000

Modernising   *Modernising Company Law*, Cm 5553, 2 vols, July 2002.

Overseas Companies   CLR, *Reforming the Law Concerning Oversea Companies*, URN 99/1146, October 1999

Strategic Framework   CLR, *The Strategic Framework*, URN 99/654, February 1999

PART ONE

INTRODUCTORY

The company, incorporated under the successive Companies Acts, is a dominant institution in our society, all the more so with the retreat in recent decades of the government-owned or public sector of the economy from a number of areas in which it previously had been a monopoly or near-monopoly provider of services or, less often, of goods. Yet, the role of the Companies Act company is not easy to describe with accuracy. Even in the area of profit-making business activity, where it is a major force, it has no exclusive position and faces competition, at least in relation to smaller businesses, from other legal forms, such as the partnership or the sole trader (if the latter is a legal form at all). Moreover, the company is not just a vehicle for making profits: it can be, and is increasingly, used in the not-for-profit sector, i.e. where the aim of the undertaking is either not to make profits or, if it is, not to distribute them to the members of the company.

Above all, the company is a highly flexible form of vehicle for carrying on business, whether for profit or not-for-profit. Although, in relation to many types of activity, the question arises whether the activity should be carried on through a company or another legal form, none of these other legal forms is available across so many types and sizes of activity as is the corporate form. In other words, the company has many competitors in the shape of other legal vehicles for carrying on business, but it is perhaps not much of an exaggeration to say that for all these other vehicles their primary competitor is the company. Thus, companies can be used to accommodate the smallest, one-person business to the largest, multi-national undertaking. The characteristics of the corporate form which give it such flexibility obviously deserve to be studied.

Finally, business today is often a multi-national activity. British companies may carry on activities in other states and companies from other jurisdictions may carry on business in the United Kingdom. The right of British companies to carry on business in other Member States of the European Community, whether directly or through a subsidiary company, and right of companies from other Member States to do so in the United Kingdom (their "freedom of establishment") are obviously matters of legitimate concern for the European Union. However, globalisation means that the international dimension of British company law is not restricted to the European Union, nor, indeed, has it ever been.

In this part we shall try to analyse the function of the modern company and its structure, discuss its advantages and disadvantages, see how it is created and introduce the international element of British company law.

CHAPTER 1

TYPES AND FUNCTIONS OF COMPANIES

USES TO WHICH THE COMPANY MAY BE PUT

Although company law is a well-recognised subject in the legal cur-   **1–1**
riculum and the title of a voluminous literature, its exact scope is not
obvious since "the word company has no strictly legal meaning".[1]
Explicitly or implicitly, many courses on "company law" solve the
problem of defining the scope of the subject by concentrating on
those companies created by registration under the Companies Acts.
That will be true of this book. Since there are more than two million
such companies existing today, in practical and pragmatic terms this
is a sensible solution, for clearly the law applying to such companies
is a matter of major concern to many people. However, to state that a
book is going to deal, principally, with companies formed under
particular Acts of Parliament does not convey much in the way of
understanding about what role such companies perform in society.
    The term "company" implies an association of a number of people

---

[1] Per Buckley J. in *Stanley, Re* [1906] 1 Ch. 131 at 134.

3

for some common object or objects. The purposes for which men and women may wish to associate are multifarious, ranging from those as basic as marriage and mutual protection against the elements to those as sophisticated as the objects of the Confederation of British Industry or a political party. However, in common parlance the word "company" is normally reserved for those associated for economic purposes, i.e. to carry on a business for gain.[2] However, to say that company law is concerned with those associations which people use to carry on business for gain would be wrong—for two reasons. First, the law provides vehicles in addition to the company in which people can associate for gainful business. Secondly, companies incorporated under the Companies Acts may be used for carrying on not-for-profit businesses or for purposes which can be only doubtfully characterised as businesses at all. Let us look at each of these matters in turn.

Companies and partnerships (limited and unlimited)

1–2 English law provides two main types of organisation for those who wish to associate in order to carry on business for gain: partnerships and companies. Although the word "company" is colloquially applied to both,[3] the modern lawyer regards companies and company law as distinct from partnerships and partnership law. Partnership law, which is now largely codified in the Partnership Act 1890, is based on the law of agency, each partner becoming an agent of the others,[4] and it therefore affords a suitable framework for an association of a small body of persons having trust and confidence in each other. A more complicated form of association, with a large and fluctuating membership, requires a more elaborate organisation which ideally should confer corporate personality on the association, that is, should recognise that it constitutes a distinct legal person, subject to legal duties and entitled to legal rights separate from those of its members.[5] This the modern company can provide easily and cheaply by being formed under a succession of statutes culminating in the principal Companies Act of 2006.[6]

The previous paragraph might be taken to imply that the difference between partnerships and companies, at least as far as business use is

---

[2] But not universally; we still talk about an infantry company, a livery company and the "glorious company of the Apostles".

[3] So that it is common for partners to carry on business in the name of "—& Company".

[4] Partnership Act 1890, s.5.

[5] It is outside the scope of this book to discuss whether this recognition is of a pre-existing fact (as contended by the Realist school, associated with the name of Gierke) or of legal fiction. Legal personality, in the sense of the capacity to be the subject of legal rights and duties, is necessarily the creation of law whether conferred upon a single human being or a group and the Realist and other theories are of no direct concern to the lawyer (as opposed to the political scientist) except in so far as they have influenced the judges in the development of the law. See further, H.L.A. Hart in (1954) 70 L.Q.R. 37 at 49–60.

[6] Most of the 2006 Act provisions discussed in this chapter are scheduled to come into force on October 1, 2009, but they are not significantly different from their 1985 Act counterparts.

concerned, is that the former is used to carry on small businesses and the latter large ones (or, better, that the former is used by a small number of people to carry on a business and the latter by a large number). It seems that the mid-Victorian legislature was animated by some such idea.[7] Thus, section 716(1) of the Companies Act 1985, re-enacting a provision first introduced by the Joint Stock Companies Act 1844 (which in fact set the limit slightly higher at 25), provided that, in principle, an association of 20 or more persons formed for the purpose of carrying on a business for gain must be formed as a company[8] (and so not as a partnership); whilst the Limited Liability Act 1855 required companies with limited liability to have at least 25 members.[9] However, the Joint Stock Companies Act 1856 quickly reduced the minimum number to seven for companies,[10] whilst the decision of the House of Lords at the end of the nineteenth century in *Salomon v Salomon*[11] in effect allowed the incorporation of a company with a single member, the other six being bare nominees for the seventh. This judicial decision preceded by nearly a century the adoption of EC Directive 89/667,[12] which required private companies formally to be capable of being formed with a single member. The 2006 Act extended this facility to public companies.[13] As for the maximum limit for partnerships, in recent years the legislature removed the 20-partner limit from a number of professions (notably solicitors and accountants,[14] who have now formed some very large, even multi-national, partnerships) and subordinate regulations removed the limit from many more professions. In 2000, the Law Commissions[15] proposed the abolition of the limit (for all types of partnership) and the Government implemented the recommendation in December 2002.[16] Thus, the 2006 Act contains no equivalent to section 716 of the 1985 Act.

Thus, since the decision in *Salomon v Salomon* small numbers of **1–3** people wishing to form a business have had a free choice between the

---

[7] Though the legislature seems to have been influenced in this view more by problems of civil procedure in relation to large partnerships than by the idea that the partnership itself was inappropriate for large numbers of joint venturers. See Law Commission and Scottish Law Commission, *Joint Consultation Paper on Partnership Law* (London, 2000), paras 5.51–5.61.

[8] It could be formed as a registered company or as a statutory or chartered one (see below, para.1–16) or indeed as an Open-Ended Investment Company under the Financial Services and Markets Act 2000 (see below, para.1–19). If it was formed as a partnership it would be automatically dissolved for illegality: Partnership Act 1890, s.34.

[9] And contained other provisions designed to restrict limited liability to relatively substantial companies, such as that each of the 25 members had to have subscribed for shares with a nominal value of at least £10, of which 20 per cent had to be paid up.

[10] And removed the capital requirements of the 1855 Act.

[11] [1897] A.C. 22. See para.2–1, below.

[12] [1989] OJ L395/40.

[13] s.7(1)—which is not confined to private companies.

[14] s.716(2) of the 1985 Act.

[15] See above, fn.7.

[16] DTI, *Removing the 20 Partner Limit: A Consultation Document* (URN 01/752), 2001; Regulatory Reform (Removal of 20 Member Limit in Partnerships, etc.) Order 2002/3203.

partnership and corporate forms, and the 2002 reform extended that choice to larger numbers of people, even outside the field of professional businesses. However, the final collapse of the Victorian attempt to segregate the two forms according to the number of people involved in them does not mean that they are equally well adapted to different sizes of business. In fact, it is clear that where a large and fluctuating number of members is involved, the company has distinct advantages as an organisational form. This is because the company has built into it a distinction between the members of the company (usually shareholders) and the management of the company (vested in a board of directors). Although this division can be replicated within a partnership, it has to be distinctly chosen by the partners,[17] whereas the division is inherent in company law and so the company legal form deals comprehensively with the consequences of the division between membership and management.

On the other hand, where a small number of persons intend to set up a business and all to be involved in running it, the distinction made by company law between shareholders and directors often becomes a nuisance, for they are the same (or nearly the same) people. The internal machinery imposed by company law often appears impossibly cumbersome in such cases. Despite the amendments made in recent years and further reforms in the 2006 Act to meet the needs of small companies,[18] Parliament was persuaded to pass the Limited Liability Partnerships Act 2000, so as to introduce a new hybrid legal vehicle. Although a hybrid, the limited liability partnership ("LLP") is much nearer to a company than to a partnership, and to that extent the title of the Act is misleading. The LLP is governed by company law, often adapted to its particular needs, rather than by partnership law, except in two crucial respects. In particular, the LLP has the separate legal personality and limited liability of the company. The exceptions are taxation (the members are taxed as if they were partners) and the internal decision-making machinery, where the division between members and directors is abandoned[19] and the members have the same freedom as in a partnership to decide on their internal decision-making structures.[20] The LLP has proved a reasonably attractive legal form, especially for professional businesses.[21]

---

[17] The default rule in partnership law is that each partner has a right to participate in the management of the partnership: Partnership Act 1890, s.24(5).

[18] Discussed throughout this book, but especially in Ch.15.

[19] Effectively, there are no directors and all members are prima facie entitled to be involved in the management of the LLP.

[20] For more detail see G. Morse *et al.* (eds), *Palmer's Limited Liability Partnership Law* (London, 2002). The LLP Regulations 2001/1090 currently apply parts of the CA 1985 to LLPs, but BERR is consulting at the time of writing on how the CA 2006 should be applied to them.

[21] Some 13,500 were on the register at the end of 2005/6 (though there were over 2 million private companies registered at the same date): DTI, *Companies in 2005–2006*, Tables A2 and E2.

The Limited Liability Partnerships Act 2000 is to be sharply distinguished from the confusingly similarly named, but much earlier, Limited Partnership Act 1907. The limited partnership is a true partnership, which is governed by the 1890 Act and the common law of partnership, except in so far as is necessary to give effect to its particular features.[22] These special features are that some (but not all) the partners of a limited partnership have limited liability,[23] and that, in return, they are prohibited from taking part in the management of the partnership business and do not have power to bind the partnership as against outsiders, and certain information about the limited partnership has to be publicly filed (in fact, with the registrar of companies).[24] The 1907 Act thus provides for the existence of a "sleeping partner", often someone who contributes assets to the company and wishes to become a member of the partnership in order to safeguard his or her investment and in order to obtain an appropriate return on it, but who does not want to be involved in its business. There were some 17,500 limited partnerships in existence in 2006.[25] Although a small number compared with the private company,[26] the number has been growing in recent years, because of the attraction of the limited partnership in certain specialised fields of commercial activity.[27] For the purposes of this book, however, there is a gulf between, on the one hand, the registered company and the limited liability partnership, which are both in essence creatures of company law, and, on the other, the partnership and the limited partnership, which are creatures of partnership law.

Not-for-profit companies

The second way in which the statement that company law is concerned with the law relating to associations formed with a view to carrying on business for gain is wrong arises out of the absence of any requirement, in the Companies Act or elsewhere, that use of a registered company should be limited to any such purpose.[28] A company may be not-for-profit in a strong sense, in that a provision

1-4

---

[22] 1907 Act, s.7.

[23] s.4(2) of the 1907 Act requires that there must be at least one general partner who is liable for debts and obligations of the firm.

[24] 1907 Act, ss.6 and 8.

[25] DTI, *Companies in 2005–2006* (2006), Table E2. However, it is not clear how many of them are active: the 1907 Act requires limited partnerships to register but provides no mechanism for de-registration.

[26] See fn.21 above.

[27] Notably, venture capital or private equity investment funds, where the investors can be limited partners distinct from the managers of the fund who are general partners; and in property investment, where tax-exempt investors may wish to be excluded from any management role. See the Law Commissions, *Limited Partnerships Act 1907: A Joint Consultation Paper*, (2001), Pt I.

[28] Unlike both the partnership and the LLP where the intention (if not the actuality) of carrying on the business for profit is part of the definition of these legal vehicles: Partnership Act 1890, s.1(1); Limited Liability Partnerships Act 2000, s.2(1).

in its constitution prohibits the distribution of profits to the members of the company, either by way of dividend or in a winding up. Or it may be so in the weak sense of not being run in order to make a profit, though it may from time to time do so and it may then distribute it to its members. "Not-for-profit" is not a term of art in British company law, in the way it is in the laws of many states of the United States.

The purposes which such companies pursue may be genuinely charitable (in which case the company will be subject to the charities legislation as well as the companies legislation)[29] or they may be public interest purposes which do not fall within the rather narrow legal definition of charitable purposes. In an Act of 2004 the Government provided an adaptation of the corporate form specially designed for those wishing to pursue public interest goals which are not charitable, in the shape of the Community Interest Company (CIC).[30] Alternatively, the purpose of the company may be to promote a private interest but that private interest may not be making a profit. A typical example is the use by the tenants of a block of flats of a company to hold the freehold title to the block or to see to the care and maintenance of the common parts of the block. These are clearly purely private purposes, but the tenants will fund the company, usually through service charges, simply to the level needed so that it can discharge its obligations and would be surprised, even indignant, if the company made a significant profit on its activities.

Companies limited by guarantee and companies limited by shares

1–5 The Companies Acts have long provided a particular form of the company which may be regarded as particularly suitable for companies which carry on a not-for-profit activity. This is the company "limited by guarantee", as opposed to the company "limited by shares",[31] the latter being the form normally used for profit-making activities and by far the more common one. The Companies Act does not permit a company to be created in which the members are free from any liability whatsoever, but, as an alternative to limiting their contribution to the amount payable on their shares,[32] it enables them to agree that in the event of liquidation they will, if required, subscribe an agreed amount.[33] The guarantee company is widely used by charitable and quasi-charitable organisations (such as schools, col-

---

[29] There is no obligation for bodies which pursue charitable objects to incorporate, though they increasingly do so today in order to obtain the benefits of limited liability, since such organisations are playing a bigger role in the delivery of welfare services previously provided directly by the Government and thus are carrying more financial risk.

[30] See below para.1–6.

[31] s.3(1).

[32] The Act even recognises a hybrid form: a company limited by guarantee but also with a share capital, but it has not been possible to create such a company since 1980: s.5.

[33] s.3(3).

leges and the "Friends" of museums and picture galleries) since incorporation with limited liability is often more convenient and less risky than a trust.[34] However, a division of such an undertaking into shares is unnecessary, since no sharing of profits is contemplated, and the creators of the company may regard membership of the company divorced from shareholding as a more appropriate expression of the objectives of the company.

It might also be thought that a company limited by guarantee places a smaller financial obligation upon the members than one limited by shares, since the members of a guarantee company do not have to put any money into the concern when it is set up, as they normally would have to if they subscribed for shares. The members of a guarantee company are under no liability so long as the company remains a going concern; they are liable, to the extent of their guarantees, only if the company is wound up and a contribution is needed to enable its debts to be paid. However, since the par value of shares can be set at a very low level (perhaps one penny)[35] and a member of a company limited by shares is obliged to buy only one share, it is doubtful whether this financial argument carries much weight in the choice between companies limited by shares and by guarantee. In fact, since the level of the guarantee is usually also set at a nominal level, the financing aspects of not-for-profit companies probably play little part in a person's decision whether to apply for membership. For this reason, companies limited by shares can be and are in fact used for non-profit purposes. For example, in the case of the service company mentioned above, often each tenant will have one share in the company.[36]

A more important advantage of the guarantee company would seem to be the fact that admission to and resignation from membership are easier than in a share company. Upon resignation from a share company, the member's share has to be allocated elsewhere, either back to the company or to a new member, whereas on admission of a new member a new share may have to be created, unless another member is resigning at exactly the same time. The issuance, transfer and repurchase of shares are all matters which are regulated by the Companies Act in the interests of creditors[37] and these provisions may make the transfer of membership in not-for-profit companies cumbersome. Where, however, membership is not attached to shares, joining and leaving can be as easy as in any club or association, i.e. normally, joining is simply a matter of agreement

---

[34] There were some 40,000 guarantee companies in existence in 1998: CLR, Developing, para. 9.12.

[35] See para.11–6.

[36] This may be convenient if the members are not to have exactly identical obligations, for example, where the obligation to contribute to the costs of the company is related to the size of the flats. In that case different contribution obligations can be attached to each share.

[37] See below, Chs 11 and 12.

between company and prospective member and leaving is a matter of unilateral decision by the member, perhaps subject to certain conditions relating to notice or discharge of obligations owed to the company.[38]

1–6   A guarantee company is, however, unsuitable where the primary object is to carry on a business for profit and to divide that profit among the members. Just as a partnership agreement will need to prescribe the shares of the partners, so will a company's constitution need to define the shares of its members, and if these shares are to be transferable it will be convenient for them to be expressed in comparatively small denominations. The members who subscribe for the shares will be under a duty to pay the company for them in money or money's worth, and the company is accordingly said to be "limited by shares", that is to say, the members' liability to contribute towards the company's debts is limited to the nominal value of the shares for which they have subscribed, and once the shares have been "paid up" (i.e. paid for) they are under no further liability.[39] A fundamental distinction between this type of company and the guarantee company is that the law assumes that in a company limited by shares its working capital will be, to some extent at any rate, contributed by the members; their contributions float the company on its launching and are not a mere life-belt to which creditors may cling when the company sinks, which is how the guarantee might be viewed. However, as we shall see,[40] since the Companies Act lays down no minimum capital requirement for private companies, the contribution of the shareholders to the initial financing of the company limited by shares may be exiguous.

Despite the long availability of the guarantee company for non-profit purposes, it does have a limitation in terms of its financing. Since there are no shares to be sold, the guarantee company must either operate on the basis that it needs no long-term working capital (many clubs can exist simply on their subscription income) or it must raise that capital by way of debt (i.e. loans to it). Partly for this reason, in Part 2 of the Companies (Audit, Investigations and Community Enterprise) Act 2004 the Government created a new type of company,[41] known as the Community Interest Company, to which the 2006 Act provisions apply subject to the modifications made in the 2004 Act.[42] Such a company can be either a company limited by shares or by guarantee, its purposes are limited to pursuit of com-

---

[38] Where membership changes are expected to be relatively rare and where a new member will always be available to replace the leaving one, as with the service company formed by the leaseholders of a block of flats, this potential disadvantage of the share company will not show itself.

[39] s.3(2) and more clearly in s.74(2)(d) of the Insolvency Act 1986, discussed further in paras 8–1 to 8–3.

[40] See below, Ch.11.

[41] s.26(1) of the 2004 Act. A company may be formed as a CIC or later convert into one.

[42] s.6(2) of the 2006 Act.

munity interests,[43] distributions to the members of the company and the payment of interest on debentures are subject to a cap and its assets otherwise "locked in",[44] and, investors having less incentive to exercise control over the company because their potential rewards are limited, a Regulator of Community Interest Companies is given potentially extensive powers of intervention in the CIC's affairs.[45] Registration as a CIC is not compatible with charitable status[46] and does not attract the tax relief afforded to charities, and so it is not clear as to how attractive the CIC would be where the community purposes were also charitable (which, of course, they might not well be).[47]

The functions of the modern company

So far, we have established two negative, and therefore not wholly helpful, propositions. First, the company form is not limited to the association of large numbers of people in the carrying on of a business, but can be used by small numbers, even by the individual entrepreneur. Secondly, the company form is not confined to the carrying on of a profit-making activity. However, a positive proposition has also emerged. This is that the comparative advantage of the company (as against, for example, the partnership or the trust) does indeed lie in the association of large numbers of people for the carrying on of large-scale business. This is for two reasons. First, company law, by insisting upon the central role of directors in the running of the company, permits a large and fluctuating body of members (the shareholders) to delegate oversight of the company's business to a small and committed group of persons (the directors). As important, over the years successive Companies Acts and the common law have developed a set of rules for regulating the relationship between shareholders and directors when authority is delegated to the directors in this way.[48] Secondly, by providing for the creation of separate legal personality, limited liability and transferable shares, company law facilitates the raising of risk capital from the public for the financing of corporate ventures. Although there are other ways of financing companies, raising funds by the sale of shares often gives companies greater flexibility than in the case of debt finance and is therefore a crucial element in financing of all businesses except those where the risk of failure is very low.[49]

This analysis is borne out by the statistics classifying businesses by

1–7

---

[43] s.35.
[44] ss.30–31.
[45] ss.41–51—subject to an appeal to an Appeal Officer (s.28).
[46] s.26(3).
[47] As at the end of 2007 some 1,500 CICs had been registered. See: www.cicregulator.gov.uk/coSearch/companyList.shtml.
[48] See Part Three, below.
[49] See Parts Six and Seven, below.

their legal type. These show that of businesses in the private sector of the economy in 2006 employing more than 500 employees (which provide about 40 per cent of both total employment and total turnover), 2895 were organised as companies and only 30 as partnerships (and none as sole traders). On the other hand, of those with fewer than five employees (providing about 10 per cent of both employment and turnover), 400,000 were companies, 130,000 were partnerships and 270,000 were sole traders.[50] This shows not only, as one would expect, that there are many more small businesses than large businesses, but also, and more relevant from our point of view, that among large businesses the company form predominates, whilst in small businesses it faces a distinct challenge from the partnership and those who make no formal distinction between their personal and business lives (the sole trader).

From a functional viewpoint it could be said that today there are three distinct types of company:

1. Companies formed for purposes other than the profit of their members, i.e. those formed for social, charitable or quasi-charitable purposes. In this case incorporation is merely a more modern and convenient substitute for the trust.

2. Companies formed to enable a single trader or a small body of partners to carry on a business. In these companies, incorporation is a device for personifying the business and, normally, divorcing its liability from that of its members despite the fact that the members retain control and share the profits. In this case, the company is often a substitute for a partnership.

3. Companies formed in order to enable the investing public to share in the profits of an enterprise without taking any part in its management. In this last type, which is economically (but not numerically) by far the most important, the company is again a device analogous to the trust, but this time it is designed to facilitate the raising and putting to use of capital by enabling a large number of owners to entrust it to a small number of expert managers.

1–8 However, this threefold categorisation needs to be treated with caution. First, there may be hybrid companies or companies which in a particular moment of their growth straddle the second and third categories. For example, a company which was formally controlled wholly by the members of a particular family may have begun to bring in one or two outside financiers (sometimes called "business

---

[50] DTI, *Small and Medium Enterprise Statistics for the United Kingdom* (2006), Table 2. The fewer than five employees figure excludes firms with no employees at all.

angels") in order to expand the business and these outsiders will naturally have wanted a share in the control of the company. At a later date, the family members may have retired from active management of the company and may have brought in professional managers to run the company (to whom shares have been allocated), but the family members may still be the predominant shareholders.

Secondly, even if a company is squarely within the third category and has a large number of shareholders, from whom the directors constitute a distinct body, there may be great variations in extent to which the shareholdings are dispersed and the ease with which those shares can be traded. At one end of the scale is a company listed on the London Stock Exchange[51] with many thousands of shareholders who are able to trade their shares with other investors with great ease; whilst at the other end is a company which does in fact have several hundred shareholders, many of whom are perhaps its employees, but which has never made a formal offer of its shares to the public and whose shares may not be traded on a public exchange.

DIFFERENT TYPES OF REGISTERED COMPANIES

Public and private companies

It follows from what has just been said that the range of functions **1–9** that may be performed by a company formed by registration under the Companies Acts is extremely wide. Yet, they are all subject to a single Act, today that of 2006. Is this at all sensible? Would it be better to have different pieces of legislation for different types of company or can sufficient differentiation among different sorts of companies be achieved within a single Act? Let us look at this matter with reference to five possible divisions among companies, the first three of which have long been recognised in British law, the fourth of which is not formally so recognised but is in practice catered for to some extent and the fifth of which can be said to have become recognised in recent years.

A division commonly found in the company laws of many states is that between public and private companies, the former being those which are permitted to offer their securities (whether shares or debentures)[52] to the public (though they may not in fact have done so) and the latter being those which are not so permitted. This distinction is important not just for the obvious one that companies which do not offer their shares to the public need not be concerned with the rules governing this process, which, today, are set out largely in the

---

[51] See Ch.25, below.
[52] On debentures see Ch.31, below.

Financial Services and Markets Act 2000 ("FSMA") and not in the Companies Act.[53] Rather, whether a company is public or private is taken more generally as an indication of the social and economic importance of the company, so that the public company is more tightly regulated than the private company in a number of ways which do not directly concern the offering of shares to the public.

The distinction between public and private companies is embodied in the Act: a private company must not offer to the public any of its securities.[54] However, unlike in many continental European countries, there is no separate legislation for public and private companies. The approach of the single Act seems to be feasible because, although British public companies are more highly regulated than private companies, the British legislation has always had less ambitious regulatory goals for public companies than our continental counterparts. Thus, for example, the German *Aktiengesetz*, applying to public companies, divides the board of directors into two bodies, the supervisory board and the management board, and deals in some detail with the allocation of functions between them and the method of appointment of their members.[55] By contrast, the British Act says very little about what the board is to do or how its members are to be appointed,[56] and certainly does not require the creation of separate supervisory and management boards.[57] These matters are left to be decided by each company itself in its constitution. Consequently, different sizes and types of company can adjust these matters to suit their own particular situation, whereas in Germany to relieve private companies of the demands of the *Aktiengesetz* has been seen to require the enactment of a separate and more flexible statute for private companies (the *GmbHGesetz*).

1–10   The British single Act approach clearly functions well if the legislative policy in question is one of leaving a matter to be decided largely by the company itself, as is the case with board structure and composition. However, one might think that this amounts to saying no more than that, if the legislature is not seeking to regulate public companies, that policy can be easily applied also to private companies. What, however, about the case where the legislative policy does involve significant regulation of public companies? Does the single Act approach work there as well? In principle, since the distinction

---

[53] See Ch.25, below.
[54] s.755. Further, s.74 of FSMA 2000 and regulations made thereunder prevent a private company from having its securities listed on an exchange, even if there has been no public offer. On listing see para.25–15, below.
[55] Other legislation requires the mandatory presence of employee representatives on the boards of large public companies, but this applies also to the boards of large private companies.
[56] Though it does contain an important provision, s.303, enabling an ordinary majority of the shareholders to remove any director at any time. See Ch.14.
[57] Typically, there is only a single board in British companies, but there is nothing in the legislation to stop them establishing a separate "management board" below the main board, and this is sometimes done. On the division within a single board between executive and non-executive directors, see para.14–29.

between public and private companies is embedded in the Companies Act, there is no formal difficulty, even within a single Act, in confining the relevant regulation to public companies, where it is thought appropriate to do so. However, the Company Law Review criticised legislative policy in the United Kingdom for historically failing to address rigorously the question of whether regulation intended for public companies should be applied, either in a modified form or at all, to private companies. It said: "Small and medium-sized companies suffer regulation that was designed for large, publicly-owned companies."[58] Its proposed remedy was not, however, the introduction of a separate Act for private companies, but rather a review, which it carried out, of the provisions applying to private companies to see which could be removed from them or applied only in a modified form.[59] It also proposed a re-ordering of the Companies Act so as to make more transparent the provisions applying to private companies,[60] a task to some considerable degree carried out by the 2006 Act.

Given the significance of the distinction between public and private companies in the present Companies Act and the likely increase in the importance of that distinction in the future, it is important to see that the choice between a public and a private company is one for the incorporators themselves or, after incorporation, for the shareholders.[61] In fact, the default rule is that the company is private: unless the company states that it is to be registered as a public company, it will be a private one.[62] In fact, the overwhelming proportion of companies on the companies register are private ones. As of March 2006 only about 11,500 companies on the register in Great Britain were public, whilst the total number of registered companies was over two million.[63]

This is a big change from the position which obtained when the notion of the private company was introduced by the Companies (Consolidation) Act 1908. The view then was that, because a private company was exempted from some of the publicity provisions of the Act, access to that status should be restricted. A company could qualify as private only if it (a) limited its membership to 50, (b) restricted the right to transfer shares and (c) prohibited any invitation to the public of its shares. Only (c) has survived into the modern law

---

[58] Final Report I, para.5.
[59] The particular proposals will be noted at the appropriate points in the book, but an important example was the removal of the prohibition on a company giving financial assistance for the acquisition of its shares from private companies. See para.13–26.
[60] Final Report I, Ch.2.
[61] A company originally incorporated as private may, subject to certain safeguards, transform itself into a public one, or vice versa. See para.4–20.
[62] s.4(2)(a).
[63] DTI, above fn.21, Tables A1 and A2. The total number of companies on the register has been increasing quite rapidly (by over one-third between 2002 and 2006), whilst the number of public companies gently declined over the same period (by about seven per cent). Now only about one in two hundred companies is a public one.

as a requirement for private status.[64] The modern approach was
introduced by the Companies Act 1980, which implemented the
Second EC Company Law Directive on the raising and maintenance
of capital.[65] Because, on the one hand, its requirements were thought
to be burdensome and, on the other, the Directive applied only to
public companies, the British legislature responded by making access
to the private company status easier to obtain. The Act also introduced new suffixes, which are a mandatory part of a company's
name, in order to distinguish private ("limited" or "Ltd") from
public ("public limited company" or "Plc") companies.[66]

Listed and other publicly traded companies

1–11   We have seen that public companies are permitted to offer their
shares to the public, but may not in fact have chosen to do so. Even if
they have, those shares may or may not be traded on a public share
exchange, such as the London Stock Exchange. Offering shares to the
public and arranging for those shares to be traded on a public market
are two separate things, though the public's willingness to buy the
shares offered is likely to be increased if the shares will be traded on a
public market. This is because a public share market makes it much
easier for a shareholder subsequently to sell his or her shares to
another investor (or to purchase more shares in the company), should
he or she wish to do so. Consequently, public offerings of shares and
the introduction of those shares to trading on a public market often
go together.[67]

By and large, the companies legislation makes very few differ-
entiations according to whether a public company's shares have
actually been offered to the public or are in fact publicly traded, and
the 2006 Act makes fewer than its predecessor. However, a company
taking either of these steps will find itself subject to the Financial
Services and Markets Act 2000 and to rules made under it by the
Financial Services Authority (FSA), as well as to an increasing set of
Community laws. This regulation, naturally, is mainly concerned
with the issues thrown up by public offers and public trading—these
are discussed later in the book—but it is important to note at this
stage a curiosity of the British approach. This is that admission to a
public market may bring with it obligations for the company of a
recognisably "company law" type, obligations which could have been
included in the Act. This is particularly true of certain parts of the
"Listing Rules" made by the FSA. A company seeking to have its
shares traded on the main market of the London Stock Exchange

---

[64] Private companies are in fact very likely to restrict the transfer of shares (see Ch.27) and to
   have fewer than 50 members, but these are no longer necessary incidents of being private.
[65] Directive 77/91/EEC, [1977] OJ L26/1. See Chs 11–13 below.
[66] Companies registered in Wales may use the Welsh equivalents. See Ch.4 below.
[67] These processes are discussed in Ch.25.

must first have them admitted to the "Official List" of securities, which list is maintained by the FSA, acting in its capacity as the UK Listing Authority ("UKLA").[68] There are about 1,100 UK-incorporated companies on the Official List. Although a main purpose of this piece of regulation is to secure proper disclosure of information about the company at the time its shares are offered to the public,[69] the UKLA is also empowered to impose on listed companies rules governing their conduct thereafter.[70] Such listing rules relate mainly to the orderly conduct of the public share market, but they also contain rules regulating the internal affairs of companies, which thus supplement the provisions of the Companies Act and the common law of companies.[71] In particular, the Listing Rules contain provisions on related party transactions[72] and significant transactions,[73] which supplement the statutory rules on directors' and controlling shareholders' conflicts of interest and set a limit on the constitutional division of powers within companies,[74] and provide the legal anchor for the Combined Code on Corporate Governance.

This last is probably the best-known example of such a "supplementary" Listing Rule. Companies subject to it must indicate to their shareholders each year how far they have complied with the Combined Code on Corporate Governance,[75] which is attached to the Listing Rules, and to explain areas of non-compliance. This Code deals with the composition and functions of the board of directors. The clue that this is more a corporate law rule than a capital markets rule is provided by the restriction of this obligation to companies incorporated in the United Kingdom. A listed company incorporated in another jurisdiction (for example, a French company whose shares are listed on the Main Market of the London Exchange) does not have to comply with this obligation because its internal affairs are regulated by the law of the place where it is incorporated.[76] In short, the fact of listing is being used to identify a small group of very important British companies[77] to which additional company law obligations are attached.

The identification of publicly traded companies as a separate group **1–12** for company law purposes has become increasingly important in

---

[68] FSMA 2000, Pt VI.
[69] See Ch.25, below.
[70] FSMA 2000, s.96.
[71] Companies whose shares are traded on secondary markets, such as the Alternative Investment Market, may also be subject to exchange rules which perform a similar function, but the rules of secondary markets are less demanding than the Listing Rules.
[72] LR 11.
[73] LR 10.
[74] See paras 14–8, 16–55 and 19–2 on these matters.
[75] LR 9.8.6. See further below, para.14–29.
[76] It will have to account for its compliance with any French code applicable to it, but, even then, only if it has primary listing in London: LR 9.8.7.
[77] There are some 2000 British companies listed on the Exchange. However, most of the Listing Rules apply to all companies with primary listings, no matter where incorporated.

recent years and it is unlikely that the importance of this category will diminish in the future. However, it is not obvious that the additional regulation of such companies should be confined to listed companies and not extend to those whose shares are traded on "secondary" markets, such as the Alternative Investment Market ("AIM").[78] Nor is it obvious that such additional regulation should be embodied in the Listing Rules rather than the Companies Act.

Because of the importance, even in core company law matters, of a company having its securities traded on a public market, an ambiguity has arisen about the term "public company". For the company lawyer it normally still means a company which for the purposes of the Companies Act is public, not private, as discussed in the previous section. For the capital markets lawyer, that is not enough to make a company public: it must also have offered its shares to the public and/ or have made a public market available for the trading of the shares. The ambiguity can be avoided by using the term "publicly traded" to refer to the latter type of company.

Unlimited companies

1–13   In a way, this is a very surprising category to find in the legislation. In an unlimited company there is no limit, provided by the shares or a guarantee, on the liability of its members. An unlimited company may have a share capital (in order to provide working capital and to measure each member's rights in the company), but that capital no longer acts as a limit on liability.[79] Since limited liability is the advantage which is said often to drive entrepreneurs' decisions to incorporate, it is notable that the Act provides a category of company in which this advantage is forgone. It is not surprising that few unlimited companies are formed,[80] and it has never been suggested that there should be separate legislation for such companies. Nevertheless, the current law does take the view that some regulation otherwise applicable to companies registered under the Act need not be applied to unlimited companies. This is true in particular of the obligation to publish the company's accounts,[81] since creditors of such companies can rely on the credit of the shareholders, and the prohibition on a company acquiring its own shares[82] (again a potential threat to creditors who are confined to the company's assets for the satisfaction of their claims). Consequently, the unlimited company may be attractive for those shareholders who are willing to

---

[78] The CLR thought the Combined Code, for example, should apply to all quoted companies: Completing, para.4.44.

[79] s.3(4). However, only a private company can be unlimited; a public company must be limited by shares or guarantee: s.4(2).

[80] Only between 100 and 200 a year over the period 1996–2001: DTI, *Companies in 2001–2002*, (2002), Table B1.

[81] s.448. See para.21–34. Unlimited companies must still produce accounts for their members.

[82] s.658. See para.13–7.

stand behind their company and for whom the advantages of privacy or flexibility of capital structure are important.

Micro companies

We now turn to two other possible classifications of companies, **1–14** which, however, are not currently embedded in the legislation. At the other end of the scale from the listed company is the very small company where the directors and the shareholders are the same people and where the size of the business carried on is also small. The Company Law Review reported research which indicated that 65 per cent of active companies have a turnover of less than £250,000, 70 per cent have only two shareholders and 90 per cent fewer than five shareholders.[83] However, the Review came out against separate legislation for companies whose directors and shareholders were identical and whose businesses were small in size (sometimes called "micro" companies) on the grounds that it would be undesirable to create a regulatory barrier to expansion, which might occur if a company became subject to different rules when its directors and shareholders ceased to be identical.[84] For the same reason, it was opposed to a distinct regime for micro companies even within a single Act.[85] Instead, it applied most of its reforms to private companies as a whole, but some of them were crafted as default rules drafted with micro companies particularly in mind, and it was expected that private companies of a larger size would opt out of them. The advantage of such an approach is that the legal regime does not formally cease to be applicable to a particular small company as it expands, though it is likely to find the regime less convenient and thus to opt out of it.

The 2006 Act took up many of the CLR's proposals in this area and, thus, it may be said that the present Act recognises the special needs of micro companies, but does not use the micro company as a formal regulatory category. Those who want a corporate form which gives more flexibility than the private company provides, especially in relation to internal decision-making structure, must go to the Limited Liability Partnership.[86]

Not-for-profit companies

The term "not-for-profit company" is not formally used in the leg- **1–15** islation, but the law has moved in recent years to provide corporate forms suitable for such use. We have noted that the Act has long provided a form of company, the company limited by guarantee, which may be suitable for carrying on a not-for-profit business, but

---

[83] Developing, paras 6.8–6.9.
[84] Strategic Framework, Ch.5.2.
[85] Developing, Ch.6; Final Report I, para.2.7.
[86] See above, para.1–3.

that the guarantee company and the company limited by shares are not regulated in fundamentally different ways.[87] Should there be a separate form of incorporation for the not-for-profit company? The principled argument in favour of a separate regime for such companies, as exists in many jurisdictions, is that company law and legislation has been designed primarily with commercial companies in mind, even if the corporate form is open to not-for-profit organisations. To some extent the community interest company, created in 2004,[88] provides a positive answer to that question. Although a CIC is either a company limited by shares or limited by guarantee and formed under the Companies Act 2006, what the Companies (Audit, Investigations and Community Enterprise) Act 2004 provides through the CIC is a set of rules into which those forming a company can opt and which is designed to meet the needs of a company whose aims are to promote the interests of the community or a section of it rather than to make a private profit for its members.[89]

In the case of not-for-profit companies which are also charities[90] there is the additional argument that they are presently subject to the burden of double regulation, under the Companies Act and the charities legislation.[91] Consequently, there is the additional argument here that a special form of charitable company should be created and made subject to a single regulatory regime, namely, that for charities. Following a lead from the Charity Commission for England and Wales, the Company Law Review recommended that a separate form of incorporation for charitable companies should indeed be introduced—the Charitable Incorporated Organisation ("CIO")—but only on an optional basis.[92] This recommendation was implemented by the Charities Act 2006 for England and Wales. A CIO is again a corporate form available to be adopted by companies whose purposes are charitable and designed for their particular needs. However, unlike a CIC, a CIO is not registered by the Registrar of Companies under the Companies Act 2006 but by the Charity Commissioners under the Charities Act 1993. Nevertheless, much of the law applicable to CIOs will be familiar to a general company lawyer and some of the decisions on the companies legislation will be capable of being read across to the rules governing the CIO.[93]

---

[87] See above, paras 1–5.

[88] See para.1–6 above.

[89] Profitable trading will be a condition for the company's survival but that profit will be devoted mainly to the promotion of the community objectives.

[90] For the categorisation of not-for-profit companies see above, para.1–4.

[91] Charities Act 1993 in England and Wales; Charities and Trustee Investment (Scotland) Act 2005. The regulation of charities is a devolved matter.

[92] Developing, paras 9.7–9.40; Completing, paras 9.2–9.7; Final Report I, paras 4.63–4.67.

[93] Charities Act 2006, s.34 and Sch.7, which operates by way of inserting into the Charities Act 1993 a new Part 8A and Sch.5B.

UNREGISTERED COMPANIES AND OTHER FORMS OF INCORPORATION

Statutory and chartered companies

We now move beyond an analysis of different types of registered **1–16** companies to look at forms of incorporation, alternative to registration under the Companies Act, which are available even for the carrying on of large-scale business. When the machinery for the formation of a company by registration under a general Act of Parliament was introduced in 1844, it supplemented, but did not replace, the existing methods of forming companies, namely by special Act of Parliament or by means of a charter granted by the Crown, either under the Royal Prerogative or under powers conferred upon the Crown by statute to grant charters of incorporation.[94] The continued effectiveness of such incorporations was implicitly recognised by section 716 of the Companies Act 1985, prohibiting partnerships of more than 20 persons.[95] This ban could be complied with by registration under the Companies Act but also by incorporation "in pursuance of some other Act of Parliament or of letters patent". In fact, in 2006 there were 50 companies in existence formed under special Acts and 798 incorporated by Royal Charter.[96]

In the past, statutory incorporation by private Acts of public utilities, such as railway, gas, water and electricity undertakings, was comparatively common since the undertakings would require powers and monopolistic rights which needed a special legislative grant. During the nineteenth century, therefore, public general Acts[97] were passed providing for standard clauses deemed to be incorporated into the private Acts, unless expressly excluded. As a result of post-war nationalisation measures, most of these statutory companies were taken over by public boards or corporations set up by public Acts (but many, if not most, of them have now been "privatised" and become registered companies). These boards and corporations fall outside the scope of this book. But some statutory companies remain and others may be formed. The statute under which they are formed need not incorporate them but today this is invariably done.

As for companies chartered by the Crown, such a charter normally confers corporate personality, but, as it was regarded as dubious

---

[94] Under many ad hoc statutes the Crown has been given power to grant charters in cases falling outside its prerogative powers. Moreover, by the Chartered Companies Acts 1837 and 1884, the prerogative was extended by empowering the Crown to grant charters for a limited period and to extend them. Thus the BBC Charter was for ten years and has been prolonged from time to time.

[95] See above, para.1–2.

[96] DTI, above fn.21, Table E3.

[97] The Companies Clauses Acts 1845–1889. These Acts, containing the general corporate powers and duties, were supplemented in the case of particular utilities by various other "Clauses Acts", e.g. the Lands Clauses Consolidation and Railways Clauses Consolidation Acts 1845, the Electric Lighting (Clauses) Act 1899, and numerous Waterworks Clauses Acts, and Gasworks Clauses Acts.

policy for the Crown to confer a full charter of incorporation on an ordinary trading concern, it was empowered by the Trading Companies Act 1834 and the Chartered Companies Act 1837 to confer by letters patent all or any of the privileges of incorporation without actually granting a charter. Today an ordinary trading concern would not contemplate trying to obtain a Royal Charter, for incorporation under the Companies Acts would be far quicker and cheaper. In practice, therefore, this method of incorporation is used only by organisations formed for charitable, or quasi-charitable, objects, such as learned and artistic societies, schools and colleges, which want the greater prestige that a charter is thought to confer.

1–17   However, there is an important regulatory policy issue arising out of the fact that statutory and "letters patent" companies are not created by registration under the Companies Act. Unless express provision is made to the contrary, the provisions of the Companies Act will not apply to such companies. This may give such "unregistered" companies an unfair competitive advantage as against companies formed by registration under the Act, and may mean that those dealing with such companies are inadequately protected. This problem was addressed, but only partially solved, by section 718 of the 1985 Act, which through Schedule 22 and regulations made under the section, applied some, but not all, of the provisions of the Act to unregistered companies. That section has been replaced by section 1043 of the 2006 Act (constituting the whole of Chapter 2 of Part 33).[98] This broadly follows its predecessor and applies to "bodies incorporated in and having a principal place of business in the United Kingdom",[99] unless they are incorporated by or under a general public Act of Parliament.[100] In addition, unregistered companies falling within the section must have been formed for the purpose of carrying on a business for gain.[101] In other words, the problems of unfair competition and inadequate protection were not perceived as arising in relation to not-for-profit companies, which, as we have seen, constitute the main type of company created by the Crown.

The section provides that those parts of the Act which apply to unregistered companies are to be set out in regulations,[102] and any charter, enactment or other instrument (e.g. letters patent) constituting the company is subordinated to those parts of the Act which

---

[98] Part 33 is scheduled to come into force on October 1, 2009.

[99] This is an interesting nod on the part of British law towards the "real seat" theory of incorporation (see para.6–15, below), for this section does not apply to a British unregistered company which does not have a place of business in the UK. By contrast, a company registered under the Companies Act will be governed by that Act even if it conducts the whole of its business outside the UK.

[100] s.1043(1)(a). This would include the Companies Act itself but also, for example, the Industrial and Provident Societies Act 1965. See below, para.1–18.

[101] s.1043(1)(b). Open-ended investment companies are also excluded (s.1043(1)(d)) as are other unregistered companies specifically excluded by direction of the Secretary of State (s.1043(1)(c)).

[102] s.1043(2) (3).

are made applicable.[103] Under the 1985 Act the main areas of regulation so applied were those relating to accounts and audit, corporate capacity and directors' authority, company investigations and fraudulent trading. This left some large and important parts of the Act which did not apply to unregistered companies, such as those dealing with the removal of directors, fair dealing by directors, distribution of profits and assets, registration of charges, arrangement and reconstructions and takeover offers, and unfair prejudice. The Company Law Review recommended that any new Companies Act should be applied more extensively to unregistered companies.[104] Regulations to be made under the 2006 Act[105] implement this policy to some considerable degree[106] by applying to unregistered companies, in addition to those provisions already applied, the whole of Part 10 (directors),[107] Part 11 (derivative actions),[108] Part 13 (resolutions and meetings),[109] Part 14 (political donations and expenditure),[110] the provisions on distributions,[111] as well as Chapters 2 and 3 of Part 28 (impediments to takeovers and squeeze out/sell out rights.[112]

An alternative policy embodied in the Act towards unregistered companies is to encourage them to register under the Act and thus become subject to its provisions in full. This encouragement is provided by enabling them to register under the Companies Act without having to form a new company and wind up the old one, although sometimes registration under the Act is a step in a plan designed to produce the winding-up of the company once it has registered. The method of doing this is dealt with in Chapter 1 of Part 33 of the Act. As far as statutory and letters patent companies are concerned, a basic distinction is drawn between those which are "joint stock companies" (essentially those with a share capital)[113] and those which are not. Only the former may make use of this special registration process and must register as a company limited by shares and not as an unlimited or guarantee company.[114] The details of the effect of registration, provisions for the automatic vesting of property, savings

---

[103] s.1043(4).
[104] Completing, paras 9.13–9.17 and Final I, paras 11.34–11.37.
[105] The (draft) Companies (Unregistered Companies) Regulations 2008.
[106] Not applied, as yet, though on the list of applicable provisions suggested by the CLR, are the rules on unfair prejudice (see Ch.20), the registration of charges (Ch.31) and company names (Ch.4).
[107] See Chs 14 and 16.
[108] See Ch.17.
[109] See Ch.15.
[110] See para.16–62.
[111] See Ch.12.
[112] See Ch.28.
[113] See s.1041.
[114] See s.1040(4), qualifying the broader provisions of s.1040(3).

for existing liabilities and rights and similar matters are to be dealt with in regulations.[115]

Building societies, friendly societies and co-operatives

1–18 Although the Victorian legislature devoted considerable efforts to the elaboration of what we today call companies legislation in order to facilitate the carrying on of large-scale business, it did not confine its efforts to this legislation. Even in the area of commercial activities, the legislature was aware that the company form, despite its flexibility, would not suit all types of business, especially where the members of the organisation were intended to have a different relationship with it than shareholders with a company. Some of these other forms of incorporation were confined to specific activities, such as the building societies,[116] whose principal purpose is to make loans secured on residential property. The building society is an incorporated body, very similar to a company—which is why it has been easy for many of them in recent years to "demutualise" by converting themselves into registered companies—but its members are those who deposit money with it or borrow from it rather than those who invest risk capital in it. A less striking example is the friendly societies legislation,[117] which until recently contemplated only the formation of unincorporated bodies, but now permits incorporation of bodies whose purposes must include the provision on a mutual basis of insurance against loss of income arising out of sickness, unemployment or retirement. The friendly society constituted, if you like, a self-help response to the perils of ordinary life before the rise of the welfare state from the beginning of the twentieth century, and still such societies have a role to play in the areas neglected by the state system.

However, probably the most important of the "non-company" incorporated bodies were those created under the Industrial and Provident Societies Acts,[118] which provide, inter alia, for the incorporation of co-operative societies, which can be deployed in a wide range of commercial settings. Membership and financial rights are accorded to people in co-operatives usually on the basis of the extent to which they have participated in the business of the society, whether

---

[115] s.1042. This Part of the Act also allows for the registration of the few remaining "deed of settlement" companies, a private law form of quasi-incorporation which was invented to avoid the costs of statutory or royal incorporation and which was overtaken by the introduction of formation by registration under a general Act in the middle of the nineteenth century. For details, see the sixth edition of this book at pp.29–31.

[116] The current legislation is the Building Societies Acts 1986–1997, but it can trace its origins to an Act of 1874.

[117] Currently, the Friendly Societies Act 1992, but that legislation can be traced as far back as the Friendly Societies Act 1793.

[118] Currently that of 2002, but again legislation traceable back to the middle of the nineteenth century.

as customers (as in retail co-operatives), producers (for example, agricultural co-operatives) or as employees (worker co-operatives). There were over 9500 societies formed under this Act in existence in 2006,[119] and they are of importance in some limited areas of commercial activity.[120] However, co-operatives, friendly societies and building societies are outside the scope of this book.[121]

Open-ended investment companies
The Victorian penchant for devising corporate vehicles for specialised   **1–19**
purposes was revived in 1996 with the creation of the Open-Ended Investment Company. It is perhaps an indication of the changes in the nature of the UK economy over the previous 150 years that, this time, the specialised purpose was that of "collective investment". Broadly, collective investment means the coming together of a number of investors, often a large number of relatively small investors, who pool their resources for the purposes of achieving better returns on their investments. Those investments will typically be the purchase of corporate securities, though the range of investments is not confined to these. This better return, it is hoped, will result partly from the greater size of the fund to be invested and partly from the employment of specialised management to discharge the investment task.[122]

Both the trust (in the shape of "unit trusts", which can trace their origin back to the 1860s) and the registered company (in the shape of the "investment company") have long been used for this purpose. In the case of an investment company the investor buys shares in a company whose resources are allocated to the purchase of investments. However, as we have noted already in relation to guarantee companies,[123] a company limited by shares suffers from the disadvantage that the repurchase of shares by the company is not freely available. An investor who wishes to dispose of his or her investment in the company will normally have to sell the shares to another investor, but the market price of the shares, depending on supply and demand, may well be less than the value of the underlying investments held by the company which the share represents. These difficulties can be avoided by the use of the unit trust, which is free to make a standing offer to buy back units from investors at a price which fully reflects the value of assets held in the trust. However, in

[119] DTI, *Companies in 2005–2006* (2006), Table E3. The registration function has now been transferred, somewhat bizarrely, to the Financial Services Authority.

[120] For a fascinating comparative attempt to explain the relative failure of the co-operatives but also their partial success see H. Hansmann, *The Ownership of Enterprise* (1996).

[121] As is the trade union, that other expression of the Victorian genius for collective self-help, but with whose legal status the legislature encountered much more difficulty.

[122] The legal definition of a "collective investment scheme" is to be found in s.235 of the FSMA 2000.

[123] See above, para.1–5.

the 1990s the trust came to be regarded as an English peculiarity which might not fare well in international competition with continental European and US investment funds, organised on a corporate basis.

The Government's response was the creation of a corporate vehicle which had the same freedom as the trust to repay to investors the value of the shares held, the value being calculated on a similar basis. Thus, s.262 of the Financial Services and Markets Act 2000 (the current governing legislation) permits the Treasury to make regulations for the creation of corporate bodies to be known as open-ended investment companies, and an essential ingredient of the definition of an OEIC is that it provides to investors in it an expectation that they shall be able to realise their investment within a reasonable period and on the basis of a value calculated mainly by reference to the value of the property held within the scheme by the company.[124] This power has been exercised in regulations,[125] which require the OEIC to provide that its shareholders be entitled either to have their shares redeemed or repurchased by the OEIC upon request at a price related to the value of the scheme property or to sell their shares on a public exchange at the same price.[126] In general, the Regulations are a combination of provisions drawn from the Companies Act 1985[127] (but without the crucial general principle to be found in the companies legislation that a company limited by shares cannot acquire its own shares)[128] and from the Financial Services and Markets Act concerning the authorisation of those wishing to engage in investment business.[129] It is perhaps an indication that the latter was regarded as the more important of the OEIC's parents that regulation of the act of formation and the task of maintaining the register of OEICs is given to the Financial Services Authority.[130]

EUROPEAN COMMUNITY FORMS OF INCORPORATION

European Economic Interest Grouping

1–20   Legislation creating corporate bodies remains mainly a matter for the Member States of the European Community, but there are now two forms of incorporation provided by European Community law. Both are concerned to promote cross-border co-operation among compa-

---

[124]   FSMA 2000, s.236(3).
[125]   Open-Ended Investment Company Regulations 2001/1228, as amended by SI 2005/923.
[126]   reg.15(11).
[127]   Pt III of the Regulations.
[128]   See para.13–7.
[129]   Pt II of the Regulations.
[130]   reg.3 and Pt IV.

nies formed in different Member States; both are in consequence rather specialised forms of incorporation; both are implemented by Regulations, which are therefore directly applicable in the Member States (though in both cases supplementary national legislation is required); but the two differ in most other respects. The European Economic Interest Grouping is based on the model of the French *Groupement d'Intérêt Economique*, and is designed to enable existing business undertakings in different Member States to form an autonomous body to provide common services ancillary to the primary activities of its members. Any profits it makes belong to its members and they are jointly and severally responsible for its liabilities. In addition, the members of the EEIG, acting as a body, may take "any decision for the purpose of achieving the objects of the grouping".[131] Although the managers of the EEIG also constitute an organ of the Grouping and may bind it as against third parties, it is clear that the Regulation does not insist upon the delegation of management authority from the members to the managers. For this reason and because of the lack of limited liability for the members, the EEIG is as much like a partnership as like a company.

The basic requirements for the formation of an EEIG are simply the conclusion of a written contract between the members and registration at a registry in the Member State where it is to have its principal establishment. The members must be at least two in number and may be companies incorporated under national laws, partnerships or natural persons, but at least two of the members must carry on their principal activities in different Member States.[132] The Regulation[133] confers upon the EEIG full legal capacity, though whether it is afforded corporate personality is left to national law,[134] which is also left with considerable scope to supplement the mandatory provisions of the Regulation. The United Kingdom supplemented the EC Regulations by the European Economic Interest Grouping Regulations 1989[135] which nominate the Companies Registrar as the registering authority. A number of the sections of the Companies Act 1985[136] and the Insolvency Act[137] are applied to an EEIG as if it were a company registered under the Companies Act and it may be wound up as an unregistered company under Pt V of the Insolvency Act.[138]

The ancillary nature of the EEIG is illustrated by the restrictions

---

[131] Council Regulation 2137/85, [1985] OJ L199/1, Art.16.
[132] Council Regulation 2137/85, [1985] OJ L199/1, Art.4.
[133] Council Regulation 2137/85, [1985] OJ L199/1.
[134] In the case of EEIG's with their principal establishment in Great Britain corporate personality is conferred by the European Economic Interest Grouping Regulations 1989 (SI 1989/638), reg.3.
[135] See previous note.
[136] reg.18 and Sch.4.
[137] reg.19.
[138] In which case the provisions of the Company Directors Disqualification Act 1986 (see Ch.10, below) apply: reg.20.

placed upon it by Article 3 of the EC Regulation. The general principle is that the EEIG's activities "shall be related to the economic
activities of its members and must not be more than ancillary to those
activities". The latter part of the restriction, in particular, is then
supplemented by prohibitions on the EEIG (a) exercising management over its members' activities or those of another undertaking; (b)
holding shares in a member company; (c) employing more than 500
workers;[139] or (d) being a member of another EEIG. Given the above,
it was always likely that the take-up of the EEIG in Britain would not
be high. That has turned out to be the case, though the number of
EEIGs with principal establishment in Great Britain has grown
steadily from 23 in 1991 to 85 in 1995[140] to 157 in 2001[141] to 185 in
2006.[142] The EEIG will receive little further discussion in this book.

The European Company (societas europaea or "SE")

1–21   The European Company,[143] by contrast, is not intended for ancillary
activities but rather to facilitate the cross-border mergers of companies and their mainstream activities, something which the creation of
a single market within the Community has promoted. Of course, a
cross-border merger does not necessarily need a European Company.
An English company could merge with a French company, so as to
produce a resulting company which was either English or French (or
indeed registered in some third State), though in fact such an exercise
has been difficult to carry out in the past, but should be facilitated by
the Cross-Border Mergers Directive.[144] Alternatively, the English or
French company can offer to buy the shares of the other company (a
process known as a takeover offer).[145] If the offer is accepted by the
shareholders of the offeree company, that company becomes a subsidiary of the offeror company, but the important point for present
purposes is that, in a takeover, there is no need for structural changes
to the pre-existing companies: the two companies continue as before
after the takeover, albeit with different shareholders in the target
company (and perhaps also in the bidder). In this way, the English or
French company could build up a string of subsidiary companies

---

[139] This restriction seems to have been motivated in part to avoid the EEIG being used by
German companies to avoid domestic worker participation legislation, which bites at the
500 employee level.
[140] DTI, *Companies in 1995–96* (1996), Table E3.
[141] DTI, *Companies in 2000–2001* (2001), Table E3.
[142] DTI, *Companies in 2005–2006* (2006), Table E3.
[143] There is also a statute for a European Co-operative Society (SCE) (Council Regulation
No.1435/2003, OJ L207/1, 18.8.2003) and an accompanying directive on the involvement of
employees (Directive 2003/72/EC, OJ L207/25, 18.8.2003). They have been transposed
domestically by the European Cooperative Society Regulations 2006/2078. These are not
discussed further in this book.
[144] Directive 2005/56/EC. See Ch.29 below.
[145] See below, Ch.28.

operating in as many Member States of the Community as was desired.

What can the European Company add to this situation? Its advantages from a company law perspective are mainly psychological. In the situation described at the end of the previous paragraph, the English (or French) company had built up a group structure which operated effectively throughout the Community, but the lead or head company in the group was clearly identified as English (or French, as the case might be). It is argued that a cross-border group might be more acceptable to those who work in or with it if it could be formed under a Community type of incorporation, which was not identified with any particular Member State,[146] and there might even be some saving of transaction costs if all the existing national subsidiaries could be folded into a single SE. Thus, the English and French companies, when they originally merge, might choose to do so by forming an SE, to replace the existing French and English companies. In addition or instead, the controllers of the group might choose to roll their various national subsidiaries into an SE, whether the top company in the group continued to be an English company or a French company or was a newly formed SE.

This was the vision of the original proponents of the SE, put forward as long ago as 1959.[147] By the time the SE was adopted by the Community (in 2001[148]) and came into force (in October 2004), however, this vision had been crucially compromised. Essential to the concept of a Community form of incorporation, divorced from the law of the Member States, is the notion that the SE law should provide a comprehensive code of company law rules for the SE. However, the adopted version of the SE not only fails to regulate adjacent legal areas such as taxation, competition law, intellectual property and insolvency,[149] even within core company law the SE law relies heavily on the national laws of the Member States. The provisions specified at Community level for the SE come near to detailed regulation in only four areas: formation, transfer of the registered office of the SE,[150] board structure and employee involvement.[151] In the latter two areas the rules applying to any particular SE will vary according to the choice made by the SE itself, any agreement made

---

[146] It is easy to overstate the force of this psychological argument: there is no guarantee that the shareholdings or management of a SE will be spread equally across the Member States in which it operates.

[147] By Professor P. Sanders of the University of Rotterdam, though the French claim co-paternity.

[148] Council Regulation 2157/2001/EC, [2001] OJ L294/1, and the accompanying Directive on worker involvement (Council Directive 2001/86/EC, [2001] OJ L294/22). The European Company must use the abbreviation SE as either a prefix or suffix to its name and in the future other types of entity will not be able to avail themselves of this acronym: Regulation, Art.11.

[149] Regulation 2157/2001, Art.63 and Preamble 20.

[150] See para.6–13.

[151] This is the matter dealt with in the accompanying Directive. See below Ch.14.

between the SE and the employee representatives or to the national origins of the companies forming the SE. Outside these four areas, the SE is to be governed by the law relating to public companies in the jurisdiction in which it is registered.[152] Thus, it seems that there will be at least as many different SEs as there are Member States of the Community. This fact is emphasised by the absence of a Community registry for the SE. The SE has to be registered in one of the Member States of the EU. Since the SE is to be embedded in the domestic law of the State of registration, this is obviously the correct technical rule, but it does make clear the fact that, for example, a German-registered SE will look rather different from a British-registered one.[153]

1–22   What the SE law achieves is only partial harmonisation of the company law applying to that body.[154] In fact, since those forming an SE apparently have a free choice of the State in which they register their SE—it does not have to be one of the States in which existing businesses operate—the SE rules may promote a certain competition among the Member States to make their rules transposing the SE, and by extension their national company laws, attractive to businesses. However, it should be noted that the requirement to have registered and head offices in the same State will constitute a break on such competition.[155]

Unlike a domestic company, the SE can be formed only by existing companies[156] and not by natural persons. In line with its cross-border objectives, those existing companies must already have a cross-border presence. The four methods of formation are: merger, formation of a holding SE, formation of a subsidiary SE and transformation.[157] The merger route is confined to public companies[158] (which in this context includes an SE) and to certain types of merger.[159] The companies must have registered and head offices in the Community and at least two of them must be incorporated in different Member States. A holding SE can be formed by public or private companies if at least two of them are incorporated in different Member States or for two years have had a subsidiary or branch in another Member State. The

---

[152] Arts 9(1)(c)(ii) and 10 of Regulation 2157/2001. It seems that this happens automatically, by force of the Regulation, without the Member State having to provide for it or to identify the applicable parts of the domestic law. For this reason the European Company statute, as adopted, is relatively short (70 articles in the Regulation and 17 in the Directive), whereas the 1975 proposal contained 284 articles.

[153] It has been unkindly remarked that the SE proposal started as a "sausage" and ended up as a "sausage skin".

[154] Klaus Hopt, *The European Company under the Nice Compromise: Major Breakthrough or Small Coin for Europe?* [2000] *Euredia* 465.

[155] See para.6–13ff.

[156] And sometimes analogous legal entities.

[157] Regulation 2157/2001, Art. 2 and ss.2–4. In addition, an established SE can set up further SEs as subsidiaries: *ibid.*, Art.3(2).

[158] Including, of course, their equivalents in other Member States.

[159] Merger by acquisition and merger by formation of a new company: see para.29–10.

SE in this case results from a form of share-for-share takeover offer, made by the new SE to the shareholders of the founding companies. A subsidiary SE may be formed by a similar set of companies, in this case by the forming companies subscribing for the shares of the SE. The most tightly regulated form of incorporation of the SE is that of transformation: a public company which for at least two years has had a subsidiary company governed by the law of another Member State may convert itself into an SE. The Regulation also provides for the conversion back of an SE into a public company governed wholly by domestic law.[160] It will be clear from this that the SE is a form of incorporation not available to companies incorporated outside the European Union.

Since the SE is so much part of domestic law, the rules applying to SEs registered in Great Britain will be referred to from time to time in this book. However, the take-up of this legal form has been rather limited. Throughout the Community as a whole only some sixty SEs had been formed as of early 2007 and only twelve of these had operations and employees (as opposed to being shelf companies).[161] There were three SEs registered in the United Kingdom, but all without operations and employees. Despite these discouraging figures the Commission has recently committed itself to producing an equivalent form of Community incorporation specifically designed for private companies.

CONCLUSION

After a period of stability in the variety of legal forms on offer to those who wish to incorporate their businesses—before 2000 the last significant innovation had been the introduction of the private company at the beginning of the twentieth century—at least four significant new forms of incorporation have been made available in less than a decade: the limited liability partnership, the community interest company, the charitable incorporated organisation and the European Company (or societas europaea). These innovations reflect different driving forces at the policy level. The LLP was a response to the desire of large partnerships to find a form of incorporation with limited liability in an increasingly litigious world which nevertheless provided the tax advantages and internal management flexibility traditionally associated with the ordinary partnership. The CIC reflected the Government's desire to encourage the deployment of **1–23**

---

[160] Regulation 2157/2001, Art. 66.

[161] See *www.seeurope-network.org/homepages/seeurope/secompanies.html#established.* The legality of forming shelf SEs has been contested on the grounds that there will have been no negotiations with the employee representatives over employee involvement.

entrepreneurial skills towards the solution of social problems and the CIO a desire to involve private bodies in the delivery of welfare state objectives. The SE reflected the goal of the European Commission and Community more generally to deepen the single European market by promoting cross-border mergers. Of the three, only the last produced an innovation in the core areas of company law, but, so far, its up-take, as we have noted, has been limited.

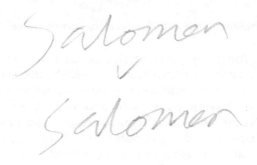

Salomon
v
Salomon

CHAPTER 2

ADVANTAGES AND DISADVANTAGES OF INCORPORATION

LEGAL ENTITY DISTINCT FROM ITS MEMBERS

As already emphasised, the fundamental attribute of corporate personality—from which indeed all the other consequences flow—is that the corporation is a legal entity distinct from its members. Hence it is capable of enjoying rights and of being subject to duties which are not the same as those enjoyed or borne by its members. In other words, it has "legal personality" and is often described as an *artificial person* in contrast with a human being, a *natural person*.[1]

2–1

As we have seen, corporate personality became an attribute of the normal joint stock company only at a comparatively late stage in its development, and it was not until *Salomon v Salomon & Co*[2] at the end of the nineteenth century that its implications were fully grasped even by the courts. The facts of this justly celebrated case were as follows:

---

[1] A company, even if it has only one member, is a "corporation aggregate" as opposed to the somewhat anomalous "corporation sole" in which an office, e.g. that of a bishop, is personified.

[2] [1897] A.C. 22, HL.

Salomon had for many years carried on as a sole trader a prosperous business as a leather merchant. In 1892, he decided to convert it into a limited company and for this purpose Salomon & Co Ltd was formed with Salomon, his wife and five of his children as members and Salomon as managing director. The company purchased the business as a going concern for £39,000—"a sum which represented the sanguine expectations of a fond owner rather than anything that can be called a businesslike or reasonable estimate of value".[3] The price was satisfied by £10,000 in debentures, conferring a charge over all the company's assets, £20,000 in fully paid £1 shares and the balance in cash. The result was that Salomon held 20,001 of the 20,007 shares issued, and each of the remaining six shares was held by a member of his family, apparently as a nominee for him. The company almost immediately ran into difficulties and only a year later the then holder of the debentures appointed a receiver and the company went into liquidation. Its assets were sufficient to discharge the debentures but nothing was left for the unsecured creditors. In these circumstances Vaughan Williams J. and a strong Court of Appeal held that the whole transaction was contrary to the true intent of the Companies Act and that the company was a mere sham, and an alias, agent, trustee or nominee for Salomon who remained the real proprietor of the business. As such he was liable to indemnify the company against its trading debts. But the House of Lords unanimously reversed this decision. They held that the company has been validly formed since the Act merely required seven members holding at least one share each. It said nothing about their being independent, or that they should take a substantial interest in the undertaking, or that they should have a mind and will of their own, or that there should be anything like a balance of power in the constitution of the company. Hence the business belonged to the company and not to Salomon, and Salomon was *its* agent. In the blunt words of Lord Halsbury L.C.:[4]

> "Either the limited company was a legal entity or it was not. If it was, the business belonged to it and not to Mr Salomon. If it was not, there was no person and no thing to be an agent at all; and it is impossible to say at the same time that there is a company and there is not."

Or, as Lord Macnaghten put it:[5]

> "The company is at law a different person altogether from the subscribers ...; and, though it may be that after incorporation

[3] [1897] A.C. 22, HL, at 49, per Lord Macnaghten.
[4] [1897] A.C. 22, HL, at 31.
[5] [1897] A.C. 22, HL, at 51.

SALOMON v SALOMON

the business is precisely the same as it was before, and the same persons are managers, and the same hands receive the profits, the company is not in law the agent of the subscribers or trustee for them. Nor are the subscribers, as members, liable in any shape or form, except to the extent and in the manner provided by the Act."[6]

The *Salomon* case established that (a) provided the formalities of the Act are complied with, a company will be validly incorporated, even if it is only a "one person" company and (b) the courts will be reluctant to treat a shareholder as personally liable for the debts of the company by "piercing the corporate veil".[7] Whereas acceptance of the former argument would have involved denying the separate legal personality of the company, the second could have been upheld without that consequence, though it would have involved undermining the concomitant of separate legal personality, i.e. limited liability (see below).

2–2

The objection of the unsecured creditors in this case was based on the overvaluation of the business which was sold to the company in exchange for shares and debentures in it. In the case of a public company today, the business would be the subject of an independent valuation so far as it was used to pay up shares,[8] but in the case of a private company, and even that of debentures issued by a public company, the main protection of unsecured creditors lies in disclosure of the company's financial position.[9] Unlike some countries, English law has developed no significant doctrine whereby loans to a company by its major shareholders are treated as equity. Even today, the best the unsecured creditors could hope for is that a floating charge securing a debenture might be invalidated if there was a successful petition for a winding-up or an administration order within two years of the creation of the charge.[10] Thus, Salomon was able to give himself protection against the downside risks of his business by taking a position as secured creditor through the debentures, whilst taking the full benefit of any upside gains through his (in effect) one

---

[6] For an early statutory recognition of the same principle, see the House of Commons (Disqualification) Act 1782, which disqualified those holding Government contracts from election to Parliament but expressly provided (s.3) that the prohibition did not extend to members of incorporated companies holding such contracts.

[7] See further Ch.8.

[8] See para.11–12. However, since Salomon was the only beneficial shareholder, it really mattered little to him whether he was issued with 20,000 or 10 shares in exchange for the business, for the value of the shares in aggregate (no matter how many or how few), would be the same, i.e. they represent the economic value (if any) of the business. However, independent valuation might protect creditors from being misled about the value of the assets contributed to the company.

[9] See ch.21 below.

[10] Insolvency Act 1986, s.245. See para.32–16.

hundred per cent. shareholding.[11] Of course, this decision does not mean that a promoter can with impunity defraud the company which he forms or swindle his existing creditors. In the *Salomon* case it was argued that the company was entitled to rescind in view of the wilful overvaluation of the business sold to it. But the House held that in fact there was no fraud at all since the shareholders were fully conversant with what was being done. Had Salomon made a profit which he concealed from his fellow shareholders the position would have been different.[12] Nor was there any fraud on Salomon's pre-incorporation creditors, all of whom were paid off in full out of the purchase price. Otherwise, they or Salomon's trustee in bankruptcy might have been entitled to upset the sale.[13]

In any event, since the *Salomon* case, the complete separation of the company and its members has never been doubted. The decision opened up new vistas to company lawyers and the world of commerce. Not only did it finally establish the legality of the "one-person" company (long before EC law required this) and showed that incorporation was as readily available to the small private partnership and sole trader as to the large public company, but it also revealed that it was possible for a trader not merely to limit his liability to the money which he put into the enterprise but even to avoid any serious risk to the major part of that by subscribing for debentures rather than shares. This result may seem shocking, and the decision has been much criticised.[14] A partial justification for it is that the public deal with a limited company at their peril and know, or should know, what to expect. In particular a search of the company's file at Companies House should reveal its latest annual accounts and whether there are any charges on the company's assets.[15] But the accounts will probably be months out of date and, in the case of a small or medium-sized company, may be rather uninformative.[16] Nor does everyone having dealings with a company have the time or knowledge needed to search the file. The experienced

---

[11] But, in this particular case, Salomon seems to have been one of the victims rather than the villain of the piece for he had mortgaged his debentures and used the money to try to support the tottering company. However, the result would have been the same if he had not, and even if he had been the only creditor to receive anything from the business which was "his" in fact though not in law.

[12] See para.5–2.

[13] Under what are now ss.423 to 425 of the Insolvency Act 1986.

[14] See, e.g. O. Kahn-Freund, "Some Reflections on Company Law Reform" in (1944) 7 M.L.R. 54 (a thought-provoking article still well worth study) in which it is described as a "calamitous decision". For a more positive assessment see D. Goddard, "Corporate Personality—Limited Recourse and its Limits" in R. Grantham and C. Rickett (eds) *Corporate Personality in the Twentieth Century* (Hart Publishing, 1998). On the rationales for limited liability, see para.8–1.

[15] But not necessarily the amount secured; most companies grant floating charges to their bankers to secure "all sums due or to become due" on their current overdrafts and the register of charges will not give any indication of the size of the overdraft at any particular time. See Ch.31.

[16] See para.21–18.

businessman can rely on trade protection associations, but the little person, whom the law should particularly protect, rarely has any idea of the risks being run when granting credit to a company with a high-sounding name,[17] impressive nominal capital (not paid up in cash), and with assets mortgaged up to the hilt.[18]

LIMITED LIABILITY

It follows from the fact that a corporation is a separate person that its **2–3** members are not as such liable for its debts.[19] Hence in the absence of express provision to the contrary the members will be completely free from any personal liability. The rule of non-liability also applies in principle to obligations other than debts: the company is liable and not the member. However, the principle applies only so long as we concentrate on the position of members as such and remains true, even for members, only so long as the company is a going concern. Members who become involved in the management of the company's business, for example as directors, will find that separate legal personality does not necessarily protect them from personal liability to third parties. Although acting on behalf of the company, they may have done things which have made them personally liable to outsiders. The most obvious example is that of a tort committed in the course of directorial duties. The extent to which those acting on behalf of companies are personally liable for their acts to third parties depends on the operation of the doctrines of agency and rules such as assumption of responsibility in tort law and identification in criminal law. These are matters we discuss in Chapter 7. For the moment we confine ourselves to the position of the member, whom the doctrine of separate legal personality normally shields from personal liability so long as the company is a going concern.

If a company enters insolvent liquidation, in theory the issue undergoes a considerable change, though in practice it does not. The question becomes whether the liquidator acting on behalf of the company can seek contributions from its members so as to bring its assets up to the level needed to meet the claims of the company's

---

[17] There are undoubtedly many who think that "Ltd" is an indication of size and stability (which "Plc" may be but "Ltd" certainly is not) rather than a warning of irresponsibility.

[18] But no sympathy was wasted on him by the House of Lords: "A creditor who will not take the trouble to use the means which the statute provides for enabling him to protect himself must bear the consequences of his own negligence": [1897] A.C. 22 at 40, *per* Lord Watson.

[19] This sentence was quoted and relied on by Kerr L.J. in *Rayner (Mincing Lane) Ltd v Department of Trade* [1989] Ch. 72 at 176 as an accurate statement of English law although, as he pointed out, it is not accurate in relation to most Civil Law countries—including Scotland so far as partnerships are concerned—or to international law: *ibid.* at 176–183.

creditors. In the case of an unlimited company,[20] section 74 of the Insolvency Act does indeed impose on the members such an obligation to contribute to the assets of the company. In the case of companies limited by shares or by guarantee,[21] however, that obligation is limited (hence, by transfer, the term "limited company") and is not, as it is with unlimited companies, open-ended.

In the case of a company limited by shares each member is liable to contribute when called upon to do so the full nominal value of the shares held in so far as this has not already been paid by the shareholder or any prior holder of those shares (which it normally will have been). In the case of a guarantee company each member is liable to contribute a specified amount (normally small) to the assets of the company in the event of its being wound up while a member or within one year after ceasing to be a member. In effect the member, without being directly liable to the company's creditors, is in both cases a limited guarantor of the company. When, therefore, obligations are incurred on behalf of a limited company, the company is liable and not the members, though in the case of a guarantee company or of partly paid shares the company may ultimately be able to recover a contribution from the members towards the discharge of its obligations. However, in the typical case of a company limited by shares with fully paid shares in issue, no further liability will arise for the member in the absence of specific statutory provision to the contrary, which provisions are rare.[22]

2–4   In contrast, an unincorporated association, not being a legal person, cannot be liable, and obligations entered into on its behalf can bind only the actual officials who purport to act on its behalf, or the individual members if the officials have actual or apparent authority to bind them. In either event the persons bound will be liable to the full extent of their property unless they expressly or impliedly restrict their responsibility to the extent of the funds of the association, as the officials may well do. Hence the extent to which the member will be liable depends on the terms of the contract of association. In the case of a club, and presumably the same applies to learned and scientific societies, there will generally be implied a term that the members are not personally liable for obligations incurred on behalf of the club. But very different is the position of members of a partnership, an association carrying on business for gain. Each partner is an agent of all the others and acts done by any one partner in "carrying on in the normal way business of the kind carried on by the firm" bind all the partners.[23] Only if the creditor knows of the limitation placed on the

---

[20] See above, para.1–13.
[21] See above, para.1–5.
[22] See Ch.9.
[23] Partnership Act 1890, s.5. This applies equally to Scotland thus largely negativing the consequence of recognising the Scottish firm as a separate person.

partner's authority will the other members escape liability.[24] More-over, an attempt to restrict the partners' liability to partnership funds by a provision to that effect in the partnership agreement will be ineffective even if known to the creditors;[25] they will be able to restrict their financial liability, in respect of acts otherwise authorised, only by an express agreement to that effect with the creditor concerned.[26] Hence the pressure, which bore fruit in 2000, for the creation of an incorporated legal entity with the internal flexibility of a partnership, i.e. the limited liability partnership.[27]

The overall result of the broad recognition by the courts of the separate legal entity of the company and of the limited liability of its members (and, usually, managers) is to produce at first sight a legal regime which is very unfavourable to potential creditors of compa-nies, a situation which they have naturally sought to readjust by contract in their favour, so far as is in their power. For large lenders, especially banks, there are a number of possibilities, to be used separately or cumulatively. Apart from the obvious commercial response of charging higher interest rates on loans to bodies whose members have limited liability, such lenders may seek to leap over the barrier created by the law of limited liability by exacting as the price of the loan to the company personal guarantees of its repayment from the managers or shareholders of the company, guarantees which may be secured on the personal assets of the individuals concerned. Instead of or in addition to obtaining personal security by con-tracting around limited liability, large lenders may seek to improve the priority of their claims by taking security against the *company's* assets. As we shall see later on in this Chapter, chancery practitioners in the nineteenth century were quick to respond to this need by creating the flexible and all-embracing instrument of the floating charge to supplement the traditional fixed charge mechanisms which were already available.

However, these self-help remedies may not be practicable for trade creditors or employees[28] and, even in the case of large lenders, there is a strong danger that, when things begin to go wrong, the controllers of the company will take risks with the company's capital which were not within the contemplation of the parties when the loan was arranged. For these reasons, although the legislature has not over-turned *Salomon v Salomon* and, indeed, under the influence of

---

[24] Partnership Act 1890, ss.5 and 8.
[25] *Sea, Fire and Life Insurance Co, Re* (1854) 3 De G.M. & G. 459.
[26] *Hallett v Dowdall* (1852) 21 L.J.Q.B. 98.
[27] Limited Liability Partnerships Act 2000. See para.1–2.
[28] Unless and to the extent that they have a statutory preference, unsecured creditors are in the worst possible world. Limited liability normally stops them suing the shareholders or directors, whilst the fixed and floating charges of the big lenders often soak up all the available assets of the company.

Community law,[29] the one-person company is now expressly recognised by domestic law, the Companies and Insolvency Acts are full of provisions whose purpose cannot be completely understood except against the background of limited liability. In particular, the extensive publicity and disclosure obligations placed upon limited liability companies[30] must be seen in this light. More recently have been added the provisions relating to wrongful trading[31] and the expanded provisions on the disqualification of directors, especially on grounds of unfitness.[32]

PROPERTY

2–5   One obvious advantage of corporate personality is that it enables the property of the association to be more clearly distinguished from that of its members. In an unincorporated society, the property of the association is the joint property of the members. The rights of the members therein differ from their rights to their separate property since the joint property must be dealt with according to the rules of the society and no individual member can claim any particular asset. By virtue of the trust the obvious complications can be minimised but not completely eradicated. And the complications cause particular difficulty in the case of a trading partnership both as regards the true nature of the interests of the partners[33] and as regards claims of creditors.[34] By contrast, on incorporation, the corporate property belongs to the company and members have no direct proprietary rights to it but merely to their "shares" in the undertaking.[35] A change in the membership, which causes inevitable dislocation to a partnership firm, leaves the company unconcerned; the shares may be transferred but the company's property will be untouched and no realisation or splitting up of its property will be necessary, as it will on a change in the constitution of a partnership firm.

However, the above does not simply permit the property of the business to be more easily identified; it also enables it to be segregated

---

[29]   See Council Directive 89/667 on single-member private limited liability companies, [1989] OJ L395, December 12, 1989.

[30]   See Ch.21, below, but note s.448 whereby the directors of unlimited liability companies are not normally required to deliver accounts and reports to the registrar for general publication.

[31]   See para.9–7.

[32]   See Ch.10.

[33]   See Partnership Act 1890, ss.20–22; *Fuller's Contract, Re* [1933] Ch. 652.

[34]   Partnership Act 1890, s.23, and the Insolvent Partnerships Order 1994 (SI 1994/2421), as amended.

[35]   "Shareholders are not, in the eye of the law, part owners of the undertaking. The undertaking is something different from the totality of the shareholdings": per Evershed L.J. in *Short v Treasury Commissioners* [1948] 1 K.B. 116, 122, CA (affd [1948] A.C. 534 HL).

from the members' personal assets. Thus, the claims of the business creditors will be against the property of the company and the claims of the members' personal creditors against the property of the member. Neither set of creditors is in competition with the other; and each has to monitor the disposition only of the assets against which its claims lie.[36]

SUING AND BEING SUED

Closely allied to questions of property are those relating to legal actions. The difficulties in the way of suing, or being sued by, an unincorporated association have long bedevilled English law.[37] The problem is obviously of the greatest practical importance in connection with trading bodies and in fact it has now been solved in the case of partnerships by allowing a partnership to sue or be sued in the firm's name. Hence, there is now no difficulty so far as the pure mechanics of suit are concerned—although there may still be complications in enforcing the judgment.   **2–6**

In the case of other unincorporated bodies (such as clubs and learned societies) not subject to special statutory provisions, the problems of suit are still serious. Sometimes its committee or other agents may be personally liable or authorised to sue. Otherwise, the only course is a "representative action" whereby, under certain conditions, one or more persons may sue or be sued on behalf of all the interested parties.[38] But resort to this procedure is available only subject to compliance with a number of somewhat ill-defined conditions, and the law, which has been inadequately explored, is obscure and difficult. The result is apt to be embarrassing to the society when it wishes to enforce its rights (or, more properly, those of its members) though it has compensating advantages when it wishes to evade its duties.[39] Needless to say, none of these difficulties arises when an incorporated company is suing or being sued; the company as a legal person can take action to enforce its legal rights and can be sued for breach of its legal duties.

---

[36] R. Kraakman and H. Hansmann, "The Essential Role of Organizational Law" (2000) 110 *Yale L J* 387.

[37] As we saw above (para.1–2) this problem seems to have lain behind the former restriction of the number of partners to a maximum of 20.

[38] CPR 19.6.

[39] "An unincorporated association has certain advantages when litigation is desired against them": per Scrutton L.J. in *Bloom v National Federation of Discharged Soldiers* (1918) 35 T.L.R. 50, 51, CA.

PERPETUAL SUCCESSION

2–7   One of the obvious advantages of an artificial person is that it is not
susceptible to "the thousand natural shocks that flesh is heir to". It
cannot become incapacitated by illness, mental or physical, and it has
not (or need not have) an allotted span of life.[40] This is not to say that
the death or incapacity of its human members may not cause the
company considerable embarrassment; obviously it will if all the
directors die or are imprisoned or if there are too few surviving
members to hold a valid meeting, or if the bulk of the members or
directors become enemy aliens.[41] But the vicissitudes of the flesh have
no direct effect on the disembodied company.[42] The death of a
member leaves the company unmoved; members may come and go
but the company can go on for ever.[43] The insanity of the managing
director will not be calamitous to the company provided that he is
removed promptly; he may be the company's brains but lobectomy is
a simpler operation than on a natural person.

Once again, the disadvantages in the case of an unincorporated
society can be minimised by the use of a trust. If the property of the
association is vested in a small body of trustees, the death, disability
or retirement of an individual member, other than one of the trustees,
need not cause much trouble. But, of course, the trustees, if natural
persons, will themselves need replacing at fairly frequent intervals
and the need for constant appointment of new trustees is a nuisance if
nothing worse. Indeed, it may be said that the trust never functioned
at its simplest until it was able to enlist the aid of its own child, the
incorporated company, to act as a trust corporation with perpetual
succession.

---

[40] s.84(1)(a) of the Insolvency Act 1986 envisages that the period of the company's duration
may be fixed in the articles, but this is rarely done in practice and, even if it were, the
company would not automatically expire on the expiration of the term; the section provides
that expiration of the term is a ground on which the members by ordinary resolution may
wind the company up voluntarily. It is otherwise with chartered companies: see para.1–16,
fn.94.

[41] *cf. Daimler Co v Continental Tyre and Rubber Co* [1916] 2 A.C. 307, HL.

[42] As Grcer L.J. said in *Stepney Corporation v Osofsky* [1937] 3 All E.R. 289 at 291, CA: a
corporate body has "no soul to be saved or body to be kicked". This epigram is believed to
be of considerable antiquity. Glanville Williams, *Criminal Law: The General Part* (2nd ed.),
p.856, has traced it back to Lord Thurlow and an earlier variation to Coke, *cf.* the decree of
Pope Innocent IV forbidding the excommunication of corporations because, having neither
minds nor souls, they could not sin: see Carr, *Law of Corporation*, p.73. In *Rolloswin
Investments Ltd v Chromolit Portugal SARL* [1970] 1 W.L.R. 912 it was held that since a
company was incapable of public worship it was not a "person" within the meaning of the
Sunday Observance Act 1677 so that a contract made by it on a Sunday was not void (the
court was unaware that before the case was heard the Act had been repealed by the Statute
Law (Repeals) Act 1969).

[43] During the 1939–1945 War all the members of one private company, while in general
meeting, were killed by a bomb. But the company survived; not even a nuclear bomb could
have destroyed it. And see the Australian case of *Noel Tedman Holding Pty Ltd, Re* (1967)
Qd.R. 561, Qd.Sup.Ct where the only two members were killed in a road accident.

Moreover, the trust obviates difficulties only when a member or his estate, has, under the constitution of the association, no right to be paid a share of the assets on death or retirement, which, of course, is the position with the normal club or learned society. But on the retirement or death of a partner, the default rule is that the partnership is automatically dissolved, so far at any rate as he is concerned,[44] and he or his estate will be entitled to be paid his share. The resulting dislocation of the firm's business can be reduced by special clauses in the articles of partnership, providing for an arbitrary basis of valuation of his share and for deferred payment, but cannot be eradicated altogether. With an incorporated company these problems do not arise. The member or his estate is not entitled to be paid out by the company. If the member, or a personal representative, trustee in bankruptcy, or receiver, wishes to realise the value of the shares, these must be sold, whereupon the purchaser will, on entry in the share register, become a member in place of the former holder.[45]

Until the Companies Act 1981 it was not permissible for the company itself to be the purchaser of the member's shares, even if it wished to acquire them, and this could be disadvantageous both to the would-be seller and to the company and the other members, especially in the case of private companies. The seller might not be able to find a purchaser and the other members might not have sufficient free capital to purchase the shares. Now, subject to stringent conditions, purchase by the company is allowed,[46] as it has long been under the laws of many other countries. **2–8**

The continuing existence of a company, irrespective of changes in its membership, is helpful in other directions also. When an individual sells a business to another, difficult questions may arise regarding the performance of existing contracts by the new proprietor,[47] the assignment of rights of a personal nature,[48] and the validity of agreements made with customers ignorant of the change of proprietorship.[49] Similar problems may arise on a change in the

---

[44] And, in the absence of contrary agreement, as regards all the partners: Partnership Act 1890, s.33.

[45] In practice, this may not be so easy as the company's articles may restrict transfer. For an unsuccessful attempt to use the unfair prejudice provisions to secure the return to the shareholder's estates of the capital represented by his shares see *A Company, Re* [1983] Ch. 178 and see also the explanation of this case in *A Company, Re* [1986] B.C.L.C. 382 para.20–6.

[46] See para.13–13.

[47] *Robson v Drummond* (1831) 2 B. & Ad. 303; *cf. British Waggon Co v Lea* (1880) 5 Q.B.D. 149.

[48] *Griffith v Tower Publishing Co* [1897] 1 Ch. 21 (publishing agreement held not assignable); *Kemp v Baerselman* [1906] 2 K.B. 604, CA (agreement not assignable if question of one party's obligation depends on the other's "personal requirements"), *cf. Tolhurst v Associated Portland Cement* [1902] 2 K.B. 660, CA.

[49] *Boulton v Jones* (1857) 2 H. & N. 564.

constitution of a partnership.[50] Where the business is incorporated and the sale is merely of the shares, none of these difficulties arises. The company remains the proprietor of the business, performs the existing contracts and retains the benefits of them, and enters into future agreements. The difficulties attending vicarious performance, assignments and mistaken identity do not arise.

Although a company may shift control of its business by means of a transfer of its shares to new investors, it does not follow that it will always choose this method of effecting the change of control. The directors or shareholders of the company could decide instead to sell the underlying business of the company to the new investors, who, perhaps, may form their own company in order to take the new business. In this case, the transferring company (rather than its shareholders) will be left holding the consideration received on the sale of its business. This method is particularly likely to be attractive to the transferring company if it is divesting itself of control of only part of its business (though even then a transfer of control by sale of shares may be possible if the relevant part of the business is held in a separate group subsidiary company). When a company disposes of the whole or part of its business (as opposed to the shareholders deciding to transfer their shares), the difficulties mentioned in the previous paragraph in relation to the sale of a business by an unincorporated entity arise in relation to companies as well. To sum up, a company,[51] unlike an unincorporated body, has the option to shift control by means of a transfer of shares, but it may choose instead to dispose of the underlying business (or even just of the assets used in the business).

TRANSFERABLE SHARES

2–9   Incorporation, with the resulting separation of the business from its members, greatly facilitates the transfer of the members' interests. Even without formal incorporation much the same end was achieved through the device of the trust coupled with an agreement for transferability in the deed of settlement. But this end could be attained only approximately since the member, even after transfer, would remain liable for the firm's debts incurred during the time when he or she was a member. Moreover, in the absence of limited

---

[50] See *Brace v Calder* [1895] 2 Q.B. 253, CA where the retirement of two partners was held to operate as the wrongful dismissal of a manager. And see also Partnership Act 1890, s.18. In practice such difficulties are often avoided by an implied novation.

[51] Of course, even in relation to companies this proposition applies only to companies limited by shares and not to guarantee companies.

liability his opportunities to transfer would in practice be much restricted.

With an incorporated company freedom to transfer of members' interests, both legally and practically, can be readily attained. The company can be incorporated with its liability limited by shares, and these shares constitute items of property which are freely transferable in the absence of express provision to the contrary, and in such a way that the transferor drops out[52] and the transferee steps into his shoes. A partner has a proprietary interest which he can assign, but the assignment does not operate to divest him of his status or liability as a partner; it merely affords the assignee the right to receive whatever the firm distributes in respect of the assigning partner's share.[53] The assignee can be admitted into partnership in the place of the assignor only if the other partners agree[54] and the assignor will not be relieved of his existing liabilities as a partner unless the creditors agree, expressly or impliedly, to release him.[55]

Even in the case of an incorporated company the power to transfer may, of course, be subject to restrictions. In a private company some form of restriction was formerly essential in order to comply with its statutory definition and, although this is no longer a statutory requirement, it is still a desirable provision if such a company is to retain its character as an incorporated private partnership. In practice, these restrictions are usually so stringent as to make transferability largely illusory. Nor is there any legal objection arising out of the Companies Act to restrictions in the case of a public company, although such restrictions, except as regards partly paid shares, are unusual, and are prohibited by the Listing Rules if the shares are to be marketed on the Stock Exchange.[56] But there is this fundamental difference: in a partnership, transferability depends on express agreement and is subject to legal and practical limitations, whereas in a company it exists to the fullest extent in the absence of express restriction. The partnership relationship is essentially personal; and in practice this is maintained in the case of the private company which in economic reality is often a partnership though in law an incorporated company.[57] On the other hand, the relationship between members of a public company is essentially impersonal and financial and hence there is usually no reason to restrict changes in membership.

[52] CA 2006, s.544. Subject only to a possible liability under ss.74 and 76 of the Insolvency Act 1986 if liquidation follows within a year and the shares were not fully paid up or were redeemed or purchased out of capital. On the latter see para.13–22.
[53] Partnership Act 1890, s.31.
[54] Partnership Act 1890, s.24(7).
[55] Partnership Act 1890, s.17(2) and (3).
[56] See para.25–16.
[57] In recent years the courts have shown a welcome tendency to recognise the economic reality in applying the legal rules to such incorporated partnerships: see especially *Ebrahimi v Westbourne Galleries Ltd* [1973] A.C. 360, HL: see Ch.20, below.

MANAGEMENT UNDER A BOARD STRUCTURE

2–10   An important feature of company law is that it provides a structure which allows for the separation of risk investment via the purchase of shares, in which many persons may participate, from the management of the company, which is delegated to a smaller and expert group of people who partly constitute and who are partly supervised by a board of directors. The separation of what is conventionally, but controversially, termed "ownership" of the company (i.e. shareholding) from its "control" (i.e. management) is a feature of large companies and it is therefore important that the organisational law governing companies should deal with its consequences. Of course, as with transferable shares, the separation of shareholders and managers is not a feature of small companies, where the two groups of people are often identical or substantially so. As we noted in Chapter 1,[58] the corporate machinery for giving effect to the separation of these roles may appear in the case of small companies to be more of a hindrance than a help, but it is a crucial element in the efficient functioning of large companies.

The legal implications of this development were first explored in the United States by A.A. Berle and G.C. Means in *The Modern Corporation and Private Property*,[59] which drew attention to the revolutionary change thus brought about in our traditional conceptions of the nature of property. Today, the great bulk of large enterprise, at least in the United States and the United Kingdom, is in the hands not of individual entrepreneurs but of large public companies in which many individuals have property rights as shareholders and to the capital of which they have directly or indirectly contributed. Direct or indirect[60] investment in companies probably constitutes the most important single item of property for most people (after home ownership), but whether this property brings profit to its "owners" no longer depends on their energy and initiative but on that of the management from which they are divorced. The modern shareholder in a public company has ceased to be a quasi-partner and has become instead simply a supplier of capital. If a person invests in the older forms of private property, such as a farm or a shop, he or she becomes tied to that property. The modern public company meets the need for a new type of property in which the relationship between the owner and the property plays little part, so that the owner can recover the wealth represented by the property, whenever needed, without removing it from the enterprise which requires it indefinitely. "The separation of ownership from manage-

---

[58] See above, para.1–14 and below, Ch.15.
[59] New York, 1933, reprinted in 1968 with a new preface.
[60] For most people the investment is indirect, perhaps even not conscious, as in the case of contributions to occupational pension schemes.

ment and control in the corporate system has performed this essential step in securing liquidity."[61] Even when, as is increasingly the case, shareholding in large companies is concentrated in the hands of institutional shareholders, such as pension funds and insurance companies, which do have a more significant potential for intervention in management than individual shareholders, such participation is discontinuous or episodic and usually precipitated by some crisis in the company's affairs rather than a day-to-day way of managing the company.[62]

Despite the fact that the board, and especially the "managing director" or, in the increasingly common Americanism, the "chief executive officer", is the driving force behind the operation of the large company, the British Act, unlike its continental counterparts, says very little about the board of directors. The Act insists there be directors, but only two are required in the case of a public company and, in the case of a private company, one will do.[63] Many sections of the Act impose administrative burdens on the directors or assume in some other way the existence of a board of directors, but the composition, structure and functions of the board are left to a very high degree to companies to decide themselves, through their articles of association[64] or through mere corporate practice. In the case of listed companies, however, this private ordering by companies themselves has been somewhat qualified by the development in the last fifteen years of the Combined Code on Corporate Governance.[65] In the face of this "hands off" approach on the part of the Act, can the claim be made good that British company law provides machinery, except in the most rudimentary way, whereby the separation of ownership and control can flourish? The most obvious answer to this question consists in pointing to the duties created originally by the common law, but now restated in the Act, which aim to require the directors to exercise the powers conferred upon them competently and loyally in the interests of the company, which is normally to be seen as the interests of the shareholders.[66] Thus, one may say that the approach of company law to the regulation of the separation of ownership from control is to allow companies maximum freedom to decide on the division of powers between shareholders and board and on the functions of the board, but then to concentrate on the regulation of the way the board discharges the powers conferred upon it, whatever they may be. How successfully this is done is the topic of later chapters. All we need note here is the importance of the fact that in

---

[61] See above, fn.59 at p.284.
[62] See P. Davies, "Institutional Investors in the United Kingdom" in D. Prentice and P. Holland (eds), *Contemporary Issues in Corporate Governance* (Clarendon Press, 1993).
[63] s.154.
[64] See below, Ch.14.
[65] Para.14–29.
[66] See Ch.16, below.

large companies there are two decision-making bodies, shareholders in general meeting and the board of directors, and that in terms of management functions the board is invariably the more important organ.

BORROWING

2–11 Hitherto we have considered only the advantages or disadvantages which flow inevitably, or at any rate naturally, from the fact of incorporation. There are, however, two further respects, borrowing and taxation, in which incorporation has important consequences.

At first sight one would suppose that a sole trader or partners, being personally liable, would find it easier than a company to raise money by borrowing. In practice, however, this is not so since a company is often able to grant a more effective charge to secure the indebtedness. The ingenuity of equity practitioners led to the evolution of an unusual but highly beneficial type of security known as the floating charge; i.e. a charge which floats like a cloud over the whole assets of the company from time to time falling within a generic description, but without preventing the mortgagor from disposing of those assets in the usual course of business until something occurs to cause the charge to become crystallised or fixed. This type of charge is particularly suitable when a business has no fixed assets, such as land, which can be included in a normal mortgage, but carries a large and valuable stock-in-trade. Since this stock needs to be turned over in the course of business, a fixed charge is impracticable because the consent of the mortgagee would be needed every time anything was sold and a new charge would have to be entered into whenever anything was bought. A floating charge obviates these difficulties; it enables the stock to be turned over but attaches to whatever it is converted into and to whatever new stock is acquired.

In theory, there is no reason why such charges should not be granted by sole traders and ordinary partnerships as well as by incorporated companies (and now, LLPs). But, until recently, there have been two pieces of legislation which have effectively precluded that. The first was the "reputed ownership" provision in the bankruptcy legislation relating to individuals.[67] This, however, under the reforms resulting from the report of the Cork Committee,[68] was repealed by the Insolvency Act 1986. It never applied to the winding-up of companies. The second, which still remains, is that the charge,

---

[67] Bankruptcy Act 1914, s.38(1)(c).
[68] (1982) Cmnd. 8558, Ch. 23. Its repeal had been recommended in the Report of the Blagden Committee 25 years earlier: (1957) Cmnd. 221.

in so far as it related to chattels, would be a bill of sale within the meaning of the Bills of Sale Acts 1878 and 1882 which apply only to individuals and not to companies.[69] Hence it would need to be registered in the Bills of Sale Registry,[70] and, what is more important, as a mortgage bill it would need to be in the statutory form[71] which involves specifying the chattels in detail in a schedule. Compliance with the latter requirement is obviously impossible, since in a floating charge the chattels are, *ex hypothesi*, indeterminate and fluctuating.

When, belatedly, we get round to reforming, as many common law countries have done, our antiquated law relating to security interests in movables, we shall be able to repeal the Bills of Sale Acts and thus make it practicable for unincorporated firms to borrow on the security of floating charges[72] or some comparable form of security on the lines of that provided by Article 9 of the American Uniform Commercial code. In the meantime, use of this advantageous form of security is in practice restricted to bodies corporate. By virtue of it the lender can obtain an effective security on "all the undertaking and assets of the company both present and future" either alone or in conjunction with a fixed charge on its land.[73] By so doing the lender can place himself in a far stronger position than if merely the personal security of the individual trader supported the loan. It therefore happens not infrequently that a business is converted into a company solely in order to enable further capital to be raised by borrowing. And sometimes, as the *Salomon* case[74] shows, a trader by "selling" his business to a company which he has formed can give himself priority over his future creditors by taking a debenture, secured by a floating charge, for the purchase price.[75]

---

[69] This was always accepted in relation to mortgages in the light of s.17 of the 1882 Act. It was later held, after an exhaustive review of the conflicting authorities, that both Acts apply only to individuals: *Slavenburg's Bank v International Natural Resources Ltd* [1980] 1 W.L.R. 1076. See further para.32–27.

[70] For some reason registration of a bill of sale against a tradesman destroys his credit, whereas registration of a debenture against a company does not. This can only be explained on the basis that the former is exceptional, whereas the latter is usual and familiarity has bred contempt.

[71] 1882 Act, s.9. Nor could it cover future goods: see *ibid.*, s.5. S.6(2), *ibid.*, allows a limited power of replacement but not anything as fluid as a floating charge.

[72] Farmers can already do so under the Agricultural Credits Act 1928 which permits individuals to grant to banks floating charges over farming stock and agricultural assets and excludes the application of the former reputed ownership provision and the Bills of Sale Acts: see ss.5 and 8(1), (2) and (4). Farming stock and agricultural assets are more readily distinguishable from a farmer's other assets (than, say, the stock of an antique dealer who lives over his shop) thus meeting the difficulty referred to in the text.

[73] The implications of floating charges are discussed more fully in Ch.32, below.

[74] [1897] A.C. 22, HL.

[75] The ability of the fixed and floating chargeholder to "scoop the pool" of the company's assets has now been restricted, after long debate, by the Enterprise Act 2002, which requires "a prescribed part" of the company's assets to be kept available for the unsecured creditors. See Ch.32, below.

TAXATION

2–12 Once a company reaches a certain size the attraction of limited liability is likely to outweigh all other considerations when business people are considering in what form to carry on their activities. Investors are unlikely to be willing to put money into a company where their liability is not limited if they are to have no or little control over the running of the company. However, with small businesses, where it is feasible to give all the investors a say in management, it is likely that tax considerations play a major part in determining whether the business shall be set up in corporate form or as a partnership, especially as in such cases where, as we have seen, limited liability may not be available in practice vis-à-vis large lenders.[76] This is not the place to examine the tax considerations which may cut one way or another at different times on this issue. What we should note, however, is that in the case of small companies, the investors' return on their capital may take the form of the payment of directors' fees rather than dividends, so that participation in the management of the company may be the means for the investor both to safeguard the investment and to earn a return on it.[77]

FORMALITIES, PUBLICITY AND EXPENSE

2–13 Incorporation is necessarily attended with formalities, loss of privacy and expense greater than that which would normally apply to a sole trader or partnership. A sole trader is a person who already exists. A partnership cannot exist without some form of agreement, but this can be written on a half-sheet of notepaper or be an informal oral agreement. An unincorporated firm can conduct its affairs without any formality and publicity beyond that which may be prescribed by the regulations (if any) applying to the particular type of business. If the business is carried on under a name different from the true name of the sole trader or those of all the partners, it will have to comply with the provisions on business names (as would a company trading under a pseudonym)[78] but these are not onerous. The business, unless it is insolvent, can eventually be wound up equally cheaply, privately and informally. An incorporated company, on the other hand,

---

[76] As noted, in the case of professional businesses the rules of the governing professional body may require the partnership form, though in fact many professional bodies have become more flexible on this issue in recent years.

[77] See further Ch.20, below.

[78] See para.4–13.

necessarily involves formalities, publicity and expenses at its birth, throughout its active life and on its final dissolution.

The costs of formation, at least of a private company (and most companies are formed as private even if they become public later in life), are very low. A competent incorporation agent should be able to set up a basic company for about £200. It is particularly important that British law does not require a private company, unlike a public one, to have a minimum share capital.[79] Consequently, the incorporators can borrow what money they need to set the company up and do not need to sink their own money into it, which, indeed, they may not have. However, the combination of no minimum capital and limited liability could be an invitation to trading at the expense of the creditors, and so British law, even if it has no *ex ante* minimum capital requirement, has developed significant *ex post* controls on those who behave in this way after the company has been formed.[80] The costs of incorporation also come with the much greater publicity required of a company as against a partnership, since the former is required, but the latter is not, to make their annual accounts available publicly through filing at Companies House.[81] Until recently, small companies were required, in addition, to produce accounts in what was an over-elaborate format and to have those accounts audited, but these requirements have now been relaxed.[82] Finally, we have noted at a number of points in this chapter that the requirement of two separate decision-making organs, shareholders' meeting and board of directors, may seem over-elaborate for small companies, though something has now been done to alleviate this problem without, however, going to the extent of permitting small companies to adopt a single decision-making body.[83]

CONCLUSION

The balance of advantage and disadvantage in relation to incor- **2–14** poration no doubt varies from one business context to another, at least as far as small firms are concerned; for large trading organisations, the arguments in favour of incorporation are normally conclusive. This may reflect the firms' respective needs for capital to finance their operations. For large firms the division between board

[79] See para.11–4.
[80] See Chs 9 and 10, below.
[81] Public filing is seen to be a consequence of limited liability. Thus, unlimited companies are not required to file their accounts publicly (s.441) whereas the limited liability partnership (above, para.1–3) is subject to the publicity regime applied to companies: Limited Liability Partnerships Regulations 2001 (SI 2001/1090), Pt II.
[82] See Chs 21 and 22, below.
[83] See below, Ch.15.

and shareholders, transferable shares and the conferment of limited liability on the shareholders are helpful for the raising of capital. As for the large firm which does not have a large capital requirement, such as large professional firms, these have happily traded as partnerships in the past and were, indeed, often required to do so by the rules of the relevant profession, most of which have now been relaxed. Unlimited liability was seen as a badge of professional respectability. However, the threat of crippling damages awards for professional negligence led the accountancy profession in particular to press for an appropriate form of limited liability vehicle for the conduct of their businesses. As we saw in Chapter 1,[84] this led to the creation of the limited liability partnership, which combines the limited liability of the company with the flat internal hierarchy of the partnership. However, where the large firm means also a need for a large amount of risk capital, the corporate form predominates.

The main policy issue, therefore, has been how far small firms should have easy access to the corporate form. Ever since the decision in *Salomon v Salomon*[85] English law has leant in favour of not restricting access, and the Company Law Review endorsed that approach.[86] As we shall see in Part Two, the issue is essentially about the access of small business to limited liability, since that feature of incorporation has a major potential impact on third parties who deal with the company, whilst separate legal personality, management under a board structure and transferable shares seem either benign, as far as third parties are concerned, or of concern only to those within the company.

---

[84] See above, para.1–3.
[85] See above, para.2–1.
[86] Developing, paras 9.61–9.71.

CHAPTER 3

SOURCES OF COMPANY LAW AND THE COMPANY'S CONSTITUTION

SOURCES

As far as domestic companies are concerned, the immediate sources **3–1** of the rules applicable to them, and the hierarchy of those sources, are the ones familiar to students of other bodies of law. They are: primary legislation, secondary legislation, rule-making by legislatively recognised bodies, the common law of companies, and the company's own constitution (in particular, its articles of association). Of these, the last may perhaps appear unfamiliar, but students of contract law are used to idea that the rules applicable in any particular situation are as likely to be found in the terms of the parties' agreement as in legislative or common law rules, and students of trade union law or of the law of other types of association know that the particular association's rule-book is an important source of law, at least for its members. As to the third category, legislation may delegate to bodies outside the legislature the power to make rules relevant to companies. These bodies may themselves be agencies created by statute or they may be pre-existing bodies which the legislature recognises for the purposes of rule-making.

Finally, and standing outside the above hierarchy but with links to it, there may be examples of "self-regulation" where the relevant rules have no legislative or common law foundation, but are nevertheless observed in practice, as a result of non-legal pressures, including the threat that Government might intervene with legislation if the self-regulatory rules were not obeyed. However, the leading example of this phenomenon in our area, the City Panel on Takeovers and Mergers and the Code it administers, were put on a statutory basis by the Companies Act 2006, implementing the Community Directive on takeovers, though its non-statutory methods of working have survived to a considerable extent.[1] Thus, self-regulation is a less obvious feature of company law than it used to be.

Whatever the source of the rule, one should also note that its content may be located on a spectrum running from "hard" to "soft". At the "hard" end the obligation may be imposed by the rule without giving those to whom it applies any choice as to whether they comply with it (a "mandatory" rule). Moving along the spectrum, the rule may permit those to whom it prima facie applies to modify or remove the obligation. Such rules, conventionally called "default rules", are in fact quite common in company law. What is the function of such a rule, given that the parties themselves are apparently free to deprive it of regulatory force? Where the obligees can easily remove the obligation, the rule may nevertheless have the important function of relieving parties of the task of working out the best rule for themselves. In formulating the default rule, the legislature will have tried to identify the rule which most parties in the relevant situation would devise for themselves. Only if the particular parties want something different from that normally adopted will they have to go through the process of altering the rule. Thus, a number of provisions in the Act on shareholder meetings apply only "subject to any provision in the company's articles".[2] Since it is relatively easy for companies to make different provisions in their articles upon formation of the company or later, these provisions may be regarded as a pure type of default rule.

3–2   In other cases the procedure for amending the position produced by the default rule may be more demanding and the regulatory objectives of such a rule may also be more sophisticated. For example, many rules relating to the duties of directors may be disapplied by the shareholders, by majority vote, either before or after the breach of duty.[3] The purpose of such a rule may be to induce the directors to bargain with the shareholders over the handling of conduct which would otherwise be in breach of duty. This rule contains a more demanding procedure because those upon whom the obligation is imposed (the directors) need to obtain the consent of

[1] See below Ch.28.
[2] See Ch.15 below.
[3] See Ch.16, below.

another group of people within the company (the shareholders) for the modification of the rule, and are thus forced to disclose to the shareholders their actual or potential wrongdoing. Such a rule may be useful where the rule-maker cannot predict what the result should be in a particular class of case (otherwise it could use a mandatory rule) nor does it think it wise to leave it to the directors themselves to modify the rule (because of their conflict of interest).

Finally, the procedure for amending the rule may be so demanding that in practice little use is made of it. In such a case, it is doubtful whether the rule should be regarded as in substance a default rule. This may be true of the example given in the previous paragraph. Thus, if the only way in which directors can secure shareholder modification of the default rule is to call a meeting of the share-holders to discuss each case of breach of duty as it arises, then in a large company they may regard such a procedure as so cumbersome and unpredictable that they treat the default rule as in fact manda-tory.[4] Whether they then choose to comply with it or to break the rule and hide the breach is a different question.

At the "soft" end of the spectrum are "rules" which are in fact only recommendations or exhortations. No sanction is attached to the breach of the rule. Each obligee decides for itself whether and how far to comply with the recommendation. A possible way of injecting some bite into recommendations is to put them on a "comply or explain basis". In this situation, the only formal obligation imposed by the rule is to explain publicly how far the recommendations have been complied with and the reasons for any areas of non-compliance. Such disclosure meets all the formal obligations of the rule, even if it shows that the recommendations have not been complied with at all, but publicity may generate extra-legal pressures on the company to comply (or to comply more fully) with the recommendations. The primary example of such a mechanism in British company law is the Combined Code on Corporate Governance,[5] in relation to which a "comply or explain" obligation is imposed.

Primary legislation

The principal piece of legislation with which this book is concerned is the Companies Act 2006, the latest in a line of Acts produced as the original legislation of the mid-nineteenth century has been reformed periodically. In 1998, the then Secretary of State, Margaret Beckett, commissioned an independent review of company law,[6] which was described as "although technical ... fundamental to our national

3–3

---

[4] For an insightful discussion of default rules see S. Deakin and A. Hughes, "Economic Efficiency and the Proceduralisation of Company Law" (1999) 3 C.F.I.L.R. 169.

[5] See below, Ch.14.

[6] DTI, *Company Law Reform: Modern Company Law for a Competitive Economy*, (1998).

competitiveness".[7] That review was carried out, with the support of DTI civil servants, by a Project Director,[8] a permanent Steering Group chaired by the Director of the Company Law and Investigations Directorate of the DTI,[9] a permanent Consultative Committee, and a series of ad hoc Working Groups, in the operation of which many people with expertise in the area were involved.[10] The Steering Group produced a number of consultative documents, some very large, and a two-volume final report.[11] In its Final Report it declared its aims to have been to produce a company law that was "primarily enabling or facilitative" and to "strip out regulation that is no longer necessary". This would not mean an absence of statutory law for the framework of company law "should provide the necessary safeguards to allow people to deal with and invest in companies with confidence".[12] It was no part of the CLR's view that opportunism should be encouraged.

The immediate response of the Government (in 2002) was enthusiastic.[13] There was then something of a hiatus within Government,[14] but eventually a further White Paper was produced in 2005.[15] A Bill was introduced into Parliament in November 2005 and received the Royal Assent a year later. It is to be introduced in parts over a period of time, ending in October 2009.[16] The Bill was introduced as the Company Law Reform Bill, dealing only with those parts of the previous legislation intended to be changed, but under Parliamentary pressure it became the Companies Bill, indicating an intention to bring within the 2006 Act nearly the whole of statutory company law, whether intended to be changed or not. This is a much more convenient approach (and was what the CLR had assumed would happen) than that initially contemplated which would have left large chunks of the earlier Acts in place. However, the "unchanged" provisions were re-drafted in order to fit them into the style and structure

---

[7] DTI, *Company Law Reform: Modern Company Law for a Competitive Economy*, Foreword.

[8] Mr Jonathan Rickford.

[9] The principal editor of this edition was a member of that Steering Group (from March 1999) and so comments on the Review in this book should be read in the light of that fact.

[10] See Final Report II, Annex E for details.

[11] This output is referred to at the appropriate points throughout this work.

[12] Final Report I, para.9.

[13] See *Modernising Company Law*, Cm. 5553, July 2002—also in two volumes.

[14] What went on in that period is probably better not closely investigated, but a person centrally involved in the production of the Bill (but not in the CLR) has said: "the (highly commendable) wide inclusive process of the Review, seeking to build a consensus, made it comprehensible only to those involved in any particular issue. It was a closed book for anyone coming from outside ..." (P. Bovey, "A Damn Close Run Thing: the Companies Act 2006" (2008) *Statute Law Review* forthcoming. This suggests a remarkable lack of policy continuity in the Department before and after the CLR's Report. After all, the CLR was serviced by DTI staff, held nearly all its meetings in the DTI, and was kept in close touch with ministerial and departmental thinking on issues germane to its functions. To purport to begin again as if the CLR had not reported would be eccentric—and probably not what is intended by this passage.

[15] *Company Law Reform*, Cm. 6456, March 2005.

[16] Though this book is written, as far as possible, on the assumption that it is all in force.

of the 2006 Act, without any intention that their meaning should be changed. This occurred over the summer of 2006 so that a considerable amount of new material was added to the Bill at a late stage.[17] The result is an Act of some 1,300 sections and sixteen schedules, said to be the longest Act produced by Parliament. This may seem an odd result for a legislative process aimed to be facilitative. Two points can be made in mitigation of its length. First, enabling legislation is not to be confused with the absence of statutory law: often confining law narrowly takes more statutory words than a sweeping prohibition. Secondly, the Act is drafted in a lengthy way, paradoxically to make it more user-friendly. Few people read an Act from beginning to end. What they need to be able to do is to find quickly the provisions relevant to their problem. Setting out the provisions in a disaggregated form (for example, separate provisions for public and private companies on a particular topic, even if the provisions are similar) is helpful in that regard.

However, ever since the middle of the 1980s, if not earlier, the whole of the law relevant to companies has ceased to be contained in companies legislation. Provisions relating to the insolvency of companies were hived off into an Insolvency Act of 1986, which also contains a number of provisions having their practical effect in the period before the company enters insolvency and intended to protect creditors in that period.[18] In the same year, a Financial Services Act (now replaced by the Financial Services and Markets Act 2000) took over the provisions relating to the public offering and listing of shares, and the 2000 Act has been modified subsequently to take account of the burgeoning Community law in this area.[19] These two developments illustrate perennial problems of classification. Should rules on the insolvency of companies go in a company law consolidation or an insolvency law consolidation; equally, should rules of share issuance by companies go in a company law consolidation or a capital markets or securities law consolidation? Whatever the decisions taken by Government, we cannot ignore the fact that, functionally, important parts of the law relating to companies are not to be found in Acts which contain the word "company" in their title.[20]

---

[17] On July 21, 2006 new clauses, covering some 200 columns of Hansard, were added on the last day of the Committee stage in the House of Commons (H C Debs, Standing Committee D, Twenty First Sitting, 21 July 2006, cols.890ff).

[18] See Ch.9.

[19] See para.6–12 and Chs 25 and 26.

[20] Other important examples of separate legislation are the Business Names Act (applying not just to corporate businesses—see below, para.4–13) and the Company Directors Disqualification Act 1986 (see below, Ch.10), which at least has the word "Company" in its title and seems to have become a separate Act because it consolidates provisions previously found partly in the Companies Acts and partly in the Insolvency Act.

Secondary legislation

3-4 One major difficulty attending legislation as long as the Companies
Act is that a major commitment of Parliamentary time by the Government is required to get such legislation onto the statute book.
Once there, ministers are likely to take the view that company law has
had its turn for some while and will be reluctant to devote additional
Parliamentary time to proposals for its further reform. This can be a
distinct disadvantage for those parts of the Act which relate to
matters where the technical or economic context is changing rapidly
and fairly frequent updating of the legislation would be desirable.
One solution to this problem is greater use of subordinate legislation,
amending primary legislation but for which the process of Parliamentary scrutiny is much reduced and which therefore is much less
time-consuming.[21] The 2006 Act contains important examples of this
technique in particular areas, for example, companies' accounts[22] or
share capital,[23] both areas likely to be affected by changes occurring
outside the United Kingdom (whether at Community or broader
international levels) to which it was desirable for the Government to
be able to respond quickly. The original version of the Act, following
the CLR,[24] contained a general power to use secondary legislation to
amend the Act, but this was dropped after opposition from
Parliament.[25]

It is also the case that the Community obligations of the United
Kingdom in relation to company law may be implemented by secondary legislation under general powers conferred by the European
Communities Act 1972, which powers are not confined to the company law area. However, it is not absolutely clear how far this power
extends beyond the minimum necessary to transpose, for example, a
Directive into domestic law.

Delegated rule-making

3-5 Although quicker than primary legislation, secondary legislation
suffers from two defects. The first is that the rules are subject to less
democratic scrutiny than an Act of Parliament. For this reason, the
Company Law Review, whilst proposing greater use of secondary
legislation, also recommended that "the basic principles and archi-

---

[21] Instead of three readings and a committee stage in each House of Parliament over several
months, as in the case of an Act, there will be only a single short debate, and in the case of
subordinate legislation subject to "negative resolution", there will not even be a debate
unless MPs take the necessary steps to initiate one.

[22] s.468.

[23] s.657.

[24] Final Report I, paras 5.7 and 5.10 and Modernising, I, p.9.

[25] H L Debs, vol.680, Grand Committee, Twelfth Day, March 30, 2006, cols. 405–406. Some
power to reform by statutory instrument is now given to Government across legislation
generally by the Legislative and Regulatory Reform Act 2006.

tecture of the new framework would be set out in primary legislation".[26] The second is that secondary legislation may not be as expert
as rules produced by rule-makers closer to the regulated, despite the
conscientious consultation process in which the relevant Department
engages before making secondary rules. This second defect can be
overcome by delegation of law-making powers to a more expert body
than the Department.

The Financial Services Authority

A primary example of delegation beyond central government in the **3–6**
current law is the rule-making power conferred upon the Financial
Services Authority. The FSA makes three types of rule which are of
particular interest to us. First, it took over from the Stock Exchange
the long-standing and originally self-regulatory task of laying down
Listing Rules for companies whose securities have been entered onto
the 'official list'.[27] Some of the Community obligations of the United
Kingdom are implemented through the LR, but, as we have noted in
Chapter 1, they have been used to promote purely domestic policies
and thus to introduce for listed companies an additional set of core
rules that are not applied to non-listed companies. More recently, the
FSA has introduced further sets of rules—Prospectus (PR) and
Disclosure and Transparency (DTR) Rules—which are, indeed,
heavily driven by the need to transpose Community law in the United
Kingdom. However, the transposition of the EU requirements has
had the further impact of shifting some topics from the companies
legislation to the FSA's rules.[28] Here it is interesting that Parliament
has proceeded with transposition not primarily by way of direct
amendment of the FSMA, but by giving the FSA extended rule-
making powers. Finally, the FSA was required in FSMA to produce a
Code of Market Conduct (MAR) to flesh out the meaning of the
statutory prohibition on market abuse, which we consider in chapter 30.

In short, the FSA has exercised its powers to issue elaborate sets of
rules, without the need for formal approval by either Parliament or a
Governmental Department.[29] The public interest is protected, however, by the specification in the legislation of a set of general objectives by which the Authority is bound and which could be used as a
basis for judicial review of the rules;[30] the statutory requirement to
publish a statement of policy on the imposition of sanctions for
breaches of the Rules;[31] and the power of the Treasury to appoint and

---

[26] Final Report I, para.5.4.
[27] For the meaning of this term see para.25–8.
[28] Mainly the rules on disclosure on interests in shares on the part of directors and 'major'
shareholders. See Chapter 26.
[29] As ss 73A and 119 of FSMA 2000 contemplate.
[30] s.73.
[31] ss.93–94.

remove the members of its governing body,[32] to enquire formally into the FSA's activities[33] and even to transfer its functions elsewhere.[34] Thus, although the FSA is a private company formed under the Companies Act, in fact a company limited by guarantee,[35] and is financed by a levy on those who engage in financial services business, it has extensive public functions and is itself subject to controls thought to be appropriate to a public body.

Financial Reporting Council

3–7   The second area where delegated rule-making is to be found on a substantial scale in the present law is in relation to accounting standards, the accuracy of accounts, auditing standards and the regulation of auditors and accountants. This is an area where the Financial Reporting Council and its various subsidiaries are immensely important and their functions were much enhanced as a result of reforms implemented in the United Kingdom in the wake of the Enron and related scandals in the United States.[36] These functions are analysed in Chapters 21 and 22 and that analysis need not be anticipated here. What needs to be noted, however, is that, like the FSA, the FRC acquires its powers by way of delegation from the Secretary of State (who can therefore re-allocate them).[37] Like the FSA, the FRC and its subsidiaries are companies limited by guarantee, but its directors are appointed by the Secretary of State, so that the FRC, although more expert than a Government Department (and partly financed by those it regulates), is tied into the governmental machinery.

Common law

3–8   In spite of the bulk of the Companies Act and its satellite legislation, it does not contain a code of company law. The British Companies Acts have never aspired to lay down all the rules which sustain the core features of company law, as identified in the previous chapter. However, the 2006 Act goes further in that regard than previous Acts. The Law Commissions recommended that there should be a statutory statement of the common law duties of directors (though not of the remedies for breach)[38] and the English Law Commission that the law relating to the enforcement of those duties should be both reformed

---

[32] Sch.1, para.2(3).
[33] ss.14–18.
[34] Sch.8.
[35] See above, para.1–5.
[36] The main legislative expression of these reforms was the Companies (Audit, Investigation and Community Enterprise) Act 2004, some parts of which have survived the 2006 Act.
[37] ss 457 and 1217 and Sch.10 of CA 2006.
[38] *Company Directors: Regulating Conflicts of Interest and Formulating a Statement of Duties*, Cm. 4436, 1999.

and stated in legislative form.[39] Both these sets of recommendations were broadly endorsed by the Company Law Review, and were included in the 2006 Act, thus effecting a major extension of statutory company law.[40] Although these reforms significantly altered the balance between statute law and common law in company law, they may have a much less pronounced effect upon the role of the judges in developing company law. Although the statutory statement largely replaces the existing common law and equitable rules on directors' duties, it is drafted as a relatively "high level" statement. Consequently, the pre-existing case-law will remain relevant where the statement simply repeats, rather than reforms, the common law. More important, the recourse throughout the statement to broad standards, rather than precise rules, means the judges will have an important role in developing and applying the standards, just as they have had in respect of those standards which were embodied in statute from the beginning.[41] As to the enforcement of directors' duties, the reform creates a greater judicial discretion to allow or refuse derivative actions, so that the judges are, if anything, more important under the Act than the prior common law.

Review and reform

It is clear that company law consists of a complex and diverse body of rules. Keeping this law under review has been the task of, mainly, the Department of Trade and Industry ("DTI")—now re-named the Department for Business, Enterprise and Regulatory Reform (BERR)—which is the Government Department responsible for, among many other matters, company and insolvency law. As for financial services law, including public offerings of securities and their listing, the Treasury is the leading source of policy.

3–9

   The CLR, referred to above, may be seen as the latest in a series of reviews of company law carried out by the DTI, or its predecessors, since the introduction of incorporation by registration in the middle of the nineteenth century. Its method of operation was rather different from that of its predecessors, which had consisted of small committees of enquiry which took formal evidence but did not engage in widespread consultation. They also tended to concentrate on particular aspects of the subject, thought to need reform, rather than upon a comprehensive review. The two most recent Committee reports of this older type, which are still important for an understanding of the current law, are the Jenkins[42] and Cohen[43] Committee reports (so referred to after the names of their chairmen). As noted

[39] *Shareholder Remedies*, Cm. 3769, 1997.
[40] See Chs 16 and 17 below. Both extensions were controversial.
[41] For example, the unfair prejudice provisions, discussed in Ch.20.
[42] Report of the Company Law Committee, Cmnd. 1749, 1962.
[43] Report of the Committee on Company Law Amendment, Cmnd. 6659, 1945.

above, in recent years the Law Commissions (English and Scottish) have also played an important part in company law reform. In the long term, however, the CLR was unconvinced that periodic, ad hoc, comprehensive reviews of the type it had undertaken were the best way forward, because they depend so heavily upon governmental commitment to devote the necessary resources to the exercise. It recommended instead that a standing Company Law and Reporting Commission should have the remit of keeping company law under review and reporting annually to the Secretary of State its views on where, if anywhere, reform was needed. In addition, the Secretary of State would be obliged to consult the Commission on proposed secondary legislation.[44] In this way, it was hoped, company law reform would become a continuing and expert process, so that less weight would need to be placed on ad hoc, across-the-board reviews. However, the Government rejected the proposal for a standing Commission.[45]

THE COMPANY'S CONSTITUTION

The significance of the constitution

3–10   A remarkable feature of British company law is the extent to which it leaves regulation of the internal affairs of a company to the company itself through rules laid down in its constitution and, in particular, in its articles of association. In fact, the principle is that the articles may deal with any matter which is not, or to the extent that it is not, regulated through any of the sources mentioned above. This is not stated explicitly in the Act, but is rather an assumption upon which the Act is drafted, too obvious to be worth stating. However, the crucial point is not just the formal relationship between the articles and the other sources of company law, especially the Act, but the extent to which substantive matters, central to the company's operation, are left to be regulated by the articles. Examples of important matters which are regulated mainly by the articles are the division of powers between the shareholders and the board of directors, and the composition, structure and operation of the board of directors.[46] Many jurisdictions regulate these matters through their companies legislation, rather than the company's constitution, and this is true of systems as otherwise different as those of Germany and the United States.[47]

---

[44]   Final Report I, para.5.22.
[45]   Modernising, I, pp.48–49.
[46]   For listed companies, the Combined Code has now begun to trespass upon the autonomy of the company. See below, Ch.14.
[47]   See for Germany the *Aktiengesetz*, Pt Four, subdivisions One and Two, and for the United States, the Model Business Corporation Act, Ch.8.

In the American case, however, the legislation often uses default rules, which can be changed by appropriate provisions in the company's constitution, so that, where this is the case, the shareholders can ultimately adopt the set of rules they want, as is the case in Britain. For example, paragraph 8.01 of the Model Business Corporation Act gives a broad management power to the board of a US company, but allows the shareholders, in the constitution or by shareholder agreement, to cut down that provision if they wish and allocate decisions to themselves; whereas the directors of a British company have management powers only to the extent that they are given to the board by the articles (as, normally, they are).[48] The ultimate division of powers between board and shareholders, in similar types of company, may thus be equivalent in the two countries. Nevertheless, since the shareholders control the constitution (see below) the British approach can be said to represent the view that the shareholders constitute the ultimate source of managerial authority within the company and that the directors obtain their powers by a process of delegation from the shareholders, albeit a delegation of a formal type which, so long as it lasts, may make the directors the central decision-making body on behalf of the company.[49] By contrast, the German and, even, the American approach can be said to be based on the principle that the allocation of powers to the organs of the company is the result of a legislative act, even if, within limits, the shareholders may alter the initial legislative allocation.

The importance of the articles of association in the British scheme is perhaps reflected in the provisions in the Act authorising the Secretary of State to promulgate model articles of association for companies of different types[50] and, in particular, in the default status conferred upon the statutory models.[51] This power is of long standing and under it have been issued from time to time lettered "tables" of model articles, that for companies limited by shares being invariably "Table A". Many companies exist whose articles are based on the Table A of 1985 or the earlier one of 1948 or, conceivably, even earlier versions. The current statutory instrument creating the models[52] has abandoned the device of denoting the models by lettered tables, but the Act and the statutory instrument in fact demonstrate that an even greater importance is now placed on the models. Following the CLR,[53] the present Act gives the power to produce sepa-

---

[48] See the (draft) model articles for public companies, art.2: "Subject to the articles, the directors are responsible for the management of the company's business, for which purpose they may exercise all the powers of the company." The model article for private companies limited by shares is in similar terms.

[49] See below, Ch.14.

[50] s.19.

[51] s.20.

[52] The (draft) Companies (Model Articles) Regulations available on the BERR web-site.

[53] Final Report II, Ch.17.

rate model articles for private and public companies limited by shares (as well as for companies not limited by shares) and this power has been exercised. The model for private companies limited by shares is in Schedule 1 to the draft Regulations and that for public companies in Schedule 3. Given the range of companies falling under the companies legislation, it is surprising that a single model set of articles for companies limited by shares was thought for so long to be adequate.[54]

3–11   When a limited company is formed,[55] it will be treated as having adopted the relevant model articles, except to the extent that it chooses to have different articles, either in whole or in part.[56] That choice may be expressed by adopting articles which, in one or more respects, are inconsistent with the model, but the model will still apply to govern matters which are not dealt with in the articles specified by the company, i.e. the model performs a gap-filling role in such a case. If the company wishes to avoid this impact of the model, it must include in its articles an article which specifically excludes the whole of the model. This is sometimes done, but it was in fact common for companies to register articles which, by contrast, explicitly adopted Table A, but stated that Table A should operate in relation to the company subject to a list of specific amendments. This meant that the full articles of the company could be established only through the laborious process of taking Table A and applying the specified changes to it, hardly a transparent process. This approach no longer seems permissible, in view of the requirement that the articles "must be contained in a single document".[57] Thus, it appears that the company must deliver to the registrar a complete set of its articles contained within a single document—not a significant burden in these days of electronic word processing. However, saying anything about the articles is not obligatory. Those registering the company could say nothing, in which case the model will apply in full.[58] At the other extreme, they could exclude the model entirely and adopt a set of articles which contains very different provisions.

The version of the model which is implied into the company's articles (unless excluded) is that which is extant when the company is formed. The subsequent promulgation of a revised version of the model will not affect companies already registered but only those registered in the future.[59] Hence the fact, noted above, that there are many companies in existence for whom the relevant model is Table A of 1948. For the practitioner, therefore, the replacement of one model

---

[54] Probably the facility of company formation agents in developing their own standard model articles for different classes of company met much of the need in practice.

[55] Whether limited by shares or not; s.8(2) of CA 1985 created a default only in the case of companies limited by shares.

[56] s.20(1).

[57] s.18(3)(a).

[58] s.20(1)(a)—unless there is no model prescribed, in which case it must register articles of association: s.18(2).

[59] s.20(2).

by another is not a reason to forget one's learning about the former model.

The aim of the models might be thought to be to reduce the costs faced by those forming companies. Under the British structure the company cannot work effectively without fairly elaborate articles and the models aim to supply that need for those who do not wish, or cannot afford, to work out their own internal regulations.

What constitutes the constitution?

Unlike its predecessors the 2006 Act defines the company's con-   **3–12**
stitution.[60] The term includes the articles of association but is not limited to them. Also included are "any resolutions or agreements to which Chapter 3 [of Part 3] applies".[61] Chapter 3 applies to special resolutions of the shareholders (whether passed as such or by virtue of unanimous agreement among the members);[62] any resolution or agreement of a class of members binding all the members of the class (for example, a resolution varying class rights);[63] any unanimous resolution or agreement adopted by the members of a class provided that it would not otherwise be binding on them unless passed by a particular majority or in a particular manner; and any other resolution or agreement to which the chapter applies by virtue of any enactment.[64] In practice, the most important category is special resolutions of the shareholders. Thus, it is important to ascertain whether a particular provision of the Act applies only to the company's articles or to its constitution more generally. Given its much reduced legal status, it is not surprising that the memorandum of association does not feature as part of the company's constitution.[65]

The legal status of the constitution

The common law tends to classify the rule-books of associations,   **3–13**
whether they are clubs, trade unions, friendly societies or other, as contractual in nature. The articles of association are no exception to this principle, though in this case the classification is done by the Act. Section 33 of the Act provides that "the provisions of the company's constitution bind the company and its members to the same extent as if there were covenants on the part of *the company and* of each member to observe it." The wording of this section can be traced back with variations to the original Act of 1844 which adopted the

---

[60] The provisions of the Companies Act 2006 relating to its constitution are scheduled to come into force on October 1, 2009.

[61] s.17.

[62] See para.15–25.

[63] See Ch.19. This could be an ordinary resolution of the class, if it binds all the members of the class.

[64] s.29.

[65] For the residual function of the memorandum see para.4–14.

existing method of forming an unincorporated joint stock company by deed of settlement (which did, of course, constitute a contract between the members who sealed it) and merely superimposed incorporation on registration. The 1856 Act substituted the memorandum and articles for the deed of settlement. Unhappily, full account was not taken of the vital new factor (namely that the incorporated company was a separate legal entity) and the words (in the previous versions of the provision) "as if ... signed and sealed by each member"[66] did not have added to them "and by the company". Thus, the Acts appeared to say that the articles bound only the members, a very odd result since the observance of the "rule-book" is one of the cornerstones of the member's protection against the company (whether it is the directors or a majority shareholder who currently controls the company). This oddity had survived into the modern Acts and would have survived into the 2006 Act, had not the Opposition spokesman in the Commons picked up and pressed the amendment Lord Wedderburn had advanced in the Lords to make the whole matter clear through the simple step of inserting the words italicised above into the provision.[67]

The Company Law Review wondered whether it was any longer appropriate to regard the articles of association as a contract, but in the end decided that the issue did not call for immediate resolution,[68] and the Act in fact retains the contractual approach. What is clear, however, is that the articles constitute a rather particular form of contract, and the peculiarities of that contract need to be noted here.

(i) The parties to the contract

3–14   In the light of what has just been said, it is now clear that the articles constitute a contract between the company and each member. Further, the contract is enforceable among the members *inter se*. The principal occasions on which this question is likely to be important arise when articles confer on members a right of pre-emption or first

---

[66] The treatment of the articles as a deed has also been removed from the current section, thus removing the consequence that a debt owed by the member to the company was a "specialty" debt, with its special limitation period, rather than an ordinary one. Contrast s.14(2) of CA 1985 and s.33(2) of CA 2006 and *cf. Compania de Electridad de Buenos Aires, Re* [1980] Ch. 146 at 187.

[67] H C Debs, Standing Committee D, Third Sitting, 20 June 2006, cols.87–89—the so-called "Wedderburn-Djanogly" amendment. The Bill as introduced had adopted the old formula despite the fact that the CLR had said that the former provision (s.14 of the CA 1985) was "obscurely drafted ... [and] clearly cannot just be re-enacted and no one supports that approach" and that "we propose therefore that the replacement for section 14 should make it clear that the constitution confers mutual rights, obligations and powers between the company and its members ..." (Completing, paras 5.64 and 5.65) Practitioners had long treated the articles as binding as between member and company, although on the basis of only a first instance authority: *Hickman v Kent or Romney Marsh Sheepbreeders Association* [1915] 1 Ch. 881.

[68] Completing, paras 5.68–5.69.

refusal when another member wishes to sell his shares[69] or, more rarely, impose a duty on the remaining members or the directors to buy the shares of a retiring member.[70] A direct action between the shareholders concerned is here possible; and for the law to insist on action through the company would merely be to promote multiplicity of actions and involve the company in unnecessary litigation. Thus, the contract created by section 33 is a multi-party contract, not that this feature in itself distinguishes it from many other types of contract found in the commercial world.

(ii) The contract as a public document

Although the articles of association have a contractual status, they are clearly more than a private bargain among the company and its members. The company's articles become a public document at the moment of formation, either because the relevant model articles, themselves a public document, will apply or because the company supplies to the registrar for public registration its own articles which amend or even fully replace the statutory model.[71] Publicity of the company's constitution has always been a requirement of British company law and is now in any event a requirement of Community company law.[72] Thus, those who deal with the company have a legitimate expectation that the registered articles represent an accurate statement of the company's internal regulations. From this situation the courts have concluded that standard contract law should be applied to the articles only with certain qualifications. The courts are reluctant to apply to the statutory contract those doctrines of contract law which might result in the articles subsequently being held to have a content substantially different from that which someone reading the registered documents would have understood them to have. Thus, the Court of Appeal has held that articles cannot later be rectified to give effect to what the incorporators actually intended but failed to embody in the registered document, since the reader of the registered documents could have no way of guessing that any error had been made in transposing the incorporators' agreement into the document.[73] Equally, that Court has refused to imply terms into the statutory contract from extrinsic evidence of surrounding circumstances, since that evidence would probably not be known to third parties who would thus have no basis for

3–15

---

[69] *Borland's Trustee v Steel* [1901] 1 Ch. 279 (member seeking declaration that rights of pre-emption in articles were valid); *cf. Lyle & Scott v Scott's Trustees* [1959] A.C. 763, HL and see para.27–7.

[70] *Rayfield v Hands* [1960] Ch. 1, where Vaisey J. was prepared to make an order in effect for specific performance.

[71] ss. 9(5)(b) and 14.

[72] Directive 68/151/EEC, [1968] O.J. 41, Art.2(1)(b).

[73] *Scott v Frank F. Scott (London) Ltd* [1940] Ch. 794, CA.

anticipating that any such implication was appropriate.[74] Further, in this case Steyn L.J. was of the view that for the same reasons the statutory contract "was not defeasible on the grounds of misrepresentation, common law mistake, mistake in equity, undue influence or duress".[75] These decisions by the courts on the meaning of the company's constitutional documents support the policy underlying the statutory provision on the conclusiveness of the certificate of incorporation.[76] Both conduce to protection of third parties by enabling the third party to rely on what he or she finds upon a search of the public registry.[77]

However, the policy behind these cases is somewhat undermined by those decisions which have allowed the doctrine of informal, unanimous shareholder consent to be applied to changes to the company's constitution. Under this doctrine, which is discussed further in Chapter 15, decisions taken informally by shareholders will nevertheless be effective, if taken unanimously. Although the Act appears to provide for such informal resolutions altering the articles to be communicated to the Registrar,[78] alterations to the articles taken informally are likely in fact not to be communicated, so that the registered constitution fails to reflect the actual set of articles.[79] Failure to inform the registrar is a criminal offence and may attract civil penalties, but the validity of the alteration appears not to be affected by non-compliance.[80]

(iii) Who can enforce the contract?

3–16   The standard answer to this question at common law is: the parties to the contract.[81] Since it is members who are party to the contract with the company, it follows that non-members cannot enforce the contract, even if they are intimately involved with the company, for

---

[74] *Bratton Seymour Service Co Ltd v Oxborough* [1992] B.C.L.C. 693, CA. In this case the majority were in effect seeking to avoid the prohibition on alterations to the constitution without individual shareholder consent which have the effect of increasing the shareholder's financial liability to the company (see s.25 and below, para.19–1). See also *Towcester Racecourse Co Ltd v Racecourse Association Ltd* [2003] 1 B.C.L.C. 260, where, in any event, the judge regarded the suggested implied terms as inconsistent with the express terms of the articles.

[75] [1992] B.C.L.C. 693, CA at 698. On the other hand, investor protection was not inconsistent with the implication of terms based on the construction of the language used in the articles, for here the basis of the implication was available to those who read the company's constitution.

[76] See below, para. 4–17.

[77] A further and important restriction on the remedies available in respect of breaches of the corporate constitution, namely the supposed rule that damages were not available to a shareholder in an action against his company so long as he remained a member, seems to have been removed by what is now s.655, originally inserted by the 1989 Act.

[78] ss. 29 and 30.

[79] *Cane v Jones* [1980] 1 W.L.R. 1451; *Home Treat Ltd, Re* [1991] B.C.L.C. 705.

[80] ss. 26 and 27.

[81] The Contracts (Rights of Third Parties) Act 1999 does not apply to the company's constitution: s.6(2) of that Act.

example, as directors. Suppose, however, a person is both a member of the company and one of its directors. Can he or she enforce rights conferred by the articles, even if that right is conferred upon the claimant in his or her capacity as director of the company? The answer appears to be in the negative. The decisions have constantly affirmed that the section confers contractual effect on a provision in the articles only in so far as it affords rights or imposes obligations on a member *qua*, or as a, member.[82] As Astbury J. said in the *Hickman* case:[83]

> "An outsider to whom rights purport to be given by the articles in his capacity as such outsider, whether he is or subsequently becomes a member, cannot sue on those articles, treating them as contracts between himself and the company, to enforce those rights."

The same applies to the contract between the members *inter se*.[84] On the wording of the section it would be difficult to interpret it as creating a contract with anyone other than the company and the members. Furthermore, there is obvious sense in restricting the ambit of the section to matters concerning the affairs of the company. The question is whether it is justified to restrict the statutory wording still further, so that it applies only to matters concerning a member in his capacity of member.[85] As a consequence of this interpretation, a promoter, who becomes a member, cannot enforce a provision that the company shall reimburse the expenses he or she incurred[86] nor a solicitor, who becomes a member, a provision that he or she shall be the company's solicitor.[87] More important, this approach to the section apparently prevents a member who is also a director or other officer of the company from enforcing any rights purporting to be conferred by the articles on directors or officers. Only if he or she has a separate contract, extraneous to the articles, will the director have contractual rights and obligations vis-à-vis the company or fellow members. For this reason, executive directors will be careful to enter into service contracts with their company (into which it is entirely permissible to incorporate provisions from the articles of associa-

[82] But not necessarily *qua* shareholder: in *Lion Mutual Marine Insurance v Tucker* (1883) 12 Q.B.D. 176, CA, the provision concerned the members' liabilities *qua* insurers.
[83] *Hickman v Kent or Romney Marsh Sheepbreeders' Association* [1915] 1 Ch. 881 at 897.
[84] *London Sack & Bag Co v Dixon & Lugton* [1943] 2 All E.R. 763, CA.
[85] The *Hickman* case may reflect the high regard in which the courts then held the doctrine of privity of contract.
[86] *English & Colonial Produce Co, Re* [1906] 2 Ch. 435.
[87] *Eley v Positive Life Association* (1876) 1 Ex. D. 88, CA.

tion)[88] in order to safeguard their remuneration, and non-executive directors would be well advised to do so also.[89]

It is somewhat anomalous to treat directors as "outsiders" since for most purposes the law treats them as the paradigm "insiders" (which members, as such, are not) and they will breach their fiduciary duties and duties of care if they do not act in accordance with the company's constitution.[90] It also produces some strange results. *Hickman*'s case concerned a provision in the articles stating that any dispute between the company and a member should be referred to arbitration and this was enforced as a contract. But in the later case of *Beattie v Beattie Ltd*,[91] where there was a similar provision, the Court of Appeal, relying on the dictum in *Hickman*, held that a dispute between a company and a director (who was a member) was not subject to the provision because the dispute was admittedly in relation to the director *qua* director. In the still later case of *Rayfield v Hands*,[92] the articles of a private company provided that a member intending to transfer his shares should give notice to the directors "who will take the said shares equally between them at a fair value". A member gave notice but the directors refused to buy. Vaisey J. felt able to hold that the provision was concerned with the relationship between the member and the directors as members and ordered them to buy.[93]

3-17   However, academic argument has been made to the effect that the *Hickman* principle can be side-stepped, in most or all cases, by the identification of an appropriate membership right. In 1957, Lord Wedderburn, in his seminal article on *Foss v Harbottle*,[94] pointed out that, in *Quinn & Axtens Ltd v Salmon*,[95] the Court of Appeal and the House of Lords allowed a managing director, suing as a member, to obtain an injunction restraining the company from completing transactions entered into in breach of the company's articles, which provided that the consent of the two managing directors was required in relation to such transactions. This, in effect, showed that a member had a membership right to require the company to act in accordance

---

[88] Relatively little is needed for the court to conclude that the articles have been incorporated into the service contract, but there must be something: see *Globalink Telecommunications Ltd v Wilmbury Ltd* [2003] 1 B.C.L.C. 145.

[89] On directors' contracts see Ch.14.

[90] s.171. See para.16–20.

[91] [1938] Ch. 708, CA.

[92] [1960] Ch. 1.

[93] What he would have held had one of the directors not been a member is unclear.

[94] See "Shareholders' Rights and the Rule in *Foss v. Harbottle*" in [1957] C.L.J. 193, especially at 210–215. See also Beck in (1974) 22 Can.B.R. 157 at 190–193.

[95] [1909] 1 Ch. 311, CA; affirmed [1909] A.C. 442, HL. For subsequent dicta in support of this view see, e.g. *Harmer Ltd, Re* [1959] 1 W.L.R. 62 at 85 and 89, CA, *Richmond Gate Property Co, Re* [1965] 1 W.L.R. 335 (see (1965) 28 M.L.R. 347 and (1966) 29 M.L.R. 608 at 612); *Hogg v Cramphorn* [1967] Ch. 254; *Bamford v Bamford* [1970] Ch. 212; *Sherbourn Park Residents Co Ltd, Re* (1986) 2 B.C.C. 99 at 528; *Breckland Group Holdings v London & Suffolk Properties* [1989] B.C.L.C. 100 (see (1989) 52 M.L.R. 401 at 407–408); *Guinness Plc v Saunders* [1990] 2 A.C. 663, HL; *Wise v USDAW* [1996] I.C.R. 691 at 702.

with its articles, which right could be enforced by the member even though the result was indirectly to protect a right which was afforded to him as director. If this is correct, the supposed principle, that there is a statutory contract between the company and its members only in respect of matters affecting members *qua* members, is effectively outflanked—though presumably it still applies to the statutory contact between members *inter se*.[96]

Despite the criticisms which can be levelled against the *Hickman* principle, when the Company Law Review consulted on the question of whether this aspect of the Act required reform,[97] a positive response was not forthcoming and the recommendation from the CLR was accordingly to leave the law as it is.[98] Perhaps this indicates that, although the *Hickman* principle may not be wholly desirable, it is a clear rule and the costs of contracting around it are not high. Consequently, practice has accommodated itself to the rule, and this may also explain the lack of pressure to change the rule when the common law of privity of contract was reformed.[99]

(iv) Which provisions can be enforced by the members?

Although the Company Law Review was content to let the "member **3–18** *qua* member" aspect of the statutory contract remain undisturbed, the same cannot be said of a related aspect of the contract with which we must deal. Even though a member sues as a member and even though he or she sues to enforce a provision in the articles which appears to confer a right on the member, he or she may nevertheless be defeated by the argument that the provision does not confer a personal right on the member but creates only an obligation on the company, breach of which constitutes "a mere internal irregularity" on the company's part. The consequence of the categorisation of the breach of the articles as an internal irregularity is that the decision whether to sue to enforce the provision is a matter for the shareholders collectively, whereas personal rights, not surprisingly, can be enforced by individual shareholders.

The issue has tended to arise particularly in relation to those provisions dealing with the convening and conduct of meetings of shareholders or the selection of members of the board. These are areas where there are statutory provisions, but they are of a limited nature and much is left to be regulated in the company's articles.[100] If, for example, the chairman of a shareholders' meeting acts in breach

---

[96] For subsequent academic discussion of the principle, see Goldberg in (1972) 33 M.L.R. 362; G.N. Prentice in (1980) 1 Co.Law 179; Gregory in (1981) 44 M.L.R. 526; Goldberg (replying) in (1985) 48 M.L.R. 121; and Drury in [1989] C.L.J. 219.

[97] Formation, paras 2.6–2.8.

[98] Completing, paras 5.66–5.67.

[99] See above, fn.81.

[100] See Chs 14 and 15, below.

of the provisions of the articles governing meetings, is that an infringement of the shareholders' personal rights or a mere internal irregularity? There are a number of decisions of the courts over the past one hundred and fifty years putting such breaches in one category or the other, but it is difficult to discern the principled basis on which the classification was carried out. The importance, if not the nature, of the distinction is shown by two ultimately irreconcilable cases from the 1870s, *MacDougall v Gardiner*[101] and *Pender v Lushington.*[102] In the former the decision of the chairman of the shareholders' meeting wrongfully (i.e. in breach of the articles) to refuse a request for a poll was held to be an internal irregularity, whilst in the latter the refusal of a chairman to recognise the votes attached to shares held by nominee shareholders was held to infringe their personal rights. Each decision has spawned a line of equally irreconcilable authorities. In truth, there is a conflict here between proper recognition of the contractual nature of the company's constitution and the traditional policy of non-interference by the courts in the internal affairs of companies. As Smith has suggested,[103] ultimately the only satisfactory solution is to choose which policy is to have priority. Moreover, it is surely clear today that it ought to be the former. It can hardly be argued in modern law that it is an example of excessive interference by the courts to hold a company (or any other association) to the procedures which it itself has adopted in its constitution for its internal decision-making (until such time as it decides to change those internal rules according to the procedures set down for that to occur).[104] Indeed, it might even be suggested that effective protection of this procedural entitlement of members is basic to any satisfactory system of company law.[105]

Part of the confusion may have arisen because of a failure to appreciate that the same situation may give rise to wrongs both by and against the company, and the individual shareholder's position will vary according to which wrong he seeks to redress. Thus, the chairman of a shareholders' meeting who breaches the relevant provisions of the articles may both put the company in breach of its contract with the members and him- or herself be in breach of duty to

---

[101] (1875) 1 Ch.D. 13.
[102] (1877) 6 Ch.D. 70.
[103] R.J. Smith, "Minority Shareholders and Corporate Irregularities" (1978) M.L.R. 147.
[104] This argument would lack force only if, as is *not* usually the case for companies or, indeed, most associations, the procedure for amending the rules on how decisions are to be taken was the same as the one for taking substantive decisions.
[105] Such a statement would surely be regarded as uncontroversial if made in relation to trade union law. *Cf. Kahn-Freund's Labour and the Law* (3rd ed., 1983), pp.286 *et seq.* The courts do not lack techniques for dealing with members whose complaints are purely "technical", i.e. where it is clear that the same result would have been arrived at even if the proper procedure had been followed: *Harben v Phillips* [1974] 1 W.L.R. 638.

the company for not observing the provisions. An analogy is provided by the decision in *Taylor v NUM (Derbyshire Area)*.[106] The plaintiff successfully sued his trade union[107] in a personal capacity to obtain an injunction restraining the officials of the union from continuing a strike which it was a breach of the union's rule-book (in fact, beyond its capacity) to conduct, but failed in his claim for an order requiring the same officials to restore to the union the funds already expended on the strike, because he did not have standing to bring a derivative action on behalf of the union.[108] The same analysis may often be applicable to breaches of the articles.[109] In other words, the company may be regarded as breaching its contract with the member if it seeks to act upon a resolution improperly passed and should be restrainable by the member, but for the loss (say the wasted costs of organising the meeting) caused to the company by the chair of the meeting in not conducting it in accordance with the company's regulations, the company is the proper plaintiff.[110]

An alternative line of attack on the above decisions might be **3–19** provided by the general membership right, postulated by Professor Wedderburn and noted above, to have the affairs of the company conducted in accordance with the articles, for that right was also put forward by him as a personal right. Consequently, this general right, if recognised by the courts or the legislature, would defeat both the "outsider right" argument and the "mere internal irregularity" argument against shareholder enforcement of the articles of association. After some hesitation, the Company Law Review decided to take a bold approach which amounted, in effect, to the acceptance of Professor Wedderburn's argument, at least on the matter of the range of provisions enforceable by the member as member. All duties imposed in favour of members under the constitution should be enforceable by individual shareholders.[111] In principle, if the company acted in breach of such duties, then the member would be able to bring an action to enforce the company's rule-book. Or the member would be able to sue another member if the obligation was laid by the articles on that member. This would not mean that every breach of the articles by a corporate officer would entitle each shareholder to

---

[106] [1985] B.C.L.C. 237. For the application of the distinction between personal and derivative actions to companies in an ultra vires context, see *Moseley v Koffyfontein Mines* [1911] 1 Ch. 73, CA.

[107] To which this distinction between personal rights and mere internal irregularities also applies.

[108] See Ch.17 for a discussion of derivative actions in relation to companies.

[109] But note *Devlin v Slough Estates Ltd* [1983] B.C.L.C. 497, refusing to recognise that the particular article in question, relating to the preparation of the company's accounts, conferred a right upon individual shareholders (as contrasted with "the company").

[110] There is some suggestion in the language used in *MacDougall v Gardiner* and *Pender v Lushington* (see above, fn.101 and 102), respectively, that the decisions are to be explained on the basis that the two courts simply fastened on two different legal aspects of a single situation.

[111] Completing, para.5.73; Final Report I, paras 7.34–7.40.

sue the company for damages. Damages would be an available remedy only if the shareholder personally[112] had suffered loss as a result of the breach. In the case of a breach of procedure in the conduct of a meeting, a remedy other than damages might well be more appropriate, for example, an injunction preventing the company from acting on an improperly passed resolution. In other cases no remedy at all might be ordered. If the breach of procedure had been purely technical and it was clear that the resolution would have been passed even if the correct procedure had been followed, the court should not grant any remedy at all and might even award costs against the complainant shareholder. This proposal was subject to one qualification: it would be possible for the shareholders to opt, by an appropriate provision included therein, for some or all of the articles not to be enforceable. In such a case, the relevant articles would not be enforceable as a contract,[113] even if they would be under the current law. Thus, general contractual enforcement of the articles would be the default rule, and in any case it should be clear which articles were enforceable and which not.

However, the 2006 Act does not take up this proposal and so the uncertainties of the case-law, discussed above, remain.

(v) Altering the contract

3–20   It is crucial that the articles, as part of the constitution of an ongoing organisation, be capable of amendment from time to time. Section 21 expressly provides that "a company may amend its articles by special resolution."[114] Thus, a member enters into a contract on terms which are alterable by the other party (the company, acting through the shareholders collectively),[115] rather in the same way as a member of a club agrees to be bound by the club rules as validly altered from time to time by the members as a whole, or a worker agrees to be employed on the terms of a collective agreement as varied from time to time by the employer and trade union. That a majority of the members should normally be able to alter the articles by following a prescribed procedure and thus alter for the future the contractual rights and obligations of individual shareholders is hardly surprising. It reflects the fact that the company is an association and that some process of collective decision-making is needed, in relation to its constitution, if it is to be able to adapt to changing circumstances in

---

[112] On the distinction between corporate and individual loss, see para.17–13.

[113] Though they could still be used as the basis for an unfair prejudice remedy: see Ch.20, below. That remedy today is probably the mechanism by which complaints of breaches of the articles are most often litigated.

[114] Changes in the articles must be notified to the registrar: s.26. In the case of charitable companies the power to amend the articles is subject to the requirement of the charities legislation operating in the three UK jurisdictions: s.21(2), (3).

[115] *Shuttleworth v Cox Bros & Co (Maidenhead) Ltd* [1927] 2 K.B. 9 at 26, per Atkin L.J., CA; *Malleson v National Insurance and Guarantee Corp* [1894] 1 Ch. 200 at 205, per North J.

the business environment. The alternative would be constitutional change only with the consent of each individual shareholder, which would be very difficult to obtain in many cases and which would give unscrupulous individuals golden opportunities for disruptive behaviour.

On the other hand, the ability of the majority to bind the minority through decisions which alter the articles of the company creates the potential for opportunistic behaviour on the part of the majority towards the minority. As we shall see in Chapters 19 and 20, company law has developed some general standards which address this problem, which arises in all situations where the majority may bind the minority, whether the matter at issue is an amendment to the articles or not. Here we need note only two particular restrictions on the majority's power to alter the articles. One is highly precise. The consent of the individual member is required for him or her to be bound by an alteration which requires him to subscribe for further shares in the company or increases his or her liability to contribute to the company's share capital or pay money to the company.[116]

The other provision is of a procedural nature and enables the shareholders to contract around the principle of majority rule for alteration of the articles. The normal rule is that the company cannot contract out of its power to alter the articles.[117] However, section 22 enables the shareholders to "entrench" provisions of the company's constitution, i.e. to make them capable of amendment or repeal "only if conditions are met, or procedures complied with, that are more restrictive than those applicable in the case of a special resolution."[118] Those additional restrictions may not make the articles completely unalterable[119]—probably a wise provision, because even a member who insists on such a provision may subsequently change his or her mind. However, amendment or repeal could be made conditional on the consent of a particular member or a higher percentage of the members than a special resolution requires. Entrenched status can be conferred upon provisions in the articles either upon the formation of the company or subsequently, but in the latter case only with the unanimous consent of the members.[120] The registrar must be given notice of the adoption of entrenchment provisions and of their removal;[121] and the company must certify compliance with the

[116] s.25(1).

[117] On the impact of this principle on contracts outside the articles, see para.19–24.

[118] Under the prior law, entrenchment could be achieved by placing the provision in the memorandum of association and subjecting it to restrictive alteration conditions—and the prior law did seem to permit making a provision unalterable in any circumstances (other than a court order). See CA 1985, s.17(2)(b). The new scheme follows that proposed by the CLR: Formation, para.2.27.

[119] s.22(3)(a) expressly provides that entrenchment cannot prevent alteration by agreement of all the members.

[120] s.22(2). On formation all the subscribers in effect agree to the contents of the articles and subsequent members join on the basis of what those articles provide.

[121] s.23.

entrenchment provisions whenever it alters its articles.[122] Thus, the principle that the constitution of the company can be altered by a three-quarters majority of the members can in fact be set aside by using the entrenchment provisions, though for most companies it would be unwise to do so on a significant scale.[123]

Shareholder agreements

3–21   The freedom of the shareholders to fashion the company's constitution facilitates the input of a significant element of "private ordering" into the rules governing the company, but the articles of association are not the only method whereby the shareholders can generate their own rules for the governance of their affairs. An alternative method is an agreement, concluded among some or all the shareholders, but existing outside and separate from the articles and to which the company itself may or may not be a party. Such an agreement is not normally treated as part of the constitution of the company, though it may have an effect which is rather similar to a provision in the articles.[124] The main advantages of the shareholders' agreement over the articles are that the agreement is a private document which does not have to be registered at Companies House and that it derives its contractual force from the normal principles of contract law and not from the Act, so that the limitations discussed above on the statutory contract do not to apply to the shareholders' agreement.

The main disadvantages are that the shareholders' agreement does not automatically bind new members of the company, as the articles do.[125] A new member of the company will not be bound by the agreement unless that person assents to it and so the shareholder agreement may not continue to bind all the members. Securing the assent of new members may or may not be easy to bring about. Nor does the Act provide an overriding mechanism for majority alteration to the shareholders' agreement. The parties to that agreement may provide such a mechanism, but if they do not do so, then the consent of each party to the agreement would apparently be necessary to effect a change. In short, a shareholders' agreement displays both the advantages and disadvantages of private contracting. We shall further discuss the shareholders' agreement and other methods of protecting minority shareholders, such as the issuance of shares with special rights attached to them, in Chapter 19.

---

[122] s.24.

[123] The entrenchment provisions can be overridden by a court order: s.22(3)(b), (4). See, for example, ss 899–901 and Ch.29.

[124] Perhaps for this reason shareholder agreements are included within the meaning of the constitution of the company for the purposes of s.40: see s.40(3)(b) and para.7–10.

[125] s.33(1) says that the articles bind the company and the members, meaning those who at any one time are the members of the company.

THE EUROPEAN COMPANY

As far as the European Company is concerned, a hierarchy of a   **3–22**
sources of rules is set out in the European Company Statute.[126] The
primary source of rules for the SE is Community law, as one would
expect, in the shape of the European Company Statute, which applies
directly in the Member States without the need for transposition,
which a Directive requires.[127] The second source of law for the SE is
its own statutes (or constitution or articles of association, as we might
term them), but only to the extent that the Regulation expressly
permits the SE through its statutes to regulate a particular matter. In
fact, some highly significant choices are expressly given by the Regulation to the SE, to be made through its statutes, for example, the
choice between a one-tier and a two-tier board.[128] However, as we
noted in Chapter 1,[129] the European Regulation does not aim to
provide a comprehensive code of company law for the SE. Much is
referred to the law of the State in which the SE is registered, and so
domestic law becomes an important source of rules for the SE. The
Regulation contemplates two types of domestic law as being relevant.
The third source is thus domestic law passed specifically in order to
embed the Regulation in the domestic company law or to exercise
choices conferred by the SE Statute on the Member States in relation
to the SE.[130] For example, Member States may, but need not, lay
down rules about the maximum and minimum number of members of
a one-tier board (if the SE chooses this system of governance)[131] or a
Member State may reduce below 10 per cent the figure for the proportion of shareholders who are entitled to insist that an item be
added to the agenda of a meeting of the SE's shareholders.[132]

However, the more important domestic (and fourth) source of rules
for the SE is likely to be the rules applying to public companies in the
jurisdiction of registration. These rules will apply to the SE automatically and without the need for special national implementing
legislation. Often, the SE Statute says in relation to a particular
subject-matter that these domestic rules shall apply (for example, in
relation to the legal capital of the SE)[133] but this is declared generally

---

[126] Council Regulation 2157/2001/EC, Art.9.
[127] However, since the provisions on worker involvement in the SE are contained in a Directive, which needs transposition, the Regulation applies in the Member States only together with the national provisions transposing the Directive. For the UK see European Public Limited-Liability Company Regulations, SI 2004/2326, Part 3 (hereafter European Company Regulations).
[128] Regulation 2157/2001/EC, Art.38. See further below, para.14–25.
[129] See above, para.1–21.
[130] See the European Company Regulations, Part 4 (exercising options) and Parts 2 and 5–7 doing various types of "embedding".
[131] SE Statute, Art.43(2).
[132] SE Statute, at Art.56.
[133] SE Statute, at Art.5.

to be the principle in relation to matters not governed, or to the extent not governed, by the Regulation itself.[134] Thus, much of the law governing domestic public companies limited by shares will apply to the SE. Indeed, the main interest of the SE as a legal form can be said to lie in those, relatively limited, areas where the domestic rules are trumped by rules emanating from Community law and the Community rules are significantly different from those which domestic law applies to its public companies,[135] and it is on those aspects that the later chapters in this book will concentrate. An obvious example is the requirement for the domestic legislature to make a two-tier board model of governance available for the SE to take up, if it so wishes.

The final source of rules for the SE under the Regulation brings the statutes of the SE back into the picture once again. They are a source of law "in the same way as for a public limited-liability formed in accordance with the law of the Member State in which the SE has its registered office."[136] As we have seen, the domestic law makes the articles a major source for the rules governing the internal affairs of the public company, and this will be the case also for the SE, except to the extent that the Regulation itself has occupied ground which the domestic company law leaves to the articles of association. This will probably mean that the statutes of a British-registered SE will be an important source of rules, but a less important source than for a domestic public company, because Title III of the Regulation governs the structure of the European Company (board of directors and shareholders' meeting) more extensively than does the Companies Act or the common law in relation to a domestic company.

However, the Community rules relating to the SE are not to be found wholly in the Regulation. The crucial issue of employee involvement in the SE[137] is dealt with at Community level by a Directive.[138] Directives do require transposition into domestic law. Moreover, if the Directive is properly transposed, the domestic law becomes the source of obligation in the national legal system, not the Directive. Consequently, the employee involvement Directive, despite the importance of its subject-matter, has no greater impact on the sources of domestic company law than do any of the many other EC Directives which have played a part in shaping modern British company law,[139] and so it need not be considered further here.

---

[134] SE Statute, at Arts 9(1)(c) and 10.
[135] Of course, some of the mandatory rules to be found in the Regulation may in fact track the domestic rules with perhaps minor changes.
[136] Regulation 2157/2001/EC, Art.9(1)(c)(iii).
[137] See further below, Ch.14.
[138] Directive 2002/14/EC, [2002] OJ L80/29.
[139] Discussed generally in Ch.6.

FORMATION PROCEDURES

As we have seen,[1] today there are three basic types of domestic **4–1** incorporated company—statutory, chartered and registered—and the formalities attending formation vary fundamentally as between each type. Detailed consideration is necessary only in respect of the last, companies registered under the Companies Act, for these are over-whelmingly the most common and important.

TYPES OF COMPANY

Statutory companies

These are formed by the promotion of a Private Act of Parliament. **4–2** Details of the procedure therefore appertain to the field of Private Bill

---

[1] See above, para.1–16.

legislation rather than to a manual of company law and the reader who is concerned in the formation of such a company should refer to the specialised works on the former topic. In practice the work is monopolised by a few firms of solicitors who specialise as parliamentary agents and by a handful of counsel at the parliamentary bar. The numbers of both promotions and specialist practitioners are dwindling, having regard to the curtailment of work resulting first from nationalisation and now from privatisation, both of which are achieved under Public Acts.

Chartered companies

4–3   It is unlikely that there will be any further creations of chartered trading companies but the grant of charters to charitable or public bodies is not uncommon. The procedure in such cases is for the promoters of the body to petition the Crown (through the office of the Lord President of the Council) praying for the grant of a charter, a draft of which is normally annexed to the petition. If the petition is granted the promoters and their successors then become:

> "one body corporate and politic by the name of—and by that name shall and may sue or be sued plead and be impleaded in all courts whether of law or equity ... and shall have perpetual succession and a common seal."

Sometimes a charter will be granted to the members of an existing guarantee company registered under the Companies Acts in which event the assets of the company will be transferred to the new chartered body and the company wound up unless the Registrar can be persuaded to exercise his power to strike it off the register, thus avoiding the expense of a formal liquidation.[2]

Registered companies

4–4   In the vast majority of cases the company, whatever its objects, will today be formed under the Companies Act, and it may be helpful to set out the practice in such cases in some detail. For ease of explanation we shall also assume that those forming the company (the "promoters") are natural persons, though this need not be the case. An existing company may form a new company by following the procedures set out below. Indeed, it is common to do so, since all but the smallest businesses are carried through groups of companies,

---

[2] See Appendix, below.

rather than single companies.[3] In the case of the European Company, however, introduced in 2004, it is formed under the relevant Community Regulation, as supplemented by domestic law, though Companies House acts as the registration body for SEs registered in Great Britain. However, as we have already noted,[4] the European Company cannot be formed by natural persons but only by existing companies (or analogous bodies) in the ways specified in the Regulation: merger, joint subsidiary, joint holding company, transformation. In what follows references will be made to the functions of the Registrar of Companies and of the Secretary of State in the formation of companies, but it should be noted that, in the modern fashion, power has been taken to delegate these functions to such persons as may be authorised by them.[5] In practice, most of the powers described in this Chapter will be exercised by Companies House, which is an executive agency of the DTI (now BERR).[6]

Choice of type of registered company

The promoters will first have to make up their minds which of the several types of registered company they wish to form, since this may make a difference to the number and types of documents required, and will certainly affect their contents.   **4–5**

First, they must choose between a limited and an unlimited company.[7] The disadvantage of the latter is that its members will ultimately be personally liable for its debts and for this reason they are likely to be wary of it if the company intends to trade. If, however, the company is merely to hold land or investments, the absence of limited liability may not matter and may confer certain advantages, for example, as regards returning capital[8] to the members and escaping from having to give publicity to the company's financial position.[9] The absence of limited liability may also render the company more acceptable in certain circles (for example, the turf).

If the promoters decide upon a limited company they must then

---

[3] The establishment of a group does not necessarily involve the creation of a new company. Rather, the group could be formed by the acquisition of the shares of an existing company, which is likely to be the procedure used if the expanding company is acquiring an established business rather than setting up its own new business from scratch.

[4] See above, para.1–22.

[5] Contracting Out (Functions in Relation to the Registration of Companies) Order 1995 (SI 1995/1013) made under the Deregulation and Contracting Out Act 1994.

[6] Most of the provisions of the Companies Act 2006 discussed in this chapter are scheduled to come into force on October 1, 2009, but the new provisions on challenges to a company's name (see below, para.4–11) are to be in force from October 1, 2008.

[7] An alternative, which in practice was very rarely adopted, was a limited company with unlimited liability on the part of the directors (s.306 of CA 1985) but the 2006 Act no longer provides for this.

[8] The prohibition against a company acquiring its own shares applies only to limited companies (s.658(1) and Ch.13).

[9] An unlimited company is not required to file its annual accounts and reports (and so make them publicly available): s.448 and Ch.21.

make up their minds whether it is to be limited by shares or by guarantee, and as already explained,[10] this is really a matter which will be decided for them by the purpose which the company is to perform. Only if it is to be a non-profit-making concern are they likely to form a guarantee company which is especially suited to a body of that type.

4–6   Overlapping these distinctions, but closely bound up with them, is the further point of whether or not the company should have a share capital. If, as is most probable, the company is to be limited by shares this question does not arise. Likewise, if it is to be limited by guarantee.[11] But if the company is unlimited it may or may not have its capital divided into shares. Once more, the decision is dependent on the company's purpose; if the company is intended to make and distribute profits a share capital will be appropriate.

They will further have to make up their minds whether the company is to be a public or private one. As we have seen,[12] public and private companies essentially fulfil different economic purposes; the former to raise capital from the public to run the corporate enterprise, the latter to confer a separate legal personality on the business of a single trader or a partnership. Once again, therefore, the choice will in practice be clear-cut and normally it will be to form a private company. The incorporators may have the ultimate ambition of "going public" but rarely will they be in a position to do so immediately. If, however, they are, then the company will have to be a company limited by shares, the certificate of incorporation will have to state that it is to be a public company and special requirements as to its registration will have to be complied with.[13] Any other type of company will, perforce, be a private company.

Finally, and again cutting across the above distinctions, is the question of whether the company's objectives are to be restricted to charitable purposes so as to make it a charitable company.[14] Moreover, since 2004 it has been possible for a limited company to be formed as a "community interest company" under the provisions of Part 2 of the Companies (Audit, Investigations and Community Enterprise) Act 2004. Such companies must have the pursuit of a community interest as their objective (but not be charitable companies) and their articles must contain restrictions on the payment of dividends and, generally, on the transfer of corporate assets other than for full consideration.[15]

In practice, the vast majority of companies formed are private

---

[10] See Ch.1, above.
[11] Since the coming into force of the Companies Act 1980 no further companies limited by guarantee and having a share capital can be formed: s.5.
[12] See Ch.1, above.
[13] s.4(2).
[14] See Ch.1 at para.1–15.
[15] 2004 Act, ss. 30 and 32 and the Community Interest Company Regulations 2005/1788, regs. 7–11.

companies limited by shares which are neither charitable nor community interest companies.[16]

<h2 style="text-align:center">COMPANY NAMES</h2>

The incorporators must next decide on a suitable name. This is of **4–7** some importance in identifying an artificial person[17] and the Act provides that an application for registration of a company must state the company's proposed name[18] and the Secretary of State has power to require companies to give appropriate publicity to their names thereafter at their places of business and on business correspondence and related documentation.[19] It is advisable, therefore, that it should be kept as short as possible.[20] Nor, once the company has been registered, can it change its name as informally as can a natural person.

Warning the public about limited liability

There are restrictions on the incorporators' freedom to formulate the **4–8** corporate name. The first of these is the obvious one, already referred to,[21] that if the company is a limited company its name must end with the prescribed warning suffix—"limited" if it is a private company or "public limited company" if it is a public one.[22] These expressions

---

[16] Full statistics are difficult to come by but DTI, *Companies in 2005–2006*, 2006, shows that only 1,000 public companies were newly incorporated in that year (though nearly 4,000 were created by conversion from private company status (see below) but some 370,000 private companies (of all types) were newly formed in that year (and a further 5,500 by conversion from public status). See Table A2.

[17] Though less so now that the Registrar has to allot each company a registered number (s.1066) which it has to state on its business letters and order forms: s.82(1)(a) and regulations made thereunder.

[18] s.9(2)(a).

[19] s.82(2)(a). The name must also be on the company's seal: s.45.

[20] Under the 2006 Act, largely for reasons of convenience of the Companies House computer system, a limit has been set on the number of characters of which a company's name may consist (no more than 160) and permitted characters have been prescribed as well as matters relating to the format of the name: s.57 and the draft Companies (Company and Business Names) (Miscellaneous Provisions) Regulations 2007, regs. 2 and 3 (hereafter "Names Regulations"). The DTI consultation document (below, fn.28), para.2.38, revealed that the longest registered name at that time had 159 characters. Like the famously long Welsh place name, Llanfairpwllgwyngyllgogerychwyrndrobwllllantysiliogogogoch, it is more a description than a name.

[21] Ch.1 at para.1–10.

[22] ss.58–59. In the case of a Welsh company (i.e. one which is registered on the basis that its registered office is to be in Wales—see s.88(1) and below, para.4–15) the Welsh equivalents ("cyfyngedig" or "cwmni cyfyngedig cyhoeddus") may (not must) be used instead. And in the case of a community interest company that term (or its abbreviation "cic") must be used as the suffix, if it is a private company, and "community interest public limited company" (abbreviated to "community interest plc") in the case of a public company: 2004 Act, s.33. The Welsh equivalents are "cwmni buddiant cymunedol" (cbc) and "cwmni buddiant cymunedol cyhoeddus cyfyngedig" ("cwmni buddiant cymunedol ccc").

may be abbreviated to "Ltd" or "Plc"[23] and the company may subsequently use those abbreviations even if it has registered with the full suffix.[24] The purpose of this requirement is to warn a person dealing with the company that it is a body with limited liability, though whether it is very effective in this regard is another matter.

To the requirement that a private limited company must have "limited" at the end of its name, the Act provides exemptions but only on a narrow basis. Charitable companies are exempted from the requirement.[25] So are certain companies under the "grandfather" provision applying to companies which were exempted from the requirement under the DTI licence system which was phased out in the early 1980s.[26] The current exemption, going beyond charities, depends upon regulations made by the Secretary of State,[27] which largely reproduce the exemption previously provided by the 1985 Act.[28] The draft regulations exempt a company limited by guarantee and engaged in "the promotion of commerce, art, science, education, religion, charity or any profession," the articles of which require its income to be devoted to the promotion of these objects, forbid the payment of dividends or any return of capital to members and require its assets on a winding-up to be transferred to a body with like objects or to a charity.[29] In effect, the exemption is available only to charitable companies or those with public interest objectives which cannot be used as vehicles for making a profit for their members.

More important than what the name must contain is what it must not. Certain expressions are banned. If, in the opinion of the Secretary of State, the name is such that its use would constitute a criminal offence or be "offensive", it cannot be adopted.[30] Further, the name must not include, except at the end, any use of "public limited company", "community interest company" or "community interest public limited company" or their abbreviations or Welsh equivalents; and the company may not use "limited" or "unlimited" (or their

---

[23] See fn.22, (the Welsh equivalents are "cyf" or "ccc").

[24] s.82(3)—if regulations allow this.

[25] s.60(1)(a).

[26] ss.60(1)(c) and 61.

[27] s.60(1)(b) and the Names Regulations, reg.4.

[28] The Department had originally proposed to confine the exemption to statutory regulators established as companies (for example, the Financial Services Authority) on the grounds that the community interest company form catered for other companies for which exemption was appropriate, but it changed its mind after consultation. See DTI, *Implementation of the Companies Act 2006: Consultation Document*, February 2007, para.2.47; BERR, *Government Response to consultation on Companies Act 2006: Company and Business Names*, para.2.8 (URN 07/1244/GR).

[29] If the company was already subject to this exemption under the 1985 Act, it retains it: s.62.

[30] s.53. An example of the use of a particular name being a criminal offence would be where the name holds out the company as carrying on a business which requires a licence or authorisation (for example, as a bank) which the company does not have.

abbreviations or Welsh equivalents) anywhere in the name, unless the company is in fact a limited or unlimited company.[31] This is done primarily to prevent any blurring of the warnings implied by "Ltd" or "Plc".[32]

Prohibition on using a name already allocated

The name must not be the same as any name already on the Registrar's index of names.[33] This is likely to present the severest obstacle because there are over two million names on that index. It is an index not just of names of companies incorporated under the 2006 or earlier Companies Acts but also of unregistered companies, overseas companies which have registered particulars in the United Kingdom, limited liability partnerships, limited partnerships, European Economic Interest Groupings registered in the United Kingdom, open-ended investment companies and bodies incorporated under the Industrial and Provident Societies Acts.[34] Certain differences are to be disregarded when judging whether a name is the same and certain expressions are to be treated as the same,[35] thus expanding the scope of the prohibition. Hence a Smith, Jones, Brown or Davies who has carried on an unincorporated business under his or her name may have difficulty in finding an available way of continuing to use that name on incorporating the business.[36] However, there is a new power to permit registration of a name that would otherwise be prohibited and this power is likely to be exercised to cover the situation where the company seeking registration is part of the same group as the body already registered with the same name and the body already registered agrees to the registration of the new company.[37] Because of the requirement that the two bodies with the same name be part of the same group, the risk of confusion of the public is reduced[38] and the consent required of the body already registered serves to protect its interests.

4–9

---

[31] s.65(1) and Names Regulations, reg.5. Nor may the company use the terms "open ended investment company", "investment company with variable capital" or "limited liability partnership" (or their abbreviations or Welsh equivalents).

[32] However, the inclusion of "unlimited" (for which, incidentally, there is no authorised abbreviation) would presumably prevent a moneylender from incorporating as "Unlimited Loans Ltd".

[33] s.66.

[34] s.1099.

[35] s.66(3) and the Names Regulations, reg.7 and Sch.2. For example, the words "company" and "cwmni" appearing at the end of the name are to be disregarded in judging whether the name is the same (so that if the only difference between the names is this one, they will be held to be the same) and "@" and "at" are to be treated as the same.

[36] Those with less common surnames can often surmount this difficulty by, for example, inserting an appropriate place-name: e.g. Gower (Hampstead) Ltd.

[37] s.66(4) and Name Regulations, reg.8. If the body already registered subsequently withdraws its consent, that will not affect the registration of the company.

[38] Though surely not eliminated, for example, where one of the two companies with the same name is a well capitalised parent company and the other an undercapitalised subsidiary.

Names requiring approval

4–10 Certain names may be adopted only with the express approval of the Secretary of State. These are names which would be likely to give the impression that the company is connected in any way with the Government, a local authority or other specified public authority.[39] Regulations may also be made which specify other sensitive words or expressions for which approval is required.[40] In both cases, the Secretary of State is empowered to require the person asking for permission to seek comments from the government department or other body which is thought to have an interest in the matter and, in particular, to ask that body whether it objects and, if so, why.[41] The relevant regulations[42] list some 90 words[43] and, in relation to about a third of them, specify a body which has to be invited to object.[44] When a request is made, the application for registration must contain a statement that the body has been asked and a copy of any response.[45]

It will, therefore, be apparent that it may be difficult to find a name acceptable to both the incorporators and the Registrar or Secretary of State. But until it is achieved, it will be impossible to complete the documents required to obtain registration and unsafe to order the stationery which the company will need once it is registered. We have never introduced a system, comparable to that in some other common law countries, whereby a name can be reserved for a prescribed period. Prior to 1981, however, it was possible and usual to write to the Registrar submitting a name (or two or three alternative names) and asking if it was available. If the reply was affirmative it was usually safe to proceed so long as one did so promptly. Now, however, the incorporators or their professional advisers will have to search the index[46] and make up their own minds.

---

[39] s.54.

[40] s.55.

[41] s.56.

[42] No new regulations have been issued at the time of writing under these sections and so the Company and Business Names Regulations, 1981/1685, as subsequently amended, will continue to apply by virtue of s.1297(3). The most recent amendment to the 1981 Regulations was by the Company and Business Names (Amendment) (No.2) Regulations, 2007/3152, adding, among others, the term "NHS" to the list.

[43] Mainly those implying some official or representative status but ranging from "Abortion" to "Windsor" and including, for example "University", "Trade Union" and "Stock Exchange". A listed word should be avoided unless the incorporators are prepared to face delay and possible rejection.

[44] e.g. if the name includes "Charitable" or "Charity", the Charity Commission must be asked; if "Dental" or "Dentistry", the General Dental Council, and if "Windsor" (because of its royal associations) the Home Office or the Scottish Home and Health Dept.

[45] s.56(3).

[46] And, ideally, also the Register of Trade Marks to ensure that the name proposed is not someone's registered trademark.

Requirements to change a name

Even if the promoters do secure registration of their company under a **4–11** particular name they cannot be certain that they will not be forced to change it. The main risk is that the Secretary of State will, within 12 months of the company's registration, direct it to change its name on the ground that it "is the same as, or in the opinion of the Secretary of State, *too like*[47] a name appearing at the time of registration in the registrar's index of company names ... or which should have appeared in that index at the time".[48] The object of the provision is twofold: (a) to enable a mistake to be rectified when the name of an existing company has been registered, either because the name had not then been entered on the index or because the fact that it was the same as that of the new company had escaped detection; and (b) to extend, by the words italicised above, the ambit of "the same as" to "too like" that of another. If another company finds that the new company is trading with a name so similar to its own as to cause confusion and face it with unfair competition, that company can, as a cheaper alternative to a "passing-off action", complain to the Registrar asking that the Secretary of State should exercise his powers to direct the new one to change its name.[49] If the Secretary of State does so, the company must comply within such period as he may direct. Non-compliance is a criminal offence on the part of the company and every officer in default, but it appears that the Secretary of State cannot simply order the Registrar to alter the company's name.[50] But this course will be effective only if the complaint is in time for a direction to be made within 12 months of registration of the second company.[51] Otherwise, the only remedy available to the first company will be a passing-off action[52] which will not be successful merely because the two names are identical or "too like". It will have to be established that both companies are carrying on the same of type of business and that the second is, in effect, cashing in on the reputation of the first and appropriating its goodwill and connection.[53]

There is a balance to be struck here. A company which begins trading under its name is likely to acquire goodwill in that name and to suffer loss if it is later required to change it. That is a possible justification for removing the administrative power to require a

---

[47] For a case where the names were not thought "too like" although they were sufficiently alike to have caused a petitioning creditor to obtain a winding up order against the wrong company with damaging consequences to it, see *Calmex Ltd, Re* [1989] 1 All E.R. 485.

[48] s.67.

[49] 310 directions were made in 2005–2006: *Companies in 2005–06*, Table D4 (but 374 requests for directions were refused). But an interlocutory application in a passing off action may provide speedier relief: *Glaxo Plc v Glaxowellcome Ltd* [1996] F.S.R. 388.

[50] cf. *Halifax Plc v Halifax Repossessions Ltd* [2004] 2 B.C.L.C. 455, CA, below.

[51] s.68(2).

[52] Unless the name conflicts with the older company's registered trademark, in which event it may also have a right of action in that respect.

[53] See, e.g. *Tussaud v Tussaud* (1890) 44 Ch.D. 678; *Panhard et Levassor v Panhard Levassor Motor Co* [1901] 2 Ch. 513.

change of name after 12 months and for requiring the complainant thereafter to challenge the newly established company in the courts, alleging passing off. If passing off is shown, the new company will be enjoined from continuing to trade under its name and will either have to go out of business or change its name, which it can easily do by special resolution,[54] though the new name will have to pass the same tests as the original one. However, a passing-off action requires the claimant company to demonstrate that the new company's choice of name presents a serious threat to the claimant's business. The Company Law Review, which thought the law on names broadly satisfactory, was attracted by the idea that the Registrar should have a new basis for ordering a name change, namely, that the registration had constituted an abuse of the registration process.[55] The classic case is where X, knowing or guessing that Y is likely to want to form a company with a particular name, gets in first and then offers to sell the company, which has never traded and was never intended to trade, to Y at an inflated price.

The Act responds to this concern by setting up a new procedure whereby a person (including another company) may object, apparently at any time, to a registered company's name on the ground that it is the same as a name associated with the applicant and in which the applicant has goodwill or it is sufficiently similar to such a name that its use in the United Kingdom would be likely to mislead by suggesting a connection between the respondent company and the applicant.[56] The mechanism is thus one whereby the applicant can seek to protect its goodwill in a name. If either of these conditions is made out, then the applicant will succeed unless the respondent company can bring itself within one of five categories.[57] The first is that its name was registered before the commencement of the activities upon which the applicant relies to show goodwill. This does not necessarily mean the respondent has to have been registered first. For example, the applicant may have been registered first but may have remained dormant until after the respondent was registered, and in such a case the respondent would be able to bring itself within this category. The second is that the respondent company is operating under the name, or has formerly operated under it and is now dormant, or is proposing to do so and has incurred substantial start-up costs. This is an important defence for the respondent because it means that operating under the name (or even incurring substantial costs in preparation for so doing) protects the respondent (subject to the qualification set out below) against the requirement to change its

---

[54] s.77(1)—or by any other means specified in its articles. Getting on for 60,000 name changes were approved in 2005/6 and only 251 refused: above, fn.49, Table D4.
[55] Completing, para.8.30.
[56] s.69(1). This new procedure is in force from 1 October 2008, whilst the remaining 2006 Act provisions on names come into force on 1 October 2009.
[57] s.69(4).

name. Thirdly, the respondent shows that the name was registered in the ordinary course of a company formation business and is available for sale to the applicant on the standard terms of that business. In this case the applicant can solve its problem by simply buying the respondent company for a modest sum. The fourth category is that the respondent acted in good faith and the fifth that the interests of the applicant have not been affected to any significant extent. However, in the first three cases the applicant will succeed nevertheless if the applicant shows the main purpose of the respondent was to obtain money or other benefit from the applicant or to prevent the applicant from registering the name.[58] Thus, beginning to operate will not protect the respondent from the applicant's challenge if the main purpose of the respondent was to extort a large sum of money from the applicant in exchange for giving up its rights to the name.

These disputes will not be handled within the Governmental **4–12** Department but by independent adjudicators.[59] If the adjudicator upholds the complaint, an order must be made requiring the respondent to change its name to an acceptable one and to take all steps within its power to achieve that end, including not forming another company with a similar offending name.[60] The adjudicator's order may be enforced in the same way as an order of the High Court (or decree of the Court of Session)[61] and, if the name is not changed by the respondent, the adjudicator can effect the change.[62] There is an appeal to a court from the adjudicator's decision.[63]

The Secretary of State has a further power to direct the company to change its name, namely, where it appears to him that misleading information has been given in connection with the company's registration with a particular name or that undertakings or assurances which have been given for that purpose have not been fulfilled;[64] and in this case the direction may be given within five years of registration.[65] Further, the Secretary of State may at any time direct a company to change its name if, in his or her opinion, it gives so misleading an indication of the nature of the company's activities as to be likely to cause harm to the public.[66] Little use of this power has been made;

---

[58] s.69(5).

[59] s.70.

[60] s.73(1). Although the company is the primary respondent, the applicant may make its directors or members respondents as well (s.69(3)), which will be important for the range of persons caught by the adjudicator's order.

[61] s.73(3)—including therefore by way of an order for contempt of court.

[62] s.73(4). Thus avoiding the problem which arose in *Halifax Plc v Halifax Repossessions Ltd* [2004] 2 B.C.L.C. 455, CA, where, after a successful trademark infringement and passing-off action, the court was held to have no power of its own motion to alter the defendant company's name but only to order the shareholders to secure such a change.

[63] s.74.

[64] s.75(1). This is likely to arise only when approval of the name has been obtained under the provisions discussed above.

[65] s.75(2).

[66] s.76.

undoubtedly the names of many companies give totally misleading indications of the nature of their activities but this, on its own, has apparently not been thought "likely to cause harm to the public".[67]

On a change of name, whether voluntarily or because of a direction,[68] the Registrar must be notified and will enter the new name on the register in place of the old and issue an amended certificate of incorporation.[69] The change is effective from the date on which that certificate is issued.[70] But the company remains the same corporate body and the change does not affect any of its rights or obligations or render defective any legal proceedings by or against it.[71]

Business names

4–13 Overall, the effect of the statutory provisions is to afford a registered company something approaching an exclusive right to corporate trading under its registered name, since another company should not be registered with the same name and may be forced to change its name if that is too like the first company's name. That, however, does not protect it against the use of the name by unincorporated businesses. The use of names by such businesses will be regulated from October 2009 by Part 41 of the Companies Act 2006, having previously been governed by the Business Names Act 1985. Unincorporated businesses are free from any statutory restraints so long as they use the true names of their proprietors.[72] However, if the unincorporated business trades under another name, those in charge of it become subject to the rules discussed above relating to names suggesting connection with government or public authority,[73] sensitive words or expressions requiring approval,[74] and names giving an inappropriate indication of company type or legal form[75] or activities.[76] In relation to the business name, however, the convenient administrative sanction of refusing to register a company with a non-compliant name is not available, since unincorporated businesses do not need to be registered in order to carry on business. Consequently, contravention of the rules on business names is made a criminal offence.[77]

---

[67] In 2005/6 two directions were given under what is now s.75 and five under what is now s.76: above, fn.49, Table D4.

[68] s.77.

[69] s.80.

[70] s.81(1).

[71] s.81(2), (3). Hence contracts entered into prematurely under the new name will not be pre-incorporation contracts on which the individual who acted will be personally liable (see paras 5–8ff).

[72] s.1192.

[73] s.1193.

[74] ss.1194–1196.

[75] s.1197.

[76] s.1198.

[77] See ss.1193(4), 1194(3), 1197(5), 1198(2) and 1207.

In addition, the unincorporated business will have to observe the provisions of Chapter 2 of Part 41, regarding disclosure of the identity of the proprietors, which are the equivalent of the trading disclosure rules applied to companies.[78] However, there is nothing in Part 41 which empowers the Secretary of State or an adjudicator to direct the change of a business name because it is the same as, or too like, the name of an existing business, corporate or incorporate.

The names rules of Part 41 apply to any person carrying on business in the United Kingdom. Thus, they apply to a registered company (or any other registered body) which carries on any business under a name other than its registered name (for example because it has acquired an existing business with a goodwill attached to the name of that business). There is no requirement for a company to use its registered name as its trading name, but, if it does use a different name for that purpose, it too will have to comply with the provisions of Part 41 about its choice of business name.[79]

REGISTRATION

Registration documents

The next step is to prepare the registration documents, of which the most important are the company's articles of association, for which, as we saw in the previous chapter, the legislature has provided model versions.[80] The articles provide many of the rules governing the internal operation of the company and, as we also noted, are particularly important under British law because of the range of matters it leaves to be regulated by the articles.

4–14

A significant change under the 2006 Act was the downgrading to a vestigial role of the memorandum of association, which, under the procedures introduced in the early days of modern company law, had contained the most important information about the company and had, originally, been largely unalterable after the registration of the company.[81] Under the 2006 Act the memorandum, which must still be delivered to the Registrar as a necessary step in the formation process,[82] simply has to state that the subscribers to it (of whom there need only

---

[78] Chapter 2 of Part 41. The same civil sanction is applied as in the case of companies: s.1206 and para.9–3.

[79] The disclosure provisions of Chapter 2 of Part 41 apply only to individuals and partnerships (s.1200), because s.82 (trading disclosure) performs the same function for companies.

[80] See above, para.3–10.

[81] The CLR had recommended that the memorandum be abolished entirely (Final Report I, para.9.4) but this was thought in some quarters, oddly, to raise the question of whether it was intended to alter the nature of the company as an incorporated association. Hence, apparently, the vestigial role for the memorandum.

[82] s.9(1).

be one)[83] wish to form a company under the Act and agree to become members of the company upon its formation and, in the case of a company having a share capital, agree to take at least one share each.[84] The memorandum has to be authenticated by each subscriber,[85] the Registrar being empowered to specify the method of authentication, but not in such a way as to impede electronic delivery of the memorandum (and the other registration documents) to the Registrar.[86]

More time is likely to need to be devoted to the drafting of the articles of association. The main question for consideration is the extent to which the appropriate model should be adopted.[87] The option of not registering any articles and relying entirely on the model[88] is rarely chosen because most companies on initial registration will be private ones and the incorporators will wish to include the sort of restrictions on freedom to transfer shares which were a pre-condition for qualifying as a private company prior to the Companies Act 1980. Although the model articles for private companies limited by shares give the directors a discretion to refuse to register a transfer of shares,[89] the incorporators are likely to want more elaborate provisions, such as ones requiring the shares to be offered to the existing shareholders if a member wishes to sell. Company formation agents normally have their own standard forms, which formally exclude the model altogether, though the agent's standard form may itself be a development of the statutory model (which, in turn, was influenced by the agents' models existing at the time the model was drafted).

4–15   Other than these documents the application for registration must state the following things.

The company's proposed name.[90]

Whether its registered office is to be in England and Wales, Wales, Scotland or Northern Ireland.[91]

Whether the liability of the members is to be limited and, if so, whether by shares or guarantee.[92] In the latter case a statement of guarantee must be part of the application[93] and that must

---

[83] s.7(1).
[84] s.8(1). S.112(1) deems the subscribers to have agreed to become members of the company and provides that, upon registration of the company, they do become members of it.
[85] s.8(2). Bizarrely, for such a simple document, the memorandum is required to be in the prescribed form, and very straightforward forms are prescribed, for companies with and without share capital respectively, in Schs 1 and 2 to the draft Companies (Registration) Regulations 2007 (hereafter "Registration Regulations").
[86] s.1068(3), (5).
[87] See previous Chapter at para.3–11.
[88] s.9(5)(b).
[89] Art.26 of sched.1 to the draft Companies (Model Articles) Regulations 2007.
[90] s.9(2)(a).
[91] s.9(2)(b).
[92] s.9(2)(c).
[93] s.9(4)(b).

state the amount which each member of the company agrees to contribute to the company on its winding up[94] and it must contain the names and addresses of each of the subscribers to the memorandum (who, of course, become its first members).[95]

In the case of a company having a share capital[96] a statement of capital and initial shareholdings must be part of the application.[97] This must give particulars of the nominal value of and amount paid up on the shares taken by the subscribers on formation (both in aggregate and individually).[98]

Whether the company is to be public or private.[99]

A statement of the proposed officers of the company,[100] meaning its first directors or secretary (if any), containing the consent of each person named to act.[101]

None of this is very demanding.[102] A good deal of the information previously had to be contained in the company's memorandum of association. Other information, for example about shareholdings and officers, is the first expression of an obligation which will continue throughout the company's life periodically to inform the Registrar about these matters.[103]

Only if the company is to be a community interest company will something more be required. First, in order to meet the restrictions which the 2004 Act places on such companies, especially in relation to the distribution of assets, the company's freedom of action in relation to its articles is restricted. It must include in its articles the provisions set out in the appropriate Schedule to the Community Interest Company Regulations 2005.[104] Further, it may be registered as a CIC only if the Regulator accepts that its objectives constitute the furtherance of a community interest. This test requires those seeking registration to provide a further document to the Registrar, namely, a "community interest statement", which is to be signed by each person

---

[94] s.11.

[95] Registration Regulations, reg.3.

[96] If the company has a share capital, it will normally be limited by shares but not necessarily so. This would not be the case with an unlimited company having a share capital.

[97] s.9(4)(a).

[98] s.10 and the Registration Regulations, reg.3. The company's power to issue shares of various classes will be set out, of course, in the articles of association. See Ch.24 for the rules governing the exercise of this power.

[99] s.9(2)(d).

[100] s.9(4)(c).

[101] s.12. The Act has abolished the requirement for a private company to have a secretary and so all that will probably be provided is the name of the first director of the company.

[102] There must also be a "statement of compliance" delivered to the Registrar that the registration requirements have been complied with, which statement the Registrar can accept as sufficient evidence of compliance.

[103] See para.14–10 and para.23–6.

[104] SI 2005/1788.

who is to be a first director of the company and which declares that the company will carry on its activities in order to benefit the community and indicates how the company's activities will benefit the community.[105] Only if the Regulator concludes that the proposed company satisfies the community interest test will the Registrar register the company as a CIC.[106] This test is in fact a rather open-ended one—"a company satisfies the community interest test if a reasonable person might consider that its activities are being carried on for the benefit of the community"[107]—and so there may be some scope for debate about its application and for appeals from the Regulator to the Appeal Officer.[108]

Purchase of a shelf-company

4–16 If the incorporators have no immediate special requirements regarding the company's constitution or name, but want their business to be incorporated as rapidly as possible as a private company limited by shares, an alternative to registering a new company is to buy one off-the-shelf from one of the agencies which provide this service. Its great advantage is speed because all the incorporators have to do is to pay the agency and to take transfers of the subscribers' shares and custody of the company's registers. They will, of course, then have to send to the Registrar notices of changes of the directors (with the required consents) and of the situation of the registered office. Any other changes (e.g. alterations of the articles or a change of name) can be effected at leisure. The main disadvantage is that until they make changes, the company's name is unlikely to bear any relationship to them or to the business being carried on.

Certificate of incorporation

4–17 If the Registrar is satisfied that the requirements for registration are met and that the purpose for which the incorporators are associated is "lawful",[109] the Registrar will register the document submitted[110]

---

[105] SI 2005/1788, regs. 2 and 11. Note the decision not to require an "objects clause" in the company's constitution for this purpose. See further para.7–2.

[106] Companies (Audit, Investigations and Community Enterprise) Act 2004, s.36(3)–(6).

[107] s.35(2).

[108] The Regulations give some further guidance (see regs. 1–3), notably by excluding political activites.

[109] See s.7(2): "A company may not be formed for an unlawful purpose." This is interpreted as banning both purposes which are criminal and those which are regarded as contrary to public policy: *R. v Registrar of Joint Stock Companies* [1931] 2 K.B. 197, CA; *R. v Registrar of Companies, Ex p. HM's Attorney-General* [1991] B.C.L.C. 476. In the light of the decision in *Yuen Kun Yeu v Attorney-General of Hong Kong* [1988] A.C. 175, PC, it seems clear that a member of the public subsequently defrauded by the company could not successfully sue the Registrar on the ground that he was negligent in registering the company (or, in the case of a public company, issuing the trading certificate).

[110] s.14.

and will issue a certificate of incorporation.[111] This states that the company is incorporated and gives its name and registered number, the date of incorporation, states whether it is limited and, if so, how, whether it is public or private and in which jurisdiction its registered office is situated.[112] Section 15(4) declares that the certificate is conclusive evidence that the requirements of the Act as to registration have been complied with and that the company is duly registered under the Act. The effect of incorporation is that "the subscribers to the memorandum, together with such other persons as may from time to time become members of the company, are a body corporate by the name stated in the certificate of incorporation."[113] Further, the subscribers to the memorandum become the holders of the shares specified in the statement of capital and the directors and secretary (if any) named in the statement of proposed officers are appointed to their offices.[114]

The functions of the Registrar in deciding whether or not to register the company are administrative, rather than judicial, but a refusal to register can be challenged by judicial review, albeit with scant hope of success.[115] However, normally, the registration of a company cannot be challenged because of the conclusive effect of the certificate. This, happily, has rendered English company law virtually immune to the problems arising from defectively incorporated companies which have plagued the United States and many continental countries.[116] But the decided cases on section 15(4) (or its predecessors under earlier Acts) and the review of them by the Court of Appeal[117] in a case concerning the, then, comparable provision relating to a certificate of registration of a charge on a company's property, show that this immunity is not complete. Since section 15 and its predecessors in earlier Companies Acts are not expressed to bind the Crown, the Attorney-General can apply to the court and may obtain certiorari to quash the registration.[118]

This was successfully done in *R. v Registrar of Companies, Ex p.*   **4–18**

---

[111] s.15—signed by the registrar and authenticated by the registrar's official seal (s.15(3)).

[112] s.15(2).

[113] s.16(2)—thus making clear the company's nature as an incorporated association.

[114] s.16(5),(6).

[115] *R. v Registrar of Joint Stock Companies* [1931] 2 K.B. 197, CA where an application for *mandamus* to order the Registrar to register a company formed for the sale in England of tickets in the Irish Hospital Lottery was rejected on the ground that the Registrar had rightly concluded that such sales were illegal in England.

[116] See Drury, "Nullity of Companies in English Law" (1985) 48 M.L.R. 644. The First Company Law Directive contains three Articles dealing with nullity.

[117] *R. v Registrar of Companies, Ex p. Central Bank of India* [1986] Q.B. 1114, CA. Reversing the decision at first instance, the Court of Appeal held that, even on judicial review, the effect of s.98(2) of the Companies Act 1948, under which the certificate of registration of a charge was "conclusive evidence that the requirements—as to registration have been satisfied", was to make evidence of non-compliance inadmissible, thus precluding the court from quashing the registration.

[118] *Bowman v Secular Society* [1917] A.C. 406, HL where, however certiorari was denied as the Society's purposes were held not to be unlawful.

HM's Attorney-General,[119] where a prostitute had succeeded in incorporating her business under the name of "Lindi St Claire (Personal Services) Ltd" (the Registrar having rejected her first preference of "Prostitutes Ltd" or "Hookers Ltd" and shown no enthusiasm for "Lindi St Claire (French Lessons) Ltd") and, with scrupulous frankness, she specified its primary object in the constitution as being "to carry on the business of prostitution".[120] The court, on judicial review at the instance of the Attorney-General, quashed the registration on the ground that the stated business was unlawful as contrary to public policy.[121] It is unlikely, however, that the Attorney-General (or any other Crown servant) will take action unless public policy is thought to be involved and will not do so if all that has occurred is a technical breach of the formalities of incorporation.

Nevertheless, there is one other situation in which the certificate does not seem to be conclusive of valid incorporation. This results from what is now s.10(3) of the Trade Union and Labour Relations (Consolidation) Act 1992 (repeating similar provisions in earlier Acts) which declares that the registration of a trade union under the Companies Acts shall be void. In the past, parties other than the Crown have been held entitled to rely on this; for example as a defence to a claim by a registered company whose objects make it a trade union. The reported cases[122] related to versions of what is now s.15(4), which were less comprehensive and which were not thought to cover substantive matters but only ministerial acts leading to registration.[123] Hence, it seems doubtful if they would be followed today. However, the researches of Mr Drury[124] have unearthed a more recent example of a company's removal from the register because its objects made it a trade union. The company in question was one formed by junior hospital doctors to represent their interests. It was later realised that its objects made it a trade union within the statutory definition. The Department of Trade took the view that the labour law provision overrode what is now s.15(4) of the Companies Act and accordingly the Registrar removed the company from the

---

[119] [1991] B.C.L.C. 476.

[120] Had she been less frank, for example by stating the primary object as "to carry on the business of masseuses and to provide related services", she would probably have got away with it.

[121] Notwithstanding that, as she indignantly protested, she paid income tax on her earnings. Since prostitution can be carried on without necessarily committing any criminal offence and since she continued, without incorporation, to practise her profession (for which she has become a well-known spokeswoman), some may think that this was an example of the "unruly horse" of public policy unseating its judicial riders.

[122] *Edinburgh & District Water Manufacturers Association v Jenkinson* (1903) 5 Sessions Cases 1159; *British Association of Glass Bottle Manufacturers v Nettlefold* [1911] 27 T.L.R. 527 (where, however, the company was held not to be a trade union).

[123] (1911) 27 T.L.R. 528 at 529.

[124] Drury, *op. cit.*, fn.116, above, at pp.649 and 650.

register for "void registration".[125] This, apparently, was done without any court order[126] and without challenge by the doctors. Presumably this action by the Registrar could be regarded as having been taken on behalf of the Crown and as the correction of a mistake which he, or one of his predecessors, had made and therefore as rectifiable.[127]

Hence, it now seems probable, but not certain, that in no circumstances can anyone other than the Crown plead the nullity of a registered company unless and until it has been removed from the register as a result of action by or on behalf of the Crown. Removal as a result of that action is tantamount to a declaration that it never existed as a corporate body. This is not likely to be a satisfactory outcome if it has in fact been carrying on business as what both its members and its creditors believed to be a registered company; it should be wound up[128] rather than declared never to have existed.[129]

COMMENCEMENT OF BUSINESS

From the date of registration mentioned in the certificate of incorporation, the company, if it is a private company, becomes "capable of exercising all the functions of an incorporated company."[130] However, it may choose not to do so. Indeed, in the case of a shelf company it is inherent in the arrangement that the company will remain dormant and begin trading only some time after registration. In the case of a public company there is in any event a further legal obstacle to its beginning trading. It needs to obtain a further certificate from the Registrar (a "trading certificate") certifying that the amount of its allotted share capital is not less than the required minimum.[131] Without it, the public company must not do business or exercise any borrowing powers unless it has re-registered as a private company. The certificate of trading is "conclusive evidence that the company is entitled to do business and exercise any borrowing

4–19

---

[125] See *Companies in 1976*, Table 10.

[126] Notwithstanding that the First Company Law Directive provides by Art.11.1 (a) that "Nullity must be ordered by a decision of a court of law."

[127] But, presumably, unless the company agreed, he could not take this action unless the incorporation was void (as in the case of a trade union or where the purposes were unlawful), rather than voidable (which would seem to be the case where, for example, registration had been secured by fraudulent misrepresentations).

[128] But as what? As a registered company, which it ostensibly is? Or as an unregistered compay under Pt V of the Insolvency Act 1986?

[129] As the First Directive appears to envisage: see Art.12.2.

[130] s.16(3).

[131] s.761. This is discussed further at para.11–4. In the more usual case where original registration was as a private company but it later converts to a public one, similar requirements will first have to be met, but there is no suspension of business during the process of conversion.

powers".[132] However, by analogy with the decisions referred to above in relation to the certificate of incorporation, it appears that, as this section is not expressed to bind the Crown, the Registrar's decision could be quashed on judicial review at the instance of the Attorney-General. This, in contrast with quashing registration, would not have the undesirable effect of nullifying the incorporation. A more likely course, however, would be for the Secretary of State, if he had grounds for suspecting that the share capital had not been properly allotted, to institute an investigation[133] and, if his suspicions proved well-founded, petition the court to wind up the company under ss.124 or 124A of the Insolvency Act.

RE-REGISTRATION OF AN EXISTING COMPANY

4–20   A company may wish, at some stage, to convert itself into a company of a different type. This, in most cases, it may do without the expense of effecting a complete re-organisation of the types referred to in Chapter 29, below, and without having to form a brand new company. The circumstances and methods whereby conversions may be achieved are now collected together in Part 7 of the Act.

(i) Private company becoming public
4–21   Under sections 90 to 96 a private company limited by shares can become re-registered as a public company, by passing a special resolution that it should be so re-registered, satisfying three conditions and then making an application to the Registrar.[134] The three conditions all relate to the legal capital rules which apply in a much more onerous way to public than to private companies. In brief they are, first, that the nominal value of the company's allotted share capital must be not less than the authorised minimum (currently £50,000) and the associated rules as to the payment for those shares must have been met.[135] Secondly, the company must produce unqualified recent accounts which show, as certified by the auditor, that its net assets (assets less liabilities) are not less than the aggregate of its called-up share capital and undistributable reserves.[136] Although there is no precisely equivalent rule applying to public companies on

---

[132] s.763(4).
[133] See Ch.18.
[134] s.90(1).
[135] s.91. See Chapter 11 below.
[136] s.92. Note that this is not a rule about minimum capital but about the relationship between the company's net assets and the legal capital it has chosen to raise.

formation, this will be the factual situation before a company formed as public begins to trade.[137] Thirdly, if the company allots shares in the period after the accounts just mentioned were drawn up and before the special resolution is passed and those shares were issued wholly or partly other than for cash, then the rules applicable to non-cash consideration received by a public company have been complied with.[138]

If the Registrar is satisfied on the above matters on the basis of the documents the company is required to include in its application to re-register,[139] then the company shall be re-registered as a public company, with an amended certificate of incorporation,[140] the alterations in the articles take effect, and the company becomes a public company.[141] In effect, the certificate is a combined certificate of incorporation and trading certificate which would have been needed had the company been initially registered as a public company.

Since, as we noted above,[142] it is more common for a public company to be formed by conversion from private status than by direct formation as a public company, the above rules are of some importance.

If the private company, which wishes to convert to a public one, is an unlimited company it will have to become limited, that being one of the essential elements of the definition of a public company. This it is enabled to do in the conversion operation—and rather more simply than if it first re-registered as limited under (iv) below, and subsequently re-registered as a public company. It merely has to add to the special resolution the necessary changes to its articles.[143]

(ii) Public company becoming private

To convert from public to private (an operation which must not be confused with ceasing to have securities traded on a public market, which does not necessarily involve any change in the company's status under the Act, or with "privatisation" in the sense of de-nationalisation) is comparatively simple unless there is disagreement among the members. It can convert to a private company limited by

4–22

---

[137] All that s.831 provides is that a public company which is not in this position cannot make a distribution to its members.

[138] s.93. In addition, the rules requiring independent valuation of transfers of non-cash assets to a public company in the "initial period" (see para.11–16) apply to a company re-registered as public, but with the members of the company being substituted for the subscribers to the memorandum as the persons in respect of whom the rule applies (see s.603(a) and para.5–3). These rules apply after re-registration and so are not a condition of it.

[139] s.94 (including a statement of proposed secretary, if the company does not already have one, which, as a private company, it was not required to: ss.94(1)(b) and 95).

[140] Which is conclusive evidence that the requirements have been met: s.96(5). On "conclusiveness", see paras 4–17ff, above.

[141] s.96.

[142] fn.16.

[143] s.90(4).

shares or by guarantee[144] by passing a special resolution making the necessary alterations in its name and its articles and applying, in the prescribed form, to the Registrar.[145] But special safeguards are prescribed since loss of public status may have adverse consequences to the members, especially as regards their ability to dispose of their shares. Hence, members who have not consented to, or voted in favour of, the resolution can, within 28 days of the resolution, apply to the court for the cancellation of the resolution if they can muster the support of:

(a) holders of not less than 5 per cent in nominal value of the company's share capital or any class of it; or

(b) if the company is not limited by shares,[146] not less than 5 per cent of the members; or

(c) not less than 50 members.[147]

The Registrar must not issue a new certificate of incorporation until the 28 days have expired without an application having been made or, if it has been made, until it has been withdrawn or dismissed and a copy of the court order delivered to the Registrar.[148] The court has broad powers to cancel or confirm the resolution, on such terms and conditions as it thinks fit, including ordering the company to purchase the shares of any members.[149] Thus, the court may grant dissenting shareholders an exit right rather than require them to accept the company's change of status. Unless the court cancels the resolution, the Registrar issues a new certificate of incorporation with the usual conclusive consequences.[150]

A public company will have to re-register as a private company if, under s.648,[151] the court makes an order confirming the reduction of its capital which has the effect of reducing the nominal amount of its allotted share capital below "the authorised minimum". In such circumstances that order will not be registered and come into effect (unless the court otherwise directs) until the company is re-registered

---

[144] For obvious reasons it cannot, by this simple process, convert to an unlimited company: s.97(1).

[145] s.97.

[146] The category (b) of objectors is somewhat puzzling since, until the Registrar issues a new certificate, the company remains a public company which it could not be unless it had a share capital. Presumably (b) is to cater for an "old public company" which has still not re-registered under the transitional provisions, now in the Companies Consolidation (Consequential Provisions) Act 1985, ss.1–9. As there can now be few, if any, such companies that have not re-registered under the transitional provisions either as Plcs or as private companies, this book ignores them.

[147] s.98.

[148] s.97(2).

[149] s.98(3)–(6).

[150] s.101.

[151] See para.13–3, below.

as a private company.[152] The court may (and, in practice will) authorise this to be done through an expedited procedure without the need to resort to the provisions just discussed. Instead of the company having to pass a special resolution, the court will specify in the order the alterations to be made in the articles and, on application in the prescribed form the Registrar will issue the new certificate of incorporation. In this case there can be no application to the court by dissenting members since the company has no option but to become private.

(iii) Private limited company becoming unlimited

The conversion which presents the greatest dangers to the members   **4–23** is, obviously, that from a limited company to an unlimited one. Nevertheless, it is not completely banned since the members of a small private company may legitimately conclude that forfeiting the advantages of limited liability is worthwhile, as enabling them to operate with much the same flexibility (particularly as regards withdrawal of their capital) and privacy of their financial affairs as a partnership, while yet retaining all the advantages of corporate personality other than limited liability. Hence, the Act provides that a private limited company may re-register as an unlimited company if *all* the members agree.[153] As with other conversions, an application, in the prescribed form, has to be lodged with the Registrar, together with supporting documents.[154] Those documents must contain a statement by the directors of the company that the persons by or on whose behalf the application form is authenticated constitute the whole of the membership of the company and that, in the case of authentication through an agent, the directors have taken all reasonable steps to satisfy themselves that the agent was authorised to act on behalf of the member.[155] The Registrar then issues a new certificate of incorporation with the usual conclusive effect.[156]

(iv) Unlimited company becoming a private limited company

In this, the converse of case (iii), it is not the members who need   **4–24** special safeguards but the creditors. Surprisingly, however, under the provisions under which this conversion is effected the only protection afforded them is that the new suffix, "Ltd", to the company's name should alert them to the fact that it has become a limited company. Their real protection is afforded by what is now s.77 of the Insolvency

---

[152] ss.650–651.
[153] s.102(1)(a). This provision does not apply to public companies, since they must be limited by either shares or guarantee: s.4(2).
[154] s.102(1)(c).
[155] s.103(4).
[156] s.104.

Act 1986. The effect of this is that those who were members of the company at the time of its re-registration remain potentially liable in respect of its debts and liabilities contracted prior thereto if winding up commences within three years of the re-registration. The Act permits re-registration as a limited company, whether limited by shares or by guarantee. As far as the members are concerned the crucial requirement is the passing of a special resolution stating which of these the company is to be and making the necessary alterations to its name and articles.[157]

(v) Public company becoming private and unlimited

4–25 This new conversion option was introduced in the 2006 Act following the recommendation of the CLR.[158] It enables a public company to do in one step what was previously possible only through two steps (i.e. steps (ii) and (iii)). All the members of the company have to consent to this step (since the company will lose its limited liability status)[159] and the usual changes must be made to the company's name and articles.[160]

Ban on vacillation between limited and unlimited

4–26 What a company is not permitted to do is to chop and change more than once between limited and unlimited. Once a limited company has been re-registered as unlimited it cannot again re-register as a public company[161] or as a private limited company.[162] Once an unlimited company has been re-registered as a limited company, it cannot be re-registered as an unlimited company, whether it was immediately before the second attempted re-registration a private[163] or a public[164] limited company. There is, however, no ban on switching back and forth between private limited company and public limited company status.

(vi) Becoming or ceasing to be a community interest company

4–27 A limited company, whether limited by shares or guarantee and whether public or private, may convert to a community interest

---

[157] s.105.
[158] Final Report I, para.11.16. The suggestion that a feasibility study should be made into providing for private companies limited by shares to convert to companies limited by guarantee and vice versa has not borne legislative fruit.
[159] s.109(1)(a).
[160] s.109(3).
[161] s.90(2)(e).
[162] s.105(2).
[163] s.102(2).
[164] s.109(2).

company.[165] This step requires a special resolution of the members, making the probably quite extensive changes to its constitution which are necessary for this purpose,[166] and the approval of the Regulator of Community Interest Companies, who needs to be satisfied that the company satisfies the community interest test.[167] However, a CIC cannot simply revert to not being a CIC. Unless it opts to be dissolved, the CIC's choices are limited to becoming a charity or an industrial and provident society.[168] Otherwise, the constraints on distributions to members by a CIC could be easily avoided by shedding that status.

(vii) Converting to a charitable incorporated organisation

Following the creation of the charitable incorporate organisation (CIO) by the Charities Act 2006,[169] it is now possible for a charitable company to convert to a CIO. This requires a special resolution of the members of the company,[170] and also the consent of the Charity Commissioners, who must be satisfied that the proposed CIO's purposes are charitable and that its constitution is in the required form. In this case, however, the body ceases to be registered with the registrar of companies and becomes registered with the Charity Commissioners.[171] Although this process seems to mean that the company becomes a new body corporate (rather than simply continuing with a new status), it is provided that this shall not affect any liability it was under before conversion.[172] No provision is made for the reversal of this process: the CIO form is clearly felt to be the more appropriate for a charity which wishes to be an incorporated body. The minister is also empowered to make regulations for the conversion of a CIC into a CIO.[173]

4–28

CONCLUSION

Despite the potential problems caused by the company names rules, the process of registration of a company in the United Kingdom is

4–29

---

[165] s.37 of the Companies (Audit, Investigations and Community Enterprise) Act 2004. Being limited is a necessary part of the definition of a CIC: s.26. However, if the company wishing to convert to CIC status is unlimited, it can first become limited under (iv) above. More important in this respect is the prohibition on a CIC re-registering as an unlimited company: s.52(1).

[166] See paras 1–6 and 1–15.

[167] s.38(3)–(6).

[168] s.53.

[169] See para.1–15.

[170] s.69G(6) of the Charities Act 1993, inserted by Sch.7 of the Charities Act 2006.

[171] s.69I.

[172] s.69I(9). Nothing is explicitly said about its rights.

[173] s.69J.

both speedy and cheap, especially if a pre-registered company is bought off the shelf from a company formation agent. The rules on changing company status are not complex either, despite their detail, and are probably used on a large scale only for transfer from private limited to public limited status and vice versa.

CHAPTER 5

PROMOTERS

MEANING OF "PROMOTER"

If, in a psychoanalyst's consulting room, we were asked to say what **5–1** picture formed in our minds at the mention of the expression "company promoter", most of us would probably confess that we envisaged a character of dubious repute and antecedents who infests the commercial demi-monde with a menagerie of bulls, bears, stags and sharks as his familiars, and who, after rising to affluence by preying on the susceptibilities of a gullible public, finally retires from the scene in the blaze of a sensational suicide or Old Bailey trial.[1] In other words, we should envisage someone whose profession it was to form bogus companies and foist them off on the public to the latter's detriment and his own profit. Such figures have existed and it is probably too much to hope that they will ever be entirely eradicated, but even in their Edwardian heyday they formed only the minutest fraction of those whom the law classifies as promoters. A much more typical, if less romantic, example, would be the village grocer who converts his business into a limited company. He, of course, is in no sense a professional company promoter, always and increasingly a rare bird,[2] but

---

[1] It is perhaps a tribute to the law that we definitely picture him as coming to a sticky end; *cf.* Lord MacNaghten in *Gluckstein v Barnes* [1900] A.C. 240, at 248 HL.

[2] As pointed out in Ch.25, the handling of public issues is now virtually monopolised by reputable investment bankers. It is the close scrutiny by these and the FSA, often by reference to standards set these days by Community law, which has caused the virtual disappearance of the old-time promoter. Moreover, the nineteenth-century practice of seeking public subscription before the company is formed has been abandoned. A company seeking listing on the Main Market of the Stock Exchange, or even a quotation on the Alternative Investment Market, must be able to show some track record. Consequently, the duties of the promoters are often swallowed up in such cases in those of the directors.

he would be the promoter of his little company, and a moment's
thought will make it clear that the difference, however great, between
him and a professional promoter is basically one of degree rather than
of kind. Both create or help to create the company and seek to sell it
something, whether it be their services or a business. Both are
obviously so placed that they can easily take advantage of their
position by obtaining a recompense grossly in excess of the true value
of what they are selling.[3] The only difference is that the grocer is less
likely than the professional to abuse his position since he will probably
continue to be the majority shareholder in his company, whereas the
promoter, if a shareholder at all, will intend to off-load his holdings
onto others as soon as possible.

It will have been apparent from the foregoing that the expression
"promoter" covers a wide range of persons. Indeed, it is still wider.
Both the professional promoter and the village grocer are promoters
to the fullest extent, in that each "undertakes to form a company with
reference to a given project, and to set it going and ... takes the
necessary steps to accomplish that purpose".[4] But a person may be a
promoter who has taken a much less active and dominating role; the
expression may, for example, cover any individual or company that
arranges for someone to become a director, places shares, or
negotiates preliminary agreements.[5] Nor need he or she necessarily be
associated with the initial formation of the company; one who subsequently helps to arrange the "floating off" of its capital (in the
manner explained in Ch.25) will equally be regarded as a promoter.[6]
On the other hand, those who act in a purely ministerial capacity,
such as solicitors and accountants, will not be classified as promoters
merely because they undertake their normal professional duties;[7]
although they may if, for example, they have agreed to become
directors or to find others who will.[8]

Who constitutes a promoter in any particular case is therefore a
question of fact.[9] The expression has never been clearly defined either
judicially[10] or legislatively, despite the fact that it is frequently used
both in decisions and statutes. So far as the promoter is concerned

---

[3] A good (or rather, bad) example of the *modus operandi* is *Darby, Re* [1911] 1 K.B. 95.
[4] Per Cockburn C.J. in *Twycross v Grant* (1877) 2 C.P.D. 469 at 541 CA.
[5] *cf. Bagnall v Carlton* (1877) 6 Ch.D. 371, CA; *Emma Silver Mining Co v Grant* (1879) 11
Ch.D. 918, CA; *Whaley Bridge Printing Co v Green* (1880) 5 Q.B.D. 109; *Lydney & Wigpool
Iron Ore Co v Bird* (1886) 33 Ch.D. 85, CA; *Mann v Edinburgh Northern Tramways Co*
[1893] A.C. 69, HL; *Jubilee Cotton Mills v Lewis* [1924] A.C. 958, HL and cases cited, below.
[6] *Lagunas Nitrate Co v Lagunas Syndicate* [1899] 2 Ch. 392 at 428, CA.
[7] *Great Wheal Polgooth Co, Re* (1883) 53 L.J. Ch. 42.
[8] *Lydney & Wigpool Iron Ore Co v Bird* (1886) 33 Ch.D. 85, CA; *Bagnall v Carlton* (1877) 6
Ch.D. 371, CA.
[9] For an excellent discussion of this question, see J.H. Gross (1970) 86 L.Q.R. 493, and his
book *Company Promoters* (Tel-Aviv, 1972).
[10] For attempts, in addition to Cockburn C.J.'s description (above), see those of Lindley J. in
Emma Silver Mining Co v Lewis (1879) 4 C.P.D. 396 at 407, and of Bowen J. in *Whaley
Bridge Printing Co v Green* (1880) 5 Q.B.D. 109 at 111.

this imposes no particular hardship; as we shall see, the relevant duty is merely to act with good faith towards the company and this should occur, whether legally compelled or not. But from the point of view of the company the vagueness of the term is apt to be embarrassing when legislation requires promoters to be named or transactions with them to be disclosed.[11]

DUTIES OF PROMOTERS

The early Companies Acts contained no provisions regarding the **5–2** liabilities of promoters, and even today legislation is largely silent on the subject, merely imposing liability for untrue statements in listing particulars or prospectuses to which they are parties.[12] Since these rules apply only to public offers and not to company formations unaccompanied by a public offer or the introduction of the securities to a public market, discussion of them is postponed to Chapter 25. The courts, however, were conscious of the possibilities of abuse inherent in the promoter's position and in a series of cases in the last quarter of the nineteenth century they laid it down that anyone who can properly be regarded as a promoter stands in a fiduciary position towards the company with all the duties of disclosure and accounting which that implies; in particular he must not make any profit out of the promotion without disclosing it to the company. These duties, which to some extent track the fiduciary duties of directors,[13] have not been restated in the 2006 Act, as directors' duties have been, and so they remain regulated by the common law.[14] However, the two sets of rules are likely to continue to influence each other.

The main difficulty, however, is to decide how to effect this duty of disclosure—the company being an artificial entity. The first leading case on the subject, *Erlanger v New Sombrero Phosphate Co*,[15] suggested that it was the promoter's duty to ensure that the company had an independent board of directors and to make full disclosure to it. In that case Lord Cairns said[16] that the promoters of a company:

---

[11] e.g. under s.762(1)(c) (in relation to obtaining a trading certificate: see para.4–19, above). Community law seems to prefer the term "founders" which is not really any clearer: Commission Regulation (EC) No. 809/2004 of April 29, 2004 (the Prospectus Regulation) Annex I, para.14.1.

[12] FSMA 2000, s.90 (see para.25–31). But note s.90(8) which makes it clear that in respect of the duty of disclosure a promoter is in no worse position than any other person responsible for the prospectus.

[13] See Ch.16 below.

[14] Indeed no Part or Chapter title of the 2006 Act contains the word "promoter".

[15] (1878) 3 App.Cas. 1218, HL.

[16] (1878) 3 App.Cas. 1218, HL at 1236.

"stand ... undoubtedly in a fiduciary position. They have in their hands the creation and moulding of the company; they have the power of defining how, and when, and in what shape, and under what supervision, it shall start into existence and begin to act as a trading corporation ... I do not say that the owner of property may not promote and form a joint stock company and then sell his property to it, but I do say that if he does he is bound to take care that he sells it to the company through the medium of a board of directors who can and do exercise an independent and intelligent judgment on the transaction."

This rule, however, was obviously too strict; an entirely independent board would be impossible in the case of most private and many public companies, and since *Salomon v Salomon*[17] it has never been doubted that a disclosure to the members would be equally effective. In that famous case it was held that the liquidator of the company could not complain of the sale to it at an obvious over-valuation of Mr Salomon's business, all the members having acquiesced therein. "After *Salomon*'s case I think it impossible to hold that it is the duty of the promoters of a company to provide it with an independent board of directors if the real truth is disclosed to those who are induced by the promoters to join the company."[18] But the promoter cannot escape liability by disclosing to a few cronies, who constitute the initial members, when it is the intention to float off the company to the public or to induce some other dupes to purchase the shares. This was emphasised by the speeches of the House of Lords in the second great landmark in the development of this branch of the law— *Gluckstein v Barnes*.[19] "It is too absurd", said Lord Halsbury with his usual bluntness, "to suggest that a disclosure to the parties to this transaction is a disclosure to the company. ... They were there by the terms of the agreement to do the work of the syndicate, that is to say, to cheat the shareholders; and this, forsooth, is to be treated as a disclosure to the company, when they were really there to hoodwink the shareholders."

5–3   The position therefore seems to be that disclosure must be made to the company either by making it to an entirely independent board or to the existing and potential members as a whole. If the first method is employed the promoter will be under no further liability to the company, although the directors will be liable to the subscribers if the information has not been passed on in the invitation to subscribe; indeed, if the promoter is a party to this invitation,[20] he or she too will

---

[17] [1897] A.C. 22, HL: see para.2–1, above.

[18] Per Lindley M.R. in *Lagunas Nitrate Co v Lagunas Syndicate* [1899] 2 Ch. 392 at 426, CA.

[19] [1900] A.C. 240 at 247, HL.

[20] In which event he will find some difficulty in persuading the court that the directors were truly independent of him.

be liable to the subscribers.[21] If the second method is adopted disclosure must be made in the prospectus, or otherwise, so that those who are or become members, as a result of the transaction in which the promoter was acting as such, have full information regarding it. A partial or incomplete disclosure will not do; the disclosure must be explicit.[22] As indicated, however, where the promotion of the company is linked today with an offer of its shares to the public, the extensive disclosure rules set by Community law are likely to overtake any issue of liability at common law. Where, on the other hand, a sole trader or partners intend to incorporate their business but continue as the only persons involved in it, the disclosure obligation has no meaning. Only in the rare case which falls within these two extremes will the common law rules be relevant, for example, the formation of a company whose shares are then offered to a narrow group of people not constituting "the public".

It is sometimes stated that the duty of a promoter may be even heavier than that of making full disclosure of any profit made. The suggestion is that if the promoter acquires any property after the commencement of the promotion he or she is presumed to do so as a trustee for the company so that it must be handed over to the company at the price paid for it, unless the promoter discloses not merely the profit which is proposed to be made but also informs the company of its right to call for the property at its cost price. In theory this is undoubtedly sound. If the promoter broke the duty by attempting to acquire the property beneficially when it should have been acquired for the unborn company,[23] then the breach of duty was not merely failure to disclose the profit but was the attempted expropriation of the company's property. Indeed, if this is the situation, it appears that nothing short of unanimous consent of all the shareholders of the company, when formed, should entitle the promoter to retain the ill-gotten gains, for not even a resolution of a general meeting can authorise an expropriation of the company's property.[24] But in fact the English decisions cited in support of this suggestion[25] do not go anything like so far (although certain dicta in them do).[26] There seems to be no case in which, *full disclosure of the profit having been made*, the promoter has been held liable to account. The judgments acknowledge the possibility that the promoter may have

---

[21] See above, fn.6 and Ch.25, below.

[22] *Gluckstein v Barnes* [1900] A.C. 240, HL.

[23] There seems to be no objection in principle to the establishment of a trust in favour of an unformed company—for there can certainly be a trust in favour of an unborn child and this might have alleviated the problem of pre-incorporation contracts dealt with below at paras 5–8ff, but the decisions display a reluctance to invoke this principle.

[24] *cf. Cook v Deeks* [1916] 1 A.C. 554, PC and see para.16–86.

[25] *Tyrrell v Bank of London* (1862) 10 H.L.C. 26; *Ambrose Lake Tin Co, Re* (1880) 14 Ch.D. 390, CA; *Cape Breton Co, Re* (1885) 29 Ch.D. 795, CA, affirmed sub nom. *Cavendish Bentinck v Fenn* (1887) 12 App.Cas. 652. HL; *Ladywell Mining Co v Brookes* (1887) 35 Ch.D. 400, CA.

[26] See especially (1887) 35 Ch.D. at 413.

acquired the property as trustee, but they seem to require something more than the mere acquisition of property after the commencement of the promotion with the intention of re-selling it to the company.[27] In principle it should suffice if the company can show that the promoter acquired the property for him- or herself when under a duty to acquire it for the company.[28] But in practice all seems to turn on the intentions of the promoter at the time of purchase; on whether he intended to buy for himself for re-sale *to* the company or to buy initially *for* the company.[29] In the former case the only duty is to disclose; in the latter the promoter cannot subsequently change direction and seek to act as vendor rather than as trustee.

It seems clear that a promoter cannot effectively contract out of his duties by inserting a clause in the articles whereby the company and the subscribers agree to waive their rights.[30] Moreover, Article 11 of the Second Company Law Directive was intended to ensure that, when a public company acquired a substantial non-cash asset[31] from its promoters within two years of its entitlement to commence business, an independent valuation of that asset and approval by the company in general meeting should be required. But, as we shall see,[32] as implemented by the United Kingdom this applies only to acquisitions from the subscribers to the memorandum who need not be the true promoters and generally are not.[33] However, when a private company re-registers as a public one (a more common occurrence than initial formation as a public company) a similar requirement applies to such acquisitions from anyone who was a member on the date of re-registration[34] and that may well catch a promoter. This, therefore, affords an additional statutory protection against the risk that promoters will seek to off-load their property to the company at an inflated price, but one which can be avoided by the promoters ceasing to be members prior to the re-registration.

Remedies for breach of promoters' duties

5–4   Since the promoter owes a duty of disclosure to the *company*, the primary remedy against him in the event of breach is for the company to bring proceedings for rescission of any contract with him or for the

---

[27]   See especially, *Omnium Electric Palaces v Baines* [1914] 1 Ch. 332, CA.

[28]   *cf. Cook v Deeks*, fn.24, above.

[29]   See especially, per Sargant J. in [1914] 1 Ch. 347.

[30]   *Gluckstein v Barnes* [1900] A.C. 240, HL; *Omnium Electric Palaces v Baines* [1914] 1 Ch. 247, per Sargant J. Such "waiver" clauses used to be common and, except as regards actual misrepresentations (on which see Misrepresentation Act 1967, s.3), there is still no statutory prohibition of them: s.232 (invalidating exemption clauses) covers only directors.

[31]   One for which the consideration paid by the company was equal to one-tenth or more of the company's issued share capital.

[32]   s.598. See para.11–16, below.

[33]   See para.4–21. Had the Act followed the CLR's recommendation to abolish the memorandum of association, the drafters would have had to reconsider this point.

[34]   s.603(a).

recovery of any secret profits which he has made. So far as the right to rescind is concerned, this must be exercised on normal contractual principles, that is to say the company must have done nothing to show an intention to ratify the agreement after finding out about the non-disclosure or misrepresentation[35] and *restitutio in integrum* must still be possible.[36] In view of the wide powers now exercised by the court to order financial adjustments when directing rescission, it is doubtful whether the *restitutio in integrum* rule operates as any real restraint, at any rate where the promoter has been fraudulent or where he himself is responsible for the dealings alleged to have resulted in restitution being impossible.[37] The only circumstances where this requirement seems likely to impose a serious limitation is where innocent third parties have acquired rights to the property concerned, and even there a monetary adjustment will often enable the third parties' rights to be satisfied.[38] The mere fact that the contract had been performed never seems to have destroyed the right to rescind a contract of this type[39] and since the Misrepresentation Act 1967 any suggestion to that effect seems unarguable.[40]

If the contract is rescinded the promoter's secret profit will normally disappear as a result, but if a profit has been made on some ancillary transaction there is no doubt that this too may be recovered. Moreover, a secret profit may be recovered although the company elects not to rescind. The classic illustration of this is *Gluckstein v Barnes*[41] itself. In that case a syndicate had been formed for the purpose of buying and reselling Olympia, then owned by a company in liquidation. The syndicate first bought up at low prices certain charges on the property and then bought the freehold itself for £140,000. They then promoted a company of which they were the directors, and to it they sold the freehold for £180,000 which was raised by a public issue of shares and debentures. In the prospectus the profit of £40,000 was disclosed. But in the meantime the pro-

---

[35] *Lagunas Nitrate Co v Lagunas Syndicate* [1899] 2 Ch. 392, CA. Here again "the company" must mean the members or an independent board; clearly ratification by puppet directors cannot be effective.

[36] *Leeds & Hanley Theatre of Varieties, Re* [1902] 2 Ch. 809, CA; *Steedman v Frigidaire Corp* [1933] 1 D.L.R. 161, PC; *Dominion Royalty Corp v Goffatt* [1935] 1 D.L.R. 780, Ont.CA, affirmed [1935] 4 D.L.R. 736, Can, SC.

[37] *Erlanger v New Sombrero Phosphate Co* (1878) 3 App.Cas. 1218, HL and *Spence v Crawford* [1939] 3 All E.R. 271, HL. These cases suggest that the courts have more restricted powers of financial adjustment when there is no fraud: *sed quaere, cf. Armstrong v Jackson* [1917] 2 K.B. 822.

[38] As, perhaps, in *Leeds & Hanley Theatre of Varieties, Re* above, where the property had been mortgaged to a bank.

[39] As pointed out in the 10th Report of the Law Reform Committee (Cmnd. 1782), paras 6–9, the extent, if any, of any such rule was doubtful except as regards contracts relating to land. The Misrepresentation Act 1967 is based on this Report.

[40] s.1 of that Act expressly provides that a contract can be rescinded for misrepresentation notwithstanding that the misrepresentation has become a term of the contract or that the contract has been performed.

[41] [1900] A.C. 240, HL. And see *Jubilee Cotton Mills v Lewis* [1924] A.C. 958, HL.

moters had had the charges on the property repaid by the liquidator out of the £140,000 and thereby made a further profit of £20,000. This was not disclosed in the prospectus, though reference was there made to a contract, close scrutiny of which might have revealed that some profit had been made. Four years later the new company went into liquidation and it was held that the promoters must account to the company for this secret profit.

There is, however, authority for saying that if the property on which the profit was made was acquired before the promoter became a promoter, there can be no claim for the recovery of the profit as such.[42] According to this view it may be necessary for this purpose to make the, admittedly difficult, determination of the exact moment of time at which the promotion began. Normally, however, this rule works fairly enough. If the company freely elects to affirm the purchase, there would be an element of injustice in making the promoter disgorge the whole of the difference between the purchase price—perhaps paid many years previously—and the sale price.

5–5   No doubt the court could assess the market value at the date of the sale and on that basis force the promoter to account, but this, it has been argued,[43] would be to make a new contract for the parties. On the other hand, the rule could work grave injustice to the company on the rare occasions when *restitutio in integrum* had become impossible so that the company had lost the right to rescind through circumstances beyond its control. In practice, the courts avoided this injustice either by finding that the promoter was fraudulent, and accordingly liable to an action for deceit, or that the promotion had commenced when he acquired the property; indeed, they have often found both.[44] They have even suggested that, in the absence of common law fraud, the promoter would be liable in damages for his failure to disclose,[45] or negligence in allowing the company to purchase at an excessive price,[46] the damages being the difference between the market value and the contract price. As a result of the Misrepresentation Act 1967 there is a clear legal basis for awarding damages in all cases where the promoter has made an actual mis-

---

[42] *Ambrose Lake Tin Co, Re* (1880) 14 Ch.D. 390, CA; *Cape Breton Co, Re* (1885) 29 Ch.D. 795, CA, affirmed sub nom. *Cavendish Bentinck v Fenn* (1887) 12 App.Cas. 652, HL; *Ladywell Mining Co v Brookes* (1887) 35 Ch.D. 400, CA; *Lady Forrest (Murchison) Gold Mine* [1901] 1 Ch. 582; *Burland v Earle* [1902] A.C. 83, PC; *Jacobus Marler Estates v Marler* (1913) 85 L.J.P.C. 167n.; *Cook v Deeks* [1916] 1 A.C. 554 at 563, 564, PC; *Robinson v Randfontein Estates* [1921] A.D. 168, S.Afr.S.C.App.Div.; *P & O Steam Nav. Co v Johnson* (1938) 60 C.L.R. 189, Austr. HC.

[43] *Cape Breton Co, Re* (1885) 29 Ch.D. 795, CA.

[44] *Olympia Ltd, Re* [1898] 2 Ch. 153, affirmed sub nom., *Gluckstein v Barnes*, above; *Leeds and Hanley Theatre of Varieties, Re*, above. But the mere non-disclosure of the amount of the profit is not misrepresentation; *Lady Forrest (Murchison) Gold Mine* [1901] 1 Ch. 582; *Jacobus Marler Estates Ltd v Marler* (1913) 85 L.J.P.C. 167n.

[45] *Leeds & Hanley Theatre of Varieties, Re*, above; see especially per Vaughan Williams L.J. in [1902] 2 Ch. at 825.

[46] Per Lord Parker in *Jacobus Marler Estates v Marler* (1913) 85 L.J.P.C. at 168.

representation (which may or may not be the case) and cannot prove that he or she had reasonable grounds to believe, and did believe up to the time the contract was made, that the facts represented were true.[47] When there is any misrepresentation the Misrepresentation Act makes any exclusion clause ineffective to bar any remedy, "except in so far as it satisfies the requirement of reasonableness ...".[48]

In addition to the remedies of the company, the promoter may be liable to those who have acquired securities of the company in reliance on misstatements in listing particulars or prospectuses to which the promoter was a party. The remedies available against him are the same as those against the officers of the company or others responsible for the listing particulars or prospectuses and are dealt with in Chapter 25.

REMUNERATION OF PROMOTERS

A promoter is not entitled to recover any remuneration for his ser-   **5–6**
vices from the company unless there is a valid contract to that end between promoter and company. Indeed, without such a contract the promoter is not even entitled to recover preliminary expenses or the registration fees.[49] In this respect the promoter is at the mercy of the directors of the company. Until the company is formed it cannot enter into a valid contract[50] and the promoter therefore has to expend the money without any guarantee of repayment. In practice, however, recovery of preliminary expenses and registration fees does not normally present any difficulty. The directors will normally be empowered to pay them and will do so. It may well be, however, that the promoter will not be content merely to recover his expenses; certainly a professional promoter will expect to be handsomely remunerated. Nor is this unreasonable. As Lord Hatherly said,[51] "The services of a promoter are very peculiar; great skill, energy and ingenuity may be employed in constructing a plan and in bringing it out to the best advantages." Hence it is perfectly proper for the promoter to be

---

[47] Misrepresentation Act 1967, s.2(1). Moreover, under s.2(2) damages may be awarded in lieu of rescission.
[48] Misrepresentation Act 1967, s.3, as substituted by s.8 of the Unfair Contract Terms Act 1977, s.11 of which defines the requirements of reasonableness for this purpose as "the terms shall have been a fair and reasonable one to be included having regard to the circumstances which were, or ought reasonably to have been, known to or in the contemplation of the parties when the contract was made". The onus is on those seeking to show that the requirement is satisfied: ss.8 and 11.
[49] *English and Colonial Produce Co, Re* [1906] 2 Ch. 435, CA; *National Motor Mail Coach Co, Re* [1908] 2 Ch. 515, CA.
[50] See below.
[51] In *Touche v Metropolitan Ry Warehousing Co* (1871) L.R. 6 Ch.App. 671 at 676.

rewarded, provided, as we have seen, that there is full disclosure to the company of the rewards to be obtained.

The reward may take many forms. The promoter may purchase an undertaking and promote a company to repurchase it at a profit, or the undertaking may be sold directly by the former owner to the new company, the promoter receiving a commission from the vendor. A once-popular device was for the company's capital structure to provide for a special class of deferred or founders' shares which would be issued credited as fully paid in consideration of the promoter's services.[52] Such shares would normally provide for the lion's share of the profits available for dividend after the preference and ordinary shares had been paid a dividend of a fixed amount. This had the advantage that the promoter advertised his or her apparent confidence in the business by retaining a stake in it; but all too often the stake (which probably cost the promoter nothing anyway) was merely window-dressing. And if, in fact, the company proved an outstanding success the promoter might do better than all the other shareholders put together. Today, when the trend is towards simplicity of capital structures, founders' shares are out of favour and, in general, those old companies which originally had them have got rid of them on a reconstruction.[53] A more likely alternative is for the promoter to be given warrants or options entitling him to subscribe for shares at a particular price (e.g. that at which they were issued to the public) within a specified time. If the shares have meanwhile gone to a premium this will obviously be a valuable right.

PRELIMINARY CONTRACTS BY PROMOTERS

5–7 Until the company has been incorporated it cannot contract or do any other act. Nor, once incorporated, can it become liable on or entitled under contracts purporting to be made on its behalf prior to

---

[52] The promoter should obtain a contract with the company prior to rendering the services, for past services are not valuable consideration: *Eddystone Marine Insurance, Re* [1893] 3 Ch. 9, CA. Hence if the services are rendered before the company was formed the promoter will have to pay for the shares. Moreover, in the case of a public company an undertaking to perform work or supply services will no longer be valid payment: s.585(1) and see para.11–14. But provided the shares are given a very low nominal value this may not be a serious snag.

[53] There have been many interesting battles between holders of founders' shares and the other members. If the holdings of founders' shares are widely dispersed there is obviously a risk of block being acquired on behalf of the other classes in the hope of outvoting the remaining founders' shareholders at a class meeting to approve a reconstruction. To safeguard their position, in a number of cases the founders' shareholders formed a special company and vested all the founders' shares in it, thus ensuring that they were voted solidly at any meeting.

incorporation,[54] for ratification is not possible when the ostensible principal did not exist at the time when the contract was originally entered into.[55] Hence, preliminary arrangements will either have to be left to mere "gentlemen's agreements" or the promoters will have to undertake personal liability. Which of these courses will be adopted depends largely on the demands of the other party. If our village grocer is converting his business into a private company of which he is to be managing director and majority shareholder he will obviously not be concerned to have a binding agreement with anyone. In such a case a draft sale agreement will be drawn up and the main object of the company will be to acquire the business as a going concern "and for this purpose to enter into an agreement in the terms of a draft already prepared and for the purpose of identification signed by . . .". When the incorporation is complete the seller will ensure that the agreement is executed and completed.

If, however, promoters are arranging for the company to take over someone else's business, the seller will certainly, and the promoters will probably, wish to have a binding agreement immediately. In this event the sale agreement will be made between the vendor and the promoters and it will be provided that the personal liability of the promoters is to cease when the company in process of formation is incorporated and enters into an agreement in similar terms.

COMPANIES' PRE-INCORPORATION CONTRACTS

What, in practice, is a not infrequent source of trouble is that those **5–8** engaged in the formation of a company cause transactions to be entered into with third parties ostensibly by the company but before it has in fact been formed. The company, when formed, cannot ratify or adopt the contract,[56] but prior to the European Communities Act 1972 the legal position of the promoter and the other party seemed to depend on the terminology employed. If the contract was entered into by the promoter and signed "for and on behalf of XY Co Ltd" then, according to the early case of *Kelner v Baxter*,[57] the promoter would be personally liable. But if, as is much more likely, the promoter signed the proposed name of the company, adding his own to authenticate it (e.g. XY Co Ltd, AB Director) then, according to

---

[54] See below.

[55] Contrast the position when a public company enters into transactions after its registration but before the issue of a trading certificate (see para.11–4) or when a company changes its name (above, para.4–12).

[56] Unless it enters into a new contract. This, of course, does not mean that, in the absence of a new contract, the company or the other party can accept the delivery of the goods or payment without being under any obligation.

[57] (1866) L.R. 2 C.P. 174. See also *Natal Land Co v Pauline Syndicate* [1904] A.C. 120, PC.

Newborne v Sensolid (Great Britain) Ltd,[58] there was no contract at all.

However, on the entry of the United Kingdom to the European Community it was necessary to implement Art.7 of the First Company Law Directive. The relevant provision is now section 51 of the Act, which reads:

> "(1) A contract which purports to be made by or on behalf of a company at a time when the company has not been formed, has effect, subject to any agreement to the contrary, as one made with the person purporting to act for the company or as agent for it, and he is personally liable on the contract accordingly."

The aim of this provision, in line with that of the First Company Law Directive, is to increase security of transactions for third parties by avoiding the consequences of the contract with the company being a nullity. This protection is provided by giving the third party an enforceable contractual obligation, not against the subsequently formed company, but against the promoter, unless the third party agrees to forgo that protection. In its first decision on the new provision the Court of Appeal held that such consent could not be deduced simply from the fact that the promoter signed as the agent of the company; an express agreement, presumably either in the contract itself or subsequently, on the part of the third party, that the promoter should not be personally liable was required.[59]

However, the presence of the statutory provision has also had an effect on the courts' perception of the common law in this area. In the same case, Oliver L.J. said that the "narrow distinction" drawn in *Kelner v Baxter* and the *Newborne* case did not represent the true common law position, which was simply: "does the contract purport to be one which is directly between the supposed principal and the other party, or does it purport to be one between the agent himself— albeit acting for a supposed principal—and the other party?"[60] This question is to be answered by looking at the whole of the contract and not just at the formula used beneath the signature. If after such an examination the latter is found to be the case, the promoter would be personally liable at common law, no matter how he signed the document.

[58] [1954] 1 Q.B. 45, CA. In that case it was the promoter who attempted to enforce the agreement but it appears that the decision would have been the same if the other party had attempted to enforce it, as was so held in *Black v Smallwood* [1966] A.L.R. 744 Aust. HC: see also *Hawkes Bay Milk Corporation Ltd v Watson* [1974] 1 N.Z.L.R. 218; *cf. Marblestone Industries Ltd v Fairchild* [1975] 1 N.Z.L.R. 529. But it is difficult to see why the promoter should not be liable for breach of implied warranty of authority.

[59] *Phonogram Ltd v Lane* [1982] 1 Q.B. 938, CA.

[60] [1982] 1 Q.B. 938, CA, at 945. This approach was applied by the Court of Appeal in *Cotronic (UK) Ltd v Dezonie* [1991] B.C.L.C. 721 and in *Badgerhill Properties Ltd v Cottrell* [1991] B.C.L.C. 805.

On this analysis the difference between section 51 and the common **5–9** law is narrowed, but not eliminated. At common law, if the parties intend to contract with the non-existent company, the result will be a nullity and the third party protected only to the extent that the law of restitution provides protection. Under the statute, a contract which purports to be made with the company will trigger the liability of the promoter, unless the third party agrees to give up the protection. In other words, the common law approaches the question of the third party's contractual rights against the promoter as a matter of the parties' intentions, with no presumption either way, whereas the statute creates a presumption in favour of the promoter being contractually liable. The common law is still important in those cases which fall outside the scope of the statute.[61]

Despite the improvements which the statute has effected, there are still some problems with its operation. First, perhaps as a consequence of the legislature's concern with the promotion of third-party protection, the section did not make it clear whether the promoter acquires a right under the statute to enforce the contract, as well as contractual obligations. It was submitted in earlier editions of this book that normal principles of contractual mutuality should lead to this latter result and this conclusion was confirmed by the Court of Appeal.[62]

Secondly, the section bites only when the contract "purports" to be made on behalf of a company which has not been formed. Both limbs of this proposition must be satisfied. Thus, where the parties thought the company existed, though it had in fact been struck off the register, the Court of Appeal held[63] that the contract did not purport to be made on behalf of the company of the same name which was hurriedly incorporated when the parties later discovered their mistake. Since all were in blissful ignorance when the contract was drawn up and signed, it could not be said that the contract purported to be on behalf of the new company, the need for whose existence was not appreciated at the time. The contract in truth purported to be made on behalf of that company which had been struck off, but that was not a company of which it could be said it "has not been formed". Ensnared in this conundrum, the claimant failed. Thus, the section has not been construed as protecting third parties in all situations where they in fact attempt to contract with non-existent companies, but only in those situations where the contract identifies a specific

---

[61] As was the situation in the two cases cited in the previous note.
[62] *Braymist Ltd v The Wise Finance Co Ltd* [2002] Ch. 273, CA. However, since this means a contract purportedly made by the company may be enforced by its agent (the promoter), the third party may be able to resist enforcement where the identity of the counterparty is important. The Government in the debates on the Act rejected the opportunity to deal with this point expressly, preferring to leave it to the courts: H C Debs, Standing Committee D, Third Sitting, July 20, 2006, cols. 99–101.
[63] In *Cotronic*, above, fn.60.

company as the purported contracting party and where that company
is one which has not been formed.[64]

Thirdly, and undoubtedly the most serious,[65] the reforms have
done nothing to make it simpler for companies to "assume" the
obligations of a pre-incorporation transaction. While one can
understand that the Directive preferred to leave that to each Member
State, the United Kingdom has not got round to doing anything
about it. Many common law countries have recognised, either by
judge-made law or by statute, that a company when formed can
effectively elect to adopt pre-incorporation transactions purporting to
be made on its behalf without the need for a formal novation and that
the liability of the promoter ceases when the company adopts it. In
1962, the Jenkins Committee recommended this reform (and clause 6
of the aborted Companies Bill 1973 would have implemented that
recommendation) but it still has not happened.[66] At present the only
way in which the company can adopt the contract is by entering into
a post-incorporation agreement in the same terms. Even if the company does so, that will not relieve the promoters of personal liability
(at any rate while the new agreement remains executory)[67] unless they
are parties to the new agreement, which expressly relieves them of
liability under the pre-incorporation agreement. The need for all this
is frequently overlooked. This may not matter much if all those
concerned remain able and willing to perform their obligations under
the pre-incorporation agreement. But it can be calamitous if one or
more of them becomes insolvent or wants to withdraw because
changes in market conditions have made the transactions disadvantageous to him or them.

As pre-incorporation transactions are inevitable features of every
new incorporation it ought to be made as easy as possible to achieve
what the parties intend (or would have intended if they had realised
that the company was not yet incorporated and had understood the
legal consequences). In this case, if not generally, the legal techni-
cality that ratification dates back to the date of the transaction so that
it is not effective unless, at that time, the ratifying person existed and
had capacity to enter into the transaction, should not apply.

---

[64] See also *Badgerhill* (above, fn.60). On the other hand, it is submitted that the decision in
Oshkosh B'Gosh Inc v Dan Marbel Inc Ltd [1989] B.C.L.C. 507, CA, that s.51 does not apply
to a company which trades under its new name before completing the statutory formalities
for change of name, is correct, since a change of name does not involve re-incorporation. See
para.4–12.
[65] Also serious from the point of view of the harmonising objectives of the First Directive is the
decision of Harman J. in *Rover International Ltd v Cannon Film Sales Ltd* [1987] B.C.L.C.
540, that s.36C does not apply to companies incorporated outside Great Britain, a view
from which the Court of Appeal did not dissent ([1988] B.C.L.C. 710).
[66] The CLR, curiously, left this issue untouched.
[67] If the new contract has been fully performed by the company, after incorporation, and by
the other party, that clearly will end any liability under the pre-incorporation contract.

CHAPTER 6

OVERSEAS COMPANIES, COMMUNITY LAW AND JURISDICTIONAL MIGRATION

British courts might have refused to recognise companies not incor- **6–1** porated under the Companies Act 1985, its predecessors or under some other method of incorporation contained in our law,[1] thus putting in jeopardy the validity, under our law, of transactions entered into by such companies. In fact, the British courts have never adopted such an approach. As Lord Wright said in 1933: "English courts have long since recognised as juristic persons corporations established by foreign law in virtue of the fact of their creation and continuance under and by that law."[2] Indeed, as far as companies incorporated in other Member States of the European Community are concerned, to adopt such a rule today would be a breach of the EC Treaty. Art.43 EC prohibits restrictions on the freedom of establishment of nationals of one Member State in the territory of another Member State and adds that such prohibition also applies "to restrictions on the setting up of agencies, branches or sub-sidiaries".[3] Just to make things absolutely clear, Art.48 EC requires companies "formed in accordance with the law of a Member State

---

[1] See Ch.1 for a discussion of the various forms of incorporation available in Great Britain.

[2] *Lazard Bros v Midland Bank Ltd* [1933] A.C. 289 at 297, HL.

[3] The right of a company established in another Member State to set up an agency, branch or subsidiary in Great Britain is normally referred to as the right of "secondary establishment". The right of a company to transfer its head or registered office to another Member State is referred to as the right of "primary establishment" and is dealt with at paras 6–13ff, below.

and having their registered office, central administration or principal place of business within the Community"[4] to be treated in the same way as natural persons who are nationals of a Member State. Thus, as a general rule,[5] a company incorporated outside the United Kingdom need not form a subsidiary company incorporated under the Act in order to do business in the United Kingdom. It may trade through an agency or branch in this country or, indeed, simply contract with someone in the United Kingdom without establishing any form of presence in this country.[6] Of course, when a company incorporated elsewhere intends to carry on a substantial business in the United Kingdom, it is likely to form a British subsidiary in order to do so. This might be regarded as a sign of commitment to the British economy, and it also allows the foreign parent company to ring-fence its British operations by putting them in a separate subsidiary with limited liability.[7] The legal point, however, is that the foreign company is not obliged to take this route; it can do business here in its own right, if it so wishes.

However, recognition by British law of companies incorporated elsewhere immediately gives rise to a policy problem which we have already encountered in relation to British companies which are incorporated other than under the Companies Acts.[8] In principle, such companies are not subject to the regulatory requirements of the Act and this generates, potentially, problems both of unfair competition with companies which are so registered and problems of inadequate protection for third parties which deal with the non-British company. However, whereas trading companies incorporated in Britain but otherwise than under the Act (or its predecessors) are a small and declining number, companies incorporated outside the United Kingdom but doing business in this country are likely to constitute a growing number, given the establishment of a Single Market within the European Community and the world-wide pressures for the liberalisation of international trade (a process sometimes referred to as "globalisation"). A number of linked issues arise in connection with such companies, which we address in this chapter.

---

[4] On the significance of these various "connecting factors" see below, para.6–15.

[5] In particular industries a company operating in the United Kingdom may be required to do so through a British subsidiary. Thus, banks from (non-EC) countries with a poor record of banking supervision were reported to have been required by the FSA to withdraw from the business of taking retail deposits in the United Kingdom, unless they incorporated their branches as subsidiaries, which would be required to have their own capital: *Financial Times*, June 25, 2002, p.2. However, such national requirements must not infringe Community law on freedom of establishment. See Case C-221/89, *Factortame* [1991] E.C.R. I-3905.

[6] For example, where the contract is concluded over the telephone or the internet by someone in Great Britain with a company established in another country.

[7] See Ch.8, below. In the future the multinational parent might put all its European operations (perhaps of a particular type) into an SE—see above, para.1–21—and the SE might or might not be registered in the United Kingdom.

[8] See above, para.1–16.

First, which parts, if any, of the Act should be applied to companies incorporated outside the United Kingdom? Secondly, should the answer to that question depend on how far the company law of the state of incorporation is similar to British law? Thirdly, should British companies be permitted to shift their jurisdiction of incorporation? Fourthly, should businesses be permitted to incorporate in another jurisdiction (or to migrate to that jurisdiction) if their intention is to carry on business wholly within the United Kingdom? We shall see that, by and large, the attitude of British law is one of tolerance, subject to the provision of some basic safeguards for third parties dealing with companies.

In the previous paragraphs we have talked about "British" companies and the law of the "United Kingdom". This is because the Act applies to England and Wales, Scotland and, unlike its predecessors since 1929, to Northern Ireland. However, the United Kingdom is not a single jurisdiction but rather three separate jurisdictions. It follows that the issue of jurisdictional migration arises, not only between the United Kingdom jurisdictions and other jurisdictions, but also among the three legal jurisdictions which constitute the United Kingdom.

OVERSEAS COMPANIES[9]

The primary answer to the question of which aspects of the Act apply   **6–2**
to companies not incorporated in the United Kingdom is to be found in its Part 34 and regulations (to be) made under it. This Part is entitled "overseas companies",[10] a term that might be thought to conjure up a picture of companies formed in some distant and exotic location, though in fact it may be only the Straits of Dover or the Irish Sea which separate the country of incorporation from the United Kingdom. An overseas company is simply "a company incorporated outside the United Kingdom."[11] The regulatory objectives of this Part are relatively modest. They are principally to ensure that there is available in the United Kingdom some basic information about a company incorporated elsewhere which has established a presence in this country from which it does business. That information is, essentially, the information a British company would have to provide on incorporation[12] or as part of its annual financial returns,[13]

---

[9] The provisions of the Companies Act 2006 relating to overseas companies are scheduled to come into force on October 1, 2009.

[10] Before 2006 the even more quaint term "oversea" company was used.

[11] s.1044.

[12] See above, Ch.4.

[13] See below, Ch.21.

plus some information relating to those who represent it in the United Kingdom. However, some provisions go beyond disclosure.

Immediately prior to the 2006 Act this was an area of law which, despite its modest objectives, was overly complicated, because there were two sets of provisions, each containing slightly different disclosure requirements, for overseas companies. This arose in part because the companies legislation does not attempt to regulate all overseas companies which do business in the United Kingdom (for example, over the internet) but only those which have some sort of base in the United Kingdom (short, of course, of setting up a British subsidiary company, to which all the requirements of the Act would apply). However, this in itself would not have prevented the previous law from adopting a single connecting factor for determining which overseas companies should be subject to the disclosure requirements. In fact, the two sets displayed slightly different connecting factors. One set was the result of the UK's implementation of the Eleventh Company Law Directive[14] which used the concept of a "branch" to define the connection which an overseas company needed to have to fall within the Act. The other set consisted of the traditional domestic rules, based on the connecting factor of having a "place of business" in Great Britain. Even this might not have been problematic if both connecting factors had been linked to the same set of disclosure requirements. However, the two sets of rules did not contain exactly the same disclosure requirements, so that companies could not simply proceed on the basis that they did not need to decide whether they operated a branch or a place of business. Rather, they had to decide between the two, in order to determine which disclosure regime applied.[15] Although it was clear that a company subject to both regimes must comply with the Community rules if they were more demanding than the domestic ones (which was generally the case), companies might be far from clear whether the Community regime applied to them or only the domestic one.[16]

The CLR recommended,[17] and the Government accepted,[18] that a single regime should be re-established. This would be based on a single set of disclosure requirements, derived from the Eleventh Directive, but using the "place of business" as the connecting factor, defined in such a way as to ensure that it incorporated the Community concept of a "branch". However, the 2006 Act did not

---

[14] Directive 89/666/EEC, [1989] OJ L395/36.

[15] The situation seems to have arisen because the then Government was unwilling to allocate Parliamentary time for primary legislation on overseas companies (which would have allowed for the integration of the two regimes) but decided instead to implement the Eleventh Directive by secondary legislation under the European Communities Act 1972.

[16] In this connection it is important to note that the Eleventh Directive applies, not only to Community companies setting up branches in the United Kingdom, but to all foreign companies so doing.

[17] Oversea Companies (1999) and Final Report I, paras 11.21–11.33.

[18] Modernising Company Law, 2002, Cm 5553-1, para.6.17.

commit itself to a particular connecting factor in its definition of an overseas company and in its consultation document on the implementation of the 2006 Act the DTI proposed to adopt the alternative proposition that the concept of the branch should be used as the connecting factor.[19] However, after consultation the Government reverted to the CLR's proposal to use the "place of business" as the connecting factor whilst making sure that the definition of that concept was wide enough to embrace all examples of branches.[20] The decisive factor in this reversion to the CLR's view seems to have been that, otherwise, those dealing with overseas companies with a place of business in the United Kingdom (but not a branch) would lose the protection of the disclosure provisions they previously enjoyed. Consequently, the draft Overseas Companies Regulations 2008[21] are expressed to apply whenever an overseas company opens an "establishment" in the United Kingdom; and "establishment" is defined to mean a branch within the meaning of the Eleventh Directive or a place of business which is not a branch. Thus, either a branch or a place of business will trigger the operation of the provisions relating to overseas companies, but the crucial point is that the disclosure rules will not now vary according to whether the "establishment" test is met on the basis of a branch or a place of business.[22]

Establishment: branch and place of business

The terms "branch" and "place of business" obviously overlap to a large extent, but it seems that both at the top and at the bottom of the spectrum a place of business may exist even though a branch does not. To take the bottom end, this situation may arise because, it seems, activities ancillary to a company's business may constitute a place of business but not a branch. It is difficult to be absolutely certain about this, because the Eleventh Directive does not define a "branch" whilst the Regulations do not define a "place of business",[23] but it seems to be the case. It has been said in case-law that establishing a place of business, as opposed to merely doing business,

6–3

---

[19] DTI, *Implementation of the Companies Act 2006: A Consultation Document*, Ch. 2K, February 2007. This was apparently on the basis that imposing disclosure requirements on a wider basis than the Eleventh Directive required might be a breach of the freedom of establishment rights of companies from other Community countries.

[20] BERR, *Government Response to Consultation on Companies Act 2006: Overseas Companies*, December 2007, URN 07/1704GR, para.2.52.

[21] Available on the BERR web-site.

[22] Though, as we shall see, the requirements do vary somewhat according to whether the place of incorporation of the company is within the EEA or not.

[23] The CA 1985 expressly included "a share transfer or share registration office" (s.744), which the CLR thought was wrong in principle if the office would not otherwise constitute a place of business: Oversea Companies, para.25.

in this country requires "a degree of permanence or recognisability as being a location of the company's business".[24] However, it is not fatal to the establishment of a place of business that the activities carried on there are only subsidiary to the company's main business, which is carried on outside the United Kingdom, or are not a substantial part of the company's overall business.[25] As to the meaning of a branch some clues may be derivable from the Community legislation referring to bank branches.[26] This does contain a definition of a bank branch, from which some guidance may be obtainable. That definition refers to a place of business through which the bank "conducts directly some or all of the operations inherent in the business".[27] So it may be that purely ancillary activities, such as warehousing or data processing, do not constitute the establishment of a branch though they could amount to a place of business. To like effect is the definition of a branch adopted by the European Court of Justice for the purposes of the Brussels Convention: a branch has the appearance of permanency and is physically equipped to negotiate business with third parties directly.[28] At the other end of the spectrum, a company incorporated outside the United Kingdom but which has its head office here,[29] clearly has a place of business in the United Kingdom, but it might be argued that this is not a branch, since a branch supposes that the head office is elsewhere.[30]

Disclosure obligations

6–4   The Act and the draft Overseas Companies Regulations impose disclosure requirements on overseas companies having an establishment in the United Kingdom in all phases of its life. An overseas company which opens an establishment must file with the Registrar ("deliver a return") within one month information relating to both

---

[24] *Oriel Ltd, Re* [1986] 1 W.L.R. 180 at 184. See also *Cleveland Museum of Art v Capricorn Art International SA* [1990] B.C.L.C. 546.

[25] *South India Shipping Corp v Export-Import Bank of Korea* [1985] 1 W.L.R. 585, CA; *Actiesselskabat Dampskib "Hercules" v Grand Trunk Pacific Railway Co* [1912] 1 K.B. 222, CA. However, the business must be the business of the company, not of its agent or subsidiary: *Rakusens Ltd v Baser Ambalaj Plastik Sanayi Ticaret AS* [2002] 1 B.C.L.C. 104, CA; *Matchnet Plc v William Blair & Co LLC* [2003] 2 B.C.L.C. 195.

[26] This Community legislation is not otherwise dealt with here.

[27] See, for example, Directive 94/19/EC on deposit guarantee schemes, Art.1(5).

[28] Case 33/78, *Etablissements Somafer v Saar-Ferngas* [1978] E.C.R. 2183.

[29] In principle, British law accepts such an arrangement, though not all European countries do: see paras 6–15ff, below.

[30] However, in the *Centros* case (Case C-212/97, [1999] E.C.R. I-1459) the ECJ seems to have treated as a branch, for the purposes of Art.43 EC, the British company's place of business in Denmark, even though it carried on no business anywhere else, including the UK, which was simply its place of incorporation. Putting the matter the other way around, this might suggest that the British head-office of a company incorporated elsewhere would also be a "branch" for the purposes of the Eleventh Directive.

itself and the establishment.[31] Subsequent alterations in the registered particulars must also be notified.[32] Failure to do so constitutes a criminal offence on the part of both company and any officer or agent of the company who knowingly and wilfully authorises or permits the default,[33] but, apparently, does not affect the validity of transactions the company may enter into through its unregistered operation. There is no need in a book of this nature to go into the detail of what is required, but it should be noted that the requirements are more limited where the company is incorporated in a Member State than where this is not so.[34] This reflects the approach of the Eleventh Directive.[35] Overall, the policy can be said to be to put the person dealing with the overseas company through its establishment in a similar informational position as would obtain if the company were one incorporated under the Act.

A crucial concern of those who deal with overseas companies is how to serve legal documents on the company. The particulars relating to the establishment must give the name and service address of every person resident in the United Kingdom authorised to accept service on behalf of the company in respect of the establishment or a statement that there is no such person.[36] In addition, the return must state the extent of the powers of the directors of the overseas company to represent the company in dealings and in legal proceedings[37] and, in relation to the establishment, give a list of those authorised to represent the company as a permanent representative of the company in respect of the branch.[38]

On-going disclosure requirements fall into two categories. First, **6–5** the "trading disclosure" rules which apply to domestic companies[39] are adapted so as to apply to overseas companies "carrying on business in the United Kingdom."[40] These rules are, rightly, not

---

[31] s.1046 and the draft Overseas Companies Regulations 2008, regs. 4–6. The information about the company must include a certified copy of its constitution (reg.8(1)(a)). Although the disclosure obligation applies in principle each time the overseas company opens an establishment in the United Kingdom (reg.3), the company need not repeat the company-specific information each time, but simply cross-refer to it (reg.4(2)(3)). This applies even though the establishments are in different UK jurisdictions.

[32] Regulations Part 3.

[33] Regulations 10 and 15.

[34] Reg.5.

[35] *cf.* Arts. 2 and 8 of the Eleventh Directive. The theory, presumably, is that the more extensive information about the company is available from the national registries of EC Member States, under the provisions of the First Directive.

[36] s.1056 and reg.6(1)(e). If there is no such person or if the registered person refuses to accept service, then service can be effected at any place of business in the United Kingdom (s.1139(2)). However, if the overseas company has not registered particulars, it is unclear how service is to be effected (*cf.* ss.694A(3) and 695(2) of CA 1985).

[37] Reg.5(1)(e).

[38] Reg.6(1)(f). Part 9 applies provisions equivalent to those operating in relation to domestic companies for the protection of directors' residential addresses from public disclosure. See para.14–10.

[39] See para.9–3.

[40] s.1051 and Regulations, Part 6.

confined to those overseas companies which have an establishment in the United Kingdom, though doing business "in" the United Kingdom is not defined. The aim of the rules is to provide third parties with certain information at the point at which they deal—or are likely to deal—with overseas companies. Thus, the company must display its name and country of incorporation at every location at which it carries on business;[41] its name on its business letters and a wide range of analogous documents;[42] and, where it has an establishment in the United Kingdom, a range of further information on such documents.[43] There are penalties for non-compliance,[44] but non-compliance also carries civil consequences on the same basis as that applied to domestic companies.[45]

Secondly, annual reporting requirements are applied to overseas companies, but, in this case, only if they have an establishment in the United Kingdom.[46] These requirements vary according to whether the overseas company is required by the law of the country in which it is incorporated (its parent law) to prepare, have audited and to disclose annual accounts.[47] In such a case the overseas company discharges its disclosure obligations by delivering to the Registrar a copy of the accounting documents prepared in accordance with the parent law.[48] The "accounting documents" include not only the accounts themselves (including the consolidated accounts, if relevant) and auditors' report but also the directors' report.[49] The company has the relatively generous period of three months from the date the documents were first disclosed under the parent law to file them with the Registrar.[50] Where the parent law does not impose the requirements indicated above, the overseas company is subject to a version of the

---

[41] Reg.48 (and at the service address of every person authorised to accept service on behalf of the company in respect of the branch).

[42] Reg.50.

[43] Reg.53.

[44] Reg.54.

[45] Reg.53. For a discussion of those civil consequences see para.9–3.

[46] s.1049 and Regulations, Part 4. Unlimited overseas companies are exempted (as domestic ones are) from this obligation, and special rules (not considered here) apply to credit or financial institutions (reg.16).

[47] Reg.17. If the overseas company is incorporated in an EEA state, it falls within this category even if it is exempted by its parent law from the requirements to have its accounts audited or to deliver them (reg.17(1)(b)). Such exemptions are controlled by the relevant Community law, which is discussed in Ch.21.

[48] The most recent accounting documents have to be included with the initial return to the Registrar (reg.8(1), (2)). Thereafter, Part 4 applies (reg.18(5)). The accounts delivered to the Registrar must identify the legislation under which the accounts have been prepared, which GAAP has been used, if any; and whether they have been audited and, if so, according to which Generally Accepted Auditing Standards. Previously, an overseas company subject to the "place of business" test alone could not rely on its parent law.

[49] Reg.18. The auditors' report, of course, is not required in the case of an EEA company if the company is exempted from audit: reg.18(3).

[50] Reg.21.

accounting and filing requirements applied to domestic companies.[51] However, in addition to the option, available to domestic companies, to file accounts in accordance with International Accounting Standards, the overseas company may prepare its accounts in accordance with its parent law.[52] Further, in this case the accounts of the overseas company are not subject to an audit requirement. Despite the absence of an audit requirement, the obligation to produce annual accounts is clearly a burdensome one for overseas companies which are not required by their parent law to do so—though there must now be few countries in the world which do not require their companies to produce annual financial statements.

Finally, if an overseas company closes an establishment in the United Kingdom, it must give notice to the Registrar.[53] As to the overseas company itself, it must give information to the Registrar if it is wound up or becomes subject to insolvency proceedings.[54]

The Act lays down a general rule that documents delivered to the Registrar must be in English.[55] However, the company's memorandum or articles of association may be delivered in another language, provided they are accompanied by a certified translation into English.[56]

Obligations going beyond disclosure

Although the overseas companies provisions are primarily concerned with disclosure, there are two sets of further provisions going beyond this. One set is largely facultative. It applies, with appropriate modifications, the domestic rules about execution of documents and seals to overseas companies, whether or not that company has an establishment in the United Kingdom or even whether or not it can be said to do business "in" the United Kingdom.[57] The second set applies to company names and is regulatory in intent.[58] An overseas company is

6–6

---

[51] Part 4, Ch.3. See Ch.21 below. This is a considerable improvement on the previous law which applied, in such cases, a modification of an out-dated set of accounting rules to overseas companies, based on the 1948 Act.

[52] s.395, as applied to overseas companies by reg.26. This assumes, of course, that the parent law does not *require* preparation, audit and filing of the accounts of the overseas company, in which case it will fall within the first category of companies.

[53] s.1058 and Regulation 88—transfer of an establishment from one jurisdiction of the UK to another counts as the closure of one establishment and the opening of another.

[54] s.1053(2) and regs. 67 and 68.

[55] s.1103(1).

[56] s.1105 and the draft Companies (Registrar of Companies) Regulations 2008, reg.6. This power may be more widely used in the future.

[57] s.1045 and reg.90. See para.7–22. Without this, there might be some argument to the effect that the UK was in breach of its obligations in respect of freedom of establishment or freedom to provide services under Community Law. The application of s.51 (pre-incorporation contracts; see para.5–8) can be argued not to be facultative, but this provision is itself derived from the First Directive, Art.7.

[58] The rules on company charges created by overseas companies (s.1052) are also regulatory and are considered in para.32–22ff.

required to register its name on its creation of an establishment in the United Kingdom. That name may be its corporate name or the name under which it proposes to carry on business in the United Kingdom (its alternative name).[59] In principle, the domestic rules on company names[60] are applied to the overseas company's registered name.[61] Despite apparent contravention of the domestic rules, however, an overseas company which is registered in an EEA Member State is exempt from the domestic name controls over its corporate name, except those relating to permitted characters in a corporate name.[62] The Eleventh Directive does not provide for controls on the choice of name by overseas companies and the virtual non-application of such controls to the corporate names of EEA companies seems to have been the result of a fear that to impose them would infringe the freedom of establishment rules of the Community.[63]

Other mandatory provisions

6–7   In the final analysis, Part 34 applies the equivalent of only a small part of the British Act to overseas companies and, as we have seen, where the home state requires the production of public, audited accounts, even Part 34 relies on the rules of the state of incorporation rather than on the rules of the British Act. Some further protection for third parties, based on British law, may apply as a result of provisions in the Insolvency Act 1986. Thus, the rules restricting the re-use by successor companies of the name of a company which has gone into insolvent liquidation[64] apply to overseas companies. This is achieved by use of the formula that the relevant sections of the 1986 Act apply also to companies "which may be wound up under Part V of this Act".[65] Part V of the 1986 Act permits the court in certain circumstances compulsorily to wind up an unregistered company, the definition of which is broad enough to include overseas companies.[66]

---

[59]   ss.1047(1),(2) and 1048—and it may alter its alternative name and toggle between its corporate and alternative names.

[60]   See para.4–7ff.

[61]   s.1047(4), (5)—and to any alteration of the registered name.

[62]   s.1047(3), (5). These controls are set out in s.57 (see above, para.4–7) and regulations made thereunder.

[63]   Case C-167/01, *Kamer van Koophandel en Fabrieken voor Amsterdam, v Inspire Art Ltd* [2003] E.C.R. I-10155, where the ECJ struck down Dutch "pseudo-foreign company" requirements applied to an overseas (in fact, British) company which went beyond the Eleventh Directive. However, the Court recognised the possibility of justification which, one would have thought, would have been applicable in principle to the domestic name requirements, on the grounds of third-party protection, not involving a disproportionate cost to the company. However, this conclusion cannot be firmly arrived at without knowing the nature and extent of the name controls applied in the Member State of incorporation. The approach of the Act simply side-steps these difficulties.

[64]   See below, para.9–12.

[65]   IA 1986, ss.216(8) and 217(6).

[66]   s.220 ("any company", except, of course, those incorporated under the British companies legislation). See *Paramount Airways Ltd, Re* [1993] Ch. 223 at 240, CA. Voluntary winding-up of an unregistered company, however, is not permitted: s.221(4).

To fall within Part V the overseas company need not have an established place of business in Great Britain nor, indeed, any assets here at the time the application for winding up is made.[67] The courts have also accepted that the jurisdiction to wind up unregistered companies brings into play certain other sections of the Insolvency Act, even though those sections do not in terms apply to "Part V" companies.[68] These include the important provisions relating to fraudulent and wrongful trading.[69] Important though these provisions may be, they apply only to companies which are being or have been wound up in the United Kingdom, which in the case of an overseas company may well not happen.[70] Finally, the Company Directors Disqualification Act 1986[71] also applies to a company incorporated outside Great Britain if it is a company capable of being wound up under the Insolvency Act 1986.[72]

COMPANY LAW AT COMMUNITY LEVEL

Company law

Despite Part 34 of the Companies Act 2006 and the application of **6–8** some sections of the Insolvency Act 1986 to overseas companies, such companies are regulated, as far as corporate law is concerned, mainly by the law of their state of incorporation. Is this a cause for worry? This approach has the clear benefit of promoting freedom of establishment and it is an approach which British law has long adopted.[73] It does not excuse overseas companies established in the United Kingdom from compliance with domestic rules not contained in company law, relating, for example, to consumer protection. Nevertheless, when the European Community was established in the

---

[67] *Stocznia Gdanska SA v Latreefers Inc (No.2)* [2001] 2 B.C.L.C. 116, CA. However, the company must have some connection with Great Britain and there must be some good reason for winding it up here.

[68] [2001] 2 B.C.L.C. 116, CA.

[69] See *Latreefers* (above, fn.67) and IA 1986, ss.213 and 214. See also Ch.9, below. Whether the application of ss.213 and 214 to EC companies could be challenged under the Treaty provisions relating to freedom of establishment is unclear. It could be argued that these provisions, which apply equally to British companies, do not impede freedom of establishment but only the subsequent conduct of an established business.

[70] In the case of insolvent companies with the centre of their main interests in another EU Member State, Council Regulation 1346/2000/EC on insolvency proceedings ([2000] OJ L160/1), Art.3(2) favours the opening of insolvency proceedings in that other Member State.

[71] See Ch.10.

[72] s.22(2). See also *Seagull Manufacturing Co Ltd (No.2), Re* [1994] 1 B.C.L.C. 273—Act applicable to foreigners outside the jurisdiction and to conduct which occurred outside the jurisdiction, though presumably only in relation to a company falling within the Act. In the case of undischarged bankrupts the connecting factor is instead whether the company has an established place of business in Great Britain.

[73] See above, para.6–1.

middle of the 1950s, with the expectation that companies based in one Member State would penetrate more readily the economies of other Member States, without necessarily establishing subsidiaries in those States, it was decided that this was acceptable only if accompanied by a programme for the mandatory harmonisation of the company laws of the Member States.[74] In other words, in the minds of the drafters of the original EC Treaty, freedom of establishment for companies and harmonisation of company laws in the EC were closely linked. The resulting programme for extensive mandatory harmonisation, from the top down, of Member States' domestic company laws got off to an impressive start, but by the middle 1990s, if not earlier, had run out of steam. After a period in which it seemed entirely to have lost its way, the company law programme of the Community is now seemingly more securely based on the identification of those matters which can better be regulated at Community level and those which can safely be left to the Member States. However, the lines of future development of Community company law cannot be said to have been laid down to the complete satisfaction of all those involved.

Art.44(2)(g) EC, as amended, permits the Council of Ministers by qualified majority vote, on a proposal from the European Commission and under the joint decision-making procedure with the European Parliament,[75] to adopt Directives which aim to protect the interests of members "and others"[76] by "co-ordinating to the necessary extent the safeguards which ... are required by Member States of companies and firms ... with a view to making such safeguards equivalent throughout the Community". By the 1970s, the Commission had an ambitious programme of company law harmonisation under way, and the period from the middle of the 1970s to the end of the 1980s may be regarded as its golden age, with some nine directives being adopted. These were the First (safeguards for third parties),[77] Second (formation of public companies and the maintenance and alteration of capital),[78] Third (mergers of public companies),[79] Fourth (accounts),[80] Sixth (division of public companies),[81] Seventh (group

---

[74] See Wouters, "European Company Law: *Quo Vadis?*" (2000) 37 C.M.L.R. 257 at 269 and Wolff, "The Commission's Programme for Company Law Harmonisation" in Andenas and Kenyon-Slade (eds), *EC Financial Market Regulation and Company Law* (London, 1993), p.22. This position was adopted in particular by France.

[75] Art.251 EC.

[76] This includes creditors and, probably, employees. Basing the Directive on employee involvement in the SE (see above, para.1–21) on Art.44 was controversial and it was eventually adopted on the basis of Art.308, which requires unanimity. However, the controversy was as much about whether the SE rules could be regarded as a harmonising measure as about the subject-matter of the Directive.

[77] Council Directive 68/151, [1968] OJ 68.

[78] Council Directive 77/91, [1977] OJ L26/1.

[79] Council Directive 78/855, [1978] OJ L295/36.

[80] Council Directive 78/660, [1978] OJ L222/11.

[81] Council Directive 82/891, [1982] OJ L378/47.

accounts),[82] Eighth (audits),[83] Eleventh (branches)[84] and Twelfth (single-member companies) Directives,[85] though they were not adopted in that precise order.

The impact of these Directives on the company law of any Member State turns partly on the pre-existing condition of the domestic law of that State and partly on whether the transactions regulated by a particular Directive are important in that State's practice. As far as the United Kingdom is concerned, the most important Directives have been the First (which triggered a review of the common rules on ultra vires and agency as they apply to companies);[86] the Second (which led to a tightening of the rules on dividend distributions and other changes and which, unlike the First, has proved to be an obstacle to radical domestic reforms);[87] and the Fourth (which led to a re-think on the relationship between the law and accountancy practice).[88] Of lesser impact were the Eighth on audits[89] and the Eleventh on branches.[90] The impact of Community law on domestic company law has thus been substantial, but not comprehensive, and it has had a particular impact in the areas of financial reporting and capital maintenance.

After 1990, however, the harmonisation programme seemed to lose impetus. There were a number of factors contributing to this state of affairs. First, it proved difficult to obtain the necessary level of Member State support for the more controversial proposed harmonisation measures. This was true, in particular, of the proposed Fifth Directive which dealt with two sensitive topics upon which Member States are pretty equally split: should the board be a one-tier structure (as is the practice in the United Kingdom) or a two-tier one, consisting of separate supervisory and management boards, and, even more controversially, should employee representation on the board (whether one-tier or two-tier) be mandatory?[91] The Fifth Directive was never adopted. For many years, the issue of mandatory employee representation also held up agreement on the European Company and on a Directive on cross-border mergers, and the issue was resolved there only by abandoning any significant commitment to uniformity, or even equivalence, of rules on employee representation. Instead, the matter is regulated, mainly though not exclusively, according to the model required by the law of the State from which

6–9

---

[82] Council Directive 83/349, [1983] OJ L193/1.
[83] Council Directive 84/253, [1984] OJ L126/20.
[84] Council Directive 89/666, [1989] OJ L395/36.
[85] Council Directive 89/667, [1989] OJ L395/40.
[86] See Ch.7, below.
[87] See Chs.11–13 below.
[88] See Ch.21, below. The Seventh on group accounts was less important since domestic law already recognised the principle of group accounting.
[89] See Ch.22, below, but the Eighth has recently been overhauled by the Community and its second version is more sigificant.
[90] See above.
[91] See Ch.14 below.

the merging company with the highest level of representation comes.[92] Equally controversial has been the draft Ninth Directive on corporate groups, where the majority of States deal with group problems through general mechanisms of company law, whereas Germany has developed a separate regime for addressing issues of minority shareholder and creditor protection in group situations.[93] The inability of the Community to make headway on these particular issues over long periods of time[94] has to some extent undermined the whole process of harmonisation.

Secondly, in both corporate law scholarship and governmental policy-making, the role of mandatory rules in the area of company law came under forceful criticism. Whilst there is undoubtedly a proper place for mandatory corporate law rules (for example, in providing the necessary infrastructure of information through mandatory disclosure or to deal with issues of market failure) it is by no means clear that the legislature is uniformly able to design more appropriate rules than the parties themselves. In that context, the role of default company law rules becomes more prominent. Although there is no reason in principle why Community-level rule-making should not adapt itself to these new policy imperatives,[95] the new approach did significantly undermine the rationale of the original programme of Community law-making which was based on the deployment of mandatory rules[96] so as to ensure convergence of Member States' company laws.[97] For those less theoretically minded it may also have been important that there was little empirical evidence that "members and others" were suffering in the Community's single market from the lack of harmonised company laws. Closely linked to these points was the third criticism that, once a policy had been embodied in Community legislation, it was more difficult to change it than in the case of domestic legislation, at least for the majority of Member States. In other words, the Community legislative process was more "sticky" than national ones.

Such was the state of uncertainty into which the company law harmonisation programme had fallen by the end of the twentieth

---

[92] See para.14–28.

[93] See paras 9–14ff, below.

[94] The draft Fifth Directive was put forward in 1972 ([1972] OJ C13/49), though it has been fundamentally revised on a number of subsequent occasions. The Commission was considering drafts of the Ninth Directive in the early 1980s, but it could not even agree on a version to be put forward to the Council of Ministers.

[95] See G. Hertig and J. McCahery, "Optional rather than Mandatory EU Company Law: Framework and Specific Proposals" (2006) 3 ECFR 341.

[96] The early Directives might permit the Member States to go further than the Directives in laying down mandatory rules but did not allow them to fall below the Community standards. In this sense the Directives are sometimes referred to as containing "minimum" standards, but the standards were not necessarily minima in the substantive sense.

[97] Sometimes the Directives might confer options on the Member States (not normally on companies in the early Directives) but this was usually the result of difficulties in obtaining agreement among the Member States rather than the result of a philosophical questioning of the role of mandatory rules.

century that, at the end of 2001, the Commission appointed a High Level Group of Experts with the brief of providing "recommendations for a modern regulatory European company law framework". The HLG's Final Report[98] proposed a "distinct shift" in the approach of the Community to company law. Instead of the emphasis being, as hitherto, on the protection of members and creditors, the focus in future should be on what the Group saw as the "primary purpose" of company law: "to provide a legal framework for those who wish to undertake business activities efficiently, in a way they consider to be best suited to attain success."[99] Although the proper protection of members and creditors was an element of an efficient system of company law, those protections themselves should be subject to a test of efficiency. The Commission responded to the Group's Report in 2003 by producing a company law Action Plan which largely accepted the Group's recommendations.[100] In 2005 the Commission began public consultation on future priorities under the Action Plan, the outlines of which had become clear by the autumn of 2007.[101]

What are the main features of the new approach? First, the role of the Community in the area of company law has become a more modest, though still significant, one. So long as the Community's task was viewed as one of harmonising Member States' company laws so as to produce equivalent protections across the Member States, no serious question could be raised about the central role of the Community in this process. By definition, harmonisation of national systems (if it is to be achieved by legislative fiat) is something which only Community law can guarantee and national laws cannot (though, even on a harmonisation rationale, it is possible to argue that some areas do not need Community harmonisation ("from the top") because harmonisation is occurring in fact as national systems converge (harmonisation "from the bottom")).[102] However, once the goal is put in terms of identifying an efficient framework for company law, the issue of subsidiarity[103] is clearly raised. It is not obvious that the Community, in principle, is better equipped to identify an efficient system of company law than the Member States, especially as national contexts differ substantially. An important implication of this new approach therefore is that the Community should con-

6–10

---

[98] *Final Report of the High Level Group of Company Law Experts on a Modern Regulatory Framework of Company Law in Europe*, Brussels, November 4, 2002.

[99] Final Report, Ch.II.1.

[100] Communication from the Commission to the Council and the European Parliament, COM(2003) 284, May 21, 2003.

[101] Speech by Commissioner McCreevy to the European Parliament on October 3, 2007.

[102] See K. Hopt in B. Markesinis (ed.) *The Coming together of the common law and the civil law* (Oxford: Hart, 2000).

[103] Art.5 EC. Where both the Community and the Member States have competence, the Community should take action "only if and insofar as the objectives of the proposed action cannot be sufficiently achieved by the Member States and can therefore, by reason of the scale or effects of the proposed action, be better achieved by the Community".

centrate, as far as new Directives are concerned, on those areas of company law where it has an especial legislative advantage, principally in relation to cross-border corporate issues.[104] The most significant Directives adopted in the company law area since the adoption of the Action Plan have fitted this pattern: the Cross-Border Mergers Directive (2005)[105] and the Directive on Shareholder Rights (2007).[106] However, it should be noted, in relation to the latter, that although the driving concern of the Commission was the difficulties facing a shareholder in Member State A wishing to exercise voting rights in a company incorporated in Member State B, the Directive approaches this issue by conferring minimum rights on all shareholders in companies whose shares are traded on a regulated market. It is the limitation of the Directive to companies with publicly traded shares which really indicates the cross-border impetus of the Directive.

An even more important conclusion which was drawn from taking subsidiarity seriously was that the creation of a single financial market in Europe was a more appropriate area for Community activity than a harmonised company law (see below). The focus on securities law, however, did tend to favour the adoption of some Directives which could be, and had been, regarded as creations of the company law reform process—the line between company and securities law being inexact. Thus, a Directive on takeover bids[107] was adopted in 2004, which had originally been proposed as the Thirteenth Directive in the company law series, but it eventually emerged without that formal designation. Equally, rules on disclosure of financial information by companies, a traditional area of Community company law activity when viewed through the lens of shareholder protection, could be re-packaged in a securities market context and presented as investor protection measures. Thus, in 2002 the Community adopted a Regulation requiring companies with securities traded on a regulated market to produce their accounts in accordance with International Accounting Standards, thus, it was hoped, making the accounts of such companies more easily comparable, no matter in which Member State they were incorporated. In the same light can, perhaps, be viewed the revised and substantially extended Eighth Directive on auditors (2006).[108] However, here should be noted the significant impact, not just of theories of law-making and subsidiarity, but also of concrete financial scandals (notably those in the United States involving the Enron Corporation and other companies and the Parmalat scandal in Europe). The result was to release a considerable regulatory impulse, the revised Eighth Directive, like its

[104] See above, fn.98, Ch.II.1.
[105] Directive 2005/56/EC, OJ L310/1, 25.11.2005. See Ch.29 below.
[106] Directive 2007/36/EC, OJ L184/17, 14.7.2007. See Ch.21 below.
[107] Directive 2004/25/EC, OJ L142/12, 30.4.2004. See Ch.28 below.
[108] Directive 2006/43/EC, OJ L157/87, 9.6.2006. See Ch.22 below.

predecessor, applying to all companies, whether traded on a public market or not.[109]

A further implication of the new approach was that Community law-making, where this was required, should be less reliant on detailed Directives of the traditional type and make more use of Recommendations[110] and of instruments which imposed disclosure requirements rather than substantive rules.[111] This has been particularly apparent in the sensitive area of corporate governance. Thus, the topics of board structure[112] and directors' remuneration[113] have been dealt with at Community level in this way—indeed through Commission rather than Community recommendations—with the recommendations again confined to publicly traded companies. Further, the Community rules on corporate governance codes take the form of a comply or explain obligation (as indeed is typical of national corporate governance codes) but with the content of the code being determined, not by the Community, but by national-level bodies.[114]

Steps have also been taken to address the point about the **6–11** "stickiness" of Community legislation. In fact, the Commission moved on this front ahead of the High Level Group's Report. It adopted in 1996 the Simpler Legislation for the Single Market ("SLIM") initiative. This was a general initiative, not confined to company law, but the First, Second and Third Directives have been amended through the SLIM process, albeit with only modest results.[115] In the middle of 2007 the Commission issued a Communication on simplification in the area of company law,[116] which raised two more radical possibilities. One was the abandonment of certain areas of Community company law on the precise ground that Community action was not needed where cross-border issues were not entailed; and the other was moving from detailed Directives to principles-based drafting, which would give Member States more freedom in adapting them to their national situations. It is not clear at the time of writing which approach the Commission will favour. The acid test for this initiative seems likely to be the reform of the Second Directive, already lightly reformed under the SLIM initiative,

---

[109] Though there are some additional requirements for such companies. See para.22–27.
[110] "Recommendations ... shall have no binding force": Art.249 EC.
[111] See HLG, above, fn.98, Ch.II.2 and 3.
[112] Commission Recommendation of February 15, 2005 on the role of non-executive or supervisory directors of listed companies and on committees of the (supervisory) board, OJ L52/51, 25.2.2005.
[113] Commission Recommendation of December 14, 2004 fostering an appropriate regime for the remuneration of directors of listed companies, OJ L385/55, 29.12.2004.
[114] See Art.46A of the Fourth Directive, inserted by Directive 2006/46/EC, Art.1(7).
[115] See Directive 2003/58/EC, OJ L221/13, 4.9.2003 (amending the First Directive); Directive 2006/68/EC, OJ L264/32, 25.9.2006 (amending the Second Directive); Directive 2007/63/EC, OJ L300/47, 17.11.2007 (amending the Third and Sixth Directives).
[116] Communication from the Commission on a simplified business environment for companies in the areas of company law, accounting and auditing, COM(2007) 394 final, July 2007.

but a candidate for substantial simplification or even repeal, in view of the criticisms which have been made of it.[117]

Finally, the new approach has led to a reluctance on the part of the Commission to press ahead with new initiatives in areas which are likely to be controversial among the Member States and whose benefits in terms of the efficient functioning of companies are not clear. The most high profile victim of this approach has been the dropping by the Commission of proposals for a mandatory "one share, one vote" rule, which had been suggested by the High Level Group, after an empirical investigation found that the case for reform was unclear.[118] This was a significant retreat on the part of the Commission, since it is strongly arguable that the OSOV rule would have heightened the contestability of control of companies in Europe and thus facilitated the creation of a single market. However, just as the Directive on takeover bids could be agreed only after it had been emasculated by Member State opt-outs, the Commission no doubt feared the same result for an OSOV proposal. The proposal for a Fourteenth Directive on the transfer of the registered office also fell under the same pressures,[119] whereas the suggestion that the SE should be complemented by a European Private Company survived, though whether it will emerge in a form which is likely to lead to the greater use of this Community form of incorporation than the SE has generated remains to be seen.

Regulation of securities markets

6–12 Whilst the Commission's programme for company law was searching for a new rationale, its activities in the area of financial markets were gathering strength. As we have explained,[120] whilst this is not a book about the regulation of financial markets in general, some aspects of that regulation impact upon the core features of company law, in particular the regulation of public offerings by companies of their securities and the facilitation of the transfer of those securities through trading on public securities markets. The Community has come to concentrate on these matters since the integration of the national capital markets has been seen as a crucial aspect of the

[117] See para.12–10. The Commission commissioned a study on the utility of the Second Directive but, after receiving that report in January 2008, decided that no further reform of the Second Directive was needed.
[118] See Shearman and Sterling, ISS and ECGI, *Report on the Proportionality Principle in the European Union*, May 2007 (Report commissioned by the European Commission); Statement of the European Corporate Governance Forum on Proportionality, August 2007; Adams and Ferreira, *One Share, One Vote: The Empirical Evidence*; Burkhardt and Lee, *The One Share One Vote Debate: A Theoretical Perspective* (all available from http://ec. europa.eu/internal_market/company/shareholders/indexb_en.htm).
[119] Commission Staff Working Document, *Impact Assessment on the Directive on the cross-border transfer of registered office*, SEC (2007) 1707, 12.12.2007, to which the Commissioner responded by dropping further work on the proposal.
[120] See above, paras 3–3.

construction of the Single Market, more so than company law har-monisation, which was, so to speak, the price for freedom of estab-lishment (also an essential feature of the Single Market) rather than a direct contributor to the Single Market. Although the securities markets Directives are often also based, in part, on Art.44 EC, these Directives are not included in the numbered company law series precisely because they cover all types of issuer (including govern-ments or other public authorities) and not only company issuers.

The Directives deal with three main areas of concern: the initial process of raising capital through public offers and the admission of securities to trading on public markets; subsequent disclosure to the market by issuers and, to some extent, their shareholders; and ensuring the non-distorted functioning of securities and other mar-kets. The first two sets of Directives are discussed in more detail in Chapters 25 and 26 below and the third in chapter 30. All that need be noted here is that the first area (public offers and admission to trading) became a focus of Community action as long ago as 1979, so that for some time the company law and securities law programmes of the Community have proceeded in parallel. However, a major change of gear was produced by the adoption in 1999 of a Financial Services Action Plan (FSAP),[121] which led to a significant level of legislative activity in the succeeding years and to the production, in particular, of Directives on prospectuses,[122] on disclosure by issuers,[123] and on market manipulation,[124] as well as the Directive on takeovers referred to above. The FSAP was accompanied by an innovation in legislative procedure at Community level, known as the "Lamfalussy" procedure for the regulation of European securities markets,[125] under which the Directive contains only the principles of the legislation and the detail is laid down subsequently by the Commission, after consultation with a Committee of European Securities Regulators (CESR), but without the need to go through the full Community legislative process.[126] Consequently, the above Directives have to be read along with various implementing instru-ments (Directives or Regulations) issued by the Commission, which constitute a very significant part of the legislative process. The Commission recently announced that it had achieved the main goals set by the FSAP and that it did not intend to introduce a second

---

[121] Financial Services, *Implementing the Framework for Financial Markets: Action Plan*, COM (1999) 232, May 11, 1999.

[122] Directive 2003/71/EC, OJ L345/64, 31.12.2003.

[123] Directive 2004/109/EC, OJ L390/38, 31.12.2004.

[124] Directive 2003/6/EC, OJ L96/16, 12.4.2003.

[125] See the *Final Report of the Committee of Wise Men on the Regulation of European Securities Markets*, Brussels, February 2001.

[126] *cf.* the discussion of primary, secondary and delegated legislation in the United Kingdom (above, paras 3–3 and 3–4). In EU jargon the subsequent procedure for law-making by the Commission is known as "comitology".

FSAP, but it is clear that securities law will continue to be a main area of Commission interest.

MIGRATION OF COMPANIES AND REGULATORY COMPETITION

Registered office

6–13   When a domestic company applies to be registered, it must state in which of the three United Kingdom jurisdictions its registered office is to be situated: England and Wales, Scotland or Northern Ireland.[127] There is no provision for its registered office to be changed subsequently from the jurisdiction of incorporation to another.[128] Thus, a company which is formed with its registered office in England and Wales cannot decide to transfer its registered office to Scotland, still less to some other Member State of the European Community or to a state outside the European Community. It may be possible to produce this result indirectly. For example, a company may be formed in the new jurisdiction and the English company merged with it, though, until very recently, such mergers across borders were often very difficult or impossible to bring off, because national merger procedures were not well adapted to use by non-domestic companies.[129] Alternatively, without a formal merger, a contractual solution may be available: the assets of the old company could be transferred to the new company or the new company could offer to acquire the shares of the English company, in exchange for its own shares or cash.

None of these mechanisms amounts to a simple transfer of the company to another jurisdiction. On the other hand, they contain a reasonably high level of protection for shareholders, creditors and perhaps other interests. These protections are built into a statutory merger procedure.[130] When contractual mechanisms are used, the English company is valued at the time of transfer and that value is paid by the new company to the English company or its shareholders, via the new company's acquisition of the English company's shares or underlying business. The English company's creditors are protected

---

[127] s.9(2)(b).

[128] The facility for companies whose registered office is in fact in Wales to alter the statement so as to toggle between "Wales" and "England and Wales" does not involve a change of legal jurisdiction. The change has an impact on the availability or otherwise on the use of Welsh in the company's official documents and in communications with Companies House. See s.88.

[129] See now the Cross-border Mergers Directive (above, fn.105), discussed further below at para.29–12. The ECJ had earlier attacked the more obvious national obstructions to cross-border mergers in its decision in Case C-411/03, *SEVIC Systems AG* [2005] E.C.R. I-10805, noted by Siems (2007) 8 EBOR 307.

[130] See Ch.29 below.

in either case, because the English company will have the proceeds of the sale[131] (if its business has been sold) and will still have the same assets, if the new company has bought the English company's shares. In either case, there will still be an English company, with assets (at least in the immediate aftermath of the sale), against which they can assert their claims. As for the shareholders in the English company, they will have been able to exit the company, if the new company offered to buy their shares for cash; only if they accept shares in the new company will something like the result of a simple transfer have been achieved from their point of view.

This account of the rather complex situation which prevails at present perhaps explains why simple transfer of the registered office has not traditionally been permitted. The present rules provide a high degree of protection, certainly for creditors and to some extent for shareholders as well. By contrast, if the directors of a company could resolve by board resolution to migrate to another jurisdiction, this might have an adverse impact upon both groups. This is because a change in the jurisdiction in which the company has its registered office changes the internal company law to which the company is subject. In British private international law, the connecting factor used to determine the company law to which a company is subject in regard to its formation, internal affairs and dissolution is the law of the jurisdiction of (purported) incorporation, signified by the jurisdiction in which the company has its registered office. Consequently, freely to permit a company to change the jurisdiction in which its registered office is located (sometimes referred to as its "domicile") might be to permit it to make a change adverse to the existing legal rights of its members or creditors.[132] As between England and Wales, Northern Ireland and Scotland these changes may be small (albeit important in certain specific cases) but as between a British jurisdiction and a non-British one, they could be highly significant.

However, it is difficult to believe that adequate protection for   **6–14** members and creditors could not be provided through a set of rules which fall short of a prohibition on transfer. The Company Law Review proposed such a scheme,[133] which was based on that laid down in the European Company Statute,[134] for the SE is empowered to move its registered office from one EU State to another. However, the CLR proposals envisaged the possibility of transfer of the registered office outside the European Community and also within the

---

[131] Since the English company and the new company are separate legal entities, the directors of the English company could not, consistently with their duties to its shareholders and creditors, simply give the assets of the English company to the new company.

[132] In so far as the creditors' rights are embodied in contracts with the company, migration will not affect the law by which those contracts are governed, but migration will probably change the jurisdiction in which those rights have to be enforced.

[133] *Completing*, paras 11.54–11.70 and *Final Report I*, Ch.14.

[134] Regulation 2157/2001/EC, Art.8.

United Kingdom (which is not a matter for Community regulation). The basis of the proposal was that transfer in principle should be permitted (i.e. the opposite of the present law) but subject to adequate safeguards for shareholders and creditors. The main elements of protection for members would be the requirement that the board draw up a detailed proposal about the transfer, that the proposal should require approval by special resolution of the shareholders (thus requiring a three-quarters majority approval) and that dissenting members should have the power to apply to the court which might order such relief as it thought appropriate. Thus, for shareholders, the protective techniques invoked were disclosure, supermajority approval and court control.

For the protection of creditors, it was additionally proposed that the directors would have to declare the company to be solvent and able to pay its debts as they fell due for the twelve months after emigration, the creditors would have the right to apply to the court to challenge the proposal and the company would have to accept service in the United Kingdom even after emigration in respect of claims arising from commitments incurred before emigration.[135] Transfer would be permitted, on compliance with these rules, to any EU or EEA Member State, but transfer to a non-EU state would be dependent upon the Secretary of State having approved that state for this purpose, the criteria for approval being related mainly to levels of creditor protection, especially for creditors resident outside the state. Finally, for emigration within the United Kingdom a less detailed proposal would need to be developed by the board and the right of dissenting shareholders to apply to the court would be removed. The full range of creditor protections, however, would apply since there are significant differences in security and property law between the three jurisdictions.[136]

However, the Government rejected the CLR's proposals for international migration, on grounds of feared loss of tax revenues.[137] Since, as we have seen above, the European Commission has now abandoned its proposal to make available a procedure for moving the registered office within the Community, it seems that a simple mechanism for the transfer of registered office will continue to be unavailable to British companies, except as an incident to a cross-border merger,[138] unless the ECJ fashions such a mechanism on the

---

[135] If the company, after emigration, maintained a place of business in the United Kingdom it would become subject to the information provision rules for overseas companies (above); if not, it would in any event have to file with Companies House contact details relating to its new jurisdiction.

[136] Immigration would also be permitted but there the regulatory burden would fall mainly on the former state of registration. The British requirements would parallel those for a domestic company which re-registers: Final Report I, para.14.12 and above, paras 4–20ff.

[137] Modernising, pp.54–55.

[138] See Ch.29 below.

basis of the right to freedom of establishment for companies provided by the EC Treaty (see below).

Regulatory competition

Why should a company wish to choose a particular jurisdiction for its **6–15** registered office or move its registered office to another jurisdiction? The most obvious reason is in order to take the benefit of the set of rules for the internal affairs of the company which is regarded as the most beneficial for the company. In other words, choosing the jurisdiction of the registered office represents a choice about the internal company law to be applied to the business. In this perspective, the power to migrate would put some pressure on those responsible for company law in a particular jurisdiction to ensure that it remained attractive to businesses. The CLR thought this was the correct approach in principle: "In general, it is desirable that businesses should remain in Great Britain because it is attractive for them to do so, and not because company law in some sense locks them in."[139] In any event, that pressure is already present in some considerable degree, since, as we have seen earlier in this chapter, a company can form itself under a foreign law but carry on business in the United Kingdom as an overseas company. The power to move the registered office elsewhere would give companies greater freedom of action, especially to respond to changes in the law in Britain or elsewhere, but would not introduce an entirely new element.

In order for this choice of law to be made available to the maximum extent, however, it is necessary that legal systems should respect the choice made by the company when it is formed in or later moves to a particular jurisdiction. British law to some extent does so.[140] Because British private international law uses the place of incorporation (i.e. the site of the company's registered office) as the connecting factor for determining by which law the internal affairs of a company are governed, choice of internal law by choice of jurisdiction for the registered office is well-protected. It does not matter that the choice of jurisdiction for the registered office produces a divorce between the jurisdictional locations of the company's registered and head offices: the applicable law will still be governed by the jurisdiction in which the registered office is located. This is known as the "incorporation theory" for determining the applicable company law. Thus, in principle, a company may have its registered office in

---

[139] Completing, para.11.55.

[140] Though, given the difficulties about moving registered office, the practical force of the incorporation theory has been demonstrated to date mainly in relation to company formation rather than subsequent movement of the registered office. See below.

another state and its head office in the United Kingdom, and the British courts will still regard that company's internal affairs as governed by the law of the foreign state.[141] Or, the other way around, it may have its registered office in a United Kingdom jurisdiction but its head office elsewhere and still be regarded as a British company. Equally, in principle a company with both registered and head offices in the United Kingdom may move its head office to another state, without the British courts ceasing to regard it as a company formed under and regulated by the British Act, as far as its internal affairs are concerned. Consequently, a company which moves its head office outside the United Kingdom does not need to move its registered office as well, unless it wishes to change the law to which it is subject. One reason why the prohibition of movement of the registered office has lasted so long under the Act may be precisely that it does not prevent the movement of the company's head office to another jurisdiction. All this is true of company law. However, it may be that other parts of domestic law, especially tax law, make the movement of the company's head office out of the United Kingdom a difficult matter. Thus, a company which moves its central management elsewhere may cease to be resident in the United Kingdom for tax purposes, even if it is still incorporated in the United Kingdom (indeed, this may be the objective of the move) and so the British tax authorities may regard such a move as a taxable event in itself.[142]

However, the incorporation theory is not adopted by all legal systems and its competitor is less respectful of the company's choice of law. The majority of Member States of the Community do not in fact use the incorporation theory as the basis of their private international law rules but rather the "real seat" (*siège réel*) theory. On this approach the courts will regard a company as governed by the law of the jurisdiction in which its central management is located. If a company is not in fact incorporated in that jurisdiction but in another one (as would be the case with a British company moving its head office, but not its registered office, to another state), then the company in question will suffer from a number of legal risks. At worst, the courts of the host state might regard the company as not being properly formed, so that its members no longer had limited liability and the "company" would not be permitted to enforce its rights in that country's courts. Even if the British company moved its head office to another Member State which used the incorporation theory, that company might encounter legal problems when seeking to enforce its rights in a third state which operated on the basis of the real seat theory. By tying the choice of registered office to the choice

---

[141] And the courts of that State are likely also to be the appropriate forum for pursuing claims against the company: *Reeves v Sprecher* [2007] 2 B.C.L.C. 614. Of course, such a company will be subject to the rules on overseas companies discussed earlier in this chapter, if it has an establishment in the United Kingdom.

[142] See the *Daily Mail* case, discussed below.

of jurisdiction for the company's head office or central management, the real seat theory adds a substantial cost to the company's choice of internal company law: a particular jurisdiction for the applicable law will be attractive for a company only if the benefits of that applicable law outweigh the costs of locating the company's central management in that state. Frequently, that will not be the case and so the company's choice of applicable law is substantially constrained. Further, in the absence of a common rule in this area, the incorporation theory is undermined in practice: a company which chooses a jurisdiction for its registered office without also locating its central management there needs to be sure that not only the state of incorporation but also other states will respect its choice, and it cannot be sure of that in relation to states which adopt the real seat theory.

Since this is clearly a cross-border issue of some importance, it is **6–16** not surprising that the European Community has shown an interest in it. Indeed, the drafters of the original Treaty foresaw the problem and provided in Art.220 EC (now Art.293) that the Member States would enter into negotiations for a Convention laying down the principles upon which companies formed under the law of one Member State would be recognised in the others, but no such Convention was ratified because even the then six Member States could not agree.[143] However, the issue has been taken up more recently by the European Court of Justice, whose decisions have addressed the issue on the basis of the principle of freedom of establishment established by the EC Treaty. Of the three central decisions of the ECJ two have dealt with the issue of the initial choice of jurisdiction for incorporation and one with the subsequent movement of the company's central administration to another Member State, without an accompanying movement of the registered office. Given the difficulties of moving the registered office, the converse case of movement of the registered office without movement of the head office has not yet fallen to be considered by the ECJ.

In *Centros*,[144] the Court held that Denmark had infringed a company's freedom of establishment, when that company was incorporated in England, but carried on all its business in Denmark and the Danish authorities refused to register its Danish operations as a branch. It was clear that the British incorporation had been effected in order to avoid the Danish minimum capital requirements. However, the significance of the ruling is perhaps reduced by the fact that the Danish authorities admitted that the branch would have been registered, if the company had carried on some business in the United Kingdom, even though its main business was in Denmark. This reduced the force of the argument that the minimum capital rules

---

[143] For an account of these negotiations see V. Edwards, *EC Company Law* (Clarendon Press, 1999), pp.384–386.

[144] Case C-212/97 *Centros Ltd v Erhverus-og Selkabsstyrelsen* [1999] E.C.R. I-1459.

were a necessary protection for Danish creditors. More important was the decision in *Inspire Art*,[145] involving an incorporation theory state, the Netherlands. Dutch law thus had no difficulty about recognising the existence of a company incorporated in another Member State (again the United Kingdom) and so did not refuse to register it. However, Dutch law did apply to "pseudo-foreign" companies (i.e. those incorporated elsewhere but for the purpose of doing business wholly in the Netherlands) certain rules of Dutch law, notably its minimum capital rules. The ECJ held that creditor protection did not justify the imposition of requirements additional to those imposed by the State of incorporation: creditors were sufficiently protected by the fact that the company in question did not hold itself out as a Dutch company but as one governed by English law.

Überseering[146] involved the transfer by a company of its centre of administration from an incorporation theory State (in this case the Netherlands) to a real seat theory State (in this case Germany). The German courts refused to recognise the company's legal personality under Dutch law and so it could not sue to enforce its contractual rights in a German court. The ECJ held that this was a clear infringement of the Dutch company's freedom of establishment.[147] Although the Court accepted that in principle considerations of the "general good" might justify the imposition of restrictions on companies' freedom of establishment, the technique of denying legal capacity to a company transferring its centre of administration was not an appropriate response. It is interesting to speculate what the result would be if the transferring company had been formed originally in a real seat theory State, for in that case the removal of the centre of administration to Germany would have caused the company to cease to be subject to the domestic law of the State of original incorporation (unlike in the actual case where the company's existence under Dutch law was not put in doubt by the events which occurred). In such a case, would the German courts be entitled to require reincorporation under German law or would the state of incorporation have to continue to recognise the transferring company as subject to its laws, thus requiring that State to adopt, at least in part, an incorporation theory?

On the other hand, in an earlier case involving a English-incorporated company which wished to transfer its central administration outside the United Kingdom, whilst keeping its registered office in the United Kingdom, and which was prevented from doing

---

[145] *Kamer van Koophandel en Fabrieken voor Amsterdam v Inspire Art Ltd* [2003] E.C.R. I-10155.

[146] Case C-208/00, *Überseering BV v Nordic Construction Company Baumanagement GmbH* [2002] E.C.R. I-9919.

[147] "The requirement of reincorporation of the same company in Germany is tantamount to outright negation of freedom of establishment." (at para.81.)

so unless it complied with a swingeing domestic tax demand, the domestic restrictions were upheld.[148] This case may be explicable on the grounds that restrictions imposed by the "departing" state are viewed more lightly than restrictions imposed by the "receiving" state[149] (which seems wrong in principle) or on the grounds that the tax demands of the British authorities were justifiable under Community law.[150]

It has been argued that the effect of the above cases has been to   **6–17** abolish the real seat theory. Certainly, its cruder manifestations, as in *Überseering*, are incompatible with Community law. However, it must be remembered that restrictions of freedom of establishment by national legislatures are permitted, provided they meet the "*Gebhard* test",[151] that is, they are non-discriminatory, pursue a legitimate objective in the public interest, are appropriate to ensuring the attainment of that objective and do not go beyond what is necessary to attain it. Even here, the significance of *Inspire Art* is that it suggests a fairly rigorous approach on the part of the Court to the question of justification. By contrast, in the Community legislature the real seat doctrine has received a fairer wind. On the one had, the SE may move its registered office freely from one Member State to another (subject to certain shareholder and creditor safeguards), but its registered office must be in the same Member State as its head office.[152] If this cease to be the case, the state of registration must take steps to require the SE either to move its head office back to the state of registration or to move its registered office to the State where its head office now is; failing either of these things, the state of registration must have the SE wound up.[153] However, this provision of the SE Statute has all the hallmarks of a temporary arrangement, arrived at for the purpose of getting a version of the SE Statute through the Community's legislative process.[154] Thus, Recital 27 of the Preamble makes it clear that the rule for the SE is not intended to require Member States which follow the incorporation theory to adopt the real seat theory for domestic companies nor is it to be regarded as pre-empting any decision which may be made on the matter in future Community company legislation. In addition, Art.69 requires the Commission to initiate a review of the Regulation within five years of its coming into force and one of the subjects specified for review is "allowing the location of an SE's head office and registered office in different Member States".

[148] Case C-81/87, *Daily Mail and General Trust* [1988] E.C.R. 5483.
[149] This was the argument apparently accepted by the Court in *Überseering*.
[150] On which particular issue the ECJ's attitudes may also be changing: Case C-9/02 *Hughes de Lasteyrie du Saillant v Ministère de l'Economie* [2004] E.C.R. I-2409.
[151] Case C–55/94, [1995] ECR 1–4165.
[152] SE Regulation, Arts 7 and 8.
[153] Art.64, implemented by the Insolvency Act 1986, s.124B.
[154] And one of doubtful legality, given the ECJ's case law: see Ringe, "The European Company Statute in the Context of Freedom of Establishment" (2007) 7 JCLS 185.

With the emergence of a choice for companies as to the Member State jurisdiction in which they will incorporate, divorced from the question of which Member State they will select for their head office or, indeed, any other operational base, the original idea of top-down harmonisation via Community law is replaced by its opposite, i.e. regulatory competition. This is based on the premise that a single legislature often cannot identify in advance the most efficient mandatory rule and so it is better to give companies a choice among a menu of rules—or at least among a menu of sets of rules—so that the best format will emerge from the choices which companies make in practice. This process may in fact lead to a form of harmonisation, as Member States which do not offer the most attractive set of rules move to amend their laws so as to conform to the model which has revealed itself in practice as the favourite; or to a form of "specialisation" in which different Member States offer somewhat different corporate laws, each adapted from the dominant form of business organisation to be found in their jurisdiction.[155] In the first case, it is said, one achieves a better form of harmonisation; in the second, a demonstration that harmonisation is not the objective which should be pursued, at least not beyond certain basic provisions.

That such competition has begun to emerge in the European Community at the level of company formation seems clear. Firms from other Member States, not intending to do business in the United Kingdom, have chosen to incorporate in the United Kingdom in order to avoid minimum capital requirements and expensive formation formalities in their home jurisdictions;[156] and this has begun to produce the expected response in the shape of other Member States seeking to reduce or remove their minimum capital requirements for private companies.[157] It is not clear whether regulatory competition at the point of formation extends significantly beyond the minimum capital rules. For mature companies to make a new choice of applicable company law, however, has not been feasible. The SE Statute, as we have seen, is designed so as at present not to offer this possibility and the Commission has dropped its proposal for a Directive on the transfer of the registered office.[158] There is thus little experience with "re-incorporations" of mature companies in the Community. The incentives for mature companies to change jurisdictions will be very different from those operating at the time of initial incorporation. Nevertheless, it has been argued that the incentives for such companies to choose England and Wales as their

[155] J. Armour, *Who Should Make Corporate Law? EC Legislation versus Regulatory Competition*, ECGI Working Paper Series in Law, No.54/2005.

[156] See M. Becht, C. Mayer and H. Wagner, *Where Do Firms Incorporate? Deregulation and the Costs of Entry*, ECGI Working Paper Series in Law, No.70/2006.

[157] For France see J. Simon, "A Comparative Approach to Capital Maintenance: France" (2004) 15 E.B.L.R. 1037.

[158] Above, para.6–14.

company law jurisdiction are strong and that the incentives for the United Kingdom to offer attractive company law for such companies are compelling,[159] unlike in the case of the start-up company, where the absence of a minimum capital requirement in English law was historically due to a scepticism about the value of such a rule rather than being part of a policy to attract foreign incorporations.

The contrary argument to those put forward in favour of reg-   **6–18** ulatory competition, and which constitutes the basis of the real seat theory, is that to allow a company to choose a jurisdiction for incorporation, even though it carries on no substantial economic activities in that state or perhaps even no economic activities at all, weakens the power of the state where those activities are carried on to impose mandatory rules on companies for the benefit of members, creditors or employees. If a company does not like the rules of the state where it has based its operations, it will simply choose the law of another Member State for its incorporation.[160] What will then ensue is a "race to the bottom" among the Member States of the Community as they compete to provide company laws which companies find attractive.

Although these fears are not fanciful, they can be exaggerated and may even be misplaced. First, as a result of the Community's initial company law harmonisation programme (discussed above in this Chapter), there are minimum standards in place below which no Member State's company law can go. Secondly, and most importantly, competition does not necessarily result in a reduction of protection. In the case of financial markets, competition among stock exchanges for investors' funds has led to a raising of standards, especially in areas such as insider dealing, market abuse and corporate governance. The crucial question is who decides on the distribution of the good (in this case, the incorporation decision) for which the competition exists. In the United States, where incorporations are a matter for each State, where the incorporation theory prevails and where a high proportion of public companies choose to incorporate in Delaware, even though their businesses may have no connection with Delaware, the argument that this situation has produced a race to the bottom seems to be based on the proposition that re-incorporations are in practice the result of a board decision, so that Delaware has a strong incentive to produce a corporate law which is too favourable to management and which provides too little

---

[159] J. Armour, above, fn.155. Whilst not disputing that the revenue-raising incentives operating on the state of Delaware have no counterpart in the case of the United Kingdom, he sees the incentive as located with the "magic circle" law firms based in London.

[160] Of course, this is a risk even for incorporation theory States whose company law contains some feature which incorporators do not like and which some other available jurisdiction does not insist on. See the *Inspire Art* case, above, fn.145. Real seat theory states seek to protect themselves against competitive pressures through a private international law rule, whereas incorporation theory States will have to use some other technique to address the threat, such as a "pseudo-foreign" company statute.

protection for shareholders and creditors.[161] One way of addressing this problem is not to make the incorporation decision a purely managerial one. It is relatively easy to build into the re-incorporation decision a substantial role for shareholders, creditors and employees, as the cross-border mergers Directive does. Moreover, in the case of listed companies, it is probably the rules and mechanisms of the exchange which are more important for the protection of shareholders than the provisions of company law as such.

Conclusion

6–19 British company law has traditionally adopted a welcoming stance towards companies incorporated elsewhere. This is shown both by the limited extent to which it applies the provisions of the British Act to such companies and its acceptance of incorporation as the connecting factor in its private international law rules. It has preferred the goals of maximising freedom of movement and promoting a degree of competition among jurisdictions to ensuring that those dealing with foreign companies do so on the basis of a framework of law with which they are familiar. Within the European Community these two objectives have been reconciled to some degree through the programme for the harmonisation of company laws, though that initiative has perhaps now run its course. However, free movement and jurisdictional competition cannot be achieved by one state alone, since the migrating company is dependent also on the laws of the country to which or from which it moves. For this reason, corporate migration is undoubtedly a proper subject for the attention of the Community legislator, or failing that, of the European Court of Justice.

---

[161] It is much controverted whether the Delaware law maximises managerial freedom or shareholder value. For a convenient short account of the, now very large, literature, see R. Romano, *The Foundations of Corporate Law* (New York: Oxford University Press) at pp.87–99.

PART TWO

SEPARATE LEGAL PERSONALITY AND LIMITED LIABILITY

We saw in Part One that the separate legal personality of the company is a necessary feature of the creation of a company and that limited liability, although optional, is overwhelmingly chosen by those who incorporate a company. Having created an artificial person, the law has to decide how that person acts and knows. This can be done only by attributing the acts and knowledge of natural persons to the company in appropriate situations. The delineation of those situations has proved to be a taxing exercise, mainly because the rules of attribution need to vary from one area of liability to another. There is no reason to suppose that the rules should be the same in relation to, for example, contractual and criminal liability—and in fact every reason to suppose that they should not be. The first chapter in this part analyses the rules of attribution.

The remainder of this part deals with limited liability. Opinions continue to differ on the question of whether limited liability is a natural consequence of separate legal personality or a perversion of the ordinary and proper state of affairs. Nevertheless, it is clear that British company law is firmly committed to the principle and that it is only rarely that the common law will set that principle aside. Statute law has shown some greater willingness to do so in recent years (or to disqualify directors from acting through the corporate form in the future), where limited liability has been abused, especially in the context of small companies, where the interposition of a company between the entrepreneur and his or her creditors can seem, on occasion, artificial.

The traditional response of company law to the risks of limited liability, however, has been not to set that principle aside but rather to lay down rules on "legal capital", which in British law turn out to be mainly rules restricting the freedom of the controllers of companies to move assets out of the company when this might prejudice the company's creditors. This is an area where the British rules have been particularly influenced by Community law in the shape of the Second Company Law Directive. Again, opinions differ on the efficacy of legal capital rules in protecting creditors and on whether the statutory rules, mentioned in the previous paragraph, are a better solution to the problem, though, in general, increasingly penetrating criticisms of the concept of legal capital in general, and of the Second Directive in particular, have been advanced in recent years.

CORPORATE ACTIONS[1]

One consequence of the artificial nature of a company as a legal **7–1** person is that inevitably decisions for, and actions by, it have to be taken for it by natural persons. Decisions on its behalf may be taken either (a) by its primary organs (the board of directors or the members in general meeting) or (b) by officers, agents or employees of the company; acts done on its behalf will perforce be by (b). In either event a question may arise as to whether the decisions or acts have been taken or done in such a way that they can be attributed to the company. Similar problems of attribution arise where the question is simply whether the company "knew" about a certain fact or situation: whose knowledge in which circumstances should be attributed to the company?

As far as third parties are concerned, the answer to these questions depends upon the normal principles of vicarious liability and agency,

---

[1] Most of the 2006 Act provisions discussed in this chapter are scheduled to come into force on October 1, 2009.

which it is not the purpose of this book to expound in detail. The relevant principles can be summarised as follows:

    (i) A principal is bound by the transactions on his behalf of his agents or employees if the latter acted within either:

        (a) the actual scope of the authority conferred upon them by their principal prior to the transaction or by subsequent ratification;[2] or

        (b) the apparent (or ostensible) scope of their authority.[3]

    (ii) A principal, *qua* employer, may also be vicariously liable in tort for acts of his employees or agents which, though not authorised, are nevertheless sufficiently connected with their employment but, in general, is not criminally liable for their acts.[4]

Obviously, application of these principles is more complicated when the principal is a body corporate which cannot confer authority on agents or employees except through the action of natural persons who constitute its organs or agents. However, before turning to the application of these principles to companies, we need to look at one additional issue, which has played a large part in the history of British company law, but which now needs only brief treatment.

THE OBJECTS CLAUSE AND CORPORATE CAPACITY

7–2   The rules summarised above about the company's liability for or through the acts of its agents and employees assume that the company has legal capacity to engage in the activities in the furtherance of which it has deployed its agents and employees. The same issue arises

---

[2] Actual authority may be conferred expressly or impliedly. Authority to perform acts which are reasonably incidental to the proper performance of an agent's duties will be implied unless expressly excluded and an agent who, on previous occasions, has been allowed to exceed the actual authority originally conferred upon him may thereby have acquired actual authority to continue so to act. Ratification of a contract entered into by an agent in excess of his authority enables the principal to sue the other party if the agent had disclosed that he was acting for an identifiable principal.

[3] This consists of (i) the authority which a person in his position and in the type of business concerned can reasonably be expected to have and (ii) the authority which the particular agent has been held out by the principal as having unless, in either case, the other party knows or ought to have known that the agent was not actually authorised. The liability of the principal in both cases rests on estoppel; but in case (ii) the principal cannot be estopped unless the other party knows that the agent is acting as agent whereas in case (i) the other party may believe the agent to be the proprietor of the business and the principal, having allowed him to appear as such, is estopped from denying his power so to act: see *Watteau v Fenwick* [1893] 2 Q.B. 346.

[4] Unless the employer has initiated, or participated in, the crime.

in relation to natural persons as principals and employers but, whereas adult natural persons normally have full legal capacity and so the issue is not a significant one, the courts in the nineteenth century developed the doctrine that the company's legal capacity was limited by its objects. A company was required by the legislation to include a statement of its objects in its memorandum of association and from that the courts deduced that the company did not have legal capacity to act outside its objects. Any such action was in principle void. This was normally referred to as the ultra vires doctrine.[5] If the company had no capacity to engage, for example, in the manufacture of widgets, the fact that it had expressly authorised its agents to contract with third parties for the supply of the parts necessary for the manufacture of widgets would not save the contract with the supplier from the operation of the ultra vires doctrine.[6]

The doctrine of ultra vires was developed by the nineteenth century courts on grounds of both shareholder and creditor protection, i.e. that shareholders and creditors should not find that the company in which they had invested or to which they had advanced credit was engaged in a different business (with a higher level of risk) than they had expected at the time of the investment or loan. Unfortunately, both policy and legal technique were misplaced. The value of the company might in fact be enhanced, to the benefit of both shareholders and creditors, by moving into new fields of operation, so that a prohibition on such a step was too strong a rule.[7] As to technique, the rule proved avoidable through the device of companies adopting lengthy and sometimes subjectively-worded objects clauses.[8] By the early twentieth century it was doubtful if the rule ever constrained the well-advised company and therefore its main role was as a trap for the unwary.

Law reform took an unconscionable length of time to catch up with practice. A first step at conferring protection on third parties from the ultra vires doctrine was taken in section 9(1) of the European Communities Act 1972, since compliance with the First Company Law Directive[9] was necessary for the United Kingdom's

---

[5] Ultra vires is a Latin expression which lawyers and civil servants use to describe acts undertaken beyond (ultra) the legal powers (vires) of those who have purported to undertake them. In this sense its application extends over a far wider area than company law. For example, those advising a Minister on proposed subordinate legislation will have to ask themselves whether the enabling primary legislation confers vires to make the desired regulations.

[6] There was a regrettable tendency in the cases to use the term ultra vires to include situations where the company did have capacity to act but the particular agent did not have the appropriate authority, i.e. it was sometimes said that the act was "ultra vires the agent". This language should be avoided, if only because the consequences of an agent acting beyond authority are quite different from those the law attached to an action outside the legal capacity of the company.

[7] Originally, the objects clause of the memorandum was incapable of change after the formation of the company; and ultra vires acts could not be ratified by the shareholders.

[8] Accounts of these developments are given in earlier editions of this book.

[9] Directive 68/151/EEC.

admission to the European Community. This was a rather limited, though important, reform, probably because the last thing the Government promoting the 1972 Act wanted was that the issue of admission to the Community should be side-tracked or delayed by questions of company law. In 1989, the Department of Trade and Industry commissioned Professor Dan Prentice to undertake a review of the position and to make recommendations, and what the Department described as a "refined" (i.e. a more complicated but less far-reaching) version, of his recommendations was enacted in the Companies Act 1989. The 1989 reform had the merit, as far as third parties were concerned, of containing the clear statement that "the validity of an act done by a company shall not be called into question on the ground of lack of capacity by reason of anything in the company's memorandum."[10] However, if the "external" effect of the ultra vires doctrine was thus abolished, it continued to have effect "internally" i.e. as between directors and the company or between shareholders and the company.[11]

The 2006 Act, largely following the recommendations of the CLR which in turn picked up some of the unimplemented reforms proposed by Professor Prentice, takes a more radical approach by removing the doctrinal underpinnings of the ultra vires rule. It is no longer necessary for a company to set out its objects.[12] Unless it chooses otherwise, its objects will be unrestricted, i.e. it will have unlimited capacity.[13] Even if a company chooses to adopt restrictions on its objects (which will appear today necessarily in the articles rather than the memorandum of association),[14] those restrictions will not affect the validity of the acts of the company: section 39(1) repeats the provision previously found in section 35(1) of the 1985 Act, as amended, with the substitution of the word "constitution" for

---

[10] s.35(1) of the CA 1985, as amended.

[11] See s.35(2)–(5).

[12] This is based on an interpretation of Art.2(b) of the Second Directive (Directive 77/91/EEC) as requiring the company's articles to state its objects (if it has them) but not as requiring the company to have objects.

[13] s.31(1). The company may add, remove or amend objects at any time by altering its articles, subject to certain restrictions for charitable companies (s.31(2)–(5)) but without any special right of appeal to the court for dissentient minorities as previously provided for in relation to alteration of objects clauses (CA 1985, s.5). Section 31 preserves the operation of section 64 of the Charities Act 1993, applying in England and Wales. The broad effect of that section is that where a charity is a company, no alteration which has the effect of the body ceasing to be a charity will affect the application of any of its existing property unless it bought it for full consideration in money or money's worth. In other words, although the company is not prevented from changing its objects (so long as it obtains the prior written consent of the Charity Commission) in such a way that they cease to be exclusively for charity, its existing property obtained by donations continues to be held for charitable purposes only. In effect, the company will be in an analogous position to an individual trustee of a charitable trust; part of its property will be held for charitable purposes only and part of it not. And, presumably, it will have to segregate the former. In Scotland the relevant legislation is the Charities and Trustee Investment (Scotland) Act 2005.

[14] See para.4–14.

"memorandum".[15] Crucially, this rule applies also to the objects clauses of existing companies.[16] Section 39 does not attempt to deal with the internal aspects of the ultra vires doctrine, thus underlining that these are matters to be dealt with according to the ordinary rules on directors' duties[17] or the enforcement of the articles as between shareholder and company.[18] Thus, as far as third parties dealing with the company are concerned, they may act on the basis that the company's capacity is unlimited (even if it has restricted objects).[19] However, they do need to be concerned about the authority of those with whom they deal on behalf of the company, to which topic we now turn. Here the provisions of the company's articles may again be relevant; but it is the relationship between the articles and the authority of the company's agents which should concern third parties, not their impact on the company's capacity.

THE AUTHORITY OF AGENTS

The company's constitution and the authority of agents

The law relating to the authority of corporate agents is the result of an interaction between the general law of agency (applying to all principals, whether companies or not) and specific rules of company law, which may affect the way the general law applies to corporate agents. The general law we briefly summarised above. The authority of an agent is derived either from its express or implied conferment on the agent by the principal or, in the case of ostensible or apparent authority, from action taken by the principal which leads the third party to believe the agent has the appropriate authority, even though the agent does not. In the first case, it is uncontroversial that the third party can rely on the agent's authority (typically, when the agent purports to contract on behalf of the principal). In the second, the principal, unusually, is held to a contract which the principal has not authorised the agent to conclude on the basis that the principal induced the third party to believe the agent was authorised to the relevant extent. Such "holding out" of the agent by the principal

7–3

---

[15] Again subject to qualifications in the case of charitable companies.

[16] Objects clauses set out in the memorandums of existing companies are to be treated as provisions in the articles, by virtue of s.28(1), and as such will benefit from s.39 and also from the new alteration/removal regime.

[17] s.171(a) requires a director to act in accordance with the company's constitution. See para.16–20.

[18] See para.3–13.

[19] Unless the company is a charity. S.39 does not apply to charitable companies except in favour of a person who does not know the company is a charity or who gives full consideration and does not know the act is not permitted by the company's constitution: s.42(1). The charitable status of a company would obviously be in jeopardy if it could freely act outside its objects.

normally flows from either the appointment of the agent by the principal to a position whose holders normally have the relevant authority, or by dealing with the third party over a period as if the agent were authorised, even though the agent is not.

A principal will often have good reasons for not giving an agent unlimited authority to enter into legal obligations on the principal's behalf. There are many ways by which a principal can limit the authority of an agent, but where the principal is a company, an obvious method of limitation is the inclusion of a provision in the company's articles of association. Thus, the articles may say that contracts over a certain value must be approved by the shareholders in general meeting and cannot be entered into by the board alone, or the articles may give a particular director authority to act on behalf of the company in relation to certain types of contract but not others. There is no reason why a provision in the company's constitution should not normally be effective to limit the agent's actual authority. A more contentious topic is the impact of such a limitation on the agent's ostensible authority. The "holding out" rationale for the agent's authority in this case indicates that the function of the law is to protect the reliance interest of the third party. However, if the third party knows that the agent does not have the relevant authority, even though, for example, the agent has been appointed to a position the holders of which normally do have it, the third party has no reliance interest which the law needs to protect. If the third party contracts with an agent who, the third party knows, does not have the appropriate authority, there is no reason why the normal rule should not apply under which a principal is not liable for the unauthorised acts of an agent. Thus, if the third party has read and understood the articles, there would seem to be no good reason for not allowing the articles to shape the ostensible authority of the agent as well as the agent's actual authority.[20]

Constructive knowledge

7–4 Suppose, however, the third party is unaware of the contents of the company's articles. Here, the rules of agency interact with the rules of company law. A second rule developed by the courts in the nineteenth century, in fact before the ultra vires doctrine was applied to registered companies, was that anyone dealing with a company registered under the companies legislation was deemed to have notice of its "public documents", a term which certainly included its articles

---

[20] An (apparent) exception might be where the third party knows the articles restrict the agent's authority but the company has honoured the contracts made by the third party through the agent over a period of time in breach of the provisions of the articles. Here the third party can be said to have a reliance interest which the law should protect.

and memorandum of association, which are required to be filed at Companies House.[21] By developing this version of the doctrine of "constructive notice" the courts substantially enhanced the restrictive impact of provisions in the articles upon agents' ostensible authority. By treating third parties as knowing that which they would have known had they read the articles, the courts in many cases deprived the third party of a plausible claim to a reliance interest which the law should protect.

What are the consequences for the third party if the agent lacked authority to deal with the third party, for example, by way of contracting with the third party on behalf of the company? Unlike with the ultra vires doctrine, the transaction in this case is not void. Rather, it is not binding on the company unless the company ratifies it, i.e. unless it is approved by the body which does have authority, actual or ostensible, to approve such transactions on behalf of the company, or it is approved by ordinary resolution of the share-holders.[22] Thus, if a director purports to contract with a third party on a matter where only the board as a whole has authority to contract (and the third party cannot establish the requisite ostensible authority on the part of the director), the third party will be at the mercy of the board, which, in effect, has an option whether to commit the company to the contract or not. This may be marginally better for the third party than in the ultra vires case (because the law places no obstacle in the way of the transaction if, in fact, both third party and board wish to proceed with it), but the security of the third party's transaction is undermined, nevertheless, by his or her inability to rely on the agent's apparent commitment of the company to the contract.

Given that the effect of the constructive notice doctrine was to increase the insecurity of the third party's transaction with the company, it is not surprising that it has been the focus of much attention and criticism over the years. As we shall see below, the courts have developed qualifications to the constructive notice doctrine from which a third party may be able to benefit. However, in recent decades the legislature has become sceptical about the utility of allowing constitutional provisions to restrict agents' ostensible authority at all. The view has been taken that commerce will be promoted by relieving third parties of the need to check the company's constitutional documents before engaging with the company's representatives. This is not to say that the company is not free to limit the authority of its agents as it wishes, but the constitution is no longer seen as an obviously appropriate way to communicate such limitations to third parties. Other and more direct methods must be employed. Hence the legislature has moved to provide statutory

[21] *Royal British Bank v Turquand* (1856) 6 E. & B. 327, Exch.Ch.; *Ernest v Nicholls* (1857) 6 H.L.C. 401, HL.
[22] *Grant v United Kingdom Switchback Railway Co* (1888) 40 Ch.D. 135, CA.

protections which override the constructive notice doctrine, at least in relation to some situations where third parties deal with the company. The reforms of 1972 and 1989 to the ultra vires doctrine (discussed above) were accompanied by reforms to the rules dealing with the impact of restrictions in the articles upon the authority of corporate agents. The modern version of those rules is to be found in section 40, which makes only minor changes from the previous law. However, section 40 and its predecessors have given rise to a number of difficult points of interpretation which we examine below.

Statutory protection for third parties

7–5   Subs. (1) of section 40 provides:

> "(1) In favour of a person dealing with a company in good faith, the power of the directors to bind the company, or authorise others to do so, shall be deemed to be free of any limitations under the company's constitution."

(a) "In good faith"

7–6   This qualification in the section immediately makes it clear that not all third parties are to benefit from the section. Only "good faith" third parties will do so. But other provisions make it clear that "bad faith" is going to be difficult to establish. Section 40(2) provides a three-tiered set of protections for third parties. First, it provides that a person dealing with the company "is not bound to enquire as to any limitation on the powers of the directors to bind the company or authorise others to do so."[23] This provision completely undermines the rationale for constructive notice which was, in effect, that the presence of information which was publicly available created a duty to find out what was available from that source. The fact the third party could have found out what was in the company's articles by making appropriate enquiries is not now to be treated as putting the third party in the "bad faith" category. Secondly, the third party is presumed to have acted in good faith, unless the contrary is proved, so that the burden of proof falls on the company rather than the third party.[24] Thirdly, and most startling, the section provides that the third party is not to be regarded as acting in bad faith "by reason only of his knowing that an act is beyond the powers of the directors under the company's constitution." It appears to contemplate that a person dealing with directors with actual knowledge that they are exceeding their powers will not necessarily be found to be in bad faith. The section does not provide, of course, that actual knowledge

---

[23] s.40(2)(b)(i).
[24] s.40(2)(b)(ii).

cannot be an ingredient in the establishment of bad faith, but it does seem to prohibit the simple equation of knowledge and bad faith. As Nourse J. said of the same phrase in section 9 of the European Communities Act, 1972:

"What it comes to is that a person who deals with a company in circumstances where he ought anyway to know that the company has no power to enter into the transaction will not necessarily act in good faith. Sometimes, perhaps often, he will not. And a fortiori where he actually knows."[25]

(b) "Dealing with a company"
Subs. (2) gives help in the interpretation of dealing. It provides: **7–7**

"(2) For this purpose—

(a) a person 'deals with' a company if he is a party to any transaction or other act to which the company is a party."

A person deals with the company so long as he is a party to a transaction (e.g. a contract) or an act (e.g. a payment of money) to which the company is also a party. Despite this, the courts remain reluctant to bring gratuitous transactions with the meaning of the subsection.[26]

(c) The directors
The section begins by stating that it applies "in favour of a person **7–8** dealing with a company", i.e. without any restriction relating to the person who represents the company in the dealings with the third party. This recognises that many transactions will be decided upon by executive officers appointed by the board of directors rather than by the board itself. However, the section does not give comprehensive protection, because it then goes on to take back some of the broad protection which its opening words seem to promise. This is because

---

[25] *Barclays Bank Ltd v TOSG Trust Fund Ltd* [1984] B.C.L.C. 1 at 18. This dictum might be thought to put the emphasis the wrong way around: a person with actual knowledge will not necessarily be regarded as acting in bad faith. See also *Wrexham Associated Football Club Ltd v Crucialmove Ltd* [2007] B.C.C. 139, CA, where the court refused to give a third party the benefit of this provision where he had every reason to believe that those acting on behalf of the company did not have authority from the company to act as they did.

[26] *EIC Services Ltd v Phipps* [2004] 2 B.C.L.C 589, CA at [35], excluding an issue of bonus shares on the grounds that the subsection requires either a bilateral transaction or an act to which both company and third person are parties and which is binding on the company, if s.40 is to apply. See also *International Sales and Agencies Ltd v Marcus* [1982] 3 All E.R. 551 at 560, but decided on different wording.

the section does not say that, in favour of a person dealing with the company in good faith, the powers of the person acting on behalf of the company shall be deemed to be free of any limitation under the company's constitution. Rather, what it says is that "the power of the *directors* to bind the company, or to authorise others to do so" shall be free of any limitation under the company's constitution. Thus, a person who deals with the company through its shareholders in general meeting would seem not to obtain much benefit from the section, for example, where the company's constitution provides that the shareholders cannot commit the company to a particular type of contract without the approval of X, who might be a shareholder of the company, a director or neither. Here, the limitation in the constitution relates to the power of the shareholders, not the directors, to bind the company. So, those who deal with the shareholders are still subject to the perils of the common law.

Of course, it is unusual for third parties to deal with companies through the shareholders as a body, and hardly feasible except in the case of small companies. How does the section operate where the third party deals with the company other than through the shareholders? For example, the third party may deal with the board of directors. This seems to be the core case with which the section deals. Even if the articles provide that the board needs the shareholders' approval for contracts above a certain value, the good faith third party may treat the board's power to bind the company as not subject to this limitation. Suppose, however, that the board has purported to act on behalf of the company but is for some reason unable to act, for example, because it is inquorate. Will the third party still have the protection of the section? This was a matter of some doubt under the previous version of the section,[27] but section 40, by substituting the word "directors" for the phrase "board of directors" in the provision quoted in the previous paragraph, seems designed to settle the point in the third party's favour. Nevertheless, the underlying problem remains. It can hardly be the case that third parties, dealing with persons with no connection with the company, can claim the benefit of section 40 on the grounds that the failure of those persons to be elected directors by the company is a "limitation under the company's constitution" which third parties are entitled to ignore, even if they are good faith third parties. As has been said, the "irreducible minimum" for section 40 to operate must be "a genuine decision

---

[27] *Smith v Henniker-Major & Co* [2002] B.C.C. 544, upheld on appeal ([2002] 2 B.C.L.C. 655, CA) but with only Carnwath L.J. fully supporting the judge's reasoning on this point and Robert Walker L.J. taking the contrary view. In other words, the quorum requirement is to be treated as one of the limitations in the company's constitution which the section is designed to override.

taken by a person or persons who can on substantial grounds claim to be the board of directors acting as such..."[28]

With large companies, however, many contracts will be entered into at sub-board level, the board having more important things to do than authorise every contract the company enters into. The person then acting on behalf of the company may then be an individual director (in his or her managerial capacity) or someone who is not a director of the company at all. In this situation the power of the individual agent to bind the company is not deemed to be free of any limitation under the company's constitution.[29] However, the section recognises the frequency of such contracting by providing that the power of the directors *to authorise others* to bind the company shall be free of any limitation under the company's constitution. Thus, if the board authorises X to contract on behalf of the company in breach of a provision in the company's constitution which either limits the board's contracting power or its power to delegate the power to contract to others, the good faith third party will be able to proceed on the basis that this limitation does not apply.

However, it should be noted that the section does not say that the directors shall be deemed to have exercised the power to authorise others to bind the company. Suppose the constitution provides that no director shall enter into a contract worth more than £1 million, without the board's approval. The director enters into a contract worth £2 million. Can the third party claim the protection of the section? If the board has not conferred any authority on the director to contract on behalf of the company, the answer would appear to be in the negative. The section does not deal at all with the question of whether a particular agent has been authorised by the board to act on behalf of the company but only with the question of whether an authority which has apparently been conferred is to be subject to a limitation derived from the articles. If, even apart from any limitations in the company's constitution, the person purporting to act on behalf of the company would not be regarded as a duly authorised agent of the company, the company will not be bound. Thus, where the board has conferred no actual authority on the alleged agent, the first question to answer is whether that individual has ostensible authority. As we shall see below,[30] the authority which the law regards an individual director as having simply as a result of his or

7–9

---

[28] *Smith v Henniker-Major & Co* [2002] 2 B.C.L.C. 655 at [41] per Robert Walker L.J. Under the current law the word "directors" should be substituted for "board of directors".

[29] This appears to be so even if the individual is a director, since s.40(1) refers to the power of "the directors" not of "a" or "any" director to bind the company.

[30] Para.7–19.

her appointment as a director is limited, though the ostensible authority arising out of appointment to a senior management position may well be much greater.[31]

A variation on the above example would be where the board has authorised a particular director to contract on behalf of the company but no mention is made of the £1 million limitation. Or suppose the board, without any reference to the director's authority, has simply appointed one of their number to a position where it would be usual for such a director to have unlimited contracting authority. Is the director's ostensible authority limited by the provision in the company's constitution? It is unclear whether the section operates automatically to override the limitations in the company's constitution, whenever the board confers authority on an agent, or whether the board must expressly or by necessary implication make an appointment which is inconsistent with the provisions in the company's constitution. It is suggested that the former interpretation will better effect security of third parties contracting with large companies.[32]

Another variation is the situation of a junior manager given authority to act by a middle manager, in circumstances where the constitution limits the authority of all agents of the company in some particular way. Can such an agent be said to have been authorised by the board? Presumably, this will be possible if the authority of the middle manager to authorise agents can be traced back, perhaps through intervening layers of management, to an original delegation of authority by the board to the senior managers of the company.

The conclusion from this section is that it is possible for third parties to contract with companies in situations in which section 40 does not apply because the agent is neither one of the directors nor someone authorised by the directors. In such a case, the impact of provisions in the company's constitution on the agent's authority is determined by the common law, to which we turn after the conclusion of our analysis of section 40.

---

[31] The same point could theoretically arise in relation to the powers of the board itself. Normally, of course, the articles will confer upon the board wide management powers. But this is not obligatory and the board appears to have no inherent powers apart from those conferred on it by the articles. Does s.40 need to be read in the following way: "In favour of a person dealing with the company in good faith the board of directors shall be deemed to have authority to exercise all the powers of the company, except such as the Act requires to be exercised by some other organ, and to authorise others to do so, notwithstanding, in either event, any limitations in the company's constitution on the board's authority." Only if the courts so construe it, will it achieve its aim. The Company Law Review's proposed re-draft of the section adopted this approach: for the purpose of directors' authority to bind the company to third parties, the board would have authority to exercise "any power of the company (except a power which this Act requires to be exercised otherwise than by the board)" (*Modernising Company Law*, clauses 17(2) and (7).

[32] Suppose the board, in making the appointment, expressly reaffirms the limitation contained in the constitution. Could it then be said that the limitation derives not from the constitution, because that limitation has been overridden by s.40, but from the board resolution, which falls outside the section?

(d) Any limitation under the company's constitution

The company's constitution includes its articles of association,[33] but for the purposes of section 40 the statute includes also resolutions of the company, resolutions of classes of shareholders and agreements among the members of the company or any class of them.[34] In short, the constitution here means any formal rules laid down by the shareholders generally (or any class of them) for the conduct of the company's affairs, whether taking the form of the adoption or alteration of the company's articles or not.

7–10

(e) Persons

Section 40 seems to apply quite generally to "persons" dealing with the company in good faith. However, there is an obvious policy question about whether corporate insiders (especially directors) should be permitted to take advantage of the section. Are they truly third parties or should they be treated as persons in relation to whom the principle that they should know and understand the limitations contained in the company's constitution is a perfectly reasonable and practicable one? The answer appears to be given in section 41, which indeed adopts the principle that the protections of section 40 should not be available to corporate insiders.

7–11

Section 41 applies where the company enters into a transaction which exceeds a limitation on the powers of the directors under the company's constitution and the other parties to the transaction include a director of the company or its holding company or a person connected with such a director.[35] In such circumstances the transaction, far from being enforceable against the company, is voidable at the instance of the company[36] and, whether or not it is voided, such parties *and* any director who authorised the transaction are liable to account to the company for any gains they make and to indemnify the company against any loss it suffers.[37] The transaction ceases to be voidable in any of the four events[38] set out in subsection (4) but this, in principle, does not affect the company's right to be indemnified, at any rate unless the transaction is affirmed by the company.[39] The section does not affect the operation of section 40 in relation to any

---

[33] s.17(a).

[34] s.40(3). This considerably adds to the standard definition of the "constitution" in ss.17 and 29.

[35] s.41(2), (7)(b). The meaning of "connected person" is discussed in para.16–51.

[36] s.41(2).

[37] s.41(3). There is a defence for non-director defendants (i.e. connected persons who are not directors) if they can show they did not know the directors were exceeding their powers: s.41(5).

[38] (a) *restitutio in integrum* is no longer possible, (b) the company has been indemnified, (c) rights of a bona fide purchaser for value (other than a party to the transaction) would be affected or (d) the transaction is affirmed by the company.

[39] s.41(4)(d)—or unless the reason for the transaction ceasing to be voidable is that the company has been indemnified: s.41(4)(b).

party to the transaction other than a director or a person with whom the director is connected but where that other party is protected by section 40 and the director is not, the court may make such order affirming, severing or setting aside the transaction on such terms as appear to be just.[40]

Despite the presence of section 41, a majority of the Court of Appeal (Robert Walker L. J., as he then was, dissenting on this point) held in *Smith v Henniker-Major*[41] that section 40 was not available to the director, at least on the facts of that case, where the director in question dealing with the company was also chairman of the company and therefore under an obligation to see that its constitution was properly applied and was himself responsible for the error in the transaction with himself (a rare legal recognition of the importance of the chairman of the board). The point may seem an arcane one, since the director in that case clearly fell within what is now section 41, but it has some importance, because a transaction within section 40 but caught by section 41 is binding unless set aside by the company, as section 41 provides; whereas if the transaction is outside section 40 and governed by the common law, it will not be binding on the company unless ratified by it. It is submitted that the reasons given by Robert Walker L.J. are the more convincing, i.e. that, in the light of the fact that the legislature has expressly addressed the issue of corporate insiders in section 41, there is no need for the courts to give the word "person" an unnaturally limited meaning in section 40.[42] In short, it is submitted that corporate insiders, dealing with the company in good faith, do have the protection of section 40 (unlike at common law),[43] but that that protection is very substantially qualified by the provisions of section 41.

(f) The internal effects of lack of authority

7–12 As the opening words of section 40 make clear, the purpose of the section is to protect good faith third parties dealing with the company. Its aim is not to alter the internal effect of a directors' decision to act without authority, except in so far as such amendment is needed to protect third parties. Thus, subsection 40(4) preserves individual shareholders' power to bring an action to restrain the company from doing an act to which the directors have committed the company in excess of their powers.[44] Such relief cannot be

---

[40] subs. (6). See *Torvale Group Ltd, Re* [1999] 2 B.C.L.C. 605.

[41] [2002] 2 B.C.L.C. 1, CA.

[42] For the same reason it is submitted that the dicta in *EIC Services v Phipps* [2004] 2 B.C.L.C. at [37], CA to the effect that even shareholders are not intended to be protected by s.40, should not be followed. Since Parliament dealt with the position of directors in s.41, it is unlikely it would not have dealt with that of shareholders, if it had wished to qualify the protection conferred on them by s.40.

[43] See below, para.7–16.

[44] On the extent of those powers see para.3–16.

granted, however, if it would impede the fulfilment of the company's legal obligations to the third party. Section 40, unlike its predecessor, says nothing about the potential liability of directors who cause the company to contract in breach of limitations contained in its constitution. However, this matter is dealt with in section 171 as one of the general duties of directors, i.e. whether the breach of the constitution is of this type or some other type altogether.[45] Likewise, it seems likely that the section does not affect the liability of a third party who receives corporate property knowing (to the appropriate extent) that it has come to him or her in breach of the directors' duties to return that property or its value to the company as a constructive trustee.[46]

Special cases

Charitable companies

The 1989 Act made special provision regarding charitable companies. **7–13** In principle and following the 1989 Act, section 40 does not apply to charitable companies, so that, in particular, the third party dealing with the charitable company will be deemed to have constructive notice of the limitations on authority contained in its articles. However, the third party will be able to claim the protection of section 40 if he or she does not know the company is a charity or has given full consideration and does not know the act is beyond the powers of the directors.[47] Furthermore, even if the protection of section 40 is not available, this does not affect the title of any person who subsequently acquires an interest in property transferred by the company to a third party so long as the acquirer gave full consideration and did not have actual notice of the circumstances affecting the validity of the transfer. It is clear that "know" in the above rules connotes actual (not constructive) knowledge. The above provisions do not apply to Scotland, but equivalent ones are made for Scotland by section 112 of the Companies Act 1989, which remains in force. The reason for the stricter rules applying to charities appears to be that donors to a charity are not well-placed or under a strong incentive to secure that their money is appropriately deployed, as compared to members of a non-charitable company.

Finally, s.42(4) provides that, in the case of a company which is a charity, affirmation of an act to which s.41 applies shall be ineffective without the prior written consent of the Charity Commission.

---

[45] See para.16–20.

[46] *International Sales and Agencies Ltd v Marcus* [1982] 3 All E.R. 651.

[47] s.42(1). The burden of proving these matters is on the person asserting them, i.e. not normally the third party: s.42(3). Given the publicity requirements applying to charitable companies, the burden of proving lack of knowledge that the company was a charity will normally be a heavy one: s.68 of the Charities Act 1993.

Provision for employees

7–14   In *Parke v Daily News*[48] it was held to be beyond the capacity of a
company, about to go into liquidation, to pay voluntary severance
payments to its employees, on the grounds that it had no continuing
interest in the goodwill of its employees. This was thought to be an
undesirable rule and statutory changes were made to allow such
payments to be made, in appropriate conditions. The aim was to deal
with the legal obstacles to such payments whether they arose out of
the doctrine of ultra vires (no longer an important problem except for
charitable companies),[49] the powers of directors or the general duties
of directors. Under what is now section 247 the powers of the
directors of a company include, "if they would not otherwise do so",
power to make provision for employees or former employees of the
company or any of its subsidiaries in connection with the cessation or
transfer of the undertaking of the company or that subsidiary.[50] In
order for the statutory power to be exercised, it must have been
sanctioned by a resolution of the members or a resolution of the
directors, but in the latter case only if the articles authorise the
directors to adopt such a resolution and, even then, not so as to
authorise payments to directors, former directors or shadow directors.[51] Moreover, the articles may add further restrictions on the
exercise of the power, which must be complied with.[52] Further, the
payment must be made out of profits available for the payment of
dividends,[53] so that the provision creates a power to allocate resources
from shareholders to employees (hence the need, directly or indirectly, for shareholder approval) and not from creditors to employees.

In addition to giving the directors a power which they might not
otherwise have, the section protects the directors who exercise the
power from challenge on the grounds that the treatment of the
employees constitutes a breach of their duty to promote the success of
the company for the benefit of its members.[54] The location of this
provision in Part 10 of the Act may reflect the draftsman's view that
this was the major legal risk faced by directors in such a case.
Nevertheless, the restrictions with which the section is hedged about
show that the well-advised employee will negotiate, individually or
collectively, for such payments to be contractually due in the circumstances in question, in which case the absence of shareholder
approval or distributable resources will not stand in the way of
enforcement of the contract. The questions then would be whether

[48] [1962] Ch. 927.
[49] In the case of a charity protection is given against any challenge, whether based on directors'
powers or corporate capacity, arising out of the charitable company's objects clause:
s.247(3).
[50] s.247(1).
[51] s.247(4),(5).
[52] s.247(6).
[53] s.247(7)(b). On distributable profits see Ch.12.
[54] s.172. See para.16–33.

the directors had power to enter into the contract containing the severance entitlement, to which the answer normally will be in the positive, on the grounds that it was an exercise of their power to manage the company by hiring employees, and whether they had acted in accordance with section 171, to which again a positive answer would normally be forthcoming, unless the severance payments were of a particularly outlandish kind.[55]

If the directors' powers under the articles do include the power to make such payments (say, by virtue of an express clause conferring this power), then the directors may act in favour of the employees without observing the statutory requirement for shareholder approval or the limitation on the sources of payment (distributable profits), since they are not exercising the statutory power. However, they would still be subject to their general duty to promote the success of the company for the benefit of the members.

Finally, section 247 requires the payment or other provision to be made before the commencement of the winding up of the company.[56] If this does happen, the liquidator may make the payment which the company had previously agreed to pay under the provisions discussed above[57] or exercise the statutory power him- or herself under conditions which, taking account of the commencement of the winding up, parallel those contained in section 247.[58]

Cases outside section 40: the rule in Turquand's case

The objective of the foregoing statutory changes was to draw the sting of the constructive notice doctrine, thus improving the position of those who dealt with the company externally, while making as few alterations as possible to the position as between the company and its members, directors and other agents. However, the scope of section 40 is not entirely clear. If a transaction with a third party acting in good faith is effected on behalf of a company by the board of directors or by a person who, in fact, the board has authorised, limitations on the board's authority may normally be ignored by the third party. But, except where the company is very small or the transaction is very large, the third party will probably not have had dealings through the board. The dealings will be in practice more often with someone who is an executive of the company or even a comparatively lowly employee of whom the directors may never have heard. Suppose there is a limitation in the company's constitution on the authority of such a person. Section 40 may not always protect the

7–15

---

[55] As we have seen in relation to directors' remuneration, the courts are normally reluctant to scrutinise the substance of remuneration decisions (para.14–14).

[56] s.247(7)(a).

[57] IA 1986, s.187(1).

[58] IA 1986, s.187(2). In both cases the payment may be made only out of assets available to the members on winding up: s.187(3).

third party. This will depend on the view which the courts take of the provision that "the power of the directors ... to authorise others [to bind the company] is deemed to be free of any limitation under the company's articles."[59] If that provision is interpreted so as to apply whenever the agent has ostensible authority to act on behalf of the company, on the basis that the board—or someone authorised, directly or indirectly by the board—has appointed the agent to a position which gives them the relevant ostensible authority, then the only question to be considered is whether the agent has such authority (which question is discussed in the next section).[60] If, however, the provision is more narrowly construed, then the situation may arise in which a person would be regarded as appropriately authorised were it not for a limitation on his or her authority contained in the company's constitution, but section 40 will not protect the third party dealing with that person, because not authorised by the board. In that situation, however, the common law in the shape of the rule in *Royal British Bank v Turquand*[61] may then come to the aid of the third party.[62]

This rule was enunciated by the courts in the middle of the nineteenth century to mitigate the effects of the constructive notice doctrine, so that it was an earlier and common law response to the problem addressed by section 40, which now covers much of the ground previously occupied by the *Turquand* rule. However, the *Turquand* rule is not confined to limitations in the company's constitution on the authority of the directors. It is a general qualification of the constructive notice doctrine and so applies for the benefit of third parties whenever they fall within the scope of that doctrine. Like section 40, the rule also operates to protect those who have actual knowledge of the company's constitution, as well as those who have constructive knowledge. Starting from the common law proposition that a person dealing with a company is bound to read its constitution and will be treated as having done so whether this is the case or not, the *Turquand* line of authority goes on to limit the further enquiries which the third party is expected to make on the basis of his or her (deemed or actual) knowledge. In *Turquand*[63] itself a security for a loan had been given by a company through its directors (so that

---

[59] s.40(1).

[60] See para.7–18, below.

[61] (1856) 6 E. & B. 327, Exch. Ch.

[62] At one stage it seemed that the legislature would attack the problem root and branch, because a provision was introduced into the CA 1985 (s.711A) by the 1989 Act generally abolishing constructive notice arising out of public filing. In fact, the provision was not brought into force and there appears to be no equivalent in the 2006 Act. The CLR had recommended an equivalent provision should be incorporated into the legislation and its draft clause declared, sweepingly, that "in determining any question whether a person has ostensible authority to exercise any of the company's powers in a given case, no reference may be made to the company's constitution" (Final Report II, cl.16(7)).

[63] The account in the text of the facts has been somewhat altered to relate the holding to a modern company.

today section 40 would apply) but the articles provided that the directors could borrow only such sums as were authorised by the shareholders in general meeting and the requisite authority had not been given. Jervis C.J. said that a third party reading the company's articles would discover "not a prohibition on borrowing, but a permission to do so under certain conditions. Finding that the authority might have been made complete by a resolution, he would have a right to infer the fact of a resolution authorising that which on the face of the document appeared to be legitimately done". This was a benign interpretation of the constructive notice doctrine, since the courts might have said that the constructive notice of the articles put the third party on notice to enquire whether the shareholders had in fact given the requisite authority.

In *Mohoney v East Holyford Mining Co*,[64] the *Turquand* doctrine was approved and applied by the House of Lords in an even more difficult case. Here, a bank had honoured the company's cheques, signed by two of three named directors, after having received from the company's secretary a copy of a board resolution giving cheque-signing powers to the three directors, to which their signatures had been appended. Unfortunately, neither "secretary" nor "directors" had been properly appointed, but the bank successfully resisted an action for the repayment of the money. Provided nothing appeared which was contrary to the articles, the bank was entitled to assume that the directors had been properly appointed. This protection for third parties was partially re-affirmed by statute which originally provided[65] that the acts of a director were valid "notwithstanding any defect that may afterwards be discovered in his appointment or qualification". However, in *Morris v Kanssen*[66] the House of Lords held that the section applies only when there has been a defective appointment and not where there has been "no appointment" at all. In the light of this, section 161 of the 2006 Act provides a somewhat expanded protection, applying not only in the case of the subsequently discovered defect in the appointment but also where the director is disqualified from holding office, has ceased to hold office,[67] is not entitled to vote on the matter in question or (which was already part of the statutory protection) the appointment was in breach of the requirement that appointments of directors be voted on individu-

---

[64] (1875) L.R. 7 H.L. 869. Note also s.249 (minutes of directors' meetings as evidence of the proceedings of the meeting if purporting to be authenticated the chairman of the meeting or of the next directors' meeting) which could strengthen reliance on the *Turquand* rule when minutes of meetings have been kept.

[65] See, for example, s.285 of the 1985 Act.

[66] [1946] A.C. 459, applied in *New Cedos Engineering Co Ltd, Re* [1994] 1 B.C.L.C. 797, a case decided in 1975.

[67] This was the issue in *Morris v Kanssen* itself, where an originally valid appointment had expired without being renewed and this was treated as "no appointment at all" when the director continued to act as such.

ally.[68] That case also establishes that the protection of what is now section 161 does not apply to a third party who knows of the facts giving rise to the invalidity of the director's act (i.e., it carries with it a concept of good faith, which is rather stronger than that applied by section 40).

7–16   Even with this somewhat more expanded statutory protection in section 161, the *Turquand* principle will still be needed where the defect in the agent's authority results from a provision in the articles which relates to something other than the validity of the appointment of a director, as was the case in *Turquand* itself. Although immensely important in keeping the doctrine of constructive notice within some sort of bounds, the rule in *Turquand's* case does have its limitations. First, *Turquand* does not protect the third party if the constitution simply provides that a particular type of contract cannot be entered into by the person purporting to act on the company's behalf. To vary the facts of *Turquand* slightly, if the articles had provided that loans above a certain amount could not be contracted for on behalf of the company by the directors at all, the rule would not have protected a lender whose contract was approved by the board alone, even if the restriction on the board's powers was an unusual one.[69] Today, of course, section 40 would probably protect the third party. In other words, *Turquand* was a benign interpretation of the constructive notice doctrine, not its abolition.

Secondly, the benefits of the rule are not available to corporate insiders, at least to insiders who are directors acting as such. In *Morris v Kanssen*[70] the third party sought to rely on the *Turquand* rule (as well as on the statutory provision) arguing that as a third party he was entitled to assume that the directors had been properly appointed and thus the allotment by them of shares to him was valid. Unfortunately for him, at the time of the allotment the third party had assumed the functions of a director of the company and was thus under a duty to see that the company's articles were complied with. This duty was inconsistent with his taking the benefit of the *Turquand* rule. As we have seen, this approach of the common law has recently influenced the courts' interpretation of section 40.[71] However, in *Hely-Hutchinson v Brayhead Ltd*[72] Roskill J. interpreted the exclusion

---

[68]   The extensions result from the incorporation into the Act of provisions previously found in art.92 of Table A, the current model articles containing no provisions of this type. On the requirement for voting individually see para.14–11.

[69]   *cf. Irvine v Union Bank of Australia* (1877) 2 App. Cas. 366, PC—in many ways an even stronger case. The directors' authority to borrow was limited to a certain amount unless a "special vote" of the shareholders had enlarged their powers. If there had been such a special vote, it would have been required to be notified to the Registrar of companies and be made publicly available in the same way as the articles. The court refused to apply *Turquand* on the ground that inspection of the company's registered documents would have revealed whether the directors' powers had been enlarged or not.

[70]   [1946] A.C. 459. See also *Howard v Patent Ivory Manufacturing Co* (1888) 38 Ch.D. 156.

[71]   Above, para.7–11.

[72]   [1968] 1 Q.B. 549.

more narrowly: a director was an "insider" only if the transaction with the company was so intimately connected with his position as a director as to make it impossible for him not to be treated as knowing of the limitations on the powers of the officers through whom he dealt.

Thirdly, and perhaps most importantly, the *Turquand* rule does not apply if the third party has been put on notice or on enquiry as to the lack of authority. Obviously, this position cannot arise simply out of the third party's constructive or even actual notice of the company's constitution, for that would be entirely to negate the *Turquand* rule. Something else is required. In the leading case on this point, *B. Liggett (Liverpool) Ltd v Barclays Bank*,[73] where the third party bank had actual knowledge of the articles, the question was whether the bank was entitled to assume that the appointment of a third director had been properly made. Such appointment required the consent of both existing directors. The letter informing the bank of the appointment was signed by only one existing director (L). The other existing director (M) had for a long time made it clear to the bank that it should not meet cheques which were not signed by himself, in line with the articles' requirement for two signatory directors, because he thought that L was improperly withdrawing money from the company's account. Nevertheless, after the "appointment" of the third director by L, the bank met cheques which carried the signatures of L and the purported third director. The prior dealing between M and the bank as to the signing of company cheques was the "something else" which put the bank on enquiry to establish whether M had in fact consented to the appointment of the third director; the bank was not entitled to assume such consent.

Knowledge of the constitution as an aid to third parties?

So far, we have considered knowledge (actual or constructive) of the company's constitution as something negative from the third party's point of view, as something which could deprive him or her of the security of the transaction with the company. Can a third party rely on his or her knowledge of the articles as a building block in a claim against the company? As far as constructive knowledge of the constitution is concerned, the courts have held that the fact that the third party was deemed to have notice of the contents of the articles did not mean that he or she could rely on something in those documents to estop the company from denying the ostensible authority of an officer of the company who would not usually have had authority of the relevant type. Constructive notice was a negative doctrine curtailing what might otherwise be the apparent scope of the authority and not

7–17

---

[73] [1928] 1 K.B. 48. For a more modern example see *Wrexham Associated Football Club Ltd v Crucialmove Ltd* [2007] B.C.C. 139, CA.

a positive doctrine increasing it.[74] The position may be different, however, if the third party had actual knowledge of the articles and had relied on some provision in them. Even here, however, what is clear is that mere knowledge that the board of directors might have delegated authority to a particular person does not estop the company from denying that it has done so. It would be necessary for the other party also to establish that "the conduct of the board, in the light of that knowledge, would be understood by a reasonable man as a representation that the agent had authority to enter into the contract sought to be enforced".[75] Obviously, it will be unlikely that the board will so conduct itself if it has neither conferred that authority nor decided to ratify what the agent has done. It is, no doubt, theoretically possible to conceive of a provision in the articles which, if known to and relied on by, the third party, might estop the company, but there seems to be no reported case in which that has occurred. If this sort of estoppel is to be relied on, it will generally be because of conduct by the company's primary decision-making bodies and not because of any provision in its articles.[76]

Establishing the authority of agents

7–18   Both section 40 and the *Turquand* rule operate so as to deprive the company of an argument which would otherwise defeat the third party's claim against the company. By virtue of the third party's actual or constructive knowledge of the company's constitution the company would otherwise be able to argue that the third party knew the agent's authority was limited, so that the third party's reliance on the agent is not one the law should protect because the third party knew that reliance was misplaced. This is the argument upon which company law books concentrate, because it represents the point at which the rules of company law intersect with the general law of agency. However, this argument arises only if, apart from the limitations in the company's constitution, the agent would otherwise be

---

[74] Any doubt on this point was finally dispelled by the Court of Appeal in *Freeman & Lockyer v Buckhurst Park Properties Ltd* [1964] 2 Q.B., especially Diplock L.J. at 504. It had formerly led to much judicial (and academic) disputation: see *Houghton v Nothard Lowe & Wills* [1927] 1 K.B. 246, CA; *B.T.H. v Federated European Bank* [1932] 2 K.B. 176; *Clay Hill Brick Co v Rawlings* [1934] 4 All E.R. 100; *Rama Corp v Proved Tin & General Investments* [1952] 2 Q.B. 147. For the academic discussion see (1934) 50 L.Q.R. 469; (1956) 11 Univ. of Toronto L.J. 248; (1966) 30 Conv. (N.S.) 128; (1969) 18 I.C.L.Q. 152.

[75] Per Diplock L.J. in *Freeman & Lockyer v Buckhurst Park Properties*, above, at 508. See also Atkin L.J. in *Kreditbank Cassel v Schenkers*, above, at 844.

[76] *Mercantile Bank of India v Chartered Bank of India* [1937] 1 All E.R. 231 is sometimes misunderstood in this regard. The headnote is misleading in suggesting that it was the fact that the articles expressly empowered the board to delegate by powers of attorney that brought about the estoppel. It was the actual exercise of that power by the board that did so. The only relevance of the articles (of which third parties were deemed to have notice) was that they did not preclude the grant of such powers of attorney.

regarded by the law as authorised by the company to act on its behalf. To take an absurd example, if a third party contracts with a person it knows to be the company's caretaker to supply goods to the company to the value of ten million pounds, the court is unlikely to hold the company to the contract, whether or not anything is said in the articles about the contracting power of employees, unless the caretaker has been actually authorised to enter into the contract. This is because the court would be very unlikely to hold that a caretaker had ostensible authority to contract on behalf of the company. In short, the problem which section 40 and the *Turquand* rule address arises only if the agent, considered apart from the provisions in the articles, has the authority to contract on behalf of the company. If ostensible authority were not a prerequisite of the *Turquand* rule, in a company whose articles permitted the board to confer upon any person the power to sell the company's assets on its behalf the rule might have the absurd consequence that a third party could assume that any person had such authority, even if in fact unconnected with the company and known to be so. In such a situation the company would be at the mercy of any plausible rogue, even though the company had done nothing to put the rogue in a position to carry out the deception.

In other words, neither section 40 nor its predecessor at common law, the *Turquand* rule, purport to set out a complete code defining when a third party can safely assume that those dealing with the third party have power to bind the company. They are aimed, rather, at the more limited question of the interrelationship of limitations on authority in the constitution and the general principles of agency. However, those general principles of agency law need to be satisfied even apart from any limitations in the articles. Logically, those principles need to be considered before section 40 or *Turquand*. Although ostensible authority is a matter dealt with by the general principles of the law of agency on which company law has had little impact, those principles need to be considered briefly in a book on company law. Of course, the company will be bound if it has conferred actual authority upon the agent, but in practice it is the rules of ostensible authority which are commercially important. Since third parties often do not in fact check—and do not want to be required to check—the alleged agent's actual authority, it is the rules on ostensible authority which facilitate or hinder third parties in their dealings with sub-board agents.

Ostensible authority and holding out
The essence of the principle underlying ostensible authority is a **7–19** holding out of the alleged agent by the company to the third party as someone who has the authority of the company to enter into the transaction in question. A common example is where the person through whom the third party dealt occupies a position in the

company[77] such that it would be usual for an occupant of that position to have authority to bind the company in relation to the transaction concerned. The third party dealing with the company in good faith will be entitled to assume that that person has authority (unless, of course, he knows the contrary or knows of facts which would have put a reasonable person on inquiry). This is so both where the company appoints the agent to the position with the intention that third parties shall rely on the representation arising out of the appointment, but also where it is reasonable for the third party to understand the appointment as constituting such a representation.[78]

From the above it follows that an officer or agent of the company cannot confer ostensible authority on himself by representing that he has actual authority.[79] It can be conferred only by conduct of the company, acting through an agent of the company, such as the board or the managing director, with actual or apparent authority to make representations as to the extent of the authority of the company's officers or agents. If the company has made such representations on which the third party has acted in good faith, the company may be estopped.[80]

Thus, if the person acting for the company is its chief executive or managing director, then, despite the fact that the Act refuses to treat him or her as an "organ" of the company equivalent to the board of directors, unless there are suspicious circumstances, or the transaction is of such magnitude as to imply the need for board approval, that person may safely be assumed to be authorised. In practice, that person will probably have actual authority[81] but, even if not, he or she will have ostensible authority and his or her acts will bind the company.[82] Moreover, it is not uncommon for the board of directors to allow one of their number to assume the position of managing director even though never formally appointed to that position and in these circumstances the courts have treated that person as if he or she were the managing director.[83]

7–20   Much the same applies to other executive directors except that, if the descriptions of their posts suggest particular areas of responsi-

---

[77] Whether formally appointed to it or merely allowed by the company to assume it; that is a matter of "internal management".

[78] *ING Re (UK) Ltd v R&V Versicherung AG* [2007] 1 B.C.L.C. 108 at [104].

[79] *Armagas Ltd v Mundogas SA* [1986] A.C. 717, HL.

[80] Contrary to what was thought at one time, this is so even if the officer or agent has forged what purported to be a document signed or sealed on behalf of the company: *Uxbridge Building Society v Pickard* [1939] 2 K.B. 248, CA, explaining dicta in *Ruben v Great Fingall Consolidated* [1906] A.C. 439, HL; *Kreditbank Cassel v Schenkers* [1927] 1 K.B. 826, CA and *S London Greyhound Racecourses v Wake* [1931] 1 Ch. 496.

[81] *Hely-Hutchinson v Brayhead Ltd* [1968] 1 Q.B. 549, CA.

[82] *Freeman & Lockyer v Buckhurst Park Properties Ltd* [1964] 2 Q.B. 480, CA, especially the judgment of Diplock L.J. at 506.

[83] See, e.g. *Biggerstaff v Rowatt's Wharf Ltd* [1896] 2 Ch. 93, CA; *Clay Hill Brick Co v Rawlings* [1938] 4 All E.R. 100; *Freeman & Lockyer v Buckhurst Park Properties Ltd*, above.

bility ("finance director", "sales director" or the like), they cannot be assumed to have authority outside those areas. Even though individual non-executive directors have no managerial responsibility unless the board delegates it to them,[84] they may be assumed to have some individual authority, beyond that of sharing in the exercise of the board's collective authority at meetings of the board or its committees. It is usual, for example, for them to be authorised signatories of the company's cheques or attestors of the affixing of its seal.[85] And whilst section 45 removes the need for a company to have a common seal, section 44 provides that in favour of a purchaser[86] a document shall be deemed to be duly executed by a company if it purports to be signed by a director in the presence of a witness[87] or by two directors or by a director and secretary.

Some decisions have even suggested that a non-executive chairman of the board has, as such, individual authority equating with that of a managing director.[88] But why the right to take the chair should imply a right to manage out of the chair is difficult to understand and the proposition has been doubted.[89] This is not to deny that the chair of the board has important corporate governance responsibilities[90] but rather to question whether those responsibilities involve contracting on behalf of the company. Nor is it to deny that a company might appoint someone to a chairman post with executive responsibilities, though the corporate governance rules frown on the cumulation of the positions of chief executive and chair of the board.[91]

When the third party deals with an officer or employee below the level of director the position is more problematical and, until recently, the courts have shown a marked reluctance to recognise any ostensible authority even of a manager.[92] But this is now changing and it may be taken that a manager, even if he does not have actual

---

[84] *Rama Corp v Proved Tin & General Investments Ltd* [1952] 2 Q.B. 147.

[85] Articles normally provide that the seal shall be affixed only pursuant to the authority of the directors and attested by a director or other authorised person: model articles for public companies, art.81. But this seems clearly to be a matter of the company's internal management despite suggestions to the contrary in *S London Greyhound Racecourses Ltd v Wake* [1931] 1 Ch. 496: see *County of Gloucester Bank v Rudry Merthyr Colliery Co* [1895] 1 Ch. 629, CA.

[86] Defined as "a purchaser in good faith for valuable consideration [including] a lessee, mortgagee or other person who for valuable consideration acquires an interest in property": s.44(5). There is no presumption in favour of the purchaser that the purchaser has acted in good faith.

[87] s.44(5),(2)—it may also be signed by two authorised signatories.

[88] *B.T.H. v Federated European Bank* [1932] 2 K.B. 176, CA; *Clay Hill Brick Co v Rawlings*, above.

[89] In *Hely-Hutchinson v Brayhead* [1968] 1 Q.B. 549, CA, per Roskill J. at first instance at 560D, and per Lord Wilberforce at 586G.

[90] See para.14–33.

[91] Ibid.

[92] *Houghton & Co v Nothard, Lowe & Wills* [1927] 1 K.B. 246, CA, affirmed on other grounds [1928] A.C. 1, HL; *Kreditbank Cassel v Schenkers* [1927] 1 K.B. 826, CA; *S London Greyhound Racecourses v Wake* [1931] 1 Ch. 496; see also the observations of Willmer L.J. in *Freeman & Lockyer v Buckhurst Park Properties Ltd* [1964] 2 Q.B. at 494.

authority, will generally have ostensible authority to undertake everyday transactions relating to the branch of business which he is managing (though probably not if they are really major transactions)[93] and that the secretary will similarly have such authority in relation to administrative matters.[94] Indeed, almost every employee of a trading company must surely have apparent authority to bind the company in some transactions, though the extent of that may be very limited. For example, the men or women behind the counter in a departmental store clearly have ostensible authority to sell the goods on display for cash and at the marked prices. Whether their apparent authority extends beyond that (for example, to accept a cheque not supported by a cheque-card or to take goods back if the customer returns them) we shall probably never know, for it is unlikely to be litigated—at any rate against the customer.

It is normally the case that what the third party seeks to show is that the alleged agent had ostensible authority to contract on behalf of the company. However, it is clear that in some cases the showing of a lesser degree of ostensible authority will be enough to secure the third party's position. Thus, in *First Energy (UK) Ltd v Hungarian International Bank Ltd*[95] a senior manager was held to have ostensible authority to communicate to a third party head office approval of a loan application, even though he did not have authority to contract on the bank's behalf, as the third party knew. Once the third party had accepted the offer, it could sue the bank on the resulting contract. Again, it has been held that a company can be bound as a result of a representation, made by an agent with ostensible authority to make it, to the effect that another agent of the company was authorised to contract with the third party on behalf of the company. When the third party purported to contract with the company through the second agent, the company was bound, even though neither first nor second agent had actual or ostensible authority to enter into the contract in question.[96]

Ratification

7–21 We have already noted that the legal effect of a lack of authority on the agent's part is that the transaction is not binding on the company

---

[93] See *Armagas Ltd v Mundogas SA* [1986] A.C. 717, HL. There an employee who bore the title of "Vice-president (Transportation) and Chartering Manager" was held not to have authority to bind his company to charter back a vessel which it was selling. But there were complicating factors in that case for the employee was colluding with an agent of the other party in a dishonest arrangement and did not purport to have any general authority to bind the company but merely alleged that he had obtained actual authority for that particular transaction.

[94] *Panorama Developments Ltd v Fidelis Furnishing Fabrics Ltd* [1971] 2 Q.B. 711, CA. How far, if at all, the secretary's ostensible authority extends to the commercial side of the company's affairs is still unclear; see, per Salmon L.J. at 718.

[95] [1993] B.C.L.C. 1409, CA.

[96] *ING Re (UK) Ltd v R&V Versicherung AG* [2007] 1 B.C.L.C. 108.

unless it is ratified by the company. The company thus has an option to take up the transaction or to treat it as not binding on it. Determining who has the power to ratify the transaction is a matter for the company's constitution. There is no requirement in the Act, as there is for breaches of directors' duties, that ratification must be by the shareholders.[97] Normally, it is a matter of finding who, under the company's constitution, does have actual authority to enter into the transaction and securing their approval of it. However, it is not necessary that ratification should take the form of an express decision to approve the transaction. Ratification can be implied from conduct[98] and the conduct may amount to ratification if the company has knowledge of the essentials of what the agent has done, even if it did not know that the agent had acted without authority.[99] If there is ratification, it has retrospective effect, i.e. it renders the transaction with the company binding on it as from the time it was entered into by the agent. It is sometimes difficult to distinguish a subsequent ratification (which is a unilateral act of the company) from the entering into by the company and the third party of a new transaction which replaces the one entered into by the agent without authority.[100] There is also a time limit on the ratification process in the sense that ratification will not be permitted if it would unfairly prejudice a third party.[101]

The company's seal

We have assumed above that the company has entered into the contract in question through an agent. The Act provides as an alternative that a contract may be made by a company, in England and Wales or Northern Ireland, "by writing under its common seal".[102] In early times the use of a seal seems to have been seen as a piece of formalism designed to answer the question of how a company acts. However, the use of a seal does not achieve this purpose, because it simply raises the question of whether the person who attached the seal to the document had authority from the company to do so. Today, it is no longer obligatory for a company to have a common seal.[103] If it does have one, however, it may execute a document by affixing its common seal to it.[104] As indicated above,

7–22

---

[97] See para.16–83.
[98] *Mawcon Ltd, Re* [1969] 1 W.L.R. 78.
[99] *ING Re (UK) Ltd v R&V Versicherung AG* [2007] 1 B.C.L.C. 108.
[100] This was the point upon which the "ratification" failed in *Smith v Henniker-Major* (above, fn.41).
[101] See the discussion *ibid*.
[102] s.43(1).
[103] s.45(1)—though that section requires that, if it does have one, the company's name must be engraved on it in legible characters, failure to meet this requirement being a criminal offence on the part of both the company and every officer in default, as is the use of the seal without the name an offence on the part of the user or person who authorises its use.
[104] s.44(1).

execution may be also effected simply by signatures from the appropriate persons,[105] and in favour of a purchaser in good faith for valuable consideration a document which purports to be signed as the Act requires is deemed to have been duly executed by the company[106]—another piece of protection for third parties.

Tort and Crime

7–23 In the previous part of this chapter we have discussed the security of third parties transactions with the company, that is, the extent to which a company is contractually bound by a transaction entered into by or on behalf of the company by some one or more natural persons. However, the separate legal personality of the company gives rise to questions, not just about how it acquires contractual liability and entitlements, but also about how it becomes liable in tort or criminally. As we shall see below, the law handles the tortious and criminal liability of companies in rather different ways. In the case of tortious liability the general doctrine of vicarious liability for the acts of employees or agents provides a ready basis for holding the company liable. However, vicarious liability plays a much more restricted role in criminal law, and the development of bases upon which to hold companies criminally liable, at least in respect of crimes requiring *mens rea*, has proved a complex task.

There is an additional important question in relation to tort and crime, which does not normally arise in relation to the contractual liability of the company. This is the question of the liability of those who act on the company's behalf. In contract, the normal operation of the rules of agency produces the result that an agent acting within the scope of his or her authority brings about contractual relations only between the third party and the company. The agent is neither entitled nor liable on the contract, to which he is not a party.[107] Since, however, torts or crimes are wrongful acts, it would be odd if the agent escaped liability on the grounds that he or she was acting on behalf of a principal. Normally, therefore, both agent and principal will be liable in tort and crime. Indeed, if the basis of the principal's liability is vicarious, it is inherent in the theory that this should be the

---

[105] See above, para.7–20.

[106] s.44(5).

[107] Within company law, the major exception to this statement occurs when the contract purports to be made on behalf of an unformed company. See above at paras 5–08ff. As far as general agency law is concerned, it is always open to an agent to contract on the basis that he is personally liable or entitled, as well as the principal, and there is a limited range of cases where agency law treats the agent as liable, of which the most significant is where the agent has not disclosed to the third party that he or she is acting on behalf of a principal.

case. The principal is liable for the wrong of the agent and so, if the agent has committed no wrong, the principal cannot be liable. Where, however, the basis of the principal's liability is not vicarious liability, as it sometimes is not in tort and often is not in crime, the question will arise whether the agent is liable as well as the company.

Tortious liability
General approach

Although, historically, the doctrine of ultra vires strictly limited the **7–24** contractual liability of a company,[108] neither it nor the fact that the act was an unlawful one for the company to commit has operated to relieve the company of vicarious liability arising out of tortious acts.[109] This is not surprising. Under the ultra vires theory of the common law, those contracting with the company could protect themselves by reading the objects clause. Those who suffer from tortious or criminal acts of a company's agent may be in no position to take this step, for example, where a pedestrian is knocked down by a van recklessly driven by an employee engaged in the company's ultra vires business. In the case of illegal acts, it would seem perverse to give the company an advantage (i.e. escape from the doctrine of vicarious liability) which it would not have, had it conducted its business in a lawful way.

Nevertheless, there must be some connection between the company and the tortfeasor if the company is to be held liable as well. This link is what the doctrine of vicarious liability provides. Over the years, the nature of the link has been broadened by the courts. From an early date, the courts were unwilling to confine the scope of the company's (or any principal's) vicarious liability to those actions actually authorised by the company. Thus, it has been clear for some time that a company or other employer does not escape vicarious liability simply because the agent has done an act which the agent or employee has been prohibited from doing or even because the agent has done a deliberate act for his own benefit which has prejudiced the employer.[110] This led to the famous (but unclear) dichotomy between doing an unauthorised act (no vicarious liability) and doing an authorised act in an unauthorised way (vicarious liability). In its most recent decisions on the doctrine,[111] the House of Lords has moved beyond that distinction and imposed vicarious liability when there was a sufficiently close connection between the wrongful acts of the

---

[108] Above, para.7–2.
[109] *Campbell v Paddington Corp* [1911] 1 K.B. 869.
[110] *Lloyd v Grace, Smith & Co* [1912] A.C. 716, HL (fraud on client by solicitors' clerk); *Morris v C W Martin & Sons Ltd* [1966] 1 Q.B. 716, CA (theft by employee of customer's coat).
[111] *Lister v Hesley Hall Ltd* [2001] 2 All E.R. 769, HL (sexual abuse of children in a care home by the staff employed to look after them); *Dubai Aluminium Company Ltd v Salaam* [2003] 1 B.C.L.C. 32, HL (firm vicariously liable for knowing assistance by a solicitor in a breach of trust). See *Deakin* (2003) 32 I.L.J. 97.

agents or employees and the activities which those persons were employed to undertake. The fact that the wrongful acts were clearly unauthorised and not for the employer's benefit would not prevent the imposition of liability, if this test was satisfied.

At a general level, the doctrines of a "sufficiently close connection" in tort and of ostensible authority in the law of agency perform a similar role, i.e. the protection of the legitimate interests of third parties coming into contact with businesses. However, they are not identical doctrines: ostensible authority turns on a holding out by the principal of the agent to the third party,[112] whereas vicarious liability does not depend upon what the third party understood to be the agent's connection with the company but upon an objective assessment of the relationship between the agent's actions and the company's activities. In other words, the focus is on the relationship between the employee or agent and the company in the case of vicarious liability, not on the relationship between the company and the third party. Furthermore, as we have already noted, there is the crucial difference between agency law and vicarious liability in tort that the former produces a contractual relationship which normally exists only between third party and company, whereas vicarious liability operates so as to make both agent and company liable in tort. Since the law of contract is designed to facilitate transactions and the law of tort to deter wrongdoing or provide compensation for it, the difference in approach is not in itself surprising.

Assumption of responsibility

7–25   However, difficult problems can arise when the law of tort and the law of contract come together to regulate the process of contracting. Suppose an agent acting for a company makes negligent statements during the contracting process. If the third party subsequently sues in contract, only the company will be liable; if the third party sues in tort, the maker of the statement might be thought to be primarily liable and the company liable only vicariously. The company will be liable on either theory, but the choice of claim will be important if the company is not available to be sued (for example, because it is insolvent). The issue is particularly important in small companies, for example, where the shareholder, director and main employee are the same person. If that person can be successfully sued in tort as an employee, he or she will lose the protection of limited liability which, as shareholder, would be available if the third party sued the company.

---

[112] See above, para.7–3.

After some uncertainty, the House of Lords[113] avoided that adverse result for the one-person company[114] by holding that a person who makes negligent misstatements whilst contracting on behalf of a company does not assume personal responsibility for the truth of the statements made, because responsibility is to be treated as assumed (in the usual case) only on behalf of the company. Thus, it is the company which has committed the tort (by making the false statement through the agent) rather than the agent; the company's liability is thus direct, not vicarious.[115] As the court made clear, this approach applies not only to negligent misstatements but also to cases of negligent delivery of services due under a contract, where again contractual and tortious duties coincide. However, two points should be noted about the scope of this decision. First, it is a statement only of the starting point for the courts' analysis. The presumption of no personal assumption of liability may be rebutted on the facts of the case. A director or other agent of the company may on the facts be treated as having assumed personal responsibility for the negligent misstatement or the negligent provision of services.[116] Moreover, the test for assumption of personal responsibility is not the subjective one of what the agent believed to be the case; rather the test is objective, something along the lines of whether it was reasonable for the third party to conclude that the director or other agent had accepted personal responsibility.[117] The principle of *Williams* may thus apply in different ways to different types of business.[118]

Secondly, the result in *Williams* was achieved, not by applying any special doctrine of company law, but by relying on the requirement for an assumption of responsibility as a necessary ingredient of liability under the tort of negligence in the relevant contexts. It follows that a director or other agent would not escape liability where

---

[113] *Williams v Natural Life Health Foods* [1998] 1 W.L.R. 830, HL.

[114] The decision applies, of course, to all sizes of company, but it is suggested that the one-person company was the difficult case. With large companies, it will be even more difficult to find that the agent assumes personal responsibility.

[115] The decision is not explicit on whether the company was liable in the tort of negligent misstatement, but it is submitted that it is inherent in the view that responsibility was accepted on behalf of the company that this was the case.

[116] Thus, *Fairline Shipping Corp v Adamson* [1975] Q.B. 180 is now to be seen as a case where the director did personally assume responsibility for the performance of the services which the company had contracted to provide, despite the rather thin evidence of such an assumption. See also para.28–56 for the application of this principle to statements made by target boards in takeover bids.

[117] *Williams*, above at fn.113.

[118] Thus, the courts have been reluctant to exempt from personal responsibility agents who are professionally qualified. See *Merrett v Babb* [2001] Q.B. 1174, CA (surveyor employed by a partnership); *Phelps v Hillingdon LBC* [2001] 2 A.C. 619, HL (educational psychologist employed by LEA), though neither case involved any threat to the separate personality of a company or to the principle of limited liability. These cases, especially the first, may contribute to the debate whether the *Williams* principle will be applied by the courts to LLPs (see para.1–2). It is submitted that it will but perhaps not with the same benefits for agents of LLPs running professional businesses as it provides for non-professional businesses.

assumption of responsibility is not a necessary ingredient for tortious liability, for example, deceit.[119] Thus, as far as tortious liability is concerned, the personal liability of directors of companies is crucially dependent upon the common law of tort rather than upon any provisions in the Companies Act or even the common law of companies. Since, however, vicarious liability is discussed at length in the tort books, it is not proposed to consider it further here, except for one matter. This concerns the application of vicarious liability and associated principles to fraudulent conduct.

Fraud

7–26   At one stage, it seems to have been thought that a company could not be held vicariously liable for fraudulent conduct on the part of an employee or agent, at least where the fraud was directed at benefiting the agent rather than the company.[120] However, the clear view today is that such cases are to be explained on the basis that the agent or employee was acting outside the scope of their authority when carrying out the fraud and that, had this not been the case, the company or principal would have been liable for the fraud.[121] As far as liability towards third parties is concerned, the tort of deceit and other torts based on fraudulent conduct are thus to be treated in the same way as other torts. There is no special exclusionary rule for such conduct. It is still necessary, of course, to show that the individual was acting in the course of his or her employment when committing the fraud, but the introduction of the "sufficiently close connection" test for establishing this relationship has also made this task easier for the claimant. Indeed, the denial of a special exclusionary rule for fraud and the introduction of the "sufficiently close connection" test for determining the scope of employment both point in the same direction: the company or other employer carries (and thus has an incentive to control) the risks to third parties generated by its business activities, even if some of the risks in question harm the company as well.

Whilst the principle just articulated provides a basis for extending the company's liability to third parties, it is hardly applicable should the company sue the fraudulent agent or employee to recover for the harm done to the company, on the grounds that it was a victim of the

---

[119] *Standard Chartered Bank v Pakistan National Shipping Corp (No.2)*, [2003] 1 A.C. 959, HL.
[120] See in particular *Ruben v Great Fingall Consolidated* [1906] A.C. 439, HL.
[121] *Uxbridge Permanent Benefit Building Society v Pickard* [1939] 2 K.B. 248, CA; *Armagas Ltd v Mundogas SA* [1986] 1 A.C. 717, HL; *Credit Lyonnais Bank Nederland NV v Export Credit Guarantee Department* [2000] 1 A.C. 486, HL; and see the cases cited in fn.110 above.

fraud committed by the former, just as much as the third party was.[122] A potential obstacle to such a claim is the common law doctrine that knowledge of an agent is attributed to the principal, which, if applied to the fraudulent agent, would defeat the company's claim against its agent. Sensibly, however, the courts have generally refused to apply the attribution of knowledge rule to the fraudulent agent.[123] Although this is sometimes said to be inconsistent with the rule that a company is liable to third parties for the fraud of the agent, it is submitted that this is not so, either doctrinally or in principle. It is entirely proper to use different rules to govern the liability of the company to the third party, on the one hand, and of the agent or employee to the company, on the other. There is no reason why rules developed to protect third parties against losses caused by fraudulent agents should also operate to protect those same fraudulent agents against the company. Nor is there anything in the doctrine of vicarious liability which compels such a consequence. The problem arises, in fact, from the separate common law rule which attributes knowledge of an agent in particular circumstances to the principal. As we have seen, vicarious liability does not operate by means of attributing knowledge (or acts) of agents to principals but by attributing a liability.

There is yet a third relationship in which the fraud of an agent or employee may be relevant. Suppose the company sues a third party (for example, its auditors), in either tort or contract, and the third party responds by pleading the contributory fault of the company as a partial defence to the company's claim. Can the third party rely on the fraud of the company's agents or employees (who committed the wrongs the auditors failed to discover) as constituting the fault of the company, so as to produce an apportionment of the loss suffered by the company between the company and the third party under the provisions of the Law Reform (Contributory Negligence) Act 1945? Here, the third party is now tortfeasor, rather than victim, but the company is attempting to prevent the third party from relying on the fraud of the company's agents so as to reduce the third party's liability. In principle, there seems no reason why the third party should not rely on the fraud of the company's employees, and where that fraud amounts to the tort of deceit on the third party, the third party will have a complete defence against the company's claim.[124]

---

[122] Since, in all cases of vicarious liability, agent and company are joint tortfeasors (*New Zealand Guardian Trust Co Ltd v Brooks* [1995] 1 W.L.R. 96, PC), the company could alternatively claim a contribution from the agent towards the damages payable to the third party and, since the company is a wholly innocent party (subject to the doctrine of imputed knowledge discussed below), that contribution will usually be a complete one, i.e. an indemnity (Civil Liability (Contribution) Act 1978, s.1; *Lister v Romford Ice and Cold Storage Co* [1965] A.C. 555, HL).

[123] *Hampshire Land Co, Re* [1896] 2 Ch. 743; *Belmont Finance Corporation Ltd v Williams Furniture Ltd* [1979] Ch. 250, CA.

[124] *Barings Plc v Coopers & Lybrand* [2002] 2 B.C.L.C. 410, Ch. D. and see para.22–39.

Authorisation of tortious acts

7–27 So far, we have discussed the respective liabilities in tort of the company's agents (who may be its directors or who may be, and often are, more junior members of the organisation) and the company, on the assumption that the agent is a tortfeasor. However, the question has been raised in a number of cases of whether a director of a company, who is not the tortfeasor, can be liable in tort to a third party simply by virtue of his directorship of the company. Many of the cases concern tortious acts consisting of infringements by the company's agents of another person's intellectual property rights, such as patents or copyright. It seems clear that the answer is in the negative, even if the tortfeasors are other directors of the company. As long ago as 1878, Fry J. said in a case of fraudulent mis-representation[125] that two classes of person could be responsible for the fraud (the agents who actually made the fraudulent mis-representations and the principal on the basis of vicarious liability) but that "one agent is not responsible for the acts of another agent". This principle has been confirmed in a number of subsequent cases.[126] However, the cases also recognise that there would be liability on the part of the director if the director, whilst not committing the tort him- or herself, authorised or procured the commission of the tortious act in question, whether that act was deceit or some other tort. Moreover, it is not necessary that that the director authorising or procuring the tortious acts should realise their tortious nature or display any other particular mental element in relation to the acts, unless this is a requirement of the tort being so authorised or procured.[127] This rule obviously creates some risks of personal liability for directors who, in the course of running the company's business, authorise action which turns out to be tortious. However, the rule imposes on directors who authorise or procure the tortious act no more stringent rule than that which applies outside the corporate context, for the rule that those who authorise or instigate tortious acts are joint tortfeasors with those who commit the tort is a general principle of tort law.[128] In

---

[125] *Cargill v Bower* (1878) 10 Ch. D. 502 at 513–514.

[126] *Rainham Chemical Works Ltd v Belvedere Fish Guano Company Ltd* [1921] 2 A.C. 465, HL; *Performing Right Society Ltd v Ciryl Theatrical Syndicate Ltd* [1924] 1 K.B. 1, CA; *British Thomson-Houston Company Ltd v Stirling Accessories Ltd* [1924] 2 Ch. 33.

[127] *C Evans & Sons Ltd v Spritebrand Ltd* [1985] 1 W.L.R. 317, CA; *Mancetter Developments Ltd v Garmanson Ltd* [1986] Q.B. 1212, CA; *MCA Records Inc v Charly Records Ltd* [2003] 1 B.C.L.C. 93, CA; *cf. White Horse Distilleries Ltd v Gregson Associates Ltd* [1984] R.P.C. 61.

[128] Nevertheless, the attempt by Nourse J. in the *White Horse* case (see previous note) to restrict the director's personal liability to those situations where he acted "deliberately or recklessly and so as to make [the tortious conduct] his own, as distinct from the act or conduct of the company" seems to have been motivated by a desire to preserve the benefits of limited liability, especially in a one-person company. In other words, Nourse J. proposed a general "assumption of responsibility" test (for all torts) in the case of tortious conduct authorised by the directors. *Cf. MCA Records* (see previous note) where the court drew a distinction between control exercised through the constitutional organs of the company (e.g. voting at board meetings—not attracting tortious liability) and control exercised otherwise (potentially attracting tortious liability).

effect, the rule provides an incentive for directors to acquaint themselves with, and to secure observance by the company's agents of, the tort rules which impinge upon the company's business.

Criminal liability

As we have just seen, vicarious liability provides the bedrock upon which companies are held liable in tort, though it is not the only basis upon which tortious liability is attributed. In criminal law, by contrast, vicarious liability is shunned by the common law. Consequently criminal law has had to work out a different set of starting points for the imposition of liability on companies. Two main sources have emerged. First, the courts have treated some regulatory statutory offences as imposing liability directly on the company, albeit that the acts which put the company in breach of its duty are the acts of its employees or agents. Secondly, the common law has developed a basis for attributing liability to companies (the "identification" doctrine) which is narrower than vicarious liability but which nevertheless goes beyond providing that the company be liable only for criminal acts authorised or endorsed by the board of directors or the shareholders in general meeting. We shall look at each in turn and then at proposals for reform.

7–28

Of course, Parliament may override the presumption against vicarious criminal liability and it is therefore a matter of construction of the statutory offence in question whether Parliament intended to do so. In the case of regulatory offences based on strict liability, it will be relatively easy to convince the court that this is indeed what Parliament intended. Doctrinally, this result is achieved by viewing the statute as imposing a non-delegable duty on the company (rather than by treating the company as vicariously liable for the agent's crime), but, as far as the company is concerned, the result is similar. In an important decision the Court of Appeal was prepared to go further and apply this approach in the case of a hybrid offence, where the strict liability was qualified by a "reasonably practical" defence.[129] In this case, it was not a defence for the company that the senior management had taken all reasonable care to avoid a breach of the statutory duty; it was necessary that those actually in charge of the dangerous operation should have done so. Where liability is imposed, then on usual principles the fact that the employees were acting

---

[129] *R. v British Steel Plc* [1995] I.C.R. 586, CA. This case only opens up the potential for imposing liability for hybrid offences. Whether a particular statute does so is again a matter of construction. See the Court of Appeal's distinguishing of the decision in *Tesco Supermarkets Ltd v Nattrass* [1972] A.C. 153 as concerning a differently worded statute in a different area of regulation (consumer protection as against health and safety at work). See also *Seaboard Offshore Ltd v Secretary of State for Transport* [1994] 1 W.L.R. 541, HL (not imposing liability) and *Tesco Stores Ltd v Brent LBC* [1993] 2 All E.R. 718, CA, imposing it.

contrary to their instructions does not necessarily provide the company with a defence.[130]

Identification

7–29   However, if the crime clearly does require *mens rea* on the part of the company, the courts will not attribute the necessary guilty state of mind to the company by using the doctrines of vicarious liability or non-delegable duty.[131] Similar issues may arise under statutes dealing with civil law matters, a fruitful source of litigation having been attempts to limit liability under the merchant shipping legislation where this was possible only if the damage was caused without "actual fault or privity"[132] on the part of the person seeking to limit liability. If vicarious liability is not to be used, what rules of attribution are available? It is always possible to look at what was known to the company's "organs", especially its board of directors. Rules of attribution derived from the company's own constitution have been referred to, indeed, as the "primary" rules of attribution.[133] However, if the company's knowledge were to be confined to what the board or the shareholders collectively knew, then the operation of many rules of law, not least in the criminal sphere, would be unacceptably narrow in their relation to companies.

In consequence, from the beginning of the twentieth century onwards the courts began to develop rules of attribution which in appropriate cases "identify"[134] the acts and knowledge of those in control of the company as those of the company. Developed first in the area of civil law,[135] in the period immediately after the Second World War the same idea was applied in the criminal law.[136] The effect of this development was to create a set of rules of attribution which operated more broadly than the primary rules but more narrowly than rules based upon the general notions of agency and vicarious liability. The crucial question is, precisely where in the gap between the primary and the general rules are the rules of identifi-

---

[130] *Supply of Ready Mixed Concrete (No.2), Re* [1995] 1 A.C. 456, HL.
[131] Though this approach has been adopted in many United States jurisdictions, provided the crime in question is of a type for which companies may be held liable. See Law Commission, *Legislating the Criminal Code: Involuntary Manslaughter*, Law Com. No. 237, H.C. 171, 1996, para.7.28.
[132] These were the words used in the Merchant Shipping Act 1894. See *Lennard's Carrying Co Ltd v Asiatic Petroleum Co Ltd* [1915] A.C. 705, HL; *The Truculent* [1952] P. 1; *The Lady Gwendolen* [1965] P. 294, CA.
[133] *Meridian Global Funds Management Asia Ltd v Securities Commission* [1995] 2 A.C. 500 at 506, PC.
[134] Law Commission, *op. cit.*, para.6.2.
[135] See *Lennard's Carrying Co Ltd v Asiatic Petroleum Co Ltd*, above, fn.132.
[136] *DPP v Kent & Sussex Contractors Ltd* [1944] K.B.146; *R. v ICR Haulage Ltd* [1944] K.B. 551, CCA; *Moore v Bresler* [1944] 2 All E.R. 515. The application of the principle in the criminal law was approved by the House of Lords in *Tesco Supermarkets Ltd v Nattrass* [1972] A.C. 153.

cation intended to operate or, in other words, what is the theory behind the idea of identification?

It is possible to find in the cases varying formulations of the underlying principle, and the most recent definitions suggest that the courts are prepared today to give the rule of attribution based on identification a somewhat broader scope. In the original formulation in the *Lennard's Carrying Company* case[137] Lord Haldane based identification on a person "who is really the directing mind and will of the corporation, the very ego and centre of the personality of the corporation".[138] This was a narrow approach to the notion of identification. Recently, however, such an approach has been castigated by the Privy Council through Lord Hoffmann in the *Meridian Global* case[139] as a misleading "general metaphysic of companies". The true question in each case was who, as a matter of construction of the statute in question, or presumably other rule of law,[140] is to be regarded as the controller of the company for the purpose of the identification rule. In appropriate cases, that might be a person who was less elevated in the corporate structure than those Lord Haldane had in mind. In *Meridian* itself, where the question was whether the company was in breach of the New Zealand laws requiring disclosure of substantial shareholdings knowingly held by an investor,[141] the controllers were held to be two senior investment managers who were not even members of the company's board. Given the purpose of the statute—speedy disclosure of shareholdings—it was appropriate to treat those in charge of dealing in the markets on behalf of the company as its "controllers" in this respect.

Welcome and more straightforward though the new approach is, it inevitably leaves uncertainty as to who will be regarded as the relevant person within the corporate hierarchy for the purposes of the identification rule in any particular case. That it should not be any agent or employee of the company acting within the scope of his or her authority is clear, for, as we have seen, there is need to resort to the identification rule of attribution only where the general rules of attribution based on agency and vicarious liability are inappropriate in the particular context. Since, however, a precise answer to the question of whose acts and knowledge are to be attributed to the company depends *ex hypothesi* on an analysis of the context of the

7–30

---

[137] See above, fn.135.

[138] *Lennard's Carrying Co Ltd v Asiatic Petroleum Co Ltd*, above, fn.135, at 713. See also *Bolton (Engineering) Co Ltd v Graham & Sons* [1957] 1 Q.B. 159 at 172, per Lord Denning, CA. Lord Haldane's dictum was probably influenced by the clear distinction drawn between agents and organs in German company law, Haldane having studied in his youth in Germany.

[139] See above, fn.133, at 509. The case is noted by Sealy [1995] C.L.J. 507, Wells (1995) 14 I.B.F.L. 42 and Yeung [1977] C.F.I.L.R. 67.

[140] See *El Ajou v Dollar Land Holdings Plc* [1994] 2 All E.R. 685, CA, where the Court of Appeal, including Hoffmann L.J., as he then was, applied a similar approach to the question of whether a company was in equity in knowing receipt of trust property.

[141] For the equivalent British rules see Ch.26, below.

particular rule with which the court is dealing, it is doubtful whether more certainty can be provided at a general level.

The identification theory has been carried to the logical conclusion that a company and an individual, who is its directing will, cannot be successfully indicted for conspiracy since this requires the meeting of two or more minds.[142] But it has not been carried to absurd extremes. If those who constitute the controllers are engaged in defrauding the company they cannot successfully defend a civil action by the company[143] or a criminal prosecution[144] by saying "we were the controlling organs of the company and accordingly the company knew all about it and consented". Were such a defence to prevail, it would wholly negate the duties which the controllers owe to the company. So far as concerns the internal relationship between the company and its officers, dishonest acts directed against the company by its organs are not attributed to the company.

Manslaughter and corporate killing

7–31   However, the Court of Appeal refused either to apply the "personal duty" notion or to extend the more generous *Meridian* approach to identification to the common law crime of manslaughter by gross negligence. Accordingly, for this important common law crime a company could be convicted only if an identifiable human being could be shown to have committed that crime and that individual met the strict common law test for the identification of that person with the company (i.e. the "directing mind and will" test).[145] Consequently, it was difficult to secure the conviction of anything other than small companies where serious fatalities occurred in the course of the company's business, because the gross negligence required could rarely be located sufficiently high up in the corporate hierarchy. As long ago as 1996, the Law Commission proposed a solution to this difficulty in its recommendation that a company should be criminally liable if management failure was a cause of a person's death, without the need to show that any human being was guilty of manslaughter or, indeed, any other crime.[146] The focus would be on the quality of the operating systems deployed by the company rather than the guilt of individuals.

After a remarkably tortuous legislative passage, extending over a number of years, the Corporate Manslaughter and Corporate Homicide Act 2007[147] eventually reached the statute book. It creates

---

[142] *R. v McDonnell* [1966] 1 Q.B. 233.

[143] *Belmont Finance Corp v Williams Furniture Ltd* [1979] Ch. 250.

[144] *Attorney-General's Reference (No.2 of 1982)* [1984] Q.B. 624, CA; *R. v Phillipou* (1989) 89 Cr.App.R. 290, CA; *R. v Rozeik* [1996] B.C.C. 271, CA.

[145] *Attorney-General's Reference (No.2 of 1999), Re* [2000] Q.B. 796, CA.

[146] See above, fn.131.

[147] The offence is corporate manslaughter in England, Wales and Northern Ireland; corporate homicide in Scotland.

an offence for companies[148] to cause a person's death as a result of the way its activities are organised or managed where that organisation or management amounts to a gross breach of a duty owed by the company to the deceased. The new statutory offence replaces the common law as far as companies are concerned.[149] The requirement for a gross breach of duty owed to the deceased[150] reflects the common law of manslaughter by gross negligence. From the point of view of the above discussion the crucial point is that no individual has to be identified whose acts constitute the offence of corporate manslaughter and who can then be identified with the company. The company can be convicted on its organisational failings alone, irrespective of the guilt of any individual person. However, the notion that the company should be found guilty only for failings at a senior level is retained in the provision that corporate guilt arises "only if the way in which its activities are managed or organised by its senior management is a substantial element in the breach ..."[151] If the failings are wholly at subordinate level, the company will not be guilty. However, significant failings at lower levels are bound to raise the question of whether the senior levels of management should have picked up these lower level failings.

The offence is triable on indictment but only, in England, Wales and Northern Ireland, with the consent of the DPP, and the company, if convicted, is liable to a unlimited fine.[152] The financial penalty thus falls on the shareholders rather than on the senior management whose failings led to the criminal offence. Whether the penalty will have a deterrent effect on management will depend in part on the nature of the shareholder/management relations in the company. A greater deterrent impact may result from the reputational harm the management will likely suffer if the company is found guilty of corporate manslaughter whilst they were in charge of it. In this respect, the court's power to order the company to give publicity to the fact of its conviction may be helpful.[153] At one stage it had been mooted that convictions would be required to be reported in the company's Operating and Financial Review.[154] Although neither the 2007 Act nor the provisions governing the Business Review (which replaced the OFR) in terms require this, such publication could be required as part of a court's publicity order.

---

[148] And for other bodies, which need not concern us here, though the question of how far public sector bodies should be the brought within the scope of the Act was one of the most contentious in Parliament.

[149] s.20.

[150] The existence of the duty is a question of law for the judge (s.2(5)); whether the breach of the duty is "gross" a question for the jury (s.8). The duty in question must be a duty under the law of negligence falling into one of the categories listed in s.2, though these categories are widely defined.

[151] s.1(3).

[152] ss.1(6) and 17.

[153] s.10. Non-compliance with a publicity order is itself a criminal offence.

[154] See below, para.21–23.

7–32   The court has a further power—which may operate more directly on the management of the company—to order a convicted company to take steps, not only to remedy the breach and any matter resulting from it which were a cause of the death, but also "any deficiency, as regards health and safety matters, in the organisation's policies, systems or practices of which the relevant breach appears to the court to be an indication." The application for the order may be made only by the prosecution, which must consult the relevant enforcement authority (for example, the Health and Safety Executive) about what should be asked for. The order will set a time limit for the specified steps to be taken and may require the company to provide evidence to the relevant enforcement authority that those steps have been taken.[155] However, the enforcement authority is given no greater monitoring role in relation to the management of the company than this, though it may think it appropriate to use its general inspection powers more vigorously in relation to a company which has been convicted of corporate manslaughter than one which has not.

However, the fact that formally the above sanctions fall on the company led to extensive debate during the passage of the Act about whether it should impose penalties—whether by way of criminal sanctions or by way of disqualification—on those members of the senior management of the company who were to blame for the organisational failings. In this debate, the wheel thus came full circle: under the directing mind and will doctrine the crimes of individual managers made the company liable; now the question was how far corporate crime should make individual managers liable. The Government resisted strongly any moves in this direction, even to the extent of excluding the normal accessory offences of aiding, abetting, counselling or procuring the offence of corporate manslaughter, at least as far as individuals are concerned.[156] However, individuals remain liable for the common law offence of manslaughter by gross negligence and for various offences under regulatory legislation, such as that under section 37 of the Health and Safety at Work Act 1974. This applies where a body corporate commits a criminal office under certain of the sections of that Act "with the consent or connivance of, or [where the corporate offence was] attributable to any neglect on the part of, any director, manager, secretary or other similar officer of the body corporate ..."[157] Disqualification of directors is also avail-

---

[155] s.9.

[156] s.18.

[157] See *R. v P* [2007] EWCA Crim 1937—the commission by the company of the regulatory offence will not suffer from the problems arising out of the identification doctrine (see above, para.7–28) and the 2007 Act preserves the possibility of the company being convicted under both that Act and the 1974 Act: s.19.

able upon their conviction of an indictable offence in connection with the management of the company or, conceivably, even without conviction, on grounds of unfitness.[158]

CONCLUSION

As we observed at the beginning of this chapter, since the company is a separate but artificial legal person, it can act only through natural legal persons. Thus, the central issue becomes the determination of which people in which circumstances can be regarded as having acted as the company. We have explored that question in relation to corporate liability in contract, tort and crime, and also the question of whether those acting on behalf of the company become personally liable or entitled as a result of their actions. Although these questions are central to a core feature of company law, that of separate legal personality, in fact the answers to them are to be found, predominantly, not in special doctrines of company law, but in the general rules of the law of contract (and agency), tort and crime respectively. The nearest to special rules of company law that we have come across are the ultra vires, constructive notice and directing mind and will doctrines. **7–33**

Since, however, this is a book on company law, rather than a book on contract, tort or crime, we have focussed on those areas where the general doctrines intersect with the rules of company law. In relation to the law of contract, the agency rules have long been skewed in their application to companies by the doctrines of ultra vires and constructive notice. As a result of the reforms of 1989, somewhat expanded in the 2006 Act, however, these distortions have largely been removed. Turning to the tort liability of the company, none of the doctrines which have caused problems in relation to the application of the rules of agency to companies have had a significant impact upon the rules of vicarious liability which are the bedrock of the law in the tort area. Rather, the main area of debate has been whether the liability of the individual acting on behalf of the company (on which the doctrine of vicarious liability depends) operates to undermine another central feature of company law, that of limited liability. So far, the requirement of an assumption of responsibility in the law of negligence has operated so as to avoid serious clashes between this corporate principle and rules on tort liability, though the requirement of an assumption of responsibility has not been applied

---

[158] See Ch.10. Though such provisions are rarely used: Health and Safety Executive, *A survey of the use and effectiveness of the Company Directors Disqualification Act 1986 as a legal sanction against directors convicted of health and safety offences* (by Alan Neal and Frank Wright, 2007).

generally to the tort liability of directors, for example, not in the area of liability arising out of the authorisation or procurement by directors of the commission of torts by others.

Only in the criminal area, and only then in respect of crimes requiring *mens rea*, has a fully satisfactory theory of attribution of liability to the company not been worked out. The identification theory has been made more supple as a result of the *Meridian* decision,[159] but the courts seem wedded to the view that this decision depends upon statutory construction and so has no application to serious common law crimes. However, the most obvious area of criminal liability where the identification doctrine caused difficulties has now been addressed in the 2007 Act on corporate manslaughter.

---

[159] See above, fn.133.

CHAPTER 8

LIMITED LIABILITY AND LIFTING THE VEIL AT COMMON LAW

THE RATIONALE FOR LIMITED LIABILITY

The company laws of all economically advanced countries make **8–1** available corporate vehicles through which businesses can be carried on with the benefit of limited liability for their members. For shareholders this means that their liability for the company's debts is limited to the amount they have paid or have agreed to pay to the company for its shares. For most shareholders this means that, once the shares have been paid for, whether they were acquired directly from the company or from an existing shareholder, the worst fate that can befall them if the company becomes insolvent is that they lose the entire value of their investment.[1] However, their other assets—their homes, pension funds, domestic goods—will be unaffected by the collapse of the company in which they have invested. To put the matter from the creditors' perspective, their claims are limited to the assets of the company and cannot be asserted against the shareholders' assets. This can be regarded as a strong rule because, if the opposite economic development occurs and the company is highly successful, the shareholders are likely to receive all the residual

---

[1] IA 1986, s.74(2)(d). In the case of a company limited by guarantee the member's obligation will be limited to the amount of the guarantee (normally minimal): *ibid.*, s.74(3).

193

benefit of that success, once the creditors have been satisfied.[2] This, at least, is the rule which is applied in the admittedly unlikely event of such a successful company being wound up; whilst it is a going concern they will receive healthy dividends or capital appreciation of their shares. So, there is an apparent disparity in the risks and rewards which are allocated to shareholders: they benefit, through limited liability, from a cap of their down-side risk, whereas the chance of up-side gain is unlimited. Since, however, all modern company law systems permit trading on this basis, it might be wondered whether the rationale for limited liability is worth further analysis. It is suggested that some further analysis is worthwhile because the rationale so identified is likely to be helpful in determining the terms and conditions upon which limited liability is made available and, more importantly the protections which should be put in place to guard against the abuses of limited liability.

During the battle for legislative acceptance of the principle of limited liability in the middle of the nineteenth century,[3] the argument which seems to have weighed most heavily with the legislator was that limited liability would facilitate the investment by members of the public, who were not professional investors, of their surplus funds in the many large capital projects which companies were being set up to carry out at that time, in particular the construction of a national network of railways. Members of the public, whose primary activity and expertise did not lie with the running of companies, would be much less likely to be willing to buy shares in such companies, if the full range of their personal assets were to be put at risk. They might be prepared to become lenders of money to such companies,[4] but not necessarily to become shareholders, and it was the flexibility of investment of risk capital through shares which those companies sought.[5]

More recently, Halpern, Trebilcock and Turnbull[6] have pointed out that limited liability, in addition, facilitates the operation of public securities markets, because it relieves the investor of the need to be concerned about the personal wealth of fellow investors. Under a rule whereby the shareholders were jointly and severally liable for a company's debts, my shares would be more valuable to me if the

---

[2] IA 1986, s.107.

[3] For an account, see the sixth edition of this book at pp.40–46.

[4] Nobody has seriously argued that a lender of money to, or depositor of money with, an organisation, whether it be a company or a building society or a bank, should be liable beyond the amount of the loan or deposit, if the borrower becomes insolvent. This rule is less surprising than the shareholders' position, since the lender or depositor is normally entitled to a fixed return, by way of interest, and does not benefit from the economic success of the company beyond that fixed return. However, where a person is both a major shareholder in and lender to the company, the law may respond to the potential for abuse in such a situation (*cf. Salomon v Salomon*, discussed above at paras 2–1ff), by, in effect, treating the loan as if it were an equity investment. See below, para.9–9.

[5] The distinction between equity and debt is discussed further in Ch.31, below.

[6] "An Economic Analysis of Limited Liability" (1980) 30 *University of Toronto* L.J. 117.

wealth of my fellow investors increased (because I would be less likely to have to pay more than the proportion of the company's debts which my shares constituted of the company's total share capital), and vice versa if the wealth of my fellow shareholders decreased. So limited liability facilitates the trading of the company's shares at a uniform price on the public exchanges. This adverse effect of unlimited liability could be mitigated, of course, by making the shareholders liable only on a proportionate basis (i.e. liability on the part of each investor only for his or her "share" of the company's debts).[7]

Two things are apparent about these two rationales for limited **8–2** liability. The first is that they support limited liability for companies which have offered their shares to the public, but are hardly persuasive for companies which have not and do not plan to do so, i.e. for all private companies (which constitute the overwhelming number of companies on the register)[8] and even for some public companies. Yet, as we saw in Chapter 2, a great deal of effort was expended on the part of practitioners in the second half of the nineteenth century in securing the extension of limited liability to all companies, including the smallest, a goal achieved when the House of Lords handed down its decision in *Salomon v Salomon*,[9] and the legislature did not reverse that decision. That decision has remained controversial,[10] but so entrenched in our law is the principle of limited liability for all companies, large or small, that nobody seriously advocates the reversal of *Salomon*. Rather, there are two lines of contemporary debate. One is the argument that the flexibility of organisational rules, which those running small businesses seek, should be provided outside company law, through a new and optional organisational form with unlimited liability, whilst those who seek limited liability should have to accept the burdens of company law, which indeed might well be somewhat enhanced, especially in relation to minimum capital requirements.[11] The Company Law Review, anxious not to place barriers in the way of the organic growth of small companies, rejected the arguments for a separate form of incorporation,[12] and in fact, under the banner "Think Small First", proposed some further deregulation of company law as it applies to small companies.[13] However, as we saw in

---

[7] Though the current rule of insolvency law, if limited liability does not apply, is joint and several liability: IA 1986, s.74(1).

[8] See above, Ch.1.

[9] [1897] A.C. 22, above, para.2–1.

[10] In (1944) 7 M.L.R. 54, Otto Kahn-Freund described it as "calamitous".

[11] This case has been put in its most attractive form by A. Hicks, R. Drury and J. Smallcombe, *Alternative Company Structures for the Small Business*, ACCA Research Report 42 (1995). On minimum capital requirements see Ch.11, below.

[12] Strategic Framework, Ch.5.2.

[13] Final Report I, Ch.2.

Chapter 1,[14] the Government can be said to have provided a separate and highly flexible form of business organisation—but, crucially, with limited liability—through the limited liability partnership, introduced by the Act of 2000. Within company law proper the debate, therefore, moved on to a second area, which is the nature of the provisions which should be included within company law to counteract the potential abuse of limited liability. In particular, there is an interesting discussion between those who would like to strengthen the rules which apply at the point of incorporation (*ex ante* protection) and those who prefer to rely on rules which come into play only if limited liability is abused (*ex post* protection). We shall look at these rules in the subsequent chapters of this Part of the book.

The second matter which is apparent about the rationales for limited liability, identified above, is that they work better, perhaps even assume, that the shareholders are natural persons. However, very many businesses are today carried on through a group of holding and subsidiary companies rather than through a single company.[15] This raises the question of whether the doctrine of limited liability should apply only as between the holding company and its shareholders or also within the group, i.e. between the holding group and the subsidiaries and among the subsidiary companies. In fact, the doctrine does apply within groups, a conclusion which the courts have arrived at without any deep consideration of the matter as an inevitable consequence of the doctrine of separate legal personality.

However, a rationale for limited liability has been advanced which would justify its application within groups and, to some extent, to small companies. This is the "asset partitioning" rationale.[16] What limited liability facilitates, it is said, is the segregation of collections of assets, between investors and the company, in the case of a single company, or as among different companies in corporate groups. Although this situation is normally presented as one which hinders the enforcement of claims by creditors, it can be argued that it works to their benefit. Just as a creditor of a company, or of one of a number of companies in a group, cannot assert its claims against that company's shareholders, individual or corporate, so also the creditors of a shareholder, individual or corporate, cannot assert their claims against that company. In other words, a creditor of the company does not have to face competition from the shareholder's creditors, in exchange for not competing with the creditors of the shareholder. Each set of creditors is thus safe in confining their monitoring efforts to the company or the shareholder, as the case may be, and creditors may be expected to specialise in these different forms of monitoring. Of course, the proponents of this rationale do not deny that the

---

[14] See above, para.1–3.
[15] See further below at paras 8–8 and 9–14.
[16] H. Hansmann and R. Kraakman, "The Essential Role of Organizational Law" (2000) 110 Yale L.J. 387.

operation of limited liability within a corporate group may give rise to possibilities for abuse, which the law should control,[17] but they do argue that the application of limited liability within groups is in principle justified.

An alternative or supplementary way of looking at limited liability **8–3** departs from the fact that it is not a mandatory rule. The incorporators themselves may opt out of limited liability across-the-board, by forming an unlimited liability company—though this argument to some degree conflicts with that based on partitioning assets.[18] Alternatively, particular creditors may contract with the company and its shareholders on the basis that both will be liable on the obligations undertaken. Where the rationales for limited liability are most in question, in relation to groups and small companies, it is in fact common for some creditors to contract out of limited liability. Those setting up small companies, into which they are not willing to inject a significant amount of legal capital, will usually find that a bank will not lend money to the company unless the shareholders give a personal guarantee of the loan to the company.[19] In this way, the personal assets of the shareholders become available to the bank if there is default on the loan and it is not confined to the assets of the company. Equally, those dealing with an undercapitalised company in a group of companies may obtain a guarantee from the parent company[20] or, less securely, the parent company may issue a "letter of comfort" to the subsidiary's auditors, allowing them to certify the subsidiary's accounts on a going concern basis, or to a third party contemplating contracting with the company.[21] The implication of the contractual approach might be thought to be that there is no need for the law to control limited liability for it lies in the hands of those contracting with the company to protect their interests themselves. In the case of large or frequent creditors this is very often true. But not all creditors can adjust their contractual relations with the company so as to reflect the riskiness of their situation and for such "non-adjusting" creditors, notably tort victims, the default rule of the law is a crucial determinant of the legal position.[22]

The contractual approach permits one further insight. The third

---

[17] See Ch.9, below.

[18] See para.1–13.

[19] On the definition of legal capital see below para.11–1, *cf.* the facts of *Regal (Hastings) Ltd v Gulliver* [1942] 1 All E.R. 378, HL, one of the leading cases on directors' fiduciary duties, but where the underlying problem arose out of the third party's request for a personal guarantee which the directors were unwilling to give.

[20] See *Polly Peck International Plc (in administration), Re* [1996] 2 All E.R. 433 (involving a single purpose finance vehicle which had no substantial assets of its own).

[21] *Augustus Barnett & Son Ltd, Re* [1986] B.C.L.C. 170; *Kleinwort Benson Ltd v Malaysia Mining Corp Bhd* [1989] 1 W.L.R. 379, CA (letter of comfort not intended in this case to create legal relations).

[22] It has been suggested that limited liability should not apply to involuntary creditors: H. Hansmann and R. Kraakman, "Towards Unlimited Shareholder Liability for Corporate Torts" (1991) 100 Yale L.J. 1879.

party should not be allowed to pursue the shareholders, on this view, because it has contracted on the basis that its claims will be limited to the assets of the company. If this is so, however, it is not only the shareholders' personal assets which should be protected from creditors' claims, but also those of its directors, managers and employees.[23] The doctrine of limited liability is traditionally conceived of as concerning itself with the protection of the shareholders' assets, but functionally it can be seen as a wider doctrine. As we saw in the previous chapter, however, the protection of agents of the company from personal liability for actions done on the company's behalf is delivered through different doctrinal mechanisms and less securely than the protection of shareholders' assets which is the focus of this chapter. However, we shall return to the personal liability of directors in the succeeding chapters, since the abuse of shareholders' limited liability may take the form of actions taken by the shareholders in their capacity as directors of the company, and the law may take the view that the most appropriate response is to impose liability upon those shareholders in their capacity as directors or managers.

Legal Responses to Limited Liability

8–4 Although the wide availability of limited liability is entrenched in current company law and although the Company Law Review chose not to dissent from that position, no serious commentator on the subject supposes that limited liability cannot be the subject of abuses which the law ought to seek to regulate. In this section, we shall sketch out a number of possible responses by the law to such abuses, before going on to consider them in a little more detail in this and subsequent chapters. The first and most obvious response is that of publicity, since that is needed as a basis for any effective self-help action on the part of outsiders. The legislature has always made it an essential condition of the recognition of corporate personality with limited liability that it should be accompanied by wide publicity. Although third parties dealing with the company will normally have no right of resort against its members, they are nevertheless entitled to see who those members are, what shares they hold and, in the case of a listed company, the beneficial interests in those shares, if substantial. They are also entitled to see who its officers are (so that they know with whom to deal), what its constitution is (so that they know what the company may do and how it may do it), and what its capital

---

[23] David Goddard, "Corporate Personality—Limited Recourse and its Limits" in R. Grantham and C. Rickett (eds), *Corporate Personality in the Twentieth Century* (Hart Publishing, 1998), Ch.2.

is and how it has been obtained (so that they know whether to trust it). And unless it is an unlimited company they are also entitled to see its accounts, or at least a modified version of them—again in order to know whether to trust it. The exemption of the unlimited company from the obligation to file accounts with the Registrar[24] is a particularly strong illustration of the link between publicity and limited liability.

Normally, however, third parties are neither bound nor entitled to look behind such information as the law provides shall be made public; in addition to the veil of incorporation, there is something in the nature of a curtain formed by the company's public file in the companies registry, and what goes on behind it is concealed from the public gaze.[25] But sometimes this curtain also may be raised. For example, inspectors may be appointed to investigate the company's affairs,[26] in which case they will have the widest inquisitorial powers; indeed they may even be appointed for the purpose of going behind the company's registers to ascertain who are its true owners.

Moving beyond disclosure, the most direct response to abuses of limited liability is to remove the veil of incorporation and make the shareholders (or directors) liable for the debts and other obligations of the company where abuse occurs. There are two ways in which this may happen: as a result of judicial creativity and as a result of explicit legislative policy. The former has been rather haphazard and of limited impact, as we shall see later on in this chapter. The latter became of increasing importance after the insolvency reforms of the 1980s in consequence of the Cork Committee's Report.[27] Or some other sanction may be imposed on those who abuse limited liability. The Act has long used criminal sanctions in the case of intentional abuse, but, again since the report of the Cork Committee, the sanction of disqualification from being a director of a company or otherwise involved in its management has become increasingly widely deployed, a sanction that is aimed at protecting the public during the period of disqualification as well as potentially deterring such conduct in the first place. Finally, since limited liability restricts creditors' claims to the company's assets, a different attack on the problem would be to take steps to ensure that assets are not improperly removed from the company before those claims are made.

We shall look at each of these strategies in turn, beginning, in this chapter, with judicial efforts to lift the veil and render shareholders personally liable.

---

[24] s.448.
[25] As we saw in the previous chapter, this may sometimes benefit the third party: the limitation of the outsider's knowledge to what is stated in the constitution is the foundation of the rule in *Royal British Bank v Turquand*, above, para.7–15.
[26] See below, Ch.18.
[27] Insolvency Law and Practice, Cmnd. 8558 (1982).

LIFTING THE VEIL UNDER CASE LAW

Under statute or contract

8–5   When analysing the judicial decisions on lifting the veil, it is crucial to distinguish between those situations where the court is applying the terms of a statute (other than the Companies Act) or, less often, a contract, from those where, as a matter of common law, the veil is lifted. The reason is that the justification for lifting the veil in the former group of cases is to be found in the policy of the statute or the intention of the contracting parties. As we have noted, it is perfectly in line with the doctrine of limited liability that parties should contract out of it and so there is nothing remarkable in the courts' deciding that this has occurred in a particular case, provided the parties' intention has been accurately identified. Equally, Parliament is free to decide that the policy of a particular statute requires that the doctrine of limited liability needs to be overruled, though it is doubtless the case that if Parliament took this step routinely, one would begin to have doubts about its commitment to the doctrine of limited liability.

In looking at the statutory cases, it is also crucial to distinguish between those cases where the courts decide that the separate legal personality of the company should be disregarded and those where, in consequence of this disregard, the additional consequence follows that the shareholders are made liable for the company's debts or other obligations. There are in fact very few, if any, cases where the courts have concluded that the policy of the statute requires the separate legal personality of the company to be ignored so that personal liability can be imposed on shareholders, except where the statute in express terms requires this approach. Typically, as a result of ignoring the separate legal personality of the company, some legal issue other than the limited liability of the shareholders is determined in a way which is different from the way in which it would have been determined, had the separate legal personality been maintained. Thus, in *FG (Films) Ltd, Re*[28] a US company had incorporated a shell company in Britain for the purposes of claiming a declaration that a film it produced was British. The result of the failure by the courts to uphold the separation between the British and US companies was that the film was not classified as British—a fact then relevant to the financing of film-making. In some cases, in fact,

[28] [1953] 1 W.L.R. 483.

ignoring the separate legal personality of the company has been for the benefit of the shareholders.[29]

In deciding whether to lift the veil in such cases, the courts ought to be guided by the policy of the statute in question, and so the decision arrived at is likely to vary from statute to statute. Nevertheless, it is difficult to avoid the conclusion that the courts are committed to the preservation of separate legal personality of companies except where the statutory wording clearly requires this. The classic illustration is the refusal of the House of Lords in *Nokes v Doncaster Amalgamated Collieries*[30] to construe what is now section 900 of the Companies Act 2006 as meaning that an order made thereunder transferring the property and liabilities of one company to another on a reconstruction could operate to transfer a contract of personal service; and this notwithstanding that the section specifically provides that "property" includes property, rights and powers of every description. To Lord Atkin the contrary interpretation would have been "tainted with oppression and confiscation"[31] and would have subverted "the principle that a man is not to be compelled to serve a master against his will ... [which] is deep-seated in the common law of this country".[32] Yet, had the whole share capital of the transferor company been transferred instead of the undertaking, the worker would have been compelled to serve what, in reality, was a new employer. The employee is better protected by recognising the continuation of the enterprise but providing him with a right to transfer or with rights to payments for redundancy or unfair dismissal if he is not kept on. And this is now recognised in respect of transfers of the undertaking (where the effect of the *Nokes* decision has been reversed) under the influence of EC social law.[33]

Another example of a refusal to lift the veil is afforded by *Lee v Lee's Air Farming Ltd*.[34] There Lee, for the purpose of carrying on his business of aerial top-dressing, had formed a company of which he beneficially owned all the shares and was sole "governing director". He was also appointed chief pilot. Pursuant to the company's stat- **8–6**

---

[29] *Trebanog Working Men's Club and Institute Ltd v MacDonald* [1940] K.B. 576 (incorporated club treated in the same way as an unincorporated one for the purposes of an exemption from the liquor licence rules); *DHN Food Distributors Ltd v Tower Hamlets LBC* [1976] 1 W.L.R. 852, CA (ignoring separate legal entity of subsidiary permitted parent to claim compensation under the planning legislation); *Smith Stone & Knight Ltd v Birmingham Corp* [1939] 4 All E.R. 116 (*ditto*) but *cf. Woolfson v Strathclyde Regional Council* 1978 S.L.T. 159, HL (*DHN* not followed in a case on similar facts).

[30] [1940] A.C. 1014, HL (reversing the unanimous decisions of the courts below).

[31] [1940] A.C. 1014, HL, at 1030.

[32] [1940] A.C. 1014, HL, at 1033.

[33] See the Transfer of Undertakings (Protection of Employment) Regulations, SI 2006/246. It is true that these Regulations have been construed by the ECJ so as not to require an employee to go across to the transferee employer but so as to give him or her an option to do so, but the Member States are free to make it economically very unattractive for the employee to choose to stay with the transferor. See Joined Cases C-132, 138 and 139/91, *Katsikas* [1992] E.C.R. I-6577, noted in (1993) 22 I.L.J. 151.

[34] [1961] A.C. 12, PC.

utory obligations he caused the company to insure against liability to pay compensation under the Workmen's Compensation Act. He was killed in a flying accident. The Court of Appeal of New Zealand held that his widow was not entitled to compensation from the company (i.e. from their insurers) since Lee could not be regarded as a "worker" within the meaning of the Act. But the Privy Council reversed that decision, holding that Lee and his company were distinct legal entities which had entered into contractual relationships under which he became, *qua* chief pilot, an employee of the company. In his capacity of governing director he could, on behalf of the company, give himself orders in his other capacity of pilot, and hence the relationship between himself, as pilot, and the company was that of servant and master. In effect the magic of corporate personality enabled him to be master and servant at the same time and to get all the advantages of both (and of limited liability). No doubt the court was influenced by the fact that the company had acted in pursuance of a purported statutory obligation and had in fact paid the necessary contributions over a period of time, thus forgoing the opportunity of making alternative insurance arrangements. More recent cases in Britain have shown the courts willing to accept that in principle it might not be appropriate to treat someone as within the employment protection legislation if he or she could, in effect, take the crucial decisions affecting the continuance of the employment, even though the employment relationship with the company was not a sham.[35]

At common law

8–7   Challenges to the doctrines of separate legal personality and limited liability at common law tend to raise more fundamental challenges to these doctrines, because they are formulated on the basis of general reasons for not applying them, such as fraud, the company being a "sham" or "facade", that the company is the agent of the shareholder, that the companies are part of a "single economic unit" or even that the "interests of justice" require this result. However, the courts seem, if anything, more reluctant to accept such general arguments against the doctrines than arguments based on particular statutes or the terms of particular contracts. The leading case is *Adams v Cape Industries Plc*.[36] That case raised the issues in a sharp fashion. It concerned liability within a group of companies and the purpose of the claim to ignore the separate legal personality of the subsidiary was to make the parent liable for the obligations of the subsidiary towards involuntary tort victims. Thus, the case encapsulated two features—internal group liability and involuntary cred-

---

[35] *Secretary of State for Trade and Industry v Bottrill* [2000] 2 B.C.L.C. 448, CA, but the point is far from settled (see *Clark v Clark Construction Initiatives Ltd* [2008] UKEAT 0225/97, where a more sophisticated approach was adopted).
[36] [1990] Ch. 433, Scott J. and CA (pet. dis. [1990] 2 W.L.R. 786, HL).

itors—where limited liability is most in question. The facts of the case were somewhat complicated but for present purposes it suffices to say that what the Court had ultimately to determine was whether judgments obtained in the United States against Cape, an English registered company whose business was mining asbestos in South Africa and marketing it worldwide, would be recognised and enforced by the English courts. In the absence of submission to the foreign jurisdiction on the part of Cape, this depended on whether Cape could be said to have been "present" in the United States. On the facts, the answer to that question depended upon whether Cape could be said to be present in the United States through its wholly owned subsidiaries or through a company (CPC) with which it had close business links. The court rejected all the arguments by which it was sought to make Cape liable.[37]

The "single economic unit" argument
The first of these, described as the "single economic unit argument", **8–8** proceeded as follows: Admittedly there is no general principle that all companies in a group of companies are to be regarded as one; on the contrary, the fundamental principle is unquestionably that "each company in a group of companies ... is a separate legal entity possessed of separate rights and liabilities".[38] Nevertheless, it was argued, the court will, in appropriate circumstances, ignore the distinction between them, treating them as one. For this proposition a number of authorities were cited, but the court distinguished them all as turning on the interpretation of particular statutory or contractual provisions.[39] After reviewing these authorities the Court in *Cape* expressed some sympathy with the claimants' submissions and agreed that:

> "To the layman at least the distinction between the case where a company trades itself in a foreign country and the case where it trades in a foreign country through a subsidiary, whose activities it has power to control, may seem a slender one."[40]

It also accepted that the wording of a particular statute or document

---

[37] Note, however, the alternative legal approach to the problem, by-passing the separate legal personality issue by postulating a duty owed in tort by the parent company directly to the asbestos victims: *Connelly v RTZ Corp Plc* [1998] A.C. 854, HL; *Lubbe v Cape Plc* [2000] 1 W.L.R. 1545, HL.

[38] At 532, quoting Roskill L.J. in *The Albazero* [1977] A.C. 744, CA and HL at 807.

[39] *The Roberta* (1937) 58 L.L.R. 159; *Holdsworth & Co v Caddies* [1955] 1 W.L.R. 352, HL; *Scottish Co-operative Wholesale Society Ltd v Meyer* [1959] A.C. 324, HL (Sc.); *DHN Food Distributors Ltd v Tower Hamlets LBC* [1976] 1 W.L.R. 852, CA (probably the strongest case in the tort victims' favour, because it was strongly arguable that the court there did not base itself on the particular statutory provision but on a more general approach founded on the idea of single economic entity); *Revlon Inc v Cripp & Lee Ltd* [1980] F.S.R. 85; and the Opinion of the Advocate General in Cases 6 and 7/73, [1974] E.C.R. 223.

[40] At 536B.

may justify the court in interpreting it so that a parent and subsidiary are treated as one unit at any rate for some purposes.[41] However, beyond that it was unwilling to go. It seems, therefore, that in aid of interpretation (of statute or contract) the court may have regard to the economic realities in relation to the companies concerned. But that now seems to be the extent to which the "single economic unit" argument can succeed.

Facade or sham

8–9   In *Cape* the court accepted that "there is one well-recognised exception to the rule prohibiting the piercing of the 'corporate veil'".[42] This exception today is generally expressed (and was in *Cape*) as permitting disregard of the company when the corporate structure is a "mere facade concealing the true facts"—"facade"[43] or "sham" having replaced an assortment of epithets[44] which judges have employed in earlier cases. The difficulty is to know what precisely may make a company a "mere facade".

In general, the court felt that it was "left with rather sparse guidance as to the principles which should guide the court in determining whether or not the arrangements of a corporate group involve a façade ..." but, unfortunately, it declined to "attempt a comprehensive definition of those principles".[45] It did, however, decide that one of Cape's wholly owned subsidiaries (AMC incorporated in Liechtenstein) was a facade in the relevant sense. Scott J. had found as a fact that arrangements made in 1979 regarding AMC and other companies concerned in the marketing of Cape's asbestos "were part of one composite arrangement designed to enable Cape asbestos to continue to be sold into the United States while reducing, if not eliminating, the appearance of any involvement therein of Cape or its subsidiaries".[46] Although he had thought that motive was irrelevant, the Court of Appeal thought it might be highly relevant, though apparently this particular motive alone would not have sufficed to make AMC a mere facade. What seems to have been regarded as decisive was the fact that AMC was not only a wholly owned subsidiary of Cape but also no more than a corporate name which Cape or its subsidiaries used on invoices.[47] However, the implications of

---

[41] At 536D.

[42] At 539.

[43] Used, clearly, in its secondary meaning (the primary one being "the face of a building"), i.e. "an outward appearance or front, especially a deceptive one".

[44] Such as "device", "creature", "stratagem", "mask", "puppet" and even (see *Bugle Press, Re* [1961] Ch. 270 at 288, CA) "a little hut".

[45] At 543D.

[46] At 478F, approved by the Court of Appeal at 541G–H, 544A and B.

[47] At 479E and 543E. If the motives of those setting up the companies are dishonest, that will make it easier for the court to conclude that the company is a sham: *Kensington International Ltd v Republic of the Congo* [2006] 2 B.C.L.C. 296.

that were not pursued because all the court was concerned with was whether Cape could be regarded as present in the United States and "on the judge's undisputed findings AMC was not in reality carrying on any business in the United States",[48] and therefore could not cause Cape to be regarded as present there. Presumably, however, those who, as a result of the invoices, thought they were dealing with AMC would, if AMC failed to perform the contract, have been able to sue Cape.

What mattered in relation to establishing that Cape was present in the United States was whether another company, CPC, incorporated and carrying on business in the United States, was a facade. Despite the fact that CPC was a party to the same arrangement as AMC and that it probably had been incorporated at Cape's expense, that did not in itself make it a mere facade. On the facts the court was satisfied that it was an independent corporation, wholly owned by its chief executive and carrying on its own business in the States and not the business of Cape or its subsidiaries.

Moreover the court declared[49] that it did not accept that:

> "as a matter of law the court is entitled to lift the corporate veil as against a defendant company which is the member of a corporate group, merely because the corporate structure has been used so as to ensure that the legal liability (if any) in respect of particular future activities of the group (and correspondingly the risk of enforcement of that liability) will fall on another member of the group rather than the defendant company. Whether or not this is desirable, the right to use a corporate structure in this manner is inherent in our corporate law."[50]

And the court added:[51]

> "[Counsel for the plaintiffs] urged on us that the purpose of the operation was in substance that Cape would have the practical benefit of the group's asbestos trade in the United States ... without the risks of tortious liability. This may be so. However, in our judgment Cape was in law entitled to organise the group's affairs in that manner and (save in the case of AMC to which special considerations apply) to expect that the court would apply the principle of [the *Salomon* case]."

---

[48] At 543G.
[49] At 544D, E.
[50] Hence Cape's wholly owned American subsidiary NAAC which, prior to its winding up, had performed a similar role to that undertaken thereafter by CPC had equally to be regarded as a separate entity: see at 538.
[51] At 544E–F.

The agency argument

8–10   A company having power to act as an agent may do so as agent for its parent company or indeed for all or any of its individual members if it or they authorise it to do so. If so, the parent company or the members will be bound by the acts of its agent so long as those acts are within the actual or apparent scope of the authority.[52] But there is no presumption of any such agency relationship between company and shareholders and in the absence of an express agreement between the parties,[53] it will be very difficult to establish one. In *Cape* the attempt to do so failed.[54] While it was clear that CPC rendered services to Cape and in some cases acted as its agent in relation to particular transactions, that did not suffice to satisfy the conditions which the Court had held to be necessary if Cape was to be regarded as "present" in the United States. CPC had carried on its own business from its own fixed place of business in the United States.

The interests of justice

8–11   Although the interests of justice may provide the policy impetus for creating exceptions to the doctrines of separate legal personality and limited liability, as an exception in itself it suffers from the defect of being inherently vague and providing to neither courts nor those engaged in business any clear guidance as to when the normal company law rules should be displaced. Consequently, it is difficult to find cases in which "the interests of justice" have represented more than simply a way of referring to the grounds identified above in which the veil of incorporation has been pierced.[55]

Impropriety

8–12   In a number of recent cases the courts have considered the principle that the corporate veil can be set aside on the grounds that the company has been used to carry on an unlawful activity or in order to avoid the impact of an order of the court. Usually, in such cases, if the veil is lifted, the principle of shareholders' limited liability is not affected. Rather, it is the company which is being made liable in some way for the obligations of the shareholder. The clearest case is *Re H*,[56]

---

[52] See Ch.7, above.
[53] As in *Southern v Watson* [1940] 3 All E.R. 439, CA, where, on the conversion of a business into a private company, the sale agreement provided that the company should fulfil existing contracts of the business as agents of the sellers, and in *Rainham Chemical Works v Belvedere* [1921] 2 A.C. 465, HL where the agreement provided that the newly formed company should take possession of land as agent of its vendor promoters.
[54] Both in relation to CPC (at 547–549) and to its predecessor, NAAC (fn.50, above) despite the fact that it had been Cape's wholly owned subsidiary (at 545–547). See also *Yukong Line Ltd of Korea v Rendsburg Investments Corp of Liberia (No.2)* [1998] 1 W.L.R. 294.
[55] See the rejection of this ground in *Cape* at 536.
[56] [1996] 2 All E.R. 291, CA.

where restraint orders under the Criminal Justice Act 1988 were made in respect of assets held by companies completely owned and controlled by individual defendants who had been convicted of excise duty fraud. However, the companies had not been convicted nor were the companies a facade in the *Cape* sense of the word, since they carried on businesses of their own, albeit partially unlawful businesses. However, the case is also explicable on the grounds that ignoring the separate legal personality of the companies was necessary for the implementation of the statutory policy underlying the 1988 Act.

More straight-forward are those cases where a company is used to avoid a court order, though again it is not clear that lifting the veil is an idea needed to explain the decisions in the cases. In *Gilford Motor Co Ltd v Horn*,[57] a director of a company sought to avoid a post-employment competition restraint by setting up the rival business through a company which he controlled, rather than conducting it personally, but the Court extended the injunction to the company. That result seems explicable on the basis that the director's agreement covered carrying on business both directly and indirectly through a company. Again, in *Jones v Lipman*[58] a defendant sought to avoid a decree of specific performance by conveying the land in question to a company he owned. The company was held bound by the order, but again the result can be explained without recourse to the doctrine of lifting the veil. Since the defendant controlled the company, the company took the property with notice of the equity of the person in whose favour the order had been made and so was bound by it.[59]

Somewhat analogous are cases where directors have sought to avoid liability by allocating assets to companies they control. Where a director had misappropriated corporate assets or opportunities, but those assets had been taken by a company owned or controlled by the director rather than the director personally, the court preferred to hold the director personally liable on the grounds that the company in question was a facade[60] rather than the company liable for knowing receipt of the corporate assets.[61] However, it is not obvious that a director should be able to escape liability to account just because the company carries on an independent business as well as receiving the assets misappropriated by the director.[62] In fact, it may be possible to analyse such cases without recourse to the doctrine of lifting the veil, on the grounds that the common rule about misappropriation of corporate assets by directors encompasses both

[57] [1933] Ch. 935, CA.
[58] [1962] 1 W.L.R. 832.
[59] This is the explanation favoured by Toulson J. in *Yukong Line Ltd of Korea v Rendsburg Investments Corp of Liberia (No.2)* [1998] 1 W.L.R. 294.
[60] *Gencor ACP Ltd v Dalby* [2000] 2 B.C.L.C. 734.
[61] See para.16–97.
[62] Lawrence Collins J. in *CMS Dolphin Ltd v Simonet* [2001] 2 B.C.L.C. 704 at 736 implied that he saw no good reason for such a distinction.

assets taken personally and those taken through entities which they control.[63]

8–13   What the courts have been unwilling to countenance, however, is ignoring the separate legal personality of the company in the converse case, i.e. where a company takes steps to avoid the practical effect of a court judgment against it by transferring assets to another person in advance of judgment. Despite some initial willingness on the part of courts to add the second person to the litigation, this approach has now been firmly rejected.[64] This does not mean that the claimant is without protection in such a situation, but rather that he or she has to rely on the rules of company and insolvency law which control the transfer of assets out of the company[65] rather than the doctrine of lifting the veil.

In short, impropriety seems not much more established than the "interests of justice" as a ground for lifting the veil, though the courts have secured just results, by and large, by recourse to other rules, often from outside company law. It may be that, as with the "interests of justice", the courts are unclear where the boundaries of an "impropriety" exception would lie. Some very clear cases have been considered in the previous paragraphs, but more difficult issues can be imagined. After all, in *Cape* itself the company was aware of the risk of negligence liability which was inherent in its activities and took steps to quarantine the impact of such liability on its business activities. The court took the view that, far from being improper, this was an entirely legitimate use of the group corporate structure.[66]

CONCLUSION

8–14   The doctrine of lifting the veil plays a small role in British company law, once one moves outside the area of particular contracts or sta-

---

[63] This was the preferred approach of Lawrence Collins J. in the case cited in the previous note, relying on *Cook v Deeks* [1916] 1 A.C. 554, PC (see below, Ch.16). But *cf. Trustor AB v Smallbone* [2001] 1 W.L.R. 1177 where the issue was, as in *CMD Dolphin*, whether the director had to account for money received by the company and the Vice Chancellor preferred to see the issue as involving lifting the veil, which he was prepared to do on the basis of the facade argument.

[64] *Yukong Line Ltd of Korea v Rendsburg Investments Corp of Liberia (No.2)* [1998] 1 W.L.R. 294; *Ord v Belhaven Pubs Ltd* [1998] 2 B.C.L.C. 447, CA, overruling the reasoning in *Creasey v Breachwood Motors Ltd* [1992] B.C.C. 638.

[65] Some of the corporate rules are discussed in Ch.12, below. Whether these other doctrines are as effective is not clear. *Creasey* (see previous note) was a very disreputable case. The day after a writ for wrongful dismissal was issued by an employee, the company transferred its business to another company controlled by the same persons and was wound up, without any provision being made for the employee's contingent claim. It is conceivable that, where evidence of the necessary intention could be shown, the controllers of the company could be held liable, criminally or civilly, for fraudulent trading: below, para.9–5).

[66] See above, para.8–12.

tutes. Even where the case for applying the doctrine may seem strong, as in the undercapitalised one-person company, which may or may not be part of a larger corporate group, the courts are unlikely to do so. As Staughton L.J. remarked in *Atlas Maritime Co SA v Avalon Maritime Ltd, The Coral Rose*:[67]

"The creation or purchase of a subsidiary company with minimal liability, which will operate with the parent's funds and on the parent's directions but not expose the parent to liability, may not seem to some the most honest way of trading. But it is extremely common in the international shipping industry and perhaps elsewhere. To hold that it creates an agency relationship between the subsidiary and the parent would be revolutionary doctrine."

This is in contrast to the law in the United States where the veil is lifted more readily.[68] However, even in the United States it seems the courts have never lifted the veil so as to remove limited liability in the case of a public company and will not do so as a matter of routine in private companies.[69] Probably, the most significant addition to the grounds for lifting the veil which US law adds to the categories recognised by British law is that of inadequate capitalisation. As we shall see in the next chapter, British law has approached that problem through the statutory doctrine of wrongful trading rather than through lifting the veil. Indeed, at a more general level, the approach of British law to regulation of the abuse of limited liability is a combination of facilitating self-help and *ex post* statutory constraints. The doctrine of piercing the veil is a technique available to the courts but it has not been developed in such a way as to be the central legal strategy for addressing abuses of limited liability.

---

[67] [1991] 4 All E.R. 769 at 779.

[68] See Blumberg, *The Multinational Challenge to Corporate Law* (Oxford University Press, 1993), especially Pt II.

[69] See Robert B. Thompson, "Piercing the Corporate Veil: An Empirical Study" (1991) 76 Cornell L.J. 1036. On these points the findings of Dr Charles Mitchell in a study of English cases do not differ ("Lifting the Corporate Veil in the English Courts: an Empirical Study" (1999) 3 C.F.I.L.R. 15). "No case was found in which the English courts have even been asked to fix the shareholders of a public company with liability for its obligations." (pp.21–22) On the various factors influencing veil lifting in private companies, see p.22 (Table 4), but in no case was it routine.

CHAPTER 9

STATUTORY EXCEPTIONS TO LIMITED LIABILITY

From the beginnings of modern company law in the middle of the   **9–1** nineteenth century, the legislature has been ready, in a small number of appropriate cases, to remove the shield of limited liability and impose responsibility for the company's obligations on the shareholders or directors personally. Some of the examples which survived into modern law were surprising, because the sanction of personal liability seemed disproportionate to the importance of the rules which the sanctions upheld. A good example was the imposition of personal liability where the number of members was reduced below one, a provision not repeated in the 2006 Act. In other words, our views about how best to protect creditors from the abuse of limited liability have changed over the years. In other cases, however, for example personal liability for fraudulent trading, the original idea was expanded in recent years so as to apply to a much wider range of situations, in this instance to catch negligent as well as fraudulent trading.

REDUCTION OF NUMBER OF MEMBERS

Under what was section 24 of the Companies Act 1985, if a public   **9–2** company carried on business for more than six months with fewer than two members any person who was a member after that six months became liable, jointly and severally with the company, for the payment of its debts. This rule was the final remnant of a legislative policy which attached significance to the number of members of a company as a protection for those who dealt with it. The Limited Liability Act 1855 applied only to companies (public or private) with at least 25 members, and as late as 1980 public companies had to have at least seven members. But the requirement was effectively undermined by the decision in *Salomon*'s case in 1897,[1] and since Parliament chose not to reverse that decision, the requirement as to numbers was capable since that date of being met through the use of bare nominees rather than shareholders who held the shares beneficially as well as legally. The rule was all but abolished by the Twelfth Company Law Directive on single-member private limited liability companies[2] which had the consequence that private companies limited by shares or by guarantee were excluded from section 24. Following the proposals of the Company Law Review any company—public or private—is now capable of being formed by a single person[3] and so section 24 of the 1985 Act has no equivalent in the Act of 2006.

MISDESCRIPTION OF THE COMPANY AND TRADING DISCLOSURES

9–3 A second example of a provision imposing personal liability on officers of the company, which the 2006 Act no longer retains, arose out of misdescription of the company's name on cheques and related instruments or orders for goods signed by an officer (or even employee) of the company. By what was section 349(4) of the Companies Act 1985, if the correct and full name of the company did not so appear, the signatory would be personally liable to pay if the company did not.[4] And it seemed clear that it made no difference that the third party concerned had not been misled by the description. The requirement to state the company's name correctly on cheques etc. was only one of a number of disclosure requirements imposed by the legislation on companies in relation to those who deal or might deal with them (known as "trading disclosures"), but it was the only one in relation to which personal liability was imposed on an officer of the

---

[1] [1897] A.C. 22. See above, para.1–2.
[2] Council Directive 89/667, implemented in Britain by the Companies (Single Member Private Limited Companies) Regulations 1992 (SI 1992/1699).
[3] CA 2006, s.7.
[4] See *Atkins v Wardle* (1889) 5 T.L.R. 734, CA; *Scottish & Newcastle Breweries Ltd v Blair*, 1967 S.L.T. 72; *Civil Service Co-operative Society v Chapman* [1914] 30 T.L.R. 679; *British Airways Board v Parish* [1979] 2 Lloyd's Rep. 361.

company. Those requirements are re-stated in Chapter 6 of Part 5 of the 2006 Act, where the Secretary of State is given power to make regulations requiring the company to give specified information, not only in "specified descriptions of documents or communications" but also in specified locations (such as the company's place of business or its website) or to those who deal with them when the latter so request.[5]

Although the sanction of personal liability has been removed for failure to state the company's name correctly on cheques etc., such a failure is not devoid of civil consequences, though they are now visited wholly on the company.[6] Moreover, these civil consequences apply to any breaches of the trading disclosure requirements, whether involving the misstatement of the company's name on a cheque, etc. or some other failure to conform with them.[7] Where a company seeks to enforce a right arising out of a contract made in the course of business and the company was in breach of the requirements at the time, the court is required to dismiss the company's claim if the defendant shows that he or she has a claim against the company which the defendant is unable to pursue because of the company's breach of the trading disclosure requirements or that he or she has suffered a financial loss by reason of the company's breach. Even in these two cases, the court may permit the company's claim to continue if it thinks it just and equitable to do so.[8] Thus, not only are the civil consequences of misdescriptions confined to the company but the company will bear them only where the misdescription has caused harm to the defendant and, even then, the court may permit the company's claim to proceed (for example, where the harm to the defendant was out of proportion to the harm the company might suffer by being denied its contractual rights and the defendant's loss could be taken into account in calculating the company's damages).

Although the trading disclosure rules no longer contain an exception to the doctrine of limited liability, they are intimately connected with that doctrine. As the Company Law Review put it, because of limited liability "it is essential that the company's legal identity ... is revealed to all who have, or may wish to have, dealings with it so that they are warned as to its status and can discover all the other information which the company is required to reveal about

---

[5] s.82(1) and the Companies (Trading Disclosure) Regulations 2008/495.

[6] This is a more radical response than that recommended by the CLR which would have kept personal liability but on a narrower basis: Final Report I, paras 11.55–11.57.

[7] This is new: previously, other than as provided by s.349(4), the sanctions for breach of the disclosure requirements were only criminal. However, the civil liability imposed by s.83 is modeled on that imposed by s.5 of the Business Names Act 1985 which already applied to companies trading other than under their corporate name. The criminal sanctions are retained in s.84 of the 2006 Act.

[8] s.83(1),(2). The restriction does not apply if the company seeks to enforce its contractual rights in proceedings brought by another person (for example, by way of counter-claim): s.83(3).

itself."[9] However, the thrust of the disclosure rules is now on fostering self-help on the part of those dealing with the company[10] rather than with providing them with an additional avenue of civil redress against company officers or employees.

PREMATURE TRADING

9–4　Our third example of personal liability is one which the 2006 Act has retained. Under the Act, a public limited company, newly incorporated as such, must not "do business or exercise any borrowing powers" until it has obtained, from the Registrar of Companies, a certificate that it has complied with the provisions of the Act relating to the raising of the prescribed minimum share capital or until it has re-registered as a private company.[11] If it enters into any transaction in contravention of this provision, not only are the company and its officers in default liable to fines,[12] but if the company fails to comply with its obligations in relation to the transaction within 21 days of being called upon to do so, the directors of the company are jointly and severally liable to indemnify the other party in respect of any loss or damage suffered by reason of the company's failure to comply.[13]

Whether this is a true example of lifting the veil is questionable; technically it does not make the directors liable for the company's debts but rather penalises the directors for any loss the third parties suffer as a result of the company's default in complying with the section. But the effect is much the same. It is, however, unlikely to be invoked often since it is unusual for companies to be formed initially as public ones. Usually, companies are formed as private companies and later convert through re-registration to public status. If this way of proceeding is adopted, however, obtaining the required minimum share capital is made a pre-condition to re-registration[14] and so trading without the authorised minimum is avoided in that way.

---

[9] Final Report I, para.11.52.
[10] Hence the importance of disclosure of the company's name, not only in correspondence, but on its web-site and at any place of business: Trading Regulations, regs.4 and 6(2).
[11] See s.761 and para.11–4.
[12] s.767(1),(2).
[13] s.767(3). The validity of the transaction, however, is not affected.
[14] ss. 90 and 91.

FRAUDULENT AND WRONGFUL TRADING

Fraudulent trading

An example of far greater practical importance has long been affor- **9–5**
ded by provisions on fraudulent trading. These provisions recognise
that the separate entity and limited liability doctrines are capable of
being abused and that the benefit of them should be removed from
the abusers. They come in both a criminal and a civil liability form.
Section 993 (constituting the single-section Part 29 of the Act) creates
a specific, but widely defined, criminal offence of carrying on the
business of a company with intent to defraud the creditors[15] of the
company or of any other person or for any other fraudulent purpose.
Every person knowingly party to the carrying on of the business in
this manner commits a criminal offence.[16]

The civil liability is to be found in section 213 of the Insolvency Act
1986.[17] This lays down the same test for liability as that in section 993
of the Companies Act, but section 213 also requires that the company
be in the course of winding up (which the criminal section does not).[18]
The court, on the application of the liquidator (alone), may declare
the persons who were parties to carrying on[19] the business in this way
"liable to make such contributions (if any) to the company's assets as
the court thinks proper."[20] Since the company in winding up will be in
need of such a contribution only where its assets are insufficient to
meet its liabilities, this is in effect an indirect way of making the
persons in question liable for the company's debts (to at least some
degree).[21] It is enough to establish liability that only one creditor was

---

[15] The section embraces fraud on future, as well as present, creditors: *R. v Smith* [1996] 2
B.C.L.C. 109, CA.
[16] Fraud is a general criminal offence, of course, but it has been regarded as less confusing for
juries to face them with a single charge of fraudulent trading rather than with numerous
charges of individual acts of fraud: see *R. v Kemp* [1988] Q.B. 645, CA. (pet. dis. [1988] 1
W.L.R. 846, HL.). The legislature thought so well of the offence that it enacted in s.9 of the
Fraud Act 2006 a similar offence in respect of those businesses carried on by persons falling
outside the scope of s.993, including sole traders. This shows that the absence of limited
liability is not a guarantee of the absence of fraud.
[17] The shift of the civil liability out of the companies legislation and into the insolvency
legislation occurred as a result of the recommendations of the Cork Committee on Insolvency Law (Cmnd. 8558 (1981), Ch. 44).
[18] The fraudulent trading, of course, will have occurred in nearly all cases before the company
went into liquidation. In fact, there is no limit in the section on the prior period which may
be scrutinised for evidence of fraudulent trading. But the company being in liquidation is a
condition for the claim being brought.
[19] A business may be regarded as "carried on" notwithstanding that the company has ceased
active trading: *Sarflax Ltd, Re* [1979] Ch. 592.
[20] s.213(2).
[21] Unlike the situation before 1985, it is no longer possible to impose liability under s.213 in
respect of particular debts or in favour of particular creditors: *cf. Cyona Distributors Ltd, Re*
[1967] Ch. 889, CA.

defrauded and in a single transaction.[22] However, in the case of a one-off fraud there is a risk that the court will not be able to conclude that the business of the company was carried on for fraudulent purposes, in which case liability under section 213 will not arise.[23]

9–6   Section 213 does not confine liability to directors. Hence banks and parent companies have at times felt inhibited from providing finance to ailing companies, fearing that they may thereby fall foul of these provisions. Their fears, however, seem unfounded so long as they play no active role in running the company with fraudulent intent.[24] However, a crucial question is who counts as the bank or other third party for the purpose of the section. In *Bank of Credit and Commerce International SA (No.15), Re*[25] the Court of Appeal rejected the proposition that only the knowledge of the board was to be attributed to a third party bank and instead attributed the knowledge of a senior manager who had been given authority by the board to set the terms of transactions with a client (in fact, another bank) whose business was being carried on in breach of section 213 to the knowledge of the manager. Moreover, as was already clear and as this case illustrates, a third party can fall within section 213 if it participates, with knowledge,[26] in the fraudulent activity of a company, even though that party could not be said to have taken a controlling role within the company.[27] Overall, therefore, these rules encourage third parties, whose dealings with a company might assist the fraudulent running of that company's business, to have in place internal controls designed to identify at an early stage situations

---

[22] *Cooper Chemicals Ltd, Re* [1978] Ch. 262 (only one creditor defrauded). Indeed, for criminal liability to arise it is not clear that it is necessary for any person actually to be defrauded provided that the business of the company was carried on with intent to defraud (*R. v Kemp* [1988] Q.B. 645, CA—only potential creditors defrauded).

[23] *Morphitis v Bernasconi* [2003] 2 B.C.L.C. 53, CA. The defrauded person will have remedies under the general law of fraud.

[24] In *Maidstone Building Provisions Ltd, Re* [1971] 1 W.L.R. 1085 an attempt to obtain a declaration against the company's secretary, who was also a partner in its auditors' firm, failed because, although he had given financial advice and had not attempted to prevent the company from trading, he had not taken "positive steps in the carrying on of the company's business in a fraudulent manner". In *Augustus Barnett & Son Ltd, Re* [1986] B.C.L.C. 170 an attempt against its parent company (Rumasa) failed on the same ground.

[25] [2005] 2 B.C.L.C. 328, CA, following the lead given in *Meridian Global Funds Management Asia Ltd v Securities Commission* [1995] 2 A.C. 500, PC (above, at para.7–29). This step was facilitated by the separation of the criminal and civil liability for fraudulent trading, so that there is no implication from this decision that the same attribution rule would be applied if criminal liability were in question: at [107] and [129].

[26] The required degree of knowledge has been stated to be "blind eye" knowledge, i.e. "a decision to avoid obtaining confirmation of facts in whose existence the individual has good reason to believe" (*Bank of Credit and Commerce International SA (No.15), Re* (previous note) at [14] quoting Lord Scott in *Manifest Shipping Co Ltd v Uni-Polaris Shipping Co Ltd* [2003] 1 A.C. 469 at [116]).

[27] In *Gerald Cooper Chemicals Ltd, Re* [1978] Ch. 262 it was held that a declaration could be made against a creditor who refrained from pressing for repayment knowing that the business was being carried on in fraud of creditors and who accepted part payment out of money which he knew had been obtained by that fraud. *Gerald Cooper Chemicals* was followed in *Bank of Credit and Commerce International SA (No.14), Re* [2001] 1 B.C.L.C. 263.

where the relevant officer or employee of the third party has acquired the requisite level of knowledge of the fraudulent activities within the company so as to make the third party liable to contribute under section 213 in the company's liquidation.[28]

As to whether those conducting business are doing so fraudulently, it has been said that what has to be shown is "actual dishonesty involving, according to current notions of fair trading among commercial men, real moral blame".[29] That may be inferred if "a company continues to carry on business and to incur debts at a time when there is, to the knowledge of the directors, no reasonable prospect of the creditors ever receiving payment of those debts",[30] but it cannot be inferred merely because they ought to have realised it. It was this need to prove subjective moral blame that led the Jenkins Committee in 1962 vainly to recommend the introduction of a remedy for "reckless trading"[31] and the Cork Committee, 20 years later, successfully to promote it under the name of "wrongful trading".

Wrongful trading

Abuse in the shape of hiding behind limited liability to effect fraud is easy to identify as something the law should address, as the long-standing provisions against fraudulent trading indicate. More significant are the recently added provisions on wrongful trading which, in effect, make access to limited liability dependent upon objective standards of proper conduct on the part of controllers of companies, at least during the period when insolvency threatens and the controllers are under the greatest incentive to take advantage of the company's creditors.[32] The wrongful trading provisions constitute what is probably the most extreme departure from the rule in *Salomon*'s case yet achieved in the United Kingdom. However, it is to be noted that the persons potentially made liable are the directors (and shadow directors) of the company rather than its shareholders. The latter will fall within the scope of the provisions only if they fall within the category of a "shadow director" (see below). The wrongful

9–7

---

[28] In *Bank of Credit and Commerce International SA (No.15), Re* (above, fn.25) it was left open whether the third party's liability could not be more simply and widely established on the basis of the third party's vicarious liability for breaches of section 213 by its employees. See *Dubai Aluminium Co Ltd v Salaam* [2003] 2 A.C. 366, HL and para.7–24.

[29] *Patrick Lyon Ltd, Re* [1933] Ch. 786 at 790, 791.

[30] *William C Leitch Ltd, Re* [1932] 2 Ch. 71 at 77, per Maugham J. See also *R. v Grantham* [1984] Q.B. 675, CA, where the court upheld a direction to the jury that they might convict of fraudulent trading a person who had taken an active part in running the business if they were satisfied that he had helped to obtain credit knowing that there was no good reason for thinking that funds would become available to pay the debts when they became due or shortly thereafter. That dishonesty may be inferred in these cases does not mean, of course, that it can never be established in other cases: *Aktieselskabet Dansk Skibsfinansiering v Brothers* [2001] 2 B.C.L.C. 324, H.K.C.F.A.

[31] Cmnd. 1749, para.503(b).

[32] As indicated at para.16–12 the provisions of s.214 had a major influence on the reformulation of the general duty of care of directors in the 2006 Act.

trading provisions thus constitute an exception to the principle of limited liability if that principle is formulated as being that the claims of the creditors are confined to the assets of the company. It is less obviously an exception to the more narrowly formulated proposition that the liability of the shareholders for the debts of the company is limited to the amount due as payment for their shares (or under a guarantee, where the company is so limited).

"Wrongful trading" is dealt with in s.214 of the Insolvency Act. It empowers the court to make a declaration similar to that under s.213 where the company has gone into *insolvent* liquidation.[33] The contribution declaration can be made only against a person who, at some time before the commencement of the winding up, was a director or shadow director of the company and so, at first sight, the issue of third party liability, discussed above in relation to fraudulent trading, does not arise. However, in fact the inclusion of "shadow directors" brings the issue of third party liability back into play, although in a less extended way, as we see below. The basis for imposing the obligation to contribute is that the director (or shadow director) knew, or ought to have concluded, at that time that there was no reasonable prospect that the company would avoid going into insolvent liquidation.[34] However, the declaration is not to be made if the court is satisfied that the person concerned thereupon took every step with a view to minimising the potential loss to the company's creditors as, on the assumption that he knew there was no reasonable prospect of avoiding insolvent liquidation, he ought to have taken.[35] In judging what facts the director ought to have known or ascertained, what conclusions the director should have drawn and what steps should have been taken, the director is to be assumed to be a reasonably diligent person having both the general knowledge, skill and experience to be expected of a person carrying out the director's functions in relation to the company[36] and the general knowledge, skill and experience that the director in fact has.[37]

There are thus two questions which have to be answered, both on an objective basis. Should the director have realised there was no reasonable prospect of the company avoiding insolvent liquidation and, once that stage has been reached, did the director take all the steps he or she ought to have taken to minimise the loss to the company's creditors, especially, no doubt, by seeking to have the company cease trading? Both these judgments will depend heavily on

---

[33] s.214(6). S.213 formally applies in any winding up (solvent or insolvent) but in practice it is needed in insolvent winding ups as well.

[34] s.214(2).

[35] s.214(3).

[36] This includes functions entrusted to the director even if the director has not carried them out: IA 1986, s.214(5). If the director has failed the objective test he or she cannot be excused by the court, under Companies Act 2006, s.1157, on the ground that the director has acted honestly and reasonably: *Produce Marketing Consortium Ltd, Re* [1989] 1 W.L.R. 745.

[37] Insolvency Act 1986, s.214(4).

the facts of particular cases: what sort of company was involved, what were the functions assigned to or discharged by the director in question, what outside advice was taken and what was its content?[38]

Shadow directors

Section 214 applies to shadow directors as well as to directors, i.e. a **9–8** person, other than a professional adviser, in accordance with whose directions or instructions the directors of a company are accustomed to act.[39] This considerably widens the class of persons against whom a declaration can be made, though not as widely as under section 213 which brings in any person who is party to the fraudulent trading (see above). A shadow director catches only the person who influences at least a certain category of board decisions on a continuing basis.[40] The two potential defendants of greatest interest are, once again, banks and parent companies. As far as the former are concerned, the courts have so far taken a cautious line, initially on the grounds that the definition of a shadow director requires that the board cede its management autonomy to the alleged shadow director and that the taking of steps by a bank to protect itself does not induce such a cession, if the company retains the power to decide whether to accept the restrictions put forward by the bank, even though the company may be thought to have no other practicable alternative.[41] In relation to parent companies, such a degree of cession of autonomy by the subsidiary may be more easily found, but much will still depend upon how exactly intra-group relationships are established. The degree of control exercised by parent companies may vary from detailed day-to-day control to virtual independence, with many variations in between. It would seem that the establishment of business guidelines within which the subsidiary has to operate would not make the parent inevitably a shadow director of the subsidiary.[42] However, subsequently, albeit in a case involving individuals rather than banks or

---

[38] The directors are likely to be treated with a particular lack of sympathy by the court if they have not abided by the statutory requirements for keeping themselves abreast of the company's financial position: *Produce Marketing Consortium Ltd (No.2), Re* [1989] B.C.L.C. 520 at 550, which requirements Knox J. referred to as the "minimum standards". This case, the leading one to date, and the underlying statutory provisions are analysed by Oditah [1990] L.M.C.L.O. 205 and Prentice (1990) 10 O.J.L.S. 265.

[39] IA 1986, s.251—the same definition as is used in the Companies Act which is discussed further at para.16–8.

[40] *Secretary of State for Trade and Industry v Becker* [2003] 1 B.C.L.C. 565; *Secretary of State for Trade and Industry v Deverell* [2000] 2 B.C.L.C. 133, CA.

[41] *Hydrodan (Corby) Ltd, Re* [1994] 2 B.C.L.C. 180; *PFTZM Ltd, Re* [1995] B.C.C. 280; *cf. A Company Ex p. Copp, Re* [1989] B.C.L.C. 13.

[42] In *Hydrodan (Corby) Ltd, Re* [1994] 2 B.C.L.C. 180 the judge was prepared to treat the indirect parent as a shadow director of a company, but that was because the directors of the company in question were corporate bodies and so must have received their instructions from elsewhere. Even here, the *directors* of the indirect parent were held on the facts not to be shadow directors.

parent companies and applying the rules on disqualification of directors[43] rather than the wrongful trading rules, the Court of Appeal rejected the proposition that it was necessary for the board to cast itself in a subservient role or surrender its discretion in order for the alleged shadow director to be found to be such.[44] Thus, whether the courts will take the opportunity afforded by the wrongful trading provisions to rationalise the legal position of groups of companies still remains to be seen, but it is suggested that in both cases (parent companies and banks) the courts are likely to maintain their initial caution.

The declaration

9–9   Section 215 contains certain procedural provisions common to both fraudulent and wrongful trading. Both sections 213 and 214 are to have effect notwithstanding that the person concerned may be criminally liable.[45] Further, the court may direct that the liability of any person against whom the declaration is made shall be a charge on any debt due from the company to that person or on any mortgage or charge in that person's favour on assets of the company, thus enabling the company to set off what it owes to the director against what the director is declared liable to contribute to the company, which may prove valuable in the bankruptcy of the director.[46] In addition, and this is a new provision from 1985, section 215[47] provides that the court may direct that the whole or any part of a debt, and interest thereon, owed by the company to a person against whom a declaration is made, shall be postponed to all other debts, and interest thereon, owed by the company. Thus, even if, for example, the court makes only a small contribution order, which the director is able to meet, the director may suffer a further financial loss by having his or her debts due from the company subordinated to those of the company's other debtors, a potentially important provision since the company *ex hypothesi* is insolvent.

The central question, however, is the amount of the contribution, a matter with which section 215 does not deal. Both sections 213 and 214 simply say that the amount of the contribution shall be "as the court thinks proper".[48] It is now established that contribution orders

---

[43] See Ch.10.

[44] *Secretary of State for Trade and Industry v Deverell* [2000] 2 B.C.L.C. 133, CA, where the precise definition of "shadow director" was determinative of the appeal. The court also decided that the central question was whether the board in fact did what the alleged shadow directors proposed and not whether those proposals were couched as directors or instruction or mere "advice"; nor was it necessary to prove the subjective expectations of the alleged shadow director and directors as to whether the advice would be followed.

[45] s.215(5).

[46] Including any assignees from that person: IA 1986, s.215(2) and (3).

[47] s.215(4).

[48] ss.213(2) and 214(1).

in relation to both wrongful and fraudulent trading are intended to be compensatory.[49] The outer boundaries of the compensation are thus set by the amount by which the company's assets have been depleted by the director's conduct. Within that, the court has a discretion to fix the amount to be paid as it thinks proper. Despite this method of calculating the upper limit on the contribution, it seems that the contribution from the directors is to the assets of the company generally and not for the particular benefit of those who became creditors of the company during the period of wrongful or fraudulent trading.

Impact of s.214

The wrongful trading provisions are capable of playing a central role **9–10** in re-orienting the duties of directors as the company's insolvency becomes overwhelmingly likely.[50] As insolvency looms, the shareholders' equity in the company will have disappeared and those with the prime interest in the company's economic performance become its creditors, secured and unsecured, who fear that, when the company is wound up, there will be insufficient assets to pay the whole of their claims. The directors, however, may not direct their minds to the interests of the creditors. In particular, they may try to keep the company going at a time when it is in the creditors' best interests for the company to engage in an orderly retreat from its activities. Although there may be only a small chance of the company trading out of its difficulties, the directors may prefer to take that chance because, if they are successful, they will save their jobs and will recover some value for their shares (if, as is often the case in small companies, the directors are also the main shareholders), whereas, if they fail, the doctrine of limited liability will protect them as shareholders from any further loss and the rules, discussed in Chapter 7, may well do the same for them as directors of the company. The threat of personal liability for the company's obligations, which section 214 creates, does something to provide a counter-incentive for the directors to give appropriate regard to the interests of the creditors in this situation.

Since the Insolvency Act creates a statutory duty to consider the interests of creditors, it is conceivable that the same result could be achieved through an appropriate element in the general statutory duties of directors, which are considered in Chapter 16. Indeed, the Company Law Review regarded section 214 as constituting so important a part of the overall framework of directors' duties that it

---

[49] See *Produce Marketing, Re* above, fn.38, for wrongful trading and *Morphitis v Bernasconi*, above, fn.23, for fraudulent trading, the latter reversing the previous understanding in relation to fraudulent trading where a penal element was thought appropriate in some cases.

[50] See Davies, "Directors' Creditor-Regarding Duties in Respect of Trading Decisions Taken in the Vicinity of Insolvency" (2006) 7 EBOR 301.

included it within its draft of the "General Principles by which Directors are Bound".[51] The Government removed it from its draft, but seemingly not on the grounds of its lack of importance, but because it thought the duty was better left embedded in the insolvency legislation, upon whose mechanisms its enforcement depends.[52] Thus, the specific creditor-regarding statutory duty created by the insolvency reforms of the middle 1980s continues to exist separately from the general statutory duties of directors enacted in 2006. However, there is another strand of authority to be considered. Prior to 2006 the common law contained certain inchoate developments by way of creditor-regarding duties, inchoate because much of the ground had already been occupied by section 214 and other elements of the insolvency legislation (such as the rules on conveyances at an undervalue or fraudulent preferences). In the formulation of the general statutory duties in the 2006 Act it was decided neither to incorporate these developments in the statutory re-statement nor to overrule them, and so they are left to be developed by the courts.[53]

9–11   Although section 214 can be justified in general terms along the lines discussed above, the section is in fact careful not to specify the precise action directors are required to take to meet its requirements. The section lays down a standard, not a rule, to which the director must conform in order to avoid liability, i.e. "to take every step with a view to minimising the potential loss to the company's creditors as (assuming him to have known that there was no reasonable prospect that the company would avoid going into insolvent liquidation) he ought to have taken."[54] The central question is, perhaps, whether in this situation the section requires the directors in all cases to cause the company to cease trading or even to put the company into liquidation. Certainly, one of the commonest forms of wrongful trading is to keep the company's business on foot even after the accounts or other management information have clearly revealed that the company is in a chronically loss-making position.[55] However, there are good reasons for not requiring this response across the board. In the interests of both creditors (higher recovery of their debts) and of shareholders and other stakeholders (such as employees) it may well be better if the company can be turned around or its business disposed of in some other way, which an immediate cessation of trading or a liquidation might jeopardise. The courts can adjust the section to the needs of the "rescue culture" either by postponing the point at which they say the directors ought to have realised the company had no reasonable

---

[51] Final Report I, Annex C, Principle 9.
[52] Modernising, paras 3.12–3.14.
[53] s.172(3) and see para.16–34. It is to be noted that these matters are left to the courts by way of a supplement to the directors' core duty of loyalty, whereas the duty created by s.214 of the 1986 Act is negligence-based.
[54] s.214(3).
[55] See *Produce Marketing, Re* (above, fn.38); *Brian D. Pierson (Contractors) Ltd, Re* [2001] 1 B.C.L.C. 275.

prospect of avoiding insolvent liquidation or by taking a broad view of the appropriate actions of the directors in such a case. An example of the first approach can be seen in *The Rod Gunner Organisation Ltd, Re*,[56] where the court refused to find "no reasonable prospect" for a period of six months after the company became unable to meet its debts as they fell due, on the grounds that the directors reasonably thought an outside investor was going to come in with substantial funding (though that analysis no longer held once it became clear that the investor would not live up to the directors' expectations of him). Similarly, in *Continental Assurance Co of London Plc (No.4), Re*,[57] where a substantial insurance company had suffered unexpected losses, the court refused to find "no reasonable prospect" during a period of some six months in which the directors commissioned a report as to the company's solvency and decided to continue trading on the basis of the report received, until it later became clear that the company was in fact insolvent. Park J. was very aware of the dangers of judging the directors' conduct on the basis of hindsight, and he remarked pithily in relation to the general issue that "ceasing to trade and liquidating too soon can be stigmatised as the cowards' way out."[58]

However, any analysis of the impact of section 214 also requires an assessment of the effectiveness of its enforcement. In contrast to litigation under the disqualification provisions discussed in the next chapter, where the public purse pays for the cases and there has been a high level of activity, litigation under section 214 seems to have been sparse and certainly there are few reported cases. As we have seen, this section places the initiation of litigation in the hands of the liquidator, who does not have access to any public funds to support any litigation he or she may propose to bring. Assuming the insolvent company does have some realisable assets, the liquidator may contemplate using those to fund the litigation in order to swell the amount available for distribution to the creditors. However, even if the liquidator can secure solicitors who will take the case on a conditional fee basis—not always possible—the litigation is likely to involve some costs (for example, for the insurance to meet the other side's costs if the litigation is unsuccessful), and so the liquidator is likely to be unwilling to risk the company's already inadequate assets

---

[56] [2004] 1 B.C.L.C 110.
[57] [2007] 2 B.C.L.C. 287. See also *Sherborne Associates Ltd, Re* [1995] B.C.C. 40, in which the judge held that the liquidator had to identify and then stick to a particular date by which it was argued the directors should have realised the company had no reasonable prospect of avoiding insolvent liquidation.
[58] At [281].

on litigation unless there is a very strong chance of success.[59] The liquidator might conceivably seek funding for the litigation from a secured creditor, but one thing that does seem to be established in this troubled area is that the proceeds of "officer-holder" claims go to benefit the unsecured creditors, not the holders of a floating charge,[60] and so secured creditors have no incentive to fund wrongful (or indeed fraudulent) trading claims.

The obvious step for the liquidator to take, faced with this uncertainty, is to assign some part of the fruits of the litigation to a third party, in exchange for that party's undertaking wholly to finance the litigation. A third party whose business consists of funding such claims is in a position to take a more adventurous view of which claims may be litigated, because it spreads its risks across a number of such claims, unlike the liquidator who has only "one shot" on behalf of the unsecured creditors of any particular company. However, the Court of Appeal has held that such arrangements are champertous and thus illegal and are not saved from illegality by the provisions of the Insolvency Act empowering liquidators to sell the assets of the company.[61] In this situation, it is perhaps not surprising that there is little reported litigation on section 214 and, one suspects, less recovery through section 214 for the benefit of creditors would occur were the liquidator able to make a credible threat of such litigation.

PHOENIX COMPANIES AND THE ABUSE OF COMPANY NAMES

9-12   The Company Law Review described the "Phoenix company" problem in the following terms:

> "The 'phoenix' problem results from the continuance of a failed company by those responsible for that failure, using the vehicle

---

[59] The issue that the costs of the s.214 litigation might not count as costs of the liquidation has been determined in favour of their so being by an amendment to r.4.218 of the Insolvency Rules 1986/1925, made in 2002; and s.176ZA of the Insolvency Act 1986, inserted by s.1282 of the Companies Act 2006, gives liquidation expenses priority over both preferential debts and assets secured by a floating charge (subject to exceptions to prevent abuse), thus overruling the result of *Buchler v Talbot* [2004] 2 A.C. 298, HL. Thus, the disincentive to liquidator litigation arising from the risk of the liquidator being left to bear the litigation costs has been considerably reduced, if not eliminated.

[60] *Yagerphone Ltd, Re* [1935] 1 Ch. 395.

[61] *Oasis Merchandising Services Ltd (in liq), Re* [1998] Ch. 170, CA. Contrast the position in relation to the assignment by a liquidator of corporate claims arising before the liquidation, for example, against a director for breach of duty, where the provisions of the Insolvency Act apply: *Whitehouse v Wilson* [2007] B.C.C. 595, CA. For the argument that *Buchler v Talbot* (previous note) impliedly overrules *Oasis Merchandising* see Armour and Walters, "Funding Liquidation: a Functional View" (2006) 122 LQR 295.

of a new company. The new company, often trading under the same or similar name, uses the old company's assets, often acquired at an undervalue, and exploits its goodwill and business opportunities. Meanwhile, the creditors of the old company are left to prove their debts against a valueless shell and the management conceal their previous failure from the public."[62]

However, it also went on to point out that the actions just described are not necessarily improper. They will be so where their purpose is to deprive the creditors of the first company of the value of that company's assets by transferring them at an undervalue to the second company; or where the purpose of the actions is to mislead the creditors of the second company by disguising the lack of success of the business when it was carried on by the first company. In other cases, where such purposes are lacking, however, the lack of success of the first company may be for reasons outside the control of its directors and, further, "the only way to continue an otherwise viable business and their own and their employees' ability to earn their livelihood may be for them to do so in a new vehicle using the assets and trading style of the original company".[63] Thus, the regulation of the Phoenix company is not an easy matter: too light a regulation may permit abuses to continue; too heavy a regulation may lead to the cessation of otherwise viable businesses.

As will be clear, the Phoenix problem needs to be tackled from two angles. One is the transfer of the assets of the first company at an undervalue to a new company controlled by the same persons. Within company law, the regulation of such an event is primarily the function of sections 190ff (substantial property transactions with directors), which we discuss in Chapter 16. Here the CLR recommended reforms but they were not taken up in the Companies Act 2006.[64] So, the law continues as before. The second angle is the re-use of the first company's name by the second company, where substantial reform, involving the imposition of personal liability for the debts of the second company, was effected by the Insolvency Act 1986. The Act does not in terms attempt to distinguish between acceptable and non-acceptable transfers, but proceeds rather by laying down a broad prohibition (to which both criminal and civil sanctions are attached) and then providing certain exceptions to it. Its primary objective

---

[62] Final I, para.15.55.

[63] Final I, para.15.56. The facts giving rise to the application to use a similar name in *Lightning Electrical Contractors Ltd, Re* [1996] 2 B.C.L.C. 302 might be thought to be an example of this: the administrative receivership of a medium-sized company was brought about by the failure of two large client companies to pay the money due from them; the successor company's use of the similar name was supported by the receivers since it enable them to maximise the value of the first company's assets.

[64] CLR Final I, paras 15.65–15.72. The problem with the existing law is perhaps demonstrated by the background facts of *Secretary of State for Trade and Industry v Becker* [2003] 1 B.C.L.C. 565.

seems to be to prevent the creditors of the new company from being misled about the history of the company with which they are dealing. Hence, it exposes those connected with the management of the transferee company to personal liability for that company's debts, if they do not comply with its provisions. Again, like the wrongful trading provisions, these provisions are not aimed primarily at the shareholders of the transferee company.

9–13   Section 216 of the Insolvency Act makes it an offence (of strict liability)[65] for anyone who was a director or shadow director of the original company at any time during the 12 months preceding its going into insolvent liquidation[66] to be in any way concerned (except with the leave of the court or in such circumstances as may be prescribed) during the next five years in the formation or management of a company, or business, with a name by which the original company was known or one so similar as to suggest an association with that company (known as a "prohibited name"). The name in question may be the company's name or a name under which the company carries or carried on business.[67] In addition to the criminal offence, a person acting in breach of section 216 is personally liable, jointly and severally with the new company and any other person so liable, for the debts and other liabilities of the new company incurred while he or she was concerned in its management in breach of section 216.[68] So is anyone involved in its management who acts or is willing to act on the instructions given by a person whom he knows, at that time, to be in breach of section 216.[69] It is to be noted that section 217 does create a personal liability for the debts of the company and not, as under the fraudulent and wrongful trading provisions, an obligation to contribute to the assets of the company. Nor need the new company (unlike the original company) be in liquidation or any other procedure for handling companies in financial difficulties (thought it often is) when the creditor brings the claim against those personally

---

[65] *R. v Cole* [1998] 2 B.C.L.C. 234, CA.

[66] On the shifts to which the directors can resort to put themselves outside this timeframe and thus avoid the offence and associated civil liability, see *Morphitis v Bernasconi*, above, fn.23.

[67] s.216(6)—an important extension, for otherwise the prohibition could be easily avoided by the transferee company's registered name being quite dissimilar from the transferor company's but by the transferee then carrying on business under a similar name. See *R (Griffin) v Richmond Magistrates Court* [2008] EWHC 84 (Admin). The CLR found that this was a practice used effectively to avoid the impact of the provisions, even though ostensibly caught by them.

[68] s.217. That the liability was restricted to debts incurred by the company in the period during which the person was in breach of s.216 (and did not extend to the whole debts incurred whilst that person was a director of the company) was accepted by Arden L.J. in *ESS Productions Ltd v Sully* [2005] 2 B.C.L.C. 547 at [75].

[69] Though such a person does not commit a criminal offence. For the purpose of both ss.216 and 217, "company" includes any company which may be wound up under Pt V of the Insolvency Act, i.e. virtually any company or association: s.220.

liable. For this reason the use of section 217 seems somewhat higher than the use of section 214.[70] Claims to enforce this personal liability are thus brought by individual creditors rather than the liquidator. Whether the similarity of names is made out is to be judged by the court in the circumstances in which the companies with the allegedly similar names operate and so is a highly fact-specific determination. It is clear that no person needs to have been misled by the prohibited act; it is enough to show that the names had a tendency to mislead.[71]

The policy behind the provisions is perhaps most clearly revealed in the three prescribed cases, set out in the Insolvency Rules,[72] where liability is not imposed. The first, and probably most important, of the cases is where a successor company purchases the whole of the insolvent company's business from an insolvency practitioner acting for the company and gives notice of the name the successor company intends to use to all the creditors of the insolvent company. The Court of Appeal held that this exception is available only where the directors of the insolvent company were not already directors of or involved in the management of the successor company at the time the notice was given, on the grounds that the warning function (see below) of the rules would be undermined.[73] This ruling caused difficulty in two situations. First, where the successor company (with common directors) bought the business from a company, which although insolvent, was not in liquidation, but, for example, in administration, it was common for the successor company to give the requisite notice in case, not in itself unlikely, the first company should go into liquidation after the administration. Secondly, and more limited, this first case, as originally drafted, would not apply if the directors were already directors of the successor company at the time notice was given, even if at that time the successor company was not known by a prohibited name (though it subsequently acquired one). In 2007 the Insolvency Rules were amended so as to extend the first case to these two situations.[74]

Overall, the first case might be thought to suggest that the aim of the section is partly the protection of the creditors of the insolvent company. This is because the insertion of the insolvency practitioner is intended to ensure that the sale by the insolvent company is not at an undervalue and the notice to the creditors ensures that they are not

---

[70] The CLR reported that the Official Receiver was aware of 134 cases of breaches of s.216 in 1999/2000, which led to 118 warning letters and 9 convictions, but these figures apparently relate only to criminal liability under the section: Completing, para.13.105.

[71] *Ricketts v Ad Valorem Factors Ltd* [2004] 1 B.C.L.C. 1, CA; *Revenue and Customs Commissioners v Walsh* [2005] 2 B.C.L.C. 455, though in the former case there was a disagreement among the judges as to whether the facts needed only to "suggest" an association or give rise to a probability that members of the public would associate the two companies.

[72] Insolvency Rules (SI 1986/1925), rr. 4.228 to 4.230 and the Insolvency (Scotland) Rules (SI 1986/1915), rr. 4.78 to 4.82.

[73] *First Independent Factors and Finance Ltd v Churchill* [2007] 1 B.C.L.C. 293, CA.

[74] The Insolvency (Amendment) Rules 2007 SI, 2007/1974.

misled into thinking that they may assert their claims against the new company.[75] However, if the requirements of this case are not met, the liability of the directors is not to the creditors of the transferor company but to those of the successor company, as indicated above. Nor is the successor company itself, which simply falls outside section 216, liable for the debts of the first company. The CLR considered, but rejected, a proposal that the liability of the successor company and those acting in breach of section 216 should be extended in this way, but rejected it.[76] So, by contrast, this aspect of section 216 suggests its aim is protection of the creditors of the successor company.

The third case[77] excepts from section 216 the situation where the "new" company has been known by the prohibited name for the whole of the twelve months ending with the liquidation of the first company.[78] The purpose of this provision is, in particular, to permit the transfer of businesses within an existing group of companies. The risk of the creditors being misled, although it exists, is not in this case the result of action taken after the liquidation of the original company but of decisions taken in advance of the liquidation by a period of at least one year—a period thought to be enough to prevent opportunistic use of this exception.[79] This exception has been given a broad interpretation by the courts: it is not necessary to show that the company was known during the twelve-month period by the prohibited name it had at the time the debt arose (provided it was known during that period by one or more prohibited names) or that it used the prohibited name in relation to the whole of its business.[80]

COMPANY GROUPS

Limited liability

9–14   The final area for consideration of the principle of lifting the veil by statute so as to qualify the doctrine of limited liability is within groups of companies. Even relatively modest businesses often operate through groups of companies and large businesses invariably do so,

---

[75] See *Penrose v Secretary of State for Trade and Industry* [1996] 1 W.L.R. 482.

[76] Final Report I, para.15.62.

[77] The second case (r.4.229) is ancillary to the provision permitting a person to act in breach of s.216 if the court gives permission. The second case permits a director, who applies for leave within seven days of the first company going into liquidation, to continue to act in breach of s.216 for a period of six weeks or until the court disposes of the application for leave, whichever is the shorter.

[78] Rule 4.230—and has not been a dormant company. Otherwise, a shelf company could be formed purely for the purpose of triggering this exception.

[79] Though *cf. Morphitis v Bernasconi* (above, fn.23). The company names rules will necessarily have been met: see para.4–7.

[80] *ESS Production Ltd v Sully* [2005] 2 B.C.L.C. 547, CA.

and so the issue is one of great practical importance. We saw, as well, at the beginning of this chapter that only the rationale of asset partitioning provides a pervasive reason for the extension of limited liability to intra-group relations, since, at least within wholly-owned groups,[81] the raising of equity capital and the trading of shares on public exchanges could effectively occur with limited liability confined to the shareholders of the parent company. In fact, however, British law does apply the doctrine of limited liability to intra-group shareholders as much as to extra-group shareholders and, as we saw in the previous chapter,[82] the courts will not pierce the veil within a group of companies simply on the grounds that the group constitutes a single economic entity. However, from time to time there have been proposals for statutory provisions to pierce the veil within groups, both at Community level and domestically, but, so far, without result.

How might creditors of a subsidiary be disadvantaged as a result of the company becoming, or being, a member of a group of companies? In general the answer is because, at least in a group with an integrated business strategy,[83] business decisions may be taken on the basis of maximising the wealth of the group as a whole, or of the parent company, rather than of the particular subsidiary of which the claimant is a creditor. This phenomenon may show itself in a variety of ways. Three examples may be given. Most obviously, the parent may instruct the board of the subsidiary to do something which is not in the best interests of the subsidiary, because that decision will maximise the benefits of the group. Again, the parent may allocate new business opportunities to the subsidiary which can maximise the benefit for the group, even though another subsidiary could develop the opportunity effectively, if less profitably. Finally, if a subsidiary falls into insolvency, the parent may refrain from rescuing it, even though the group has sufficient funds to do so.

Three points can be made about these examples. First, these actions are likely to have an adverse effect upon any outside shareholders of the subsidiary (i.e. where it is not wholly owned by the parent or some other group company) as well as upon the subsidiary's creditors. Indeed, except in the third example, the adverse effect is likely to be felt first by the outside shareholders. Thus, it follows that, as in single companies which are going concerns, the protection of creditors often follows as an indirect consequence of measures taken to protect the interests of shareholders. Protection of minority shareholders, both within and without groups, is discussed

---

[81] Where a subsidiary has external shareholders and raises capital independently, then the other rationales for limited liability will apply to it as much as to the parent company.

[82] At para.8–8.

[83] This does not include all groups of companies: in conglomerate groups (i.e. groups of diversified businesses) the advantages of common ownership may well reside in something other than the imposition of a single business strategy (for example, access to sources of finance or managerial expertise).

in a later chapter, since it is typically based on techniques other than the qualification of limited liability.[84] Secondly, it is far from clear that the actions described above in the second and third examples do, or ought to, involve any illegality on the part of those involved. Unless the business opportunity had been generated by a particular subsidiary,[85] it is not clear that it has, or ought to have, any claim to take all the opportunities arising within the group which it could effectively develop. Nor is it obvious that the descent into insolvency of a properly capitalised subsidiary which has fully disclosed the risks of its business should be allowed to threaten the economic viability of the remainder of the group's operations. In short, the overruling of limited liability within corporate groups is likely to require sophisticated and nuanced regulation if it is to make sense in policy terms.

9–15   Thirdly, and this is the heart of the policy discussion, it is debated whether, or to what extent, such sophisticated regulation requires the development of distinct rules for corporate groups or whether it is better based on the extension of existing creditor-protection rules to deal with this particular situation of group creditors. We have already noted in this chapter an important example of this latter technique, namely, the application of the rules against fraudulent trading to all those party to it and of wrongful trading to shadow directors, both of which extensions may bring in parent companies, at least in some circumstances.[86] To date, British law has operated wholly in this way, i.e. it does not deny that serious issues for creditors can arise within groups but aims to cope with them through the general mechanisms of creditor protection, including, of course, self-help. A contrasting approach is to be found in German law dealing with public companies which contains a separate section dealing with the issue of creditor and minority shareholder protection within groups,[87] though even these provisions do not purport to deal comprehensively with group issues but focus predominantly on the first example of disadvantageous behaviour given above. Even within Germany, however, these provisions are not thought to work effectively.[88]

---

[84] See Ch.20, below.

[85] On "corporate opportunities" see para.16–64.

[86] For an example of the use of the strategy of disqualifying directors (discussed in the following chapter) see *Genosyis Technology Management Ltd, Re* [2007] 1 B.C.L.C. 208—directors disqualified for causing debts due to subsidiary to be paid to parent company.

[87] *Aktiengesetz*, Book Three.

[88] For a discussion of German "*Konzernrecht*", see V. Emmerich and J. Sonnenschein, *Konzernrecht* (1997, 6th ed.); Klaus J. Hopt, *Legal Elements and Policy Decisions in Regulating Groups of Companies*, in Clive M. Schmitthoff and Frank Wooldridge (eds), *Groups of Companies* (Sweet & Maxwell, 1991), p.81; Herbert Wiedemann, "The German Experience with the Law of Affiliated Enterprise", in Klaus J. Hopt (ed.), *Groups of Companies in European Laws, Legal and Economic Analyses on Multinational Enterprises*, Vol. II (Walter de Gruyter, 1982) 21. For a comparative perspective, see Peter Hommelhoff, Klaus J. Hopt and Markus Lutter (eds.), *Konzernrecht und Kapitalmarktrecht* (Verlag C.H. Beck, 2001) and V. Priskich, "Corporate Groups: Current Proposals for Reform in Australia and the United Kingdom and a Comparative Analysis of the Regime in Germany" in (2002) 4 I.C.C.L.J. 37.

The German statutory regulation of public companies provides two models of regulation, one of which is contractual and thus optional. Under the optional provision, in exchange for undertaking an obligation to indemnify the subsidiary for its annual net losses incurred during the term of the agreement, the parent acquires the power to instruct the subsidiary to act in the interests of the group rather than its own best interests. This option has been taken up only by a small number of companies, presumably because the incentive to do so (i.e. protection from the potential liabilities for ignoring the separate legal personality of the subsidiary) is too small. The Company Law Review proposed something similar: in exchange for a guarantee of the liabilities of its subsidiary, the parent should be freed from the obligation to publish separate accounts relating to that subsidiary.[89] However, the proposal was not proceeded with, partly because it was again thought that the incentive provided was not large enough to induce a substantial take-up of the option and, partly and conversely, because there were fears about loss of information about subsidiary companies if the option were taken up, especially where the subsidiary was the main British operating company of a foreign parent.[90]

The second strand of the German statutory regime is mandatory and applies to de facto groups. The core provision[91] is that the parent is liable for the damage to the subsidiary if the parent causes the subsidiary to enter into a disadvantageous transaction, unless, within the fiscal year, the parent has compensated the subsidiary for the loss or agreed to do so. The provision has proved less effective than expected seemingly because of difficulties of proof, both in relation to identifying particular disadvantageous transactions, where there is a continuous course of dealing between parent and subsidiary, and to identifying the loss caused by that transaction. This weakness of the de facto group regime undermines also the contractual group rules, since it is escape from the former which could provide a major incentive for companies to enter into the optional regime.[92]

Nevertheless, the German model, which has been followed within the European Community only by Portugal, was used by the European Commission in its preliminary consideration of a draft Ninth Company Law Directive on groups in the early 1980s. However, so

---

[89] Completing, Ch.10. On parent and subsidiary company reporting requirements see immediately below.

[90] Final Report I, paras 8.23–8.28.

[91] Akt, para.317.

[92] A possible partial solution, which the German courts have used for private companies (GmbH), would be to use the contractual group model under which exercise of influence to disadvantageous ends would make the parent liable for all the subsidiary's losses, whether they could be related to a particular disadvantageous contract or not.

remote from the traditions of the other Member States was this idea that the draft was never adopted by the full Commission. The Report of the High Level Group of Company Law Experts,[93] whilst not proposing a revival of the Ninth Directive, did propose that Member States should be required to introduce into their company laws the principle that the management of the parent company should be entitled to pursue the interests of the group, even if a particular transaction was to the disadvantage of a particular subsidiary, provided that, over time, there was a fair balance of burdens and advantages for the subsidiary. The modalities of the incorporation of this principle into national law would be for each Member State to decide. The Report thus put as much stress on the need for group management to be able to run a coherent group policy as it did on the protection of creditors and minority shareholders in the subsidiary. This principle has received only limited acceptance in English law, where the separate legal personality of each group company has meant that the starting point is that the directors of a particular group company are not entitled to sacrifice the interest of that company. This starting point is qualified only to the extent that, if the directors of the group company have acted in the best interests of that company, the fact that they did so inadvertently, because they actually considered only the interests of the group as a whole, will not put them in breach of duty.[94] The High Level Group also proposed greater disclosure of information about the group, both of a financial and, more important, of a non-financial kind, relating, in particular, to control relations within the group and the types of dependency created. Although the latter proposal has achieved some legislative result in the Takeovers Directive,[95] the proposals for action beyond disclosure have not been taken up at Community level and seem unlikely to be so.

Finally, in some jurisdictions, part of the solution to the group problem, especially in the case of the third example given above, is to be found in insolvency law, where the court may be given a discretion in certain circumstances to bring a solvent group company into the insolvency of another group company.[96] The High Level Group also supported this principle.

---

[93] Brussels, November 4, 2002, Ch. V. See above, para.6–9. For more detailed consideration of the options, see Forum Europaeum, *Corporate Group Law for Europe* (Corporate Governance Forum, 2000).

[94] *Charterbridge Corporation Ltd v Lloyds Bank Ltd* [1970] Ch. 62, a decision on an ultra vires issue, but a decision, it is thought, that would also be followed in a case of breach of directors' duties. See further para.16–30.

[95] See para.28–27.

[96] On New Zealand law and Australian proposals, see R. P. Austin, "Corporate Groups" in R. Grantham and C. Rickett (eds), *Corporate Personality in the Twentieth Century* (Hart Publishing, 1998), especially at pp.84–87; on French law, M. Cozian, A. Viandier and Fl. Deboissy, *Droit des Sociétés* (Litec, 18th ed., 2005), pp.602–604.

Ignoring separate legal personality

If it is rare for British law to ignore the principle of limited liability **9–16** within groups, it would be completely wrong to conclude that the law is not prepared to override the separate legal personality of companies within groups where this does not involve any infringement of the principle of limited liability. There are many instances in which domestic company law takes account of group structures, though these instances tend to be rather ad hoc, rather than the result of the application of a single general principle.

Perhaps the best known example is in the area of financial reporting. It has long been recognised that, in relation to financial disclosure, the group phenomenon cannot be ignored if a "true and fair" view of the overall position of the company is to be presented, and that accordingly when one company (the parent or holding company) controls others (the subsidiary and sub-subsidiary companies) the parent company must present group financial statements as well as its own individual statements, thus avoiding the misleading impression which the latter alone might give.[97] The subordinate companies in the group must also produce individual accounts. This is discussed more fully in Chapter 21.

The Companies Acts have also long used the concept of the parent-subsidiary relationship in areas other than that of financial disclosure. Clearly if one is to ban or control certain types of transaction between a company and its directors it is essential to ensure that this cannot be easily evaded by effecting the transactions with or through another company in the group. Hence many of the sections in Chapter 4 of Part 10 (Transactions with Directors Requiring Approval of Members) so provide.[98] Similarly, the prohibition on financial assistance for the purchase of a company's own shares extends to financial assistance by any of its subsidiaries.[99]

In non-legal and much legal discourse, the expressions "parent" and "holding" company are used interchangeably. Until the Companies Act 1989, UK company legislation used the latter, but the EC Company Law Directives the former, which seems preferable since "holding" suggests that the sole function of the parent is to control the operations of subsidiaries whereas it too may well be undertaking one or more of the trading activities of the group. Now, in the Act, they have slightly different meanings, the definition of a "parent" company being broader than that of a "holding" company; and the term "parent" company being used in relation to company accounts

---

[97] To take a simplified example: if a parent company A has two wholly-owned subsidiaries, B and C, and in a financial year B makes a loss of £100,000 while C makes a distributable profit of £10,000 all of which it pays to A by way of dividend, the individual accounts of A (assuming it has broken even) will show a profit of £10,000 whereas in fact the group has made a loss of £90,000.

[98] See para.16–51.

[99] See para.13–26.

and that of "holding" company elsewhere where the Act recognises group situations.[100] This came about because, when the Seventh Directive compelled a change in the definition for the purposes of accounts, it was represented that to apply the whole of the extended definition to other cases would introduce an unreasonable degree of uncertainty.[101] Hence it was decided to adopt a narrower definition in the non-accounts area, albeit one based on the Community definition. While it is a pity that it was thought necessary to have different definitions for what is essentially the same concept, there is no doubt that both are considerable improvements on the previous definition[102] since they recognise that what counts is "control" and not majority shareholding which, because of non-voting shares or weighted voting, will not necessarily afford control.

Under section 1159 the definition of "holding" and "subsidiary" company now is:

> "A company is a 'subsidiary' of another company, its 'holding company', if that other company
>
> (a) holds a majority of the voting rights in it, or
> (b) is a member of it and has the right to appoint or remove a majority of its board of directors, or
> (c) is a member of it and controls alone, pursuant to an agreement with other members, a majority of the voting rights in it.
>
> or if it is a subsidiary of a company which is itself a subsidiary of that other company."

CONCLUSION

9–17 Since the Cork Committee[103] reported in 1982, statutory willingness to lift the corporate veil and reduce the importance of the principle of limited liability has achieved a new lease of life, especially in relation to small companies where the shareholders with limited liability typically also provide the directors of the company. Both the wrongful trading provisions and those dealing with the re-use of corporate names were a response to primarily small company pro-

---

[100] "Parent company" is defined in s.1162 and Sch.7 (see para.21–8) and "holding company" in s.1159.
[101] For purposes of consolidation a measure of uncertainty is acceptable because, when in doubt, one can play safe and consolidate.
[102] 1948 Act, s.154. Under the former s.154(10)(a)(ii) holding more than half in nominal value of a company's equity share capital (voting or non-voting) made it a subsidiary.
[103] See above fn.17.

blems. Together with the provisions on the disqualification of directors,[104] also aimed primarily at small companies, they may be said to constitute the legislature's preferred alternative to compulsory minimum capital requirements[105] for dealing with the abuses of limited liability in small companies. These provisions, however, are not formally limited to small companies; and the wrongful trading provisions, through the use of the idea of shadow directors, are capable also of catching abuses outside small companies, in particular within corporate groups. However, the issue of limited liability within groups has not received the same degree of legislative attention. Like the judges, whose decisions on lifting the veil we examined in the previous chapter, the legislature has touched on limited liability within groups only gingerly, whilst showing itself perfectly able to recognise group structures in other areas of company law. In the end, the Company Law Review failed to break out of that mould, which thus remains that in which the current law is cast.

[104] Discussed in the next chapter.
[105] See Ch.11.

CHAPTER 10

DISQUALIFICATION OF DIRECTORS

In the previous chapter we saw that the most important modern **10–1** statutory exception to the principle of limited liability is that based on the notion of "wrongful trading" by directors in the period preceding the insolvency of their company. The Cork Committee, which recommended this reform in 1982, went further, however, and argued that "proper safeguards for the public" required that wrongful trading be supplemented by provisions which ensure that "those whose conduct has shown them to be unfitted to manage the affairs of a company with limited liability shall, for a specified period, be prohibited from doing so".[1] In particular, they thought the law should "protect the non-executive directors in large enterprises, while severely penalising those who abuse the privilege of limited liability by operating behind one-man, insufficiently capitalised companies".[2] Their proposed remedy was an extension and reform of provisions already to be found to some extent in the law which prohibited certain persons in certain situations from being involved in the management of companies. In particular, they proposed a radical reform of the rules relating to the disqualification of directors of insolvent

---

[1] Report of the Review Committee on Insolvency Law and Practice, Cmnd. 8558 (1982), para.1808.
[2] Cmnd. 8558, para.1815.

companies on grounds of "unfitness". Their proposals received statutory embodiment, though not quite in the form intended by the Committee, in the insolvency law reforms of the mid-1980s and, soon after, the disqualification provisions were consolidated in the Company Directors Disqualification Act 1986. This is still the principal legislation (and references in this chapter to sections will be to that Act, unless otherwise indicated), but there was further significant reform in the Insolvency Act 2000, which inserted new provisions into the 1986 Act. In particular, the reforms of 2000 introduced the notion of an out-of-court "disqualification undertaking" to supplement the "disqualification order", which only a court can make.[3]

In addition to the general ground of unfitness, revealed in the company's insolvency,[4] there are a number of more specific cases in which disqualification can be imposed. In these cases, however, disqualification by court order alone is provided for.[5] These more specific cases seem also to have the protection of creditors as their primary goal, though disqualification based on failure to make the required returns to the Registrar of companies might also operate so as to protect minority shareholder or investor interests. The specific instances can best be analysed as falling within the following categories:

(a) commission of a serious offence, usually involving dishonesty, in connection with the management of a company;

(b) being found liable to make a contribution to the assets of the company on grounds of fraudulent or wrongful trading;

(c) failure to comply with the provisions of the companies or insolvency legislation relating to the filing of documents with the Registrar.

Finally, there is a long-standing provision in the companies legislation which disqualifies an undischarged bankrupt from being involved in the management of companies, to which were added in 2002 the notion of "bankruptcy restriction orders". We shall examine first the provisions relating to disqualification on grounds of unfitness, before proceeding to the specific instances of the disqualification power.

---

[3] ss.1 and 1A. See further below, para.10–2.
[4] Or where the Department of Business, Enterprise and Regulatory Reform (BERR) has received information from an investigation: see para.10–4, below.
[5] s.1A(1).

DISQUALIFICATION ORDERS AND UNDERTAKINGS

The power to disqualify has generated a high level of activity. In the **10–2** years 1997–1998 to 2000–2001 between 1,250 and 1,500 directors were disqualified each year by court order and in 2001–2002, when disqualification undertakings were introduced, the total of orders and undertakings was nearly 2,000.[6] After rising for a further year, the total of orders and undertakings has slowly declined so that in 2005–2006 the total was 1,200, of which 900 were undertakings and 135 were disqualification orders on grounds other than unfitness.[7] Thus, the Act has been the basis of a considerable activity on the part of the relevant government department. The rationale behind the introduction of undertakings in unfitness cases by the Insolvency Act 2000 was the fact that, under the previous legislation, even clear in cases, where the Insolvency Service and the director could reach agreement on how the provisions of the Act should apply in the particular case, it was necessary to go to court to obtain an order and it was doubtful whether the court could simply accept, and rubber-stamp, the agreement between them.[8] The amended Act makes it clear that the Secretary of State and the director can reach an agreement out-of-court on a disqualification undertaking, which will restrict the director's future activities in the same way as a disqualification order, but without the need for a court hearing.[9] The director can always trigger a court hearing by refusing to agree terms for an undertaking, though he or she will normally be liable for the Secretary of State's costs, as well as his or her own costs, if the court makes an order. Alternatively, a director who has accepted an undertaking may subsequently apply to the court, apparently at any time, for the period of the disqualification to be reduced or for the undertaking to cease to apply.[10] This is equivalent to the power which the court has under the Insolvency Rules to review, vary or rescind disqualification orders.[11] Although the power is broadly framed, the courts are likely to find it appropriate to alter the undertaking for the future (the court has no power to declare that it ought not to have been made) only in limited circumstances. In particular, it would be likely to undermine

---

[6] DTI, *Companies in 2001–2002* (2002), Table D1.
[7] DTI, *Companies in 2005–2006* (2006), Table D1.
[8] Though the courts had developed a summary procedure for dealing with non-contested cases: *Carecraft Construction Co Ltd, Re* [1994] 1 W.L.R. 172 and Practice Direction [1999] B.C.C. 717. The summary procedure has effectively been overtaken by the out-of-court undertaking, though in principle it is still available.
[9] ss.1 and 1A.
[10] s.8A. This is separate from the director's power to apply to the court for leave to act notwithstanding the undertaking, a power which applies also to orders: s.17. See below, para.10–3.
[11] Insolvency Rule r.7.47(1).

the undertaking procedure if directors, having entered into an undertaking, were able freely to invoke the section.[12]

Scope of disqualification orders

10–3 The scope of the disqualification order or undertaking is obviously a crucial matter in the design of the legislation. It would be too limited for such an order to prohibit a person from acting only as director of a company, since there are many ways of controlling a company's management without being a director of the company. A way forward might have been to extend the prohibition to being a shadow director of a company but the Act in fact avoids the difficulties of that definition and takes an even broader approach. The prohibition imposed by a disqualification order or undertaking extends to "in any way, directly or indirectly, be[ing] concerned or tak[ing] part in the promotion, formation or management of a company".[13] The courts have taken a broad approach to what being concerned or taking part in the management of a company may embrace.[14] In addition, the disqualified person is prohibited from acting as an insolvency practitioner,[15] without which he or she might have a role in relation to insolvent companies. Finally, the disqualified person is denied access to limited liability through some corporate form other than a registered company, such as a limited liability partnership, a building society or an incorporated friendly society.[16]

Adherence to a disqualification order, once made, is secured by criminal penalties[17] and, probably much more important, by personal liability for the debts and other liabilities of the company incurred during the time the disqualified person was involved in its manage-

---

[12] *INS Realisations Ltd, Re* [2006] 2 B.C.L.C. 239—director not normally able to use the section to challenge the facts on which the undertaking was premised, but in the particular circumstances of that case the power was used to cause the undertaking to cease to operate.

[13] ss.1(1) and 1A(1). If a court makes a disqualification order, it must cover all the activities set out in the statute, but the court could give the disqualified director limited leave to act despite the order. See *Gower Enterprises (No.2), Re* [1995] 2 B.C.L.C. 201 and *Seagull Manufacturing Co Ltd, Re* [1996] 1 B.C.L.C. 51 and below.

[14] Management of a company is thought to require involvement in the general management and policy of the company and not just the holding of any post labelled managerial, though in small companies it may not be possible to distinguish between policy-setting and day-to-day management: *R. v Campbell* (1983) 78 Cr.App.R. 95, CA (acting as a management consultant); *Drew v HM Advocate* [1996] S.L.T. 1062; *Market Wizard Systems (UK) Ltd, Re* [1998] 2 B.C.L.C. 282.

[15] ss.1(1)(b) and 1A(1)(b).

[16] ss.22A and 22B and the Limited Liability Partnership Regulations 2001 (SI 2001/1090), reg.4(2). Indeed, the whole Act applies to these bodies (and to NHS foundation trusts (s.22C)), so that a disqualification order may be imposed or an undertaking agreed on the basis of activities in relation to these bodies alone. The disqualified director is also prohibited from acting as the trustee of a charitable trust, whether that trust is incorporated or not: Charities Act 1993, s.72(1)(f), though the charity commissioners may give leave to act.

[17] ss.13 and 14. The equivalent offence in relation to acting when bankrupt has been held to be one of strict liability (*R. v Brockley* (1993) 92 Cr.App.R. 385, CA) and the arguments used to support that conclusion would seem equally applicable to the offence of acting when disqualified.

ment in breach of the order.[18] This demonstrates that it is misuse of the facility of limited liability which lies at the basis of disqualification orders. Personal liability is also extended to any other person involved in the management of the company who knowingly acts on the instructions of a disqualified person.[19] Conversely, entrusting the management of a company to someone known to be disqualified might well be a basis for disqualifying the entrusting director on grounds of unfitness.[20]

The rigour of the prohibition imposed by the Act is mitigated by two factors. First, as we shall see below, the disqualification is for a limited period of time, and the maximum period of time (15 years) will be imposed only in the most serious cases. Secondly, the prohibition (except that part of it which relates to acting as an insolvency practitioner) may be relaxed by the court, which may give leave to the disqualified person to act in a particular case. In the case of disqualification on grounds of unfitness under section 6, it is the practice to consider such applications at the same time as the disqualification order is made (in those, now minority, cases in which the disqualification is imposed by the court).[21] The leave granted, which obviously must not be so wide as to undermine the purposes of the Act,[22] often relates to other companies of which the applicant is already a director, which are trading successfully and whose future success is thought to be dependent on the continued involvement of the applicant. Often the leave is made conditional upon other steps being taken to protect the public, such as the appointment of an independent director to the board.[23] Overall, what the court has to do is to balance the need to protect the public, especially creditors, as demonstrated by the conduct which has rendered the director unfit, with the interest of the director or other persons in the director having access to trading with limited liability.[24]

---

[18] s.15(1)(a).

[19] s.15(1)(b). The various people made personally liable by s.15 are jointly and severally liable with each other and with the company and any others who are for any reason personally liable: s.15(2).

[20] See *Moorgate Metals Ltd, Re* [1995] 1 B.C.L.C. 503.

[21] *Secretary of State for Trade and Industry v Worth* [1994] 2 B.C.L.C. 113, CA, which indeed puts the applicant under some costs pressure to apply then, if his application is based on circumstances existing at the time of the order. If disqualification is by undertaking, a separate application for leave will, of course, be necessary.

[22] *Secretary of State for Trade and Industry v Barnett* [1998] 2 B.C.L.C. 64; *Britannia Homes Centres Ltd, Re* [2001] 2 B.C.L.C. 63: leave refused where director with history of insolvencies wished to incorporate a new and wholly-owned company to carry on trading in same line of business.

[23] *Cargo Agency Ltd, Re* [1992] B.C.L.C. 686; *Chartmore Ltd, Re* [1990] B.C.L.C. 673. The practice has been followed in Scotland despite doubts whether the power to give leave confers upon the courts the power to specify conditions: *Secretary of State for Trade and Industry v Palfreman* [1995] 2 B.C.L.C. 301. If the conditions attached by the court are not strictly complied with, the director is in breach of the disqualification order and so exposed to personal liability: *Brian Sheridan Cars Ltd, Re* [1996] 1 B.C.L.C. 327.

[24] *Barings Plc (No.3), Re* [2000] 1 W.L.R. 634; *Tech Textiles, Re* [1998] 1 B.C.L.C. 259.

DISQUALIFICATION ON GROUNDS OF UNFITNESS

10–4   There are in fact two provisions of the 1986 Act relating to disqualification on unfitness grounds, the initiative in both cases lying with the Secretary of State. Under sections 6 and 7 the Secretary of State (or the Official Receiver in the case of a company being wound up by the court in England and Wales) may apply to the court to have a director[25] or shadow director[26] of an insolvent[27] company disqualified where the Secretary of State thinks it is expedient in the public interest to do so.[28] Alternatively, the Secretary of State may accept a disqualification undertaking from the director in such circumstances.[29] Under section 8 the Secretary of State may apply to the court or accept an undertaking in relation to a similar range of people, whether the company is insolvent or not,[30] if he or she decides it is in the public interest to apply, after consideration of the results of an official investigation of the company.[31] The former sections (but not section 8) have the unique feature that, if unfitness is established to the satisfaction of the court, disqualification is mandatory (for a period of two years, though the court may impose a longer period).[32] Thus, although in the wake of the Cork Report business opposition fought off the idea of automatic disqualification in the case of directors of insolvent companies, the Government managed to avoid leaving the issue entirely to the discretion of the courts.[33]

It should be noted that section 6 does not permit the court to disqualify *any* person whose conduct seems to the court to make him or her unfit to be a director. Only directors (including de facto and shadow directors) may be disqualified. On the other hand, once the company has become insolvent, the director is liable to have the whole of his or her conduct as director of that company scrutinised for evidence of unfitness. Unlike the wrongful trading provisions

---

[25] Including a de facto director (s.22(4)), i.e. a person who acts as a director even though he has not been validly appointed as a director or even though there has been no attempt at all to appoint him as director: *Kaytech International Plc, Re* [1999] 2 B.C.L.C. 351, CA.

[26] s.22(5). On the meaning of "shadow director" see the previous chapter at para.9–8 and Ch.16 at para.16–8.

[27] A company is insolvent if it goes into liquidation with insufficient assets to meet its liabilities, if an administration order has been made in relation to the company or if an administrative receiver is appointed: s.6(2). Thus, the disqualification provisions are not confined to companies which go into insolvent liquidation. The court is specifically given power to look at the director's conduct post-insolvency.

[28] s.7(1).

[29] s.7(2A).

[30] Which perhaps explains why the Official Receiver is given no role under s.8.

[31] The investigation may be one initiated under the Companies Act (see Ch.18) or under the Financial Services and Markets Act 2000 (some aspects of which are discussed in Chs. 25 and 26). In 2005–6 only 26 undertakings were accepted (and no orders were made) on this ground: above, fn.7.

[32] s.6(1) and (4)—the maximum period is 15 years.

[33] See Hicks, "Disqualification of Directors—Forty Years On" [1988] J.B.L. 27 at 35 and 38–40.

considered in the previous chapter, that scrutiny is not confined to the director's conduct in the period immediately before the insolvency. Moreover, section 6(1) includes within the scrutiny the director's conduct of the insolvent company "taken together with his conduct as a director of any other company or companies". These other companies may not have fallen into insolvency and there need be no particular business or other link between the "lead" company and the other companies in order for the director's conduct in relation to them to be taken into account.[34] In short, once a company falls into insolvency, the disqualification provisions are capable of reaching out into the whole of the activities of the directors of that company in their capacity as directors.[35]

Before embarking upon an analysis of section 6 and the case law it has generated, it is necessary to address an underlying question about the purpose of the section. That it is there to protect the public against being involved, whether as shareholders or, more likely, as creditors, with companies run by people who have shown themselves to be unfit to be directors is clear.[36] What is less clear is how that protection is to be effected. The issue has arisen in relation to the calculation of the period of disqualification. Should that be assessed on a forward- or a backward-looking basis? In other words, is the question which the court has to answer: for what period in the future will the director be a danger to the public? Or is the question: how far below the conduct expected of a director did the respondent fall in the activities which have been examined by the court? After some lack of clarity in the cases the Court of Appeal has opted for the latter approach. In other words, the public is to be protected by the imposition of sanctions on directors for falling below the standard required by section 6, the sanction being gradated according to the seriousness of the director's lapse.[37] As we have noted, the minimum and maximum periods of disqualification under section 6 are set at two and 15 years respectively. In *Sevenoaks Stationers (Retail) Ltd, Re*[38] the Court of Appeal divided that period into three brackets,

---

[34] *Secretary of State for Trade and Industry v Ivens* [1997] 2 B.C.L.C. 334, CA. However, it would seem that a director cannot be disqualified on the basis of his conduct of the non-lead companies alone.

[35] And, indeed, post-insolvency activies: s.6(2).

[36] *Sevenoaks Stationers (Retail) Ltd, Re* [1991] Ch. 164 at 176, CA.

[37] *Grayan Building Services Ltd, Re* [1995] Ch. 241, CA. In this case the Court of Appeal held that the respondent could not reduce the period of disqualification by showing that, despite past shortcomings, he was unlikely to offend again. Such evidence, however, could be taken into account on an application for leave. See also *Westmid Packing Services Ltd, Re* [1998] 2 All E.R. 124 at 131–132, CA.

[38] [1991] Ch. 164 at 176, CA.

reflecting different levels of seriousness, though it cannot be said that it drew the dividing line between them very clearly.[39]

The role of the Insolvency Service

10–5 When recommending what is now section 6, the Cork Committee[40] said that its aim was to "replace by a far more rigorous system the present ineffective provisions ...". The effectiveness in practice of section 6 can be said to depend upon two matters. The first is the assiduity of the Insolvency Service, an executive agency of the DTI, in bringing applications for disqualification orders before the court; and the second is the courts' approach to section 6, especially their interpretation of the central concept of unfitness.

In order to maximise the chances of applications being made, the Cork Committee[41] recommended that applications by liquidators or, with leave, other creditors should be permitted, and so confining applications to the Secretary of State and the Official Receiver was regarded at the time of the passage of the Insolvency Act 1986 as a retrograde step. There are two reasons why the Insolvency Service might not prove effective. The first is lack of information about directors' conduct, especially when the company is being wound up voluntarily, so that the Official Receiver is not involved.[42] This is addressed by the imposition of a requirement on liquidators, administrators and receivers to report to the Secretary of State on the conduct of directors and shadow directors of companies for whose affairs they are responsible, if they think such conduct falls within section 6,[43] though the quality of the information provided is not always high.[44]

Secondly, there was doubt about the quantity and quality of the resources the DTI would devote to the enforcement of the legislation.

---

[39] The court distinguished between a top bracket of over ten years for "particularly serious" cases; a middle bracket of six to ten years for serious cases "which do not merit the top bracket"; and a minimum bracket for "not very serious" cases. See also *Westmid Packing Services Ltd, Re* [1998] 2 All E.R. 124, CA: fixing of length of disqualification to be done on the basis of "common sense")—*ibid.*, at 132.

[40] See above, fn.1 at para.1809.

[41] See above, fn.1 at para.1818.

[42] In Scotland, where there are no Official Receivers, even compulsory liquidations are handled by insolvency practitioners and the potential scope of the problem is accordingly greater.

[43] s.7(3) and the Insolvent Companies (Reports on Conduct of Directors) Rules 1996 (SI 1996/1909) and the Insolvent Companies (Reports on Conduct of Directors)(Scotland) Rules 1996 (SI 1996/1910). The Secretary of State may also take the initiative to ask for information, including the production of documents (s.7(4)), something most often done, presumably, when the report under s.7(3) suggests unfitness but does not contain enough detail to form the basis of an application.

[44] See Wheeler, "Directors' Disqualification: Insolvency Practitioners and the Decision-making Process" (1995) 15 L.S. 283. Moreover, the statutory scheme does not bite if the company is simply struck off the register (see below, paras A–12 to A–13) without going through any of these procedures.

Although the early efforts of the Insolvency Service were criticised,[45] by the middle of the 1990s it was securing the disqualification of some 400 directors a year, about 40 per cent on reports from Official Receivers, the remainder on reports from insolvency practitioners.[46] Nevertheless, it is clear that the Service still experiences difficulties in commencing insolvency applications within the two-year period permitted by the statute[47] and in prosecuting them with sufficient vigour to avoid striking out on grounds of delay or infringement of the director's human rights (i.e. the right to have one's civil rights and obligations determined within a reasonable time, as required by Article 6(1) of the European Convention on Human Rights).[48]

However, if the increasing efficiency of the Insolvency Service means it is less likely to infringe the human rights of directors on grounds of delay, there is the emerging risk that the human rights of directors will be threatened by the disparity between the state resources available to the Insolvency Service and those available to the director, who, in the case of a small company, may be virtually bankrupt. In particular, there is a danger that the impoverished director will give a disqualification undertaking because he or she cannot afford the costs of a full-scale court examination of the issues. So far, these issues have been addressed rather little in litigation, though appreciation of the situation may lie behind the courts' unwillingness to impose too high a level of competence on directors under the disqualification provisions.[49] As far as the European Convention on Human Rights is concerned, both the domestic courts and the European Court of Human Rights seem agreed that disqualification proceedings are civil in nature, not criminal, so that a lower, but not negligible, standard of fairness is required in conducting them.[50] In particular, the domestic courts have concluded

---

[45] National Audit Office, *The Insolvency Service Executive Agency: Company Director Disqualification* (1993) H.C. 907.

[46] Insolvency Service, *Annual Report 1994–95*, p.11. 67 per cent of disqualification orders were in the lowest bracket; 30 per cent in the middle bracket; and 3 per cent in the highest bracket. See fn.39, above. In 1996, 946 directors were disqualified as unfit.

[47] s.7(2). The court may give leave to commence the application out of time, though the Secretary of State must show a good reason for any extension: *Copecrest Ltd, Re* [1994] 2 B.C.L.C. 284, CA.

[48] *Manlon Trading Ltd, Re* [1996] Ch. 136, CA; *Davies v UK* [2006] 2 B.C.L.C. 351, ECtHR (a case decided in 2002); *Eastaway v UK* [2006] 2 B.C.L.C. 361, ECtHR. However, in the last of these cases the Court of Appeal refused to set aside the disqualification agreement entered into by the director under the *Carecraft* procedure (above, fn.8), even though the ECtHR had held the proceedings to have taken too long: *Eastaway v Secretary of State for Trade and Industry* [2007] B.C.C. 550. The National Audit Office, above, fn.45 para.18; found that the Insolvency Service in most cases took nearly the full two-year period permitted to bring an application and that up to a further four years might elapse before a disqualification order was made, during which period the director was free to carry on business with limited liability.

[49] See para.10–7, below and the extra-judicial remarks of Lord Hoffmann, Fourth Annual Leonard Sainer Lecture in (1997) *Company Lawyer* 194.

[50] *R. v Secretary of State for Trade and Industry Ex p. McCormick* [1998] B.C.C. 379, CA; *DC v United Kingdom* [2000] B.C.C. 710, ECtHR.

that the Human Rights Convention does not require the automatic exclusion of evidence against the director which was obtained from him or her under statutory powers of compulsion.[51] However, the exclusion of such evidence has been achieved in fact, as a matter of interpretation of the domestic law, in the case of the statutory provisions most likely to be of use to Official Receivers and the Insolvency Service. Under ss.235 and 236 of the Insolvency Act 1986 the liquidator of a company and the Official Receiver are empowered to require answers to questions which they put to directors of companies in insolvent liquidation and to require the production of documents, but the Court of Appeal has held that these provisions cannot be used for the purpose of supporting disqualification applications.[52]

Breach of commercial morality

10–6 As far as the role of the courts is concerned, it seems possible to divide the cases in which the courts have found unfitness into two rough categories: probity and competence.[53] However, it must be remembered that the concept of unfitness is open-ended, so that it cannot be claimed that all potential, or even actual, disqualification applications can be forced into one or other of these categories. Further, in the nature of things, many disqualification cases display aspects from both categories. Nevertheless, it is thought that identifying the two categories is a useful starting point, if nothing more.

The first category, breach of commercial morality, has at its centre the idea of conducting a business at the expense of its creditors. A leading example, though only an example, of such conduct was described by the Cork Committee in terms of a person who sets up an undercapitalised company, allows it to become insolvent, forms a new company (often with assets purchased at a discount from the liquidator of the old company), carries on trading much as before, and repeats the process perhaps several times, leaving behind him each time a trail of unpaid creditors.[54] More generally, the courts have been alert to find unfairness where the directors have apparently attempted to trade on the backs of the company's creditors.[55] Part II of Schedule I indeed requires the court, when assessing unfitness, to have regard to the extent of the directors' responsibility for the

---

[51] *Official Receiver v Stern* [2000] 1 W.L.R. 2230, CA. Contrast the decision in *Saunders v United Kingdom* [1998] 1 B.C.L.C. 362, ECtHR.

[52] *Pantmaenog Timber Co Ltd, Re* [2001] 4 All E.R. 588, CA.

[53] "Those who trade under the regime of limited liability and who avail themselves of the privileges of that regime must accept the standards of probity and competence to which the law requires company directors to conform" (per Neill L.J. in *Grayan Building Services Ltd, Re* above, fn.37).

[54] Cork Committee, para.1813. This is the so-called "Phoenix" syndrome. For the operation of the rule forbidding re-use of corporate names in this situation, see Ch.9, above. For examples in the disqualification case law, see *Travel Mondial (UK) Ltd, Re* [1991] B.C.L.C. 120; *Linvale Ltd, Re* [1993] B.C.L.C. 654; *Swift 736 Ltd, Re* [1993] B.C.L.C. 1.

[55] *Keypak Homecare Ltd, Re* [1990] B.C.L.C. 440.

company becoming insolvent, for the failure of the company to provide goods or services which have already been paid for or for giving a preference to one group of creditors over another or entering into a transaction at an undervalue.[56] It was thought at one time that particular obloquy attached to directors who attempted to trade out their difficulties by using as working capital in the business monies owed to the Crown by way of income tax, national insurance contributions or VAT, on the grounds that the Crown was an involuntary creditor. Although that view has been rejected by the Court of Appeal, the same court has affirmed that, in relation to any creditor, paying only those creditors who pressed for payment and taking advantage of those creditors who did not, in order to provide the working capital which the company needed, was a clear example of unfitness.[57] If the directors of the financially troubled company were at the same time paying themselves salaries which were out of proportion to the company's trading success (or lack of it), the likelihood of a disqualification order being made is only increased.[58]

Recklessness and incompetence

In the previous section the cases considered highlighted the improper **10–7** treatment by directors of the creditors of the company. The cases considered in this section focus on the recklessness or incompetence of the directors' conduct of the business. It may often be that the creditors are the ones who suffer from the maladministration, but here it is the competence of the directors which is at issue, rather than the fact that they have improperly used monies owed to creditors to finance the business, or otherwise acted improperly in relation to the creditors. In many cases, of course, both aspects of unfitness can be found.

The early cases put liability on the basis of recklessness,[59] but more recently it has been said that "incompetence or negligence to a very marked degree"[60] would be enough. The danger which the courts have to avoid in this area is that of treating any business venture which collapses as evidence of negligence. To do so would be to discourage the taking of commercial risks, which must be the lifeblood of corporate activity. However, creating a space for proper

---

[56] paras 6–8.
[57] *Sevenoaks Stationers (Retail) Ltd, Re* [1991] Ch. 164, CA; *Secretary of State for Trade and Industry v McTighe (No.2)* [1996] 2 B.C.L.C. 477, CA.
[58] *Synthetic Technology Ltd, Re* [1993] B.C.C. 549; *Secretary of State v Van Hengel* [1995] 1 B.C.L.C. 545.
[59] *Stanford Services Ltd, Re* [1987] B.C.L.C. 607.
[60] *Sevenoaks Stationers (Retail) Ltd, Re* above, fn.57, at 184.

risk-taking is no longer thought to require relieving directors of all objective standards of conduct. In *Barings Plc (No.5), Re*[61] the Court of Appeal gave guidance on what constitutes a high degree of incompetence in the common situation of the directors having properly delegated functions to lower levels of management. Provided the articles of association permit such delegation, as they inevitably will in large organisations, delegation in itself is not evidence of unfitness. However, the responsible director may be found to be unfit if there is put in place no system for supervising the discharge of the delegated function or if the director in question is not able to understand the information produced by the supervisory system. In other words, in large organisations directors must ensure there are in place adequate internal systems for monitoring risk.

However, the proposition that directors "have a continuing duty to acquire and maintain a sufficient knowledge and understanding of the company's business to enable them properly to discharge their duties as directors"[62] applies not just to delegated duties but also to reliance by directors on their board colleagues to take responsibility for particular functions and duties. Although such reliance is again in principle acceptable, so that there can be a division of functions on the board, most obviously between executive and non-executive directors, all directors must maintain a minimum level of knowledge and understanding about the business so that important problems can be identified and dealt with before they bring the company down. Thus, in *Richborough Furniture Ltd, Re*[63] a director was disqualified for three years, on the basis of "lack of experience, knowledge and understanding ... She did not have enough experience or knowledge to know what she should do in the face of the problems of pressing creditors, escalating Crown debts and lack of capital. It seems that she was not sufficiently skilful as regards the accounts functions to see that the records were inadequate."

10–8   In this area, particular importance is attached by the courts to failure by directors to file annual returns, produce audited accounts and to keep proper accounting records.[64] These are the practical expressions of a more general view that all directors must keep themselves *au fait* with the financial position of their company and make sure that it complies with the reporting requirements of the

---

[61] [2000] 1 B.C.L.C. 523, CA. The case involved the insolvency of an old and respected merchant bank brought about by the huge losses generated by the unauthorised trading activities of a junior employee whose activities were neither well understood nor effectively monitored by his superiors.

[62] [2000] 1 B.C.L.C. 523 at 536. See also *Westmid Packing Services Ltd, Re* [1998] 2 All E.R. 124 and *Vintage Hallmark Plc, Re* [2007] 1 B.C.L.C. 788.

[63] [1996] 1 B.C.L.C. 507.

[64] These may be ingredients in a finding of unfitness, even though, as we see below, para.10–11, non-compliance with the reporting requirements of the legislation is a separate ground of disqualification, albeit only for up to five years. For further discussion of what is required in this area see Ch.21.

companies legislation, for otherwise they cannot know what corrective action, if any, needs to be taken.[65] Although this duty may fall with particular emphasis on those responsible for the financial side of the company, all directors must keep themselves informed about the company's basic financial position.[66]

Disqualification of incompetent directors has become a crucial tool in the enforcement of directors' standards of competence, perhaps more so than actions for breach of the director's duty of care, which must be funded by private litigants. With the adoption of an objective standard of care for the directors' general duties[67]—a development in itself partly due to the experience in the disqualification area—the substantive test for liability under the general duty has become at least as attractive as the standard under the disqualification legislation—perhaps more so—and the two areas of law will no doubt continue to influence each other.

On the other hand, seeking and acting on competent outside advice when financial difficulties arise will be an indication of competence, even if the plan recommended does not pay off and the company eventually collapses.[68] It should also be remembered that, in the disqualification area, the courts have required a "marked degree" of negligence[69] before declaring a director unfit. There is a contrast here with wrongful trading and the standard of care under the directors' general duties[70] where there is no suggestion that a particularly enhanced standard of care is to be applied to directors.[71] It is suggested that this contrast is explained by the fact that a disqualification order can often have the effect of depriving the director of his livelihood and that, once unfitness is found, a two-year disqualification is mandatory.

---

[65] *Firedart Ltd, Re* [1994] 2 B.C.L.C. 340; *New Generation Engineers Ltd, Re* [1993] B.C.L.C. 435.

[66] *City Investment Centres Ltd, Re* [1992] B.C.L.C. 956; *Secretary of State v Van Hengel* [1995] 1 B.C.L.C. 545; *Majestic Recording Studios Ltd, Re* [1989] B.C.L.C. 1; *Continental Assurance Co of London Plc, Re* [1977] 1 B.C.L.C. 48; *Kaytech International Plc, Re* [1999] 2 B.C.L.C. 351, CA.

[67] See para.16–12.

[68] *Douglas Construction Services Ltd, Re* [1988] B.C.L.C. 397. Conversely, ignoring a plan produced by outside accountants is likely to be characterised as "obstinately and unjustifiably backing [the director's] own assessment of the company's business": *GSAR Realisations Ltd, Re* [1993] B.C.L.C. 409.

[69] See above, fn.60.

[70] See para.9–11 and para.16–12.

[71] Of course, keeping an insolvent company going can be grounds for disqualification for being unfit but only in strong cases. See, for example, *Living Images Ltd, Re* [1996] 1 B.C.L.C. 348, where the directors were aware of the company's parlous condition and keeping it going was described as "a gamble at long odds" and "the taking of unwarranted risks with creditors' money", so that there was a lack of probity involved and not just negligence. *cf.* the refusal to make a disqualification order in *Dawson Print Group Ltd, Re* [1987] B.C.L.C. 601; *Bath Glass Ltd, Re* [1988] B.C.L.C. 329; *CU Fittings Ltd, Re* [1989] B.C.L.C. 556; and *Secretary of State v Gash* [1997] 1 B.C.L.C. 341.

NON-MANDATORY DISQUALIFICATION

Serious offences

10–9 The remaining provisions of the 1986 Act permit, but do not require, the court to disqualify a director, on various grounds. Disqualification here is based on a court order. Disqualification by means of undertaking is not available outside the area of unfitness. These other grounds of disqualification will be dealt with briefly, partly because they have not generated as much controversy as the unfitness ground. Disqualifications under section 2 (disqualification on conviction of an indictable offence) apparently constitute the second most common source (after unfitness) for disqualification orders.[72]

In relation to serious offences, there are two routes to a disqualification order, depending upon whether the person concerned has actually been convicted of an offence. If there has been a conviction, a disqualification order may be made against a person, whether a director or not, who has committed an indictable offence in connection with the promotion, formation, management, liquidation or striking off of a company or in connection with the receivership or management of its property.[73] Usually, the disqualification will be ordered by the court by which the person is convicted and at the time of his or her conviction. However, if the convicting court does not act, the Secretary of State or the liquidator or any past or present creditor or member of the company in relation to which the offence was committed may apply to any court having jurisdiction to wind up the company to impose the disqualification.[74] Here, too, the courts have taken a wide view of what "in connection with the management of the company" means in this context.[75]

Where there has not been a conviction, but the company is being wound up, then if it appears that a person has been guilty of the offence of fraudulent trading[76] or has been guilty as an officer[77] of the company of any fraud in relation to it or any breach of duty as an

---

[72] A. Hicks, *Disqualification of Directors: No Hiding Place for the Unfit?* (ACCA Research Report 59, 1998), p.35, found that in 1996 about one quarter of those at that time disqualified were in that position as a result of a s.2 disqualification. The proportion has probably fallen since then, with the rise of unfitness disqualifications, especially via undertakings. The DTI figures (above, fn.7) do not distinguish among disqualifications on any of the grounds laid down in ss.1–5 of the Act.

[73] s.2.

[74] s.16(2).

[75] *R. v Goodman* [1994] 1 B.C.L.C. 349, CA (insider dealing by a director in the shares of his company); *R. v Georgiou* (1988) 4 B.C.C. 625; *R. v Ward, The Times*, April 10, 1997 (conspiracy to defraud by creating a false market in shares during a takeover bid); *R v Creggy* [2008] EWCA Crim 394 (facilitating criminal activity by third parties).

[76] See para.9–5.

[77] Also included are the usual cast of liquidators, receivers and administrative receivers and also shadow directors: s.4(1)(b) and (2).

officer, then the court having jurisdiction to wind up the company may impose a disqualification order.[78]

Disqualification in connection with civil liability for fraudulent or wrongful trading

In addition to the array of orders which the court may make under **10–10** ss.213 and 214 of the Insolvency Act 1986 in cases of fraudulent or wrongful trading,[79] section 10 of the Disqualification Act adds the power to make a disqualification order. The court may act here on its own motion, that is, whether or not an application is made to it by anyone for an order to be made. Since there are only low levels to litigation over fraudulent and wrongful trading, the number of disqualifications is also low.[80]

Failure to comply with reporting requirements

Again, there are separate provisions according to whether the person **10–11** to be disqualified has been convicted or not. If he or she has been convicted of a summary offence in connection with a failure to file a document with or give notice of a fact to the Registrar, then the convicting court may disqualify that person if in the previous five years he has had at least three convictions (including the current one) or default orders against him for non-compliance with the reporting requirements of the Companies and Insolvency Acts.[81] If the current conviction is on indictment, then the provisions of section 2 (above) apply, though naturally, where the current conviction is summary, the fact that the earlier convictions were on indictment does not prevent the convicting summary court from disqualifying.[82]

Where there has been no conviction, the Secretary of State and the others mentioned in s.16(2)[83] may apply to the court having jurisdiction to wind up the companies in question for disqualification orders to be made on the grounds that the respondent has been "persistently in default" in complying with the reporting requirements of the Companies and Insolvency Acts.[84] The "three convictions or defaults in five years" rule applies here too, but without prejudice to proof of persistent default in any other manner.[85] Since the offences involved in these sections may be only summary ones, the

---

[78] s.4, upon application by those listed in s.16(2). It is unclear whether the breach of duty referred to must involve the commission of a criminal offence, but the use of the word "guilty" suggests so.

[79] See para.9–9, but the court is not obliged to disqualify.

[80] None in the period 2001–2006: DTI, above, fn.7.

[81] s.5. Those listed in s.16(2) may apply for a disqualification order to be made.

[82] Contrast the wording of subs. (1) and (2) of s.5.

[83] See above, text attached to fn.74.

[84] s.3.

[85] s.3(2).

maximum period of disqualification is limited to five, instead of the usual 15, years. Nevertheless, the fact that these provisions are in the Act at all is a testimony to the importance attached recently to timely filing of accounts and other documents. However, the improvement recorded in this area may be due more to the introduction of late filing penalties than the disqualification orders.

Register of disqualification orders

10–12 Crucial to the effective operation of the disqualification machinery is that publicity should be given to the names of those who have been disqualified. Thus, the Act requires the Secretary of State to create such a register of orders and undertakings, which register is open to public inspection.[86] The register should also contain details of any leave given to a disqualified person to act despite the disqualification. However, either because of doubts about the accuracy of the register or to relieve the Registrar of the need to check it, the 2006 Act contains a power for the Secretary of State to make regulations about the returns which companies have to make to the Registrar about the appointment of directors and secretaries. The regulations may require the return to contain the statement in relation to a disqualified person that the leave of the court to act has been obtained.[87]

BANKRUPTS

10–13 The prohibition on undischarged bankrupts acting as directors or being involved in the management of companies can be traced back to the Companies Act 1928. Although bankruptcy does not necessarily connote any wrongdoing, the policy against permitting those who have been so spectacularly unsuccessful in the management of their own finances taking charge of other people's money is so self-evident that it has not proved controversial. The prohibition is contained in section 11 of the 1986 Act, which makes so acting a criminal offence,[88] and the main point of interest about it for present purposes is that it is an automatic disqualification, not dependent upon the making of a disqualification order by the court. In 2002 the prohibition was extended to include acting in breach of a bankruptcy restriction order or undertaking, themselves creations of the legisla-

---

[86] s.18 and the Companies (Disqualification Orders) Regulations 2001 (SI 2001/967).
[87] s.1189 of the CA 2006.
[88] Acting in breach of the prohibition also attracts personal liability for the company's debts (s.15—though this may not be of much utility in relation to bankrupts) and could, apparently, give rise to the making of a disqualification order under s.2 (above, para.10–9): *R. v Young* [1990] B.C.C. 549, CA).

tive reforms of that year.[89] Bankruptcy restriction orders and undertakings, clearly modelled to some extent on directors' disqualification orders and undertakings, put restrictions on a former bankrupt's activities after discharge from bankruptcy, in general an earlier event than had previously been the case.

However, the disqualification is not absolute, because the bankrupt or previous bankrupt may apply to the court for leave to act in the management of a company, other than as an insolvency practitioner.[90] In other words, the statute really reverses the burden of taking action, by placing it upon the bankrupt to show that he or she may be safely involved in the management of companies rather than upon some state official to demonstrate to a court that the bankrupt ought not to be allowed to act.

IMPACT OF DISQUALIFICATIONS UNDER FOREIGN LAW

The Disqualification Act applies not only to companies incorporated **10–14** under the companies legislation or even to companies otherwise incorporated in Great Britatain, but also to companies capable of being wound up under Part V of the Insolvency Act 1986, a phrase which includes at least certain overseas companies operating in Great Britain.[91] The conduct of directors of such companies may lead to the British courts making disqualification orders against them. However, this does not necessarily cover the situation where a person has been disqualified under the law of a jurisdiction outside the United Kingdom and subsequently becomes involved in a company registered in the United Kingdom. This will not be a breach of the Disqualification Act (because the person has not been disqualified under it) and, if the foreign law is drafted in the same way as the Disqualification Act, it may not be a breach of the foreign law either.[92] Given the ease with which persons may cross boundaries, especially within the European Community, in order to carry on business, this was a serious lacuna in the Disqualification Act.

However, Part 40 of the Companies Act 2006[93] empowers the Secretary of State to apply the equivalent of the domestic rules to a person who, under the law of a non-United Kingdom jurisdiction, is, by reason of misconduct or unfitness, disqualified to any extent from

---

[89] These changes were effected by Sch.20 to the Enterprise Act 2002, introducing a new Sch.4A into the Insolvency Act 1986.

[90] ss.11(1) and 390(4)(a) of the IA 1986.

[91] s.22(2) of the Disqualification Act. See para.6–7.

[92] The Disqualification Act does not prevent a disqualified person from acting in relation to an overseas company which has no connection with the United Kingdom.

[93] Scheduled to be brought into force on October 1, 2009.

acting in relation to the affairs of a company incorporated in that jurisdiction or can do so only subject to permission or condition.[94] That person may be prohibited from acting in relation to a company incorporated under the domestic legislation and that prohibition may arise automatically as a result of the foreign disqualification, as a result of an order of a court in the United Kingdom or as a result of an undertaking given to the Secretary of State.[95] Where the disqualification is the result of a court order in the United Kingdom the court must take into account whether the conduct on the basis of which the person was disqualified abroad would have led a United Kingdom court to impose disqualification.[96] The same criminal and civil sanctions may be applied as in the case of a Disqualification Act disqualification.[97] In addition, the regulations may provide that a person, subject to a foreign disqualification order but not disqualified under the 2006 Act, must send a statement to the Registrar every time he or she does something which would be breach of a disqualification order made under the 2006 Act.[98]

CONCLUSION

10–15 For many years the disqualification provisions of the successive Companies Acts seemed to make little impact. Important in principle as a technique for dealing with corporate wrongdoing of one sort or another, especially on the part of directors, the practical consequences of the provisions were limited. The combination of the substantive reforms recommended by the Cork Committee and of acceptance by Government that the promotion of small, and not-so-small, businesses needed to be accompanied by action to raise the standards of directors' behaviour and to protect the public from the scheming and the incompetent, brought the disqualification provisions to the fore. Indeed, disqualification is now increasingly used as a sanction against directors in areas outside company law, for example, under the Enterprise Act 2002 in support of competition law. Further, as we have seen in Chapter 7,[99] controversy about whether directors whose companies are convicted of the proposed new corporate killing offence should be disqualified from acting in connection with businesses delayed progress on that reform proposal, though in the end the legislation did not make use of the dis-

---

[94] s.1182.
[95] ss.1183–1184.
[96] s.1185(3)(a).
[97] ss.1186 and 1187.
[98] s.1189.
[99] see above, para.7–32.

qualification technique. As to disqualification orders in company law, judged by the level of disqualification orders and undertakings, the provisions now have a substantial impact. An independent survey[100] found a widespread consensus that the provisions performed a useful role and should be retained, although they were certainly capable of improvement, especially at the level of securing compliance with the disqualification orders made.[101]

---

[100] By Andrew Hicks; see fn.72, above. The report makes a number of interesting and thought-provoking suggestions for reform. For a more sceptical account see Williams, "Disqualifying Directors: a Remedy Worse than the Disease?" (2007) *J.C.L.S.* 213.

[101] *Companies in 2005–2006* (above, fn.7) reveals that some 90 prosecutions for breach of disqualification orders or of the prohibition on bankrupts acting as directors were launched in that year, producing 81 convictions. It is difficult to know whether this relatively modest total indicates a high level of compliance with the disqualifications or a low level of detection of breaches.

CHAPTER 11

LEGAL CAPITAL AND MINIMUM CAPITAL

MEANING OF CAPITAL

In the previous two chapters we saw how the law applies sanctions to **11–1** the controllers of companies who abuse the facility of limited liability. In particular, personal liability for the company's obligations and disqualification from being involved in the management of a company are applied in these cases. The most important examples of the imposition of these sanctions arise out of situations where the controllers have infringed some broad and general standard laid down for the assessment of their conduct, for example, engaging in "wrongful" trading or displaying "unfit" conduct. In this chapter and the next two we turn to a rather different approach to the abuse of limited liability. The legal mechanisms discussed in these chapters take as their starting point the fact that, where limited liability operates, the creditors' claims are confined to the assets of the company. Consequently, a method of protecting creditors can consist in ensuring that a company operates only with an appropriate level of assets, so as to increase the chances that it will be able to meet the claims of its creditors. This idea can be given expression in a number of ways, which will be explored in these chapters. It will be seen, as well, that this policy is given effect mainly through detailed rules rather than through broad standards.

The traditional protective mechanism of company law in this area, which is as old as limited liability itself, involves laying down rules about the raising and maintenance of "capital". "Capital" is a word of many meanings,[1] but in company law it is used in a very restricted sense. It connotes the value of the assets contributed to the company by those who subscribe for its shares. By and large, the value of what the company receives from investors in exchange for its shares constitutes its capital.[2] One talks about the value of what is received, rather than the assets themselves, because those assets will change form in the course of the business activities of the company. If the company receives cash in exchange for its shares, the directors will turn that cash into other types of asset in order to promote its business: indeed, if they did not, they would probably be in breach of duty.

The value of the assets which the company receives in exchange for its shares may represent less than the total value of the company's assets. Even where the company has not yet begun to trade, it may have raised money from sources other than in exchange for its shares. For example, it may have borrowed money from a bank or a group of banks. The value of such loans does not count as its capital, however. This is because the aim of the definition of the capital of the company is to protect creditors as a class and only assets contributed by shareholders do this effectively. This arises from the principle that in an insolvency the creditors are paid before the shareholders.[3] Thus, assets contributed by shareholders go fully to satisfy the claims of the creditors before any return is made to the shareholders.[4] Once a company has begun trading and if it has done so profitably, it will have assets which represent the profits made and these, too, do not count as part of the company's legal capital (though the shareholders will have a lively interest in them since they may provide the basis for dividend payments to the shareholders).[5] In short, the value of the company's legal capital and the net value of the assets held in the

---

[1] *cf.* capital punishment, capital letter, capital ship, capital city, capital of a pillar, capital and labour, capital and income, and "capital!".

[2] In *Kellar v Williams* [2000] 2 B.C.L.C. 390, the Privy Council accepted that it was possible for an investor to make a capital contribution to a company, other than in exchange for the purchase of shares, in which case the contribution is to be treated in the same way as a share premium (see below, para.11–8). Such a procedure is very unusual, of course, since the contributor is left substantially in the dark as to what he or she is getting in exchange for the contribution. However, one can see that an existing shareholder in a company wholly controlled by him might act in this way. The difficulty is to distinguish between such a capital contribution and a loan to the company.

[3] IA 1986, s.107.

[4] Of course, a contribution made by a creditor may in fact benefit other creditors, for example, a loan made to a company just before insolvency may mean the creditors as a class obtain a larger percentage pay out than if the loan had not been made, but that the benefit to the earlier creditors is paid for by the later lender.

[5] See Ch.13, below.

company (i.e. assets minus liabilities) are not necessarily or even typically equivalent. In the above examples, the value of the total assets is greater than the value of the company's legal capital; if the company trades unsuccessfully, the value of those assets may fall, of course, below the value of its legal capital. This is the situation where the legal rules are engaged.

What then are the rules about legal capital which company law lays **11–2** down for the protection of creditors?[6] Most obviously, the law could require the company to have a certain level of legal capital before it begins trading. British law requires this of public companies, since the implementation of the Second Company Law Directive,[7] which imposes this requirement, but it has not traditionally attached much importance to minimum capital requirements, as they are called. Alternatively, or in addition, the law could leave the company free to decide its own level of legal capital, but attach legal consequences to the company's decision. At a basic level it could take steps to ensure that creditors were not misled by the company in relation to its apparent levels of capital. This could involve ensuring that the company had actually received the value it showed in its accounts in respect of its legal capital. Going further, the law could restrict the freedom of the company subsequently to distribute assets to its shareholders if the result would be that its net asset value fell below that of its legal capital. This is generally referred to as the doctrine of "capital maintenance". As we shall see, this is something of a misnomer. The rules do not require the net asset value of the company to at least equal its legal capital at all times. Rather, the rules restrict the distribution of its assets by the company to the shareholders so long as the company's net asset value is less than its legal capital. We will deal in this chapter with the legal capital rules which apply when the company decides to raise capital (whether voluntarily or to meet minimum capital requirements). The following chapter will deal with the payment of dividends and the making of distributions generally to members, and the chapter after that with the maintenance of capital doctrine.[8]

---

[6] Legal capital is also important in company accounts, because it provides a basis for measuring the success of the company from the shareholders' point of view or for fixing the distribution of dividends. For this reason the concept may also be used in the accounts of partnerships, whose members do not benefit from limited liability, but the movement of assets in and out of partnerships is not controlled as it is in companies.

[7] Council Directive 77/91/EC, [1977] OJ L26/1. See para.6–8.

[8] Most of the provisions of the 2006 Act referred to in this chapter and Chapter 13 are scheduled to come into force on October 1, 2009.

FROM AUTHORISED CAPITAL TO STATEMENT OF CAPITAL

11–3   When a company is formed, assuming it is limited by shares, the
application for registration must contain a statement of capital and
initial shareholdings, i.e. of the total number of shares to be taken on
formation by the subscribers to the memorandum of association,
their aggregate nominal value, the prescribed particulars of the rights
attached to them,[9] the number of shares taken by each subscriber and
the amount immediately paid up on the shares.[10] In practice, the
answer will often be one £1 share taken by each of two people, upon
which nothing is paid up, the two people being employees of a
company formation business, which has created a shelf private
company. When more serious amounts of shares are issued at a later
date, similar information has to be given to the Registrar of companies via a "return of allotments".[11] Thus, data about those to
whom shares of various classes have been issued[12] and the main rights
and obligations attached to those shares is public information, but
this is a disclosure provision, not a provision which regulates the
amount or type of share the company issues.

However, the new Act does away with the former concept of
"authorised capital", as recommended by the CLR.[13] This was a
concept which sounded important but which fulfilled no identifiable
creditor-protection role. Under the old law, in the case of a company
with a share capital (unless it was an unlimited company) its memorandum was required to "state the amount of the share capital with
which [it] proposes to be registered and the division of that share
capital into shares of a fixed amount".[14] Until the authorised capital
was allotted, i.e. an investor agreed to take some shares in exchange
for a consideration provided to the company, the authorised capital in
no way increased the company's assets. The company's authorised
capital might have been 10 million shares of £1 each, but if only two of
those shares had been issued, say at par, then its legal capital was £2.

The new Act does not contain an equivalent requirement.[15] If
anything, authorised capital served to confuse the potential investor.
In fact, the requirement for authorised capital had more to do with

---

[9] Prescribed are details of the right to vote, to receive a distribution either by way of dividend
or capital, and provisions about redemption: the draft Companies (Shares, Share Capital
and Authorised Minimum) Regulations 2007 (hereafter "Shares Regulations").
[10] s.10.
[11] s.555 and see para.23–6.
[12] As we see in para.26–18, those who take the shares may be nominees for others who have the
financial interest in them, but this is perhaps of less moment to the creditors whose main
interest is in the amount of shares issued, rather than data about their holders. Since the
shareholders' liability is limited, it does not matter to the creditors whether the shareholders
are rich or poor, at least once the shares are fully paid up.
[13] *Modernising*, para.6.5.
[14] s.2(5)(a) of the 1985 Act.
[15] Or, rather, is scheduled not to as from October 1, 2009.

relations between directors and shareholders than with creditor relations. The directors could not issue more than the amount of the company's authorised capital without returning to the shareholders for approval of an increase in the authorised amount.[16] However, since shareholder control of share issues is now effected by other sections of the Act and since shareholders, if they wish, can put stronger controls in the company's constitution, authorised capital is not needed for the protection of shareholders either.[17]

Minimum Capital

Thus, what we need to focus on is the company's issued share capital, **11–4** i.e. the shares it has allotted in exchange for a consideration from an investor who has now become a shareholder in the company.[18] An obvious form of creditor protection might seem to be a rule which requires the company to raise a minimum value of assets from the allotment of its shares (its minimum legal capital) before it commences trading. Despite the longevity of rules about legal capital in British law, historically it has not in fact attached much significance to minimum capital (as opposed to capital maintenance) rules.[19] However, as a result of the Second Directive,[20] a minimum capital requirement was introduced for public companies. This was set at the derisory level (for a public company) of £50,000 (or €65,000),[21] though that is above the level required by the Directive.[22] Moreover, that £50,000 (or assets of equivalent value) does not have to be handed over to the company at the time of issue of the shares. It is enough, as with all share issues by public companies, that one quarter of the nominal value of the share and the whole of any premium be paid at the time of issue.[23] The rest may remain unpaid, though of course subject to being called up by the company at a later date or in its liquidation. However, the Act retains its traditional aversion to minimum capital requirements in respect of private companies, where none is imposed. This is said to have been a major factor behind the incorporation in England of companies from other Community

---

[16] s.121 of the 1985 Act.
[17] See Ch.24.
[18] For a more detailed discussion of the issuance of shares see Ch.24.
[19] Minimum capital requirements tend to be common in Continental European systems but are not used extensively in the United States or Commonwealth countries. See M. Lutter, "Business and Private Organizations" in *International Encyclopedia of Comparative Law* (Mohr Siebeck, 1998), Vol. XIII, Ch.2, Table.
[20] See above, fn.7, Art.6.
[21] s.763 and the Companies (Authorised Minimum) Regulations 2008/729, reg.2.
[22] Art.6: €25,000.
[23] On nominal value and premia see below.

countries which do apply minimum capital requirements to their equivalents of private companies.[24]

In the relatively unusual case of a company being formed directly as a public company, the minimum capital requirement operates, not as a condition of its formation, but as a condition of its commencing business.[25] In order to commence business (or to exercise any borrowing powers—an important addition) it must apply to the Registrar for a "trading certificate"[26] (in addition to the formation certificate which it will already have obtained); and the condition for the issuance of a trading certificate is that the nominal value of the company's allotted share capital must be not less than the required or "authorised" minimum.[27] The company is under some pressure to obtain the trading certificate, because if it does not do so within a year from incorporation, it may be wound up by the Court and the Secretary of State may petition for that to happen.[28] A public company which trades or borrows without a certificate is liable to a fine, as is any officer of the company (including therefore its directors) who is in default.[29] However, the interests of third parties are properly protected in this case. Transactions entered into by the company in such a case are valid, and further, if the company fails to comply with its obligations, the directors of the company are jointly and severally liable to indemnify the third parties in respect of any loss or damage suffered.[30] Thus, personal liability of the directors, criminal and civil, operates to give them a strong incentive not to trade without a trading certificate.

In the more usual case of a company becoming public upon conversion from private status, the requirement that the company's allotted capital be not less than the authorised minimum operates as a condition for the re-registration of the private company as a public one.[31]

---

[24] See Becht, Mayer and Wagner, "Where do Firms Incorporate? Deregulation and the Cost of Entry" available on: http://papers.ssrn.com/sol3/papers.cfm?abstract_id=906066.

[25] s.761.

[26] The form of the application, containing a statement of compliance on the part of the company, is set out in s.762. It is not demanding and the Registrar may accept the company's statement of compliance as sufficient evidence of the matters stated in it, and the Registrar must issue the certificate if satisfied the minimum capital requirements are met: s.765(2). The trading certificate, once issued, is conclusive evidence that the company is entitled to commence business: s.761(4). However, by analogy with the decisions referred to in para.4–18 in relation to the certificate of incorporation, it appears that, as this section is not expressed to bind the Crown, the Registrar's decision could be quashed on judicial review at the instance of the Attorney-General.

[27] s.761(2). A company's capital may be stated in euros in which case s.763 deals with the fixing of the equivalent prescribed euro amount. Where a company has some share capital denominated in pounds and some in euros, the company's application for a certificate must be made by reference to the sterling capital or to the euro capital alone and not by reference to a mixture of the two types of capital: s.765.

[28] Insolvency Act 1986, ss.122(1)(b) and 124(4)(a).

[29] s.767(1),(2).

[30] s.767(3),(4).

[31] ss.90(1)(b), (2)(b) and 91(1)(a).

If the nominal value of the company's allotted share capital meets the authorised minimum, on either of the occasions described above, it will normally remain at that level thereafter. It will not be affected by a rise or fall in the net asset value of the company or the market value of the company's shares. The minimum capital rule is concerned with the nominal value of allotted share capital at the initial stage, not with the subsequent trading history of the company and the effect of that history on the market value of its shares and assets— a possible criticism of the minimum capital rules (see below). However, in relatively rare cases the nominal value of the company's allotted capital might subsequently fall below the authorised minimum. There is no general provision in the Act dealing with this eventuality. Rather, provision is made on an ad hoc basis. Thus, if under the reduction of capital procedure[32] the company's capital is reduced below the authorised minimum, the normal requirement is that the company must re-register as a private company before the reduction of capital order is finalised.[33] Further, the Secretary of State has power to alter the authorised minimum by regulation (subject to affirmative resolution).[34] Were that alteration to be in an upward direction, the Secretary of State also has the power to require existing public companies to bring their nominal values into line with the new authorised minimum or to re-register as a private company.[35]

Objections to the minimum capital requirement

There are two objections which can be made to minimum capital rules. First, company laws normally set only one (as in the United Kingdom) or a small number of minimum capital rules (for example, one for private and another for public companies), but in fact, to be effective, the minimum capital requirement ought to be related to the riskiness of the business which the company undertakes. General minimum capital requirements tend either to be too low effectively to protect creditors (as in the case of the current British requirement) or too high, in which case they simply reduce competition (by discouraging new entrants into the field) whilst over-protecting creditors. However, adjusting capital requirements to the riskiness of the company's business would be a complex and continuing activity, as is shown by the special regulation necessary to implement such a principle in those industries, for example banking and insurance, where capital adequacy requirements are taken seriously. Thus, it is not surprising that the approach of company laws to minimum

11–5

---

[32] See Ch.13.
[33] s.650(2). The court may order otherwise. S.651 provides an expedited procedure for re-registering as a private company in such cases. See also s.662(2)(b), dealing with the consequences of a forced cancellation by a public company of its own shares.
[34] s.764(1),(4).
[35] s.764(3)—no doubt through an expedited procedure.

capital requirements is relatively crude; and in practice in developed economies tends towards the "too low" end of the spectrum, thus conferring no substantial protection on creditors but conceivably discouraging the incorporation of companies.

If, therefore, the minimum capital requirement has no claim to be a genuine assessment of the amount of risk capital the company needs to survive the vicissitudes of its business, could it nevertheless be justified as a "cushion" of assets provided by the shareholders for the protection of the creditors? This is also a difficult argument to sustain. The creditors need the protection of an asset cushion when the company begins to trade unprofitably. A minimum capital requirement imposed at the time the company commences trading does not guarantee any particular level of assets being available for the creditors at this later date or when the company goes into an insolvency procedure. For example, a minimum capital requirement of, say, £3,000 for a private company, even if paid in cash, could soon be returned quite legitimately to the incorporators by means of salary payments for services rendered to the company[36] or it could be satisfied by the contribution to the company by the incorporators of a depreciating asset, such as a second-hand car. Thus, minimum capital rules are likely to be ineffective beyond a very short initial period unless coupled with rules which require the directors to take action if the net value of the company's actual assets declines below the value of its legal capital.

Section 656 requires a public company to convene an extraordinary meeting of the shareholders if the net value of its assets falls below one half of its called-up share capital.[37] Where the company has allotted shares well beyond the authorised minimum, this requirement may bite even though the company's assets are still above the level of that minimum. However, the section does not require the shareholders or the directors to take any particular action in this situation (for example, cause the company to cease trading). This section seems not to be very important in practice, probably because, before it becomes operative, large lenders will have exercised rights under their loan contracts to replace the failing management or otherwise to redress the situation[38] or the wrongful trading provisions[39] will have required the directors to take corrective action. Consequently, it can be argued that, at the initial stage, the minimum capital requirement is too low to confer substantial protection on creditors; that, subsequently, the relationship between the amount of

---

[36] As we shall see below at para.12–4, directors' remuneration would not normally be caught by the rules controlling distributions by companies.
[37] This implements domestically Art.17 of the Second Directive. Art.17 refers to the company's "subscribed" capital, which probably means the nominal value of the issued share capital.
[38] See para.31–1 and para.32–35.
[39] See paras 9–7ff.

the authorised minimum and the value of the company's assets is not normally central to the operation of the legal rules which seek to protect creditors; and that it is to those other mechanisms which seek to protect creditors as trading becomes unsuccessful that creditors need to look.[40]

NOMINAL VALUE AND SHARE PREMIUMS

Nominal value

We have just seen that the authorised minimum is expressed in terms **11–6** of the "nominal" value of the company's allotted share capital. Before proceeding further, we need to examine this concept—of doubtful utility—of "nominal" or "par" value, as it is sometimes also called. This is not a concept which is peculiar to the area of the authorised minimum capital. Rather it pervades the law on legal capital. Thus, the Act requires that shares in a limited company "must each have a fixed nominal value" and that an allotment of shares not meeting this requirement is void.[41] In other words a monetary value needs to be attached to the company's shares. In consequence, one talks of the company having issued a certain number of "£1 shares" or "10p shares" and so on. The par value is a doubtfully useful concept because it does not indicate in any way the price at which the share is likely to be issued to investors—still less the price at which the share is likely to trade in the market after issue. Very often, the issue price will be higher than the nominal value, and rightly so. Suppose a company has issued a tranche of shares at par, has traded successfully, re-invested the profits and seeks capital for further expansion. The second tranche of shares will naturally be issued at a price higher than par; otherwise, the second set of shareholders would obtain a disproportionately large interest in the company. In effect, they would be obtaining an interest in the profits earned in the past without having contributed any of the capital which was used to earn them. The situation can be rectified by setting the share price on the second issue so that it reflects the total value of the shareholders' interest in the company and not just the legal capital.

Even when a company is issuing shares for the first time, it is under no obligation to set the par value near the level of the price which it will obtain for the shares. Indeed, one of the central oddities of the nominal or par value requirement is that, whilst being obliged to attach one to its shares, the company is not constrained by the Act in

---

[40] See Chs 9 and 10 above.
[41] s.542(1),(2). This implements the requirements of the Second Directive.

fixing the amount of the nominal value. In fact, since there are some legal rules which could impair the company's freedom of action if it sets a high nominal value, notably the rule against issuing shares at a discount to their nominal value (see below), the company is under some incentive to set a low nominal value (relative to the price at which the shares are to be issued). For both the above reasons, the issue price of a share may well be very much in excess of its nominal value.

In addition to proposing the abolition of authorised capital, the CLR contemplated taking the additional step of abolishing par value for private companies,[42] but eventually resiled from the proposal. The Second Directive was thought to require the retention of par value, or something very much like it,[43] for public companies, and the transitional difficulties likely to arise when a company moved from private to public were thought to militate against this reform.[44] So, unless and until the Second Directive is amended on this point, par values will remain part of the law.

Share capital and choice of currency

11–7   The Act requires the minimum capital requirement for public companies to be satisfied at the time the trading certificate is issued by shares denominated in either pounds sterling or euros.[45] However, apart from this, the company has considerable freedom to denominate shares in such currency as it wishes. It has never been doubted that this was possible in relation to the share premium account (and other capital reserves) but the issue was debated in relation to the share capital account until it was decided in favour of giving the

---

[42] Strategic, paras 5.4.26–5.4.33. The Gedge Committee, Cmnd. 9112, had recommended as long ago as 1954 that no-par equity shares should be introduced and the Jenkins Committee (Cmnd. 1749, 1962, paras 32–34) recommended this reform in relation to all classes of share. The reform has been widely introduced in North America, but now seems unlikely to be introduced here unless the Second Directive is amended on this point. Introduction of no-par shares would require some matters to be expressed differently or regulated differently in the contract of issue. For example, the dividend on a preference share is normally expressed as a percentage of its nominal value (but could as easily be expressed as so many pence per share) and surplus assets are distributed on a winding in accordance with nominal values, so that a different formula would have to be adopted. See *Birch v Cropper* (1889) 14 App. Cas. 525.

[43] The Directive refers to "accountable par" as a permitted alternative to "nominal value" (but without defining it). The concept appears to be that one takes the total consideration raised through the issue of shares and divides it by the number of shares in issue at any time. Two consequences follow: the shares do not have a fixed nominal value (because the accountable par would change on a new share issue at a different price) but a par value does exist at all times; and the company has no freedom to set the nominal value: it is simply the result of an arithmetical exercise. See Bank of England, *Practical Issues Arising From the Euro*, Issue 8, June 1998, Ch.6 at paras 24–28.

[44] Completing, para.7.3.

[45] s.765(1).

company this freedom in *Scandinavian Bank, Re*.[46] The Act now puts the point beyond doubt.[47] Moreover, the Act adds to this freedom by providing a simple procedure for re-denominating share capital from one currency to another (into or out of sterling or from one non-sterling currency to another), including the re-denomination of the shares used to satisfy the minimum capital requirement when trading began. Formerly, this could be achieved only by the cumbersome and potentially expensive procedure of a reduction of capital and an issue of new shares in the desired currency.[48] Now any limited[49] company, subject to contrary provision in its articles, may re-denominate its shares by ordinary resolution of the members.[50] Such re-denomination does not affect the currency in which dividends are required to be paid by the company or calls on shares met by the shareholder.[51]

Such re-denomination, which must be carried out at prevailing rates of exchange,[52] could produce new nominal values of a rather awkward kind, for example, \$2.24. The company may respond in two ways: by capitalising distributable reserves so as to increase the nominal values to a more acceptable level, for which no special statutory permission is needed,[53] or by reducing the nominal values so as to achieve the same result, which the statute permits without the need to follow the full reduction of capital procedure. All that is required is a special resolution of the members, provided the decision is taken within three months of the re-denomination resolution and does not reduce the company's share capital by more than 10 per cent.[54] Further, the amount of the reduction must be carried to a "re-denomination reserve" which is a new undistributable reserve created by the Act.[55] It is also conceivable that the reduction following re-denomination could produce the result that neither the euro nor the sterling requirements for the authorised minimum capital of a public company is met, in which case the company will have to re-register as a private company.[56]

---

[46] [1988] Ch. 87. Of course, until the rules on share capital were brought into line with those on share premium, the company was not in a position to exercise freedom of choice in relation to currency.

[47] s.542(3): shares "may be denominated in any currency and different classes of shares may be denominated in different currencies" (subject, of course, to s.765, above, fn.45).

[48] As happened in *Scandinavian Bank, Re* (previous note). For the reduction of capital procedure see para.13–2.

[49] Unlimited companies had the freedom already.

[50] s.622(1). The section requires the actual conversion to take place within 28 days of the adoption of the resolution (s.622(5),(6)).

[51] s.624(1). Other rights and obligations of members under the constitution or the terms of issue of the shares are also expressly preserved.

[52] s.622(3).

[53] On capitalisation issues see below, para.11–18.

[54] s.626. Thus, in the example in the text, the company would not be able to use this procedure to reduce the nominal value to \$2, but it would be able to if the unreduced nominal value were \$2.20. There must also be notification to the Registrar: s.627.

[55] s.628. For the significance of this for the payment of dividends see para.12–1.

[56] s.766 and the draft Companies (Shares, Share Capital and Authorised Minimum) Regulations 2007, regs 3–7. A speedy method of re-registration is provided.

The share premium

11–8   An immediate question which arises is how should the law treat the
extra amount above par (referred to as the "premium") which the
company receives in exchange for the shares. Should it be treated in
the same way as the par value for the purpose of the legal capital
rules? As we have seen, the rules on the authorised minimum do
distinguish between the nominal value and the premium. Only the
nominal value of the shares counts towards meeting the authorised
minimum.[57] To this extent, a public company, not wishing in fact to
raise through a share issue much more than £50,000, has some
incentive, contrary to the one identified in the previous paragraph, to
bring the nominal value near to the likely issue price, because any
premium received will not count towards meeting the authorised
minimum. In general, however, public companies' share issues are of
a much larger character and meeting the authorised minimum
through nominal value alone does not pose a problem.

More significant is the question of whether the law on capital
maintenance should operate on the basis of nominal capital alone or
on the basis of the total proceeds received by the company from the
issuance of its shares (i.e. nominal value plus premium). The question
is more significant because the law's capital maintenance rules have
always been more demanding than its minimum capital rules. The
essence of the capital maintenance rules is that they restrict the
freedom of the company to return assets to its shareholders (most
obviously by way of dividend payments, but also in other ways, such
as share buy-backs) so long as its net value of its assets is less than the
value of its legal capital.[58] Contrary to the minimum capital rules, the
rules on capital maintenance are more constraining if they embrace
the full value of the consideration received for the shares, because
that sets a higher threshold of assets which must be kept within the
company than would a rule which focussed solely on nominal values
(especially given the company's control over setting the level of the
nominal value of the share). The current law does apply the capital
maintenance principle to the full value received for the shares, though
it has not always done so.

Prior to 1948, when companies issued shares at a premium (i.e. at
above their nominal value), the premiums were treated totally differently from share capital. Legal capital was regarded as determined
by the nominal or par value of the shares; if they had been issued at a
price above par the excess was not "capital" and, indeed, constituted
part of the distributable surplus which the company, if it wished,
could return to the shareholders by way of dividend.[59] This was, of
course, a ridiculous rule, except on the basis that it might be an

---

[57] s.761(2).
[58] See Chs. 12 and 13 below.
[59] *Drown v Gaumont British Corp* [1937] Ch. 402. See C. Napier and C. Noke "Premiums and
Pre-acquisition Profits" (1991) 54 M.L.R. 810.

indirect way of getting rid of the capital maintenance requirements. If the price paid for the shares was £100,000, the true capital of the company was £100,000 and it should have made no difference to the company or to the shareholders whether the £100,000 was obtained by issuing 100,000 £1 shares at par or by issuing 100,000 1p shares at £1 (i.e. at a premium of 99p per share). In either case, the issue price (£1 in both cases) determines the amount raised by the company, whilst the par value, set by the company, is a figure determined in order to give the company maximum flexibility under the Act.[60] This situation was changed, however, by the 1948 Act. The rule, now stated in section 610 of the 2006 Act, is that a sum equal to the aggregate amount or value of the premiums shall be transferred to a "share premium account" which, in general, has to be treated as if it were part of the paid-up share capital. However, the Act does not fully assimilate share capital and the share premium. It is still necessary to refer expressly to both, and for the company, in its annual accounts and reports, to distinguish between the share capital account and the share premium account What, if it were not for arbitrary par values, would be a single item—capital—has to be treated as two distinct items, albeit for most purposes treated identically.

The choice made in 1948 to treat both the nominal value and the **11–9** share premium as varieties of legal capital was highly significant, because, as indicated, it makes the capital maintenance rules more demanding than they would otherwise have been. However, it is far from clear that the Second Directive's rules on minimum capital and capital maintenance extend beyond nominal capital; indeed, the contrary seems to be the case.[61] This certainly seems to have been the interpretation of the British drafters who transposed the authorised minimum requirement so as to make it a rule about the amount of nominal capital.[62] It is certainly the case that a number of Member States of the Community base their capital maintenance rules on the nominal value of the share (rather than the full consideration received), thus making the capital maintenance rules in those countries largely optional.[63]

However, even in domestic law share capital and share premim are not treated as wholly identical, though the 2006 Act has narrowed

---

[60] In some cases, the nominal value of the share has a more substantial significance. The dividend entitlement of a preference share is normally set as a percentage of the nominal value of the share, so that choosing a low nominal value for a preference share might imply a high percentage dividend. To produce the equivalent of a 10% dividend on a £1 share, the dividend entitlement on a 1p share would have to be 1000%! In general with preference shares, given their bond-like characteristics (see para.23–7), the nominal value will be set much closer to the issue price, since the nominal value will also determine what the preference shareholder receives in a reduction of capital or liquidation, at least if the holder has no right to participate in surplus assets.

[61] See J. Rickford (ed), *Reforming Capital* (2004) 15 EBLR at 939–941.

[62] The Directive does not use the terms nominal capital or share premium but talks simply of "subscribed" capital.

[63] Rickford, *ibid.* fn.61.

some of the differences between them. Section 610 provides two "exceptions" and two "reliefs" for the share premium account which do not apply to the capital account. The first exception is that a company may apply the share premium account in paying up bonus shares.[64] A bonus share is a share issued to the existing shareholders, without requiring any payment from them, but is paid for, in this case, by using the share premium account.[65] Since the effect of this transaction is simply to reduce the share premium account but to increase the share capital account by an equivalent amount, it is wholly unobjectionable from the creditors' point of view,[66] and it is hardly an exception to the main rule laid down by section 610. It would, of course, be impossible thus to apply share capital account but to apply share premium account in this way is unobjectionable since the only effect is to convert it, or a part of it, to share capital proper. The second exception is that the share premium account may be applied in writing off the expenses of or the commissions paid on the issue of the shares which generated the premiums.[67] This is a real exception, but now is a relatively minor contrast with share capital. Within limits, share capital may also be used to pay commission.[68] Although the rule in relation to the share premium account is somewhat more broadly phrased, the rule is now tighter than it was previously.[69]

More important (and more interesting) are the "reliefs". Section 610 (as did its predecessors) expressly applies to issues at a premium "whether for cash or otherwise". The result of this was held to be that if, say, on a merger one company (A) acquired the shares of another (B) in consideration of an issue of A's own shares and the true value of B's shares exceeded the nominal value of those issued by A, a share premium account had to be established in respect of the excess.[70] The result of this was that B's undistributed profits formerly available for distribution by way of dividend ceased to be distributable. This caused something of a furore in commercial circles. However, in 1980 the question was again litigated and the earlier decision fully upheld.[71]

---

[64] s.610(3).

[65] The bonus issue could also be funded by distributable profits. See below at para.11–18.

[66] The issuance of a bonus share has little impact on the shareholders either in the normal case. The shareholder now has more shares, but since the value of the company is not increased by this exercise, the market price of each share in the expanded class will fall. Sometimes bonus shares are issued precisely to achieve this result because it is thought that the market value of the share has become so large that it is an obstacle to trading them. See *EIC Services Ltd v Phipps* [2004] 2 B.C.L.C. 589, CA, where the (botched) bonus issue was aimed at reducing the trading price of the shares. A similar result can be obtained by effecting a "stock split" under s.618, an exercise which is possible no matter whether the company has a share premium account of any size.

[67] s.610(2).

[68] s.553 and see below, para.11–13.

[69] Under the 1985 Act the share premiums account could be written off against a wider range of share issue expenses which, in particular, did not necessarily have to have been incurred in relation to the shares generating the premiums.

[70] *Head & Co Ltd v Ropner Holdings Ltd* [1952] Ch. 124.

[71] *Shearer v Bercain Ltd* [1980] 3 All E.R. 295.

In consequence, "merger relief" was introduced in the Companies Act 1981. The general effect of the merger relief provisions[72] is that the premium does not have to be transferred to the share premium account when, pursuant to a merger arrangement, one company has acquired at least 90 per cent of *each*[73] class of equity shares[74] of another in exchange for an allotment of its equity shares at a premium.

The Act also modifies (rather than removes) the requirement for a transfer to the share premium account in certain cases of reconstruction within a group of companies.[75] The relief applies in the case of issues at a premium by a wholly-owned subsidiary in consideration of a transfer to it of non-cash assets from another company in the group comprising the holding company and its wholly-owned subsidiaries. In this case the company issuing the shares is permitted to value the assets received, not by reference to their market value, but by reference to the cost of their acquisition by the transferor company or their value in the books of the transferor company. In this way, the value of the assets received in exchange for the shares will often be reduced, but, to the extent that this reduced value exceeds the nominal value of the shares issued, the excess must be transferred to the share premium account.[76] If this relief is available on the facts of a particular case, the more extensive merger relief is not.[77]

Finally, the Secretary of State is empowered by section 614 to make regulations providing further relief in relation to premiums other than cash premiums or for modifying the reliefs in the Act.

LEGAL CAPITAL AND SHARE ISSUANCE

The legal capital rules have an impact on the terms upon which shares **11–10** can be issued and, especially, on the consideration which may be accepted for them by the company. The impact on the pricing of the shares flows from the rule that shares cannot be issued at a discount to their nominal or par value. The rules on acceptable consideration play a wider role. In part, these rules buttress the authorised minimum requirement. There is not much point in requiring a public company not to commence trading until it has allotted shares with an aggregate nominal value of £50,000, unless there is some reason to

---

[72] ss.612–613.
[73] s.613(3).
[74] Which will include preference shares if they have a right to participate in either dividends or surplus on a winding up beyond a fixed amount: ss.616(1) and 548.
[75] s.611.
[76] s.611(2)–(5), defining the "minimum premium value".
[77] s.612(4).

suppose it has received assets of that value in exchange for the shares. More generally, however, creditors need to be assured that a company has received assets whose value is equivalent to that stated in the company's share capital and share premium accounts. Otherwise, they may mis-price the loans they make to the company. This is the case irrespective of whether any authorised minimum concerns arise in a particular case. However, there can also be an issue of fairness between groups of shareholders in such cases, for example, where one group has provided assets which are clearly equivalent to the price asked for the shares whilst another group has or may not have done so. The shares, if of the same class, confer the same rights on the two groups of shareholders, but the consideration per share provided by one group may be less than that provided by the other. We now look at the rules which address these issues.

No issue of shares at a discount

The real bite of the par value requirement appears when a company wishes to issue shares at less than par. It was established by the courts in the nineteenth century[78] that shares must not be issued at a discount to their nominal par value. This is now stated in the Act,[79] which specifically provides that, if the shares should be so issued, the allottee is liable to pay to the company the amount of the discount with interest.[80] This provision is of some value to creditors, but of only limited value. The creditor is probably less interested in whether the company has received assets equivalent to the nominal value of its shares than in whether it has received assets to the value of the price it claims the shares were issued at, normally higher than the nominal value. The par value rule does not address this concern, though the rules considered below do. Even if the shares are issued at par, the comfort the creditor can derive from the rule will apply only during a limited period. Once the company begins trading, there is no reason why the company's net asset value should be the same as its share capital. In other words, if the creditor is interested in the company's net asset value at a particular point in time, he or she would be better advised to look at the assets and liabilities in the balance sheet rather than try to deduce the position from the company's capital account.

In fact, it could be argued that the rule against discounts to nominal value harms creditors, at least where the company nears insolvency. Suppose that, because of the unsuccessful trading of the company, its shares are in fact trading on the market at less than par. The company needs to raise new capital. No sensible investor will pay more than the market price for the shares and yet the Act seems to

---

[78] Finally in *Ooregum Gold Mining Co v Roper* [1892] A.C. 125, HL.
[79] s.580(1).
[80] s.580(2).

prevent the company from recognising the economic reality of its situation in the pricing of any new issue, which may help it back to solvency. Yet, in this situation creditors will benefit if the legal capital of the company is increased, no matter how little the company receives for its shares. Any contribution from shareholders increases the amount available to satisfy the claims of the creditors. Will the creditor be misled if the company issues shares at a discount to nominal value where that reflects its market position? It is suggested that this will be true only if the creditor has failed to grasp that the market value of the shares is less than their nominal value, in which case it is doubtful whether such creditors will be protected by any technique which requires them to understand a balance sheet.

In fact, there are a number of ways around this problem, though it **11–11** cannot be guaranteed that in every situation one will be available. For example, a new class of share may be created with a lower par value but otherwise with rights substantially the same as the existing shares. This new class of share can be issued without infringing the prohibition on issuing shares at a discount. Nevertheless, as noted, the risk that the par value rule will hamper the company in the future gives companies some incentive to fix low par values initially and to raise most of the consideration for the shares by way of premium, so that the par value displays an even more remote relationship to the issue price than it might otherwise do.

It might be argued that the rule is better understood as a protection for the shareholders. The rule, it might be said, was intended to protect existing shareholders from directors who proposed to devalue (or "dilute") their interest in the company by issuing shares to new shareholders too cheaply. However, dilution arises only if the shares are issued to new investors at a price which is lower than the current market price of the shares, so that the "no shares at a discount" rule does not seem well adapted to shareholder protection either. It will be under-protective of shareholders where the market price is above nominal value and over-protective where it is below. Indeed, what is surprising from a shareholders' perspective is that there is no precise statutory obligation laid on the company to issue shares at a premium, where the market will bear one.[81] This is probably because the company may have a number of good reasons to contract on the basis that the share will be issued at less than its full market price.[82] No doubt, the directors' duty to promote the success of the com-

---

[81] *Hilder v Dexter* [1902] A.C. 474, HL. The argument was there rejected that failing to obtain the premium amounted to the payment of a commission, contrary to what is now s.552 (see below). The decision was undoubtedly right on its facts, since the right to purchase further shares at par was an explicit part of the contract under which the investor had originally become a shareholder in a corporate rescue.

[82] See the previous note and directors' share option schemes, the essence of which is that the director has the right to subscribe in the future for shares in the company at today's share price.

pany[83] will normally require the directors to issue shares at the best obtainable price, though it is far from clear that the company, as opposed to the shareholders, suffers a loss if this is not done.[84]

Consideration received upon issue

11–12 The rules considered below focus on the quality and even the reality of the consideration received by a company upon the issuance of its shares, irrespective of whether that consideration is referable to the nominal value of the share or the premium payable. Before 1980 the domestic rules in this area were exiguous, but they were strengthened as a result of the Second Directive, which, however, has itself been somewhat relaxed recently.[85] As a result, there is a marked divergence between the rules applying to all companies and to public companies only.

Rules applying to all companies

11–13 We should first note that the law does not require that the consideration promised for the shares be immediately due to the company. There is thus a distinction between paid-up capital and uncalled capital, the former being, for example, the amount paid on allotment and the latter the amount payable when the company calls upon the shareholder for the payment in accordance with the terms of the allotment.[86] Long-term uncalled capital could be a valuable indication of creditworthiness since, in effect, it affords a personal guarantee by the members, but it is doubtful whether it is extensively used in private companies.[87]

Whilst the rule prohibiting the issue of shares at a discount doubtfully promotes creditor protection, the rules restricting the use

---

[83] See para.16–24.

[84] "If the share stands at a premium, the directors *prima facie* owe a duty to the company to obtain for it the full value which they are able to get. It is true that it is within their powers under the Companies Acts to issue it at par, even in such a case, but their duty to the company is not to do so unless for good reason." (Per Lord Wright in *Lowry v Consolidated African Selection Trust Ltd* [1940] A.C. 648, 679.) See also *Shearer v Bercain Ltd* [1980] 3 All E.R. 295: "Those who have practised in the field of company law for any length of time will have spent many hours convincing directors that it is wholly wrong for them ... to issue to themselves and their friends shares at par when they command a premium, however great the company's need for capital may be." (Per Walton J.)

[85] A set of relaxations to the Second Directive was made by Directive 2006/68/EC ([2006] OJ L264/32). However, in relation to the issues discussed below the Government took the view that the permitted relaxations were so minor and so hedged about with qualifications that it was not worth taking them up: DTI, *Implementation of the Companies Act 2006: A Consultation Document*, February 2007, para.6.23.

[86] s.547 defines called-up capital so as to include that amount represented by calls which have been made, whether or not they have been met, and the amount payable under the articles or the terms of allotment on a specified future date, even though that date has not arrived.

[87] Or, indeed, by public ones. As the CLR proposed, the Act no longer contains provisions which permit a company to determine by special resolution that any part of its capital which has not been called up shall be incapable of being called up except in a winding up.

of capital to pay commissions etc. undoubtedly do. Payment by way of commissions, brokerage or the like to any person in consideration for subscribing or agreeing to subscribe is prohibited,[88] even if the shares are issued at a premium, except to the limited extent to which they are explicitly permitted. Without this rule, the amount actually received by the company from an investor in exchange for its shares might be substantially less than appears. However, the Act permits commission for subscribing for shares (or procuring others to do so) to be paid out of capital provided it is limited to 10 per cent of the issue price and is authorised by the articles (which may set a lower percentage).[89] It would be logical if this restriction on the payment of commission did not apply to payments out of distributable profits, since creditors have no claim to limit what the company does with such funds. This is what section 552 appears to say, since it provides that a company "must not apply any of its shares or capital money" in the payment of commissions etc.[90] However, the section no longer attempts to do that which earlier drafts of the statute attempted, i.e. to make clear the consequences of infringing the prohibition. They provided that, if there were an agreement to pay commission etc. in breach of the prohibition, the agreement was to be void; if the payment had been made, the amount of the inducement was to be recoverable, either from the person to whom it was paid or any third party who knew of the circumstance constituting the contravention and benefited from it.[91]

Moreover, payment does not have to be in cash; it can instead be made in kind[92] and very frequently is.[93] But, except in relation to public companies, it seems that the parties' valuation of the non-cash consideration will be accepted as conclusive[94] unless its inadequacy appears on the face of the transaction[95] or there is evidence of bad faith.[96] Hence on an issue for a non-cash consideration it is possible to some degree to "water" the shares by agreeing to accept payment in property which is worth less than the value of the shares.

---

[88] s.552.

[89] s.553. S.552(3) also permits the payment of "such brokerage as has previously been lawful"—an obscure and potentially wide permission. On the use of the share premium account to pay commissions etc. see above, para.11–9.

[90] Of course, for a company to make such a payment, even out of distributable profits, might infringe the prohibition on a company giving financial assistance towards the purchase of its own shares, but the latter rule no longer applies to private companies: see para.13–26, below.

[91] *Modernising Company Law—Draft Clauses*, Cm 5553-II, July 2002, cl. 28.

[92] s.582(1) restates the general rule that "shares allotted by a company may be paid-up in money or money's worth (including goodwill and know-how)" but this is followed by exceptions and qualifications relating to public companies only. Again, bonus shares are specifically allowed.

[93] For example, when the proprietor of a business incorporates it by transferring the undertaking and assets to a newly formed company in consideration of an allotment of its shares.

[94] *Wragg, Re* [1897] 1 Ch. 796, CA; *Park Business Interiors Ltd v Park* [1992] B.C.L.C. 1034.

[95] *White Star Line, Re* [1938] Ch. 458.

[96] *Tintin Exploration Syndicate v Sandys* (1947) 177 L.T. 412.

Public companies

11–14   Shares allotted by a public company must be paid up (in cash or in kind) at least as to one quarter of their nominal value and the whole of any premium due.[97] If this does not occur, the share is nevertheless to be treated as if this had happened and the allottee is liable to pay the company that amount, with interest. This provision reduces the company's and creditors' exposure to the continuing solvency of its shareholders, although it is relatively uncommon for companies not to require full payment upon allotment. If the company does want to stagger the payments for the shares, this is a situation in which there is a penalty for setting the nominal value of the shares well below the issue price, because the whole of the premium must be paid up on allotment.

The remaining rules for public companies concern the regulation of non-cash issues, but before turning to them it is important to note the width of the definition of "cash consideration" in section 583(3), for the rules do not apply where the consideration falls within this section. The section includes within the definition of "cash consideration" an undertaking to pay cash to the company in the future, thus putting the company at risk of the insolvency of the shareholder,[98] and also the release of a liability of the company for a liquidated sum.[99] The latter is a useful provision in facilitating equity for debt swaps whereby the creditors of an insolvent company forgo their claims as debtors against the company in exchange for the issue to them of equity shares. The company is thereby released from an often crippling burden of interest payments and the removal of the debt may even produce by itself a surplus of assets over liabilities. This will be to the immediate benefit of the shareholders and unsecured creditors, though if the company prospers in the future the original shareholders will naturally find that their equity interest has been extensively diluted. It seems that no infringement of the rule forbidding issuing shares at a discount to par value occurs where the face value of the debt is taken for the purposes of paying up the new shares, even though the market value of the debt at the time of the swap was less than its face value because of the debtor's insolvency.[100]

---

[97] s.586.

[98] s.583(3)(d). There is no apparent limit on the future date which may be fixed for the actual payment, for the five-year limit in s.587 (see below) applies only to non-cash payments, but the undertaking must be one given to the company in consideration of the allotment of the shares: *System Controls Plc v Munro Corporation Plc* [1990] B.C.C. 386. And the "cash" must be given to the company, not a third person: s.583(5).

[99] s.583(3)(c). So, if the company owes the investor a sum of money, the release by the investor of the company from that obligation in exchange for the shares amounts to the provision of a cash consideration for them: *EIC Services Ltd v Phipps* [2004] 2 B.C.L.C. 589 at [36] to [52] (Neuberger J.).

[100] *Mercantile Trading Co, Schroeder's Case, Re* (1871) L.R. 11 Eq. 13; *Pro-Image Studios v Commonwealth Bank of Australia* (1990–1991) 4 A.C.S.R. 586, though it should be noted that in this case both the debt and the consideration for the new shares were immediately payable.

A public company may not accept, in payment for its shares or any premium on them, an undertaking by any person that he or another will do work or perform services for the company or any other person.[101] If it should do so, the holder of the shares[102] at the time they are treated as paid up (wholly or partly) by the services is liable to pay the company an amount equal to the nominal value of the shares plus the premium or such part of that amount as has been treated as paid up by the undertaking.[103] Nor may the company allot shares as fully or partly paid-up if the consideration is *any* sort of undertaking which need not be performed until after five years from the date of the allotment.[104] If the undertaking should have been performed within five years but is not, payment in cash then becomes due immediately.[105] And (though this is of minimal importance) shares taken by a subscriber to the memorandum of association in pursuance of his undertaking in the memorandum must be paid for in cash.[106]

Valuation of non-cash consideration

Finally, the possibility of "share-watering" by placing an inflated value on the non-cash consideration is tackled in the case of public companies by requiring it to be independently valued. Under Chapter 6 of Part 17 a public company may not allot shares as fully or partly paid-up (as to their nominal value or any premium) otherwise than in cash unless:—(i) the consideration has been valued in accordance with the provisions of the Part, (ii) a report is made to the company in accordance with that section during the six months immediately preceding the allotment and (iii) a copy is sent to the proposed allottee.[107] To this there are exceptions in relation to bonus issues[108] and in relation to most types of takeovers and mergers.[109] But, in other cases, if the allottee has not received the copy of the valuation report or there is some other contravention of the Part, which he knew, or ought to have known, amounted to a contravention, once

11–15

---

[101] s.585. But this section (nor s.587 below) does not prevent the company from enforcing the undertaking: s.591. If a private company wishes to convert to a Plc such undertakings must first be performed or discharged: s.91(1)(d).

[102] Including the holder of the beneficial interest under a bare trust: s.585(3).

[103] s.585(2).

[104] s.587(1). If contravened the consequences are similar to those for contravention of s.585, except that the liability falls on the allottee: s.587(2). If a contract of allotment does not offend s.587(1) but is later varied so as to produce this consequence, the variation is void: s.587(3).

[105] s.587(4). And see s.91(1)(d) regarding a private company converting to a Plc.

[106] s.584.

[107] s.593(1).

[108] s.593(2).

[109] ss.594–595. The rules of the Act, the Takeover Panel or the FSA will normally ensure that there has been professional assessment of value in such cases.

again he or she is liable to pay in cash with interest.[110] These provisions clearly protect existing shareholders as well as creditors.

The valuation has to be made by a person "qualified to be appointed, or continue to be, an auditor of the company"[111] and that person must meet statutory tests of independence from the company.[112] The expert has a similar right to an auditor to require from officers of the company the information and explanations required to produce the valuation.[113] The expert may, however, arrange for and accept a valuation from another person who appears to him to have the requisite experience and knowledge and who is not an employee or officer of any company in the group.[114] In practice, therefore, the report will be by the company's auditor supported by another professional valuation of any real property or other consideration which the auditor does not feel competent to value on his own. The report has to go into considerable detail[115] and must support the conclusion that the aggregate of the cash and non-cash consideration is not less than the nominal value and the premium.[116]

A private company proposing to convert to a public one cannot evade these valuation requirements by allotting shares for a non-cash consideration shortly before it re-registers as a public one. In such a case, the Registrar cannot entertain the application to re-register unless the consideration has been valued and reported on in accordance with the above provisions.[117]

11–16   This relatively straightforward mandatory valuation rule, imposed where a public company issues shares for a non-cash consideration, is extended by the Act to a category of cases where the company acquires a non-cash asset in exchange for something other than the issuance of shares.[118] This rule applies only during the period of two years after the company has been issued with a trading certificate;[119] only to agreements on the part of the company to acquire non-cash assets from anyone who was a subscriber to the memorandum on the company's formation or a member of it on its conversion to a public company;[120] and only where the consideration to be provided by the company is at least equal to one tenth of its issued share capital. This

---

[110] s.593(3). As is a subsequent holder unless he is or claims through a purchaser for value without notice: s.605(1),(3). See *Bradford Investments, Re* [1991] B.C.L.C. 224.

[111] ss.596(1) and 1150. For these qualifications, see Ch.22, below.

[112] ss.1151–1152.

[113] s.1153. Knowingly or recklessly making a false statement under the section is a criminal offence: s.1153(2)–(4). Unlike the auditor's right, the independent expert's does not extend to employees of the company. See para.22–3.

[114] s.1150(2).

[115] s.596(3)–(5).

[116] s.586(3)(d).

[117] s.93.

[118] s.598.

[119] s.598(2)—the "initial period". For the requirement for a public company to obtain a trading certificate see above, para.11–4.

[120] ss.598(1)(a) and 603.

provision is aimed at a purchase by the company of property from the promoters of the company at an excessive price, though it seems relatively easy to avoid by simply not becoming a member of the company until just after either of the two dates which trigger the mandatory valuation rule. Again, these controls protect both creditors and "outside" shareholders, but a significant feature of the extended rule is that it places greater emphasis on the protection of the shareholders through the imposition of the additional requirement that the shareholders approve of the proposed transaction.

Unless the transaction is in the ordinary course of the company's business or the agreement is entered into under the supervision of the court,[121] the following conditions will have to be complied with:

(i) the consideration to be received by the company and any consideration (other than cash) to be given by the company must be independently valued;

(ii) the valuer's report must have been made during the six months immediately preceding the agreement;[122]

(iii) the terms of the agreement must have been approved by an ordinary resolution, a copy of the valuer's report having been circulated to the members in advance, and a copy of the proposed resolution and valuer's report being sent to the other party to the transaction.[123]

If the other party to the transaction does not receive a copy of the valuer's report or there has been some other contravention of the above requirements which that person knew or ought to have known constituted a contravention, the agreement, so far as not carried out, is void.[124] Moreover, the company can normally recover the consideration given by it or its value.[125] However, if the agreement included provision for the allotment of the company's shares, that provision is not void but the consequences are similar to those on contravention of an allotment without valuation, i.e. the allottee becomes liable to pay cash with interest.[126]

The valuation requirements, especially on a small issue of shares, are potentially time-consuming and expensive. However, they are required by the Second Directive.[127] In 2006 the Directive was amended so as to permit certain assets to be valued without an

---

[121] s.598(4),(5).
[122] s.599. S.600 adapts the provisions of ss.1150–1153 to meet the requirements of the valuation here required.
[123] ss.599(1)(c) and 601.
[124] s.604(2)(b).
[125] s.604(2)(a).
[126] s.604(3).
[127] Arts.10 and 11.

independent expert's report.[128] Although the Act contains a power for
the Secretary of State to make regulations to modify the independent
valuation requirements,[129] the Government did not propose to take
up the options offered by the amendment to the Directive, on the
grounds it was not clear the amendments did relax the provisions of
the Directive and, in any event, they would not simplify the
legislation.[130]

Further provisions as to sanctions

11–17   The above provisions, both those relating to all companies and those
applying to public companies alone, impose civil liability in most
cases on the allottee towards the company, as we have seen. However,
by the time the company comes to enforce that liability, it is not
unlikely that the shares will be in the hands of someone else. The
general policy of the Act is to impose liability jointly and severally
with the allottee on the subsequent holder[131] of the shares, but subject
to a major defence.[132] Following normal equitable principles, that
defence is that the holder is a purchaser for value in good faith (i.e.
without actual knowledge of the contravention concerned) of the
securities or someone who derives title from such a purchaser.[133]
Consequently, if the shares have been traded in the normal way on a
public market, the current holder will not be liable. On the other
hand, a donee of the shares would be jointly and severally liable.

The liability which the above provisions impose on the allottee or
the current holder of the shares is potentially substantial, in respect of
what might be only a technical breach of the statute, for example, the
allottee has not been sent a copy of the valuer's report, though the
allottee is in fact aware of its contents. Even where there has been a
more than technical breach, the liability imposed may be penal. For
example, a failure to have non-cash assets valued makes the allottee
liable to pay the whole of the consideration due for the shares in cash
with interest,[134] without any account being taken of the actual value
of the non-cash assets transferred. Consequently, the court has the
power to grant relief against liability to make a payment to the

---

[128] Arts.10A and 10B.

[129] s.657(1).

[130] DTI, above, fn.85, para.6.23.

[131] "Holder" is defined to include not just the registered holder of the share but also a person
who has the unconditional right to be included in the company's register of members or to
have a transfer of the share executed in his favour: ss.588(3) and 605(4). See Ch.27 below.

[132] ss.588 and 605.

[133] ss.588(2) and 605(3). The requirement for "actual notice" is favourable to the subsequent
holder. On the possible meanings of "actual knowledge" see *Eagle Trust Plc v SBC Securities Ltd* [1991] B.C.L.C. 438.

[134] s.593(3).

company in most cases,[135] but that power to grant relief is limited.[136] In particular, the court must have regard to two "overriding principles", namely:

(a) that a company which has allotted shares should receive money or money's worth at least equal in value to the aggregate of the nominal value of those shares and the value of the premium or, if the case so requires, so much of that aggregate as is treated as paid-up;[137] and

(b) that when the company would, if the court did not grant exemption, have more than one remedy against a particular person it should be for the company to decide which remedy it should remain entitled to pursue.[138]

Capitalisation Issues

"Capital", in the sense of the net worth of a business, will fluctuate   **11–18** from time to time according to whether the company makes profits and ploughs them back or suffers losses. But a company's legal capital, i.e. the issued share capital plus share premium account (if any) does not automatically fluctuate to reflect this. It remains unaltered until increased by a further issue of shares, which must be made in conformity with the rules dealt with above, or reduced in accordance with the rules dealt with in Chapter 13. If, however, the company has made profits and not distributed them as dividends, a necessary consequence of the static nature of its capital accounts is that its net asset value will exceed its legal capital. This is not necessarily something either company or shareholders need worry about—in fact, they should welcome the profits—but an accounting device is needed to bring the company's books back into balance. This is to be found in a further (notional) liability on the balance sheet in order to balance the "assets" and "liabilities". This is normally described as a "reserve", an expression which may confuse those unaccustomed to accounting practice since it may suggest

---

[135] There is no such power in the case of the issuance of shares at a discount, so that the relief powers apply to the public company rules only.

[136] ss.589 and 606.

[137] The importance of which is demonstrated in *Bradford Investments Plc (No.2), Re* [1991] B.C.L.C. 688.

[138] ss.589(5) and 606(4). For other matters which the court should take into account, see ss.589(3),(4) and 606(2),(3). When proceedings are brought by one person (e.g. a holder of the shares) against another (e.g. the original allottee) for a contribution in respect of liability the court may adjust the extent (if any) of the contribution having regard to their respective culpability in relation to that liability: ss.589(6) and 606(5). And see s.606(6) for exemption from liability under s.604(3)(b).

(falsely) that the company has set aside an actual earmarked fund to meet some potential or actual liability. The crucial point is that this reserve is a distributable reserve, unlike the capital accounts, i.e. the company can distribute assets to its shareholders up to the value in the reserve, and keep its books in balance by reducing the reserve accordingly.

Should a profit-rich company wish to bring its legal capital more into line with its net worth, it can do so by making a "bonus" or "capitalisation" issue[139] to its shareholders. The former expression is likely to be used by the company when communicating with its shareholders (in the hope that they will think that they are being treated generously by being given something for nothing) and the latter when communicating with the workforce (which might otherwise demand a bonus in the form of increased wages). In fact, such an issue is merely a means of capitalising reserves by using them to pay-up shares newly issued to the shareholders.[140] We have already noted one form of bonus issue, where the shares are paid up out of the share premium account, which is accordingly reduced to the extent of the nominal value of the bonus shares. Here, however, the bonus shares are paid up out of the distributable profits reserve. For example, suppose that before the issue the net worth (taking book values) of the company was £2 million and the issued capital one million shares of £1 each. The shares, on book values, will be worth £2 each.[141] The company then makes a one-for-one bonus issue paid up out of the distributable profits reserve. The immediate effect on a shareholder is that for each former £1 share worth £2 he or she will now have two £1 shares each worth £1.[142] However, a more significant change has occurred, which may have implications for the future. The formerly distributable profit can no longer be distributed because it has been converted into share capital. The company is thus signalling a need to have greater permanent risk capital than might previously have been

---

[139] The two expressions mean the same thing and, indeed, so does a third ("scrip" issue) which is sometimes used.

[140] Technically, there is a two-stage process. First, the undivided profits of the company are capitalised and then there is the appropriation to each member who would have been entitled to a distribution of the profits by way of dividend of the amount needed to pay up as fully paid the shares to be issued. See *Topham v Charles Topham Group Ltd* [2003] 1 B.C.L.C. 123, especially at pp.139–141, where the failure of a parent company to carry out the first step (because its accounts in fact showed no distributable profits, though its subsidiary did have such profits) meant that the issue of the bonus shares was ineffective to create any right in the shareholders to receive the shares. *Cf. Cleveland Trust, Re* [1991] B.C.L.C. 424, where the company's accounts erroneously showed a distributable profit (in fact the profit so shown was repayable to a subsidiary) and the issue of the bonus shares was held to have been effective, as far as the statute was concerned, but rendered void by the common law doctrine of common mistake.

[141] This does not mean that listed shares will be quoted at that price: that will depend on many other factors, including in particular the expected future profits and dividends. And the book values, of fixed assets in particular, may not reflect their present values.

[142] The *quoted* price is not likely to fall by a half because it is to be expected that the company will seek to maintain approximately the same rate of dividend per share as before the issue.

understood to be the case. Further, it is likely to stop short of capitalising undistributed reserves to an extent which would impair its freedom to pursue an appropriate dividend policy in the future. Thus, a bonus share paid up out of distributable reserves is a potentially more significant event than such shares paid up from the share premium account, where the decrease in one undistributable account is balanced by the increase in another.

CONCLUSION

The requirement that a public company have a minimum allotted **11–19** capital when it begins trading is of doubtful utility to creditors, given the low level at which it is set. Protections of creditors which take as their base the nominal value of the share (notably the rule against issues at a discount to nominal value) are also of doubtful utility, given the company's freedom to set the nominal value of the share, and may even be harmful to their interests in certain circumstances. The rules designed to ensure that a company receives assets of a value equal to the price at which it has issued the shares are more useful to creditors and also promote equal treatment of different groups of members holding the same class of share. However, such rules do not depend for their effectiveness on a concept of legal capital. Such rules could be equally well-formulated and enforced even if there were no legal capital rules. The main claim that the legal capital rules have to remain part of our company law must rest, therefore, on their role in constraining the payment of distributions to the members of the company to which we turn next.

CHAPTER 12

DIVIDENDS AND DISTRIBUTIONS

THE BASIC RULES

The rules on legal capital discussed in the previous chapter have their **12–1**
main impact as a control on the amount a company may pay by way
of dividend or other form of distribution to its shareholders. That is
to say, these rules set a maximum limit on what may be so distributed. Whether the company chooses to make the maximum distribution permitted by the distribution rules is, in most
circumstances, a matter for it. Where a company has substantial
distributable profits, it will often not pay them all out to the shareholders but will keep some for re-investment. The legal rules have
their bite where the company does in fact hold enough cash to make a
dividend but the rules to be discussed in this chapter prevent a distribution at the level the company would desire. The internal procedure which a company has to follow when declaring a dividend is
left to the articles of association, but the model articles for both
private and public companies limited by shares require both a
recommendation from the board and shareholder approval, but with
the shareholders not permitted to approve a level of dividend above
that recommended by the directors.[1] If the articles, unusually, say
absolutely nothing about the mechanism for determining dividends,
then on normal principles that decision would rest with the share-

---

[1] Draft model articles for private companies, art.30(2); for public companies, art.69(2).

holders alone. There is no apparent reason why the articles should not give the dividend decision entirely to the directors, though it is rare to do so, and it is thought that that would require very clear words in the articles, i.e. the court would be unlikely to deduce this result from a general grant of management powers to the board.

The inter-relationship between the legal capital rules and the rules on distributions appears most clearly in the rule applicable to public companies and set out in section 831 of the Act.[2] It applies a balance-sheet test for the legality of a distribution. A company must not make a distribution if its net assets (assets minus liabilities) are (or would be after the distribution) less than its called up share capital and undistributable reserves.[3] Its undistributable reserves include its share premium account.[4] Thus, to take a simple example, a company which has issued as fully paid up 200 £1 shares at an issue price of £1.50 will have a share capital of £200 and a value of £100 in its share premium account. Consequently, for such a company it will not be enough to permit a distribution of, say, 10p per share that it has positive net assets of £20, so that it can pay the dividend and still have assets in balance with its liabilities. Instead, it must have positive net assets of £320 before it pays the dividend. The legal capital rules thus lead to greater conservatism in the payment of dividends than would a "bare" net assets test for the legality of dividend payment (which test is obviously not the only potential alternative to the current test). One can also see from this example the significance of the share premium account being classified as an undistributable reserve in domestic law.[5] If, as before 1948, the share premium account were a distributable reserve, the company would need to have positive net assets of only £220 before it made the dividend payment. And had the company chosen to set the par value at 10p (but still issued the shares at the same price, generating a premium of £1.40 per share), it would have needed positive net assets of only £40 before it made the dividend payment.

However, the undistributable reserves include not only the share premium account. Also added is the "capital redemption reserve" which we shall consider in the following chapter.[6] That is created when a company re-purchases or redeems its shares, and it simply replaces the reduction in the share capital account which the re-purchase or redemption brings about. In other words, the capital redemption reserve operates so as to hold legal capital constant in this situation but it does not increase it. Further, there is added any

---

[2] The rule is derived from Art.15(1)(a) of the Second Directive (77/91/EEC).
[3] s.831(1),(2).
[4] s.831(4)(a). On the share premium account see para.11–8.
[5] s.610 and para.11–8.
[6] Below, para.13–3.

other undistributable reserve created by an enactment other than Part 23 of the Act.[7] The company itself may also add restrictions in its articles by creating an undistributable reserve.[8] There is one final item in the list of undistributable reserves which, however, is best examined after looking at the rule which applies to all companies.

This further rule is set out in section 830[9] and states that a company may "make a distribution only out of profits available for the purpose". It then defines "profits available for the purpose" as the company's "accumulated realised profits, so far as not previously utilised by distribution or capitalisation, less its accumulated, realised losses, so far as not previously written off in a reduction or reorganisation of capital duly made."[10] This second rule, unlike the first one, seems focussed on the company's profit and loss account, rather than its balance sheet. The thrust of the rule is on two points. First, the company needs to assess its accumulated profits and losses over the years to determine whether, at the point a dividend is under consideration, there are profits to support it. Thus, what are sometimes called "nimble dividends" are not permitted, i.e. the paying of dividends out of profits earned in a particular year, even though in previous years the company has made losses, which have not been replaced.[11] More fully, the company must subtract from the profits it has made over the years any amounts already paid out by way of dividend or any profits which have been capitalised,[12] but it may also deduct from its losses it has made over the years any amount properly written off through a reduction or reorganisation of capital.[13] If the company's aggregate profits over the years exceed its aggregate losses over the years, it may make a distribution under this rule to the extent of the surplus profit, subject, however, to one further qualification.

12–2

The second feature of section 830 is that it applies to only "realised" profits and "realised" losses. "Unrealised" profits and losses are left out of account in the calculation required by section 830.[14]

---

[7] An example of a undistributable reserve created elsewhere in the Act is the re-denomination reserve created by s.620 of the Act. See para.11–7. This operates in the same way as the CRR.

[8] Which was the cause of the problems in *Cleveland Trust Plc, Re* [1991] B.C.L.C. 424 where the company's constitution provided that certain realised profits "shall be dealt with as capital surpluses not available for the payment of dividends", which provision, however, was overlooked.

[9] Derived from Art.15(1)(c) of the Directive.

[10] s.830(2). With one exception, the Act does not distinguish between trading profits and capital profits, such as that made on the ad hoc disposal of the company's head office, and both are distributable. In the case of investment companies, however, only revenue profits are in principle distributable: ss.832–835.

[11] This reverses the common law: *Lee v Neuchatel Asphalte Co* (1889) 41 Ch. D. 1, CA; *Ammonia Soda Co v Chamberlain* [1918] 1 Ch. 266, CA.

[12] See para.11–18.

[13] See Ch.13.

[14] This again reverses the English common law rule which allowed unrealised profits on fixed assets to be distributed: *Dimbula Valley (Ceylon) Tea Co Ltd v Laurie* [1961] Ch. 353. Scots law took a stricter view: *Westburn Sugar Refineries v I R C* 1960 S.L.T. 297.

"Realised" profits and losses are not defined in the Act which delegates the solution to accounting practice.[15] In fact, the precise line
between the two is a matter of some controversy, particularly on the
question of whether realisation requires a transaction with a third
party,[16] but for present purposes it is perhaps enough to give two
clear examples, one on each side of the line. Suppose a company has a
piece of real property which it acquired some years ago for £1 million.
Because of an inflation in asset prices, the property is now worth £5
million. If the company sells the property at its current valuation,
receiving £5 million in cash in exchange, it will report a profit of £4
million (assuming no taxes or transaction costs) which it may distribute in whole to its shareholders (assuming it has no accumulated
realised losses from the past which it must set against the profit). If,
however, the company simply re-values the property in its books at
£5 million (but does not dispose of it), which is something it might do
in order to demonstrate that a takeover bidder was offering too low a
price for the company or because it has adopted accounting principles
which systematically deal with its assets and liabilities on a "mark to
market" basis, it has recorded simply an unrealised profit.[17] Since the
property will be reflected in the balance sheet at a higher value, a
counterbalancing entry is needed, which will probably take the form
of a "revaluation reserve".[18] The same principles apply to losses: only
realised losses count against the amount of distributable profit.

12–3   A troubling issue is understanding the interrelationship between
the two rules laid down in sections 830 and 831. Since the former
applies to all companies and the latter to public companies alone, the
latter presumably prevents certain amounts contributing towards a
distribution which would count under the former. But what are those
amounts or items? At first sight, the rules seem to have an entirely
different focus, the general rule looking at successive profit and loss
accounts and the public company looking at the current state of the

---

[15] s.853(4): they are "such profits or losses of the company as fall to be treated as realised in
accordance with principles generally accepted at the time when the accounts are prepared
..." However, s.841 does lay down that provisions in the accounts (other than revaluation
provisions) should be treated as realised losses (for example, depreciation provisions); s.844
requires development costs to be treated as a realised loss, even if stated as an asset in the
accounts; and s.843 makes provisions about the realised gains and losses of long-term
insurance businesses.

[16] See CLR, *Capital Maintenance: Other Issues*, paras 62–66; ICAEW, *Guidance on the
Determination of Realised Profits and Losses in the Context of Distributions under the
Companies Act 1985*, Tech 7/03.

[17] If, however, the re-valued asset is later distributed *in specie* to its shareholders (a perfectly
possible, if not common, course of action, because distributions do not have to be in cash)
the amount of the unrealised profit is treated as a realised profit for the purpose of determining the legality of the distribution: s.846. The purpose of this provision is to make it
possible for the company to distribute assets at book value, even if the value to be found in
the company's accounts represents a revaluation of the assets. See further below at para.12–
4. The provision was driven initially by a perceived need to facilitate de-mergers, in which
assets or shares held by a company might be distributed to its shareholders.

[18] Which is a undistributable reserve unless it represents realised gains: Fourth Directive (78/
660/EEC), Art.33(2)(c).

balance sheet. The profit and loss account records the company's financial success (or lack of it) over a period of a year, the balance sheet its assets and liabilities at the end of the year.[19] However, the two are clearly interrelated over time. Take a simple example: if a company at the end of a year shows a profit of £1 million and it decides to distribute none of that profit to the shareholders, then the profit will be reflected in the asset items on the balance sheet and a balancing item, probably by way of a running profit and loss entry, will have to appear on the balance sheet as well. Thus, it is probably not helpful to regard the two tests as focussing on different aspects of the company's performance, once one understands that the general rule applies across successive profit and loss accounts. Both tests are, in effect, balance sheet tests.

However, this analysis gives rise to a different problem. If the results of the company's profits and losses over the years are identified in the balance sheet, how does the rule for public companies constrain a public company from distributing the whole of the amount revealed in the running profit and loss account? Since share capital, share premium account and capital redemption reserve are liabilities, a rule that distributions may be made only out of net profits does not permit the company to ignore legal capital when determining distributions. In other words, the "dividends out of profits" rule also requires the company's net assets after the payment of the dividend to be equal to or exceed legal capital. The difference between the two rules seems in the end to come down to the final item in the list of undistributable reserves in section 831 which we have not yet mentioned. The section renders undistributable "the amount by which its accumulated unrealised profits ... exceed its accumulated, unrealised losses ..."[20] Since unrealised profits are not distributable in any event under the general rule, as we have just seen, it may not be obvious why this provision is important. This can perhaps be seen if we take the situation where the figure under this heading is a minus amount, because unrealised losses exceed unrealised profits. In other words, a public company must take unrealised losses into account when determining the maximum amount payable by way of dividend, but a private company need not.

DEFINITION OF A DISTRIBUTION

The above rules apply to "distributions" by companies. Beyond **12–4** making it clear that a distribution need not be in cash and that the

---

[19] See further, Ch.21 below.
[20] s.831(4)(c).

definition is intended to be extensive, the statutory definition is not very helpful: "every description of distribution of a company's assets to its members, whether in cash or otherwise".[21] No doubt, this is sufficient to catch the most common form of distribution, the yearly or semi-yearly payment of a dividend by a company to its share-holders, usually in cash but sometimes with the alternative of sub-scribing for additional shares in the company. The statutory definition is clearly intended to go beyond that simple situation, by its reference to non-cash dividends, but how far? One thing that is clear is that not all payments received from a company by a person who is in fact a shareholder fall within the statutory definition. If that were so, corporate life would be difficult to organise. Suppose a share-holder is also a director of the company and has a service contract with it, remuneration due under the contract does not have to satisfy the statutory tests for distributions. A company can pay its directors under their service contracts, even if it has no distributable profits and even if the directors are members of the company. However, if the object of the contract is to achieve a result which undermines the statutory rules laid down for the protection of creditors[22] or if the payment is not a genuine payment of remuneration,[23] the contract will be unenforceable and payments made will be recoverable.

Some further guidance can probably be gained from the common law decisions on the meaning of a distribution, where a wide view was also taken. However, this raises a second fundamental issue, namely the relationship between the common law and the statutory rules on distributions. The Act makes it clear that the statutory rules do not displace any more restrictive common law rules, which therefore operate in tandem with the statutory rules on distributions.[24] The

[21] s.829(1). Certain transactions are specifically exempted from the term: an issuance of bonus shares (for the reasons given at para.11–18); transactions regulated elsewhere in the Act (reductions of capital and redemption or re-purchase of shares (see the following chapter); and distributions on a winding up (regulated by the Insolvency Act 1986): s.829(2). The exclusion of bonus shares permits companies to capitalise unrealised (and thus undis-tributable) profits, assuming they have power in the articles so to do (as art.36 of the draft model articles for private companies and art.77 of those for public companies provide). S.848 gives statutory authority to this end for pre-1980 companies whose powers under the articles might otherwise have been involuntarily restricted by the changes made in the Companies Act 1980.

[22] *MacPherson v European Strategic Bureau Ltd* [2000] 2 B.C.L.C. 683, CA. In this case, the contract sought to produce the result for the shareholder/directors which would obtain on a winding up (which is a permitted exception to the distribution rules: see fn.21 above), except that no provision was made for the creditors, which is a central objective of the winding-up rules.

[23] See *Halt Garage (1964) Ltd, Re* [1982] 3 All E.R. 1016—payment of remuneration where no services rendered held to be a disguised return of capital. However, if the payment is genuinely remuneration, the court will not investigate its adequacy under the distributions rule.

[24] s.851(1). After some havering, the Company Law Review proposed to reverse the position that the common law and statutory regimes operate in tandem and to make the statute the exclusive source of rules in this area (see Formation, para.3.66; Maintenance, Pt II; Com-pleting, para.7.21), but this proposal was not taken up in the Act.

relevant common law rule is that a company cannot return capital (or perhaps any corporate assets) to its shareholders, except to the extent authorised by or under a relevant statutory procedure or by way of a contract for full consideration.[25] These two issues came together in the decision of Hoffmann J. in *Aveling Barford Ltd v Perion Ltd.*[26]

In that case, the company, which was solvent (in the sense that it could pay its debts as they fell due) but had accumulated heavy losses, and so was not in a position to meet the general rule requiring distributions only out of accumulated profits, transferred to another company, controlled by the same person as was its controlling shareholder, an important asset at an undervalue as compared with its current market value. There was no doubt that this was a breach of duty on the part of the directors of the transferring company and that the receiving company became a constructive trustee of the company's property.[27] However, it was also held that the transfer was unlawful as being an unauthorised return of capital to the controlling shareholder, the fact that the payment was made to a company controlled by its main shareholder rather than to the shareholder directly being regarded as "irrelevant".[28] This decision caused considerable alarm in commercial circles about the legality of inter-group transfers of assets, which are, of course, a common occurrence as a result of the carrying on of business through groups of companies.[29] Such transfers are usually effected on the basis of the value of the asset as stated in the company's accounts (its "book" value), which may not reflect the current market price of the asset.[30] These problems arose, it is suggested, because the common law does not provide detailed rules for the operation of its principle, unlike the statute which operates, in particular, by reference to the company's published accounts (see immediately below). Advice was given that the common law rule might strike down a transaction where a company transferred an asset at book value to another group company, if the asset was in fact worth more than its book value, and even where the transferring company had distributable reserves (which was not the case in *Aveling Barford* itself).

The 2006 Act deals with this problem by laying down rules about distributions in kind which apply to both the statutory restrictions on distributions and any other rule of law restricting distributions.[31] The

---

[25] *Ridge Securities Ltd v IRC* [1964] 1 W.L.R. 479 at 495.

[26] [1989] B.C.L.C. 626.

[27] See below, para.16–79.

[28] At p.632, *cf.* the cases discussed above at para.8–12.

[29] The nature of the reaction to the decision is set out by the CLR in Maintenance, Pt II.

[30] Since accounts are often, even today, constructed on a "historical" basis, an asset is likely to be shown in the company's balance sheet at the price paid for it (or perhaps less, if it has been depreciated), rather than at its current market value, which might be higher.

[31] s.851(2)—thus embracing not only the common law rules but also rules contained in a statute other than the Act (unless that Act overrides the Act explicitly or by necessary implication).

central and new provision[32] applies where a company has profits available for distribution of sufficient amount to cover the distribution proposed.[33] Where this is not the case, the common law will continue to apply unamended, with the apparent requirement that the asset would have to be transferred at market value to be sure of avoiding the risk of infringing the common law rules on distributions. Given the risk of opportunism on the part of controlling shareholders where the company has no distributable profits, this restriction in the new section is probably wise. Assuming distributable profits, the amount of the distribution is assessed under the section at zero, provided the consideration received for the asset is at least equivalent to its book value, and otherwise is restricted to the amount by which the book value exceeds the consideration.[34] If, by contrast, the consideration received upon the transfer of the asset exceeds its book value, the distributable profits of the company are increased by the amount of the excess.[35] Of course, the rules relating to directors' fiduciary duties[36] are unaffected by these changes.

RELEVANT ACCOUNTS

12–5   It will probably have been apparent from the foregoing that, in determining whether there are profits from which distributions can be made in accordance with the statutory rules, what counts in most cases are the relevant figures in the company's accounts. This is explicitly stated in section 836. This may seem an obvious step to take: companies are normally required by the Act to produce accounts annually and, except for small companies, to have them audited,[37] thus providing a degree of verification; and the declaration of a dividend is normally one of the decisions for the annual general meeting of the shareholders, at which the accounts will be considered as well. However, the use of the numbers in the accounts as an inflexible basis for determining the permitted amount of a distribution has come under question in some quarters as a result of the changing nature of companies' accounts. Under modern develop-

---

[32] s.846 (above, fn.17) is also added to the common law rules.
[33] s. 845(1)—assuming the amount of the distribution to be assessed in accordance with the section.
[34] s.845(2).
[35] s.845(3).
[36] On the duty of directors to have regard to the interests of creditors, see para.16–34, below.
[37] See Chs 21 and 22 below. Dividends are paid by individual companies and so what counts here are the relevant accounts of the paying company, not the accounts of the group of which the company is a member. For an example of the problems that ignoring this point can cause see *Inn Spirit Ltd v Burns* [2002] 2 B.C.L.C. 780.

ments in accounting there is an increasing emphasis on using the current market valuations, rather than historic ones, in the accounts. Such an approach can produce considerable volatility in companies' profits from year to year, and it is now less clear that the accounts should be the almost sole basis for determining distributions, as opposed to a significant element in that decision.[38] However, at least for public companies, such an approach is mandated by the Second Directive in respect of the net asset restriction in section 831[39] and it probably also applies—though this is less clear from the wording of the Directive—to the accumulated net profits rule of section 830. Certainly, the Directive has been interpreted by the drafters in the United Kingdom as requiring both tests to be applied by reference to the numbers in the accounts, and that approach has been applied to private companies as well.

The main thing which the distribution rules have to achieve on this point is the identification of the accounts (the "relevant" accounts) which are to be used for assessing the legality of the distribution. The general rule is easy to state: the most recent statutory accounts should be used.[40] When that is so, the distribution is lawful so long as it is justified by reference to those accounts and the accounts have been properly prepared in accordance with the Act, or have been properly prepared subject only to matters not material for determining whether the distribution would be lawful.[41] These accounts must have been duly audited, if subject to audit, and, if the auditors' report is qualified, the auditors must also state in writing whether the respect in which the report was qualified is material in determining whether the distribution would be lawful. This statement must have been laid before the company in general meeting, or sent to the members where no meeting is held.[42]

Interim and initial accounts

In two cases, however, special accounts will be needed. The first is **12–6** where the distribution would contravene the statutory distribution

---

[38] See J Rickford (ed), *Reforming Capital* (2004) 15 EBLR 1, especially Ch.4 dealing with pension scheme deficits.

[39] See Art.15(1)(a) but *cf.* Art.15(1)(c).

[40] s.836(2).

[41] s.837(2). If the directors knew or ought to have known of a serious defect in the company's accounts, they will not be "properly prepared" nor give a true and fair view, so that any distribution by the company will be unlawful: *Cleveland Trust Plc, Re* [1991] B.C.L.C. 424.

[42] s.837(3), (4). The auditor's statement may be made whether or not a distribution is proposed at the time when the statement is made and may refer to all or any types of distribution; it will then suffice to validate any distributions of the types covered by the statement: s.837(5). This rule also applies if the directors choose to have an audit, although not obliged to do so. The need for the auditors' statement where the accounts are qualified is frequently overlooked and the resulting distribution will be unlawful: *Precisions Dippings Ltd v Precious Dippings Marketing Ltd* [1986] Ch. 447, CA; *BDS Roof-Bond Ltd v Douglas* [2000] 1 B.C.L.C. 401.

rules if reference were made only to the last annual accounts. In that event the company may be able to justify the distribution by reference to additional "interim accounts".[43] The second is where it is proposed to declare a dividend during the company's first accounting period or before any accounts have been presented in respect of that period.[44] In that event it will have to prepare "initial accounts". Initial accounts enable the company to make a distribution before its first set of financial statements is produced; interim accounts allow the company to take advantage of an improvement in its financial position since the previous statutory accounts were produced. This might occur, for example, when a realised profit had been made on the sale of fixed assets after the date of the last annual accounts and the company wanted to distribute part or all of it to its shareholders without waiting until the next annual accounts are prepared. It could also occur if the net trading profits in the current year are seen to be running at a rate considerably higher than formerly and the directors wished to give the shareholders early concrete evidence of this by paying an immediate dividend. In both these examples the last year's accounts might well not justify the payment and would have to be supplemented by interim accounts.

The interim or initial accounts must be those necessary to enable a reasonable judgment to be made on the items needed to be considered in order to determine the legality of the distribution.[45] So far as *private* companies are concerned, that is the only requirement laid down regarding interim or initial accounts; presumably it was thought that it sufficed in relation to them and that it would be unreasonable to impose on them the specific obligations appropriate (and necessary to comply with the Directive) in relation to public companies. In the case of a public company the accounts must have been properly prepared in accordance with the Act, with such modifications as are necessary because the accounts are not prepared in respect of the company's accounting reference period, or have been so prepared subject only to such matters as are not material for determining whether the proposed distribution would contravene the relevant section.[46] And, like annual accounts, a copy of the accounts must be delivered to the Registrar[47] with an English translation if they are in a foreign language.[48] Initial accounts must be audited and, if the auditors' report is qualified, must, as in the case of annual accounts, be accompanied by a written statement on whether the qualifications are material in relation to determining whether the distribution rules

[43] s.836(2)(a).
[44] s.836(2)(b).
[45] ss.838(1) and 839(1).
[46] ss.838(3),(4) and 839(3),(4).
[47] ss.272(4), 273(6).
[48] ss.838(6) and 839(7).

have been complied with.[49] There are no such auditing requirements in relation to interim accounts.[50] Hence a public company with listed shares is unlikely to be put to much additional expense in preparing interim accounts when they are needed since it will have to prepare half-yearly financial statements in order to comply with the FSA's rules.[51]

The term "interim accounts", although now well established in the **12–7** Act, is potentially confusing because it might lead one to suppose that such accounts are needed whenever it is proposed to declare interim or special dividends in addition to the normal dividend for the year. That is not so. So long as the company has duly complied with its obligations under the Act in respect of its annual accounts for the past year, it can, in the current year, pay interim or other special dividends in addition to the final dividend for that year so long as these dividends, in total, do not exceed the amount (as determined from the relevant annual accounts) which it can distribute without contravening the distribution rules.[52] It is only when the last annual accounts would not justify a proposed payment that it is necessary to prepare interim accounts. Normally, however, it will not be necessary to prepare interim accounts merely because the company pays quarterly or half-yearly interim dividends, in anticipation of the final dividend for the year, to be declared by the company when the year's accounts are presented. The articles normally provide for interim dividends to be paid on the authority of the directors alone, there not being any regularly scheduled meeting of the shareholders to which the matter could be put.[53]

The need for interim accounts arises out of the time that may well have passed since the last statutory accounts were drawn up and the proposed dividend payment and the possible improvements in the company's financial position which may have occurred in the interim. What, however, about the opposite situation? What is the position if, before the date of actual payment, the directors realise or suspect that the company would not be in a position to meet the distribution requirements, if interim accounts were now drawn up? The normal practice regarding dividend payments is that a directors' recommendation as to the level of the dividend is an essential part of the

---

[49] s.839(5),(6).

[50] But, in contrast with initial accounts, there will be published audited annual accounts which the interim accounts supplement.

[51] See para.26–3.

[52] The legitimacy of this approach to interim dividends is recognised by section 840, which requires that all previous distributions made by reference to the same set of accounts have to be treated as added to that proposed for the purpose of determining whether the latter will be lawful. For this purpose, "distributions" include not only dividends but also payments made since the date when the relevant accounts were prepared, in respect of financial assistance for the acquisition of the company's shares or as the purchase price for the acquisition by the company of its own shares (unless such payments were lawfully made otherwise than out of distributable profits). On these matters see Ch.13.

[53] As do the draft model articles for both public (art.69(1)) and private (art.30(1)) companies.

dividend-setting process. Whether they should, in the light of their then knowledge, refrain from recommending a dividend will depend on the nature of that knowledge. If they have discovered that the relevant accounts were so seriously inaccurate that they did not in fact give a true and fair view of the state of the company's affairs and its profits or losses at the time the accounts were signed,[54] they clearly should not recommend a dividend, and should withdraw any recommendation they have made; for the dividend, if paid, would be unlawful.[55] If, however, the relevant accounts truly reflected the position as at their date and the only reason why the requisite conditions are no longer met is some calamity occurring thereafter, payment of the dividend would not, seemingly, be unlawful under the statute. Payment in such circumstances might constitute a breach of the directors' fiduciary duties or an act of wrongful trading, and this is also a situation in which the common law rule prohibiting a return of capital to shareholders might bite.[56] The Company Law Review recommended[57] that the statute itself should provide that subsequent losses, of which the company was aware at the time of taking the decision to declare a dividend, should be deducted from the distributable profits shown in the relevant accounts, but this has not been implemented.

CONSEQUENCES OF UNLAWFUL DISTRIBUTIONS

12–8 No criminal sanctions are provided in the case of unlawful distributions covered by the Act but something (though precious little) is said about the civil consequences. This is done by section 847 which provides that, when a distribution[58] is made to a member which the member knows, or has reasonable grounds for believing, is made in contravention (in whole or in part) of the statutory distribution rules, that person is liable to repay it or, if the distribution was otherwise than in cash, its value.[59] Thus, by virtue of this section, the payment, though "unlawful", is neither void nor voidable but can nevertheless be recovered from any recipient of it who knew or ought to have known that it was unlawful.

---

[54] *Cleveland Trust Plc, Re* [1991] B.C.L.C. 424.
[55] And the accounts should be revised; there are now statutory provisions for this: see para.21–30.
[56] See above, para.12–4. See *Peter Buchanan Ltd v McVey* [1955] A.C. 516 at 521–522, HL.
[57] Maintenance, para.38.
[58] Other than a distribution which constitutes financial assistance for the acquisition of the company's own shares given in breach of the Act (see para.13–35) or any payment made in respect of the redemption or purchase of shares in the company (para.13–7): s.847(4).
[59] s.847(2).

This provision has been interpreted to mean that there is liability to repay the dividend if the recipient knows it has not been paid out of distributable profits, even if that person is unaware that such distributions are illegal.[60] The section is thus potentially wide-ranging in its impact on shareholders if this limited definition of what has to be known is coupled with a broad approach to what "knowledge" consists of. This raises the question of whether "reasonable grounds for believing" means that a shareholder is treated as knowing those facts which would have been discovered through proper enquiries (constructive knowledge) or only those to which the recipient turned a blind eye.[61] On the former approach it might be argued that a shareholder who had received the annual reports should be treated as knowing, for example, that the company had no distributable profits or that the auditor had not included the required statement in the case of a qualified report,[62] even if he or she had not in fact read them, and that such knowledge is all that is required to trigger the repayment obligation.[63]

However, this section does not constitute the only basis on which a claim for repayment of dividend can be made against a shareholder. The company may claim repayment at common law.[64] This is on the basis that the payment of an unlawful dividend amounts to a misapplication by the directors of corporate property and where "the transferee of the assets has knowledge of the facts rendering the disposition ultra vires, that party is under a duty to restore those assets to the company because he is deemed to hold them as

---

[60] *It's A Wrap (UK) Ltd v Gala* [2006] 2 B.C.L.C. 634, CA, a case which illustrates the arbitrary nature of many of the legal capital rules. The defendants, who ran a small business which was unsuccessful, paid themselves a modest remuneration, which they could have received entirely lawfully as salary under their service contracts with the company or as directors' fees. See para.12–4 above. However, they were diverted from this course of action by advice that it would be more tax efficient for the remuneration to be paid by way of dividend.

[61] Arden and Chadwick L.JJ. were divided on this issue in *It's A Wrap* (above, fn.60)—the point not being relevant to the decision in that case. The former is a more natural reading of the language of the section and conforms to the approach of the common law (see below), whilst the latter is a more natural reading of the language of the Directive (an irregularity of which the recipient "could not in view of the circumstances have been unaware"), which the section implements in the UK.

[62] Above, para.12–5 and see *Precision Dippings Ltd v Precison Dippings Marketing Ltd* [1986] Ch. 447.

[63] It seems fanciful to suppose that any court would hold that a small shareholder in a listed company should study the relevant accounts and the documents accompanying them and read them with an understanding of the Act to check that their dividends are lawfully payable, no matter how much that court may be committed to the doctrine that ignorance of the law is no excuse. In relation to an institutional investor, however, or a "business angel" who has invested in a start-up company, the proposition is not so fanciful.

[64] This basis of claim is specifically preserved by s.847(3).

constructive trustee."[65] The common law claim, which may or may not be broader than the statutory claim in terms of its definition of knowledge,[66] operates by making the recipient a constructive trustee of the distribution. However, it is in fact unclear whether this gives the company only a personal or a proprietary claim against the recipient. If the latter, the company will not have to compete with the other creditors of the shareholder but can simply recover the amount paid on the grounds that it is, and has always been, the property of the company.[67]

12–9   The statute provides for no specific remedy against the directors, who authorised the unlawful distribution, but here again the common law of directors' duties provided a remedy against directors.[68] It has been clear since the decision in *Flitcroft*'s case[69] in the nineteenth century that directors who pay dividends improperly may in certain circumstances be liable to compensate the company for the loss thereby caused. In *Bairstow v Queens Moat Houses Plc*[70] the principle was applied to hold directors liable where the accounts failed to give a true and fair view[71] of the company's financial situation as a result of accounting irregularities of which the directors were aware. Under the statutory schema, improper payment of dividends might constitute the exercise of a power given by the constitution for an improper purpose, a failure to promote the success of the company or an act of negligence.[72] The principle that the directors should compensate the company for the loss suffered is potentially a much broader one than the claim that a shareholder should return to the company dividends improperly paid to that shareholder. The director might have received no dividends him- or herself and yet be liable, in principle, to compensate the company for the whole of the amount wrongfully paid out of the company's assets. However, in *Bairstow* the court showed little interest in confining the scope of the directors' liability. The principle in *Flitcroft*'s case, the court held, was not limited to companies which were insolvent at the time of the claim against the director (where the directors' payment would go to benefit the creditors) but applied also to solvent companies, so that the

---

[65] *Rolled Steel Products (Holdings) Ltd v British Steel Corporation* [1986] Ch. 246, 303–304 per Browne-Wilkinson L.J. The principle applies equally where the transferee is the director him- or herself, receiving the dividend in the capacity as shareholder: see *Allied Carpets Plc v Nethercott* [2001] B.C.C. 81, following the earlier case of *Precision Dippings Ltd v Precison Dippings Marketing Ltd* [1986] Ch. 447. Indeed, a director of the company or of another group company is the person in respect of whom the knowledge requirements can most easily be met.

[66] Constructive knowledge appears to suffice for liability at common law: see the *Rolled Steel* case (previous note) at pp.297–298, per Slade L.J.

[67] See further at para.16–97.

[68] If the director is a recipient shareholder, then, of course, he or she may be liable in that way. See fn.65.

[69] *Exchange Banking Co, Re* (1882) 21 Ch. D. 519, CA.

[70] [2001] 2 B.C.L.C. 531, CA.

[71] On the meaning of this phrase see para.21–13.

[72] See Ch.16.

directors might end up putting the company in funds whereby it could pay the dividend all over again.[73] Nor was the directors' liability confined to the amount by which the improper dividend exceeded the amount which the company could lawfully have paid out: the directors were liable for the full amount of the improper dividend.[74]

However, this last point has been somewhat qualified in subsequent cases. In *Bairstow*, there were no accounts in existence (i.e. properly prepared in accordance with the Act), at least in relation to the 1991 financial year, by which the dividend payments could have been justified.[75] Where there is a properly drawn set of accounts in existence which justify a distribution up to a particular level but the company exceeds that level, it seems that the requirement to make "a distribution out of profits available for the purpose" means that the directors act improperly only to the extent of the excess.[76] Further, since the directors' obligation to recompense the company derives from a breach of their duty to the company, they can appeal to the court to grant them relief under section 1157 of the Act, provided they have acted "honestly and reasonably."[77]

The upshot of these rules is that directors who make improper distributions are more likely to be held liable to compensate the company than the shareholders who receive them are likely to be to restore them to the company. If directors cannot meet the requirements of section 1157, it is probably right that they are liable to the company for the full amount of the unlawful dividend, since the dividend rules, being tied to the accounting numbers, are not difficult to comply with. Although recovery of small amounts of dividend from numerous shareholders is probably not practicable, it is not clear that recovery should be confined to those who receive the dividend with knowledge of its unlawfulness where this practical objection does not apply.[78]

Finally, one should not forget the possibility of an action by the

---

[73] At pp.545–548. The so-called "windfall" objection to the principle of repayment. The objection works, of course, only if the directors have the resources to repay the dividend and if the company could lawfully pay out the money restored by the directors. The court did leave open the possibility that the directors could claim an equitable contribution from the shareholders who had received the improper dividend with notice of the facts.

[74] At pp.548–550, distinguishing *Target Holdings v Redferns* [1996] A.C. 421, HL. See also *Inn Spirit Ltd v Burns* [2002] 2 B.C.L.C. 780.

[75] See also *Inn Spirit Ltd v Burns* [2002] 2 B.C.L.C. 780, where a subsidiary had paid a dividend directly to the shareholders of the parent company and the court refused to entertain the question of whether the same amount of dividend could have reached the shareholders' pockets by way of a distribution to the parent and then a distribution by the parent.

[76] *Marini Ltd, Re* [2004] B.C.C. 172.

[77] See para.16–96.

[78] For an attractive argument that shareholders should always be liable to repay the dividend, subject to a defence of change of position, see J. Payne, "Unjust Enrichment, Trusts and Recipient Liability for Unlawful Dividends" (2003) 119 LQR 583.

company against its auditors if it can be shown that their negligence led the directors to approve a defective set of accounts.[79]

CONCLUSION

12–10   This chapter has shown that that British law has developed a complex set of rules for the purpose of setting the maximum level of dividend (or other form of distribution) payable by a company in respect of a particular financial period. Those rules take as their central idea that a distribution should be made only if, after it has been made, the company will retain assets whose value exceeds its liabilities by the amount of the company's legal capital. It is not enough that, post the distribution, the company's assets should exceed its liabilities (i.e. that it should have positive net assets). As it has been put, the requirement is that the assets should exceed the liabilities by a "margin" and that margin is set by the amount of the company's legal capital.[80] It is clearly a sensible measure of creditor protection that a company should be subject to constraints on its freedom to transfer assets to shareholders by way of a distribution (for which it receives nothing tangible in return). There would be little point in giving the creditors priority over the members in a winding up if there were no limits on the company's freedom to return assets to members whilst it is a going concern, and the rules of insolvency law, operating only in the vicinity of insolvency, can be argued not to fill the whole of this regulatory need. The question, however, is whether basing those constraints around the notion of legal capital is the most appropriate technique.

It is sometimes said that the present inflexibilities with the distribution rules are the result of the Second Directive. This is only partly true. British law adopted the notion of distribution rules based on legal capital at a very early stage of its development in the nineteenth century.[81] And it was in 1948 that domestic law adopted the position that the share premium must be treated in virtually the same way as the nominal value of the share for the purposes of legal capital rules,[82] probably the single most important step in making the distribution rules an effective constraint on companies. Whilst the Second Directive undoubtedly did tighten the previously applicable distribution rules, for example, by ruling out "nimble" dividends,[83] it

---

[79] See para.22–37.
[80] J.Rickford (ed), "Reforming Capital: Report of the Interdisciplinary Group on Capital Maintenance" [2004] EBLR 1, 51.
[81] See, for example, *Flitcroft's Case* (1882), above, fn.69.
[82] Above, para.11–8.
[83] Above, para.12–2.

did not introduce a fundamentally new approach into domestic law. The inflexibility of the Second Directive relates rather to any fundamental reform of the distribution rules. As far as public companies are concerned, it is not possible for the United Kingdom to move away radically from the test of positive net assets plus a margin represented by legal capital for the legality of dividends, without a reform at Community level.[84] Without reform of the public company rules, it is in general not attractive to the United Kingdom to put the rules for private companies on a new basis.[85] Reform at Community level, of course, could take the form either of the adoption by Community law of a test for distributions no longer based on legal capital or of a decision that the setting of distribution rules is a matter for the Member States in which matter the Community has no or only a limited interest.[86]

Whether reform takes place primarily at Community or at domestic level, the question still remains of the strength of the case for reform. There are really three questions which need to be considered, which can only be sketched out here. First, do the current rules provide creditor protection effectively? There are reasons to think that they do not, for the reason that many, perhaps all, classes of creditor do not rely on them. Sophisticated (i.e. large-scale and repeat) creditors, such as banks, place their trust in the terms of the loan contracts, which deal with many risks other than excessive distributions.[87] Trade creditors use other protective techniques, such as retention-of-title clauses or simply not becoming heavily exposed to a single debtor. Finally, involuntary creditors (notably tort victims) necessarily do not rely on the company's balance sheet and really need a guarantee that their claims will be met, which the legal capital rules do not provide but compulsory insurance would—and does in some cases.[88] In other words, it is not at all easy to identify the

12–11

---

[84] Arguably, this statement is subject to the strong qualification that the Second Directive does not require the share premium to be treated as part of legal capital, in which case the impact of the current distribution rules could be heavily reduced by reducing the margin to the amount of the nominal value of the shares. A legal capital test for distributions would be left in place but it would be largely ineffective. See above, para.11–9. On the pros and cons of such an approach see Rickford, above, fn.80, at pp.70ff.

[85] The one area where this step has been taken is in relation to financial assistance (see para.13–26), but it can be argued that the financial assistance rules are not a necessary consequence of distribution rules based on legal capital.

[86] The Commission has carried out a feasibility study on alternatives to the current capital maintenance regime, whilst the Communication from the Commission on a simplified business environment for companies in the areas of company law, accounting and auditing (COM(2007) 394 final, 10.7.2007) raises the question (at p.5) as to whether the Second Directive is still needed. But see para.6–11, fn.117.

[87] See para.31–1.

[88] The most pressing classes of claim (from road accident victims and employees) are subject to mandatory insurance, which, suggestively, is required to be taken out by all those engaged in the relevant activity, whether they operate with limited liability or not.

beneficiaries of the current rules or, therefore, those who would be harmed if those rules were substantially amended.[89]

Secondly, however, it might be argued that, although the distribution rules may not do much good, they cause little harm and so should be left in place to pick up those cases where self-help or mandatory insurance, for one reason or another, do not deal with the problem. This approach would be acceptable if it were clear that the current distribution rules carry with them no costs—or at least fewer costs than benefits. The second question therefore relates to the costs of the current distribution rules. The argument that the current rules do carry considerable costs has been vigorously argued in the Rickford Report.[90] At the centre of its argument is a change in the role of the company accounts to which, as we have seen, the present distribution rules are tightly linked. The trend from historic cost accounting to reporting on the basis of current values for assets and liabilities, associated with the adoption of International Financial Reporting Standards,[91] is designed to make the accounts more helpful for shareholders and investors, but can be argued to have distorted the creditor protection function of the accounts. Reported profits have become more volatile, whilst retention of the "realised profits" rule for distributions[92] does not permit the company to take advantage of the upward fluctuations in asset values when considering distributions.

Even so, the case for reform is still not made out unless a workable alternative test for the legality of distributions can be advanced. As it happens, there is considerable comparative experience with alternative tests, since the United States jurisdictions abandoned legal capital a long time ago and so have had to devise alternative tests, and some Commonwealth countries, notably New Zealand, have taken the same step. The Rickford Report, which gives an account of alternatives, recommends an approach based on a solvency test.[93] This is not an entirely new technique even in domestic law, where it is used in certain limited areas.[94] However, its adoption as the test for the legality of distributions would be novel. In essence, the directors would have to form a judgment about what level of dividend the company could appropriately pay, without endangering its solvency. The directors already take a similar decision at present when deciding, within the limits set by the distribution rules, what level of dis-

---

[89] See J. Armour, "Share Capital and Creditor Protection: Efficient Rules for a Modern Company Law" (2000) 63 MLR 355 and "Legal Capital: An Outdated Concept" (2006) 7 EBOR 5.

[90] Above, fn.80, especially Chs 3 and 4.

[91] See para.21–12.

[92] Above, para.12–12.

[93] Above, fn.80, Ch.5. For counter-argument see W. Schön, "Comment: Balance Sheet Tests or Solvency Tests—or Both?" (2006) 7 EBOR 181.

[94] For the operation of such a scheme in relation to reductions of capital out of court by private companies see para.13–20.

tribution it is appropriate to make to shareholders and how much to keep in the company for investment in future projects. Under the reform proposal the role of the directors' judgment would be expanded to embrace creditors' as well as shareholders' interests. Since company law is structured so as to require the directors to put the shareholders' interests first, so long as the company is a going concern, the obvious risk with this proposal is that the directors will undervalue the interests of the creditors and overvalue those of the shareholders when taking this new or expanded decision. At present, the rule-based distribution test gives directors no discretion about the maximum which is distributable; under the reform proposal that issue would become a matter of the directors' judgment as to the impact of the proposed distribution on the company's ability in the future to meet its debts as they fall due. In order to counteract a pro-shareholder bias the directors would be required to certify (through a public "solvency statement") that the proposed distribution would not affect the company's ability to meet its debts, either immediately or for a period after the distribution (probably one year). Sanctions (probably both criminal and civil) would be attached to directors whose statement was made negligently. The debate is thus about whether ex ante rules (the current distribution test) should be replaced by an ex post standard (the solvency test), both in terms of their comparative effectiveness and, indeed, their comparative attractiveness to directors, who might perceive themselves as personally exposed to a more extensive liability under the solvency test than under the current rules.[95]

---

[95] That there is personal liability for directors even under the current rules is clear (above, para.12–9) but directors might consider a rule-based system as easier to comply with than one based on a standard.

CHAPTER 13

CAPITAL MAINTENANCE

The rules regarding distributions, discussed in the previous chapter, **13–1** would be pointless if the company were free to adjust its legal capital as it wished. In particular, the requirement that a distribution not be made if the company's net asset value does not exceed its legal capital and other undistributable reserves by the appropriate amount, would have little bite if the company could easily adjust downwards the amounts standing in its share capital, share premium and other accounts declared to be undistributable. On the other hand, there may be good reasons to allow the adjustment in certain cases. Thus, the question for this chapter is the identification of the legal freedom the company has to adjust downwards these amounts.

Suppose the company has traded unsuccessfully, the value of its assets is well below the level of its legal capital, but the company has found a new investor who is prepared to inject funds into the company so that it can try an alternative business plan. In return, however, the new investor wants to make sure that any profits made in the future can be paid out immediately and that he or she obtains the fair share of those profits, and so the investor requires that, before the issue of new shares is made, the value of the company's legal capital accounts are reduced to reflect the value of its actual assets. This is only an example of a potentially legitimate transaction which has the

305

effect of reducing the company's legal capital We need in fact to analyse a number of transactions a company might want to carry out which have the consequence that the value attached to its legal capital in its balance sheet is reduced. We shall look in this chapter not only at the rules on formal reductions in capital but also at those which govern the situations in which a company can acquire, redeem or re-purchase its own shares. Finally, we shall examine the rules on the granting by a company of financial assistance towards the purchase of its own shares, which is conventionally dealt with in this context, though it is not obvious that such action raises primarily creditor-protection concerns. The CLR made extensive proposals for reform in the areas covered by this chapter, taking the view that in some cases the current rules were over-protective of creditors and pre-vented or rendered more costly for companies legitimate commercial transactions.[1] Some of those suggestions for reform, though not the majority, were taken up in the Act.[2]

REDUCTIONS OF CAPITAL

13–2 The starting point of the statute is that a company cannot reduce its share capital, except in accordance with the procedures laid down in Chapter 10 of Part 16 of the Act.[3] Although this rule and Chapter 10 refer in terms only to "share capital", in fact the rule is applied also to the share premium account, the capital redemption reserve and the re-denomination reserve, i.e. to all the elements of the company's legal capital.[4] Reduction of capital is to be distinguished from the situation where the company simply divides its share capital into shares of a smaller nominal value or consolidates them into shares of a larger nominal value, where the aggregate nominal value of the shares (and thus the company's share capital) remains the same, though there is a smaller or a larger number of shares representing that aggregate. These steps present no creditor protection issues and the matter is one for the shareholders alone. Subject to contrary

---

[1] CLR, *Company Formation and Capital Maintenance*, 1999.

[2] Most of the provisions of the 2006 Act discussed in this chapter are scheduled to come into force on October 1, 2009. However, the new method for reductions of capital by private companies (below, para.13–5) and the abolition of the financial assistance rule for private companies (below, para.13–26) are scheduled for October 1, 2008.

[3] s.617(2)(b). In fact, s.617(1) begins with a broader proposition, to the effect that a company cannot *alter* its share capital except as permitted by that section, but it then goes on to list the situations where the Act permits such alteration, including the reduction procedure.

[4] For the share premium account (see s.610(4) and Ch.11 above at para.11–8); the capital redemption reserve (s.733(6) and below, para.13–11); and the re-denomination reserve (see s.628(3) and Ch.11 above at para.11–7).

provisions in the articles of association, the shareholders may authorise the directors by ordinary resolution to take these steps and that authorisation can be formulated in fairly broad terms.[5]

Before the passage of the 2006 Act the general principle was that a company might reduce its capital only by a formal reduction of capital confirmed by the court in accordance with the Act. However, a private company rarely needed to resort to that procedure. The main situation in which such a company might wish to reduce capital is when it needs to buy out a retiring member of the company or to return to the personal representatives of a deceased member his share of the capital, but has insufficient profits available for dividend to enable it to do so except out of capital. As pointed out below,[6] when companies were empowered to purchase their own shares special concessions were made to private companies to enable them to do so out of capital and without the need for a formal reduction. This provided a substitute for capital reduction which met the needs of private companies in many cases.[7] However, the Act introduces an alternative procedure for the reduction of capital by private companies, for which court confirmation is not needed, but leaves in place the special rules enabling private companies to re-purchase shares out of capital. On the other hand, in the case of public companies, where formal reductions may well be necessary or desirable especially in the light of the stricter rules regarding payment of dividends,[8] the previous law is unchanged.

Whichever procedure is used, the Act provides that a company may reduce its share capital "in any way"[9] but it then sets out three typical situations, which are important because of their different implications for creditor protection. The three situations are: (a) by reducing or extinguishing the amount of any uncalled liability on its shares;[10] (b) by cancelling any paid-up share capital "which is lost or unrepresented by available assets";[11] (c) by paying off any paid-up share capital which is in excess of the company's wants.[12] In situation (a) a shareholder's liability to the company is terminated and in (c)

---

[5] s.618. In particular authority may be given to exercise the powers "on more than one occasion": s.618(4)(b). Notice of division or consolidation must be given to the Registrar after it has been effected: s.619. For the minority oppression potential of this power see *Greenhalgh v Arderne Cinemas* [1946] 1 All E.R. 512, CA and para.19–15.

[6] At para.13–19.

[7] s.617(5) makes it clear that a repurchase or redemption of shares in accordance with the Act does not fall foul of the prohibition on altering share capital contained in that section.

[8] See para.12–2.

[9] s.641(3).

[10] s.641(4)(a)—in the unlikely event of its having uncalled capital.

[11] s.641(4)(b)(i). Technically share capital (a notional liability) cannot be "lost" (see Ch.11, above) but may well be "unrepresented by available assets". However, this does not seem to have bothered the courts which have interpreted "lost" to mean that the value of the company's net assets has fallen below the amount of its capital (i.e. its issued share capital, and, if any, its share premium account and capital redemption reserve) and that this "loss" is likely to be permanent.

[12] s.641(4)(b)(ii).

assets are returned by the company to the shareholder.[13] In both these cases, therefore, creditors are potentially worse off. In situation (b) the shareholder's position is not necessarily and immediately improved or the creditor's worsened by the reduction. All that has happened is that the company's legal capital is brought into line with the company's net asset position. Suppose that a company, having initially raised £1 million by way of a share issue, has traded relatively unsuccessfully, so that its assets now exceed its liabilities by only £500,000. A reduction of the company's legal capital by half would mean that any profits earned in the future would be distributable, whereas, without the reduction, the excess assets would have to be built up to £1 million again before a distribution was possible. Thus, in case (b) the reduction itself does not benefit the shareholder but only if it is coupled with a further decision to make a distribution, either at once or in the future.[14]

Procedure applying to all companies

13–3   Under the procedure applying to all companies a reduction of capital requires a special resolution of the members and confirmation by the court.[15] It is the requirement for court approval which is supposed to provide the necessary protection for creditors (as well as for minority shareholders). The obtaining of shareholder consent is most likely to raise tricky issues where there is more than one class of share and the reduction does not affect all the classes rateably. In particular, companies have often wanted to cancel the shares issued to preference shareholders, whose entitlement to a fixed preference dividend has moved out of line with interest rates in the market, so that the contribution of those shareholders can be re-financed more cheaply. The courts have been prepared to let companies do this, provided the preference shareholders are treated in accordance with their class rights, i.e. the rights they would have on a winding up of the

---

[13] Where there is a reduction of capital of this type, it is normal accounting practice to create a reserve to reflect the reduction. There is some doubt about how this reserve relates to the requirement for realised profits which is the central test for lawful distributions (see para.12–2). The result of the combination of s.654 and reg.9 of the draft Companies (Shares, Share Capital and Authorised Minimum) Regulations 2007 is that, for limited companies, the reserve will be distributable if the reduction results from the court-based procedure (unless the court orders otherwise) and in the case of the out-of-court procedure will be distributable unless "the reserve is not treated as a realised profit"—the treatment in question being apparently a reference to accounting practice.

[14] For the difficulties arising where, in the above example, the company reduces its capital by three-quarters, thus creating a distributable reserve of £250,000 immediately, see para.13–4.

[15] s.641(1)(b). The previous requirement that the company have power under its articles to reduce its capital has been removed.

company.[16] Thus, the question becomes whether the reduction of the preference shares meets this test. Although the court probably has a discretion to approve a reduction of shares which infringes class rights and which has not secured the consent of that class, it is highly unlikely to do so.[17] The operation of the class rights procedure is discussed in Chapter 19. Where there is only one class of share, the minority's protections are less extensive,[18] though they do have the chance to oppose the confirmation of the reduction by the court under the reduction procedure.

Creditor protection is provided when company applies to the court for an order confirming the resolution.[19] The practical pressure generated by the former procedure was towards making the company discharge or secure all the creditors' claims outstanding at the time of the reduction. The Company Law Review thought that the interests of creditors were over-protected by the statute, because in effect creditors obtained either payment of or security for their debts, which put them in a better position than the one they had been in before the reduction.[20] It put forward proposals to change this situation, and an early draft of the Act addressed the issue.[21] However, this provision did not make its way into the Act. Nevertheless, the story does not end there. In 2006 the Community amended the Second Directive's provisions on reduction of capital[22] so as to make them less protective of creditors. The Government's initial reaction was not to take advantage of this new flexibility,[23] but after consultation changed its mind.[24] The reduction of capital provisions of the 2006 Act were then to be amended by statutory instrument[25] so as to make the procedure

---

[16] The proposition that the preference shareholders are treated unfairly through deprivation of a favourable dividend entitlement if their shares are reduced was decisively rejected by the House of Lords in *Scottish Insurance Corp Ltd v Wilsons and Clyde Coal Co Ltd* [1949] A.C. 462, so that the issue has become whether they have been treated on the reduction in accordance with the rights which they would have on a winding up. The effect of the decision was to make preference shares in effect redeemable by the company, even if not formally issued as redeemable, provided the company could satisfy the requirements of the reduction procedure.

[17] s.645 in terms requires only a resolution of the company, not of the class in question.

[18] These possibilities are also discussed in Ch.19.

[19] s.645(1).

[20] Strategic, para.5.4.5.

[21] This contained a provision authorising the court to confirm the reduction, even though creditors have not consented to it or had their claims secured, where the court thought these safeguards unnecessary "in view of the assets the company would have after the reduction": Modernising Company Law—II, draft clause 61(3)(c).

[22] Directive 2006/68/EC amending Art.32 of Directive 77/91/EEC.

[23] DTI, *Implementation of the Companies Act 2006*, February 2007, Ch.6.

[24] *The Government response to the consultation on the implementation of amendments to the 2nd Company Law Directive*, October 28, 2007.

[25] The draft Companies (Reduction of Capital) Regulations 2007. The Secretary of State has power under s.657 to amend a number of the elements in Part 17 of the Act, in addition to the usual powers under s.2 of the European Communities Act 1972. SI 2008/719 makes equivalent changes in the 1985 Act, pending implementation of this element of the 2006 Act in October 2009.

less protective of creditors, thus achieving, albeit by slightly different wording, the policy recommended by the CLR.

The crucial change proposed is that it is no longer the case that every creditor is entitled to object to the reduction of capital who, at the relevant date, has a debt or claim which would be admissible were the company being wound up. Under the prior law this was the position at least where the reduction fell within cases (a) or (c) above or analogous cases.[26] Now, in all cases, in order to obtain a right of objection the creditor, upon whom the burden of proof lies, must demonstrate not only an admissible debt or claim but, in addition, "a real likelihood that the proposed reduction will put at risk the due discharge of the debt or claim."[27] Moreover, even such a creditor must remain alert, for the court is required to set a date or dates by which the claim must be notified to it or the creditor loses the right to object to the reduction.[28] The list of objecting creditors will, in future, thus consist of those who have demonstrated that their claim is subject to real risk of non-payment if the reduction goes ahead, so that the pressure on the company to settle the claims of all creditors should be mitigated, if not eliminated. In the past, companies often felt obliged, in order to avoid the difficulty of identifying every one of a fluctuating body of trade creditors, to arrange for a sufficient sum to be deposited with or guaranteed by a bank or insurance company to meet the claims of all the unsecured creditors. However, a provision remains for the protection of any creditor, entitled to object, who was not entered on the list of objecting creditors through ignorance of the reduction proceedings. If, after the reduction, such a creditor is not paid and the company goes into insolvent liquidation, the court on the application of that creditor may order members, whose uncalled liability has been reduced (i.e. case (a) above), to contribute, as if it had not been, to the extent necessary to pay the creditor.[29]

13–4   Once the list of objecting creditors has been settled, the principle to be applied by the court is that it may not confirm the reduction unless all the objecting creditors have consented to the reduction or their claims have been discharged or secured.[30] Knowing this, the company is likely to seek to deal, in one way or another, with the claims of those creditors who are entitled to object to the reduction in advance of the confirmation hearing. However, even if there are no objecting

---

[26]   See s.645(2)—now to be repealed. In case (b) there appeared to be no right of objection, unless the court so ordered: s.645(4).

[27]   s.646(1)(b).

[28]   s.646(3).

[29]   s.653.

[30]   s.648(2). See also s.646(4). See *Lucania Temperance Billiard Halls (London) Ltd, Re* [1966] Ch. 98, dealing with the difficult issue of long-term obligations of the company. The court rejected the argument that the company must have sufficient liquid assets to cover the whole of the rent due under long leases but nevertheless insisted on 10 years' coverage. Although a decision on a part of the statute which will be repealed by the Regulations, it may give some guidance on the courts' understanding of "secured".

creditors or their objections have been dealt with, it appears that the court must still have regard to creditor interests when deciding whether to confirm the reduction "on such terms and conditions as it thinks fit". This is shown by the prior case-law concerning reductions of capital because that capital was not represented by available assets (i.e. case (b) above). Here, even under the previous law, there was no right of objection for creditors, unless the court so ordered, as the 2006 Act continues to provide. Nevertheless, the courts might regard the interests of creditors in such a case as requiring protection at the confirmation stage. A standard situation falling within case (b) is where a company is required to write down the value of an asset in its accounts (for example, a loan which the company now thinks is unlikely to be re-paid), thus extinguishing its distributable profits. It then wishes to reduce its share capital (and probably its share premium account) so as to permit the distribution of future profits. However, a variation on this theme is where, on the facts, it is possible (and foreseeable at the time of the write-down) that the asset may recover in value. In that case the court may impose a condition that any amount recovered in the future should be put in an undistributable reserve. However, it seems that this will be required only if needed to protect the creditors existing at the time of the write-down[31] and that future creditors are sufficiently protected by the publicity requirements for the reduction of capital.

Those publicity requirements consist, now,[32] mainly of the requirement that the company deliver a copy of the court order and a statement of its capital,[33] as now reduced, to the Registrar, who must register and certify them;[34] the registration must be publicised; and the reduction takes effect only upon registration.[35]

Minority shareholders as well may seek—or the court may provide—protection at the confirmation stage, even if any requirements for class meetings have been met at the point at which the company adopted the resolution for the reduction of capital. The two main requirements for shareholder protection which the court will insist on are that the reduction treat the shareholders equitably and that the reduction proposal be properly explained to the shareholders who approved it. It is established that the court must be satisfied on these matters, even if the petition for confirmation is unopposed, as it often

---

[31] *Grosvenor Press Plc, Re* [1985] B.C.L.C. 286, *cf. Jupiter House Investments (Cambridge) Ltd, Re* [1985] B.C.L.C. 222.

[32] The courts' former powers to require publicity ad hoc at the time of confirmation are to be repealed by the draft Regulations.

[33] Equivalent to that required on an allotment of shares.

[34] Giving "conclusive evidence" that the statutory reduction requirements have been complied with and that the company's share capital is as stated in the statement of capital: s.649(6).

[35] s.649. There is more flexibility about the effective date where the reduction is part of a scheme of arrangement because that is normally upon delivery of the order to the Registrar, a matter under the control of the company (see Ch.29 and CLR, Final Report, para.13.11): s.649(3)(a).

will be.[36] However, it will be necessary before a conclusion of inequitable treatment is reached to identify a significant risk to those shareholders arising out of the reduction. Thus, in *Ransomes Plc, Re*[37] a substantial reduction in share premium account was permitted over the objections of preference shareholders, in order to permit a distribution to the ordinary shareholders, on the grounds that the preference shareholders' entitlements to dividend and return of capital (non-participating in both cases) were not put at risk by the proposed distribution. Even after the proposed distribution, the company would have assets and projected profits well in excess of what was required to meet the preference shareholders' entitlements. In other words, the protection for both creditors and shareholders now revolves around the same general notion: their objections will be plausible if the reduction is likely significantly to harm their entitlements. The apparently strict procedural requirements of proper explanation have been somewhat qualified by the adoption of a "no difference" rider, i.e. the court may forgive procedural inadequacies if convinced that following the correct procedure would have led to the same result.[38]

Procedure available to private companies only

13–5　The provisions for reduction of capital without court confirmation apply only to private companies. These were introduced to mitigate the delay and cost involved in court confirmation. The CLR wished to make this procedure available to public companies as well, but with the rider, needed to meet the requirements of the Second Directive, that creditors entitled to object to the reduction could invoke the court to veto or modify the reduction.[39] In place of court confirmation reliance would be put on a solvency statement made by the directors. For both types of company the procedure with court confirmation (above) would be kept as an alternative, because it allows directors to avoid the potential liabilities arising out of the solvency statement.[40] However, in the event the Act makes the procedure of reduction without court approval available to private

---

[36] *Ransomes Plc, Re* [1999] 2 B.C.L.C. 591, 602, CA.

[37] [1999] 1 B.C.L.C 775 (affirmed on appeal; see previous note). See also *Ratners Group Plc, Re* [1988] B.C.L.C. 685 and *Thorn EMI Plc, Re* (1988) 4 B.C.C. 698 (reduction of share premium account to write off goodwill arising out of the same transaction as generated the premium).

[38] See previous note—a hypothetical and sometimes difficult judgment, which the courts should use sparingly.

[39] Company Formation and Capital Maintenance, para.3.27. However, in the absence of creditor objection, court involvement would not be necessary.

[40] Completing, para.7.9.

companies only (which retain the option of using the court-based procedure).[41]

Under the procedure available to private companies only, a resolution of the members is still required,[42] as discussed above, with the need to hold separate meetings of each class of shares whose rights are varied by the proposed reduction. However, the resolution of the members is to be supported by a solvency statement from the directors rather than confirmed by the court. The essence of the solvency statement is that to some degree it transfers responsibility for the reduction from the court to the directors of the company. This is a gain for the company in terms of speed and cost, but a potential risk for the directors, in so far as personal liability attaches to their approval of the solvency statement.[43] The solvency statement, which must accompany the resolution, is not an entirely novel device in British company law. It was required as part of the (now repealed) "whitewash" procedure available to private companies wishing to give financial assistance for the purchase of their own shares.[44] Something similar is also to be found in the rules governing share repurchases by private companies from capital.[45] However, the solvency statement on a reduction of capital is not required to be audited.

The solvency statement is a statement by each director of the company, who must each sign it.[46] Each director asserts in it that he or she has formed an opinion on two matters. The first relates to the company's current financial position at the time the statement is made and is to the effect that "there is no ground on which the company could ... be found unable to pay (or otherwise discharge) its debts."[47] The second relates to the future and covers a period of one year after the date of the statement. The second opinion comes in two alternative forms.[48] If it is intended to commence the winding up

---

[41] DTI, *Company Law Reform*, Cm. 6456, para.4.8 rejected the application of the alternative procedure to public companies. It was thought that the possibility of creditor objection and thus court involvement would lead public companies to opt for the court-confirmation route, though it is not clear that this is a strong argument against making the option available to public companies.

[42] s.641(1)(a). The private company procedure is scheduled to come into force on 1 October 2008, in advance of the rest of chapter 10.

[43] Under the court procedure, liability (for example, in negligence) could attach to the directors for proposing the reduction, but they would be protected to a considerable extent against such liability in practice by the subsequent examination of the scheme by the court.

[44] s.155 of the Companies Act 1985. The financial assistance rules no longer apply to private companies: see below, para.13–26.

[45] See below, para.13–20.

[46] s.643(1),(3) and the draft Companies (Shares, Share Capital and Authorised Minimum) Regulations 2007, reg.13 (hereafter "Shares Regulations"). Although the section does not extend to shadow directors, the term "director" does include de facto directors: see s.250. In *In A Flap Envelope Co Ltd, Re* [2004] 1 B.C.L.C. 64, a case arising under the financial assistance whitewash procedure, a director who resigned for part of a day in order that the statement could be signed by his replacement, was held to be a de facto director during this period and thus liable to make the statement required under those provisions.

[47] s.643(1)(a).

[48] s.643(1)(b).

of the company within a year,[49] then the required opinion is that the company will be able to pay or otherwise discharge its debts within twelve months of the winding up. In any other case, it is that the company will able to pay (or discharge) its debts as they fall due within the twelve months after the date of the statement. The required opinion relates only to the payment or discharge of debts (i.e. claims on the company to pay a liquidated sum). However, the directors are required to take into account contingent and prospective liabilities when forming their opinions.[50] The obligation to take into account prospective liabilities is hardly surprising, since these are liabilities which will certainly become due in the future (though it may not be clear precisely when). Contingent liabilities are those which may arise in the future because of an existing legal obligation or state of affairs. In other words, directors have to take account of contingent and prospective liabilities which may become debts payable by the company and imperil its ability to pay its debts, either at the date of the statement or, more likely, as they fall due over the twelve-month period required to be considered under the second opinion.[51]

13–6   The transfer of responsibility to the directors is most graphically illustrated by the provision in the Act that it is a criminal offence for a director to make a solvency statement without having reasonable grounds for the opinions expressed in it—unless the solvency statement is not delivered to the Registrar, so that the reduction does not take effect.[52] This criminalises purely negligent conduct on the part of the director, an unusual step, for the Act normally confines criminal sanctions to knowing or reckless misstatements. The greater liability imposed by the Act is an indication of the importance attached by the legislature to the accuracy of the solvency statement. The Act is silent on the civil liabilities of the directors for making an inaccurate solvency statement. The CLR had recommended that there should be an express civil liability on the directors to pay up the capital reduced,[53] but this suggestion is not taken up in the Act. However, it seems clear, at least where the reduction involves a return of assets to the shareholders, that the directors could be liable to the company for the loss suffered on the grounds that they are in breach of their general duties to the company; and that those who receive the assets with knowledge of the breach, whether directors or shareholders, would be liable to restore them to the company, under the principles discussed

---

[49] So that the reduction of capital is a prelude to a winding up, as in the *Scottish Insurance* case (above, fn.16).

[50] s.643(2).

[51] The language of s.643 reflects to some considerable degree the language to be found in s.123(1)(e) of the Insolvency Act, on which see Roy Goode, *Principles of Corporate Insolvency Law* (London: Sweet & Maxwell, Student Edition, 2005) paras 4–15 to 4–23 and 4–28 to 4–29.

[52] s.643(4). The offence is punishable by imprisonment, whether tried summarily or on indictment: s.643(5).

[53] *Company Formation and Capital Maintenance*, para.3.35.

in relation to unlawful dividends.[54] It is further arguable that the reduction is ineffective where the directors have not made a solvency statement in accordance with the requirements of the Act, in particular where they do not have reasonable grounds for the opinions expressed in it.[55] In this case, the recipients could be said to be liable to return the company's assets, whether they know of the breach or not, subject only to defences such as change of position.[56]

A copy of the solvency statement must be provided to the members voting on the reduction resolution (in different ways according to whether the vote is at a meeting or by written resolution),[57] but it is expressly provided that failure to observe these requirements does not affect the validity of the resolution passed.[58] The solvency statement must precede the date on which the resolution is passed by no more than 15 days and, if this is not the case, it appears the resolution cannot be said to be supported by a solvency statement. Thus, if the date for passing the resolution slips for one reason or another, the directors will be required to review and re-issue their solvency statement. After the passing of the resolution, the company has a further 15 days to file the copy of the resolution and the solvency statement and a current statement of the company's capital with the Registrar.[59] It is only with the registration of these documents by the Registrar (thus making them publicly available) that the reduction is effective.[60] Failure to deliver the documents to the Registrar on time does not affect the validity of the resolution but it does constitute an offence on the part of every officer of the company in default.[61]

Provided a private company observes the requirements of the Act, especially the requirement laid upon the directors to have reasonable grounds for the beliefs stated in the solvency statement, it is provided with an inexpensive and quick method of reducing its capital. Where those provisions are not complied with, and especially where the directors do not have reasonable grounds for those beliefs, the civil consequences of this failure are to some degree uncertain but potentially far-reaching.

---

[54] See para.12–8. However, the specific statutory rules on distributions will not be relevant since a reduction of capital in cases (a) and (c) does not amount to a distribution for the purposes of Part 23: s.829(2)(b).

[55] If a solvency statement is not made in accordance with s.643, the resolution for the reduction of capital appears not to be "supported by a solvency statement" as s.642(1) requires and no other provision of the Act explicitly saves the resolution from this defect.

[56] *cf. MacPherson v European Strategic Bureau Ltd* [2000] 2 B.C.L.C. 683, CA.

[57] s.642(2),(3). On these different methods of shareholder decision-making see Ch.15.

[58] s.642(4). However, it is an offence on the part of every officer in default to fail to comply with this requirement: s.644(7)–(8), but liability is restricted to a fine.

[59] s.644(1),(2) and the Shares Regulations, reg.10.

[60] s.644(3),(4).

[61] s.644(6),(7).

ACQUISITIONS OF OWN SHARES

The general principle

13–7 It was held by the House of Lords in the nineteenth century that a company could not purchase its own shares, even though there was an express power to do so in its memorandum, since this would result in a reduction of capital.[62] Assuming that on purchase the shares were cancelled and nothing put in their place this would necessarily reduce the capital yardstick represented by issued share capital and it could also be regarded as objectionable as a diversion of the company's assets to the shareholder whose shares were purchased. Nevertheless, the rule thus laid down was stricter than in some common law countries (for example the United States and Canada) and many civil law ones (and than was required by the Second Directive). Section 658(1)[63] confirms, but does not replace, the common law rule that a limited company "shall not acquire its own shares whether by purchase, subscription or otherwise."[64] If it purports to do so, the company and every officer in default is liable to a fine and the purported acquisition is void.[65]

Moreover, this central prohibition is buttressed by three further statutory restrictions. First, this prohibition could be avoided in certain cases if the company acquired the shares through a nominee. Accordingly, in such a case the shares are treated as held by the nominee on his or her own account and the company is regarded as having no beneficial interest in them.[66] Further, if the nominee does not meet the financial obligations attached to the shares, then that liability will fall on the other subscribers to the memorandum (where the nominee is a subscriber) and in the other cases it will fall on the directors of the company at the time the shares were issued to or acquired by the nominee.[67] In both cases it is a joint and several liability.

However, this liability rule is applied only where the nominee for the company acquires the shares as a subscriber to its memorandum, where the shares are issued by the company to the nominee and where the nominee acquires the shares partly paid from a third person.[68] It does not apply if the nominee acquires fully paid shares from a third

---

[62] *Trevor v Whitworth* (1887) 12 App.Cas. 409, HL.

[63] Which applies to a company, public or private, whether limited by shares or by guarantee if it has a share capital.

[64] s.658(1)—the exemption of unlimited companies from this prohibition shows the connection between the rule and creditor protection.

[65] s.658(2).

[66] s.660(2). Unless the company has no beneficial interest in the shares: s.660(3)(b).

[67] s.661(2), but the court has the power to relieve a director or subscriber who has acted honestly and reasonably from the whole or part of the liability: s.661(3)–(4).

[68] s.660.

party, even if the nominee does so with funds provided by the company.[69] This suggests that the rationale of the section is to ensure that the company receives the full price of the shares as an addition to its assets, which in the case of the acquisition of fully paid shares by a nominee will necessarily have occurred before the nominee's acquisition of the shares. The contrast between the law's treatment of a nominee acquisition and acquisition by the company (where even the acquisition of fully paid shares is in principle prohibited) is that the shares remain in the hands of the nominee (i.e. are not cancelled) so that the company's capital account remains unaffected.

Secondly, following Article 24 of the Second Directive, a public company is prohibited from taking a lien or charge over its own shares (it is treated as void), except to cover the unpaid liability on a partly paid share.[70]

Thirdly, the prohibition on acquisition of own shares is supplemented by section 136 which provides that a company cannot be a member of its holding company, either directly or through a nominee,[71] and any allotment or transfer of shares in the holding company to the subsidiary or its nominee is void. Section 136 is aimed at preventing the de facto reduction of capital which would result from a subsidiary company acquiring shares in its holding company. The company, through its subsidiary, would be returning assets to a shareholder.[72] Nevertheless, section 136 does not apply where company A, at the time of acquisition of the shares in company B, is not a subsidiary of company B, but later becomes so, for example, where company B later takes over company A by purchasing its shares.[73] The upshot of the exception is that the capital of company B may be expended in buying (in effect) its own shares (i.e. when it completes the takeover), but it has been held, nevertheless, that this result cannot be prevented by relying on the general prohibition on a company acquiring its own shares (section 658) rather than section 136.[74] Presumably the desire to permit a useful commercial transaction was thought, in this instance, to outweigh the policy behind the prohibition on the acquisition of own shares.

---

[69] Though the financial assistance rules, below, para.13–26, may apply.

[70] s.670. There are also exceptions for companies whose ordinary business includes the lending of money and the charge is part of that business, and for charges taken by a private company before it re-registered as public.

[71] s.144.

[72] However, if such a transaction were permitted, the parent's legal capital account would not be reduced by the fact that one of its members is a subsidiary—any more than in the case of shares held by a nominee—so that it would not become easier for the parent to make distributions.

[73] s.137(1)(b), (c). Company A may not exercise the voting rights attached to the shares, once it becomes a subsidiary of Company B (s.137(4)), but this does little to help creditors.

[74] *Acatos & Hutchinson Plc v Watson* [1995] 1 B.C.L.C. 218. Technically, the basis of the decision was that the acquiring company was acquiring the shares of the acquired company, not its own shares, which were held by the acquired company, and so s.658 was not infringed.

13–8   This apparently comprehensive set of prohibitions is, however, subject to a number of exceptions. Thus, a company may acquire its own shares by way of gift[75] or by way of forfeiture for non-payment of calls.[76] In the latter case, however, a public company must cancel the shares and reduce its capital account accordingly if the shares are not disposed of within three years of the forfeiture.[77] Both these exceptions are of long-standing. In 1983 there was added a further complex set of rules to deal with possible problems faced by public companies in relation to shares acquired by the trustees of a company's employees' share scheme or pension scheme.[78] These do not need to be further analysed in a work of this kind. There are also scattered throughout the Act provisions which permit the court to order that a company acquire shares from a shareholder, as a remedy for some wrong which has been done to that shareholder. The best known example is a compulsory purchase order made by the court under the unfair prejudice provisions, considered in Chapter 20.[79] Finally, an acquisition of shares by the company under a reduction of capital carried out under the provisions discussed above is exempted from the prohibition.[80]

However, the most obvious exception to the prohibition on a company acquiring its own shares is to be found in Chapters 3 and 4 of Part 18 of the Act, which permit a company to redeem or re-purchase its own shares. We turn to these provisions below. Before we do so, it is important to note one important creditor protection arising out of any of the above relaxations of the prohibitions. Where a public company is permitted to acquire its own shares, whether directly or through a nominee, then so long as it holds those shares (i.e. does not cancel or dispose of them) and decides to show those shares as an asset in its balance sheet, an amount equal to the value of the shares must be transferred out of profits available for dividend to an undistributable reserve.[81] In effect, the amount available for distribution will be reduced by the value of the purchase. Thus, suppose a public company acquires through a nominee fully paid shares from a third party, providing the nominee with the funds to effect the purchase. The company's net asset value will remain the same, the reduction in cash being offset by the value of the shares acquired.

---

[75] s.659(1)—"otherwise than for valuable consideration". This was held to be permissible at common law in *Castiglione's Will Trust, Re* [1958] Ch. 549, where the acquisition was through a nominee, but the Act permits direct acquisition in such a case.

[76] s.659(2)(c).

[77] s.662(1)(a),(2),(3)(a).

[78] These problems were originally tackled by the Companies (Beneficial Interests) Act 1983: see now the 2006 Act, ss.671–676. The acquisition of such shares is likely to be financed by the company and the company may have a residuary beneficial interest in them which, under these provisions, may be disregarded.

[79] s.659(2)(b), which also lists three other situations where the court may order the purchase of shares, i.e. under ss.98, 721(6) and 759.

[80] s.659(2)(a).

[81] s.669.

However, by virtue of the requirement to create an undistributable reserve, the amount of the profit available for distribution will be reduced, thus protecting creditors.[82] To put the matter another way, the purchase of the shares is treated as a distribution to the shareholder whose shares the nominee acquired.

Redeemable shares

Redeemable shares are shares which are issued on the basis that they **13–9** are to be or may be redeemed (i.e. bought back) at a later date by the company. The basis of issue may be that the shares will be redeemed at a certain point or that they may be, and in the latter case the option to redeem may be allocated to the shareholder or the company or both. The process of redemption is thus different from the process of re-purchase (discussed below), where the Act, under certain conditions, permits the company to re-purchase shares, something which would otherwise have been unlawful on its part, but there is no obligation upon either company to make an offer to re-purchase or, if one is made, upon the shareholder to accept it.

Redeemable shares have been permissible since the Companies Act 1929. This introduced a method whereby redemption could take place without a reduction of the capital yardstick—a method which was adopted when, many years later,[83] companies were empowered to purchase their own shares, whether or not they were issued as redeemable. Prior to the 1981 Act only preference shares could be issued as redeemable.[84] Now, however, section 684 provides that a company may issue shares of any class which are to be redeemed or are liable to be redeemed, whether at the option of the company or the shareholder. The provisions governing redeemable shares are set out in Chapter 3 of Part 18 and, unlike many of the other provisions relating to legal capital, which simply re-state the law, Chapter 3 contains certain reforms proposed by the CLR.

Redeemable shares may not be issued unless the company has also issued shares which are not redeemable.[85] This provision eliminates the risk of the company ending up with no members if and when all

---

[82] This result will be achieved as a result of the requirement in s.831 that a public company may make a distribution only to the extent that its net assets (unchanged in this example) exceed its legal capital and undistributable reserves (increased in the example by the value of the share purchase).

[83] By the Companies Act 1981.

[84] As we have seen, preference shares were also effectively redeemable by the company through the reduction procedure, on the basis of their rights in a winding up. See above, para.13–3.

[85] s.684(4).

the redeemable shares are redeemed.[86] However, the Act makes no stipulation as to the number or value of the non-redeemable shares which are required to have been issued, and so the main form of equity financing for the company could be via redeemable shares.

13–10   Further, in the case of a public company redeemable shares may not be issued unless the company is authorised in its articles to do so and, in the case of a private company, the articles may exclude or restrict the issue of redeemable shares. Thus, the default rule is in favour of the private company having the power to issue redeemable shares and against it in the case of public companies. This requirement is additional to the provisions discussed in Chapter 24 which, in some cases, require the directors to seek the authorisation of the shareholders before they take advantage of a share issue power in a particular situation. The provisions on redeemable shares address the logically prior question of whether the company has power to issue redeemable shares at all. Nevertheless, both sets of rules create a requirement for shareholder consent. The main difference between them appears to be that, in the case of a public company, authority to issue shares can be given to the directors by ordinary resolution,[87] whereas a provision in the articles conferring power on the company to issue redeemable shares must either be there from the beginning, and thus be consented to by all the subscribers to the memorandum, or have been introduced at a later date by special resolution of the members altering the articles. This higher level of shareholder consent might be thought to be justified by the drain on the company's cash resources that redemption is likely to entail, thus reducing the cash available to pay dividends to the other shareholders or to invest in projects for the benefit of the shareholders as a whole.

Concern for the impact of the redemption on the non-redeemable shareholders also lies behind a long-running problem concerning the setting of the terms of the redemption. Under the 1985 Act, in order to protect the shareholders whose shares are not to be redeemed (and indeed the offerees of the redeemable shares), the terms and manner of the redemption were required to be set out in the company's articles, so that all would know the position.[88] However, this was thought to be an inflexible requirement and the rule now embodied in the Act is somewhat more flexible.[89] Fixing the terms in the articles

---

[86] Moreover, after issue, the non-redeemable shares cannot be re-purchased so as to produce the result that the company has only redeemable or treasury shares in issue: s.690(2). Nor may a private company reduce its share capital through the solvency statement regime so as to produce the result that it has only redeemable shares in issue: s.641(2). In the case of the court-centred reduction, the court could permit such a reduction but, presumably, would be unlikely to do so.

[87] s.551 and see para.24–4.

[88] s.160(3) of the 1985 Act.

[89] Though not as flexible as the CLR's recommendation, which would have given the directors an unconditional power to set the terms of the redemption: Final Report—I, para.4.5.

remains the default rule,[90] but, provided either the articles or an ordinary resolution of the company permit it, the directors may fix the terms and conditions of the redemption.[91] Protection for the shareholders is maintained by the requirement that the directors, if they set the terms, must do so before the shares are allotted and the company's return of allotments to the Registrar must include the terms of the redemption.[92]

The Act contains two specific provisions about the terms of redemption (which are generally a commercial matter for company and investors), one restrictive, the other facultative. First, redeemable shares may not be redeemed until they are fully paid.[93] This avoids redemption wiping out the personal liability of the holders in respect of uncalled capital. Secondly, the terms of redemption may provide that, by agreement between company and shareholder, the amount due be paid on a date later than the redemption date.[94]

Once the redemption is effected, the Registrar must be informed in the usual way and supplied with an updated capital statement.[95]

Creditor protection

Turning to the creditor protection aspect of redemptions, the rules for **13–11** public companies are, in brief, that redeemable shares can be redeemed only out of distributable profits or out of the proceeds of a fresh issue of shares made for the purpose.[96] Any premium payable on redemption must be paid out of distributable profits alone, unless the redeemed shares were issued initially at a premium, in which case the redemption premium is payable out of the proceeds of a new issue, up to the amount of the premium received on issue or the value of the company's current share premium account, whichever is the less.[97] Once the shares have been redeemed, they are treated as cancelled and the amount of the company's issued share capital is diminished by the nominal value of the shares redeemed.[98] Finally, the company must create an (undistributable) "capital redemption reserve" (CRR) equivalent to the amount by which the company's issued share capital is diminished by a purchase wholly out of profits;[99] or, where the redemption is financed partly by the proceeds of a new issue and partly by distributable profits, the company must

---

[90] s.685(4).
[91] s.685(1),(2).
[92] s.685(3).
[93] s.686(1).
[94] s.686(2)—otherwise the shares must be paid for on redemption: s.686(3).
[95] s.689.
[96] s.687(2).
[97] s.687(3),(4).
[98] s.688.
[99] s.733(2).

create a CRR equal to the amount by which the proceeds of the new issue fall short of the amount paid on redemption.[100]

Much more difficult is to explain why the rules are as they are. Let us assume, first, a redemption without premium to the nominal value of the shares, which the company finances wholly out of distributable profits. The creditors cannot object to the use by the company of its distributable profits to redeem the shares, for the very reason that they are distributable (though the other shareholders may have grounds for unhappiness—see above). The company could have distributed those profits by way of dividend,[101] and so the creditors have no grounds for objection if the profits are returned to a particular group of shareholders through this different route. However, the obligation upon the company to cancel the redeemed shares means that the company's share capital account is diminished. Thus, if no countervailing step were taken, the company's distributable profits, after the redemption, would be increased, compared to what would be available for distribution had there been a dividend payment of an amount equivalent to that used for the redemption. This is because a dividend payment has no impact on the company's share capital account. This problem is dealt with by the CRR, to which the company must transfer an amount equal to that by which its share capital account is diminished by the cancellation. This step maintains the company's overall capital yardstick at the level it was before the payment out of profits to redeem the shares. The CRR is treated as if it was paid-up capital of the company[102] but it may be applied in paying up bonus issues,[103] thus converting it to paid-up share capital. Unless and until this is done the company's "capital" will consist not just of issued share capital plus share premium account (if any) but of issued share capital plus share premium account (if any) plus capital redemption reserve. Overall, there is no reduction of the capital yardstick: one type of "capital" (CRR) is substituted for another (share capital). By the same token, the full amount of the profits used to redeem the shares is taken out of the company's distributable profits.

Let us assume, secondly, a redemption without premium to the nominal value of the shares, which the company finances wholly out of the proceeds of a new issue, also not issued at a premium. Since the issue of new shares will increase the company's share capital account by the amount of the proceeds of the issue, there is no need to create a CRR in this case. The increase in the share capital account from the

---

[100] s.733(3).

[101] See para.12–1.

[102] s.831(4)(b) brings it into account for the purpose of the net asset restriction on distributions by public companies (see para.12–1) and s.733(6) applies the reduction of capital rules, discussed above, to this reserve.

[103] s.733(5). The capital redemption reserve is thus more restricted than the share premium account, to which it is otherwise closely analogous. See para.11–18.

new issue will balance the reduction in that account brought about by the cancellation of the redeemed shares. In effect, the company, once again, has substituted one sort of capital (whatever the new issue consists of) for another (the redeemable shares). For the same reason, creditors need not worry that funds raised from one set of shareholders has been handed over (distributed) immediately to another group of shareholders, for the company's net asset position, as well as its capital yardstick, remain as before. Where the assumptions are as above, but the redemption is financed partly out of distributable profits and partly out of the proceeds of a fresh issue, the CRR is needed only to cover the distributable profits part of the financing.

Thirdly, let us assume a redemption of the shares at a premium to their nominal value, the redeemable shares having been issued initially at par. The basic rule is that the premium on redemption is payable only out of distributable profits.[104] The proceeds of a fresh issue may not be used for this purpose. Why not? The answer appears to be that the use of the proceeds of fresh issue to pay the premium would amount to making a distribution to the redeemable shareholders in breach of the policy behind the dividend rules. To see this, let us suppose that, immediately before the redemption, the company has net assets exactly equivalent to its then legal capital. Thus, it has distributable profits of zero.[105] It then raises money by issuing 100 new shares at par at £2 per share. Its share capital account will increase by £200. It then uses the money to redeem 100 redeemable £1 shares at a premium of £1, the redeemable shares having been originally issued at par. After cancellation of the redeemable shares, the company's share capital will be reduced by £100 (the nominal value of the redeemable shares) so that there is a net increase in its legal capital of £100 (the increase arising out of the new issue (£200) less the cancellation of the redeemable shares (£100)). However, the company will have distributed £200 to the redeemable shareholders, even though the result of the new issue was to raise the company's net assets by only £100 above its (new) capital yardstick. In effect, it has made an unlawful distribution. No such objection arises, of course, if the company uses distributable profits to pay the premium.

The same reasoning explains the amelioration of the rule that the **13–12** premium on redemption may be paid only out of distributable profits where the redeemable shares were issued initially at a premium. Here the proceeds of the fresh issue may be used to finance the redemption premium to the extent of the premium received by the company on the issue of the redeemable shares or, if less, the amount of its current share premium account, no matter which issues that amount reflects.[106] In this case, upon cancellation of the redeemable shares,

---

[104] s.687(3).
[105] See para.12–1.
[106] This amount includes any premium arising on the issue of the new shares: s.687(4)(b).

not only is the company's share capital account reduced but so also is its share premium account by the amount of the permitted payment.[107] If the redemption premium is less than the issue premium and the company's share premium account at least equals the redemption premium, the company can pay the whole of the premium out of the proceeds of a fresh issue. In this way the increase in the company's capital yardstick as a result of the fresh issue is balanced by the reduction (in share capital and share premium accounts) brought about by the cancellation of the redeemable shares, so that the problem noted in the previous paragraph does not arise.

There is one final puzzle to be examined. Where a company funds the redemption out of distributable profits, the amount that has to be transferred to the CRR is based on the nominal value of the shares redeemed.[108] This appears to be the rule, even if the redeemable shares were issued at a premium, perhaps a large one, or were redeemed at a premium. The explanation is to be found in section 688 which provides that, when the redeemable shares are cancelled, only the "amount of the company's issued share capital is diminished accordingly". The share premium account is unaffected so that only the equivalent of the nominal value of the redeemable shares has to be replaced through the CRR.[109]

The above rules apply to both public and private companies. However, if a private company can meet certain requirements, it may redeem shares out of capital (i.e. not out of distributable profits or the proceeds of a new issue).[110] Since, however, this facility is available to a private company in respect of share purchases as well, we shall postpone discussion of it until we have examined the share purchase rules.

---

[107] s.687(5).

[108] s.733(2)—"the amount by which the company's share capital account is diminished". This wording clearly excludes the share premium account.

[109] This might appear inconsistent with s.687(5), providing for the reduction of the company's share premium account and discussed in the previous paragraph. However, s.687(5) applies only to the specific case of a payment out of the proceeds of a fresh issue to meet a premium arising on redemption and can thus be seen as a particular exception to the general rule stated in s.688. Moreover, substantively the distinction seems supportable. Where redeemable shares, initially issued at a premium, are redeemed out of distributable profits, a diminution of the share premium account by an appropriate amount and its transfer to the CRR would achieve nothing by way of creditor protection and would simply complicate the legislation. However, where the shares are redeemed out of the proceeds of a new issue, a diminution of the share premium account is necessary in order to prevent the inflation of the company's overall capital yardstick, as explained in the previous paragraph, but no transfer to the CRR is necessary because the new issue itself increases the company's capital accounts.

[110] s.687(1).

Purchase of own shares

Although introducing an element of flexibility, the redemption pro-   **13–13**
visions do require the company to decide at the time of issue whether
the shares are to be redeemable. After issue, the company cannot
simply decide to re-purchase some of its shares, under those provisions. Nevertheless, until the 1981 Act, redemption was the only type
of purchase by a company of its own shares permitted by English law
without a court order (and even redemption was confined to preference shares). So far as capital maintenance is concerned there was
no reason for so restricting purchases; the creditor-protection solution adopted in relation to redeemable shares could equally well be
applied to other purchases. But undoubtedly the opportunities for
other abuses are then greater: for example, the directors, by causing
the company to repurchase shares of other members, could, without
any personal expense, enhance the value of their own holdings and
their control of the company. But these dangers too could be guarded
against and it was widely felt that the former restrictions were anachronistic. Hence, in 1980 the Department of Trade published a
Consultative Document (a Green Paper)[111] canvassing the possibility
of widening a company's powers. This met with an enthusiastic
reception and was implemented by the 1981 Act, both in relation to
private companies and, to the extent permitted by the Second
Company Law Directive, to public companies. The power has been
widely used by both and seems to have given rise to few problems.

The essential difference between redemption and purchase is that,
under the latter, agreement of the parties (the selling shareholder and
the buying company) will be needed at the time of the purchase.
Neither party can force the other to sell or buy if one or other does
not want to and, even if both agree in principle, the terms and conditions of the purchase will have to be agreed at the time of the
purchase. In contrast, as we have seen, in the case of redeemable
shares the terms and conditions of redemption will have been set out
in advance at the time the shares were issued. However, many of the
provisions relating to the implementation of the two transactions are
similar.

Section 690 provides that a company may purchase its own shares
(including redeemable shares),[112] subject to any restriction or prohibition in the company's articles.[113] Thus, the default rule for both
public and private companies is that the company does have power to
re-purchase its shares. A re-purchase cannot be made if the result
would be that there were no longer any members of the company

---

[111] *The Purchase by a Company of its own Shares*: Cmnd. 7944.
[112] Thus enabling the company to "redeem" them prior to a date fixed in the terms and
conditions if it can reach agreement with the holder.
[113] A purported re-purchase in breach of the articles would be void, because the company
would no longer be protected from the operation of s.658(2) (above, para.13–7); *cf. Hague v
Nam Tai Electronics Inc* [2007] 2 B.C.L.C. 194, PC.

holding non-redeemable shares or only treasury shares remained.[114] There is the same restriction on the re-purchase of shares which are not fully paid as exists in the case of redemptions.[115] The requirement that the shares be paid for on purchase is unqualified.[116]

13–14   From the point of view of creditor protection, the crucial point about the re-purchase provisions is that they apply the same rules about the permissible sources of finance for the re-purchase as apply in the case of a redemption,[117] and the same rules about the creation of a CRR are applied.[118] It is in fact the issue of shareholder protection which has proved more problematic in relation to re-purchases than in relation to redemptions, precisely because in redemptions the terms and method of redemption are set in advance, whereas with re-purchases there is greater scope for inequitable treatment of shareholders in the implementation of the re-purchase. Further, there was pressure in relation to re-purchases to relax the rule that the shares re-purchased be cancelled and instead to allow companies to hold onto the shares re-purchased (to hold them "in treasury", as it is usually called) with a view to later selling them to investors. Although not part of the original 1981 reforms, treasury shares were admitted in 2003, subject to safeguards. We will look at each issue in turn.

Protection for shareholders

13–15   It is clear that re-purchases have implications for the relations of shareholders among themselves. Controlling shareholders may be given the opportunity to sell their shares when minority shareholders are excluded, or may be given the opportunity to sell on more favourable terms. The Act contains some provisions aimed at controlling such abuses. These protections vary according to whether the purchase is to be an "off-market" or a "market" purchase. The essential distinction between the two situations is whether the purchase takes place on a "recognised investment exchange", i.e. one authorised by the Financial Services Authority.[119] In broad terms this means that it is a market purchase if it takes place on the main market of the London Stock Exchange, on the Alternative Invest-

---

[114] s.690(2). On treasury shares, see below.
[115] s.691(1).
[116] s.691(2) *cf.* the position on redemption: see para.13–10 above. And for the problems to which this lack of flexibility can give rise see *Peña v Dale* [2004] 2 B.C.L.C. 508; *Kinlan v Crimmin* [2007] 2 B.C.L.C. 67 (though in the latter case the judge managed to avoid requiring the shareholder to return to the company the money received by resort to the defence of a good faith change of position).
[117] s.692 tracks s.687, discussed above.
[118] s.733 (discussed above) applies to both redemptions and re-purchases.
[119] s.693(2), (5). See para.25–5.

ment Market or on Plus Market.[120] Market purchases create fewer risks of abuse since the rules of the FSA or the Exchange will apply and purchases will be effected at an objectively determined market price. If there is no market, a shareholder who needs to sell is likely to find that the company (or its directors) is the only potential purchaser and the shareholder will have to accept the price that it is prepared to pay.

Under section 694 an off-market purchase can be made only in pursuance of a contract the terms of which have been authorised by a special resolution of the company before it is entered into.[121] The contract so approved may take the form of what used to be called a "contingent purchase contract", i.e. one which does not amount to a binding contract to purchase shares but under which the company may become entitled or obliged to purchase them.[122] Where contingent purchase contracts may be particularly useful is to enable the company to bind or entitle itself to purchase the shares of a director or employee upon termination of employment, or, as an alternative to the creation of a new class of redeemable shares, to meet the requirements of a potential investor in an unquoted company who wants assurance that he or she will be able to find a purchaser if the investor needs to realise his investment. The authorisation can subsequently be varied, revoked or renewed by a like resolution.[123]

In the case of a public company the authorising resolution must specify a date on which it is to expire and that date must not be later than 18 months after the passing of the resolution,[124] so that directors may not subsequently act on a "stale" authority. Moreover, on any such resolution, whether of a public or private company, a member, holding shares to which the resolution relates, may not exercise the voting rights of those shares[125] and if the resolution would not have been passed but for his votes the resolution is ineffective.[126] This is an interesting example of the extension of the rule that directors must not vote at directors' meetings on matters in which they have a personal financial interest—a rule which normally does not apply to members voting as such.[127] The resolution is also ineffective unless a

[120] However, even if the trade takes place on a RIE it will not count as a market purchase if the market authorities have given only restricted permission for trading in the shares: s.693(3)(b).

[121] The contract may be entered into before approval, but in that case no shares may be purchased in pursuance of it before approval is obtained: s.694(2)(b).

[122] s.694(3).

[123] s.694(4).

[124] s.694(5).

[125] Or, on a written resolution, vote any shares held: s.695(2).

[126] s.695 which also provides (a) that it applies whether the vote is on a poll or by a show of hands, (b) that, notwithstanding any provision in the company's articles, any member may demand a poll and (c) that a vote and a demand for a poll by a member's proxy is treated as a vote and demand by the member.

[127] s.695 does not exclude only directors holding shares to which the resolution relates.

copy of the contract or a memorandum of its terms is available for inspection by members, and in the case of a resolution passed at a meeting it must be available at the company's registered office for not less than 15 days before it is held.[128] The same requirements apply on a resolution to approve any variation of the contract.[129]

Essentially, the shareholder protection technique deployed in the case of an off-market purchase is the requirement for super-majority approval by the shareholders in advance of the terms of the re-purchase contract.

13–16   Under section 701 a company (which, in practice, will be a public one) cannot make a market purchase of its own shares unless the making of such purchases has first been authorised by the company in general meeting.[130] In this case, however, an ordinary resolution suffices because the process of market purchase is more protective of shareholders. Nor are those whose shares are to be purchased to be excluded from voting, for the very good reason that, with a market purchase, their identities will not be known in advance. For the same reason what the shareholders are asked to approve in this case is not a contract (even a contingent one) for the purchase of the shares of specified members but an authorisation to the company (in practice, its directors) to go into the market in the future and acquire its shares on certain terms. The authorisation may be general or limited to shares of any particular class or description and may be conditional or unconditional[131] but it must specify the maximum number of shares to be acquired, the maximum and minimum prices,[132] and a date on which it is to expire, which must not be later than 18 months after the passing of the resolution.[133] Moreover, a copy of the resolution required by the section has to be sent to the Registrar within 15 days,[134] so that the market is formally aware of the company's intentions or at least its powers. Thus, the directors are given a re-purchase authority but one which is exercisable only within the specified limits as to price, amount and timing.

In the case of a re-purchase effected by a company listed on the Main Market of the London Stock Exchange, the Listing Rules of the

---

[128] s.696. In the case of a written resolution the information is sent to the members at or before the copy of the proposed resolution: s.696(2)(a). In either case the names of members holding shares to which the contract relates must be disclosed. These rights, being for the benefit of the shareholders, may be waived by their unanimous agreement: *Kinlan v Crummin*, above, fn.116, and see para.15–8.

[129] ss.697–699.

[130] As in the case of off-market purchases, the authority may be varied, revoked or renewed by a like resolution: s.701(4).

[131] s.701(2).

[132] s.701(3). The resolution may specify a particular sum or a non-discretionary formula for calculating the price (for example, by reference to the market price of the shares): s.701(7).

[133] s.701(5). But the purchase may be completed after the expiry date if the contract to buy was made before that date and the authorisation permitted the company to make a contract which would or might be executed after that date: s.701(6).

[134] s.701(8), applying Chapter 3 of Part 3 of the Act to this ordinary resolution.

FSA add a further and significant set of rules relating to the exercise by the company of the authority conferred upon it under the statutory provisions. In order to provide some degree of equality of treatment of shareholders in relation to substantial market re-purchases, which might affect the balance of power within the company, the Listing Rules require re-purchases of more than 15 per cent of a class of the company's equity shares[135] to be by way of a tender offer to all shareholders of the class.[136] A tender offer is an offer open to all the shareholders of the class on the same terms for a period of at least seven days, capable of being accepted by the shareholders *pro rata* with their existing holdings, and setting a fixed or maximum price for the purchase.[137] Thus, in a fixed price tender a shareholder holding two per cent of the class may sell shares to the company up to the amount of two per cent of the shares the company is offering to purchase. Where the tender is at a maximum (but not a fixed) price, the shareholder has to indicate the price at which it is prepared to sell its shares to the company (a price not exceeding the maximum set by the company) and the company will implement the tender by accepting the lowest-priced offers first and continue up the price curve until it has fulfilled its tender. Even where the purchase is of less than 15 per cent, the company must either use the tender offer procedure or limit the price it is offering to not more than 5 per cent above the market price of the shares over the five days preceding the purchase.[138] This limits the possibilities for favoured shareholders to sell their shares to the company at an attractive price.

In fact, the Listing Rules add in a variety of ways to the statutory rules on share re-purchases, even where the transaction is to be implemented off-market. Thus, whether the purchase is to be on- or off-market, the Listing Rules require the prior consent of any class of listed securities convertible or exchangeable into equity shares of the class to which the re-purchase proposal relates, unless there was provision at the date of issue of the convertibles that the company could re-purchase the relevant equity shares.[139] Thus, in principle, the holders of convertible bonds will need to consent to a re-purchase of the equity shares into which the bonds are convertible. Further, where an off-market transaction is contemplated, the Listing Rules apply their rules concerning related-party transactions.[140] These may exclude from voting on the resolution a wider range of persons than would the statute, because the statute excludes only those whose shares are to be re-purchased, whereas the Listing Rules also exclude

---

[135] This includes preference shares which are participating in either dividend or distributions on a winding up: LR, Glossary Definition, "equity share capital".
[136] LR 12.2.2.
[137] LR, Glossary Definition, "tender offer".
[138] LR 12.2.1.
[139] LR 12.4.7.
[140] LR 12.3.1.

their associates.[141] Finally, the FSA's Rules not surprisingly address market issues, such as the need for the market to be informed immediately of all the stages of a share re-purchase, from proposal to results;[142] and the need to avoid insider trading by excluding re-purchases during prohibited trading periods, except when the purchases are outside the control of the company, and other forms of market abuse.[143]

Treasury shares

13–17 Although treasury shares were not permitted under the original reforms of 1981, in 1998, in advance of the Company Law Review, the Government began consultation over the proposition that companies should be able to retain re-purchased shares and re-issue them, as required.[144] The main argument in favour of this reform was that it would permit companies to raise capital in small lots but at a full market price by re-selling the re-purchased shares as and when it was thought fit to do so. The argument against was that the freedom to re-sell would give boards of directors opportunities to engage in the manipulation of the company's share price, i.e. an argument based on investor protection rather than creditor protection. In 2001, the Government issued a further consultation document which accepted the idea in principle, but only for companies whose shares were traded on a public market, and consulted on further issues related to its implementation.[145] The manipulation danger was thought to be addressed by the separate provisions, contained in the FSMA 2000, dealing with market abuse,[146] and by the restriction on the amount of the treasury shares to 10 per cent of any class (as then required by the Second Directive).[147] These proposals were implemented in 2003[148] and Chapter 6 of Part 18 of the 2006 Act re-states them without substantive change. However, where a company cannot fit its situation into the rules on treasury shares, the principle remains that the re-purchased shares must be cancelled and the amount of the company's share capital account reduced by the nominal value of the cancelled shares.[149]

---

[141] LR 11.1.7(4)(b). "Associate" is defined widely in LR, Glossary Definition, "associate".

[142] L.R. 12.4.4–6. In addition the legislation requires ex post disclosure of the shares purchased in the directors' annual report: SI 2008/410 Sched.7, Part 2.

[143] See paras 30–4 and 30–35.

[144] See DTI, *Share Buybacks*, URN 98/713 (1998).

[145] DTI, *Treasury Shares*, URN 01/500 (2001).

[146] FSMA 2000, Pt VIII, especially s.118 and the Financial Services and Markets Act 2000 (Prescribed Markets and Qualifying Investments) Order 2001 (SI 2001/996). See Ch.30.

[147] Art.19. Under the Directive as amended in 2006 the imposition of this limit is no longer required of Member States.

[148] By the Companies (Acquisition of Own Shares) (Treasury Shares) Regulations 2003, (SI 2003/1116) and the No.2 Regulations, SI 2003/3031. See Geoffrey Morse, "The Introduction of Treasury Shares into English Law and Practice" [2004] J.B.L. 303.

[149] s.706.

The permission granted to companies to hold shares in treasury is subject to three conditions. First, the shares ("qualifying shares") must be listed shares (either in the UK or another EEA state) or traded on AIM or traded on a regulated market, which might also be a market outside the UK in another EEA state.[150] In short, the shares must be shares admitted to trading on a public market which meets certain standards of quality.[151] A consequence of this approach to the definition of qualifying shares is that private companies[152] are excluded from holding shares in treasury, which, given the rationale for permitting them, is not surprising. Secondly, the shares must have been purchased out of distributable profits (not out of the proceeds of a new issue, whether wholly or partly).[153] This limitation seems to have been imposed because it was thought that there would be little demand for re-purchases out of new issues and because their exclusion enables the legislation to take a much simpler approach to the accounting consequences of treasury shares.[154]

Thirdly, the aggregate nominal value of the shares held in treasury must not exceed 10 per cent of the nominal value of the issued share capital of the class in question at any time during the period they are held in treasury.[155] If that limit is breached, the "excess" shares must be disposed of or cancelled within twelve months of the contravention, but the original acquisition of the shares by the company is not rendered void.[156] This limit was derived from the Second Directive, which, however, no longer makes the rule mandatory on Member States. However, it is far from clear that the British Government intends to take advantage of the relaxation.[157]

The underlying rationale of the treasury share scheme is given **13–18** effect by the provision that treasury shares may at any time be sold by the company for cash.[158] When this happens, there is a sale by the company of existing shares, not an allotment of new shares. Consequently, the rules about the shareholder authorisation of directors to

---

[150] For the meaning of these terms see para.25–5. Although the shares must be traded on a public market (in the sense defined) to count as qualifying shares, the actual re-purchase could be effected by means of an off-market purchase of those shares, although it would be rare for a listed company to effect a re-purchase in this way.

[151] s.724(1),(2).

[152] As indeed will public companies unless their shares have actually been admitted to trading on one of the specified public markets.

[153] s.724(1)(b).

[154] Some indication of the complexities which arise when new issues are the source of finance have been given above at para.13–11.

[155] s.725(1),(2).

[156] s.725(3),(4). This obligation appears to bite even if, as a result of a later increase of the number of shares of the class in issue, the limit is no longer exceeded. See the definition of "excess shares" in s.725(3).

[157] See DTI, *Implementation of the Companies Act 2006*, February 2007, para.6.23.

[158] s.727(1)(a). Cash is widely defined in s.727(2). There is one minor restriction: where a company has been the subject of a successful takeover offer (which included the treasury shares) and the bidder is using the statutory squeeze-out procedure, the transfer of the shares can be only to the bidder: s.727(4) and see para.28–61.

allot shares do not apply,[159] thus facilitating speedy action by the directors. The same argument would be applicable to pre-emption rights for shareholders on allotment, but the Act artificially extends the statutory concept of allotment so as to make pre-emption rights applicable on sales of ordinary shares held in treasury.[160] Although shareholders can waive pre-emption rights in advance, their application to treasury shares is another example of the attachment of institutional shareholders to pre-emption rights.[161]

Where the proceeds of the sale are equal to or less than the purchase price paid by the company, the money received by the company is to be treated as a realised profit and so potentially distributable by the company.[162] Since the shares will have been acquired out of distributable profits, which were thereby diminished, there can be no creditor-protection objection against the proceeds of the sale being treated as a realised profit. Any excess of the price received by the company over that paid by it, however, must be transferred to the share premium account.[163] This again seems correct. The increase in the price of the shares presumably represents an increase in the value of the company since the shares were purchased, so that the portion of the price obtained on re-sale which represents that increase in value should be treated as legal capital, just like the consideration received by the company on the initial issue of shares.[164]

Alternatively, the company may transfer treasury shares to meet the requirements of an employees' share scheme.[165] Or it may do what it could have done when it originally acquired the shares, i.e. cancel them.[166] In this latter case its share capital account must be reduced by the amount of the nominal value of the shares cancelled.[167] In the usual way the company has to inform the Registrar when it disposes of the shares (in either of the permitted ways) or cancels them, giving the necessary particulars.[168]

Whilst the shares are still held by the company, it may not exercise any of the rights attached to them (notably the right to vote) and any such purported exercise is void,[169] so that the directors cannot strengthen their position in the general meeting of the company

---

[159] See para.24–4.
[160] s.560(2)(b).
[161] See para.24–13.
[162] s.731(2).
[163] s.731(3). On the share premium account see para.11–8.
[164] Of course, normally what is transferred to the share premium account is the excess above the nominal value of the share (see para.11–8), whereas what is being transferred here is the excess above the purchase price.
[165] s.727(1)(b).
[166] s.729. It may be obliged to cancel them if the shares cease to be "qualifying shares": s.729(2), (3).
[167] s.729(4). The directors may do this without following the reduction of capital procedure: s.729(5).
[168] ss.728 and 730.
[169] s.726(1),(2).

through the use of the treasury shares. Nor may a dividend be paid or any other distribution be made on the treasury shares.[170] However, the company may receive (fully paid) bonus shares in respect of the treasury shares, for otherwise the proportion of the equity represented by the treasury shares would decline, and the bonus shares so allotted are to be treated as treasury shares purchased by the company at the time they were allotted.[171] On a subsequent sale of the bonus shares their purchase price is to be treated as nil, so that the full amount received for them must be transferred to the share premium account.[172] This seems correct, since the purpose of issuing bonus shares is to capitalise profits and so the sale price of the bonus shares needs to be added to the company's capital accounts and not be treated as a realised profit.[173]

Private companies: redemption or purchase out of capital

In relation to both redemptions and re-purchases of shares, special **13–19** concessions were made to private companies in the 1981 reforms. It was recognised that it would frequently be impossible for a private company to redeem or purchase its own shares unless it could do so out of capital and without having to incur the expense of a formal reduction of capital with the court's consent. The whole concept of raising and maintaining capital is, in relation to such companies, of somewhat dubious value. Hence it was decided that, subject to safeguards, they should be empowered to redeem or buy without maintaining the former capital yardstick. In particular, the aim was to permit entrepreneurs to withdraw assets from their company to fund their retirement rather than by selling control to a larger competitor. The relevant provisions are now contained in Chapter 5 of Part 18 of the Act. They have been retained even though there has now been provided to private companies a non-court based method of reducing capital.[174]

Section 709 provides that, subject to what follows, a private company, unless restricted or prohibited by its articles from so doing, may make a payment in respect of the redemption or purchase of its shares otherwise than out of its distributable profits or the proceeds of a fresh issue of shares. Such a payment is termed a payment "out of capital".[175] This is a very wide definition and may explain why it was thought there might be some cases where a redemption or re-purchase "out of capital" would be available, whereas a reduction of

---

[170] s.726(3)—including a distribution on a winding up.
[171] s.726(4)(a), (5). On capitalisation issues see para.11–18.
[172] s.731(4)(b).
[173] By the same token, the value treasury shares acquired by purchase will be reduced by the bonus issue, thus reducing the amount of realised profit arising on their re-sale.
[174] See para.13–5 above.
[175] s.709(2).

capital would not. Suppose a company wishes to acquire shares for a price above their nominal value but has no share premium or capital redemption reserve. No matter how much the share capital account is reduced, this will not free up a sufficient amount of assets to be distributed so as to meet the desired purchase price. Assuming, however, that the company has sufficient cash, it may be able to engage in a redemption or re-purchase by making a payment "out of capital" under section 709. This helpfully says that a payment other than out of distributable profits or the proceeds of a fresh issue is a payment out of capital (and so in principle permitted) "whether or not it would be regarded apart from this section as a payment out of capital". Provided the company has the necessary cash and follows the provisions of this part of the Act, that is all it needs to be concerned with.[176]

The extent of any such payment out of capital must, however, be restricted to what is described as "the permissible capital payment" (PCP).[177] In brief, the rule is that any distributable profits and any proceeds of fresh issue made for the purpose of the redemption or purchase must first be used before resort may be had to a payment out of capital. The rules for determining distributable profits are those considered in the previous chapter in relation to dividends, but there are certain amendments,[178] perhaps the most important of which is that the accounts by reference to which the profits are calculated must be prepared within a period of three months ending with the date of the statutory declaration which the directors are required to make.[179]

The principal protective techniques used in the Chapter in respect of the PCP are, in the case of creditors, the requirement for a solvency statement from the directors; in the case of shareholders, the requirement for approval of the proposed redemption or re-purchase by special resolution; and, in both cases, the availability of a right of objection to the court.

Directors' statement

13–20 As far as the solvency statement is concerned, the requirements of the Act are similar to those applied in the case of a solvency statement upon a reduction of capital out of court by a private company, including the requirement for the directors to take into account contingent and prospective liabilities.[180] However, they are not the

---

[176] HL Debs, Grand Committee, Tenth Day, March 20, 2006, cols. 31–32.
[177] s.710.
[178] s.711.
[179] s.712(6), (7). The available profits so determined have then to be treated as reduced by any lawful distributions made by the company since the date of the accounts and before the date of the statutory declaration: s.712(3),(4).
[180] s.714(4). On the requirements for a capital reduction see para.13–5 above.

same. In particular, the directors are apparently unable to make the required forward-looking statement in the case of a purchase out of capital, if they intend to wind the company up within twelve months of the proposed payment.[181] And the forward-looking statement, even where no winding up is contemplated, is required to be a little fuller. The form of the required statement is that, having regard to the "the amount and character of the financial resources" which will be available to the company in the directors' view, the directors have formed the opinion that the company will be able to carry on business as a going concern throughout that year (and accordingly will be able to pay its debts as they fall due).[182] The emphasis is thus on an opinion which envisages a continuing business, not just the ability of the company to pay its debts.[183] Perhaps because of these differences the statement required on a purchase or redemption is termed a "directors' statement" in the Act, whilst the term "solvency statement" is reserved for the statement required of directors under the out-of-court reduction procedure, though both statements are, substantively, statements about the solvency of the company.

The Act applies to the directors' statement the same criminal liability for negligence as is applied to the solvency statement.[184] There is also a limited statutory civil liability in negligence to the company if the company goes into winding up within one year of the payment being made to the shareholder.[185] However, a major difference with the solvency statement is that the directors' statement needs to be accompanied by a report from the company's auditors stating their opinion that the amount of the PCP has been properly calculated and that they are not aware of any matters, after inquiry into the company's affairs, which renders the directors' statement unreasonable in all the circumstances.[186]

The special resolution is required to be passed within a week of the directors' statement and on the basis of prior disclosure to the members of the directors' statement and auditors' report,[187] but in this case it is explicitly provided that the resolution is ineffective if

---

[181] Presumably on the grounds that a re-purchase to enable the founding entrepreneur to retire is in those circumstances unnecessary: the withdrawal can take place as part of the winding up. The section does not make provision for a statement to be made if a winding up is contemplated, and the forward-looking statement which the directors are required to make requires them to "have regard to their intentions with respect to the management of the company during the year", so that they could not honestly make the required statement if they contemplated a winding up.

[182] s.714(3)(b). S.643 (above, para.13–5) refers only to the payment of debts as they fall due.

[183] As to the opinion about the current position, that relates to the position "immediately following" the date on which the PCP is proposed to be made (s.714(3)(a)) rather than the date of the statement (*cf.* s.643(1)(a)), so that the current statement in the case of a purchase requires a small degree of foresight.

[184] s.715 *cf.* s.643(4) (see above, para.13–6).

[185] s.76 of the Insolvency Act 1986. See fn.200 below.

[186] s.714(6).

[187] s.718(1), (2)—the method of disclosure varying according to whether a written resolution or a resolution at a meeting is contemplated.

these requirements are not complied with.[188] The same restrictions on voting by the member of the company whose shares are to be redeemed or bought are applied as in the case of an off-market purchase.[189]

Appeal to the court

13–21 To protect creditors, the Act requires that within a week following the passing of the resolution the company must cause to be published in the *Gazette* and, unless it notifies each of its creditors in writing, in an "appropriate national newspaper",[190] a notice giving details about the resolution and the intended purchase or redemption out of capital and stating where the directors' and auditors' statements may be inspected and that any creditor may within five weeks of the resolution apply to the court for an order prohibiting the payment.[191] Not later than the date of the first publication of the notice the company must deliver to the Registrar a copy of the directors' statutory declaration and the auditors' report and the originals of these must be kept at the company's registered office for the next five weeks and be open to inspection by any member or creditor.[192]

The final protective device (for both creditors and dissenting members) is court scrutiny. The Act entitles any member of the company, who has not consented to or voted for the resolution, and any creditor of the company, within five weeks of the passing of the resolution to apply to the court for the cancellation of the resolution.[193] The court is given the widest powers. For example, it can cancel the resolution, confirm it, or make such orders as it thinks expedient for the purchase of dissentient members' shares or for the protection of creditors, and may make ancillary orders for the reduction of the company's capital.[194]

If there is no court objection, the PCP must be made between five and seven weeks after the adoption of the resolution.[195] Upon the re-purchase of the shares, the company's share capital account will be reduced accordingly, but, because this is a permitted payment out of capital, there will be no need to transfer a corresponding amount to the CRR, as would happen in the case of a purchase out of distributable profits.[196] A transfer to CRR will be needed only to the

---

[188] s.718(3), *cf.* s.642(4) applying to solvency statements where the validity of the resolution is expressly preserved (see para.13–6, above) and reliance is placed instead on criminal sanctions to produce compliance with the disclosure obligation: s.644(7).

[189] s.717, *cf.* s.695 and see above, para.13–15.

[190] i.e. a newspaper circulating throughout the part of the United Kingdom in which the company is registered in: s.719(3).

[191] s.719(1),(2).

[192] s.719(4) and 720.

[193] s.721(1),(2).

[194] s.721(3)–(7).

[195] s.723.

[196] See para.13–11 above.

extent that distributable profits have been used in part to fund the purchase of the shares.[197] Where the PCP is greater than the nominal value of the purchased shares (i.e. they are being purchased at a premium), the company is given permission to reduce its CRR, share premium account and its revaluation reserve accordingly.[198] In other words, the company's capital yardstick will in all probability be reduced to the extent of the PCP.[199] This is, after all, the object of the exercise. Overall, indeed, the effect of the foregoing provisions is that a private company may be able to make a return to one or more of its members which will exhaust its accumulated profits available for dividend and reduce both its assets and its capital yardstick.

As far as the Companies Act is concerned, this is the end of the procedure. However, the Insolvency Act contains a limited mechanism for unscrambling the acquisition. If the company goes into liquidation within one year of the payment being made to the shareholder, that person is liable to return to the company the amount of the payment out of capital, to the extent that this is needed to meet any deficiency of the company's assets in relation to its liabilities.[200]   **13–22**

Given that private companies are provided by the Act with both a simplified procedure for reduction of capital without court approval and one for a re-purchase or redemption out of capital, which will prove more popular where both mechanisms are available? Re-purchase out of capital has the virtue of familiarity and may continue to be used quite widely, at least initially, but the procedure for reduction out of court seems simpler and cheaper. No auditors' report is required on the directors' solvency statement, no special accounts have to be prepared[201] and there is no right of objection to the court on the part of creditors or non-approving members.

Failure by the company to perform

Suppose the company has incurred an obligation to redeem shares under the terms of their issue or to re-purchase shares as a result of a contract entered into with the shareholder, but does not meet its obligations. This may occur because the company decides to break the contract or because it cannot lawfully perform it since, for example, the new issue of shares has not raised the proceeds expected   **13–23**

---

[197] s.734(4).
[198] s.734(3). S.734(4) deals with the complication where the purchase is partly by way of PCP and partly by way of the proceeds of a fresh issue.
[199] But note the example given above where the PCP is greater than the company's CRR and share premium account.
[200] s.76. The directors of the company who signed the statement are jointly and severally liable with the shareholders unless the director can show reasonable grounds for the opinion set out therein.
[201] Though the directors can hardly make the required statement unless they have at least up-to-date management accounts.

and the company has inadequate available profits.[202] What are the remedies of a shareholder if the company does not perform the contract to redeem or purchase his shares? Section 735 provides that the company is not liable in damages in respect of any failure on its part to redeem or purchase.[203] It was thought that damages were not an appropriate remedy; that would result in the seller retaining his shares in, and membership of, the company and yet recovering damages (paid perhaps out of capital) from the company.[204] Any other right of the shareholder to sue the company is expressly preserved, but, even then, it is provided that the court shall not grant an order for specific performance (perhaps a more appropriate discretionary remedy) "if the company shows that it is unable to meet the costs of redeeming or purchasing the shares in question out of distributable profits".[205] Apart from this, the section gives no indication of what "other rights" the shareholder might have. There is little doubt that these would include the right to sue for an injunction restraining the company from making a distribution of profits which would have the effect of making it unlawful for the company to perform its contract.

However, the ban on the recovery of damages can be circumvented by using an indirect procedure to this end. In *British & Commonwealth Holdings Plc v Barclays Bank Plc*[206] a consortium of banks had promised to take the shares from the shareholder if the company could not redeem them and the company had promised to indemnify the banks in respect of actions by it which made it impossible for it to redeem. It was held that the section did not prevent the banks suing the company on the covenants, even though the aim of the whole scheme was to ensure that the shareholder would be able to redeem even if the company had no distributable reserves. The case strongly suggests, but does not finally decide, that the section is concerned only with the range of remedies available to the shareholder rather than with ensuring that a company never in effect redeems shares out of capital.

A second issue which arises is the position if the company goes into liquidation before the shares have been redeemed or purchased. Generally, the terms of redemption or purchase may then be enforced against the company and when the shares are accordingly redeemed

---

[202] The company could, presumably, protect itself from being in breach by expressly providing in the contract that the purchase is conditional upon its having the needed proceeds or sufficient profits.

[203] s.735(2).

[204] In any event, the section does not protect the company against paying damages in all cases as a result of its failure to redeem. See *British & Commonwealth Holdings Plc v Barclays Bank Plc* [1996] 1 W.L.R. 1, CA, below.

[205] s.735(2),(3). This ignores the possibility that it has adequate proceeds of a fresh issue but has nevertheless decided to break the contract. Surely the seller should then be entitled to specific performance?

[206] [1996] 1 W.L.R. 1, CA.

or purchased, they are cancelled.[207] However, the shareholder will gain little or nothing by enforcing the contract if the winding up is an insolvent liquidation since the member is a deferred creditor. Any claim in respect of the purchase price is postponed to the claims of all other creditors—and, indeed, to those of other shareholders whose shares carry rights (whether as to capital or income) which are preferred to the rights as to capital of the shares to be redeemed or purchased.[208] Moreover, even this limited right may not be enforced in liquidation if the terms of redemption or purchase provided for performance to take place at a date later than that of the commencement of the winding-up; or if during the period beginning with the date when redemption or purchase was to take place and ending with the commencement of the winding-up, the company did not have distributable profits equal in value to the redemption or purchase price.[209] In this case it appears the member is treated in the winding-up as if there were no obligation on the company to redeem or purchase the shares and as if he or she were still a member of the company.

Subsequent dealings over the contract to purchase

In the case of a re-purchase, but obviously not in relation to redemptions, it is possible that subsequent dealings in relation to the contract of purchase could give rise to abuses, especially where the other party to the contract is an insider of the company (director or large shareholder). To limit these possibilities, the Act provides that the rights of a company under a contract to purchase its own shares are not capable of being assigned.[210] This is designed to minimise the risk that the company will speculate on its own shares or attempt to rig the market. Further, an agreement by the company to release its rights under an off-market purchase is void unless approved in advance by a special resolution in relation to which the requirements for the original contract are observed.[211] The sort of abuse struck at here is when the company has agreed to purchase the shares of a director who, when the time to complete the purchase arises, finds that he has made a bad bargain and persuades his fellow directors to release him. A variation of the contract would require prior approval by special resolution; so should a release. There is no similar requirement in the case of market purchases; it is not needed since a

13–24

---

[207] s.735(4). Hence in respect of these shares the seller will cease to be a member or "contributory" and will become a creditor in respect of the price.

[208] s.735(6). In a solvent liquidation the shareholder may be worse off than if shares not been redeemed or purchases, if the share gave a right to participate in surplus assets but the purchase or redemption price did not reflect the value of this right.

[209] s.735(5).

[210] s.704.

[211] s.700(1)—in particular the rules as to voting and disclosure.

bargain, once struck on the Stock Exchange, cannot be cancelled at the whim of the parties.[212]

As we have seen, the price for any of its shares purchased by the company must normally be paid out of distributable profits or the proceeds of a new issue of shares made for the purpose.[213] The Act applies a similar, but stricter, rule to any payment (other than the purchase price) made by the company in consideration of:

    (a) acquiring any right (for example an option) to purchase under a contingent purchase contract;

    (b) the variation of any off-market contract; or

    (c) the release of any of the company's obligations under any off-market or market contract.[214]

Although such payments are not strictly part of the purchase price,[215] none of them is normal expenditure in the course of the company's business but rather a distribution to a member or members, and the payment would not have been made but for the fact that the company was minded to agree to purchase its shares. Such payments ought therefore to be treated, so far as practicable, in the same way as the purchase price. It is highly unlikely that a company would contemplate making a new issue of shares for the purpose of financing any such payment.[216] Hence the Act provides that they must be paid for out of distributable profits only. If this is contravened, in cases (a) and (b) above, purchases are not lawful, and in case (c) the release is void.[217]

Conclusion

13–25   Even if one takes the view that legal capital is a central doctrine of company law, the above discussion has shown that it is relatively easy to reconcile it with the acquisition by a company of its own shares, provided certain conditions are met. In particular, acquisitions out of distributable profits, coupled with an appropriate adjustment to the company's capital accounts, present no threat to the integrity of the doctrine of legal capital. Since share re-purchases became lawful a quarter of a century or so ago, share buybacks have become a routine method of utilisation of their profits by listed companies, supple-

---

[212] But if, in consideration of a payment made by the company, the contract is reversed, s.705 (discussed immediately below) will apply.

[213] See above, para.13–11.

[214] s.705(1).

[215] Though, in case (a), the division of the total price between that paid for the option and that paid on its exercise may be arbitrary.

[216] Which, in case (a) and perhaps (b), would be made some time before any actual purchase and which in cases (a) and (c) might never be made at all.

[217] s.705(2).

menting the alternative of a dividend payment (considered in Chapter 12). There are a number of reasons why a company might wish to proceed by way of a share buyback rather than a dividend distribution. By reducing the number of shares in issue, the price of the remaining shares may increase, because supply is restricted. Even if that is not so, the directors may take the view that the company has need of a smaller equity capital base in the future and that, for example, by replacing equity with debt, the company will be able to improve the returns to the remaining equity shareholders after the buyback. Or the directors may simply think that the company has more equity capital than it can usefully put to work. As for the shareholders, a buy-back offer gives them the choice of a partial exit from the company, at a modest premium to the current market price, or in effect increasing their exposure to the company by remaining invested at the same level in monetary terms but, in future, holding an increased percentage of the equity.

FINANCIAL ASSISTANCE

Section 678 prohibits a public company (or its subsidiary) from **13–26** giving financial assistance to a person for the acquisition by that person of the company's shares, whether the assistance is given in advance of or after the acquisition. The history of this rule does not constitute one of the most glorious episodes in British company law. The rationale for its introduction was under-articulated; it has proved capable of rending unlawful what seem from any perspective to be perfectly innocuous transactions; and it has proved resistant to a reformulation which would avoid these problems. The Company Law Review eventually decided that, for private companies, the only way forward was to take them out of the scope of the rule altogether, which reform proposal was implemented in the 2006 Act. The CLR also proposed a series of amendments to the rule as it applies to public companies,[218] but most of these were not implemented in the 2006 Act. The Government took the view that the Second Directive, whose provisions the then British Government unwisely insisted should contain a rule against financial assistance, was said to prevent significant changes to the rule as it applies to public companies.[219] Since then, the Second Directive itself has been amended,[220] but the

---

[218] *Company Formation and Capital Maintenance*, paras 3.42 and 3.43. These proposals were derived in the main from proposals for reform made earlier by the DTI itself.

[219] DTI, *Company Law Reform*, Cm. 6456, March 2005, paras 42–43.

[220] See new Arts. 23(1) and 23A introduced into the Second Directive by Directive 2006/68/EC.

Government regarded the relaxations introduced as not significant[221] and pinned its hopes on a more radical reform of the Directive in the future.

The rule against financial assistance for acquisitions of the company's shares was not developed by the nineteenth century judges as part of the capital maintenance regime. Rather, it was a statutory reform introduced in the 1929 Act as a result of the recommendations of the Greene Committee.[222] Although conventionally dealt with, as in this work, under the heading of legal capital, it is clear that in formal terms financial assistance may have no impact on the company's legal capital. If a company lends £100,000 to someone to purchase its shares, the company's share capital, share premium account and capital redemption reserve will not be in any way altered by that loan or the subsequent purchase of the shares. The Greene Committee seems to have thought that financial assistance offended against the spirit, if not the letter, of the rule in *Trevor v Whitworth* (company prohibited from acquiring its own shares),[223] but the Jenkins Committee commented that, had the ban "been designed merely to extend that rule, we should have felt some doubt whether it was worth retaining".[224]

Nor does financial assistance necessarily reduce the company's net asset position. If in the above example the borrower is fully able to repay the loan, the company is simply replacing one asset (cash) with another (the rights under the loan) and possibly the latter will earn the company a higher rate of return. For obvious reasons, there is no general principle of creditor protection in company law which prohibits the company from altering the risk characteristics of its assets,[225] and it is by no means clear that the rule against financial assistance can be singled out for justification on this ground.

13–27 In fact, the Greene Committee seems to have been heavily, perhaps inappropriately, influenced by the use of financial assistance in schemes which it disapproved of for more general reasons. That Committee thought, in particular, that it was abusive to finance a takeover by a bridging loan and immediately repay it by raiding the coffers of the cash-rich company which is taken over.[226] Now that highly leveraged takeovers are a common event, this worry looks somewhat overdone. More to the point, as it has operated in recent

---

[221] DTI, *Implementation of Companies Act 2006: A Consultative Document*, February 2007, para.6–26

[222] Cmnd. 2657 (1926).

[223] See fn.62 above.

[224] Cmnd. 1749 (1962), para.173. Of course, if the shares are held by the person to whom the assistance is given, not beneficially, but as a nominee for the company, then the provisions discussed above at para.13–7 will apply (so that the financial assistance rules are not necessary to address the nominee situation).

[225] Lenders may impose such constraints by contract, of course. See para.31–2.

[226] On variations on this theme see *Selangor United Rubber Estates v Cradock (No.3)* [1968] 1 W.L.R. 1555; *Karak Rubber Co v Burden (No.2)* [1972] 1 W.L.R. 602; and *Wallersteiner v Moir* [1974] 1 W.L.R. 991, CA (pet. dis.) [1975] 1 W.L.R. 1093, HL.

years, the financial assistance rule has not proved a major hindrance to such takeovers. In particular, the legislation has for some time permitted a payment of cash from the new subsidiary to the parent provided it is made by way of lawful dividend.[227] This suggests that, at least under the current law, the objection is not to the use of the subsidiary's cash balances to repay the loan as a desire to allow this to happen only in a way which protects both creditors (by requiring the dividend to be paid out of profits)[228] and minority shareholders, since dividends are paid *pro rata* to the proportion of the share capital held.[229] In other words, the financial assistance prohibition does not express a policy about desirable and undesirable takeovers but more general concerns about creditor and minority shareholder protection. However, the financial assistance rule seems too broad to be supported on a simple creditor or minority shareholder rationale, as the above example of a loan to purchase shares suggests. For example, if the loan were for some purpose other than the purchase of shares, the rule would not bite, yet the borrower might be less able to repay the loan than the borrower for the share purchase.

However, the Greene Committee's recommendations were enacted as s.45 of the 1929 Act, which was re-enacted with amendments as s.54 of the 1948 Act. However, s.45 immediately revealed the difficulties involved in drafting a prohibition that was properly targeted on the perceived abuses. That section, despite its relative brevity, became notorious as unintelligible and liable to penalise innocent transactions while failing to deter guilty ones. The Jenkins Committee[230] suggested an alternative approach very similar to that eventually adopted in 1981 in relation to private companies, but at the time no action was taken on that suggestion and, when the Second Company Law Directive was adopted, it became impracticable in relation to public companies.[231]

However, in 1980 two reported cases[232] caused considerable alarm in commercial and legal circles, suggesting, as they did, that the scope of the section was even wider, and the risk of wholly unobjectionable transactions being shot down even greater, than had formerly been thought. Hence it was decided that something had to be done about it in the 1981 Act which was then in preparation. Probably more midnight oil was burnt on this subject than on all the rest of that Act, and the resulting elaborate provisions were certainly some improvement on section 54. However, they still did not produce the holy grail of a precisely targeted prohibition and, after the controversy gener-

[227] s.681(2).
[228] See para.12–1.
[229] See para.19–1.
[230] Cmnd. 1749 (1962) paras 170–186.
[231] See Art.23 of Directive 77/91, [1977] OJ L26/1.
[232] *Belmont Finance Corp v Williams Furniture Ltd (No.2)* [1980] 1 All E.R. 393, CA; *Armour Hick Northern Ltd v Whitehouse* [1980] 1 W.L.R. 1520.

ated by the House of Lords decision in *Brady v Brady*,[233] the Government made proposals for the further relaxation of the provisions.[234] However, before these proposals could be implemented, the Company Law Review was established, with the results described above. In the meantime, the difficulty of producing a targeted formula continued to be demonstrated in litigation, for example, in the decision of the Court of Appeal in *Chaston v SWP Group Ltd*[235] in 2002.

The prohibition

13–28 Section 678 distinguishes between assistance given prior to the acquisition and that given afterwards.[236] Its subs. (1) says that, subject to exceptions:

> "where a person[237] is acquiring or is proposing to acquire[238] shares in a public company, it is not lawful for that company, or a company that is a subsidiary of that company,[239] to give financial assistance directly or indirectly[240] for the purpose of that acquisition before or at the same time as the acquisition takes place."

Subsection (3) provides that, subject to the same exceptions, when a person has acquired shares in a company and any liability has been incurred (by that or any other person) for that purpose, it is not lawful for the company or any of its subsidiaries to give financial assistance, directly or indirectly, for the purpose of reducing or discharging that liability, if at the time the assistance was given the

---

[233] [1989] A.C. 755, HL.

[234] DTI, *Company Law Reform: Proposals for Reform of Sections 151–158 of the Companies Act 1985* (1993); DTI, *Consultation Paper on Financial Assistance* (November 1996).

[235] [2003] 1 B.C.L.C. 675, helpfully considered by Ferran, "Corporate Transactions and Financial Assistance: Shifting Policy Perceptions but Static Law" (2004) 63 C.L.J. 225.

[236] On the other hand, the drafters seem to have thought of financial assistance, whether given before or after the event, as a one-off transaction. For the difficulties involved in calculating the impact of the assistance on the company's net assets where the assistance is continuing, see *Parlett v Guppys (Bridport) Ltd* [1996] 2 B.C.L.C. 34, CA.

[237] The Government's interpretation of the section is that the person must be someone other than the company itself: HC Debs, Standing Committee D, July 20, 2006, cols. 856–857 (Vera Baird).

[238] In contrast with s.54 of the 1948 Act, which used the expression "purchase or subscription", this section refers to "acquire" or "acquisition" thus extending the ambit of the section to non-cash subscriptions and exchanges.

[239] The sections do not apply to financial assistance by a holding company for the acquisition of shares in its subsidiary; in such a case there is less likelihood of prejudice to other shareholders or to creditors. The subsidiary must be a "company" within the meaning of the Act (see s.1) so that foreign subsidiaries are not caught by the prohibition. This was the view taken previously: see *Arab Bank Plc v Merchantile Holdings Ltd* [1994] Ch. 755.

[240] A charge given by a company to secure a loan to the company which both lender and company knew was to be on-lent to the purchaser of a company's shares to finance the purchase constitutes indirect financial assistance: *Hill and Tylor Ltd, Re* [2005] 1 B.C.L.C. 41; *Central and Eastern Trust Co v Irving Oil Ltd* (1980) 110 D.L.R. (3d) 257 (Sup Ct. Can.).

company in which the shares were acquired was a public company. Thus, if A (probably a bank) lends B (a bidder) £1 million to enable B (an acquisition vehicle) to make a takeover of a company and C (probably B's parent company) guarantees repayment, it will be unlawful for any financial assistance to be given by the company, when taken over, to A, B or C towards the repayment of the £1 million. However, the test is whether the company whose shares were acquired and which is now giving the financial assistance is a public company at the time the assistance is given by it. Thus, in this example, if the target company were a public company, it could nevertheless give financial assistance after the acquisition, provided it had by then been re-registered as a private company. This step is commonly taken in private equity buy-outs.

Section 683 provides that a reference to a person incurring a lia- **13–29** bility includes:

> "his changing his financial position by making an agreement or arrangement (whether enforceable or unenforceable and whether made on his own account or with any other person)[241] or by any other means"

and it adds that reference to a company giving financial assistance to reduce or discharge a liability incurred for the purposes of acquiring shares includes giving assistance for the purpose of wholly or partly restoring the financial position of the person concerned to what it was before the acquisition. This results in an enormous extension of the normal meaning of "liability" and seems to mean that before a company can give any financial assistance to *any* person (whether or not the acquirer) it must assess his overall financial position before and after the acquisition[242] and if, afterwards, it has deteriorated, must refrain from any form of financial assistance which is not covered by one of the exceptions—at any rate if there is a causal connection between the deterioration and the acquisition.

The scope of the prohibition depends crucially on what is meant by "financial assistance". This is widely defined by the Act, certainly more widely than is required by the Second Directive. In addition to such obvious assistance as gifts, loans, guarantees, releases, waivers and indemnities,[243] the definition includes any other agreement under

---

[241] The words "or with any other person" are somewhat puzzling; one would have expected "or that of any other person". Can there be an agreement or arrangement which is not made with some other person? And, if there can, would it not be covered by "or by any other means"?

[242] The difficulty of doing this after a takeover is mind-boggling.

[243] s.677(1)(a)–(c)—other than an indemnity given in respect of the indemnifier's own neglect or default.

which the obligations of the company giving the assistance are to be fulfilled before the obligations of another party to the agreement,[244] and the novation of a loan or of other agreement; or the assignment of rights under it. If the assistance is of one or more of these types, it is irrelevant whether or not the net assets of the company are reduced by reason of the assistance.[245]

However, this is not all. The definition concludes with "any other financial assistance given by a company, the net assets[246] of which are thereby reduced to a material extent, or which has no net assets". The effect of this is that, even if the financial assistance does not fall within the specific types that the drafter was able to foresee, it will nevertheless be unlawful if the company has no net assets or if the consequence of the assistance is to reduce its net assets "to a material extent". Only in this last case, where the company has net assets, does it seem to be a requirement of the definition of financial assistance that the company giving it should suffer a detriment. Clearly "materiality" is to be determined to some extent by the relationship between the value of the assistance and the value of the net assets: assistance worth £50 would reduce the net assets materially if they were only £100 but immaterially if they were £1 million. But how far is that to be taken? A company with net assets of £billions might regard a reduction of £1 million as immaterial, but it seems unlikely that judges (most of whom are not accustomed to disposing of £millions) would so regard it. At the other end of the scale, it was held in *Chaston*[247] that an expenditure of £20,000 by a subsidiary was material whose net assets were only £100,000 and even though the assistance was in relation to the purchase of the shares of the parent at a price of some £2.5 million.[248]

13–30   Assistance, however, will not be unlawful unless it is "financial". Merely giving information (even financial information) is not financial assistance.[249] Moreover, even if financial, the assistance must fall within the admittedly wide definition if it is to be unlawful. In other words, the definition of "financial assistance" seems intended to be exhaustive. Thus, timely repayment of a debt due, even if done in

---

[244] e.g. where a company which is a diamond merchant sells a diamond to a dealer for £100,000, payment to be 12 months hence, the intention being that the dealer will sell the diamond at a profit or borrow on its security thus putting him in funds to acquire shares in the company.

[245] In some cases (e.g. gifts) they will be; in others (e.g. loans or guarantees) they may or may not.

[246] Defined as "the aggregate of the company's assets, less the aggregate of its liabilities" and "liabilities" includes any provision for anticipated losses or charges: s.677(2).

[247] Above, fn.235.

[248] If the assistance had been provided by the parent, as it could well have been, no question of financial assistance would probably have arisen.

[249] But reimbursement of the costs of digesting and assessing the information could be, as in *Chaston*.

order to assist the creditor in the purchase of the debtor's shares, would not seem to be caught,[250] but it might be if the debt were paid early because it could then be said to have an element of gift in it.[251]

Finally, the impugned transaction must actually be capable of assisting the acquirer to obtain the shares. In the *British & Commonwealth Holdings* case,[252] the promises, made by the company to banks which could be required to acquire the shares from the shareholder if the company did not redeem them, were regarded as an "inducement" to the shareholder to acquire the redeemable shares in the first place but not as financial assistance to it to do so. However, in *Chaston*[253] this decision was explained on the basis that the company did not expect to have to meet its obligations at the time the promises were made and it was held that there was no general rule that an inducement could not constitute financial assistance. In that case the subsidiary of the target had paid for an accountant's report on the target, which was an inducement to the potential bidder to make the offer, but it was also financial assistance in the sense that it reduced the costs the potential bidder incurred in investigating the worth of the target.

Chaston is another example of the financial assistance prohibition striking down an entirely innocuous transaction. The company (or rather its subsidiary) spent a modest amount of money to further a sale of the company to a purchaser—a sale which was clearly in the shareholders' interests (as the subsequent litigation showed) and which carried no additional risks (probably the opposite) for its creditors. For this exemplary business decision the directors of the company were found to be in breach of their fiduciary duties to the company (by providing the unlawful financial assistance) and held personally liable to restore the amount of the assistance to the company, i.e. to the purchaser, which sued as assignee of the subsidiary's claim.[254]

The exceptions
The Act provides a number of exceptions to the prohibitions. Some **13–31** are more or less what one would have expected. They include allot-

---

[250] *cf. MT Realisations Ltd v Digital Equipment Co Ltd* [2003] 2 B.C.L.C 117, CA—enforcement of security rights was recovery of a legal entitlement rather than the receipt of financial assistance.

[251] See *Plaut v Steiner* (1988) 5 B.C.C. 352, but note also the insistence by the Court of Appeal in *British & Commonwealth Holdings Plc v Burclays Bank Plc* [1996] 1 W.L.R. 1, CA that the terms used in the definition must be given their technical meaning (in this case in relation to the meaning of an "indemnity").

[252] Above, para.13–23.

[253] Above, fn.235.

[254] In *Anglo Petroleum Ltd v TFB (Mortgages) Ltd* [2007] B.C.C 407, a differently constituted CA took a more commercially robust line, notably in rejecting the argument that any payment by a company which "smoothed the path to the acquisition" of its shares constituted financial assistance.

ment of bonus shares, lawful distributions, anything done in accordance with a court order, reductions of capital or redemptions or purchases of shares under the provisions discussed above, and anything done under the reconstruction provisions discussed in Chapter 29.[255] Also excepted are lending money in the ordinary course of business when lending is part of the company's ordinary business, and contributions to employees' share schemes and the like; but, in the case of a public company, only if it has net assets which are not thereby reduced or, to the extent that they are thereby reduced, if the assistance is provided out of distributable profits.[256]

The main and most debated exception is to be found, however, in section 678 itself. This was intended to allay the fears aroused by two decisions in 1980.[257] The section relates to the purposes for which the financial assistance was given. It is a necessary pre-condition for liability under section 678 that the financial assistance should have been given for the purpose of the acquisition of the shares. In some cases the company will be able to show that, although the financial assistance was given in connection with an acquisition of shares, it was not given for that purpose.[258] However, the exceptions come into play where that cannot be shown, i.e. where the purpose of the financial assistance was to facilitate the acquisition of shares. Under section 678(2) the prohibition on a company from giving financial assistance before or at the time of the acquisition nevertheless does not apply if:

(a) the company's principal purpose in giving the assistance is not to give it for the purpose of any such acquisition; or

(b) if the giving of the assistance for that purpose is only an incidental part of some larger purpose of the company; and

the assistance is given in good faith in the interests of the company.

Subsection (4) provides similarly that the prohibition does not apply to assistance given subsequently to the acquisition if:

(a) the company's principal purpose in giving the assistance is not to reduce or discharge any liability incurred by a person for the purpose of the acquisition of shares in the company or its holding company; or

---

[255] s.681. There is no express exemption for the expenses of share issues (for example, commissions—See para.11–13), but there clearly should be.

[256] s.682. Distributable profits are defined in s.683(1). For the need to include private companies within this exception, see below, para.000.

[257] *Belmont Finance Corp v Williams Furniture Ltd (No.2)* and *Armour Hick Northern Ltd v Whitehouse*: above, fn.232.

[258] *Dymont v Boyden* [2005] 1 B.C.L.C. 163, CA.

  (b) the reduction or discharge of any such liability is only an
      incidental part of some larger purpose of the company; and

the assistance is given in good faith in the interests of the company.
On the meaning of these difficult subsections[259] there is an   **13–32**
authoritative ruling from the House of Lords in the case of *Brady v
Brady*,[260] a case remarkable both because of the extent of the judicial
disagreement to which it gave rise and because it was ultimately
decided on a ground not argued in the lower courts. It related to
prosperous family businesses, principally concerned with haulage and
soft drinks. The businesses were run and owned in equal shares by
two brothers, Jack and Bob Brady, and their respective families,
through a parent company, T. Brady & Co Ltd (Brady's), and a
number of subsidiary and associated companies. Unfortunately Jack
and Bob fell out, resulting in a complete deadlock. It was clear that
unless something could be agreed amicably, Brady's would have to be
wound-up—which was the last thing that anyone wanted. It was
therefore agreed that the group should be reorganised, sole control of
the haulage business being taken by Jack and that of the drinks
business by Bob. As the respective values of the two businesses were
not precisely equal, this involved various intra-group transfers of
assets and shareholdings which became increasingly complicated as
the negotiations proceeded. It suffices to say that, in the end, one of
the companies had acquired shares in Brady's and the liability to pay
for them thus incurred was to be discharged by a transfer to it of
assets of Brady's. Bob, however, contended that further valuation
adjustments were needed and refused to proceed further unless they
were made. Jack then started proceedings for specific performance
which Bob defended on various grounds among which was that it
would require Brady's to give unlawful financial assistance.

  It was conceded that the transfer of assets would be unlawful
financial assistance unless, in the circumstances, the prohibition was
disapplied by what is now section 678(4). On the face of it one might
have thought that the circumstances afforded a classic illustration of
the sort of situation that the above provisions were intended to
legitimate. And, at first instance, that view prevailed. In the Court of
Appeal,[261] however, while all three judges thought that the conditions

---

[259] Which hardly seem to be compatible with Art.23 of the Second Directive.
[260] [1989] A.C. 755, HL. This case is an illustration (of which *Charterhouse Investment Trust v Tempest Diesels Ltd* [1987] B.C.L.C. 1, is another) of how, all too often, parties agree in principle to a simple arrangement which on the face of it raises no question of unlawful financial assistance but then refer it to their respective advisers who, in their anxiety to obtain the maximum fiscal and other advantages for their respective clients, introduce complicated refinements which arguably cause it to fall foul of the prohibition on financial assistance. In the *Charterhouse* case, where the former s.54 applied, Hoffmann J., by exercising commonsense in interpreting the meaning of "financial assistance", was able to avoid striking down an obviously unobjectionable arrangement. But the elaborate definition of that expression in the present Act leaves less scope for commonsense.
[261] [1988] B.C.L.C. 20, CA.

relating to "purpose" were satisfied, the majority thought that those relating to "good faith in the interests of the company", were not. In contrast, in the House of Lords it was held unanimously that the good faith requirements were complied with but that the purpose ones were not. Hence the contemplated transfer would be unlawful financial assistance if carried out in the way proposed.

Lord Oliver, in a speech concurred in by the other Law Lords, subjected the purpose requirements to detailed analysis.[262] He pointed out that "purpose" had to be distinguished from "reason" or "motive" (which would almost always be different and wider) and that the purpose requirements contemplated alternative situations. The first is where the company has a principal and a subsidiary purpose: the question then is whether the principal purpose is to assist or relieve the acquirer or is for some other corporate purpose. The second situation is where the financial assistance is not for any purpose other than to help the acquirer but is merely incidental to some larger corporate purpose.[263] As regards the first alternative, he accepted that an example might be where the principal purpose was to enable the company to obtain from the person assisted a supply of some product which the company needed for its business.[264] As regards the second, he offered no example, merely saying that he had "not found the concept of larger purpose easy to grasp" but that:

> "if the paragraph is to be given any meaning that does not provide a blank cheque for avoiding the effective application of [the prohibition] in every case, the concept must be narrower than that for which the appellants contend."[265]

13–33 The trial judge, and O'Connor L.J. in the Court of Appeal,[266] had thought that the larger purpose was to resolve the deadlock and its inevitable consequences and Croom-Johnson L.J.[267] had found it in the need to reorganise the whole group. But if either could be so regarded, it would follow that, if the board of a company concluded in good faith that the only way that a company could survive was for it to be taken over, it could lawfully provide financial assistance to the bidder—the very "mischief" that the legislation was designed to prevent. The logic is, of course, impeccable. But the result seems to reduce the purpose exceptions to very narrow limits indeed and to

---

[262] [1989] A.C. 755 at 778. Agreeing with O'Connor L.J. in the Court of Appeal ([1988] B.C.L.C. 20 at 25) he described the paragraph, with commendable restraint, as "not altogether easy to construe".

[263] The layout of subsections 678(2) and (4) now reflects this analysis more clearly than did the previous legislation.

[264] A situation envisaged by Buckley L.J. in his judgment in the *Belmont Finance* case [1980] 1 All E.R. at 402, as giving rise to doubts under the former s.54 of the 1948 Act.

[265] [1989] A.C. 755 at 779.

[266] [1988] B.C.L.C. 20 at 26.

[267] [1988] B.C.L.C. 20, at 32.

make one wonder whether the midnight oil burnt on the drafting of the two subsections has achieved anything worthwhile.

The transaction was in fact saved by application of the special provisions then applying to private companies (now repealed). However, the (eventually) successful outcome in that particular case did not get rid of the awkward issues raised by it. The DTI[268] floated the ideas of substituting "predominant reason" for "principal purpose" or relying solely on the test of good faith in the interests of the company. The CLR supported the first of these suggestions.[269] Quite apart from the question whether the Second Directive gives us the freedom to apply such a broad exemption in the case of public companies, these suggestions do nothing to address the arguments put forward in the House of Lords in favour of giving the purpose requirements a strict interpretation, if the prohibition is to remain a meaningful restriction. In any event, the 2006 Act retains the former wording.

Relaxation for private companies

While the Second Company Law Directive curtails the freedom of 13–34 action of the United Kingdom in relation to public companies, it does not do so in relation to private companies and in the 1981 Act advantage was taken of this to introduce a more relaxed regime for private companies. The basic rule was that for private companies financial assistance could be given if this did not involve a reduction of the company's net assets or if the financial assistance was given out of distributable profits.[270] The effect of this provision was to tie the financial assistance rule more clearly to the concerns of the legal capital rules, certainly as they apply to distributions.[271] Even then, however, the financial assistance had to be supported by a directors' solvency statement (which had to be audited)[272] and a special resolution of the members (with a facility for non-approving shareholders to appeal to the court).[273] These additional requirements might be thought to be excessive, since they would not be required for a distribution or for financial assistance given by the company other than for the purchase of its shares.

In the event, the 2006 Act removed the financial assistance prohibition from private companies, as the CLR recommended. Section 678 applies only to financial assistance given to a person who is proposing to acquire shares in a public company or, in relation to an

---

[268] *Company Law Reform: Proposals for Reform of Sections 151–158 of the Companies Act 1985* (1993).
[269] *Completing*, para.7.14.
[270] s.155(2) of the 1985 Act.
[271] See Ch.12.
[272] s.156 of the 1985 Act.
[273] s.157.

acquisition which has occurred, where the company whose shares have been acquired is at the time of the assistance a public company. Consequently, where a public company is taken over and then re-registered as a private company, it may give financial assistance by way of reducing or discharging the liabilities of the (new) parent incurred for the purpose of the acquisition.[274] The focus of section 678 is thus on the private status of the company whose shares are subject to the acquisition. Consequently, if a private subsidiary gives financial assistance for the purchase of the shares to its public parent, as in the *Chaston* case,[275] that situation will be caught by section 678. The converse case, however, will not be caught by section 678, except that the prohibition is extended by section 679 to catch financial assistance given by a public company towards the acquisition of shares in its private holding company—a less usual but not impossible situation.[276] In this case the status of the provider of the assistance as a public company subsidiary is enough to trigger the rule.

Civil remedies for breach of the prohibition

13–35   The only sanctions prescribed by the Act for breaches of the prohibition are fining the company[277] and fining or imprisoning (or both) its officers in default.[278] More important are the consequences in civil law resulting from the fact that the transaction is unlawful. Unfortunately, precisely what these consequences are has vexed the courts both of England and of other countries which have adopted comparable provisions and it is a pity that the current Act did not attempt to clarify the position.[279]

What has caused the courts to make heavy weather of this is the somewhat curious wording of the prohibition down the years. Since the object of the section is to protect the company and its members and creditors, one would have expected it to say that it is not lawful for any person who is acquiring or proposing to acquire shares of a company to receive financial assistance from the company or any of

---

[274] Something which was previously possible but only by following the "whitewash" procedure. Of course, the directors of the (new) subsidiary will need to continue to comply with their fiduciary duties to their company.

[275] Above, fn.00.

[276] s.679. An example might be where a target public company in a takeover is re-registered as a private company (to avoid the ban on its giving financial assistance to its new parent) but still has subsidiary companies which are public companies. Section 679 prevents the subsidiaries giving financial assistance to their immediate parent (unless an exception applies). At least this is what s.679(3) appears to say.

[277] Since the prohibition is intended to protect the company and its members and creditors it is difficult to conceive of a more inappropriate sanction than to reduce the company's net assets (still further than the unlawful financial assistance may have done) by fining the company. The CLR had proposed that the criminal sanction on the company be removed: Formation, para.343(d).

[278] s.680.

[279] The remedies for an unlawful distribution are specifically excluded from the area of unlawful financial assistance: s.847(4)(a).

its subsidiaries. That would have pointed the courts in the right direction to work out the consequences. But instead it declares that it is unlawful for the company to give the assistance, and follows that by imposing criminal sanctions on the company and (the one thing that makes good sense) on the officers of the company who are in default. This could be taken to imply (and was so taken by Roxburgh J. in *Victor Battery Co Ltd v Curry's Ltd*)[280] that the object of the prohibition was not to protect the company but to punish it and its officers by imposing fines. This calamitous decision continued to be accepted in England, and was cited with apparent approval by Cross J. (subsequently a Law Lord) 20 years later,[281] though rejected by the Australian Courts whose decisions helped those in England eventually to see the light. The decision has now been disapproved or not followed in a series of cases[282] and is accepted to be heretical.

Freed from the fetters of that heresy the courts have since given the section real teeth and it is submitted that the following propositions can now be regarded as reasonably well established: **13–36**

(a) An agreement to provide unlawful financial assistance, being unlawful, is unenforceable by either party to it. This proposition is undoubted and authority for it is the decision of the House of Lords in *Brady v Brady*.[283] However, if the contract could be performed legally (i.e. without giving unlawful financial assistance), but unlawful financial assistance is in fact provided, then the legality of the contract depends on whether the other party to it was party to a common design to act unlawfully.[284]

(b) However, the illegality of the financial assistance given or provided by the company normally does not taint other

---

[280] [1946] Ch. 242.
[281] *Curtis's Furnishing Stores Ltd v Freedman* [1966] 1 W.L.R. 1219. But he ignored it in *S. Western Mineral Water Co Ltd v Ashmore* [1967] 1 W.L.R. 1110.
[282] *Selangor United Rubber Estate Ltd v Cradock (No.3)* [1968] 1 W.L.R. 1555; *Heald v O'Connor* [1971] 1 W.L.R. 497; and Lord Denning M.R. in *Wallersteiner v Moir* [1974] 1 W.L.R. at 1014H–1015A. The modern view helped Millett J. to conclude in *Arab Bank Plc v Mercantile Holdings Ltd* [1994] Ch. 71 that the legislation applies to assistance provided by a subsidiary of an English company only where the subsidiary is not a foreign company, on the grounds that the protection of the shareholders and creditors of a company is a matter for the law of the place of incorporation. By the same token, the giving of assistance by the English subsidiary of a foreign parent ought to be regulated by the Act, though it is by no means clear that it is.
[283] Above, fn.260. See also *Hill and Tyler Ltd, Re* [2005] 1 B.C.L.C. 41.
[284] *Anglo Petroleum Ltd v TFB (Mortgages) Ltd* [2007] B.C.C 407, CA: a contract to lend money to a company where the contract did not require the sum advanced to be used to provide unlawful financial assistance but where the lender knew the money lent was to be used to repay monies due to the company's former parent from the purchaser of the company's shares from the former parent. The CA thought there was no public policy in forcing the lender to investigate whether the proposed use of the loan would constitute unlawful financial assistance and so held the contract of loan enforceable (though this view was, strictly, *obiter*).

connected transactions, such as the agreement by the person assisted to acquire the shares. It would be absurd if, for example, a takeover bidder which had been given financial assistance by the company, or by a subsidiary of the company, could escape from the liability to perform purchase contracts which it had entered into with the shareholders. Clearly, it cannot.

(c) This, however, is subject to a qualification if the obligation to acquire the shares and the obligation to provide financial assistance form part of a single composite transaction. The obvious example of this would be an arrangement in which someone agreed to subscribe for shares in a company (or its holding company) in consideration of which the company agreed to give him some form of financial assistance. In such a case the position apparently depends on whether the terms relating to the acquisition of shares can be severed from those relating to the unlawful financial assistance. If they can, those relating to the acquisition can be enforced. If they cannot, the whole agreement is void.

The authorities supporting this proposition are the decisions of Cross J. in *South Western Mineral Water Co Ltd v Ashmore*[285] and of the Privy Council in *Carney v Herbert*.[286] In essence, the facts of both were that shares of a company were to be acquired and payment of the purchase price was to be secured by a charge on the assets of, in the former case, that company and, in the latter, its subsidiary. The agreed security was, of course, unlawful financial assistance. In the former case, the shares had not been transferred or the charge executed; in the latter, they had. In the former it was held that unless the sellers were prepared to dispense with the charge (which they were not) the whole agreement was void and that the parties must be restored to their positions prior to the agreement. In the latter it was held that the unlawful charge could be severed from the sale of the shares and that the sellers were entitled to sue the purchaser for the price. Despite the different results, the Privy Council judgment, delivered by Lord Brightman, cited with approval the decision of Cross J. in the earlier case. In both cases a fair result seems to have been arrived at and certainly one preferable to that for which the assisted share-purchaser contended in *Carney*, namely that he should be entitled to retain the shares without having to pay for them.[287] It is therefore to be hoped

---

[285] [1967] 1 W.L.R. 1110.

[286] [1985] A.C. 301, PC, on appeal from the Sup. Ct. of N.S.W.

[287] Yet Lord Brightman seemed to think that this would be the consequence if severance was not possible: see [1985] A.C. at 309.

that even in a single composite transaction the courts will permit severance or order *restitutio in integrum* unless there are strong reasons of public policy[288] why the whole transaction should be treated as unlawful so as to preclude the court from offering any assistance to any party to it.

(d) If the company has actually given the unlawful financial assistance, that transaction will be void. The practical effect of that depends on the nature of the financial assistance. If it is a mortgage, guarantee or indemnity or the like, the party to whom it was given cannot sue the company upon it.[289] It is that party who suffers,[290] and the company, so long as it realises in time that the transaction is void, need do nothing but defend any hopeless action that may be brought against it. If, however, the unlawful assistance was a completed gift or loan, the company will need to take action if it is to recover what it has lost. And a long line of cases has established that, in most circumstances, this it will be able to do.[291] Its claim may be based on misfeasance, when recovery is sought from the directors or other officers of the company, or on restitution, conspiracy, or constructive trust, when the claim is against them or those to whom the unlawful assistance has passed or who have otherwise actively participated in the unlawful transaction. The most popular basis seems to be constructive trust, the argument being that the directors committed the equivalent of a breach of trust when they caused the company's assets to be used for the unlawful purpose and the recipients became constructive trustees thereof. The constructive trust is discussed further in Ch.16, below.

(e) In the light of propositions (a)–(d) it would also seem to follow that if the unlawful assistance given by the company is a loan secured by a mortgage or charge on the borrower's property[292] then, so long as the company has rights of

---

[288] In support of this caveat, see [1985] A.C. at 313 and 317.

[289] See the cases discussed under (c) and *Heald v O'Connor* [1971] 1 W.L.R. 497, where the unlawful assistance was a mortgage on the property of the company whose shares were being acquired, the purchaser guaranteeing the payment of sums due under the mortgage. The mortgage was unlawful. Hence the purchaser escaped liability on the guarantee (though that was lawful) since no payments were lawfully due under the mortgage. It would have been different had the guarantee been an indemnity.

[290] Since the mortgage is illegal and void (not merely voidable) presumably a bona fide purchaser of it without notice could not enforce it either.

[291] *Steen v Law* [1964] A.C. 287, PC; *Selangor United Rubber Estates v Cradock (No.3)* [1968] 1 W.L.R. 1555; *Karak Rubber Co v Burden (No.2)* [1972] 1 W.L.R. 602; *Wallersteiner v Moir* [1974] 1 W.L.R. 991 CA; *Belmont Finance Corp v Williams Furniture Ltd (No.2)* [1980] 1 All E.R. 393, CA; *Smith v Croft (No.2)* [1988] Ch. 114; *Agip (Africa) Ltd v Jackson* [1991] Ch. 547, CA.

[292] Unless the company is a public company and the charge is on shares in it, for then the charge may be void under s.670: see above, para.13–7.

recovery from the borrower under proposition (d), it should be able to do so by realising its security. This would certainly be so if the mortgage or charge could be severed from the unlawful loan—which, however, might be regarded as impossible since the consideration given for the mortgage or charge *was* the unlawful loan. But, since the effect of the recent case law is to recognise that the object of the prohibition, despite its wording, is to protect the company, the courts ought not to boggle at the conclusion that the security given to the company can be realised to recover what is due to it by the borrower.

(f) The above points all go to the validity of the financial assistance transaction and transactions associated with it. In addition, the directors who cause the company to give the unlawful finance assistance may be found to have been in breach of their duties to the company and the company is not prevented from enforcing those duties against the directors (normally to recover any loss suffered) by virtue of the fact that the company's act in providing the assistance was unlawful.[293]

It will therefore be seen that we have come a long way from the time when it was believed that the only likely sanctions were derisory fines on the company and its officers in default. These developments have caused the banking community some alarm, for there is no doubt that banks could find themselves caught out—as indeed they have been in the past.[294] The fact that money passing in the relevant transactions is likely to do so through banking channels inevitably exposes banks to risks.[295] The government proposed, in consequence, that transactions in breach of the prohibition should no longer be void for that reason alone,[296] but the Act did not take up this proposal.

---

[293] *Steen v Law* [1964] A.C. 287; *Selangor United Rubber Estates v Cradock (No.3)* [1968] 1 W.L.R. 1555; *Chaston v SWP Group Plc* [2003] 1 B.C.L.C. 675, CA. The same principle is applied to actions the company may have against third parties who are implicated in the provision of the financial assistance: *Belmont Finance Corp Ltd v Williams Furniture Ltd* [1979] Ch. 250, CA.

[294] See, for example, the *Cradock* and *Burden* cases, fn.293 above.

[295] But they are afforded special protection since the prohibition does not invalidate a loan "where the lending of money is part of the ordinary business of the company" and the loan is "in the ordinary course of its business": s.682(2)(a). This recognises that it would be absurd if, on a public issue of shares by one of the major High Street banks, its branches had to refuse to honour applicants' cheques if they were customers who had been granted overdrafts.

[296] DTI, *Consultation Paper on Financial Assistance* (1996), para.14.

CONCLUSION

The elaborate rules on preservation of legal capital, discussed in this **13–37** chapter, can be justified only if the role of legal capital in controlling distributions by companies is regarded as a valuable one. This was discussed in Chapter 12. If some form of distribution rule, not based on legal capital, were to be adopted, the Act could be simplified substantially by largely removing the rules on reduction of capital or redemption or re-purchases of shares—or at least by confining them to their shareholder protection aspects. Creditor protection would then turn on other concepts. The financial assistance rules, by contrast, are a candidate for reform even if the concept of legal capital is maintained, since they have no necessary connection with that doctrine in their current form. Further, the other goals which the financial assistance rules might be thought to promote are, these days, probably better targeted by other provisions with less potential for disruption of innocuous transactions. For example, where a target company in a takeover lends money to, or indemnifies against loss, known sympathisers who buy its shares or where, on a share-for-share offer, either or both of the target and predator companies do so to maintain or enhance the quoted price of their own shares, such practices are now regulated by the provisions on market abuse or by the rules of the Takeover Panel.[297] Again, in the case of abuses in the period prior to insolvency the provisions on wrongful trading may be better targeted.[298]

Progress on either front, however, requires changes to Community law in the shape of the Second Directive. In 2006 the Directive was amended so as to put the financial assistance provisions more clearly on a legal capital basis. New Article 23(1) permits financial assistance to be granted provided the net-assets-plus-legal-capital test for distributions by public companies is met.[299] However, even if this test is met, further requirements are imposed. An amount equal to the financial assistance must be transferred to an undistributable reserve, so that the company's undistributable reserves are increased, even though the payment of a dividend would not have this consequence.[300] Shareholder approval by way of written resolution would also be required (on the basis of a report by the board, dealing among other things with the solvency risks of the financial assistance, and the board must investigate the creditworthiness of the recipient of the

---

[297] See Chapters 28 and 30 below.
[298] See Ch.9 above.
[299] See para.12–1.
[300] Presumably this requirement is imposed because many forms of financial assistance will have no impact on the company's net asset position, for example a loan to a creditworthy borrower, but the Directive still treats such assistance with suspicion. Presumably also this reserve would be written down if, for example, a loan to acquire shares were repaid.

financial assistance). The transaction with the person receiving the assistance must be "at fair market conditions" and the actual acquisition of the shares must be "at a fair price". The Government's reaction was that this was not a sufficiently attractive set of relaxations for the United Kingdom to seek to adopt it.[301]

---

[301] Above, fn.221, para.6.23. Ch.6. Their adoption is not obligatory for the Member States.

PART THREE

CORPORATE GOVERNANCE: THE BOARD AND SHAREHOLDERS

Over recent decades, corporate governance has been a highly fashionable topic in company law and has generated an enormous literature.[1] The subject came to prominence in the United States with the work leading to the publication of the American Law Institute's *Principles of Corporate Governance* in 1994 and in the United Kingdom the topic is associated above all with the Cadbury Committee Report of 1992 and its associated Code of Best Practice,[2] which has provided a focal point for the subsequent spread of corporate governance codes throughout Europe.[3] However, one could say that corporate governance, whether recognised under that name or not, is a topic which is as old as the large company. The fact which the corporate governance debate takes as its starting point is the appearance, in large companies, of a group of senior managers who are separate and distinct from the shareholders. There are good reasons why, in economically large companies with large groups of shareholders, the functions of investment and management should be carried out by separate, though possibly overlapping, groups of people. Where there are large numbers of shareholders, taking management decisions through the shareholders, meeting would be impossibly cumbersome. Further, where the company's capital needs have led to a public offering of its shares, there is no reason to sup-

---

[1] It is too vast to cite, but for a representative sample of this work at its highest level see K. Hopt *et al.* (eds), *Comparative Corporate Governance* (Oxford: Clarendon Press, 1998); Hopt *et al.* (eds), *Corporate Governance in Context* (Oxford: OUP, 2005).

[2] *Report of the Committee on the Financial Aspects of Corporate Governance* (1992). See further below, para.14–29.

[3] Such codes have become a standard feature in continental Europe: see Weil, Gotshal and Manges (on behalf of the European Commission), *Comparative Study of Corporate Governance Codes Relevant to the European Union and its Members* (January 2002).

pose that those who buy the shares have the necessary expertise or commitment to run a large business organisation, and this is likely to be just as true of professional fund managers as it is of individual members of the public. In such a situation, the emergence of a specialist cadre of corporate managers is a natural development, managers who do not simply do as the shareholders say but who develop and implement corporate strategy on their own responsibility. In order for such managers to exercise these functions, it is necessary that a very broad set of discretionary powers be conferred upon them. In some jurisdictions this is done through the companies legislation itself, but in the United Kingdom this result is achieved by the practice of including provisions in the company's articles of association giving the board of directors extensive power to manage the company's business and to exercise the company's powers.

Thus arises the central issue of the corporate governance debate, which is the accountability of the senior management of the company for the extensive powers vested in them. Since the historical development was, or is perceived to have been, one of a movement from a situation in which shareholders were both investors and managers to one in which management became a separate function from that of investment, it is natural to think of the accountability issue as being one of the accountability of the managers to the shareholders. This is the tradition in British company law, tempered only by the qualification, which we noted at several points in Part Two and will see again in Part Three, that, as the company nears insolvency, accountability to the creditors is as important as, and even replaces, accountability to the shareholders. However, the separation out of management as a distinct function creates the possibility of imposing lines of accountability on management towards other groups who have a long-term interest in the company (usually referred to as "stakeholders"). One group of such stakeholders, the employees, has become the beneficiary of the accountability rules of corporate law (mainly through board representation) in about half of the Member States of the European Union.[4] Though once proposed by an official committee for the United Kingdom,[5] board representation is not an idea which has in fact taken root within British company law, though traces of it can be found. In its recent examination of company law the Company Law Review did not find sufficient support for the stakeholder model to justify a major shift in the accountability rules,[6]

---

[4] Final Report on the Group of Experts on European Systems of Worker Involvement (Davignon Report), Brussels, 1997, Table I. The split seems to have remained largely the same even after the enlargement of the Community: N. Kluge and M. Stollt, *Board-level Representation in the EU-25* (Brussels, European Trade Union Institute, 2004). The proportion of countries with board level representation is greater if those with representation only in public sector companies are taken into account.

[5] *Report of the Committee of Inquiry on Industrial Democracy*, Cmnd. 6706 (1975) (the "Bullock Report").

[6] Strategic, Ch.5.1; Developing, Ch.2.

and so it concentrated its efforts on promoting a modernised and inclusive version of the tradition of accountability to shareholders.[7] That "enlightened shareholder value" approach found its way into the Companies Act 2006.

Some ("managerialists") have even gone so far as to argue that elaborate accountability structures are not necessary because management will function so as to adjudicate neutrally and impartially among the competing claims of the various stakeholder groups on the company. This vision, however, ignores the fact that management itself is an important stakeholder group and it is difficult to see why, in the absence of accountability rules, managers would not give in to the temptation to overvalue their own claims on the company and undervalue those of other groups, for example, in the setting of their own remuneration. However, the managerialists make a better point when they argue that the accountability rules will be self-defeating if they operate so as to prevent or discourage managers from discharging effectively the tasks which the institution of centralised management entrusts to them. In other words, the accountability rules, no matter to whom the accountability lies, must not be so restrictive as to stifle the entrepreneurial talents of the managers, which talents constitute the rationale for conferring the wide discretion upon them in the first place.

Since the emergence of specialised management is not a phenomenon of just the last twenty years—large companies with such managements can be traced back at least as far as the late nineteenth century—it is not surprising that company law has always contained some mechanisms whereby the accountability issue can be addressed. The very requirement that a company appoint directors[8] provides a rudimentary mechanism for accountability. Unlike a partnership, where all the partners are prima facie entitled to participate in the management of the partnership,[9] in a company the requirement for directors presupposes that directors will play an important role, at least in large companies. In short, the default rule in partnerships is management by the partners; in companies, it is management by the directors. However, since British company law, unlike the corporate governance codes, says little or nothing about the structure and composition of the board of directors, the board's position in company law is deeply ambiguous. The board is the point of contact between the shareholders as a group and the senior management of the company, but whether, in any particular company or in companies generally, it acts predominantly as a monitor of the management on behalf of the shareholders or mechanism through which the

---

[7] Final Report, Ch.3. For what this might entail, see para.16–25, below.

[8] s.154 (at least two for public companies and one for private companies).

[9] Partnership Act 1890, s.24(5); LLP Regulations 2001, reg.7(3). However, the partners are free to create, by agreement, delegation structures akin to those found in companies and in large partnerships normally do so.

managers promote their control of the company is a matter for empirical investigation—and the situation may vary from company to company and from time to time. As we shall see in the following chapter, in order to reduce the likelihood of boards acting purely as instruments of management domination modern corporate governance codes have been concerned to restrict the proportion of board seats held by the managers of the company by requiring the presence of a proportion of "non-executive" directors on the board.

Despite the ambiguous role of the board, it constitutes a convenient focus for the legislature and the courts when developing rules to constrain the exercise by management of the discretion vested in them. Whether the board monitors management or does the managing itself (or does a bit of each), imposition of accountability rules on the board should have an impact, directly or indirectly, on the way the management function is discharged. The underlying aim of the law may be control of the management function, but the subjects of the legal rules are the directors. The issue of how far those controls extend to managers who are not directors is, as we shall see, controversial. By the same token, when the articles delegate a wide discretion from the shareholders, they do so by conferring power, not on the company's managers as such, but on the board of directors. The rules conferring the powers and the rules constraining the exercise of the powers focus on the board rather than on the senior management as a whole. Thus, although the corporate governance debate starts from the functional differentiation between investment and management, company law operates by regulating the actions, not of managers in general, but of the board of directors.

In this Part we look at three sets of rules which the courts, the legislature and business bodies have created to constrain the exercise by directors individually and the board collectively of the discretion vested in them. The first set concerns the extent to which the shareholders have the power to appoint or, more importantly, remove the directors of the company. How easy is it, for example, for the shareholders to remove directors who exercise their powers in a way of which the shareholders disapprove? The second concerns the structure and composition of the board of directors, matters upon which the Companies Acts and the common law have traditionally had little to say but which are a central focus for the corporate governance codes. Should the board be structured in such a way as to facilitate control over the managers of the company by the board? Thirdly, we consider a set of rules which the common law and the legislature have spent much effort in elaborating, from the very beginnings of modern company law in the first half of the nineteenth century. This is the law of "directors duties" and, as important, the law relating to the enforcement of those duties. These duties operate directly upon the directors so as to control the ways in which they exercise their discretion. When these duties are broken, the decision which the directors have taken may be ineffective or at least capable of being set aside or the director may have to compensate the company for any harm it has suffered, or account to the company for profits made from the breach of duty or some other remedy may be available.

Although the rules discussed in this Part are a central part of company law and the subject of public controversy, it is important to stress that the problem they aim to deal with is premised upon a distinction between those who are shareholders in the company and those who are its directors. In the case of economically small companies—the majority in fact on the register of companies—this situation does not obtain, because the shareholders and the directors are the same people. For such companies, the rules analysed in this Part are of less significance. It would be wrong to say that they are of no significance because those who are the owner/controllers of a small company may fall out with one another and one faction may be tempted to act in a way which is in breach of their duties as directors, for example, by diverting corporate opportunities away from the jointly-owned company to another controlled wholly by themselves. However, even when there is a falling out among the owner-controllers, the situation is probably better analysed as a conflict between one group of shareholder/directors and another group, rather than a conflict between shareholders on the one hand and directors on the other. We discuss this issue further in Part 4 of the book.

Finally, even when one is dealing with an economically large company with shareholders who are distinct from the managers, the complexity of the problems thrown up by the shareholder/director relationship depends significantly upon the structure of the company's shareholdings, in particular on whether they are concentrated or dispersed. Where there is concentrated shareholding (for example, one shareholder who holds a block of shares which gives him or her de facto control of the company), there will normally be little difficulty in that shareholder ensuring that the directors do as he wishes. The more problematic issue is likely to be whether the controlling shareholder takes appropriate account of the interests of the non-controlling shareholders. In this case, again, the potential conflict is one between controlling and non-controlling shareholders rather than between shareholders and directors, though again some aspects of directors' duties, for example, those concerning related-party transactions, may be relevant here. However, block-holder control of economically large companies is relatively uncommon in the United Kingdom, where a more dispersed pattern of shareholding prevails. Consequently, the issue of shareholder and director relationships is a crucial one.

THE BOARD

THE ROLE OF THE BOARD

The board of directors is the most important decision-making body **14–1** within the company. The first Principle of the Combined Code on Corporate Governance[1] states: "Every company should be headed by an effective board, which is collectively responsible for the success of the company." The Supporting Principles to this main principle add the following explanation about the role of the board:

"The board should set the company's strategic aims, ensure that the necessary financial and human resources are in place for the company to meet its objectives and review management performance. The board should set the company's values and stan-

---

[1] Financial Reporting Council, *The Combined Code on Corporate Governance*, June 2006, hereafter "Combined Code".

dards and ensure that its obligations to its shareholders and others are understood and met."

Even after making allowances for the fact that the Combined Code applies formally only to companies listed on the Main Market of the London Stock Exchange, and that in small companies things may appear very differently, this is a formidable specification for the board's role.

However, it would be difficult to glean any similar understanding of the importance of the board from a reading of the Companies Act. Although section 154 requires all public companies to have two directors and private companies one,[2] it leaves the determination of the role of the board very largely to the company's constitution, which is, of course, under the control of the shareholders. Unlike in many, perhaps most, other jurisdictions, the division of powers as between board and the shareholders is a matter for private ordering by the members of the company rather than something to be specified mandatorily in the companies legislation. This may reflect the partnership origins of British company law (under partnership law the partners are given a very broad freedom to arrange the internal affairs of the partnership as they wish) and it certainly facilitates the use of a single Act to regulate all manner and sizes of company. Jurisdictions which specify the role of the board for large companies in legislation often have a separate statute for smaller companies which gives the members in the latter class of company a freedom nearer to that enjoyed by the members of a British company.[3] It is also a point of some theoretical (even ideological) importance: the directors' authority is derived from the shareholders through a process of delegation via the articles and not from a separate and free-standing grant of authority from the State. This helps to underline the shareholder-centred nature of British company law.

The default provision in the model articles

14–2   Since the division of powers between board and shareholders is a matter for the articles (subject to a limited range of matters where the statute requires the participation of the shareholders in the decisions, discussed below), it is difficult to generalise about the patterns of

---

[2] After the 2006 Act at least one of those directors must be a natural person (s.155)—as opposed to a corporate director—in order to improve the enforceability of directors' obligations. The Act also now contains a mechanism for dealing with the situation where the company does not comply with ss.154 or 155. The Secretary of State may issue a direction to the company, specifying the action the company must take and failure to comply with the SS's direction constitutes a criminal offence on the part of the company and any officer in default, including a shadow director: s.156.

[3] Contrast, for example, Part 4, Divisions One and Two of the German *Aktiengesetz* for large companies and §37 of the statute for the *Gesellschaft mit beschränkter Haftung* (private company).

division found in practice. However, some limited help can be gained from the model sets of articles which apply unless excluded by the incorporators in a particular case.[4] For both public and private companies, the default provision is the same and it is one which gives substantial authority to the board: "Subject to the articles, the directors are responsible for the management of the company's business, for which purpose they may exercise all the powers of the company."[5] This follows quite closely the provision found in earlier sets of articles.

It is perhaps surprising that the model article for public companies refers to "management" quite generally, since it is clear that, in a large company, the totality of its management is something quite beyond the grasp of even the most talented set of directors. The provision of the Combined Code, quoted above, is more realistic for large companies when it gives the board the functions of setting the corporate strategy and reviewing management performance, thus indicating that the task of executive management is otherwise not for it but rather for the full-time senior employees of the company. This approach causes no formal difficulty for the model set of articles, since the model gives the board a wide power of delegation of the powers conferred upon them by the articles "to such person ... to such an extent ... and on such terms and conditions as they think fit."[6] Thus, delegation of powers by the board to the senior management of the company is provided for in the model articles. The point rather is that the strategy followed in the model set of articles for public companies of a broad grant of management power to the board which is then permitted a wide power of delegation does not tell one what pattern of division of function is in fact adopted in large companies between the board and senior (and, indeed, other) management.[7] On that, the Combined Code may be a better guide.

Turning to private companies, here discharge of the full management function by the board is often in fact possible, but it is equally possible in small companies for the shareholders to play a larger role in decision-making than in large companies. Often in such companies important shareholders who are not also directors will expect to have such a role. In quasi-partnership companies in particular the incorporators may wish to reproduce the rule which would apply if the entity were a partnership rather than a company. This rule is that "any differences arising as to ordinary matters connected with the partnership business may be decided by a majority of the partners,

---

[4] See para.3–10.

[5] Article 2 of the draft model articles in each case.

[6] Article 4 of the draft model articles for public companies. The same provision is included in the draft model set for private companies limited by shares: para.4.

[7] Exercise of the delegation power also raises questions of compliance by directors with their general duties, notably in relation to the degree of supervision they should maintain over delegated functions. See para.16–14.

but no change may be made in the nature of the partnership business without the consent of all existing partners."[8] Such a desire again creates no formal problem for the model articles, since the grant of management authority to the board is "subject to the articles". It is thus possible for the articles to provide that certain types of decision shall either not be given to the board at all or shall be subject to the shareholders' consent (even though such consent is not required by the Act). Again, however, the model articles provide no hint as to the ways in which or the extent to which this power is in fact used in small companies to move away from the default rule.

Thus, in both public and private companies (though for different reasons) the model articles provide only a starting point in determining the role of the board which may be modified substantially through either board decisions to delegate authority to management (in public companies) or modifications of the articles in the case of private companies so as to confer decision-making authority on the shareholders. One may wonder how useful such a default provision is, but the truth is that the variations from the default are so many and so varied (depending on the circumstances of the particular company) that it is impossible to identify a better default provision.

The legal effect of the articles
The board and shareholders

14–3 If it is not possible to make general statements about the division of authority between shareholders and the board and management, because that is, in the main, the function of the articles of association of each company, it is possible, nevertheless, to analyse the legal effect of the articles. As far as the shareholders are concerned, for many years it was disputed whether the effect of the delegation of authority in the articles to the directors was simply to confer authority on the directors or also, at the same time, to restrict the authority of the shareholders in general meeting to take decisions in the delegated area. Was the relationship between company and shareholders simply one of principal and agent[9] or did the articles effect something in the nature of a constitutional division of powers as between the shareholders in general meeting and the board? At one level, this was simply a matter of choosing the appropriate default rule. A principal conferring authority on an agent does not normally restrict its own authority to act, but there is no reason why the principal should not contract on the basis that the agent has authority to the exclusion of

---

[8] Partnership Act 1890, s.24(8).

[9] i.e., in legal terms. It is clear that, in terms of the functional analysis of economists, directors are agents and shareholders principals because the former have the factual power to affect the well-being of the latter. But this does not mean the authority of the directors is conferred upon them in such a way as to make them the legal agents of the shareholders.

the principal. Equally, a constitution normally divides up authority among the various relevant bodies, but there is no legal reason why a constitution should not confer concurrent competence on two or more bodies. However, the choice between these two legal analyses did affect very strongly the way in which the courts approached the interpretation of provisions in the articles of particular companies.

Until the end of the nineteenth century, it seems to have been generally assumed that the proposition remained intact that the general meeting was the supreme organ of the company and that the board of directors was merely an agent of the company subject to the control of the company in general meeting. The implication of this analysis was that the shareholders could at any time by ordinary resolution give the directors binding instructions as to how they were to exercise their management powers. Thus, in *Isle of Wight Railway v Tahourdin*,[10] the court refused the directors of a statutory company an injunction to restrain the holding of a general meeting, one purpose of which was to appoint a committee to reorganise the management of the company. Cotton L.J. said:

> "It is a very strong thing indeed to prevent shareholders from holding a meeting of the company when such a meeting is the only way in which they can interfere if the majority of them think that the course taken by the directors, in a matter *intra vires* of the directors, is not for the benefit of the company."[11]

In 1906, however, the Court of Appeal in *Automatic Self-Cleansing Filter Syndicate Co v Cuninghame*,[12] made it clear that the division of powers between the board and the company in general meeting depended in the case of registered companies entirely on the construction of the articles of association and that, where powers had been vested in the board, the general meeting could not interfere with their exercise. The articles were held to constitute a contract by which the members had agreed that "the directors and the directors alone shall manage".[13] Hence the directors were entitled to refuse to carry out a sale agreement adopted by ordinary resolution in general meeting where that decision fell within the management powers conferred upon the board. *Tahourdin*'s case was distinguished on the ground that the wording of s.90 of the Companies Clauses Act 1845 was different—though that section does not in fact seem to have been relied on in the earlier case.

[10] (1883) 25 Ch.D. 320, CA.
[11] (1883) 25 Ch.D. 320, CA, at 329.
[12] [1906] 2 Ch. 34, CA.
[13] Per Cozens-Hardy L.J. at 44.

The new approach, though cited with apparent approval by a differently constituted Court of Appeal in 1908,[14] did not secure immediate acceptance[15] but since *Quin & Axtens v Salmon*[16] it appears to have been generally accepted that where the relevant articles are in the normal form exemplified by successive model sets of articles, the general meeting cannot interfere with a decision of the directors unless they are acting contrary to the provisions of the Act or the articles.[17]

In *Shaw & Sons (Salford) Ltd v Shaw*,[18] in which a resolution of the general meeting disapproving the commencement of an action by the directors was held to be a nullity, the modern doctrine was expressed by Greer L.J. as follows:[19]

"A company is an entity distinct alike from its shareholders and its directors. Some of its powers may, according to its articles, be exercised by directors, certain other powers may be reserved for the shareholders in general meeting. If powers of management are vested in the directors, they and they alone can exercise these powers. The only way in which the general body of the shareholders can control the exercise of the powers vested by the articles in the directors is by altering their articles, or, if opportunity arises under the articles, by refusing to re-elect the directors of whose actions they disapprove.[20] They cannot themselves usurp the powers which by the articles are vested in the directors any more than the directors can usurp the powers vested by the articles in the general body of shareholders."

And, in *Scott v Scott*[21] it was held, on the same grounds, that resolutions of a general meeting, which might be interpreted either as directions to pay an interim dividend or as instructions to make loans, were nullities. In either event the relevant powers had been delegated to the directors, and until those powers were taken away by an amendment of the articles the members in general meeting could not interfere with their exercise. As Lord Clauson[22] rightly said, "the

[14] *Gramophone & Typewriter Ltd v Stanley* [1908] 2 K.B. 89, CA; see especially, per Fletcher Moulton L.J. at 98, and per Buckley L.J. at 105–106 (despite the fact that the then current edition of his book took the opposite view).
[15] *Marshall's Valve Gear Co v Manning Wardle & Co* [1909] 1 Ch. 267.
[16] [1909] 1 Ch. 311, CA; [1909] A.C. 442, HL.
[17] But for contrary views, see Goldberg in (1970) 33 M.L.R. 177; Blackman in (1975) 92 S.A.L.J. 286; and Sullivan in (1977) 93 L.Q.R. 569.
[18] [1935] 2 K.B. 113, CA. See also *Rose v McGivern* [1998] 2 B.C.L.C. at p.604.
[19] [1935] 2 K.B. 113, CA, at 134.
[20] They can now remove the directors by ordinary resolution: s.168, below.
[21] [1943] 1 All E.R. 582. See also *Black White and Grey Cabs Ltd v Fox* [1969] N.Z.L.R. 824, NZCA, where the cases were reviewed, as they were by Plowman J. at first instance in *Bamford v Bamford* [1970] Ch. 212, CA.
[22] [1943] 1 All E.R. 582, at 585D. Lord Clauson was sitting as a judge of the Chancery Division.

professional view as to the control of the company in general meeting over the actions of directors has, over a period of years, undoubtedly varied".[23]

From 1985 onwards the model set of articles sought to make the **14-4** position clear, for those companies adopting them, on the lines indicated in the above cases. Thus, in the draft current model sets for both private and public companies, the grant of authority to the board is qualified by the phrase "subject to the articles" and there is now a specific article dealing with the "members' reserve power."[24] This makes it clear that the members may by special resolution (i.e. as would be needed to change the articles) instruct the directors "to take, or refrain from taking, specified action". By implication, any instruction given by the shareholders by ordinary majority to the board within the area of authority delegated to the directors is not binding on the directors.

To some considerable extent, however, this development of the case-law has been overtaken by a change made to the statute in 1948 when the power, presently in section 168, was introduced, giving the shareholders the ability to remove directors at any time by ordinary resolution (as discussed below). Thus, at the very moment when the new interpretation became fully accepted in the case-law, the legislature changed the rules so as to give shareholders a removal power exercisable by ordinary majority. Although a removal power is different from a power to give instructions, the two overlap to a considerable extent, for the disgruntled shareholders can say, in effect, to the directors: if you choose not to follow our views, we will by ordinary majority seek to remove you from office. That can be a powerful inducement to the directors to follow the line of action preferred by the shareholders.

The board and senior management

The directors' power of delegation to senior management has not **14-5** given rise to any equivalent debate as to its legal effects. This is partly because that power of delegation is broadly drafted (see above) and

---

[23] This is clearly seen if the judgments in the above cases are compared with that in *Foss v Harbottle* (1843) 2 Hare 461; see below, para.17–7. The modern view was reiterated at first instance in *Breckland Group Holdings Ltd v London and Suffolk Properties Ltd* [1989] B.C.L.C. 100, noted by Wedderburn in [1989] 52 M.L.R. 401 and Sealy in [1989] C.L.J. 26.

[24] Article 3 in each case. However, the special resolution altering the articles or giving instructions to the directors does not have the effect of invalidating anything done by the directors before the passing of the resolution: art.3(2). If the directors have merely resolved to take course X before the shareholders resolve by special resolution to take contradictory course Y, then presumably the shareholder resolution constitutes a binding instruction to the directors not to implement their prior resolution. However, if in implementation of their prior resolution the directors have contracted on behalf of the company with a third party, that third-party contract would remain binding on the company. If extensive powers of direction are exercised by the shareholders, it is conceivable that they might come to be regarded as de facto or shadow directors of the company. See para.16–8.

includes an express power to "revoke any delegation in whole or part, or alter its terms and conditions". Partly, the absence of legal argument is due to the fact that managers, unlike shareholders, have no formal place in the company's legal structure. Partly, it is due to the fact that the delegation takes place through a resolution of the board and does not require an alteration of the articles. Rather the board, when delegating, is exercising a power conferred upon it by the articles. In practice, powers will be delegated on the basis that the delegation continues only at the pleasure of the board. The board can normally revoke its grant of authority as readily as it made it. However, although alteration or revocation of authority by the board may be effective, as we shall see below it may also constitute a breach (perhaps even a de facto termination) of the service contract entered into by the manager with the company, giving rise to claims for compensation on the part of the manager against the company, sometimes of a substantial character.

Nevertheless, in practice such delegation is of enormous importance in large companies. In particular, there is normally a very large grant of managerial power to the most senior of the company's managers, who will invariably be a member of the board of directors as well. Such a person, traditionally known in the British parlance as the "managing director" but more often today, following US terminology, as the "chief executive officer" (CEO), is the driving force behind the formulation and implementation of the company's strategy. Of increasing importance as well is the "chief financial officer" (CFO). As we shall see below, the major motivation behind the development of the Combined Code was the desire to place the CEO within a framework of accountability to the board, a problem created, but not solved, by use of the extensive delegation power contained in the articles.

Default powers of the general meeting

14–6   Despite what has been said above about the powers of the board and their impact on the powers of the shareholders, it seems that, if for some reason the board cannot exercise the powers vested in them, the general meeting may do so. On this ground, action by the general meeting has been held effective where there was a deadlock on the board;[25] where there were no directors;[26] where an effective quorum

---

[25]   *Baron v Potter* [1914] 1 Ch. 895. Contrast situations in which a board cannot do what the majority of the directors want because of the opposition of a minority acting within its powers under the articles: see, e.g. *Quin & Axtens v Salmon* [1909] A.C. 442, HL and the decision of Harman J. in *Breckland Group Holdings v London & Suffolk Properties* [1989] B.C.L.C. 100.

[26]   *Alexander Ward & Co v Samyang Navigation Co* [1975] 1 W.L.R. 673, HLSc, per Lord Hailsham at 679 citing the corresponding passage from the 3rd edition of this book.

could not be obtained;[27] or the directors were disqualified from voting.[28] These exceptions are convenient, but difficult to reconcile in principle with the strict theory of a division of powers. Their exact limits are not entirely clear. However, there seems good sense in the proposition that the shareholders may take the substantive decision only where the articles do not give them some effective way of reconstituting the board so as to remove the impediment to board decision-making.[29]

It is generally assumed that it is perfectly in order for the board of directors, if it so wishes, to refer any matter to the general meeting either to ratify what the board has done or to enable a general meeting to decide on action to be taken. It is quite clear, as was affirmed by the Court of Appeal in *Bamford v Bamford*,[30] that an act of the directors which is voidable because, for example, it is in breach of their fiduciary duties, can be ratified by the company in general meeting if the act is within the powers of the company and the meeting acts with full knowledge and without oppression of the minority. It is, perhaps, less clear whether the board, without taking a decision on a matter within its powers, can initially refer it to the general meeting for a decision there. In an elaborate discussion at first instance in the *Bamford* case,[31] Plowman J. had held that the general meeting then had power to act under residual powers, but he suggested that this might depend on the terms of the articles of the company concerned. The Court of Appeal considered that this question was irrelevant to the issue before them and expressed no view on it. It seems absurd if the directors are forced to take a decision and then to ask the general meeting to whitewash them, but perhaps the safest course is for them to resolve on action "subject to ratification by the company in general meeting". Alternatively, asking the general meeting to decide might be regarded as a delegation by the board of their powers on the particular issue (back) to the shareholders.

If the directors have purported to exercise powers reserved to the company in general meeting their action can be effectively ratified by the company in general meeting. And for the purpose of ratifying past actions of the board, as opposed to conferring powers on the board for the future, it is not necessary to pass a special resolution altering the article; normally an ordinary resolution will suffice.[32]

---

[27] *Foster v Foster* [1916] 1 Ch. 532.
[28] *Irvine v Union Bank of Australia* (1877) 2 App.Cas. 366, PC.
[29] *Massey v Wales* (2003) 57 NSWLR 718, NSWCA.
[30] [1970] Ch.D. 135, CA.
[31] [1970] Ch.D. 135, CA.
[32] *Grant v UK Switchback Rys* (1888) 40 Ch.D. 135, CA.

Unanimous consent of the shareholders

14-7   Under the rules discussed in the previous section, the shareholders have power to act, despite provisions in the articles apparently conferring exclusive authority on the directors. They allow the shareholders to take, or participate in the taking of, a corporate decision if the board is unable to exercise its powers, if the board's decision is in some way defective or, perhaps, if they are invited by the board to participate in the decision. However, it is also established in case-law that the shareholders may bind the company by unanimous agreement—"unanimous" here meaning all the shareholders entitled to vote, not just all those who turn up at a meeting. The main function of this rule, which is discussed below,[33] is to permit shareholders in small companies to take the decisions allocated to them without the need to hold a meeting (for example, by circulating a resolution, to which they individually indicate their consent) or without observing all the formalities (for example, as to notice) which shareholder meetings entail, though this common-law facility has now been overtaken in the normal case by more extensive statutory provisions.

However, there are also dicta in the cases which suggest that the unanimous consent of the shareholders binds the company, even on matters which the constitution allocates to the board.[34] Nevertheless, none of the decided cases clearly present the situation of the shareholders unanimously taking a decision which had been allocated by the constitution to the board. The nearest case is *Express Engineering Works Ltd, Re*,[35] where the decision in question was the purchase of certain property and thus would clearly have fallen within the clause conferring general management powers on the board, but in fact all the directors were disqualified from acting on the purchase, and so the shareholders could be said to have had default powers to take this decision, under the principle discussed above. The Company Law Review proposed that the unanimous consent rule should be codified and that this should be done on the basis that "the members of the company may, by unanimous agreement, bind or empower the company, regardless of any limitation in its constitution".[36] However, the Government decided against codification, though the new companies legislation preserves the common law rule,[37] so that it appears that the question of whether the unanimous consent rule operates within or outside the constitutional division of powers produced by

[33] Ch.15.

[34] See, for example, *Salomon v Salomon & Co Ltd* [1897] A.C. 22 at 57, per Lord Davey.

[35] [1920] 1 Ch. 466, CA. To similar effect is *Euro Brokers Holdings Ltd v Monecor (London) Ltd* [2003] 1 B.C.L.C. 506, CA, where the decision in question (under a shareholders' agreement) required a resolution of the board but unanimous shareholder agreement was treated as a substitute. Again, however, the board was disabled from acting and so the case could be seen as one in which the shareholders had a default power to act.

[36] Final Report I, para.7.17. The Report states that this is how the rule is recognised at common law, though this may rather overstate things.

[37] Modernising, paras 2.31–2.35; CA 2006, s.281(4).

the articles will be left for the courts to decide. As to the merits of allowing the shareholders unanimously to depart from the constitution, the requirement of unanimity means that there is no issue of the protection of minority shareholders, which was one of the factors which weighed with the courts when they introduced the doctrine that shareholders, by ordinary resolution, could not give directors instructions on matters within their competence. Allowing unanimous shareholder consent to override the articles would further emphasise the primacy of shareholders as against the directors. Shareholders would be able to tell the directors what to do, even within the area of competence granted by the articles to the board, provided only they acted unanimously.

The mandatory involvement of shareholders in corporate decisions

Despite the flexibility which British company law gives the company   **14–8** to divide decision-making powers between shareholders and the board, there are a number of situations where the legislation requires shareholder approval of the board's decision (and sometimes even permits the shareholders to initiate a decision). The main category of such cases is where decision is likely to have an impact upon the shareholders' legal or contractual rights, even if the practical impact of that change on the member in a particular case is small (as with many changes to the articles). Without giving an exhaustive list of such situations, the following can be said to constitute the main examples of this policy:

- alterations to the company's articles;[38]

- alteration of the type of company, for example, from public to private or vice versa;[39]

- decisions to issue shares[40] or to disapply pre-emption rights on issuance;[41]

- decisions to reduce share capital, re-purchase shares; redeem or re-purchase shares out of capital in the case of private companies or give financial assistance in the case of private companies;[42]

- alterations to the class rights attached to shares;[43]

---

[38] As discussed in Ch.3, above. The adoption of the initial constitution is also an act of the shareholders, since the incorporators become members of the company: above, para.4–14.
[39] Discussed in Ch.4, above.
[40] s.549 (below, Ch.24).
[41] s.569ff *(ibid.)*
[42] All these matters are discussed in Ch.12, above.
[43] ss.630 *et seq.*, discussed below in Ch.19.

- adoption of schemes of arrangement;[44]
- decisions to wind the company up voluntarily.[45]

All these provisions place limits on the extent to which the articles may authorise the board to proceed solely on its own initiative. They probably reflect the view that shareholder interests are potentially involved in such decisions, that shareholders are probably as well-equipped to take the decisions as the board, and that they are not decisions which occur frequently in the life of the company, but, beyond that, the provisions do not contribute directly to the development of good corporate governance. There are, however, four further cases where the requirement of shareholder approval is aimed at contributing directly to good corporate governance:

- the requirement that the appointment of the company's auditors be approved by the shareholders;[46]

- the requirement of shareholder approval for certain transactions entered into by directors or their associates with their company;[47]

- the requirement of prior shareholder approval at common law for the taking by directors of corporate opportunities.[48]

- the requirement for shareholder approval of defensive measures to be taken once a takeover offer is imminent—a requirement contained in the rules of the City Code on Takeovers and Mergers but those rules now having statutory force.[49]

The first of these requirements is designed to promote the independence of the company's auditors from its management (though it is far from clear that it always successful in doing so) and the others deal with conflicts of interest between the director and his or her company.

Finally, the Listing Rules, applying to companies quoted on the Main Market of the LSE, introduce a third basis for shareholder approval, namely the size of the transaction. Under those Rules significant transactions which meet the test of being "Class 1" transactions require shareholder approval. In brief, the Class 1 criteria are met if the transaction in question involves assets being

---

[44] ss.895 *et seq.*, discussed below in Ch.29.
[45] IA 1986, s.84.
[46] Part 16, Ch. 2, discussed below at paras 22–17ff.
[47] Part 10, Chapter 3, discussed below at paras 16–49ff.
[48] Discussed below at paras 16–69ff. See also the "advisory" role of shareholders on board remuneration: below in this chapter.
[49] See paras 28–18ff.

acquired, the profits attributable to the business ~
consideration being paid under the transaction or u.
company being acquired exceeding one quarter of the ed, the
existing assets, profits or capital, as the case may be.[50] The fi. 's
behind the provision seems to be that a big transaction is as much h.
an investment decision as a management decision and so the shareholders are to be involved in the taking of the decision, along with the
management. This ground for insisting on shareholder involvement
in a decision has no counterpart in the Act.

Mandatory functions of the directors

14–9

Just as the Act requires shareholders to be involved in some corporate decisions, so, scattered throughout the Act, are functions which
are imposed on the directors of companies and which therefore may
not be given to the shareholders. It would be too tedious to list them
all. What needs to be noted, however, is that they relate to two main
areas of corporate life, the production of the annual accounts and
reports and the regular administration of the company, in particular
its communications with Companies House. Thus, the directors are
under a duty to prepare accounts and reports each year; having done
that, to approve them and to send copies to the Registrar; and, in
most cases, to lay them before the shareholders in general meeting.[51]
What these statutory provisions do not purport to do is to stipulate
the division of decision-making about the company's business
activities as between the shareholders in general meeting, the board
and the management. That is left for stipulation in or under the
company's constitution. The statutory provisions relate essentially to
the administrative obligations of the company.

One further point should be made about these obligations. In many
cases, the obligation is laid not only on the director, but upon any
"officer" of the company, and the sanction for non-compliance,
normally a minor criminal sanction, is laid on any "officer who is in
default". Examples are where the company fails to carry out its third
task with respect to the annual accounts, i.e. fails to send a copy to
every shareholder,[52] or where the company fails to keep an accurate
record of its members.[53] The Act defines "officer"[54] as including "a
director, manager or secretary" and now goes on to add "any person

---

[50] LR 10. The FSA has the power to dispense from the application of this rule. The Jenkins
Committee (Report of the Company Law Committee, 1962, Cmnd. 1749, paras 117 and
122(e)) recommended the introduction of a mandatory statutory rule to this effect, but the
LR provision seems to have constituted the response to its recommendation.
[51] Part 16, discussed further in Ch.21, below.
[52] s.425.
[53] s.113.
[54] s.1121. Where the director or officer is itself a company, there is no liability unless one of the
latter's officers is in default, in which case he or she is criminally liable as well as the
corporate officer or director: s.1122.

378

... treated as an officer of the company for the purposes of ~~wh~~ ....sion in question". These are thus cases where the Act ~~p~~ses liabilities on sub-board managers. This is sensible in prin- ....ple, given that such administrative tasks are likely to be delegated to levels of management below the board.[55] The CLR recommended that the definition of manager should be restricted normally to a person who "under the immediate authority of a director or secretary is charged with managerial functions which include the relevant function"[56] but this limitation has not been adopted. The CLR also recommended that, for all those covered by the definition of officer, i.e. including directors, default should be taken to have occurred only where the person had authorised, actively participated in, knowingly permitted or knowingly failed to take active steps to prevent the action in question, and this recommendation is reflected in the Act.[57]

APPOINTMENT AND REMUNERATION OF DIRECTORS

Appointment

14–10 The Act itself says little about the means of appointing the directors, leaving this to the articles of association. Its main concern is to give publicity to those who are appointed rather than to regulate the appointment process. On initial registration the company must send to the Registrar of Companies particulars of the first directors[58] with their signed written consents to act. Thereafter there must be sent particulars of any changes with signed consent to act by any new directors.[59] The company must also maintain a register giving particulars of its directors.[60] Both registers are open to inspection by members of the public and so the public can obtain information about who the directors are either from Companies House or from the company's registered office. This is a crucial provision, enabling people to know who controls what might otherwise appear to be faceless companies and facilitating the enforcement of the obligations to which directors are subject, whether by creditors, the public authorities or others.

---

[55] To some extent the statute is following the lead given by the decision in *Meridian Global Funds Management Asia Ltd v Securities Commission* [1995] 2 A.C. 500, PC. The CLR reported that, under the previous law, the uncertainty as to who was a manager meant that prosecution of sub-board managers was rarely attempted: Final Report, Ch.14, fn.296.

[56] Final Report, para.15.54, though for particular offences it would be possible to cast the net wider. It would not be necessary for such a manager to be employed by the company, as where the particular administrative function had been out-sourced to an independent organisation.

[57] s.1121(3).

[58] s.12.

[59] s.167.

[60] ss.162ff.

However, as a result of the threats, or actual infliction, of violence by protestors on the persons or property of the directors of companies carrying on lawful activities to which the protestors objected, the scope of the information on the public registers has been reduced. No longer does the company's public register have to contain the director's usual residential address but only a service address (which might be the company's registered address), though the company must maintain a register of the directors' residential addresses which is not open to public inspection. Moreover, the company is prohibited from disclosing, except in limited circumstances, the residential address of a director or former director.[61] Equally, whilst the company must give to the Registrar the information which is contained in both its public and non-public registers, the Registrar must omit this "protected information" from the Registrar's public register and not otherwise disclose it, except in limited circumstances.[62]

As far as appointment is concerned, and contrary to popular belief, the Act requires neither that directors be elected by the shareholders in general meeting nor that they submit themselves periodically to re-election by the shareholders. This may often be the case, though it is far from universal practice, but, if it is, it is a consequence of the provisions of the company's articles, not of the Act's requirements. Equally, there is nothing to prevent articles providing that directors can be appointed by a particular class of shareholders, rather than the shareholders as a whole, by debenture holders or, indeed by third parties. In the case of community interest companies section 45 of the Companies (Audit, Investigations and Community Enterprise) Act 2004 explicitly empowers the Regulator of CICs to appoint a director of a CIC and for that person not to be removable by the company. In fact, the articles of public companies normally provide for retirement of board members by rotation on a three-year cycle and for the filling of the vacancies at each annual general meeting.[63]

---

[61] ss.163, 165 and 241. The company, on the application of a member, liquidator or creditor or other person with a sufficient interest, may be ordered by the court to disclose the residential address if there is evidence that service of documents at the service address is ineffective or it is necessary or expedient to do so in connection with the enforcement of a court order: s.244.

[62] ss.240 and 242. The Registrar may use protected information for the purposes of disclosure to a public authority specified in regulations or, again subject to regulations, a credit reference agency, for otherwise the company might not be able to obtain credit: s.243 and the draft Companies (Particulars of Usual Residential Address) Regulations 2008. Further, the Registrar may put the director's address on the public record if communications sent to the director by the Registrar remain unanswered or there is evidence that service of documents at the director's service address is ineffective. The director and the company must be consulted before this step is taken. If it is, the company must alter its public record as well: ss.245 and 246.

[63] Model public company articles, art.20. The draft model set for private companies makes no such provision. The board has power to appoint directors but directors appointed by the board come up for re-election at the next AGM (arts.19 and 20). This is a useful power for filling vacancies arising unexpectedly between annual general meetings.

14–11 The Act provides that each appointment in a public company shall be voted on individually[64] unless the meetings shall agree *nem. con.* that two or more shall be included in a single resolution. However, there are often provisions in the company's articles (as to notice to be given by shareholders to the company of their proposed candidates etc.) which make it difficult for shareholders, if they are so minded, to put up candidates against the board's nominees. So, the crucial decisions for the shareholders in public companies are normally whether to accept the board's nominees for election at the annual general meeting and whether subsequently to exercise their removal rights, as discussed below.

Unless the articles so provide, directors need not be members of the company. At one time it was customary so to provide,[65] but now the possibility of a complete separation of shareholders and directors is recognised and the model articles no longer provide for a share qualification. Of course, it is common for directors of public companies to become shareholders, often in a major way, under a share-option or other incentive scheme (discussed below), but even in these cases being a shareholder is not a formal condition of being a director.

14–12 As to age requirements, the law has undergone a complete reversal in recent years. The Cohen Committee tried to ensure that directors should normally retire when they attained the age of 70,[66] but as finally enacted this provision was so riddled with exceptions that it has proved to have little impact. It no longer appears in the Companies Act, as recommended by the CLR.[67] However, there was introduced into the 2006 Act a minimum age requirement of 16, apparently because of evidence that appointment of young directors was being used in order to exploit their immunity from prosecution or the unwillingness of public authorities to prosecute young persons.[68] Any such appointment is void, though the person appointed remains subject to the duties of directors under the Act.[69] This may mean that the company will no longer be in compliance with the requirements as to the minimum number of directors and thus be open to a direction from the Secretary of State as to the action it must take to remedy this situation.[70] However, the Secretary of State has power to make regulations permitting the appointment of classes of

---

[64] s.160. This is designed to prevent the members being faced with the alternative of either accepting or rejecting the whole of a slate of nominees.
[65] Companies Act 1929, Table A, art.66.
[66] Cmnd. 6659, para.131.
[67] Completing, paras 4.42–4.43.
[68] s.157.
[69] s.157(4) (5). Existing under-age directors cease to be directors on the section coming into force (s.159(2)).
[70] See above, fn.2.

person under the age of 16, which regulations may make different provisions for different parts of the United Kingdom.[71] Other than this, no positive qualifications are required of directors—though, as we saw in Chapter 10, they may be disqualified on the ground of misconduct or unfitness.

Sometimes the articles entitle a director to appoint an alternate director to act for him at any board meeting that he is unable to attend. The extent of the alternate's powers and the answer to such questions as whether he is entitled to remuneration from the company or from the director appointing him will then depend on the terms of the relevant article.[72]

Finally, it should be noted that not everyone who is a called a director is a director in the terms of the Act and some people who are not called directors are directors in terms of the Act. The law does nothing to control the growing and potentially misleading practice of giving employees the title of director, even though they perform none of the central management functions of a director and are thus not directors under the Act. On the other hand, a person who is a director, as meant by the Act, need not be so called, for the term director, as used in the legislation, includes any person occupying the position of director, by whatever name called,[73] and directors of some guarantee companies are still called "governors" or the like.

Remuneration

14–13 The remuneration of directors comes from two sources: fees paid to them for acting as directors and, in the case of executive directors, money and other benefits receivable under the service contract entered into by them as managers with the company. The latter is by far the greater source of income of the executive directors of companies, especially of large companies, and it has been a source of both controversy and regulatory action in recent years. Reflecting the trust origins of the company, a director is not entitled to a fee for acting as such, unless the articles or a resolution of the company makes provision for such payments, as they invariably will. By contrast, a person who provides additional services as a manager to the company, even if also a director, is entitled to reasonable remuneration on a quantum meruit basis for services actually accepted by the company, even in the absence of a contract, though the two situations

---

[71] s.158. This particular aspect of the regulation-making power is necessary because, under devolution, the age of criminal responsibility could vary within the United Kingdom.

[72] See the draft model articles for public companies, arts.14 and 24–29, which, if adopted, go far to clarify the alternate's position. The model articles for private companies make no provision for alternates.

[73] s.250.

may not be easy to distinguish.[74] In practice, these difficulties rarely arise, since the company will have express power under its articles to remunerate directors and employ managers and an explicit contract is made in both cases.

In either case, a director dealing with the company as to fees and remuneration is in a stark position of conflict of interest, and the traditional common law rule in such a case was that the sanction of the shareholders was needed for the agreement between director and company.[75] However, directors found this rule inconvenient and, for more than a century, it has been common to provide in the articles that the board shall have power to set directors' remuneration as executives, though the director whose remuneration is at issue is not usually permitted to vote on the matter.[76] The current model article applies this rule also to directors' fees, even though under the 1985 model articles the default rule was that fees required shareholder approval.[77] Setting remuneration in this way is a classic case where the risk of "mutual back scratching" arises: directors may not scrutinise too closely the remuneration of a fellow director in the expectation of similar treatment in return when their cases are considered. The increase in the levels of executive remuneration has been a matter of considerable public controversy in recent years, not simply because of the growing gap between executive salaries and the average incomes of others in society, but also because of the unsatisfactory negotiating process through which executive salaries are set under the typical form of articles. If directors, directly or indirectly, sit on both sides of the table when their remuneration is determined, then the results cannot be justified as emerging from a market process. Since this defect may characterise pay-setting in most companies with large shareholder bodies, it amounts to an example of a market failure, which justifies regulatory intervention.

14–14   What sort of regulation, however, should be adopted? The courts have been unwilling to scrutinise directors' remuneration decisions on grounds of excess or waste, refusing even to prescribe that pay must be set by reference to market rates, provided the decision on remuneration is a genuine one and not an attempt, for example, to make distributions to shareholders/directors where there are no

---

[74] *Craven-Ellis v Canons Ltd* [1936] 2 K.B. 403, CA, *cf. Richmond Gate Property Co Ltd, Re* [1965] 1 W.L.R. 335, which is probably based on a misunderstanding of the earlier case.
[75] See para.16–40.
[76] Draft model articles for public companies, arts.12 and 22 (a widely expressed power). Similar provisions are to be found for private companies. For the problems which arise if the company seeks to fix the terms of executive remuneration without complying with its articles, see *Guinness v Saunders* [1990] 2 A.C. 662, HL; *UK Safety Group Ltd v Hearne* [1998] 2 B.C.L.C. 208 and below, para.16–46.
[77] Table A, art.82.

distributable profits.[78] This is probably a wise decision on the part of the courts, which might otherwise find themselves saddled with developing a general policy about the remuneration of directors of large companies. Neither has the legislature shown any enthusiasm to grasp the nettle of determining, substantively, what the level, or rate of increase, of directors' pay should be.

In this situation of abstention from settling the substantive issue, attention focuses on the procedure within the company for the setting of directors' remuneration. One strategy is further to exclude executive directors from the process of remuneration setting, so that, not only is the executive whose remuneration is at issue forbidden from voting on the decision, but executive directors are side-lined in the remuneration-setting process. Under this strategy, remuneration decisions are allocated principally to a committee of the board consisting of non-executive directors. We examine this strategy further when we look more generally at the role of non-executive directors later in this chapter. The doubts about it relate principally to the question of how independent even non-executive directors are when it comes to the setting of executive remuneration.

Incentive pay schemes
A further, and perhaps complementary, strategy is to revive the common law principle of shareholder approval of directors' contracts.[79] We shall see later in this chapter that the companies legislation has reintroduced the principle of shareholder approval in relation to some decisions which are particularly relevant to the amounts paid to directors when their contracts are terminated. However, the legislation has stopped short of making the level of directors' remuneration and benefits whilst they are in office dependent upon shareholder approval. Nevertheless, such approval is required under the Listing Rules for certain share option schemes and other long-term incentive plans for directors, in the case of companies admitted to the Official List and traded on the Main Market of the London Stock Exchange.[80] Under a share option scheme a director is given the right to subscribe at some time in the future (normally after

14–15

---

[78] *Halt Garage (1964) Ltd, Re* [1982] 3 All E.R. 1016. This case involved a decision by shareholders as to the remuneration to be paid to themselves as directors. It seems likely that the same principle would be applied to a directors' decision, except that the directors would also have to meet their core duty of loyalty (see below at para.16–24). In the context of unfair prejudice petitions (that is, in cases of disputes between shareholders) the courts have struck out more boldly and have been willing to assess whether the remuneration paid to the controllers as directors was appropriate: see below at para.20–11.

[79] Though one should note the argument of Professors Cheffins and Thomas that such approval is more likely to be effective in relation to sudden leaps in executive pay in a particular company than in controlling a steady, general upward drift in pay across all companies: "Should Shareholders Have a Greater Say over Executive Pay? Learning from US Experience" (2001) 1 J.C.L.S. 277.

[80] LR 9.4. For the meaning of the "Official List" see below at para.25–8.

a period of years) for shares in the company and to pay for them (the "exercise price") the price which the shares had at the time the option was granted. The theory is that the director is thus incentivised to increase the price of the shares over the intervening period for the benefit of the shareholders. In order to meet the obvious objection that the increase in the stock price may have little to do with the efforts of the directors, long-term incentive plans (ltips) substitute some other form of incentive to be provided by the company in place of the shares.

The payment of performance-related remuneration to executive directors is now recommended as best practice by the Combined Code. Its Main Principle on remuneration now includes the statement: "A significant proportion of executive directors' remuneration should be structured so as to link rewards to corporate and individual performance."[81] However, the CC also suggests that payouts under incentive schemes "should be subject to challenging performance criteria reflecting the company's objectives. Consideration should be given to criteria which reflect the company's performance relative to a group of comparator companies in some key variables such as total shareholder return."[82] Thus, a simple increase in the price of the company's shares should not trigger the options (or not all of them) but only an increase which is better than that of comparator companies.

Originally because the granting of share options could dilute the position of the other shareholders, the LR made their grant subject to shareholder approval.[83] The principle was later extended to other forms of ltip and it now provides a convenient mechanism for the shareholders to express concerns about whether, for example, the performance criteria attached to the ltip are "challenging". However, because obtaining shareholder approval is time-consuming and leaves the director in doubt as to what ltip the remuneration package will include, the company is given permission to dispense with shareholder approval where the option scheme or other ltip is "established specifically to facilitate, in unusual circumstances, the recruitment or retention of the relevant individual". This permission is subject to disclosure in the company's next annual report of the principal terms

---

[81] Above, n.1 at B.1.
[82] Above, n.1, Sch. A, para.4.
[83] It should be noted that the statutory pre-emption rights of shareholders (see below at para.24–6) might lead to a similar requirement for shareholder approval, but the statutory rights (a) do not apply to an allotment of securities under an employees' share scheme (s.566), which might include a scheme for executive directors, and (b) can be disapplied in advance by shareholder vote (ss.569–571), whereas the rights under the LR may not be. It should also be noted that the LR do not require shareholder approval for share option schemes or other long-term incentive plans which are open to all or substantially all the company's employees (provided that the employees are not coterminous with the directors), presumably on the grounds that the wide scope of the scheme is protection against directorial self-interest: LR 9.4.2.

of the scheme and the reasons why the circumstances in question were viewed as unusual.[84]

The directors' remuneration report

Despite the importance of shareholder approval for share option schemes and other ltips, the Listing Rules fall short of reviving a general rule of shareholder consent for directors' remuneration packages. Nor does the CC recommend this as best practice. As, however, public concern over levels of directors' pay continued to rise, the Government decided to take a bolder line and in 2002 amended the companies legislation so as to require (a) that the directors of quoted companies produce an annual remuneration report[85] and (b) an advisory vote of the shareholders on the report.[86] The definition of a quoted company goes somewhat wider than those incorporated in the United Kingdom and subject to the Listing Rules by virtue of being included in the Official List, which are the companies caught by the relevant provisions of the LR. The statute embraces as well British-incorporated companies if they have been included in the official list of any Member State of the European Economic Area or if their securities have been admitted to trading on the New York Stock Exchange or Nasdaq.[87] The purpose of this broader definition is to remove any incentive for British companies to escape the new requirements by listing their securities elsewhere than in London. The Secretary of State has the power to alter the definition of a quoted company by regulation,[88] which, presumably, he might do if admission to trading on an exchange other than those mentioned above were to become a practical possibility for British companies.

The crucial innovation was the requirement for an advisory vote of the shareholders, for much of the information required to be included in the directors' remuneration report (DRR) was already required to be disclosed under the LR.[89] An advisory vote is a novel creature in the companies legislation. Under section 439, the directors must give notice to the shareholders of their intention to move an ordinary resolution approving the DRR at the meeting at which the accounts are laid before the members, and they must ensure that the resolution is put to the vote at that meeting. Not to do so is a criminal offence on the part of every officer in default (but, rightly, not on the part of the company). However, "no entitlement of a person to remuneration is

---

[84] LR 9.4.2–3.
[85] See now s.420. The changes were made originally by the Directors' Remuneration Report Regulations 2002, (SI 2002/1986).
[86] See now s.439.
[87] s.385.
[88] s.385(4)–(6).
[89] For the current requirements see LR 9.8.8.

made conditional on the resolution being passed by reason only of the provision made by this section."[90] Thus, even if the shareholders overwhelmingly reject the DRR, the remuneration of the directors continues as before, at least as far as the law is concerned.

It may thus be wondered what it is that the advisory vote adds to a simple disclosure requirement. The answer to that is that the advisory vote gives the shareholders a guaranteed opportunity to express their views on the directors' remuneration, which, without section 439, they would be able to do only if they requisitioned a resolution to be added to the agenda of the accounts meeting or requisitioned an extraordinary meeting of the shareholders, neither of which is necessarily easy to arrange.[91] Under section 439 the burden of action in relation to the approval resolution lies on the directors, not the shareholders. It may still be asked what is the value to the shareholders of this guaranteed opportunity for the expression of their views if the directors' contractual entitlement to remuneration is unaffected by an adverse vote. However, the legal position does not reveal the practical impact of an adverse vote of the shareholders or even of a vote in which a substantial minority vote against the DRR. Those companies which have experienced such a vote have moved quickly to diffuse shareholder discontent by amending their remuneration arrangements. Probably the major impact of the reform, coupled with the support of the institutional shareholders, has been to encourage boards to discuss with their leading shareholders potentially contentious changes in remuneration before the policy is adopted and thus has to be voted on.[92]

14–17 The DRR is required to be drawn up and approved by the directors and to contain the information prescribed by the Secretary of State in regulations.[93] Crucially, where the regulations require information to be given in relation to a particular person (for example, "each director"), that person must be identified by name.[94] The regulations divide the remuneration report into two parts: one, which is not subject to audit, relates to the company's remuneration policy and another, which is subject to audit, concerns payments actually made to directors in the financial year in question.[95] The legislative requirement for the disclosure of remuneration policy is the more interesting aspect of the DRR, for it in effect requires the board to justify, rather than simply report, the company's remuneration arrangements. The first part includes disclosure of:

[90] s.439(5). The director and company could agree of course that some item of the remuneration package should be so conditional.

[91] See paras 15–29 and 15–32.

[92] See Deloitte, *Report of the impact of the Directors' Remuneration Report Regulations*, November 2004 (available on: http://www.berr.gov.uk/files/file13425.pdf).

[93] Large and Medium-Sized Companies and Groups (Accounts and Reports) Regulations 2008/410, Sch. 8.

[94] Para.1(2).

[95] Parts 2 and 3 of the Schedule respectively.

- The composition of the remuneration committee (considered below), if any, which has considered the issue of directors' remuneration during the relevant financial year and the names of those, including non-directors such as remuneration consultants, who have provided services to the committee.

- For each person who has served as a director in the period between the end of the financial year and the holding of the meeting, there must be disclosure of the performance criteria, if any, applied to the director's entitlement to share options or under long-term incentive schemes, together with the justification for the choice of such criteria and of the methods used to assess whether the criteria were met. If no performance criteria are applied, that decision must be explained. Any significant amendments proposed to a scheme in place must be described and explained. The relative importance of the performance-related and non-performance-related elements in the remuneration package must be explained.

- There must be a statement of how the pay and conditions of employees in the company (and group companies) was taken into account in determining the directors' remuneration.[96] This represents an attempt to persuade directors and shareholders to focus on the issue of widening pay dispersal within companies, with the multiples by which executive directors' remuneration exceeds the average remuneration of employees increasing dramatically.

- The report must contain a graph plotting the total shareholder return for each class of the company's listed securities over a period of five years and comparing that return with the total shareholder return on some appropriate general index of company shares.[97] The aim here is to put the members in possession of information by which to assess, inter alia, the appropriateness of the performance criteria chosen for directors' incentive schemes.

- An explanation of the company's policy on the length of directors' contracts, notice periods and termination payments (discussed further below).

- For each director who served as such during the financial year, the length of any unexpired term and details of notice periods and compensation payable on early termination and

---

[96] Para.4. This is a new provision as from 2008 and shows the continuing pressure in relation to directors' pay.

[97] The appropriate comparator index is to be selected by the company, which must justify its choice: para.5(1)(b). The five-year period is appropriately reduced in the case of new companies: para.5(3).

of any other provisions necessary to form a view of the company's liability upon early termination.

The audited part of the remuneration report concerns payments actually made to persons who served as directors during the financial year. This part covers, for each director:

- Salary, bonuses,[98] expenses, compensation for loss of office or other termination payments and non-cash benefits, together with a comparison with the previous financial year;

- information about the terms of share options, distinguishing between those awarded during the year, those exercised during the year and those still unexpired;

- similar information in relation to long-term incentive schemes;

- details of pension benefits, giving in particular the transfer value of the director's accrued benefits under a defined benefit scheme (a way of assessing their value); and

- retirement benefits or other compensation paid to previous directors and remuneration paid to third parties in relation to a director's services.

Even unquoted companies cannot remain entirely silent on the subject of directors' remuneration. However, the relevant rules do not require a shareholder advisory vote, there is no equivalent to the first part of the DRR, and the equivalent to the second part is less detailed and requires the disclosure of aggregate remuneration only, or, where the data is further broken down, does not require recipients to be identified by name.[99]

In an extension of the usual role of the auditor, if the auditor concludes that the information required, of either a quoted or unquoted company, in relation to directors' remuneration has not been provided, then a statement giving the required particulars must be contained in the auditor's report, so far as the auditor is reasonably able to provide it.[100] This is presumably thought to be a more

---

[98] Annual bonuses are not subject to the share option and ltip provisions discussed above and so the criteria for the payment of such bonuses do not have to be disclosed or justified. This is apparently on the grounds that such criteria are commercially sensitive, as disclosing the company's short-term strategy. A natural consequence of such exclusion, however, has been a shift upwards in the importance of annual bonus payments as compared with ltips.

[99] Large and Medium-Sized Companies and Groups (Accounts and Reports) Regulations 2008/410, Sch.5. Para.1 requires the disclosure of aggregate remuneration (a rule applied to quoted companies as well), para. 2 of the amount paid to the highest paid director (but without naming that person) if the aggregate remuneration exceeds £200,000, and paras 3–5, the aggregates paid by way of early retirement benefits, compensation for loss of office and to third parties by way of directors' services.

[100] s.498(4). On the role of the auditor see Ch.22.

effective remedy than fining the directors for failure to produce proper accounts and reports, though that sanction is available as well.

REMOVAL OF DIRECTORS

Accountability of the directors to the shareholders is obviously **14–18** enhanced if shareholders can influence directly the choice of those who sit on the board. As we have seen above, company law does little to enhance shareholders' control over the appointment process, which is regulated predominantly by the company's articles of association. As far as company law is concerned, it would not be a breach of any mandatory rule for the articles to provide that none of the directors should be required to stand for re-election and that the existing directors, again without shareholder sanction, should choose any replacements for directors who resigned or were removed. In other words, shareholders could be wholly written out of the appointment process. In practice such extreme cases are rare, though for reasons that reflect market rather than legal constraints: large companies might find it difficult to sell their shares to institutional investors on the basis of such articles. This fact of life is reflected in the CC whose "best practice" provision is that "all directors should be submitted for re-election at regular intervals, subject to continued satisfactory performance".[101]

When we turn to the removal of directors, however, we find that the legal rules are entirely different, though this has been the case only for the past half century or so. Until 1948, the power of the shareholders to remove directors depended, as with their appointment powers, on the provisions of the articles of association. However, under what is now section 168 of the Companies Act 2006, a director can be removed by ordinary resolution of the shareholders at any time. This expressly applies notwithstanding anything to the contrary in any agreement between the company and the director.[102] The

---

[101] CC, section A.7, Main Principle. Even as late as 1985 the model set of articles (Table A) provided that "a managing director and a director holding any other executive office shall not be subject to retirement by rotation" (art.84). The current draft set of model articles for public companies contains no such provision (that for private companies contains no provision for regular re-election at all, whether for executive or non-executive directors).

[102] s.168(1). The previous version of the section (s.303 of the 1985 Act) also explicitly overrode anything to the contrary in the articles. This is not repeated in s.168, presumably on the grounds that it was unnecessary so to provide. The statute will override the articles, unless otherwise provided in the statute, although one would have thought that the same was true of a private agreement. In the case of a community interest company the Regulator is empowered to remove a director at any time, but not apparently so as to give the director a claim for compensation against the company. Instead, the director can appeal to the court against the Regulator's decision, apparently with the effect of reinstating the director if the appeal is successful: Companies (Audit, Investigations and Community Enterprise) Act 2004, s.46.

articles may provide additional grounds for the removal of directors, the most common being a request from fellow directors.[103] In comparative terms, this is a very strong provision. It means that the notion of a term of office for a director has little meaning. The articles may in fact provide that directors shall be appointed for three years at a time and things may be carefully arranged so that no more than one third of the board comes up for election in any one year,[104] but these provisions cannot be relied upon because the shareholders may intervene at any time to secure a removal. It means also that there is little point in the board securing the appointment of a director over the vigorous opposition of the shareholders, since this may simply provoke them to remove those of whom they disapprove. Finally, as we have already noted,[105] there is now a certain policy tension between the common law decisions, discussed above, which prevent the shareholders from giving directions by ordinary resolution to directors on matters within their exclusive competence and the statutory provisions permitting the removal of directors at any time by ordinary resolution. In practice, presumably, the latter overshadows the former: directors may commit no legal wrong if they refuse to obey such instructions, but they will be aware that disobedience may trigger their removal from office.

There are two qualifications to the powers contained in s.168 which need to be noted: the courts have authorised provisions in the articles which provide an indirect way around the section, at least in relation to private companies; and the section itself preserves certain rights for directors upon removal, notably their right to compensation for breach of contract. On the first, it has been held by the House of Lords in *Bushell v Faith*[106] that the object of the section can be frustrated by a provision in the articles attaching increased votes to a director's shares on a resolution to remove him, thus enabling him always to defeat such a resolution. This apparently indefensible decision can perhaps be justified on the ground that in a small private company[107] which is, in effect, an incorporated partnership, or in a joint-venture company it is not unreasonable that each "partner"

---

[103] See the draft model articles for public companies, art.21(g). No similar provision is included in the model articles for private companies. See also *Bersel Manufacturing Co Ltd v Berry* [1968] 2 All E.R. 552, HL (power of life directors to terminate the appointment of ordinary directors); *Lee v Chou Wen Hsien* [1984] 1 W.L.R. 1201, PC (power of majority of directors to require a director to resign).

[104] Such arrangements are what in the United States are referred to as "staggered boards".

[105] See above, para.14–4.

[106] [1970] A.C. 1099, HL. The shares in a private company were held equally by three directors and the articles provided that in the event of a resolution to remove any director the shares held by that director should carry three times their normal votes, thereby enabling him to outvote the other two. It was held that: "There is no fetter which compels the company to make voting rights or restrictions of general application and—such rights or restrictions can be attached to special circumstances and to particular types of resolution": per Lord Upjohn at 1109.

[107] A similar article would scarcely be practical in most other cases.

should, as under partnership law, be entitled to participate in the management of the firm in the absence of his agreement to the contrary and to protect himself against removal by his fellow partners. Moreover, it has been recognised that the removal of a director in the case of such "quasi-partnerships" (as they have come to be called) may so strike at the essential underlying obligations of the members to each other as to justify a remedy on grounds of unfair prejudice or even the compulsory winding-up of the company on the ground that it is "just and equitable" to do so.[108] Nevertheless, the decision was much criticised[109] but has not been reversed in subsequent legislation. In effect, for private companies s.168 is only the default rule.

Director's rights on termination

Even where the articles contain no provisions as to weighted voting rights, the successful operation of the section requires some pretty stringent conditions to be met. Special notice has to be given of any resolution to remove a director (and to appoint someone else instead, if that is proposed).[110] This means the proposer must give 28 days' notice to the company of the intention to propose the resolution.[111] The company must supply a copy to the director, who is entitled to be heard at the meeting.[112] Further, the director may require the company to circulate any representations which that person wishes to

14–19

---

[108] See *Westbourne Galleries Ltd, Re* [1973] A.C. 360, HL, and Ch.20, below. It also seems that the court could enjoin the breach of a binding agreement between members and a director on how they should vote on any resolution to remove a director, thus, in effect, affording another method of circumventing s.168. See *Walker v Standard Chartered Bank Plc* [1992] B.C.L.C. 535, CA. Such an agreement would not be caught by s.168(1) which refers only to agreements between the director and the company.

[109] See the forthright dissenting opinion of Lord Morris of Borth-y-Gest at 1106 and Prentice (1969) 32 M.L.R. 693 (a note on the Court of Appeal's judgments). The development of the unfair prejudice protection further reduces the need for the decision—but it equally reduces its adverse consequences, since the exercise of the legal right to remove a director may nevertheless constitute unfairly prejudicial conduct. See para.20–6.

[110] s.168(2). This gives rise to a potential ruse for avoiding the impact of s.168. Shortly before the meeting the directors whose removal is sought resign, having added to the board new members under their gap-filling powers (see above fn.63). The removal resolution is now unnecessary in relation to the directors who have resigned and will be ineffective in relation to their replacements (even if the resolution states as one of its objectives the removal of the replacements) because special notice will not have been given by the proposers to the company about the removal of the replacements, since the proposers will not have known who the replacements were to be at the time they served notice on the company: *Monnington v Easier Plc* [2006] 1 B.C.L.C. 283.

[111] s.312. The company must then give notice to the members in the notice convening the meeting or, if that is not practicable, by newspaper advertisement or other mode allowed by the articles, normally not less than 14 days before the meeting: *ibid.*

[112] s.169(1),(2). In this case a private company cannot use the written resolution procedure: a meeting has to be held.

make.[113] The object of these restrictions is to prevent a director from being deprived of an office of profit on a snap vote and without having had a full opportunity of stating the contrary case.[114]

A more serious restraint on the members' powers of dismissal is the provision that the section shall not deprive a director of any claim for compensation or damages payable in respect of the termination.[115] This provision applies to both the termination of the directorship as such and of "any appointment terminating with that as director". Thus, compensation for termination of the executive director's service contract is included where, as is invariably the case, both directorship and service contract are terminated at the same time. In fact, the continuation of the service contract is often made conditional on the holding of the directorship, so that the service contract terminates automatically upon cessation of the directorship.

The importance of the service contract

14–20 Thus, if there is a contract of service between the director and the company, as will be the case with managing and other executive directors, the probability is that the members will be able to sack the director only at the risk of imposing on the company liability to pay damages or a sum fixed by the contract as compensation. This, it may be said, is also fair, because the company has freely bound itself by contract. However, once again, we encounter the risk that the director may have been present on both sides of the bargaining table when the provisions were negotiated which are now relied upon to provide compensation at the point of termination.[116] The members may therefore find that the directors have entrenched themselves by contracts of service, as a result of which the company has to pay them substantial sums if it exercises its statutory power to dismiss them by ordinary resolution—or indeed dismisses them in any other way[117]— other than for serious misconduct.

It must be emphasised, however, that the dismissed director will have a legal claim for damages for breach of contract only if there

---

[113] s.169(3). If those representations are not received in time to be circulated, the director can require them to be read out at the meeting (s.169(4)). The same rule applies if the company does not comply with its obligations under s.169(3), but the resolution is not invalidated in such a case. This would provide an easy way for the company to avoid the director's removal.

[114] But apparently the director can be deprived of this protection if the articles contain an express power to remove a director by ordinary resolution and the company acts under that power. S.169 is expressly limited to removals "under section 168" and s.168(5)(b) provides that s.168 does not "derogate from any power to remove a director that may exist apart from this section".

[115] s.168(5)(a).

[116] See above, para.14–13.

[117] The board of directors can normally terminate a director's contract of service as an executive but, under the usual provision in the articles, so can the general meeting by removing him as a director: see *ibid.*

exists a binding contract entitling the director either to hold that position for a fixed term or to be dismissed only after a prescribed or reasonable notice and that notice requirement is not observed by the company (as it rarely will be). Further, the director will be entitled to a payment upon termination other than by way of damages for breach of contract only if the contract specifically so provides for such payment. As has been pointed out,[118] the articles do not constitute a contract between the company and a director, so they cannot be the basis of a claim by the director. The director will have to show that there exists a separate contract of service or for services, whether formal or informal,[119] which, however, may incorporate provisions from the company's articles. If there is such a contract, the company cannot evade its terms by altering the articles, unless, of course, the company has contracted on the basis that the terms of the contract will change automatically if the articles are altered.[120] If the alteration of the articles gives the company a power of dismissal contrary to the terms of an existing agreement, the exercise of this power will constitute a breach of contract.[121] This is so even though the articles at the time of the director's appointment provided that an "appointment shall be automatically determined if he ceases from any cause to be a director", since, on entering into a contract for a given period, the company impliedly undertakes during that period not to revoke the appointment as director.

If, however, the director's contract does not contain any provisions about its duration and the articles of association at the time of appointment provide that the contract shall terminate automatically on ceasing to be a director, it appears from the decision of the Court of Appeal in *Read v Astoria Garage (Streatham) Ltd*[122] that, on ceasing to be a director from any cause, the contract will also be terminated without that being a breach of contract. Accordingly it would seem that the company in such circumstances can sack a managing director (without breaking the contract) by exercising its powers under s.168 (or under any other power in the articles)—and equally that the director can resign the directorship and walk out without any period of notice.[123]

---

[118] See above, paras 3–16 *et seq.*

[119] For the complications which are liable to occur in the latter event, see *James v Kent* [1951] 1 K.B. 551, CA, and *Pocock v ADAC Ltd* [1952] 1 All E.R. 294n.

[120] Even then, the alteration will normally operate only for the future: *Swabey v Port Darwin Gold Mining Co* (1889) 1 Meg. 385, CA; *Bailey v Medical Defence Union* (1995) 18 A.C.S.R. 521, H. Ct Australia.

[121] *Southern Foundries v Shirlaw* [1940] A.C. 701, HL; *Shindler v Northern Raincoat Co Ltd* [1960] 1 W.L.R. 1038, per Diplock J. In the light of the observations in the earlier case it seems that the court will not grant an injunction to restrain the alteration of the articles.

[122] [1952] Ch. 637, CA.

[123] Assuming no provisions in the articles explicitly controlling resignation.

Control of termination payments

14–21 However, the problem of the director who can be dismissed without notice or compensation for breach of his or her service contract, as discussed in the previous paragraph, is not the issue which has occupied policy-makers in recent years, at least in relation to public companies. That problem can be, and has been, solved by the careful drafting of service contracts, so that they have an existence independent of the articles. Directors of companies have a strong incentive to ensure that such contracts are in place. The current concern is with the opposite problem: the director who is removed from a failing company but nevertheless receives a very large payment either under the contract or by way of compensation for breach of contract. This has been referred to as the problem of "rewards of failure".

A director's contract can employ a number of devices which operate so as to enhance the levels of compensation payable upon termination, in particular, entering into a long fixed-term contract, perhaps one with a rolling fixed term;[124] including long notice periods for the lawful termination of the contract by the company;[125] and including express entitlements to compensation if the contract is terminated.[126] None of these provisions would operate to protect a director were the company entitled to terminate the service contract without notice on grounds of a serious breach of contract on the part of the director. However, it is unlikely that mere lack of economic success on the part of the company would amount to a fundamental breach of contract and, even where there has been clear wrongdoing by the director, the company may prefer to pay the director to go quietly, rather than insist on its contractual rights. Moreover, economic failure by the company does not necessarily betoken lack of effort or commitment on the part of the directors. If directors were entitled to no contractual protection on termination, they might take too cautious an approach to risky business ventures.

---

[124] Under a rolling fixed-term contract, the fixed term is renewed from day to day, so that the full length of the term always remains to run. Under an ordinary fixed term, a director removed, for example, in the last three months of a fixed five-year term, would not receive much benefit from the fixed term; under a "five-year roller" the director will always have the full protection of the five-year term. Moreover, it is possible to structure the contract so that, although the company is bound by the fixed term, the director is permitted to terminate the contract by giving relatively short notice.

[125] In *Runciman v Walter Runciman Plc* [1992] B.C.L.C. 1084 the directors' service contracts required five years' notice for lawful termination, a provision which had been increased from three years in the face of the prospect of a takeover bid.

[126] This express provision may be, but need not be, a liquidated damages clause. It may give the director an entitlement which goes far beyond any compensation which would otherwise be payable to him for breach of contract. The CC provides, however, that "the aim [when agreeing provisions which determine termination payments] should be to avoid rewarding poor performance" (B.1.5).

Disclosure

Company law tries to steer a course between these competing con-   **14-22**
siderations by a combination of disclosure and shareholder approval
requirements, both advisory and binding. Formerly, the members,
contemplating removal, might know nothing about the directors'
service contracts. In this respect their position was improved some
time ago: each director's service contract, or a memorandum of its
terms if it is an unwritten contract, have to be available for their
inspection at any time. This applies also to shadow directors and to
service contracts with subsidiary companies.[127] The previous exemptions for service contracts with less than twelve months to run or for
directors required to work wholly or mainly outside the United
Kingdom have been removed.

In relation to quoted companies, as we have seen above,[128] the Act
now requires, in addition, that directors produce an annual remuneration report (DRR), which, like the other annual reports, must be
provided to the members and the Registrar.[129] For present purposes,
the crucial points about the DRR are as follows. It must disclose to
the shareholders the details of the company's policy on the duration
of directors' contracts, on notice periods and on termination payments.[130] As a check that this policy is being implemented in practice,
the report must give, in respect of each director, details of the length
of the unexpired term, notice periods, compensation payable on
termination and, generally, such information as will enable a shareholder to estimate the company's liability to the director, should the
service contract be terminated prematurely.[131] By way of a further
check, the report must reveal payments actually made in the financial
year to which it relates to directors or former directors by way of
compensation for breach of service contract with either the company
or a subsidiary.[132] The report must not only give information about
such payments but also explain them (if significant).[133] Finally, as we
have also seen, the remuneration report must be put to a vote of the
shareholders at the meeting which considers the annual accounts,[134]
but the vote is advisory only, in the sense that no director's entitle-

---

[127] ss.228 and 229. Failure to comply constitutes a criminal offence on the part of every officer
of the company who is in default. Section 228 refers to "service contracts", unlike its
predecessor (s.318 of the 1985 Act) which referred to "contracts of service". It is suggested
that this change makes it clear that both contracts of service and contracts for services are
covered. S.230 brings in shadow directors (on the meaning of which see para.16–8).

[128] At para.14–17.

[129] ss.423(1) and 441(1).

[130] SI 2008/410, sch.8, para.3(4).

[131] para.6(1).

[132] paras 7(1)(d), 14 and 15. In fact, these provisions are drafted so as to catch not only
contractual payments but also non-contractual ones. See immediately below. Information
about termination payments actually made must also be disclosed by non-quoted companies
(Sch.5, para.4), but only on an aggregate basis, whereas Sch.8 requires the information to be
shown separately for each director.

[133] para.6(2).

[134] s.439.

ment to remuneration is conditional on a positive vote. It is difficult to believe, however, that an adverse vote, or even a substantial "no" vote in the case of a resolution which is approved, would not produce a change in the company's policy on termination payments.[135]

Shareholder approval

14–23 The advisory vote on the DRR moves the law nearer to the position where certain terms in a director's service contract depend upon shareholder approval. However, this is in fact required only in relation to contractual terms governing the length of the contract, whether those terms take the form of notice periods or fixed or rolling contractual terms. If such a term has the effect that the contract cannot be terminated by the company within a two-year period (referred to as the "guaranteed term"), prior approval by a resolution of the general meeting is required.[136] In the absence of shareholder approval, the provisions establishing the guaranteed term are void and the contract can be terminated at any time by the company on reasonable notice.[137] The section applies to shadow directors and to service contracts with subsidiaries.[138]

Despite the changes made, the sections are still open to criticism on two grounds. First, by concentrating on the length of employment, section 188 seems not to catch contractual provisions which give the company the contractual right to terminate the director's employment at any time but then provide for substantial payments to be made to the director under the contract, if termination takes place. The CLR proposed that contractual covenants for severance payments "should be void to the extent that they provide for more compensation than would be available by way of compensation for breach of contract",[139] but this suggestion seems not to have been taken up.

Secondly, it is arguable that for public companies the period of two years is too long. The Greenbury Committee thought there was a strong case of reducing the period to one year.[140] As a consequence,

---

[135] The first company to suffer a defeat on an advisory resolution, GSK, roused the ire of its shareholders mainly in respect of the amounts payable on termination.

[136] s.188. S.188(3) sets out a complex definition of the "guaranteed period" so as to prevent a company circumventing the legislative policy through a combination of fixed terms and notice periods, each shorter than two years but cumulatively longer. S.188(4) performs the same role for guaranteed terms made up of more than one contract. Under the previous legislation the relevant period was the very long one of five years, but both the Law Commission and the CLR had recommended a reduction.

[137] s.189. That period of reasonable notice might be less than two years. Thus, the director pays a potential penalty for failing to secure shareholder approval, in that the contract may become subject to a notice period shorter than the two years which the contract could have contained without shareholder approval.

[138] ss.188(1) and 223.

[139] Final I, para.6.14.

[140] *Directors' Remuneration, Report of a Study Group* (Gee, 1995), para.7.13.

the Listing Rules[141] now require boards to report to the shareholders annually giving "the details of any director's service contract with a notice period in excess of one year or with provisions for pre-determined compensation on termination which exceeds one year's salary and benefits in kind, giving the reasons for such notice period." This provision catches both notice periods and contractual severance payments and applies a one-year limit, but requires only disclosure and justification, not shareholder approval. To similar effect, the Combined Code, also applying to listed companies, provides: "Notice or contract periods should be set at one year or less. If it is necessary to offer longer notice or contract periods to new directors recruited from outside, such periods should reduce to one year or less after the initial period."[142] The CC is enforceable on a "comply or explain" basis, as discussed below, and so its provisions are not mandatory, though they are generally observed.

So far, we have been considering compensation payments received by directors, removed from office under s.168, because the removal from office as director also brings to an end some other contract the director has with the company or a subsidiary, normally a service contract, and the termination of that contract amounts to a breach of contract by the company. However, it is not impossible that the remaining members of the board might choose to make a gratuitous payment to one of their number removed from office by shareholder vote, perhaps to ensure the director goes quietly, perhaps to encourage similar treatment of themselves, should they suffer the same fate in the future. This, however, is a matter where the Act has required shareholder approval since 1948. What is now s.217 makes it unlawful for a company to give a director of the company (or of its holding company) any payment by way of compensation for loss of office or as consideration for or in connection with his retirement from office,[143] without particulars of the proposed payment (including its amount) being disclosed to members of the company and the proposal being approved by the members (and the members of the holding company, where appropriate). In other words, the directors cannot increase the cost of a removal without the consent of the shareholders. The section does not apply, however, to payments by way of compensation for breach of contract, to payments to which the director is contractually entitled (unless the contract was entered into in connection with the termination) or pension payments in respect of past services, apparently whether contractually required or

---

[141] LR 9.8.8(9).
[142] CC, para.B.1.6.
[143] The circumstances in which the section bites are widely defined in s.215. There are specific provisions in ss.218 and 219 dealing with compensation payments made in connection with takeover bids or transfers of the company's assets, which are discussed in para.28–31.

not.[144] An unauthorised payment to the director is held by the recipient on trust for the company and any director who authorised the payment is jointly and severally liable to indemnify the company for any loss suffered (for example, where the payment is not recoverable from the recipient).[145]

STRUCTURE AND COMPOSITION OF THE BOARD

14–24 When we looked at the role of the board in the first section of this chapter, we saw that, broadly, the range of business decisions to be conferred upon the board is left by the law to be determined by the company's articles of association. By contrast, in the third section we saw that the law plays a crucial role in setting the rules governing the removal of board members. In this fourth and final section of the chapter we look at the rules on board structure and composition. Here again the law leaves matters to be determined by the company's constitution, but this is an area in which the "corporate governance" movement of the past decade has made a significant impact on listed companies, but through "soft law", in the shape of the Combined Code, rather than through legislation.

Structure

14–25 Before turning to the composition of the board, let us look at its structure. An important difference between legal systems is whether they require one-tier or two-tier boards. In Germany, for example, as we have already noted, a two-tier board is mandatory for public companies (*Aktiengesellschaften*), and so the relevant statute (*Aktiengesetz*), besides requiring both a supervisory and a managing board, stipulates the functions of each and the methods of appointment of each board. The task of running the company (in the sense of setting and executing its strategy) is entrusted to the managing board, and the supervisory board monitors the discharge by the managing board of its functions. A person may not be a member of both

---

[144] s.220. The exclusion of covenanted payments, in the standard case, is in line with the previous law (*Taupo Totara Timber Co v Rowe* [1978] A.C. 537, PC; *Lander v Premier Pict Petroleum* 1997 S.L.T. 1361) and was recommended by the Law Commission (*Company Directors: Regulating Conflicts of Interests and Formulating a Statement of Duties*, Cm. 4436 (1999), para.7.48). But it makes all the more peculiar the exemption from shareholder approval of covenanted payments equivalent to more than two years' salary.

[145] s.222(1), thus at last implementing the report of the Cohen Committee: Report of the Committee on Company Law Amendment, Cmnd. 6659 (1945), p.52. The recipient will normally be the director but the legislation covers compensation payments to persons connected with the director or at the direction of the director or a person connected with the director: s.215(3).

boards. By contrast, in Britain the one-tier board is the norm, with managing and supervisory functions being discharged by a single body.

However, although the single tier board is what is normally found in Britain, it is not obvious that the law requires a single board. The Act, as we have noted, does not require the directors to act as a board and so it hardly needs to address the further question of whether the board is to be a one-tier or a two-tier board.[146] In fact, the CLR found some evidence that "the practice of delegating [from 'the board'] day to day management and major operational questions to a 'management board' is becoming increasingly common in this country".[147] This infringes no provision of the statute, and, provided the articles permit such further delegation by the board and provided the board monitors effectively the functioning of the "management board", it involves no breach by the directors of their duties or risk of disqualification on grounds of unfitness.[148] The single board remains the norm in Britain, the United States and the Commonwealth.

However, domestic law does formally recognise the possibility of a two-tier structure for one class of company. This is the SE (European Company) which opts to register in Britain. Under the SE Regulation of the European Community, which is directly applicable in the United Kingdom, an SE may choose in its statutes (as its equivalent to the articles are termed) whether to have a one-tier board or a two-tier board, consisting of a supervisory organ and a management organ.[149] Where this structure is adopted a German-style division of function between the two boards is applied: the management organ (MO) "shall be responsible for managing the SE";[150] and the supervisory organ (SO) "shall supervise the work of the management organ", but the SO may not "itself exercise the power to manage the SE".[151] However, the statutes of the SE must list the categories of transaction (which may be extensive or limited) which require the authorisation of the SO.[152] Thus, there is some flexibility in fixing the line between supervision and management, since an extensive list of matters requiring SO authorisation would give that body a significant influence over the management of the company. Further, the SO itself (or its individual members) may require the MO to provide the information it requires for the discharge of its functions and may

---

[146] For the same reason the Act says nothing about the division of function between the board and its committees nor about the role of the chair of the board.

[147] *Developing*, para.3.139.

[148] See above at para.10–7 and below at para.16–14

[149] Council Regulation 2157/2001/EC, Art.38 and Recital 14 (see above at para.1–21).

[150] Art.39(1).

[151] Art.40(1).

[152] Art.48. The UK Government decided not to take up the option available under the Regulation for the SO itself to determine the list of matters requiring its authorisation.

arrange for investigations to the same end.[153] Thus, the SO has some flexibility as to how vigorously it discharges its functions.

14–26   With one small exception, no person may be a member of both bodies.[154] The members of the MO are appointed by the SO, whose members, in the absence of employee representatives, will be appointed by the general meeting.[155] What goes for appointment must apply to removal. Consequently, the shareholders' power of removal under section 168 applies to members of the SO alone, so that the members of the MO will be removable by the shareholders only indirectly.

However, the provisions in the Regulation relating to the two-tier board provide only a skeleton of the structure. That has to be fleshed out by reference to national law. Where the Regulation does not deal with a matter or deals with it only partly, then the rules of the Member State in which the SE is registered, as they apply to public limited companies, will apply to the SE. Hence the relevance of section 168 of the 2006 Act, just mentioned. This will be the case unless the Regulation requires or empowers the Member States to adopt implementing legislation specifically for the SE, in which case that implementing legislation will prevail over general public company rules as regards the matters it deals with.[156]

There are relatively few areas where specific implementing legislation is required or permitted but one of them is in relation to the two-tier board. Where in the domestic law of a Member State "no provision is made for a two-tier board system", that Member State "may adopt the appropriate measures in relation to the SE".[157] It might be thought that the UK was quintessentially such a State and that specific implementing measures for the two-tier board were thus required. However, the Government took the view that, since the domestic companies legislation does not require the directors to form a board in any particular way, the law permitted domestic companies to establish one-tier or two-tier boards, as they wished. The fact that UK boards were one-tier rather than two-tier in form was a result of practice, rather than legal requirement, as the CLR's evidence could be taken to suggest.

14–27   In the end, the Government moved a little way away from this stance in relation to the duties laid on directors by statute, including now their general duties under the 2006 Act. The domestic imple-

---

[153] Art.41(3), (4). The right of individual members of the SO to information is a Member State option which the UK has exercised. See the European Public Limited-Liability Company Regulations 2005, (SI 2005/2326), reg.63.

[154] Art.39(3). The exception is where the SO nominates one of its members to fill a vacancy on the MO, during which period that person's supervisory functions are suspended.

[155] Arts 39(2) and 40(2). There is a Member State option for members of the MO to be appointed directly by the shareholders, but the UK felt unable to take it up. Art.47(4) preserves appointing rights under national law of minority shareholders or other persons.

[156] Art.9(1)(c).

[157] Art.39(5).

menting regulations do make specific provisions in relation to such duties. Their general approach is to apply the statutory duties of directors indifferently to the members of both the organs in a two-tier system, but not so as to impose on the SO a function which is managerial and so within the sole competence of the MO.[158] An example might be the production of the annual accounts, though other duties might be more difficult to classify.

The adoption by SEs registered in the UK of two-tier board structures is potentially an exciting development, since it may create a "spill over" effect from the SE into domestic law. Will large companies regulated by national law press for domestic law to be altered so as to give them this option as well, as is the case in, for example, the domestic company laws of France and Italy? However, such an impact is a long way off: at the time of writing only very few SEs have been registered in the United Kingdom.

Composition
Employee representatives

If the division between one-tier and two-tier board structures is an **14–28** important dividing line in European jurisdictions, an even more crucial one is the requirement for employee representatives on the board. There is an inaccurate view that most continental European company laws require employee representation on the model adopted for large companies in Germany (that is, an equal division between employee and shareholder representatives), whereas that model is unique to Germany. Nevertheless, about half the Member States of the European Union require minority shareholder representation on the boards of private sector companies.[159] The United Kingdom, of course, is among the half which does not have mandatory board representation for employees, i.e. does not use company law to regulate the process of contracting for labour but leaves that task to labour law and contract law. In this context, the SE is again of interest, since Community law requires SEs, even when registered in the UK, in some situations to have employee representatives at board level. This will arise when at least one of the companies forming the SE was subject to mandatory employee representation rules under its

---

[158] European Public Limited-Liability Company Regulations 2005, (SI 2005/2326) reg.78(3) and (5). Nor must the application of the statutory duties require the SO and MO to take a decision jointly: reg.78(4). For the Government's views on whether domestic rules were required at all and their extent see DTI, *Implementation of the European Company Statute: A Consultative Document*, October 2003, pp.22–23 and 25 and DTI, *Implementation of the European Company Statute: Results of Consultation*, July 2004, pp.2–4.

[159] Group of Experts, *European Systems of Worker Involvement: Final Report*, Brussels, May 1977, Annex III. The subsequent enlargement of the Community has not affected this statistic.

domestic laws.[160] The experience of UK-registered companies operating a system of employee representation at board level might be
instructive, but again the low level of SE registrations in the United
Kingdom—with or without employee representation—makes this
possibility not of immediate interest.

The Cadbury Report and non-executive directors

14–29 Despite the lack of change in the United Kingdom in the area of
board representation for employees, there has been a lively debate
over the past two decades about board composition, at least of listed
companies, albeit a debate conducted within the framework of a
single-tier board without employee representatives. That debate has
focused on the proportion and role of non-executive directors on the
board and the regulatory results have shown themselves in the
Combined Code on Corporate Governance, rather than in legislation. Before these changes got underway the non-executive director
was not regarded in a particularly prestigious light. He (and it was
normally a he) was generally chosen by the CEO and expected to do
little or nothing other than to attend a reasonable number of board
meetings and, perhaps, some of the committees that the board may
establish, and, broadly, to do as the CEO wished.[161] As such they
were to be modestly rewarded by directors' fees.[162] The executive
directors were the dominant force within the company, with the CEO
as the embodiment of managerial authority.

This may still be the way in which non-executive directors function
in some companies, but in the case of non-executive directors of
companies subject to the CC a considerable change in the role and
prestige of the non-executive director has occurred in recent years,
though the impact of these changes on the business success of the
company is still debated.[163] The corporate governance movement in

---

[160] Council Directive 2001/86/EC supplementing the Statute for a European Company with
regard to the involvement of employees, implemented in the UK by the European Public
Limited-Liability Company Regulations 2005, (SI 2005/2326) Part 3. The provisions of this
directive are notoriously complex and include a option for the employee representatives not
to take up their representation rights. For an attempt at analysis see Davies, "Workers on
the Board of the European Company?" (2003) 32 I.L.J. 75. Despite the attempt to protect
countries with mandatory employee representation requirements from having them undermined by the formation of an SE, it seems that some German companies have found the SE
attractive because it enables them to escape some aspects of their domestic laws. Although
the proportion of employees may be the same, the size of the board may be reduced for the
SE, as compared with, the domestic German rules, (small boards being regarded as more
efficient than large ones) and all the SE's employees will be represented at board level, not
just the German ones, thus arguably diluting the employees' influence. Thus, when Allianz
merged with its Italian subsidiary to form an SE its supervisory board was reduced from 20
to 12 and, of the six board members for employees, four were German, one French and one
British.
[161] The articles invariably make provision for delegation to committees.
[162] See para.14–13.
[163] S. Bhagat and B. Black, "The Uncertain Relationship between Board Composition and
Firm Performance" (1999) 54 *Business Lawyer* 921.

the United Kingdom can be said to have begun with the report of the Cadbury Committee in 1992.[164] As is often the case with company law reform, the Cadbury Committee was appointed as a result of scandal, in this case the sudden descent into insolvency of major companies which had only recently issued annual financial statements which revealed nothing of the horror to come.[165] However, the Committee concluded that the causes of these problems were not to be found in the narrow area of accounts and auditing, though it gave attention to the role of auditors, but reflected more widespread defects in the corporate governance systems of large British companies. In consequence, its proposed reforms heralded a general reform of board composition and functioning in large UK companies, for which the scandals constituted the precipitating factor but to which they did not set a limit. This was well understood in the report of the Hampel Committee,[166] which, as recommended by the Cadbury Committee, was set up to review the operation of the Code of Best Practice which the earlier committee had put in place. The Hampel Committee regarded the Cadbury Code as a general prescription for good corporate governance and evaluated it in that light.[167] In this connection it is interesting to note that, whilst the Cadbury Committee described its report as being concerned with the "financial aspects" of corporate governance, the Hampel Committee was called simply a committee "on corporate governance", despite the fact that the scope of the latter's enquiries was set by the former's report.

What was the corporate governance problem which Cadbury sought to address? Although it identified a number of problems, the central one might be thought to have been the domination of companies, not just by top management, but by a single over-powerful managing director or chief executive officer (CEO). The fact that other executives may take up seats on the board gives, of course, only the illusion of constraint on the CEO in such a company, because the other directors are the latter's managerial subordinates, whilst non-executive directors may equally owe their board positions to the patronage of the CEO. Whilst not taking the view that all or even a majority of large British companies were governed in this way, the thrust of the Committee's proposals was towards putting in place a board structure which would render such dominance by a single person less likely, through the introduction of various counter-balances to the executive management of the company.

---

[164] *Report of the Committee on the Financial Aspects of Corporate Governance*, 1992.
[165] *Report of the Committee on the Financial Aspects of Corporate Governance*, Preface.
[166] *Final Report of the Committee on Corporate Governance* (Gee, 1998).
[167] However, the Cadbury Committee treated one fundamental matter as outside its remit: it assumed that the directors should be accountable to the shareholders of the company and not, in addition or instead, to any other group of stakeholders.

14–30   From the point of view of top management, therefore, the Cadbury Code could be presented as an attack on their discretion.[168] Indeed, the Hampel Committee Report can be seen as a failed attempt by management to win back some of the ground which it had conceded to the Cadbury Committee. The Preliminary Report of the Hampel Committee[169] struck a distinctly sceptical note, asserting that "there is no hard evidence to link success to good governance", a phrase which was not repeated in the Final Report, and implicitly criticising Cadbury for giving rise to a "box ticking" approach to corporate governance. Past debate on corporate governance, it said, had focused too much on accountability and not enough on the governance contribution to business prosperity, and the Committee wished to "see the balance corrected".[170] Only in the final report could the Hampel Committee bring itself to say that it endorsed the "overwhelming majority"[171] of the recommendations of the Cadbury Committee (and of the Greenbury Committee[172] which had reported in the interim on the particular and still controversial subject of directors' remuneration). Hampel's main contribution was to propose, as indeed happened, that the recommendations of the Cadbury and Greenbury Committees, as refined by Hampel, should be brought together in a "Combined Code".

Following a further set of corporate failures, but this time in the United States and forever to be associated with the name of the Enron company, the Government commissioned another review of the CC, which was carried out by Derek Higgs. The Government's overt role in the appointment of Mr Higgs was an innovation, since the earlier bodies had been appointed by private associations, such as the Confederation of British Industry and the accounting bodies, though they were generally observed or even serviced by civil servants. The Higgs report constituted a ringing endorsement of the approach of the Cadbury committee and contained recommendations for the strengthening of the CC, but along the lines already established by that Committee.[173] For example, it contained proposals, later implemented, for an increase in the proportion of non-executive

---

[168] Which, however, can be seen as a general trend in corporate law and regulation and by no means a British peculiarity: G. Hertig, "Western Europe's Corporate Governance Dilemma" in T. Baums, K. Hopt and N. Horn (eds), *Corporations, Capital Markets and Business in the Law* (Kluwer Law International, 2000), pp.276–278.

[169] Committee on Corporate Governance, *Preliminary Report* (August 1997).

[170] This sentiment does survive to the Final Report: *op. cit.* n.7, para.1.1.

[171] Final Report, para.1.7.

[172] See above, fn.140.

[173] Derek Higgs, *Review of the Role and Effectiveness of Non-Executive Directors* (London, The Stationery Office, January 2003). In the preface to his report Mr Higgs stated: "From the work I have done, I am clear that the fundamentals of corporate governance in the UK are sound, thanks to Sir Adrian Cadbury and those who built on his foundations." For a review of the Higgs Report (and of the contemporaneous Report by Sir Robert Smith on the role of the audit committee) see Davies, "Enron and Corporate Governance Reform in the UK and the European Community" in J. Armour and J. McCahery (eds), *After Enron* (Oxford, Hart Publishing, 2006).

directors (NEDs) on the board from one third to one half, at least in the largest listed companies. Thus, remuneration apart, the new principles of corporate governance in the United Kingdom are in essence the product of the Cadbury Committee whose recommendations, without much violation of the truth, are often treated as a proxy for the whole set of corporate governance reforms in the United Kingdom since the 1990s.

Enforcement of the Combined Code
We referred above to the Combined Code as "soft law". This is **14–31** perhaps misleading. At the centre of the CC there is a perfectly "hard" obligation. The Listing Rules require UK-registered companies with a primary listing in the United Kingdom to disclose in their annual report the extent to which they have complied with the Combined Code in the previous 12 months and to give reasons for areas of non-compliance (if any).[174] More precisely, the company must explain how it has complied with the principles set out in the CC (i.e. compliance at the level of principle is obligatory) but it must also state whether it has complied with the lower-level specific "provisions" of the CC relating to the board and explain any areas of non-compliance. The sanctions which can be applied to both companies and directors for non-compliance with the listing rules are extensive.[175]

The "softness" of the law is a result of the lack of legal consequences if compliance with the disclosure obligation imposed by the LR reveals non-compliance with the CC. It would be perfectly in compliance with the listing rules for the company to report that it has not complied with the Code in any respect, provided it also gave reasons for its wholesale rejection of the Code. Any further action on the basis of the reported non-compliance is for the shareholders, as the recipients of the annual reports, not for the FSA or any other Governmental body. This has been called the principle of "comply or explain". It suggests that, even in relation to the relatively small group of listed companies, UK regulators still feel hesitant about their ability to devise governance structures which will be suitable for all the companies in the identified population. The possibility of not

---

[174] LR 9.8.6(5) and (6). A company not incorporated in the UK but with a primary listing in the UK must explain whether it complies with the corporate governance code of its country of incorporation and how that code differs from the CC, but it is not required to explain areas of non-compliance: LR 9.8.7. That such a provision should be thought to be worth including demonstrates the international spread of the corporate governance code phenomenon. (Companies incorporated within the EEA and whose securities are traded on a regulated market have to make full disclosure about compliance with their national code as a result of Art.46A of the Fourth Directive on accounts (see para.21–22), as inserted in that Directive by Art.1(7) of Directive 2006/46/EC and see FSA, *Implementation of the 8th Company Law Directive*, CP 07/25, December 2007, proposed DTR 7.2.3. This will apply to UK-incorporated companies traded on a regulated market anywhere in the EEA.)

[175] See para.25–40.

complying fully with the Code gives the companies in question flexibility in adapting the provisions of the Combined Code to their particular circumstances, whilst the need to "explain" gives the Code a somewhat greater force than a recommendation which companies are free to accept or reject. The freedom to explain rather than comply in full with the Code has been used in particular by small listed companies.[176] "Comply or explain" clearly puts shareholders in a pivotal position in determining whether the Code's requirements will bite in practice, and much of its impact is due to the support which institutional shareholders have given to the Code.[177]

However, the restriction of the Combined Code to listed companies can be criticised as being too narrow. Certainly, the Cadbury Committee recommended that its Code of Practice should be observed by all large companies;[178] the restriction to listed companies seems to have resulted from the fact that the Listing Rules provided a convenient enforcement mechanism. Companies whose securities are traded on a public market but are not admitted to the Official List (for example, companies traded on the Alternative Investment Market) are not required to comply with the CC.

14–32   How effective is this regime? There is evidence that there is some degree of non-compliance with even the "hard" obligation of the LR. Some companies fail to explain all areas of non-compliance and a somewhat greater number give explanations which can hardly be considered as adequate.[179] The level of enforcement by the FSA is relatively low. Non-compliance with the CC is a more slippery concept, since there is no obligation to abide by it, if non-compliance is adequately explained. In general, companies have chosen to comply with the CC rather than to explain non-compliance. Further, in areas of inadequate explanation, the move has often been from inadequate explanation of non-compliance to full compliance rather than to adequate explanation.[180] This may suggest that the comply or explain mechanism operates rather in the manner of a transitional period. On the other hand, some companies do make proper use of the explanation mechanism to give good reasons why in their particular case one or more provisions of the CC is inappropriate.[181]

---

[176] Pensions and Investment Research Consultants Ltd, *Compliance with the Combined Code* (September 1999).
[177] On the role of institutional shareholders see paras 15–10ff.
[178] See above fn.164.
[179] S. Arcot and V. Bruno, *In Letter but not in Spirit: An Analysis of Corporate Governance in the UK*, (available on: http://papers.ssrn.com/sol3/papers.cfm?abstract_id=819784).
[180] See previous note.
[181] And such companies do not suffer in market terms from using such an approach and seem in fact to perform well: S. Arcot and V. Bruno, *One Size Does Not Fit All After All: Evidence from Corporate Governance* (available on: http://ssrn.com/abstract=887947).

The requirements of the Combined Code

What, concretely, does the Combined Code recommend to listed **14–33** companies as far as board structure is concerned? The main points are as follows, and they revolve around two central ideas. The main one is enhancement of the role of non-executive directors and the other is splitting the role of CEO and chair of the board.

- At least one half of the board as a whole should be non-executive directors [NEDs], all of whom should be independent.[182] However, there should be "a balance of executive and non-executive directors"[183] and "to ensure that power and information are not concentrated in one or two individuals, there should be a strong presence on the board of both executive and non-executive directors."[184] As with the board as a whole the NEDs have a role both in setting the company's strategy and supervising its implementation. In the case of the non-executive directors, however, "supervising" includes monitoring the performance of the company's executive directors.[185] The CC provides a definition of independence, which is essentially conceived of as independence from the management. Thus, a person who has been an employee of the company within the previous five years or has had a material business relationship with it in the previous three years is not categorised as independent.[186]

- The board should have nomination, remuneration and audit committees on which the NEDs should be the only or the majority (in the case of the nomination committee) of the members.[187] These three committees clearly deal with the three most sensitive governance matters. The whole scheme will fail if the executive directors can control the appointment of the NEDs; remuneration decisions place the executive directors in a position of acute conflict of interest; and assessment by the shareholders of the performance of the management will be impossible in the absence of accurate financial data about the company but, by the same token, this is an area where the management has the greatest incentive to

---

[182] CC, A.3.2. In companies below the FTSE 350 the requirement is only for two independent NEDs.

[183] CC, A.3—Main Principle.

[184] CC, A.3—Supporting Principle. However, there is some evidence of British boards now going in the same direction as in the US and having only one or two executive directors on them: *Financial Times*, UK edition, December 31, 2007, p.2.

[185] CC, A.1.

[186] CC, A.3.1.

[187] The nomination committee may have the chair of the board as a member, provided he or she was independent upon appointment, but must otherwise consist of two or three independent NEDs (B.2.1).

put an unduly optimistic interpretation on the company's position.

- The CEO and the chair of the board should not be the same person.[188] The role of the chair of the board is distinct from that of the CEO. The chair of the board, whose role is nowhere specified or indeed hardly recognised in statutory company law, "is responsible for leadership of the board, ensuring its effectiveness on all aspects of its role and setting its agenda. The chairman is also responsible for ensuring that the directors receive accurate, timely and clear information. The chairman should ensure effective communication with shareholders. The chairman should also facilitate the effective contribution of non-executive directors in particular and ensure constructive relations between executive and non-executive directors."[189] An illustration of the importance attached to the chairmanship of the board is the provision that in the largest companies (the FTSE 100) a person should hold only one chairmanship.[190]

  The CC, reflecting the views of Mr Higgs, treats the chair of the board as falling into neither the executive or non-executive category. Although not having executive responsibilities within the company, the CC wisely recognises that the chair will have such extensive contact with the executive management that he or she cannot be treated as wholly independent of them and so should not count as an independent NED.[191] On the other hand, the chair should be independent upon appointment. From this follows one of the most contentious, and disregarded, provisions of the CC, namely, that a retiring or recently retired CEO should not move on to become chair of the board.[192]

- The chairman should meet the NEDs without the executives being present (it is not stipulated how often) and once a year the NEDs should meet without the chair to appraise the latter's performance.[193]

- A senior independent director should be identified and be available for shareholders to contact if they think that contact through the CEO or chair of the board would be inappropriate. All non-executive directors should be offered the opportunity to attend meetings with shareholders (and should attend them if requested by the shareholders). However, a

---

[188] CC, A.2.1.
[189] CC, A.2.
[190] CC, A.4.3. This restriction is currently under review by the FRC.
[191] CC, A.3.2.
[192] CC, A.2.2.
[193] CC, A.1.3.

particular obligation falls on the senior NED to "attend sufficient meetings with a range of major shareholders to listen to their views in order to help develop a balanced understanding of the issues and concerns of major shareholders".[194]

- There should be a formal statement of the matters on which the board's decision is necessary (i.e. of matters which are not simply left for management to decide and subsequently report to the board).[195]

- The NEDs should have access to appropriate outside professional advice and to internal information from the company.[196]

There are two points to be made about these provisions of the Combined Code. The first is that the stress on the monitoring role of the independent NEDs has the effect of reproducing within the single-tier board the distinction between management and supervision (or monitoring) that is to be found within the two-tier board system, except that in the single-tier system the NEDs are necessarily involved in the formulation of company strategy. Whether it is better to extend this functional distinction into a structural division between managing and supervisory boards depends on whether one thinks that monitoring is carried out more effectively if the executives set strategy together with the monitors or separately from them. The former provides the monitors with more information, but facilitates their capture by the executive directors.[197] In any event, one can conclude that the functions performed by one-tier and two-tier boards are not fundamentally different from one another.[198]

Second, although independent NEDs may no longer be the cat's-paws of the CEO, which in the past they often were, it is far from clear that the Combined Code provisions provide the independent NEDs with effective incentives to exercise control over strong-minded CEOs. Since executive management is unlikely easily to accept supervision by the non-executives, the non-executives may well have a battle on their hands to impose their will where there is a divergence of view. Even when explicitly trained, as Higgs recommended, why should the non-executives fight this battle rather than opt for a quiet life? Self-esteem will provide some incentive to this end, no doubt, but the acceptance, at least tentatively, in the current version of the CC,

---

[194] CC, A.3.3 and D.1.1.
[195] CC, A.1.1 *cf.* the similar provision relating to the role of the SO in an SE (above, para.14–25).
[196] CC, A.5.2.
[197] See P. Davies, "Board Structure in the United Kingdom and Germany: Convergence or Continuing Divergence" (2000) 2 I.C.C.L.J. 435.
[198] What will change board methods of operation is the presence of employee representatives on them, whether on a one-tier or a two-tier board.

following the Higgs Report, of some greater degree of direct accountability on the part of the NEDs to the shareholders, especially the institutional shareholders, may add to their incentives.

CONCLUSION

14–34 The board of directors has long been the "black box" of British company law. In large companies, with numerous and dispersed shareholding bodies, the central management of the company's business is necessarily in the hands of the board. Yet company law has traditionally specified very little about how this body should operate. That the board is central to the operation of companies was recognised from the beginning by the development of a wide range of duties (considered in Chapter 16) which apply to directors who undertake to act on behalf of the company. However, the question of which functions should be assigned to the board and the question of how the board should organise itself for the effective discharge of those duties were ones that company law did not seek to answer. All that constituted the "internal management" of the company which it was for the shareholders to design.

Other than for listed companies, that still remains largely the case, though the case-law on the disqualification of directors (considered in Chapter 10), conceived with the interests of creditors in mind, has begun to lead to the formulation of principles about the proper conduct of directors of companies at the other end of the corporate scale. For listed companies, however, things have changed over the past quarter of a century. Now there is not only a small-scale corporate governance industry in existence, but the central tenets of its beliefs have been given regulatory expression in the Combined Code on Corporate Governance which, with the support of the institutional shareholders, exerts a real, if not completely inflexible, pressure on companies to conform to a particular model of board composition and operation. A company whose business is producing outstanding profits can probably afford to ignore the CC to some large extent, but should its business performance falter, it is likely to find the pressures to conform to that model irresistible.

CHAPTER 15

SHAREHOLDER DECISION-MAKING

We saw in the previous chapter that, in large companies, most **15–1**
decisions about the company's business will be taken by the board.
Nevertheless, shareholders' decision-making still has an important,
indeed crucial, role to play in the governance of companies. Quite
apart from those decisions for which the Act requires shareholder
consent,[1] the traditional model of directorial accountability to the
shareholders depends heavily upon the ability of the shareholders to

---

[1] See above, para.14–8.

review the performance of the board (notably when the annual report and accounts are presented to them) and to take decisions if they think that performance has not been adequate, for example, by removing the existing directors and installing a new board.[2] Nevertheless, the shareholder meeting has had a bad press in recent years. In small companies it is argued that the meeting is an unnecessary encumbrance, because the shareholder/directors frequently meet together informally, whilst in large companies shareholders do not show sufficient interest in using the general meeting and often allow it to be captured instead by single-issue pressure groups, whose primary objective is to advance the policies they stand for rather than their interests as shareholders. In recent years, the Act has been amended to address the first set of concerns, and the CLR proposed to take that policy further. The second, and more intractable, set of problems the CLR proposed to tackle head on, with "a sharper focus on the shareholder".[3] A "more effective machinery for enabling and encouraging shareholders to exercise effective and responsible control" was one of three core policies of the CLR in the corporate governance area,[4] an approach which chimed in with policy initiatives emerging at the same time from the Treasury.[5]

We shall begin with the first set of problems. Before we do so, however, it is important to address one preliminary issue, which is the question of who is entitled to vote on shareholder decisions. It should not be supposed that all shareholders, not even all ordinary shareholders, necessarily have the right to vote on shareholder resolutions or, even if they do, that they have voting rights as extensive as those attached to other shares which apparently carry the same level of risk. As we shall see,[6] the rights to be attached to classes of shares, including the number of votes to be attached to the shares, are matters for the company to determine in its articles of association or in the terms of issue of the shares. The exclusion of preference shareholders from voting rights, except in limited circumstances, is common and the issuance of non-voting ordinary shares is not unknown, though it is fiercely opposed by institutional shareholders.[7] Thus, "shareholder democracy", which is in any event a democracy

---

[2] See above para.14–18.

[3] Final Report I, para.1.56.

[4] Final Report I, para.3.4. The other two were the proposed statement of directors' duties, discussed in the following chapter, and improved disclosure and transparency provisions, discussed in a number of places in this work but especially in Ch.21.

[5] See below, para.15–12. From a governmental point of view, putting pressure on shareholders to regulate boards of directors reduces the pressure on the Government to regulate substantively in the contested area. See the example of the recent re-regulation of directors' remuneration, discussed in the previous chapter at paras 14–16ff.

[6] See below, Ch.23.

[7] On whom, see below. Additional voting rights may be confined to certain types of resolution, for example, the "golden share" held by the Government after some recent privatisations may operate so as to allow the Government to out-vote all other shareholders on certain specified resolutions: see Graham (1988) 9 Co. Law. 24.

of shares rather than of shareholders, is, or may be, an imperfect one. Company law does not require equal voting rights for shares carrying the same risk nor equivalent rights for shares of different classes of risk.[8]

There is a risk that where voting and cash-flow rights are not proportionate, then the controlling shareholder (controlling in terms of votes but not necessarily in terms of capital committed to the company) will take excessive risks with the company's business at the expense of the non-controlling shareholders (who may be the majority contributors to the company's capital). This is because the controlling shareholder does not bear a proportionate part of the downside if the strategy is unsuccessful. Alternatively, disproportionate voting structures may be used to maintain the existing directors of the company in office, because the controllers elect themselves or their nominees to the board and are reluctant to abandon their control. However, it is also the case that the price of the non-controlling shares (at least where these are traded on public markets) can and usually do adjust to reflect these risks. These problems have not tended to generate lengthy discussion in the United Kingdom, mainly because the pricing mechanism, reflecting the views of the institutional shareholders, does tend to discourage large companies from issuing non-voting or weighted-voting shares or to introduce proportionality where it was previously lacking. However, such capital structures are not unknown in the United Kingdom and a minority report of the Jenkins Committee in 1962 recommended a ban on non- and restricted-voting shares.[9] More recently, the issue has been given attention by the European Commission, whose concern was mainly with the management entrenchment qualities of disproportionate capital structures, which could operate to slow down the creation of a market in corporate control within the Community. However, its proposals were introduced into the Takeovers Directive on only an optional basis and its general study of the issue seems to be tending towards enhanced disclosure of voting arrangements, rather than more detailed regulation of them.[10]

---

[8] s.284 lays down a rule of "one share, one vote" (for all shares, whether ordinary or preference), except where the vote is taken on a "show of hands" (see below, para.15–46), but allows the articles to make alternative provisions, so that the distribution of voting rights (including the creation of classes of non-voting ordinary shares) is under the control of the shareholders: s.284(4). See *Savoy Hotel Ltd, Re* [1981] Ch. 351 (discussed at para.29–5) where the company had created A and B shares, ranking *pari passu* except in relation to voting rights, with the effect that the holders of the B shares, who owned 2.3 per cent of the equity, could exercise 48.55 per cent of the votes.

[9] *Report of the Committee on Company Law Amendment*, 1962, Cmnd. 1749, "Note of Dissent", *cf.* the main report at paras 123–136. The dissentients were mainly influenced by the inconsistency between the development of a market for corporate control and the issuance of non- or restricted-voting shares.

[10] For the "break-through rule" in relation to takeovers, see paras 28–19ff. For the Commission's study of the general issue see para.6–11.

DECISION-MAKING WITHOUT MEETINGS

The nature of the problem

15–2   In small companies where shareholders and directors are the same people, requiring them to distinguish between the decisions they take as directors and those which they take as shareholders can seem unduly burdensome. They will tend in fact to take all decisions as directors, since the rules about board meetings are largely under their control, whereas the Act contains some mandatory rules about shareholder meetings, for example, as to the length of notice required.[11] However, this approach generates legal risks, because the rules for the two types of meeting are not the same. For example, voting is normally on the basis of "one person, one vote" on the board, but on the basis of "one share, one vote" at a shareholders meeting. If the shares are not equally divided among the directors, the outcomes in the two situations may not be the same. Normally, this does not matter as long as all is going well, because decisions will in fact be taken unanimously. However, if relations between the entre-preneurs begin to deteriorate, as in small companies they often do,[12] clear decision-making mechanisms are required.

One straightforward way of resolving this problem would be to permit companies where shareholders and directors are the same people to operate with only a single decision-making organ, probably the board. This facility is provided by many state laws in the United States, but when the CLR consulted on this proposal,[13] it did not find enough support for the idea to take it forward in Britain. Consultees seem to have been put off by the apparent complexity of the pro-posals, designed to deal with the transitional problems which arise when the directors and shareholders cease to be exactly the same people (for example, where, upon the death of a member, either the person to whom the shares have been left does not want to participate in running the company or the existing members do not want to have that person join them). Instead, the CLR proposed a further exten-sion of the relaxations originally introduced in the Companies Act 1989 for private companies. The 1989 reforms aimed to make it easier for small companies to operate with two decision-making bodies, but they fall short of formally permitting the board and the shareholders' meeting to be rolled into one. If incorporators wish to have that facility, whilst still retaining limited liability, they will have to operate as a Limited Liability Partnership.[14]

---

[11] See below, para.15–36.
[12] See Ch.20, below.
[13] Developing, paras 7.95f *et seq*.; Completing, paras 2.35–2.36.
[14] See above, para.1–3.

Written resolutions

As a result of reforms introduced in 1989 a private company was **15–3** permitted, first, to elect to dispense with the need to hold an annual general meeting (AGM) of its shareholders and instead to take the statutory decisions normally taken at the AGM by written resolution (i.e. without a meeting). However, any member could require the company to hold an AGM in a particular year, provided notice of the requirement was given in time. Secondly, for other decisions, the written resolution method was made available without any need to opt for it. The 2006 Act provides a simpler and more far-reaching system for taking decisions within private companies by written resolution rather than by resolutions passed at a meeting of the shareholders. The default obligation on private companies to hold an AGM is abolished and resolutions of the members of a private company may either be taken as a written resolution or be adopted at a meeting of the members.[15] Both forms of taking shareholder decisions are of equal validity and (with two limited but important exceptions, discussed below) any decision may be taken in either manner. The main consequences of this change are three-fold:

(i) The private company does not have to opt into the process for dispensing with the AGM and taking the relevant statutory decisions by written resolution. That method for taking shareholder decisions, subject to the exceptions, will be available automatically to all such companies and for all decisions put to its members, whether under the Act or its articles or otherwise.

(ii) With the disappearance of the opting in procedure, there has disappeared the right of the single member to call for an AGM.[16] If a member of a private company wishes to have a meeting of its members—and the board is unwilling to convene one[17]—then a meeting will be held only if the general provisions on the calling of meetings by members have been observed. These general provisions normally require the requisitionists to hold 10 per cent of the company's share capital which carries voting rights.[18]

(iii) As part of these reforms, though not logically required, the previous unanimity rule for members to adopt a written resolution has been replaced by the rule that the written resolution be adopted by the same percentage of support as

---

[15] s.336, requiring an AGM, applies only to public companies (it is discussed below at para.15–28) and s.281(1) provides for private companies to take resolutions in either way.

[16] Previously provided under s.366A(3) of the 1985 Act.

[17] s.302 makes it clear that the directors may always call a general meeting of the company.

[18] ss.303–306, discussed below at para.15–29.

is needed for a resolution adopted at a meeting.[19] This last change has necessitated a certain greater formalisation of the rules governing written resolutions, since it can no longer be taken as given that all the members are in favour of the written resolution.

Overall, the policy of the legislature can be said to have been to remove most of the obstacles to the taking of members' decisions by written resolution, rather than at a meeting, thus encouraging private companies to proceed in that way, since the meeting procedure is necessarily more cumbersome.

Where written resolutions not available

15–4   The two situations where the written resolution procedure was not available under the prior law are maintained. These are for the removal of a director[20] or an auditor[21] before the expiration of their period of appointment.[22] In the case of a director, if the Act did not insist on a meeting, the director's entitlement[23] to be heard on the removal resolution at the meeting would be nugatory. However, the auditor does not have a right to be heard at the removal meeting, but only to make written representations to it.[24] Thus, the rationale for insistence upon a meeting seems to be to subject those shareholders who favour the removal to face-to-face questioning by the other shareholders, if they wish to put questions, presumably on the grounds that both events are potentially significant changes of the personnel in central parts of the company's corporate governance structure.

These are the only two situations where the written resolution procedure is not available to the private company in respect of a decision required, or provided for, by the Act, and where the company has to proceed by means of a meeting of members. Section 300 makes it clear that the articles may not deprive the company of its right to take other such statutory decisions by written resolution, though the articles could require a meeting for decisions which are wholly within the jurisdiction of the articles. It is unclear that there are good reasons for making the written resolution procedure mandatory.

[19]   s.296(4), discussed below at para.15–5.
[20]   s.168. See the previous chapter at para.14–18.
[21]   s.510. See para.22–19.
[22]   s.288(2).
[23]   s.169(2).
[24]   s.511(3)–(6).

The procedure for passing written resolutions

The major change made by the 2006 Act in relation to the adoption **15–5** of a written resolution was the move from a requirement for unanimous shareholders' consent to that which would be needed to pass a resolution if it were proposed at a meeting.[25] This means either 50 per cent or 75 per cent, depending upon whether the resolution required is an ordinary or a special resolution.[26] Of course, in the case of a meeting the percentage figures refer to those who vote, whether in person or by proxy, whereas in the case of a written resolution they refer to those entitled to vote.[27] In practice, therefore, normally the consent of a higher percentage of the members needs to be obtained for the passing of a written resolution than a resolution at a meeting, where typically fewer than half the members attend, in person or by proxy. However, the advantages of not having to call a meeting outweigh that potential disadvantage.

The statute requires a copy of the proposed written resolution to be sent at the same time (as far as is reasonably practical) to every member entitled to vote. However, if this can be done without "undue delay", the company may submit the same copy to each member in turn (or different copies to each of a number of members in turn) or employ a combination of simultaneous and consecutive circulation.[28] It is submitted that the courts should take a rather strict view of what constitutes "undue delay". Near-simultaneous circulation is important because it prevents the proposers circulating the resolution first to its likely supporters or those with no strong view on the matter, thus securing their support before the opponents have had the opportunity to put their case to the other members. In this connection it is worth noting that the written resolution is passed at the point at which it secures the requisite majority of the members, whether or not all those members to whom the resolution has been sent have voted at that time, whether the period for voting has expired or whether, indeed, all the members have been sent copies of the resolution at that point.[29] If a proposed ordinary resolution is sent to a 51 per cent shareholder and he or she signifies assent to it, before any of the other shareholders have opened their emails, the resolution will be adopted at that point.

A member signifies agreement to a proposed resolution when the

[25] s.296(4).
[26] See below, para.15–25.
[27] Referred to in s.292(4) as the "eligible" members, but s.289 defines the eligible members as those members who would have been entitled to vote on the date the resolution was circulated. The written resolution provisions do not alter the rules on the distribution of voting rights, discussed above at para.15–1.
[28] s.291(3) for resolutions proposed by directors and s.293(2) for resolutions proposed by members.
[29] s.296(4). The period for voting is 28 days from the date of circulation or whatever other period is fixed in the company's articles: s.297. If the requisite support is not achieved by that date, the resolution lapses. The circulation date is the first date on which a copy of the resolution is sent or submitted to a member: s.290.

company receives from the member or someone acting on the member's behalf a document indicating agreement, the method of signifying agreement having been indicated when the resolution was circulated.[30] Once given, the consent cannot be revoked.[31] This is another consideration in favour of simultaneous circulation. Despite the importance of simultaneous circulation, non-compliance with the provisions of section 291 (which includes the requirements for informing the members of the method of signifying consent and the final voting date) does not affect the validity of the resolution, if it is passed, though it does constitute a criminal offence on the part of every officer in default.[32]

Written resolutions proposed by members

15–6 Resolutions may be proposed as written resolutions by the directors or by the members.[33] The express provision for member initiation of written resolutions is new. The central requirement is that members holding at least 5 per cent of the total voting rights exercisable on the resolution in question request the circulation of the resolution, unless the articles fix a percentage lower than 5 per cent for this purpose.[34] The requisitionists may also require the company to circulate with the proposed resolution a statement of up to 1,000 words in support of the resolution.[35] Once a request has been made by the appropriate proportion of members, the company must, within 21 days of receiving the requisition, initiate the written resolution procedure in the manner described above, including with the resolution the members' statement in support, if any.[36]

This requirement is subject to three exceptions.

> (i) The requisitionists must tender a sum necessary to cover the costs of the circulation, which should not be large if electronic circulation is possible, unless the company has resolved otherwise.[37]

---

[30] s.291(2)(a). The statement accompanying the proposed resolution must also indicate the final date for voting: s.291(2)(b). Voting may be electronic: ss.296(1), (2) and 298.

[31] s.291(6),(7).

[32] s.296(3).

[33] s.288(3).

[34] s.292(4),(5). The 5 per cent figure tracks that for requiring a public company to add a resolution to the agenda of its AGM (see below, para.15–33), for which section 292 is the functional substitute, since it is not expected that private companies will typically hold AGMs. However, the original Draft Clauses had proposed that any member might require the company to initiate the written resolution procedure: *Modernising Company Law—Draft Clauses*, Cm. 5553-II, July 2002, cl. 174.

[35] s.292(3).

[36] s.293(1),(3). Non-compliance is a criminal offence on the part of every officer in default but again the validity of the resolution, if passed, is not affected by non-compliance: s.293(6), (7).

[37] s.294.

(ii) The resolution must not be ineffective "whether by reason of inconsistency with any enactment or the company's articles or otherwise".[38] There is no point in securing a resolution for the company to do something which the company may not lawfully do, but, in the case of inconsistency with the articles, this may simply affect the level of support the resolution needs, i.e. it must be enough to alter the articles.[39] Nor need the company circulate the resolution if it is defamatory of any person or is frivolous or vexatious.[40]

(iii) The company or any other aggrieved person may apply to the court for an order that the company is not obliged to circulate the members' statement on the grounds that the members' circulation rights are being abused.[41]

Written resolutions under the articles
Section 381C(1) of the 1985 Act explicitly preserved the power of **15–7** companies to adopt provisions in their articles on the taking of resolutions, and art.53 of Table A 1985 contained a procedure for consenting to written resolutions unanimously without a meeting. Although section 300 of the 2006 Act does not retain this explicit authorisation and although the current draft model sets of articles do not deal with written resolutions, it is difficult to see why the 2006 Act should be construed as taking this power away from public companies, which do not fall within the statutory provisions. This facility may be useful to those few public companies with small shareholding bodies. For private companies, the incentive to create a special procedure in the articles is now much less, since the statutory procedure has dropped the requirement of unanimous consent. Even so, section 300 is concerned with restraining the company's power to exclude a written resolution procedure rather than its power to have a more generous one than the statutory procedure.

Unanimous consent at common law
We touched on the common law rules on unanimous consent in the **15–8** previous chapter,[42] where we saw that their main purpose is to allow

---

[38] s.292(2)(a).
[39] See para.3–20.
[40] s.292(2)(b),(c).
[41] s.295. The requisitionists may have to pay the company's costs (s.295(2)) and presumably the normal rules as to costs will apply if the application is by a person aggrieved, i.e. the requisitionists will have to pay if they lose. This is a new section, though it mirrors the provision which now appears in relation to meetings (see s.317).
[42] See above, para.14–7.

shareholders to decide informally on matters within their competence. However, it may be asked what the purpose is of the common
law rule, now that there is statutory provision for written resolutions,
especially as the statute has been amended to permit written resolutions on a basis of less than unanimity. Part of the answer is that the
unanimous consent rules of the common law appear to apply to
public as well as private companies, but the main advantage of the
common law over the statute is that it does not require even consent
to a written resolution. Wholly informal consent, given by all the
members entitled to vote, may bind the company. For example, in
Wright v Atlas Wright (Europe) Ltd[43] the managing director of the
parent company had discussed, indeed negotiated, with the managing
director of its wholly-owned subsidiary the terms of a consultancy
agreement which the latter was proposing to enter into with the
subsidiary, and this was found, without difficulty, to amount to
informal unanimous consent on the part of the parent. Thus, as its
name suggests, the written resolution procedure allows shareholders
to adopt resolutions outside meetings; the unanimous consent rule
permits wholly informal methods of giving shareholder consent. The
common rules operating to this effect are preserved under the 2006
Act.[44]

The unanimous consent principle is now well-established in the
law. In a series of cases, the courts have come to recognise that
"individual assents given separately" by all the members entitled to
vote are "equivalent to the assent of a meeting" and that the assent
may be no more than passive acquiescence in the result. This development started with a recognition that a resolution of a board
meeting bound the company, notwithstanding that it was beyond the
directors' powers, when the directors were the company's only
members and all were present.[45] It was then extended to a recognition
that the members might waive the normal period of notice for convening meetings[46]—a view later adopted and extended by the companies legislation. Finally, the courts have recognised that there need
be no sort of "meeting" or "resolution", or, indeed, unanimous
agreement of all members. It suffices if all the members entitled to
vote on the matter concerned have informally ratified or acquiesced
and this seems to be so irrespective of the nature of the resolution and
the size of the majority that would have been needed had the formal

---

[43] [1999] 2 B.C.L.C. 301, CA. The issue in this case was not the informality of the consent as
such, but the failure to comply with the procedural requirements of the relevant section. See
below.
[44] s.281(4)(a): "nothing in this Part affects any enactment of rule of law as to things done
otherwise than by passing a resolution". s.281(4)(c) also preserves the estoppel-based version of the common law rules, discussed below: "nothing in this Part affects any enactment
or rule of law as to ... cases in which a person is precluded from alleging that a resolution
has not been duly passed."
[45] *Express Engineering Works Ltd, Re* [1920] 1 Ch. 466, CA.
[46] *Oxted Motor Co Ltd, Re* [1921] 3 K.B. 32.

procedures been observed.[47] In addition, the principle appears to apply whether the formal decision-making requirements are to be found in the Act or the company's articles or a shareholders' agreement.[48] However, it does appear that the consent which is required is the consent of the registered, rather than of the beneficial, shareholders and so, to that extent, an element of formality, but also of simplicity, is built into the rules.[49]

The problem which has troubled the courts in recent years has been the relationship between the common law principle and the procedural formalities required by the Act to be observed in many cases where the Act requires a shareholder resolution. Given the centrality of written resolutions in decision-making by shareholders of private companies, the Act now generally deals expressly with the issue by setting out different procedures for written resolutions and resolutions adopted at meetings. A good example is the frequent requirement that certain information be provided to the members before they take their decision. To take an example discussed in the previous chapter, section 188(5), dealing with shareholder approval of long-term service contracts, requires the terms of the proposed contract to be disclosed to the members before they decide whether to approve it or not. The subsection simply says that, in the case of a written resolution, a document containing the terms must be sent to each member at or before the time when proposed resolution is circulated; and in the case of a resolution to be proposed at a meeting, the document must be available at the company's registered office for the fifteen days before the meeting and at the meeting itself.

However, in the nature of things, informal processes are likely to end up ignoring the procedural formalities laid down for resolutions, whether written or adopted at meetings. If all the statutory formalities for resolutions need to be observed at common law, the unanimous consent rule will have little scope for operation in relation to many of the decisions required by the Act. In fact, the courts seem to be moving towards the principle that unanimous consent can operate to waive formalities required for the protection of shareholders, but not those required for the protection of other parties, notably creditors. Thus, in *Precision Dipping Ltd v Precision Dipping Marketing Ltd*[50] the requirement of auditor approval of a dividend, where the

15–9

---

[47] See, in addition to the *Atlas Wright* case (above, fn.43), *Parker & Cooper Ltd v Reading* [1926] Ch. 975; *Pearce Duff & Co Ltd, Re* [1960] 1 W.L.R. 1014; *Duomatic Ltd, Re* [1969] 2 Ch. 365; *Bailey Hay & Co Ltd, Re* [1971] 1 W.L.R. 1357; *Gee & Co (Woolwich) Ltd, Re* [1975] Ch. 52; *Cane v Jones* [1980] 1 W.L.R. 1451; *Moorgate Mercantile Holdings Ltd, Re* [1980] 1 W.L.R. 227 at 242G; *Multinational Gas Co v Multinational Gas Services* [1983] 1 Ch. 258 especially at 289, CA. The unanimous consent rule is often referred to as "the *Duomatic* rule", although that case was not the first to formulate it.

[48] *Torvale Group Ltd, Re* [1999] 2 B.C.L.C. 605; *Euro Brokers Holdings Ltd v Monecor (London) Ltd* [2003] 1 B.C.L.C. 505 at [62], CA.

[49] *Domoney v Godinho* [2004] 2 B.C.L.C. 15 at [45].

[50] [1985] B.C.L.C. 385, CA. See Ch.12, above at para.12–5.

company's accounts were qualified, could not be waived by unanimous consent of the shareholders, because the provision was clearly one aimed at protecting creditors (possibly as well as shareholders). By contrast, in the *Atlas Wright* case,[51] the Court of Appeal was prepared to permit unanimous shareholder consent to override the procedural requirements set out above for the approval of a long service contract.[52] However, it may not always be easy to categorise the function of particular statutory requirements.[53] For example, it seems unlikely that the courts would permit the unanimous consent rule to operate in the two cases excepted from the written resolution procedure (removal of a director or auditor from office before the expiration of their term), since, it might be said, the purpose of these rules is to protect the director or officer by permitting him or her to make representations against the proposal. However, it could also be argued that the purpose of these provisions is solely to promote the interests of the members (enabling them to be better informed about the reasons for the proposed removal), so that the unanimous consent rule should operate even here.[54]

There are also certain post-decision formalities which have to be complied with, most importantly, the notification of certain resolutions to the Registrar and the making a record of them in the company's minute book. The obligation to notify the Registrar seems to apply to informal decisions,[55] but the requirement as to recording in the minute book seems not to.[56] Non-compliance involves a criminal sanction but the decision itself is not invalidated.

A final area of unclarity is whether, at common law, something less than agreement of all members entitled to vote can be treated as equivalent to a resolution passed at a general meeting. Obiter dicta in a decision of the Privy Council in 1937[57] suggest that it cannot. The decision which, at first sight, comes closest to holding that something less will suffice is *Bailey Hay & Co Ltd, Re*[58] There, a resolution was passed by two votes in favour and three abstaining at a meeting attended by all the members of the company but of which the requisite length of notice had not been given. One of the grounds for

---

[51] See above, fn.43.
[52] This was a strong decision because s.319(3) of the Companies Act 1985 could be read as requiring a resolution in any event in this case, so that the principle of informal unanimous consent had no operation at all.
[53] Note the contrasting approaches of Lindsay J. in *R W Peak (King's Lynn) Ltd, Re* [1998] 1 B.C.L.C. 183 and Park J. in *BDG Roof-Bond Ltd v Douglas* [2000] 1 B.C.L.C. 401 to the construction of the rules relating to the purchase of own shares. See further *Kinlan v Crimmin* [2007] 2 B.C.L.C. 67.
[54] This is what the CLR recommended: Final Report I, para.7.22.
[55] See s.29(1)(b): "any resolution or agreement agreed to by all the members of the company" that would otherwise need to be a special resolution.
[56] s.356(2), referring only to "a resolution".
[57] *EBM Co Ltd v Dominion Bank* [1937] 3 All E.R. 555 (cited with apparent approval by the House of Lords in *Williams & Humbert v W & H Trade Marks* [1986] A.C. 368 at 429).
[58] [1971] 1 W.L.R. 1357. See also *Peña v Dale* [2004] 2 B.C.L.C. 508 at [120].

denying a challenge three years later to the validity of the resolution was delay (or "laches") in making the claim. The delay made it "practically unjust" now to upset the resolution (which had been for the appointment of a liquidator). This argument did not involve holding that the resolution was an act of the company, but simply that certain individuals, those who had delayed, could not bring proceedings to challenge the resolution. Hints can be found that the courts might be prepared to hold that it could be "practically unjust" to allow anyone to complain of an irregularity if an unreasonable length of time had elapsed since the irregularity occurred.[59] If that is so, laches, unlike estoppel, would not merely ban proceedings by particular complainants but, like unanimous agreement of members, would, in effect, validate the transaction.

INSTITUTIONAL INVESTORS

15–10 We turn now to shareholder decision-making through meetings. This is the only method section 281 provides for the adoption of resolutions by public companies and it is open to private companies to use it instead of the written resolution method, which it may wish to do where it has a large shareholding body.

The first matter to note is the changing composition of the shareholding body, at least in listed companies. Although the exact historical development is still unclear,[60] there is general agreement that three distinct periods of shareholder structure in such companies can be identified. There was an initial period, beginning with the development of the large company in the nineteenth century, when the shareholdings were held mainly by the founding entrepreneurs and their families. At this time, therefore, the shareholdings were in "concentrated" form and establishing the wishes of the shareholders was relatively easy. However, as the capital needs of such companies grew, some shares were offered to the public, with the outside shareholders being, however, in the minority and with most of them

---

[59] See *Phosphate of Lime Co v Green* [1871] L.R. 7 C.P. 43, where it was held that "acquiescence" by members of a company could be established without proving actual knowledge by each individual member so long as each could have found out if he had bothered to ask, and *Ho Tung v Man On Insurance Co* [1902] A.C. 232, PC, where articles of association, which had never been adopted by a resolution but had been acted on for 19 years and amended from time to time, were held to have been accepted and adopted as valid and operative articles.

[60] Interesting work on the issue has been carried out by Professor Cheffins. See "Putting Britain on the Roe Map: the Emergence of the Berle-Means Corporation in the United Kingdom" in J. McCahery and L. Renneboog (eds), *Convergence and Diversity in Corporate Regimes and Capital Markets* (OUP, 2002) and "Does Law Matter?: The Separation of Ownership and Control in the United Kingdom", Working Paper 172, ESRC Centre for Business Research (University of Cambridge, 2000).

holding only small stakes. By the middle of the last century, family shareholdings had declined and the small outside shareholders, collectively, made up the bulk of the shareholders. This is the second period, so brilliantly analysed by Berle and Means (see below), where the shareholdings in large companies were typically "dispersed", so that the shareholders' ability to act together in a meaningful way was doubtful. Since the 1960s, however, there has been a partial re-concentration of shareholdings, not into the hands of entrepreneurial families, but into the hands of "institutional" shareholders, especially pension funds and insurance companies. These different patterns of shareholding have significant implications for the ability and willingness of shareholders to exercise effectively the governance rights which the law confers upon them.

Ever since Berle and Means wrote their classic study of patterns of share ownership in large American corporations in the 1930s,[61] it has been common to think that shareholders are not in general interested in using the rights which the law or the company's articles confer upon them to hold the management of their company to account. The authors' thesis was that in large companies shareholdings had become so widely dispersed that it was not worth the while of most shareholders to devote time, effort and resources to seeking to change the policies of the managements which they thought were ineffective. The return on their relatively small investment, which success might bring, would be outweighed by the certain costs of seeking to achieve such change in a large company where co-ordination of shareholder action would be intensely difficult. Since large companies were likely to be listed on a stock exchange, the alternative and cheaper responses of accepting a takeover offer or simply selling in the market the shares in the company with whose management one had become disenchanted were likely to prove more attractive. Shareholders in large companies were thus "rationally apathetic" towards their general meeting rights.

Whether this was ever an entirely correct picture is controversial, but in any event it has been altered by the concentration over recent decades of shares in public companies in the hands of institutional investors, especially pension funds and insurance companies.[62] Institutional shareholders now hold about 60 per cent of the equity shares of companies listed on the London Stock Exchange, and this implies a considerable re-concentration of shareholdings. Although it is unusual for a single institution to hold more than 5 per cent of the equities of the largest quoted companies, nevertheless the situation is one in which a small group of institutional shareholders can often

---

[61] A.A. Berle and G.C. Means, *The Modern Corporation and Private Property* (revised ed., New York, 1968).

[62] See P.L. Davies, "Institutional Investors in the United Kingdom" in T. Baums *et al.* (eds), *Institutional Investors and Corporate Governance* (1994); E. Boros, *Minority Shareholder Remedies* (Oxford, 1995), Ch.3; and G.P. Stapledon, *Institutional Shareholders and Corporate Governance* (Oxford, 1996), Ch.2.

bring decisive influence to bear on the management of ailing companies. Of course, they may not always wish to do so. Even institutional shareholders will not exercise their general meeting rights simply for the sake of it. If a takeover offer provides a cheaper remedy for the problem, they may be inclined to accept that, rather than take on the incumbent management of the under-performing company themselves. Nevertheless, "shareholder activism" on the part of the institutions is now a bigger part of the corporate scene than it was, say, 20 years ago. However, the make-up of the institutional investors and their associated attitudes towards activism cannot be expected to remain unchanged. For reasons which do not need to be explored here, UK institutional shareholders have been tending to reduce their exposure to UK equities, whilst foreign institutions and hedge funds have been increasing them. Some types of hedge fund in particular can be expected to be even more interventionist in relation to their portfolio companies, often identifying specific business decisions which they wish the board to take.[63]

Shareholder activism is crucially underpinned by the rights of **15–11** shareholders at general meetings. Although most intervention by institutional shareholders takes place in private and will move into the public arena of the general meeting only if private pressure is unsuccessful, the pressure which the institutions can bring to bear privately depends in large part upon the prospect of their being able to get their way in the public meeting if the private pressures are unsuccessful. No doubt, the crucial factors, if it comes to a public fight between the incumbent management and the institutional shareholders, are the ability of an ordinary majority of the shareholders at any time to remove the directors under the provisions of s.168,[64] coupled with the institutions' long-held opposition to non-voting equity shares. Nevertheless, the detailed legal rules governing the holding and conduct of meetings of shareholders can also be significant if it comes to a public fight. When all is going well, the institutional shareholders tend not to attend and to leave the AGM to the pressure groups and querulous individual shareholders, so that many managing directors regard the AGM "as presently constituted as an expensive waste of time and money".[65] But that is to underestimate its value, at least in the background, when things are not going well.

---

[63] See M. Kahan and E. Rock, "Hedge Funds in Corporate Governance and Corporate Control", ECGI Law Series 76/2006 (suggesting that some hedge funds make investments in order to become activists rather than in order to protect an investment which has turned out not to perform as expected) and W. Bratton, "Hedge Funds and Governance Targets", *ibid.*, 80/2007.

[64] See above, paras 14–18ff.

[65] City/Industry Working Group, *Developing a Winning Partnership* (1995), p.14. Some reformers have proposed that institutional investors be obliged to vote at, though presumably not to attend, shareholder meetings.

The organisation of institutional investment

15–12 Both the Company Law Review and the Myner's Report,[66] commissioned by the Treasury, concluded that the level of institutional intervention in the affairs of their portfolio companies[67] was less than was optimal in the interests of those on whose behalf the institutions invested. This was, the CLR thought, not only a matter of concern to those investors, but also "a matter of corporate governance, impinging on the properly disciplined and competitive management of British business and industry".[68] In order to understand the possible reasons for sub-optimal intervention and the reforms proposed, it is necessary to say a bit more about the way in which pension funds are organised. This is because law reform proposals have focussed in particular upon pension funds, though, as we shall see, they are not the only significant form of institutional investment. In simplified form,[69] a pension scheme is normally promoted by an employer, who sets up a trust into which both employer and, normally, employees pay regular contributions and out of which pensions are paid.[70] Both the pensioners and the contributing employees may be seen as beneficiaries of the trust. The trustees see to the investment of the contributions, but normally do not discharge that task themselves, but contract it out one or more specialist fund managers. The fund managers may be freestanding institutions, but, today, they are likely to be part of larger financial groups (for example, investment banks) which offer other services in addition to fund management. The contract between the pension fund and the fund manager is likely to give the manager the right to vote the shares it purchases on behalf of the fund, though the trustees may reserve the right themselves to take voting decisions, either generally or in specific classes of case. Finally, for reasons of both efficiency and prudence, the manager is not likely itself to hold the shares it purchases on behalf of the fund, but to have them held by a separate custodian company, which may well be part of a different group of companies from that in which the fund manager sits.

---

[66] *Institutional Investment in the United Kingdom: A Review* (London, 2001).

[67] i.e. companies in which the institution has investments.

[68] Final Report 1, para.3.54.

[69] More detail can be found in Ch.5 of the Myners Report, above, fn.66.

[70] The fund may promise a certain level of benefits on retirement ("defined benefit" schemes) or only that the pensioner will be entitled to his or her share of the fund at retirement in order to purchase an annuity ("defined contribution" schemes). The distinction, though enormously important for employees in terms of the allocation of investment risk, is not significant for present purposes, though the present trend is firmly away from DB and towards DC. The proposed "activism" obligation (see below) is the same for both types of scheme.

Conflicts of interest and inactivity

There are three main types of argument which have been put forward **15–13**
to explain the under-use by pension funds or, more often, their fund
managers of the corporate governance rights which the law gives
them: conflicts of interest; a desire for a quiet life; and technical
difficulties of voting. The conflicts of interest arise mainly where the
group of which the fund manager is part provides other financial
services to corporate clients. The management of a portfolio company may be unwilling to buy, or continue to buy, these other
financial services, for example in connection with public share
offerings,[71] if some part of the same group is using its corporate
governance rights on behalf of a pension fund to make life difficult
for that management.[72] Indeed, the management of the portfolio
company may actively threaten to withdraw its custom from the
group if the intervention on behalf of the pension fund continues. In
extreme cases, such conduct may amount to the offence of corrup-
tion, but that is likely to be very difficult to prove. After floating a
number of proposals the best the CLR could come up with was a
requirement that quoted companies be required to disclose in annual
reports the identity of their major suppliers of financial services. This
would reveal potential conflicts of interest within financial services
groups, though it would not eliminate them nor, by itself, guarantee
the appropriate handling of the conflicts.[73]

Inactivity on the part of fund managers may, as we have just seen,
result from conflicts of interest, but it may also result, the Myners'
Report thought,[74] from a lack of incentives for the fund managers to
be active, for example, because the costs of intervention would
depress the manager's short-term performance whilst the benefits of
intervention would be reaped only in the medium term or because the
benefits of intervention would accrue to all shareholders, whether
they participated in the intervention or not, including rival fund
managers. The CLR's response was a proposed requirement that
managers disclose to trustees their voting record in portfolio companies on demand and a reserve power for the Secretary of State to
require the publication of the voting record, so that the beneficiaries
of the pension fund would be aware of it as well.[75] This proposal was
controversial, to the point where the clauses were removed from the
Bill in the House of Lords against the Government's wishes, but were
reinstated in the Commons and are now to be found in sections 1277
to 1280. In line with the CLR's recommendation, the power is one to

---

[71] See below, Ch.25.
[72] Even a stand-alone fund manager may suffer from conflicts of interest, for example, where it
manages the pension fund of a company in which another pension fund under its management is invested.
[73] In any event, the Government was not minded to pursue this particular recommendation:
Modernising, para.2.47.
[74] See above, fn.66 at paras 5.83 to 5.88.
[75] Final Report, I, para.6.39.

make regulations, in relation to which the Government said that it was "willing to see how market practice evolves before choosing whether and how to exercise the power".[76] Those regulations may require institutional investors (broadly defined in section 1278) to disclose, either to the public (a particularly controversial point) or specified persons only, information about the exercise or non-exercise of voting rights by the institution or any person acting on its behalf, about the voting instructions given by the institution or person on its behalf and about the delegation of voting functions (section 1280) in relation to shares which are publicly traded and in which the institution has an interest (section 1279).

15–14   The Myners Report was bolder, proposing a substantive obligation, derived from US law, on the fund manager to monitor and attempt to influence the boards of companies where there is a reasonable expectation that such activity would enhance the value of the portfolio investments.[77] This would include, but not be limited to, the exercise of the right to vote at shareholder meetings. This would not amount to an obligation to vote the shares in portfolio companies on each and every occasion. On the one hand, voting on routine proposals might be neither here nor there in corporate governance terms; on the other, merely to vote might be an inadequate form of intervention, if, for example, a private meeting with the management might solve the problem at an earlier stage and avoid an adverse vote.

The Myners Report did not propose the embodiment of these rules in legislation, but only in voluntary Statements of Investment Principles, which the fund management industry was to observe on a "comply or explain" basis,[78] with the threat of legal regulation if voluntarism did not work. The Government, however, committed itself to legislation on the point,[79] but, for the time being, the institutional investors seem to have headed off the threat by adopting a voluntary code of practice under which they undertake to maintain and publish policies on active engagement with portfolio companies; to monitor the performance of such companies and to maintain a dialogue with them; to intervene where necessary; and, in the case of investment managers, to report back to clients on whose behalf they invest.[80] Of course, it is strongly arguable that the fiduciary duties of pension fund trustees already require them to exercise their corporate governance rights actively, if they judge that this will enhance the

[76] HL Debs, vol. 682, col. 787, May, 23 2006 (Lord Sainsbury).
[77] See above, fn.66 at para.5.89.
[78] See para.14–29.
[79] H. M. Treasury and Department for Work and Pensions, *Myners Review: The Government's Response*, para.11.
[80] Institutional Shareholders' Committee, *The Responsibilities of Institutional Shareholders and Agents—Statement of Principles* (2002). In December 2004 the Treasury published *Myners principles for institutional investment decision-making: review of progress*, concluding that progress had been made, that more needed to be done but that legislation was not required at that stage.

value of the trust's assets and, therefore, to secure that a similar obligation is laid upon those to whom they contract out the exercise of their corporate governance rights. However, it may be very difficult to show that any particular piece of inaction or even a course of inaction over a period of time reduced the value of the trust's assets.

"Fiduciary investors"

The generation of an obligation of activism in the case of pension **15–15** funds takes as its starting point, as we have seen, the fact that the trustees of pension funds owe fiduciary obligations to the beneficiaries of the fund.[81] However, it is not the case that the relationship between investors and those who invest the money on their behalf is necessarily a fiduciary one. The relationship between investors and insurance companies, which are as important as pension funds in the collective investment area, is predominantly contractual. Yet, insurance companies play an important role in the provision of pensions, especially to those who are not part of occupational schemes. However, the Myners Report makes no recommendations about the activism responsibilities of insurance companies.[82] The situation is not satisfactory. Occupational pension schemes took the form of trusts originally because of insistence by the Revenue that the funds of the scheme be separated from those of the company promoting the scheme, but it would be wrong to use that tax-based requirement to determine the extent to which institutional shareholders should be legally obliged to make use of their corporate governance rights. If the value of investments will be increased by voting, or other forms of exercise of their governance rights, by institutional shareholders, it is difficult to see why this should not be required of all intermediaries, whether established as trusts or not, which acquire funds on the basis that they can manage them more effectively on behalf of investors than the investors can themselves. It is interesting that the new code of practice from the Institutional Shareholders Committee applies to all institutional investors, whether pension funds or not, as does the reserve disclosure power contained in the 2006 Act.

Cross-border voting

Increasingly an institutional investor based in one Member State of **15–16** the EU will hold shares in a company incorporated in another Member State and wish to exercise its voting rights in relation to that company. This is a natural area for regulation by Community law

---

[81] Though the Myners Committee seems to have forgotten this for it proposed to impose its obligation on the fund managers only. The mistake was corrected by the Government: see above, fn.79, para.60.
[82] See above, fn.66, Ch.9.

and in 2007 the Community adopted Directive 2007/36/EC on the exercise of certain rights of shareholders in listed companies.[83] Although confined neither to cross-border voting nor to voting by institutional shareholders—though it is confined to shares traded on a regulated market[84]—the Directive lays down certain minimum standards relating to the holding of meetings. Many of its provisions were already met by the domestic companies legislation and some of the others were anticipated in the enactment of the 2006 Act, but there is a third group, noted as appropriate below, where reform will be required in the United Kingdom.

INDIRECT INVESTORS

15–17   Under the typical arrangement for pension funds, described above, the shares in the portfolio company are held by a custodian company. That custodian company will appear on the portfolio company's share register as the holder of the shares, even though it holds them as a nominee, either for the fund manager or for the pension fund. Clearly, the custodian has no interest in voting the shares in question. Rather, the law is that, if the custodian is a bare nominee for a beneficial owner, the beneficial owner can instruct the nominee how to deal with the shares.[85] In order to bring this about, however, the custodian must confer with the fund manager and, perhaps, through the fund manager with the trustees. However, the registered holder is not placed under any obligation by company law to engage in this process, which, in any event, may not prove to be possible within the notice period for the meeting,[86] though there may be contractual arrangements in place between the member and others with an interest in the shares which require this consultation. It can be argued that this process would operate more smoothly if the company communicated directly with the beneficial owner or, going further, if the governance rights attached to the shares could be exercised by the beneficial (or "indirect") owner.

The CLR proposed to remove any impediments which existed to the creation of contractual arrangements for giving non-members an input into the exercise of the governance rights attached to the shares, together with a fall-back power for the Government to require such

---

[83] OJ L184/17, 14.7.2007.
[84] On the definition of a "regulated market" see para.25–6. In the UK this means in effect the Main Market of the London Stock Exchange. The Directive thus does not impinge on the domestic policy of relieving private companies from the need to hold meetings.
[85] *Kirby v Wilkins* [1929] 2 Ch. 444. If the nominee votes the shares without instructions, that right must be exercised in the interests of the beneficiary.
[86] See below, para.15–37.

transfers of governance rights if contractual arrangements did not continue to develop on an adequate scale.[87] The Companies Bill followed this formula but in the debates in Parliament the position of institutional investors was linked to that of many private investors who also hold shares through nominee accounts, partly as a result of the dematerialisation of shares and partly because government tax relief on private investment is often available only in relation to shares held in this way.[88] Thus, the governance rights of indirect investors became a politically much more significant matter than had been initially anticipated. The Government's fall-back proposals were defeated in the Lords.[89] The Government then consulted with those affected on alternative provision, which contain an element of compulsion, though they are still have a significant fall-back element. They were introduced at a very late stage in the Parliamentary process and received little debate.[90]

Voluntary arrangements for all companies
The reforms now contained in Part 9 fall into two groups. As recommended by the CLR, some are purely facultative. They help companies to reassign governance rights to indirect shareholders, but do not require it. These provisions apply to all companies. The other group contains the element of compulsion, which at present relates only to shareholders' information rights in companies whose securities are traded on a regulated market, in effect the Main Market of the London Stock Exchange.[91] However, the Secretary of State has power by regulation to expand the scope of this second class of provisions so as to expand the rights provided or the types of company covered by the Act.[92]

15–18

Turning first to the facultative provisions applying to all companies, the view was taken in some quarters that s.126,[93] by providing that "no notice of any trust ... shall be entered on the register [of members] or be receivable by the registrar",[94] and a parallel provision in the articles dealing with the position of the company,[95] prevented the transfer of governance rights between the company and the holders of the beneficial interests in the shares. The CLR proposed

---

[87] Final I, paras 7.1–7.4.
[88] See para.27–12.
[89] HL Debs, vol. 681, cols. 813ff, May 9, 2006.
[90] HC Debs, Standing Committee D, Twenty First Sitting, cols. 875ff, July 21, 2006.
[91] For the meaning of a "regulated market" see para.25–6.
[92] s.151. The regulations are subject to affirmative resolution by Parliament.
[93] The register of members is discussed below, at para.27–16.
[94] This section does not apply in Scotland.
[95] Thus art.44 of the draft model set of articles for public companies: "Except as required by law, no person shall be recognised by the company as holding any share upon any trust, and except as otherwise required by law or the articles, the company shall not in any way be bound by or recognise any interest in a share other than the holder's absolute ownership of it and all the rights attaching to it."

that, if this was so, what is now s.126 be amended so as to make clear that it permits the transfer of corporate governance rights to third parties.[96] Such transfers would not be compulsory, but were to be left to contractual arrangements between those holding shares on behalf of others and the persons on whose behalf the shares were held.

The drafters of the Act clearly took the view that section 126 was not an impediment to the transfer of governance rights for it does not deal with the issue. However, section 145(1) is drafted on the basis that a company in its articles may (and always has been able to) make provision enabling a member to nominate another person to enjoy all or any of the governance rights of the member in relation to the company. That other person need not in fact be the holder of the beneficial interest in the shares, so that, for example, a custodian could nominate a fund manager as entitled to vote the shares, even though the beneficial interest is held by the pension trust. The person to whom the rights are transferred is the "nominated person".[97]

15–19   The section does not in any way require such a transfer of governance rights to be made. Its purpose rather is to ensure that the statutory provisions discussed below in relation to meetings (and, indeed, those discussed above in relation to written resolutions) work properly where contractual governance rights are held by a nominated person. In other words, where rights under the articles are transferred to a nominated person, so are the linked statutory rights. A good example is the right to vote. As we have seen above,[98] voting rights in a company are not allocated by the statute but by the company, normally through its articles. If the articles permit or require[99] those voting rights to be transferred to a nominated person and the right to vote is so transferred by a particular member, then section 145(3)(f) ensures that the statutory right to appoint a proxy to vote at the meeting on behalf of the voter[100] is also transferred to the nominated person.

Precisely which statutory rights are transferred under the section to a nominated person will depend upon which contractual rights have been transferred to the nominated person under the articles. The section potentially transfers eight statutory rights,[101] but operates only "so far as necessary to give effect to" a transfer of rights effected

[96] Completing, paras 5.2–5.12 and Final Report I, paras 7.3–7.4.
[97] An obvious, but perhaps potentially confusing, term to employ, since the nominator will often be a nominee shareholder! Any custodian of relevant shares may use the power, whether in a pension-fund context or otherwise.
[98] At para.15–1.
[99] Although the section is permissive as to the adoption of "transfer" articles by the company, there seems no reason why the articles should not be mandatory as against the member in appropriate cases.
[100] On proxies see below, para.15–41.
[101] The rights to be sent a proposed written resolution; to require circulation of a written resolution; to require directors to call a general meeting; to require notice of a general meeting; to require circulation of a statement; to appoint a proxy; to require circulation of a resolution for the AGM of a public company; to be sent the annual report and accounts.

under the company's articles.[102] Where the right to vote is transferred, it seems that most of the listed statutory rights will also be transferred. Even so, if the company is a public company, the rights in relation to written resolutions will not be transferred and if the company is a private company, the right to propose a resolution at an AGM will not be transferred, since these rights are specific to private or public companies.[103]

If the linked statutory right is transferred to the nominated person, then anything the member might have done may instead be done by the nominated person and any duty owed by the company to the member is owed instead to the nominated person.[104] Thus, there is a genuine transfer of statutory powers and rights to the nominated person and away from the member, not the creation of a parallel set of provisions. However, no rights enforceable against the company by anyone other than the member are so created by the section *or* by the provisions in the articles creating the transfer system.[105] In fact, the primary sanction for many of the rights covered by the section is a criminal one, to which this provision is irrelevant, but civil rights could arise also, for example, to challenge the validity of a resolution because of an inaccuracy in the circular sent out in support of it.[106] Although the section is not absolutely crystal clear on the point, presumably its implication is that the right of the member to enforce a right against the company is not affected by the fact that the right has been transferred to a nominated person. To hold otherwise would mean a reduction in the enforceability of members' rights where there was a transfer to a nominated person.

Whether section 145 will mean much in practice will depend on the willingness of companies to adopt articles permitting or requiring the transfer of governance rights, that of nominee shareholding organisations to exercise the power of transfer (if it is permissive) and that of beneficial shareholders to put pressure on nominee shareholders to transfer rights to them and to pay for any associated costs.[107]

A further piece of apparent facilitation is to be found in section 152. This makes it clear that a member of a company holding shares on behalf of more than one person (as will typically be the case with nominees, whether they hold on behalf, ultimately, of institutional or private investors) need not exercise all the shareholders' rights

15–20

---

[102] s.145(2).
[103] s.145(4)(b) makes it clear that the section does not affect the requirements relating to the transfer of the shares themselves.
[104] s.145 (2).
[105] s.145(4)(a). Thus, the articles may not confer enforceable rights on third parties, even if the company wishes to do so, a somewhat strange restriction.
[106] See below, para.15–39.
[107] For an excellent survey of practice as of a few years ago and proposals for reform going beyond what the CLR recommended, see R. C. Nolan, "Indirect Investors: A Greater Say in the Company?" (2003) 3 J.C.L.S. 73.

(whether given under the contract of issue or provided by statute) in the same way—nor indeed need all of them be exercised on any particular occasion. Thus, the holder is enabled to give effect to the different views which the various beneficial owners may hold on the issue in question. It is doubtful whether this provision changes the previous law. What may be new, therefore, is the further provision that, if the member does not inform the company that not all the rights are being exercised or that some are being exercised in one way and some in another, the company is entitled to assume that all are being exercised and all in the same way.[108] Thus, this section may be more protective of the company than anything else.

Mandatory transfer of information rights

15–21   The rules on information rights are mandatory as against the company. This means that a member of a company whose shares are admitted to trading on a regulated market may nominate another person to enjoy those information rights, whether the company has provided in its articles for this to happen or not. However, it is not mandatory for the shareholder to confer this right on someone else. Further, the rights conferred upon the other person do not deprive the nominating shareholder of his or her right to the same information.[109] The fact that the provisions are mandatory as against the company and increase, at least marginally, the company's costs in relation to the circulation of information was a strong argument in the Government's eyes against introducing them, and the provisions are crafted so far as possible to reduce those costs. Those costs are confined to the largest companies because the provisions, at present, apply only to companies listed on a regulated market.[110] However, there are a number of other provisions which aim to cut down the cost implications of the new rule, even for these large companies.

First, the right to nominate a recipient of information rights is restricted to those members who hold shares on behalf of another person and where the recipient is that other person.[111] Secondly, the only rights which may thus be conferred are "information rights", i.e. essentially the right to receive the communications which a company sends to its members (including its annual accounts and reports) or

---

[108] s.152(2)–(4). Though the provisions do not indicate the content of the assumption the company is entitled to make or require it to be a reasonable one.

[109] s.150(5)(a).

[110] s.146(1). That regulated market may be located in any Member State but the company must be one subject to the domestic companies legislation. In other words, a company registered in any jurisdiction of the UK will not escape this obligation by listing on a regulated market in, for example, France or Germany, but a company incorporated in Germany and listed on a regulated market in the UK will not be subject to the obligation.

[111] s.146(2). As we saw above, s.145 is not restricted in this way, though the articles are most likely to provide for transfers of rights in such a case.

any class of them which includes the nominating shareholder.[112] No other governance rights may be transferred compulsorily as against the company. Thirdly, a company need not accept the conferment of only some of the shareholder's information rights.[113] The company can thus insist on an "all or nothing" conferment of information rights. Fourthly, unless the shareholder, on behalf of the nominated person, requests circulation in hard copy and provides the company with an address, the company may meet its obligation to the nominated person through website publication.[114] Fifthly, all nominations are suspended when there are more nominations in force than the nominator has shares in the company, so that the burden of sorting out the errors is moved away from the company.[115] Sixthly, the company may enquire of a nominated person once every twelve months whether it wishes to retain information rights and the nomination will cease if the company does not receive a positive response within twenty-eight days. Seventhly, to relieve the company of the burden of staying on top of things, if the nomination is terminated or suspended for any reason,[116] the company may continue to abide by it "to such extent or for such period as it thinks fit".[117] Eighthly, the rights conferred upon the nominated person are enforceable only by the member, the rights to be treated for this purpose as if they were conferred by the company's articles.[118]

The right to enjoy information rights is thus, it may be said, rather grudgingly conferred. The main non-restrictive provision is the one which tracks section 145 and provides that any enactment or anything in the company's articles relating to communications with members has corresponding effect in relation to communications with nominated persons.[119]

The compulsory information provisions discussed above do not in any way touch on the relationship between the nominated person and the member after the information has been received. As we have seen above, the nominated person, having received notice of a meeting, for example, has power to instruct the member how to vote, if the member holds the share on a bare trust for the nominated person.[120]

15–22

---

[112] s.146(3)(a),(4). Rights to require copies of the accounts and reports or to require hard copies of documents are also included within the notion of "information rights": s.146(3)(b).

[113] s.146(5).

[114] s.147. The right to request hard copy will also give way if the company has adopted electronic communication as its way of communicating with its members generally: s.147(4) and see below, para.15–54.

[115] s.148(6). S.148(7) deals with the class right variation of this problem.

[116] Besides the two situations just described, the nomination will be terminated at the request of the member or nominated person, and will cease to have effect on the death or bankruptcy of an individual or the dissolution or the making of a winding-up order of a corporate shareholder: s.148(2)–(4).

[117] s.148(8).

[118] s.150(2).

[119] s.150(3)—and even that provision is subject to qualifications in s.150(4).

[120] Above, fn.85.

But there is no legal obligation upon the member, in this case or more generally, to seek the views of the nominated person before voting, in the absence of an instruction, contrary to the position in some other legal systems. Such an obligation may be created by contract, however, either between the nominated person and the member or, conceivably, between the company and the member.

An example of the latter form of contract can be found in some companies in relation to "American Depositary Receipts" (ADRs). A UK company acquiring a US company in a share exchange deal may not wish to issue its shares directly to the US investors, partly in order to avoid some of the complications of US securities laws and partly in order to give the US investors a security denominated in dollars. One way of achieving these consequences is the ADR, the shares being issued to a depositary institution, which in turn issues to the US investors a "depositary receipt"—one for each share—denominated in dollars, which becomes the security which is traded in the US.[121] In some cases, the company's articles may then require the depositary institution to appoint the ADR holder as its proxy, possibly just for voting purposes but possibly for all governance purposes, including the receipt of communications from the company.[122] In such a case, one sees the company using its contracting power through the articles, as facilitated by section 145, to overcome the limitations of the mandatory conferment of a governance right which is restricted to information. However, there is no legal obligation upon companies to treat the holders of ADRs in this way.

THE MECHANICS OF MEETINGS

15–23 We turn now to the various issues arising where a meeting is sought to be held, so that resolutions of the shareholders can be voted upon. These issues appear in their sharpest form where a group of shareholders wish to use the shareholders' meeting to challenge some aspect of the management of the incumbent directors. Therefore, we shall generally adopt this perspective in our analysis of the rules, though, of course, those rules may also be relevant in the more usual case where the meeting is called by the board to discuss a matter which the shareholders find relatively uncontentious.

---

[121] Such provisions also prevent the depositary institution becoming a significant holder of voting rights at the company's meetings.

[122] Nolan, above, fn.107, analyses such a set of provisions in the articles of BP.

What happens at meetings?

It is a rare shareholders' meeting which does not end up passing a resolution on some matter or another. As we have seen in Chapter 14, the Act requires the shareholders' consent before certain decisions can bind the company, and the articles may add to that list. By assenting to a resolution the shareholders give the consent which is necessary to make the act an act of the company. Once the shareholders have adopted an effective resolution on a particular matter, the board is empowered, and normally obliged, to take the necessary steps to put the resolution into effect. Some decisions are routinely required of shareholders, though in particular cases the decision may be anything but routine, such as the re-appointment of directors[123] or of auditors[124] or the granting of powers to directors to issue a certain amount of shares without pre-emption rights.[125] Others occur irregularly. However, the business of general meetings does not consist entirely of the consideration of proposals for resolutions. For example, the Act requires the annual reports and accounts to be laid before the company in general meeting,[126] but does not require the meeting to consider any resolution in relation to them. The exercise is not pointless, however, because it gives the shareholders an opportunity to question the board generally on the progress of the company and to express their views on the matter. Often, this item on the agenda provides the opportunity for a wide-ranging debate, which specific resolutions would not permit. Indeed, there is no reason why an item should not be placed on the agenda simply for the purposes of having a debate, without any resolution being proposed. Nevertheless, apart for the consideration of the annual reports and accounts, it is the consideration of resolutions with which the general meetings of the shareholders largely deal.

15–24

Types of resolution

The 2006 Act has reduced the types of resolution which the members may take to two: an ordinary resolution and a special resolution.[127] An ordinary resolution is one passed by a simple majority of those voting, and is to be used for all decisions required under the Act, unless the Act specifies a special resolution. However, the articles may specify a higher level of approval, up to and including unanimity,

15–25

---

[123] See above, para.14–10.
[124] See below, para.22–17.
[125] See below, para.24–9.
[126] See below, para.21–41.
[127] ss.282 (ordinary resolutions) and 283 (special resolutions). The relatively recently introduced "elective resolution" is no longer necessary in light of the simplified regime for private companies, whilst the longer standing "extraordinary resolution" has been abolished, as the CLR recommended.

obviously in the case of resolutions required by the articles but also in the case of resolutions required by the companies legislation.[128]

A special resolution is one passed by a three-fourths majority.[129] A special resolution is required before any important constitutional changes can be undertaken; and as a result of the legislation in the 1980s the number of such cases has greatly increased. In the case of a special resolution the notice of the meeting must specify the intention to propose the resolution as a special resolution.[130]

In both cases, the requisite majority on a poll[131] is that of the votes attached to the shares voted by members entitled to vote and actually voting either in person or by proxy, where proxy voting is allowed.[132] In the case of a meeting of a class of shareholders, where the same rules apply, this means the appropriate majority is of the votes of the class in question.[133] As we shall see below, many votes at meetings are taken on a show of hands, and may never proceed further if no one challenges the result. The statute facilitates the continued use of such votes, though they are controversial, by providing that the majorities are then to be calculated by reference to those entitled to and actually voting, rather than to the votes attached to their shares.[134] Overall, the higher majority required for special resolutions obviously constitutes a form of minority protection, as compared with the simple majority required for an ordinary resolution. It means, for example, that a person with more than 25 per cent of the votes, and in practice often with many fewer votes, can block the adoption of a special resolution.[135]

15–26   The distinction between ordinary and special resolutions is important also in relation to the question of amendment of proposed resolutions at the meeting held to consider them. This, one might have supposed, would be entirely legitimate so long as the amendment was not such as to take the resolution beyond the scope of the business notified to the members in the notice of the meeting. However, as a result of the decision of Slade J. in *Moorgate Mercantile*

---

[128] s.281(3).

[129] s.283(1). Confusingly, this was previously the definition of an extraordinary resolution, a special resolution being one for which a "special" notice period was required. Thus, in effect, the category of special resolution has been abolished and the extraordinary resolution renamed a special resolution.

[130] s.283(6). And include the text of the proposed special resolution. In the case of a written resolution the text of the resolution must state that it is proposed as a special resolution (s.283(3)).

[131] On a poll the votes attached to the shares are counted (see below, para.15–46) so that a single shareholder with 100 shares will outvote 99 shareholders with one vote each.

[132] ss.282(4) and 283(5). On proxy voting see below, para.15–41.

[133] s.281(1) and (2) make it clear that the same rules apply to voting at class meetings.

[134] ss. 282(3) and 283(4). On a show of hands, it is not known how many shares each voter represents.

[135] See further, Ch.19, below.

Holdings Ltd, Re,[136] it seems that, in relation to special resolutions, no amendment can be made if it in any way alters the substance of the resolution as set out in the notice. Grammatical and clerical errors may be corrected, or words translated into more formal language, and, if the precise text of the resolution was not included in the notice,[137] it may be converted into a formal resolution, provided always that there is no departure whatever from the substance as stated in the notice.[138]

The learned judge thought that his decision was desirable on policy grounds,[139] as well as being demanded by the terms of the Act, and that it would prevent the substantial embarrassment to the chairman of the meeting and to any persons holding "two-way" proxies on behalf of absent members,[140] that any less strict rule would cause. Slade J. emphasised that his decision had no relevance to ordinary resolutions and that in relation to them the criteria for permissible amendments might well be wider.[141] This is clearly so if the precise terms of the resolution are not set out in the notice but come within a statement of "the general nature of the business to be dealt with at the meeting".[142] But even if the terms of an ordinary resolution are set out in the notice it seems that some amendments may be made at the meeting, and that if the chairman refuses to allow a permissible amendment to be moved the resolution will be invalid.[143] It is submitted that an amendment is permissible if, but only if, the amended resolution is such that no member who had made up his mind whether or not to attend and vote and, if he had decided to do so, how he should vote, could reasonably adopt a different attitude to the amended version.[144] The criticisms of that test by Slade J.[145] apply equally to an ordinary resolution but it is difficult to find any other test short of applying to ordinary resolutions that applied to special resolutions, i.e.that no amendment of substance, however trivial, may be made. And does the suggested test really face the chairman and

---

[136] [1980] 1 W.L.R. 227. The case concerned the confirmation of a special resolution reducing the company's share premium account which had been "lost". The notice of the meeting proposed that the whole of it (£1,356,900.48) "be cancelled". Before the meeting was held it was realised that £327.17 resulting from a recent share issue could not be said yet to have been "lost". Accordingly, at the meeting the resolution was amended and it was resolved that the share premium a/c be reduced to £327.17. Confirmation was refused on the ground that the resolution had not been validly passed. But in a later case (unreported, but see (1991) 12 Co. Law. at 64, 65), where the facts were virtually identical, a reduction was confirmed because the "substance" (i.e. the amount of the reduction) remained unchanged.

[137] As is now in any event required by s.283(6).

[138] At 242C.

[139] At 242A–243.

[140] At 243F.

[141] At 242H, citing *Betts & Co Ltd v Macnaghten* [1910] 1 Ch. 430.

[142] s.311(2).

[143] *Henderson v Bank of Australasia* (1890) 45 Ch.D. 330, CA.

[144] This was the advice given to the chairman in the *Moorgate* case; see [1980] 1 W.L.R. at 230A.

[145] *Moorgate* case, at 243D–G.

two-way proxy-holders with the substantial embarrassments that Slade J. foresaw?[146]

There may, nevertheless, be one type of ordinary resolution to which the stricter rule applies. This is when "special notice" of the ordinary resolution is required. Special notice is defined by section 312 as notice to be given to the company by the proposers of the resolution (not by the company to the members in general) and the length of the notice is at least 28 days before the meeting at which the resolution is to be moved. The wording of s.312(1) bears a close resemblance to that considered in *Moorgate Mercantile Holdings, Re* and makes it arguable that no amendment of substance, however trivial, can be made to the resolution stated in the special notice. Hence, if, say, special notice has been given of a single resolution to remove all the directors[147] (under s.168) or both of two joint auditors (under s.510), an amendment seeking to exclude from the resolution some or one of them may be impermissible. If so, this seems a regrettable emasculation of such powers as members have (and which the relevant sections were intended to enhance) and also seems unfair to the directors or auditors whom the members may wish to retain.[148] Even where an amendment to an ordinary resolution may be proposed on the above principles, the company's articles may aim to restrict the shareholders' freedom, say, by providing that, where the text is fully set out in the notice of the meeting, the Chairman has a discretion not to consider amendments of which at least 48 hours' notice in writing has not been given to the company.

Convening a meeting of the shareholders

15–27   However, in the above discussion of amendments to resolutions we are getting rather ahead of ourselves. No resolution can be debated until there is a meeting. Clearly, therefore, the shareholders' meeting is not of much value as a vehicle of shareholder control if the meeting cannot easily be convened. The law distinguishes between annual general meetings ("AGMs") and any other meeting of the shareholders.[149] The advantage of the former from our perspective is that,

---

[146] If the articles say (as did Table A 1985, art.82) that directors' fees shall be such as "the company may by ordinary resolution determine" and the directors give notice of an ordinary resolution to increase the fees by £10,000 p.a., surely a member should be entitled to move an amendment to reduce the increase (though the directors clearly should not be permitted to move an amendment to increase it further)?

[147] This seems to be permissible—the singular "director" includes the plural—and s.160 relates only to voting on *appointments*, not to *removals*.

[148] Nor should proxy-holders have any doubts on how they should vote. If instructed to vote for the resolution they would vote against the amendment but, if that was passed, for the amended resolution. If instructed to vote against, they would vote for the amendment but against the resolution as amended. If given a discretion they would exercise it.

[149] The law used to distinguish between AGMs and extraordinary general meetings (EGMs) but the Act no longer uses the latter term, no doubt because in the case of a private company it is the only type of meeting that can be held.

in principle, it must be held on a regular annual basis, whereas the Act provides procedures for the convening of other meetings but says nothing about their frequency. Even the AGM is not compulsory if the company is a private one.[150]

Annual general meetings
The law, rather oddly, whilst requiring the holding of AGMs by public companies, does not prescribe the business which has to be transacted at the AGM and in particular does not say that the annual directors' report and the accounts must be laid before the AGM[151] or that the directors due for re-election must be considered then. In fact, it is normal for these matters to be taken at the AGM and for the shareholders to have an opportunity to question the directors generally on the company's business and financial position.[152] This is the result of the practice, however, rather than of law, a practice which is encouraged by the Combined Code, applying to Listed Companies,[153] which states that "boards should use the AGM to communicate with private investors and encourage their participation".[154] Of course, the business of a particular AGM may go far beyond these matters: in fact, there seems to be no limit on the business which may be transacted at an AGM, assuming only that it is business properly to be put before the shareholders.[155]

15–28

Following the recommendations of the CLR, the timing of the AGM is now tied to the company's annual reporting cycle. The AGM must be held yearly within the six-month period following its accounting reference date,[156] which determines the beginning and end of its financial year.[157] One of the considerations behind the CLR recommendation was that this rule would facilitate the procedure by which shareholders may introduce their own resolutions onto the agenda of the AGM. However, as we shall see below,[158] the Government failed to pick up this opportunity. If a company fails to comply with this requirement, every officer in default is liable to a

---

[150] ss.336–340, concerning AGMs, apply only to public companies. See s.336(1).
[151] But see fn.154 below.
[152] The Shareholders' Rights Directive (Directive 2007/36/EC), Article 9, will give shareholders the right to ask questions related to items on the agenda of a general meeting as from August 2009.
[153] See below, para.25–8.
[154] Para.D.2. In particular the Code suggests that companies propose a resolution in relation to the report and accounts (para.D.2.1). The Code envisages that the company's relationship with institutional investors will take the form of continuing dialogue which will extend beyond the general meeting: para.D.1.
[155] In particular, the fact that a special resolution is required to transact a particular piece of business does not mean that that business cannot be considered at an AGM.
[156] s.336(1).
[157] s.391. See below, para.21–6. Subsection (2) deals with the situation where the company changes, as is permitted, its accounting reference date.
[158] At para.15–34.

fine.[159] The persons most obviously at risk are the directors since they have the power to convene a meeting of the shareholders at any time.[160] However, the power, previously contained in the legislation,[161] for the Secretary of State, on the application of any member, to call or direct the calling of a meeting has been removed. Thus, the member has no direct and easy way of securing compliance with the AGM requirement, but must rely on the indirect impact of the criminal sanctions.

Other general meetings

15–29 As for the convening of meetings, other than the AGM of a public company, such meetings are not required at any specific time. As we have just noted, the board may convene a meeting of the members of a private or public company at any time. The articles may make further provision for the calling of meetings, but they are unlikely to give the members an extensive right to do so, for the management would like nothing better than to be able to call meetings when it suited them, but to be under no obligation to do so when it did not. In fact, the draft model set of articles for public companies provides for members to convene meetings only where the number of directors falls below two and the remaining director (if any) is unwilling to appoint a further director so as to restore the board's power to act in this area;[162] and no provision for members to convene meetings is made in the model articles for private companies.

However, the Act provides that the directors must convene a meeting on the requisition of holders of not less than one-tenth of the paid-up capital carrying voting rights.[163] However, that fraction is reduced to one-twentieth in the case of a private company which has not held a meeting convened by the members under their statutory powers within the previous twelve months.[164] This is the substitute for the previously available right of any member to insist on the holding of an AGM in a private company. The request must state the general nature of the business to be dealt with at the meeting. It may include the text of a resolution intended to be moved at the meeting, which facility the members will normally be well advised to take up.[165]

---

[159] s.336(3),(4).

[160] s.302.

[161] s.367 of the CA 1985.

[162] art.27.

[163] s.303. In the case of a company without shareholders the threshold is members holding at least one-tenth of the voting rights of the members: s.303(2)(b).

[164] s.303(3). The fraction remains at one-tenth also if a meeting has been held other than under the section at which the members had rights to circulate a resolution (however arising) at least as extensive as those arising under the section.

[165] s.303(4). This is because (a) that makes their intentions clearer and (b) if what is proposed is a special resolution, notice of it has to be given to the shareholders (see above, para.15–26). The company must then give the notice to the shareholders required for a special resolution: s.304(4).

However, the resolution must be one which may be "properly moved" at the meeting and, if it is not, it appears the directors are under no obligation to circulate it.[166]

If the directors fail to convene a meeting within 21 days of the deposit of the requisition, the meeting to be held within a further 28 days of the notice convening it, the requisitionists, or any of them representing more than half of the total voting rights of all of them, may themselves convene the meeting, and their reasonable expenses must be paid by the company and recovered from fees or remuneration payable to the defaulting directors.[167]

The provisions for requisitioning a meeting work reasonably well in private companies and also in public companies where, for example, the co-operation of only two or three institutional shareholders is required to get across the 10 per cent threshold.[168] However, small individual shareholders in public companies are likely to find it a matter of considerable difficulty and expense to enlist the support of a sufficient number of fellow members to be able to make a valid requisition.

Meetings convened by the court

Finally, section 306(1) gives the court power to convene a meeting "if for any reason it is impracticable to call a meeting … in any manner in which meetings of that company may be called or to conduct the meeting in manner prescribed by the articles or this Act". This power may be exercised by the court "of its own motion or on the application—(a) of any director of the company or (b) of any member who would be entitled to vote at the meeting".[169] The meeting can be "called, held and conducted in any manner the court thinks fit" and the "court may give such ancillary or consequential directions as it

15–30

---

[166] The resolution is not "properly moved" if it falls within any of the three categories of resolution which the directors may refuse to circulate as a written resolution: s.303(5) and see above, para.15–6. For an example of the operation of this principle under the prior legislation see *Rose v McGivern* [1998] 2 B.C.L.C. 593. Here a proposed resolution "to elect a new board of not more than ten members" was held to be ineffective on the grounds that it did not provide for the removal of the existing board and there were otherwise no vacancies to which the ten could be elected (quite apart from the failure to state whether the number was in fact to be ten or some lesser number and to state who the ten were to be). The leaders of the requisition subsequently submitted 25 individual resolutions to the company, removing each of the 16 existing directors and appointing nine new ones, but the company refused to circulate the individual resolutions on the grounds they were too late.

[167] s.305(1),(6),(7). The effect of this is that, if more than 10 per cent requisitioned the meeting, the percentage needed to call a meeting directly is itself increased. The requisitionists may act not only where the directors fail to act in time but also where they fail to include a proposed resolution in the notice of the meeting or fail to give notice of the proposed resolution as a special resolution, if such it is: ss.304(3),(4) and 305(1)(b).

[168] Activist shareholders seeking to obtain changes in the board's policy have recently made use of it.

[169] s.306(2). The section does not make the addition originally proposed of the personal representative of a deceased member of the company who would have had the right to vote at the meeting.

thinks expedient and these may include a direction that one member of the company present in person or by proxy be deemed to constitute a meeting".[170]

Most of the litigation under this section has revolved around quorum requirements for shareholder meetings. In the absence of a required quorum, no resolution can be effectively passed. In contrast to many other jurisdictions, the quorum requirements set by the British Act are not demanding, except in relation to class[171] meetings: two members only are required for meetings of the shareholders as a whole, unless the company's constitution sets a higher figure,[172] and only one member in the case of a single-member company.[173] It is not even clear that the Act requires the quorum to be present throughout the meeting.[174] However, staying away can in principle be an effective way of preventing a meeting from being held in a private company with only two shareholders. If the board consists of the same two persons (or their nominees) and also has a quorum requirement of two, the company may become completely deadlocked. The question the courts have had to address is whether the provisions of s.306 can be used to overcome this deadlock.

After a certain amount of litigation in recent years, the position which the courts seem to have reached as to the exercise of their discretion under the section is as follows. In principle, the section is available to break a deadlock created by quorum requirements, because, where the shareholdings are not held equally, the normal principle of majority rule is being frustrated by the quorum requirement.[175] However, it may be that the quorum requirements have been deliberately adopted in order to produce deadlock if the parties cannot agree, and in that case the section should not be used to overrule the parties' agreement. The court is likely to conclude that this is the purpose of the quorum requirement where that takes the form of a class right attached to the shares of one of the parties.[176] Other than that perhaps unusual situation, the question of whether the quorum provision was intended to create deadlock in the case of disagreement is a matter of construction of the articles or shareholders' agreement so as to provide a context for an understanding of

---

[170] s.306(2)–(4).
[171] See below, para.15–53.
[172] s.318(2).
[173] s.318(1) (in this case, the rule overrides anything to the contrary in the articles).
[174] Table A 1985, art.41 made it clear that this was required. The present draft model articles revert to ambiguity.
[175] *El Sombrero Ltd, Re* [1958] Ch. 900 where the applicant shareholder held 900 of the company's 1,000 shares, the remaining 100 being held by the two directors whom the applicant wished to remove in exercise of his statutory powers under what is now s.168 and who refused to attend the meeting. The court directed that one member present in person or by proxy should constitute a quorate meeting. See also *Opera Photographic Ltd, Re* [1989] 1 W.L.R. 634 and *Sticky Fingers Restaurant Ltd, Re* [1992] B.C.L.C. 84.
[176] *Harman v BML Group Ltd* [1994] 1 W.L.R. 893, CA. On class rights generally see below, para.19–11.

the quorum provisions, whether contained in the articles or share-holders' agreement or applied by the Act.[177]

It might be noted that, in future, the quorum requirement will not be effective in private companies in producing deadlock where the shareholdings of the two contestants are not equal (and, of course, the quorum provision is unnecessary if they are). This is because the holder of the majority will be able to secure the passing of at least an ordinary resolution through the written resolution procedure, discussed above, without the need for a meeting. Some different protection in the articles will be required, such as a requirement for the consent of all shareholders to some or all resolutions of the company.

On the other hand, where the court takes the view that the provisions of the articles or the Act are being cynically exploited by a group of shareholders to block an effective meeting, it may exercise its s.306 powers in the broadest way. Thus, in *British Union for the Abolition of Vivisection, Re*[178] a company whose articles required personal attendance in order to vote had had a general meeting badly disrupted by a minority of members, and the committee feared that other members would in future be deterred from attending. On an application by a majority of the committee the court ordered that a meeting be held to consider a resolution for the abolition of the personal attendance rule, at which meeting the personal attendance rule itself would not apply and personal attendance would be permitted only to the members of the company's committee.

What is a meeting?

Thanks to modern technology it is no longer necessary that a meeting should require all those attending to be in the same room. If more turn up than had been foreseen, a valid meeting can still take place if proper arrangements have been made to direct the overflow to other rooms with adequate audio-visual links enabling everyone to participate in the discussion to the same extent as if all had been in the same room.[179] However, a meeting requires two-way, real time communication among all the participants. If relaxation of the real-time requirement is sought, it is necessary for the company, if a

15–31

---

[177] *Ross v Telford* [1998] 1 B.C.L.C. 82, CA; *Union Music Ltd v Watson* [2003] 1 B.C.L.C. 453, CA; *Woven Rugs Ltd, Re* [2002] 1 B.C.L.C. 324; *Vectone Entertainment Holding Ltd v South Entertainment Ltd* [2004] 2 B.C.L.C. 224.

[178] [1995] 2 B.C.L.C. 1. Contrast *Monnington v Easier Plc* [2006] 2 B.C.L.C. 283, where the judge took the view that a meeting to remove a director could be convened and conducted in accordance with the Act, but the result, as a consequence of the drafting of the removal section, would be ineffective. In that case the court had no jurisdiction to use its s.306 power to reform the Act.

[179] *Byng v London Life Association* [1990] Ch.170, CA. The Company Law Review proposed that this be made clear in legislation, if there was any doubt about the principle: Final Report, para.7.7.

private one, to take decisions through the use of written resolutions.[180]

Getting items onto the agenda and expressing views on agenda items

15–32   Rather than going through the process of requisitioning a meeting in order to discuss a particular piece of business, the shareholders may wish simply to add an item to the agenda of a meeting which the board has called in any event. This is most likely to be attractive in relation to the AGM, which, as we have seen, a public company is obliged to hold. The CLR proposed to make this facility of much greater utility to shareholders, but in the end the Government backed away from the proposal. Alternatively, some shareholders may simply wish to make known to other shareholders in advance of the meeting their views on a particular item which is already on the agenda, thereby hoping to encourage the other shareholders to attend the meeting, in person or by proxy, and support those views. We shall look in turn at these two possibilities.

Placing an item on the agenda

15–33   As we have seen, the AGM is normally convened by the board and, as part of that process, the board will be able to stipulate the items which it wishes to have discussed at the meeting. Under s.338 members representing not less than one-twentieth of the total voting rights of the members entitled to vote on the proposed resolution,[181] or 100 members holding shares on which there has been paid up an average sum per shareholder of not less than £100, may require the company to give notice of their resolutions which can then be considered at the next AGM. In a company with a large shareholding body shareholders with small shareholdings may find this second criterion easier to meet than the first, whereas a small number of institutional shareholders (perhaps even one) may be able to meet the first criterion. The second criterion for requiring a resolution to be placed on the agenda has also benefited from the steps which the Act has taken to protect the interests of "indirect" investors, i.e. those who hold their shares through nominees. Subject to safeguards, the 100 "members" may include those who are not members of the company but whose interest in the shares arises from the fact that a member of the company holds the shares on their behalf in the course

---

[180] See above, para.15–3.
[181] Thus, the section operates on the basis of the distribution of voting rights in the company. Non-voting shares do not count, and multiple voting shares will make the 5% target easier or more difficult to reach according to whether or not their holders support the requisition.

of a business and—a very important limitation—the indirect investor has the right to instruct the member how to exercise the voting rights.[182]

However, the company is not bound to give notice of the resolution unless certain of the conditions are met. First, the standard conditions, discussed above in relation to member's written resolutions, about the effectiveness of the resolution and so on must be met.[183] Secondly, the requisition, identifying the resolution of which notice is to be given, must be received by the company at least six weeks before the AGM or before the company gives notice to the members of the AGM.[184]

The third condition relates to the costs of circulating the resolution. In principle, those requesting the circulation must pay for it (unless the company resolves otherwise).[185] This was the previous law. However, the Company Law Review proposed that members' resolutions received in time to be circulated with the notice of the AGM should be circulated free of charge.[186] The Act does not accept that proposal and makes only the limited concession that circulation shall be free if the request is received before the end of the financial year preceding the meeting, which may be up to six months before the meeting is held.[187] The limited nature of this concession can be more fully understood when put in the context of a further reform proposal from the CLR which was rejected entirely.

One major problem with the members' resolution procedure is that **15–34** it is all too likely that something in the AGM circulation from the board will trigger the wish to place a shareholders' resolution on the agenda, but, since the minimum period of notice for calling the AGM is 21 days,[188] though the company may in fact give longer notice, there may well not be time for the members to respond to the AGM documentation and get their resolution to the company within the six week limit. In addition, the company's costs of circulation would be much greater in such a case, for the proposed resolution would have to be circulated separately. The Company Law Review proposed to

---

[182] s.153. The right to instruct the member as to the exercise of voting rights is most likely to arise by way of contract between the registered and beneficial owners. The safeguards are designed to verify that the non-members are indirect investors and that there is no double-counting of shares.

[183] s.338(2). See above, para.15–6. Besides being effective, the resolution must not be defamatory or frivolous or vexatious.

[184] s.338(4). Thus, the board cannot frustrate the requisitionists by convening a meeting on less than six weeks' notice after the receipt of the request or by giving very long notice of the AGM.

[185] s.340(2).

[186] Completing, paras 5.33–5.35.

[187] ss.340(1), 437 and 442. However, the costs of circulation should not be large if the members' resolution can be circulated along with the general circulation for the AGM. The company is obliged to circulate the resolution with the notice if this is possible: s.339(1).

[188] s.307(2). For listed companies the recommended period is rather longer (20 working days), but still not long enough to obviate the problem under discussion: Combined Code, para.D.2.4. On notice periods see below, para.15–37.

address the problem, at least in part, by requiring quoted companies to put their annual reports and accounts on their website within 120 days of the end of the financial year, after which there would be a "holding period" of 15 clear days, during which the company would be obliged to accept a members' resolution (having the support presently required) for circulation with the notice of the AGM and at the company's cost.[189] However, this opportunity for enhanced debate over the annual reports and accounts of large companies proved too much for management interests, who secured that this reform was not adopted.

For meetings other than AGMs there is no statutory procedure whereby members can add an item to the agenda of a meeting called by the board. However, as we have noted above, the members do have a statutory power to convene a meeting at any time (without costs to themselves) and to require circulation of a resolution to be considered at that meeting, though normally shareholders holding one-tenth of the voting rights are needed to secure the convening of such a meeting.[190] The fact that a statutory procedure is not available for adding an item to the agenda of a meeting, other than an AGM, convened by the board probably reflects the impracticability of so doing, when the minimum notice period for convening such a meeting is only 14 days and such meetings are often held urgently.

Circulation of members' statements

15–35 However, it is not enough for the shareholders to have their resolution circulated in advance of the AGM. It will have much more effect if it is accompanied by a statement from the proposers setting out its merits. Alternatively, the shareholders may wish to circulate only a statement and not a resolution, for example, where they wish to oppose a resolution from the board rather than to propose one of their own. The directors will undoubtedly make use of their power to circulate statements in support of their resolutions. Even if the directors do not directly control many votes, they are for the moment in control of the company and they can get their say in first and use all the facilities and funds of the company in putting their views across. They will have had all the time in the world in which to prepare a polished and closely reasoned circular and with it they will

---

[189] Final Report, paras 8.66 and 8.100–101. One can find only a pale reflection of this idea in the provisions enabling five per cent of the shareholders to require the company to place on its website a statement about the audit of the company's accounts or an auditor's ceasing to hold office for discussion at the company's accounts meeting (normally its AGM): ss.527–531, discussed at para.22–26.

[190] See above, para.15–29.

have been able to dispatch stamped and addressed proxy forms in their own favour.[191] And all this, of course, at the company's expense.[192]

Until the 1948 Act members opposing the board's resolution or proposing their resolutions had none of these advantages and, even now, only timid steps have been taken towards counteracting the immense advantage enjoyed by those in possession of the company's machinery. Such steps as have been taken are included in sections 314–316. These sections track the provisions of sections 338–340 dealing with members' requests for the circulation of resolutions and add the right, under similar conditions,[193] to have a statement of up to 1,000 words circulated to the members. It may be wondered why both matters are not dealt with in sections 338–340. The answer is that the earlier sections have a broader scope. They apply to any meeting of the company, including those of private companies (i.e. not just to AGMs), and the statement need not be tied to a proposal by the members of their own resolution.

In practice, however, this provision is of limited value, except where the statement is in support of a shareholders' resolution and is dispatched with it. The expense still has to be borne by the members—unless the company otherwise resolves[194]—and no substantial saving will result from the use of the company's facilities. In other cases (for example, when the circulars are designed to oppose proposals already forwarded by the board), little extra cost will be incurred by acting independently of the company and this will have a number of advantages. It will avoid any difficulty in obtaining sufficient requisitionists and will prevent delay, which may be fatal if notices of the meeting have already been dispatched. It will also obviate the need to cut the circular to 1,000 words and will enable the opposition to accompany it with proxies in their own favour.[195] Moreover, and from a tactical point of view this is vital, the board

---

[191] On proxies, see below.

[192] *Peel v LNW Railway* [1907] 1 Ch.5, CA. For an excellent description of the relative weakness of the opposition, see per Maugham J. in *Dorman Long & Co, Re* [1934] 1 Ch.635 at 657–658.

[193] Including the extension of the "100 member" right to indirect investors: s.153(1)(a). The main differences are that the request for the circulation has to be received only one week before the meeting: (s.314(4)(d)) and the company, or any person aggrieved, can make an application to the court for exemption from the obligation to circulate on grounds of abuse (s.317), as in the case of members' statements in support of written resolutions (above, para.15–6).

[194] s.316—subject to the limited concession where the request is received before the end of the financial year preceding the meeting. The company is likely so to resolve if the members' resolution is passed (which is unlikely) and may conceivably do so even if it is lost. In cases where it has not so resolved, there have sometimes been disputes on precisely what are properly to be regarded as "the company's expenses in giving effect" to the requisition—e.g. does it include the costs of a circular opposing the members' resolution? It ought not to.

[195] There is clearly no reason why the members' circular should not invite recipients to cancel any proxies previously given to the board but it seems that the company could refuse to despatch the members' proxy forms unless, perhaps, the words in them were counted against the 1,000 words allowed.

will not obtain advance information about the opposition's case, nor be able to send out at the same time a circular of its own in reply. Moreover, in the case of large companies the institutional investors will have mechanisms for communicating with each other which are not dependent upon the company's good offices and the financial press will often report the shareholders' concerns, thus encouraging prior communication among the shareholders and attendance at the meeting.

Notice of meetings and information about the agenda

15–36   In most cases, as we have seen, shareholder meetings are convened by the board. The main protection for the shareholders in such a case lies in the information made available to them in advance of the meeting and the length of notice required. On the basis of this information and during this period, they should be able to form a view whether the matter is sufficiently important for them to vote at the meeting or to attend it, and perhaps even to form an alliance with other shareholders to oppose the board, though, as we have noted, the shareholders start off on the back foot and will not have much time to organise their opposition. Naturally, these rules apply also to meetings convened by the members, for the requsitionists may not represent a majority of the members, who, in such a case, need to be protected against being "rail-roaded" into unwise decisions, whether the proposal emanates from the board or a minority of the members.

Length of notice

15–37   Prior to the 1948 Act, the length of notice of meetings, and how and to whom notice should be given, depended primarily on the company's articles. The only statutory regulation which could not be varied was that 21 days' notice was required for a meeting at which a special resolution was to be proposed. In other cases the Act of 1929 provided that, unless the articles otherwise directed (which they rarely did) only seven days' notice was needed. This left far too short a time for opposition to be organised.[196] Hence, it is now provided by s.307 of the 2006 Act that any provision of a company's articles shall be void in so far as it provides for the calling of a meeting by a shorter notice than 21 days' notice in the case of an annual general meeting or 14 days' notice in other cases. The company's articles may provide for longer notice but they cannot validly provide for shorter.[197] The

---

[196] Particularly as the period might be reduced still further by provisions requiring proxy forms to be lodged in advance of the meeting: see below, para.15–41.

[197] s.307(3). The previous requirement of 21 days' notice in the case of special resolutions has been removed. S.360 makes it clear that in this and related contexts "days" means "clear days", i.e. excluding the day of the meeting and the day on which the notice is given.

Shareholders Rights Directive[198] will require companies whose shares are traded on a regulated market to give 21 days' notice for all meetings (not just the AGM), unless the company offers the facility of voting by electronic means, in which case the shareholders in general meeting may decide to reduce the period to 14 days for meetings other than the AGM.[199] In practice, neither the statutory provisions nor those in the Directive have much significance for the AGMs of listed companies, since the Combined Code[200] suggests 20 working days' notice (in effect, 28 days' notice in statutory terms) for the AGM. However, the rules in the Directive will be significant for other meetings of listed companies.

However, if a meeting is called on shorter notice than the Act or the articles prescribe, it is deemed to be duly called if so agreed, in the case of an AGM, by all the members entitled to attend and vote.[201] In other cases a somewhat lower level of agreement will suffice.[202] This is a majority in number of those having the right to attend and vote[203] who must also hold the "requisite percentage" of the nominal value of the shares giving the right to attend and vote. That percentage is 95 per cent in the case of a public company and 90 per cent in the case of a private company (unless the article increases the percentage, which they may do but not beyond 95 per cent).[204] The effect of requiring, other than for AGMs where unanimity is the rule, the agreement of both a majority in number of members as well as a high percentage of the voting rights is that, where there is one or a small number of major shareholders and a number of small ones, at least some of small shareholders will need to concur in the major shareholders' view that short notice is appropriate.

Special notice

As we have seen, in certain circumstances a type of notice, unim- **15–38** aginatively and unhelpfully designated a "special notice", has to be given, the principal examples being when it is proposed to remove a director or to remove or not to reappoint the auditors.[205] In the light of the discussion of these examples in Chapters 14[206] and 22[207] respectively, little more needs to be said here except to emphasise that special notice is a type of notice very different from that discussed

---

[198] Above, fn.152, art.5.
[199] Art.5 does not apply to meetings of shareholders called to approve defensive measures proposed by management in a takeover. See para.28–19.
[200] Para.D.2.4. On the Combined Code, see above, para.14–29.
[201] s.337(2).
[202] s.307(4),(7).
[203] s.307(5).
[204] s.307(5),(6). In the case of companies without share capital the percentages relate to the total voting rights of all the members at the meeting.
[205] ss.168 and 510.
[206] At paras 14–18ff.
[207] At paras 22–19ff.

hitherto in this chapter. It is not notice of a meeting given *by* the company but notice given *to* the company of the intention to move a resolution at the meeting. Under s.312, where any provision of the Act requires special notice of a resolution, the resolution is ineffective unless notice of the intention to move it has been given to the company at least 28 days before the meeting.[208] The company must then give notice (in the normal sense) of the resolution, with the notice of the meeting or, if that is not practicable,[209] either by newspaper advertisement or by any other method allowed by the articles, at least 14 days before the meeting.[210]

All this achieves in itself is to ensure that the company and its members have plenty of time to consider the resolution but in the two principal cases where special notice is required supplementary provisions enable protective steps to be taken by the directors or auditors concerned. Under this heading it is also to be noted that the company's articles may require notice of certain types of resolution to be given to the company in advance of the meeting, and this requirement may limit shareholders' freedom of action at the meeting itself. For example, the articles may provide that no person shall be appointed as a director at a meeting of the company unless he or she is a director retiring by rotation, a person recommended by the board or a person of whose proposed appointment the company has been given at least 14 days' (and not more than 35 days') notice, together with the proposed appointee's consent.[211] At the general meeting of such a company it is thus not open to dissenting shareholders to put forward an alternative candidate for director on the spur of the moment, though it appears that the board could do so.

The contents of the notice of the meeting and circulars

15–39   Having previously left this matter to the articles,[212] statute now lays down some basic requirements. The notice of the meeting must give the date, time and place of the meeting; a statement of the general nature of the business to be transacted at the meeting; and any other matters required by the company's constitution.[213] The second of these three requirements is obviously the crucial one, for the member is entitled to be put in receipt of sufficient information about the

---

[208] s.321(1). This applies whether the resolution is proposed by the board or by a member. But the notice is effective if the meeting is called for a date 28 days or less after special notice has been given, so that the board can, in effect, forgive its own tardiness: s.312(4).

[209] e.g. if notices of the meeting have already been despatched.

[210] s.312(2),(3). But it seems that this notice has to be given only if the resolution is to be put on the agenda and that the mover cannot compel the company to do this unless he can and does invoke s.338, above: *Pedley v Inland Waterways Ltd* [1971] 1 All E.R. 209.

[211] Such a provision was included in Table A 1985, art.76, but it no longer appears. See the difficulties caused for the requisitionists by such a provision in *Rose v McGivern* [1998] 2 B.C.L.C. 593, above, fn.166.

[212] See, for example, Table A 1985, art.38.

[213] s.311.

business of the meeting to determine whether he or she will attend it.[214] But how specific must the notice be? If the meeting is an AGM at which all that is to be undertaken is what former Tables A described as "ordinary business",[215] all that is necessary is to list those matters. If, however, resolutions on other matters are to be proposed it is customary to set out the resolutions verbatim and to indicate that they are to be proposed as special or ordinary resolutions as the case may be. In the case of special resolutions s.283(6) requires that the notice of the meeting contains the text of the resolution and indicates the intention to propose it as a special resolution. The notice may also indicate that the resolution shall not be passed unless passed as a special resolution. This apparently curious provision follows from the further provision that anything that may be done by ordinary resolution may also be done by special resolution.[216] In effect, this gives the proposers of the resolution an ad hoc method of raising the majority required for the passing of an ordinary resolution to that required for a special resolution.

The CLR proposed that the requirement to set out the text of the resolution should be applied to all resolutions,[217] but this suggestion was not taken up. In all cases, the directors should ensure that, if the effect of the proposed business will be to confer a personal benefit on the directors, that should be made clear either in the notice or in a circular sent with it.[218]

In practice, the notice of a meeting will be of a formal nature but, if anything other than ordinary business is to be transacted, it will be accompanied by a circular explaining the reasons for the proposals and giving the opinion of the board thereon. Indeed, it is arguable that the common law principle that members should be put in a position to determine whether to attend the meeting requires such circulars, except where the nature of the business will be obvious to all the members from what is said in the notice of the meeting. Normally, therefore, the circular will be a reasoned case by the directors in favour of their own proposals or in opposition to proposals put forward by others. In deciding whether the nature of the business has been adequately described, the notice and circular can be

---

[214] Contrast *Choppington Collieries Ltd v Johnson* [1944] 1 All E.R. 762, CA with *Batchellor & Sons v Batchellor* [1945] Ch.169.
[215] The distinction between "ordinary" and "special" business of an AGM disappeared from Table A of 1985.
[216] ss.283(6)(b) and 282(5).
[217] Developing, para.4.45.
[218] On circulars and the cases applying this principle to circulars, see below.

read together.[219] But the circular must not misrepresent the facts; there have been many cases in which resolutions have been set aside on the ground that they were passed as a result of a "tricky" circular.[220] Misleading circulars may not only influence the vote at the meeting but also the decisions of the members whether to attend. For this reason, the fault in the circular should not be capable of cure even if the truth emerges at the meeting. For the same reason, it has been suggested that the notion of a "tricky" circular should embrace all misleading documents, whether the misinformation is the result of opportunism on the part of those putting it out or a genuine error on their part; and that the same principles should be applied to communications from shareholders to fellow members seeking their support for the requisition of a meeting of the company.[221]

If there is opposition to the board's proposals, the opposers will doubtless wish to state their case and a battle of circulars will result. It is here, however, that the superiority of the board's position becomes manifest. Even if the directors do not directly control many votes, they are for the moment in control of the company and they can get their say in first and use all the facilities and funds of the company in putting their views across. Even institutional shareholders, who may be able to stand the cost of the circulation, may find themselves on the back foot, whilst smaller shareholders may be unable to respond effectively at all. As we have seen,[222] the statutory provisions permitting 5 per cent of the members to require the company to send a statement of their views to all the members are singularly ineffective in practice.

Communicating notice of the meeting to the members

15–40 Having prescribed the basic content of the notice, the Act now goes on to specify to whom it should be given, thus giving statutory form to something previously contained in the model articles.[223] Those entitled to receive notice of the meeting are every member of the company (whether entitled to vote or not) and every director.[224] Members include those entitled to a share on the death or bankruptcy

---

[219] *Tiessen v Henderson* [1899] 1 Ch.861 at 867; *Moorgate Mercantile Holdings Ltd, Re* [1980] 1 W.L.R. 227 at 242F.

[220] *Kaye v Croydon Tramways Co* [1898] 1 Ch.358, CA; *Tiessen v Henderson* [1899] 1 Ch.861; *Baillie v Oriental Telephone Co* [1915] 1 Ch.503, CA; and see *Prudential Assurance v Newman Industries Ltd (No.2)* [1981] Ch.257; [1982] Ch.204, CA. The circular must be construed in a commonsense way. In the case of listed companies there is a further safeguard in the requirement that non-routine circulars have to be approved in advance by the FSA: see Listing Rules, 13.2 but also the exceptions set out in LR 13.8.

[221] *Rose v McGivern* [1998] 2 B.C.L.C. 593, on the former point following the Australian case of *Bain and Company Nominees Pty Ltd v Grace Bros Holdings Ltd* [1983] 1 A.C.L.C. 816.

[222] See above, para.13–35.

[223] s.310. For the former model provision see Table A 1985, art.38.

[224] s.310(1).

of a member, if the company has been notified of their entitlement.[225] However, these statutory provisions are subject to any provision in the company's articles (for example, excluding non-voting members from entitlement to receive notice). This also enables companies which need to, to deal with exceptional cases (such as that where holders of share-warrants to bearer are entitled to attend and vote).[226] The articles may also contain more prosaic matters, such as the rules identifying the address which the company will use to communicate with the members and removing the member's entitlement to be notified if the address so identified proves ineffective.[227] Accidental failure to give notice to one or more members shall not affect the validity of the meeting or resolution, and the company's articles can expand this relaxation, except for meetings or resolutions required by the members.[228]

Attending the meeting
Proxies

One of the important features of company meetings is that the members do not have to appear at the meeting in person; they may appoint another person (a proxy) to attend and vote on their behalf. At common law attending and voting had to be in person,[229] but it early became the normal practice to allow these duties to be undertaken by an agent or "proxy".[230] It should be noted that the system of proxy voting is not the same as that of postal voting. With postal voting the vote is cast directly by the member who holds the vote and he or she votes without attending a meeting. With proxy voting, the proxy votes on behalf of the member and at a meeting. In practice, there may not be much difference between the two when the proxy is given precise instructions and follows them, for then the member in effect makes up his or her mind on how the vote is to be cast in advance of the meeting. The Shareholders' Rights Directive requires Member States to permit companies to offer voting "by correspon-

15–41

---

[225] s.310(2).

[226] The usual practice is to give notice by a newspaper advertisement. The Listing Rules require this form of communication. On bearer shares see para.24–17, below.

[227] See arts.78–80 of the draft model set of articles for public companies.

[228] s.313. The "accidental omission" provision, of course, would not cover the deliberate omission to give notice to a troublesome member, nor does it cover a deliberate omission based on a mistaken belief that a member is not entitled to attend the meeting: *Musselwhite v Musselwhite & Son Ltd* [1962] Ch.964. But, if the omission is "accidental", it applies even if the meeting is called to pass a special resolution: *West Canadian Collieries Ltd, Re* [1962] Ch.370.

[229] *Harben v Philips* (1883) 23 Ch.D. 14, CA, and see *Woodford v Smith* [1970] 1 W.L.R. 806 at 810, per Mcgarry J.

[230] The word "proxy" is used indiscriminately to describe both the agent and the instrument appointing him.

dence in advance of the general meeting" to their shareholders, but does not require companies to adopt this procedure.[231]

Until the 1948 Act, however, the right to vote by proxy at a meeting of a company was dependent upon express authorisation in the articles. In practice this was almost invariably given; but not infrequently it was limited in some way, generally by providing that the proxy must himself be a member. Where there was such a limitation the scales were further tilted in favour of the board, for a member wishing to appoint a proxy to oppose the board's proposals might find difficulty in locating a fellow member prepared to attend and vote on his behalf. It was also customary to provide that proxy forms must be lodged in advance of the meeting. While this is a reasonable provision, in as much as it is necessary to check their validity before they are used at the meeting, it too could be used to favour the board if the period allowed for lodging was unreasonably short. Moreover, as already pointed out, it had become the practice for the board to send out proxy forms in their own favour with the notice of the meeting and for these to be stamped and addressed at the company's expense.

For all these reasons, although proxy voting gave an appearance of stockholder democracy, this appearance was deceptive and in reality the practice helped to enhance the dictatorship of the board. In recognition of this the Stock Exchange required that listed companies should send out "two-way" proxies, i.e. forms which enable members to direct the proxy whether to vote for or against any resolution. The FSA's listing rules currently require "three-way" proxies (i.e. for, against or abstain).[232]

15–42　The statutory provisions relating to proxies are now to be found in sections 324–331 of the Act. They show a further development in the movement of the proxy provisions from the articles to the Act. The effect is in many cases to make the proxy rules mandatory. Unless the Act expressly allows derogation from its provisions, the articles cannot reduce the statutory entitlements, though the Act gives the articles a general permission to improve them.[233] Any member is entitled to appoint another person (whether a member of the company or not) as his proxy to attend, speak and vote instead of himself at a meeting of the company.[234] In the case of a company having a

---

[231] Above, fn.152, Art.12. The articles may already provide for portal ballots under domestic law: see fn.256, below.

[232] LR 9.3.6. Notwithstanding recommendations that this should be a statutory requirement in all cases (e.g. by the Jenkins Committee, Cmnd. 1749, para.464) it still is not. An abstention from supporting a management proposal on the part of a larger shareholder is taken as a significant event in the case of listed companies.

[233] s.331.

[234] s.324(1). The restrictions under the previous law as to (a) the proxy's right to speak at meetings of public companies (b) the proxy's right to vote on a poll or (c) the member's right to appoint a proxy at all in a company not having a share capital, have all been swept away. The proxy may also demand a poll (s.329) and may even be elected the chair of the meeting (s.328).

share capital the member may appoint more than one proxy, provided each proxy is appointed to exercise rights attached to different shares.[235] Previously, this facility was subject to the articles of the company permitting it. It is now mandatory and is useful in the case for fund managers or nominee custodians[236] who may hold shares on behalf of a number of different beneficial owners who may hold different views on the matters at issue.

The members must be informed of their statutory rights to attend, speak and vote by proxy (and of any more extensive rights provided under the company's articles) in the notice convening the meeting.[237] Moreover, if proxies are solicited at the company's expense the invitation must be sent to all members entitled to attend and vote.[238] Thus, the board cannot invite only those from whom it expects a favourable response. Finally, the articles may not require that proxy forms (or other documents required to validate the proxy) must be lodged more than 48 hours before a meeting or adjourned meeting.[239]

It cannot be said, however, that these provisions have done much to curtail the tactical advantages possessed by the directors. They still strike the first blow and their solicitation of proxy votes is likely to meet with a substantial response before the opposition is able to get under way. Even if their proxies are in the "two-way" form, many members will complete and lodge them[240] after hearing but one side of the case, and only the most intelligent or obstinate are likely to withstand the impact of the, as yet, uncontradicted assertions of the directors. It is, of course, true that, once opposition is aroused, members may be persuaded to cancel their proxies, for these are

---

[235] s.324(2).

[236] See above, para.15–12.

[237] s.325. Failure to comply does not affect the validity of the meeting or anything done at it, but does constitute a criminal offence on the part of every officer in default: s.325(2)–(4). This notice is not given to the person nominated under s.146 to receive communications from the company (see above, para.15–21). That person is told that he or she may have a right to appoint a proxy or to instruct the member how to vote, depending on the agreement between the nominated person and the member (s.149). This is not a very useful notice but it is the best that can be provided.

[238] s.326(1), unless a proxy form or other information is issued at the request of the member and is available to all members upon request: s.326(2). As with s.325 (previous note) non-compliance is a criminal offence. Nothing is said about the impact of non-compliance on the validity of what is done at the meeting, presumably because s.326, unlike s.325, does not concern the content of the notice of the meeting.

[239] s.327. Hence proxies may now validly be lodged between the original date of the meeting and any adjournment for more than 48 hours. In the case of votes taken on polls, which are sometimes delayed, the relevant time is the time the poll is demanded or, if the poll is not to be taken within 48 hours of being demanded, 24 hours before the time appointed for the taking of the poll.

[240] Encouraged by the fact that postage is prepaid. Most two-way proxies provide that if neither "for" nor "against" is deleted the proxy will be used as the proxy thinks fit (i.e. as the board wish). LR 9.3.6 requires this to be expressly stated.

merely appointments of agents and the agents' authority can be withdrawn.[241] But in practice this rarely happens.

15–43   The issue of termination of the proxy's authority is now partly addressed in section 330. The aim of the provisions is to protect things done by the proxy from being brought into question if the company[242] has not received notification of the termination of the proxy's authority before the meeting. Thus, the proxy's vote will still be valid and the proxy will still count towards the quorum and can still validly join in demanding a poll, unless the company receives notice of termination of the authority before the commencement of the meeting.[243] The company's articles may set an earlier time for the notification of the termination, but not so as to make it earlier than 48 hours before the meeting (excluding non-working days).[244] However, the section deals only with the termination of the proxy's authority by "notice of termination". It has been held that a member may attend and vote in person and the company must then accept his vote instead of the proxy's,[245] i.e. that the proxy's authority may be terminated by a personal vote. However, two points should be noted about that case. First, it was based on the construction of the particular articles of the company in question, and so does not purport to lay down a general rule. Secondly, the company was aware the shareholder had voted in person and that the votes held by the proxy were accordingly reduced—indeed the company in that case wished positively to insist on the proxy's votes having been reduced. Thus, outside the matters covered by the section, the terms of the articles and the company's knowledge seem to be the crucial determinants of the ability of the proxy to exercise his or her voting rights as against the company, despite the withdrawal of the member's authority.

As between the member and the proxy, on ordinary agency principles a revocation is always effective if notified to the proxy before he has voted.[246] Conversely, it can be asked whether proxies are compelled to exercise the authority conferred upon them. Unless there is a binding contract or some equitable obligation compelling them to do so, the answer appears to be in the negative. Normally, there is only a gratuitous authorisation imposing no positive obligation on the

---

[241] Unless it is an "authority coupled with an interest" (e.g. when given to a transferee prior to registration of his transfer) or is an irrevocable power of attorney under the Power of Attorney Act 1971, s.4.

[242] Or someone other than the company if the articles require or permit the notice to be given to someone else: s.330(4).

[243] s.330(2),(3). In the case of voting at a poll to be held more than 48 hours after it is demanded the relevant time is the time appointed for the poll (s.330(3)(b)).

[244] s.330(5)–(7). In the case of polls the relevant point is as indicated in fn.?? for the lodging of proxies.

[245] *Cousins v International Brick Co* [1931] 2 Ch.90, CA.

[246] Unless the agency is irrevocable, see fn.241, above.

agent, but merely a negative obligation not to vote contrary to the instructions of his principal if he votes at all.[247] But there may be a binding contract, if, for example, the proxy is to be remunerated. Or there may be a fiduciary duty, if, for example, the proxy is the member's professional adviser. Although the directors are not normally in a fiduciary relationship to individual members, it seems that if they are appointed proxies and instructed how to vote they must obey their instructions.[248] If it were otherwise the two-way proxy would be valueless, for the board would only use the favourable proxies and ignore the others. Similarly, anyone who solicits proxies stating that he will use them in a certain way or as instructed, will, it is thought, be under a legal obligation to do as he has stated. But failing any such statement or definite instructions from his principal he will have a discretion and if he exercises it in good faith he will not be liable, whichever way he votes or if he refrains from voting.

Corporations' representatives

Since a company or other corporation is an artificial person which **15–44** must act through agents or employees, it might be supposed that, when a member is another company, it could attend and vote at meetings only by proxy. This, however, is not so. Section 323 provides that a body corporate may, by a resolution of its directors or other governing body,[249] authorise such person or persons as it thinks fit to act as its representative at meetings of companies of which it is a member (or creditor) and that the representative may exercise the same powers as could the body corporate if it were an individual.[250] With the expansion of the powers of the proxy, on the one hand, and the removal of the previous restriction that a company could appoint only a single corporate representative, it is unclear whether the proxy or the corporate representative is the more attractive mechanism for the corporate shareholder. The representative may have the slight advantage that, unlike a proxy, he or she can simply turn up at the meeting and is not subject to any requirement for documentation to be lodged with the company in advance of the meeting, as a proxy is. This may be particularly valuable where institutional investors are in discussion with the company's management right until the last minute

---

[247] This was discussed, but not decided, in *Oliver v Dalgleish* [1963] 1 W.L.R. 1274, which also left open the question of how far the company is concerned to see whether the proxy is obeying his instructions.

[248] Per Uthwatt J. in *Second Consolidated Trust v Ceylon Amalgamated Estates* [1943] 2 All E.R. 567 at 570. So held in the case of proxies solicited under an order of the court in connection with a scheme of arrangement in *Dorman Long & Co, Re* [1934] Ch.635 (this case contains an admirable discussion of the general problems of proxy voting). But in both the cases the proxy-holders were present at the meeting: *quaere* whether they can be compelled to attend: see [1934] Ch.664 at 665.

[249] e.g. its liquidator: *Hillman v Crystal Bowl Amusements Ltd* [1973] 1 W.L.R. 162.

[250] s.323(2). This is really a statutory example of an officer acting as an organ of the company rather than as a mere agent.

about the acceptability or otherwise of a resolution to be proposed at a meeting and, if those discussions break down, where it will be too late to appoint a proxy.[251]

Voting and verification of votes

15–45   Company law has traditionally proceeded on the basis that voting at a general meeting is a property right for those shareholders who have voting shares. This gives rise to two problems. Shareholders may choose not to exercise their votes at all; or they may vote at the behest of a non-shareholder. Both responses are capable of undermining the legitimacy of shareholder decisions, in the first case because the result is not representative of the shareholding body as a whole and in the second because it may reflect the interests of non-shareholders.

As to the first problem, we have seen above that for "fiduciary" investors the law of trusts may impose a duty to give consideration to the question of whether voting rights should be exercised in order to promote the interests of the beneficiaries of pension trusts. Under government pressure, the institutional shareholders generally have adopted a voluntary code on active engagement, including voting, with portfolio companies, so that for such shareholders voting is coming close to being a duty.[252] This is not a duty enshrined in the law but a "duty" resulting from the need to ward off proposals to enshrine such a duty in the law—the typical set of factors which produces what is often referred to as "self-regulation", though that is arguably an inappropriate term. Nevertheless, these developments address to some degree the problem of non-voting. Voting levels at general meetings of large companies improved from one-half to over sixty per cent in the three years 2004 to 2007.[253]

Votes on a show of hands and polls

15–46   This development has naturally led institutional shareholders to look closely at the rules on voting and to criticise rules which make their task difficult. Companies' articles normally provide for voting to be on a show of hands, unless a poll is demanded under the provisions discussed below, i.e. those present indicate their views by raising their hands. Proxies may vote on a show of hands, though previously this

---

[251] For the former restrictions on the proxy's powers, now removed, see fn.234 above. S.323 (3) and (4) deal with the situation where more than one representative is authorised to act on behalf of the company, but it is unclear that representatives can be assigned voting rights in respect of different parcels of shares held by the corporate shareholder in the way that is explicitly provided for in the case of a proxy. See s.324(2) and above para.16–41; and ICSA, *Guidance on Proxies 2 Corporate Representatives at General Meetings*, January 2008.

[252] See paras 15–14ff.

[253] *Review of the impediments to voting UK shares*, Report by Paul Myners to the Shareholder Voting Working Group, July 2007 (hereafter Myners 2007 Report). The issue of "empty" voting is considered at para.15–50, below.

was a matter left to be regulated by the articles, though a proxy holding instructions both for and against a resolution may find it very difficult to know how to act. The result on a show of hands may give a very imperfect picture of where the majority of the voting rights lie. The alternative voting mechanism is that of the poll in which members and proxies vote the shares which they represent, though a person is not obliged to vote all the shares represented or to vote them all the same way.[254] The voting process usually involves signing slips of paper indicating how many votes are being cast in each direction and the number of abstentions. This is a more cumbersome, if more accurate, voting process, and in large meetings it may not be practical to complete it during the meeting, because of the need to check proxy forms and the votes cast, though there must be scope for increasing the speed of the voting process by use of electronic technology.[255] What is not permitted, unless the articles specifically provide for it, is voting by postal ballot.[256] The latter may be thought strange since clearly such a referendum would be a better way of obtaining the views of the members. But the fiction is preserved that the result is determined after oral discussion at a meeting, although everybody knows that in the case of public companies the result is normally determined by proxies lodged before the meeting is held.[257]

Given the potential inaccuracy of the vote on the show of hands, its retention requires some explanation, especially as it is not common in other jurisdictions and so is often misunderstood by foreign investors.[258] The main argument in its favour is its speed and simplicity, enabling the company to take uncontroversial decisions quickly, though for completely uncontroversial decisions other techniques would do equally well, such as taking decisions without a vote, if no person present demands one. Where the resolution is controversial and where the voting process therefore comes under the strongest pressure, the show of hands has two main defects. The first is that it may disguise the level of opposition to the resolution, even if the show of hands produces the same result as a poll would have done. For example, a resolution may be passed on a show of hands by 80 to 20, but if a poll had been taken it might have been revealed that 500

---

[254] s.322. See also s.152. Thus, the chairman of the meeting, under a typical three-way proxy, will hold some votes for and some against the resolution to be voted on and some instructions to abstain, and can give effect to each set of instructions.

[255] If proxies have been gathered only by the company and have been lodged with, for example, the chairman of the meeting, calculating the vote will be easy. It is where there have been multiple proxy solicitations that the process can extend beyond the meeting.

[256] *McMillan v Le Roi Mining Co* [1906] 1 Ch.338. The articles rarely do so provide except in the case of clubs or other associations formed as companies limited by guarantee.

[257] As was well said in an American case (*Berendt v Bethlehem Steel Corp* (1931) 154 A. 321 at 322), statements made to a meeting of proxy-holders fall "upon ears not allowed to hear and minds not permitted to judge: upon automatons whose principals are uninformed of their own injury".

[258] Nevertheless, the second sub-paragraph of Art.14 of the Shareholders Rights Directive (above, fn.152) appears to permit the UK to keep it.

votes were in favour of the resolution and 400 against. It is particularly likely that the chairman of the meeting will not vote on a show
of hands and yet he or she may have been appointed the person to
receive the proxies solicited by the company. Such situations in
particular discourage institutional shareholders from voting by
proxy, because they feel their votes have no impact. In the case of
companies subject to the Combined Code these adverse consequences
are somewhat mitigated by the recommendation that companies
should display on their websites the proxies lodged for and against a
resolution where the vote was taken on a show of hands.[259]

The second, and more serious, defect in the show of hands is that it
may produce a result different from that which would be revealed by
a poll. This situation is addressed by the legislation through rules
dealing with the question of who can demand that a poll be taken,
even though a result has been achieved on a show of hands, or can
demand a poll even before a decision on a show of hands has been
taken.[260] The articles of companies invariably direct that a demand by
the chairman shall be effective.[261] This again strengthens the position
of the directors, for they run no risk of not being able to use their full
voting power. Further, the Act provides that the articles must not
exclude the right to demand a poll on any question, other than the
election of a chairman or the adjournment of the meeting. Nor may
the articles make ineffective a demand by not less than five members
having a right to vote on the resolution; or by members representing
not less than one-tenth of the total voting rights on the resolution; or
by members holding shares having a right to vote on which a sum has
been paid up equal to not less than one-tenth of the total sum paid up
on all the shares conferring that right.[262] Further, a proxy may
demand or join in demanding a poll.[263] This makes it difficult for the
articles to hamstring a sizeable opposition by depriving them of their
opportunity to exercise their full voting strength. Moreover, it is the
duty of the chairman to exercise his right to demand a poll so that
effect is given to the real sense of the meeting, and, if he realised that a

---

[259] Combined Code D.2.2. For the coverage of the CC see above at para.14–29.
[260] It is a question of construction of the relevant article whether a poll can be demanded before
there has been a vote on a show of hands: *Carruth v ICI* [1937] A.C. 707 at 754–755, HL;
Holmes v Keyes [1959] Ch. 199, CA. The draft model set of articles for public companies,
article 35, does provide for a poll to be demanded in advance of the meeting or at the
meeting but before the show of hands decision has been taken, as well as immediately after
the result has been declared of the show of hands vote.
[261] See art.35 of the draft model set of articles for public companies, which also allows the
directors to call for a poll, which facilitates the calling for a poll by the company in advance
of the meeting.
[262] s.321. In the absence of anything in the articles any member may demand a poll (*R. v
Wimbledon Local Board* (1882) 8 Q.B.D. 459, CA), and, of course, the articles may be more
generous than s.321: see art.35 of the draft model public company articles, which entitles
two members, rather than the statutory five, to demand a poll.
[263] s.329.

poll might well produce a different result, it seems that he would be legally bound to direct that a poll should be taken.[264]

Verifying votes

The Company Law Review received evidence that the reliability of **15–47** the results produced on a poll might not always be all it should be, because votes are "lost" somewhere in the chain between the person holding the voting power giving instructions as to how the votes are to be cast and the recording of those votes at the meeting.[265] Following this, the Act gives the same percentage of the members (including indirect members) as can place a resolution on the agenda of an AGM the right to requisition an independent assessor's report (normally from the company's auditors) on a poll at a general meeting of the company (but without any cost to the requisitionists).[266] This right applies only within "quoted companies" i.e. companies incorporated in one of the jurisdictions of the UK and listed on the Main Market of the London Stock Exchange or listed in another Member State of the EEA or having their shares traded on the New York Stock Exchange or Nasdaq.[267] The report must give the assessor's opinion, with supporting reasons, on a number of matters, notably whether the procedures adopted in connection with the poll were adequate, whether the votes (including proxy votes) were fairly and accurately recorded and whether the validity of the members' appointment of proxies was fairly assessed.[268] The context in which the right is set strongly suggests that the assessor is required to look only at the company's practices and procedures, so that defects in the passing of voting instructions down the chain before those instructions reach the company will not be picked up.

Certainly, the rights which the assessor is given to support the discharge of reporting function are all rights against the company and associated persons. The assessor has the right to attend the meeting of the company at which the poll is to be taken or any subsequent proceedings if the poll is not taken at the meeting itself and to be given copies of the documentation sent out by the company in connection with the meeting.[269] The assessor has a right of access to the company's records relating to the meeting and the poll and a right to

---

[264] *Second Consolidated Trust v Ceylon Amalgamated Estates* [1943] 2 All E.R. 567. In this case the chairman held proxies (without which there would have been no quorum) which, if voted, would have defeated the resolutions passed on a show of hands.

[265] Final Report, para.6.25. See also the Myners Report 2007 (above fn.253) pp.1–4.

[266] s.342. The right extends to class meetings at which it is proposed to vary the rights of any class of member: s.352. On variation of class rights see para.19–11.

[267] s.385. s.354 gives the Secretary of State the power by regulations, subject to affirmative resolution in Parliament, to extend the types of company to which the assessor's report requirement applies (but also to limit them).

[268] s.347(1).

[269] s.348.

require directors, officers, employees, members and agents of the company (including the operators of its share register) to provide information and explanation (unless this would involve a breach of legal professional privilege).[270] Non-compliance with the request for information or giving knowingly or recklessly misleading information in response to a request is a criminal offence.[271] The company must put on its website a copy of the report as soon as is reasonably practicable and keep the information there for two years and, at an earlier stage, must post some information about the appointment of the assessor.[272]

Non-compliance with the requirements for an assessor's report appears to have no impact on the validity of the resolution passed, though it is a criminal offence on the part of every officer in default for the company not to respond within one week of receiving a valid request by appointing an independent assessor to produce the report.[273] The request will normally be made before the meeting at which the poll is likely to be requested or conducted but a valid request may be made up to one week after the date on which the poll is held.[274] The appointed person must meet the statutory requirements for independence, which, however, are drawn so as not to exclude necessarily the company's auditors,[275] and the assessor must not have any other role in relation to the poll upon which a report is to be made.[276]

Record dates

15–48 One final issue, which should be mentioned, is the apparently fundamental one of establishing who is entitled to vote when the shares in a company are constantly traded. This can only sensibly be done by establishing some date prior to, but not too far in advance of, the meeting as the "record date". Those who are members on that date may vote, even if by the date of the meeting they have disposed of their shares, and those who have acquired shares since that date may not (except by instructing the shareholder on record how to vote). This is not an entirely satisfactory situation and in some continental European countries it is dealt with by "share-blocking" i.e. prohibiting trading between the record date and the date of the meeting. However, the disadvantages of this device, in terms of loss of liquidity, outweigh the advantages, and it has not been used in the United Kingdom and is now in any event to be prohibited by Article

---

[270] s.349.
[271] s.350.
[272] ss.351 and 353.
[273] s.343.
[274] s.342(4)(d).
[275] s.344. See notably s.344(2).
[276] s.343(3)(b).

7 of the Shareholders' Rights Directive.[277] The alternative is to set the record date close to the meeting date, so as to minimise the effect of trading post the record date, but to accept that some misallocation of voting rights will inevitably occur. This is the United Kingdom approach where the record date is set at not more than 48 hours before the meeting by the Uncertificated Securities Regulations, which are determinative in the case of publicly traded companies.[278]

Publicity for votes and resolutions

Whether or not an independent assessor is requested by the members, **15–49** a quoted company is required to post on its website the text of any resolution voted on through a poll at a general meeting and give the details of the votes cast in favour of or against it.[279] This will include resolutions which are not passed. Again, failure to do so does not affect the validity of the resolution but does constitute a criminal offence on the part of every officer in default. The Combined Code[280] goes a little further and suggests website publication of votes directed to be withheld and of the number of shares in respect of which valid proxy appointments were made. The purpose of the latter piece of information is presumably to indicate how important or, more likely, unimportant attending the meeting actually was.

Apart from this new requirement for quoted companies, the publicity requirements for the results of meetings are of a more traditional kind. Section 355 requires every company to keep records containing the minutes of all proceedings of general meetings and copies of resolutions passed otherwise than at meetings (for example, as written resolutions or by unanimous consent), and to keep those records for ten years.[281] Those records must be open to inspection by any member of the company (but not by the public) free of charge, who, for a prescribed fee, may require a copy of them.[282] The place of inspection is the company's registered office or some other place permitted under regulations made by the Secretary of State.[283] However, some resolutions of the company will be available publicly because they have to be supplied to the Registrar. This is true in particular of special resolutions, including such resolutions passed by unanimous consent.[284]

The minutes of the meetings and the records of the resolutions have some legal significance. A record of a resolution passed other than at

---

[277] Above, fn.152.
[278] The Uncertificated Securities Regulations 2001 (SI 2001/3755) reg.41(1). See below at para.27–4.
[279] s.341. This meets the requirements of Art.14 of the Shareholders' Rights Directive.
[280] D.2.2.
[281] The provisions apply also to class meetings: s.359.
[282] s.358(3).
[283] ss.358(1) and 1136.
[284] ss.29–30.

a meeting, if signed by a director or the company secretary, is evidence of the passing of the resolution, and the minutes of a meeting, if signed by the chair of that meeting or the following one, are evidence of the proceedings at the meeting. A record of proceedings at a meeting is deemed, unless the contrary is proved, to establish that the meeting was duly held, was conducted as recorded and all appointments made at it were valid. A record of a written resolution produces the same effect as to the requirements of the Act for passing written resolutions.[285]

"Empty" voting

15–50 The second problem identified above was that of members voting at the behest of non-members. In some cases this is entirely legitimate. We have noted, for example, that a nominee shareholder must vote as instructed by the beneficial owner.[286] This is unproblematic because the effect of the rule is to reunite the voting right with the person who has the economic interest in the share.[287] The issue with "empty" voting is that the right to vote is in fact exercised by a person with no or only a limited economic interest in it, to the exclusion of the person with the greater economic interest. There are two principal ways in which voting by those with no or only a limited economic interest in the shares can come about: contracts for differences (CfDs) and stock "lending".[288] Both are fairly sophisticated market arrangements, which do have a legitimate role, but whose impact on the allocation of voting rights has not been fully thought through.

In the first case, a person typically contracts with a counterparty for the difference in the price of a security at two points in time, and the counterparty, at least in a "long" CfD, will purchase the security in question as a hedge against its exposure under the CfD. In practice, though not as a matter of law, the holder of the CfD can often determine the way in which the counterparty exercises the votes attached to the shares acquired as a hedge. In this way a non-owner with a limited economic exposure to the share becomes in practice able to vote it. We discuss CfDs further below when dealing with takeovers, which is the one area where regulation (relating to disclosure of interests in shares) has addressed them.[289]

---

[285] s.356.

[286] Above, fn.85.

[287] Though perhaps less clear, other rules conferring voting rights on non-members can be justified as giving the vote to the person with the primary economic interest in the share. See, for example, the unpaid vendor of shares (*Musselwhite v C H Musselwhite & Sons Ltd* [1962] Ch. 964 but *cf. Michaels v Harley House (Marylebone) Ltd* [2000] 1 Ch. 104). Or the law may be indifferent as to the allocation by contract of the voting right as between two people each with an economic interest in the share: *Puddephatt v Leith* [1916] 1 Ch. 200 (mortgagor and mortgagee).

[288] ADRs (above, para.15–22) can also give rise to empty voting unless the depository is required to pass the governance rights onto the holder of the depository receipt.

[289] See para.28–43.

The second main form of "empty" voting arises out of stock "lending". This is a misnomer. With stock lending the shares are not lent by their holder to someone else but are transferred to that person on the basis that the transferee undertakes to re-transfer an equivalent number of shares (together with any dividend paid on them in the interim) upon demand to the transferor. The economic result may be near that of a loan of securities but because the legal form is an outright transfer of the shares to the other person, the right to vote is transferred to that other person as well. By the same token, because the economic effect of the transaction is that of a loan, for the transferee to exercise the voting rights leads to a disjunction between the voter and the person with the long-term economic interest in the shares (i.e. the lender). Again, there is no formal regulation of the voting rights issues arising with stock lending. The Myners Report 2007[290] reiterated its earlier recommendation that in the case of contentious votes the transferor should exercise its right to have shares re-transferred to it in order to be able to exercise the right to vote. However, it noted that, in the case of institutional shareholders, where, often, the shares were held by a custodian under a direct contract with the institution, whilst the right to vote the shares was delegated to a fund manager under a separate contract with the institution, the fund manager might be unaware whether the shares held by the custodian had been "lent" (perhaps under an automatic stock lending programme) and so would not be in a position to ask for the re-transfer of their equivalent.[291]

Miscellaneous matters

Chairman

Every meeting needs a person to preside over it, if it is not to descend **15–51** into chaos. The Act lays down the default rule that a member may be elected at the meeting by resolution to be its chair, but states that this provision is subject to any provisions in the articles as to how that person is to be chosen.[292] The articles invariably do deal with the matter. The draft model articles for public companies[293] sensibly take the view that the chairman ought to be a member of the board and accordingly provide that the chairman of the board shall also be the chairman of the meeting, which is what normally happens. However, if the chairman of the board is not present with ten minutes of the time appointed for the start of the meeting, the directors present must

---

[290] Above, fn.253. The Commission has consulted on a provision to be included in a Commission Recommendation which would say that "borrowed" shares should be voted only on instructions from the "lender".

[291] This situation could also lead to the fund manager purporting to vote shares the custodian did not hold at the relevant time and to the manager's proxy instructions to the company being rejected by the company on the grounds that they related to more shares than were held.

[292] s.319.

[293] art.30.

appoint a director or member to preside and, if there are no directors present, then those constituting the meeting do that job.

The position of chairman is an important and onerous one, for he or she will be in charge of the meeting and will be responsible for ensuring that its business is properly conducted. As chairman, he owes a duty to the meeting, not to the board of directors, even if he is a director.[294] He should see that the business of the meeting is efficiently conducted and that all shades of opinion are given a fair hearing. This may entail taking snap decisions on points of order, motions, amendments and questions, often deliberately designed to harass him, and upon the correctness of his ruling the validity of any resolution may depend.[295] He will probably require the company's legal adviser to be at his elbow, and this is one of the occasions when even the most cautious lawyer will have to give advice without an opportunity of referring to the authorities.

Adjournments

15–52 One situation in which it may be necessary to adjourn is when the meeting is inquorate, but this is a rare situation in public companies, because the quorum requirement is so low, i.e. two persons. What may present problems is the converse case where those attending the meeting are too many rather than too few, and the meeting becomes chaotic. It should be emphasised that an adjournment of a meeting is to be distinguished from an abandonment of it. In the latter case the meeting ends. If a new meeting is convened, new business, as well as any unfinished at the abandoned meeting, may be undertaken so long as proper notice is given of both. In contrast, if a meeting is adjourned, the adjourned meeting can undertake only the business of the original meeting[296] or such of it which had not been completed at that meeting. Indeed, it was thought necessary specifically to provide by what is now section 332 of the Act that where a resolution is passed at an adjourned meeting it shall "for all purposes be treated as having been passed on the date on which it was in fact passed and is not to be deemed to be passed on any earlier date".[297]

---

[294] See *Second Consolidated Trust v Ceylon Amalgamated Estates*, above, fn.264. Conversely, it seems a director may act as chairman of the meeting even though a resolution to be debated is critical of the board's policy: *Might SA v Redbus Interhouse Plc* [2004] 2 B.C.L.C. 449.

[295] For the sort of situation with which the chairman may have to cope if the members of a public company turn up in far larger numbers than the board has foreseen, see the case of *Byng v London Life Association Ltd* [1990] Ch. 170, CA (below) where his well-meaning efforts were in vain and the company had to convene a new meeting.

[296] Model articles for public companies, art.32(6). But a meeting can be adjourned despite the fact that it was not a meeting at which any substantive resolution could be passed: see *Byng v London Life Association Ltd* [1990] Ch. 170, CA. This must be right for otherwise an inquorate meeting could not be adjourned, as all Tables A have provided that they can.

[297] Were it otherwise, the company might unavoidably contravene the obligation to deliver to the Registrar a copy of the resolution within 15 days of its passage, as required, in the case of a considerable number of resolutions, under s.380.

The grounds for adjournment are normally set out in the articles. Article 32 of the draft model set for public companies provides for adjournment if those present agree, either at the chairman's suggestion or by adopting a resolution to that effect off their own motion. Basically this gives effect to the common law rule under which the chairman has no general right to adjourn a meeting if there are no circumstances preventing its effective continuance.[298] However, responding to the difficulties demonstrated in the *Byng* case,[299] the model article now further provides that the chairman may unilaterally adjourn a meeting if "it appears to the chairman of the meeting that an adjournment is necessary to protect the safety of any person attending the meeting or ensure that the business of the meeting is conducted in an orderly manner." However, this part of the model article does no more than reflect the position at common law. Helpfully, in the *Byng* case[300] this element of the common law power was held to continue to operate, even though the company's articles, reflecting the earlier model sets of articles, contained an express power to adjourn only with the consent of the meeting. But the power and duty must be exercised bona fide for the purpose of facilitating the meeting and not as a ploy to prevent or delay the taking of a decision to which the chairman objects;[301] and the chairman's exercise of the common law power must be a reasonable one.[302]

Finally, under article 32 no notice has to be given if a meeting is adjourned for less than 14 days; otherwise, seven days' clear notice must be given. Clearly if the adjournment is a temporary one and the meeting is resumed at the same place on the same day, this is fair enough; but otherwise it seems unfair to members who may, perhaps through no fault of their own, have found themselves unable to attend the meeting as they had intended. As a result they may not know that it has been adjourned and may be prevented from exercising their rights to attend the adjourned meeting.

Class meetings

In addition to general meetings it may be necessary to convene **15–53** separate meetings of classes of members or debenture-holders (for example, to consider variation of rights) or of creditors (for example, in connection with a reconstruction or in a winding up). Here again, the rules to be observed will depend on the company's articles con-

---

[298] *National Dwellings Society v Sykes* [1897] 3 Ch. 159; *John v Rees* [1970] Ch. 345 (which concerned, not a company meeting, but one of a Divisional Labour Party); *Byng v London Life Association Ltd*, above, fn.295.

[299] Above, fn.295.

[300] Above, fn.295.

[301] If the chairman purports to adjourn for such a reason, the meeting may elect another chairman and continue.

[302] *Byng*, above, fn.295.

strued in the light of the general law relating to meetings. However, the Act does provide that, for meetings of classes of shareholder, the statutory rules apply as they apply to general meetings, with some modifications.[303] The most important of the shareholder protections which are not applied are the members' power to require the directors to convene a meeting and the power of the court to order a meeting.[304] As we see in Chapter 19, the company, if it wishes to take certain steps, may be obliged to seek the consent of a class of shareholders and convene a meeting for that purpose, but the class has no general right on its own to meet to consider issues which concern it. On the other hand, some protections are more extensive at class meetings called to vary the rights of the class members: the two people constituting the quorum must represent at least one-third of the nominal value of the class of shares in question, except at an adjourned class meeting;[305] and any one member may demand a poll.[306]

In practice, very similar arrangements are incorporated in debenture trust deeds to regulate the conduct of meetings of debenture-holders.

At class meetings all members other than those of the class ought to be excluded, but if for convenience a joint meeting is held of the company and all separate classes, followed by separate polls, the court will not interfere if no objection has been taken by anyone present.[307]

Forms of communication by the company

15–54   Much of this chapter has concerned information (about meetings, for example) which is required to be supplied by the company to its members. In the case of AGMs of public companies that material will typically include the company's annual accounts and reports (considered in more detail in Chapter 21) which are today quite bulky documents. One important issue, therefore, is the form that the communication takes. That may be by traditional hard copy, electronically or by publication on the company's website. The Act takes some tentative steps towards encouraging the use of the latter two forms of communication, whilst not depriving members of their traditional supply of hard copy, if they wish to have it. Thus, section 1145 provides that where a member has received a communication otherwise than in hard copy (i.e. electronically or via a website), that

---

[303] ss.334 and 352 (and s.335 deals with class meetings of companies without share capital).
[304] ss.334(2) and 335(2) and above, paras 15–27 to 15–30.
[305] ss.334(4) and 335(4). At an adjourned meeting one person holding shares of the class or his proxy suffices. This makes sense only if the adjournment is because there was no quorum at the original meeting.
[306] ss.334(6) and 335(5).
[307] *Carruth v I C I* [1937] A.C. 707, HL.

member is entitled to be sent, without charge, a hard copy version of the document upon request within 21 days.

More generally, before a company can validly communicate with a member[308] otherwise than in hard copy, the consent or deemed consent of that member must be obtained. Electronic communication of documents is permitted only if the member has consented to that form of communication, either generally or for a specific class of documents.[309] As to website communication, that is permitted only if there has been actual agreement by the particular member,[310] as for electronic communication, or there has been deemed agreement. Deemed agreement arises where (a) the company's articles provide for website communication or the members have resolved to permit it and (b) the particular member has been asked by the company to agree to website communication for all or a particular class of documents and the company has not received a response within 28 days.[311] The deemed agreement may be revoked at any time by the member, but the burden is on the member to take this step.[312] To the extent that the deemed consent provisions apply to website communication only, it can be said that the Act puts more pressure on members to accept that form of communication than to accept electronic documents.

However, website communication has a number of disadvantages for the member over receiving an electronic document, which the Act aims to redress. First, unless the member constantly monitors the relevant website, he or she may not be aware of the availability of the document. Thus, the company is required to notify the member of the availability of the document, the address of the website and how to access the document.[313] This communication could be via an electronic document, if the member has consented to that form of communication. (Evidently, notification via the website itself will not do!) Secondly, hard copy or electronic communication gives the member their own copy of the document, whereas, unless downloaded, the member will lose access to the document when it is removed from the website. Thus, minimum rules are set for the period

---

[308] "Person" is the term used in Schedule 5 in relation to actual consent, so that its provisions embrace not just members but also those to whom governance rights have been transferred or information rights have been given (see above, para.15–17). The deemed consent provisions (see below) apply only to "members" but that term is expanded to include the two groups mentioned in the previous sentence: Sch.5, para.10(1).

[309] Sch.5, para.6.

[310] Sch.5, para.9(a).

[311] Sch.5, para.10(2) (3). The request may be repeated at twelve-monthly intervals if it does not produce acceptance or deemed acceptance. Similar provisions exist for debenture-holders: para.11.

[312] Sch.5, para.9(b).

[313] Sch.5, para.13(1).

during which the document must be available on the website. This is 28 days from the date on which the member was notified, as above, unless a specific section of the Act sets a different period.[314] There are a number of such specific provisions relating to the passing of resolutions.[315]

Forms of communication to the company

15–55 Where the company is the communicator, it is likely to be anxious to move away from the obligation to supply hard copy. When it is the potential receiver of communications, it may not be as anxious to facilitate the members' task. With members' communications to the company, we are necessarily concerned with their freedom to use electronic communications, rather than website based communication. The general rule in the Act is that the company is not obliged to accept electronic communications from other persons unless it has actually consented to this method of communication or is deemed to have accepted it.[316] Important for our purposes is that section 333 provides, where a company gives an electronic address in a notice calling a meeting or in a document from the company inviting the appointment of proxies, it is deemed to have agreed that any document relating to the meeting or proxy solicitation may be sent to it electronically at that address. In some other cases, the Act simply imposes a mandatory obligation on the company to accept communication in electronic form, for example, with regard to communication of assent to a written resolution.[317] Of course, a difficulty with electronic communications is authentication. What is the equivalent of a signature on a hard copy? Section 1146 provides that an electronic communication is authenticated if the identity of the sender is confirmed in the manner specified by the company or, in the absence of such specification, the document contains a statement of the identity of the sender and the company has no reason to doubt the truth of the statement.

CONCLUSIONS

15–56 At the beginning of this chapter we pointed out that the CLR recommended reforms to improve the governance rights of share-

---

[314] Sch.5, para.14. The Act does often require a longer period, for example, quoted companies being required to maintain web-site availability of the annual accounts and reports until the next set is available: s.430. There are also minimum standards set for the quality of the website: para.12.

[315] For example, s.299 (written resolutions: period is from date of circulation to date resolution lapses); s.309 (general meetings: date of notification to date of conclusion of meeting, which would include any adjournment of it). The latter section is also a little more prescriptive about the detail of the notification to be given when it concerns website documents for a general meeting.

[316] Sch.4, para.6.

[317] s.296(2).

holders, as part of its policy of making a shareholder-centred system of company law operate properly. The exercise of governance rights by shareholders may not be the only or even the most effective way of providing accountability on the part of management to shareholders—the threat of a takeover bid is probably more potent—but governance rights are certainly an important element of the accountability structure of company law. Having looked at the detail of the current law, how have the proposals of the CLR fared?

There has certainly been a great deal of tidying up and modernisation, notably the facilitation of electronic communication. Beyond that, in relation to private companies the written resolution provisions are now much simpler and likely to be more attractive, with the abandonment of the requirement of unanimity. For public companies, a major focus of concern was voting by the institutional shareholders, in terms of both the importance institutions attached to voting and the technical difficulties faced by indirect shareholders in casting their votes. The CLR proposed to rely mainly upon market developments and governmental suasion, rather than mandatory legal rules, to deal with both problems. Thus, there were to be fall-back powers only for the Secretary of State to require disclosure of voting by institutional shareholders[318] or to facilitate voting by indirect shareholders. As a result of pressure in Parliament, the fall-back powers designed to overcome the technical barriers to voting by indirect shareholders were given a slightly harder edge, in relation to information provision by quoted companies, but remain otherwise of a fall-back nature.[319] Meanwhile, policy-makers' understanding of the technical problems of voting has expanded with the development of the idea of "empty voting", a topic hardly touched on by the CLR, but it is not clear, even to the Shareholder Voting Working Party, consisting of those professionally involved in the area, what the correct solution should be.[320]

Finally, the CLR placed great store on the alignment of the AGM cycle with that for company reporting. Formally, that has been achieved, but the Government did not implement the further reform intended to take advantage of the alignment. This was the statutory "pause" of two weeks after circulation of the accounts and reports, during which members would be able to formulate resolutions, to be circulated by the company free of charge, to be debated at the AGM. This is undoubtedly a lost opportunity to turn the AGM into a more significant event.

---

[318] Now ss.277ff. See above, para.15–14.
[319] See above, para.15–21.
[320] See the Myners' Report 2007, above, fn.253.

CHAPTER 16

DIRECTORS' DUTIES

16–1   In Chapter 14 we saw that it is common for the articles of large companies to confer extremely broad discretionary powers upon the boards of such companies. The arguments in favour of giving the centralised management a broad power to run the company are essentially arguments of efficiency. At the same time, the grant of a broad discretion creates a real risk that the powers will be exercised by the directors other than for the purposes for which they were conferred, and in particular will be exercised more in the interests of the senior management themselves than of anyone else. A central part of company law is thus concerned with providing a framework of rules which, on the one hand, constrains the potential abuse by directors of their powers, whilst on the other hand does not so constrain the directors that the efficiency gains from having a strong centralised management are dissipated. This is an age-old problem for company law and one that is constantly re-visited by successive generations of rule-makers, for no one approach can be shown to have struck the balance in an appropriate manner. It was a major issue in the debates leading up to the passage of the Companies Act 2006.

On the part of the rule-makers a number of distinct responses to this intractable problem can be identified. In Chapter 14 itself we examined the extent to which rules relating to the structure and composition of the board itself and to the power of the shareholders to remove members of the board are used to constrain the exercise by the board of its powers and to produce accountability to the members of the company. In the previous chapter, we analysed the opportunities which the shareholders have to intervene directly in the management of the company by securing the passing at general meetings of resolutions binding the company or by subjecting the performance of the management to critical review. The taking of managerial decisions by the shareholders themselves is necessarily an activity of limited potential in large companies, since it flies in the face of the efficiency arguments for centralised management in the first place, but well-directed criticism of board performance may be more effective, especially if accompanied by an implicit or explicit threat of removal if performance is not improved.

In addition to rules on board structure and the governance rights of the members of the company there is a third set of rules of great longevity in our law which are intended to operate so as to constrain the board's exercise of its powers. These are the duties which company law lays directly on the members of the board as to limits within which they should exercise their powers. These rules for directors were developed by the courts at an early stage, often on the basis of analogy with the rules applying to trustees. The substantial corpus of learning on the nature and scope of these general fiduciary duties and duties of skill and care has remained until now largely within the common law. Both the Law Commission and the Company Law Review,[1] however, recommended a "high level" statutory restatement of the common law principles. This recommendation, controversial though it was, made its way into the Companies Act 2006, Chapter 2 of Part 10 of which is headed: "General Duties of Directors".

The main aim behind the proposal for a "high level" statutory **16–2** statement of directors' duties was to promote understanding of the basic principles underlying this area of law, especially among directors themselves. It was thought that this objective would be furthered if there was a relatively brief statutory statement of those principles in place of the previous situation whereby those principles had to be deduced from an elaborate body of case-law. The behavioural premises upon which this view was based were never extensively investigated. An objection to this move, which was heavily contested in particular by the Law Society and some of the leading commercial firms of solicitors in the City of London, was that such a reform was in danger of "freezing" the law of directors' duties and impeding its further development as circumstances changed. This contention could be refuted by the argument that the statutory statement was intended to be, and in the Companies Act 2006 is, a "high level" statement, which gives the courts plenty of interpretative scope when applying the principles to the changing circumstances of commercial life.

The CLR and the Law Commission did differ, however, on whether the statutory statement should be comprehensive, in the sense of setting out at a high level all the duties to which directors were subject (the CLR's view) or only the principal duties, leaving the courts to develop those duties which had not yet been clearly formulated in the cases (the Law Commissions' view).[2] In the end the Act comes closer to the Law Commissions' view. For example, section 173(3) makes it clear that that the issue of directors' duties to consider the interests of creditors is not dealt with comprehensively in Part 10 of the 2006 Act and the courts remain free to develop this aspect of the law, even at the level of general principle.[3] However, whilst the Act is not absolutely clear on this point, it seems likely that the statutory

---

[1] *Company Directors: Regulating Conflicts of Interest and Formulating a Statement of Duties*, Law Commission No.261 and Scottish Law Commission No.173, Cm. 4436 (1999); CLR, Final Report, Ch.3 and Annex C.

[2] *cf.* Developing, para.3.82 and Completing, para.3.31, on the one hand, and Law Commissions, above, fn.1 at para.4.28, on the other.

[3] See below, para.16–34.

enactment of the general duties of directors prevents or at least strongly discourages the courts from developing new general duties at common law, except where the legislation specifically contemplates such judicial creativity. However, this "freezing" of the general duties, if such it is, is probably not a significant restriction on the creativity of the courts. The seven general duties which are set out in Chapter 2 of Part 10 have been long established at common law and the courts have been able to deal with new problems by development of those general duties rather than by seeking to create new ones.

There was a second objection, which was more substantial, that a high-level statutory statement would cause confusion or uncertainty about the relationship between the statutory statement and existing or future decisions of the courts at common law. These matters are dealt with in subsections 170(3) and (4). The first subsection establishes the proposition that the general duties replace ("have effect in place of") the common law principles on which they are based. Consequently, in future, any allegation of breach of duty by the director to the company needs to be identified as a breach of one or more of the general duties set out in the statute, except in so far as the statutory statement preserves, as it does in relation to creditors' interests, the common law duties. However, the second subsection goes on to add two further propositions: first, the statutory general duties "shall be interpreted and applied in the same way as the common law duties or equitable principles", so that the existing case-law on the common law duties will remain, in most cases, relevant to the interpretation of the statutory duties. The second proposition is that "regard shall be had to the corresponding common law rules and equitable principles in interpreting and applying the general principles". This second proposition is less obvious in its purpose, which seems, however, to be as follows. The law relating to directors was often developed by the courts by analogy with the rules relating to the duties of trustees to their beneficiaries and agents to their principals. Those rules continue to be embodied largely in the common law. The second proposition enables the courts, in developing the statutory duties of directors, to take into account developments in the equivalent common law duties applying to trustees and agents.[4] Thus, there was no desire on the part of the legislature to cut the law of directors' duties off from its historical roots in the duties applying to other persons acting in a fiduciary character.

16–3   However, there is a difficulty underlying subsections 170(3) and (4), arising from the fact that, as we shall see, the statutory statement is more than simply a restatement of the common law. In some cases it clarifies areas of uncertainty in the common law, for example, in relation to the standard of care expected of directors, whilst in other cases it adopts a different approach from that of the common law, for

---

[4] HL Debs, vol. 678, col. 244, February 6, 2006 (Grand Committee), Lord Goldsmith.

example, in relation to the authorisation by independent directors of conflicts of duty. Where there is a departure in the statutory statement from the previous common law, it will obviously be inappropriate for the courts to refer to that common law in the interpretation of the statutory duties.[5] Since, however, the Act does not on its face reveal where it is confirming and where it is departing from the common law, it will be necessary to understand when the statute departs from the common law in order to determine the relevance of common law decisions to the interpretation of the statute.

The seven duties set out in Chapter 2 of Part 10 cover only the substantive content of the directors' duties. The Company Law Review hoped to be able to recommend codification of the remedies for breaches of duty as well, but did not have enough time to produce a workable schema. The Government initially continued with this work after the Review's final report but eventually abandoned the idea. However, the considerable work done in this direction has not been entirely lost since the interesting paper of Mr Richard Nolan, written for the Review, has been published.[6] The failure to carry through this project is regrettable, since the remedies for breach of duty constitute an area where the law is confused and inconsistent and where practitioners as well as business people would have benefited from reform and restatement. In the result, the Act simply provides in section 178 that the civil consequences of breaches of the statutory duties are to be those which would apply at common law.

To Whom and by Whom are the Duties Owed?

To whom are the general duties owed?

The company

Before turning to the substance of directors' duties, we need to ask **16–4** who are their beneficiaries, i.e. to whom are they owed? The answer in British law is clear: the common law formulation was that the duties of the directors were owed to "the company" and that is repeated in section 170(1) in respect of the statutory duties. The importance of this point arises mainly in relation to the enforcement of those duties. First, it tells you that those duties are not owed to persons other than the company, for example, individual shareholders or employees. Secondly, it tells you that only those who are able to act as or on

---

[5] "The courts should continue to refer to existing case law on the corresponding common law rules and equitable principles, except where it is obviously irreconcilable with the statutory statement." (HC Debs, Standing Committee D, Thirteenth Sitting, July 6, 2006, col. 536 (The Solicitor-General)).

[6] R. C. Nolan, "Enacting Civil Remedies in Company Law" (2001) 1 J.C.L.S. 245.

behalf of the company can enforce the duties. As we shall see in Chapter 17, the issue of who can act on behalf of the company to enforce its rights, and in particular the question of whether an individual shareholder can do so through the so-called "derivative action", has caused considerable controversy ever since the emergence of modern company law in the nineteenth century. That is also an area where the Companies Act 2006 has introduced a major reform.

Individual shareholders

16–5 We shall leave the derivative action until Chapter 17. However, we need to touch briefly on the question of duties owed by directors directly to individual shareholders. It is clear that the statutory duties are owed only to the company, but equally clear that the Act does not purport to answer the question whether fiduciary or other duties are owed by the directors to shareholders individually. That issue is left to the common law. Traditionally, and still today, the common law has been reluctant to recognise directors' general duties as being owed to shareholders individually. This is hardly surprising. Recognition of duties owed individually would undermine the collective nature of the shareholders' association in a company. It would also undermine the rule that the duties are owed to and are enforceable by the company. If the directors owed to individual shareholders a set of duties parallel to those owed by them to the company, the restrictions on the derivative action could easily be side-stepped by means of the individual shareholder suing to enforce, not the company's rights, but his or her own rights.[7]

However, the precept that directors' duties are not owed to individual shareholders applies only to those duties which directors are subject to simply by virtue of their appointment and actions as directors. There may well be in a particular case dealings between one or more directors and one or more of the shareholders as a result of which a duty of some sort becomes owed by a director to one or more shareholders. This principle has now been fully accepted in English law as a result of the recent decision of the Court of Appeal in *Peskin v Anderson*,[8] where Mummery L.J. distinguished clearly between the fiduciary duties owed by directors to the company which arise out of the relationship between the director and the company, and fiduciary duties owed to shareholders which are dependent upon establishing "a special factual relationship between the directors and the shareholders in the particular case".

The crucial question, therefore, is what sort of dealing needs to

---

[7] On similar grounds the court rejected an attempt to create a parallel set of duties owed by directors to individual shareholders via implied terms in the articles of association: *Towcester Racecourse Co Ltd v The Racecourse Association Ltd* [2003] 1 B.C.L.C. 260.

[8] [2001] 1 B.C.L.C. 372 at 379.

take place between director and shareholder in order to trigger a fiduciary or other duty owed to an individual shareholder by the directors. Such a duty will certainly arise where, on the facts, the directors place themselves, as against shareholders individually, in one of the established legal relationships to which fiduciary duties are attached, such as agency. This may arise, for example, where the shareholders authorise the directors to sell their shares on their behalf to a potential takeover bidder.[9] If, in the course of such a relationship, the directors come across information which is pertinent to the shareholders' decision whether or on what terms to sell the shares, they would normally be obliged to disclose it to the shareholders on whose behalf they are acting. On the other hand, in *Percival v Wright*,[10] which is the leading authority for the proposition that the directors' duties as directors are not owed to the shareholders individually, the directors purchased shares from their members without revealing that negotiations were in progress for the sale of the company's undertaking at a favourable price. They were held not to be in breach of duty through their non-disclosure. Here, the shareholders approached the directors directly and sought to persuade the directors to purchase their shares themselves rather than to act as the shareholders' agents to sell the shares to third parties.

Nevertheless, there is no doubt that the directors of a company are likely to have much more information at their disposal about the company and so are likely to be at an advantage when dealing with the members about their shares. The law of agency, as we have just seen, will cover some, but not all of this ground. Can the doctrine of a "special factual relationship" be extended beyond the law of agency? Commonwealth authority established some time ago that it can. In *Coleman v Myers*[11] the New Zealand Court of Appeal found that a fiduciary duty of disclosure arose, even in the absence of agency, in the case of a small family company where there was a gross disparity of knowledge between the directors and the shareholders and where the shareholders of the company had traditionally relied on the directors for information and advice. When the directors negotiated with the shareholders for the purchase of their shares and, therefore, were clearly *not* acting on behalf of the shareholders, they were nevertheless held to be subject to a fiduciary duty of full disclosure of relevant facts about the company to the shareholders. The New

16–6

---

[9] *Briess v Woolley* [1954] A.C. 333, HL; *Allen v Hyett* (1914) 30 T.L.R. 444, PC.

[10] [1902] 2 Ch.421. This applies even if all the shares are owned by a holding company with which the directors have service contracts: *Bell v Lever Bros* [1932] A.C. 161, HL.

[11] [1977] 2 N.Z.L.R. 225, NZCA. In the Supreme Court (*ibid.*) Mahon J. had held that *Percival v Wright* was wrongly decided but the Court of Appeal distinguished it. See also *Brunningshausen v Glavanics* (1999) 46 NSWLR 538, CANSW.

Zealand decision was approved by the English Court of Appeal in *Peskin v Anderson*,[12] though the English decision also reveals the limits of the rule. In the English case, directors were not obliged to disclose to shareholders their plans for the company, even though the shareholders' decision on the sale of their shares would have been affected by the knowledge, where the directors were not parties to or otherwise involved in the sale of the shares, and the company's interests arguably required the directors' plans to be kept secret until they matured.

Despite the recent significant developments in English law, based on a "special relationship" exception to the general proposition that directors do not owe duties directly to the shareholders, the exception is essentially one of significance for family or small companies, and does not substantially reduce, within companies with large shareholder bodies, the significance of the general proposition. The only situation where the expanded notion of directors' fiduciary duties is likely to apply to a company with substantial numbers of shareholders is where advice is given by directors in the course of a takeover bid. In *A Company, Re*[13] Hoffmann J. held that directors were not obliged to offer their shareholders advice on the bid, but, if they did so, they must do so "with a view to enabling the shareholders ... to sell, if they so wish, at the best price" and not, for example, in order to favour one bid, which the directors supported, over another, which they did not.[14] The directors, fiduciary-like, must in this case give advice in order to further the interests of the shareholders.

Other stakeholders

16–7 If British company law has been reluctant to recognise general duties owed by directors to individual shareholders, it perhaps goes without saying that it has not recognised such duties owed to individual employees or creditors or other groups upon whom the successful functioning of the company depends. It is important to distinguish this issue (duties owed directly to stakeholder groups) from the question of how far directors' duties owed to the company require the directors to take into account the interests of stakeholder groups. Explicit duties of this latter kind were recommended by the Company

---

[12] See above, fn.8, following the decisions of Browne-Wilkinson V.-C. in *Chez Nico (Restaurants) Ltd, Re* [1991] B.C.C. 736 at 750 and, though not cited, of David Mackie Q.C. in *Platt v Platt* [1999] 2 B.C.L.C. 745 (the Court of Appeal in that case did not deal with the point: [2001] 1 B.C.L.C. 698).

[13] [1986] B.C.L.C. 382. The case involved an application under s.459 (see Ch.20, below), but the judge's analysis appears to have related to the common law.

[14] Even then, the decision is likely to be of interest only to private companies with large shareholder bodies, since bids for public and listed companies will be governed by the City Code on Take-overs and Mergers (below, Ch.28), which both requires directors to give advice and attempts to ensure that that advice is given in the interests of the shareholders. The more demanding provisions of the Code will in practice overtake those of the common law.

Law Review and were embodied in the 2006 Act. We shall deal with them below in our analysis of the statutory duties.

By whom are the general duties owed?
De facto and shadow directors
The general statutory duties to be discussed in this chapter are clearly owed by those who have been properly appointed as directors of the company. From the early days, however, the courts have applied the common law and statutory duties also to persons who act as directors, even though they have not been appointed as such—normally referred as "de facto directors".[15] There seems to be no doubt but that the general statutory duties apply to de facto directors.[16] However, some years ago the legislature created a third category of director—the "shadow director". This is a person in accordance with whose directions or instructions the directors of a company are accustomed to act,[17] whether or not the person giving the instructions has been formally appointed as director or acts as such. A number of the specific statutory duties, which supplement the general duties and are to be found in Chapters 3 and 4 of Part 10, are expressed to apply also to shadow directors. However, in relation to the general duties contained in Chapter 2 section 170(5) unhelpfully provides that they apply to shadow directors "to the extent that the corresponding common law rules or equitable principles apply". To what extent does the common law apply rules corresponding to the statutory general duties to shadow directors? This is an issue on which there is surprisingly little authority. In *Ultraframe (UK) Ltd v Fielding*[18] Lewison J. took the view that directors' fiduciary duties did not apply to shadow directors, on the grounds that a shadow director, unlike a de facto or properly appointed director, had not undertaken to act on behalf of the company and so had not put him- or herself in a fiduciary relationship with the company. This decision shows the continuing influence of the trustee analogy in the development of directors' duties, but it is submitted that in this case it is an unfortunate one. The judge's approach provides a relatively easy route for

16–8

---

[15] *Canadian Land Reclaiming and Colonizing Co, Re* (1880) 14 Ch. D. 660—director not properly appointed because of his failure to take up shares in the company which action its articles stipulated to be a condition for appointment as director. For a more detailed discussion in a modern context of what makes a person a de facto director see *Secretary of State for Trade and Industry v Tjolle* [1998] 1 B.C.L.C. 333. This case shows that the important question is whether the person is factually engaged in the central management of the company; if not, then he or she will not be a de facto director, even if the title of "director" has been conferred on the person in question.

[16] There is some statutory support for this view in the definition of a director in section 250 as including "any person occupying the position of director, by whatever name called".

[17] s.251.

[18] [2005] EWHC 1638 (Ch) at paras 1279ff—the case went on appeal but the CA did not consider this issue. *Cf. Yukong Line Ltd v Rendsburg Investments Corp of Liberia* [1998] 1 W.L.R. 294, in which Toulson J., in a brief and unargued dictum, took the opposite view.

the true mover behind the company's strategy to distance him- or herself from liability for the decisions taken, by appointing a compliant board and giving it instructions at crucial points.[19] More important, if the purpose of the law of directors' duties is to constrain the exercise of the discretion vested in the board, it would be unfortunate if those rules did not reach all those involved in that exercise.

The source of the difficulty here may be the firm distinction which the courts have sought to draw between a de facto and a shadow director. Although the language used to define a shadow director is of some antiquity,[20] the term "shadow director" was applied as a shorthand way of referring to the definition only in the Companies Act 1980. As we have indicated, this was done in order to make clear the scope of application of the specific duties created by that Act which apply to certain transactions entered into by directors with their companies, the modern forms of which we discuss below. The 1980 Act set the courts off on the task of defining the difference between a de facto and a shadow director. In *Hydrodam (Corby) Ltd, Re*[21] Millett J. took the view that in nearly all cases the two categories were mutually exclusive.

> "A *de facto* director ... is one who claims to act and purports to act as a director, although not validly appointed as such. A shadow director, by contrast, does not claim or purport to act as director. On the contrary, he claims not to be a director. He lurks in the shadows, sheltering behind others who, he claims, are the only directors of the company to the exclusion of himself."

Although doubts have subsequently been expressed about whether the categories are mutually exclusive, nevertheless there is agreement that they do not overlap extensively. It is important to draw this distinction in a statutory context because some statutory provisions apply to shadow directors and directors whilst others apply only to directors, in which category, as said, the courts have long included de facto directors. However, it is not clear that the differences between the two categories of directors should be the main focus of attention when deciding the applicability of the common law, now the general statutory, duties of directors. As Robert Walker L. J. pointed out in

---

[19] The judge did accept that the shadow director might attract liability under the rules relating to the involvement of third parties in breaches of directors' duties (see below, para.16–97), but these provisions are relatively restrictive.

[20] It seems to have been introduced by the Companies (Particulars as to Directors) Act 1917, s.3.

[21] [1994] 2 B.C.L.C. 180, 183.

Kaytech International Plc, Re[22] "the two concepts do have at least this much in common, that an individual who was not a *de jure* director is alleged to have exercised real influence ... in the corporate governance of a company." It is submitted that in terms of the application of the common law duties of directors, the element of commonality (the "real influence") between shadow and de facto directors is more important then the elements of difference. In principle, therefore, the general duties should apply to shadow directors. Of course, the common law duties should be applied to shadow directors only to the extent that they have exercised control over the board: it is not inherent in the definition of a shadow director that he or she should have controlled all the activities of the board.[23]

It should be noted that, even if the courts conclude that the general duties apply to shadow directors in appropriate circumstances, nevertheless section 250(3) provides one exception. A company is not to be regarded as the shadow director of its subsidiary for the purpose of the general duties by reason only that the directors of the subsidiary are accustomed to act on the instructions of the parent. A parent company can thus impose a common policy on the group of companies which it controls without placing itself in breach of duty to the subsidiary (for example, because the group policy is not in the best interests of the subsidiary). This provision does not answer the question whether the directors of the subsidiary can agree to implement the group policy without placing themselves in breach of duty to the subsidiary, which is discussed in para.16–30 below.

Senior managers

The general statutory duties set out in Chapter 2 of Part 10 clearly do **16–9** not apply to managers who are not directors of the company. However, it is important to note that, when applying the law relating to directors' duties, the courts do not distinguish between the actions of the director as director and actions *qua* manager, where the director is an executive director of the company. Those duties will apply to both aspects of the directors' activities.[24] In consequence, some actions by senior managers of the company, provided they are also directors of the company, will be subject to the controls of the

---

[22] [1999] 2 B.C.L.C. 351, 424, CA. The Law Commissions took the view that the shadow director was subject to the common law duties and certainly ought to be "where he effectively acts as a director through the people he can influence". (Law Commission and Scottish Law Commission, *Company Directors: Regulating Conflicts of Interest and Formulating a Statement of Duties, A Joint Consultation Paper*, 1998, para.17.15); and the CLR took a similar view: Completing, para.4.7.

[23] *Secretary of State for Trade and Industry v Deverell* [2001] Ch.340 at para.35, CA.

[24] For a recent example see *Item Software (UK) Ltd v Fassihi* [2005] 2 B.C.L.C. 91, CA, where the consequence of this approach was to subject the director to a higher standard of fiduciary duty than would have been applicable, had he only been an employee, albeit a senior one.

general statutory duties. Although management theory may posit that it is the role of the board in large companies to set the company's strategy and to oversee its execution, rather than to execute it itself, the law of directors' duties does not make this distinction in the case of a director who has both a board position and a non-board executive function. This is consonant with the traditional provision in companies' articles that the management of the company is a matter for the board of directors.

However, it can be asked whether the fiduciary duties apply as a matter of common law to the senior managers of the company who are not directors. In *Canadian Aero Services Ltd v O'Malley* the Canadian Supreme Court approved a statement from an earlier edition of this book that directors' duties apply to those "officials of the company who are authorised to act on its behalf and in particular to those acting in a senior management capacity".[25] That view has not been adopted expressly in any English court. Moreover, it is clear that, in principle, the employment relationship is not a fiduciary relationship, so that it would be inappropriate to apply the full range of directors' duties to even senior employees. However, this proposition is subject to a number of qualifications. First, a senior employee who does in fact discharge the duties of a director may be classed as a de facto director, under the principles discussed above. Secondly, the courts have held that, as a result of the specific terms of an employee's contract and of the particular duties undertaken by him or her, a fiduciary relationship may arise between employee and employer, even in the case of employees who are not part of senior management, though the fiduciary duty may be restricted to some part of their overall duties.[26] The view of the Canadian Supreme Court is not inconsistent with these developments, since it too was derived from an analysis of the functions of the employees in question as senior management employees, though there will be scope for argument on the facts of each case about how extensive the fiduciary aspects of the employee's duties are. It goes without saying that, should a senior manager place him- or herself in an agency relationship with the company, then the normal fiduciary incidents of that relationship would arise. Thirdly, the implied and mutual duty of trust and confidence which is imported into all contracts of employment can in some cases operate in the same way as directors' fiduciary duties. This is particularly the case in relation to competitive activities on the part of an employee or the non-disclosure by senior

---

[25] (1973) 40 D.L.R. (3d) 371 at 381.
[26] *University of Nottingham v Fishel* [2000] ICR 1462; *Shepherds Investments Ltd v Walters* [2007] IRLR 110; *Helmet Integrated Systems Ltd v Tunnard* [2007] IRLR 126, CA. However, the duty of care (which is not dependent upon the existence of a fiduciary relationship) imposed on employees seems to be similar to that now required of directors.

managers of the wrongdoing of fellow employees and in some cases their own wrongdoing.[27]

The exclusion of senior managers as such from the statutory general duties of directors probably depends upon the continuation of the UK practice, as recommended in the Combined Code,[28] that the board should contain a substantial number of executive directors. If British practice were to move in the US direction of reducing the number of executive directors on the board, sometimes to one (the CEO), confining the statutory duties to members of the board might become a policy which needed to be re-considered.

Finally, the above discussion has concerned the fiduciary duties of employees and directors. In relation to the statutory duty of care (see below), which equally applies only to directors, the common law duty of care required of employees seems to come very close to that now required of directors (taking account of the fact that the application of the reasonable care standard will produce different results in different circumstances).[29]

Former directors

At common law the general duties of directors attach from the date **16–10** when the director's appointment takes effect[30] but do not necessarily cease when his appointment ends. The second part of the common law position is explicitly confirmed by section 170(2) which provides that a person who ceases to be a director continues to be subject to two of the seven general duties, namely those relating to corporate opportunities of which he had become aware whilst still a director and the taking of a benefit from a third party in respect of acts or omissions whilst still a director. However, those two duties are to be applied by the courts to former directors "subject to any necessary adaptations", for example, to take account of the fact that the former director may no longer have up-to-date knowledge of the conduct of the company's affairs. In this way it can be said that liability is

---

[27] *Shepherds Investments Ltd v Walters* (previous note) at paras [129]–[130]; *Sybron Corp v Rochem Ltd* [1984] Ch.112, CA; *Tesco Stores Ltd v Pook* [2004] IRLR 618. On disclosure of wrongdoing the main difference between a senior manager and a director concerns the extent to which they are obliged to disclose their own wrongdoing: see *Bell v Lever Bros* [1932] A.C. 161, HL (suggesting an employee is never under a duty to disclose his own wrongdoing) and *Item Software (UK) Ltd v Fassihi* [2005] 2 B.C.L.C. 91, CA, taking a narrower view.

[28] See para.14–29.

[29] For employees see *Lister v Romford Ice and Cold Storage Co Ltd* [1957] A.C. 555, HL and *Janata Bank v Ahmed* [1981] I.C.R. 791, CA and for the duty of care required of directors see the following section. For a case where the defendant was sued for breach of his duty of care both as a director and as an employee see *Simtel Communications Ltd v Rebak* [2006] 2 B.C.L.C. 571.

[30] In *Lindgren v L & P Estates Ltd* [1968] Ch.572, the Court of Appeal rejected an argument that a "director-elect" is in a fiduciary relationship to the company.

imposed in respect of actions which straddle the time before and after the director ceased to hold office.[31]

Particularly difficult issues can arise in relation to the analysis of actions by directors, whilst still directors, but after they have given notice of resignation. In such cases the director is not (yet) a former director and the issue is discussed below under "Competing with the company".

Directors of insolvent companies

16–11   When a company enters into an insolvency procedure (liquidation, administration or receivership), the situation under British law, unlike that in the US, is that the powers of the directors are substantially curtailed and the direction of the business passes into the hands of the insolvency practitioner appointed to act in one or other of these roles and who acts in the interests of the creditors. This is likely to have a substantial impact on what the law of directors' duties requires of the directors in practice, but does not in principle relieve the directors of their obligations to the company.[32]

DIRECTORS' DUTIES OF SKILL, CARE AND DILIGENCE

Historical development

16–12   We turn now to the substance of the duties which directors assume when they take up office. It is common in comparative analysis of company law systems to divide those duties into duties of loyalty and duties of care. Although the line between these two sets of duties is not absolutely clear, they broadly correspond to the two main risks which shareholders run when management of their company is delegated to the board. The board may be active, but not in the direction of promoting the shareholders' interests; or the board may be slack or incompetent. We shall adopt this division here, for it corresponds also to the two basic common law sources of the rules on directors' duties in English law: duties of loyalty based on fiduciary principles, developed initially by courts of equity, and duties of skill and care which rest, with some particular twists, on the principles of the law of negligence. However, it should be noted that the general duties laid out in Chapter 2 of Part 10 are not divided in this way. The

---

[31] This point is discussed further below in relation to the taking of corporate opportunities, which is where it most often arises.

[32] Directors cannot, for example, be held liable for the failure to exercise powers which they no longer have. In *Ultraframe (UK) Ltd v Fielding* [2005] UKHC 1638 at [1330] Lewison J. suggested the "no conflict" rule would not apply either (though the "no profit" and basic loyalty duties would continue to bite).

duty of care appears as the fourth of the seven duties. It is with this duty that we begin.

The issue in this area which has long been debated is that of the appropriate standard of care to be required of directors. Historically, the common law was based upon a very low standard of care, because it was subjectively formulated. The traditional view is to be found in a stream of largely nineteenth-century cases which culminated in the decision in 1925 in *City Equitable Fire Insurance Co, Re*.[33] Those cases seem to have framed the directors' duties of skill and care with non-executive rather than executive directors in mind and, moreover, on the basis of a view that the non-executive director had no serious role to play within the company but was simply a piece of window-dressing aimed at promoting the company's image.[34] The result was a conceptualisation of the duty in highly subjective terms. The proposition was famously formulated by Romer J. in the *City Equitable* case that "a director need not exhibit in the performance of his duties a greater degree of skill than may reasonably be expected from a person of *his* knowledge and experience."[35] The courts were also influenced by a model of corporate decision-making which gave the shareholders effective control over the choice of directors. If the shareholders chose incompetent directors, that was their fault and the remedy lay in their hands. As we have seen,[36] that is no longer an accurate picture of the degree of control exercised by shareholders over boards of directors in most public companies. Furthermore, the proposition formulated by Romer J. was highly inappropriate for executive directors, appointed to their positions and paid large, sometimes very large, sums of money for the expertise which they assert they can bring to the business. The implicit view of the role of the non-executive director also became anachronistic after the development of the corporate governance codes in the 1990s, which allocated a major role to the non-executive directors in the monitoring of the executive directors.[37]

Even before the enactment of the Companies Act 2006 this was an area of the law of directors' duties which was beginning to change. The courts were influenced by the development of more demanding and objective statutory standards for directors whose companies were

---

[33] [1925] Ch.407, a decision of the Court of Appeal but always quoted for the judgment of Romer J. at first instance, because the appeal concerned only the liability of the auditors.

[34] The most famous example of this is perhaps *Cardiff Savings Bank, Re* [1892] 2 Ch.100, where the Marquis of Bute, whose family, despite its Scottish antecedents, owned, indeed had largely rebuilt, Cardiff Castle, was appointed president of the Bank at the age of six months and attended only one meeting of the board in his whole life. He was held not liable.

[35] At 427 (emphasis added). This test contains *an* objective element because the director could be held liable for failing on a particular occasion to live up to the standard of which he or she is in fact capable of reaching, but the stronger element in the proposition is the subjective one, meaning that the director can never be required to achieve a standard higher than that which he or she is personally capable of reaching.

[36] See above, Ch.15.

[37] See above, para.14–29.

facing insolvency[38] and began to develop the common law requirements by analogy with those specific statutory provisions. The
beginnings of the modern approach at common law can be found in
Dorchester Finance Co v Stebbing,[39] but it was a pair of first instance
decisions by Hoffmann J.[40] in the 1990s which marked a move
towards a fully objective approach. He explicitly adopted as an
accurate expression of the common law the test contained in s.214(4)
of the Insolvency Act in relation to wrongful trading.[41] This inchoate
change in the common law was endorsed by both the Law Commissions and the Company Law Review and now finds expression in
section 174 of the 2006 Act. This section first requires that "a director
of a company must exercise reasonable care, skill and diligence" and
then goes on to define what is meant by reasonable care, using a
formulation which tracks very closely section 214 of the Insolvency
Act 1986.

> "This means the care, skill and diligence that would be exercised
> by a reasonably diligent person with (a) the general knowledge,
> skill and experience that may reasonably be expected of a person
> carrying out the same functions carried out by the director in
> relation to the company, and (b) the general knowledge, skill and
> experience that the director has."

However, it should be noted that in one particular area the statute
has exempted directors from liability for negligence. In the case of
misstatements in or omissions from the directors' report and the
directors' remuneration report liability arises on the part of directors
to the company only on the basis of knowledge or recklessness.[42]

The statutory standard

16–13 The crucial difference between the statutory formulation and that of
Romer J. is that in the latter the director's subjective level of skill sets
the standard required of the director, whereas under the 2006 Act the
director's subjective level does so only if it improves upon the
objective standard of the reasonable director. Limb (a) of the statu-

---

[38] Principally the wrongful trading provisions to be found in s.214 of the Insolvency Act 1986,
above, para.9–7.

[39] Decided in 1977 but fully reported only in 1989: [1989] B.C.L.C. 498.

[40] *Norman v Theodore Goddard* [1991] B.C.L.C. 1027 (where the judge was "willing to assume"
that s.214 of the Insolvency Act represented the common law) and *D'Jan of London Ltd, Re*
[1994] 1 B.C.L.C. 561 where the director was found negligent on the basis of an objective
test, though it has to be said that the director could probably have been found liable on the
facts on a subjective test of diligence (he signed an insurance proposal form without reading
it). See also *Cohen v Selby* [2001] 1 B.C.L.C. 176 at 183, CA.

[41] See above, para.9–7.

[42] s.463. See below, para.21–26. It should be noted that this clause exempts the director only in
respect of statements in the relevant reports and not in respect of any negligent conduct to
which the statements inaccurately refer.

tory formula sets a standard which all directors must meet and it is not one dependent on the particular director's capabilities; limb (b) adds a subjective standard which, however, can operate only to increase the level of care required of the director.[43] Whether the statutory provision is to be regarded as simply endorsing the current common law or, probably better, as effecting a change in the common law which was under consideration but not fully accepted by the courts, this is clearly an area where a court applying section 174 should be cautious in its use of the older common law authorities as an aid to interpretation under section 170(4).

What does this all mean or not mean for directors? First, although directors, executive and non-executive, are subject to a uniform and objective duty of care, what the discharge of that duty requires in particular cases will not be uniform. As the statutory formulation itself recognises, what is required of the director will depend on the functions carried out by the director,[44] so that there will be variations, not only between executive and non-executive directors[45] but also between different types of executive director (and equally of non-executives) and between different types and sizes of company.

Secondly, the imposition of an objective duty of care does not necessarily require a directorship to be regarded as a profession. The vexed issue of what constitutes a profession does not have to be addressed; all that is required is an assessment of what is reasonably required of a person having, as the statute puts it, the knowledge, skill and experience which a person in the position of the particular director ought to have. Given the enormous range of types and sizes of companies, it would be odd if all directors were to be regarded as professional. On the other hand, as was pointed out by the Court of Appeal of New South Wales, an objective approach does require even non-executive directors, as a minimum, to "take reasonable steps to place themselves in a position to guide and monitor the management of the company".[46] The days of the wholly inactive or passive director would thus seem to be numbered—or, at least, a director who is so runs a high risk of being held negligent.

Thirdly, directors are permitted to engage in substantial delegation **16–14** of management functions to non-board employees. This is an inevitable reflection of the fact that companies are organisations, some-

[43] The section attributes to the director the knowledge, skill and experience of *both* the reasonable person and the particular director in question, so the latter is important only when it *adds* to the attributes of the reasonable person.

[44] One potentially significant omission from section 174 of the Companies Act in comparison with the Insolvency Act is that s.214(5) of the latter extends the meaning of "carried on" to include functions entrusted to the director as well as those actually carried out.

[45] Note how in the Australian case of *Daniels v Anderson* (1995) 16 ACSR 607 the Court of Appeal of NSW, applying an objective test, found that the non-executive directors were not liable for the failure to discover the foreign exchange frauds being committed by an employee, but the chief executive officer was so held.

[46] *Daniels v Anderson*, above at 664. The language of monitoring fits in well with the views of the Cadbury and Greenbury Committees on the proper role for the board of directors.

times very big organisations, the running of which may require a large staff. In *City Equitable, Re* Romer J. put this point in very robust terms. He said that "in respect of all duties that, having regard to the exigencies of business, and the articles of association, may properly be left to some other official, a director is, in the absence of grounds for suspicion, justified in trusting to that official to perform such duties honestly."[47] In the recent cases of *Daniels v Anderson* and *Norman v Theodore Goddard*,[48] where objective tests were applied, at least some of the directors escaped liability as a result of the application of this proposition. However, in so far as this dictum suggests that, once an appropriate delegate has been chosen and the task delegated to that person, the director is under no further duties, it cannot stand with recent developments in the law, as the next point indicates.

Fourthly, an objective standard of care is not inconsistent with extensive delegation nor, however, does it permit the directors to escape from the second requirement of always being in a position to "guide and monitor" the management. These two things are to be reconciled by the directors ensuring that there are in place adequate internal control systems which will throw up problems in the delegated areas whilst there is still time to do something about them. As it has been put, the freedom to delegate "does not absolve a director from the duty to supervise the discharge of the delegated functions".[49] The need for adequate internal control systems was stressed by the Report of the Turnbull Committee,[50] one of the lesser known of the reports which contributed to the Combined Code, but arguably the most important for what it has to say about directors' responsibility for sub-board structures of control. Although neither the Turnbull Report nor the Combined Code are legislative instruments binding the courts, it is likely that, in appropriate cases, the courts' view of what an objective standard of care requires will be influenced by these provisions. Indeed, one can already see that process at work in the adjacent area of disqualification of directors on grounds of unfitness. Thus, in *Barings Plc (No.5), Re*[51] directors were disqualified for

---

[47] See above at 429. See also *Dovey v Cory* [1901] A.C. 477, HL. But the matter must not be delegated to an obviously inappropriate employee or official, as was the case in *City Equitable, Re* itself.

[48] See above.

[49] *Barings Plc (No.5), Re* [2000] 1 B.C.L.C. 433, 489 (per Jonathan Parker J.), approved by the CA at p.536. See also *Equitable Life Assurance Society v Bowley* [2004] 1 B.C.L.C. 180, 188–189.

[50] Institute of Chartered Accountants in England and Wales, *Internal Control: Guidance for Directors on the Combined Code* (1999). The Report fleshes out the bare principles contained in the Combined Code (Provision C.2) that boards should maintain sound systems of internal control "including financial, operational and compliance controls and risk management systems", should annually review them and should report to the shareholders that they have done so. In October 2005 the Financial Reporting Council issued revised guidance: *Internal Control: Revised Guidance for Directors on the Combined Code*.

[51] [2000] 1 B.C.L.C. 523, CA. See above, para.10–7.

failing to have such internal controls in place in relation to trading activities in an overseas subsidiary, whose losses eventually caused the demise of the bank.

Fifthly, the principles relating to delegation to sub-board managers apply also to the division of functions among the directors themselves. Inevitably, executive directors will carry a greater load of management responsibility than non-executive directors and, even within the executive directors, there will be specialisation (for example, the chief financial officer will carry particular responsibility in that area). However, all directors "have a continuing duty to acquire and maintain a sufficient knowledge and understanding of the company's business to enable them properly to discharge their duties as directors" and certainly no board may permit itself to be dominated by one of their number.[52]

Sixthly, however, it follows from the inevitable acceptance of **16–15** extensive delegation, at least in large companies, that directors cannot be guarantors that everything is going well within the company. Subordinate employees may be fraudulent or negligent and the directors may not discover this in time, but this does not necessarily mean that the directors have been negligent. That conclusion will depend on the facts of the situation, including the quality of the internal controls. Further, although nearly all decided English cases have arisen out of alleged failures by directors to act or to act effectively, negligence suits could arise where the directors have clearly acted, but with disastrous consequences for their company. Here too, however, since companies are in business to take risks, the fact that a business venture does not pay off and even leads the company into financial trouble does not necessarily indicate negligence, though it may encourage the shareholders to replace the directors. In the United States, where an objective standard for directors' competence is well-established, the "business judgment" rule generally operates to relieve the directors of liability in such cases. The business judgment rule involves the specification of a set of procedural steps, which, if followed, will give the directors the benefit of a presumption that they were not negligent. The Law Commissions thought such a rule unnecessary in the United Kingdom;[53] and there is certainly a risk with the business judgment rule that the courts will come to regard cases where the procedural standards have not been met as presumptively negligent.[54] The Commissions thought that one could expect the courts to be alive to the probability that they are better at dealing with conflicts of interest than with the assessment of

---

[52] *Barings, Re*, above, fn.49 and *Westmid Packaging Services Ltd, Re* [1998] 2 B.C.L.C. 646, 653.

[53] Law Commission and Scottish Law Commission, *Company Directors: Regulating Conflicts of Interest and Formulating a Statement of Duties*, Cm. 4436, 1999, Pt 5.

[54] *cf. Smith v Van Gorkam* (1985) 488 A. 2d 858.

business risks and to the desirability of avoiding the luxury of substituting the courts' hindsight for the directors' foresight.[55]

Finally, as with auditors,[56] showing breach of a duty of care is one
thing; showing that the loss suffered by the company was a consequence of the breach of duty may be quite another. Thus, the true
explanation of the finding of no liability in *Denham & Co, Re*[57] is only
in part that the director was entitled to rely on others. Equally
important was the judge's view that, even if the director had made the
inquiries he should have made, he would probably not have discovered the fraud.

Overall, it can be said that the recent developments at common law
and, now, in the Act, have brought the standard of care, skill and
diligence required of directors into line with that required generally in
other areas of social life by the law of negligence. However, an
inevitable result of the move from a subjective to an objective test will
be to give the courts a greater role in defining the functions of the
board, no matter how sensitive the courts are to the need to avoid the
use of hindsight. For example, the courts' decisions on the rigour
with which the board has to supervise the discharge of delegated tasks
will help to define the monitoring role of the board, whilst decisions
about whether the audit committee of the board has sufficiently
scrutinised the tasks carried out by the external auditors will help to
define the relationships between audit committee, auditors and
management. Twenty years ago one might have predicted that the
courts would either be ineffectual in the discharge of these responsibilities (through a desire to avoid reliance on hindsight) or produce
undesirable interventions. However, today, as a result of developments associated with the emergence of the Combined Code, discussed in Chapter 14, there is a body of best practice available, on
which the courts can draw, though not be bound by, at least in the
case of large companies. A striking example of the creative use of
such material is to be found in the judgement of Austin J. in *ASIC v
Rich*[58] in which the Australian court had recourse to a wide range of
"best practice" material, including corporate governance reports
from the UK, in holding that the duties of the chair of the board of a
listed company extended beyond responsibility for simply chairing
meetings of the board.

[55] For a critique see C.A. Riley, "The Company Director's Duty of Care and Skill: the Case
   for an Onerous but Subjective Standard" (1999) 62 M.L.R. 697.
[56] See below, para.22–37.
[57] (1883) 25 Ch.D. 752. See also *Cohen v Selby* [2001] B.C.L.C. 176, CA, stressing the need at
   common law to show that the negligence caused the loss suffered by the company. The
   classic statement of the problem is that by Learned Hand J. in *Barnes v Andrews* (1924) 298
   F. 614 at 616–617.
[58] [2003] NSWSC 85. The judge referred in particular to Annex D of Mr Derek Higg's review
   of the role of non-executive directors: above, para.14–30.

Remedies

The standard remedy for breach of a director's duty of care is com-   **16–16**
pensation to recompense the company for the harm caused to it by
the director's breach. Even though the director is in a fiduciary
position as against the company, mere breach of the duty of care does
not give the company restitutionary or restorative remedies for
breach of fiduciary duty against the director. As Millett L.J. said in
Bristol and West Building Society v Mothew,[59] "it is inappropriate to
apply the expression [breach of fiduciary duty] to the obligation of a
trustee or other fiduciary to use proper skill and care in the discharge
of his duties". This is so even if the duty of care to which the fiduciary
is subject was developed, historically, by the courts of equity rather
than at common law. This led to the use of different terminology
("compensation" in equity; "damages" at common law), different
standards of care and different rules on causation, remoteness and
measure of damages. However, the modern tendency is to assimilate
the requirements for liability for breach of the duty of care in equity
and at common law.[60] In any event, breach of a duty of care arising
historically in equity gives access only to compensatory remedies.

DIRECTORS' FIDUCIARY DUTIES

As remarked above, the duties of loyalty which the law requires of   **16–17**
directors were developed by the courts by analogy with the duties of
trustees. It is easy to see how, historically, this came about. Prior to
the Joint Stock Companies Act 1844 most joint stock companies were
unincorporated and depended for their validity on a deed of settlement vesting the property of the company in trustees. Often the
directors were themselves the trustees and even when a distinction
was drawn between the passive trustees and the managing board of
directors, the latter would quite clearly be regarded as trustees in the
eyes of a court of equity in so far as they dealt with the trust property.
With directors of incorporated companies the description "trustees"
was less apposite, because the assets were now held by the company, a

---

[59] [1998] Ch. 1, CA. The case provides a good example of the difference between a compensatory and a restitutionary remedy. A building society had advanced money to a purchaser,
who defaulted on the loan, after receiving negligent information from its solicitor. A restitutionary claim would have required the solicitor to put the building society back in the
position in was in before it made the loan (i.e. to meet the whole of the society's loss),
whereas the compensatory claim required him only to compensate the society for the loss
caused to it by his negligence. This might have been nil if the solicitor's negligence had not
affected the ability of the purchaser to keep up the repayments on the loan.

[60] In the *Mothew* case (see previous footnote) Millett L.J. referred to the distinction between
equitable compensation and common law damages for breach of the duty of care as "a
distinction without a difference".

separate legal person, rather than being vested in trustees. However, it was not unnatural that the courts should extend it to them by analogy. For one thing, the duties of the directors should obviously be the same whether the company was incorporated or not; for another, courts of equity tend to apply the label "trustee" to anyone in a fiduciary position. Nevertheless, to describe directors as trustees seems today to be neither strictly correct nor invariably helpful.[61] In truth, directors are agents of the company rather than trustees of it or its property. But as agents they stand in a fiduciary relationship to their principal, the company. The duties of good faith which this fiduciary relationship imposes are virtually identical with those imposed on trustees, and to this extent the description "trustee" still has validity. Moreover, when it comes to remedies for breach of duty, the trust analogy can provide a strong remedial structure. Directors who dispose of the company's assets in breach of duty are regarded as committing a breach of trust, and the persons (including the directors themselves) into whose hands those assets come may find that they are under a duty to restore the value of the misapplied assets to the company.[62]

Even the analogy of directors as agents of the company is less than perfect. As we saw in Chapter 7, the authority of the directors to bind the company as its agents normally depends on their acting collectively as a board, unless authority has specifically been conferred under the company's constitution upon an individual director.[63] By contrast, their duties of good faith are owed by each director individually. One of several directors may not as such be an agent of the company with power to saddle it with responsibility for his acts, but he will be a fiduciary of it. To this extent, directors again resemble trustees who must normally act jointly but each of whom severally owes duties of good faith towards the beneficiaries. Moreover, when the directors act collectively as a board, the modern view is not so much that they are agents of the company but that, so long as they remain within their powers, they act as the company.[64]

Perhaps all that needs to be established, which is indisputable, is that directors individually owe fiduciary duties to their company and sometimes are regarded as acting in breach of trust when they deal improperly with the company's assets.

16–18   Turning now to the main elements of the directors' fiduciary duties,

---

[61] *City Equitable Fire Insurance Co, Re* [1925] Ch. 407 at 426, per Romer J.

[62] "It follows from the principle that directors who dispose of the company's property in breach of their fiduciary duties are treated as having committed a breach of trust that a person who receives that property with knowledge of the breach of duty is treated as holding it upon trust for the company. He is said to be a constructive trustee of the property." Per Chadwick L.J. in *J J Harrison (Properties) Ltd v Harrison* [2002] 1 B.C.L.C. 162, 173. In this situation the trustee-like nature of the directors' duties affects also the legal position of third parties. See further below, at para.16–97.

[63] See above, para.7–20.

[64] See above, para.14–3.

we divide them below into six sub-groups, following the scheme of the Act. Three of these categories seem distinct. They are:

(1) that the directors must remain within the scope of the powers which have been conferred upon them;

(2) that directors must act in good faith to promote the success of the company;

(3) that they must exercise independent judgment.

The final three categories are all examples of the rule against directors putting themselves in a position in which their personal interests (or duties to others) conflict with their duty to the company. However, it is useful to sub-divide the "no conflict" principle in this way because the specific rules implementing the principle differ according to whether the conflict arises:

(4) out of a transaction with the company (self-dealing transactions);

(5) out of the director's personal exploitation of the company's property, information or opportunities; or

(6) out of the receipt from a third party of a benefit for exercising their directorial functions in a particular way.

For the purposes of statutory enactment and analysis it is inevitable that the duties are separated out in some such way as that adopted in the 2006 Act. However, section 179 provides that, except where a duty is explicitly excluded by something in the statute, "more than one of the general duties may apply in any given case". This provision applies also to the duty of care. In practice, many situations will raise issues regarding more than one of the duties and, where this is so, the claimant can choose to pursue all or any of them.

Duty to Act within Powers

A duty upon the directors to remain within the powers which have **16–19** been conferred upon them is a very obvious duty for the law to impose. Section 171 deals with two manifestations of this principle: the director must "act in accordance with the company's constitution" and must "only exercise powers for the purposes for which they are conferred". We shall look at each in turn.

Acting in accordance with the constitution

16–20   As we saw in Chapter 3,[65] in contrast to many other company law jurisdictions, the main source of the directors' powers is likely to be the company's articles, and the articles, therefore, are likely also to be a source of constraints on the directors' powers. The articles may confer unlimited powers on the directors, but they are likely in fact to set some parameters within which the powers are to be exercised, even if the limits are generous, as they typically will be. So, it is perhaps not surprising that section 171 contains the obligation "to act in accordance with the company's constitution". However, it should be noted that the term "constitution" goes beyond the articles. It includes resolutions and agreements which are required to be notified to the Registrar and annexed to the articles, notably any special resolution of the company.[66] It also embraces any resolution or decision taken in accordance with the constitution and any decision by the members of the company or a class of members which is treated as equivalent to a decision of the company.[67] Thus, the duty includes an obligation to obey decisions properly taken by the shareholders in general meeting, for example, giving instructions to the directors without formally altering the articles.[68]

This duty was recognised in the early years of modern company law and is reflected in a number of nineteenth-century decisions, usually involving the purported exercise by directors of powers which were ultra vires the company[69] or payments of dividends or directors' remuneration contrary to the provisions in the company's articles.[70] The directors break this duty if they act in fact in breach of the requirements of the company's constitution; it is not necessary that they should be shown to be subjectively aware of the unconstitutional nature of their actions.[71] In other words, directors are under a duty to acquaint themselves with the terms of the company's articles and to abide by them. Moreover, this is one of the situations where the trust

---

[65]   See above, para.3–10.

[66]   ss.17 and 29–30.

[67]   s.257.

[68]   As we saw at para.14–4 under the draft model articles the shareholders by special resolution may give directors instructions as to how they should conduct the management of the company, even in areas where the articles confer managerial powers upon the directors.

[69]   *Lands Allotment Company, Re* [1894] 1 Ch. 616, CA. On ultra vires see above at paras 7–2ff.

[70]   *Oxford Benefit Building and Investment Society, Re* (1886) 35 Ch. D. 502 (an early example of a company's accounts recognising profits which had not been earned); *Leeds Estate Building and Investment Company v Shepherd* (1887) 36 Ch. D. 787. It might be said that the requirement upon the directors to repay the dividends was based on the illegality of their payment as a matter of statute or common law, but the directors were also required to repay their remuneration, the payment of which was objectionable only because it was done in breach of the company's articles. (The articles entitled the directors to remuneration only if dividends of a certain size were paid, a rule which, perhaps naturally, encouraged the directors not to be too careful about observing the restrictions on their dividend payment powers.)

[71]   See the cases cited in fn.70.

analogy is used to strong effect. If the contravention of the constitution has involved the improper distribution of the company's assets, the directors are regarded as in breach of trust and are liable to replace the assets, whether or not they were the recipients of them.[72] This gives the directors a strong incentive to remain within the company's constitution.[73]

At common law, an act or decision of the directors which is outside the company's constitution is void, i.e. of no effect. However, where the directors simply exceed an authority which has been conferred on them, the decision is only voidable.[74] A decision which is void necessarily has a bigger impact upon third parties than a rule that the act or decision is merely voidable, i.e. valid until set aside by the company and incapable of being set aside if third party rights have intervened. Even in the case of voidable decisions, however, the impact of this rule on third parties' interests has now been substantially softened by the statutory protections (especially section 40) for those dealing with the company in good faith.[75] In favour of such persons the powers of the directors to bind the company are treated as free of any limitation contained in the company's constitution. However, this will not help the directors, for section 40(5) makes it clear that liability on the part of the director to the company may be incurred under section 171, even if the third party with whom the directors dealt on behalf of the company is able to enforce the transaction against the company.[76] In fact, to the extent that section 40 protects the position of third parties as against the company it increases in importance the company's potential remedy against the director. Companies now restricted in their ability to escape from transactions with third parties on the grounds that the directors have exceeded their powers may be tempted to look to the directors to recover compensation for the loss suffered as a result of entering into them.

It is also worth recalling at this point the provisions of section 41, which applies where the third party contracting with the company is a director of the company or a person connected with the director. In

---

[72] See the cases cited in fn.70.
[73] They might escape liability, however, where, for example, the provisions of the constitution were not clear and see also the discussion of s.1157, below, para.16–96.
[74] *Hogg v Cramphorn* [1967] Ch. 254—a decision to attach multiple voting rights to shares issued to the company's pension fund, in breach of the company's articles, ineffective; *Guinness v Saunders* [1990] 2 A.C. 663, HL—fixing of directors' remuneration by a board committee, rather than the full board, in breach of the articles meant that the recipient director had to repay the money; *Smith v Henniker-Major Co* [2003] Ch. 182 at para.48—inquorate board meeting. *Cf. Hely-Hutchinson v Brayhead Ltd* [1968] 1 Q.B. 549, where the correct body acted but the director was in breach of his obligation under the articles to comply with disclosure provisions based on section 317 of the 1985 Act: here the decision was voidable but not void.
[75] See above, at para.7–5. Unless the third party is a director of the company or a person connected with the director. See s.41 and above, para.7–11.
[76] s.40(1).

that case the protection afforded by section 40 does not apply and instead section 41 imposes liability both on directors who authorise such transactions (as section 171 does)[77] *and* on the director[78] (or connected person) who enters into the transaction with the company.[79] Both sets of directors are liable to account to the company for any gain made from the transaction and to indemnify the company for any loss which it suffered as a result of the transaction. Section 41 in its specific area of operation thus reinforces the principle underlying section 171 that directors should observe the limitations on their constitutional powers.

Improper purposes

16–21 The second proposition contained in section 171 is that a director must "only exercise powers for the purposes for which they are conferred."[80] Often the improper purpose will be to feather the directors' own nests or to preserve their control of the company in their own interests, in which event it will also be a breach of the duty, considered below, to act in good faith to promote the success of the company.[81] But it is clear that, notwithstanding that directors have acted honestly to promote the success of the company, they may nevertheless be in breach of duty if they have exercised their powers for a purpose outside those for which the powers were conferred upon them. Thus, the improper purposes test, like the requirement to act in accordance with the company's constitution, is an objective test.[82]

The statutory formulation of the duty reflects the prior common law case-law. That case-law was reviewed by the Privy Council in *Howard Smith Ltd v Ampol Petroleum Ltd*,[83] which considered the decisions on this subject of courts throughout the Commonwealth. It concerned, as have many of the cases, the power of directors to issue

---

[77] Liability under section 172 is preserved by section 41(1) but it would seem more attractive to proceed under s.41 where this is possible.

[78] Including a director of the company's holding company.

[79] The transaction itself is voidable by the company (s.41(2) and (4)), but not void, as it would be at common law. It will cease to be avoidable if (a) restitution of the subject-matter of the contract is not possible; (b) the company has been indemnified for the loss suffered; (c) the rights of bona fide purchasers without notice have intervened; or (d) the shareholders in general meeting have ratified the transaction.

[80] s.171(b).

[81] Para.16–24.

[82] See *Howard Smith Ltd v Ampol Ltd* [1974] A.C. 821 at 834, PC, citing *Fraser v Whalley* (1864) 2 H.C.M. & M. 10; *Punt v Symons & Co Ltd* [1903] 2 Ch. 506; *Piercy v S Mills & Co Ltd* [1920] 1 Ch. 77; *Ngurli v McCann* (1954) 90 C.L.R. 425, Aust. HC; *Hogg v Cramphorn Ltd* [1967] Ch. 254 at 267 (in respect of the issuance of the shares even without the multiple voting rights—see fn.74, above). The "improper purpose" test, as a requirement distinct from good faith, has been rejected, however, in British Columbia: *Teck Corporation Ltd v Millar* (1973) 33 D.L.R. (3d) 288.

[83] See previous note.

new shares.[84] In the case a majority shareholder (Ampol) in a company called Millers made an offer to acquire the shares in Millers it did not already own. However, the directors of Millers preferred a takeover offer from Howard Smith, which could not succeed so long as Ampol retained a majority holding. Consequently, the directors caused the company to issue sufficient new shares to Howard Smith that Ampol was reduced to a minority position and Howard Smith could launch its offer with some hope of success, since it was higher than Ampol's. It was argued that the only proper purpose for which a share-issue power could be exercised was to raise new capital when the company needed it.[85] This was rejected as too narrow.[86] There might be a range of purposes for which a company might issue new shares—a view reflected in the statutory reference to proper purposes in the plural. It might be a proper use of the power to issue shares to do so to a larger company in order to secure the financial stability of the company[87] or as part of an agreement relating to the exploitation of mineral rights owned by the company.[88] Provided the purpose of the issue was a proper one, the mere fact that the incidental (and desired) result was to deprive a shareholder of his voting majority or to defeat a takeover bid would not be sufficient to make the purpose improper. But if, as in the instant case, the purpose of the share issue was to dilute the majority voting power so as to enable an offer to proceed which the existing majority was in a position to block,[89] the exercise of the power would be improper despite the fact that the directors were not motivated by a desire to obtain some personal advantage and considered that they were acting in the best interests of the company.

Frequently, as in this case, the directors will not be actuated by a single purpose, for the company did have a need for fresh capital. Then the test of legality must be applied to the dominant or primary purpose which the directors had and which, naturally, the court must first identify.[90] In this case the facts showed rather clearly that the

---

[84] But the principle applies generally. For examples in relation to other powers, see *Stanhope's Case* (1866) L.R. 1 Ch.App. 161, and *Manisty's Case* (1873) 17 S.J. 745 (forfeiture of shares); *Galloway v Halle Concerts Society* [1915] 2 Ch. 233 (calls); *Bennett's case* (1854) 5 De G.M. & G. 284 and *Australian Metropolitan Life Association Co Ltd v Ure* (1923) 33 C.L.R. 199, Aust. HC (registration of transfers); *Hogg v Cramphorn Ltd*, above, fn.74 (loans); *Lee Panavision Ltd v Lee Lighting Ltd* [1992] B.C.L.C. 22, CA (entering into a management agreement); *Criterion Properties Plc v Stratford UK Properties LLC* [2003] B.C.C. 50, CA (giving joint venture partner an option to be bought out at a favourable price).

[85] This has often been assumed and the directors had apparently been so advised and sought, unsuccessfully, to show that this was their purpose.

[86] At 835–836.

[87] *Harlowe's Nominees Pty Ltd v Woodside Oil Co* (1968) 121 C.L.R. 483, Aust. HC.

[88] *Teck Corp Ltd v Miller* (1972) 33 D.L.R. (3d) 288, BC Sup.Ct.

[89] Or, conversely, to block a bid: *Winthrop Investments Ltd v Winns Ltd* [1975] 2 N.S.W.L.R. 666, NSWCA.

[90] *Hirsche v Sims* [1894] A.C. 654, PC; *Hindle v John Cotton Ltd* (1919) 56 S.L.T. 625; *Mills v Mills* (1938) 60 C.L.R. 150, Aust. HC.

predominant purpose of the directors in making the share issue under challenge was to defeat the takeover by Ampol rather than to raise fresh capital. The case comes close to deciding that it is always a breach of the directors' duties to exercise their powers to promote or defeat a takeover offer, which decision should be left to the existing body of shareholders. This is certainly the proposition upon which the City Code on Take-overs is based, whose provisions will prevail once a bid for a listed company is imminent.[91] However, in *Criterion Properties Plc v Stratford UK Properties LLC*[92] neither Hart J. nor the Court of Appeal ruled out the possibility that in some cases it might be a proper purpose of the exercise of directors' powers for them to be used to block or discourage a takeover. However, the issue was not presented in a sharp fashion in that case since both courts were agreed that the "poison pill" adopted by the directors in that case was disproportionate to the threat faced by the company.

16–22   Perhaps the greatest puzzle in this area is to know by what criteria the courts judge whether a particular purpose is proper. This is generally stated to be a matter of construction of the articles of association.[93] In *Smith v Ampol*, however, the clause giving the directors power to issue shares was drawn in the widest terms. The "purposes" limitation which the Privy Council read into the directors' powers derived not from a narrow analysis of that clause, but from placing the share issue power within the company's constitutional arrangements as a whole, as demonstrated in particular by the terms of its articles of association. In essence, to do what the directors did in that case was regarded as undermining the division of powers between shareholders and the board which the articles had created.[94] It follows from this approach that in a different type of company with

[91] See below at para.28–17.
[92] [2002] 2 B.C.L.C. 151 (Hart J.); [2003] 2 B.C.L.C. 129, CA. The issue was not analysed by the House of Lords: [2004] 1 W.L.R. 1846. The "poison pill" arrangement entitled the joint venture partner of the potential target company (Criterion) to require Criterion to buy out its interest in the venture on terms which were very favourable to the partner and thus very damaging economically to Criterion. However, this arrangement was capable of being triggered not only by a takeover but also by any departure of the existing management of Criterion, even in circumstances, which in fact arose, which were wholly unconnected with a takeover.
[93] *Smith and Fawcett Ltd, Re* [1942] Ch. 304 at 306.
[94] "The constitution of a limited company normally provides for directors, with powers of management, and shareholders, with defined voting powers having to appoint the directors, and to take, in general meeting, by majority vote, decisions on matters not reserved for management. Just as it is established that directors, within their management powers, may take decisions against the wishes of majority shareholders, and indeed that the majority of shareholders cannot control them in the exercise of these powers while they remain in office ... so it must be unconstitutional for directors to use their fiduciary powers over the shares in the company purely for the purpose of destroying an existing majority, or creating a new majority which did not previously exist. To do so is to interfere with that element in the company's constitution which is separate from and set against their powers" ([1974] A.C. 821 at 837, PC). This principle was applied by the Court of Appeal in *Lee Panavision Ltd v Lee Lighting Ltd* [1992] B.C.L.C. 22 where the incumbent directors entered into a long-term management agreement with a third party knowing that the shareholders were proposing to exercise their rights to appoint new directors.

a different constitution, in which, say, ownership and control were not separated, a broader view might be taken of the directors' powers under the articles.

This seems to be the explanation of the decisions in *Smith and Fawcett Ltd, Re*,[95] where the clause in question (regarding the admission of new members to a small company) was widely construed so as to produce the effect equivalent to the partnership rule of strict control by the board over the admission of new members. Similarly, in a company limited by guarantee and formed for the purpose of campaigning for the adoption of a particular policy in a certain area of social life, it was held that the directors' powers to expel members with contrary views should not be cut down on the grounds that the directors were seeking to control the composition of the general meeting.[96] Even in relation to a large commercial company limited by shares the proper purposes doctrine could be invoked if the articles contained an express limitation on the purposes for which a power conferred on the directors could be exercised. The burden would be on those who favoured the restriction to obtain its inclusion in the articles, but, subject to that, the articles may in principle shape the directors' powers through limitations of purpose, just as they can do so by not conferring a power on the directors at all. The Company Law Review thought it should be left open for judicial development whether the proper purposes rule should continue to be grounded solely in an interpretation of the company's constitution or whether wider criteria for the identification of improper purposes should be developed, and the proposed statutory statement appears to leave that issue to the courts.[97]

Where the directors act for an improper purpose, at common law their act is voidable by the company, not void, as it is in the case where the directors purport to exercise a power they do not have. Thus, third parties are safe if they act before the shareholders set aside the directors' decision; and, of course, the third party will also have the wider benefit of section 40, discussed above.[98]

Finally, we should note that, although both duties stated in section 171 are, as with the other statutory duties, owed to the company, this

[95] [1942] Ch. 304, CA, where in a quasi-partnership company it was held that the directors, in exercising a power to refuse to register a transfer of shares, could "take account of any matter which they conceive to be in the interests of the company ... such matters, for instance, as whether by their passing a particular transfer the transferee would obtain too great a weight in the councils of the company or might even perhaps obtain control" (at 308). In modern law the position would now have to be considered in the light of any "legitimate expectations" enforceable under s.994. See below, Ch.20.

[96] *Gaiman v National Association of Mental Health* [1971] Ch. 317.

[97] Completing, para.3.14. The issue which arises if one moves away from the articles is how the courts should test propriety of purpose. For a suggestion, see R. Nolan, "The Proper Purpose Doctrine and Company Directors" in B. Rider (ed.), *The Realm of Company Law* (Kluwer Law International, 1998).

[98] *Bamford v Bamford* [1970] Ch. 212, CA (ratification by shareholders of decision taken for an improper purpose) and *Criterion Properties Plc v Stratford UK Properties LLC* [2004] 1 W.L.R. 1846 (on the application of the statutory protection for the benefit of third parties).

does not necessarily mean that the shareholders cannot bring claims asserting breaches of their own rights arising out of directors' actions. Thus, a failure on the part of the directors to observe the limits on their powers contained in the company's constitution may put *the company* in breach of the contract with the shareholders created by the articles. As we saw in Chapter 3,[99] at least some breaches of the articles by the company can be complained of by a shareholder, who might, for example, obtain an injunction to restrain the company from continuing in breach of the articles—in effect restraining the directors from causing the company to act in breach of its articles. However, it has been controversial whether the exercise for an improper purpose of the powers conferred on the directors by the articles amounts to a breach of them. In a case concerning the improper exercise of the directors' share issue powers, Hoffmann J. held in a brief judgment that the complaint should be regarded primarily as an infringement of the shareholder's contractual rights. He said:

"The allotment is alleged to be an improper and unlawful exercise of the powers granted to the board by the articles of association, which constitute a contract between the company and its members. These are fiduciary powers, not to be exercised for an improper purpose ... An abuse of these powers is an infringement of a member's contractual rights under the articles."[100]

Whilst not denying that "the alleged breach of fiduciary duty by the board is in theory a breach of its duty to the company", the judge held that "the wrong to the company is not the substance of the complaint". However, it should be noted that the learned judge was not saying that the result of his analysis was to create a right in the shareholders as against the directors (as opposed to a contractual right against the company).[101]

Other situations?

16–23 Besides limitations on the directors' powers which are to be found in the company's constitution, the general law may limit what directors may do (or what companies may do, which will necessarily control the actions of the board) or the limitations may be found in the Companies Act or the common law of companies. Very often these

---

[99] Above, para.3–13.
[100] *Sherborne Park Residents Co Ltd, Re* (1986) 2 B.C.C. 528. For the contrary view that acting for an improper purpose is an abuse of power but not a breach of the articles see *Winthrop Investments Ltd v Winns Ltd* [1975] 2 N.S.W.L.R. 666, NSWCA.
[101] In the particular case the claim was brought under the unfair prejudice provisions (see Chapter 20) and the judge's argument was used to deny the petitioner access to the company's funds to finance the litigation, which funds would normally be available if the action had been brought to enforce the company's rights. See below, Chapter 17.

provisions will specify the consequences of failure to abide by the relevant rules, and where this is the case, those rules will prevail and the directors' duties of loyalty have no role to play. However, sometimes the consequences of breach of the rules are not specified or not fully specified, so that the question of the extent of the civil liability of the director to the company for breach of the rule is not answered. In such a case the law of directors' duties may be called upon to provide an answer. We have already seen an example of this situation in Chapter 12 where the directors, in breach of the Act, made a distribution to shareholders otherwise than out of profits. In the absence of statutory specification of the liabilities of the directors to the company in that situation, the courts have had recourse to the notion that if directors, "as quasi-trustees for the company, improperly pay away the assets to the shareholders, they are liable to replace them".[102] Another example is to be found in Chapter 13[103] where directors are regarded as having acted in breach of trust when they used the company's assets to give financial assistance for the purchase of the company's shares in breach of the statutory prohibition. In this way, directors who apply the company's assets in breach of restrictions contained in the Act are made liable to replace them. It is not thought that these liabilities, derived from the trustee-like duties imposed on directors in the handling of the company's assets, have been overtaken or displaced by the statutory duties set out in Chapter 2 of Part 10 and in section 171 in particular.

A somewhat more general application of this approach can be found in the decision of the Court of Appeal in *MacPherson v European Strategic Bureau Ltd.*[104] Here the directors of an insolvent company caused it to enter into a number of contracts which, the court found, amounted to an informal winding up of the company. Under the contracts, the directors as creditors were the primary beneficiaries rather than the creditors of the company as a whole, as would have been the case had the company been wound up formally under the provisions of the Act and the insolvency legislation. Chadwick L.J. said that it was a breach of the duties which directors owe to the company for them to attempt such a scheme:

> "It is an attempt to circumvent the protection which the 1985 Act aims to provide for those who give credit to a business carried on, with the benefit of limited liability, through the vehicle of a company incorporated under that Act."[105]

---

[102] Per Sir George Jessel M.R. in *Flitcroft*'s case (1882) 21 Ch. D. 519, quoted with approval by the Court of Appeal in *Bairstow v Queen's Moat Houses Plc* [2001] 2 B.C.L.C. 531. See para.12–9, above.

[103] At para.13–36. See also the discussion of *Duckwari (No.2), Re* [1998] 2 B.C.L.C. 215, CA, below at fn.223.

[104] [2000] 2 B.C.L.C. 683.

[105] [2000] 2 B.C.L.C., at 683, at 701.

In consequence, the contracts were not enforceable by the directors (who were obviously aware of the facts giving rise to the breach of duty) against the company. This case can thus be seen as demonstrating a limitation on the directors' powers derived from the statutory rules on limited liability and payments to shareholders out of capital. It could also be seen as a breach of the directors' core duty of loyalty (discussed immediately below) as it applies in the vicinity of insolvency where the creditors' interests are predominant.

DUTY TO PROMOTE THE SUCCESS OF THE COMPANY

Reformulating the common law

16-24 The duty to promote the success of the company is the modern version of the basic loyalty duty of directors. It is the core duty to which directors are subject, in the sense that it applies to every exercise of judgment which the directors undertake, whether they are pressing on the margins of their powers under the constitution or not and whether or not there is an operative conflict of interest. Together with the non-fiduciary duty to exercise care, skill and diligence, the duty to promote the success of the company expresses the law's view on how directors should discharge their functions on a day-to-day basis. Thus, it is not surprising that the proper formulation of the directors' duty of loyalty was a matter of considerable controversy, both during the deliberations of the Company Law Review and during the passage of the 2006 Act through Parliament. That controversy was all the more intense because this was an area of directors' duties where it was not proposed that the statute should simply repeat the common law. The common law duty was typically formulated as one which required the directors to act in good faith in what they believed to be "the best interests of the company". This is clearly a significantly different formulation from that which is to be found now in section 172(1) of the Act. This section requires the director to act "in the way he considers, in good faith, would be most likely to promote the success of the company for the benefit of its members as a whole"; and then sets out a non-exhaustive list of six matters to which the directors must "have regard" when deciding on the appropriate course of action.

The reasons for making the change were two-fold, though closely linked with one another. They both related to the fundamental question of whose interests the directors are required to pursue when exercising their powers. Given the concentration of economic power in large companies, this was necessarily a question of considerable interest and controversy across the political spectrum. Ironically, as we shall see, the answer to the question is of limited significance in terms of litigation, since there continues to be a high level of subjectivity in the formulation of the duty, which subjectivity cuts against the duty becoming a powerful weapon in litigation. Nevertheless, the theoretical or even ideological significance of the debate about the correct formulation of the basic loyalty duty cannot be easily over-estimated.

The first of the two linked reasons for proposing a change from the common law formulation was that the existing common law duty was thought to be insufficiently precise in the guidance it gave to directors about whose interests should be promoted in the exercise of their discretion. Although, as we have seen, the statement that the duties of directors are owed to the company is valuable because it indicates that only those who can claim to act as or on behalf of the company can enforce the duties, a requirement, as in the common law, that directors must act *in the interests of* "the company" comes close to being meaningless. This is because the company is an artificial legal person and it is impossible to assign interests to it unless one goes further and identifies with the company the interests of one or more groups of human persons. As Nourse L.J. has remarked, "The interests of a company, as an artificial person, cannot be distinguished from the interests of the persons who are interested in it."[106] To say, without more, that directors must exercise their powers in the interests of the company is thus to give very imprecise guidance to those directors about what the law requires, unless it is further specified which group or groups of persons are to be identified as "the company". The contrary view of the Law Society[107] that "the concept of the company as a legal entity separate from its members, and in whose interests the directors must act, is well understood" seems unsupported and unsupportable, except on the basis that the common law normally identified the interests of the company with those of its shareholders and thus took the further step envisaged by Nourse L.J.

In any event, the first move by the drafters of the statutory statement was to reformulate the common law test in such a way as to omit any reference to the "interests of the company" but also to make it clear, as was the dominant view at common law, that the shareholders or members are to be the primary object of the directors' efforts, as far as company law is concerned. Hence, the current formulation that the director must act "in the way he considers, in good faith, would be most likely to promote the success of the company for

16–25

---

[106] *Brady v Brady* [1988] B.C.L.C. 20 at 40, CA. Is it suggested that it is not possible to say whether it is in the interests of the company as a separate legal entity distinct from all those involved in its success that, over a given time period, it is desirable to maximise the company's profitability, size, number of employees or any other business objective, assuming that, as will be the case, these objectives are not all compatible one with the other, at least at the margin. However, identify the company with its shareholders, its managers, its employers or some other group, then the question becomes much easier to answer.

[107] The Law Society, *Company Law Reform White Paper*, June 2005, p.6.

the benefit of its members as a whole". The persons who are to benefit from the directors' efforts to promote the success of the company are clearly identified as the company's members, i.e., normally its shareholders. This is the central duty imposed by the section: the obligation, discussed in the following paragraph, to have regard to the interests of other stakeholders is clearly subordinate to the central duty to promote the success of the company for the benefit of its members. This is made clear by the words "in doing so", i.e. in discharging the central duty. The shareholders' position as the object of the directors' efforts is not shared with other groups of persons upon whose success the company's business may be thought to depend, for example, its employees or other stakeholders. To this extent, the rule of shareholder primacy is reiterated in the section.

Although this first step on the part of the drafters provides greater clarity to directors as to the interests they should promote, by identifying the interests of the members as the relevant interests, it was precisely that clarity which was controversial. In contrast, the common law formula, because of its conceptual ambiguity, obscured the extent to which shareholders' interests were in the forefront of the common law duty. The statutory formulation clearly rejects the "pluralist" approach to the law of directors' duties, under which the interests of a range of other stakeholders are given equal status with the shareholders as groups whose interests are to be promoted when the directors exercise their discretion. However, the rule of shareholder primacy was not intended by the Government to be adopted in an unsophisticated way. Instead, the degree of overlap between the interests of the members and those of other stakeholders is emphasised through the directors' duty to "have regard" to the interests of other stakeholders. In the words of the Company Law Review, from whom the strategy of rejecting pluralism but adopting a modernised version of shareholder primacy emerged, the philosophy behind the statutory formula was to be one of "enlightened shareholder value (ESV)".[108] Thus, in promoting the success of the company for the benefit of its members, the director:

in doing so [must] have regard (amongst other matters) to—

(a) the likely consequences of any decision in the long term,
(b) the interests of the company's employees,
(c) the need to foster the company's business relationships with suppliers, customers and others,
(d) the impact of the company's operations on the community and the environment,

---

[108] See Developing, ch.3 and Completing, ch.3.

    (e) the desirability of the company maintaining a reputation for high standards of business conduct, and

    (f) the need to act fairly as between members of the company. (s.172(1))

The ESV approach can be said to embody the insight that the interests of the shareholders are not likely to be advanced if the management of the company conducts its business so that its employees are unwilling to work effectively, its suppliers and customers would rather not deal with it, it is at odds with the community in which it operates and its ethical and environmental standards are regarded as lamentable. However, it is crucial to note that the interests of the non-shareholder groups are to be given consideration by the directors only to the extent that it is desirable to do so in order to promote the success of the company for the benefit of its members. The non-shareholder interests do not have an independent value in the directors' decision-making, as they would have under a pluralist approach. For this reason, it seems wrong in principle to regard the section as requiring the directors to "balance" the interests of the members with those of the stakeholders. The members' interests are paramount, but the interests of stakeholders are to be taken into account when determining the best way of promoting the members' interests.

It may be asked whether the ESV approach amounts to a development or a repetition of the common law. The answer is that it represents a development, but a modest one. At common law it was seemingly permissible for the directors to take into account stakeholder interests when acting in the interests of the company, i.e. the shareholders. The point was made a long time ago, albeit in the context of ultra vires, by Bowen L.J., who famously said: "The law does not say that there are to be no cakes and ale, but there are to be no cakes and ale except such as are required for the benefit of the company."[109] What the Act adds to the common law is a *duty* on the part of the directors to take account of stakeholder interests when it is in the interests of the members to do so. However, the statutory restatement of the duty may have an impact, even if it is largely based in the common law, because it may disabuse directors, and their advisers, of unduly narrow interpretations of the duty previously held.

    16–26

However, if the move from permission to obligation is what lies at the root of the ESV approach, it becomes of great importance to know how the duty is to be enforced. It is argued immediately below

---

[109] *Hutton v West Cork Railway* (1883) 23 Ch.D. at 673, the "cakes and ale" being in this case gratuitous benefits for the employees. For this reason directors can normally justify modest, business-related political or charitable donations on the part of their companies, though the broader public policy issues arising out of such donations are recognised in the requirement that such donations be disclosed in the directors' report and in some cases approved by the shareholders: see below, paras 16–62 and 21–22.

that section 172 imposes mainly a subjective test so that litigation will have only a minor place in its enforcement, just as litigation to enforce the common law duty of loyalty was relatively uncommon and even less often successful. This is because it is very difficult to show that the directors have broken the duty of good faith, except in egregious cases or cases where the directors, obligingly, have left a clear record of their thought processes leading up to the challenged decision.[110] Instead, a major role in giving some degree of practical substance to the ESV duty will lie in the extended reporting requirements to shareholders by directors which have recently been introduced, as we shall see in Chapter 21. Originally, the major reporting role in relation to listed companies was to be played by the Operating and Financial Review, but, after the Government's surprising change of mind on that issue, the burden will be borne by the new Business Review. Nevertheless, in the thinking of the Company Law Review the ESV approach to directors' duties and enhanced reporting requirements were closely linked.[111]

Finally, and for the avoidance of doubt, it should be stated that the duties laid out in Chapter 2 of Part 10 and, in particular, the core duty of loyalty do not override any obligations specifically laid upon management or the board in other legislation, whether it be employment, consumer or commercial legislation. The 2006 Act adds to those duties; it does not replace them. The duty of the directors to promote the success of the company for the benefit of its members does not exempt the company from compliance with, for example, health and safety or discrimination legislation, even if it could be shown that non-compliance would promote the company's success.

Interpreting the statutory formula
Defining the company's success

16–27 A number of important points arise on the interpretation of the new language contained in this section. First, it is to be noted that corporate *success* for the benefit of the members is the word used to identify the touchstone for the exercise of the directors' discretion. Success is a more general word than, for example, "value", which it might have been thought was what the shareholders are interested in.

---

[110] The classic case where the directors did all too clearly reveal their reasoning is *Dodge v Ford Motor Co* (1919) 170 N.W. 668. Henry Ford openly took the view that the shareholders had been more than amply rewarded on their investment in the company and so proposed to declare no further special dividends but only the regular dividends (of some 60 per cent per annum!) in order to reduce the price of the cars, to expand production and "to employ still more men, to spread the benefits of this industrial system to the greatest possible number, to help them build up their lives and their homes" (at 683). This was held to be "an arbitrary refusal to distribute funds that ought to have been distributed to the stockholders as dividends" (at 685).

[111] "The key components are the inclusive duty and broader accountability, in particular the inclusive operating review in the case of companies with real economic power ... They are mutually reinforcing." (CLR, *Developing*, para.2.22.)

However, the more general word is clearly the appropriate one, because not all companies formed under the Act are aimed at maximising the financial interests of their members. Companies may be charitable, for example, collecting money from donors to support activities which, whilst in the public interest, are not financially self-sustaining. They may have non-profit-making objectives, without being charities, as in the case of a company formed by leaseholders to hold the freehold of a block of flats; and sometimes a company is set up within a group of companies simply to hold a particular asset rather than to exploit it, even though the overall purpose of the group is to make profits. The company may be commercially-oriented without aiming to distribute profits, in which case it may, but is not obliged to, be incorporated as a CIC. In all these cases maximising the value of the company is not the primary objective of its members and perhaps not even an objective at all. Section 172(2) makes it clear that:

> "where or to the extent that the purposes of the company consist of or include purposes other than the benefit of its members, subsection (1) has effect as if the reference to promoting the success of the company for the benefit of its members were to achieving those purposes."

The underlying thrust of the section is that it is the members who are to define the purposes of the company against which the directors can give meaning to the requirement to promote its success. The definition of the purpose of the company may be set out in its constitution. This is less likely to be the case now that the company is no longer required to have an objects clause, but certainly in the case of companies with non-commercial or non-profit objectives this fact is likely to appear clearly enough from the company's articles. In other words, the position may turn out to be that the company is to be regarded as a commercial company, unless its constitution indicates otherwise, and so in the typical case the directors will define success in commercial terms.

A more important underlying question is the extent to which the section is intended to constrain directors' decisions about precisely how to pursue the success of the company. Should the company aim for expansion through a series of takeovers or by organic growth? Should the company be aiming for expansion or for exploitation of a niche position? It seems clear that the section does not intend to address this sort of issue at all, which is to be left to the directors, who in turn are accountable to the shareholders for their decisions through the company's corporate governance mechanisms rather than through the courts. To this end, the section imposes a subjective test for compliance: the director must act "in the way he considers, in good faith, would be most likely to promote the success of the company". This aspect of the statutory duty is one shared with the previous common law formulation and that was interpreted by the courts in such a way as to leave business decisions to the directors. As Lord Greene M.R. put it in *Smith & Fawcett Ltd, Re*, directors were required to act "bona fide in what they consider—not what a court may consider—is in the interests of the company . . ."[112] In most cases, it is true, compliance with the rule that directors must act in good faith was tested on commonsense principles, the court asking itself whether it was proved that the directors had not done what they believed to be right, and normally accepting that they had unless satisfied that they had not behaved as honest men of business might be expected to act. However, even where the director had not acted as an honest business person might be expected to act, this is not necessarily a demonstration of breach of the duty of good faith. Thus, in a recent case, where the directors' decision had caused substantial harm to the company, it was held that this was merely a piece of evidence, perhaps a strong piece, against their contention that they had acted in good faith rather than proof absolute that they had not.[113] These decisions on the meaning of good faith in the context of the core duty of loyalty at common law seem equally applicable to the statutory duty.

Failure to have regard to relevant matters

16–28 However, in order to give effect to the concept of ESV, the statutory duty contains the important element which the common law duty did not, namely, the obligation on the director to "have regard" to the list of factors set out in subsection 1(a) to (f). Does this requirement on the part of the directors give rise to a requirement on the part of the courts to scrutinise the decisions of the directors to establish whether, on an objective basis, they have in fact taken appropriate account of the relevant factors? It was already the case at common law that there was a minor strand in judicial thought which consisted of applying the public law doctrine of "*Wednesbury* unreasonableness" in the company sphere, notably where there had been a failure by the directors in exercising their powers under the articles to take into account factors or an alternative course of action which the court thought should have been taken into account. A number of comments need to be made about these cases. First, in the area of the

---

[112] [1942] Ch. 304 at 306, CA.

[113] *Regentcrest Plc (in liquidation) v Cohen* [2001] 2 B.C.L.C. 80. See also *Extrasure Travel Insurances Ltd v Scattergood* [2003] 1 B.C.L.C. 598 at [90]. It is to be noted that in neither the formulation of Lord Greene M.R. nor in section 172 is there a requirement upon the director to act "honestly" as well as "in good faith", though the word "honestly" is used in a number of court decisions in this area. However, the CLR did not believe that the adverb "honestly" added anything of importance to the requirement of good faith and its use might create uncertainty, and so it did not recommend its use either here or elsewhere in the statutory restatement: Completing, para.3.13.

exercise of directors' discretionary powers under the articles, this novel approach of appeal to the principles of public law has been used in only a small number of cases. The most authoritative statement of this approach, that of Lord Woolf in *Equitable Life Assurance Society v Hyman*,[114] was not part of the arguments of the other two judges in that case (or in the House of Lords on appeal). Secondly, the analogy between the powers conferred upon public authorities and powers conferred by the articles on directors is not close. It is notable that the architect of the *Wednesbury* principle, Lord Greene M.R., was also the judge who in *Smith & Fawcett, Re* (quoted in the previous paragraph) was concerned to stress the freedom of directors from control by the courts in the exercise of their judgment. Thirdly, it is of course the case that, as a general matter of fiduciary law, powers must be exercised for the purposes for which they have been conferred, but, as we saw in our discussion of section 171, that principle is already recognised in company law without the need to bring in the full panoply of the *Wednesbury* doctrine. Fourthly, those few cases where the *Wednesbury* principle has been invoked involved disputes among members of the company about the rights and interests as shareholders rather than disagreements about the setting of the company's business strategy.[115] It may turn out, therefore, that the inclusion in subsection 1(f) of "the need to act fairly as between the members of the company" as one of the factors of which the directors need to have regard will turn out to be significant. Fifthly, in so far as unfair treatment of minorities by controlling persons is the mischief which is to be dealt with, a remedy can often be provided under the unfair prejudice provisions discussed in Chapter 20, without developing a more stringent standard for judicial review of directors' decisions.

Sixthly, and perhaps most importantly, it seems clear that the Government did not intend in its formulation of section 172 to introduce a wide-ranging judicial review of the decisions of directors. In an earlier version of what became section 172 the duty to act in good faith was set out in subsection 1 and the list of ESV factors in subsection 3. Later they were brought together in subsection 1. As the Minister for Industry and the Regions explained in the Parliamentary debates,

> "In [the House of Lords], the clause was amended to bring together what are now its subsections and make even clearer—I

---

[114] *Equitable Life Assurance Society v Hyman* [2000] 2 All E.R. 331 at [17]–[21], CA (per Lord Woolf). In the House of Lords ([2002] 1 A.C. 408) Lord Steyn dealt with the case as a matter of an implied term in a contract, whilst Lord Cooke, dealing with it as a matter of the exercise of a discretion for a proper purpose, did not cite the *Wednesbury* principle but confined himself to mention of the *Smith v Ampol* case (see fn.82 above). See also *Hunter v Senate Support Services Ltd* [2005] 1 B.C.L.C. 175 at [165]–[232].

[115] See the previous note and the cases referred to therein. However, it should also be noted that *Smith & Fawcett Ltd, Re* was itself an intra-member dispute.

hope to hon. Members and certainly to those outside who will have to use the law—our intention that, while a director must have regard to the various factors stated, that requirement is subordinate to the overriding duty to promote the success of the company."

In addition, the Minister continued, the bringing together of the two previously separate subsections involved the deletion "from the clause of a second 'must', which we considered could be perceived as creating a separate duty". Finally, and most importantly,

"we believe it essential for the weight given to any factor to be a matter for a director's good faith judgment. Importantly, the decision is not subject to the reasonableness test that appears in other legislation ... That is in sharp contrast to, for example, decisions on public law, to which courts often apply such a test."[116]

16–29   For the reasons given above, it appears that the deferential approach of the common law to directors' judgments in relation to the core duty of loyalty was intended to be applied also to its statutory reformulation. Nevertheless, a proper reading of the section does lead to the conclusion that a failure by a director to have regard to each item on the list of factors would constitute a breach of duty and render the directors' decision challengeable, even if the weight to be attached to each factor and the extent to which it is appropriate to consider it in the circumstance of the case remain matters for the director's judgment. Indeed, this principle was already established at common law. Notwithstanding that it was for the directors and not the court to consider what was in the interests of the company, the directors might break that duty where they failed to direct their minds to the question whether a transaction was in fact in the interests of the company, even though a board which had considered the company's interests might have come to the same conclusion. A good illustration of the principle is afforded by *W & M Roith Ltd, Re*.[117] There the controlling shareholder and director wished to make provision for his widow. On advice he entered into a service agreement with the company whereby on his death she was to be entitled to a pension for life. On being satisfied that no thought had been given to the question whether the arrangement was for the benefit of the

---

[116] HC Debs, Standing Committee D, Company Law Reform Bill, Fifteenth Sitting, July 11, 2006 (Afternoon), all quotations from cols. 591–2. At one stage the duty of the director to take into account the listed factors was qualified by the phrase "so far as reasonably practicable" but this was deleted, perhaps because of the suggestion in the phrase of an objective test for review of the directors' decision. See also HL Debs, vol. 681, cols. 845–846, May 9, 2006 (Lord Goldsmith, on Report).

[117] [1967] 1 W.L.R. 432.

company and that, indeed, the sole object was to make provision for the widow, the court held that the transaction was not binding on the company.[118]

Finding a breach of the duty of loyalty on the grounds that not all the relevant interests have been taken into account will be somewhat more likely under the ESV approach. This is because the section is much clearer about the range of matters to which directors must have regard in the discharge of their duty to promote the success of the company for the benefit of its members. Indeed, since the statutory list of factors is non-exhaustive, it would follow that a director would be in breach of duty in failing to take account of any matter which he or she considered relevant to the decision in question. However, it needs to be remembered that the obligation to consider the impact of a proposed decision on non-shareholder interests arises only in the context of the directors' judgment as to what is necessary to promote the success of the company for the benefit of its members. Since the common law was broadly understood to be shareholder-focussed, the statutory formulation can be said simply to make explicit what was already implicit in the prior law; it does not require boards to approach decision-making, or to document their decisions, in a totally novel fashion. Of course, to the extent that boards previously ignored adverse impacts on shareholders' interests arising out of a failure to analyse the impact of a proposed decision on non-share-holders, the section should produce a change of practice.

Groups of companies

However, it is worth noting one situation where the objective test can come to the rescue of a director who has failed to take into account relevant interests. This exception arises in relation to decisions by directors of companies which are members of a group of companies. Under the statute, as at common law, the duty of loyalty is for-mulated in relation to the company of which the person in question is a director. In group situations it is common for directors to take decisions in the interests of the group as a whole (or some part of it), without considering the interests of the particular company to which they have been appointed. In *Charterbridge Corp v Lloyds Bank*[119] the directors of a company forming part of a group had considered the benefit of the group as a whole without giving separate consideration to that of the company alone when they caused the subsidiary com-pany of which they were directors to give security for a debt owed by the parent company to a bank. It was held that "the proper test . . . in

16–30

---

[118] Following *Lee, Behrens & Co Ltd, Re* [1932] 2 Ch. 46; but *cf. Lindgren v L & P Estates Ltd* [1968] Ch. 572, CA, where it was held that there had been no failure on the part of the directors to consider the commercial merits.

[119] [1970] Ch. 62. A similar approach has been adopted in the area of unfair prejudice. See *Nicholas v Soundcraft Electronics Ltd* [1993] 1 B.C.L.C. 360, CA.

the absence of actual separate consideration must be whether an intelligent and honest man in the position of a director of the company concerned could ... have reasonably believed that the transactions were for the benefit of the company." The challenge to the directors' decision failed in this case because the collapse of the parent company would have been "a disaster" for the subsidiary.[120] Despite the *Charterbridge* decision, it must be said that the core duty of loyalty does not recognise a duty "to the group" or to other companies in the group, for it insists that the main focus of the directors should be on the interests of the subsidiary, even if it accepts that the interests of the subsidiary are in many cases intimately related to the continuing existence of the group.[121]

A duty to disclose wrongdoing

16–31   In an interesting recent decision, *Item Software (UK) Ltd v Fassihi*[122] the Court of Appeal held that a director was under a duty to disclose his own breaches of fiduciary duty, an obligation apparently derived from, i.e. was an aspect of, the core duty of loyalty. At first sight this is a draconian duty. However, in many cases it will add little to the director's potential liability for breaches of fiduciary duty, though in some cases, as in this one, it will. The director had committed a breach of the corporate opportunity rule (discussed below) by attempting to persuade a client of the company to renew a contract with him personally rather than with the company. In the end, the client renewed the contract with neither the director nor the company. The company sued for damages but failed in respect of the breach of the corporate opportunity doctrine, because the court at first instance found the client did not take the director's offer seriously. However, it also found that, had the company known of the director's activities, it would have accepted an offer to renew from the

---

[120]   *cf. Extrasure Travel Insurances Ltd v Scattergood* [2003] 1 B.C.L.C. 598, accepting the law as stated in the *Charterbridge* case, but coming to a different conclusion on the facts because (a) the directors of the subsidiary never considered whether the survival of the parent was crucial to the subsidiary and (b) no reasonable director would have concluded that the steps taken by the directors would lead to the survival of the parent.

[121]   See also *Lindgren v L & P Estates Co Ltd* [1968] Ch. 572, 595 per Harman L.J. (no duty owed by director of holding company to subsidiary) and *Bell v Lever Bros Ltd* [1932] A.C. 161 at 229 per Lord Atkin (no duty owed by director of subsidiary to the parent company). The statutory qualification to the definition of a "shadow director" in section 250(3) (above, para.16–8), excluding a company in relation to its subsidiaries, supports this approach. The cases do not distinguish between wholly-owned subsidiaries and those with outside minority shareholders. Only in the latter case does the imposition of a group policy potentially have an adverse effect on the interests of the shareholders, for which the unfair prejudice provisions may now provide a remedy (see Chapter 20). It should also be noted that it is apparently legitimate for the company's articles to permit or require the directors to take into account the interests of other companies in the group, because in that way it could be said that the articles have defined what is to be regarded as "success" for the company in question.

[122]   [2005] 2 B.C.L.C. 91.

client which it in fact rejected. Thus, the company's loss was the profit it would have made on this admittedly not favourable contract, but that loss could be recovered only if the director should have told the company of his underhand activities, a duty which the court found to exist.

The case has been thought in some quarters to create a new and free-standing "duty of disclosure" on directors, but it is submitted that this is not the case. In fact, seen as a part of the core duty of loyalty, rather than as a free-standing duty of disclosure, the decision seems unproblematic. The core duty must require a director to bring to the attention of the board threats to its business of which the director becomes aware. The twist in this case was that the duty was imposed even though the threat arose out of the director's own wrongdoing, but it would be odd if the director's wrongdoing could relieve him or her from a course of action which would otherwise have to be taken.[123] The main obstacle in reaching this result was the earlier decision of the House of Lords in *Bell v Lever Bros Ltd*,[124] which had been interpreted by some as laying down a general principle that a director's own wrongdoing never had to be disclosed. The court was able to accept the result in that case by confining it to the situation where the director was negotiating compensation for the termination of his or her services with the company or an improvement in the terms of his or her employment, on the grounds that disclosure in such a case would be "contrary to the expectations of the parties".[125] However, outside the context of the director negotiating terms of service with the company, a duty to disclose others' or one's own wrongdoing can be regarded as a normal incident of the core duty of loyalty, where the director is aware that the facts of which he or she is in possession should be given to the company if it is to protect and further its own interests.

The timeframe for decisions

There was a widespread but, it is submitted, erroneous view that the   **16–32**
common law not only required directors normally to act in the interests of the shareholders but also to prioritise their short-term interests. However, it is suggested that the better view was that the directors were not bound to any particular timeframe within which to promote the shareholders' interests; on the contrary, they must take into account both the long- and the short-term interests of the

---

[123] See *Shepherds Investments Ltd v Walters* [2006] IRLR at [132].
[124] [1932] A.C. 161.
[125] At para.[57]—presumably because the parties were on opposite sides of a negotiation.

shareholders and strike a balance between them.[126] The Company
Law Review proposed in its draft statement of directors' duties to
specify an obligation on the directors to take into account "the likely
consequences (short and long term) of the actions open to the
director".[127] As we have seen, section 172 refers merely to "the likely
consequences of any decision in the long term". If anything, the
omission of the reference to short-term interests in the non-exhaustive
list emphasises the importance of long-term consequences.

Employees

16–33   Among the factors to which a director of a company must have
regard under section 172(1) are "the interests of the company's
employees". This is as one would expect: any list of stakeholder
interests will include the employees. However, in the case of the
employees this is no improvement on their position under the 1985
Act and constitutes, arguably, a worsening of it. This is because
under section 309 of the 1985 Act—a provision introduced in the
Companies Act 1980 by a Conservative Government—the matters to
which directors[128] were to have regard in the performance of their
functions "include the interests of the company's employees in general, as well as the interests of its members". That section has no
counterpart in the 2006 Act, other than the reference to employees'
interests in section 172. However, it never became clear whether
section 309 recognised the interests of the employees as something
separate from the interests of the members (a pluralist standpoint) or
whether it required the directors simply to take account of the
interests of the employees in the course of promoting the interests of
the shareholders (an ESV standpoint). If the former was the correct
interpretation of section 309, then the current position is less
favourable to the employees. This lack of clarity persisted under the
1985 Act in large measure because section 309(2) provided that:
"Accordingly the duty imposed by this section on the directors is
owed by them to the company (and the company alone) and is
enforceable in the same way as any other fiduciary duty owed to a
company by its directors", which meant enforcement by or on behalf
of the company and that the employees as such had no special means
of enforcing it. Indeed, it may be that one effect of section 309 was to

---

[126] See Counsel's Opinion quoted in the Report by Mr Milner Holland of an investigation
under s.165(b) of the Companies Act 1948 into the affairs of the Savoy Hotel Ltd and the
Berkeley Hotel Company Ltd, Board of Trade, 1954. This somewhat obscure source has
long been regarded as the *locus classicus* on this point. See also *Gaiman v National Association for Mental Health* [1971] Ch. at p.330: "both present and future members".

[127] CLR, Final 1, p.345 (Principle 2, Note (1)).

[128] Including shadow directors: s.309(3)—a strong indication that the drafters of the 1985 Act
thought that the common law duties of directors applied to shadow directors, since the
purpose of the section was to expand the common law duties otherwise applying to
directors.

dilute directors' accountability to shareholders rather than to strengthen their accountability to employees. Employees found it difficult to use the section offensively, whilst directors could make some use of the section defensively when sued by shareholders by arguing that a decision apparently unfavourable to the shareholders was unchallengeable because it was taken in the interests of the employees.[129] Writ large, this is an example of an argument against the pluralist approach to the duty of loyalty. So long as that duty is perceived subjectively, increasing the number of equal-status groups whose interests the directors must promote makes proof of breach of the core duty of loyalty difficult, almost to the point of impossibility. Correcting that defect by making the duty objective, however, paves the way for excessive judicial intervention in the taking of board-level decisions, thus inducing caution on the part of those who ought to be risk-takers. The best view is probably that a section like 309 of the 1985 Act or a more broadly-formulated pluralist section cannot by itself operate so as to alter the decision-making processes of a board, unless coupled with further changes in company law, such as board-level representation for the relevant stakeholder groups.

There is, however, one particular derogation from the core duty of loyalty which is made in favour of employees. This is to be found in section 247, involving the power to make gratuitous payments to employees on the cessation of the company's business and has been discussed in Chapter 7 at para.7–14.

Creditors

There is one surprising omission from the statutory list of matters to   **16–34**
which the directors must have regard, namely, the interests of the creditors. To be sure, so long as the company's business is flourishing, the creditors' position is not prejudiced by such an omission. Their contractual rights against the company plus the company's desire to preserve its reputation and thus access to future credit will act so as to protect the creditors. However, once the company's fortunes begin to decline, conflict between the interests of the shareholders and the creditors may emerge in a strong form. This is especially so under the British insolvency law which replaces the board with an insolvency practitioner responsible to the creditors when the company enters into insolvency. Consequently, the directors have an incentive to take excessive risks to protect their own and the shareholders' position before that point is reached, knowing that, if the company is already in the vicinity of insolvency, the downside risk will fall wholly on the creditors, whilst the upside benefit will get the company out of

---

[129] *cf. Saul D. Harrison & Sons Plc, Re* [1995] 1 B.C.L.C. 14, CA, where s.309 was prayed in aid to undermine the shareholder petitioning under s.459 against the board/majority shareholders of the company (at 25).

trouble. To be sure, insolvency law itself has long recognised this danger and has developed doctrines, notably those dealing with fraudulent preferences or transactions at an undervalue, which enable the liquidator to reverse some opportunistic transactions entered into by the directors in the period before insolvency. We are not concerned with those doctrines in this book. We have also seen in Chapter 9 that, relatively recently, the insolvency legislation developed the doctrine of wrongful trading (section 214 of the Insolvency Act 1986), which in effect creates a duty of care owed by the directors to the creditors, enforceable by the liquidator, to take all reasonable steps to minimise further loss to the creditors, once there is no reasonable prospect of the company avoiding insolvent liquidation. The CLR proposed that section 214 should be reflected in the statutory statement of directors' duties.[130] However, the Government rejected this proposal on the grounds that decoupling the substantive provisions at present in section 214 from the remedies available under the 1986 Insolvency Act would be "incongruous".[131] Consequently, section 172(3) merely provides that the duty imposed under that section "has effect subject to any enactment ... requiring directors, in certain circumstances, to consider or act in the interests of creditors of the company." Thus, the duty imposed by section 172(1) on directors to promote the success of the company for the benefit of its members will be severely qualified by the duty of care towards creditors contained in section 214 of the Insolvency Act, once there is no reasonable prospect of the company's avoiding insolvent liquidation.

However, the test of "no reasonable prospect of avoiding insolvent liquidation" has been argued not to identify accurately the point at which creditors' interests become at risk. They may well be at risk before section 214 bites. This argument was considered by the Company Law Review. It considered the proposition that directors should be required "where they know or ought to recognise that there is a substantial probability[132] of an insolvent liquidation, to take such steps as they believe, in their good faith judgement, appropriate to reduce the risk, without undue caution and thus continuing also to have in mind the interests of members."[133] The qualified way in which this proposition is put indicates the lack of agreement among the members of the Steering Group of the CLR about the attractiveness of the idea. Those in favour thought the principle expressed simply what good directors ought to do; those against that fears of personal liability would lead to excessive caution on the part of directors and

---

[130] CLR, Final 1, p.348 (Principle 9).
[131] *Modernising Company Law*, Cm. 5533-I, July 2002, para.3.12.
[132] To be defined as meaning more probable than not.
[133] CLR, Final I, para.3.17. The s.214 duty would remain in place and bite where there was no reasonable prospect of avoiding insolvent liquidation.

induce premature decisions to end or scale down trading, especially as the trigger point for the new duty might well be difficult to identify. The Steering Group simply put the idea forward for further consideration by the relevant Government Department, which later, and probably rightly, rejected it as inconsistent with its policy of promoting a "rescue culture" for companies in financial difficulty.[134] Certainly, in the form quoted above, the court would be given a very difficult balancing decision between reducing the risk that the company will be unable to pay its debts as they fall due and promoting the success of the company for the benefit of its members, because of the lack of guidance as to how to strike the balance. Consequently, this (new) principle relating to creditors did not find its way into Chapter 2 of Part 10 of the 2006 Act.

However, the common law also provides a potential source of creditor-regarding duties on directors, operating before section 214 of the Insolvency Act bites, and section 172(3) preserves not only existing statutory enactments protecting creditors, but also "any rule of law" having the effect specified in that subsection. In other words, the question of how far creditor-protecting duties on directors should be developed to supplement section 214 of the Insolvency Act 1986 has been remitted by the legislature to the courts as a matter of common law. What does the common law say about this matter? Starting in Australia in the 1970s,[135] the notion of a duty upon directors to take account of the interests of creditors as insolvency approaches has been widely accepted throughout the common-law world, including in the United States.[136] As with most significant common-law developments in their early stages, there is considerable uncertainty about the conceptual boundaries of the new doctrine. For example, it is clear that creditor-regarding duties are being developed by extension of the traditional common law duties of directors. However, it is not always clear whether the duty being developed is a fiduciary duty of loyalty or a duty of care. It would be conceptually possible to extend either or both of these duties to creditors. The former is a more demanding duty: in exercising their discretionary powers, directors would be required to give priority to promoting the interests of the creditors, either exclusively or, more likely, along with the interests of the shareholders. The latter would permit the directors

---

[134] *Modernising Company Law*, Cm. 5553-I), July 2002, para.3.11.

[135] *Walker v Wimborne* (1976) 137 C.L.R. 1.

[136] The current state of play is conveniently summarised by Andrew Keay, "Another way of skinning a cat: enforcing directors' duties for the benefit of creditors", (2004) 17 *Insolvency Intelligence* 1.

to continue to exercise their discretion so as to promote exclusively the shareholders' interests, but impose the constraint that their action should not, as a by-product, damage creditors' interests.[137]

16–35   Equally unclear from the decisions is the definition of the trigger point for the creditor-regarding duty, except that there appears to be general acceptance that the duty can bite in advance of the company being in a state of insolvency. In *Brady v Brady* Nourse L.J. said that the interests of the company were really the interests of the creditors when the company was "doubtfully solvent",[138] whilst in *Nicholson v Permakraft (NZ) Ltd*[139] the judge conceivably was prepared to go a bit further by suggesting the duty was triggered by "a course of action which would jeopardise solvency". Given the difficulty of defining in operational terms the point at which the creditor-regarding duty should be triggered, it seems likely that the courts will continue to experiment with different formulations of the trigger point for some time to come.

On the other hand, the majority view is that this duty is not in fact owed directly to creditors individually,[140] but is an extension of directors' duties as traditionally understood and so is a duty owed to the company.[141] The importance of this point is that it is thus a duty which can be enforced only by the company (or in a derivative action on its behalf) and not directly by creditors, so long as the company has not entered into a formal insolvency procedure. Even at that point, the duty is enforceable only by the creditors collectively (for example, by the liquidator) and not by individual creditors. As Gummow J. said in the Australian High Court, "the result is that there is a duty of imperfect obligation owed to creditors, one which the creditors cannot enforce save to the extent that the company acts on its own motion or through a liquidator."[142]

Breach of the duty opens up the possibility of challenges at common law, on behalf of creditors, to dispositions of the company's

---

[137] There is some authority in favour of the view that English law supports the duty of care approach. See *Welfab Engineers Ltd, Re* [1990] B.C.L.C. 833: when insolvency threatens, the directors may not take a course of action which will clearly leave the creditors in a worse position, but they are not bound to give creditors' interests absolute priority. On the other hand, the remedies granted for breach of the duty, see below, include the typical remedies for breach of fiduciary duty.

[138] [1988] B.C.L.C. 20, 40, CA.

[139] [1985] 1 NZLR 242.

[140] Or, even, to a section of the creditors with special rights on a winding up: *Pantone 485 Ltd, Re* [2002] 1 B.C.L.C. 266, though the case does not explore whether there is a duty on directors to act fairly as among different classes of creditor.

[141] In this respect the dictum of Lord Templeman in *Winkworth v Edward Baron Development Co Ltd* [1986] 1 W.L.R. 1512 at 1517 goes too far. However, the matter is not settled. See the recent decision of the Supreme Court of Canada, *Peoples Department Stores v Wise* [2004] 3 S.C.R. 461, adopting the notion of direct duties to individual creditors (criticised by Stéphane Rousseau, correctly it is submitted, on the basis that the case involved a reversal of "a fundamental principle of corporate law": "Directors" Duty of Care after *Peoples*: Would it be Wise to Start Worrying about Liability? (2005) 41 *Canadian Business Law Journal* at p.225).

[142] *Sycotex Pty Ltd v Baseler* (1994) 122 ALR 531, 550.

assets by the board when insolvency was in prospect which reduce the pool of assets available to satisfy the creditors, especially if the duty is regarded as fiduciary in nature and not a mere duty of care. A resolution of the directors passed in breach of this duty will be void.[143] Further, and contrary to the normal situation,[144] a breach of duty on the part of the board cannot be authorised or ratified by the shareholders in general meeting, since the creditors are now the residual beneficiaries of the directors' efforts, so that the cause of action against the directors survives to be enforced or not as the liquidator or administrator chooses. That officer may seek damages from the directors for the harm their actions have inflicted on the creditors (by way of reduction of the company's assets) or an accounting of profits made.[145] Before the recognition of creditor-regarding duties, there was a strong risk that directors would seek authority or forgiveness from the shareholders for their actions, which the shareholders would presumably be only too happy to give since the action was aimed to promote their interests. The main disadvantage of the common law duty—and it is a significant one—is that its proceeds would appear not to go primarily to the unsecured creditors. Since the company's cause of action against the directors exists at the point the company goes into liquidation, the proceeds of its enforcement will be caught by any security interests the company has granted. However, it does not follow from the above that the common law, any more than section 214 of the Insolvency Act, requires the directors to cease trading once it becomes clear that the company is in financial difficulty. As Scott V.-C. recognised in *Facia Footwear Ltd v Hinchliffe*[146] "a continuation of trading might mean a reduction in the dividend eventually payable to creditors but it represented the creditors' only chance of full payment. It is, therefore, not in the least obvious that in continuing to trade ... the directors were ignoring the interests of the creditors."

Donations

In the abstract, a decision on the part of the directors to give the company's assets away would appear to be a clear example of a decision not taken in good faith to promote the success of the company for the benefit of its members. On the other hand, companies are always being approached to support various causes, worthy or less worthy, and, these days, not only by individual citizens but even

16–36

---

[143] *Colin Gwyer & Associated Ltd v London Wharf (Limehouse) Ltd* [2003] 2 B.C.L.C. 153.

[144] See below, para.16–83.

[145] See *Liquidator of West Mercia Safetywear v Dodd* [1988] B.C.L.C. 250, CA; *Official Receiver v Stern* [2002] 1 B.C.L.C. 119 at [32]; *MDA Investment Management Ltd, Re* [2004] 1 B.C.L.C. 217.

[146] [1998] 1 B.C.L.C. 218 (an application for summary judgment). On the courts' interpretation of section 214 see above, para.9–10.

by various agencies of the State; and do in fact make donations of various sorts. Company law has sought to distinguish between donations which promote the company's business (legitimate) and those which do not (illegitimate). Traditionally, that distinction has been drawn by the law relating to ultra vires, but with the decline of the ultra vires doctrine, the issue tends today to be viewed as one of directors' powers: in the absence of an express provision in the articles or elsewhere conferring upon directors the authority to make donations, is there an implied power to do so in order to further the company's business?[147] However, even if in principle the directors have the power to make donations, any particular donation must still be justified by reference to the core duty of loyalty (and any other duties of the directors, if relevant).[148] In fact, the courts often run together tests for the existence of an implied power and tests for the proper exercise of the power. Thus, in *Lee, Behrens and Co Ltd, Re*,[149] where the company's constitution in fact conferred an express power on the directors to make the gift in question, Eve J. identified the relevant tests as follows: "(i.) Is the transaction reasonably incidental to the carrying on of the company's business? (ii.) Is it a bona fide transaction? and (iii.) Is it done for the benefit and to promote the prosperity of the company?"

In practice, the courts have tended not to examine very closely the link between the donation and the company's business when it seemed to them that the donation was in the public interest, so that a substantial donation by a large chemical company to promote scientific tertiary education was upheld even though the gift might not be used to promote the study of chemistry in particular and the company had no greater claim on the graduating students than any of its rivals.[150] It seems unlikely that this approach will change in the future, in the light of pressures on companies to be "good citizens" in their communities and of the recognition that companies may secure "reputational" advantages from supporting activities which seem remote from their businesses, for example, a bank sponsoring an opera production (presumably thus enhancing its reputation among wealthy potential customers).[151] By contrast, donations which shift assets away from shareholders in the direction of other stakeholders in the company have traditionally been treated with suspicion, but

---

[147] The courts are likely to give a positive answer to this question.

[148] Thus, in *Evans v Brunner, Mond & Co Ltd* [1921] 1 Ch. 359, where the question was whether a shareholders' resolution expressly conferring power on the directors to make a certain class of donation was ultra vires, Eve J. said *obiter* of the authority conferred by the resolution that it "is certainly impressed with this implied obligation on those to whom it is given, that they shall exercise the discretion vested in them bona fide in the interests of the company whose agents they are."

[149] [1932] 2 Ch. 46.

[150] *Evans v Brunner, Mond & Co Ltd*, above.

[151] The donation can then be presented as a contract: a payment in exchange for exposure of the company's name before a valued target audience, in fact a form of advertising.

that attitude may also be undergoing a change and, in any event, it is normally possible to present such apparent gifts as part of an exchange where the company is a going concern.[152]

The upshot of the law in this area is that directors probably have some leeway to steer donations or other similar arrangements (such as sponsorship) in the direction of their favourite charities or pastimes, without serious threat of legal challenge, provided such donations are not of excessive size and provided there is some link with the company's business. However, in one area, that of corporate political donations such leeway is arguably constitutionally objectionable. Consequently, in that area, as we shall see, the law has required shareholder approval of donations since reforms made in 2000.[153]

DUTY TO EXERCISE INDEPENDENT JUDGMENT

At common law, and in the previous edition of this book, this issue is **16–37** often discussed under the heading of the director's duty not to fetter the exercise of his or her discretion. However, the duty is better put in positive terms, as it is in section 173, as a duty to exercise independent judgment. At the level of principle the requirement is uncontroversial. However, there are four points relating to the practical working of this principle which need to be considered.

First, and perhaps most obviously, the principle does not prevent directors seeking and acting on advice from others. The board will frequently seek advice from outsiders (investment bankers, lawyers, valuers) and rely on it. Indeed, the board might well infringe its duty to take reasonable care if it proceeded to a decision without appropriate advice. However, the board will step over the mark if it treats the advice as an instruction, though in complex technical areas the advice may leave the board with little freedom of manoeuvre, for example, where lawyers advise that the board's preferred course of action would be unlawful. The board must regard itself as taking responsibility for the decision reached, after taking appropriate advice.

Secondly, just as the duty of care does not prevent a board from delegating its functions to non-board employees (provided it has in

---

[152] Thus, in *Parke v Daily News Ltd* [1962] Ch. 927 the payments to the employees failed because it could not be argued that a company about to enter liquidation any longer had a (shareholder) interest in fostering good relations with its employees. The specific decision in that case was reversed, within limits, by what is now s.247, which confers a power on the company, if it would otherwise not have it, to make provisions for the benefit of employees on the cessation or transfer of its business, which power is exercisable "notwithstanding the general duty imposed by section 172 (duty to promote the success of the company)."

[153] Below, para.16–62.

place appropriate internal controls—see above), so the duty to exercise independent judgment does not prohibit such delegation. However, it seems that section 173 was not intended to overrule the common law rule that *delegatus non potest delegare*, i.e. that a person to whom powers are delegated (as powers are to directors under the articles) cannot further delegate the exercise of those powers, *unless* the instrument of delegation itself authorises further delegation.[154] In practice, wide powers of further delegation are conferred on the directors by the articles, and it is indeed difficult to see how the board of a large company could otherwise effectively exercise its powers of management of the company. However, this rule means that the articles may effectively prevent further delegation beyond the board by simply not providing for this.

Exercise of future discretion

16–38   Thirdly, it was debated at common law whether the non-fettering rule prevented a director from contracting with a third party as to the future exercise of his or her discretion. The answer ultimately arrived at was that this was permissible in appropriate cases. The starting point at common law, despite the paucity of reported cases on the point,[155] seems to be that directors cannot validly contract (either with one another or with third parties) as to how they shall vote at future board meetings or otherwise conduct themselves in the future.[156] This is so even though there is no improper motive or purpose and no personal advantage reaped by the directors under the agreement. This, however, does not mean that if, in the bona fide exercise of their discretion, the directors have entered into a contract on behalf of the company, they cannot in that contract validly agree to take such further action at board meetings or otherwise as is

---

[154] *Cartmells'* case (1874) L.R. 9 Ch.App. 691. On the Government's intention to preserve this rule see HC Debs, Standing Committee D, Company Law Reform Bill, Fifteenth Sitting, July 11, 2006 (Afternoon), col. 600 (the Solicitor-General).

[155] But see *Clark v Workman* [1920] 1 Ir.R. 107 and an unreported decision of Morton J. in the *Arderne Cinema* litigation, below, at paras 19–7ff and the Scottish decision in *Dawson International Plc v Coats Paton Plc* 1989 S.L.T. 655 (1st Div.) where it was accepted that an agreement by the directors would be subject to an implied term that it did not derogate from their duty to give advice to the shareholders which reflected the situation at the time the advice was given.

[156] Contrast the position of shareholders who may freely enter into such voting agreements: below, paras 19–26ff. What if the directors and the members enter into an agreement which fetters the directors' discretion? This was discussed, but not clearly settled, by the Canadian Supreme Court in *Ringuet v Bergeron* [1960] S.C.R. 672, where the majority held the voting agreement valid because, in their view, it related only to voting at general meetings. The minority held that it extended also to directors' meetings and was void, but they conceded that the position might have been different had all the members originally been parties to the agreement: see *ibid.*, at 677. But *cf. Fulham Football Club Ltd v Cabra Estates Plc* [1994] 1 B.C.L.C. 363 at 393.

necessary to carry out that contract. As was said in a judgment of the Australian High Court[157]:

> "There are many kinds of transaction in which the proper time for the exercise of the directors' discretion is the time of the negotiation of a contract and not the time at which the contract is to be performed ... If at the former time they are bona fide of opinion that it is in the best interests of the company that the transaction should be entered into and carried into effect, I can see no reason in law why they should not bind themselves to do whatever under the transaction is to be done by the board."[158]

The principle in *Thorby v Goldberg* was applied by the English Court of Appeal in *Cabra Estates Plc v Fulham Football Club*,[159] so as to uphold an elaborate contract which the directors had entered into on behalf of the company for the redevelopment of the football ground and under which, inter alia, the club was entitled to some £11 million and the directors agreed to support any planning application the developers might make during the coming seven years. This is surely correct: if individuals may contract as to their future behaviour in these matters, it is desirable that companies should be able to do so too. The application of the "no fettering" rule would make companies unreliable contracting parties and perhaps deprive them of the opportunity to enter into long-term contracts which would be to their commercial benefit.

Section 173(2)(a) now provides that the duty to exercise independent judgment is not infringed by a director acting "in accordance with an agreement duly entered into by the company that restricts the future exercise of discretion by its directors." In the Parliamentary debates this provision was described as enshrining the *Cabra Estates* decision,[160] including presumably the rider that the agreement must be one entered into by the directors in the bona fide opinion that it is in the best interests of the company to do so (i.e. "duly" entered into). Section 173(2)(b) goes on to state that no breach of the independent judgment rule arises if the director acts "in a way authorised by the company's constitution". Thus, the articles may authorise restrictions on the exercise of independent judgment, which might be a useful facility in private companies.

However, section 173(2)(a) protects the directors only from the argument that they have failed to exercise independent judgment by entering into the agreement which restricts their future freedom of action. Can the subsequent exercise of their powers as the contract

---

[157] *Thorby v Goldberg* (1964) 112 C.L.R. 597, Aus.HC.
[158] *Thorby v Goldberg* per Kitto J. at 605–606.
[159] [1994] 1 B.C.L.C. 363, CA, noted by Griffiths [1993] J.B.L. 576.
[160] See HC Debs, Standing Committee D, Company Law Reform Bill, Fifteenth Sitting, July 11, 2006 (Afternoon), col. 600 (the Solicitor-General).

demands be said to be a breach of their core duty of loyalty, if at that time they no longer believe it to be in accordance with their core duty to act in accordance with the contract? There are a number of cases in which, where shareholder consent has been required for a disposal of assets or for a takeover, the courts have been reluctant to construe agreements on the part of the directors not to co-operate with rival suitors or to recommend a rival offer to the shareholders as binding the directors, if they come to the view that the later offer is preferable from the shareholders' point of view.[161] This line of cases might be justified on the basis that shareholders are peculiarly dependent upon the advice of their directors and that they might find themselves in a poor position to take the decision which had been put in their hands, if they were given advice by the directors which did not reflect the situation as the directors saw it at the time it fell to the shareholders to take their decision. The continuing validity of the no fettering rule in this context could be reconciled with the provisions of section 173 on the basis that that section deals only with the fiduciary duties owed by the director to the company (see section 170(1)), whereas the situation just mentioned triggers the fiduciary duty owed by directors to the shareholders to give them advice in the shareholders' best interest, if they choose to give them advice at all.[162]

Nominee directors

16–39   Finally, the independent judgment principle could cause difficulties for "nominee" directors, i.e. directors not elected by the shareholders generally but appointed by a particular class of security holder or creditor to protect their interests. English law solves such problems by requiring nominee directors to ignore the interests of the nominator,[163] though it may be doubted how far this injunction is obeyed in practice. The Ghana Companies Code 1973 adopted what might be regarded as the more realistic line by permitting nominee directors to "give special, but not exclusive, consideration to the interests" of the nominator, but even this formulation would not permit the "mandating" of directors and thus the creation of a fettering problem.

---

[161] *John Crowther Group Plc v Carpets International* [1990] B.C.L.C. 460; *Rackham v Peek Foods Ltd* [1990] B.C.L.C. 895; *Dawson International Plc v Coats Paton Plc* 1989 S.L.T. 655. The correctness of these decisions was left open by the Court of Appeal in *Cabra Estates*. Even here it must be accepted that the shareholders may in consequence lose a commercial opportunity which would otherwise be open to them. See the discussion below at paras 28–36ff.

[162] See above, para.16–6.

[163] *Boulting v ACTT* [1963] 2 Q.B. 606 at 626, per Lord Denning M.R.; *Kuwait Asia Bank EC v National Mutual Life Nominees Ltd* [1991] 1 A.C. 187, PC. The latter case shows that this principle has the advantage of not making the nominator liable for any breaches of duty to the company by the nominee director.

TRANSACTIONS WITH THE COMPANY (SELF-DEALING)

Introduction

As fiduciaries, directors must not place themselves in a position in **16–40** which there is a conflict between their duties to the company and their personal interests or duties to others.[164] Good faith must not only be done but must manifestly be seen to be done, and the law will not allow a fiduciary to place him- or herself in a position in which judgment is likely to be biased and then to escape liability by denying that in fact it was biased. At common law, the "no conflict" rule was probably the most important of the directors' fiduciary duties. As we have seen, the core loyalty rule is overwhelmingly subjective and so difficult to enforce, whilst, given the width of the powers conferred upon directors by the articles, the requirement that they stay within their powers under the constitution tends to have only a marginally constraining impact upon directors' activities.

It can be argued that the "no conflict" principle underlies all three of the remaining general duties of directors set out in the Act: the self-dealing transaction rules discussed in this section; the principle that a director must not make personal use of the company's property, information or opportunities; and the requirement that he or she must not receive benefits from third parties in exchange for the exercise of directorial powers, discussed in the following two sections. At a broad level, it is undoubtedly true to say that the purpose of all three duties is to discourage directors from putting their personal interests ahead of those of the company. However, the more specific rules under each duty have now developed sufficiently separately, especially, as we shall see, in terms of the action required of the director to comply with the duty, that it is convenient to consider them separately.[165] The separate nature of the three situations is emphasised by their separate treatment in sections 175 to 177 of the 2006 Act. This approach emerged because the sources of the conflict are somewhat different in each of the three cases. In the situations discussed in this section (self-dealing) the conflict arises because the director is in some sense on both sides of the transaction with the company. In the case of directorial exploitation of corporate property or opportunity, by contrast, the director uses for his or her own ends property or opportunities, to the exclusion of the company. Finally, in the case of what the common law called "bribes" the risk is that the

---

[164] Overwhelmingly, the conflict is between the director's personal interest and his duty to the company of which he is director, but where the same person is director of two competing companies, he or she may then be subject to competing duties. See *Transvaal Lands Co v New Belgium (Transvaal) Land and Development Co* [1914] 2 Ch. 488—conflict between duty as trustee and duty as director.

[165] On the importance of distinguishing between conflicted transactions and personal exploitation of corporate opportunities see *Bell v Lever Bros Ltd* [1932] A.C. 161, HL, per Lord Blanesburgh.

director exercises his or her powers in the interests of the third party rather than the company because of the personal benefit conferred on the director by that third party.

The structure of the Act is somewhat more complex than the above would suggest, partly because the three situations identified above do not exhaust the possibilities of conflict situations, which are endless. Section 175 is an apparently general section dealing with, as the side-note says, "the duty to avoid conflicts of interest". However, self-dealing transactions are excluded from section 175 by section 175(3): "this duty does not apply to a conflict of interest arising in relation to a transaction or arrangement with the company." Consequently, we shall deal in this section with self-dealing transactions before returning to the general duty created by section 175 below.

As far as self-dealing transactions are concerned, by the middle of the nineteenth century it had been clearly established that the trustee-like position of directors was liable to vitiate any contract which the board entered into on behalf of the company with one of their number. This principle received its clearest expression in *Aberdeen Railway v Blaikie*[166] in which a contract between the company and a partnership of which one of the directors was a partner was avoided at the instance of the company, notwithstanding that its terms were perfectly fair. Lord Cranworth L.C. said[167] on that occasion:

> "A corporate body can only act by agents, and it is, of course, the duty of those agents so to act as best to promote the interests of the corporation whose affairs they are conducting. Such agents have duties to discharge of a fiduciary nature towards their principal. And it is a rule of universal application that no one, having such duties to discharge, shall be allowed to enter into engagements in which he has, or can have, a personal interest conflicting, or which possibly may conflict, with the interests of those whom he is bound to protect. ... So strictly is this principle adhered to that no question is allowed to be raised as to the fairness or unfairness of a contract so entered into...."

16–41 It is important to note that this principle means that a director is in breach of duty, provided there is a conflict of interest which is not just fanciful, whether or not the conflict had an effect upon the terms negotiated between the parties to the transaction and whether or not the terms of the transaction could be regarded as fair, even if affected by the conflict of interest. It is therefore a strict rule: proof that exactly the same terms would have been negotiated, had there been no conflict of interest, will not save the director. Strict though this rule is from the director's point of view, it makes the task of the

---

[166] (1854) 1 Macq. H. L. 461, HL Sc.
[167] (1854) 1 Macq. H. L. 461, HL Sc., at 471–472.

courts somewhat easier. The British courts do not scrutinise self-dealing transactions, as they do in some jurisdictions, to see if they are fair, despite the conflict of interest. If there is a conflict of the type covered by the self-dealing rules, there is a breach of duty on the part of the director (though the company's remedy may be affected by the fairness of the transaction because no loss has been suffered).[168]

However, the lesson that might have been drawn from Lord Cranworth's statement that directors should not contract with their company was not necessarily correct or wise, even from the company's point of view. The director may in fact be the best source of a particular thing which the company wishes to acquire, and so a prohibition on interested contracting would cut against the company's interests. An obvious example is a contract between a director and the company for the provision of the full-time services of the director to the company. A ban on interested contracting would mean that executive directors[169] became a thing of the past. The crucial issue underlying the rule thus became, even at common law, the identification of the procedure which the director needed to observe in order to rid him- or herself of the taint of conflicted contracting. At common law the rule was that disclosure of the conflict in advance to, and approval of the contract by, the shareholders was the appropriate procedure whereby an interested director could enter into a contract with the company. This was because the shareholders, acting as the company and thus as the beneficiaries of the directors' duty, could waive compliance with it, if they wished.

Thus, from the beginning, the British self-dealing rules did not depend upon the application by the courts of a standard of fairness to judge whether the transaction should be upheld. Rather, the law sought to find a body within the company to which that judgment could be entrusted, and the common law allocated that decision to the shareholders. The search for the appropriate internal decision-maker to approve the transaction is an aspect of the self-dealing rules which is shared with the other no-conflict rules, as we shall see. Moreover, this approach had a corollary which somewhat mitigated the apparent strictness of the rule against self-dealing. If the shareholders did approve the transaction, it would be virtually impossible to challenge it in court. In other words, shareholder approval (or "whitewash" as it is sometimes called) was a robust technique for protecting the director. Shareholder approval did not, for example, simply create a presumption of fairness which a court might overturn, as it does in some other systems, but rather it insulated director and transaction from challenge. The robustness of the "whitewash"

---

[168] Even then, the company may be able to avoid, or capture the profit made by a director out of, a fair self-dealing transaction. See the discussion of remedies below at para.16–76.

[169] See above at para.14–29.

provisions is again a feature of other British no-conflict rules, as we
shall see.

16–42   Nevertheless, directors found shareholder approval an inconvenient rule and one which they regarded as in many cases tantamount to a prohibition on contracting with the company. They
sought through provisions in the articles to substitute the more
congenial requirement of mere disclosure, rather than disclosure and
approval; and disclosure to the board rather than to the shareholders
in general meeting. Just as the normal restraints on trustees can be
modified by express provisions in the will or deed under which they
were appointed,[170] so (at common law) can the normal fiduciary
duties of directors be modified by express provision in the company's
articles, which of course bind all the members of the company. Such
provisions became common-form in the articles of registered companies. However, there was no reason why provisions in the articles
should insist even on disclosure to the board and in some cases
articles giving directors permission to engage in conflicted transactions without any form of disclosure were adopted. This caused the
legislature to step in and require (in a provision which was introduced
in 1929 and became section 317 of the 1985 Act) that directors disclose conflicts to the board, irrespective of any provisions in the
articles. Thus, the board would be aware of the conflict and could
decide what to do about it, especially where the conflicted transaction
required board approval (under the company's internal decision-
making arrangements or as a result of an external rule). Thus,
through a combination of common-law principle, provisions in the
articles of association and statutory enactment the requirement for
directors in relation to conflicted transactions became one of disclosure of the conflict to the board. Section 177 of the 2006 Act cuts
through that complicated set of interactions among rules from different sources to impose directly a rule of disclosure to the board.
Because the statute endorses the rule of mere disclosure to the board
it was apparently thought appropriate to exclude conflicted contracting from the "duty to *avoid* conflicts of interest" which is the
heading for section 175.

Thus, the modern rule on self-dealing has become, in principle,
simply a requirement of disclosure to the board; and approval by
others, whether shareholders or fellow directors, is not formally
required. Unlike section 317 of the 1985 Act and earlier versions of
the statutory disclosure requirement, the 2006 Act deals in separate
places with disclosure of interests in proposed transactions (section
177) and disclosure in relation to existing transactions (section 182).
We shall look at each in turn. The duty of disclosure in relation to
proposed transactions constitutes one of the general duties imposed

---

[170] The most common example is a "charging clause" enabling professional trustees and their
firms to charge fees for acting as trustees or executors.

on directors by Chapter 2 of Part 10, whereas the duty of disclosure in relation to existing transactions constitutes Chapter 3 of Part 10. The reason for this division seems to have been the view that the common law applied only to disclosure of interests in proposed transactions and section 177, dealing with proposed transactions, is the statutory version of the previous common law (though very differently formulated) and so should be placed in Chapter 2. Disclosure of interests in existing transactions, by contrast, was a purely statutory invention (from 1929) and so its modern version should appear in Chapter 3. Beyond doctrinal elegance, however, the division is important in relation to the sanctions for breach of the two disclosure duties, for the categories of directors who are bound by the two duties and to some extent for the methods of disclosure.

Duty to declare interests in relation to proposed transactions or arrangements

The interests to be disclosed

A director who is "in any way, directly or indirectly" interested in a proposed transaction or arrangement with the company must declare to the other directors the "nature and extent" of that interest and do so before the company enters into the transaction or arrangement (section 177(1)). If the declaration, once made, becomes or proves to be inaccurate or incomplete, a further declaration must be made (section 177(3)). The term "transaction or arrangement" clearly includes a contract, which will be the paradigm example of a transaction or arrangement, but it embraces non-contractual arrangements as well.[171] The aim of the section is to put the other directors on notice of the conflict of interest, so that they may take the necessary steps to safeguard the company's position. It should be noted that the disclosure duty applies to any transaction or arrangement with the company, whether one to be entered into by the company through its board or through a subordinate manager.[172] What steps the other directors should take, once put on notice, is not dealt with in the section or, indeed, in precise terms elsewhere in the Act. No doubt, they will be in breach of their duties of care and, perhaps, loyalty if they take no or inadequate steps, but such a conclusion would require

16–43

---

[171] *cf. Duckwari (No.2), Re* [1998] 2 B.C.L.C. 315, 319, interpreting the word "arrangement" in what is now section 190. Section 317 of the 1985 Act made this point clear (see section 317(5)—"whether or not constituting a contract"). This subsection was an amendment first introduced by section 60 of the 1980 Act to section 199 of the 1948 Act, which had referred only to interests in contracts. It is not thought that the omission of the words "whether or not constituting a contract" from section 177 indicates an intention to confine the section to contractual transactions or arrangements.

[172] The arguments in favour of this view, given in the fifth edition of this book at p.577, in relation to section 317 seem equally applicable to section 177. Those arguments were approved by the judge in *Neptune (Vehicle Washing Equipment) Ltd v Fitzgerald* [1996] Ch. 274, whose decision was treated as authoritative by the Law Commissions, above, para.16–01, fn.1, at para.8.38 and was approved on consultation.

analysis of the other directors' actions (or inaction) under the principles discussed above. It is not difficult to envisage a board culture in which the steps taken on the basis of the declaration are minimal, especially if all the directors from time to time make such disclosures and trust that their disclosure will be readily accepted if they readily accept disclosures by others. It is also to be noted that the Act leaves to the company's articles the task of deciding whether, if the proposed transaction is to be entered into by the board, the interested director is entitled to vote or count towards the quorum at the meeting at which the decision is taken.[173]

The extension of the section to "indirect" interests means that the director need not himself be the other party to the transaction. It is enough, for example, that he is a shareholder in the company which is the other party or a member of a contracting partnership. This is not a novel development: the common law had recognised indirect conflicts of interest during the nineteenth century.[174] The requirement that the declaration disclose not only the nature but also the extent of the interest is a welcome improvement on section 317 of the 1985 Act which referred only to the nature of the interest.[175] It is obviously more informative to be told, not simply that X is a shareholder in the contracting party, but also whether X is a 1 per cent shareholder or holds a controlling interest.

On the other hand, a number of restrictive clarifications of the scope of the disclosure principle are contained in the section. The words of Lord Cranworth, quoted above, that the common law embraced personal interests "which possibly may conflict" with the director's duty were thought to be too broad, and in consequence section 177(6)(a) provides that a director does not have to declare an interest "if it cannot reasonably be regarded as likely to give rise to a conflict of interest".[176] It is doubtful if in fact this does other than restate the common law.[177] Section 177(5) does not require the director to disclose an interest in relation to a transaction unless he is aware *or* ought reasonably to be aware of both the interest and the transaction. Section 317 did not contain this qualification, which seems a sensible one. A director might be excusably unaware of an interest he or she

---

[173] The draft model articles for both public and private companies exclude the director from both, but subject to important exceptions where the director can both be counted and vote.

[174] See, for example, *Transvaal Lands Co v New Belgian Land Co* [1914] 2 Ch. 485, CA and more recently, *Newgate Stud Co v Penfold* [2008] 1 B.C.L.C. 46, suggesting the common law rule catches transactions between the company and any person whose relationship with the director is such as to create "a real risk of conflict between duty and personal loyalties".

[175] However, the courts when interpreting provisions in companies' articles have long required disclosure of extent as well as the nature of interests. See, for example, *Imperial Mercantile Credit Association v Coleman* (1873) L.R. 6 H.L. 189.

[176] A similar provision is to be found in section 175(4)(a) in relation to the statutory duty to avoid conflicts of interest.

[177] *cf. Boardman v Phipps* [1967] 2 A.C. 46 at 124 per Lord Upjohn: "In my view [the phrase] means that the reasonable man looking at the relevant facts and circumstances of the particular case would think that there was real sensible possibility of conflict..."

has in a third party who is contracting with the company (for example, where the managers of a unit trust in which the director holds units have recently bought a large stake in the third party) or in the transaction (for example, where it is to be entered into at sub-board level). Nor need the director disclose interests of which the other directors are or ought reasonably to be aware, on the grounds that such disclosure is or ought to be unnecessary (section 177(6)(b)). The courts in interpreting section 317 had reached the same position in relation to interests actually known to the other directors,[178] but they had got into some difficulties where there was only one director of the (private) company. That might have been thought to be the paradigm case of the director knowing of the interest in question, but the courts had required disclosure under section 317.[179] Section 177 will no longer require disclosure in the case of single-member boards.[180]

Also excluded is the need for a director to disclose an interest in the **16–44** terms of his service contract that is being or has been considered by a meeting of the directors or the appropriate committee of the board (section 177(6)(c)). It might be thought that this last exception is covered by the previous one and in most cases this will be so. However, where the service contract is to be decided on by a committee of the board, for example, its remuneration committee, it is conceivable that not all the other directors would be aware of the director's interest.

The above changes, as compared with section 317, are largely as recommended by the Law Commissions and the Company Law Review. However, the legislature did not accept their recommendations that the director should be obliged to disclose the interests of "connected persons", if aware of them.[181] The director need disclose only his or her own interests, though since that interest is defined as

---

[178] *Runciman v Walter Runciman Plc* [1992] B.C.L.C. 1084; *MacPherson v European Strategic Bureau Ltd* [1999] 2 B.C.L.C. 203 at 219 (the case was disposed of by the Court of Appeal on different grounds).

[179] *Neptune (Vehicle Washing Equipment) Ltd v Fitzgerald* [1996] Ch. 274. The judge thought that, if the secretary were not present, the director could even make the declaration silently.

[180] In the case where there is a single member who is also a director of the company (and may be the only director) and the company contracts with that member other than in the ordinary course of the company's business, section 231 requires that the terms of the contract are either set out in a written memorandum or recorded in the minutes of the first meeting of the directors following the making of the contract. This section aims to reduce the uncertainties which might later arise about the terms of the contract if there were to be no contemporaneous written record of it and no other person had been involved in its approval on the part of the company. This could be important, for example, if the company subsequently went into liquidation and a liquidator had to establish the extent of the company's liabilities. The section is enforced by a summary criminal sanction but breach of it does not affect the validity of the contract (section 231(4) and (6)). However, the requirement is applied expressly to shadow directors, i.e. where the sole member is a shadow director, in which case some other person(s) will constitute the board (section 231(5)). The section implements in domestic law the requirements of Art.5 of Directive 89/667 on single-member private limited-liability companies ([1989] OJ L395/40).

[181] Above, fn.1, at para.8.62. In fact, section 177 contains no equivalent to section 317(6) which made some limited interests of connected persons disclosable by the director under the 1985 Act.

an interest "in any way", some interests of connected persons will be disclosable on the grounds that they are indirect interests of the director. Furthermore, section 177 may involve a retreat as compared with section 317 as regards the categories of directors to whom it applies. Section 317 was explicitly applied to shadow directors, as is section 182 of the 2006 Act in relation to disclosure of interests in existing transactions.[182] As we have seen, however, section 177 will apply to shadow directors only "where and to the extent that the corresponding common law rules or equitable principles so apply", a matter about which there is considerable doubt.[183] This is an unhappy state of affairs. The arguments for requiring disclosure of interests in relation to proposed transactions seem even stronger than those relating to existing transactions, since in relation to a proposed transaction, the company will always be legally free to withdraw from the transaction on its current terms.[184]

Methods of disclosure

16–45   Assuming the duty to disclose does bite, section 177(2) lays down three methods of making the disclosure. In the case of a proposed transaction, these methods are said to be non-exhaustive, whereas in the case of existing transactions, where they also apply, the list is exhaustive of the permitted methods of disclosure.[185] The three statutory methods of disclosure are:

— at a meeting of the directors;

— by written notice to the directors;

— by a general notice.

The scheme of the statute seems to be that the first two methods are methods of giving notice in relation to an identified proposed or actual (in the case of Chapter 3) transaction, whereas a general notice is not given in respect of an identified transaction. The difference between the first two methods is that notice given outside a meeting must be sent to each director and the notice is deemed to be part of the proceedings of the next directors' meeting and so must be

---

[182]   See section 317(8) of the 1985 Act and section 187 of the 2006 Act.

[183]   Section 170(5) and see above, para.16–8.

[184]   The argument that disclosure to the board is pointless in the case of a shadow director, because the board by definition does what the shadow director wants, needs to be qualified because (a) the definition of a shadow director requires only that the board be accustomed to do what the shadow director wants, not that it does it on every occasion (see section 251) and (b) because, if the argument is correct, it is not clear why shadow directors are required to disclose interests in relation to existing transactions.

[185]   *cf.* s.177(2) "but need not" and s.182(2). It thus appears that an oral declaration of interest to other directors outside a directors' meeting is permissible in respect of proposed transactions.

included in the minutes of that meeting.[186] A general notice is one in which the director declares that he is to be regarded as interested in any transaction or arrangement which is subsequently entered into by the company with a specified company, firm or individual because of the director's interest in or connection with that other person.[187] As usual, the nature and extent of the interest has to be declared. Unlike a specific notice, however, a general notice must either be given at a meeting of the directors or, if given outside a meeting, the director must take reasonable steps to ensure that it is brought up and read out at the next meeting after it is given.[188] Thus, in relation to a general notice, the board must positively be given the opportunity to discuss the notice, though there is no obligation on the board actually to do so. The giver of a general notice is not exempted from the requirement to provide a further declaration if the first notice becomes inaccurate, as it might if the nature or extent of the director's interest in the third party altered, for example, if the director's shareholding in the third party increased significantly. Thus, even a general notice cannot simply be given once and forgotten.

Remedies

Although it was unclear whether breach of section 317 of the 1985 **16–46** Act by itself gave rise to civil sanctions,[189] breach of section 177 (proposed transactions) is subject to civil sanctions, but those sanctions are defined only generally. They are "the same as would apply if the corresponding common law rule or equitable principle applied".[190] The corresponding sanctions are presumably those which applied if the common law rule of shareholder approval (as modified by the articles) were not followed. Conversely, section 317 did have a criminal penalty attached to it for non-disclosure to the board in relation to proposed transactions. There is no criminal sanction for breach of section 177. By contrast, the Act confines the sanctions for non-disclosure in relation to existing transactions to criminal ones, as we shall see.

The civil sanctions available at common law and now provided by the Act in relation to proposed transactions seem to be as follows. Where the director acts in breach of the disclosure rule, the trans-

---

[186] ss.184 and 248.
[187] s.185.
[188] s.185(4).
[189] See (in favour of civil liability flowing from mere breach of s.317, independently of the articles), per Lord Denning at 585 and Lord Wilberforce at 589 in *Hely-Hutchinson v Brayhead* [1968] 1 Q.B. 549, CA, per Fox L.J. in the Court of Appeal in *Guinness v Saunders* ([1988] 1 W.L.R. 869) and per Lord Templeman in the House of Lords in that case ([1990] 2 A.C. 663); and against independent civil liability per Lord Pearson (probably) in *Hely-Hutchinson*, per Lord Goff at 697 in *Guinness*, per Harman J. in *Lee Panavision Ltd v Lee Lighting Ltd* [1991] B.C.L.C. 575 at 583 (the Court of Appeal did not commit itself on the point).
[190] s.178.

action is voidable by (i.e. not binding on) the company, unless third party rights have intervened. In addition, the director will be liable to account to the company for profits earned in breach of duty; to compensate the company for any loss suffered by the company; and will be a constructive trustee of any of the company's property which has come into his hands as a result of the breach of duty and thus be liable to restore it, or its value, to the company.[191] The third of these remedies is capable of acting in a harsh manner. It creates the risk that a director, who contracts with his or her company in breach of section 177 and finds that the transaction goes wrong in a commercial sense, will have the commercial loss thrown on him or her, even though that breach was not causally significant in the company's decision to enter into the transaction.[192]

Duty to declare interests in relation to existing transactions or arrangements

16–47 Section 182 applies the principle of disclosure to the board to existing transactions, unless the interest has already been declared in relation to a proposed transaction.[193] This section catches situations such as the interests of a newly appointed director in the company's existing transactions or interests in existing contracts which an established director has just acquired, for example, because he or she has become a shareholder in one of the company's suppliers. But why should a board wish to know about the interests of its directors in concluded transactions? What practical use can it make of the information? An example might be where the company has a power under an existing contract (for example, to terminate it unilaterally) to which knowledge of the director's interest is relevant. The rules applicable to proposed transactions (discussed immediately above) apply here as well, with the following amendments and exceptions. First, the disclosure must be made "as soon as is reasonably practicable".[194] Secondly, as already noted, the statutory methods of giving notice are the only ones permitted in relation to existing transactions.[195] Thirdly, a sole director is required to make a declaration only where the company is required to have more than one director but that is not the case at the time of the disclosure. That declaration must be recorded in writing and is deemed to be part of the proceedings at the

---

[191] See *Costa Rica Railway Co Ltd v Forward* [1901] 1 Ch. 746; *Imperial Mercantile Credit Association v Coleman* (1873) L.R. 6 H. L. 189; *J J Harrison (Properties) Ltd v Harrison* [2001] 1 B.C.L.C. 158, Ch.D. and [2002] 1 B.C.L.C. 183, CA.

[192] *cf. Duckwari Plc (No.2), Re* [1998] 2 B.C.L.C. 315, CA, discussed below at fn.222.

[193] s.182(1).

[194] s.182(4). The formulation in section 177(4)—before the company enters into the transaction—is clearly not available.

[195] s.182(2).

next meeting of the directors after it is given.[196] Fourthly, the obligation applies explicitly to shadow directors.[197] However, not surprisingly, the method of giving notice at a meeting of the directors is not available to a shadow director nor is a general notice required to be given or brought up at a meeting of directors. Instead a general or specific notice is to be given in the case of a shadow director by notice in writing to the directors, though that will then cause the notice to be treated as part of the proceedings of the next directors' meeting and minuted accordingly.[198] Finally, only a criminal sanction (a fine) is provided in respect of breaches of this statutory duty to disclose.[199]

A continuing role for the articles

We know from section 170(3) that the duties laid out in Chapter 2 of Part 10 "have effect in place" of the common law rules and equitable principles on which they are based. Consequently, in a conflicted transaction, a director who complies with the provisions of section 177 and discloses his or her interests to the board will not be in breach of duty if the company enters into the proposed transaction; and no liability will fall on that director. However, it might be argued that the common law rule requiring shareholder approval still has effect as far as the validity of the transaction is concerned. If there has been no shareholder approval, it could be suggested, the transaction will not be binding on the company, because equity says that directors are disabled from contracting on behalf of the company in such a case (whether or not they are in breach of duty).[200] Section 180(1), however, blocks this argument, for it provides that compliance with section 177 means that "the transaction or arrangement is not liable to be set aside by virtue of any common law rule or equitable principle requiring the consent or approval of the members of the company." Thus, in the standard case, compliance with section 177 will mean both that the director avoids a breach of duty and that the transaction is binding on the company.

16–48

However, section 180(1) operates without prejudice to any "provision of the company's constitution requiring such consent or approval." Thus, the company's articles may reinstate the common law principle of shareholder approval and, where this is done, a transaction entered into without such approval will not be binding on

---

[196] s.186. In the case of a proposed transaction the declaration has no point (if a further director is appointed before the transaction is completed, the section 177 obligation will arise at that point) but an interest in an existing transaction will be of continuing relevance and the declaration will be available to the new director immediately when appointed. Indeed, in most cases the sole director will have to make disclosure as soon as the proposed transaction is completed.

[197] s.187(1).

[198] s.187(2)–(4).

[199] s.183.

[200] *Movitex Ltd v Bulfield* [1988] B.C.L.C. 104.

the company, subject to the protections for third parties contained in section 40.[201] Will non-compliance with a requirement in the company's articles that a certain class of conflicted transactions be subject to shareholder approval also have an impact on the director's duties (as well as on the validity of the transaction)? It seems that it will. As we have seen, section 171(a) puts a director under a duty to "act in accordance with the company's constitution", so that in principle the members of a board which proceeds to enter into a transaction, without obtaining the consent of the shareholders as required by the articles, acts in breach of this duty. The directors could be required to compensate the company for any harm suffered in consequence or to account to the company for any profit made out of the breach of duty.

Again, the articles might add to the requirements for board disclosure as laid down in section 177, for example, by requiring it in relation to existing transactions. As we have seen, the articles of association of many companies require, directly or indirectly, disclosure to the board of interests in relation to existing contracts, because they ape or incorporate the provisions of the old section 317.[202] Non-compliance with such an article would be a breach of section 171(a), though it might be difficult to show that the company had suffered any loss or the director made any profit as a result of the non-disclosure. The impact of provisions in the articles of the above types upon the validity of the transaction would seem to vary according to whether the breach had the consequence that the wrong body within the company took the decision on the conflicted transaction. In that case the decision will be void; in other cases voidable.[203]

In short, at least in theory, the shareholders remain masters of the rules on conflicted transactions but now the onus is on those who want to move away from board disclosure and require shareholder approval or some other additional control, whereas under the prior law the burden of action lay on those who wished to introduce into the articles provisions modifying the common law requirement of shareholder approval.

---

[201] See para.7–5 above.
[202] The draft model articles for neither public nor private companies now contain any disclosure obligations in respect of conflicted transactions, but this will not affect the articles of existing companies, unless those articles are changed by the shareholders.
[203] See *Guinness Plc v Saunders* [1990] 2 A.C. 663, HL, where the wrong body under the company's articles (a committee of the board rather than the full board) acted to pay a bonus to the director so that the decision to pay the bonus was void, the committee being without power to act, and the money repayable by the director. *Cf. Hely-Hutchinson v Brayhead Ltd* [1968] 1 Q.B. 549, where the correct body acted but the director was in breach of his obligation under the articles to comply with disclosure provisions based on section 317: here the decision was voidable but not void.

TRANSACTIONS WITH DIRECTORS REQUIRING APPROVAL OF MEMBERS

The move over the years from shareholder approval of conflicted   **16–49**
transactions (as required by the common law) to mere board disclosure amounted to a significant dilution of the legal controls over
this class of conflicts of interest. The move, which had been substantially achieved by the first quarter of the last century, was later
shown to have weaknesses in those areas where the temptation to give
way to conflicts of interest was high and scrutiny of the terms of the
conflicted transaction by the other members of board could not be
relied upon to be effective. Consequently, not only did the legislature
introduce what became section 317 of the 1985 Act but it also went
further and, at various times, introduced statutory provisions which
restored the common law principle of shareholder approval in certain
specific classes of case. Sometimes the legislature went even further
and prohibited a particular class of conflicted transaction, though the
2006 Act has replaced the prohibitions with requirements for shareholder approval. These provisions were gathered together in Part X
of the 1985 Act and are now in Chapter 4 of Part 10 of the 2006 Act.
Consequently, a complete understanding of the law relating to conflicted transactions requires knowledge not only of section 178 and
Chapter 3 of Part 10 of the 2006 Act but also of its Chapter 4.

Relationship with the general duties
Where Chapter 4 applies, then compliance with the general duties is   **16–50**
not enough to put the director in compliance with the requirements of
the Act (s.180(3)). Indeed, without this rule, Chapter 4 would have
little point. In the interests of avoiding having to obtain multiple
approvals, however, the same subsection provides that securing
shareholder approval under Chapter 4 will relieve the director from
having to comply with sections 175 (the duty to avoid conflicts of
duty and interest) and 176 (duty not to accept benefit from third
party).[204] The subsection also applies even if the situation is one which
in principle falls within Chapter 4 but no shareholder approval is in
fact required under that Chapter, for example, because the transaction is one of small value. In such a case neither Chapter 4 nor
sections 175 and 176 apply. However, since the paradigm transaction
falling under Chapter 4 is a transaction *with* the company, in the
usual case sections 175 and 176 would not bite, even if applicable.
Shareholder approval is to be given by ordinary resolution of the

---

[204] Both duties discussed below.

shareholders unless the articles of association require a higher level of approval, which might extend to unanimity (section 281(3)).[205]

However, the other general duties will apply to transactions falling within Chapter 4 (s.180(2)). Thus, the duty of the directors to promote the success of the company and to act within their powers will still apply and crucially will apply to all the directors, not just the conflicted one. This is important because transactions within Chapter 4 will typically require both board and shareholder decisions. The board in the exercise of its powers under the articles takes the decision whether to enter into the proposed transaction and the shareholders then decide whether to approve the proposal under statute.[206] Thus, it is important that directors taking the decision whether to enter into the proposed transaction should be under the core duty of loyalty and be required to stay within their powers. Further, the conflicted director will remain under the duty to disclose the nature and extent of his or her interest to the board under section 177. This may seem unnecessary because such disclosure will be part of the process of seeking shareholder approval. However, the board decision may well precede the shareholder decision by some time. In any event, the board decision will be the only one in the case of a transaction falling within Chapter 4 but not requiring shareholder approval under its provisions. In either case, disclosure of the conflict to the board in advance of the board decision, as section 177 requires, is obviously desirable.

Chapter 4 of Part 10 brings within its scope three types of transaction: (a) substantial property transactions, (b) loans and analogous transactions, and (c) two sets of decisions affecting the remuneration of directors, namely, decisions about the length of directors' service contracts and decisions about gratuitous payments to directors upon loss of office. These situations were reviewed by the Law Commission which made various proposals for reform, mainly of a detailed nature.[207] A problem of overlap among the Chapter 4 approval requirements arises which is analogous to the overlap between the Chapter 4 requirements and the general duties; and the same solution is applied. If approval is required under more than one set of provisions in Chapter 4, the requirements of each set must be met, but it is not necessary to pass more than one resolution (section 225).

---

[205] If approval is required under more than one of the sets of statutory provisions discussed below, the requirements of each must be met, but not so as to require separate resolutions for each: s.225. In the case of charitable companies in England and Wales prior written consent on the part of the Charities Commission is also required, even where the transaction is exempted from shareholder approval by the provisions of Chapter 4 itself: ss.66 and 66A of the Charities Act 1993, inserted by s.226 of the 2006 Act.

[206] The shareholders' meeting could in principle both approve the transaction and instruct the board to enter into it, but if the transaction falls within the managerial powers of the directors, such an instruction would have to take the form of a special resolution. See above, para.14–4.

[207] Law Commissions, above, fn.1

Unlike with the general duties the statute here takes the plunge and applies all the provisions of Chapter 4 to shadow directors (section 223), though with the qualification that a company is not to be regarded as the shadow director of its subsidiary simply because the directors of the subsidiary are accustomed to act in accordance with its instructions or directions (section 251(3)).[208] A further and helpful characteristic of Chapter 4, in comparison with the general duties of Chapter 3, is that it stipulates not only the duties to obtain shareholder approval, but also the consequences of failure to obtain it, in terms of both the directors (and others) being in breach of duty and of the validity of the transaction in question. The provisions of Chapter 4 apply only to "UK registered companies".[209] These are defined as companies registered under the 2006 Act or its predecessors, but excluding oversea companies.[210] The exclusion of companies registered in other jurisdictions is not surprising. However, confining the statutory provisions to companies registered under the Companies Acts excludes also companies incorporated in the UK but in some other way than under the Companies Acts, for example, companies formed by royal charter or Act of Parliament.[211]

A number of the provisions discussed below contain financial limits. These are capable of being altered by statutory instrument as the Secretary of State sees fit, subject to negative resolution in Parliament (section 258).

Substantial property transactions
The scope of the requirement for shareholder approval
The law governing this situation is nearly the same as that contained   **16–51**
in the 1985 Act, with some minor improvements recommended by the Law Commissions. Section 190 requires prior shareholder approval of a substantial property transaction between the company and its director. It has been said of the predecessor of section 190:

> "The thinking behind that section is that if directors enter into a substantial commercial transaction with one of their number, there is a danger that their judgment may be distorted by conflicts of interest and loyalties, even in cases of no actual dishonesty ... It enables members to provide a check ... It does

---

[208] The statute leaves it up to the courts to decide how far the general duties apply to shadow directors, but does exclude holding companies in the circumstances set out in section 251, if the shadow director principle applies at all. See above, para.16–8.

[209] ss.188(6)(a), 190(4)(b), 197(5)(a), 198(6)(a), 201(6)(a), 203(5)(a), 217(4)(a), 218(4)(a), and 219(6)(a).

[210] ss.1158 and 1.

[211] Above, para.1–17.

make it likely the matter will be more widely ventilated, and a more objective decision reached."[212]

A substantial property transaction is an arrangement (note the vagueness of this term) in which the director acquires[213] from, or has acquired from him or her by, the company a substantial non-cash asset[214] of a value which exceeds £100,000 or 10 per cent of the company's net assets (provided the latter figure exceeds £5,000) (section 191).[215] The approval must be given either before the director enters into the transaction or the transaction must be conditional upon the approval being given, i.e. everything can be agreed between the parties but the transaction must not become binding on the company until the shareholders give their consent. If this principle is not followed the director in question, the contracting party (if different) and the directors who authorised the transaction are all potentially liable to civil sanctions (as set out in section 195). However, the company itself is not subject to any liability by reason of the failure to obtain the necessary approval (section 190(3)), a necessary provision since the purpose of the rules is to protect the company's assets. Although section 190 requires prior approval of the transaction, nevertheless approval by the members of the company within a reasonable period after the transaction has been entered into will mean that the transaction can no longer be avoided by the company, but the other civil consequences of breach of section 190 will follow (section 196). Those civil consequences are dealt with below.

It will be noted that the section does not preclude the conflicted director from voting as a member at a general meeting to approve or affirm the transaction.

Approval is also required if the contracting party is a director of the company's holding company or a person connected with the director (of the company or the holding company). The extension of the section in this way is in order to pre-empt rather obvious avoidance devices. In the case of the director of a holding company (and a person connected with that director), the section requires the

---

[212] *British Racing Driver's Club Ltd v Hextall Erskine & Co (a firm)* [1996] 3 All E.R. 667 at 681–682. The case is a good illustration of the operation of both the dangers and their remedy. Technically, the transaction is not between the directors and one of their number but rather between a director and the company, but of course the decision on behalf of the company is taken by the other directors.

[213] Defined in s.1163 to include the creation or extinction of an estate or interest in, or right over, any property and the discharge of any person's liability other than for a liquidated sum.

[214] Also defined in s.1163 and meaning "any property or interest in property other than cash". See *Duckwari Plc (No.1), Re* [1997] 2 B.C.L.C. 713, CA and *Ultraframe (UK) Ltd v Fielding* [2005] UKHC 1638, where the term was held to include a lease, a licence to exploit intellectual property, a supply of assets, and a sale of stock, but not a supply of services.

[215] The value of the net assets is to be determined by the latest accounts or, if none have been laid, by reference to its called-up share capital: s.192(2). Non-cash transactions need to be aggregated to test for their compliance with the statutory thresholds: s.191(5).

approval of the members of the holding company as well as of the members of the company, unless the company is a wholly-owned subsidiary of the holding company, in which case, for obvious reasons, the authorisation of the subsidiary's members is dispensed with (section 190(2) and (4)(b)).[216] The policy here appears to be that the director of the holding company may be in an institutional position to influence the actions of the subsidiary, so that the risk of unfair dealing with the subsidiary's property arises here as well. On the other hand, such a policy explains why the section is not extended to transactions between the company and a director of its subsidiary or of a sister company in the group, because those directors have no institutional position of influence over the company. If, in the particular case, such a situation of influence does exist, then it may be that the director of the subsidiary will fall within the definition of a shadow director in relation to the parent or will be regarded as a connected person in relation to a director of the parent.

The provisions on connected persons deal with a different set of avoidance devices, applicable to free-standing companies as well as companies which are members of groups, whereby the contract is diverted to a person with whom the director is connected, such as the director's spouse. However, to cover all possibilities, the resulting definition of a "connected person" is highly complex. Section 252 puts into that category members of the director's family, as widely defined in section 253. It adds companies (in fact, "bodies corporate")[217] with which the director is "connected", and section 254 defines the necessary connection as being where the director and persons connected with him or her are interested in at least 20 per cent of the equity shares of the company or control at least 20 per cent of the voting power at a general meeting. Section 252 then adds a person who is a trustee of a trust the beneficiaries (including discretionary beneficiaries) of which include the director or a person who is connected with the director under the above provisions and, finally a (business) partner of the director or of a person connected with the director. The detail need not be further examined here, but it will provide many hours of delight for those trying to avoid the provisions of Chapter 4 of Part 10 of the Act.

Because of the width of the connected person definition certain **16–52** transactions have to be taken out of the requirement for shareholder approval, notably certain transfers of property between group companies. Here, no director or indeed any other individual is a party to the transaction, but one of the companies might be a person connected with the director, for example, where a holding company, in

---

[216] Section 190(4)(a) dispenses with the requirement for shareholder approval if the company is not a UK-registered company. So, if the only British company is a wholly-owned subsidiary of a foreign company, the requirements for shareholder approval, if any, will be determined by the system of company law governing the foreign company.

[217] Section 1173(1), so that bodies incorporated outside the United Kingdom are included.

which a person has a 20 per cent shareholding, enters into a substantial transaction with a subsidiary company of which that person is a director (section 192(b)). To provide a safe harbour, also excluded from section 190 are transactions between a company and a person in his character as a member of the company (even if that person is also a director of the company), thus protecting substantial distributions *in specie* to its members by the company (section 192(a)). Also excluded are transactions by a company in insolvent winding up or administration (section 193—though not transactions by a company in administrative receivership), presumably because the directors are no longer in control of the company; and certain transactions on a recognised stock exchange effected through an independent broker (section 194), presumably because the broker and the market provide the assurance that the terms of the trade are fair. Finally, section 190 does not apply to anything the director is entitled to under his or her service contract or any payment for loss of office falling under the provisions discussed below (section 190(6)).

Remedies

16–53 Section 195 provides an extensive suite of civil remedies for breach of section 190, which at one stage looked likely to provide a template for the remedies to be made available for breach of the general duties.[218] The transaction or arrangement is voidable at the instance of the company unless restitution of the subject-matter of the transaction is no longer possible, third party rights have intervened, an indemnity has been paid (section 195(2)) or the arrangement has been affirmed within a reasonable time by a general meeting (section 196). It should be noted that a third party is one who "is not a party to the arrangement or transaction" entered into in contravention of section 190 (section 195(2)(c)). So, a connected person who is a party to the transaction will not count as a "third party" even if that person did not know of the connection with the director. Consequently, the connected person will not be able to prevent the transaction being avoided by the company by claiming to be a good faith third party without actual knowledge of the contravention—even though such a connected person may be relieved of liability to the company, as we see below.

As to the liability of those involved in the transaction, section 195(3) contemplates liability to account to the company for any gain which has been made by the defendant (directly or indirectly)[219] and (jointly and severally with any others liable under the section) to

---

[218] See fn.6 above.

[219] Thus, the duty to account is confined to the profit made by the person who is so accountable (though indirect profit is taken into account): there appears to be no duty on a director to account, for example, for a profit made solely by a connected person, though the connected person may be liable to account.

indemnify the company from any loss resulting from the arrangement or transaction. In the normal case, a gain will be made by the director where the director acquires an asset from the company and a loss suffered by the company where the company acquires an asset from the director.[220] A notable feature of the section is the range of persons made potentially liable. Under section 195(4)(a) and (b) liability is imposed upon the director who entered into the transaction (including the director of the holding company where the transaction is with him or her) and on the connected person if that person was the party to the transaction. This is to be expected. However, section 195(4)(c) extends liability to a director (of the company or the holding company) with whom the party to the arrangement is connected, where the transaction was with the connected person. In other words, by using a connected person to effect the transaction the director does not escape personal liability to indemnify the company against losses or to account for profits, if the director made a profit thereby— though the subsection is not confined to such instrumental cases. Finally, and this is most important, section 196(4)(d) extends liability to any director of the company who authorised the arrangement, or any transaction in pursuance of it, even if neither that director nor a person connected with him entered into the arrangement. Thus, section 195 creates incentives not only for directors not to break section 190 but also for directors to monitor compliance with the requirements of that section on the part of their fellow directors and, even more difficult, of persons connected with fellow directors. These liabilities arise whether or not the arrangement has been avoided by the company so that they continue even if, for example, the company confirms the arrangement under section 196.

This is a wide-ranging remedial scheme, for three reasons. First, the potential defendants are not just the director who was in a position of conflict of duty and interest and entered into the transaction, but also the person connected with him or her and the director so connected (where the transaction was with the connected party) and the non-conflicted directors of the company who authorised the transaction. For this reason, two defences are provided against the liabilities created by section 195(3) and (4).

Where the arrangement is entered into by a connected person, the **16–54** director with whom the connection exists is not liable if the director shows that he or she took "all reasonable steps to secure the company's compliance" with section 190 (section 195(6)). This defence does nevertheless require the director to be active, by taking "reasonable steps". For example, a director with a controlling holding in another company, which might engage in substantial property

---

[220] *NBH Ltd v Hoare* [2006] 2 B.C.L.C. at [44] to [49]: director not liable for profit made on subsequent sale of an asset acquired at an undervalue but only for the loss suffered by the company on the undervalue sale. *Cf.* fn.81 below.

transactions with the company, would appear to be required at least to disclose to the company of which he is a director the existence of the connection and to warn of the need for shareholder approval, should a transaction be contemplated. Moreover, the director would seem required to take reasonable steps to monitor developments in both business and personal life which might give rise to "connections" of a statutory kind, so as to be able to disclose them.[221]

A further defence is provided for the connected person and an "authorising" director. They are not liable if they show that they "did not know the relevant circumstances constituting the contravention" (section 195(7)), which, given the width of the connected person definition, is not a fanciful situation. This wording does seem wide enough to cover the situation where the connected person (an estranged step-son, for example) does not know of the step-father's directorship. In this case, the connected person does not appear to be under any legal pressure to monitor the activities of the person with whom he or she is connected so as to ascertain, for example, of which companies the other person has become a director. The defence in section 195(7) is one based on simple ignorance. However, if the connected person does know of the connection, it does not appear that he or she escapes liability on the basis that there was a failure to understand that the law requires shareholder approval in such a case.

A second example of the width of the remedial structure is that section 195(3) makes the remedy of accounting of profits additional to the right to avoid the transaction. Thus, any profit made by the director, but not captured by the company through avoidance of the transaction, can still be sought by the company; or the company may seek an accounting of profit even though the transaction cannot any longer be avoided. In the case of losses, actual payment of an indemnity, by any person, removes the power to avoid the transaction. However, if the transaction has been avoided, the company could still sue for an indemnity against any losses not recovered by the reversal of the transaction. Further, the Court of Appeal has deduced from the fact that an indemnity deprives the company of its power to avoid the transaction that the indemnity, in relation to assets acquired by the company, must include losses incurred after the completion of the transaction in question, even if those losses were not caused by the absence of shareholder consent, provided the losses result from the acquisition. This means that the director is at risk of having to indemnify the company for losses caused by post-

---

[221] It would not seem a legitimate reading of the section to interpret it so as to require the taking of reasonable steps only in relation to connections of which the director is actually aware, though the more remote the connection, the less the taking of reasonable steps would require.

transaction adverse movements in the market.[222] Where a transaction is avoided, the company, by restoring the situation prior to the transaction, protects itself against both transaction losses and post-transaction losses, and it was held that an indemnity must go as far.

Finally, section 195(8) preserves any other remedy the company may have against the director or to avoid the transaction, for example, under the common law or any other provisions of the Act. It might be wondered what common law remedies would not be covered by the comprehensive provisions of section 195. One answer is that the remedies created by section 195 are not proprietary, because the section applies to Scotland which does not recognise proprietary remedies in this situation. However, so far as the common law applying in other parts of the United Kingdom confers a proprietary character on the company's remedies against directors,[223] section 195 preserves it.

Additional rules for listed companies
In the case of companies whose shares are listed on the main market **16–55** of the London Stock Exchange, and so need to meet the requirements of the Listing Rules[224] drawn up by the Financial Services Authority, there are further requirements for shareholder approval. The Listing Rules apply to "related-party" transactions, a term which includes transactions with a director or shadow director of the listed company or of another company within the same corporate group (not just of the holding company) or a person who has been such a director within the previous twelve months or an associate of such a director.[225] On the other side of the transaction is the listed company or any of its subsidiaries. The requirement for shareholder approval also applies to transactions between the listed company and any person, the purpose and effect of which is to benefit a related party.[226] The requirement for shareholder approval applies to *any* related-party transaction (other than a transaction of a revenue nature in the ordinary course of business, small transactions and certain specified

---

[222] Contrast *Duckwari (No.2), Re*, [1998] 2 B.C.L.C. 315, CA and *Duckwari (No.3), Re*, [1999] 1 B.C.L.C. 168, CA. In these cases, the company recovered by way of indemnity the loss (with interest) suffered after the acquisition of a piece of land (at a fair price) from a director without shareholder approval when the property market subsequently collapsed, but not the higher rate of interest actually paid by the company on the funds borrowed to effect the purchase. The court in the former case based its decision that the post-acquisition loss was recoverable also on the argument that, if the statute had not made express provision for the company's remedies, the director would have been liable to restore to the company the money paid for the property (less its residual value) on the grounds that the payment amounted to receipt of corporate assets paid to the director in breach of trust on the part of the directors; and there was no suggestion in the statute that Parliament wished to give the company remedies inferior to the common law ones.
[223] See below, para.16–79.
[224] LR 11.1.
[225] LR 11.1.4.
[226] LR 11.1.5.

types of transaction),[227] so that the FSA rules have a wider range than those contained in Chapter 4 of Part 10 of the 2006 Act. Crucially, on the approval resolution the related party may not vote and the related party must also take all reasonable steps to ensure any associates do not vote either.[228] The principle of shareholder approval and disinterested voting is thus taken much further in the Listing Rules than in the Act.

Loans, quasi-loans and credit transactions

16–56   As in other areas of life—a recent example being the funding of political parties—loans constitute an easy way of avoiding the rules governing the disposition of assets. A transaction can be presented as a loan when it is in effect a gift, either because the loan is never expected to be re-paid or because the terms of the loan are non-commercial. Given their control over the company's day-to-day activities, the directors are in a good position to effect such transactions for their own benefit, thus indirectly increasing their remuneration; and history has shown that from time to time they give into the temptation to do so. Consequently, loans have long been subject to special regulation by the Companies Acts. In 1945 the Cohen Committee[229] recommended that the legislation move beyond requiring disclosure of the loans to directors to prohibiting them. It said: "We consider it undesirable that directors should borrow from their companies. If the director can offer good security, it is no hardship for him to borrow from other sources. If he cannot offer good security, it is undesirable that he should obtain from the company credit which he would not be able to obtain elsewhere." The 1948 Act introduced a prohibition on loans to directors. Now in the 2006 Act the prohibition has been re-cast in terms of a requirement for prior shareholder approval (section 197).[230] At the same time, the criminal sanctions previously attaching to these provisions were removed so that the sanctions are now purely civil. The result is to produce a much greater degree of parallelism between the provisions on loans and those on substantial property transactions, discussed above. On the other hand, the change arguably downgrades the protection available to creditors. In owner-controlled companies making a loan to the directors can be used as a way of siphoning assets out of the company to the shareholders where the company

---

[227] LR 11.1.5–6. The specific exemptions are set out in LR 11 Annex 1.

[228] LR 11.1.7.

[229] Report of the Committee on Company Law Amendment, Cmnd. 6659, 1945, para.94. It is interesting to note that one of the corporate governance reforms made in US federal law in the aftermath of the Enron affair was to introduce in the Sarbanes-Oxley Act 2002 a ban on loans by companies to their directors: s.402(a).

[230] This has removed a doubt arising under the old law about whether the company could seek to enforce its rights of civil recovery under the statute, on the grounds that it was seeking to rely on an illegal transaction.

does not have distributable profits. If the company becomes insolvent, the administrator or liquidator will not be able to sue the directors for the recovery of the loans under the 2006 Act, unless either the controllers, acting as shareholders, have forgotten to approve their decision to make the loans, taken as directors (which may happen), or the insolvency practitioner can discharge the greater burden of showing a breach of the directors' core duty of loyalty or some other duty, such as the wrongful trading provisions or the common law creditor-regarding duties.[231]

As with property transactions, a headache for the legislature has been the need to predict and pre-empt avoidance devices on the part of directors. The 2006 Act, as the 1985 Act before it, brings within its compass loans to both the directors of holding companies[232] and persons connected with directors (of both the company and its holding company)[233] but also extends the rules to transactions analogous to loans. Thus, the provisions extend to what are called "quasi-loans", to "credit transactions" and to "related arrangements". The extension of the provisions to analogous transactions was effected, originally, by the 1980 Companies Act and produced a tortuous set of provisions. The 2006 Act sets out the current law in somewhat less complex, but hardly simple, form. Initially in the drafting of the 2006 Act, some additional simplicity was to be achieved by applying the rules uniformly to both public and private companies, whereas the "analogous transactions" rules introduced in 1980 applied only to public companies. As late as July 2006, the Bill made no distinction between public and private companies, but in the event the Act reintroduces the exemption for private companies in respect of analogous transactions.[234]

Arrangements covered and method of approval
Section 197 applies to loans and section 198 to quasi-loans. The **16–57** former applies to any company, the latter only to a public company or a company, even if private, which is "associated with" a public company. Two companies are associated if one is subsidiary of the other or both are subsidiaries of the same body corporate.[235] It does not matter which is the public and which the private company. A loan is a well-known concept. A quasi-loan is not. Essentially, quasi-loans are transactions, to which the company is a party, resulting in a

---

[231] See above, para.16–34.
[232] ss.197(1), 198(2) and 201(2).
[233] See ss.200 and 201(2).
[234] See HC Deb, vol. 450, col. 797ff (October 17, 2006), seemingly as part of a bidding war with the opposition as to who could be the more deregulatory.
[235] Section 256. The reference to "body corporate" brings in companies incorporated outside the UK (s.1173(1)), so two British subsidiaries of a foreign company will be associated. If one is public and the other private, both will be caught by the quasi-loans provisions, even though the rules on quasi-loans do not apply to the holding company (see s.198(6)).

director or a connected person obtaining some financial benefit for which the director is liable to make reimbursement to the company.[236] An example might be the company providing a credit card to the director, the company undertaking the obligation to meet the payments due to the credit card issuer and the director having an obligation to reimburse the company. This is not a loan because no funds are advanced by the company to the director, but the effect is the same as if the director took out the credit card in his or her own name and the company lent the director the money to pay the card issuer. The sections require disclosure to the shareholders of the core elements of the proposed transaction and approval from the members before the company enters into a loan or quasi-loan transaction with a director or director of the holding company or a person connected with such a director. Approval is also required if the company, instead of making the loan or quasi-loan, gives a guarantee or provides security in relation to loan or quasi-loan made by a third party. Thus, if an unconnected bank makes a loan to the director, but the company guarantees the loan, approval will be required.

Section 201 deals with credit transactions, and also applies only to public companies or associated private companies. A credit transaction is one in which goods, services or land are supplied to the director but payment for them is left outstanding, including hire-purchase, conditional sale, lease or hire agreements (section 202). Again, such a transaction is not a loan, because no funds are advanced to the director, but the economic effect is the same as if the company had made a loan to the director and the director had then used those funds to obtain the goods, land or services in question. The section applies to both credit transactions entered into by the company with the director (i.e. the company provides the goods, services or land) and transactions entered into by a third party with the director but the company gives a guarantee or security to the third person (section 201(2)).

Finally, section 203(1) requires shareholder approval for a further set of "arrangements" entered into, not by the company, but by a third party with or for the benefit of a relevant director or connected person. In order for such an arrangement to be caught it must be one which (a) would have required shareholder approval if it had been entered into by the company and (b) the third party acquires a benefit from the company or a body corporate associated with it. Thus, the company cannot induce a third party to do without shareholder approval something which, if done by the company, requires such approval, where the third party obtains a benefit from the company for doing that thing. Section 203(1) also brings within the shareholder approval requirement situations where the company assumes responsibility under an arrangement previously entered into by a

---

[236] s.199.

third party which, if entered into by the company, would have required the shareholders' approval. Thus, if a bank makes a loan to the director, but later the company assumes the obligation to repay the loan, the assumption of obligation by the company will require shareholder approval. By virtue of section 203 the company cannot avoid shareholder approval by doing indirectly what it cannot do directly.

Shareholder approval is by ordinary resolution, unless the articles   **16–58** impose a higher requirement.[237] Because of the potential complexity of the transactions covered by the provisions, it is not surprising that the Act requires full details of the proposed arrangement to be disclosed to the shareholders in writing in advance of their consideration of the approval resolution. Those details must disclose in particular the value the director will receive under the transaction and the amount of the company's liability.[238] As usual, approval is not required of the members of a wholly-owned subsidiary.[239]

The previous additional disclosure obligation in the annual accounts issued at the end of the relevant financial year is carried forward in section 413, but in a modified way. Under section 232 of the 1985 Act details of loans, quasi-loans, credit transactions etc. were required to be given in notes to the annual accounts.[240] Section 413 applies to "advances and credits" granted by the company to its directors and "guarantees of any kind" entered into by the company on behalf of its directors. The new wording does not map easily onto the transactions dealt with in Chapter 4 of Part 10 of the Act and is in fact derived from the Directives on companies' accounts.[241] It was possibly thought that, disclosure to the shareholders now being a function of the need to obtain their approval to the proposed arrangements, there was less need for the accounts provisions to mimic the provisions of the sections discussed above. Indeed, it is possible that nothing specific about disclosure of the above transactions in the accounts would have been required by the Act, had the Directives not required otherwise.

Exceptions
Having brought a wide range of transactions within the net of those   **16–59** needing shareholder approval, the statute then proceeds to provide "safe harbours" i.e. to identify certain situations where the member approval requirement is not required because the transaction is thought to be legitimate or to raise only a small risk of abuse. First, the requirement does not apply to anything done by the company to

---

[237] s.281(3).
[238] ss.197(3),(4), 198(3),(5), 200(4),(5), 201(4),(5), and 203(3),(4).
[239] ss.197(5)(b), 198(6)(b), 200(6)(b), and 203(5)(b).
[240] Detail was provided in Part II of Schedule 6 to the 1985 Act.
[241] Articles 43(1) and (13) of Directives 78/660/EEC and 83/459/EEC.

put the director or connected person with funds to meet expenditure incurred for the purpose of the company or to perform properly the duties of an officer of the company or to enable the person to avoid incurring such expenditure. However, a cap of £50,000 is placed on the value arrangements falling within the exemption (section 204).[242] Thus, if the credit card mentioned above is confined to business expenditures, and has an appropriate credit limit, it will not require shareholder approval.

Secondly, shareholder approval is not required for arrangements designed to put the director of the company or holding company in a position to defend civil or criminal proceedings alleging breach of duty, to apply for relief in relation to such an action,[243] or to defend regulatory proceedings, in relation to the company or any associated company (sections 205–206). However, other than in the case of regulatory proceedings, the arrangement must be reversed (for example, the company repaid a loan) if the defence is not successful. Thirdly, certain minor value arrangements are exempted (under £10,000 for loans and quasi-loans; under £15,000 for credit transactions) (section 207(1), (2)).

Fourthly, credit transactions entered into by the company in the ordinary course of its business on no more favourable terms than it is "reasonable to expect" the company would offer to an unconnected person are exempted (section 207(3)). Fifthly, loans and quasi-loans by money-lending companies are exempted if made in the ordinary course of the company's business and no more favourable terms[244] than it is "reasonable to expect" the company would offer to an unconnected person (section 209).[245] Finally, arrangements for the benefit of associated companies[246] are permitted, even if they are connected persons, in order to facilitate intra-group transfers (section 208).

---

[242] The cap is the only survivor of a number of restrictions placed on such arrangements by its predecessor, s.337 of the 1985 Act. In practice, this is likely to be a heavily used exception. Transactions have to be aggregated for the purpose of determining whether monetary thresholds have been crossed (s.209) and section 210 gives some guidance on the valuation of different types of arrangement.

[243] See below, para.16–96.

[244] However, a loan to purchase or improve a main residence for the director may be on non-commercial terms if the company has a home-loan scheme for its employees, it regularly makes such loans to its employees and the terms of the loan are the standard ones under the scheme: s.208(3), (4).

[245] s.208(2). This is a somewhat narrower exception than that for credit transactions because credit transactions are exempted when entered into by any company (provided this is done in the ordinary course of the company's business) whereas the loan exception applies only to money-lending companies, i.e. those whose ordinary business includes the making of such loans. So, if the ordinary course of a company's business requires it to enter into a one-off credit transaction, it may make use of section 206(3), whether or not its ordinary business includes entering into this class of transaction.

[246] See para.16–57 above.

Remedies

The civil remedies provided under section 213 are similar to those **16–60** under section 195 in relation to substantial property transactions, i.e. avoidance of the transaction,[247] recovery of profits made and an indemnity against loss, the latter two remedies being exercisable against the director receiving the loan, etc., those connected with that director and the directors authorising the loan.[248] The same defences are provided.

Directors' service contracts and gratuitous payments to directors

A director contracting with his or her company in relation to the **16–61** remuneration to be received constitutes a paradigm example of a conflict of interest, which is likely to exist in a very strong form. However, Chapter 4 of Part 10 does not in general require share-holder approval of directors' remuneration. It does so only in two specific areas. Approval is required for directors' service contracts of more than two years' duration (section 188) and of gratuitous payments for loss of office (sections 215ff). These provisions are discussed elsewhere in the book, as part of our more general discussion of the control of directors' remuneration and in relation to takeovers.[249]

Political donations and expenditure

It may be convenient here to deal briefly with a final situation where **16–62** shareholder approval of directors' acts is required, namely for political donations and expenditure. These provisions are to be found in Part 14 of the Act, rather than Part 10, though they can be presented as aiming to control a potential conflict of interest. That conflict is between the personal interests of the directors in promoting a particular political party and the interests of the shareholders as a body in not having corporate assets spent in ways which do not help to promote the success of the company. Of course, the provisions also have a wider constitutional significance, which is not a concern for this book, especially in the light of the long-standing regulation of the use by trade unions of their funds for political purposes.[250] One reason why the requirement for shareholder approval of political expenditure is to be found in Part 14 may be that what is required is

---

[247] And section 214 makes the same provision as s.196 in relation to affirmation.

[248] It has been held that it is sufficient to impose liability on the director who authorised the loan (s.213(4)(d)), jointly and severally with the director who received it, that the director was aware from the annual accounts of the practice of making loans to the recipient director, even if he was unaware of the precise amounts. See *Neville v Krikorian* [2007] 1 B.C.L.C. 1, CA (followed in *Queensway Systems Ltd v Walker* [2007] 2 B.C.L.C. 577). In that case the authorising director was also held to be in breach of his general duties to the company by not seeking to recover the loans (which were repayable on demand) as soon as he knew of their existence.

[249] See paras 14–23 and 28–32.

[250] See now the Trade Union and Labour Relations (Consolidation) Act 1992, Chapter III, Part VI.

not, as in Part 10, shareholder approval of a particular transaction but shareholder approval of a company policy. The shareholder resolution approving political expenditure "must be expressed in general terms" and in fact "must not purport to authorise particular donations or expenditure."[251] If passed, the resolution has effect for four years, though the articles may impose a shorter period.[252]

The Act requires an authorising resolution for (a) corporate donations to political parties registered under the relevant British legislation or those which participate in elections to public office in other EU Member States, to other political organisations and to independent candidates;[253] and (b) other political expenditure.[254] The latter is expenditure of a promotional type and other corporate activities which are "capable of being reasonably regarded as intended to affect public support for a political party or other political organisation",[255] even though there is no direct donation to a political party. A resolution is required of the shareholders (by ordinary resolution unless the articles impose a higher standard) in the case of a free-standing company; and of the shareholders of the (ultimate) holding company as well if the company is part of a group. However, in a group situation some relief is provided from the need to obtain multiple authorisations in that a resolution is not required of the company itself if it is a wholly-owned subsidiary.[256] There is one exception to this relief: even a wholly-owned subsidiary requires a resolution of its shareholders, if the parent company is not "UK registered", i.e. registered under the Act or any of its predecessors.[257] This is because a holding company which is not UK registered is not required to pass a resolution conferring approval on the political expenditure of its UK subsidiaries, so that, in such a case, the obligation on the wholly-owned subsidiary revives.[258] This may often be a rather pointless formality, but at least it will require the directors of the UK subsidiary to explain to the foreign parent the provisions of the Act on political donations.

The resolution may give authority for political expenditure generally or confine it to one or more of the following: donations to

---

[251] s.367(5).

[252] s.368.

[253] s.364. A donation to the political fund of a trade union is included, but not any other type of donation to a union: s.374.

[254] s.366. There is an exemption for small donations (no more than £5,000 over any period of twelve months): s.378.

[255] s.365. Also included is expenditure on activity designed to influence voters' attitudes in referendums.

[256] s.366(3),(4). Provision is made for a single resolution to be passed in groups of companies, for example, covering donations by a holding company and any of its subsidiaries (even where those subsidiaries change during the period of the validity of the resolution): s.367(1), (2),(4),(7).

[257] ss.1158 and 1.

[258] s.366(4)(b). The 1985 Act had a series of more complex provisions attempting to deal with non-UK holding and subsidiary companies, but these have been abandoned.

political parties and independent candidates, donations to other political organisations and political expenditure. In any event, the resolution must set a monetary limit for the expenditures during the period to which it applies.[259]

Where a free-standing company makes a political payment or incurs expenditure without the required shareholder approval the directors of the company making the payment will be jointly and severally liable to restore to the company the expenditure (with interest) and to compensate the company for any loss or damage it has suffered in consequence, though this second head of loss might be difficult to show.[260] The liability provisions of Part 14 also extend to shadow directors.[261] Where the company in default is a subsidiary, the directors of the ultimate UK holding company will also be liable (to the subsidiary) but only if they failed to take all reasonable steps to prevent the breach by the subsidiary.[262]

There is anecdotal evidence that the effect of these provisions of the Act (introduced in 2000) has been to persuade the directors of many companies not to make political donations from corporate funds, rather than to seek to shareholder approval to do so. Of course, wealthy business figures make large donations to political parties, but do so out of their personal wealth, which may be derived from the activities of businesses they control.

CONFLICTS OF INTEREST AND THE USE OF CORPORATE PROPERTY, INFORMATION AND OPPORTUNITY

The scope and functioning of section 175

Section 175(1) states that "a director must avoid a situation in which **16–63** he has, or can have, a direct or indirect interest that conflicts, or possibly may conflict, with the interests of the company".[263] Section 175(7) makes it clear that a conflict of interests includes a conflict of duties. Subject to a restriction in relation to charitable companies,[264]

---

[259] s.367(3),(6).
[260] s.369(1),(2),(3). If the donation is repaid by the recipient, presumably the first head of loss falls away. This was made explicit under the previous law.
[261] s.379(1).
[262] s.369(3)(b),(4).
[263] Subject to the exception—"not reasonably regarded as likely" to give rise to a conflict—in section 175(4)(a), which parallels the provision in section 177(6)(a). See para.16–43 above.
[264] In the case of charitable companies self-dealing transactions fall within s.175, unless the articles permit the s.175 duty to be disapplied and, even then, the articles may not effect a blanket disapplication but may do so only "in relation to descriptions of transactions or arrangements specified" in the articles (section 181(2)). Thus, for charitable companies board or shareholder authorisation will be required in many cases for directors' conflicted transactions with the company. The tougher rules for charitable companies are probably based on the premise that monitoring of the directors by the members of a charitable company is generally less effective than in the case of a non-charitable company and that the Charity Commission cannot make up the whole of the monitoring deficit.

section 175(3) excludes from the scope of the section one central type of situation involving conflict of interest, namely, "a conflict of interest arising in relation to a transaction or arrangement with the company". Self-dealing transactions are covered by section 177, discussed above, rather than by section 175. However, it should be noted that s.175(3) has the effect of excluding self-dealing transactions even if section 177 does not apply its normal rule of disclosure to the board of the conflicted transaction in question, for example, decisions on directors' remuneration. Having excluded self-dealing transactions, section 175 applies, as is expressly stated in section 175(2), "in particular to the exploitation of any property, information or opportunity" of the company. However, it is important to note that section 175 imposes a general obligation to avoid conflicts of interest. Any conflict situation, not excluded by section 175(3), will fall within its scope, whether or not it involves the exploitation of property, information or opportunity of the company. The example of a person acting as a director of competing companies is discussed below.

As with the self-dealing transactions discussed above, the aim of the rules in this area is to identify the appropriate body or bodies to handle the conflict situation on behalf of the company. As with self-dealing transactions, again, the common law rule was shareholder approval.[265] Section 175 introduces, as we shall see, the mechanism of approval by the uninvolved members of the board, as an alternative to shareholder approval. However, unlike section 177 which imposes simply an obligation of disclosure to the board for self-dealing transactions, section 175 requires the board, assuming it wishes to act, to approve the director putting him- or herself in a position of conflict of duty and interest. This difference in the roles of the board is necessary because, unlike with self-dealing transactions, situations falling within section 175 will not necessarily generate a transaction to which the company is party. An example would be where a director diverts a corporate opportunity for personal use. The decision for the board thus becomes not whether to enter into the transaction (the typical question in the self-dealing case), but whether to approve the director's breach of duty.

We will look first at corporate opportunities, to which section 175 applies "in particular" and then at other conflict situations falling within the section.

---

[265] In *Queensland Mines Ltd v Hudson* [1978] 52 ALJR 379 the Privy Council appeared to accept a board decision as releasing the corporate interest in an opportunity, but in that case the only members of the company were two other companies, each represented on the board of the company in question.

Corporate opportunities

It follows from the placing of references to corporate opportunities **16–64** and related transactions within a section 175 whose subsection (1) lays down a general principle about the avoidance of conflicts of interest that the rules on corporate opportunities are to be viewed as an expression of the "no conflict" principle rather than, as some have argued, as a free-standing prohibition on the making of profits by directors out of their office as director, without the sanction of the shareholders. This should not worry us. As was argued above,[266] sections 175 and 177 (and, indeed, section 176) all deal with different manifestations of the no-conflict principle. The reason for depriving a director of a profit made from unauthorised exploitation of a corporate opportunity is not an objection to directors making profits as a result of or in connection with or whilst holding their office, but rather that the prospect of a personal profit may make the director careless about promoting the company's interest in taking the opportunity. If taking the opportunity personally does not involve any conflict with the interests of the company, there is no reason to deprive the director of his or her profit. It follows that some of the prior case-law on corporate opportunity, which seemed to be based on a free-standing "no profit" rule, is to be regarded with caution under the new statutory provisions. However, as we shall see below, there is a high degree of overlap between a "no conflict" approach and a "no profit" approach, if the former is given a rigorous interpretation. That the approach of section 175 to the "no conflict" principle is rigorous is suggested by two features of the section. First, section 175(1), echoing Lord Cranworth L.C. in *Aberdeen Rly Co v Blaikie Bros*,[267] includes within the principle a personal interest which "possibly may conflict" with that of the company. Secondly, section 175(2), referring to corporate opportunities etc., says that "it is immaterial whether the company could take advantage of the property, information or opportunity." On the other hand, the primacy of the conflict approach is asserted by section 175(4)(a), which provides that the section is not infringed if "the situation cannot reasonably be regarded as likely to give rise to a conflict of interest." These parts of the section are to some degree in tension with one another. One thing is clear: it is certainly not enough for the director to escape liability under this section that he or she acted in good faith (i.e. had honestly formed the view that the company's interests were not capable of being harmed by what was done), for the question of whether an actual or potential conflict of interest has arisen is one for the court.

There are two crucial questions to be answered in the area of corporate opportunities: first, how does the law identify an oppor-

---

[266] At para.16–40. For a trenchant pre-Act elaboration of the "no conflict"—"no profit" contrast see D Kershaw, "Lost in Translation: Corporate Opportunities in Comparative Perspective" (2005) 25 OJLS 603.

[267] (1854) 1 Macq. 461, HL.

tunity as a "corporate" one and, secondly, what processes does it specify for the company to give authority for the taking of the corporate opportunity by the director personally? The statute deals with the second issue in part but with the first issue hardly at all, where reliance is placed on the common law. Overall, recent developments in the case-law[268] seem to have brought a wider range of opportunities within the corporate category, whilst the statute has made it easier for directors to obtain approval for the exploitation of a corporate opportunity personally, by permitting the non-involved members of the board to give approval (subject to safeguards). We look at each issue in turn.

The identification of the corporate opportunity

16–65 Section 175 applies in particular to exploitation by the director of "property, information or opportunity" of the company. Misuse of corporate assets generally presents no particular problem;[269] even the most unsophisticated director should realise that he or she must not use the company's property as if it was his own (although even this is frequently overlooked or ignored in a "one-man" company). It is misuse of corporate information or a corporate opportunity—in practice the two are likely to overlap—which gives rise to difficulties. The main difficulty in the law relating to the misuse of corporate information and opportunities (hereafter to be referred to simply as corporate opportunities) is isolating the criteria for the identification of a corporate opportunity (as opposed to one the director is free to exploit personally without seeking any authorisation from the company). To put it another way, what sorts of linkages between the opportunity and the company are needed to make the opportunity a corporate one, for whose exploitation personally the director needs the authorisation of the company? In a recent decision the Court of Appeal has taken a broad view of the criteria, but we need to put that decision in the context of the prior case-law.

In a famous decision during the Second World War, *Regal (Hastings) Ltd v Gulliver*,[270] the House of Lords, following the law relating to trustees,[271] held directors liable to account to the company for the profit made from their personal exploitation of a corporate opportunity once it was established:

---

[268] Notably *Bhullar v Bhullar* [2003] 2 B.C.L.C. 241, CA.

[269] Except the problem of knowing when "corporate assets" end and "corporate information" or "corporate opportunity" begin. The present law does not clearly draw a distinction between them and the decisions frequently treat the latter as "belonging" to the company, i.e. as being its "property" or "asset". As we shall see, the distinction may be important in relation to ratification by the company.

[270] [1942] 1 All E.R. 378; [1967] 2 A.C. 134n.

[271] Notably *Keech v Sandford* (1726) Scl. Cas. Ch.61.

"(i) that what the directors did was so related to the affairs of the company that it can properly be said to have been done in the course of their management and in utilisation of their opportunities and special knowledge as directors; and (ii) that what they did resulted in a profit to themselves."[272]

Although this case is based on a "no profit" rationale which the Act now apparently rejects, it is not difficult to re-cast it in conflict terms. The facts, briefly, were as follows: company A owned a cinema and the directors decided to acquire two others with a view to selling the whole undertaking as a going concern. For this purpose they formed company B to take a lease of the other two cinemas. But the lessor insisted on a personal guarantee from the directors unless the paid-up capital of company B was at least £5,000 (which in those days was a large sum). The company, the directors concluded, was unable to subscribe more than £2,000 and the directors, although initially willing to do so, changed their minds about giving personal guarantees. Accordingly the original plan was changed; instead of company A subscribing for all the shares in company B, company A took up 2,000 and the remaining 3,000 were taken by the directors and their friends. Three weeks later, all the shares in both companies were sold, a profit of nearly £3 being made on each of the shares in company B. The new controllers then caused company A to bring an action against the former directors to recover the profit they had made.

It is not difficult to see a conflict of interest in these facts. It was the directors who decided not to give personal guarantees, thus creating the opportunity for them to participate personally in the financing of the acquisition and to share in the profits from the re-sale and depriving the company of the ability to take the whole of the profit on the sale of the subsidiary. It was the directors who, with the same result, decided not to obtain additional finance for the company to capitalise the subsidiary at the required level, even though the subsequent sale three weeks later was in contemplation when the additional cinemas were being acquired, so that it is difficult to believe that it would have been impossible for the company to obtain bridging finance for such a short period. These facts were emphasised in the judgment of Lord Russell of Killowen, even though he, like the other judges, based his reasoning on the "no profit" principle noted above.

Thus, it is submitted that a modern court, applying the "no conflict" principle, could come to the same result as the House of Lords in this case, especially as section 176(2) provides that "it is immaterial whether the company could take advantage of the property,

---

[272] Per Lord MacMilan at [1967] A.C. 153.

information or opportunity."[273] This seems at first sight a very odd provision: was it not the possibility that the company could have taken up the opportunity itself which in *Regal* provided the basis for the conflict of interest, so that the existence of that possibility can hardly be characterised as "immaterial"? However, the rule can be justified as relieving the court of having to make a judgment it was not well-placed to make, i.e. whether the company was genuinely unable to raise the finance itself. It may be also be justified as a prophylactic rule. It is the duty of the director to obtain the opportunity for the company. If the director is to be relieved of this duty and made free to take the opportunity personally where there is only a low chance of the company obtaining the opportunity itself, this will give the director an incentive not to strive as hard as he or she might to promote the company's interests. Section 176(2) removes this incentive.

16–66 It will be observed, however, that the claim in *Regal* was wholly unmeritorious. Recovery by the company benefited only the purchasers, who in this way received an undeserved windfall resulting, in effect, in a reduction in the price which they had freely agreed to pay. It also appears that the directors had held a majority of the shares in company A so that there would have been no difficulty in obtaining authorisation or ratification of their action by the company in general meeting;[274] but acting, as it was conceded they had, in perfect good faith and in full belief in the legality and propriety of their actions it had not occurred to them to go through this formality. Nor does this account exhaust the anomalies inherent in the decision. The chairman (and, apparently, the dominant member) of the board, instead of agreeing himself to subscribe for shares in company B, had merely agreed to find subscribers for £500. Shares to that value had, accordingly, been taken up by two private companies of which he was a member and director, and by a personal friend of his. It was accepted that the companies and friend had subscribed beneficially and not as his nominees and, accordingly, he was held not to be under any liability to account for the profit which they had made.[275]

The company's solicitor also escaped; though he had subscribed for

---

[273] More difficult to explain in this way might be the trusts case of *Boardman v Phipps* [1967] 2 A.C. 46, HL, where two of their lordships found against liability on the grounds that there was no conflict of interest on the part of the trustees, who made a profit out of confidential information obtained from the trust, which the trust itself was prohibited from acting on, whilst the majority found in favour of liability on the basis of confidential information plus profit. However, Lord Cohen (in the majority) also found that there was a conflict of interest, so that it might be argued that the majority view was that a conflict needed to be found for liability to be established. Lord Upjohn, dissenting, said that for a conflict of interest to arise there must be "a real sensible possibility of conflict" in the eyes of a reasonable person, a dictum which seems to be reflected in s.176(4)(a) of the Act.

[274] See the cogent editorial note in [1942] 1 All E.R. at 379. It was conceded that had this been done, there could have been no recovery: see further on this question, paras 16–83ff, below.

[275] The companies and friend had not been sued. Recovery might have been obtained from them if they had fallen within the rules relating to third parties' involvement in breaches of directors' duties. And in that case could the director be made liable for the third party's profits? See below, para.16–98.

shares and profited personally, he could retain his profit because he had acted with the knowledge and consent of the company exercised through the board of directors. The directors themselves could avoid liability only if a general meeting had approved,[276] but the solicitor, not being a director, could rely on the consent of the board. And this despite the fact that the board had acted throughout on his advice. Hence the two men most responsible for what had been done escaped liability, while those who had followed their lead had to pay up. What seems wrong with the application of the basic principle in this case is that recovery was not from all the right people and, more especially, was in favour of quite the wrong people.[277] Had it not been for the change of ownership it might well have been equitable to order restoration to the company, thus, in effect, causing the directors' profits to be shared among all the members. As it was, the case can be seen as one in which equitable principles were taken to inequitable conclusions.

Of the many subsequent decisions that have followed or com- **16–67** mented on the *Regal* case, three are of particular interest: *Industrial Development Consultants v Cooley*,[278] *Canadian Aero Service v O'Malley*[279] (a decision of the Canadian Supreme Court in which the judgment was delivered by Laskin J.—later the C.J.) and *Bhullar v Bhullar*.[280] The facts in the first two cases were very similar. In both, the companies concerned had been eager to obtain, and in negotiation for, highly remunerative work in connection with impending projects. In both, it was unlikely that the companies would have obtained the work, but in each there was a director whose expertise the undertaker of the project was anxious to obtain. Accordingly, each of the directors concerned resigned his office and later joined the undertaker of the project, in *Cooley* directly, in *Canadian Aero Service* indirectly through a company formed for the purpose which entered into a consortium with the undertaker. In both they were held liable to account for the profits which they made.

In neither case is it difficult to analyse the facts through a conflict-of-interest prism, since both directors were under a duty to obtain the opportunity for the company, unlikely though it was that they would succeed, though the reasoning of the courts involved was not expressed exclusively in this way. In *Cooley*, liability was based on misuse of information,[281] the defendant, while managing director,

---

[276] This would continue to be the case even under the Act because there appear to have been no uninvolved directors who could have given authorisation.

[277] Some American jurisdictions, in like circumstances, allow what is there known as "pro rata recovery" by those shareholders who have not profited. We, unfortunately, lack any such procedure.

[278] [1972] 1 W.L.R. 443, per Roskill J.

[279] [1973] 40 D.L.R. (3d) 371, Can. SC.

[280] [2003] 2 B.C.L.C. 241, CA.

[281] Roskill J. presumably chose this rather than the more obvious loss of opportunity because the chance that the company could have secured the opportunity was minimal: Roskill J. assessed it at not more than 10 per cent: [1972] 1 W.L.R. at 454.

having obtained information and knowledge that the project was to be revived and deliberately concealed this from the company and taken steps to turn the information to his personal advantage. It was irrelevant that the approach had been made to him and that his services were being sought as an individual consultant and would be undertaken free from any association with the company.[282] "Information which came to him while he was managing director and which was of concern to the plaintiffs and relevant for the plaintiffs to know, was information which it was his duty to pass on to the plaintiffs." It might be remarkable that the plaintiffs should receive a benefit which "it is unlikely that they would have got for themselves had the defendant complied with his duty to them" but "if the defendant is not required to account he will have made a large profit as a result of having deliberately put himself into a position in which his duty to the plaintiffs who were employing him and his personal interests conflicted."[283] This is an expression of the policy, as noted above, which now finds expression in section 175(2) of the Act. The quotation also demonstrates that the basis of the decision was not a mere misuse of information but the conflict of interest and duty to which the use gave rise.

In *Canadian Aero Service*, the decision was based firmly on misuse of a corporate opportunity, conceived of as generating a conflict of interest. On this Laskin J. said:[284]

> "An examination of the case-law ... shows the pervasiveness of a strict ethic in this area of the law. In my opinion this ethic disqualifies a director or senior officer[285] from usurping for himself or diverting to another person or company with whom or with which he is associated a maturing business opportunity which his company is actively pursuing; he is also precluded from so acting even after his resignation where the resignation may fairly be said to be prompted or influenced by a wish to acquire for himself the opportunity sought by the company, or where it was his position with the company rather than a fresh initiative which led him to the opportunity which he later acquired."

Another feature of the *Cooley* and *O'Malley* cases was that the directors in question resigned, but were nevertheless held liable to account to the company for the profits subsequently made. The issue was considered by Lawrence Collins J. in *CMS Dolphin Ltd v*

---

[282] So that, "in one sense, the benefit ... did not arise because of the defendant's directorship: indeed, the defendant would not have got this work had he remained a director": [1972] 1 W.L.R. at 451.

[283] [1972] 1 W.L.R. 443, at 453.

[284] (1973) 40 D.L.R. (3d) at 382.

[285] See above, para.16–9 on the question of how far English fiduciary principles apply to non-board senior managers.

Simonet[286] who concluded that the answer lay in the proposition that the opportunity is treated as the property of the company, so that a director who resigns after learning about such an opportunity "is just as accountable as a trustee who retires without properly accounting for trust property". As we have seen above,[287] this approach to the issue of resignation has been confirmed in section 170(2)(a) of the Act—but without the need to characterise the opportunity as the property of the company. It follows, of course, that if what the director has learned before his or her resignation does not fall within the category of a corporate opportunity, it is no breach of this aspect of their fiduciary duty to exploit the information personally thereafter.[288] Indeed, in order to encourage the exploitation of directors' talents, the general policy of the courts is not to put executive directors of a company in any worse position than employees in terms of restraints on their post-resignation activities.[289] This means that, in the absence of explicit contractual restraints on the director, he or she is free to exploit after resignation even confidential information carried away in his or her head, unless this information amounts to knowledge of trade secrets.

Bhullar v Bhullar[290] is in many ways the most interesting of the cases. In contrast to *Cooley* and *Canaero*, in *Bhullar* the defendants did not seek to divert to themselves an opportunity which their company was actively pursuing. On the contrary, the two families which had set up the company to acquire properties having fallen out, the family which constituted the claimant side of the litigation informed the family which formed the defendant side of the litigation that it did not want the company to acquire further properties. Subsequently, the defendant directors, by chance and without reliance on any information confidential to the company, discovered that a property adjacent to one of the company's properties was for sale and purchased it themselves. The claimants succeeded in their argument that the opportunity to purchase the property should have been made available to the company, whose property would have been much more valuable if joined with the adjacent property, and that the

16–68

---

[286] [2001] 2 B.C.L.C. 704 at 733. Alternatively, it can be said that the conflict of personal interest and duty to the company arises at the moment the opportunity emerges and that subsequent resignation does not operate retrospectively to cure the breach (indeed, it is often an expression of the director's preference for his or her personal interest). It is true that the profit arising out of the breach is made after resignation, but there is no reason why the company should not recover this if the breach occurred before resignation, just as a director who takes a decision adverse to the company in breach of the core duty of loyalty or duty of care does not reduce his or her liability to the company by resigning immediately after taking the decision. *Cf. Lindsley v Woodfull* [2004] 2 B.C.L.C. 131 at [28]–[30], CA.

[287] Para.16–10.

[288] *Island Export Finance Ltd v Umunna* [1986] B.C.L.C. 460; *Balston Ltd v Headline Filters Ltd* [1990] F.S.R. 385; *Framlington Group Plc v Anderson* [1995] 1 B.C.L.C. 475.

[289] *Dranez Anstalt v Hayek* [2002] 1 B.C.L.C. 693. This is a reason why it is desirable not to explain *Cooley* simply on the grounds of use of confidential information.

[290] [2003] 2 B.C.L.C. 241, CA.

defendants accordingly held the property on trust for the company.[291] This is a notable decision on two grounds. First, it seems to move English law in the direction of the US "line of business test", i.e. if the opportunity falls within the company's existing business activities as well as where the company is actively pursuing a particular type of opportunity, then an opportunity the director comes across is a corporate one, even if no property or information of the company was deployed by the director to obtain the opportunity. There was no suggestion in *Bhullar* that the directors had used their position in the company to bring the opportunity to maturity and then diverted it for themselves, as in *Canaero*. For this reason, the decision can be seen as effecting a significant extension of the criteria for identifying a corporate opportunity. This is probably a desirable development. It recognises that, for the purpose of the conflict of interest and duty rule, the duties of a director are pervasive, not ones arising only in specific and limited circumstances.

Secondly, however, the application of the extended understanding of a corporate opportunity to the facts of the case was questionable, for the court attached no weight to the fact that, before the opportunity arose, the board decided, albeit informally, at the initiative of the claimants and for reasons which were apparent not to acquire any more properties.[292] Nevertheless, the claimants were, in effect, able to reverse their decision once a particularly attractive opportunity arose. It is not clear why the claimants should have been permitted to act in such an opportunistic way. In *Regal*, where the claimants' behaviour was also opportunistic, as we have seen, it could be said that it was the directors who decided that the company could not afford the opportunity who were the ones who later took it themselves and that such behaviour is necessarily suspect. In *Bhullar* it was found as a fact that the claimants, not the defendants, took the initiative to restrict the scope of company's future activities.[293] The second point is not unrelated to the first. If the courts are, rightly it is submitted, to extend liability beyond the maturing business opportunity so as to embrace opportunities within the company's line of business, a director needs to be able to establish what the company's business actually is. Companies' business models change from time to time, often quite rapidly, and the obvious place for a director to look for a current definition is in the decisions of the board setting its business strategy. It would seem undesirable to extend the corporate opportunity doctrine to any business opening which a director comes across

---

[291] Thus, they could be obliged to convey it to the company, subject to the company's payment to them of the costs of purchase.

[292] The issue is hardly touched upon in the reasoning of the court.

[293] It is possible that the court thought that the purchase of the adjacent property did not fall unambiguously within the decision not to purchase new properties.

and which the company could exploit, even though the company was neither already exploiting that type of opportunity nor seeking to do so.[294] To do so would come close to restoring the "no profit" rule which the section does not adopt. Such a rule would increase the costs of being a director (the director is at risk of losing the opportunity to the company) and in the case of non-executive directors in particular this might seem a high cost as against the potential rewards of the directorship.

In particular, an answer needs to be provided to the question posed in *Regal*: does the equitable principle involve "the proposition that, if the directors bona fide decide not to invest their company's funds in some proposed investment, a director who thereafter embarks his own money therein is accountable for any profits he may derive therefrom?"[295] The reason this question is unresolved, it is suggested, is to be found in the underdeveloped state of the law on the role of the board in the area of corporate opportunities, for the board performs two closely linked but conceptually distinct roles. It may authorise the taking by the director of an opportunity which is a corporate one, as section 175 contemplates, but, through its direction of the company's business strategy, its decisions may or ought to have the effect of taking some opportunities out of the category of being corporate, with the consequence that authorisation is not required, because there is no conflict of interest. As section 175(2) says, it may indeed be "immaterial" whether the company could take advantage of the opportunity, but if it is an opportunity outside the range of the company's business activities, present or in contemplation, can the situation "reasonably be regarded as likely to give rise to a conflict of interest", as section 175(4)(a) requires? It is suggested that the line of business test provides a way of reconciling these two provisions of the section, with due regard being accorded to decisions of the board in determining the company's business strategy.

Authorisation by the board

Assuming a corporate opportunity, whose permission must the director obtain for personal exploitation of it? Section 175 introduces the possibility of board approval, supplementing the common law doctrine of shareholder approval, which we discuss below in relation to direc- **16–69**

---

[294] For example, the non-executive director of a company providing business services learns on the golf course from a friend who does not know of his directorship of an opportunity to invest in a restaurant project. Does the director need the authorisation of the company to make the investment, simply because his company is financially able to take it up? It is suggested that the answer is in the negative. For some recognition of the force of this argument see *Wilkinson v West Coast Capital* [2007] B.C.C. 717.

[295] Per Lord Russell (quoting Greene M.R.) at [1967] A.C. 152. *Cf.* the answer given in *Peso Silver Mines v Cropper* (1966) 58 D.L.R. 2d 1 and the criticism of that decision by Beck in (1971) 49 *Can. B.R.* 80.

tors' duties as a whole.[296] What the common law did not contemplate was board waiver of the duty. This was because the common law rule was that the company was entitled to the disinterested advice of all its directors and, if this was not available, the board could no longer authorise by itself a course of conduct binding on the company.[297] The common law thus excluded the non-involved members of the board from a role in the authorisation process, and their use by the statute in this way under section 175 constitutes a major innovation of the 2006 Act. By virtue of section 175(4)(b) authorisation may be given by the board itself for a conflict of interest on the part of one of their number, so that no breach of duty is committed.[298]

The conflicted director him- or herself is to be excluded in the calculation of the quorum needed for the directors' meeting at which authorisation is given and the director's vote is to be disregarded in determining whether board approval has been given (section 175(6)). So, also is any "interested" director, but in which circumstances a director can be said to be interested in another director's authorisation to take a corporate opportunity is left to the courts to decide. Another director whose participation in the exploitation of the opportunity which is the subject of a separate resolution of the board would clearly be interested in the resolution on the director in question, but how far the concept of interest goes beyond that is not clear. It is also the case that, if there is no authorisation in advance of the taking of the opportunity, subsequent ratification of the director's breach of duty by the company requires a decision of the shareholders.[299] Nevertheless, it can still be asked whether this is a wise innovation. On the one hand, a requirement of shareholder approval is a heavy one and may deter directors from proceeding with courses of action which, if asked, shareholders would approve, thus imposing unnecessary restrictions on directors' entrepreneurial activities. On the other hand, the risk with board approval is that, although the approving directors may have no interest in the particular case, they may have an underlying interest in a culture of easy conflict approvals ("you scratch my back and I'll scratch yours"). No doubt, such conduct would be a breach of the other duties imposed on directors,

---

[296] Below, para.16–83.
[297] See *Benson v Heathorn* (1842) 1 Y. & C.C.C. 326, per Knight-Bruce V.-C. at 341–342, and *Imperial Mercantile Credit Association v Coleman* (1871) L.R. 6 Ch.App. 558, CA, per Hatherley L.C. at 567–568.
[298] Nor is any transaction or arrangement with the company liable to be set aside on the grounds that the shareholders have not given their approval: section 180(1). This provision applies to conflicts of interest generally under s.175, although the present discussion relates to corporate opportunities.
[299] Section 239(2)(a), on which see below at para.16–84. It is submitted that the standard use of the word "authorise" in company law is to refer to *ex ante* permission, whilst ratification refers to permission given after the breach. It is clear that the CLR's proposal, on which section 175 is based, contemplated the non-involved members of the board giving permission only in advance. See Final 1, p.346, clause 6 where the phrase adopted is "the use [of the corporate opportunity] has been proposed to and authorised by the board".

discussed above, but such breaches may be difficult to detect and prove in court.

It may be for this sort of reason that the statute allows or requires the company's constitution (notably the articles) to have some control over whether uninvolved directors can authorise conflicts of interest. In the case of private companies the board can act as the authorising body unless something in the company's articles or other parts of its constitution restricts the board from so acting. In the case of a public company or a charitable one,[300] the company's constitution must positively empower the directors to act in this way, and the articles might (but need not) then regulate in further detail the scope or manner of exercise of the authorisation power. Compliance with the articles would in either case be a pre-condition for the valid exercise of the directors' powers of authorisation (section 178(5)). The more restrictive rule applied to public companies reflects the fact that their shareholding bodies tend to be more dispersed than those in private companies and their collective action problems accordingly greater. Hence, in public companies the burden of introducing the rule of director authorisation is placed on those who want it (normally the directors themselves) rather than the burden of removing it on those who do not want it (presumably the shareholders).[301] However, the statute, surprisingly, does not adopt a proposal of the CLR that board authorisations should be reported to the shareholders in the subsequent directors' report.[302]

We shall see below that, in relation to ad hoc shareholder approval, the common law developed a doctrine that certain breaches of duty are not capable of approval by the company, the case of *Cook v Deeks* (above) being a leading authority in this area. Does such a restriction apply to authorisation given by the independent members of the board? There is no mention of such a restriction in section 176 and, since independent board approval is an invention of the statute, it would seem that this limitation cannot be imported into the board's power of authorisation. Is this surprising? There are two controls over board authorisation which do not exist in relation to shareholder authorisation at common law. First, interested directors are excluded by the statute from voting on a board resolution whereas at common law interested directors are entitled to vote as shareholders to authorise the taking of a corporate opportunity (though they may no longer vote on a ratification decision).[303] The exclusion of inter-

---

[300] s.181(2)(b).

[301] Of course, the provision may be inserted in the company's articles upon incorporation, but at least those who become its shareholders then know what they are letting themselves in for. In the case of subsequent amendments to the articles it will be interesting to see what sorts of board approval provisions institutional investors are prepared to accept in the articles of listed companies.

[302] CLR, Final 1, para.3.25.

[303] In relation to ratification s.239(3),(4) now reverse this rule, but it seems still to apply to authorisation. On ratification see para.16–85 below.

ested directors from voting might be thought to reduce the danger of unfair treatment of minority shareholders, though it does not eliminate it. Secondly, non-involved directors, unlike shareholders, are subject to fiduciary duties when exercising their votes. The core duty of loyalty would require the director to give priority to the promotion of the success of the company when deciding whether to authorise, for example, the taking of a corporate opportunity, though such a breach might be difficult to prove.[304]

A conceptual issue

16–70   Section 175 is based on the existence of a conflict of duty and interest (or a conflict of duties). In the area of corporate opportunity, this conflict arises because of the conflict between the interest of the director in personal exploitation of the opportunity and his or her duty to offer the opportunity to the company. The duty to offer the opportunity to the company arises because it has been characterised as a corporate one: that is why the identification of the criteria for making the opportunity a corporate one is so central to this body of law. However, one can ask, what is the nature of this duty? It is generally accepted that, if the director does not wish to exploit the opportunity personally, no breach of section 175 arises because there is then no personal interest conflicting with his duty to the company. In other words, a director who does nothing escapes liability under section 175. Might the director be liable for breach of some other duty, for example, the duty of care or loyalty? In principle, this possibility exists. In the case of the core duty of loyalty the director would have to form the view that the promotion of the success of the company required the opportunity to be communicated to the company and then fail to do so. The duty of care seems a more promising avenue of approach because it is based on an objective test. However, it would not necessarily be correct to infer from the existence of a duty for the purposes of the no-conflict rule a duty for the purposes of the duty of care. The courts have traditionally developed more demanding standards of loyalty than of care and that approach may continue under the statute.[305]

Competing and multiple directorships

16–71   It is common for directors to hold directorships in more than one company, certainly where the companies are part of a group but also where they are independent of one another. In such cases an issue

---

[304]   *cf.* the discussion of *Regentcrest Plc v Cohen* [2001] 2 B.C.L.C. 80 in para.16–27 above.

[305]   It is difficult to believe that the directors in *Regal*, having concluded that the company could not finance the project, would have been held liable in negligence for not putting additional money of their own into the company so that it could take up the opportunity, whereas in *Cooley* failing to follow up for the company an opportunity of the very type the director had been hired to pursue would seem to constitute a plausible case of negligence.

arises in relation to the compatibility of this practice with the no-conflict rule set out in section 175. There are two situations which need to be looked at: the first is where directorships are held in companies which are in business competition with one another or indeed where the director in any other way enters into competition with the company; and, secondly and more commonly, where the companies are not competitors but where nevertheless their interests may conflict from time to time.

Competing with the company

One of the most obvious examples of a situation which might be   **16–72**
expected to give rise to a conflict between two sets of a director's duties[306] is where the director carries on or is associated with a business competing with that of the company. Certainly a fiduciary without the consent of his beneficiaries is normally precluded from competing with them and this is specifically stated in the analogous field of partnership law.[307] Yet, strangely, it is by no means clear on the existing case-law that a similar rule applies to directors[308] of a company. Indeed, it is generally stated that it does not, and there appears to be a definite, if inadequately reported, decision that a director cannot be restrained from acting as a director of a rival company.[309] And it has been said that "What he could do for a rival company he could, of course, do for himself."[310] This view is becoming increasingly difficult to support. It has been held that the duty of fidelity flowing from the relationship of employer and worker may preclude the worker from engaging, even in his spare time, in work for a competitor,[311] notwithstanding that the worker's duty of fidelity imposes lesser obligations than the full duty of good faith owed by a director or other fiduciary agent. How, then, can it be that a director can compete whereas a subordinate employee cannot?

In the light of the above it is not surprising that in *In Plus Group Ltd v Pyke*[312] the Court of Appeal expressed some unease with the state of the law as set out above, but resisted the temptation to engage in a wholesale review of the case-law in this area in a situation where the defendant director had been wholly, and probably wrongfully, excluded from any influence over the operation of the claimant

---

[306] s.176(7) makes it clear that the section applies to a conflict of duties.

[307] Partnership Act 1890, s.30.

[308] It clearly does not apply to members, even in a private company, for members, as such, are not fiduciaries, though such conduct might give rise to a remedy under the unfair prejudice provisions. See Ch.20, below.

[309] *London & Mashonaland Exploration Co v New Mashonaland Exploration Co* [1891] W.N. 165, approved by Lord Blanesburgh in *Bell v Lever Bros* [1932] A.C. 161 at 195, HL.

[310] Per Lord Blanesburgh, *Bell v Lever Bros* (see previous note).

[311] *Hivac Ltd v Park Royal Scientific Instruments Ltd* [1946] Ch. 169, CA. If correct it must apply to an executive director: see *Scottish Co-op Wholesale Society Ltd v Meyer* [1959] A.C. 324, HL, per Lord Denning at 367.

[312] [2002] 2 B.C.L.C. 201, CA, especially the judgment of Sedley L.J.

companies, in which he was also a substantial shareholder. The Court held that the claimant companies could not obtain in such a case an account of the profits made by the director as a director of a competing company which he had established. However, the court in that case may well have indicated the way forward. The application of the rule against competition must be examined in the circumstances of each case. The *Mashonaland* case must be seen, not as one laying down a rule that competition is in principle permitted, but as one where, as in the *Pyke* case, it was inappropriate to apply the no-competition rule.[313]

It can also be argued that section 175 has made it much easier for directors to deal with such conflicts of duty. If both companies consent to the situation, there is no breach of fiduciary duty arising simply from taking up directorships in competing companies, but so long as consent required the approval of the shareholders, directors would regard the process of obtaining consent as a burdensome one. Under section 175, by contrast, the other directors of the companies involved will normally be in a position to give their consent. Indeed, an opposition Member of the House of Commons suggested in the Standing Committee debates that this was already good practice.[314]

Two difficulties remain, however. First, the section does not contemplate in the way that section 177 does a general declaration of interest. The director must seek approval from the non-involved directors for taking up the position as a director of the competing company and, should the nature of that situation change—for example, should the competing company start an additional line of business in competition with the other company—a further consent would apparently be required. However, it may not always be easy to judge when a situation has arisen which requires further consent. Secondly, even if consent is given to the taking up of the directorship, the director is likely to be faced with constant difficulties in avoiding breaches of the core duty of loyalty to the companies concerned as he or she performs the duties of the directorships. The director would be required to treat both companies equally, which might reduce his or her utility to both companies.[315] It has been recognised that one who

---

[313] As Brooke L.J. pointed out, the *Mashonaland* case was a "startling" one, but the director there had never acted as a director of the claimant company nor attended a board meeting. As for the *In Plus Group* case, Lewison J. in *Ultraframe (UK) Ltd v Fielding* [2005] EWHC 1638 suggested that the "no conflict" principle applied only to the powers a director has, so that a director excluded from exercising powers, even if wrongfully, was no longer subject to the principle—and certainly not at the suit of those who excluded him.

[314] HC Debs, Standing Committee D, Company Law Reform Bill, Fifteenth Sitting, July 11, 2006 (Afternoon), col. 611 (Mr Quentin Davies).

[315] For example, if the director came across a corporate opportunity, might he not have to offer it at the same time to both companies? Consent to acting as a director of competing companies would not of course involve consent to personal exploitation of any corporate opportunity the director might come across.

is a director of two rival concerns is walking a tight-rope and at risk if he fails to deal fairly with both.[316] However, it should be noted that the legal problem here arises not so much from the no-conflict rule as from the fact that, by becoming a director of two companies, the director owes a core duty of loyalty to each.

In practice, it is in fact rare for a director to act for competing **16–73** companies, except in the case where the director forms a new company for the purpose of competing with the current company when he ceases to be associated with it. The director's position in such a case may seem to be lacking in merit, but, as we have noted,[317] there is a public policy interest in the law not discouraging persons from exploiting their talents after their association with a company ceases, whether that association is as director or employee. Consequently, the law seems to have arrived at the position that for a director, whilst still a director, to make plans to compete with the company in the future is not a breach of fiduciary duty nor, even, is taking limited preliminary steps to implement those plans.[318] However, those preliminary steps must stop short of actual competitive activity (such as recruiting the company's employees to work in the new business). Such action will not only be a breach of the no-conflict rule but the director's core duty of loyalty will require disclosure of this threat to the company's business to its board, even if it involves the director disclosing his or her own wrongdoing.[319] Where exactly the line is to be drawn between permitted preparatory activity and prohibited competition with the company (and possibly improper personal exploitation of corporate opportunities) depends upon a fact-specific analysis of the facts of the particular case. The rigour of the fiduciary principles is, however, somewhat abated in those cases where the resignation of the directors has been forced upon him or her and the director has not actively sought to seduce the company's customers away or to exploit an opportunity belonging to it.[320] After resignation, however, the director will be able to compete freely subject to any contractual restraints, the law relating to trade secrets and the rules relating to corporate opportunities acquired before resignation (see section 170(2)).

---

[316] See, per Lord Denning in *Scottish Co-op Wholesale Society v Meyer*, above fn.311, at 366–368. This concerned an application under what is now the unfair prejudice provisions (on which see Ch.20, below) but Lord Denning obviously had doubts whether the *Mashonaland* case was still good law. See also *Bristol and West Building Society v Mothew* [1998] Ch. 1, 18 (per Millett L.J.).

[317] Above, para.16–67.

[318] *Balston Ltd v Headline Filters Ltd* [1990] F.S.R. 385.

[319] *British Midland Tool Ltd v Midland International Tooling Ltd* [2003] 2 B.C.L.C. 523 at [77] to [92]; *CMS Dolphin Ltd v Simonet* [2001] 2 B.C.L.C. 704. On the "duty to disclose" see above, para.16–31.

[320] *Foster Bryant Surveying Ltd v Bryant* [2007] 2 B.C.L.C. 239, CA (no breach of duty where director, forced to resign, agreed in notice period on the initiative of a major customer to work for it after the notice ran out). The case contains a full discussion of the authorities.

Multiple directorships

16–74   The law relating to multiple directorships of a non-competing type is
basically as set out above, though obviously a directorship of another
non-competing company creates a lesser conflict problem. Indeed, in
the case of a non-executive director of a company (i.e. one who is not
bound to devote all his time and efforts to the company) taking a
non-executive directorship in another, non-competing company can
be said not to raise a conflict issue at all. However, it is no doubt
good practice to obtain the consent of each board to the position and
in the case of an executive director such consent would seem to be
necessary. When conflicts of interest arise at a later date, for example,
where the director is on the boards of two companies which are on
opposite sides of a transaction, it is common for the director simply
to withdraw from a role on the board of either company. Provided
the articles make provision for this solution, the Act appears to
relieve the director of liability in such a case, even liability arising
under the core duty of loyalty.[321] In the absence of appropriate
provisions in the articles, however, the director's position is precarious. If a person is a director of two non-competing companies but
one makes a takeover bid for the other, how can the director discharge the core duty of loyalty to both in such a situation? Withdrawal may ensure equal treatment but can hardly be said to amount
to a discharge of the duty to promote the success of the (each)
company. In that situation, resignation from one of the involved
companies may be the only possible step. However, where the conflict
is less pressing, the strategy of withdrawal may seem appropriate.

DUTY NOT TO ACCEPT BENEFITS FROM THIRD PARTIES

16–75   Section 176 provides that a director "must not accept a benefit from a
third party conferred by reason of (a) his being a director, or (b) his
doing (or not doing) anything as a director."[322] A "third party"
means a person other than the company, an associated body corporate or a person acting on behalf of such companies. The connection
of this rule with the no-conflict principle is underlined by the standard provision in this area that the duty is not infringed if the benefit
"cannot reasonably be regarded as likely to give rise to a conflict of
interest" (section 176(3)). This being so, it may be wondered what the

---

[321] s.180(4)(b): general duties not infringed "where the company's articles contain provisions
for dealing with conflicts of interest" and the director acts in accordance with them. Again,
it will be interesting to see what types of provision are thought acceptable by the institutional shareholders in respect of listed companies.

[322] Benefits from associated companies are excluded as are benefits received by the director
from a company which supplies his or her services to the company: section 177(2) and (3).

purpose of section 176 is, for could not the situations it deals with be handled under the general no-conflict section (s.175)? The answer, and it is an important one, is that there is no provision in section 176 for authorisation to be given by uninvolved directors for the receipt of third-party benefits. The risk of such benefits distorting the proper performance of a director's duties is so high that it is rightly thought to be proper to require authorisation from the shareholders in general meeting (even though that turns the rule into a near-ban on the receipt of third-party benefits). The fact that section 175 applies to a situation does not prevent section 176 being relied upon as well, i.e. the sections are cumulative rather than mutually exclusive in their operation.[323] Although the point is not expressly dealt with in section 176, the availability at common law of shareholder authorisation is preserved by section 180(4)(a).[324]

The common law termed such payments "bribes" though that seems a misnomer. It is enough at common law that there has been the payment of money or the conferment of another benefit upon an agent whom the payer knows is acting as an agent for a principal in circumstances where the payment has not been disclosed to the principal.[325] There is no need to show that the payer of the bribe acted with a corrupt motive; that the agent's mind was actually affected by the bribe; that the payer knew or suspected that the agent would conceal the payment from the principal; or that the principal suffered any loss or that the transaction was in some way unfair. None of these matters seem to be requirements of section 176 either. Thus, the term "third party benefits" is more appropriate than the term "bribe".

At common law the remedies available in the case of third party benefits were extensive. These common law remedies continue to apply by virtue of section 178, despite the change of nomenclature, including the remedies against the third party as well as the remedies against the director. Although the section imposes a duty only on the director, the common law obligations of (and thus remedies against) the third party are presumably unaffected. Indeed, the interrelatedness of the rules governing the position of the director and of the third party is so high that it constitutes a strong reason for construing section 176 as simply re-stating the prior common law, since that common law will still apply to the third party. Thus, where the benefit has been paid to a director, the company may rescind the contract between it and the third party (provided at least the third party knew the recipient was a director of the company), whether the payer is the

---

[323] "Except as otherwise provided, more than one of the general duties may apply": section 179.

[324] "The general duties have effect subject to any rule of law enabling the company to give authority ... for anything to be done ... by the directors ... that would otherwise be a breach of duty."

[325] *Industries and General Mortgage Co Ltd v Lewis* [1949] 2 All E.R. 573; *Taylor v Walker* [1958] 1 Lloyd's Rep. 490; *Logicrose Ltd v Southend United FC Ltd* [1988] 1 W.L.R. 1257.

third party or the third party's agent.[326] In addition, or instead, both the third party and the director are jointly and severally liable in damages in fraud to the company, the amount of the recovery depending upon proof of actual loss.[327] Alternatively, the company may hold both the director and the third party jointly and severally liable to pay the amount of the benefit to the company as money had and received to its use, this liability being naturally not dependent upon proof of loss. Against the director, such a personal liability to account is straightforward: the bribe is akin to a secret profit made out the director's position. Against the third party it is a rather peculiar remedy, though one which seems to be established.[328] However, the company must choose between the remedies of damages and account, the choice no doubt depending on the amount of the provable loss which the company suffered as a result of the bribe, though it need not do so until judgment.[329]

In *Attorney-General for Hong Kong v Reid*[330] the Privy Council took the further step of recognising a proprietary remedy by way of a constructive trust in favour of the company (or other principal) against the director (or other agent) in respect of the bribe. The significance of the provision of this remedy in addition to the personal remedy to account for money had and received is that the company may claim any profit made by the director through the use of the benefit (whilst falling back on the personal claim if the investment has been unprofitable) and that the company's claim will prevail over those of the unsecured creditors in the event of the director's insolvency.

REMEDIES FOR BREACH OF DUTY

16–76   The CLR failed to carry through its suggestion that the remedies for breach of directors' duties should be stated in the statute, along with

---

[326] *Taylor v Walker*, above, previous note; *Shipway v Broadwood* [1899] 1 Q.B. 369, CA. There is not space here to explore the complications which may arise when the payer is also the director of a company and makes unauthorised use of that company's assets to effect the bribe.

[327] *Mahesan v Malaysia Government Officers' Co-operative Housing Society Ltd* [1979] A.C. 374 at 381, PC. The cause of action appears to lie in fraud.

[328] [1979] A.C. 374, at 383.

[329] [1979] A.C. 374, and *United Australia Ltd v Barclays Bank Ltd* [1941] A.C. 1, HL. Where the briber is or acts on behalf of a supplier, the damages are unlikely to be less than the amount of the bribe, but could be more.

[330] [1994] 1 A.C. 324, PC, declining to follow *Metropolitan Bank v Heiron* (1880) 5 Ex. D. 319, CA and *Lister & Co v Stubbs* (1890) 45 Ch. D. 1, CA. The decision was controversial among academic writers but mostly has been followed by the courts. See the judgment of Lawrence Collins J. in *Daraydan International Ltd v Solland International Ltd* [2005] Ch. 119 for a review of both the subsequent court decisions and the academic writings.

the substantive duties, and the Government decided not to proceed with the project.[331] In consequence, section 178 simply provides that "the consequences of a breach (or threatened breach) of sections 171 to 177 are the same as would apply if the corresponding common law rule or equitable duty applied"; and that the duties contained in the sections (other than s.174) are "enforceable in the same way as any other fiduciary duty owed to a company by its directors." It should be noted that section 178 applies only to the general duties laid out in sections 171 to 177, not to the provisions to be found in Chapter 3 of Part 10 dealing with disclosure of interests in existing transactions (for which the statute provides only criminal sanctions);[332] nor to the provisions contained in Chapter 4 of Part 10, requiring shareholder approval for certain transactions with directors, for which a self-contained statutory civil code of remedies is provided.[333] It should also be noted that the second proposition in section 178 is not applied to the duty to exercise reasonable care, skill and diligence, in line with the modern view that this is not a fiduciary duty. The remedy for that duty is normally confined to damages.[334]

For this reason, we have sought to indicate the principal remedies available for each of the duties as we have gone along. Nevertheless, it may be useful to bring them together here, since they largely overlap and so can usefully be considered together. However, there are some differences in the remedies available in relation to the different duties which do not seem logically connected to the nature of the particular duty. There are also a number of uncertainties, notably as to whether the remedy available is personal only or proprietary. To clear up these difficulties was the reason the CLR proposed that the statutory statement of directors' duties should be accompanied by a statutory code of remedies.[335]

The main remedies available are:

    (a) injunction or declaration;

    (b) damages or compensation;

    (c) restoration of the company's property;

    (d) rescission of the contract;

    (e) account of profits; and

    (f) summary dismissal.

---

[331] Final Report I, paras 15.28–15.30.
[332] See above, para.16–47.
[333] See above, paras 16–49ff.
[334] Above, para.16–16.
[335] Final Report I, paras 15.28–15.30.

(a) Injunction or declaration

16–77 These are primarily employed where the breach is threatened but has not yet occurred. If action can be taken in time, this is obviously the most satisfactory course. However, if the remedy is to be used effectively by an individual shareholder, suing derivatively,[336] he or she will need to be well-informed about the proposals of the board, which in all but the smallest companies will often not be the case. An injunction may also be appropriate where the breach has already occurred but is likely to continue or if some of its consequences can thereby be avoided.[337]

(b) Damages or compensation

16–78 Damages are the appropriate remedy for breach of a common law duty of care; compensation is the equivalent equitable remedy granted against a trustee or other fiduciary to compel restitution for the loss suffered by the breach of fiduciary duty. In practice, the distinction between the two has become blurred, and probably no useful purpose is served by seeking to keep them distinct. All the directors who participate in the breach[338] are jointly and severally liable with the usual rights of contribution *inter se*.[339]

(c) Restoration of property

16–79 Although the directors are not trustees of the company's property (which is held by the company itself as a separate legal person), we have noted at a number of points in this chapter that the courts sometimes treat directors as if they were such trustees. In particular, where a director disposes of the company's property in breach of fiduciary duty and in consequence the company's property comes into his or her own hands, the director will be treated as a constructive trustee of the property for the company.[340] This means that it can be recovered *in rem* from the director, so far as traceable, either in law or in equity; and that the company's claim will have priority over those of the director's creditors (since the property is the company's property, not the director's). Where the company's assets are paid

---

[336] See Chapter 17.
[337] For example, to enjoin the delivery up of confidential documents improperly taken away by a former director: *Measures Bros v Measures* [1910] 2 Ch. 248, CA; *Cranleigh Precision Engineering Ltd v Bryant* [1965] 1 W.L.R. 1293.
[338] Either actively or by subsequent acquiescence in it: *Lands Allotment Co, Re* [1894] 1 Ch. 616, CA. Merely protesting will not necessarily disprove acquiescence: *Joint Stock Discount Co v Brown* (1869) L.R. 8 Eq. 381.
[339] Civil Liability (Contribution) Act 1978. The application of the principle of joint and several liability is discussed more fully below at paras 22–34 *et seq.* in relation to auditors.
[340] *JJ Harrison (Properties) Ltd v Harrison* [2002] 1 B.C.L.C. 162, CA. For an early recognition of the principle see *Forest of Dean Coal Co, Re* (1879) 10 Ch. D. 450.

away improperly to third parties, the directors will still be under a duty to restore them to the company,[341] although the obligation to restore is in this case merely personal and so will rank equally with the claims of the directors' general creditors. Nevertheless, the claim for restoration of property (which, normally, is a claim for the monetary value of that property) may be more beneficial to the company than a claim for damages or equitable compensation, because the claim is not dependent upon proof of loss on the part of the company, as a damages claim would be.[342]

For the proper understanding of this principle, it is important to be able to distinguish cases where the directors are improperly handling the company's property from those where they act merely in breach of fiduciary duty without involving the company's property and thereby make a profit.[343] In the latter case the proper remedy will be an accounting of profits (below) and the remedy normally will be personal, not proprietary.[344] The "company's property" includes not only property reduced into the company's possession but also property which it was the directors' duty to acquire for the company or perhaps give the company the opportunity of acquiring. But apparently it does not include all profits made by a director or other agent for which the company has a right to call upon him to account. These profits and the investments made with them will not be regarded as belonging in equity to the company unless they flowed from a use of the company's property. As we note below,[345] the line between these two categories is not easy to draw, nor in particular is the question of when information is property one to which the courts have given consistent answers.[346]

(d) Avoidance of contracts

An agreement with the company that breaks the rules relating to contracts in which directors are interested may be avoided, provided that the company has done nothing to indicate an intention to ratify the agreement after finding out about the breach of duty,[347] that

16–80

---

[341] *Bairstow v Queen's Moat Houses Plc* [2001] 2 B.C.L.C. 531, CA.

[342] In the case cited in fn.341, the company may even have gained a windfall from its litigation, since the shareholders in practice probably kept the dividend unlawfully paid to them, whilst the cost of paying the dividend was to be made good to the company by the directors. The case does not record whether the directors satisfied the judgment against them.

[343] *Gwembe Valley Development Co Ltd v Koshy (No.3)* [2004] 1 B.C.L.C. 131 at [117] to [121], CA.

[344] For the anomalous case of bribes, see above, para.16–75.

[345] At para.16–86.

[346] See the contrasting views on this matter expressed by the judges in *Phipps v Boardman* [1967] 2 A.C. 46, HL.

[347] *Lagunas Nitrate Co v Lagunas Syndicate* [1899] 2 Ch. 392, CA, a case concerning promoters' liability, but the operative principles are the same.

restitutio in integrum is possible and that the rights of bona fide third parties have not supervened.[348] Indeed, it may be doubted how strong a bar *restitutio in integrum* really is, given the wide powers the court has to order financial adjustments when directing rescission.[349] Equally, a contract entered into by the company in breach of the directors' duties to exercise their powers for a proper purpose is in principle avoidable by the company, but again subject to the rights of good faith third parties.[350] Where, however, the directors have simply acted outside their powers, the contract will be void, not voidable.[351]

(e) Accounting for profits

16–81 This liability may arise either out of a contract made between a director and the company[352] or as a result of some contract or arrangement between the director and a third person.[353] In the former case, accounting is a remedy additional to avoidance of the contract and is normally available whether or not there is rescission. However, if a director has sold his or her own property to the company, the right to an account of profits will be lost if the company elects not to rescind or is too late to do so.[354] When the profit arises out of a contract between the director and a third party there will be no question of rescinding that contract at the instance of the company, since the company is not a party to it. Here an account of profit will be the sole remedy.

As we have seen, in neither case does recovery of the profit depend on proof of any loss suffered by the company; the profit is recoverable not as damages or compensation but because the company is entitled to call upon the director to account to it. However, in the case of trustees, where the profit arises out of transactions with a third party, it has been usual to make an allowance in the account to provide a

---

[348] *Transvaal Lands Co v New Belgium (Transvaal) Land & Development Co* [1914] 2 Ch. 488, CA.

[349] This is certainly the case when fraud is involved and perhaps even when it is not: *Erlanger v New Sombrero Phosphate Co* (1873) 3 App. Cas.1218, HL; *Spence v Crawford* [1939] 3 All E.R. 271, HL; *Armstrong v Jackson* [1917] 2 K.B. 822; *O'Sullivan v Management Agency and Music Ltd* [1985] Q.B. 428, CA.

[350] *Hogg v Cramphorn* [1967] Ch.254; *Bamford v Bamford* [1970] Ch. 212, CA; *Criterion Properties Plc v Stratford UK Properties LLC* [2004] B.C.C. 570, HL.

[351] *Guiness Plc v Saunders* [1990] 2 A.C. 663, HL. A void contract is much more threatening to the position of third parties, though in the case of third parties contracting with companies the provisions of section 40 (above, para.7–5) may save the day.

[352] *Imperial Mercantile Credit Association v Coleman* (1873) L.R. 6 H.L. 189.

[353] For example, in relation to the use of corporate information or opportunity discussed above, paras 16–64ff.

[354] *Ambrose Lake Tin Co, Re* (1880) 11 Ch.D. 390, CA; *Cape Breton Co, Re* (1885) 29 Ch.D. 795, CA (affirmed sub nom. *Cavendish Bentinck v Fenn* (1887) 12 App. Cas.652, HL); *Ladywell Mining Co v Brookes* (1887) 35 Ch.D. 400, CA; *Gluckstein v Barnes* [1900] A.C. 240, HL; *Lady Forrest (Murchison) Gold Mine, Re* [1901] 1 Ch. 582; *Burland v Earle* [1902] A.C. 83, PC; *Jacobus Marler v Marler* (1913) 85 I.J.P.C. 167n; *Hely-Hutchinson v Brayhead Ltd* [1968] 1 Q.B. 549, CA.

reasonable remuneration (including a profit element) for the work carried out by the trustee in effecting the transaction.[355]

(f) Summary dismissal

The right which an employer has at common law to dismiss an **16–82** employee who has been guilty of serious misconduct has no application to the director as such.[356] However, it could be an effective sanction against executive directors and other officers of the company, since it may involve loss of livelihood rather than simply of position and directors' fees. However, it tends to be used only in the clearest cases. Generally, the company prefers the director to "go quietly", which means that his or her entitlements on departure are calculated as if the contract were unimpeachable, even if there is scope for arguing that the company has the unilateral right to remove the director for breach of contract.[357]

Specific Shareholder Approval of Breaches of Duty

It is a normal principle of the law relating to fiduciaries that those to **16–83** whom the duties are owed may release those who owe the duties from their legal obligations. Thus, the shareholders, acting as the company, ought in principle to be able to release the directors from their duties. In principle, such approval might be given in relation to a specific breach of duty or generally i.e. where no specific breach of duty is in contemplation or has yet occurred. In the former case the release might be prospective (i.e. before the breach occurs) or retrospective. In relation to general releases the proposed release is inevitably prospective, and the obvious mechanism to use to provide such *ex ante* release from a category of duties is an appropriate provision in the articles of association. It is obvious that a general release in the articles may be regarded with more suspicion than an *ex ante* or *ex post* specific release because, provided that full disclosure of the relevant facts is made to them in advance of their decision, the

---

[355] *Phipps v Boardman* [1967] 2 A.C. 46, HL; *O'Sullivan v Management Agency and Music Ltd* [1985] Q.B. 428, CA. In *Guinness v Saunders* [1990] 2 A.C. 663 their lordships were very reluctant to entertain the possibility of an allowance for work done, but that was a case in which the claim was for return of the company's property, not for an account of profits made. See above, fn.351.

[356] The right which the shareholders have under s.168 to remove a director at any time by ordinary resolution (see above, paras 14–18ff) could be prayed in aid, and the articles sometimes provide that a director must resign if called upon by a majority of the board to do so.

[357] Hence the importance of regulating the contractual entitlements of the director when the contract is concluded. See above, para.14–19.

shareholders in the latter case will know precisely the nature of the infringement of the company's rights to which they are consenting. However, waiver of the benefit of a duty in advance in the articles is necessarily a less informed waiver and shareholders, when voting on a change to the articles, may underestimate the chances of situations arising in the future where they would not want to give approval.[358] In other words, general authorisation via the articles may be less reliable an indication of shareholder preferences than specific authorisation of the taking of a particular opportunity. In this section we are concerned with what might be called "ad hoc" approval by the company, i.e. approval of a particular actual or proposed breach of duty. We discuss in the following section whether approval can be given in advance for categories of future breaches, where no or little detail is available on the particular breaches which may occur in the future.

Although the principle that the company may waive the benefit of the fiduciary duties owed it by means of shareholder approval is well-established at common law, even so it is subject to certain limitations, in the interests of protecting creditors and minority shareholders. The principle depends upon the notion that the shareholders constitute the appropriate expression of "the company" for the purpose of approval. However, as we have seen,[359] the common law takes the view that the creditors are the persons with the primary economic interest in the company, when the company is in the vicinity of insolvency. One consequence which has been drawn from this view is that the shareholders in such a situation may no longer approve breaches of the directors' duties: that is a matter for the creditors who, however, have no means of acting until the company goes into an insolvency procedure and an insolvency practitioner is appointed to act on their behalf.[360]

A further potential problem with shareholder approval, even when the company is a going concern, is that the majority shareholders may approve a breach of duty by the directors and, in so doing, act unfairly towards the minority, most obviously where they themselves are the directors in question. It might be thought that this is simply an example of majority unfairness towards the minority which can be handled through the general mechanisms for dealing with such unfairness and which we discuss in Part 4. However, perhaps because of the underdeveloped nature of the minority protection mechanisms until fairly recently, the need to protect minorities has shaped the

---

[358] A fortiori if the change has already been made and the question for an investor is whether he or she should acquire shares in that company.

[359] Above, para.16–34.

[360] See *West Mercia Safetywear Ltd v Dodd* [1988] B.C.L.C. 250, CA; *Aveling Barford v Perion Ltd* [1989] B.C.L.C. 626; *D K G Contractors Ltd, Re* [1990] B.C.C. 903; *Official Receiver v Stern* [2002] 1 B.C.L.C. 119 at 129.

common law rules on when shareholder approval should be permitted, as we shall see.

Where approval is given in advance of the breach of duty, it is **16–84** normally referred to as authorisation and where it is given afterwards it is referred to as ratification. This terminology seems to be adopted by the Act, for example in section 263, dealing with derivative actions, which distinguishes, in respect of a breach which has yet to occur, between whether it is likely to be "(i) authorised by the company before it occurs, or (ii) ratified by the company after it occurs."[361] Both methods of giving approval were established at common law and both are recognised in, but not comprehensively regulated by, the Act. Thus, section 180(4)(a), recognising but not seeking to amend the common law rules, states that the general duties "have effect subject to any rule of law enabling the company to give authority ... for anything to be done (or omitted) by the directors ... that would otherwise be a breach of duty."[362] Section 239 of the Act recognises the common law doctrine of ratification but also seeks to regulate it in certain respects. Although the regulation introduced by section 239 is welcome, one undesirable side-effect seems to be that the rules applying to ratification are no longer in all respects the same as those applying to authorisation, so that it may matter, oddly, if the company gives its approval the day before or the day after the directors breach their duty.

A crucial feature of company authorisation or ratification at common law was that they were required to be acts of an ordinary majority of the shareholders. Section 239(2) endorses this by stipulating that the ratification decision "must be taken by the members" and "may" be taken by ordinary majority, unless the company's articles or some common law or statutory rule requires a higher level of approval.[363] The common law as regards authorisation remains undisturbed, except that we have seen above that, in relation to breaches of section 175, the Act introduces the very significant change of board authorisation (subject to the articles permitting this) as an alternative to shareholder authorisation.

Ratification and authorisation, where effective, have the result of putting the directors in a position where they do not commit a breach of duty to the company or are treated as not having been in breach. In consequence, these actions should be distinguished from affirmation, where the shareholder resolution has the effect of making binding on the company a transaction which is otherwise voidable by

---

[361] s.263(2)(c) and (3)(c). See below, para.17–10.

[362] This does not necessarily mean that the doctrine of authorisation is confined to breaches of the general duties.

[363] s.239(7). The shareholders may also act informally by unanimous consent: s.239(6)(a).

the company because of the director's breach of duty, and from adoption where the transaction is one the director had no power to enter into at all but the shareholders decide the company should enter into.[364] Affirmation (or adoption) does not put the director in a position in which his or her breach of duty has been forgiven and the company, even after affirmation of the underlying transaction, may have remedies against the director, for example, for compensation or an account of profits. However, a single shareholder resolution may both forgive the directors and make the transaction binding on the company, and it is a matter of interpretation whether any particular resolution does so. Ratification is also to be distinguished from a mere decision not to sue the director. Such a decision has no effect on the director's legal position as being in breach of duty; the company can always change its mind later and sue the director, subject to the statute of limitations or any contract the company has entered into with the director containing an undertaking not to sue.[365]

Entitlement to vote

16–85   There were two much-debated questions about ratification and authorisation at common law, only one of which the statute answers, and then only in relation to ratification. However, since the two questions are at least functionally interlinked, it may be that the statute's answer to the one question will have an impact on the courts' answer to the second. The question the section answers in relation to ratification is that of who is entitled to vote on a ratification decision. The common law view was that it was open to the directors who were in breach of duty to cast their votes as shareholders in favour of the forgiveness of the breaches of duty committed by them as directors.[366] This conclusion seems to have been

---

[364] For an example of affirmation see s.214 (above, para.16–53): shareholders making loan transaction binding on the company but not relieving the directors of their breach of duty. See generally Yeung, "Disentangling the Tangled Skein: the Ratification of Directors' Actions" (1992) 66 A.J.L.R. 343.

[365] This is the difficult case. S.239(6)(b) preserves "any power of the directors to agree not to sue, or to settle or release a claim made by them on behalf of the company" but does not tell us anything about the extent of that power. Suppose the directors in good faith enter into a contract with one of their number on behalf of the company not to sue him or her for breach of duty. Can the director obtain an injunction to stop the litigation if the shareholders in general meeting or an individual shareholder in a derivative action later institutes litigation? Since the contract gives the director nearly the whole of what is obtainable by ratification, but ratification requires shareholder approval or may not be available at all (see below), it might be thought odd policy to allow the board to enter into such a contract on behalf of the company. The problem is discussed in H Hirt, *The Enforcement of Directors' Duties in Britain and Germany*, 2004, pp.95–96.

[366] *North-West Transportation v Beatty* (1887) 12 App.Cas.589, PC; *Burland v Earle* [1902] A.C. 83, PC; *Goodfellow v Nelson Line* [1912] 2 Ch.324; *Northern Counties Securities Ltd v Jackson & Steeple Ltd* [1974] 1 W.L.R. 1133. The contrary views of Vinelott J. in *Prudential Assurance Co Ltd v Newman Industries Ltd (No.2)* [1981] Ch.257, to the effect that interested shareholders may not vote on ratification resolutions must be regarded as heretical. See Wedderburn (1981) 44 M.L.R. 202.

derived from the view that shareholders, unlike directors, were not the subject of fiduciary duties and, indeed, that their shares, and the rights attached to them, were to be regarded as the shareholders' property. There is much to be said for the view that the law in this area should start from a different point. Instead of directors being entitled to vote as shareholders to ratify their own wrongs as directors, the principle should be, as the CLR recommended,[367] that a member having an interest in an actual or threatened wrong against the company (or being under the substantial influence of such a person) should be disqualified from voting on a shareholder resolution to ratify the wrong or indeed on a resolution that action be taken by the company to enforce the company's rights. Section 239(4) now partially adopts that principle: the ratification resolution is to be regarded as passed "only if the necessary majority is obtained disregarding the votes in favour of the resolution by the director . . . and any member connected with him."[368]

It has often been objected that it would prove impossibly difficult to identify the "interested" persons who should be disqualified from voting. It is to be noted that the Act does not in fact pose this question to the court. Although the underlying policy may be to exclude interested shareholders from voting, in fact the section adopts a more easily applied, but arguably less well-targeted, rule.[369] The rule is simply that the director or directors whose conduct is up for ratification may not vote on the resolution, nor may any person "connected with" the director, as defined by the sections discussed above in the context of substantial property transactions.[370] Thus, it would appear that, where two independent entrepreneurs are pursuing a common business strategy in relation to a company, one could vote in favour of ratification of the other's breach of duty, even where that breach of duty had been committed in pursuit of the common strategy, unless they could be said to have entered into an informal partnership.

It should be noted that that the disqualification from voting is not applied by the section to the common law concerning to authorisation, even though it seems clear that the CLR used the term "ratifi-

---

[367] Completing, paras 5.85 and 5.101. The Bill as originally introduced also disqualified from voting those "with a personal interest, direct or indirect, in the ratification."

[368] Section 239(4). An equivalent provision is made for written resolutions in section 239(3).

[369] This was a change introduced on Report in the House of Lords, the Bill having originally referred to "interested" persons. The Attorney General explained that the change was intended to introduce "a more precise and narrow test" and to exclude the votes of those "most likely to be biased in favour of the director or under his influence" whilst making it "easier to identify those persons when the votes are counted." (HL Debs, vol. 681, col, 872, May 9, 2006 (Lord Goldsmith).

[370] See above, para.16–51, except that here a fellow director can be a connected person if he or she otherwise meets the criteria: s.239(5)(d). Thus, the question of what is "substantial influence", as in the CLR's formulation, or whether the shareholder will vote "bona fide in the best interests of the company", as suggested by Knox J. in *Smith v Croft (No.3)* [1987] B.C.L.C. 365 at 404 are not questions the court will have to address under section 239.

cation" to include authorisation.[371] This is consistent with the provisions of Chapter 4 of Part 10, which, as we have seen, apparently
permit interested directors to vote on the resolutions required by that
Chapter (subject to any stricter rules applying to listed companies),
but is in principle undesirable, since controlling directors will be able
to choose the timing of the shareholder resolution.[372]

Non-ratifiable breaches

16–86   The other question, which the section does not answer,[373] is whether
all breaches of duty by a director are capable of being ratified. At
common law it is clear that some breaches of directors' duties are not
ratifiable, but it is much less clear how wide that rule is. Moreover, it
would appear that the doctrine of the non-ratifiable breach restricts
the scope of authorisation as much as it does that of ratification, so
that one benefit of the section's failure to address the issue is that
parallelism between the rules applying before and after the breach is
maintained. The most commonly formulated proposition is that a
majority of the shareholders may not by resolution expropriate to
themselves company property, because the property of the company
is something in which all the shareholders of the company have a (pro
rata) interest. Consequently, a resolution to ratify directors' breaches
of duty which would offend against this principle of equality is
ineffective (unless, presumably, all the shareholders of the company
agreed to the resolution and any relevant capital maintenance rules
were complied with).[374] But it is a principle easier to formulate than
apply, because of the ambiguities surrounding the meaning of
"property". The principle was applied in *Cook v Deeks*,[375] in which
the directors had diverted to themselves contracts which they should
have taken up on behalf of the company. By virtue of their controlling interests they secured the passing of a resolution in general
meeting ratifying what they had done. It was held that they must be
regarded as holding the benefit of the contracts on trust for the

---

[371] Thus, *Completing*, para.5.101 refers to the "votes of those supporting the ratification of a
wrong done *or to be done* on the company" (italics added).
[372] Above, para.16–51.
[373] s.239(7) says it does not "affect ... any rule of law as to acts that are incapable of being
ratified by the company." Those rules would seem to apply equally to prior authorisation by
the shareholders. Section 180(4)(a) does not require otherwise, since it preserves existing
powers of authorisation only.
[374] See *Halt Garage (1964) Ltd, Re* [1982] 3 All E.R. 1016; *Aveling Barford Ltd v Perion Ltd*
[1989] B.C.L.C. 626; *Rolled Steel Products (Holdings) Ltd v British Steel Corporation* [1986]
Ch.246 at 296.
[375] [1916] 1 A.C. 554, PC. See also *Menier v Hooper's Telegraph Works* (1874) L.R. 9
Ch.App.350.

company, for "directors holding a majority of votes would not be permitted [by the law] to make a present to themselves".[376] The same may apply when the present is not to themselves but to someone else.

Where, then, is the line to be drawn between those cases where shareholder approval is ineffective, and those in which shareholder approval has been upheld? How, in particular, can one reconcile *Cook v Deeks* with the many cases in which the liability of directors has been held to disappear as a result of ratification in general meeting?[377] Why, in *Regal (Hastings) Ltd v Gulliver*,[378] did the House of Lords say that the directors would not have been liable to account for their profits had the transaction been ratified, while, in *Cook v Deeks*, the Privy Council made them account notwithstanding such ratification? A satisfactory answer, consistent with common sense and with the decided cases, is difficult (and perhaps impossible) to provide.[379] The solution may be that a distinction is to be drawn between (i) misappropriating the company's property and (ii) merely making an incidental profit for which the directors are liable to account to the company. *Cook v Deeks* came within (i) for it was the duty of the directors to acquire the contracts on behalf of the company and accordingly when they themselves acquired them they did so as constructive trustees of the company. On the other hand, in *Regal (Hastings) Ltd v Gulliver* the directors did not misappropriate any property of the company; they had instead profited from information acquired as directors of the company and made use of an opportunity of which the company might have availed itself.

Beyond the proposition that ratification is not effective where it would amount to misappropriation of corporate property, it is difficult to formulate any further limitations which command general consent. It is sometimes said that breach of the directors' core duty of loyalty cannot be ratified by ordinary resolution of the shareholders. Certainly, this would be odd where the breach consists of failure to take account of the interests of the creditors, since that would mean release of the duty by the persons other than those to whom it is owed.[380] However, it is not obvious that release should never be permitted where it is the interests of the shareholders which have been

16–87

---

[376] At 564. Followed by Templeman J. in *Daniels v Daniels* [1978] Ch.406, where he refused to strike out a claim alleging that the majority had sold to themselves property of the company at a gross undervalue. In that case, the majority had not actually sought to ratify their actions, but the question was whether the wrong was ratifiable so as to prevent the minority from suing in a derivative action by virtue of the rule in *Foss v Harbottle*. Today such a transaction might well be caught by s.190 of the Act (see above, para.16–51).

[377] e.g. *NW Transportation Co v Beatty* (1887) 12 App.Cas.589, PC; *Burland v Earle* [1902] A.C. 83, PC; *A Harris v Harris Ltd* 1936 S.C. 183 (Sc.); *Baird v Baird & Co* 1949 S.L.T. 368 (Sc.).

[378] [1942] 1 All E.R. 378; [1967] 2 A.C. 134n., HL, above, paras 16–65 *et seq.*

[379] It has troubled a number of other writers: see, in particular, Wedderburn [1957] Cam.L.J. 194; [1958] *ibid.*, at 93; Afterman, *Company Directors and Controllers* (Sydney, 1970), pp.149 *et seq.*; Beck, in Ziegel (ed.), *Studies in Canadian Company Law*, Vol. II (Toronto, 1973), pp.232–238, and Sealy [1967] C.L.J. 83 at 102 *et seq.*

[380] See above, fn.360.

ignored by the directors, and the Court of Appeal in *Bamford v Bamford*[381] proceeded on the assumption that such ratification was possible. For example, if the directors have simply failed to consider whether a particular transaction was in the interests of the shareholders,[382] there would seem to be no reason why it should not be open to the shareholders in general meeting to conclude that, on consideration, it was and so ratify it.[383]

Thus, the existence of a set of non-ratifiable wrongs is established in the case-law, but the scope of the class is unclear. Future decisions on this issue may be affected by the fact that the most obvious categories of interested shareholders are now excluded from voting on the ratification resolution. Section 239, by depriving the directors in breach of the right to vote, avoids the result which the Privy Council were desirous of avoiding in *Cook v Deeks*, where the wrongdoers held three-quarters of the votes in the company, but does so without the need to resort to the concept of a "non-ratifiable wrong". Section 239 would now exclude the directors in that case from voting and in fact would leave the ratification decision wholly in the hands of the remaining shareholder in the company, who was the claimant in the case. In the unlikely event that that person approved the wrongdoing, there would seem to be no reason why the court should not accept that result. In other words, the rule against making presents of the corporate assets seems much less strong (provided the creditors' interests are not affected) if the non-involved shareholders approve. This consideration may lead the courts in future to narrow, perhaps severely, the class of non-ratifiable wrongs.[384] However, the issue of parallelism between the rules applicable to authorisation and ratification arises again here. It would be undesirable to remove or narrow the category of breaches incapable of shareholder approval if, in relation to authorisation, the interested directors were able to vote in their own favour as shareholders.

GENERAL PROVISIONS EXEMPTING DIRECTORS FROM LIABILITY

16–88   Although directors may secure specific authorisation or ratification of their actions from the shareholders, they are likely to regard that

---

[381] [1972] Ch.212. Both judgments delivered in the Court of Appeal referred to the case as one of lack of bona fides, though in fact Plowman J. at first instance characterised it more accurately as an "improper purposes" case.

[382] See above, para.16–29.

[383] It would be different if actual dishonesty were involved: *Atwood v Merryweather* (1867) L.R. 5 Eq. 464n.

[384] For further elaboration of this complex matter see Sarah Worthington, "Corporate Governance: Remedying and Ratifying Directors' Breaches" (2000) 116 L.Q.R. 638.

route to legal absolution as uncertain and unduly public. Historically, they have sought to use the articles to obtain general shareholder approval for certain categories of, or even all, breaches of duty. We have seen above that the articles were widely used in this way in respect of self-dealing transactions. We also saw that, in fact, the legislature in the 2006 Act accepted the outcome of such provisions by re-writing the statutory duty in relation to self-dealing transactions as a duty to disclose to the board rather than as a duty to obtain the approval of the shareholders. However, in some cases the articles went further and included more general provisions exempting the directors from liability for any breaches of duty (unless fraud was involved). Parliament responded in the Companies Act 1929.[385] In the current version of that reform (section 232(1)) the principle is laid down that "any provision that purports to exempt a director[386] of a company (to any extent) from any liability that would otherwise attach to him in connection with any negligence, default, breach of duty or breach of trust in relation to the company is void." This is a very important statutory provision. Subject to its exceptions, the section turns the directors' duties provisions into mandatory rules. Although the common law may regard those duties as existing for the benefit of the shareholders and thus to be waivable by the shareholders in the articles, the section takes a different view, perhaps reflecting doubt about the reality of the consent expressed in waivers given in advance of the event.

Conflicts of interest

Despite the general prohibition in the section, section 232(4) provides that "nothing in this section prevents a company's articles from making such provision as has previously been lawful for dealing with conflicts of interest". Thus it is clear that *some* exemptions from liability in the articles are permitted in the relation to the "no conflict" duties. This conclusion is reinforced by the provisions of section 180(4)(b) to the effect that "where the company's articles contain provisions for dealing with conflicts of interest, [the general duties] are not infringed by anything done (or omitted) by the directors, or any of them, in accordance with those provisions." Neither section 180(4)(b) nor 232(4) was contained in the version of the Bill introduced into Parliament; both were added at Third Reading stage in the Lords, under pressure from the Law Society. The two changes were

16–89

---

[385] Responding to the decision in *City Equitable Fir Insurance Co Ltd, Re* [1925] Ch.407, where a provision in the company's articles exempted the directors from liability except in cases of "wilful neglect or default".

[386] The earlier provisions applied also to any auditor or officer of the company. Since the enactment of the 2004 Act the provisions on auditors have developed in a separate direction and are discussed below at para.22–40, whilst officers have now disappeared from the section as well—and have not been replaced, it should be noted, by shadow directors.

introduced together as part of a single initiative which was described as follows by the minister, "the result of these two government amendments is that everything that may currently be done in the articles for authorising or dealing with conflicts of interest will remain valid. The Bill will leave the law unchanged in this area."[387] The test for the legality of such provisions which section 232 adopts is whether the provision had "previously been lawful for dealing with conflicts of interest"; and it seems that section 180(4)(b) must be interpreted as subject to a similar restriction.

What is the meaning of this Delphic phrase? What could the articles previously (i.e. before the 2006 Act) do in relation to conflicts of interest? In order to answer this question one needs to know the history of judicial interpretation of the predecessor of section 232, namely, section 310, later section 309A, of the 1985 Act. This was a highly debated question, arising previously mainly in relation to self-dealing transactions, because that was where the problem arose in practice. The debated question was whether articles substituting informing the board for shareholder approval were compatible with the predecessors of section 232. That particular question is no longer relevant because section 177 adopts outright the principle of disclosure to the board.[388] However, the answer given to the question under the former law will tell us how to approach under the 2006 Act an article dealing with any other conflict of interest. The only intellectually respectable answer in that debate was given by Vinelott J. in *Movitex Ltd v Bulfield*.[389] His explanation drew a distinction between (1) "the overriding principle of equity" that "if a director places himself in a position in which his duty to the company conflicts with his personal interest or duty to another, the court will set aside the transaction without enquiring whether there was any breach of duty to the company" and (2) the director's "duty to promote the interests of [the company] and when the interests of [the company] conflicted with his own to prefer the interests of [the company]". While any proposed modification of (2) would infringe s.310 of the 1985 Act, the shareholders of the company in formulating the articles could exclude or modify the application of (1) "the overriding principle of equity". In doing so they did not exempt the director from, or from the consequences of, a breach of duty owed to the company.[390] In short, the articles could permit the director to put him- or herself in a position of potential conflict of interest, but if the conflict became actual the articles could not exempt the director from the obligation to prefer the company's interests.

[387] HL Debs, vol. 682, col. 721, May 23, 2006, Third Reading (Lord Sainsbury of Turville). See also vol. 681, col. 865, May 9, 2006 (Lord Goldsmith).
[388] See above, p.16–42.
[389] [1988] B.C.L.C. 104.
[390] [1988] B.C.L.C. 104, at 120–121d.

Given that the duty in relation to self-dealing transactions has **16–90** become under the 2006 Act a simple duty of disclosure, where will there be an incentive for provisions in the articles to be deployed in future which exempt directors from liability for conflicts of interest? There seem to be two main areas: corporate opportunities and multiple directorships. Translated into corporate opportunity terms, the *Movitex* approach indicates that the articles cannot exempt the director from obtaining the company's authorisation before taking personally an opportunity the company was actually pursuing (as in *Cook v Deeks*[391] and *Industrial Development Consultants v Cooley*[392]) or probably one which the company had an interest in considering because it fell within its current line of business (as in *Bhullar v Bhullar*[393]), because in that situation there would be an actual conflict of interest. However, the articles might exempt the director from taking without authorisation an opportunity which the company (normally the board) had rejected in good faith (as in *Regal*).[394] The argument would be that the director would not be in breach of the core duty of loyalty if the board had in good faith rejected the opportunity, whilst liability arising out of the potential conflict of interest arising in such a case could be removed by appropriate provisions in the articles.

Provisions seeking to exempt directors generally from liability for taking corporate opportunities are in fact relatively uncommon. It might be thought that it would take a brazen set of directors to propose such provisions and a supine set of shareholders to accept them. However, this is not to say that limited provisions of this kind cannot be found. In fact, the previous, though not the current, version of the model set of articles contained such provisions. Under Article 85 of the 1985 version of Table A,[395] it was provided that, subject to disclosure to the board, a director "may be a director or other officer of, or employed by ... or *otherwise interested in*, any body corporate promoted by the company or in which the company is otherwise interested" and was not liable to account to the company for any benefit received as a result. This provision was fairly clearly directed at protecting directors from liability to account to the company in the situation which arose in *Regal v Gulliver*.[396] It might well survive today by virtue of section 232(4).

In relation to multiple directorships, the articles might seek to provide that it was permissible for a director to take on additional directorships, rather than having to seek board or shareholder

---

[391] Above, fn.375.
[392] Above, fn.278.
[393] Above, fn.280.
[394] Above, fn.378.
[395] SI 1985/805.
[396] Above, para.16–65, where it will be recalled the directors took up shares in a company set up by the company of which they were directors.

approval in each case. However, the *Movitex* case would suggest that such an article will be upheld by virtue of section 232(4) only if there is no actual conflict of duties for the director in consequence of the taking up of additional directorships. If a situation arises in which the director's core duty of loyalty to each of two companies forces him or her in different directions, it is far from clear that section 232(4) legitimates an article which allows the director to simply withdraw from acting on behalf of either company.[397]

Provisions providing directors with an indemnity

16–91 The ban, contained in section 232, on provisions exempting directors from liability extends (subject to important exceptions) to any provision by which the company provides, directly or indirectly, an indemnity to a director or a director of an associated company in respect of these liabilities.[398] Under an indemnity arrangement the director remains in principle liable but the company picks up the financial consequences of that liability. The indemnity prohibition applies also to indemnities provided in favour of directors of associated[399] companies, thus preventing evasion of the section in group situations, whereby all the directors have the benefit of indemnity provisions, but in no case is the indemnity provided by the company of which they are a director. The provisions referred to in the section are those "contained in a company's articles or in any contract with the company or otherwise".[400] The indemnity might be provided by means of the company promising to indemnify the director or, indirectly, by the company taking out insurance on the director's behalf, so that the indemnity is to be provided by the insurance company. As we shall see, the legislation is less strict in relation to insurance than in respect of the direct indemnity.

Insurance

16–92 Since 1989 a company has been free (but of course not obliged) to buy insurance against any of the liabilities mentioned in section 232 for the benefit of its directors (section 233) and it is in fact common practice to do so, at least in large companies. At first sight, this is very odd. Insurance certainly means, assuming the policy limits are large enough, that the company receives compensation for any loss it

---

[397] See above, para.16–74.

[398] s.232(2).

[399] See above, para.16–57. This extension was effected by the Companies (Audit, Investigation and Community Enterprise) Act 2004, s.19.

[400] s.232(3). In *Burgoine v Waltham Forest LBC* [1997] 2 B.C.L.C. 612 it was held that the phrase "or otherwise" did not extend the section beyond indemnities, etc., given by the company (as opposed to a third party), though that is now subject to the extension of the indemnity prohibition to the directors of associated companies. Presumably, the force of these words is to ban such provisions in members' or directors' resolutions.

suffers as a result of the breach of duty. On the other hand, the company pays for the insurance and so, over time at least, the insurance premia will roughly equal the losses inflicted on the company by the directors, so that the company ends up paying for the directors' breaches of duty. This seems to deprive the directors' duties rules of any deterrent effect as against the directors and to mean that the insurance simply operates as a way of smoothing the losses inflicted on the company by the directors. This argument has considerable force, but needs to be assessed subject to the following qualifications. First, the impact of section 233 depends upon the extent of the cover which the insurance market is prepared to make available at any particular time. It is unlikely that insurance is available against the consequences of breach of duty involving fraud or wilful default, because of the moral hazard problem for the insurance company in providing such cover.[401] And it may be difficult to obtain cover against the liability to account for profits made as opposed to losses inflicted on the company. In any event, the policy is likely to be subject to monetary limits, so that liability remains to some extent personally with the director in the case of large claims.

Secondly, it is conceivable that insurance companies will adjust their premia according to the claims experience of the company so that a financial incentive is generated for the company to monitor the actions of its directors or refuse to insure those with a bad claims record, or insurance companies may even engage in more general monitoring of the corporate governance arrangements in the company, thus somewhat restoring the deterrent effect of the duties.[402] Finally, it may be that qualified persons will be unwilling to take on board positions without the benefit of such insurance. This might be true particularly of non-executive directors, whose financial benefits from the company may be modest (at least in comparison with the remuneration of executive directors) and whose knowledge of and control over the company is necessarily limited. They could buy such insurance themselves, for the section does not restrict the taking out of insurance against directors' liabilities by the directors them-

---

[401] The provisions to be found in such insurance contracts are analysed by Colin Baxter, "Demystifying D&O Insurance" (1995) 15 OJLS 537, now a somewhat dated, but nevertheless useful, article. The insurance may extend, of course, to protection against liabilities beyond those discussed in this chapter.

[402] Evidence from the US suggests that neither form of control by insurance companies is strong, probably because the directors, who control the decision where to place the insurance, would not welcome it. See T. Baker and S. Griffin, "Predicting Governance Risk: Evidence from the Directors' and Officers' Liability Insurance Market" 74 *Chicago L.R.* 487 (2007) and "The Missing Monitor in Corporate Governance: The Directors' and Officers' Liability Insurer" 95 Georgetown L.J. 1795 (2007). This view is concurred in by Baxter, above, fn.401.

selves.[403] However, they would no doubt expect the cost of such insurance to be reflected in their fees, and it may be cheaper and more effective for the company to provide that insurance itself.

Third party indemnities

16–93   Despite the term "third party indemnities" the indemnity under discussion here is one provided by the company in favour of the director. It is a "third party" indemnity because it relates to litigation which might be brought by a third party (i.e. someone other than the company) against the director.[404] Under an indemnity provision the company promises that the director will not be out of pocket in relation to the claim made against him or her (whether by way of a judgment against the director, a settlement of the litigation or by the incurring of legal costs), so that, to the extent of the indemnity, the cost of the director's breach of duty is borne directly by the company. As we have seen, it will be rare for breaches of the duties discussed in this chapter to lead to liability other than to the company, but this may not be the case where the liability arises under a foreign system of law, notably US law, and section 232 is not in terms confined to liabilities arising under the law of a UK jurisdiction. A director may prefer insurance to a promise of an indemnity by the company, because on insolvency the company's promise may not be worth very much, but an indemnity may be regarded by the director as better than nothing, and the company may prefer, in effect, to self-insure by promising an indemnity.

Note, however, that the company may not promise an indemnity against liability or costs incurred in an action brought by the company. This may be provided for only through the purchase of insurance by the company, as discussed above. Why is this? It may have been thought, on the one hand, that a complete indemnity would come very close to an exemption from liability, thus defeating the purpose of section 232. On the other hand, despite the failings of the insurance market, insurance requires an assessment of the extent of and the costs of the risks involved by another commercial organisation, which will exclude some risks from those it is prepared to underwrite. This provides some external control over the liabilities from which directors can be exempted, for example, where they have acted deliberately in breach of duty. Equally, the need to buy insurance will bring the cost of the protection home to the board which is arranging for it, whilst an indemnity, which carries no immediate costs for the company, might be too easy a provision to slip into the articles.

In the Companies Act 1989 a limited set of permitted indemnity

---

[403] This seems to be the implication of the *Burgoine* decision, above, fn.400.
[404] s.234(2).

provisions was introduced (essentially confined to legal costs) which was substantially extended by the 2006 Act. What is permitted by way of an indemnity is defined in section 234 by specifying what is not permitted by way of third-party indemnity: anything not prohibited is permitted. No indemnity is permitted by section 234(3) in relation to:

— a fine imposed on a director in criminal proceedings,

— the costs of defending criminal proceedings in which the director is convicted,

— a penalty payable to a regulatory authority,

— costs incurred in connection with an application for relief (see below) which is unsuccessful, or

— the costs of defending civil proceedings brought by the company or an associated company in which judgement is given against the director.

The last category of exclusion may seem surprising, given that liability to the company or associated company is not within the definition of a "third party indemnity" (section 234(2)) but it is to be noted that what section 234(3) deals with is not the director's liability to the company or associated company but the director's liability for costs incurred in defending civil proceedings brought by such a company, which liability may be incurred to a third party, i.e. the director's legal team. The exclusion thus completes the policy objective of preventing the indemnity from operating in respect of any aspect of a claim brought by the company or an associated company, but only if the company is successful in the claim. If no judgment is given against the director, either because the director is successful or because the case is settled, a provision requiring the company to indemnify the director against legal costs is permitted. The section achieves the same result in relation to criminal proceedings against the director: only the costs of successfully defending a criminal charge may be the subject of an indemnity provision. However, it appears that the costs of an unsuccessful defence in a regulatory procedure (for example, one brought by the Financial Services Authority) may be the subject of an indemnity provision (though not the cost of any penalty imposed by the FSA).

16–94 However, the real importance of the section is not revealed by what it says by way of exclusion but what it does not exclude. In the case of a civil action brought by a third party (for example, shareholders in a class action) the indemnity provision may cover both the liability of the director and the costs of defending the action, whether successfully or unsuccessfully.

An indemnity provision which meets the requirements of section 234 is termed a "qualifying indemnity provision". A qualifying indemnity provision[405] must be disclosed to the shareholders in the directors' annual report (section 236); and must be made available for inspection in the usual way by any shareholder of the company without charge, who may also require a copy of it to be provided upon payment of the prescribed fee (sections 237 and 238).

It should finally be noted that what section 234 creates is a permission for the company, not an obligation, and it is a permission to have a provision (in the company's articles or in a contract with a director, for example) which provides for an indemnity of the relevant type. The section does not deal with ad hoc decisions by boards of directors to pay an indemnity in a particular case, where there is no existing provision dealing with this matter. Such a decision is governed by the directors' duties discussed above and by the general law of the land.[406] It is also possible that a company might wish to lend the director money in advance to defend proceedings brought against him or her, whether criminal, civil or regulatory. We have already seen that a company is exempted from the normal rules on shareholder approval if it decides to make such a loan, or enter into an analogous transaction, for this purpose. However, the loan must be on terms that it is repayable if the director is unsuccessful in the proceedings.[407] A loan on different terms or for a different purpose (for example, to meet a liability in a judgment rather than to defend proceedings) would need shareholder approval.

Pension scheme indemnity

16–95 Where a company runs an occupational pension scheme (a regrettably less frequent situation these days than previously), the company may be a trustee of the trust through which the scheme is organised and the director may act on behalf of the company in its capacity as such a trustee.[408] Section 235 permits provisions indemnifying the director against any liability incurred in connection with the company's activities as trustee of the scheme, subject to the same restrictions as in section 234 in relation to criminal and regulatory

---

[405] Whether made by the company or not, so that the directors of an associated company must report it as well; and copies must be available for inspection by the shareholders of both companies.

[406] It has been suggested in a trade union case that, whereas a once-off *ex post* decision to indemnify an officer against a fine was unobjectionable (if authorised by the union's rules), "continued resolutions authorising the re-funding of fines might fairly be said to lead to an expectation that a union would indemnify its members against the consequences of future offences" and that would be against public policy: *Drake v Morgan* [1978] I.C.R. 56, 61.

[407] See above, para.16–59.

[408] Of course, the director may be appointed personally by the company to be a trustee of the scheme, but it may have been thought that, in such a case, any liability would not be incurred in the capacity of director but as trustee or appointee, so that any indemnity provision would not fall within s.232.

proceedings. However, section 235 permits indemnity arrangements in relation to civil suits, whether brought by a third party or by the company, which indemnity may extend to both costs and liability. In other words, as far as the director's activities on behalf of the company as trustee are concerned, a complete indemnity arrangement is permissible in relation to civil liability. The same reporting and copy requirements apply in relation to a qualifying pension scheme indemnity provision as in relation to a third-party indemnity provision.

RELIEF

Whether or not the director is able to secure forgiveness from the company, the director, and any officer of the company (including the auditor), has the possibility of appealing to the court to prevent the full application to him or her of the statutory duties included in Part 10 or indeed any analogous duties arising, for example, at common law. Under section 1157 the court has a discretion to relieve, prospectively or retrospectively, against liability for negligence, default, breach of duty or breach of trust, provided that it appears to the court that the director has acted honestly and reasonably and that, having regard to all the circumstances, he ought to be excused. The court may relieve on such terms as it thinks fit. The requirement of reasonableness might suggest that section 1157 is not available in relation to the directors' duties of care, skill and diligence but this appears not to be the case.[409] However, the section is not available in respect of third-party (as opposed to corporate) claims against the director,[410] and, more important for present purposes, will not be applied even to corporate claims where that would be inconsistent with the purposes underlying the rule imposing the liability against which relief is sought.[411]   **16–96**

LIABILITY OF THIRD PARTIES

Despite the wide range of civil remedies which exist to support the substantive law of directors' duties, it is to be doubted whether in   **16–97**

---

[409] *Equitable Life Assurance Society v Bowley* [2004] 1 B.C.L.C. 180 at [45]; *D'Jan of London Ltd, Re* [1994] 1 B.C.L.C. 561 at 564.
[410] *Customs and Excise Commissioners v Hedon Alpha Ltd* [1981] 1 Q.B. 818, CA.
[411] *Produce Marketing Consortium Ltd, Re* [1989] 1 W.L.R. 745 (wrongful trading liabilities excluded).

many cases the directors are in fact worth suing, at least if they are uninsured. They may once have had property belonging to the company but, by the time the company finds this out, may have it no longer. They may have made large profits which they should account to the company, but may well have spent them by the time the writ arrives. Companies are therefore likely to want to identify some more stable third party, often a bank, which is worth powder-and-shot, either instead of or in addition to the directors.[412]

But under what conditions may the company hold a third party liable in connection with a breach of duty by the directors? This is not a matter dealt with in the Act in relation to the general duties of directors. It is left to the common law, which is rather complex, though it is an area to which recent decisions of the Privy Council and House of Lords have helped to clarify. Only the briefest sketch of the relevant principles can be attempted here. It has long been recognised that there are two bases of third-party liability, one resting on receipt by the third party of company property and the other resting on complicity on the part of the third party in the director's breach of duty. The main conceptual contribution of the Privy Council in *Royal Brunei Airlines Sdn. Bhd. v Tan*[413] was to make it clear that the principles supporting the imposition of liability in these two situations are different from one another.

In the case of complicity in the breach, which the court helpfully termed "accessory" liability, the liability is a reflection of a general principle of the law of obligations. This imposes liability upon third parties who assist or procure the breach of a duty or obligation owed by another, the liability of the third party being enforceable by the person who is the beneficiary of the duty whose performance has been interfered with.[414] Since the liability is imposed on the third party in order to protect the beneficiary (in our case, the company), the liability of the third party should not depend, as had previously been thought, upon the director having acted dishonestly.[415] Provided

---

[412] See, for example, *Selangor United Rubber Estates v Cradock (No.3)* [1968] 1 W.L.R. 1555.

[413] [1995] 2 A.C. 378, PC, noted by Birks [1996] L.M.C.L.Q. 1 and Harpum (1995) 111 L.Q.R. 545. The facts of the case did not raise an issue of directors' duties. In fact, the fiduciary duty in question was owed by the company and the principle of accessory liability was used to make the director liable to the claimant for the *company's* breach of duty. But the principle of the case is clearly of general application.

[414] See at 387. For this reason, this head of third party liability should apply to all cases of breach of fiduciary duty by directors, whether misappropriation of corporate property is involved or not. See *Brown v Bennett* [1999] 1 B.C.L.C. 649, CA. Although the courts often refer to third parties who are liable as accessories in relation to breaches of directors' duties as "constructive trustees", it would seem that their liability is personal, not proprietary, and that the language of constructive trusts could be abandoned here. See Birks, "The Recovery of Misapplied Assets" in McKendrick (ed.), *Commercial Aspects of Trusts and Fiduciary Obligations* (Oxford, 1992) at pp.153–154.

[415] However, it was held in *Fyffes Group Ltd v Templeman* [2000] 2 Lloyd's Rep. 643 and in *Ultraframe (UK) Ltd v Fielding* [2005] EWHC 1638 that the accessory's liability was not confined to damages but included a liability to account for profits which the accessory had made (but not profits made by the director).

there has been a breach of duty by the director, whether committed knowingly or not, the third party will be liable to the company if that party has acted dishonestly. The focus is on the fault of the third party, not on the fault of the director. The effect of the decision was to expand the boundaries of the liability of third parties as accessories, though the House of Lords has subsequently somewhat qualified the expansion by adopting a rather traditional definition of dishonesty. In *Twinsectra Ltd v Yardley*,[416] it was held, over the dissent of Lord Millett, that, although dishonesty meant dishonesty according to the ordinary standards of reasonable people, it was also necessary for liability that the third party should realise that his conduct was dishonest according to those standards. The test of dishonesty is thus not wholly objective (as Lord Millett urged) but is qualified by an additional and subjective requirement.

In the case of solvent and respectable third parties, however, **16–98** accessory liability is less likely[417] to be available on the facts than an argument based upon "knowing receipt" of the company's property, at least if the term "knowing" is given a wide enough connotation. The essence of this claim is restitutionary. Company property has been transferred to the third party in breach of the directors' fiduciary duties and the company seeks the imposition of a constructive trust upon the third party recipient to secure the return of the value of that property to the company, even if the third party no longer has the property or its identifiable proceeds in its hands.[418] A common situation found in the cases is one where the directors have used the company's assets in breach of the statutory prohibition on the provision of financial assistance towards the purchase of its shares, and the assets in question have passed through the hands of a third party.[419]

The scope of knowing receipt liability depends heavily upon the degree of knowledge on the part of the third party which is requisite to trigger it, an issue which has been much discussed in the courts in recent years. Although the issue is far from settled, the tendency of the recent decisions has been not to impose liability on the basis of constructive knowledge in ordinary commercial transactions, on the grounds that the doctrine of constructive knowledge presupposes an underlying system of careful and comprehensive investigation of the surrounding legal context, which is typical of property transactions

[416] [2002] 2 A.C. 164, HL.

[417] Which is not to say that the first basis of liability is never available: see *Canada Safeway Ltd v Thompson* [1951] 3 D.L.R. 295.

[418] *El Ajou v Dollar Land Holdings Plc* [1994] 2 All E.R. 685 at 700, per Hoffmann L.J. If the third party does still have the property or its identifiable proceeds to hand, then a proprietary constructive trust or tracing claim may be possible. Otherwise, the liability imposed under the constructive trust seems to be personal, and again it is doubtful whether the language of "constructive trust" is really needed. See Birks, *op. cit.*, pp.154–156.

[419] See above, para.13–36, and *Belmont Finance Corporation v Williams Furniture Ltd (No.2)* [1980] 1 All E.R. 393, CA.

but atypical of commercial transactions (including the non-property aspects of commercial property transfers).[420] In *Bank of Credit and Commerce International (Overseas) Ltd v Akindele*[421] the Court of Appeal struck out on a new tack. Whilst confirming that dishonesty is not a requirement for liability under the "knowing receipt" head, the Court abandoned the search for a single test for knowledge in this area. Instead, the question to ask was whether the recipient's state of knowledge was such as to make it unconscionable for him or her to retain the benefit of the receipt. The Court thought this would enable judges to "give common sense decisions in the commercial context", though it has to be said that the test is a very open-ended one and not likely to conduce to a common approach on the part of the courts.

Third-party liability may also arise in relation to corporate opportunities. Here, the question again arises of how far a corporate opportunity constitutes an asset of the company. We have seen above[422] that this question is relevant to the question of whether the director's taking of the opportunity can be ratified by a simple majority of the shareholders. It arises again here: does receipt by a third party either of the opportunity itself or of assets arising out of its exploitation fall within the "knowing receipt" principle? What is clear is that merely entering into a contract with the company which remains executory does not put the third party in a position in which he or she can be said to be in receipt of corporate assets.[423] Where the corporate opportunity is regarded as an asset of the company, it follows that the company will be able to seek to recover profits made out of exploitation of the opportunity by the third party (provided the requirement of knowledge is met), even if the director does not make any profit, as in the case of the chairman in *Regal (Hastings) Ltd v Gulliver*.[424]

Whether in such a case the director him- or herself can be held liable for the third party's profits is much debated. This will be possible if the third party is a partnership of which the director is a member, because, the partnership not being a separate legal entity, the profit is regarded as the director's, even if the director's partners are entitled to a share of the profit. It will also be possible in the narrow circumstance where the third party is a company but the company is a sham, hiding the director, in which case the court will

---

[420] See *Eagle Trust Plc v SBC Securities Ltd* [1993] 1 W.L.R. 484; *Cowan de Groot Properties Ltd v Eagle Trust Plc* [1992] 4 All E.R. 700; *Eagle Trust Plc v SBC Securities Ltd (No.2)* [1996] 1 B.C.L.C. 121.

[421] [2001] Ch. 437, CA. See also the use of this test in *Criterion Properties Plc v Stratford UK Properties LLC*, above, fn.92.

[422] At para.16–86.

[423] *Criterion Properties Ltd v Stratford UK Properties Ltd* [2004] 1 W. L. R. 1846, HL.

[424] Above, fn.270, though it should be noted that in that case the language of the court was not noticeably proprietary in tone.

pierce the corporate veil so as to make the director liable.[425] Where the third-party company is not a sham, it is disputed whether the director can be liable with the company for the company's profits on the grounds that director and company are jointly in breach of trust or whether the position is that each is liable only for the profits made personally.[426]

LIMITATION OF ACTIONS

The question of whether directors acting in breach of their fiduciary duties have the benefit of the Limitation Acts is another area where the analogy between the director and the trustee is to the fore, the specific provisions of the Limitation Act 1980 dealing with actions by a beneficiary against a trustee being applied to actions by a company against a director.[427] The crucial question is whether there is any limitation period in such cases, for until the late nineteenth century trustees did not have the benefit of a limitation period in actions by beneficiaries.[428] Under s.21 of the 1980 Act a limitation period of six years is applied to such actions (unless some other section of the Act applies a different limitation period), but there are two exceptions where the old rule of no limitation continues to operate. These are (a) where the claim is based upon fraud or fraudulent breach of trust and (b) where the action is to recover "from the trustee trust property or the proceeds of trust property in the possession of the trustee or previously received by the trustee and converted to his use". In a standard case, therefore, of an action against a director to recover a profit made in breach of his fiduciary duties or for equitable compensation, the limitation period will be six years. Only where the claimant can go further and bring himself within either the (a) or (b) exception will the Act not apply.[429]

16–99

As to (a), it should be noted that it is a strong rule, since defendants in actions based on fraud are not generally deprived by the Limitation Act of the benefit of a limitation period. To benefit from this exception the claimant has to show not simply that the director acted in breach of duty, but that he or she intended to act either knowing

---

[425] For the third-party partnership see *Mercantile Credit Association v Coleman* (1873) L.R. 6 H.L. 189 and on the sham third-party company see *Trustor AB v Smallbone (No.2)* [2001] 1 W.L.R. 1177; *Glencor ACP Ltd v Dalby* [2000] 2 B.C.L.C. 734.

[426] Contrast *CMS Dolphin Ltd v Simonet* [2001] 2 B.C.L.C. 704 at [98] ff and *Ultraframe (UK) Ltd v Fielding* [2005] EWHC 1638 at [1516] ff.

[427] But not to claims by third parties against a director, where the normal limitation periods apply.

[428] The position was changed by the Trustee Act 1888.

[429] *Gwembe Valley Development Co Ltd v Koshy (No.3)* [2004] 1 B.C.L.C. 131, CA at [111] and [118].

that the action was contrary to the interests of the company or recklessly indifferent as to whether it was.[430]

As to (b), it means that there is no limitation period in those cases where a director has misapplied company property which has come into his or her hands and the company is seeking restoration of that property. This rule applies even though the company's property is no longer in the hands of the director.[431] As it was put some hundred years ago, the rule is intended to prevent the director from "coming off with something he ought not to have".[432] However, in recent years the scope of (b) has been debated in relation to third parties who are often called "constructive trustees" by the courts under the doctrines of accessory liability and knowing receipt discussed above. The courts have drawn a distinction between two types of constructive trustee, constructive trustees properly so-called and those in respect of whom the term would better be abandoned.[433] The first case is the case of the person who, though not expressly appointed as a trustee, has assumed the duties of a trustee by a lawful transaction which was independent of and preceded the breach of trust. Such a person falls within case (b) and this explains why a director who receives company property in breach of fiduciary duty is not subject to the six-year limitation rule.

The second case is where the trust obligation arises as a direct consequence of the unlawful transaction which the claimant challenges and where the constructive trust is imposed simply to provide an effective remedy in equity.[434] Such a person does not fall within case (b). Applying these definitions, it would seem that the case of knowing receipt is an example of the remedial constructive trust, because it is the receipt of the property by the third party in the relevant circumstances which creates the duty to restore the property to the company and not the breach of any preceding fiduciary relationship between the third party and the company. Such a third party can rely on the normal limitation periods. A similar analysis would seem to be applicable to the person made liable to the company on an accessory basis, though, as has been noted by Millett L.J., "there is a case for treating a claim against a person who has assisted a trustee in committing a breach of trust as subject to the same limitation regime as the claim against the trustee",[435] so that the matter may still be open in relation to accessory liability.

---

[430] *Gwembe Valley* (previous note) at [131].
[431] *JJ Harrison (Properties) Ltd v Harrison* [2002] 1 B.C.L.C. 162, CA; *Pantone 485 Ltd, Re*, [2002] 1 B.C.L.C. 266.
[432] *Timmis, Nixon v Smith, Re*, [1902] 1 Ch. 176 at 186.
[433] *Paragon Finance Plc v D B Thackerar & Co* [1999] 1 All E.R. 400, CA.
[434] These are the definitions of Millett L.J. in the case cited in the previous note.
[435] See above, fn.433 at p.414.

CONCLUSION

Looking at the reform elements in the statutory statement and else-   **16–100**
where in the statutory provisions on directors' duties, one can ask
whether the resulting set of rules is more or less constraining of
directors' actions than the law it replaces. This is not an easy question
to answer. The candidates in support of the view that the new rules
are more constraining are the provisions on negligence (section 174),
the core duty of loyalty (s.172) and the rules on ratification (s.239).
The objective standard of care introduced by section 174 is
undoubtedly a strong contrast with the subjective formulation of that
duty to be found in the nineteenth-century negligence cases. However, more recent common law decisions were already moving the law
in an objective direction, and so it can be said that section 174 confirms a trend which was already evident in the case-law.[436]

Section 172 contains an explicit recognition of stakeholder interests
for the first time in British company law, which had previously
referred only to employee interests.[437] However, those stakeholder
interests are to be pursued by directors only where such action is
needed to promote the success of the company for the benefit of its
members. The core duty of loyalty is thus still shareholder-centred.
Further, it seems clear that the prior common law permitted directors
to take into account stakeholder interests where promoting the
interests of the company (shareholders) required it.[438] Consequently,
the novelty of the statutory formulation of the core duty of loyalty
may be the obligation upon directors to take stakeholder interests
into account where the promotion of the success of the company
requires this. This is only a marginal change in legal obligation, but it
is possible that the statutory articulation of the need to take into
account stakeholder interests in this way will have, when coupled
with larger changes in legal rules and the social and economic context
within which companies operate, a bigger impact than might otherwise be predicted.[439]

Finally, section 239[440] introduces an important change to the rules
about who may vote on a shareholder resolution to ratify a breach of
directors' duties by excluding the votes of the directors in question
and those connected with them. This is likely to be an important
reform in closely held companies. Whether it will trigger a change in
the categorisation of wrongs as ratifiable or not remains to be seen.

---

[436] See above, paras 16–12ff.
[437] See above, paras 16–25ff and for the prior statutory law see Companies Act 1985, s.309.
[438] *Hutton v West Cork Ry Co* (1883) 23 Ch. D. 654 per Bowen L. J.: "Most businesses require liberal dealings".
[439] For example, changes within company law about narrative reporting (see paras 21–21ff) or outside company law the increasing legal and political significance of environmental issues.
[440] Above, para.16–85.

On the side of the argument that the new rules are less constraining of directors is the significant change that the independent members of the board may authorise breaches of the directors' duty not to place themselves in a position of conflict of duty and interest (or of duty and duty).[441] Although the principle of board decision-making was already established under the prior law in relation to self-dealing transactions, its extension to corporate opportunities and other conflicted situations is a new step. The argument in favour of the extension is that shareholder authorisation, as the sole method of authorisation permitted by the prior law, was in practice too uncertain and too public to be a practical form of permission, so that the prior law operated in fact so as to allow directors to pursue corporate opportunities only at the risk of the company later deciding to take from the director the profit earned from the exploitation of the opportunity. The argument against the extension is that the dynamics of board relationships mean that the uninvolved members of the board may not exercise a genuinely independent judgment on whether to release the corporate interest in the opportunity, even if this is what the law requires of them. This argument may be less strong in companies listed on the main market of the London Stock Exchange and so required to comply with the provisions of the Combined Code on Corporate Governance as to independent non-executive directors, but that is a very small proportion of the companies incorporated under the Companies Acts. In the result, outside the area of benefits received by directors from third parties,[442] the board is now the guardian of the company's position in situations of conflict, contrary to the wisdom of the common law that only the shareholders could be relied upon for this purpose.

---

[441] s.175 and see above, paras 16–69ff.
[442] See above, paras 16–75ff.

CHAPTER 17

THE DERIVATIVE CLAIM AND PERSONAL ACTIONS AGAINST DIRECTORS

THE NATURE OF THE PROBLEM AND THE POTENTIAL SOLUTIONS

The duties discussed in the previous chapter are not likely to play a **17–1** significant role in the governance of British companies if, for one reason or another, they are rarely enforced, either in actual litigation or in the threat of it. However, it is important not to jump from that banality to the conclusion that in every case where it is arguable that a director has infringed his or her duties to the company, the company should be contemplating litigation. The test, it is submitted, is whether "the interests of the company" require that litigation be instituted, and that question can be answered only on the facts of a particular case. It is easy to imagine many reasons why litigation would actually leave the company worse off than it was before. There may be doubts about whether a judgment in favour of the company will be obtained, either because of disputes about the law or because of difficulties of proving the events said to constitute the breach of duty. Or the defendants may not be in a position to meet the judgment even if the litigation is successful. Or the senior management time spent on the litigation might more profitably be used elsewhere or, finally, whilst winning the legal arguments and obtaining an enforceable remedy, the company may suffer collateral reputational harm which outweighs the gain from the litigation. In other words, the decision whether to initiate litigation in respect of an alleged breach of directors' duty will not always be an easy one, and a negative decision is not necessarily a sign that the company is being too lax towards its directors.

On the other hand, a decision not to sue a director may indeed be heavily influenced by that director's personal interests, rather than those of the company. The conflicts of interest which we analysed in the previous chapter are not magically excluded from corporate decision-making on litigation. Thus, the need is to distinguish between litigation decisions (especially decisions not to sue) which are in the interests of the company and those which are not. Given that such decisions require a close analysis of particular cases, it is impossible to specify in advance categories of case in which litigation should always be brought and categories where it should never be. The role of the law is thus to determine the person or persons who can safely be entrusted with taking the decision whether in a particular case litigation to enforce the company's rights should be initiated or not.

The board and litigation

17–2   One possible solution to this question would be to say that the litigation decision is like any other decision the company might take and so should be left to the normal decision-making processes of the company. In most cases this approach would have the consequence of putting the litigation decision exclusively in the hands of the board. That the board will have the power under the constitutions of most companies to initiate litigation against wrongdoing directors seems clear, for it will be part of its standard management powers.[1] That the board may be unwilling always to sue the wrongdoing director even when it is in the best interests of the company to do so, however, seems equally clear. The wrongdoers may be a majority of the board or may be able to influence a majority of the board, and the same incentives which operated to cause the directors to break their duties in the first place may cause them to utilise their board positions so as to suppress litigation against them. Of course, this is not always the case. The board may act in an independent-minded way[2] or, perhaps

---

[1]   See art.2 of the draft model articles for both private and public companies limited by shares.

[2]   *cf. John Shaw & Sons (Salford) Ltd v Shaw* [1935] 2 K.B. 113, CA, where the company's articles had allocated the litigation decision to a committee of the board from which the wrongdoers were excluded. This case shows that, where the board has the power under the articles and does decide to sue, the shareholders cannot by ordinary majority countermand their decision.

more likely, the directors may have lost the influential positions on the board which they had when they committed the original wrong-doing. Thus, the previous board may have been replaced by a new set of directors as a result of a takeover[3] or, the company having become insolvent, the board has been replaced by an insolvency practitioner, acting in one capacity or another on behalf of the creditors.[4] Indeed, the importance of litigation against wrongdoing directors (and other officers of the company) in this situation is recognised in section 212 of the Insolvency Act 1986, which gives liquidators in a winding up the benefit of a summary procedure for the enforcement of, inter alia, breaches of fiduciary duty and of the duty of care on the part of directors and to recover compensation by way of a contribution to the company's assets of such amount as the court thinks just. Under section 212 the liquidator sues in his or her own name but in sub-stance on behalf of the company, which will be the recipient of any recovery. Crucially, however, the courts regard the section as purely procedural so that it does not extend the range of the duties to which directors are subject.[5]

The shareholders collectively and litigation

Despite these examples of litigation against wrongdoing directors being initiated by those in charge of its management, it would obviously be unsound policy to leave such decisions exclusively with the board of the company. If the board decides to sue, all well and good, but it may result in less litigation than is optimal (i.e. than the interests of the company would dictate) if the board has exclusive control over the initiation of litigation in the company's name. In recognition of this argument, the common law seems to take the view that, even if the board does not wish to sue, it is open to the share-holders collectively by ordinary resolution to decide to do so. Although sensible enough in policy terms, the reasoning by which the shareholders collectively come to have concurrent powers with the board to initiate litigation against wrongdoing directors is something

17–3

---

[3] See *Regal (Hastings) Ltd v Gulliver* [1942] 1 All E.R. 378, HL, above, para.16–65.
[4] Indeed, the replacement of the board by an insolvency practitioner was regarded under the previous law as a good reason for not allowing the individual shareholder to sue on behalf of the company. See *Ferguson v Wallbridge* [1935] 3 D.L.R. 66, PC; *Fargro Ltd v Godfroy* [1986] 1 W.L.R. 1134. In *Barrett v Duckett* [1995] 1 B.C.L.C. 243, CA the principle was even extended to deny the possibility of bringing a derivative claim to a shareholder who turned down the opportunity to put the company into liquidation: "As the company does have some money which might be used in litigating the claims, it is in my opinion manifest that it is better that the decision whether or not to use the money should be taken by an inde-pendent liquidator rather than by [the shareholder]" (at 255, per Peter Gibson L.J.). These are still factors the court could take into account under section 263 (see below) but they would no longer be absolute bars to the derivative claim.
[5] *Cohen v Selby* [2001] 1 B.C.L.C. 176 at [20], CA. Nor does it allow the liquidator to escape from any limitation period to which the claim by the company would be subject: *Lands Allotment Co, Re* [1894] 1 Ch. 616; *Eurocruit Europe Ltd, Re* [2007] 2 B.C.L.C. 598.

of a mystery, since, as we saw in Chapter 14, the allocation of a power to the board by the articles operates, in the absence of an express reservation, to remove that power from the shareholders. Consequently, in the absence of an express provision in the articles conferring upon the shareholders the power to initiate litigation, a shareholder decision to that effect would need to be passed by a special resolution, because that is the equivalent of a resolution to alter the articles. However, the common law appears to regard an ordinary resolution to initiate litigation as sufficient. This result can be rationalised on the basis that there is a rule of law, designed to promote shareholder control of the litigation decision, which overrides in this limited respect the allocation of functions by the articles. So, despite what the articles may say about the directors having general powers of management, it may be that the decision to sue may still be taken by an ordinary majority of the shareholders.[6]

However, it is still not obvious that the test of promoting the interests of the company will always be correctly applied to the litigation decision by the shareholders collectively. It is not impossible that the directors will control the general meeting, through their own shareholdings alone or in combination with those other shareholders whose decisions they can influence. Although the CLR proposed[7] to discount the votes of interested directors and those under their influence on decisions to sue, the Act applies that rule only to ratification decisions. If the shareholders do not purport to forgive the director's wrongdoing, but simply decide not to sue him or her, it appears that the director in question is free to vote on that question.

Further, even in the absence of wrongdoer control of the general meeting, it is not obvious that the general meeting will come to consider the exercise of its power to initiate litigation. The wrongdoing directors, presumably, will not take steps to put the matter before the general meeting, unless they think the general meeting will support them, and so the shareholders as a whole may simply remain in ignorance of the fact that there is an issue for them to discuss. One or more shareholders may know of at least some of the relevant facts,

---

[6] See *Alexander Ward & Co Ltd v Samyang Navigation Co Ltd* [1975] 1 W.L.R. 673 at 679, per Lord Hailsham L.C., quoting with approval a passage from the third edition of this book at pp.136–137. Unless this is the case, the rule in *Foss v Harbottle* (see below) made no sense, because the question that rule posed was whether the individual shareholder should be allowed to sue on behalf of the company or whether the matter should be left to a simple majority of the shareholders. On the other hand, the abolition by the 2006 Act of the rule in *Foss v Harbottle*, as far as derivative claims are concerned, reduces the force of this argument. The power of the shareholders to initiate litigation may not apply in the situation identified in the cases mentioned in fn.4, i.e. where the board has been replaced by an insolvency practitioner acting on behalf of the creditors. The not fully considered decision of Harman J. in *Breckland Group Holdings Ltd v London and Suffolk Properties* [1989] B.C.L.C. 100 might seem to point in the direction of exclusive board control of the litigation, but there was in that case a shareholders' agreement in effect requiring the only two shareholders (or rather their board nominees) to support a decision to commence "material litigation".

[7] CLR, *Completing*, para.5.101 but contrast s.239 (above, para.16–85).

and may seek to use their powers, discussed in Chapter 15, to have the matter put on the agenda of an AGM or to have a meeting called to discuss the issue. In both cases, the support of substantial numbers of fellow shareholders will be required to force the company to take these steps and the support of half the shareholders present and voting at the meeting actually to pass a resolution in favour of litigation.

Derivative claims

In these circumstances, it is hardly surprising that provision is made for giving individual shareholders, subject to appropriate safeguards, standing to pursue litigation on behalf of the company against the alleged wrongdoing directors. Indeed, the principle just articulated can be said to have been accepted for since 1843, when the *Foss v Harbottle* principle was formulated, because the substance of the controversy ever since has centred, not on whether such litigation should be permitted, but on the definition of the "appropriate safeguards". On the one hand, relatively free access to the courts for individual shareholders suing on behalf of the company (or "derivatively", as the term is) will increase the levels of litigation against wrongdoing directors. If it is thought that the levels of such litigation are sub-optimal, because of the ability of the wrongdoers to influence litigation decisions at either board or shareholder level, then such an increase in litigation is likely to be welcomed. However, it is difficult to demonstrate that such litigation brought derivatively by individuals will invariably be in the interests of the company. It may be initiated more to promote the personal interests of the shareholder than the interests of the company (i.e. the shareholders as a whole). This is a particular risk because, as we shall see further below, in a derivative claim, recovery in the litigation goes to the company, not to the individual shareholder bringing the litigation. A person with a small shareholding thus has little financial incentive to sue on behalf of the company, because the return to that person will be, at most, a percentage of the recovery which reflects the percentage of the shares of the company that person holds.[8] So, litigation brought by such a person runs a risk of being motivated by concerns other than to increase the value of the company's business.[9] Of course, the larger the shareholder, the less this particular risk, but, by the same token,

17–4

---

[8] Even then, the directors may choose not to pay out the recovery by way of dividend and instead to invest it in some unsuccessful venture.

[9] For an example of a derivative claim brought for what appears to be a collateral purpose see the rather unusual case of *Konamaneni v Rolls-Royce Industrial Power (India) Ltd* [2002] 1 All E.R. 979. In the United States, where derivative claims can be brought much more freely, it is sometimes argued that the drivers of the litigation are the firms of lawyers who stand to take a handsome percentage of awards obtained under contingent fee arrangements, if the derivative litigation is successful.

the lower the obstacles are which prevent such a shareholder from using the mechanism of the general meeting.

The English common law had always been more impressed by the risk of derivative claims being motivated by personal objectives than by the risk that confining derivative claims would lead to less litigation than the company's interests required. Accordingly, the common law, whose cumulative decisions in this area were referred to as "the rule in *Foss v Harbottle*",[10] determining when individual shareholders could sue derivatively, permitted individual shareholder access to the courts on behalf of the company on only a very limited basis. The question which the rule in *Foss* set itself to answer was whether the individual shareholder should be allowed to sue derivatively or whether the litigation question could not better be left to the shareholders as a whole.[11] Unfortunately, the rule was one-sided in its operation, i.e. it was effective to exclude the derivative suit where the law took the view that a decision of the shareholders as a whole could be relied upon, but it contained no mechanism whereby a meeting of the shareholders could actually be summoned to consider the question or to deprive interested directors of their votes.[12] Consequently, the rule did nothing to correct the deficiencies of group decision-making by the shareholders, as identified above, but simply made it difficult for the individual shareholder to sue instead. These problems with the rule in *Foss v Harbottle* had become increasingly apparent over time and in 1997 the Law Commission made proposals for taking the law in a new direction, by allocating the litigation decision to someone external to the company, namely, a court.[13] These proposals were largely endorsed by the CLR and embodied in the Companies Act 2006, which gives effect to the underlying reform proposed by the Law Commission, though not quite in the way it proposed. It is now provided that derivative claims can be brought only under the statute, so that the rule in *Foss v Harbottle* need no longer be examined—to the relief of all those involved in company law except any whose main aim in life was to restrict derivative claims.

---

[10] (1843) 2 Hare 461.

[11] See in particular the classic judgment of Jenkins L.J. in *Edwards v Halliwell* [1950] 2 All E.R. 1064, CA.

[12] The technique endorsed in *Danish Mercantile Co Ltd v Beaumont* [1951] Ch. 680, CA, of commencing litigation in the name of the company (i.e. not derivatively) but without authority to do so and the court referring the issue to the shareholders for decision when the authority issue is raised, has not been used in practice (perhaps because the solicitors are personally liable in costs if the shareholders do not ratify the decision to sue), though it is consistent with the notion that, in the area of litigation, the shareholders have authority to decide, parallel to that of the board.

[13] Law Commission, *Shareholder Remedies*, Cm. 3769, 1997. The excellent study by A. Reisberg, *Derivatice Actions and Corporate Governance* (Oxford: OUP, 2007) appeared too late for detailed consideration in this book, but use has been made of his earlier work.

Other possible solutions and the statutory derivative claim for unauthorised political expenditure

Before turning to an analysis of the statutory provisions on the **17–5** derivative claim, it is perhaps worth noting that the three mechanisms noted above—board, shareholders as a whole, individual share-holders—do not exhaust the possible mechanisms for handling this problem, even within the company. Another approach might be to give the decision to a sub-set of the members of the board, such as the uninvolved members or its independent NEDs. As we have seen,[14] this is the approach taken in the Act to the authorisation of conflicts of interest, but not to the ratification of breaches of duty, where a shareholder decision is required. Since the decision not to sue is akin to a ratification decision, it seems consistent not to use a sub-set of the board to take the litigation decision either. However, the CLR did propose[15] that, where the non-involved members of the board had decided against litigation, a derivative claim should not lie and only the shareholders as a whole should be able to overrule the board. However, the Act does not impose this limitation on the derivative claim.

A further alternative legal technique would be to entrust the liti-gation decision to some group of shareholders, lying between the shareholders as a whole and the individual shareholder. The common law has not used this device and, although it has been used exten-sively in German law, the common law was perhaps right to reject it, since fixing the appropriate percentage has proved difficult.[16] How-ever, it is worth noting that in one area minority group shareholder action on behalf of the company has been introduced into British law by the legislature. Under what is now Part 14 of the Act, a company's policy to make political donations and incur political expenditure is subject to approval by the shareholders in general meeting.[17] If this requirement is contravened, every director (and shadow director) of the company at the relevant time is liable to pay to the company the amount of any donation or expenditure and damages in respect of any loss or damage suffered by the company in consequence of the unauthorised donation or expenditure.[18] Section 370 then provides for a statutory derivative claim in order to enforce the directors' liability. However, the right to sue in the name of the company is

---

[14] Above, paras 16–69 and 16–83.
[15] *Developing*, paras 5.83–5.85.
[16] T. Baums, "Empfiehlt sich eine Neuregelung des aktienrechtlichen Anfechtungs- und Organhaftungsrechts, insbesondere der Klagemöglichkeiten der Aktionären?" in *Gutachten F zum 63 Deutschen Juristentag Leipzig 2000* (Munich: 2000).
[17] See the previous chapter at para.16–62.
[18] s.369. In some cases, as we saw above in the previous chapter at para.16–62, the liability may fall upon a director of a holding company and be a liability to the subsidiary. In such a case the derivative claim to enforce the subsidiary's rights may be brought by an authorised group of the shareholders of the holding company as well as by an authorised group of the shareholders of the subsidiary: s.370(1)(b). This will be a useful facility where the subsidiary is wholly owned by the parent.

conferred, not on individual shareholders, but on an "authorised group" of members, meaning, in the case of a company limited by shares, the holders of not less than 5 per cent of the nominal value of the company's issued share capital or any class thereof; in the case of a company not limited by shares by not less than 5 per cent of its members; or, in either case, by not less than 50 members of the company.[19] It seems that the aim of confining the right to sue to a small group of shareholders was to provide a realistic chance of enforcement action being brought whilst at the same time excluding individual shareholders from suing, who might be motivated by reasons which did not relate to the company's interests.

17–6   Having conferred a statutory right of action in relation to dona-tions upon the approved group of members, the Act also takes some steps to facilitate the use of the power by the minority but also to ensure that the power is exercised by the group in the interests of the shareholders as a whole. In particular, the fact that the statutory derivative claim is brought on behalf and in the interests of the company is emphasised by a number of features of the legislation.

> (i) The same duties (of care and loyalty) are owed to the company by the authorised group as would be owed to the company if the claim had been brought by the directors of the company. However, action to enforce these duties against the minority cannot be taken without the leave of the court, presumably so as to protect the minority from the tactical use of counter-litigation by the alleged wrongdoing directors.[20]

> (ii) Proceedings may not be discontinued or settled by the group without the leave of the court and the court may impose terms on any leave it grants.[21] This provision reduces the risk of "gold digging" or "greenmail" claims where the purpose of the claim is to extract from the company a private benefit for the group in exchange for the settlement of the claim rather than to advance the interests of the shareholders as a whole.

> (iii) The group may apply to the court for an order that the company indemnify the group in respect of the costs of the litigation and the court may make such order as it thinks fit. The group is not entitled to be paid its costs out of the assets of the company other than by virtue of an indemnification

---

[19] This mechanism seems to have been chosen in the original legislation of 2000 on the basis of a somewhat bizarre analogy with the group of shareholders who have the right to complain to the court about a resolution on the part of a public company to re-register as a private one: s.98. The analogy is odd because the claim arising under section 98 is not derivative.

[20] s.371(4).

[21] s.371(5).

order or as a result of a costs order made in the litigation in favour of the company.[22] These provisions both recognise the principle that the company in appropriate circumstance should pay for derivative litigation which is brought for its benefit (as is the case with the general statutory derivative claim)[23] and make it less easy for the group to pursue "gold digging" claims in the guise of generous payments by the company to the group by way of recompense for costs incurred in the litigation.

(iv) On the other hand, there is conferred upon the group an express right to all information relating to the subject-matter of the litigation which is in the company's possession, so that the group can better decide in what way to prosecute the litigation. This right extends to information which is reasonably obtainable by the company (for example, from another group company). The court may enforce this right by order.[24]

The general derivative claim created by the 2006 Act does not follow the above model of conferring the litigation decision on a minority group of shareholders, though the views of the non-involved shareholders are a factor which the judge is required to take into account when deciding whether to consent to the individual share-holder's application to proceed with a derivative claim. Section 370(5) provides that the existence of the specific procedure does not bar access to the general statutory derivative procedure. The general procedure will normally be available because payment of an unau-thorised donation or the incurring of unauthorised expenditure by the director will usually constitute a breach of the director's general duties. Whether the specific or the general statutory derivative claim will be more attractive is not clear. The general procedure may be triggered by a single member; on the other hand, the decision whether to permit the litigation is placed under the general procedure in the hands of the court, whereas the specific procedure gives the author-ised group a right to sue to enforce the company's rights.

A final and more radical approach would be to give the right to commence a derivative action to someone outside the company altogether. This is unlikely to be a sensible approach to the general run of companies where it is difficult to identify anyone outside the company with a legitimate interest in commencing litigation on its behalf. However, some vestigial use of this technique can—or

---

[22] s.372.
[23] See below, para.17–12.
[24] s.373. However, the right to information does not arise until proceedings have been insti-tuted, and so the right seems not to aid the minority at the stage when it is considering whether to institute litigation.

could—be found in the legislation. First, the Secretary of State used to have power to institute civil proceedings in the name of the company as a result of information received from an official report or investigation.[25] Secondly, the Regulator of Community Interest Companies may bring such proceedings subject to a right of appeal by any director of the CIC to the court, which is given broad powers to confirm, discontinue or set terms for the litigation.[26] If the Regulator takes this step, the company must be indemnified by the Regulator against the costs and expenses of the litigation, unless, presumably, the court orders the costs should be borne by the company. Neither of these provisions was or is confined to acts of directors in breach of their duties to the company, though the right of appeal to the court given to the director against the Regulator's decision perhaps indicates that breaches of directors' duties were thought to be a central example of the potential use of the power.

THE GENERAL STATUTORY DERIVATIVE CLAIM

The scope of the statutory derivative claim

17–7   The novelty of the general statutory derivative claim, contained in Part 11 of the Act, is that it places the decision about whether it is in the interests of the company for litigation to be commenced in any particular case in the hands of the court, i.e. an outsider to the company. After the claim form has been issued, a shareholder seeking to bring a derivative claim must seek the permission of the court to take any further steps in the litigation, other than, in the normal case, informing the company than the claim has been issued and that the shareholder is applying to the court for permission to continue the claim.[27] It was already the case that the court had a role in the early stages of derivative claims at common law, but this was to check that the claimant had standing to sue under the rule in *Foss v Harbottle*.[28] Under the new general derivative claim the court has a broader role, namely, to exercise a constrained discretion to decide whether it is in the best interests of the company for the litigation to be brought. This new procedure has the advantages, on the one hand, that the indi-

---

[25] See s.438 of the CA 1985, repealed by s.1176 of CA 2006. On departmental investigations and reports see Ch.18 below.

[26] Companies (Audit, Investigations and Community Enterprise) Act 2004, s.44.

[27] CPR 19.9(4), 9A(2).

[28] In *Prudential Assurance Co Ltd v Newman Industries Ltd (No.2)* [1982] Ch. 204, CA the court insisted that the question of standing to bring the derivative claim should be decided in advance of and separately from the decision on the merits of the case. This approach is embodied in CPR 19.9. Under this provision the courts recently began to take a broader look at the value to the company of the proposed derivative claim: *Portfolios of Distinction Ltd v Laird* [2004] 2 B.C.L.C. 741, paras 51–68; *Airey v Cordell* [2007] B.C.C. 785.

vidual shareholder can easily obtain a decision on the central question (whether it is in the interests of the company for the litigation to be brought), whilst, on the other hand, the individual shareholder's enthusiasm for derivative litigation is subject to the filter of a judge having to be convinced that the litigation on behalf of the company is desirable. Whilst it is true that many of the policy issues which underlay the rule in *Foss v Harbottle* reappear under the statutory procedure,[29] they appear now not as absolute bars to a derivative claim, but as factors the court must take into account in deciding whether to allow the litigation to proceed. Thus, a claimant who is turned away by the court will receive a judgment explaining why a derivative claim in the particular case is not in the company's interests, whereas previously the court's decision said nothing about the desirability of the litigation from the company's point of view, but simply that the litigation decision was a decision for the shareholders generally rather than the individual shareholder.

The statute applies only to derivative claims or derivative proceedings, i.e. claims brought in respect of a cause of action vested in the company and seeking relief on its behalf.[30] Since the individual shareholder has no power to initiate litigation in the company's name, but the company is to be bound by and is the potential beneficiary of any judgment or order made in the derivative litigation, the Civil Procedure Rules require the company to be made a defendant in the litigation, even though it is the company's rights which are being enforced. Thus, the claim appears in the form of Shareholder v Director and Company.[31] This can be a cause of confusion, unless it is remembered that the company is only a nominal defendant and that the real defendants are the directors.[32]

Derivative claims can now be brought only under the Act, either **17–8** under the Part 11 provisions discussed here or as a result of a court order made in unfair prejudice provisions discussed in Chapter 20. The rule in *Foss v Harbottle* is thus consigned to the dustbin. On the other hand, not all claims a shareholder might want to bring on behalf of the company may be brought under Part 11 of the Act. The Act contemplates as derivative claims only claims "arising from an actual or proposed act or omission involving negligence, default,

---

[29] See ss.263 and 268, discussed below.

[30] s.260(1): derivative claims (for England and Wales and Northern Ireland). s.265(1) provides similarly for derivative proceedings in Scotland. Because of the intimate connection between derivative claims and civil procedure, the Act contains separate provisions for Scotland (ss.265–269) and the rest of the United Kingdom (ss.260–264). However, the underlying policies are the same.

[31] CPR 19.9(3). The reason for this oddity seems to be that anyone can make another person a defendant to a claim but making a person a claimant requires that person's consent.

[32] If the shareholder has a personal claim against the directors, the statutory procedure has no application. Personal claims are dealt with below and, as we shall see, there are great complexities about remedies where both the company and the shareholder personally have claims against a director.

breach of duty or breach of trust by a director of the company."[33]
Where the company has a cause of action arising in some other way
(for example, a claim against a non-directorial employee), the policy
seems to be that the litigation decision should be taken according to
the division of powers contained in the company's articles of association (i.e. normally exclusively by the board). It is only where the
directors themselves are in breach of duty that the statutory derivative procedure is available because that is when the risk of conflicted
decision-making by board or shareholders generally arises. However,
although the company's cause of action must arise out of breach of
duty etc. by the directors, the defendants are not necessarily limited
to and may not even include the directors themselves.[34] We have seen
above[35] that third parties may become liable to the company as a
result of their involvement in directors' breaches of duty and, in such
cases, the derivative claim may be used against the third party, even if
no director is sued.

Directors for the purpose of Part 11 include former and shadow
directors,[36] but this is less significant than it may seem. The Part 11
rules do not alter the circumstances in which former or shadow
directors owe duties to the company; they merely ensure that, where
such duties are owed, the derivative claim can be used to enforce
them. We have discussed in the previous chapter the circumstances in
which the general duties of directors do in fact fall upon former or
shadow directors.[37]

A shareholder may bring a derivative claim in respect of a cause of
action which arose before he or she became a member of the company.[38] On the other hand, only members of the company can bring
derivative claims: a former member cannot sue even in respect of a
matter which occurred when he was a shareholder.[39] This reflects the
legal position of shareholders generally: the shareholder has an
interest in the assets of the company as they stand during his or her
membership. That interest is not confined to assets acquired during
the shareholder's membership. On the other hand, once membership
is relinquished, so is the interest in the company's assets, including in
assets the shareholder or even the company were unaware were
possessed during the period of membership (for example, the shareholder who sells the week before oil is discovered below land owned
by the company just has to accept that loss). However, there is one
useful statutory extension of the notion of a "member". This term is
not confined to those who have been entered on the company's reg-

---

[33] ss.260(3) and 265(3).
[34] ss.260(3) and 265(4).
[35] Paras 16–97ff.
[36] ss.260(5) and 265(7).
[37] See above, paras 16–8 and 16–10.
[38] ss.260(4) and 265(5).
[39] ss.260(1) and 265(1).

ister of members—which is a standard requirement for membership[40]—but is extended to those to whom shares have been transferred or transmitted by operation of law, even if not entered on the register of members.[41] The usual example of transmission is on death or bankruptcy. The extension of the meaning of membership to include mere transferees is especially useful in quasi-partnership companies where the directors normally have power under the articles to refuse to admit new members and are often prepared to use the power to keep out of the company those with whom they do not wish to work. Making the derivative claim available may enable them to challenge their exclusion or, at least, to challenge action by the controllers of the company—for example, siphoning assets out of the company to the detriment of the would-be member—designed to induce the would-be member to transfer the shares to the other members at a low price. Such action by the controllers carries the risk that the would-be member will bring a derivative action to restore the company's position. A similar and even more important extension of the term "member" is to be found in the unfair prejudice provisions, discussed in Chapter 20.

Deciding whether to give permission for the derivative claim
The central issue under the new statutory procedure is the nature of   **17–9**
the discretion vested in the court to approve or not the continuance of
the derivative claim. That discretion is broad but not unconstrained.
The statute proceeds by identifying three situations in which leave
must be denied[42] and then, assuming the case does not fall within any
of those three situations, by laying down a number of factors the
court must take into account when deciding whether to give
permission.

Two of the situations where permission must be denied are
obvious: where the actual or proposed breach of duty has been
authorised or ratified in accordance with the rules set out in the
previous chapter.[43] In such a case, there is no or is no longer any
wrong by the director to the company, and, just as the company
cannot complain of it, neither can the shareholder suing derivatively.
The important prohibition is thus the third one. The court must deny
permission to continue the derivative claim where a person acting in
accordance with the directors' core duty of loyalty (to promote the
success of the company for the benefit of its members) would not seek
to continue the claim.[44] Since the core duty of loyalty, set out in
section 172, is the modern version of the notion of acting "in the

---

[40] s.112. For further discussion see para.27–5.
[41] ss.260(5)(c) and 265(7)(e).
[42] ss.263(1) and 268(1).
[43] ss.263(2)(b), (c) and 268(1)(b), (c).
[44] ss.263(2)(a) and 268(1)(a). On the director's core duty of loyalty see above, paras 16–24ff.

interests of the company", it is sensible to use it as the test in relation to the derivative claim. However, it should be noted that there is one crucial difference between the court's role when it is hearing an allegation that a director has broken the core duty of loyalty and its role in the statutory derivative claim. In the former case, provided the director has properly formed a good faith view as to what promoting the success of the company requires, the court has no power to interfere. Under the statutory procedure, however, it does not appear that such deference is to be accorded to the individual shareholder's decision to initiate derivative proceedings. Rather, the court will have to formulate its own view about whether the proposed litigation will fail to promote the success of the company.

17–10   If the proposed litigation passes the negative test (i.e. will it fail to promote the success of the company?), one might have thought that whether it should be allowed to proceed should depend on whether it can pass that test put positively, i.e. will the litigation promote the success of the company?—or, rather, that all that is required is the positive version of the test. However, the tests which are to be applied to the proposal if it passes the negative test are more varied than that. The statute sets out seven factors[45] which the court must take into account in deciding whether to allow the litigation to proceed, if it passes the negative test.[46] To be sure, one of those tests is "the importance that a person acting in accordance with section 172 ... would attach to continuing it",[47] but that is only one of the tests. The thinking behind the drafting may have been that the court should not be under pressure to allow the litigation to proceed where its financial contribution to the company was likely to be small and there were other factors pointing against the litigation, though it is doubtful if the term "success" in section 172 is to be construed solely in financial terms. Alternatively, it may have been thought desirable to give the court more guidance on the factors to be considered than a single general test would provide. The further tests, which appear not to be intended to be exhaustive of the considerations the court should take into account,[48] are as follows:

- Whether the shareholder seeking to bring the derivative claim is acting in good faith—or whether, for example, the litigation is motivated by personal interests.

- Whether the act or omission which constituted the breach of duty is likely to be ratified by the company (i.e. by the shareholders collectively) or—expressed as a separate test— whether in the case of a proposed breach of duty the act or

---

[45] To which the Secretary of State may add by regulation: ss.263(5) and 268(4).
[46] ss.263(3),(4) and 268(2),(3).
[47] ss.263(3)(b) and 268(2)(b).
[48] See the words "in particular" in ss.263(3) and 268(2).

omission is likely to be authorised or ratified by the company. Authorisation, as we saw in the previous chapter,[49] can sometimes be given by the non-involved members of the board. These two tests reflect a factor which was very important under the rule in *Foss v Harbottle*, but, whereas at common law, the possibility of shareholder approval (normally referred to as ratifiability) of the wrong normally barred access to the derivative claim,[50] under the statutory procedure the court must have regard to the likelihood of shareholder approval (not mere ratifiability) and, in any event, the prospect of ratification is not a bar to the derivative claim but simply a factor weighing against giving permission. The removal of ratifiability as a bar to the derivative claim is one of the most important changes brought about by the new procedure. Under the common law the derivative claim was largely excluded as a mechanism for the enforcement of ratifiable breaches of duty.[51]

- Whether the company (whether through a decision of the board or of the shareholders) has decided not to pursue the claim. What is at issue here is a board or shareholder resolution which, whilst not seeking to ratify the directors' breach of duty, nevertheless contains a decision not to sue the directors. Such a resolution may constitute an argument against allowing the derivative claim to continue, provided the decision was not influenced by the alleged wrongdoers, but it is only a factor to be taken into account. Thus, the statute rejects the CLR's proposal that a decision by the independent members of the board not to sue should bar the derivative claim.[52] Again, this is a significant change from the common law. Under the common law regime, even a non-ratifiable wrong could not be pursued derivatively unless the alleged wrongdoers were in control of the general meeting. Under the statutory procedure permission to continue the litigation can be granted by the court even if the alleged wrongdoers are not in control of the shareholders' meeting. No doubt, however, a decision by the shareholders, uninfluenced by the wrongdoers, not to initiate litigation will count heavily against the derivative claim.

- Whether the facts give rise to a cause of action which vests in the member personally and which he or she could pursue as

---

[49] Above, para.16–69.
[50] See *Edwards v Halliwell* [1950] 2 All E.R. 1064, CA.
[51] On the distinction between ratifiable and non-ratifiable breaches of duty see the previous chapter at para.16–86.
[52] Above, para.17–5. Only the shareholders collectively would be able to override the directors' decision under the CLR's proposal.

such rather than through a derivative claim on behalf of the company. Perhaps the most obvious claim a shareholder might bring is a petition based on unfairly prejudicial conduct by the controllers of the company, dealt with in Chapter 20. Apart from that, the possibilities for a personal action will be limited, since, normally, directors' duties are owed to the company, not to shareholders individually.[53] The shareholder may prefer a derivative claim because the costs of it will fall on the company (see below) but, given the courts' firm view, outside the area of unfair prejudice, that recovery cannot be obtained in a personal claim for loss to the shareholder which reflects the company's loss, the availability of the personal claim may not be a strong argument against allowing the derivative claim to proceed, even where both causes of action exist.[54]

- The court is required to have "particular regard" to any evidence before it of the views of the other shareholders who have no personal interest in the matter.[55] Again, this reflects an important element of the rule in *Foss v Harbottle*, which, however, appeared to say that the individual shareholder did not have standing to bring a derivative claim if a majority of the independent shareholders were against the litigation.[56] Now, those views are only a factor, but are likely to be a powerful factor for or against the derivative claim, where reliable evidence of those views can be provided to the court.

The decision whether to grant permission for the derivative claim to proceed will potentially generate a wide-ranging enquiry before the court. Although the company is a potential beneficiary of the derivative action, there was a fear, much adumbrated in the Parliamentary debates,[57] that companies would experience high levels of proposed derivative claims by shareholders who had a fanciful or even self-interested view of the likely benefits to the company from such litigation. Companies would then be distracted from more important tasks by having to explain in court why such claims should not be allowed to proceed further. In partial recognition of this issue, the statute contains a procedure whereby the court's initial consideration of the claim is on the basis of the evidence submitted by the member alone. If the court does not at this stage think the applicant has established a prima facie case for permission to be granted, the application will be refused. At this initial stage, the company is not a

[53] See above at para.16–5.
[54] See below, para.17–13.
[55] ss.263(4) and 268(3). Moreover, unlike the other matters to which the court must have regard, this one cannot be altered by the Secretary of State by regulation: s.263(5)(b).
[56] *Smith v Croft (No.2)* [1988] Ch. 114.
[57] See HL Debs, vol. 681, col. 883, May 9, 2006.

respondent to the application to the court for permission to continue the claim and so is not required to file evidence or be present at any hearing. Only if the application survives this initial examination will the company be invited to file evidence as to whether permission should be granted or not.[58]

Varieties of derivative claim

We have discussed above a derivative claim brought where the company has failed to initiate litigation. No doubt this is the core case where derivative litigation will be employed. However, the statute also specifically provides for a shareholder to apply to the court for permission to take over as a derivative claim litigation which the company has actually commenced.[59] The reasoning behind this provision seems to have been that, without it, the directors of a company might stultify any potential derivative claims by instituting litigation in the company's name but then not pursuing the claim with vigour or perhaps settling it on favourable terms. The statute deals with this problem, or at least some parts of it, by allowing a shareholder to apply to the court for permission to take over the company's litigation in derivative form. Of course, the company's claim must be one which falls within the scope of the derivative claim and the court must apply to the shareholder's application for permission to take over the claim the same criteria it would have applied had the litigation been commenced in derivative form.[60] In addition, the shareholder must show why he or she should be allowed to take over the company's claim. The permitted grounds are that the proceedings have been conducted by the company in a way which constitutes an abuse of the process of the court or that the company has not prosecuted the litigation diligently or that for other reasons it is "appropriate" for the shareholder to be substituted for the company.[61] However, if the company has already settled the case against the directors, there would appear to be no basis upon which the section could operate.

The statute even provides a mechanism for a shareholder to apply to the court to take over an existing derivative claim. The point seems to be to prevent the directors from stultifying litigation against themselves by securing a friendly shareholder to commence litigation in derivative form but then not to prosecute the claim effectively.[62] The grounds for taking over a derivative claim are the same as for taking over a claim begun in the company's name, but of course the tests for giving permission to commence a derivative claim do not have to be applied to the claim to take over an existing derivative

17–11

---

[58] ss.261(2) and 266(3). In England and Wales this procedure is fleshed out in CPR 19.9A.
[59] ss.262 and 267.
[60] ss.262(1),(3), 263(1), 267(1),(3), 268(1).
[61] ss.262(2) and 267(2).
[62] ss.264 and 269.

claim, since they will have been met at an earlier stage. It should be noted that a claim to take over an existing derivative claim can be made whether the claim was originally commenced in derivative form or was commenced by the company but later taken over derivatively; and whether the shareholder from whom the applicant wishes to take over the litigation is the originator of the litigation, took the litigation over from the company or is someone later down the chain of shareholders who have been pursuing the claim derivatively.[63]

The subsequent conduct of the derivative claim

17–12   The statutory provisions governing the general derivative claim, unlike those relating to the derivative claim arising out of unauthorised political donations or expenditure, say nothing about the subsequent conduct of the derivative claim, except that the court is given a general power to give permission for the claim to continue "on such terms as it thinks fit".[64] However, it was established in the important case of *Wallersteiner v Moir (No.2)* in 1975[65] that a consequence of the derivative claim being to enforce the company's rights is that, where permission is given, the company should normally be liable for the costs of the claim, even, in fact especially, where the litigation is ultimately unsuccessful. This decision is now reflected in the CPR which provide that "the court may order the company . . . to indemnify the claimant against any liability for costs incurred in the permission application or in the derivative claim or both."[66] This is a very important provision because, without it, the financial disincentive for a shareholder to bring a derivative claim would be very strong, no matter how relaxed the standing rules. Or, to put the matter another way, if a shareholder can obtain permission from the court to bring a derivative claim, the *Wallersteiner* case means there should be no financial disincentive to proceed.

The Civil Procedure Rules also deal with one further post-permission issue. The derivative litigation is brought to enforce the company's rights for the company's benefit, but a common perversion of the procedure, known in some quarters as "greenmail", involves the shareholder being primarily interested in obtaining some private benefit from the litigation, normally as part of the terms on which the company's claim against the directors is settled. To discourage such behaviour, the CPR empower the court to order that

---

[63]   ss.264(1) and 269(1).
[64]   ss.261(4)(a), 262(5)(a), 264(5)(a), 266(5)(a), 267(5)(a) and 269(5)(a).
[65]   [1975] Q.B. 373, CA.
[66]   CPR 19.9. However, the court is not likely to give the claimant a blank cheque but to review the company's obligation to pay stage-by-stage as the litigation proceeds. See *McDonald v Horn* [1995] 1 All E.R. 961, 974–975, CA. Moreover, such an order does not give the shareholder priority over the unsecured creditors of the company (*Qayoumi v Oakhouse Property Holdings Plc* [2003] 1 B.C.L.C. 352) so that the shareholder may be unwilling to pursue a derivative claim on behalf of a doubtfully solvent company.

the claim may not be "discontinued, settled or compromised without the permission of the court", thus giving the court the opportunity to scrutinise the terms of any settlement.[67] Nevertheless, it is odd that the subsequent conduct of the general derivative claim is less clearly regulated than that of the special derivative claim for unlawful political donations. In particular, there is no counterpart in the statute or CPR to the duties of care and loyalty which are imposed on those bringing a derivative claim in respect of unauthorised political donations.[68] It may be that the courts will develop such provisions on the basis of the quasi-agency position in which a person bringing a general derivative claim is placed.

Those bringing general derivative claim also lack the specific information right conferred by section 373 in favour of those seeking derivatively to recover an unauthorised donation from the directors. It is possible that the court might deal with this matter when setting the conditions for the conduct of the general claim. However, another avenue may be open to secure the board's co-operation with those responsible for the general derivative claim. By permitting the derivative action, the court will have determined that a director acting in accordance with the core duty of loyalty would bring the litigation and that there are no other factors which outweigh that conclusion. In that situation it will be difficult for the board, consistently with their duties, not to co-operate fully with the shareholder who has charge of the derivative claim. Indeed, it may be wondered whether its duties do not require the board to give serious consideration to bringing the claim in the company's name, though presumably the court's permission would be needed for the derivative claim to be superseded by a corporate one and the court might be reluctant to so agree if the board's previous attitude towards the claim had been one of unmitigated hostility.

Shareholders' Personal Claims against Directors

The above description of the problem underlying the rule in *Foss v Harbottle* has been couched in terms of the enforcement by individual shareholders of duties owed by directors to their company. Where the duty is owed by the director to the shareholder personally, the above analysis ought to be irrelevant. If the shareholder is also the right-holder, it would seem in principle to be entirely a matter for his or her discretion whether the right is enforced. So much is indeed recognised in the statute, Part 11 of which applies only to claims to enforce "a **17–13**

---

[67] CPR 19.9F.
[68] See above, para.17–6.

cause of action vested in the company".[69] However, there are two points which call for comment. First, the range of rights owed by directors to shareholders personally is limited. We saw in the previous chapter that the general duties of directors are only rarely owed to individual shareholders rather than to the company.[70] In addition, the shareholder may have rights against a director under the general law. In either case, the typical situation in which to find duties owed by the directors to shareholders individually is where the directors give advice to the shareholders or otherwise take action in relation to the exercise by the shareholders of the rights attached to their shares, including the sale of the shares. Duties owed by directors to the shareholders individually, under the general law or under company law, should be freely enforceable without resort to the derivative claim, but it is not often that shareholders have such rights to enforce.

Reflective loss

Secondly, where the shareholder and the company have rights against the director arising out of the same set of facts, the shareholder's damages in the personal claim may be restricted by the "no reflective loss" principle, which we consider here. The no reflective loss rule applies whether or not a derivative claim is available to enforce the company's rights and whether or not the shareholder chooses to bring a derivative claim against the director as well as a personal claim.[71] What is required to trigger the principle is that both the company and the shareholder should have a claim against the directors arising out of the same set of facts, and part or all of the shareholder's loss can be seen as mimicking the loss caused by the directors to the company. The rule also applies to claims which the shareholder may have against the director other than in his or her capacity as a member of the company (so that the rule applies to claims the shareholder brings as creditor or employee).[72] In this respect an employee or creditor who is also a shareholder is worse off than if this were not the case.

The principle can be illustrated by the decision of the Court of Appeal in *Prudential Assurance Co Ltd v Newman Industries Ltd*

---

[69] s.260(1)(a). s.265, applying in Scotland, is less explicit but, it is submitted, equally clear. More than one shareholder may have their rights infringed by the directors' claims, in which case the litigation may be brought in representative form by one shareholder as a representative of all shareholders who have the same interest in the matter (under CPR 19.6).

[70] Above, para.16–5. The cases below suggest that the shareholders' agreement adopts some or all of the general duties of directors and so makes them binding as between the director/shareholders parties to the agreement.

[71] It used to be thought that it was not possible to combine a personal and a derivative claim in the same litigation, but in *Prudential Assurance Co Ltd v Newman Industries Ltd (No.2)* [1981] Ch. 257, 303–304 Vinelott J. permitted it a first instance. The Court of Appeal [1982] Ch. 204, 222–224 did not dissent from this view.

[72] *Gardner v Parker* [2004] 2 B.C.L.C. 554, CA.

(No.2),[73] where the directors in breach of duty to the company had sold assets at an undervalue to a third party and had then obtained the shareholders' consent to the transaction by issuing a misleading circular convening a meeting of the shareholders, thus committing a wrong by way of misrepresentation against the shareholders. The Court of Appeal held that the personal claim should lead (in effect) to no recovery for the shareholder on the facts, because the only relevant loss suffered by them consisted in a diminution in the value of their shares, which was simply a reflection of the loss inflicted on the company by the sale of its assets at an undervalue, which was a wrong only to the company. The principle that a shareholder cannot recover a loss which is simply reflective of the company's loss, even though the shareholder's cause of action is independent of the company's, was confirmed by the House of Lords in *Johnson v Gore, Wood & Co.*[74]

Several rationales could be put forward for this rule limiting recovery. It might be thought to be justifiable on the grounds of preventing double recovery i.e. to prevent the wrongdoer having to compensate both the shareholder and the company for, in effect, the same loss. However, this result could be avoided simply by preventing the company from recovering if the shareholder has recovered, and vice versa. However, the rule in fact goes further than that by always subordinating the shareholder's claim to that of the company. It applies whether or not the company has recovered from the directors. Why should this be? It might be said that it addresses the following issue: if the shareholder is allowed to recover first, he or she effectively moves assets out of the company, to the potential detriment of the creditors of the company, who can sue the company but not the shareholders. This seems a good reason for often giving the company's claim priority, but, where the company has distributable assets, the creditors cannot be said to be prejudiced by this indirect form of distribution to the shareholders. A final argument might be that the initiation of a decision to distribute is normally entrusted by the articles to the board and certainly is not given to individual shareholders. The "no reflective loss" principle thus supports the principle of centralised management of the company through the board.

The strength of these arguments has to be weighed against the fact that, where the principle applies, the shareholder's recovery is limited even though the company may not recover its loss from the directors, so that the shareholder's loss is not made good through the company either. Thus, the rule applies even where the company is incapable of enforcing its claim, for example, because it has been compromised or is subject to limitation or simply because the defendant has a good

17–14

---

[73] Above, fn.71.
[74] [2002] 2 A.C. 1, HL. For a critique see Mitchell (2004) 120 L.Q.R. 457.

defence to the company's, but not to the shareholder's, claim.[75] This point led the Court of Appeal in *Giles v Rhind*[76] to refuse to apply the "no reflective loss" principle in the case where it was the wrongful act of the defendant which had put the company in a position where it could not pursue its claim. Here, if the shareholder has a separate cause of action, he or she should be able to recover damages in full, even for reflective losses.

However, the "no reflective loss" principle does not prevent the shareholder from suing to recover a loss which is distinct from that suffered by the company. The distinction between reflective and separate losses is illustrated in *Heron International Ltd v Lord Grade*,[77] where, in the context of a proposed takeover, the board preferred the lower bidder to the higher bidder and, unusually, was able to take action to enforce its choice on the shareholders. The Court of Appeal distinguished between the harm inflicted on the company's assets by this decision (because it was unclear that the relevant regulator would allow the lower bidder to operate in the industry in question) and the harm suffered directly by the shareholders individually though their inability to accept a higher takeover offer for their shares (assertable in a personal claim). However, the distinction between reflective and independent losses is not always easy to draw.

CONCLUSION

17–15   Although the new statutory derivative claim is doctrinally very different from the common law it replaces, it is not clear what its impact on the levels of derivative litigation will be. Surprisingly, the Law Commission was rather downbeat in its assessment. In its Consultation Paper it made the following remarks about the policy which underlay its proposed reforms: "a member should be able to maintain proceedings about wrongs done to the company only in exceptional circumstances" and "shareholders should not be able to involve the

---

[75] *Day v Cook* [2002] 1 B.C.L.C. 1, CA; *Barings v Coopers & Lybrand (No.1)* [2002] 1 B.C.L.C. 364; *Stein v Blake* [1998] 1 All E.R. 724, CA (this last containing the probably erroneous suggestion that the rule does not apply to claims by former shareholders).

[76] [2003] Ch. 618, CA. The defendant's wrongful act had destroyed the company's business, so that it had no funds for litigation. This was followed in *Perry v Day* [2005] 2 B.C.L.C. 405, where the directors' wrongful act (as against both shareholder and company) consisted in accepting a settlement giving up the company's claim against the defendant directors (as vendors to the company). Contrast *Gardner v Parker* [2004] 2 B.C.L.C. 554, CA where the directors' allegedly wrongful acts as against the company had put the company into administrative receivership (not by itself enough to prevent the company commencing litigation) and where the compromise of the company's claim against the directors, although on generous terms, was not improper.

[77] [1983] B.C.L.C. at 261–263.

company in litigation without good cause ... Otherwise the company may be 'killed by kindness', or waste money and management time in dealing with unwarranted proceedings."[78] Whilst the latter remark is undoubtedly true, it is unclear whether this should lead to derivative claims being available only in exceptional circumstances, because the ability of wrongdoing directors to block decisions in favour of litigation is a matter of empirical fact which has not been extensively investigated—though the unfair prejudice cases discussed in Chapter 20 below suggest it is a not uncommon feature of small companies. In its final report the Law Commission stated that "we do not accept that the proposals will make significant changes to the availability of the action. In some respects, the availability may be slightly wider, in others it may be slightly narrower. But in all cases the new procedure will be subject to tight judicial control."[79] If the common law led to sub-optimal levels of derivative litigation, one would hope that the statutory changes would have a significant impact, even whilst the judges remain fully alive to the fact that the statute, rightly, creates no entitlement in the shareholder to bring a derivative claim. All will depend on how the courts exercise their discretion. The statute does not suggest the rule in *Foss v Harbottle* should rule the courts from its grave and in due course the courts may strike out more boldly.

---

[78] Law Commission, *Shareholders' Remedies*, Consultation Paper No.142, 1996, para.4.6.
[79] Above, 13 at para.6.13.

CHAPTER 18

BREACH OF CORPORATE DUTIES: ADMINISTRATIVE REMEDIES

A distinctive feature of British company regulation for many years **18–1** has been the conferment of powers of investigation on the relevant Government Department, currently the Department of Business Enterprise and Regulatory Reform (BERR), formerly the Department of Trade and Industry (DTI) and before that the Board of Trade (BoT). Those provisions are still contained in Part XIV of the Companies Act 1985 (rather than the 2006 Act)[1] but were recently strengthened by the Companies (Audit, Investigations and Community Enterprise) Act 2004, having previously been amended by the Companies Act 1989. Those amendments did not alter the grounds on which investigations can be launched, but did upgrade the powers of the investigators and reduce the possibilities of delay or obstruction on the part of the companies under investigation. The 1985 Act, as amended, empowers the department to launch inquisitorial raids on corporate (and even unincorporated) bodies and BERR now has a sizeable Companies Investigation Branch (CIB), which in 2006 became part of the Insolvency Service Agency of the Department. Although the departmental powers are draconian, the Government's desire not to spend public money on matters which should be the concern purely of the company's members or creditors has tended to limit the scale of their use.

Originally, appointment of outside inspectors (usually a Q.C. and a

---

[1] Unless indicated otherwise, the references below are to the 1985 Act.

senior accountant) was the only form of investigation power that the Secretary of State had. But an announced appointment of inspectors is likely in itself to cause damage to the company. Hence the Department was reluctant to appoint unless a strong case for doing so could be made out and it normally made inquiries of the board of directors before doing so. Though such inquiries might cause the board to take remedial action, they might equally well provide an opportunity for evidence to be destroyed or fabricated. Hence, on the recommendation of the Jenkins Committee,[2] power to require the production of books and papers was added by the 1967 Companies Act, a power which can be exercised with less publicity[3] and which may suffice in itself or lead to a formal appointment of inspectors if the facts elicited show that that is needed. This power, now conferred by section 447 of the 1985 Act, is by far the one most commonly exercised.[4] It is sometimes referred to as the powers of "investigation", by way of contrast with the power to appoint inspectors.

Although company inspections and investigations were outside the terms of reference of the CLR, the Department conducted its own review of its powers.[5] This concluded that, overall, the reforms proposed by the CLR strengthened the case for retaining the Department's investigation and inspection powers, since the deregulation proposed by the Review in some areas of company law was likely to throw a greater weight onto the Department's administrative powers. However, the Department also concluded that the powers of investigation were too narrowly drawn to meet effectively their current role and proposed that they be expanded, whilst the powers of inspection should be streamlined, notably by introducing a new general power to appoint inspectors which would replace some of the existing, hardly used, specific powers. However, the document held out little hope of reducing either the time taken or the cost of formal inspections.[6] The Department's document also acknowledged the need to

---

[2] Cmnd. 1749 (1962), paras 213–219.

[3] The Department does not normally announce that it has mounted such an investigation and all information about it is regarded as confidential. This has its disadvantages. If a team of officials is going through the company's books and papers, this cannot be concealed from its employees and will soon become known to the Press, thus putting the company under a cloud which may never be dispersed because the ending of the inquiries will not normally be announced or their results ever be published, notwithstanding that the conclusion may be that all is well with the company.

[4] On average 180 such investigations were completed in each of the years 1997/98 to 2005/06 (though it is to be noted that the Department receives some 4,000 complaints a year which could lead to use of these powers: DTI, *Companies in 2001–2002* (2002) and DTI, *Companies in 2005–2006* (2006)). By contrast, the various powers to appoint inspectors were used only very infrequently.

[5] DTI, *Company Investigations: Powers for the Twenty-First Century* (2001).

[6] DTI, *Company Investigations: Powers for the Twenty-First Century*, which gives details of the costs and length of recent s.432 inspections. For example, the inspection into Mirror Group Newspapers Ltd took nearly nine years and cost £9.5 million. However, nearly half the time was taken up with waiting for criminal trials to be completed or with dealing with challenges in the courts to the inspectors by those sought to be inspected. See fn.48, below.

ensure that the investigatory and inspection powers comply, in both design and use, with the human rights standards of the European Convention on Human Rights, now embodied in the Human Rights Act 1998, and with the fairness standards of domestic public law. The 2004 Act expanded the departmental investigators' powers but did not put in place the more far-reaching re-formulation of the statutory provisions which the document envisaged. In particular, it did not re-cast the statutory provisions so as to reflect the modern reality, which is that investigation under section 447 is the primary form of inter-vention and that the appointment of inspectors is a rare event. Nevertheless, we will approach the powers in that order.

DISCLOSURE OF DOCUMENTS AND INFORMATION

Under section 447 the Secretary of State may require or, more likely, **18-2** authorise an investigator from the CIB to require, a company to produce at such time and place as are specified such documents[7] and information as may be specified. Authorising an investigator to impose the requirement avoids the risk of the documents being destroyed or doctored; the officer will arrive without warning[8] at the company's registered office (or wherever else the documents are believed to be held).[9] The investigator may be authorised further to impose the same requirements on "any person",[10] a power to be used where, for example, the documents concerned are in the possession of some person other than the company. The power of an investigator to impose a requirement on "any person" in relation to the production of "information" as well as documents means that, for example, an officer or employee of the company may be required to provide an explanation of a document or, if a document is not produced by the person asked, to state to the best of his or her knowledge where it is.[11]

Failure to comply with the requirements of section 447 on the part of any person may be certified by the Secretary of State or the

---

[7] s.447(8). The 1989 Act substituted documents for books of papers. "Document" is now defined as "information recorded in any form". The requirement to produce documents includes power, if they are produced, to take copies of them or extracts from them: s.447(7).

[8] The investigation is an administrative act to which the full rules of natural justice do not apply: *Norwest Holst Ltd v Secretary of State* [1978] Ch. 201 at 224, CA. But "fairness" must be observed and directions to produce should be clear and not excessive: *R. v Trade Secretary Ex p. Perestrello* [1981] 1 Q.B. 19 (a case which illustrates the problems that may be met if the documents are not held in the United Kingdom).

[9] The officer may be accompanied by a policeman with a search warrant: see s.448, below.

[10] s.447(3). But this is without prejudice to any lien that the possessor may have.

[11] See *Attorney-General's Reference No.2 of 1998, Re* [1999] B.C.C. 590, CA, decided on an earlier version of s.447 where this power was stated explicitly. However, the current version of the power is not confined to officers and employees. This extension was recommended in the 1981 proposals: see above, fn.5 at para.67.

investigator to the court and the court may treat that person as guilty of contempt of court if, after a hearing, it concludes that the defendant did not have a reasonable excuse[12] for non-compliance with the requirement.[13] In addition, providing information known to be false in a material particular or doing so recklessly is a criminal offence, punishable by imprisonment or a fine.[14] Criminal sanctions are also imposed on any officer of the company who is privy to the falsification or destruction of a document relating to the company's affairs, unless the officer shows there was no intention to conceal the affairs of the company or to defeat the law.[15] In addition, fraudulently to part with, alter or make an omission in such a document is a crime.[16]

The above provisions are all aimed at extracting information from those who may be unwilling to provide it without compulsion. It may happen, however, that a person wishes to volunteer information to an investigator, but feels constrained from so doing because the information has been imparted to him or her in confidence and so disclosure might trigger an action for breach of confidence on the part of the person who provided the information to the informer. The Act now gives a limited protection against such actions. The information must be of a kind which the person making the disclosure could be required to disclose under the Act, the disclosure must be in good faith and in the reasonable belief that it is capable of assisting the Secretary of State, must be no more than is necessary for this purpose, and must not be a disclosure prohibited by or under statute or by a banker or lawyer in breach of an obligation of confidence owed in that capacity.[17]

18–3   An investigator appointed under section 447 is not confined to turning up at premises to ask questions and demand documents, running the risk that admittance will be denied. The Act provides for the

---

[12] s.453C. *Cf. An Investigation under the Insider Dealing Act, Re* [1988] A.C. 660, HL, dealing with an analogous provision, where the court took a narrow view of reasonable excuse in the case of a journalist refusing to answer questions in order to protect his sources. This was because the information was needed for the prevention of crime, which is likely to, but need not, be the case under s.447.

[13] One effect of proceeding in this way is that the defendant is deprived of the automatic protection of legal professional privilege, which applies if, as previously, failure to comply is treated as an offence (s.1129 of the CA 2006), though the court might regard legal professional privilege as reasonable grounds for non-compliance.

[14] s.451. Prosecution requires the consent of the Secretary of State or DPP in England and Wales and Northern Ireland (s.1126(2),(3) of the CA 2006).

[15] s.450(1). The same restriction on prosecution applies as under s.451. See previous note.

[16] s.450(2).

[17] s.448A.

investigator to be given compulsory powers of entry and search.[18] The section of the Act dealing with search warrants was replaced and strengthened by the Companies Act 1989. Formerly it applied only to investigations under what is now section 447. But now it applies also to any investigations under Part XIV of the Act, i.e. to those by outside inspectors as well. It nevertheless seems better to deal with it before turning to inspectors because the full implications of section 447 cannot otherwise be appreciated. A Justice of the Peace, if satisfied on information given on oath by the Secretary of State, or by a person appointed or authorised to exercise powers under Part XIV, that there are on any premises documents, production of which has been required under that Part and which have not been produced, may issue a search warrant.[19] Under that provision a search warrant cannot be issued unless there has first been a requirement to produce the documents sought. The company, thus forewarned, could destroy the documents before the search took place, even if such action might be a crime.[20] Hence, the 1989 Act added a further provision under which a warrant may be issued if the J.P. is satisfied: (a) that there are reasonable grounds for believing that an indictable offence has been committed and that there are on the premises documents relating to whether the offence has been committed, (b) that the applicant has power under Part XIV to require the production of the documents, and (c) that there are reasonable grounds for believing that if production was required it would not be forthcoming but the documents would be removed, hidden, tampered with or destroyed.[21] Though narrowly circumscribed by the need to satisfy the J.P. of conditions (a)–(c), this enables the search for the documents to be undertaken by the police rather than by the (possibly self-interested) officers of the company.

Although the search warrant power introduced in 1989 undoubtedly increased the investigators' powers, in many cases it is not available, particularly given conditions (a) and (c) above. Where it is not, the investigator might still be left standing on the doorstep. Consequently, in the 2004 Act a right of entry to premises was

---

[18] These powers apply also to inspectors, discussed below: s.448(1). Note also that there is a power under s.1132 of the CA 2006 whereby (on application of the DPP, the Secretary of State or the police) a High Court judge, if satisfied that there is reasonable cause to believe that any person, while an officer of a company, has committed an offence in its management and that evidence of the commission is to be found in any books or papers of, or under the control of, the company, may make an order authorising any named person to inspect the books and papers or require an officer of the company to produce them: see *A Company, Re* [1980] Ch. 138, CA (reversed by the House of Lords sub nom. *Racal Communications Ltd, Re* [1981] A.C. 374, because, under the express provisions of subs.(5), there can be no appeal from the judge and it was held that this included cases where he had erred on a point of law—and, having discovered that other judges had taken a different view, had volunteered leave to appeal!).

[19] s.448(1).

[20] See fn.3 above.

[21] s.448(2).

introduced which was not dependent on a warrant issued by a J.P. nor subject to onerous conditions. Whenever authorised by the Secretary of State to do so and provided the investigator[22] thinks it will materially help in the exercise of his or her functions, the investigator may require entry to premises believed to be used wholly or partly for the purpose of the company's business and may remain there for such time as is necessary to discharge those functions.[23] The power of entry extends to accompanying persons whom the investigator thinks appropriate.[24] The section does not give the investigator powers of search but it does potentially give him or her access to relevant persons from whom the production of documents or information can be demanded. Intentional obstruction of the exercise of this power of entry is an offence, punishable with imprisonment or a fine,[25] and non-compliance with a requirement imposed under the section may be certified to the court to be dealt with as a contempt of court.[26] The power is subject to some procedural safeguards, notably a requirement that the investigator and accompanying persons identify themselves[27] and the investigator must give a written statement as soon as practicable after entry to the occupiers of the premises about the investigator's powers and the rights and obligations of the persons on the premises.[28]

The powers discussed above are cumulatively very considerable, but it is worth remembering that over three-quarters of the investigations initiated are prompted by allegations of fraudulent trading,[29] so that attempts to side-step the investigation are likely. Despite the width of the power to appoint investigators, this fact also illustrates the reluctance of the Department to use it unless wrongdoing and a strong public interest in taking action are present.[30]

Pt XIV contains further provisions common to both departmental investigations and to inspections but these are left until after a description of the latter. What should be emphasised, however, is that an investigation by the Department's officials under section 447 is very far from being merely a preliminary step towards the appointment of inspectors if the documentary evidence thus discovered justifies that. On the contrary, in most cases it will be the only

---

[22] Or inspector (see below).
[23] s.453A(1)–(3).
[24] s.453A(4).
[25] s.453A(5),(5A).
[26] s.453C(1) and see para.18–2 above.
[27] s.453B(3).
[28] s.453B(4)–(10) and the Companies Act 1985 (Power to Enter and Remain on Premises: Procedural) Regulations 2005, (SI 2005/684), which, together, go into considerably more detail than is indicated in the text.
[29] *Companies in 2005–2006*, Table 5.
[30] The two other main grounds for appointing an investigator after fraudulent trading were the involvement of a disqualified person or an undischarged bankrupt in the management of the company and using the company to promote an unlawful pyramid selling scheme: *Companies in 2005–2006*.

investigation undertaken and will lead either to a decision that no further action is needed or that some non-inspection follow-up action should be taken.[31] The time taken to decide may vary from a few days to several months and, while the investigation continues, the officials will probe deeply and in a way which from the viewpoint of the company is just as traumatic as a formal inspection.

INVESTIGATIONS BY INSPECTORS

When inspectors can be appointed

Sections 431 and 432 set out circumstances in which the Secretary of State is empowered to appoint one or more competent inspectors[32] to investigate the affairs[33] of a company and to report the result of their investigations to him; and one situation where the Secretary of State is obliged to do so. This last is where the court by order declares that the affairs of the company ought to be so investigated.[34] The courts rarely make use of this power. As to those situations in which the Secretary of State has a discretion, section 431 deals with cases where the company, formally, takes the initiative to suggest the appointment and section 432 with cases where the Secretary of State acts of his or her own motion.

Under section 431 the Secretary of State may appoint on the application of: (a) in the case of a company with a share capital, not less than 200 members or members holding not less than one-tenth of the issued shares; (b) in the case of a company not having a share capital, not less than one-fifth of the persons on the company's register of members; or (c) in any case, the company itself.[35] However, appointments under this section hardly ever occur.[36] This is due not

18–4

---

[31] See para.18–10, below.

[32] As already mentioned, the usual appointees are a Q.C. and a chartered accountant but less expensive mortals may be appointed in the rarer case when the Department appoints in relation to a private company.

[33] i.e. its business, including its control over its subsidiaries, whether that is being managed by the board of directors or an administrator, administrative receiver or a liquidator in a voluntary liquidation: *R. v Board of Trade Ex p. St Martins Preserving Co* [1965] 1 Q.B. 603.

[34] s.432(1). This seems to make the Secretary of State's refusal to appoint reviewable by the court if an application is made to it by anyone with *locus standi* and to enable a court, in proceedings before it (e.g. on an unfair prejudice petition), to make an order declaring that the company's affairs ought to be investigated by inspectors. A copy of the inspectors' report will be sent to the court: s.437(2). There was formerly another situation in which the Secretary of State had to appoint, i.e. if the company passed a special resolution declaring that its affairs ought to be so investigated, but this was removed by the 1981 Act.

[35] s.431(2)(c). This was added on the deletion by the 1981 Act of the former provision, compelling the Secretary of State to appoint if the company resolved by special resolution (see previous note) and enables an application to be instigated by a resolution of the board or, if it refuses to do so, by an ordinary resolution of the company in general meeting.

[36] It is believed that there have been no appointments since 1990.

only to the fact that, before appointing under the section, the Secretary of State may require applicants to give security to an amount not exceeding £5,000 for payment of the costs of the investigation,[37] but also because the application has to be supported by evidence that the applicants have good reason for the application.[38] If they have, the Secretary of State will normally have power to appoint of his own motion under section 432(2), below, and it is far better for those who have good reasons to draw them quietly to the attention of the Department, requesting that there should be an appointment under that section. Proceeding thus avoids the danger, inherent in section 431, that the malefactors in the company will tamper with the evidence once they learn of possible action under that section and thus frustrate effective intervention by the Department, whether by the appointment of inspectors or the appointment of an investigator under section 447 (see above).

Section 432(2) empowers the Secretary of State to appoint inspectors[39] if it appears that there are circumstances suggesting one (or more) of four grounds, the first two of which are:

> "(a) that the company's affairs are being conducted or have been conducted with intent to defraud creditors or the creditors of any other person or otherwise for a fraudulent or unlawful purpose or in a manner which is unfairly prejudicial to some part of its members;[40] or

> "(b) that any actual or proposed act or omission of the company (including an act or omission on its behalf) is or would be so prejudicial, or that the company was formed for any fraudulent or unlawful purpose."

These, it will be observed, in part adopt the wording of section 994 on unfair prejudice petitions,[41] but in addition they enable the Secretary of State to appoint where the company has been operated with intent to defraud creditors or was formed or conducted for a fraudulent or unlawful purpose.

In addition an appointment may be made on the ground:

---

[37] s.431(4). The £5,000 can be altered by statutory instrument. In the 1948 Act it was only £100 which, even then, would not have kept a competent Q.C. and chartered accountant happy for the time that most inspections take.

[38] s.431(3).

[39] Even if the company is in the course of being voluntarily wound up: s.432(3).

[40] "Member" includes a person to whom shares have been transmitted by operation of law: s.432(4).

[41] See Ch.20—except that, presumably by an oversight, the 1989 Act omitted here to change "some part of the members" (at the end of (a)) to "members generally or some part of the members", arguably, with the absurd result that, strictly speaking, the Secretary of State should not appoint inspectors if he thinks that *all* the members are unfairly prejudiced. Since, however, the precise grounds on which he has acted do not have to be stated (see *Norwest Holst v Trade Secretary* [1978] Ch. 201, CA) the omission is probably of no practical importance.

"(c) that persons concerned with the company's formation or the management of its affairs have in connection therewith been guilty of fraud, misfeasance or other misconduct towards it or towards its member; or

"(d) that the company's members have not been given all the information with respect to its affairs which they might reasonably expect."[42]

Under a new subsection (2A), inserted by the 1989 Act, inspectors **18-5** may be appointed on terms that any report they make is not for publication, in which case section 437, below, does not apply. Since, under that section, a report does not have to be published unless the Secretary of State thinks fit, it might be thought that subsection (2A) was unnecessary. But it has two advantages: it protects the Secretary of State from pressure to publish even though advised that that might prejudice possible criminal prosecutions; and, since it is an *ex ante* rule, it makes it clear to the proposed appointees that they will not be able to bask in publicity resulting from their efforts.[43]

In recent years, appointments under s.432(2) have also become less common than they were before the introduction of the investigation powers dealt with above, which, except in major cases, normally suffice and produce results more rapidly and at less expense. Had the reforms suggested in 2001[44] been implemented, this fact would have been recognised in the legislation. There would have been a re-formulation of the general inspection power, currently contained in s.432(2), so that it captured current practice, i.e. to appoint inspectors only when there are circumstances suggesting malpractice and there is a strong public interest in having an inspection. Thus, inspectors would have been appointable where it appeared that the company had been formed or used for an unlawful, dishonest, fraudulent or improper way and it was necessary in the public interest to have an inspection.[45] There would no longer be any mention, as grounds for appointment, of unfairly prejudicial treatment of members or inadequate provision of information, though these could be elements tending towards proof of the proposed grounds—in the case of inadequate provision of information only with some difficulty, however. The obligation to appoint at the request of the court would

---

[42] The wording of this implies that members may "reasonably expect" more information than that to which the Act entitles them. But it seems that s.432(2) does not entitle the Secretary of State to appoint merely because the directors or officers of the company appear to have breached their duties of care, skill or diligence: see *SBA Properties Ltd v Cradock* [1967] 1 W.L.R. 716 (which, however, was concerned with an action by the Secretary of State under what is now s.438, below).

[43] It may also tend to make the officers of the company more co-operative.

[44] See above fn.5.

[45] See above, fn.5 at para.97.

have disappeared, as would the power to appoint on the application of members.[46]

Conduct of inspections

Extent of the inspectors' powers

18–6   The Act itself contains a number of sections on the conduct of inspections. Under section 433, if inspectors, appointed to investigate the affairs of a company, think it necessary for the purposes of their investigation to investigate also the affairs of another body corporate in the same group they may do so and report the results of that so far as it is relevant to the affairs of the company.[47] Under section 434 inspectors have powers, similar to those of investigators under section 447 (above), to require the production of documents and information. They may also require any past or present officer or agent of the company to attend before them and otherwise to give all assistance that he is *reasonably* able to give.[48] In addition, they may examine any person on oath.[49] If any person fails to comply with their requirements or refuses to answer any question put by the inspectors for the purposes of the investigation, the inspectors may certify that fact in writing to the court which will thereupon inquire into the case and, subject to the important defence of reasonableness, may punish the offender in like manner as if he had been guilty of contempt of court.[50]

The inspectors may and, if so directed by the Secretary of State, shall make interim reports and, on the conclusion of the investigation, must make a final report.[51] If so directed by the Secretary of State, they must also inform the Minister of matters coming to their knowledge during their investigation.[52] The Secretary of State may, if thought fit, forward a copy of any report to the company's registered office and, on request and payment of a prescribed fee, to any member of the company or other body corporate which is the subject of the report, to any person whose conduct is referred to in the report,

---

[46] Though presumably members could have continued to draw relevant facts to the attention of the Secretary of State.

[47] Most major corporate scandals involve the use of a network of holding and subsidiary companies, the extent of which may only become apparent during the course of the investigation: s.433 avoids the need for a formal extension of the inspectors' appointment each time they unearth another member of the group. The extended power applies to bodies corporate (i.e. not just Companies Act companies) but does not extend to unincorporated bodies, which, however, may be capable of investigation on the grounds that associated unincorporated bodies are part of the affairs of the corporate body with which they are associated. The reforms proposed above (fn.5) would have filled this lacuna, if such it is.

[48] s.434(1) and (2). On the use of the "reasonableness" defence to protect a director against oppressive use by the inspectors of their powers see *Mirror Group Newspapers Plc, Re* [1999] 1 B.C.L.C. 690. Agents include auditors, bankers and solicitor (s.434(4)).

[49] s.434(3).

[50] s.436.

[51] s.437(1).

[52] s.437(1A).

to the auditors, to the applicants for the investigation[53] and to any other person whose financial interests appear to be affected by matters dealt with in the report.[54] And he or she may (and generally will, though not until after any criminal proceedings have been concluded)[55] cause the report to be printed and published.[56]

Control of the inspectors' powers

This topic can be looked at from two points of view: control over the **18–7** inspectors by the Secretary of State and control over the inspectors in the interests of third parties. The former control was considerably strengthened by Part 32 of the Companies Act 2006, inserting new provisions in the 1985 Act, though to some extent they reflect what was probably already administrative practice. In any event, the inspectors are now under a statutory obligation to comply with any direction given them by the Secretary of State as to the subject-matter of the investigation, as to the steps to be taken in the investigation and to report or not report on a particular matter or in a particular way.[57] The Secretary of State may also terminate an investigation.[58] Perhaps anticipating that exercise of these powers may lead to dissatisfaction among inspectors, they are given an express statutory right to resign and the Secretary of State a power to revoke an appointment as inspector.[59] However, former inspectors are under an obligation to produce to the Secretary of State or a replacement inspector documents and information obtained or generated in the course of the inspection.[60] These provisions make it very clear that the inspector is a creature of the Department.

As to control in the interests of the investigated, a number of matters have been established by practice and case-law. Although the inspectors may be expected to be somewhat more independent and impartial than the Secretary of State or civil servants exercising powers under section 447 in the belief that there is good reason for doing so, they too are not regarded as exercising a judicial role but an administrative one. Nevertheless, though the full rules of "natural

---

[53] This is not relevant to inspections under s.432(2) when the Secretary of State appoints of his or her own motion.

[54] s.437(3).

[55] For an unsuccessful attempt to force the Secretary of State to publish while criminal proceedings were still being considered: see *R. v Secretary of State Ex p. Lonrho* [1989] 1 W.L.R. 525, HL.

[56] s.437(3)(c). Thus making the reports available for purchase from H.M.S.O. by any member of the public so long as the reports remain in print. They often make fascinating reading for anyone interested in "the unacceptable face of capitalism".

[57] s.446A.

[58] s.446B(1)—though in the case of inspectors appointed as a result of a court order, only if matters have come to light suggesting the commission of a criminal offence and those matters have been referred to the appropriate prosecuting authority: s.446B(2).

[59] s.446C—and the Secretary of State can fill any vacancy: s.446D.

[60] s.446E. The inspector is under a duty to comply but no sanction is specified—presumably *in extremis* the Department could obtain a court order.

justice" do not apply, they must act fairly. This involves letting witnesses know of criticisms made against them (assuming that the inspectors envisage relying on, or referring to, those criticisms in their report) and giving them adequate opportunity of answering. But the inspectors are not bound to show them a draft of the parts of their report referring to them, so long as they have had a fair opportunity of answering any criticisms of their conduct. Inspectors are free to draw conclusions from the evidence about the conduct of individuals, but should do so only with restraint.[61]

Inspectors sit in private (and probably do not have the power to sit in public)[62] but allow witnesses to be accompanied by their lawyers—although the latter's role is limited since the questioning is undertaken by the inspectors and neither the witness nor his lawyers can cross-examine other witnesses. Although the range of persons whom the inspectors may question is very wide, the Act provides that such persons cannot be compelled to disclose or produce any information or document in breach of legal professional privilege, except that lawyers must disclose the names and addresses of their clients.[63] A banker's duty of confidentiality is protected more narrowly.[64] In particular, it may be overridden by the Secretary of State.[65]

The process of inspection is undoubtedly an inquisitorial one. However, as noted, since the aim of the inspection is to establish facts, rather than to determine legal rights, in domestic law the process has been characterised as administrative, rather than judicial, so that the inspectors are obliged to act fairly but are not subject to the full requirements of natural justice. The European Court of Human Rights has adopted a similar stance in relation to the applicability of Article 6 of the European Convention (right to a fair trial) to inspections.[66] Consequently, it would seem that the use of compulsion in investigations and inspections to secure information from those investigated, including compulsion to answer questions put by inspectors, is not in principle unlawful, as a matter of either domestic or European Convention law. However, as we shall see below, European Convention law has had a significant impact on what can be done subsequently, for example by the prosecuting authorities, with compelled testimony obtained by inspectors, and the Act was amended by the Criminal Justice and Police Act 2001 to take

---

[61] *Pergamon Press Ltd, Re*, [1971] Ch. 388, CA; *Maxwell v DTI* [1974] Q.B. 523, CA; *R (on the application of Clegg) v Secretary of State* [2003] B.C.C. 128, CA.
[62] *Hearts of Oak Assurance Co Ltd v Attorney-General* [1932] A.C. 392, HL.
[63] s.452(1),(5). This applies to Departmental investigations as well as to inspections: s.452(2).
[64] s.452(1A),(1B).
[65] s.452(1A)(c). The bankers' protection in relation to s.447 investigations is differently worded. It can be overridden by the Secretary of State only if he or she thinks it is necessary for the purpose of investigating the affairs of the person carrying on the banking business or the customer is a person upon whom a s.447 requirement has been imposed: s.452(4).
[66] *Fayed v United Kingdom* (1994) 18 E.H.R.R. 393.

account of the jurisprudence of the European Court of Human Rights.

POWER OF INVESTIGATION OF COMPANY OWNERSHIP

18–8 The above provisions relate to the appointment of inspectors or investigators to examine the affairs of the company in general (even if in particular cases they may be given a more limited remit). There is, however, one situation in which the Secretary of State's powers to appoint inspectors or investigators are limited by the statute to a particular topic. This is the power of investigation into company ownership.[67] This may be a controversial issue and the facts may not be clear, because, although the name of the shareholder has to be entered on the company's share register, that shareholder may be a nominee rather than the beneficial owner of the share. The circumstances in which large beneficial shareholders are required to disclose their positions or in which a company may require a person to reveal the extent of a beneficial holding in the company are discussed in Chapters 26[68] and 28.[69] The Secretary of State's investigatory powers are essentially supplementary to these provisions.

In the first instance, if the Secretary of State is persuaded that there may be good reasons for intervening, he or she will probably institute preliminary investigations under the powers conferred by section 444. Under this the Secretary of State can require any person whom he has reasonable cause to believe to have, or to be able to obtain, information as to the present and past interests in a company's shares or debentures to disclose this information.

If this fails to produce a satisfactory answer the Secretary of State may then appoint inspectors under section 442.[70] The Secretary of State may do so of his own volition and must do so, if application is made by members sufficient to instigate an appointment of inspectors under the general powers.[71] A fully-fledged investigation may afford the best chance of getting at the truth but it is expensive and time-consuming.[72] Hence, the amendments to the section made by the 1989

---

[67] There was also a power of investigation into share dealings (s.446) but this was repealed by the Companies Act 2006 from October 2007, but the Financial Services Authority has a like investigatory power and is now regarded as the more appropriate body to exercise this type of power. See para.30–46.
[68] At para.26–18.
[69] At para.28–49.
[70] This section is directed not merely to determining share and debenture ownership but "the true persons who are or have been primarily interested in the success or failure (real or apparent) of the company or able to control or materially to influence its policy": s.442(1).
[71] s.442(3) and see above, para.18–4, though under s.442(3) the appointment is mandatory.
[72] It is believed that no appointments have been made since 1992.

Act provide that the Secretary of State shall not be obliged to appoint inspectors if satisfied that the members' application is vexatious and, if an appointment is made, may exclude any matter if satisfied that it is unreasonable for it to be investigated;[73] and the applicants may be required to give security for costs as in a general investigation initiated by the members.[74]

The inspectors' powers in this area are supported by the sanctions mentioned above[75] but what makes the foregoing sections more effective than they would otherwise be is that, if there is difficulty in finding out the relevant facts on an investigation under sections 442 or 444, the Secretary of State may by order direct that the securities concerned shall, until further notice, be subject to restrictions on their transfer and the exercise of rights attached to them. These restrictions are discussed further in Chapter 28.[76]

LIABILITY FOR COSTS OF INVESTIGATIONS

18–9   Under s.439, the expenses of any investigation under Part XIV of the Act[77] are to be defrayed in the first instance by the Department, but may be recoverable from persons specified in that section, there being treated as expenses such reasonable sums as the Secretary of State may determine in respect of general staff costs and overheads. The persons from whom costs are recoverable include: anyone successfully prosecuted as a result of the investigation; the applicants for the investigation where inspectors were appointed under section 431, to the extent that the Secretary of State directs;[78] any body corporate dealt with in an inspectors' report when the inspectors were not appointed on the Secretary of State's own motion unless the body corporate was the applicant or except so far as the Secretary of State otherwise directs.[79] Thus, in the case of investigations under section 447 the only persons at risk of costs are those subsequently prosecuted and, even where inspectors are appointed, the same is true if the Secretary of State takes the initiative to appoint the inspectors.

---

[73] s.442(3A).
[74] See above, para.18–4.
[75] s.443.
[76] At para.28–50.
[77] Which in the case of inspections are likely to be heavy; the Atlantic Computers investigation cost £6.5 million and the Consolidated Goldfields one nearly £4 million, above, fn.5, Annex A, and the total costs to the companies and their officers were probably as great or greater.
[78] Or the equivalent provisions relating to ownership investigations: s.439(5).
[79] s.439(4). Inspectors appointed otherwise than on the Secretary of State's own motion may, and shall if so directed, include in their report a recommendation about costs: s.439(6). Note also the provisions regarding rights to indemnity or contribution (s.439(8) and (9)).

FOLLOW-UP TO INVESTIGATIONS

Following an investigation, whether by inspectors or otherwise, the **18–10** Secretary of State has a number of powers. Apart from the obvious one of causing prosecutions to be mounted against those whose crimes have come to light, which prosecutions may be mounted by the Department itself or by others, such as the Serious Fraud Office, the Secretary of State may petition under section 8 of the Disqualification Act for the disqualification of a director or shadow director on grounds of unfitness.[80] The Secretary of State may also petition the court for an appropriate order if unfair prejudice to all or some of the company's members has been revealed.[81] Alternatively or in addition, he or she may petition for the winding-up of the company under section 124A[82] of the Insolvency Act 1986. Under that section if it appears to the Secretary of State as a result of any report or information obtained under Part XIV of the Companies Act that it is expedient in the public interest that a company should be wound up, he or she may present a petition for it to be wound up if the court thinks it just and equitable. More than one hundred companies were wound up on the Secretary of State's petition in 2005–2006 and twenty-six disqualification orders obtained as a result of investigations.[83]

Before the 2006 Act it was the case that, if from any report made or information obtained under Part XIV it appeared to the Secretary of State that any civil proceedings ought, in the public interest, to be brought by any body corporate, he or she could bring such proceedings in the name and on behalf of the body corporate, indemnifying it against any costs or expenses incurred by it in connection with the proceedings. This power was removed by the 2006 Act,[84] perhaps on the basis that remedies for the benefit of the company should be a matter for its members.[85] By contrast taking companies off the register and disqualifying unfit persons from future involvement in the management of companies may well be steps which no member has an interest in taking.

---

[80] See para.10–4.

[81] See para.20–1.

[82] Inserted by the 1989 Act, s.60(3). In 2001 it was proposed that powers of the Secretary of State should include the power to seek from the court a restraining order as an alternative to a winding-up order, on the grounds that restraining the company from engaging in a specified business activity or carrying on business in a specified way might enable a lawful and viable part of the business to survive. See fn.5 at paras 120ff, but this reform has not been carried through.

[83] *Companies in 2005–2006*, p.10. Neither the winding-up or the disqualification application can be made on the basis of information supplied under the voluntary method (see para.18–2, above): Insolvency Act, s.124A(1)(a) and Company Directors Disqualification Act 1986, s.8(1A).

[84] s.438 of the 1985 Act was repealed by s.1176 of the CA 2006 as from April 2007.

[85] For the same reason the Department seems to make little or no use of its power to bring unfair prejudice petitions.

Since the majority of investigations and inspections are driven by allegations of potentially serious wrongdoing on the part of those involved in companies, it is hardly surprising that the Department does not simply receive the information produced by the investigation machinery, but makes use of the possibilities just described to take remedial steps of one sort or another. That this is contemplated by the Act is revealed by section 449 which contains a long list of exceptions to the starting proposition that information obtained under the section 447 investigation powers is confidential to the Department and cannot be disseminated more widely without the consent of the company.[86] These so-called "gateways" permit the information to be provided to those who are best placed to take the consequential action.

18–11   However, the possibility of subsequent action brings into sharp focus the rules which permit investigators and inspectors to secure information compulsorily. Although the domestic courts had held to the contrary (before the enactment of the Human Rights Act 1998), the European Court of Human Rights, in litigation arising out of the *Guinness* affair, concluded that evidence given to inspectors under threat of compulsion cannot normally be used in subsequent criminal proceedings against those investigated, on the grounds that this would infringe their privilege against self-incrimination.[87] The Act now provides that compelled testimony (but not documents produced under compulsion) may not be used in either primary evidence or cross-examination in a subsequent criminal trial of the person providing the testimony, unless the defendant or him- or herself brought the compelled testimony in or unless the offence in question is giving false evidence to the investigator or certain offences under the general perjury legislation.[88] However, this restriction does not apply to subsequent use of the testimony in proceedings for disqualification under section 8 of the Disqualification Act. Indeed, section 441 specifically provides that an inspectors' report can be evidence as to the opinion of the inspectors in such an application and the courts have come to the same conclusion in respect of a report by investigators under section 447.[89] Both the domestic courts and the ECtHR

---

[86] The gateways are set out in Schedules 15C and 15D of the Act. The same provisions apply to information provided voluntarily: see para.18–2 above.

[87] *Saunders v United Kingdom* [1998] 1 B.C.L.C. 362, ECtHR; *IJL v United Kingdom* (2001) 33 E.H.R.R. 11, ECtHR. For sceptical assessment, see Davies, "Self-incrimination, Fair Trials and the Pursuit of Corporate and Financial Wrongdoing" in B. Markesinis (ed.), *The Impact of the Human Rights Bill on English Law* (OUP, 1998). The House of Lords refused to quash the convictions of those involved despite the breach of the Convention: *R. v Saunders, Times Law Reports*, November 15, 2002.

[88] s.447A. Nor do the amendments specifically exclude evidence to which the prosecuting authorities were drawn as a result of the compelled testimony, where the answers themselves are not used in the criminal trial.

[89] *Rex Williams Leisure Plc, Re* [1994] Ch. 350, CA.

seem to be in agreement that disqualification applications are not criminal proceedings.[90] However, disqualification applications, if not criminal proceedings, clearly are proceedings falling within Article 6 of the European Convention because they determine the legal rights of the person to be disqualified. Unlike the investigation process itself, which lies outside Article 6,[91] disqualification proceedings will have to comply with Convention standards appropriate for civil proceedings. These standards do not specifically include a privilege against self-incrimination but they do involve general standards of fairness. Especially since disqualification has a penal element, the presumption of innocence might be relevant.[92] Presumably, the same considerations will apply where it is proposed to use compelled testimony in purely civil litigation:[93] there will be no ban in principle, but the court conducting the civil trial will need to have regard to general fairness issues. One such issue, already identified by the English courts in the context of the Insolvency Act powers of compulsory examination, is the undesirability of allowing statutory powers to give one party a litigation advantage over another in purely civil litigation which it would not have, were the company not insolvent.[94]

CONCLUSION

Since the scheme of administrative remedies under the Act is domi-nated by the power of investigation and this power is predominantly used in cases of suspected fraudulent trading or breach of the dis-qualification provisions, it is far from clear that these remedies con-stitute an important element in the British system of corporate governance, if that is defined as the accountability of the senior management to the shareholders as a whole. These provisions might be better seen as seen as supporting the provisions analysed in Part Two of this book, dealing with the abuse of limited liability. It would seem that the Department leaves allegations of breaches of the duties discussed in Chapter 16 to be pursued by companies or shareholders themselves, perhaps now through the reformed derivative action procedure,[95] unless either there is a strong public interest in favour of

18–12

---

[90] *R. v Secretary of State for Trade and Industry Ex p. McCormick* [1998] B.C.C. 379, CA; *DC v United Kingdom* [2000] B.C.C. 710, ECHR.
[91] See above, fn.66.
[92] *Albert and Le Compte v Belgium* (1983) 5 E.H.R.R. 533, ECHR. The Court of Appeal remains of the view that general fairness does not in principle require the exclusion of compelled testimony: *Westminster Property Management Ltd, Re* [2000] 2 B.C.L.C. 396, CA.
[93] Where the inspectors' report is also admissible: s.441.
[94] *Cloverbay Ltd v BCCI SA* [1991] Ch. 90, CA.
[95] See Ch.17.

intervention by the Department or the misconduct of the directors has been egregious. Nevertheless, administrative remedies are an important part of corporate law, and shareholders may benefit from them indirectly, as where inspectors' reports reveal matters which lead to the reform of company law.[96]

---

[96] As we noted in Ch.16 substantial elements in Pt X of the Act are the response to abuses revealed in inspectors' reports.

PART FOUR

CORPORATE GOVERNANCE—MAJORITY AND MINORITY SHAREHOLDERS

An important determinant of behaviour in a company is the structure of its shareholding along the continuum between highly dispersed and atomised shareholdings to one person holding all the shares. Where there are many shareholders, each with only a very small shareholding, the risk to the shareholders is that the management will be the true controllers of the company and they may not give the shareholders' interests proper consideration. We looked at the legal mechanisms which may address those issues in Part Three. On the other hand, where there is a controlling shareholder—or a small group of shareholders who can exercise control—the management will certainly be accountable to the controlling shareholders, but the latter may act opportunistically towards the non-controlling shareholders. (Where there is only one shareholder, then neither problem exists.) Some of the consequences of majority control the law should not be worried about. For example, the controlling shareholders will set the company's business policy and, in most cases, the non-controlling shareholders have to accept that this will be the case. In return, they may be able to "free-ride" on the efforts of the controlling shareholders to ensure that their policy is effectively implemented by the management of the company.

However, it might be that the majority seek to exercise their power so as to divert to themselves, in one way or another, a greater part of the company's earnings than their contribution to the company's share capital justifies. Such "private benefits of control" are probably impossible to eradicate without recourse to a set of interventionist rules whose costs would probably outweigh the rewards—and, in any event, some such benefits are a legitimate return to the majority of their monitoring efforts. Nevertheless, the law must deal with the more outrageous examples of majority opportunism, if those responsible for company law wish to encourage investors to place their money in companies which are controlled by one or a small group of shareholders. Apart from the unfairness of majority exploitation of the minority, there is a strong efficiency argument in favour of minority protection. If the holders of minority stakes of ordinary shares in companies are not so protected, they will protect themselves, probably by being prepared to buy such shares only at a lower price, thus in effect buying insurance against the majority's unfair treatment of them. This will raise the company's cost of capital, so that the cost of the unfair treatment is ultimately transferred back to the controllers of the company. On this argument, it is as much in the interests of the majority as it is of the minority shareholders that effective legal limits should be placed on the freedom of the majority to act opportunistically towards the minority.

Unfair treatment of the minority by the majority may occur, obviously, through decisions taken by shareholders in general meeting. Thus, the general meeting becomes a focus of rules designed to protect the minority, and we shall examine these rules in the next chapter. However, since in our system, as we saw in Chapter 14, a simple majority of the shareholders has the power to replace the members of the board at any time and for any reason, the majority's influence may well be articulated through decisions of the board, as well as or instead of through shareholder decisions. In fact, given the division of powers between the board and the general meeting, normally in favour of the former in all but small companies, majority shareholder influence over the company is very likely to involve some element of board decision-making. Sometimes the rules on directors' duties will catch action by directors aimed at diverting corporate assets to themselves, for example, the rules on self-dealing.[1] However, effective control of the majority therefore requires rules which operate on the "controllers" of the company, whether they act through the board or the shareholder decision-making. In recent times the legislature has tried to provide such a remedy in the shape of the "unfair prejudice" provisions. We shall examine these rules in Chapter 20.

---

[1] Above, paras 16–40ff.

CHAPTER 19

CONTROLLING MEMBERS' VOTING

INTRODUCTION

In any company law system a number of techniques are in principle **19–1** available to control the exercise by the majority of the shareholders of their voting power over the company in an unfair way. In fact, we have come across a number of relevant techniques already in this book, and it is useful to draw them together briefly, before going on to discuss in more detail some techniques not previously dealt with.

Perhaps most obviously, the legislature could specify in advance certain decisions which it should not be open to the majority to take. There are one or two examples of this approach to be found in the Act, one of which concerns a topic which will take up some considerable space in this chapter: alteration of the articles. Section 25[1] provides that a member is not bound by an alteration of the articles after the date upon which he or she became a member if its effect is to require the member to take more shares in the company than the number held on the date of the alteration or in any other way increases the member's liability to contribute to the company's share

---

[1] See above, para.3–20.

capital or otherwise pay money to the company. In other words, the size of a shareholder's investment in the company is a matter for individual, not collective, decision. Another is the admittedly controversial common law rule that the shareholders cannot ratify wrongdoing by a director which involves the appropriation by the director of corporate property.[2] However, it is impossible for the legislature or the judges to identify in advance very many substantive decisions which should be prohibited on the grounds that they will always be unfair to the minority. Normally, fairness and unfairness are fact-specific assessments and therefore not appropriate for *ex ante* decision-making on the part of the rule-maker.

An obvious response of the rule-maker in this situation is to move from substance to procedure, and in fact the legislature does make much greater use of rules which determine *how* the shareholders are to decide than it does of rules which determine *what* they shall decide. In Chapter 14[3] we gave a list of decisions which the Act requires to be taken by the shareholders. In many of those cases the decision is also required to be taken by a three-quarters majority of those voting rather than a simple majority. Although such a "supermajority" is not required in all cases where a role in decision-making is reserved by the Act for the shareholders nor is the line between ordinary and supermajority requirements drawn in an entirely consistent way in policy terms, it can be said that when the decision will affect the rights of the shareholders under the constitution, a supermajority of the shareholders is normally required. Of course, a three-quarters majority requirement does not obviate all cases of unfair prejudice of the minority, but it will reduce the incidence of such events because, under a supermajority requirement, only a quarter of the votes is needed to block the resolution.

An approach lying in between the substantive and the procedural is to leave the shareholders largely free to take what substantive decision they will, but to control those elements of the decision which are most likely to cause prejudice to the minority. This policy is often effected through an equal treatment or sharing rule. Thus, when a company repurchases its shares and does so through market purchases,[4] the Listing Rules insist on equality of treatment of the shareholders, either by controlling the price at which the repurchase is made or by requiring the repurchase to be made by way of a tender offer to all shareholders.[5] This does something to prevent insiders from taking undue advantage of the repurchase exercise or the repurchase having an effect on the balance of power within the company to the benefit of the majority. In the same vein, the common law requires dividends to be paid equally to shareholders according to

---

[2] See above, para.16–86.
[3] See above, at para.14–8.
[4] See above, at para.13–15.
[5] Listing Rules 12.4.1–2.

their shareholdings. The common law took as its test for equality the nominal value of the shares, though the articles normally adjust this so as to use the amount paid up on the shares where the nominal value differs from the amount paid up.[6] This makes it difficult for the majority to use the mechanism of dividend distribution to allocate a disproportionate share of the company's earnings to themselves.[7]

Three further minority protection techniques are worth mentioning at this stage. The new statutory derivative action procedure makes it more difficult for a controlling shareholder/director to block access to the courts by the minority to enforce the company's rights against the controller acting as director.[8] The derivative action allows the minority to side-step the majority's control of the board or shareholder decision-making and to seek court (rather than corporate) approval to initiate litigation. Of course, the derivative action is not available if the shareholders have ratified the wrong. However, the statute now prevents interested directors from voting on a shareholder resolution to ratify the wrongdoing.[9] Thus, two techniques are used. One is the essentially procedural one of structuring the vote at shareholder level by excluding the votes of those interested in the decision. The other is novel, i.e. shifting the litigation decision to an outside authority free of majority influence.

19–2

Excluding the controllers, when interested, from voting on the decision in question is a technique taken further by the Listing Rules of the Financial Services Authority and applying to companies listed on the Main Market of the London Stock Exchange. More importantly, those Rules impose a requirement for shareholder approval of transactions with significant shareholders which is not to be found in general company law. Under the rules for "related party" transactions, the Listing Rules exclude the related party from voting on the decision in question and require that party to take all reasonable efforts to ensure that associates do not vote either. Crucially, the term "related party" is widely defined so as to include a person who can control ten per cent or more of the voting rights in the company or who can exercise substantial control over the company. "Associate" is widely defined, rather in the manner of a "connected person" in section 252 of the Act. Finally, a "related party transaction" is widely defined so as to include not only transactions between the company

---

[6] *Birch v Cropper* (1889) 14 App. Cas. 525, HL, *cf.* art.71 of the draft model set of articles for public companies. The model for private companies says nothing about this point, probably because nominal values and amounts paid up are normally the same in such companies.

[7] This provides a possible rationale for the exemption of dividends from the rules on financial assistance, especially as creditors are also protected by the rule that dividends are payable only out of profits. See above at para.13–27.

[8] See above, Ch.17.

[9] See above, para.16–85.

and the related party but also transactions in which the company and related party together finance a transaction or project and any other similar transaction which benefits the related party.[10]

The final technique to be mentioned is that of giving the minority the right to exit the company at a fair price if certain decisions with which they disagree are taken by the majority. Such exit rights are usually referred to as "appraisal" rights. Crucially, they are not simply rights to exit the company, which in a listed company the shareholder hardly needs, but rights to leave at a fair price. Although in some company law systems this is a rather well-developed minority protection remedy,[11] the British legislation uses it only very sparingly. This is perhaps because, whether the right is to be bought out by the company or by the majority shareholder, the effect is to place a potentially substantial financial hurdle in the way of the decision which triggers the appraisal right. Nevertheless, an appraisal right can be found in ss.110 and 111 of the IA 1986 (reflecting provisions introduced in the nineteenth century) which deal with the reorganisation of companies in liquidation.[12] More important, it is also to be found in both the Companies Act and the Take-over Code where it provides an exit right at a fair price where there has been an acquisition or transfer of a controlling block of shares in the company. In this second situation, the exit right is not tied to the taking of a business decision but rather to a shift in the composition of the shareholder body, though the basis of the exit right is, in part, that the shift in the identity of the controller of the company may well have an adverse impact upon the minority shareholders.[13]

In this chapter, however, we shall look at two further minority protection techniques. The first consists of giving power to the court to review the decision of the majority on the grounds that it is in some sense unfair to the minority. In specific instances we have seen that the Act gives such a right of appeal to the minority. The question now is whether the common law gives such a general right. The second is treating the shareholders whose interests are at risk from the decision as a separate group whose consent is needed for the decision to go

---

[10] See Listing Rules 11.1 ff. The closest the general law comes to requiring shareholders approval of transactions with significant shareholders is where that shareholder falls within the category of "shadow director" and thus is subject to the statutory rules on self-dealing contained in Chapter 4 of Part 10 (above, paras 16–49ff).

[11] For example, the United States (see R. Clark, *Corporate Law* (Little Brown, 1986) pp.444 *et seq.*

[12] See below, para.29–15.

[13] See paras 28–40 and 28–66. The statute recognises the exit right only if the new controller holds 90 per cent of the voting rights after a takeover bid; the Code gives an exit opportunity at the 30 per cent level, no matter how the 30 per cent has been acquired and so goes much further than the statute.

ahead, whether or not under the company's constitution the separate consent of that group would be required. The first of these two techniques obviates the difficulty of having to predict in advance which decisions are acceptable and which not, for the decision is subject to *ex post* scrutiny on a case-by-case basis by the courts. The second technique is an extension of the policy of excluding interested parties from voting on a decision. Sometimes this negative technique is enough by itself. In other cases, however, the law may need to go further and specify those who are entitled to vote as well as those who are not, rather than leaving the determination of those entitled to vote to the rules contained in the company's articles.

REVIEW OF SHAREHOLDERS' DECISIONS

The starting point

Scattered throughout the reports are statements that members must exercise their votes "bona fide for the benefit of the company as a whole",[14] a statement which suggests that they are subject at common law to precisely the same basic principle as directors. But, it seems, this is highly misleading, and the decisions do not support any such rule as a universal principle. On the contrary, it has been repeatedly laid down that votes are proprietary rights, to the same extent as any other incidents of the shares, which the holder may exercise in his own selfish interests even if these are opposed to those of the company.[15] He or she may even bind him- or herself by contract to vote or not to vote in a particular way and his contract may be enforced by injunction.[16] Moreover, as we have seen, directors themselves, even though personally interested, can vote in their capacity of shareholders at that general meeting,[17] unless the Act or the Listing Rules specifically deprive them of the right to vote.[18] And this is so also as

19–3

---

[14] The original source of this oft-repeated but misleading expression seems to be Lindley M.R. in *Allen v Gold Reefs of West Africa* [1900] 1 Ch. at 671.

[15] *North-West Transportation Co v Beatty* (1887) 12 App.Cas.589, PC; *Burland v Earle* [1902] A.C. 83, PC; *Goodfellow v Nelson Line* [1912] 2 Ch. 324.

[16] *Greenwell v Porter* [1902] 1 Ch. 530; *Puddephatt v Leith* [1916] 1 Ch. 200—in which a mandatory injunction was granted. Contrast the rules on directors' fettering their discretion: above, para.16–37.

[17] *NW Transportation Co v Beatty*, above; *Burland v Earle* [1902] A.C. 83 at 93, PC; *Harris v A Harris Ltd* (1936) S.C. 183 (Sc); *Baird v Baird & Co* 1949 S.L.T. 368 (Sc). And see the remarkable case of *Northern Counties Securities Ltd v Jackson & Steeple Ltd* [1974] 1 W.L.R. 1133 where it was held that, although to comply with an undertaking given by the company to the court the directors were bound to recommend the shareholders to vote for a resolution, they, as shareholders, could vote against it, if so minded.

[18] See, for example, section 239 excluding the interested director from voting on a resolution to ratify his or her wrongdoing (above, para.16–85) or the Listing Rules provisions on related-party transactions, discussed above.

regards the transactions which, under Chapter 4 of Part 10 of the Act, require the prior approval of the company in general meeting.

Thus, it is wrong to see the voting powers of shareholders as being of a fiduciary character. Unlike directors' powers, shareholders' voting rights are not conferred upon them in order that they shall be exercised in the best interests of others, whether those others are seen to be "the company" or the minority shareholders or, indeed, any other group. However, to deny the fiduciary character of share-holders' voting rights and to assert their proprietary nature is not to say that the exercise of shareholders' voting powers is, or should be, unconstrained by the law. The controlling shareholders may not be required to exercise their powers in the best interests of the non-controlling shareholders, but this does not mean they may trample over the interests of the latter with impunity. There are many situations in the modern law, and not just within company law, where the exercise of property rights is subject to some sort of review by the courts. The issue which arises, therefore, is not the one of principle, but whether it has proved possible for the courts or the legislature to develop a set of criteria for the effective review of majority share-holders' decisions. As we shall see below, this task was addressed by the courts at an early stage in the development of British company law, but the results of that exercise have not been spectacularly successful. The courts have hovered uncomfortably between an unwillingness to determine how businesses should be run and an equally deeply felt unease that simple majoritarianism would leave the minority exposed to opportunistic treatment by the majority.

Resolutions to expropriate members' shares

19–4   The principle which the courts have found so difficult to develop and apply to shareholder decisions was articulated as early as 1900 by the Court of Appeal in *Allen v Gold Reefs of West Africa Ltd*[19] and in the context of a vote to alter the company's articles, which the Court of Appeal in the case in fact upheld. The principle was that that the power to alter the articles must be exercised "bona fide for the benefit of the company as a whole" because it was a power which enabled the majority to bind the minority. In analysing the case-law, it is useful to divide alteration of the articles into those arguably involving an expropriation of the member's shares and those not having that effect.

In expropriation (or, less pejoratively, compulsory transfer, since the expropriation is invariably accompanied by an offer of compensation) cases, the arguments for judicial intervention might seem to be at their strongest, but the law falls far short of prohibiting changes in the articles aimed at introducing such clauses. On the contrary, it is

---

[19] [1900] 1 Ch. 656, CA.

clear that compulsory transfer articles may be introduced into the company's articles, and the debate is about the level of judicial scrutiny to which such amendments will be subject. The relevant authorities start with *Brown v British Abrasive Wheel Co*,[20] a decision at first instance in which a public company was in urgent need of further capital which shareholders, holding 98 per cent of the shares, were willing to put up but only if they could buy out the 2 per cent minority. Having failed to persuade the minority to sell, they proposed a special resolution adding to the articles a provision to the effect that any shareholder was bound to transfer his shares upon a request in writing of the holders of 90 per cent of the shares. Although such a provision could have been validly inserted in the original articles,[21] and although the good faith of the majority was not challenged, it was held that the addition of such a provision in order to enable the majority to expropriate the minority could not be for the benefit of the company as a whole but was solely for the benefit of the majority. Hence an injunction was granted restraining the company from passing the resolution.

This decision, however, was almost immediately "distinguished" by the Court of Appeal in *Sidebottom v Kershaw, Leese & Co Ltd*.[22] There, a director-controlled private company had a minority shareholder who had an interest in a competing business. Objecting to this, the company passed a special resolution adding to the articles a provision empowering the directors to require any shareholder who competed with the company to sell his shares at a fair value to nominees of the directors. This was upheld on the basis that it was obviously beneficial to the company. In contrast, shortly thereafter in *Dafen Tinplate Co v Llanelly Steel Co*,[23] it was held at first instance that a resolution inserting a new article empowering the majority to buy out any shareholder as they thought proper, was invalid as being self-evidently wider than could be necessary in the interests of the company.

So far, all the decisions had implied that a resolution adding to the **19–5** articles a provision enabling the shares of a member to be compulsorily transferred would be upheld only if it was passed bona fide in the interests of the company and that this was to be judged not just by the members but also by the court. However, in *Shuttleworth v Cox Bros Ltd*,[24] a case concerning not expropriation of shares but the removal of an unpopular life director, the Court of Appeal, in

---

[20] [1919] 1 Ch. 290. For a stimulating recent analysis of these cases see Hannigan, "Altering the Articles for Compulsory Transfer" [2007] J.B.L. 471.

[21] *Phillips v Manufacturers Securities Ltd* (1917) 116 L.T. 209; in *Borland's Trustees v Steel Bros* [1901] 1 Ch. 279 an even wider article was inserted with the agreement of all the members. Presumably too a compulsory transfer article could be introduced by majority vote which would affect only shares acquired in the future.

[22] [1920] 1 Ch. 154, CA.

[23] [1920] 2 Ch. 124.

[24] [1927] 2 K.B. 9, CA.

upholding the validity of a resolution inserting in the articles a provision that any director should vacate office if called upon to do so by
the board, held that it was for the members, and not the court, to
determine whether the resolution is for the benefit of the company
and that the court will intervene only if satisfied that the members
have acted in bad faith.[25] If the same applies to expropriation of
shares, it is difficult to understand why what is now s.979 of the Act[26]
was needed. That section[27] enables a takeover bidder who has
acquired 90 per cent or more of the target company's shares to
acquire compulsorily the remainder. There would have been no need
for that section if a bidder, having acquired a controlling interest,
could then cause the target company to insert in its articles a similar
power.

Thus, it may well be that, in the case of a compulsory transfer of
shares, and despite the decision in *Shuttleworth*, the scrutiny which
the courts will exercise over the majority's decision to expropriate is
more rigorous than in other cases of alterations of the articles. But
that still leaves the task of identifying the nature of the control the
courts will exert. Of the three cases mentioned above, *Sidebottom* was
an easy case, *Dafen Tinplate* more difficult and *Brown* very difficult.
In *Sidebottom* prevention of damage to the company's business was
the object of the alteration and the compulsory transfer power was
appropriately drafted so as to apply only to competing shareholders.
The change was upheld. *Dafen Tinplate* also involved a shareholder
with an interest in a competing business who had begun to act contrary to the expectations on which the company had been founded,
but the alteration of the articles was drafted in wide terms so as to
allow the majority to transfer compulsorily the shares of any minority
shareholder. The change was invalidated but an implication might be
that a more narrowly drafted compulsory transfer power would have
been unobjectionable.

In *Brown* the company needed further financing which the majority
(holding 98% of the shares) were willing to provide if they could
obtain complete control. Astbury J. restrained the alteration on the
grounds that it was for the benefit only of the majority and not of the
company. However, it is difficult to see why the proposal could not
equally be expressed as one which was for the benefit of the company,
if, for example, the necessary financing was available to the company

---

[25] The court conceded that if the resolution was such that no reasonable man could consider it
for the benefit of the company as a whole that might be a ground for finding bad faith,
[1927] 2 K.B. 9, at pp.18, 19, 23, 26 and 27. Another, it is submitted, would be if the majority
was trying to acquire the shares of the minority at an obvious undervalue.

[26] Formerly s.429 of the 1985 Act.

[27] Dealt with in Ch.28 at paras 28–61ff, below.

only or on the best terms from the majority.[28] After all, the exclusion of the competitor in *Sidebottom* was presumably for the benefit of both the company's business and the shareholders who remained in the company after the competitor had been eliminated. The fact that, as in *Dafen Tinplate*, the proposed change was a wide one seems a highly technical objection since, once the power was exercised, the majority would have complete control, and any future shareholder, if any were allowed in, would come in on the basis of the altered article.

An issue akin to the *Brown* facts was recently considered by the High Court of Australia in *Gambotto v WCP Ltd*,[29] where it was proposed to alter the articles to allow a 90 per cent shareholder to acquire the shares of minority shareholders at a certain price (the majority holder in fact holding 99.7% of the shares). The court was unwilling to leave the issue to (super-) majority rule, coupled with a requirement of good faith on the part of the majority. There was an objective test which had to be applied, even if the price was fair and the majority had acted in good faith, which the majority found in the notion of proper purposes. This meant, in the court's view, that expropriation of shares could legitimately be used to save the company from "significant detriment or harm" (as in *Sidebottom v Kershaw, Leese and Co Ltd*) but not to "advance the interest of the company as a legal and commercial entity or those of the majority, albeit the great majority, of the incorporators" (as in this case where acquisition of the minority shares would have conferred very considerable tax advantages on the company and thus its controlling shareholders). "English authority", presumably *Shuttleworth v Cox Bros Ltd*, was disapproved on the grounds that "it does not attach sufficient weight to the proprietary nature of a share".[30]

There seem to be three ways forward in this area. The first is to **19–6** attach less weight to the proprietary nature of the share and, instead, to view it as an investment in the shape of a series of financial entitlements, notably to future dividends. This view would be favourable to the notion of compulsory acquisition at a fair price by a good faith majority, so that the test would be solely the good faith test, i.e. no special test for compulsory acquisitions.[31] The second is to keep an objective element in the test but to take a more sceptical attitude towards the distinction between harm to the company and benefit to

---

[28] It may be that the decision can be put on the basis, as found by the judge, that the majority did not think about the benefit to the company's business at all, but only their own benefit, for example, because financing was available on equivalent terms from those who did not require complete control.

[29] (1995) 127 A.L.R. 417.

[30] Above, fn.29 at paras 425–426.

[31] There is some indirect support for this approach in English law in *Citco Banking Corp N V v Pusser's Ltd* [2007] 2 B.C.L.C. 483, PC at [20], where a subjective approach was endorsed in what was admittedly not an expropriation case but which was, nevertheless, one in which a significant, if minority, shareholder was prepared to provide further financing to the company only if he were given control over it, which was achieved by altering the articles so as to assign to his shares weighted-voting rights.

the company and between the interests of the majority and the interests of the company. In many cases, the latter distinction represents two sides of the same coin. Thus, a compulsory transfer, at a fair price, which, in the court's view, will confer a significant benefit on the company's business and thus on the shareholders who remain in the company, would be permitted if put forward in good faith. The third, and least satisfactory, is to retain the distinction, implicit in the English cases and explicit in *Gambotto*, between compulsory transfers aimed to protect the company's business (and its shareholders) against harm and those which aim to confer a benefit on the company's business (and its shareholders) The second approach is perhaps reflected in the view of the minority judge[32] in *Gambotto* who was unimpressed by the distinction between harm and benefit, drawn by the majority, but agreed in the result, on the basis that the proponents of the change had not demonstrated the price to be a fair one. It is not entirely clear which way domestic law will develop, but no court has endorsed *Gambotto* as representing English law.

What does seem to be clear, in any event, is that the issue is no more easy to solve when presented in terms of improper purposes (or fraud on a power) than when presented in terms of "bona fide in the interests of the company". It is also clear, as a judge recently said with some understatement, that the current British law is "somewhat untidy".[33] Section 979 can be justified as settling doubts about the issue and providing a mechanism for effecting the compulsory acquisition of minorities in the post-takeover situation, where it is important for the parties to know where they stand.

Other resolutions

19–7   If, in cases of compulsory transfer of shares, it is not clear whether English law requires the court to form its own view of the needs of the company or to accept the majority's view, provided it has been arrived at in good faith, it is not surprising that good faith is the sole test applied in the case of alterations of the articles which fall short of compulsory transfer but which are nevertheless disadvantageous to the minority. Thus, in *Citco Banking Corporation N V v Pusser's Ltd*[34] the Privy Council upheld a change in the articles which entrenched the existing controller of the company (who before the change controlled 28% of the company's shares) by permitting the conversion of his existing shares (carrying one vote per share) into a new class of

---

[32]   McHugh J. There is in fact some difficulty in valuing the minority's shares in such a case as this, but in fact the minority conceded that the valuation put on their shares was independent and fair (at para.3).

[33]   *Constable v Executive Connections Ltd* [2005] 2 B.C.L.C. 638, the judge refusing to dispose of an expropriation claim summarily.

[34]   Above, fn.31, following *Rights & Issues Trust Ltd v Stylo Shoes Ltd* [1965] Ch.250. Nor did the court think that, as in fact happened in *Stylo Shoes*, the shareholders who might be thought to benefit from the alteration were disbarred from voting on the resolution.

share carrying 50 votes per share. This was said by those who sup-ported the alteration to be a bona fide decision in the interests of the company because it enabled the company to raise further finance for expansion, the financiers requiring that the existing controller remain in charge. The genuineness of this belief on the part of the majority was not challenged by the other party to the litigation and the court found that a reasonable shareholder could have held this view about the proposed alteration. Applying the *Shuttleworth* test and reiter-ating that the burden of proof is on those who challenge the reso-lution, the court found the test of bona fide in the interests of the company to have been met. The only element of objective control which remained—and it has probably always been inherent in the bona fides test—is that the decision be one which a reasonable shareholder could have considered to be in the interests of the company. Or, to put it another way, if the court is of the view that no reasonable shareholder could have thought that the decision was in the interests of the company, it is unlikely to accept the majority's evidence that they did so believe.

The main legal issue which remains, outside the expropriation cases, is whether the courts' deference to the views of the controller applies also in the case where it is not possible to identify a corporate benefit arising from the change in the articles and the dispute is really between two groups of shareholders as to how their relations should be regulated by the articles. An attempt to answer this question was made by the Court of Appeal in *Greenhalgh v Arderne Cinemas Ltd.*[35] This case marked the conclusion of a 10-year battle between the claimant, Greenhalgh, and one Mallard and his associates who had enlisted the aid of Greenhalgh when the company needed financial support. As a result Greenhalgh then became the controlling share-holder and a director. However, after a few years, thanks to an adroit series of manoeuvres orchestrated by Mallard (which had already led to no less than six actions, three of which had been taken to the Court of Appeal)[36] Greenhalgh had been ousted from his control and his seat on the board. But he was still a shareholder and, as such, had pre-emptive rights under the articles if any other shareholder wanted to sell to a non-member. This the Mallard faction now wished to do because Mallard had negotiated a deal with another entrepreneur to take over the company. To enable the deal to go through, they had to circumvent Greenhalgh's pre-emptive rights and this they sought to do by amending the articles by a special resolution which provided

---

[35] [1951] Ch. 286, CA and [1950] 2 All E.R. 1120 where the judgment of Evershed M.R. is reported more fully.

[36] The three are: *Greenhalgh v Mallard* [1943] 2 All E.R. 234, CA; *Greenhalgh v Arderne Cinemas Ltd* [1946] 1 All E.R. 512, CA; and *Greenhalgh v Mallard* [1947] 2 All E.R. 255, CA. A fuller account of the whole saga was recounted in earlier editions (4th ed. at pp.624–627) but is omitted here as largely of historical interest only; it is thought that today anyone treated as Greenhalgh was would be able to nip it in the bud by invoking s.994: see Ch.20, below.

that, despite the pre-emptive rights, "any member may, with the sanction of an ordinary resolution ... transfer his shares ... to any person named in such resolution as the proposed transferee and the directors shall be bound to register any transfer which has been so sanctioned". Having secured the passage of this special resolution, they then passed an ordinary resolution sanctioning transfers to the purchaser. Thereupon Greenhalgh instituted this, his seventh, action, claiming a declaration that the resolutions had not been passed bona fide in the interests of the company as a whole. This, too, went to the Court of Appeal—and, again, Greenhalgh lost.

19–8   In his judgment,[37] Evershed M.R., in a dictum which has been widely cited in judgments throughout the Commonwealth, said:[38]

> "In the first place, I think it is now plain that 'bona fide for the benefit of the company as a whole' means not two things, but one thing.[39] It means that the shareholder must proceed on what, in his honest opinion, is for the benefit of the company as a whole. The second thing is that the phrase, 'the company as a whole' does not (at any rate in such a case as the present) mean the company as a commercial entity, distinct from the corporators; it means the corporators as a general body. That is to say, the case may be taken of an individual hypothetical member and it may be asked whether what is proposed is, in the honest opinion of those who voted in its favour, for that person's benefit."

On the face of it, what this is saying is that, whenever members vote on a resolution, they must ask themselves whether the proposal is beneficial not only to themselves but to a hypothetical member who, presumably, has no personal interest apart from that of being a member and (if such be the case) a shareholder.[40] If their honest answer is that it would not be in the hypothetical member's interest they should vote against (if they vote at all) and, presumably, if their answer is that it would be for the hypothetical member's interest they should vote for it (if they vote at all), even though convinced that it would be against their own interests. If that is correct, the only safe course seems to be for every member to refrain from voting unless he is satisfied that he is the paradigm hypothetical member—for no one has yet suggested that a member is bound to exercise his votes.[41]

---

[37] With which Asquith and Jenkins L.JJ. concurred.

[38] [1951] Ch. at 291.

[39] i.e. not "(i) bona fide" and (ii) "for the benefit of the company as a whole" but a single "bona fide for the company as a whole".

[40] This interpretation was expressly adopted by McLelland J. in *Australian Fixed Trusts Pty Ltd v Clyde Industries Ltd* [1959] S.R. (N.S.W.) 33 at 56.

[41] In this respect there would seem to be a difference between the position of a member and that of a director at a directors' meeting; the latter, if present at the meeting, could not, by abstaining, evade his duty to act in the interests of the company.

One can see that such a conclusion might conceivably be reasonable (a) in relation to a small family concern which was, in reality, an incorporated partnership and (b) in relation to directors voting as members at general meetings. But in other situations it seems utterly unrealistic. Even if the onus of proof that members had not asked themselves the suggested question was placed on those attacking the validity of the resolution, there would be little difficulty in the case of a resolution voted on at a meeting of a large public company in finding numerous small shareholders honest enough to confess that it had never occurred to them to ask themselves anything of the sort. The impracticability of the formula suggested by Evershed M.R. seems to have worried him; for he went on to say:

> "I think that the matter can, in practice, be more accurately and precisely stated by looking at the converse and by saying that a special resolution of this kind would be liable to be impeached if the effect of it were to discriminate between the majority shareholders and the minority shareholders, so as to give the former an advantage of which the latter were deprived."

That, however, seems to go to the other extreme; for all it appears to do is to reiterate that members of the same class must generally be treated alike. That principle[42] seems to have no connection with the concept of "bona fide in the interests of the company" unless what Evershed M.R. meant was that resolutions could be impeached if they were intended to enable the majority to deprive the minority (but not the majority) of an advantage. But clearly he did not mean that. In all the expropriation cases that is precisely what the majority had done. In some, it was held that the resolution could not be impeached since it was in the interests of the company as a whole, while in others the resolution was impeached because it was not in the company's interests. In none was there any overt distinction, in the resolution itself, discriminating against the minority. And in the instant case the majority were given an advantage of which the minority were deprived, in the shape of the freedom to transfer their shares to whomsoever they pleased. Despite the frequency with which Lord Evershed's judgment is cited, the guidance which can be obtained from it is limited. As was pointed out by the High Court of Australia in its famous inter-war decision, *Peter's American Delicacy Co Ltd v Heath*,[43] the "bona fide in the interests of the company" test is not a

---

[42] But which Goulding J., in *Mutual Life v Rank Organisation* [1985] B.C.L.C. 11, held did not mean that there could be no discrimination so long as directors acted fairly as between different shareholders.

[43] (1939) 61 C.L.R. 457. A fortiori the test is not useful if the group in question is made up of a number of distinct sub-groups: *Redwood Master Fund Ltd v TD Bank Europe Ltd* [2006] 1 B.C.L.C. 149, not an expropriation case and involving a "class" of creditors rather than of shareholders, but applying the same principles.

useful one in the context of a conflict purely between two groups of shareholders as to how their respective rights and liabilities should be adjusted.

19–9   Overall, it is suggested:

> (a) that if it is desired to keep an objective element in the test as it applies to compulsory transfers at a fair price, then that objective test should recognise both benefits conferred on as well as the avoidance of harms to the company, and that benefits conferred on or harms avoided by the company will necessarily be benefits conferred on or harms avoided by the shareholders, as far as the increase in corporate wealth is reflected in the value of their shares.[44]

> (b) That outside the area of compulsory transfers but where the majority's purpose is to benefit the company (either positively or negatively) it should be enough that the majority has acted in good faith, as is the dominant trend in the English decisions.

> (c) That in cases of conflicts between or among groups of shareholders, where no corporate interest is engaged, the best approach is to apply a test of fairness, on the lines of the test used in the statutory unfair prejudice jurisdiction, considered in the next chapter and which, therefore, would be likely to be the forum of choice for this third class of case.[45]

Voting at class meetings

19–10   The rules discussed above apply not only to decisions by the shareholders at large but also to votes at meetings of classes of shareholders, where it is sometimes possible to give the test a more precise meaning. *Holders Investment Trust, Re*[46] concerned a capital reduction scheme requiring the confirmation of the court. Confirmation was refused because the resolution of a class meeting of the preference shareholders had been passed as a result of votes of trustees who held a large block of the preference shares but a still larger block of ordinary shares. Had the refusal been on the ground that the court was not satisfied that the scheme was fair to both classes there would

---

[44] The CLR thought that in applying the principle to alterations of the articles no attempt should be made to distinguish between alterations involving an expropriation of shares and those not: Completing, para.5.98.

[45] The CLR in fact considered excluding the principle developed in the above cases entirely from a reformed company law and relying solely on s.994 and its proposed rule to exclude interested directors from voting on resolutions whether to enforce or ratify breaches of directors' duties. In the end, however, it recommended that the principle be retained. Completing, paras 5.94–5.101; Final Report I, paras 7.52–7.62.

[46] [1971] 1 W.L.R. 583.

have been nothing remarkable about the decision; as we shall see later[47] the courts, which normally regard a majority vote of members as cogent evidence that the scheme is fair, are rightly hesitant to do so where the majority vote of one class has resulted from the votes of members who also belong to another class. But Megarry J. approached the matter on the basis that he first had to be satisfied that the resolution of the preference shareholders had been validly passed bona fide in the interest of that class. He held that it had not, because the trustees had taken advice as to how, as trustees, they should vote and had been advised that in the interest of their beneficiaries they should vote for the resolution. This they did, admittedly without any consideration of what was in the best interest of the preference shareholders as a whole.[48] This case is also interesting in that it confirms the view taken in an earlier case[49] that, in relation to class meetings, it is the interest of the class rather than that of "the company as a whole" that has to be considered.

Class Rights

We have already noted that the principle discussed in the previous **19–11** section applies to class meetings as well as to general meetings of the shareholders. Now we need to turn to the question of when separate meetings of classes of shareholders are required and how the class in question is defined. Under the company's constitution the approval of a class of shareholders may be required to make a decision binding on the company, normally in addition to a decision of the shareholders generally. However, we are interested at this point in mandatory requirements in company law for the separate consent of shareholders particularly affected by a proposed resolution. As we shall see, the principle of separate consent is well-established in relation to proposed alterations of the articles where these alterations may affect the "rights" of a class of members.

---

[47] Para.29–8.

[48] Contrast *Rights & Issues Investments Trust v Stylo Shoes Ltd* [1965] Ch. 250 where there was an unsuccessful attack on the validity of a resolution which, on the issue of further shares to one class, increased the votes of another class to preserve the existing balance of control. That other class had refrained from voting and the court held that there had been no "oppression" of or "discrimination" against some part of the members. Both classes had decided that it was for the benefit of the company to preserve the existing balance.

[49] *British American Nickel Corp v O'Brien* [1927] A.C. 369, PC which seems to suggest that the obligation of a class member to consider the interest of the class as a whole is greater than that of a member voting at a general meeting to consider the interest of the company as a whole. There seems to be no reason why that should be so and there is nothing in the judgment of Megarry J. to suggest that there is any such difference.

The procedure for varying class rights

19–12   Where the proposed alteration of the articles involves "the variation of the rights attached to a class of shares", then additional protective provisions come into play beyond the supermajority provisions of section 21. The protective technique deployed in sections 630 and 631 consists of requiring the separate consent of the class, usually by way of a 75 per cent majority, to any proposal to alter the articles in such a way as would vary their class rights. It is a very important protective technique. Without it, the protected class might be swamped by the votes of other classes of shareholders. Indeed, the class in question might not otherwise have any say in the matter at all, if, for example, they were a class of non-voting shareholders. Preference shares are often non-voting, at least if their dividends are being paid on time, and classes of non-voting ordinary shares are not unknown. The alteration of their rights would otherwise be a matter entirely for the voting shareholders. Thus, the sections ensure that the class in question have in effect a veto over the change proposed, even if the company's constitution provides them with no right to vote on the issue. Of course, the alteration of the articles must also be approved in the normal way under section 21 (approval by a three-quarters majority of those shareholders entitled to vote under the company's articles) but that is not normally a problem in the cases which we consider in this section.

The predecessors to the current sections were introduced in 1980 and were intended to clear up a problem which existed before that date about the correct procedure for the variation of class rights contained in the articles. It was clear before 1980 that if the articles contained a procedure for the variation of class rights, that procedure had to be followed if a variation was to be validly effected. Moreover, the then applicable model articles contained a variation of class rights procedure which, no doubt, was incorporated into the articles of many companies. That article required "the consent in writing of the holders of three-fourths of the issued shares of that class or ... the sanction of an extraordinary resolution passed at a separate general meeting of the holders of the shares of that class". Where, however, the model article was excluded, it was unclear whether class rights were not variable at all without the consent of each individual shareholder affected or whether they could be varied simply by using the normal variation procedure set out in what is now s.21, which would give the minority members of the class very little protection.[50]

---

[50] For example, under the articles of association of the particular company, the class affected by the proposal might have no right to attend and vote at a general meeting of the company. Nevertheless, in *Cumbria Newspapers Group Ltd v Cumberland & Westmorland Herald Ltd* [1987] Ch. 1, Scott J. took the view that this was the position, but by then the legislation had been introduced. The current draft model articles contain no variation of rights procedure, so that, in effect, the statute has become the default model.

Moreover, the Act now cures a deficiency of its predecessor by applying both to companies with share capital and those without.[51]

The statutory provisions on variation in the 2006 Act are now considerably simpler than those contained in the 1985 Act, whose provisions varied according to whether the rights were attached to the shares by the memorandum or by the articles (or, indeed, elsewhere); whether there was a variation of rights clause in the articles or memorandum of association or not; whether variation was expressly prohibited; whether the variation of rights clause, assuming there was such, was in the articles when the company was incorporated; and according to whether the variation was concerned with the allotment of shares or a reduction of capital.

Section 630 in effect lays down a single default rule, with equivalent **19–13** provision being made in section 631 for companies without shares. Variation of the rights attached to a class of shares requires the consent of three-quarters of the votes cast at a separate meeting of that class or a written resolution having the support of holders of three-quarters of the nominal value of the class (excluding treasury shares) (section 630(4)). That default rule may be displaced by explicit provisions in the company's articles, which may set a higher or a lower standard.[52] This is very straightforward and is enough to deal with most cases which will arise.

The complexity of the section, such as it is, derives from its attempt to answer the question of what rules should govern any attempt to amend the procedure in the articles for the variation of class rights, if the articles contain such a procedure. If the variation procedure in the articles could be freely amended in the same way as any other article of the company, the protection intended to be afforded by the articles to the class could easily be undermined. The section begins by stating that any amendment to the variation procedure contained in the articles itself attracts the provisions protecting class rights (section 630(5)).[53] Without this provision, a variation procedure in the articles requiring a higher level of consent could be reduced to, or even below, the level of the statutory default by simply following the requirements of section 21 for general alterations to the articles (for example, no class meeting). This will not be possible as a result of section 630(5), unless, presumably, the articles themselves expressly provide a less demanding way of amending the variation procedure than the default rule in the statute.

The same subsection also treats as a variation of class rights the

---

[51] s.630 (companies with shares) and s.631 (those without). The previous editions of this book had criticised the omission of companies not limited by shares. The CLR recommended that the legislation be extended to all companies: Final Report I, para.7.28.

[52] s.630(2). The CLR would have permitted the articles to set only a higher standard: Developing, para.4.150.

[53] Both in relation to variation of rights and amendments to variation procedures, variation includes abrogation: s.630(6). Class rights and variation procedures contained in the memorandums of existing companies are be treated as being contained in the articles: s.28.

introduction of a variation procedure into the articles, for that might set a lower standard than the statutory default rule previously applicable. Finally, the section is without prejudice "to any other restrictions on the variation of rights".[54] This appears to mean that a company could use the entrenchment mechanism of section 22[55] to set an even higher requirement for amendments to the variation procedure contained in the articles than that otherwise required by section 630. For example, the articles could provide that amendments to the variation procedure require the consent of all the members of the class.

19–14   So far, we have observed that the statutory provisions on class rights use two protective techniques, at least on a default basis: a separate meeting of the class (the main protection) and the super-majority protection of a three-quarters majority to obtain an effective decision of the class meeting. However, section 633 also makes use of a third technique analysed in the first part of this chapter, namely, court review of the majority's decision. This acknowledges the fact that, even within a class meeting, it is possible for the majority of the class to act opportunistically towards the minority of the class. Section 633 may be particularly useful where the articles adopt a variation procedure considerably less demanding than the default statutory one. As we have seen,[56] those voting at class meetings are subject to the general common law requirement to act "bona fide in the interest of the class", but s.633 (with equivalent provisions in section 634 for companies limited by guarantee) goes further. It affords a dissenting minority of not less than 15 per cent of the issued shares of a class,[57] whose rights have been varied in manner permitted by s.630, a right to apply to the court to have the variation cancelled. Application must be made within 21 days after the consent was given or the resolution passed but can be made by such one or more of the dissenting shareholders as they appoint in writing. Once such an application is made the variation has no effect unless and until it is confirmed by the court. If, after hearing the applicant "and any other persons who apply to be heard and appear to the court to be interested",[58] the court is satisfied that the variation would unfairly prejudice[59] the shareholders of the class represented by the applicant, it may disallow the variation but otherwise must confirm it.[60] It is

---

[54] s.630(3).

[55] Discussed below at para.19–21.

[56] See above, para.19–10.

[57] Provided that they have not consented to or voted in favour of the resolution—an unfortunately worded restriction which effectively rules out nominees who have not exercised all their votes in one way.

[58] This clearly includes representatives of other classes affected and of the company.

[59] This is the same expression as that used in Part 30 (see Ch.20, below) which would seem to provide a better alternative remedy not demanding 15 per cent support and strict time limits and with a wider range of orders that the court can make.

[60] s.633(5). The company must within 15 days after the making of an order forward a copy to the Registrar: s.635.

expressly provided that "the decision of the court is final",[61] which presumably means that it cannot be taken to appeal.[62]

The dearth of reported cases on s.633, and earlier versions of it, suggests that applications under it are made rarely if at all. Nevertheless, it probably serves a useful purpose in specifically drawing the attention of boards of directors to the need to ensure that variations of class rights treat classes fairly. But, should they ignore that warning, they are more likely to face an application under Part 30 rather than under s.633.

The sections analysed above provide a procedure whereby the company can vary class rights. Sometimes, a variation of class rights is effected by an order of the court. Section 632 makes it clear that the courts' powers under Part 26 of the Act (dealing with arrangements and reconstructions (see Chapter 29) and Part 30 (unfair prejudice—see the following Chapter) and, less important, section 98 (cancellation of resolution of public company to re-register as private) are not affected by sections 630 and 631.

What constitutes a "variation"

Although the Act deals at some length with the procedure to be followed to vary class rights, it tells one very little, if anything, about what a variation of class rights is or, indeed, what a class right is. Both these matters are defined principally by the common law. As a matter of logic, however, there is no need to identify the procedure for varying class rights until such time as one is sure that what one is dealing with is something which can be classified as a variation of a class right. We will look first at "variation" and then at "class right".

19–15

Prior to the enactment of the statutory provisions it seems to have been widely assumed that variation of class rights in accordance with the articles required class consent only of the class whose rights were being altered in a manner adverse to that class. Thus, if there were two classes of ordinary shares, one of which had restricted voting rights or none at all, the separate consent of that class was not

---

[61] s.633(5).

[62] This was certainly the intention of the Greene Committee on whose recommendation the section was based: Cmnd. 2657, para.23. But the need for speedy finality seems no greater than on an application under the general unfair prejudice provisions where there is no such provision and cases can be taken to the House of Lords. But if the application under s.633 is struck out on the ground that the time-limit was not complied with, that can be taken to appeal and was in *Suburban Stores Ltd, Re* [1943] Ch.156, CA. See also *Sound City (Films) Ltd, Re* [1947] Ch.169 which seems to be the only officially reported case on the predecessors to section 633. Cases in which it might have been invoked (e.g. *Rights & Issues Investment Trust v Stylo Shoes Ltd* [1965] Ch.250) have been taken instead under the unfair prejudice sections or earlier versions of those sections.

necessary if what was proposed was the enfranchisement of their shares without any reduction of their other rights.[63] But it is very difficult to believe that "variation" (even if coupled with the statement that it includes "abrogation") can reasonably be construed as "*adverse variation*" and it is submitted that, to avoid any subsequent attack on the validity of the resolution, the formal consent of the benefited class should be obtained.

However, the real problem lies where the class is adversely affected by what is proposed, but the courts, by placing an extraordinarily narrow construction on what constitutes a variation of rights, have failed to bring the proposal within the class rights provisions of the statute or the articles. Thus, the House of Lords in *Adelaide Electric Co v Prudential Assurance*[64] held that the alteration in the place of payment of a preferential dividend from England to Australia did not vary the rights of the preference shareholders notwithstanding that the Australian pound was worth less than the English. A subdivision[65] or increase[66] of one class of shares was held not to vary the rights of another class notwithstanding that the result was to alter the voting equilibrium of the classes.

19–16 It has also been held that, where preference shares were non-participating as regards dividend but participating as regards capital on a winding-up or reduction of capital, a capitalisation of undistributed profits in the form of a bonus issue to the ordinary shareholders was not a variation of the preference shareholders' rights notwithstanding that the effect was to deny them their future participation in those profits on winding up or reduction.[67] In the contrary situation, where the shares were participating as regards dividends but not in relation to return of capital on a winding-up, a reduction of capital by

---

[63] Nor, it seems, would the separate consent of a class with one vote per share be needed if another with one vote per hundred shares was to be given one vote per share. On the construction placed by the courts on the meaning of "variation" (see the cases cited in fn.64–70, below), their rights to one vote per share would not be "varied".

[64] [1934] A.C. 122, HL.

[65] *Greenhalgh v Arderne Cinemas* [1946] 1 All E.R. 512, CA, where the result of the subdivision was to deprive the holder of one class of his power to block a special resolution.

[66] *White v Bristol Aeroplane Co* [1953] Ch.65, CA; *John Smith's Tadcaster Brewery Co, Re* [1953] Ch.308, CA.

[67] *Dimbula Valley (Ceylon) Tea Co v Laurie* [1961] Ch.353. On the meaning of "participation" in this context see para.23–7 and on bonus shares see para.11-18. And see the startling decision in *Mackenzie & Co Ltd, Re* [1916] 2 Ch.450 which implies that a rateable reduction of the nominal values of preference and ordinary capital (which participated *pari passu* on a winding up) did not modify the rights of the preference shareholders notwithstanding that the effect was to reduce the amount payable to them by way of preference dividend while making no difference at all to the ordinary.

repayment of irredeemable preference shares in accordance with their rights on a winding-up (ie at their nominal value) was not regarded as a variation or abrogation of their rights, even though the share-holders were deprived of valuable dividend rights.[68] Even if the dividend rights of the preference shareholders were fixed, those rights might be valuable, if interest rates had fallen after the issuance of the preference shares. The obvious unfairness of this led to a contractual solution: the practice of providing, on issues by public companies of preference shares which are non-participating in a winding-up, that on redemption or any return of capital the amount repaid should be tied to the average quoted market price of the shares in the months before (the market price reflecting the value of the dividend rights rather than the nominal value of the shares). This, so-called "Spens formula", named after its inventor, affords reasonable protection in the case of listed companies but preference shareholders in unquoted companies still remain at risk.

Finally, an issue of further shares ranking *pari passu* with the existing shares of a class was not regarded as a variation of rights.[69] And, where there were preference and ordinary shares, an issue of preferred ordinary shares ranking ahead of the ordinary but behind the preference was not a variation of the rights of either existing class.[70] The principle applied in all the above cases was that the formal rights of the complaining shareholders had not been varied, even if the change had adversely affected the value of those rights.

Presumably the courts will continue to follow this restrictive interpretation of variation of rights clauses in the articles and will apply it in relation to section 630, for there is nothing in the wording of that section which constrains them to do otherwise. However, just as it is possible for the articles to require a variation procedure which is more demanding than the statutory default procedure in terms, for example, of the level of approval required, so it is possible for the articles to require a wider range of variations to be subject to the procedure than the statute requires. Thus, in the wake of the decisions on reduction of capital referred to in the previous paragraph, it became common to introduce special provisions into a company's

---

[68] *Scottish Insurance Corp v Wilson & Clyde Coal Co* [1949] A.C. 462, HL; *Prudential Assurance Co v Chatterly Whitfield Collieries* [1949] A.C. 512, HL; *Saltdean Estate Co Ltd, Re* [1968] 1 W.L.R. 1844; *House of Fraser v AGCE Investments Ltd* [1987] A.C. 387, HL (Sc.); *Hunting Plc, Re* [2005] 2 B.C.L.C. 211. But contrast *Old Silkstone Collieries Ltd, Re* [1954] Ch.169, CA where confirmation of the repayment was refused because it would have deprived the preference shareholders of a contingent right to apply for an adjustment of capital under the coal nationalisation legislation.

[69] This was expressly provided in Table A 1948, art.5 (but not subsequently). But the position seems to be the same in the absence of express provision: see the cases cited above, but contrast *Schweppes Ltd, Re* [1914] 1 Ch.322, CA, which, however, concerned s.45 of the 1908 Act, which forbade "interference" with the "preference or special privileges" of a class.

[70] *Hodge v James Howell & Co* [1958] C.L.Y. 446, CA, *The Times*, December 13, 1958.

articles to protect preference shareholders. In *Northern Engineering Industries Plc, Re*[71] a clause in the articles deeming a reduction of capital to be a variation of rights was upheld and enforced when the company proposed to cancel its preference shares. But very clear wording will have to be used if such a provision is to be construed as affording any greater safeguards. In *White v Bristol Aeroplane Co*[72] and *John Smith's Tadcaster Brewery Co, Re*,[73] the relevant clauses referred to class rights being "affected, modified, dealt with or abrogated". At first instance Danckwerts J.[74] held that bonus issue to the ordinary shareholders could not be made without the consent of the preference shareholders because, although their rights would not be abrogated or varied, they would be "affected" since their votes would be worth less in view of the increased voting power of the ordinary shareholders. But the Court of Appeal reversed his decisions. They said that the rights of the preference shareholders would not be affected; the rights themselves—to one vote per share in certain circumstances—remained precisely as before. All that would occur was that their holders' enjoyment of those rights would be affected. If that eventuality was to be guarded against, more explicit wording would have to be used, making it clear that the clause was intended to protect economic interests as well as rights.

It seems, therefore, that if section 630 is effectively to prevent class rights from being "affected as a matter of business",[75] it is necessary to find a formula for a variation of rights clause which will expressly operate in relation to an alteration which affects the enjoyment of their rights (as opposed to the rights themselves). In the absence of such a clause in the model articles, however, such rights are likely to be granted by companies only if it is thought that the securities on offer would not otherwise be acceptable to potential purchasers or, at least, not acceptable at the price the company wishes to issue them at.

The definition of class rights

19–17   Even before one arrives at the question of what is a variation of a class right, one needs to know what a class right is. This is a matter

---

[71] [1994] 2 B.C.L.C. 704, CA. It was for this reason that the CLR did not propose to change the approach adopted by the courts: Completing, para.5.81.

[72] [1953] Ch.65, CA.

[73] [1953] Ch.308, CA.

[74] Only his judgment in the latter case is fully reported: see [1952] 2 All E.R. 751.

[75] The words are those of Greene M.R. in *Greenhalgh v Arderne Cinemas* [1946] 1 All E.R. at 518.

upon which there is a surprising degree of doubt. Section 629 tells us that shares are to be regarded as of one class if the rights attached to them "are in all respects uniform" so that merely attaching different names to groups of shares does not turn them into different classes of share if the rights attached to them are the same.[76] This definition of a class of shares applies to the Act generally, not just in relation to the variation of class rights.

Beyond that, the statute gives no help. It does not even state expressly, as section 127(1) of the 1985 Act did, that class rights can arise only if there is more than one class of share. It seems likely that no change was intended on this point, since, where there is only one class of share, section 21 (alteration of the articles) and section 630 (variation of class rights) would overlap to an unacceptable extent, if section 630 applied in this case as well. However, assuming two or more classes of share, what is then a class right? The choices range from only the rights attached to any one of the classes which are unique to it (i.e. not held in common with any of the other classes of share) to all the rights attached to any of the classes. An intermediate position adds to the first group the core rights of shareholders (relating to voting, dividends and return of capital on a winding-up) whether or not those rights are unique to the class in that particular case. There is little authority on the choice to be made, though in *Cumbrian Newspapers Group Ltd v Cumberland and Westmoreland Newspaper and Printing Co Ltd*[77] Scott J. seemed to favour the first and narrowest view. The second view might be thought to protect more adequately the expectations of shareholders. On the first and narrowest view a shareholder seeking protection of dividend, voting and return of capital rights which were not unique to the class would have to ensure that there was a variation of rights clause in the articles and that that clause defined class rights in an appropriately broad way. This seems undesirable. The right to class consent at least for the variation of core rights would be what companies and, for example, preference shareholders would expect and the law should give effect to that expectation.

Whilst this basic issue about the definition of a class right continues unresolved, a more sophisticated aspect of the same question has been considered judicially and has received a surprisingly liberal

---

[76] This definition does not solve all the problematic cases. Suppose the only difference between the classes is a difference in par values (thought by the Court of Appeal in *Greenhalgh v Arderne Cinemas Ltd* [1946] 1 All E.R. 512, CA to be enough to create separate classes); or suppose the par values are the same but some shares are fully paid-up and others only partly. The statute provides that its definition is satisfied even if the rights to dividends of shares in the twelve months after allotment are different from those of other shares with otherwise similar rights—as they might be if additional shares were issued part-way through a financial year.

[77] [1987] Ch.1, 15. Earlier editions of this book have argued for the second view. For a full discussion see E. Ferran, *Company Law and Corporate Finance* (Oxford: OUP, 1999) pp.337–340.

response. The question is whether there are class rights where nominally the shares are of the same class but special rights are conferred on one or more members without attaching those rights to any particular shares held by that member or members. This was the question facing Scott J. in the *Cumbrian Newspapers* case.[78] Two companies, publishing rival provincial weekly newspapers in an area where it had become apparent that only one was viable, entered into an arrangement designed to ensure that one of the companies (company A) would publish that one newspaper but that it would issue 10 per cent of its ordinary share capital[79] to the other company (company B). Company B was anxious to ensure that the paper should remain locally owned and controlled and to this end the articles of company A were amended in such a way as to confer on company B pre-emptive rights in the event of any new issue of shares by company A or on a disposal by other shareholders of their shares in company A. These rights were not attached to any particular shares but conferred on company B by name. Further, another new article provided that: "If and so long as [company B] shall be the holder of not less than one-tenth in nominal value of the issued ordinary share capital of" company A, company B "shall be entitled from time to time to nominate one person to be a director of" company A. Company A's articles contained a variation of rights clause. Eighteen years later, company A's directors proposed to convene a general meeting to pass a special resolution deleting the relevant articles. Company B thereupon applied to the court for a declaration that company B's rights were class rights that could not be abrogated without its consent.

19–18   Scott J. pointed out that special rights contained in articles could be divided into three categories.[80] First, there are rights annexed to particular shares. The classic example of this is where particular shares carry particular rights not enjoyed by others, e.g. in relation to "dividends and rights to participate in surplus assets on a winding up".[81] These clearly were "rights attached to [a] class of shares" within the meaning of s.630. He also held that this category would include cases where rights were attached to particular shares issued to a named individual but expressed to determine upon transfer by that individual of his shares.

The second category was where the articles purported to confer rights on individuals not in their capacity as members or shareholders.[82] Rights of this sort would not be class rights for they would

[78] [1987] Ch.1, 15.
[79] It also had preference shares but nothing turned on that. Clearly an attempt to vary their class rights would have been subject to the equivalent of s.630.
[80] [1987] 1 Ch. at 15A–18A.
[81] [1987], 1 Ch. at 15.
[82] He instanced *Eley v Positive Life Assurance Co* (1875) 1 Ex.D. 20, on which see para.3–16, above. It seems clear that in such a case the individual will have no enforceable rights in the absence of an express contract with the company additional to the articles.

not be attached to any class of shares.[83] But company B's rights did not fall within this class; the articles in question were "inextricably connected with the issue to the plaintiff[84] and the acceptance by the plaintiff of the ordinary shares in the defendant".[85]

This left the third category: "rights that, although not attached to any particular shares were nonetheless conferred upon the beneficiary in the capacity of member or shareholder of the company".[86] In his view, rights conferred on company B fell into this category.[87] But did they come within the words in the then equivalent of section 630(1) as "rights attached to any class of shares"? After an analysis of the various legislative provisions and of the anomalies which would result if they did not,[88] he concluded that the legislative intent must have been to deal comprehensively with the variation or abrogation of shareholders' class rights and that he should therefore construe what is now section 630 as applying to categories one and three. He accordingly granted the declaration sought.[89]

It is unclear whether the decision of Scott J. survives under the new Act. In effect, the learned judge treated the expressions "the rights of any class of members" and the "rights ... attached to a class of shares" as synonymous. The former phrase was to be found in section 17(2) of the 1985 Act which has no equivalent in the 2006 Act, as a consequence of the reduction in the role of the memorandum. On the other hand, the latter phrase (now in section 630(1)) does survive and indeed is now supported by the general definition of a class in section 629 (see above) which both refer only to rights being attached to shares.[90] It can thus be argued that the current provisions solve the ambiguity noted by Scott J. by identifying class rights with rights attached to shares, not to shareholders even in their capacity as such.

Other cases

There are some statutory procedures for taking corporate decisions **19–19** which explicitly require the separate consent of each class of shares, for example, Part 26 dealing with schemes of arrangement, where the

---

[83] At 16A–E.
[84] i.e. company B.
[85] At 16G.
[86] At 16A–17A.
[87] At 17. He instanced as other examples, *Bushell v Faith* [1970] A.C. 1099 (above, para.14–18) and *Rayfield v Hands* [1960] Ch.1 (above, para.3–14).
[88] At 18A–22B.
[89] At 22F–G. But he refrained from granting an injunction on the ground that this would "prevent the company from discharging its statutory duties in respect of the convening of meetings" (instancing s.368—though there had not in fact been any requisition by its members under this section). The result was therefore that company A could hold the meeting if it wished but, if the resolution was passed, it would nevertheless be ineffective in the light of the declaration unless company B consented.
[90] A variation of the definition now in s.629 could previously be found in s.128(2) of the 1985 Act but it operated there only to define the circumstances in which notification had to be made to the Registrar of companies.

definition of a "class" of shares is interpreted functionally rather than literally, in contrast with the variation of rights cases.[91]

SELF-HELP

19–20   It is wrong to think that protection for minority shareholders is to be found only in mandatory provisions of company law. Provided the minority shareholder has sufficient bargaining power, which may be at the point the much-needed investment is made in the company, that shareholder may be able to negotiate for protections over and above those to be found in company law. These contractual protections may then be reflected in the company's constitution or in an agreement existing separately from and outside the constitution. A potential minority shareholder, reading the previous pages, would be justified in feeling somewhat gloomy about the extent to which his or her interests are truly protected by the rules there analysed and so might well feel that such contractual protections would be essential. Where class rights are not involved, the scope of the objective controls upon the voting decisions of the majority is still very unclear. Even where class rights are involved, the protection afforded still has its weaknesses, notably the limited view taken by the courts of what constitutes the variation of a class right. Indeed, the statutory class-rights procedure encourages self-help because it sets out only default rules and limited ones at that.[92] Across the board, therefore, there is a considerable incentive to shareholders themselves to provide, in advance of a dispute arising, for a substantive or procedural rule which will govern the case.

Furthermore, the techniques discussed below may be used to control in the interests of minority shareholders any corporate decision, whether that decision needs to be taken by the shareholders or may be taken by the board of the company. As such, the following discussion constitutes a bridge to the statutory unfair prejudice provisions discussed in the following chapter.

Provisions in the constitution
19–21   The articles provide an obvious place in which to locate any agreements reached for the protection of minority shareholders, because the articles bind the company and its members as they exist from time to time (section 33) so that future members are bound by the provisions of the articles protecting the minority without further ado.

---

[91] See below, Ch.29.
[92] See above, para.19–15.

The weakness with protective provisions in the articles is that they are alterable by special resolution of those entitled to vote on shareholder resolutions (section 21). This may provide a way to defeat the expectations of non-voting shareholders or even those of minority voting shareholders, because a previous protection may simply be removed from the articles, at least provided no class rights have been created. The Act itself suggests one possible solution to the risk of future amendment, namely, use of the entrenchment powers contained in section 22. Under this section a provision in the articles can be declared to be alterable only through a more restrictive procedure than that required for a special resolution under section 21. The entrenchment provision may go so far as to require unanimity for a particular change, though it cannot render the provision unalterable if all the members agree to the change (section 22(3)). Thus, section 22 provides a mechanism whereby a provision protective of the minority can be included in the company's articles and that protective provision can be declared to be alterable only in the desired way, most obviously only if those it is intended to protect agree to the change. However, the entrenchment provision may have a powerful and adverse effect on those it does not benefit and so section 22(2) provides that entrenchment provisions may be included only in the company's articles on formation or, subsequently, with the consent of all the members of the company. Entrenchment is, thus, an essentially small company facility.

Consequently, it may be more attractive to provide the required minority protection in a company already in existence by creating a new class of shares carrying the relevant protection, issuing those shares to the shareholder to be protected, and then including a broad variation of rights clause in the articles, so that, for example, the consent of the protected shareholder becomes necessary for the alteration of the protection. Alternatively, the shareholder may be given in effect control over the taking of any resolutions by the shareholders through provisions which in principle are alterable but in practice cannot be. An example would be a rule that the quorum for a meeting of the shareholders cannot be constituted unless the minority shareholder is present, either in person or by proxy. Thus, the shareholder would be given a veto over decisions of the shareholders, exercisable by refusing to participate in the meeting.[93] This provision would be ineffective where the shareholders decide by written resolution, but in that case it might be possible to provide a solution by requiring the particular shareholder's consent for a written resolution or through weighted voting rights.[94]

---

[93] As we have seen at para.15–30, the courts have been unwilling to undermine such arrangements through use of their powers under s.306 of the Act.

[94] See *Bushell v Faith* (above, para.14–18).

Enforcement of the articles

19–22 Protective provisions in the articles will be an effective way of safeguarding minorities only if they can be enforced. Often the minority shareholder will want to assert that a decision taken in breach of the protective provisions is not binding on the company and that an injunction should be granted to enjoin the company and its directors from acting on the invalid resolution. In principle, such an action should be available since, as we saw in Chapter 3,[95] the articles are enforceable as a contract.

Shareholder agreements

19–24 However, the parties may prefer to proceed by way of an agreement existing outside and separate from the articles. This has the advantage of privacy because such an agreement, unlike the company's constitution, does not have to be filed at Companies House. However, an issue immediately arises as to whether the company can effectively be made party to such an agreement, as it would be if the agreement were embodied in the company's articles. Here, there are two apparently conflicting principles: first, that a company, like any other person, cannot with impunity break its contracts and, secondly, that a company cannot contract out of its statutory power under section 21 to alter its articles by special resolution.

The second proposition was recently favoured by the House of Lords in *Russell v Northern Bank Development Corp Ltd.*[96] It was clear to their lordships that "a provision in a company's articles which restricts its statutory power to alter those articles is invalid"[97] and they applied that principle to the agreement before them, existing outside the articles among the shareholders and to which the company purported to be a party. That agreement provided that no further share capital should be created or issued in the company without the written consent of all the parties to the agreement. Consequently, it would seem that the company cannot validly contract independently of the articles not to alter those articles.[98] However, that proposition is heavily qualified by two further propositions which may render the initial proposition ineffective in practice, at least for those who are well advised.

---

[95] Though there are difficulties, see para.3–18 on "more internal irregularities".
[96] [1992] 1 W.L.R. 588, HL. See Sealy [1992] C.L.J. 437; Davenport (1993) 109 L.Q.R. 553; Riley (1993) 44 N.I.L.Q. 34; Ferran [1994] C.L.J. 343.
[97] At 593.
[98] In this case what was proposed was an increase in the company's authorised capital laid down in the memorandum. Whether the quoted principle applies to all powers conferred on the company by the statute is unclear.

Prior contracts

The first qualification is that the principle of invalidity, laid down in **19–25** *Russell*, does not apply where the company has entered into a previous contract on such terms that for the company to act upon its subsequently altered article would involve it in a breach of the prior contract. In this situation the term of the earlier contract, which would be breached if the company acted upon the altered article, is not invalid. The *Russell* principle is not relevant here because the term in the earlier contract is not broken when the company alters its articles, but only when it acts upon the altered article. Although the case-law has tended to focus on directors' service contracts, its implication for shareholder agreements is that a company would be a party to them and agree not to act in a particular way in the future, provided it did not agree to refrain from amending its articles. Thus, in *Southern Foundries (1926) Ltd v Shirlaw*[99] the company altered its articles so as to introduce a new method of removing directors from office and then used the new method to dismiss the managing director in breach of his 10-year service contract. The managing director successfully obtained damages for wrongful dismissal. The provision as to the term of the service agreement was thus clearly held by the House of Lords to be valid. Lord Porter said: "A company cannot be precluded from altering its articles thereby giving itself power to act upon the provisions of the altered articles—but so to act may nevertheless be a breach of contract if it is contrary to a stipulation in a contract validly made before the alteration."[100] In this case the contract protected a manager but the principle is equally applicable to a contract protecting a shareholder.

The unresolved issue in relation to this first qualification is whether a claimant seeking to enforce his or her contractual rights against the company is confined to the remedy of damages or whether and, if so, how far, injunctive relief is available to enforce the earlier contract. In *Baily v British Equitable Insurance Co*,[101] the Court of Appeal granted a declaration that to act on the altered article would be a breach of the plaintiff's contractual rights. More surprisingly, in *British Murac Syndicate Ltd v Alperton Rubber Co Ltd*[102] Sargant J. went so far as to

---

[99] [1940] A.C. 701, HL.
[100] At 740–741.
[101] [1904] 1 Ch. 373, CA.
[102] [1915] 2 Ch. 186. The case concerned the right of the plaintiff, under both the articles and a separate contract, to appoint two directors to the board so long as he held 5,000 shares in the company. Today, after the *Cumbria Newspaper* decision (see para.19–17, above) the claimant might be protected as the holder of a class right.

grant an injunction to restrain an alteration of the articles which would have contravened the plaintiff's contractual rights. Although Sargant J.'s decision is generally regarded as based upon a misunderstanding of the previous authorities, some sympathy with this approach was expressed by Scott J. in the *Cumbria Newspapers* case,[103] where he said that he could "see no reason why [the company] should not, in a suitable case, be injuncted from initiating the calling of a general meeting with a view to the alteration of the articles." To the extent that injunctive relief is made available in this way not simply to restrain acting upon the altered article but to restrain the operation of the machinery for effecting the alteration itself, the notion that the company cannot validly make a direct contract not to alter its articles becomes hollow. Such an extension of injunctive relief would also contradict the dictum of Lord Porter in *Shirlaw*[104]: "Nor can an injunction be granted to prevent the adoption of the new articles." However, injunctive relief merely to prevent the company acting upon the new articles would not fall foul of this principle.

Binding only the shareholders

19–26 The second qualification is that an agreement among the shareholders alone as to how they will exercise the voting rights attached to their shares is not caught by the principle that a company cannot contract out of its statutory powers to alter its articles. This rule was applied to save the agreement in *Russell*, the House of Lords benignly severing the company from the agreement in question. Lord Jauncy said that "shareholders may lawfully agree *inter se* to exercise their voting rights in a manner which, if it were dictated by the articles, and were thereby binding on the company, would be unlawful".[105] The claimant was granted a declaration as to the validity of the agreement, and it seems that their lordships would have been happy to grant an injunction had the claimant objected substantively to the course of action proposed by the company, as against wishing to establish the principle that his consent to the change was required.[106]

---

[103] See above, fn.77, at 24.
[104] See above, fn.109.
[105] [1992] 1 W.L.R. at 593.
[106] [1992] 1 W.L.R., at 595.

This conclusion flows from the more general proposition that the vote attached to a share is a property right which the shareholder is prima facie entitled to exercise and deal with as he or she thinks fit.[107] Since the company can act only through its members to alter the articles, an agreement binding all the members is as effective as one to which the company is party as well.

However, in one respect a members' agreement is less secure than one which binds the company as well. On a subsequent transfer of a shareholding covered by the agreement the new shareholder will not be bound without his or her express adherence to the agreement among the other shareholders.[108] Nevertheless, the shareholders' agreement does play an important role in establishing the requirement for minority shareholder consent to important changes in the company's financial or constitutional arrangements in situations such as management buy-outs, venture capital investments and joint ventures.[109]

Finally, a device analogous to the voting agreement should be noted. Closely associated with, but more sophisticated than, the voting agreement is the voting trust, not uncommon in the United States but less common in the United Kingdom. Under this, in effect, voting rights are separated from the financial interest in the shares, the former being held and exercisable by trustees while the latter remains with the shareholders. Voting policy then becomes a matter for the trustees, who may use their powers to protect minority shareholders, though the voting trust may be driven by other considerations, such as a desire to make a takeover bid more difficult and thus protect the incumbent management.[110]

[107] On the enforcement of shareholder agreement see *Greenwell v Porter* [1902] 1 Ch. 530 and *Puddephatt v Leith* [1916] 1 Ch. 200, where a mandatory injunction was granted to compel a shareholder to vote in accordance with his agreement. Some shareholder agreements may make their adherents "concert parties", thus triggering provisions which impose obligations on a member of the shareholder group because of the size of the group interest. See paras 26–23, 28–42 and 28–51, below.

[108] cf. *Greenhalgh v Mallard* [1943] 2 All E.R. 234, CA. Of course, the selling shareholder may be contractually bound to secure the adherence of the acquiring shareholder, but even so it is difficult to make the arrangement completely water-tight by purely contractual means, especially at the remedial level.

[109] See, for example, *Growth Management Ltd v Mutafchiev* [2007] 1 B.C.L.C. 645 and, generally, G. Stedman and J. Jones, *Shareholders' Agreements* (London: Sweet & Maxwell, 4th ed., 2004). If the power which it is sought to control is one which is exercisable by the board of directors, it may in addition be necessary to alter the articles so as to shift the power in question to the general meeting or to provide for its exercise by the board only with the consent of the general meeting or to provide that the shareholders shall take all appropriate action to prevent the company taking the steps to which a shareholder, exercising its rights under the agreement, objects.

[110] An offeror, where a trust is in operation, may acquire the majority of the shares but still not be able to dismiss the incumbent management. Such trusts are common in the Netherlands. See Ch.28, below.

CONCLUSION

19–27 The mandatory protections for minority shareholders identified in this chapter are rather patchy. They apply only to voting at general meetings and not to majority control exercised via the board and, even then, only to certain types of shareholder decision. In the case of the "bona fides" requirement for shareholder voting the protection provided manages to be, at once, both limited and uncertain in scope. It is perhaps not surprising that the legislature has attempted make more far-reaching protections available, to the development and current status of which we turn in the next chapter.

CHAPTER 20

UNFAIR PREJUDICE

INTRODUCTION

Section 994(1),[1] the first of only six sections which constitute Part 30 **20–1** of the Act, provides that any member may petition the court for relief on the grounds that:

> "(a) the company's affairs are being or have been conducted in a manner which is unfairly prejudicial to the interest of its members generally or some part of the members (including at least himself) or (b) that any actual or proposed act or omission of the company (including any act or omission on its behalf) is or would be so prejudicial."

This is a very widely drafted provision, which, however, repeats rather than reforms the provisions previously found in section 459 of

---

[1] The procedure for petitions is governed mainly by the Companies (Unfair Prejudice Applications) Proceedings Rules 1986 (SI 1986/2000), which continue in force for the purposes of the new Act (s.1297(3)), but also by the Civil Procedure Rules and the practice of the High Court, where not inconsistent with the 1986 Rules. S.994(1A), somewhat bizarrely, specifically states that the removal of an auditor in certain circumstances falls within (a). The reasons for this provision are dealt with at para.22–19.

the Companies Act 1985. It is clear that the section, by referring to the conduct of the company's affairs, is wide enough to catch the activities of controllers of companies, whether they conduct the business of the company through the exercise of their powers as directors or as shareholders or both. Controlling shareholders are not in terms excluded from using the section but normally any prejudice they are subject to will be remediable through the use of the ordinary powers they possess by virtue of their controlling position, and so the conduct of the minority cannot be said to be in such a case *unfairly* prejudicial to the controllers.[2] The section thus operates as a mechanism for minority protection—or, at least, for the protection of non-controlling shareholders, for petitions are often brought where there is an equal division of shares in the company among two persons. The section even applies to the conduct of corporate groups. Although the conduct of a shareholder, even a majority shareholder, of its own affairs is excluded from the section, nevertheless, where a parent company has assumed detailed control over the affairs of its subsidiary and treats the financial affairs of the two companies as those of a single enterprise, actions taken by the parent in its own interest may be regarded as acts done in the conduct of the affairs of the subsidiary; and in some cases conduct of the subsidiary's business may amount to conduct of the business of the parent.[3] The "outside" shareholders in the subsidiary may thus use the section to protect themselves against exploitation by the majority-shareholding parent company.

The right to petition for relief under section 994 is conferred upon the members of the company, but section 994(2) extends this right to non-members to whom shares have been transferred or transmitted by operation of law. As in the case of the derivative action, where a similar extension applies, this provision is useful in small companies where the directors of the company may exercise the power they have under the articles to refuse to register as a member a person to whom shares have been transferred, especially as section 771 now requires directors to give reasons for their refusal. If not within this extension, however, a non-member will not be able to petition under the section, for example, where the registered shareholder is a nominee and the person with the beneficial interest in the shares seeks to petition.

---

[2] *Legal Costs Negotiators Ltd, Re* [1999] 2 B.C.L.C. 171, CA; *cf. Parkinson v Eurofinance Group Ltd* [2001] 1 B.C.L.C. 720—majority shareholder, removed from the board, not able to use his shareholding to obtain redress in respect of a sale of the company's assets by the directors to a company controlled wholly by them, and so able to use the unfair prejudice provisions.

[3] On conduct of the parent as conduct of the subsidiary see *Nicholas v Soundcraft Electronics Ltd* [1993] B.C.L.C. 360, CA, expanding upon the approach taken in *Scottish Co-operative Wholesale Society Ltd v Meyer* [1959] A.C. 324, HL, by not confining the principle to companies engaged in the same type of business. See also *Dominion International Group (No.2), Re* [1996] 1 B.C.L.C. 634. On conduct of the subsidiary as conduct of the parent see *Rackind v Gross* [2005] 1 W.L.R. 3505.

However, the nominee will be a legitimate petitioner and the interests the nominee may seek to protect include those of the beneficiary.[4]

Section 995 permits the Secretary of State to petition if, as a result of an investigation carried out into a company,[5] he concludes that the affairs of the company have been carried on in a way that is unfairly prejudicial to the members (or some part of them). Finally, when an administration order is in force, section 994 is supplemented by paragraph 74 of Schedule B1 to the Insolvency Act 1986, permitting any creditor or member to apply to the court on the grounds that the administrator has acted in a way which has unfairly harmed the interests of the applicant (or proposes to do so) or on the grounds that the administrator is not performing his functions as quickly or as efficiently as is reasonably practical.[6]

In general, the statutory remedy is capable of ranging very widely **20–2** over the conduct of corporate affairs. It embraces control of both shareholders' voting powers, examined in the immediately preceding Chapter, and directors' powers, examined in Chapter 14. The section posed, moreover, when introduced in its modern form in 1980, a very considerable challenge to the traditionally non-interventionist attitudes of the judges in relation to the internal affairs of companies.[7] The extent to which the modern judges have thrown off that traditional attitude is one of the main underlying themes of this Chapter. It will be suggested that what we have witnessed is a partial revolution in judicial attitudes.

Since the right of petition is drafted in deliberately wide terms, it has presented to the courts an initial problem of defining its scope. It is suggested that three main questions have arisen. First, should the sections be seen as simply aimed at providing a more effective way of remedying harms which, independently of the unfair prejudice pro-

---

[4] *Atlasview Ltd v Brightview Ltd* [2004] 2 B.C.L.C. 191. Also, the conduct of which a petitioner may complain embraces conduct occurring before the petitioner became a member, even if that conduct is not continuing (though it must prejudice the petitioner), so that the beneficial holder will be able to petition if the shares are transferred to him by the nominee: *Lloyd v Casey* [2002] 1 B.C.L.C. 454.

[5] See Ch.18, above. A petition under s.995 may be instead of or in addition to a petition by the Secretary of State to have the company wound up under s.124A of the Insolvency Act (see para.18–10, above) but it is notable that the Companies Act power does not require the Secretary of States to be of the opinion that the public interest would be furthered by the bringing of an unfair prejudice petition. The Secretary of State's power of petition also applies to any company capable of being wound up under the Insolvency Act (including in some cases companies not incorporated in the UK), whilst the general right of petition under section 994 applies only to companies incorporated under the Companies Acts and statutory water companies: s.994(3) and (4).

[6] The Insolvency Act provision is not considered in any detail in this chapter. For administration in general see para.32–44. An unfair prejudice challenge may also be made to proposals adopted by way of a company voluntary arrangement (see s.6 of the Insolvency Act 1986) but the court's powers are here confined to setting aside the proposals adopted at the creditors' meeting and ordering meetings to consider revised proposals.

[7] See the lament of the Lord President (Cooper) in *Scottish Insurance Corp v Wilsons & Clyde Coal Co* 1948 S.C. 376.

visons, are in any case unlawful? This may be termed the "independent illegality" issue. The competing view, which, as we shall see, has
been adopted by the courts and which constitutes one of their most
important contributions to the development of the provisions, is that
the provisions are not concerned simply with better remedies but, in
addition, are designed to render unlawful some types of conduct
which, apart from the sections, are not in any way unlawful. This
approach launches the courts upon a voyage of discovery. Deprived
of the familiar landmarks of established illegalities, what criteria
should the courts deploy in determining whether conduct is unfairly
prejudicial, i.e. unlawful? This is the second main issue which has
faced the courts and it is the one which has absorbed the greatest
amount of judicial thought and effort. It is upon the courts' handling
of this issue that the suggestion that there has been a partial revolution in judicial attitudes largely depends.

However, whether or not the courts extend the range of unfairly
prejudicial conduct beyond conduct which is independently unlawful,
there remains an important issue of the relationship between the
unfair prejudice remedy and the derivative action. When a wrong has
been committed against the company, may a shareholder leap over
the restrictions on bringing a derivative action, formerly contained in
the rule in *Foss v Harbottle* and now set out in the statute[8], by presenting a petition founded upon unfair prejudice and obtaining in this
way a remedy for the company? Or is the petitioner under section 994
confined to the recovery of personal losses? In other words, are the
unfair prejudice petition and the derivative action aimed at redressing
different wrongs and, if so, how does one distinguish between them?
It is this issue with which we shall begin.[9]

UNFAIR PREJUDICE AND THE DERIVATIVE ACTION

20–3 It may seem odd at first sight that a right of petition vested in the
individual member may be used to secure the redress of wrongs done
to the company, especially those committed by its directors. Directors' duties are owed, normally, to the company, not individual
shareholders. However, the provisions are drafted so as to protect the
interests of the members and not just their rights,[10] and it cannot be
denied that a wrong done to the company may affect the interests of
its members. Before the introduction by the 1989 Companies Act of
the words "of its members generally" into s.459 of the 1985 Act, there

---

[8] Analysed in Ch.17, above.
[9] For a penetrating analysis of the problem in a Canadian context, see MacIntosh, "The
Oppression Remedy: Personal or Derivative?" (1991) 70 Can. Bar Rev. 29.
[10] A point to which the courts have attached some importance. See below, para.20–6.

was an argument that a wrong done to the company, which affected all the members equally, fell outside the section,[11] but that argument is no longer available.

The Jenkins Committee, whose report recommended the introduction of the unfair prejudice remedy, envisaged that it would have a role in relation to wrongs done to the company.

> "In addition to these direct wrongs[12] to the minority, there is the type of case in which a wrong is done to the company itself and the control vested in the majority is wrongfully used to prevent action being taken against the wrongdoer. In such a case the minority is indirectly wronged."[13]

However, there is an ambiguity here: did the Committee mean simply that, where a wrong done to the company also has inflicted harm on the shareholder, the member should be able to use section 994 to obtain redress for that personal harm? If so, that seems uncontroversial: there are a number of reported cases under the current legislation in which petitions have been entertained by the courts where the wrongdoers' conduct consisted wholly or partly of wrongs done to the company.[14] The courts have even gone so far as to refuse to accept that the actual availability of a derivative action constitutes a bar to an unfair prejudice petition.[15] As Hoffmann L.J. (as he then was) has said: "Enabling the court in an appropriate case to outflank the rule in *Foss v Harbottle* was one of the purposes of the section."[16]

Alternatively, the Committee may have meant that the court could award relief to the company in a section 994 petition to redress the harm done to it. This approach raises a difficulty in the light of the reforms to the derivative action made by the 2006 Act and discussed in Chapter 17. Thus, the question is, what sort of "outflanking" of the derivative action rules is envisaged? Whereas it may just possibly have been legitimate to view the unfair prejudice remedy as designed

---

[11] The argument was accepted by Vinelott J. in *Carrington Viyella Plc, Re* (1983) 1 B.C.C. 98, 951, though the exact scope of the point was never finally settled.

[12] "Direct wrongs", i.e. where the harm is inflicted directly on the minority and not via a diminution in the value of their stake in the company, are considered below at para.20–8.

[13] Report of the Company Law Committee, Cmnd. 1749 (1962), para.206.

[14] *Stewarts (Brixton) Ltd, Re* [1985] B.C.L.C. 4; *London School of Electronics, Re* [1986] Ch. 211; *Cumana Ltd, Re* [1986] B.C.L.C. 430 (all involving various forms of diversion of the company's business to rival companies in which the majority were interested, i.e. situations of the type found in *Cook v Deeks* [1916] 1 A.C. 553, PC, above, para.439); *A Company Ex p. Glossop, Re* [1988] 1 W.L.R. 1068 (exercise of directors' powers for an improper purpose); *Saul D. Harrison & Sons Plc, Re* [1995] 1 B.C.L.C. 14 (failure of directors to act bona fide in the interests of the company). In not all these cases was the allegation in question made out on the facts. Indeed, so long as the "independent illegality" theory held sway, proving breaches of directors' duties was a way of bringing the controllers' conduct within the unfair prejudice provisions.

[15] *A Company (No.5287 of 1985), Re* [1986] 1 W.L.R. 281; *Stewarts (Brixton) Ltd, Re*, above, fn.14; *Lowe v Fahey* [1996] 1 B.C.L.C. 262.

[16] *Saul D Harrison & Sons Plc, Re*, above, fn.14 at 18.

to overcome the excessively strict limitations on the derivative action imposed by the common law, it will hardly conduce to a coherent reading of the statute to allow the unfair prejudice provisions to be interpreted so as routinely to side-step the reformed statutory regime governing the derivative action. The statutory derivative action rules set out criteria which must be satisfied before the claimant is allowed to proceed against the directors, even if it is likely that the litigation will be successful. This is a recognition that it is not always in the company's interests to enforce its legal rights. Should a shareholder who otherwise would have to convince a judge that it was in the interests of the company that he or she should be allowed to continue a derivative action be able to secure a hearing on the merits of the corporate claim, simply by commencing the litigation by petition under section 994?

Part 11 of the Act makes it clear that derivative actions can be brought only under its provisions or "in pursuance of an order of the court in proceedings under section 994."[17] However, this is not a general permission for derivative actions to be begun by way of petition under section 994. The reference to "an order of the court" is to one of the court's remedial orders, when an unfair prejudice petition has been successful, namely the power to "authorise civil proceedings to be brought in the name and on behalf of the company by such persons and on such terms as the court may direct." (section 996(2)(c)). This point is made more clearly in the provision relating to Scotland, which says that the derivative action rules in Part 11 "do not affect ... the court's power to make an order under section 996(2)(c)." This wording in fact emphasises the difference between a petition under section 994 and a derivative action, for there would be little need for a subsequent derivative action to be authorised by the court after the petition had succeeded, if corporate relief could normally be granted in the petition itself. Where corporate relief is sought in a derivative action authorised by the court after a successful unfair prejudice petition has been brought, the problem referred to above does not arise acutely, because the court in the exercise of its discretion may have regard to the range of factors listed in Part 11 of the Act. However, it will not normally be attractive for a shareholder to bring a petition to obtain authority to commence a second piece of litigation as opposed to seeking permission directly under Part 11 to commence derivative litigation.

20–4   Even before the statutory reform of the derivative action, some courts were concerned to draw the boundary between the derivative claim and the unfair prejudice petition.[18] An attempt to address this difficult problem by distinguishing between corporate and personal

---

[17] s.260(2). The provision for Scotland is in s.265(6)(b).
[18] For a trenchant analysis of the issue on the law as it stood prior to the 2006 Act see A. Reisberg (2005) 16 *European Business Law Review* 1065.

loss was made by Millett J. in *Charnley Davies Ltd (No.2), Re,*[19] which involved a petition under the Insolvency Act claiming that the administrator had broken his duty of care to the company by selling its business at an undervalue and ought to pay compensation to the company. Whilst holding that on the facts there had been no breach of duty, he nevertheless went on to consider in dicta the relationship between a petition based on unfair prejudice and the derivative action. The learned judge thought that an allegation that the controllers as directors had broken their duties to the company was not sufficient to found a petition. What needed to be shown was that there was also conduct on the part of the controllers which was unfairly prejudicial to the minority. If the shareholder wished to complain simply of the breach of duty by the directors, this could not be done by petition. The shareholder must sue instead on behalf of the company and subject to the standing restrictions of the derivative action. In the petition the gist of the action is not the wrong done to the company but the disregard by the controllers of the interests of the minority.

The answers to the difficult questions of which complaint the petitioner is seeking to make and of whether the petition is the appropriate vehicle turn very largely on the nature of the remedy sought. In *Charnley Davies, Re* the petition sought compensation for the company, for which, it was said, an unfair prejudice petition was inappropriate, whereas a claim that the controllers purchase the petitioners' shares at an appropriate price would have indicated that the gist of the complaint was unfair prejudice to the minority.[20] In short, the suggestion was that, whilst an unfair prejudice petition might arise out of breaches of duty owed by directors to the company, unfair prejudice to the petitioner was the ground for any relief granted; and the relief that might be claimed in a petition was confined to personal remedies and might not include corporate relief. This approach might be thought to fit in well with the view of the Jenkins Committee[21] that the harm to the shareholders in such cases is "indirect" and that the wrong to them consists, not in the wrong done to the company, but in the controllers' use of their position to prevent action being taken to redress the wrong done to the company. The remedy in the petition should thus address the indirect wrong to the shareholder, not the direct wrong to the company.

Despite this initial caution, there have been a number of subsequent cases at appeal court level in which corporate remedies have been granted in an unfair prejudice petition. In *Anderson v Hogg*[22] the Inner House of the Court of Session (Lord Prosser dissenting)

---

[19] [1990] B.C.L.C. 760.
[20] This is, of course, a remedy very commonly sought by s.459 petitioners (see below, para.20–15).
[21] See above.
[22] 2002 S.L.T. 354, Inner House.

awarded relief to the company, where the unfair prejudice was based
on an unlawful payment by the respondent director of remuneration
to himself. Without detailed consideration of the point, the director
was ordered to return the money to the company. More important,
perhaps, the court came close to rejecting Millett J.'s proposition in
Charnley Davies, Re that proof of illegality on the part of the director
as against the company is not by itself enough to demonstrate unfair
prejudice to the petitioning shareholder. Since that case involved in
essence a two-person company which was in course of solvent
liquidation, the distinction between illegality to the company and
unfairness to the shareholder was in that instance very fine. *Clark v
Cutland*[23] was a somewhat similar case involving a petition about a
two-person company where the controlling director had made large
and unauthorised payments to himself, this time by way of contributions to his pension fund. Although the decision was principally
about other matters, the Court of Appeal did order the unauthorised
payments to be restored to the company and indeed was prepared to
contemplate that, as in a derivative action,[24] the costs of the litigation
should be borne by the company. However, this decision may not be
as dramatic as it seems, since the litigation began as separate derivative and unfair prejudice cases, which were later consolidated into
the unfair prejudice application.[25] Thus, at an early stage in the
derivative action the then applicable standing rules were presumably
satisfied, so that granting corporate relief in the unfair prejudice
petition would not be objectionable on the ground identified above.

20–5   In the corporate opportunity case, *Bhullar v Bhullar*,[26] which we
considered in Chapter 16 and which again concerned a two-person—
or, at least, a two-family company—the litigation was always in the
form of an unfair prejudice petition and, indeed, the petitioners
sought the traditional personal relief in such a petition, namely, the
compulsory purchase of their shares at a fair price by the respondents. However, the initial petition also sought permission to bring a
derivative action in the company's name. The trial judge refused the
compulsory purchase order but ordered direct corporate relief by
declaring the property in question to be held on trust for the company. The Court of Appeal did not demur from this way of proceeding. It may be that in this case the court took the view that the
facts upon which a derivative suit would be based and the petitioner's
standing to sue derivatively had been clearly established in the petition and that it would be simply a waste of time and money to have a
further action commenced by writ, and so corporate relief was

[23] [2004] 1 W.L.R. 783, CA (considered by Payne (2004) 67 M.L.R. 500 and [2005] C.L.J. 647).
[24] See above at para.17–12.
[25] Above, fn.23 at [2].
[26] [2004] 2 B.C.L.C. 241. The early stages of the litigation are recounted at [3]–[4]. See above at
      para.16–68.

granted immediately. However, it is notable that the Court of Appeal did not think it necessary to address this issue.

The most extensive discussion of the principles at issue in this area is to be found a decision of only persuasive authority, *Kung v Kou*, a decision of the Court of Final Appeal of Hong Kong.[27] Although petition in the case was ill-conceived and there were some differences of emphasis in the judgments of Bokhary P.J. and Lord Scott of Foscote N.P.J., the issue of whether an unfair prejudice petition could be used to avoid the standing rules of *Foss v Harbottle* was addressed head-on and answered in the negative. This answer did not mean that allegations of breaches of duty by directors are irrelevant in unfair prejudice proceedings, for example, as a basis for making out a claim for relief to be granted to the member. Nor did it mean that the court can never at the end of an unfair petition hearing grant a remedy in the company's favour. However, in order to do that the court would have to hear both the company's claim and the member's claim together. This would be appropriate only in "rare and exceptional" circumstances (per Bokhary P.J.) or where at the pleading stage of the petition it was clear that "the director's liability at law to the company can conveniently be dealt with in the hearing of the petition" (per Lord Scott of Foscote). Otherwise, the petitioner should seek an order in the petition to bring a derivative action on behalf of the company or, under the new Act, make such an application directly to the court rather than through the unfair prejudice petition.

It is submitted that the decision in *Kung v Kou* is based on the correct principles and that the unfair prejudice petition is normally confined to relief in respect of harm personal to the minority shareholder. It is to the circumstances in which personal harm may be remedied that we now turn.

INDEPENDENT ILLEGALITY

After the emergence of the unfair prejudice petition in its current **20–6** form in 1980 the first question the courts had to consider was whether it was a necessary ingredient of a successful petition that the petitioner should allege that the controllers' acts were independently

---

[27] (2004) 7 HKCFAR 579. The decision was mentioned by the Privy Council in the case of *Gamlestaden Fastigheter AB v Baltic Partners Limited* [2007] B.C.C. 272, PC, where the judgment of the PC, delivered by Lord Scott of Foscote, makes no reference to the restrictive conditions set out in the Hong Kong decision and seems to treat it as a general permission to award damages to the company. Even stranger, the company being hopelessly insolvent, the benefit to the petitioner from any payment by the directors to the company would be obtained only as lender to the company, whose loans would achieve a higher percentage recovery.

unlawful. We will examine that issue together with another limiting factor, the "*qua* member" requirement, which was also inherited from earlier legislation. The unfair prejudice provisions are not the first attempt by Parliament to provide a statutory remedy for the protection of minorities. Section 210 of the 1948 Act was aimed at the same objective, but achieved very limited success because of both limitations in its drafting and narrow interpretation by the courts. Many of those restrictions were removed when the remedy was cast into its modern form in 1980. Most notably, the test for intervention ceased to be "oppression" of the minority by the controllers and became instead that of "unfair prejudice", a clear indication that Parliament intended the courts to take a more active role.

However, the legislature did not deal expressly with two limitations which the courts had built into the oppression remedy by way of interpretation. The first was that s.210 was interpreted as applying only to oppression of the petitioner *qua* member and not in any other capacity. In an early decision under what is now section 994 it seemed that this restriction was going to be transposed with full effect,[28] but it is clear now that the courts take a more flexible view of the requirement. The point is an important one, for under s.210 a very common form of minority oppression, namely expulsion of the minority shareholder from a position on the board, could not give rise to a remedy, for that was oppression *qua* director, not *qua* member.[29] It is now clear that, although the *qua* member restriction remains as part of the unfair prejudice provisions, it is much more flexibly interpreted, so that its practical significance is very much reduced. It is now accepted that the interests of a member, at least in a small company, may be affected by his or her expulsion from the board, whether because it was expected that the return on investment would take the form of directors' fees or because a board position, even in a non-executive role, may be necessary to monitor and protect the member's investment.[30]

The second restriction suggested by judicial interpretation of s.210, although perhaps less well-established than the "*qua* member" requirement, was encapsulated in the definition of "oppression" by the House of Lords as conduct which was "burdensome, harsh *and wrongful*" (emphasis added).[31] This was the point which gave rise to the notion that the oppression section was aimed only at providing better remedies for existing wrongs, and it offered another reason for not regarding the expulsion of the minority from the board as oppressive: in most cases the removal was an exercise of the majority's statutory powers under what is now section 168.[32] The Jenkins

---

[28] *A Company, Re* [1983] Ch. 178.
[29] *Lundie Bros, Re* [1965] 1 W.L.R. 1051; *Westbourne Galleries, Re* [1970] 3 All E.R. 374.
[30] *A Company, Re* [1986] B.C.L.C. 376; *Haden Bill Electrical Ltd, Re* [1995] 2 B.C.L.C. 280.
[31] *Scottish Co-operative Wholesale Society Ltd v Meyer* [1959] A.C. 324.
[32] See above, para.14–18.

Committee recommended that the restriction, if it existed, should be removed,[33] and the courts, from an early stage, have interpreted the substitution of the words "unfairly prejudicial" for "oppressive" as intended to achieve that result.

> "The concept of unfairness which was chosen by Parliament as the basis of the jurisdiction under section [994] in my judgment cuts across the distinction between acts which do or do not infringe the rights attached to the shares by the constitution of the company."[34]

So by the middle of the 1980s the two judicial interpretations which **20–7** had hobbled s.210 had been rejected by the courts in their application of what is now section 994. These were crucial steps, without which the new section might well have been consigned to the limited place which its predecessor had occupied. They put the courts in a position to tackle the second of the tasks envisaged for the new remedy by the Jenkins Committee, that of dealing with reprehensible acts done "directly" to the minority by those in control.[35] However, they were only ground-clearing steps; they gave no clear indication of the nature of the judicial construction which was to be built in the space so cleared.

In modern law, giving courts the power by statute to control the exercise of discretion by persons or institutions on grounds of "unfairness" is hardly novel.[36] Yet such open-ended legislation, which in effect involves a sharing of the legislative function between Parliament and the courts, always presents the courts with the challenge of how to develop on a case-by-case basis criteria by which the imprecise concept of "fairness" can be given operational content. As we remarked above, the challenge was particularly acute for the courts in relation to the unfair prejudice remedy, for the tradition of the courts was not to interfere in the internal affairs of companies. It is to the issue of how that challenge has been met by the courts that we now turn.

LEGITIMATE EXPECTATIONS OR EQUITABLE CONSIDERATIONS

The important steps taken by the courts, as described in the previous **20–8** section, can be characterised by saying that the courts recognised that

---

[33] Above, fn.13, para.203.
[34] Per Hoffmann J. in *A Company (No.8699 of 1985), Re* [1986] B.C.L.C. 382 at 387. This was the position at which the courts had arrived some years previously in the case of petitions to wind up the company. See *Ebrahimi v Westbourne Galleries Ltd* [1973] A.C. 360, HL, below, para.20–17.
[35] Above, fn.13, paras 203–206.
[36] See, for example, the law relating to unfair dismissal of employees by employers, introduced in 1971 and now contained in the Employment Rights Act 1996.

section 994 protects expectations and not just rights. Borrowing from public law, it is sometimes said that the section protects the "legitimate expectations" of the petitioner, though more recently the courts have preferred the private law phrase "equitable considerations".[37] Whatever the language used, the difficult issue is to distinguish those expectations of the petitioner which are to be classified as "legitimate" or which considerations are to fall within the category of "equitable considerations", and so as deserving of legal recognition and protection, from those expectations which the petitioner may harbour as a matter of fact but which the courts will not protect. It is suggested that the decisions of the courts to date have succeeded in identifying one clear class of legitimate expectation and have hinted at a range of other situations where section 994 may be prayed in aid but without developing any of them in a comprehensive way. We shall begin with the clearly established category of legitimate expectation.

Informal arrangements among the members

20–9   This category of legitimate expectation or equitable consideration has been described as follows: it "arises out of a fundamental understanding between the shareholders which formed the basis of their association but was not put into contractual form".[38] What this principle recognises is that the totality of the agreement or arrangements among the members of the company may not be captured in the articles of association. This may be so for a number of reasons, but predominantly, it is suggested, because of a desire to avoid transaction costs when establishing a company or when admitting a new person to membership of the company. It will be cheaper to adopt some standard, or only slightly modified, form of articles rather than to bargain out in detail and then incorporate into the articles a customised set of rules dealing with every aspect of the company's present and likely future method of operation, the future being in any case inherently unpredictable. This is especially likely to be the case for small "quasi-partnership" companies where the incorporators[39] know each other well and may have worked out a

---

[37] "Legitimate expectations" was the phrase endorsed by the Court of Appeal in *Saul D Harrison & Sons Plc, Re* [1995] 1 B.C.L.C. 14 at 19, per Hoffmann L.J. but in *O'Neill v Phillips* [1999] 2 B.C.L.C. 1, HL, the same judge led the House of Lords to adopt the phrase "equitable considerations" for fear that the former phrase carried connotations which were too wide.

[38] [1995] 1 B.C.L.C. 14, at 19.

[39] Though the legitimate expectation often arises when the company is formed, it may arise at a later date, for example, when the petitioner becomes a member: *Tay Bok Choon v Tahanson Sdn Bhd* [1987] 1 W.L.R. 413, PC; *Strahan v Wilcock* [2006] 2 B.C.L.C. 555, CA. Equally, a legitimate expectation based on informal agreement among all the members is most often recognised in a quasi-partnership company, but may arise in any small company, whether the company is to be operated as an incorporated partnership or not: *Elgindata Ltd, Re* [1991] B.C.L.C. 959.

successful method of operation when trading in unincorporated form whose translation into a formal document they would see as a needless expense. However, it would seem that the correct analysis is that a company is a quasi-partnership because of the particular understandings among its members, not that the understandings exist because the company is a quasi-partnership. When things eventually go wrong—and small companies emulate marriages in the frequency and bitterness of their breakdown—the precise provisions of the articles may seem almost irrelevant to the petitioner's sense of grievance. Crucially, the understandings upon which the members of the company operate will include the assumption that, where powers are conferred upon the board, those powers will be exercised in accordance with the fiduciary duties of directors, so that breaches of fiduciary duty may be tied in this way to the shareholders' arrangements as well.[40]

The range of expectations which may be protected in this way is open-ended, though the one most commonly protected is undoubtedly the petitioner's expectation that he or she would be involved in the management of the company through having a seat on the board.[41] It is important to grasp, however, that this category of legitimate expectation does depend on the factual demonstration that an informal agreement or arrangement, generating the expectation relied upon, did exist outside the articles and supplementing them. The "starting point"[42] of the court's analysis will be the articles of association and "something more" will be required to move the court from the view that "it can safely be said that the basis of association is adequately and exhaustively laid down in the articles".[43] If that factual demonstration cannot be made, the petitioner's case will fail.[44] It follows from this that this category of protected expectations is almost wholly confined to small, even very small, companies. Beyond such companies it becomes increasingly difficult to demonstrate that all the members of the company were parties to the informal arrangement, and, if they were not, the court is unlikely to enforce it,

---

[40] *Saul D Harrison, Re*, above, fn.37 at p.18. This aspect of unfair prejudice is, of course, not peculiar to small companies but applies across the full range of companies. Hence, it is suggested, the importance of the question, discussed above at para.20–3, whether s.994 provides corporate or only personal relief to the petitioner.

[41] So that s.994 may qualify, not only the formal articles, but also the statutory powers of the majority under s.168. In this respect the s.994 decisions reinforce the decision of the House of Lords in *Bushell v Faith*, above, para.14–18.

[42] *Saul D Harrison, Re*, above, fn.37 at 18.

[43] *Ebrahimi v Westbourne Galleries Ltd*, above, fn.34, at 379.

[44] See *Saul D Harrison, Re*, above, fn.37, itself but also *Posgate and Denby (Agencies) Ltd, Re* [1987] B.C.L.C. 8; *A Company, Re* [1987] B.C.L.C. 562; *A Company, Re* (1988) 4 B.C.L.C. 80; *Ringtower Holdings Plc, Re* (1989) 5 B.C.C. 82; *Currie v Cowdenbeath Football Club Ltd* [1992] B.C.L.C. 1029; *J E Cade & Sons Ltd, Re* [1992] B.C.L.C. 213; *Murray's Judicial Factor v Thomas Murray & Sons (Ice Merchants) Ltd* [1993] B.C.L.C. 1437 at 1455.

on the grounds that the non-involved members are entitled to rely on the registered constitution of the company.[45]

This approach on the part of the courts was confirmed, indeed re-emphasised, in the first decision of the House of Lords on what is now section 994, *O'Neill v Phillips*.[46] The leading judgement was given by Lord Hoffmann, whose own rise through the judicial hierarchy has roughly coincided with that of the unfair prejudice case-law and who has had a particular influence upon its development. Their lordships' endorsement of the dominant approach in the lower courts was accompanied, however, by a shift in terminology from the public law language of "legitimate expectations" to the more traditional private law phraseology of constraining the exercise of legal rights by reference to "equitable considerations". Although on its face not obviously more restrictive than "legitimate expectations", the purpose of the phrase "legitimate expectations" was to anchor the courts' assessment of what constituted unfair conduct in an analysis of the bargain, formal and informal, struck by those who were the shareholders of the company. Their lordships feared that lower courts might treat the legitimate expectations test as a licence to "do whatever the individual judge happens to think fair."[47] Instead, the correct approach was to ask whether the exercise of the majority's powers under company law or the company's constitution should be limited by reference to the bargain which the members of the company had struck, a bargain which, in its totality, might be located in informal, non-legally enforceable understandings between the members as well as in the company's formal constitution.[48] This "contractual" approach to the assessment of unfairness under section 994 might admit not only of an approach based on analogy with breach of contract but also with other doctrines for the discharge of contracts, for example, frustration, where the majority used its legal powers to keep the association on foot in circumstances in which the original agreement between the parties had become fundamentally changed.[49]

20–10   Their lordships thought that legal certainty would be promoted by the expulsion from this area of "some wholly indefinite notion of fairness"[50] and the costs of litigation would be reduced by discouraging lengthy and expensive hearings which ranged over the full history of the company and the relationships among its members.

---

[45]   *Blue Arrow Plc, Re* [1987] B.C.L.C. 585; *Tottenham Hotspur Plc, Re* [1994] 1 B.C.L.C. 655; *Astec (BSR) Plc, Re* [1998] 2 B.C.L.C. 556.

[46]   [1999] 2 B.C.L.C. 1, HL.

[47]   At p.7e.

[48]   At pp.10–11. In *Guidezone Ltd, Re* [2000] 2 B.C.L.C. 321 at 356 Jonathan Parker J. took the equitable analogy a stage further by requiring that non-contractual understandings be relied upon by the minority before they could form the basis of an unfair prejudice petition.

[49]   At p.11b–d.

[50]   At p.9a.

They rejected the view of the Law Commission[51] that the contractual definition of unfair prejudice would unduly limit the scope of the section, but seemingly more on the grounds that some limitation was a price worth paying for legal certainty than on the grounds that all deserving cases would in fact fall within the section on the contractual approach.[52] The CLR endorsed[53] the policy balance struck by the House of Lords, although the majority of those responding to the CLR's proposals were in favour of a wider approach, and the 2006 Act thus seeks to repeat rather than to reform the unfair prejudice provisions previously contained in the 1985 Act.

In the particular case, a not-uncommon situation arose in which a founding entrepreneur, who had built up the business, increasingly handed over control to a trusted employee (the petitioner), allowing him to acquire a quarter of the shares in the company. Later the petitioner became managing director of the company, receiving half its profits and there were talks about his acquiring one-half of the share capital. However, an economic downturn occurred and the company began to falter, the founder removed the petitioner from his managing directorship, taking back the reins himself, and paid the petitioner only a salary and the dividends due on his 25 per cent. shareholding. This treatment of the petitioner, who resigned, was held not to be unfairly prejudicial because there was no agreement between the parties, even at an informal level, that the petitioner should be entitled to receive half the profits, except for so long as he acted as managing director, or that he was entitled to increase his shareholding to one-half.

So the strict legal rights of the majority, deriving from the articles of association or the Companies Act, may be subject to "equitable considerations"[54] which channel and restrict the discretion which the majority would otherwise have, where it can be shown that the members came together on the basis that those legal rights should not be entirely freely exercisable. It is suggested that putting the proposition in this way enables us to explain both the vigour with which the courts have developed this aspect of unfair prejudice and the limited conceptual nature of the development. As we have already said, the difficulty for the courts, when they abandon illegality as the touchstone of unfairness, is that the choice of criteria for judging whether section 994 has been broken seems to be at large. The "informal arrangement" category of unfair prejudice provides a partial answer

---

[51] *Shareholders' Remedies*, Cm. 3769 (1997), para.4.11. An example might be mismanagement of the company not amounting to a breach of directors' duties (see *Elgindata, Re* [1991] B.C.L.C. 959 but *cf. Macro (Ipswich) Ltd, Re* [1994] 2 B.C.L.C. 354); but with the rise in the standard of care required of directors (above at para.16–13) it may be that this is a declining problem, because such cases will fall within the category of "indirect" wrongs (above, para.20–3).

[52] At p.8g–h.

[53] Final Report I, para.7.41; Completing, paras 5.77–5.79.

[54] *Ebrahimi*'s case, above, fn.34.

to this problem. The courts can claim to be, and indeed are, using as the criteria for judging unfairness the standards laid down, albeit informally, by the members themselves, and the judges can thus avoid the more challenging task of developing their own criteria. These considerations explain, it is suggested, the emphasis in the *Ebrahimi* case[55] that the equitable considerations do not flow simply from the nature of the company as a quasi-partnership but require "something more" in the shape of proof of the existence of an informal agreement concerning, say, the participation by the minority in the management of the company. As we have seen, this requirement has been fully absorbed into the unfair prejudice case-law. The company's formal constitution is the "starting point" for judicial analysis because "keeping promises and honouring agreements is probably the most important element of commercial fairness".[56] Informal qualifications and supplements to the written constitution must be proved to have been agreed. And even when they are proved, the "extended" agreement sets the boundaries of the courts' intervention. Thus, in *JE Cade and Son Ltd, Re*[57] Warner J. denied the proposition that:

> "where such equitable considerations arise from agreements or understandings between the shareholders dehors the constitution of the company, the court is free to superimpose on the rights, expectations and obligations springing from those agreements or understandings further rights and obligations arising from its own concept of fairness. There can in my judgment be no such third tier of rights and obligations."

Dividends and directors' remuneration

20–11 Where the petitioner has never been, or has ceased to be, a director of the company, a frequent cause of dispute is the payment of excessive remuneration to the directors of the company and the failure to declare dividends payable to all the shareholders. It seems that there are no special rules about unfair prejudice applicable in this situation, but rather that the principles discussed above should be applied. Thus, minority shareholders have no legitimate expectation that dividends will be paid just because they are shareholders in a quasi-partnership company.[58] However, there may be particular circumstances in which the payment of no or only derisory dividends will amount to unfair prejudice, for example, where there was an arrangement that all the profits of the company would be taken out

---

[55] [1973] A.C. at 379. This was a winding-up case, but, as we shall see below at para.20–17, similar considerations apply there too and the winding-up case-law has strongly influenced the development of this category of unfair prejudice.

[56] *Saul D Harrison, Re*, above, fn.37, at 18.

[57] [1992] B.C.L.C. 213.

[58] *Irvine v Irvine (No.1)* [2007] 1 B.C.L.C. 349, 421.

of the company in one way or another; that the fiscally efficient way of doing this had been to pay large remuneration to the directors; and that the fact that the petitioner was not a director deprived the petitioner of any share of the profits.[59] The court has also refused to strike out a petition alleging that the non-payment of dividends produced a disparity between the petitioner and the respondents as far as their participation in the profits of the company was concerned, because the respondents obtained their return through the payment of directors' remuneration and other benefits provided by the company to the directors, whilst the petitioners were excluded from any substantial return.[60]

As far as the payment of directors' remuneration to the controllers is concerned, which is often the other side of the coin of the non-payment of dividends, it is perhaps obvious that it may be a ground for a successful petition if the directors have fixed their remuneration in disregard of the provisions of the articles governing that matter.[61] However, where the controllers have executive positions within the company and the petitioner does not, it may well be fair that the returns which the controllers receive via directors' salaries and perks exceed those of the petitioner, obtained via dividends. Perhaps surprisingly, where the proper procedures for fixing the directors' remuneration have not been followed, the courts have not shrunk from embarking on the exercise of determining whether the directors' remuneration package is excessive in order to establish whether the petitioner has suffered from unfair prejudice. The appropriate level of remuneration for the directors is to be determined by reference to "objective commercial criteria" in order to see whether the remuneration was "within the bracket that executives carrying that sort of responsibility and discharging the sort of duties [the respondent] was would expect to receive."[62]

Overall, whether what is at issue is dividends and remuneration or not, in this category of unfair prejudice petitions the court is still dealing with and enforcing the parties' agreements, formal and informal. The charge of unwarranted intervention by the courts in the internal affairs of companies can be easily rebutted, because it is the members' own standards which the courts are purporting to enforce.[63] On the other hand, because, at least in small companies, the articles systematically fail to capture the full agreement between the members, the development of this case-law has brought company law

---

[59] *Irvine v Irvine (No.1)* (previous note).
[60] *Sam Weller & Sons Ltd, Re* [1990] B.C.L.C. 80.
[61] *Irvine v Irvine (No.1)* [2007] 1 B.C.L.C. 349; *Ravenhart Services (Holdings) Ltd, Re* [2004] 2 B.C.L.C. 375.
[62] *Irvine v Irvine (No.1)* [2007] 1 B.C.L.C. 349, 420.
[63] This is not to deny that the degree of proof which the court requires of the informal arrangement may vary according to whether the alleged arrangement is usual or unusual in the type of company in question.

into much greater touch with corporate reality and, as the amount of litigation shows, has addressed a previously unmet legal need.

Other categories of unfair prejudice

20–12 Although the case-law is dominated by the informal arrangement category of unfair prejudice, the wording of the section in no way permits the courts to confine its scope to such cases. However, beyond informal arrangements and the linked argument that the controllers have committed breaches of their fiduciary duties, the issue of how to set the bounds of the courts' intervention arises in an acute way. Probably for this reason alone, no further, clearly defined categories of unfair prejudice can be found in the case law, though one can find a number of cases where allegations of unfair prejudice have been accepted outside the categories mentioned above. An examination of these cases is of particular importance in assessing the significance of section 994 outside the small company field.

A feature of some of them is reasoning by analogy from established standards, that is, using the unfair prejudice provisions to extend established rules into adjacent areas where the provisions do not formally apply. Thus, in *A Company, Re*[64] the court used the provisions of the City Code on Takeovers and Mergers as a guide to what section 994 requires the directors of a target company should do by way of communication with their shareholders, even though the target was a private company and so outside the formal scope of the Code.[65] In *McGuinness v Bremner Plc*[66] the judge found a useful analogy in art.37 of the then current version of Table A, even though the company in question had not adopted that version, when deciding whether delay on the part of the directors in convening a meeting requisitioned by the petitioners was unfairly prejudicial. Again, such reasoning by analogy plays a useful role in defending the courts against the charge of unwarranted or inexpert interference.

However, an appropriate analogy will not be available in all cases. Then the court may have to face the task of developing its own criteria of fairness. For example, the company may have adopted a

---

[64] [1986] B.C.L.C. 382. See also *St Piran Ltd, Re* [1981] 1 W.L.R. 1300 but *cf. Astec (BSR) Plc, Re* [1998] 2 B.C.L.C. 556 at 579.

[65] See below, para.28–13. The Code was used only as a guide. In particular, the judge borrowed from the Code the proposition that any advice given by the directors should be given in the interests of the shareholders, but he did not borrow the further proposition that the directors were obliged to give the shareholders their view on the bid.

[66] [1988] B.C.L.C. 673. See also *Bermuda Cablevision Ltd v Colica Trust Co Ltd* [1998] A.C. 198, PC (analogy with the criminal law, though the directors were acting, presumably, in breach of fiduciary duty). However, the courts have not in general been prepared to use the unfair prejudice petition as a way of curing defects in the statutory protections conferred upon minorities: see *CAS (Nominees) Ltd v Nottingham Forest FC Plc* [2002] 1 B.C.L.C. 613 (avoidance of minority power to block share issue—see below, para.24–4) and *Rock Nominees Ltd v RCO (Holdings) Plc* [2004] 1 B.C.L.C. 439, CA (avoidance of minority's power to reject a "squeeze out" after a takeover—see below, para.28–61).

policy of paying only low dividends, although financially able to do better and even though the controllers have been able to obtain an income from the company by way of directors' fees. Is that unfairly prejudicial to the interests of the non-director shareholders, even in the absence of any informal understanding as to the level of dividend pay-outs or as to the participation of the petitioner in the management of the company as a director (thus entitling him to directors' fees)? The courts have shown themselves willing to entertain such claims under section 994, but have not yet had to adjudicate on their merits.[67] The issue could be approached on the basis that the court undertakes the task of working out the appropriate distribution policy for the company (or for companies of that type), which seems unlikely, or by asking the question whether the policy in question unfairly discriminated between the insiders with their directorships and the outsiders who were only shareholders.[68]

Prejudice and unfairness

In a number of cases the courts have stressed that the section requires **20–13** prejudice to the minority which is unfair and not just prejudice per se. In some cases this is simply another way of putting the point that only legitimate expectations are protected by the section, not every factual expectation which the petitioner may entertain. Thus, a shareholder who needs the money may be prejudiced by the failure of the company to adopt a scheme for the return of capital to its shareholders, but it does not follow that there was anything unfair in the company's decision to retain the capital in the business, in the absence of a formal or informal understanding that the company's capital would be returned at a certain point in its life.[69]

In other and more interesting cases the petitioner appears to have a prima facie case for the protection of section 994, but his conduct means that he or she is not granted relief. There is no requirement that the petitioner come to the court with clean hands, but the petitioner's conduct might mean that the harm inflicted upon him was not unfair or that the relief granted should be restricted. Thus, in *Grace v Biagioli*[70] the petitioner had been removed from his directorship, contrary to the agreement between himself and the three other persons involved when the company was set up, which would normally be a clear example of unfair prejudice. However, the petitioner had put himself in a position of conflict by seeking to purchase

---

[67] *Sam Weller Ltd, Re* [1990] Ch. 682, where the judge refused to strike out the claim. The case was largely concerned with the now irrelevant issue of whether the dividend policy affected all the shareholders equally: *cf. A Company Ex p. Glossop, Re* [1988] 1 W.L.R. 1068.

[68] *A Company (No.004415 of 1996), Re* [1997] 1 B.C.L.C. 479.

[69] *A Company, Re* [1983] Ch. 178, as explained in *A Company, Re* [1986] B.C.L.C. 382 at 387; *Guidezone Ltd, Re* [2002] 2 B.C.L.C. 321.

[70] [2006] 2 B.C.L.C. 70, CA, following *London School of Electronics, Re* [1986] Ch. 211.

a competing company, which act was held by the Court of Appeal to justify his removal in breach of the agreement, so that the prejudice to the petitioner could not be said to be unfair to him. Again, the petitioners may have consented to, and even benefited from, the company being run in a way which would normally be regarded as unfairly prejudicial to their interests;[71] or they might have shown no interest in pursuing their legitimate interest in being involved in the company.[72]

The test of whether the prejudice was unfair is an objective one, but this means no more than that unfair prejudice may be established even if the controllers did not intend to harm the petitioners.[73] The question is whether the harm which the petitioner has suffered is something he or she is entitled to be protected from. It has been suggested that a fall in the value of the petitioners' shares is a touchstone of unfairness, but this seems to be incorrect. The exclusion of petitioners from the management of the company in breach of their legitimate expectation of involvement would not necessarily have any impact upon the value of the company's shares, whilst, on the other hand, those shares might fall in value as a result of a managerial misjudgement which was in no way unfair to the petitioners.

Finally, in rare cases it may be that what was done to the petitioner was unfair but it caused him or her no prejudice, for example, because no loss was inflicted.[74]

REDUCING LITIGATION COSTS

20–14 A major issue which has emerged under the unfair prejudice jurisdiction is the length and, therefore, the cost of trials of these petitions. Although the decision of the House of Lords in *O'Neill v Phillips*[75] has done something to reduce the scope of the issues to be explored, the court may still find itself trawling through a great deal of the history of the relations between petitioner and respondent, to establish, first, the existence of any informal understandings and, secondly, whether they have subsequently been breached. All this will

---

[71] *Jesner v Jarrad Properties Ltd* [1993] B.C.L.C. 1032, Inner House.
[72] *RA Noble & Sons (Clothing) Ltd, Re* [1983] B.C.L.C. 273.
[73] *Bovey Hotel Ventures Ltd, Re* unreported, but this view is set out and approved in [1983] B.C.L.C. 290; *Saul D. Harrison & Sons Plc, Re* above, fn.37 at 17.
[74] *Guinness Peat Group Plc v British Land Co Plc* [1999] 2 B.C.L.C. 243, CA—exclusion of petitioner from an interest in a company where the shareholder's equity was negative. However, the case was mainly concerned with the inappropriateness of making such a determination at the strike-out stage of litigation where the experts on each side were in sharp disagreement as to the applicable valuation methodology.
[75] See above, fn.46.

typically occur in relation to small companies, whose net value may not be large. Both the Law Commission[76] and the CLR investigated a number of ways of reducing the costs of unfair prejudice litigation, but all were ultimately rejected as ineffective, either by the Commission or the Review,[77] except for a suggestion that an arbitration scheme be developed as an alternative to litigation before the High Court,[78] plus reliance on the newly introduced general system of case management in the civil courts for those cases not going down the arbitral route.

However, the courts themselves have developed a technique for encouraging an agreed solution to unfair prejudice claims. Where it is clear, as it will normally be, that the relationship between the petitioner and the remainder of the members cannot be reconstituted by the court and that the only effective remedy available to the minority is to have their shares purchased at a fair price, then if a suitable ad hoc offer is made to the petitioner for the purchase of the shares or there is a suitable mechanism to this effect in the company's articles, but the petitioner decides to proceed with the petition, rather than to accept the offer or use the mechanism, that will be seen to be an abuse of the process of the court and the petition will be struck out. In *O'Neill v Phillips*[79] Lord Hoffmann was as keen to endorse and encourage this procedure as he was to set out the basis of the unfair prejudice claim itself. His lordship thought that a petitioner could not be said to have been *unfairly* prejudiced by the respondent's conduct if:

(a) the offer was to buy the shares at a fair price, which normally would be without a discount for their minority status (see below);

(b) there was a mechanism for determination of the price by a competent expert in the absence of agreement;

(c) to encourage agreement the expert should not give reasons for the valuation;

(d) both sides should have equal access to information about the company and equal freedom to make submissions to the expert; and

---

[76] See above, fn.51.

[77] These were (a) a new unfair prejudice remedy for those excluded from the management of small companies (rejected by the Law Commission, above, fn.51 at para.3.25, as likely to lead to "duplication and complication of shareholder proceedings"); (b) a presumption of unfairness in certain cases of exclusion from management (recommended by the Commission but rejected by the CLR after the proposal received little support from consultees: Developing, para.4.104); (c) the development of a model exit article (recommended by the Law Commission, above, Pt V, but rejected by the CLR, Developing, para.4.103, on the grounds that it was not likely to be used by the well-advised and would be a trap for the ill-advised).

[78] Final Report I, para.2.27 (this proposal was not confined to unfair prejudice petitions).

[79] See above, fn.46 at pp.16–17. This approach was applied to the winding-up remedy (below, para.20–17) in *CVC/Opportunity Equity Partners Ltd v Demarco Almeida* [2002] B.C.C. 684, PC.

> (e) the respondent should be given a reasonable time at the beginning of the proceedings to make the offer and should not be liable for the petitioner's legal costs incurred during that period.

Cases where an offer from the respondent has not blocked a petition have usually involved offers which did not give the petitioner all he or she would get if successful at trial[80] or have involved valuation by a non-independent expert.[81] The offer which the court has to evaluate may be an ad hoc one or may result from the application of provisions in the company's articles laying down a mechanism to be used where a shareholder wishes to dispose of his or her holding. Although the courts once took a different view, it does not now appear that an offer arising out of the mechanism contained in the articles is to be treated differently from an ad hoc offer, in terms of its effect in excluding an unfair prejudice provision.[82]

REMEDIES

20–15 Section 996 gives the court a wide remedial discretion to "make such order as it thinks fit for giving relief in respect of the matters complained of". In addition to this general grant, five specific powers are given to the court by section 996(2), of which undoubtedly the most commonly used is an order that the petitioners' shares be purchased by the controllers or the company.[83] The reason for the popularity of this remedy, with both petitioners and the courts, is linked to the fact that, as we have seen, the notion of unfair prejudice is most firmly established in relation to quasi-partnership companies. Where business and, often, personal relations between quasi-partners have broken down, they are incapable of reconstitution by a court, which

---

[80] *North Holdings Ltd v Southern Tropics Ltd* [1999] 2 B.C.L.C. 624, CA.

[81] *Benfield Greig Group Plc, Re* [2002] 1 B.C.L.C. 65, CA, where, in fact, the non-independence of the expert constituted the alleged unfair prejudice.

[82] On the original approach see *A Company Ex p. Kremer, Re* [1989] B.C.L.C. 365 and on the later developments *Virdi v Abbey Leisure Ltd* [1990] B.C.L.C. 342; *A Company Ex p. Holden, Re* [1991] B.C.L.C. 597; *A Company, Re* [1996] 2 B.C.L.C. 192.

[83] s.996(2)(e). In the latter case the company's share capital must be reduced. The statutory power is widely enough drawn to include an order that the minority purchase the majority's shares, which has occasionally been ordered: *Brenfield Squash Racquets Club Ltd, Re* [1996] 2 B.C.L.C. 184. The other specific powers are the authorisation of proceedings to be brought in the company's name (s.996(2)(c) and above, para.20–3); requiring the company to do or refrain from doing an act (s.996(2)(b)); requiring the company not to make alterations to its articles of association without the leave of the court (s.996(2)(d)); and regulating the conduct of the company's affairs in the future (s.996(2)(a)). Whatever remedy is contemplated, the court must choose what is appropriate at the time it is granted: *A Company, Re* [1992] B.C.C. 542. Ss.757 and 758 give the court a further specific power in the case where the unfair prejudice consists of a public offer of shares by a private company: see para.24–2.

can effectively operate only on the terms of the minority's exit. A share purchase order gives the petitioner an opportunity to exit from the company with the fair value of his or her investment, something which, in the absence of a court order, is often not available to the shareholder in a small company, because often no potential purchasers of the shares are available or, even if they were, the purchase price a third party would be willing to pay would reflect, rather than remedy, the harm inflicted on the seller by the unfairly prejudicial conduct.[84]

The crucial question in this buy-out process is how the court is to assess the fairness of the price to be paid for the shares. Two important issues have emerged in the valuation process. The first is whether the petitioner's shareholding should be valued *pro rata* to the total value of the company or whether its value should be discounted on the basis that it is *ex hypothesi* a minority holding and so does not carry with it control of the company. In this context the notion of a "quasi-partnership" company has become important. Although many unfair prejudice proceedings concern such companies, the statutory provisions are not confined to them. However, in relation to whether a minority shareholding should be discounted, the courts have developed a presumption that it should not in a quasi-partnership company, whereas no such presumption applies for other categories of company.

In *Bird Precision Bellows Ltd, Re*[85] it was established that the principle was *pro rata* valuation where the company could be characterised as a quasi-partnership. This is because, in a true partnership, upon dissolution of the partnership the court orders a sale of the partnership business as a going concern and divides the proceeds among the partners according to their interests in the former partnership.[86] However, the normal principle in company law of discounting a minority shareholding applies if the company is not a partnership carried on in corporate form or if the petitioner had bought the shareholding at a price which reflected its minority status or it had devolved upon him or her by operation of law.[87] The concept of a quasi-partnership involves more than simply the company having a small number of members. The members must have set up their association on the basis of mutual trust and confidence, expect

---

[84] See *Grace v Biagioli* [2006] 2 B.C.L.C. 70, CA, for a good example of the court's preference for a "clean break" via a share purchase as against a compensation order, which might have remedied the specific harm suffered by the petitioner but would have left him exposed in the future.

[85] [1984] Ch. 419, per Nourse J., approved on appeal [1986] Ch. 658.

[86] *CVC/Opportunity Equity Partners Ltd v Demarco Almeida* [2002] 2 B.C.L.C. 108 at [41]–[42]; *Strahan v Wilcock* [2006] 2 B.C.L.C. 555. The court might instead work out what the former's partner's interest would be worth upon the hypothesis of a sale, without actually holding one.

[87] *Irvine v Irvine (No.2)* [2007] 1 B.C.L.C. 445; *Elgindata Ltd, Re* [1991] B.C.L.C. 959 at 1007. See also *DR Chemicals, Re* (1989) 5 B.C.C. 37.

to be involved in the management of the company (though the existence of clearly defined "sleeping partners" would not defeat this requirement) and there must be some degree of lock-in of the members to the company.[88]

20–16   The second question is whether the valuation should be on the basis that the company will continue as a going concern, or on a liquidation or break-up basis, which would normally yield a lower value for the company. The going concern basis will normally be appropriate, but this will depend to some degree on the facts of the case, as will the precise method to be adopted for valuing the going concern.[89]

A further issue concerns timing. The value put on shares, whether on a *pro rata* or on a discounted basis, will often crucially depend on when the value of the company is assessed. The courts have given themselves the widest discretion to choose the most appropriate date. The normally competing dates are a date close to when the shares are to be purchased and the date when the petition was presented. In *Profinance Trust SA v Gladstone*,[90] the Court of Appeal thought that the former had become the presumptive valuation date, but that there were many circumstances when an earlier date might be chosen, for example, where the unfairly prejudicial conduct had deprived the company of its business, where the company had reconstructed its business or even that there had been a general fall in the market since the presentation of the petition.

Although the buy-out of the minority is the most common remedy, it is not always the appropriate one and section 996 gives the courts a wide range of other possible remedies. These include compensation, to which it is not yet clear whether the "no reflective loss" principle applies.[91]

WINDING UP ON THE JUST AND EQUITABLE GROUND

20–17   The area of general legal protection for minority shareholders is now dominated by the unfair prejudice remedy, but, despite its remedial flexibility, the court cannot thereby order the winding-up of the company in question. The Law Commission recommended that that

---

[88] These criteria are taken from *Ebrahimi v Westbourne Galleries Ltd* [1973] A.C. 360, 371 (a winding-up case considered further below, para.20–17) and applied by the Court of Appeal to unfair prejudice valuations in *Strahan v Wilcock* [2006] 2 B.C.L.C. 555.

[89] *CVC/Opportunity Equity Partners Ltd v Demarco Almeida* [2002] 2 B.C.L.C. 108; *Parkinson v Eurofinance Group Ltd* [2001] 1 B.C.L.C. 720; *Guinness Peat Group Plc v British Land Co Plc* [1999] 2 B.C.L.C. 243, CA; *Planet Organic Ltd, Re* [2000] 1 B.C.L.C. 366.

[90] [2002] 1 B.C.L.C. 141, CA, where the earlier authorities are reviewed.

[91] *Atlasview Ltd v Brightview Ltd* [2004] 2 B.C.L.C. 191. This principle is discussed above at para.17–13.

power should be added to the range of remedies available to the court for the redress of unfair prejudice,[92] but the CLR rejected it on the grounds that it was open to abuse for the reasons discussed below.[93] Nevertheless there is a separate procedure which a minority shareholder may seek to use to have the company wound up. A company may be wound up compulsorily by the court on a petition presented to it by a contributory[94] if the court is of the opinion that it is just and equitable to do so. This provision, now contained in s.122(1)(g) of the Insolvency Act 1986, has a long pedigree in the law relating to companies, and the power can be traced back to the Joint Stock Companies Winding-up Act 1848. The provision was influenced by the (then uncodified) partnership law and was originally used mainly in cases where the company was deadlocked. In the course of the twentieth century it has been moulded by the courts into a means of subjecting small private companies to equitable principles derived from partnership law when they were in reality incorporated partnerships. The apotheosis of this use of the section, the decision of the House of Lords in *Ebrahimi v Westbourne Galleries Ltd*,[95] was highly influential in the courts' development of their powers under the predecessors of section 994. Despite its remarkable substantive development, the winding up provision always suffered from a weakness at the remedial level: if the company was prospering, presenting a "just and equitable" petition was tantamount to killing the goose that might lay the golden egg (although the threat of liquidation might induce the parties to negotiate an alternative solution to their dispute). So long as the oppression remedy was hobbled by the restrictive wording and interpretation associated with s.210 of the Companies Act 1948, the winding-up petition was better than nothing. But, with the introduction of the unfair prejudice remedy, one

---

[92] See above, fn.51 at paras 4.24–4.49.

[93] Developing, para.4.105.

[94] s.124(1). Petitions may also be brought by creditors, directors or the company itself, though such applications are rare. The Secretary of State may petition under s.124A in the public interest on the basis of information received as a result of an investigation into the company's affairs. See above, para.18–10. However, public interest grounds for a winding-up are not available other than to the Secretary of State: *Millennium Advanced Technology Ltd, Re* [2004] 2 B.C.L.C. 77. The term "contributory" includes even a fully paid-up shareholder provided he or she has a tangible interest in the winding-up, which is usually demonstrated by showing that the company has a surplus of assets over liabilities, though that will not be required if the petitioner's complaint is that the controllers failed to provide the financial information from which that assessment could be made: see *Rica Gold Washing Co, Re* (1879) 11 Ch.D. 36; *Bellador Silk Ltd, Re* [1965] 1 All E.R. 667; *Othery Construction Ltd, Re* [1966] 1 W.L.R. 69; *Expanded Plugs Ltd, Re* [1966] 1 W.L.R. 514; *Chesterfield Catering Ltd, Re* [1977] Ch. 373 at 380; *Land and Property Trust Co Plc, Re* [1991] B.C.C. 446 at 448; *Newman & Howard Ltd, Re* [1962] Ch. 257; *Wessex Computer Stationers Ltd, Re* [1992] B.C.L.C. 366; *A Company, Re* [1995] B.C.C. 705. The Jenkins Committee recommended (para.503(h)) that any member should be entitled to petition, presumably on the grounds that this remedy was aimed primarily at protecting minorities rather than at winding up companies.

[95] See above, fn.88.

may argue that the role of the winding-up remedy should now be restricted.

A winding-up petition triggers s.127 of the Insolvency Act 1986, which requires the court's consent for any disposition of the company's property after the petition is presented. This ability to paralyse, or at least disrupt, the normal running of the company's business adds to the negotiating strength of the petitioner but is hardly legitimate if an unfair prejudice petition could give him or her all that is required. Consequently, a Practice Direction[96] seeks to discourage the routine joining of winding-up petitions to unfair prejudice claims, unless a winding-up remedy is what is genuinely sought. The force behind the Practice Direction is provided by s.125(2) of the Insolvency Act 1986, to the effect that the court need not grant a winding-up order if it is of the opinion that some alternative remedy is available to the petitioners and that they have acted unreasonably in not pursuing it.[97] It would seem an appropriate use of this power for the courts to insist that, where a more flexible section 996 remedy is available, the petitioner should be confined to it. That would be a natural consequence of the fact that the statutory alternative to a winding-up order has finally come of age.

The courts seem to be reinforcing this development by limiting the substantive grounds on which a winding-up order may be made. There is a long-running controversy in the cases whether the grounds of unfairness upon which a company can be wound up under s.122(1)(g) of the 1986 Act are wider than those which will found an unfair prejudice remedy under section 994 of the 2006 Act. There are reported cases in which the court has denied a petition based on unfair prejudice, because the conduct of the petitioner did not merit it, but has granted a winding-up order on the grounds that mutual confidence among the quasi-partners had broken down.[98] In other words, in these cases the mere fact of breakdown is sufficient to ground a winding-up order, whereas an unfair prejudice petition is seen as requiring some assessment of the comparative blame-worthiness of petitioners and controllers. However, in the wake of the decision of the House of Lords in *O'Neill v Phillips*[99] the view has been taken at first instance "that the winding-up jurisdiction is, at the

---

[96] CPR Practice Direction, Applications under the Companies Act and Other Legislation Relating to Companies, para.9(1). See *A Company (No.004415 of 1996), Re* [1997] 1 B.C.L.C. 479 where the judge struck out the alternative petition for winding up on the just and equitable ground on the basis that there was no reasonable prospect that the trial judge would order a winding up as against a share purchase under what is now s.996.

[97] The alternative remedy need not be a legal one. For example, it may be an offer to purchase the petitioner's shares on the same basis as the court would order on an unfair prejudice petition: *Virdi v Abbey Leisure Ltd* [1990] B.C.L.C. 342.

[98] *RA Noble (Clothing) Ltd, Re*, above, fn.72, and *Jesner v Jarrad Properties Ltd*, above, fn.71. See also *Full Cup International Trading Ltd, Re* [1995] B.C.C. 682, where the judge found himself in the presumably unusual position of being unable to fashion an appropriate remedy under section 996 but of being prepared to wind up the company.

[99] See above, fn.46.

very least, no wider than the [unfair prejudice] jurisdiction", for otherwise the effect of their lordships' decision would simply be that "of transferring business from the [unfair prejudice] jurisdiction to the winding-up jurisdiction".[100]

CONCLUSION

Part 30 of the Act does not provide, and on no conceivable inter-   **20–18**
pretation could provide, a unilateral exit right for minority shareholders, i.e. a right for minority shareholders at any time to withdraw
their capital from the company. Indeed, it might be thought that such
a right would be inconsistent with the nature of shareholding in
companies. The shareholder is locked into the investment in the
company unless he or she is able to find someone else to purchase the
shares and thus stand in the shareholder's shoes in relation to the
company.[101] Compulsory purchase appears under Part 30, not as a
right for the minority, but as a remedy—and not even a remedy the
minority can insist upon, though it is the most common—in respect
of unfair prejudice committed by the company's controllers. Thus in
Phoenix Office Supplies Ltd, Re[102] the Court of Appeal refused a
shareholder's petition to have his shares acquired at a non-discounted
value, even though he had been removed from his directorship by the
other two incorporators in breach of their common understanding.
The reason for the decision was that the conduct of the others had
been a response to the petitioner's unilateral decision to sever his
relations with the company, which could be seen as a prior and more
fundamental breach of the original understandings among the three
people involved. Of course, members may bargain for rights of unilateral exit to be incorporated in the articles of particular companies;[103] but they are rare, since a general right for minority
shareholders to withdraw their capital when they will would seem
likely wholly to undermine the financing function of shares.

Finally, there is some evidence that the unfair prejudice remedy,
whatever its imperfections, has successfully "crowded out" alternative techniques of controlling the exercise of majority power
through board decisions. Thus, the Law Commissions' draft statement of directors' statutory duties[104] included a requirement that

---

[100] *Guidezone Ltd, Re* [2000] 2 B.C.L.C. 321 at 357.
[101] Of course, if the company and the shareholder wish expressly to bargain for "redeemable" shares, they are free to do so (above, para.13–9).
[102] [2003] 1 B.C.L.C. 76, CA.
[103] See above, para.19–21.
[104] *Company Directors: Regulating Conflicts of Interest and Formulating a Statement of Duties*, Cm. 4436 (1999), Appendix A.

directors act fairly as between shareholders, a duty reflected at least at first instance in the current caselaw.[105] The CLR's initial draft statement contained the same duty,[106] but fairness between shareholders was later reduced to one of the factors to be taken into account by the directors when discharging their duty to promote the success of the company for the benefit of its members.[107] The explanation given for this development was a desire to "make it clear that fairness is a factor in achieving success for the members as a whole, rather than an independent requirement which could override commercial success".[108] It is difficult to believe that this argument would have been accepted in the absence of Part 30 as an overriding instrument of minority protection.

[105] See especially *Mutual Life Insurance Co of New York v Rank Organisation Ltd* [1985] B.C.L.C. 11.
[106] Developing, para.3.40.
[107] Final Report I, Annex C, Sch.2. On the nature of the general duty see para.16–25, above.
[108] Final Report I, Annex C, Explanatory Notes, para.18.

PART FIVE

ACCOUNTS AND AUDIT

It has been accepted since the early days of modern company law that mandatory publicity about the company's affairs was an important regulatory tool. For shareholders in large companies with dispersed shareholdings it operates to reduce the risk of management incompetence or self-seeking. The non-director shareholders of a company will have a difficult task to judge the effectiveness of the management of the company if they do not have access to relevant data about the company's financial performance. For creditors it operates to reduce the risks of dealing with an entity whose members have limited liability. A creditor of a company with limited liability[1] has a natural interest in the financial health of the body upon whose assets alone, in the normal case, he or she is able to assert claims. In fact, mandatory disclosure has long been seen as something which could legitimately be asked for in exchange for the freedom to trade with limited liability, though there has been controversy throughout the history of company law about how extensive the disclosure rules should be. Today, therefore, there is a major difference between the disclosure rules applicable to ordinary partnerships (without limited liability) and those applicable to companies, with limited liability partnerships being rightly placed in the company category for these purposes, because they benefit from limited liability.[2] Given this range of interests in mandatory disclosure of information by companies, it is not surprising that successive company scandals have provoked demands for ever more far-reaching mandatory disclosure of information, and such demands have often been successful.

---

[1] An unlimited liability company is not normally required to make its accounts available to the public: see para.21–34, below.

[2] See Morse *et al.*, *Palmer's Limited Liability Partnership Law* (Sweet & Maxwell, 2002), Ch.3.

As far as the companies legislation is concerned, the main instrument for delivering mandatory disclosure has been the annual accounts and reports—which the directors are required to produce, have verified by the company's auditors (in most cases), lay before the members in general meeting (or otherwise distribute to them in the case of private companies) and register in a public registry. This development over the years has produced an elaborate body of rules. The desire of the Company Law Review to use mandatory disclosure to promote an "enlightened shareholder value" approach to company law has led to reforms which require disclosure of information which is not directly financial, but concerns the quality of the company's relationships with those who are capable of making a major contribution to the success of the business or about the impact of the company's operations upon the community in which it operates. Further, the impact in Europe of the Enron and related scandals from the United States has only served to make those rules even more elaborate, especially in relation to the verification of the accounts through the process of audit. Accounts and audit are the subject of the two Chapters in this Part.

However, mandatory disclosure can be seen as an instrument, not only of corporate law (for the benefit of shareholders, creditors and other stakeholders) but of financial services or securities law (for the benefit of investors and the efficient functioning of the capital markets). Consequently, we shall return to the issue of mandatory disclosure in Part 6, where we analyse the additional disclosure requirements which apply to companies whose securities are traded on a public securities market.

CHAPTER 21

ANNUAL ACCOUNTS AND REPORTS

INTRODUCTION

Scope and rationale of the annual reporting requirement

On the basis that "forewarned is forearmed" the fundamental prin- **21–1**
ciple underlying the Companies Acts has been that of disclosure. If
the public and the members were enabled to find out all relevant
information about the company, this, thought the founding fathers of
our company law, would be a sure shield. The shield may not have
proved quite so strong as they had expected and in more recent times

it has been supported by offensive weapons. Basically, however, disclosure still remains the basic safeguard on which the Companies Acts pin their faith, and every succeeding Act since 1862 has added to the extent of the publicity required, although, not unreasonably, what is required varies according to the type of company concerned. Not only may disclosure by itself promote efficient conduct of the company's business, because the company's controllers (whether directors or large shareholders) may fear the reputational losses associated with the revelation of incompetence or self-dealing, but the more interventionist legal strategies, going beyond disclosure, depend upon those who hold the legal rights being well-informed about the company's position. For example, those in a position to enforce the company's rights against directors for breach of duty[1] or to bring claims of unfair prejudice[2] or shareholders holding rights to remove directors,[3] if rational persons, will not turn their minds to the exercise of those rights unless they think there are grounds for so doing. Thus, disclosure is the bed-rock of company law.

This Chapter is centred on what has always been the central disclosure mechanism of the British companies legislation, namely, the obligation laid on the directors to produce annual accounts relating to the financial position of the company and to accompany those accounts with a report on the company's activities, including their own stewardship of the company. Those accounts and reports are then typically considered by the shareholders at an annual general meeting of the company, though, as we have seen, only public companies are now required to hold an AGM.[4] Over the years, what is required of at least large companies by way of accounts and reports has expanded, as we shall see below, and the CLR proposed a further significant expansion in reporting, which, however, has been only partially implemented in the 2006 Act.[5] Furthermore, this is an area where the harmonisation programme of the European Community has had some impact, first of all in relation to the presentation of accounts,[6] and more latterly in relation to use of accounting standards[7] and the provision of non-financial information.[8]

The production of the annual accounts has seen the development of an industry of professionals to help the company meet its statutory

---

[1] See Chs.16 and 17 above.

[2] See Ch.20 above.

[3] See Ch.14 above.

[4] See para.15–3.

[5] See below, para.21–23.

[6] Notably the Fourth Council Directive on the Annual Accounts of Certain Types of Companies, Directive 78/660/EEC ([1978] OJ L222/110), as amended (hereafter "Fourth Directive") and the Seventh Council Directive on Consolidated Accounts, Directive 83/349/EEC ([1983] OJ L193/1), as amended (hereafter "Seventh Directive").

[7] Regulation (EC) No.1606/2002 on the Application of International Accounting Standards, ([2002] OJ L243/1) (hereafter "IAS Regulation").

[8] Directive 2003/51/EC ([2003] OJ L178/16) (hereafter the "accounts modernisation directive").

obligations. Notably, the accounting profession has played a major role in developing the standards which determine how the raw financial data is to be analysed and presented in the accounts, the law having rightly shied away from doing more than setting the broad parameters for this task.[9] That profession then reappears in the guise of auditors to verify that the accounts do meet those standards and the applicable legal rules and, in particular, present a "true and fair view" of the company's financial position.[10]

Those who introduced this annual reporting obligation in the **21–2** nineteenth century probably saw it as aimed at informing two groups of people: the shareholders of the company, so that they could assess whether the company's management was doing an acceptable job; and the creditors of the company, whose claims are confined to the company's assets (except in the rare case of an unlimited company) and so have a natural interest in the state of those assets. However, the modern view would probably include two further groups as having an interest in this matter. First, at least with companies whose securities are traded on a public market (usually a "stock exchange"), investors will be interested in the company's reports and accounts. The term "investors" certainly includes those who are already shareholders in the company, but it goes more broadly than that so as to embrace those who are contemplating investment in it but are not yet shareholders. Further, the term encourages us to distinguish between the two types of decision an existing shareholder might make after reading the account reports: seeking to exercise governance rights (for example, by removing directors) or selling (or buying) shares in the company. Finally, an investor might be a person who has lent or is contemplating lending money to the company, perhaps a bank contemplating a loan or someone contemplating buying or selling debentures (debt securities) issued by the company.[11]

One can conclude that, where there is a public market in the company's equity or debt securities, the company's annual reports and accounts will be avidly read, not only by existing shareholders and creditors, but by a wider investing public. In fact, a major event in the annual cycle of a publicly traded company is the point at which it makes a preliminary announcement of its financial results for the previous year (the "prelims"), the full details of which will be included in its annual statutory accounts.[12] Such announcements—and the later full accounts and reports, though they are somewhat stale news by then—are pored over by analysts, whose task it is to generate

---

[9] See below, para.21–12.
[10] See Ch.22.
[11] See Part Seven below.
[12] Such a preliminary statement used to be obligatory for listed companies, but ceased to be so in January 2007, in the light of the implementation of the Transparency Directive, though companies continue to make such announcements and the Listing Rules regulate the form they must take, if made. See LR 9.7A.1 and Chapter 26 below.

advice for investors. Thus, the statutory accounts and reports are used by a wider investment community than just the shareholders, in the case of publicly traded companies. As we shall see, the issue of corporate or auditor liability where the company's annual statements are negligently misleading but are relied upon for the purpose of taking investment decisions has been a contentious one.[13]

In this way, the annual reports and accounts have moved beyond company law to become part of securities or capital markets law as well. Since this is a development which concerns only the relatively small number of (but economically important) companies whose securities are traded on public markets, it is not surprising that further developments in the disclosure requirements applying to those companies have taken the form of rules targeted explicitly at such companies. In some cases, such additional rules are to be found in the Companies Act. For example, the directors' remuneration report, which is part of the annual reporting obligation of the board, is confined to "quoted" companies, but the rules governing it are to be found in the Companies Act 2006.[14] We shall see a similar development in relation to the "enhanced" business review later in this Chapter. More often, however, the specific additional reporting requirements for publicly traded companies are not found in the Companies Act but rather in the Financial Services and Markets Act 2000 or in rules made by the Financial Services Authority under powers conferred by that Act. Such rules include more frequent periodic reporting than the annual requirements of the Companies Act, as well as significant requirements for the episodic or ad hoc reporting of particular events. We consider those rules in Chapter 26. Here, we confine ourselves to the reporting requirements of the Companies Act 2006, even if those requirements perform an additional role in relation to investors in publicly traded companies.

Small companies

21–3   Just as there has been differentiation in the disclosure rules applying at the "top" end of the spectrum of companies, so also that phenomenon can be observed at the "bottom" end of the spectrum. There are carve outs from the full Companies Act disclosure requirements for "small" companies, both in terms of what has to be reported and, as we shall see in the next Chapter, whether it has to be verified by audit. A company which qualifies as small and is not excluded by the provisions discussed below is subject to the "small

---

[13] See paras 22–42 and 26–11.
[14] See para.14–16.

companies regime" for the accounts and reports, which is less stringent than that for larger companies.[15] The tests for small companies relate to the economic size of the company, as makes sense for reporting purposes, rather than to the number of shareholders, which is a better test for governance purposes.

The criteria concern the company's turnover (not more than £6.5 million), balance sheet total, i.e. its assets (not more than £3.26 million), and number of employees (not more than 50).[16] To qualify as small the company must meet two of the criteria; it does not need to meet all three of them. However, the company does not qualify as small unless it meets two of the three criteria in the financial year in question and in the previous financial year (unless the financial year in question is the first one). By way of amelioration of the two-year requirement it is provided that, having qualified as small, the company does not lose that status if it fails to meet the criteria in the first year after it last met the criteria; and it will also hang on to its status if in the following year it again meets the criteria.[17] The purpose of these rather complex rules is to stop the company drifting in and out of the status for successive financial years.

A company which meets the criteria nevertheless cannot count as a small company if it is a public company or carries on insurance, banking or fund management activities or is a member of a group which contains an "ineligible" member.[18] The thought here appears to be that such companies (or groups of which they are members) are engaged in sufficiently sensitive activities that full disclosure is required, especially for the benefit of the relevant regulators, and, in the case of public companies, the fact that they are free to offer their shares to the public suggests that a full financial record should be available.

Medium-sized companies

Somewhat misleadingly placed some eighty sections away from the provisions on small companies are to be found in the "supplementary provisions" to Part 15 the provisions defining a medium-sized com-   **21–4**

---

[15] s.381. The European Commission has floated the idea that "micro" companies be excluded from the European accounts regime entirely: Communication from the Commission on a simplified environment for companies in the areas of company law, accounts and auditing, COM(2007) 394 final, 10.7.2007, p.8. The criteria for a "micro" company would be a turnover below 1 million euros, a balance sheet total below 500,000 euros and fewer than 10 employees. This would mean that Member States would be permitted, but not obliged, to remove micro companies entirely from the annual reporting requirements, rather than simply to reduce the statutory burdens laid upon them.

[16] s.382(3)–(6), as amended by the Companies Act 2006 (Amendment) (Accounts and Reports) Regulations 2008/393 (hereafter "2008 Amending Regulations"). The employee number is an average over the year. These criteria reflect the maximum allowed under EU law.

[17] s.382(1), (2). Thus if in year 1 (its first) the company meets the criteria, fails to do so in year 2, but does so again in year 3, it will remain "small" throughout the three years.

[18] s.384(1). S.384(2) setting out the criteria for ineligibility in relation to a group is discussed below, para.21–9.

pany. The same types of criteria are used as in the case of small companies but they have a higher value: turnover not more than £25.9 million, balance sheet total of not more than £12.9 million and not more than 250 employees.[19] The same two-year rule applies, with its ameliorations, as in the case of small companies,[20] and there are similarly-motivated, but not identical, exclusions, amongst which, crucially, are public companies.[21] There is a similar definition of a medium-sized group to that used for a small group (discussed below), though, of course, with higher values attached to the criteria.[22] In some ways, however, placing these definitions in the "supplementary provisions" of the Part dealing with accounts is appropriate, for medium-sized companies and groups benefit from rather fewer relaxations from the full accounts requirements, as compared with small companies. The CLR recommended the removal of this category on the grounds that it was neither much used or valued, but this suggestion was not taken up.[23]

THE ANNUAL ACCOUNTS

Accounting records

21–5 The statutory provisions relating to the annual accounts begin by imposing on the company a continuing obligation to maintain accounting records.[24] This is logical enough, because, although these records are not open to inspection by members or the public, unless they are kept it will be impossible for the company to produce verifiable annual accounts. Hence, s.386 provides that every company shall keep records sufficient to show and explain the company's transactions, to disclose with reasonable accuracy at any time its financial position and to enable its directors to ensure that any balance sheet and profit and loss account will comply with the provisions of the Act or the IAS Regulation.[25]

To these general obligations are added certain specific requirements. The records must contain day-to-day entries of all money received or expended and of the matters to which that related and a record of the company's assets and liabilities.[26] If the company's business involves dealing in goods, the records must also contain a statement of stock held at the end of the financial year and statements

---

[19] s.465(3) as amended by the 2008 Amending Regulations, reg.4.
[20] s.465(1).
[21] s.467(1).
[22] s.466.
[23] Developing, para.8.35.
[24] ss.386–389.
[25] Above, fn.7.
[26] s.386(3).

of stocktakings from which that was prepared, and, except in the case of goods sold in the ordinary course of retail trade, statements of all goods sold or purchased, in sufficient detail to enable the other party to be identified.[27] None of these specific requirements seems to envisage any particularly sophisticated form of business activity. For any but the most basic businesses probably the more important requirement are the general ones.

A company which has a subsidiary undertaking to which these requirements do not apply[28] must take all reasonable steps to secure that the subsidiary keeps such records as will enable the directors of the parent company to ensure that any accounts required under the Act or the IAS Regulation comply with the relevant requirements.[29]

Failure to comply with the section renders every officer of the company (but not the company itself) who is in default guilty of an offence[30] unless he shows that he acted honestly and that, in the circumstances in which the company's business was carried on, the default was excusable.[31] More effective in practice is probably the duty laid on the auditor to check whether adequate accounting records have been kept and to reveal failure to do so in the auditor's report.[32]

Section 388 provides that accounting records are at all times to be open for inspection by officers of the company.[33] If any such records are kept outside the United Kingdom,[34] there must be sent to the United Kingdom (and be available for inspection there by the officers) records which will disclose with reasonable accuracy the position of the business in question at intervals of not more than six months and will enable the directors to ensure that the company's balance sheet and profit and loss account comply with the statutory requirements.[35] All required records must be preserved for three years if it is a private company or for six years if it is a public one.[36]

---

[27] s.386(4).

[28] e.g. because it is a foreign subsidiary or a partnership.

[29] s.386(5).

[30] Punishable by fine or imprisonment or both: s.387(3).

[31] s.387(2).

[32] s.498(2).

[33] For this reason, accountants may not exercise a lien for unpaid fees over such documents: *DTC(CNC) Ltd v Gary Sargeant & Co* [1996] 1 B.C.L.C. 529. Of course, other persons may also have the right of access to the records, for example, the company's auditors: s.499.

[34] e.g. because the company has a branch outside Great Britain.

[35] s.388(2),(3). The six-monthly requirement seems remarkably lax in the light of both modern management practice and modern electronic technology.

[36] s.388(4). An officer of the company is liable to imprisonment or a fine or both if he fails to take all reasonable steps to secure compliance with the preservation requirement or intentionally causes any default: s.389(4). If there has been villainy, destroying all record of it is all too likely.

The financial year

21–6 The first step in the production of the annual accounts is to fix the company's financial year. Sections 390–392 prescribe how this is to be done. Despite its name the financial year is not a calendar year or, necessarily, a period of 12 months. What period it is depends on its "accounting reference period" (ARP), which in turn depends on its "accounting reference date" (ARD), which is the date in each calendar year on which the company's ARP ends. For companies incorporated after April 1, 1996, the company's ARD will be the anniversary of the last day of the month in which the anniversary of its incorporation falls.[37] However, the company may choose a new ARD for the current and future ARPs and even for its immediately preceding one.[38] This it may well want to do for a variety of reasons; for instance, if the company has been taken over and wishes to bring its ARD into line with that of its new parent.[39] The new ARD may operate either to shorten or to lengthen the ARP within which the change is made,[40] but in the latter case the company may not normally extend the ARP to more than 18 months[41] and may not normally engage in the process of extending the ARP more than once every five years.[42] These are necessary safeguards against obvious abuses. The company's financial year then corresponds to its ARP, as fixed according to the above rules, except that the directors have a discretion to make the financial year end at any point up to seven days before or seven days after the end of the ARP.[43]

Individual accounts and group accounts

21–7 Section 394 imposes on the directors of every company the duty to prepare for each financial year a set of accounts of the company (its "individual accounts"). This duty applies even to the directors of small companies, though the requirements as to what the accounts have to contain in that case are less onerous. The Accounting Standards Board (ASB) (see below) has recommended that cash flow statements should also be produced by all but small companies on an

---

[37] s.391(4). For companies in Northern Ireland the relevant date is 22 August, 1997. For methods of determining the ARD for earlier incorporations see s.391(2),(3).

[38] s.292. This section applies no matter when the company was incorporated.

[39] Indeed, in this particular situation, in order to promote the production of group accounts, the directors of the parent company are under a presumptive duty to ensure that the financial years of subsidiaries coincide with that of the parent: s.390(5).

[40] s.392(2).

[41] s.392(5), unless an administration order is in force in relation to the company, presumably because the administrator, who is responsible to the court, can be trusted in a way the directors cannot.

[42] s.392(3), unless an administration order is in force (see previous note) or the step is taken to make the ARD coincide with that of an EEA undertaking which is the company's parent or subsidiary company, or the Secretary of State permits it.

[43] s.390(2),(3).

annual basis and the CLR recommended that this statement be added to the statutory list.[44] However, this has not been done.

Parent and subsidiary undertakings

Section 399 imposes a duty on directors of a company which is a **21–8** parent company additionally to prepare a consolidated balance sheet and profit and loss account ("group accounts"). Those group accounts must deal with the state of affairs of the parent company and its "subsidiary undertakings"—taken together.[45] The obligation to produce group accounts does not relieve the directors of the parent company from the obligation to produce individual accounts for the parent,[46] nor the directors of the other companies in the group from that obligation in relation to their company.[47] The individual and group accounts of companies within a group should be produced, in principle, using the same financial reporting framework.[48] This is as it should be. Creditors, in particular, may well have claims only against particular companies in the group, unless they have contracted for guarantees from other group members, and so the group picture alone might be misleading.[49]

The obligation to produce group accounts gives rise to the need to define a subsidiary undertaking, for a company may have a relationship with another company which raises a question as to whether it is to be classified as a parent/subsidiary relationship. The situation may be clear when Company A holds all the voting shares in Company B, but suppose it holds only 30 per cent of them. What is then the position? The answer is provided by sections 1161 and 1162 and Schedule 7. The term "undertaking" is used rather than "company" because consolidation of the accounts is required even if the subsidiary business does not take the form of a company or some other body corporate, but is a partnership or other unincorporated body.[50] Thus, although group accounts are required by the Act only of

---

[44] Final Report I, para.8.4. If a company runs out of cash, it is likely to be heading for insolvency on a "going concern" basis (i.e. it cannot pay its bills as they fall due), even if it is solvent on a "balance sheet" test (i.e., its assets exceed its liabilities but, for example, a large part of those assets consists of amounts due from creditors but not payable until a future date or of real property which is not easy to realise).

[45] s.404(1).

[46] s.399(2)—"as well as producing individual accounts". S.408 permits certain relaxations for the individual accounts of a company which produces group accounts, notably that the company's individual profit and loss account need not be circulated to the shareholders or filed with the Registrar, if notes to the group accounts show the profit and loss of the company for the financial year.

[47] s.394—"the directors of every company".

[48] s.407. For the meaning of "financial reporting framework" see para.21–12.

[49] Shareholders will also have rights against particular companies, but have a greater interest in the performance of the group as a whole, because profits in subsidiaries may lead to dividends to the parent which may in turn be distributed to the parents' shareholders, whereas losses may be left where they lie.

[50] s.1161(1).

entities which are companies,[51] the shareholders and creditors of and investors in those companies are to be provided with financial information relating to all the businesses the parent controls, no matter what legal form they may take.

But what is control? The Act sets out five situations where control will be found to exist. Briefly summarised, these situations are where the parent company:

(a) holds a majority of voting rights in the undertaking;[52]

(b) is a member of the other undertaking and has the right to appoint or remove a majority of its board of directors;[53]

(c) by virtue of provisions in the constitution of the other undertaking or in a written "control contract", permitted by that constitution, has a right, recognised by the law under which that undertaking is established, to exercise a "dominant influence" over that undertaking (by giving directions to the directors of the undertaking on its operating and financial policies which those directors are obliged to comply with whether or not the directions are for the benefit of the undertaking);[54]

(d) has the power to exercise or actually exercises dominant influence or control over the undertaking or the parent and alleged subsidiary are actually managed on a unified basis;[55]

(e) is a member of another undertaking and alone controls, pursuant to an agreement with other members, a majority of the voting rights in that undertaking;[56]

and sub-subsidiaries are to be treated as subsidiaries of the ultimate parent also.[57]

Despite the complexities of this definition, which arise partly out of the need to address control structures across the Community, it is clear that the most important case in the United Kingdom is (a).

---

[51] s.399(2).

[52] s.1162(2)(a).

[53] s.1162(2)(b). Membership includes "indirect" membership, i.e. where a subsidiary of the parent is a member of the undertaking in question: s.1162(3).

[54] s.1162(2)(c) and Sch.7, para.4. This situation of "contractual subordination" is probably never found in the UK, though it is provided for in Germany, where, however, it is rarely found in practice. There would be great difficulties with the legality of such a contract under the law of the United Kingdom.

[55] s.1162(4). This is a reference to actual domination and the qualifications needed to establish contractual domination do not apply here: Sch.7, para.4(3).

[56] This brings in shareholder agreements which are an established way of exercising control over companies in some continental European jurisdictions, but note that the effect of the agreement must be to give the alleged parent sole control.

[57] s.1162(5). For this reason it is important that the section refers to parent undertakings, since the immediate parent of the indirect subsidiary might not itself be a company.

Thus, the answer to our question is that a holding of 30 per cent by Company A in Company B will not, by itself, make Company B its subsidiary. However, companies are not permitted to remain entirely silent about their significant relationships with companies other than subsidiaries. Thus, companies have to disclose in their individual or group accounts certain information about companies, not being subsidiaries, in which they have nevertheless a significant holding.[58]

Small parent companies

Even if a parent/subsidiary relationship is established there are two **21–9** major and one minor exemption from the requirement to produce group accounts. First, a parent company which is subject to the small company regime is not required to produce group accounts.[59] This is undoubtedly a major benefit to small companies. However, in order to benefit from this exemption, the test is not whether the parent is small, but whether the group as a whole meets the relevant criteria.[60] Thus, a business cannot seek to benefit from the small company exemptions simply by splitting up its activities among a number of companies, headed by a small company. The size tests for a small group are the same as for a stand-alone company (discussed above) except that intra-group transactions may be eliminated when calculating turnover and balance sheet totals or the parent company may choose instead to benefit from slightly higher levels without eliminating intra-group transactions.[61] The same two-year rule, with its ameliorations, applies.[62] A somewhat wider exclusion of certain groups from eligibility also operates, and the exclusion is triggered if

---

[58] See, for example, paras 4–6 of Sch.4 to the Large and Medium-Sized Companies and Groups (Accounts and Reports) Regulations 2008/410, (hereafter "Accounts Regulations 2008") requiring a company's individual accounts to give certain information about companies in which the reporting company has a "significant holding"—defined as 20 per cent or more of any class of shares in the other company. Similar rules apply to group accounts (paras 20–22) with more detail being required in the cases where the "significant holding" makes the other company an "associated" undertaking or a joint venture with the reporting company (paras 18–19).

[59] s.399(1), though it may opt to do so: s.398. This exemption previously applied to medium-sized groups (CA 1985, s.248) but its removal was recommended by the CLR.

[60] s.383(1).

[61] s.383(4)–(7), as amended by the 2008 Amending Regulations, reg.3. The gross turnover level is £7.8 million and balance sheet total £3.9 million. The choice is available separately in relation to each of the turnover and balance sheet tests: s.383(6).

[62] s.383(1)–(3). See above, para.21–3.

any member of the group falls within the excluded cases.[63] Where the group is not a small group, then not only will the parent company have to produce group accounts, but also each company within the group will have to produce individual accounts.[64]

Parent companies which are part of a larger group

21–10 The rules for determining whether a parent/subsidiary relationship (above) exists do not exclude cases where the parent is itself the subsidiary of another company. In groups of companies this situation often exists. There may be a chain of companies in which all but the bottom company meet the statutory definition for being a parent of the company (or companies) below them in the chain. The resulting proliferation of group accounts of varying scope is not likely to be helpful. Consequently, there are exemptions which apply in such cases, aimed at producing the situation where, in general, only the ultimate holding company in the group (which may not be incorporated in a United Kingdom jurisdiction) is subject to the obligation to produce group accounts. However, it is important to note that there is no general exemption in the parent/subsidiary rules from the obligation to produce group accounts for parents which are themselves subsidiaries. Instead, the separate criteria set out in sections 400 and 401 have to be met for the exemption to be available. The rules vary slightly according to whether the immediate parent of the company seeking the exemption is or is not incorporated in a Member State of the European Economic Area.

There is one significant exclusion from the exemption. It is not available for companies whose securities (whether shares or not) are traded on a regulated market in the EEA.[65] For such securities to be admitted to trading, there will necessarily be a significant block of the company's shares which are not held by that company's parent but are in the hands of public investors. Their interests dictate that the traded company should produce accounts which cover its position

---

[63] s.384(2). Also excluded are cases where any member of the group is traded on a regulated market of an EEA state and where a member of the group is authorised to carry out regulated activities under Part IV of FSMA, unless it is independently a small company. It is not clear that either extension is of enormous importance. As to the first, as far as UK markets are concerned, the exclusion of groups containing public companies from the small companies regime listing will have the same effect, since private companies cannot be admitted to the official list: Financial Services and Markets Act 2000 (Official Listing of Securities) Regulations 2001 (SI 2001/2956) reg.3. As to the second, the effect is to require Part IV activities to be carried out through a company, rather than any other form of undertaking, because if the company undertaking this business is not small, the group is unlikely to be small either.

[64] s.384(1)(c).

[65] ss.400(4), (6) and 401(4), (6). For the definition of a regulated market see para.25–5.

together with the position of the undertakings it controls, for that is the economic entity in which the public have invested.[66]

Subject to certain further conditions, a wholly-owned subsidiary, which is also a parent company on the definition discussed above, is relieved of the obligation to produce group accounts. Where the subsidiary is not wholly owned but the parent holds more than 50 per cent of the allotted shares in the subsidiary, which would otherwise have to produce group accounts, the subsidiary's exemption from that obligation is subject to the inaction of the shareholders. If the holders of more than half of the remaining allotted shares or the holders of 5 per cent of the total allotted shares in the company serve a notice, requiring the production of group accounts, within six months of the end of the financial year in question, then group accounts must be produced.[67] Thus, a significant proportion of the "outside" shareholders can still insist on group accounts from the subsidiary which is also a parent, but the burden lies upon them to take this step.

Even where the exemption is available in principle, certain other conditions have to be met. First, the subsidiary which is also a parent must actually be included in the accounts of a larger group, those accounts must be drawn up in accordance with the standards contained in the Seventh Directive[68] or equivalent standards, and must be audited.[69] Secondly, the individual accounts of the subsidiary which is also a parent must disclose that it is exempt from the obligation to produce group accounts, must give the name of the parent undertaking that draws up the group accounts,[70] its country of incorporation (if not the United Kingdom) and, if unincorporated, its principal place of business.[71] Thirdly, the company seeking the exemption must deliver the group accounts to the Registrar, translated into English, if necessary.[72]

Companies excluded from consolidation

If a company is in principle subject to the obligation to produce **21–11** group accounts, nevertheless some subsidiary companies may be

---

[66] Of course, those investors may also be strongly interested in the traded company's relations with its parent, for fear that the parent may seek to take a disproportionate share of the company's earnings. But that is a different issue.

[67] ss.400(1) and 401(1).

[68] Above, fn.6.

[69] ss.400(2)(a)–(b), 401(2)(a)–(c). The requirement for audit is stated expressly in relation only to non-EEA parent companies, but in the case of EEA companies this requirement follows from the provisions of the Eighth Directive (see Ch.22 below).

[70] This is not necessarily its immediate holding company, since that company, by operation of the same rules, might be exempt from the need to produce consolidated accounts. Thus, where there is a chain of three wholly-owned subsidiaries, only the top company will normally have to produce consolidated accounts.

[71] ss.400(2)(c)–(d), 401(2)(d)–(e).

[72] ss.400(2)(e)–(f), 401(2)(f)–(g).

omitted from the consolidation. Subsidiaries may be omitted if (a) their inclusion is not material for giving a true and fair view of the group (for example, if they are inactive companies); (b) "severe long-term restrictions" substantially hinder the exercise of the parent's rights over the assets or management of the company (a situation most likely to arise from restrictions in foreign legal systems); (c) the necessary information cannot be obtained "without disproportionate expense or undue delay"; and (d) the parent's interest is held exclusively with a view to resale.[73] If all the subsidiaries fall within one or other of these categories, no group accounts need be produced—no doubt a rare situation.[74]

Form and content of annual accounts
Possible approaches
21–12 Broadly, there are two model approaches for the legislature to take to the rules relating to the analysis of the transactions the company has engaged in during the financial year and the presentation of the results of that analysis in the company's individual or group accounts. It could lay down one or more very general principles to be followed and leave it to the accounting profession to develop more specific rules (usually referred to as "accounting standards"), to which, however, legal force would not be attached; or the legislature could try to set out a detailed set of rules itself. The British tradition has been very much to follow the former model. However, the continental European tradition, which is closer to the second model, had an impact on British law in the 1980s, because that tradition influenced the Fourth and Seventh Directives on companies' accounts,[75] though not to the extent by any means of a complete shift to the latter approach. However, in a later development the Community moved towards giving standard setters a bigger role in the setting of the detailed rules, through the adoption of International Accounting Standards (IAS), though with provisions which meant that standard-setting was no longer purely a matter for the professions and the public interest was represented in the standard-setting exercise.

The result is that the current rules are a mixture of legislative provision and accounting standards, to which different degrees of legal recognition are accorded. Moreover, there are two sets of rules, with different mixtures. This is the significance of the term "accounting framework". A company which is under an obligation to produce individual accounts is free to do so either by reference to the rules contained in the Companies Act and regulations made there-

---

[73] s.405.
[74] s.402.
[75] See fn.6, above.

under or by reference to IAS.[76] These accounts are called, helpfully if unimaginatively, "Companies Act individual accounts" and "IAS individual accounts" respectively. The same choice is available to companies under an obligation to produce group accounts, except that companies with securities traded on a regulated market[77] must use IAS for their group accounts, as required by Community law.[78] Thus, there are also "Companies Act group accounts" and "IAS group accounts".

The IAS Regulation permits Member States to permit or require domestic companies to use IAS more widely.[79] The UK adopted the permissive approach but made it widely available, for even small companies may use IAS. There is some pressure towards the adoption of IAS because the legislation has a ratchet effect in favour of IAS. A company may be free to adopt IAS or not (if it is not obliged to do so by the IAS Regulation) but, having done so, it cannot switch back to the Companies Act rules unless "there is a relevant change of circumstance".[80] Moreover, having switched to Companies Act accounts, a re-conversion to IAS accounts will require the company to stay with IAS unless there is a further change of circumstance.[81]

We will now look at Companies Act accounts and IAS accounts in turn, but first it is necessary to look at a provision which applies to both Companies Act and IAS accounts.

True and fair view
The traditional British approach to the accounts has long focussed **21–13** around the general principle that the accounts must "give a true and fair view of the assets, liabilities, financial position and profit or loss"[82] of the individual company or the companies included in the consolidation in the case of group accounts. For many years this was virtually all the companies legislation said about the content of the accounts. It remains an overriding principle, no matter which accounting framework the directors choose for the presentation of the accounts. The directors must not approve accounts under the chapter unless they provide a true and fair view, whether these are

---

[76] s.395. A company which is a charity must provide Companies Act individual and group accounts: ss.395(2) and 403(3).
[77] See para.25–7.
[78] IAS Regulation (above, fn.7), Art.4. Since the Regulation is directly applicable in the Member States, the provisions of Art.4 are not reproduced in the Act, though s.403(1) refers to the Community obligation.
[79] IAS Regulation, Art.5.
[80] ss.395(3) and 403(4). The changes identified in the Act, and they are apparently exclusive, are becoming a subsidiary of a company which does not prepare IAS accounts and the company or its parent ceasing to have securities traded on a regulated market: ss.395(4) and 403(5).
[81] ss.395(5) and 403(6).
[82] s.393(1).

Companies Act accounts or IAS accounts.[83] If, in relation to Companies Act accounts, compliance with the Act or provisions made under it would not be sufficient to give a true and fair view, the necessary additional information must be given in the accounts or notes to them.[84] Further, if compliance with the statutory provisions would put the accounts in breach of the "true and fair" requirement, the directors must depart from the statute or subordinate legislation to the extent necessary to give a true and fair view.[85] What this qualification seems not to permit, though standard-setters have sometimes taken a different view, is the issuance of a standard which gives a general dispensation to companies to depart from a provision in or made under the Act, on the grounds that a true and fair view requires this. The provisions of the Act and of the Directives[86] seem to contemplate only ad hoc departures from the requirements of the Schedules in the case of particular companies.[87]

With regard to IAS accounts, the position is probably the same, at least on the assumption that the requirement in IAS 1 that the accounts "present fairly" the company's or group's financial position may be equated with a "true and fair view".[88] The application of IAS (or rather International Financial Reporting Standards (IFRS), as they have now become) is presumed to lead to fair presentation, but IAS 1 recognises that further disclosure may be necessary to achieve this result. Departure from IFRS in order to achieve fair presentation is recognised as permissible but only "in extremely rare circumstances".

Companies Act accounts

21–14 Other than for group accounts prepared by a company having its securities traded on a regulated market, the directors may choose to prepare Companies Act accounts and may stay with that choice unless their company becomes admitted to such a market. The accounts required to be produced are of a traditional type: a balance sheet as of the last day of the financial year and a profit and loss account.[89] The balance sheet shows the company's financial position, in terms of assets and liabilities, as at a particular point in time. The profit and loss account indicates the company's performance over the financial year.

---

[83] s.393(1).
[84] ss.396(4) and 404(4).
[85] ss.396(5) and 404(5).
[86] Fourth Directive, above, fn.6, Art.2(5); Seventh Directive, above, fn.6, Art.26(5).
[87] IAS accounts will not raise this issue, since where a company chooses to produce IAS accounts, the statutory requirements do not apply other than the obligation on the director to produce accounts which give a true and fair view.
[88] If this is not the case, then there is a flat contradiction between the requirements of s.393 and the obligations of companies which have chosen the IAS accounting framework under the Community's IAS Regulation.
[89] s.396. See the similar s.404(1) for group accounts.

With the enactment of the Fourth and Seventh Directives, which, whilst adopting the overall "true and fair" test from British law, also adopted the Continental practice of dealing with matters of form and content in the legislation itself, the provisions in the Act dealing with the accounts were expanded. Those provisions are now in the Accounts Regulations 2008.[90] Part 1 of Schedule 1 to the Regulations[91] provides two alternative formats in which the balance sheet may be presented and four possible formats for the profit and loss account. However, the directors cannot shift from the formats adopted in the previous year "unless in their opinion there are special reasons for a change."[92]

The formats concern simply the questions of how the accounting information is grouped and the order in which the information, so grouped, is presented to the reader. More important, therefore, are the provisions of the Schedule which go into issues relating to the proper accounting treatment of transactions or contain rules about the valuation of assets and liabilities. These are contained in Part 2 of the Schedule under the heading "Accounting Principles and Rules". However, these rules are (strong) default rules, for the directors may depart from them if there are "special reasons" for so doing, provided the nature of the departure, the reasons for it and its effect are stated.[93] Furthermore, the Schedule explicitly provides a choice to the directors as to the fundamental accounting approach which will be adopted. No longer is a historical cost approach mandatory (under which, for example, assets are carried in the books at their original acquisition price, less depreciation, even though their current market price is much higher) but rather various forms of "marking to market" are permitted.[94]

Finally, it is clear that the "Accounting Principles and Rules" contained in the Schedule are not sufficient to produce a set of accounts for any particular company, except perhaps one of the simplest character. More detailed accounting standards need to be deployed, which are not to be found in the Regulations implementing the Directives but in standards developed by the standard-setters, to which we now turn.

---

[90] Above, fn.58. They were previously in Schedules to the 1985 Act. For small companies less demanding requirements are set out in the Small Companies and Groups (Accounts and Directors' Report) Regulations 2008/409 (hereafter "Small Companies Accounts Regulations 2008"). This account of the regulations is necessarily brief and we shall omit entirely the special provisions applying to banking and insurance companies.

[91] Schedule 6 makes some additional provisions in relation to group accounts.

[92] Sch.1, para.2.

[93] Sch.1, para.10.

[94] See Sections C and D of Part 2. The introduction of "fair value accounting" into the Fourth and Seventh Directives was effected by Directive 2003/53/EC (OJ L178, 17.7.2003) as a direct result of the adoption by the Community of the IAS for companies on regulated markets, where this approach was required. Further amendments of the same character to the Fourth and Seventh Directives were made by Art.1(5) of Directive 2006/46/EC. In this way, the IAS have expanded as well the scope of action of purely domestic standard-setters.

Accounting standards

21–15 In the United Kingdom the professional accountancy bodies had begun as early as 1942[95] to issue accounting standards. At that time and for a long while thereafter they provided the only authoritative guidance on what the "true and fair" requirement meant in particular situations. Those standards covered ever more topics and became ever more sophisticated over time; and, as we have seen, their centrality to the accounts-producing exercise was not ended by the transposition in the United Kingdom of the Fourth and Seventh Directives. Two important developments have accompanied the expansion of the role of accounting standards. These two developments are probably not unconnected with one another, their common feature being a recognition of the quasi-public role played by accounting standards. First, accounting standards, whilst not becoming legally enforceable directly, have achieved legal backing; secondly, the professional bodies have lost their previously complete control over the standard-setting process.

The acquisition of indirect legal support was itself a twin-track process, involving both legislature and courts. In 1989 a provision was added to the Act, which is now paragraph 45 of Schedule 1 to the Accounts Regulations 2008, which provides that "it must be stated whether the accounts have been prepared in accordance with applicable accounting standards and particulars of any material departure from those standards and the reasons for it must be given."[96] This in effect puts accounting standards on a "comply or explain" basis, and it was probably the first example of the use of this technique in company law.[97] About the same time the courts accepted the professional standards (which had now become Statements of Standard Accounting Practice (SSAPs)) as the best evidence of the standard of care required by the law of negligence of accountants in the discharge of their professional duties, especially when acting as auditors, though the courts are not bound by the professionally developed standards.[98]

The second development—the interjection of a public element into the standard-setting bodies—also occurred about this time when, in 1990, the Accounting Standards Committee was replaced by the Accounting Standards Board (ASB) and, incidentally, SSAPs by Financial Reporting Standards (FRS). However, the crucial point is

---

[95] In that year the Institute of Chartered Accountants in England and Wales began to issue Recommendations on Accounting Principles.

[96] Small companies are not subject to this obligation by the Small Companies Accounts Regulations 2008 (above fn.90) and medium-sized companies are exempt from this obligation (see the Accounts Regulations 2008, reg.4(2)), though the CLR recommended that this exemption should be withdrawn: Developing, para.8.35.

[97] For its use in relation to the Combined Code, which was developed only in the 1990s, see above at para.14–29.

[98] *Lloyd Cheyham & Co v Littlejohn & Co* [1987] B.C.L.C. 303; but *cf. Bolitho v City and Hackney Health Authority* [1998] A.C. 232, HL (court not bound by professional standards where "in a rare case" it is convinced they are not reasonable or responsible).

that authority to issue accounting standards which have statutory recognition had been made by the Companies Act 1989 something which the Secretary of State confers by regulation on the body or bodies thought appropriate.[99] The ASB is an operating body of the Financial Reporting Council (FRC), whose functions we will consider in more detail later in this Chapter and the next. The FRC, is a private company (limited by guarantee), but the Chair and Deputy Chair of the FRC are appointed by the Secretary of State and the FRC directors appoint the members of the ASB board. In addition, the users of accountants' services are represented on the governing bodies of both the FRC and ASB. The Government has contributed about a third of the FRC's running costs.[100] Overall, the public authorities, through a combination of powers to confer authority on the ASB to set standards, without which it would lose the reason for its existence and to influence the membership of its board can be said to have considerable potential control over its activities. On the other hand, the governmental bodies do not interfere in the day-to-day running of the ASB. Thus, the current structure can be said to combine the technical competence and flexibility of setting rules through expert bodies exercising delegated powers with the safeguarding of the public interest which legislation should ensure.

IAS accounts

If the Fourth and Seventh Directives represented the use by the Community of (partial) legislative specification of the form of the accounts, the IAS Regulation[101] represents the Community's adoption of the alternative strategy of reliance on the standard-setters. Companies subject to the IAS, whether mandatorily or by their own choice, are to prepare their accounts in conformity with international accounting standards as laid down by the International Accounting Standards Board.[102] True it is that such companies remain subject to the Fourth and Seventh Directives, but those Directives were amended so as to ensure that they permitted companies to adopt the IAS approach.[103] A good example is the fact that IAS 1 does not require the production of a profit and loss account but rather of income and cash flow statements, which necessitated an adjustment

21–16

---

[99] Now s.464 of the 2006 Act. The ASB is prescribed by the Accounting Standards (Prescribed Body) Regulations 2008/651.

[100] Power to make grants to standard setting bodies is contained in s.16 of the Companies (Audit, Investigation and Community Enterprise) Act 2004, whilst s.17 authorises the Secretary of State to impose a levy on others to support the grant-aided setter. However, in February 2008 the government announced its decision to shift funding for the FRC's accounting, auditing and corporate governance work wholly onto market participants via the levy system.

[101] Above, fn.7.

[102] IAS Regulation, Art.2.

[103] See fn.94 above.

of the Fourth Directive.[104] In other words, compliance with the IAS produces compliance with the (amended) Fourth and Seventh Directives. Since the IAS Regulation (and hence the obligation to use IAS) applies directly in the United Kingdom to those companies required or permitted to be covered by it, without the need for transposing legislation, the Accounts Regulations 2008[105] apply only to companies producing Companies Act accounts.

The effect of the IAS Regulation is to give the standards produced by the IASB (now called International Financial Reporting Standards (IFRS)) an even stronger legal position than that afforded to FRS produced domestically by the ASB. As we have seen, the domestic standards are enforced on a "comply or explain" basis, whereas the appropriate IAS and IFRS must be followed under the terms of the IAS Regulation. Not surprisingly, and following the domestic developments, the more prominent role afforded to the international standards was accompanied by a loss of purely professional control over the setting of those standards. The IASB became an independent body in 2001, having been founded in 1973 by the professional accountancy bodies of nine leading countries. However, close ties with a particular government, as with the ASB, were hardly feasible for the IASB, which adopted a different path away from professional control. In brief, its members are appointed by the trustees of a foundation, which trustees are a self-perpetuating body (i.e. they appoint their own successors). However, the constitution of the foundation, prescribing both the initial membership of the trustee body and the choice of replacements, requires the trustees to have an international geographical spread and to "provide an appropriate balance of professional backgrounds, including auditors, preparers, users, academics, and other officials serving the public interest."[106]

21–17 Although based in London, the IASB is not a European but an international organisation, as its name suggests. Given its wider scope, on the one hand, and the obligation of companies within the IAS Regulation to apply IAS and IFRS, it is perhaps not surprising that there is a filter put in place between the adoption of a standard by the IASB and its becoming mandatory for European companies subject to the IAS Regulation. The filter is that the standard produced by the IASB must have been adopted by the Commission of the EU, as advised by an Accounting Regulatory Committee ("ARC") consisting of representatives from the Member States, before it becomes binding on companies.[107] It is perhaps less clear

---

[104] Arts.2 and 22.
[105] Above, fn.58. There is one exception, dealt with below, para.21–20, in the form of Schedule 4 to the Regulations, dealing with related party transactions.
[106] The constitution of the Foundation is set out at: http://www.iasb.org/About+Us/About+the+Foundation/Constitution.htm.
[107] IAS Regulation, Arts.3 and 6.

what is the nature of the filtration process. Adoption is not permitted if the IASB standard is contrary to the "true and fair view" principle,[108] but if the "fair presentation" principle of IAS 1 is the same as a true and fair view,[109] then that judgment will have been made already by the IASB. Nor may the Commission adopt an IASB standard if it fails to "meet the criteria of understandability, relevance, reliability and comparability" required of such standards. However, it is highly unlikely that the IASB would adopt a standard which it considered infringed this principle either. In effect, the filter operates as an opportunity for the same issues to be debated again as were considered in the adoption of the initial IAS or IFRS. Such a re-hashing of the arguments occurred in relation to the IAS standards on the valuation of financial instruments. After a long debate IAS 39 was initially adopted only with two significant carve outs.[110] The other IAS and IFRS have been adopted straightforwardly. It is clear that extensive use of the blocking power by the Commission would be likely to lead to a collapse of the IASB venture.

It may be wondered why the Community threw its weight behind the IAS and the IASB rather than keeping closer control over accounting standards itself. This seems to have constituted a recognition that producing accounting standards for the largest companies is necessarily a global rather than a regional activity.[111] Globalisation has led multinational companies to acquire not only cross-border business activities, but also cross-border groups of investors. Both investors, seeking to compare companies from different jurisdictions, and companies, seeking to raise money in more than one country, have generated a demand for international uniformity in accounting standards, so that accounts do not have to be constantly restated according to different countries' "generally accepted accounting principles" ("GAAP"). The only other contender for a global role was the spread of the US standards (US GAAP). The IASB provides a platform from which convergence may be pursued with the US standards rather than a simple adoption of them.[112]

Small company accounts
As we have seen above, a small company is not required to produce **21–18** group accounts, though it may choose to do so. In addition, the statutory format for its Companies Act accounts (individual or

---

[108] IAS Regulation, Art.3(2).
[109] See para.21–13, above.
[110] Commission Regulation (EC) No.2086/2004. The IASB later amended IAS 39 which was, as amended, adopted in full by the Community: Commission Regulation (EC) No.1864/2005.
[111] Among the countries which allow or soon will allow their companies to use IFRS are Australia, India, Japan and South Korea.
[112] The ASB also has a policy of producing convergence with IAS, so that in the end there may be relatively little difference between Companies Act and IAS accounts, though the IASB would be in the lead.

group) is simpler.[113] In particular, small companies are not required to state the extent of their compliance with ASB standards and to explain areas of non-compliance.[114] Finally, the accounting standards applying to small companies have been simplified, both by the ASB and the IASB.[115]

Notes to the accounts

21–19 Although the British tradition has been for the legislature not to specify the form and content of the accounts, but to leave that to standard-setters, the legislature has long seen the accounts as a useful place to require the disclosure of specific pieces of information. These are not required to be part of the accounts proper but are to be given in "notes" to the accounts.[116] The information required to be disclosed is designed to make the information contained in the accounts complete.[117] We have seen above the example of the requirement to give information in the notes about non-subsidiary companies in which the reporting company has a significant holding.[118] Article 43 of the Fourth Directive lists some 17 and Art.34 of the Seventh Directive some 18 matters which must be dealt with in this way.

However, the policy behind the notes requirement may be something more than just completing the picture presented by the accounts. Thus, Accounts Regulations 2008[119] require unquoted companies to give certain information about directors' remuneration in notes to their accounts, whether those accounts are drawn up under the Companies Act or IAS, as part of the Government's policy for controlling of directors' remuneration. As we have seen,[120] the directors of a quoted company are required to produce a directors' remuneration report (DRR), so the notes requirement is confined principally to unquoted companies. However, what this illustrates is that disclosure-as-regulation is a policy which appears in relation to the directors' reports as well as in relation to the notes to the accounts, as we shall see below.

---

[113] This is set out in the Small Companies and Groups (Accounts and Directors' Report) Regulations 2008/409 (hereafter Small Companies Accounts Regulations 2008).

[114] This exemption also applies to medium-sized companies. See fn.96 above.

[115] ASB, Financial Reporting Standard for Smaller Entities 2007 (FRSSE). The IASB is still working, at the time of writing, on a standard for small and medium-sized entities: IASB, *Exposure Draft of a Proposed IFRS for Small and Medium-sized Entities*, February 2007.

[116] In fact, the company may, but is not required to, put them in a separate document annexed to the accounts: s.472.

[117] Much of the information required to be disclosed in notes under Part 3 of Schedule 1 to the Accounts Regulations 2008 is of this character.

[118] Above, fn.58. This part of the Regulations is made under ss.409 and 410 of the Act and extends to information about subsidiaries as well as about affiliates.

[119] Above, fn.58, reg.8 and Sch.5, Part 2—Regulations made under s.412.

[120] See para.14–17.

Another example is the requirement in section 411 that notes to a company's accounts state, unless it is a small company, the average number of employees employed by it in the financial year (in total and by category) and the aggregate amounts paid to them by way of salary and the aggregate amount of social security and pension costs incurred.[121] This helps meet public policy concerns about two matters: the level of job opportunities created by British companies (suspected to be falling with out-sourcing to other countries) and the gap between directors' and employees' remuneration (suspected (or known) to be increasing).

Of course, the notes may contain information which is relevant **21–20** both to understanding the company's financial position and to meeting the public policy objectives of governments. An example is provided by the recent amendments to the Fourth and Seventh Directives in relation to "off-balance sheet" transactions.[122] This is a wide category of transactions, which the Directive wisely does not try to define,[123] the essence of which is that the company is subject to a risk of loss as a result of a transaction entered into with another entity (often one closely connected with the reporting entity but not counting as a subsidiary) but where that risk is not required to be shown on the company's balance sheet. Where these risks are material a person reading the accounts needs to know of them. Equally, however, public policy concerns arising out of the collapse of the Enron Corporation in the United States in 2002 are addressed in this way, a collapse in part brought about by the acquisition of liabilities towards Special Purpose Vehicles (SPVs) connected with Enron but not counting as its subsidiaries.[124] In fact, domestic rules already required disclosure of many of these transactions,[125] but the new statutory rules are more comprehensive. They are implemented through the addition of what is likely to be the first of many new sections to the Companies Act 2006, in this case section 410A.[126]

A further variant is to use disclosure to reinforce a different legal strategy adopted elsewhere. We have seen that the issue of transactions between companies and those who are in a position to influence

---

[121] See para.14–17 above, for the new requirement that this issue be directly addressed in the DRR.
[122] Art.43(7A) of the Fourth Directive and Art.34(7A) of the Seventh Directive, inserted by Directive 2006/46/EC.
[123] But see the "non-definition" provided in Recital 9 to Directive 2006/46/EC.
[124] For an analysis of the accounting implications of Enron and for some comparative discussion with the UK see W. W. Bratton, "Principles and the Accounting Crisis in the United States" in J. Armour and J McCahery (eds), *After Enron* (Oxford: Hart Publishing, 2006).
[125] As a result of FRS 5 (Reporting the Substance of Transactions).
[126] Inserted by the Companies Act 2006 (Accounts and Reports) (Amendment) Regulations 2008/393, reg.8. This disclosure is not required of small companies and only in a modified way of medium-sized companies.

the terms of those transactions or their associates is a central regulatory problem in relation to both directors and controlling shareholders. Transactions between directors and their companies are subject to special rules about disclosure to the board or even shareholder approval,[127] whilst similar transactions by controlling shareholders, though in general less well policed by British company law, may give rise to claims of unfair prejudice.[128] The Accounts Regulations 2008[129] reinforce these provisions by requiring disclosure in the accounts (other than of small and medium-sized companies) of related-party transactions, if they are material and have not been concluded "under normal market conditions", so that shareholders may be in a better position to decide whether to seek to invoke these other rules.[130] However, this is perhaps a less important change than it seems since domestic accounting standards, enforceable on a comply or explain basis, already required similar disclosure.[131]

THE DIRECTORS' REPORT

21–21 The directors' report, to accompany both the individual and group accounts, has long been a statutory requirement in the United Kingdom, and it is now a requirement of the Fourth and Seventh Directives.[132] In recent years, it has been the subject of important legislative expansion, in two areas. First, the directors of quoted companies are required to produce a directors' remuneration report (DRR). This has been dealt with in Chapter 14[133] and need not be further considered here.[134] Secondly, the directors' report (DR) has become the focus of a new requirement for the company's annual statements to include forward-looking "soft" data to accompany the

---

[127] Above, para.16–40.

[128] Above, Ch.20.

[129] Para.72 of Sch.1, implementing Art.43(7B) of the Fourth Directive, inserted by Directive 2006/46/EC. Para.22 of Sch.6 makes similar provision in relation to group accounts. These provisions apply formally only to companies preparing Companies Act accounts, but those preparing IAS accounts are under a similar obligation because of the provisions in IAS 24 (Related Party Disclosures). The two are further tied together by the adoption in para.72 of the same definition of "related party" as in the IAS—though unhelpfully it does not reproduce it.

[130] A similar role is played by s.413 in relation to a narrower range of transactions between the company and its directors. See above at para.16–40.

[131] See FRS 8 (Related Party Disclosure) and on the enforcement of domestic standards, above, para.21–14.

[132] See s.415 (the requirement is supported by criminal sanctions); and the Fourth Directive, Arts.46ff and Seventh Directive, Arts.36ff (where it is referred to as the "annual report").

[133] At paras 14–16ff.

[134] The DRR appears to be a separate document from the DR, though in practice they are usually presented together. The DR and the DRR are dealt with in separate chapters of Part 15 of the Act and the DRR is not expressed, as the business review is (s.417(1)), to be part of the DR.

backward-looking, "hard" financial data contained in the accounts. This section of the report is termed the "business review" and is sometimes referred to as "narrative" reporting, to distinguish it from the numbers-based accounts. The introduction of this requirement[135] was accompanied by moments of high farce, as the Government first introduced, then repealed, then partially re-introduced the more far-reaching recommendations which the CLR had made for an "operating and financial review".

Content of the directors' report other than the business review

First, however, we turn to the requirements for the DR other than the business review. The statute requires the report to list those who were directors of the company at any time during the year and the company's principal activities in the course of the year.[136] It must also state the amount the directors recommend to be paid by way of dividend to the shareholders.[137] However, this latter requirement does not apply to companies entitled to the "small company exemption". Presumably, this is because in small companies public disclosure of dividend recommendations may reveal the income of easily identifiable individuals, for example, where the directors are the only shareholders. This exemption is available not only to small companies falling within the small companies regime for the accounts but also to small companies which would so fall but for the fact that they are members of a group of companies which contains an ineligible member.[138] Thus, the relaxations for small companies in relation to the DR go somewhat wider than in relation to the accounts.

None of the above is very demanding. However, the directors' report is subject to further requirements as to its contents, those requirements very much reflecting the policies underlying the notes to the accounts which we examined above. Thus, the policy of using disclosure in the accounts to further strategies developed elsewhere in the legislation, either as a result of domestic or Community reform impulses, is well to the fore. The DR must contain a statement by the directors about information provided to the company's auditors, as a way of furthering the effectiveness of the audit.[139] As a result of amendments to the Fourth Directive in 2006, a company whose securities are admitted to trading on a regulated market must include a corporate governance statement in its annual report.[140] That cor-

21–22

---

[135] Now s.417.
[136] s.416(1),(2).
[137] s.416(3).
[138] s.416(3), as amended by s.415A, inserted by the Companies Act 2006 (Accounts and Reports) (Amendment) Regulations 2008/393, reg.6. For the meaning of "ineligible" companies see above, para.21–9.
[139] s.418. See the following Chapter at para.22–32.
[140] Fourth Directive, Art.46A, inserted by Directive 2006/46/EC. That statement need not be but normally will be part of the directors' report.

porate governance statement must deal, amongst other things, with the company's control structures,[141] compliance with the relevant corporate governance code,[142] and contain a description of the company's internal control and risk management systems in relation to financial reporting.[143]

Many further requirements for the DR are to be found in Schedule 7 to the Accounts Regulations 2008, which is divided into a number of parts, some of which require information which goes far beyond the purely financial. Thus Part 3 requires information to be given about the employment, training and promotion of disabled persons. Part 4 requires information about "employee involvement", i.e. the extent to which employees are systematically given information, consulted, and encouraged to join employee share schemes. Part 5 requires companies to disclose their policies and practice on the payment of creditors. None of these is strictly relevant to an appraisal of the company's financial position, except that shareholders might think that the longer creditors are kept waiting, the better. Nor, indeed, is the requirement in Part 1 for separate disclosure of the amounts of charitable or political donations; in view of the minimal amounts needed to trigger this requirement and the modest amounts normally donated, they would very rarely be material to a true and fair view of its financial affairs. In fact, Schedule 7 is used by Government, not for the purpose of financial disclosure, but in order to expose to public gaze matters which Government is unwilling to regulate prescriptively but which it hopes, perhaps optimistically, will be either promoted or contained (as the case may be) through the pressures of public opinion. If, as often happens, for example in relation to political donations,[144] governmental policy develops further so as to impose substantive obligations on companies or businesses in general, the disclosure provisions of the Schedule nevertheless act as a useful supplementary means of enforcement.

The business review

Rationale and history

21–23 Section 417 requires the DR of all companies, other than those benefiting from the small companies regime,[145] to contain a business review (BR). The requirement for a BR reflects the perception that shareholders and investors need more than financial data to under-

---

[141] Accounts Regulations 2008, Sch.7, Part 6, discussed at para.28–27. This information is relevant to the policy of promoting a European market in corporate control.

[142] Discussed above at para.14–31. In this case the obligation is to be found in the Listing Rules (LR 9.8.6 and 9.8.7).

[143] This requirement is also likely to be implemented via FSA Rules.

[144] Above para.16–62.

[145] The requirements are relaxed for medium-sized companies, but not excluded entirely. A small company excluded from the small company regime because a member of an ineligible group may also take advantage of this exemption: s.415A, inserted by 2008 Amending Regulations, reg.6.

stand fully the prospects of the company. They need also to be able to gauge the quality of the company's relationships with those upon whose contributions or cooperation the success of the company depends (sometimes called "stakeholders"). For stakeholders, as well, this information may be useful, even if company law itself gives them no particular platform from which to take action on the basis of the information.[146] The BR required by section 417 varies in its intensity according to whether the company producing it is quoted or not.[147] If it is not, the section's requirements track those of Article 46(1) of the Fourth Directive and 36(1) of the Seventh Directive, as amended in 2003.[148] If it is, the requirements for the BR go further, but not as far as recommended by the CLR in its proposals for an Operating and Financial Review (OFR) and as initially implemented by the Government. The sequence of events whereby the OFR arrived, but then disappeared, and was ultimately replaced by an "enhanced" BR is a dramatic one in an area where drama is normally in short supply.

It is possible to detect in the reports of the CLR two main reasons underlying the proposal for the requirement that major companies produce an OFR. The first was based on a re-evaluation of the information needed to assess the position and prospects of many companies by adding to the historical, financial information, already required to be reported, information relating to:

> "qualitative and intangible assets such as the skills and knowledge of their employees, their business relationships and their reputation. Information about future plans, opportunities, risks and strategies is just as important as the historical review of performance which form the basis of reporting at present".[149]

The second, less clearly articulated, was the need to provide a check on the discharge by directors of their "inclusive" duty[150] to promote the success of the company for the benefit of its members but on the basis of taking into account the company's need to foster its relationships with stakeholders, its impact upon communities affected and environment and reputational concerns. Thus, there was a close link between the shareholder-centred statement of directors' duties recommended by the CLR and the desire to provide some mechanism whereby its "enlightened" elements meant something significant in practice and were not just self-serving. That mechanism was to be disclosure via the OFR.

---

[146] Trade unions might use the information in collective bargaining with the company or they and other stakeholders might use it in making representations to government or in other ways taking political action.

[147] For the definition of a quoted company see above, para.14–16.

[148] By Directive 2003/51/EC.

[149] Final Report I, para.3.33.

[150] See above at paras 16–25ff.

At first, all seemed to be going well with the OFR proposal. In fact, it was introduced by regulation in 2005 under powers contained in the Companies Act 1985 in advance of the enactment of the 2006 Act,[151] after extensive consultation among those affected.[152] Whilst the companies affected were preparing their first OFRs, the then Chancellor of the Exchequer, in a speech to the Confederation of British Industry,[153] and apparently after exiguous consultation with the Department of Trade and Industry (the Department responsible for company law at that time),[154] announced the repeal[155] of the OFR on the grounds it was "a gold-plated regulatory requirement"—but without showing any appreciation of its place in the wider scheme of reforms proposed by the CLR. The DTI, re-stating its commitment to "strategic forward-looking narrative reporting", then undertook consultation on how far this commitment could be implemented within the BR requirement without imposing on companies "unnecessary burdens". It is the result of this process, with some last-minute amendments in Parliament, which gave rise to the present section.

Operating and Financial Review and Business Review compared

21–24   The central question about the section is, how much of the OFR does it reinstate for quoted companies, which are subject to the enhanced requirements? It is suggested that a good deal, but far from all, of the substance of the OFR requirements is applied to quoted companies, and that the quality of what is disclosed under the BR may be less than would have been the case with the OFR. To establish this one needs to analyse the section, to which we now turn.

Section 417(2) states that the purpose of the BR is to "inform members of the company" and to help them assess whether the directors have performed their duty under section 172 of the Act to promote the success of the company for the benefit of its members.[156] Although placing the emphasis on the members ties in well with the shareholder-centred focus of section 172, we have seen that the CLR proposed that the OFR should not be so narrowly targeted,[157] though

---

[151] Companies Act 1985 (Operating and Financial Review and Directors' Report etc.) Regulations 2005 (SI 2005/1011).

[152] DTI, *The Operating and Financial Review and Directors' Report: A Consultative Document*, May 2004 (URN 04/1003).

[153] Speech by the Rt. Hon. Gordon Brown MP, Chancellor of the Exchequer, at the CBI Annual Conference in London, November 28, 2005.

[154] Somewhat more is known about the internal workings of government on this issue than might be expected as a result of documents produced in judicial review proceedings brought by Friends of the Earth over the abolition decision. See *Financial Times*, UK Edition, March 8, 2006.

[155] Effected by the Companies Act 1985 (Operating and Financial Review) (Repeal) Regulations 2005 (SI 2005/3442).

[156] Above at para.16–24.

[157] Completing, para.3.33. Thus, non-shareholders would have been included among the addresses of the OFR.

the OFR as implemented did not reflect this suggestion. Section 417 requires all companies (other than those able to benefit from the small company exemption) to produce a business review containing a fair review of the company's business and a description of the principal risks and uncertainties facing it—or them in the case of group accounts.[158] The review required is "a balanced and comprehensive" analysis of the development and performance of the company's business during the financial year and of its position at the end of the year.[159] To the extent that it is necessary for an understanding of the business the review must make use of "key performance indicators", both financial and non-financial.[160] This is an attempt to inject some quantitative analysis into what might otherwise be a set of generalities. These parts of the section simply track Community law, whose requirements are indeed rather general.

For quoted companies[161] the BR must deal with further matters "to the extent necessary for an understanding" of the company's business,[162]—with KPIs where necessary. The phrase in quotes does not give the directors a discretion whether to deal with a matter: it simply recognises that not all the additional matters will be relevant to the businesses of all companies, though few will not have to comment, for example, on the employees. The list of additional matters potentially to be commented on is:

(a) "the main trends and factors" likely to affect the future of the company's business;

(b) the impact of the company's business on the environment;

(c) the employees;

(d) social and community issues;

(e) persons with whom the company has contractual or other arrangements which are essential to the company's business, unless in the opinion of the directors such disclosure would be seriously prejudicial to those persons or to the public interest.[163]

---

[158] s.417(3),(9).

[159] s.417(4).

[160] Unless the company qualifies as medium-sized, or would do were it not for the fact that it is a member of an ineligible group, in which case it need not use KPIs in relation to non-financial matters: ss.417(7) and 467(4).

[161] Above, para.14–16—a narrower set than proposed by the CLR which wished to apply the OFR requirement to most public and some large private companies as well.

[162] s.417(5).

[163] This last requirement (contained in s.417(5)(c) and the qualification in (11)) was highly controversial because it was introduced only at a very late stage in Parliament, though it had been part of the OFR. Its aim is to require information about supply chains and outsourcing arrangements, but only of course to the extent necessary to meet the shareholders' needs under s.417(2).

None of these provisions requires disclosure of impending developments or matters in the course of negotiation if, in the directors'
opinion, disclosure would be seriously prejudicial to the interests of
the company.[164]

21–25   This list in fact covers most of what was in the OFR, with the
exceptions of capital structure, treasury policies and liquidity, though
a small part of even this will be covered by the corporate governance
statement which is now required.[165] What is most noticeable in a
comparison of the OFR Regulations[166] and section 417 is the greater
generality (and thus lesser detail) with which the BR requirements are
set out. This is the case even though in relation to items (b) to (d)
above the statute requires information about any policies the company has on these matters and their effectiveness.[167] This raises the
risk that the BR will be productive of self-serving and vacuous narrative rather than analytical material which is of genuine use to those
who read the report. There are two traditional ways of dealing with
this issue. One is to require the BR to be audited. The risk with this
approach is that it will take away from the desirability of the OFR/
BR constituting the directors' view of the business rather than that of
its auditors. Consequently, the audit requirement for the directors'
report is simply that the auditors certify that the DR is consistent
with the accounts (which are required to be audited).[168]

The alternative approach is to rely on the standard-setters to
produce authoritative guidance for the BR, just as they have done
over the years for the accounts. The OFR Regulations in fact contained the familiar requirement from the accounts provisions that the
Review must state whether it had been prepared in accordance with
the relevant reporting standard and giving reasons for any departure;[169] and a "reporting standard" was defined, as with an
accounting standard, as a "statement of standard reporting practice"
relating to OFRs and issued by a body authorised by the Secretary of
State, i.e. the Accounting Standards Board.[170] The ASB duly produced its reporting standard (RS 1) in May 2005. However, the BR
provisions contain no statutory underpinning for reporting standards
and so the ASB turned RS 1 into Reporting Statement of best
practice, changing its language so as to reflect its new voluntary
status.[171] With this reduced guidance it is not clear what the quality of

---

[164] s.417(10).
[165] See above, para.21–22. A useful basis for comparing the enhanced BR and the former OFR
can be found in the Table to DTI, *Invitation to comments on the Business Review*, December
15, 2005.
[166] Above, fn.151.
[167] s.417(5)(b).
[168] s.496. The CLR proposed a more rigorous audit (Final Report I, para.8.63) and the OFR
Regulations (reg.10) required the auditors to report whether *any* matter had come to their
attention in the course of their functions which was inconsistent with the OFR.
[169] OFR Regulations (above, fn.151), reg.8.
[170] OFR Regulations, reg.11.
[171] ASB, *Reporting Statement: Operating and Financial Review*, January 2006.

the enhanced BRs will be, especially as companies may take from the sorry history of this development the conclusion that at least some parts of Government do not take it seriously.[172]

Liability for misstatements in the directors' reports

This is not a matter with which the Act has previously dealt specifi- **21–26** cally. There are two areas of potential liability which need to be considered. First, there is liability on the part of the directors to the company. Secondly, there is liability on the part of the directors or the company (and conceivably others) to third parties, including investors in the market. The issue was previously left to the law of directors' duties or the general law on misstatements, whether negligent or fraudulent. However, the introduction of the BR prompted the introduction of specific provisions, now to be found in section 463, whose aim is either to remove these potential liabilities (in the case of liability to third parties) or to confine them to fraud (in the case of liability of the director to the company).

There is a case for providing a "safe harbour" in relation to directors' forward-looking statements, on the grounds that no one can predict the future with certainty and if directors were to be exposed to litigation, or the threat of it, whenever their forward-looking statements turned out to be untrue, they would be very cautious in the statements they made, which caution might undermine the value of the BR to its users.[173] In fact, the OFR Regulations contained no such provision (perhaps because of the powers under which they were made), whilst section 463, by contrast, goes well beyond forward-looking statements, apparently on the grounds that it would be difficult to distinguish them from other types of statement. The section applies to the entire content of the DR and of the DRR (and, indeed, of the summary financial statement, so far as derived from the DR or DRR).[174]

Without section 463, the directors' liability to the company in respect of statements in the DR or DRR would most obviously be based on the general duty of directors to take care and exercise skill in the performance of their duties. As we have seen above,[175] that duty is now put on an objective basis, which creates at least the possibility of suit for damages based on negligent preparation of the DR or DRR on the part of the directors (though the company's loss might be very difficult to identify). The effect of section 463 is to exclude directors'

---

[172] In 2007 the ASB published a somewhat mixed review of experience with the statement, but it is probably too early for a definitive assessment: ASB, *A Review of Narrative Reporting by UK Listed Companies in 2006*, January 2007.

[173] CLR, Final 1, para.8.38.

[174] s.463(1). For the summary financial statement see below, para.21–40. The inclusion of the DRR is particularly bizarre, since it requires statements of policies but very little in the way of forward-looking statements. See paras 14–16ff.

[175] Ch.16 at para.16–12.

liability in negligence to the company entirely. The director is so liable in respect of untrue or misleading statements in the reports or omissions from them only if the director has been fraudulent.[176] Fraud is defined in the way it is in the common law of deceit: the maker of the statement must know it is untrue or misleading or be reckless as to whether this is the case.[177] Thus, a genuine belief in the truth of the statement, no matter how unreasonable, will save the director from liability.

21–27   If the directors' liability to the company is preserved in the case of fraud, their liability to other persons is excluded entirely, even in the case of fraud.[178] Moreover, the liability which is excluded is the liability of "any person", not just of the directors, provided it is not a liability to the company. Thus, investors (including existing shareholders) cannot impose liability on the company in respect of unsuccessful investment decisions which are based on inaccurate information in the DR or DRR. It is in fact very unclear whether, without the section, liability in negligence towards investors on the part of the company or the directors would exist under the general law. The issue has been tested at the highest levels only in respect of auditors, where, as we shall see, the starting point of the courts is one of non-liability.[179] The exclusion of liability towards third parties in the case of fraud is more questionable, since the common law does impose liability in principle for fraud and it is unclear why fraud should be condoned. In fact, however, the exclusion of liability to third parties is qualified by the provisions of section 90A of FSMA 2000, applying to companies with securities traded on a regulated market, which imposes liability in fraud (but only on the company) in relation to certain statements required of the company by the Transparency Directive, which include the DR.[180]

Section 463 excludes the third-party liability of "any person", but it is not clear who might be liable beyond the directors and the company in respect of errors in the DR or DRR. A number of professionals may be consulted and have a hand in the compilation of the DR and DRR but they are not normally identified in those reports as responsible for particular parts of it and thus as having particular statements attributed to them, since both reports are the

---

[176] s.463(2),(3). The liability excluded is only the liability to compensate the company, though it will be rare for any other liability to be in issue.

[177] Recklessness means making the statement not caring whether it is true or untrue, accurate or misleading: *Derry v Peek* (1889) L.R. 14 App. Cas. 337, HL. In the case of omissions there must be "a dishonest concealment of a material fact".

[178] s.463(4),(5). The liability here excluded is not confined to liability to compensate but embraces any civil remedy, including self-help remedies.

[179] See para.22–42.

[180] See below at para.26–11. S.90A of FSMA 2000 applies to reports published in response to the requirements of Art.4 of the TD, which article requires publication of the "management report" which is in turn defined in Art.4(5) to mean the report drawn up in accordance with Art.46 of the Fourth Directive or Art.36 of the Seventh Directive. Query whether this includes that part of the DR which goes beyond the requirements of the Directives.

reports of the directors. However, if this did occur, section 463 would protect these persons (other than in respect of their liability to the company). The auditors are required to report on the consistency of the DR with the accounts and to audit parts of the DRR, as we have seen, but the auditor's report is a separate document and so would not be covered by section 463.

APPROVAL OF THE ACCOUNTS AND REPORTS BY THE DIRECTORS

That the DR and DRR are the reports of the directors is clear from their names, let alone the provisions of the Act.[181] The accounts as well are the product of the directors: the directors must draw them up,[182] although in this case, because of the role played by the auditors in verifying the accounts and, in practice, in drawing them up, they are often misconceived as the auditors' accounts. With the collapse of the Enron Company and others renewed emphasis was placed on the directors' responsibility for the accounts. At Community level the Fourth and Seventh Directives were amended so as to require directors to "have the collective duty to ensure that the annual accounts, the annual report ... are drawn up" in accordance with the Directive or the IAS Regulation.[183] The Government took the view that this requirement was met by the existing domestic provision that the annual accounts must be approved by the directors and signed on behalf of the board by a director.[184] If the directors approve accounts that do not comply with the Act or the IAS Regulation, every director who knows that they do not comply or is reckless as to whether or not they comply and who fails to take reasonable steps to secure compliance or to prevent the accounts being approved is guilty of an offence.[185] The duty on the directors to produce the DR and DRR is likewise backed by criminal sanctions: failure to take reasonable steps to secure compliance with the duty to produce the reports is a criminal offence on the part of each of the directors.[186]

21–28

---

[181] See ss.415 and 420: directors' duty to prepare DR and DRR respectively.

[182] Ss.394 and 399.

[183] Fourth Directive, Art.50B and Seventh Directive, Art.36A.

[184] s.414(1). The signature must be on the balance sheet (s.414(2)) and must be accompanied by a statement that the accounts have been prepared in accordance with the provisions for small companies, if this is the case.

[185] s.414(4),(5). This re-states the previous law somewhat more simply by dropping the requirement that the director be a party to the approval and presuming the existing directors to be parties.

[186] s.415(4) and 420(2). Curiously, simple non-production of the accounts is not a criminal offence under ss.394 and 399, but since failure to take the steps required after production of the accounts is a criminal offence (for example, failure to circulate them to the members (s.425)) this perhaps hardly matters.

The Member States are also required to ensure that their "laws, regulations and administrative provisions on liability" to the company apply to the directors who breach their collective duty.[187] This provision does not require the Member States to have any particular liability regime in place. In the case of the United Kingdom this requirement is met presumably through the general law on directors' duties and, in the case of the DR and DRR, by the preservation of the directors' liability in fraud to the company.[188]

THE AUDITOR'S REPORT

21–29   The final document that has to accompany the annual accounts is the auditors' report thereon—assuming the company is one which is required to have its accounts audited or has chosen to do so. This has to be addressed to the company's members[189] and to state whether in the auditors' opinion the annual accounts have been properly prepared in accordance with the Act or the IAS Regulation, as appropriate and, in particular, whether they give a true and fair view.[190] The report must also state whether the auditors consider that the information given in the DR is consistent with that in the annual accounts[191] and, in the case of the auditable part of the DRR, state whether it has been properly prepared.[192] The rights and duties of the auditor in the preparation of the audit report are considered more fully in the following Chapter. The auditors' report must state the names of the auditors and be signed by them.[193] However, those names need not appear on the published copies of the report or on the copy filed with the Registrar (see below) if the company has resolved that the names should not be stated on basis that there are reasonable grounds for thinking that publication would create a serious risk of violence to or intimidation of the auditor or any other person, and has provided that information instead to the Secretary of State.[194]

---

[187] Fourth Directive, Art.50C and Seventh Directive, Art.36B.
[188] See above.
[189] s.495(1).
[190] s.495(3).
[191] s.496.
[192] s.497.
[193] s.503.
[194] s.506. The reasons for this measure or secrecy in relation to the auditors are the same as those which led to the suppression of public information about directors' residential addresses: see above at para.14–10.

REVISION OF DEFECTIVE ACCOUNTS AND REPORTS

Despite the requirements for director and auditor approval, noted **21–30**
above, it is not impossible that accounts and reports will be produced
by the company which are later discovered to be incorrect. Until the
passing of the Companies Act 1989 there were no statutory provisions for revising incorrect accounts and reports. However, it has
never been doubted that, if directors discover such defects, they can,
and should, correct them. Section 454 makes it clear that the directors
may revise the accounts and reports (both DR and DRR) on a
voluntary basis. Where the accounts have not yet been sent to the
Registrar or the members (see below), the directors have a pretty free
hand as to revisions, but if either of those events has occurred, as is
likely, the corrections must be confined to what is necessary to bring
the accounts and reports into line with the requirements of the Act or
the IAS Regulation.[195] Regulations made under the section provide
that the revised accounts or reports become, as nearly as possible, the
reports and accounts of the company for the relevant financial year,
to which the other provisions of the Act apply. For example, they will
be subject to audit.[196]

More significant are the statutory powers to compel revision of
defective accounts. The Secretary of State has power to apply to the
court for a declaration that the accounts or directors' report (but not,
it seems, the DRR) does not comply with the Act or the IAS Regulation and for an order that it be brought into line, with consequential directions.[197] The court may order the costs of the
application and of the production of the revised accounts to be borne
by the directors in place at the time of the approval of the accounts or
report, unless a director can show that he or she took all reasonable
steps to prevent approval, though the court also has power to exclude
from liability a director who did not know and ought not to have
known of the defects.[198] Notice of the application and of its result
must be given to the Registrar.[199]

However, in practice this is not an activity the Secretary of State
undertakes. There is power under section 457 for authorisation to
make applications to the court to be conferred upon persons
appearing to the Secretary of State "to have an interest in, and to
have satisfactory procedures directed to securing, compliance by
companies" with the Act and the IAS Regulation and "to have
satisfactory procedures for receiving and investigating complaints"
about annual accounts and directors' reports and otherwise to be "fit

---

[195] s.454(2).
[196] Companies (Revision of Defective Accounts and Reports) Regulations 2008/373.
[197] s.456(1)–(3).
[198] s.456(5),(6).
[199] s.456(2), (7).

and proper". Such authorisation has been conferred on the Financial Reporting Review Panel ("FRRP"),[200] an operating body of the Financial Reporting Council ("FRC"). In practice, the task of dealing with defective reports is discharged by FRRP, rather than by the Department, except in relation to small companies.[201] The FRRP has statutory authority to require the production of documents, information and explanations if it thinks there is a question-mark over the compliance of a company's accounts or report with the Act or IAS Regulation.[202] It must keep the information received confidential, except for disclosure to a list of approved recipients (relevant Government Departments and Regulators).[203]

21–31 The FRRP has been criticised in the past for being reactive, i.e. acting only on complaints or media revelations that a particular set of accounts is defective rather than checking or investigating on its own motion. Partly because of EU pressure to produce equivalent mechanisms in the Member States for the enforcement of international accounting standards, the FRRP agreed in 2002 to adopt a proactive review policy,[204] though it has not had to resort to a court order to secure the necessary changes, a threat of an application being enough.

With regard to companies with securities traded on a regulated market, the obligation to secure compliance with the reporting requirements of such companies (which include but extend beyond the annual reports and accounts)[205] is apparently allocated by Community law to the Financial Services Authority, but the relevant Directive permits the FSA to delegate the tasks conferred upon it.[206] Accordingly, the FRRP has been authorised[207] by the Secretary of State to keep under review not only the accounts and reports required by the Act but also those required to be produced by companies whose securities are traded on regulated markets under the provisions of Part 6 of the Financial Services and Markets Act 2000. In this case, there is an obvious need for close liaison with the Financial Services

---

[200] Companies (Defective Accounts and Directors' Reports) (Authorised Person) and Supervision of Accounts and Reports (Prescribed Body) Order 2008/623.

[201] Where Companies House takes the lead: CLR, Completing, para.12.48.

[202] s.459.

[203] ss.460–462.

[204] DTI, *Final Report of the Co-ordinating Group on Audit and Accounting Issues*, URN 03/567, paras 4.11 *et seq.* Such a policy, including the identification of "priority sectors" for review, has been developed and since 2006 the FRRP has included the directors' report, and so the business review, in its activities. See http://www.frc.org.uk/frrp/how/. In the year 2006/7 312 reviews were carried out: FRC, *Annual Report 2006/7*, May 2007, p.17.

[205] These requirements are discussed in Chapter 26 below.

[206] Directive 2004/109/EC, Art.24 (the Transparency Directive).

[207] See fn.200, made under s.14 of the Companies (Audit, Investigations and Community Enterprise) Act 2004. The tests laid down in s.14 of the 2004 Act are similar to those contained in s.457 of the 2006 Act.

Authority.[208] The FRRP is under a duty to report its findings to the FSA in appropriate cases and the FSA may expand the FRRP's remit.[209]

FILING ACCOUNTS AND REPORTS WITH THE REGISTRAR

The statutory requirement to produce accounts and reports would be **21–32** of little use if there were no provisions for the information so generated to reach the hands of those who might make use of it. This is done in two ways under the Act: circulation to the members (discussed below) and delivery of the accounts to the Registrar.[210] By delivery to the Registrar, the accounts and reports become public documents.

Speed of filing
A source of complaint in the past has been the length of the gap **21–33** between the end of the financial year and the date laid down for filing the accounts and reports with the Registrar. The CLR thought that modern technology permitted speedier filing than had been required in the past and recommended that the period be reduced from seven to six months for public companies and ten to seven for private companies.[211] Section 442 implements the former reform but only marginally reduces the private company period (to nine months), which is a pity.[212] For public companies whose securities are traded on a regulated market[213] the period for publication of the annual accounts and reports is four months from the end of the financial year,[214] though the core elements in the accounts may have been made

---

[208] The FRRP concluded a "memorandum of understanding" with the FSA in 2005 about their joint working, which is available on the FRRP website. Indeed, there was some debate at the time as to whether these powers should not be given directly to the FSA.

[209] s.14(2),(7). The FRRP's power to apply for a court order appears to be limited to annual accounts and reports only (s.456(1)), so that it would fall to the FSA to take action in respect of the semi-annual and quarterly reports required of companies on regulated markets.

[210] s.441.

[211] CLR, Final I, paras 4.49–4.32 and 8.80ff.

[212] s.442 deals with some exceptional cases as well.

[213] See para.25–6, essentially those traded on the Main Market of the London Stock Exchange.

[214] See FSA, Disclosure and Transparency Rule 4.1.3, implementing Article 4 of the Transparency Directive 2004/109/EC. See Ch.26 below.

available earlier through a preliminary public announcement of the results.[215]

A linked source of complaint has been non-compliance with the filing requirement, though the UK's record in this area is superior to that of some Member States of the Community. The formal sanctions are criminal liabilities on the directors and civil penalties on the company. If the filing requirements are not complied with on time, any person who was a director immediately before the end of the time allowed is liable to a fine and, for continued contravention, to a daily default fine, unless the director can prove that he took all reasonable steps for securing that the accounts were delivered in time.[216] Furthermore, if the directors fail to make good the default within 14 days after the service of a notice requiring compliance, the court, on the application of the Registrar or any member or creditor of the company, may make an order directing the directors or any of them to make good the default within such time as may be specified and may order them to pay the costs of and incidental to the application.[217]

To these criminal sanctions against directors, the Act adds civil penalties against the company.[218] The amount of the penalty is set by regulation.[219] The amount of the penalty, recoverable by the Registrar, varies according to whether the company is private or public and to the length of time that the default continues; the minimum being £150 for a private company and £750 for a public company when the default is for not more than one month, and the maximum £1,500 for a private and £7,500 for a public company when the default exceeds six months.[220] There are obvious attractions in affording the Registrar an additional weapon in the form of a penalty recoverable by civil suit to which there is no defence once it is shown that accounts have not been delivered on time. Presumably, the thought is that civil sanctions on the company will put pressure on shareholders to intervene and secure compliance on the part of the directors, but it is

---

[215] The CLR's proposals for the prelims (see above) fell away once the production of prelims ceased to be required by the Listing Rules. The LR previously required the prelims to be announced within four months, but that has now become the period for the full accounts and reports.

[216] s.451. But, to spike the guns of barrack-room lawyers, it is expressly stated that it is not a defence to prove that the documents required were not in fact prepared in accordance with the Act!

[217] s.452. If they fail to do so, they will be in contempt of court and liable to imprisonment. The subsection does not say who may serve such a notice so presumably anyone can: but in practice it is likely to be the Registrar who does so—though the subsection makes it pretty clear that a member or creditor certainly could.

[218] s.453.

[219] The Companies (Late Filing Penalties) and Limited Liability Partnerships (Filing Periods and Late Filing Penalties) Regulations 2008/497.

[220] The figures quoted apply as from 1 February, 2009. The Scheme withstood judicial review in *R. (Pow Trust) v Registrar of Companies* [2003] 2 B.C.L.C. 295.

not clear how effective this mechanism is. It may be that the share-holders simply lose profits as well as suffer from a failure on the part of the directors to perform a duty intended to protect them.[221] In recent years the rate of compliance with the filing deadlines at Companies House has been around the 95 per cent mark and just over a million pounds was raised in late filing penalties in 2005–2006.[222]

Modifications of the full filing requirements

Filing with the Registrar is such a sensitive issue precisely because the information in the accounts and reports thus becomes generally available. The Act itself makes some concessions to the fear of publicity in the case of small, medium-sized and unlimited companies, by way of derogations from the full filing regime. That regime requires filing of the annual accounts, the directors' report and (in the case of a quoted company) the directors' remuneration report, and the auditor's report on those accounts and reports.[223] If the company has been required to produce group accounts, then the full regime applies to both the group and individual accounts.[224] The balance sheet must contain the name of the person who signed it on behalf of the board.[225]

21–34

Unlimited companies are in principle exempt from filing any accounts and reports, provided the unlimited company is not part of a group containing limited companies and is not a banking or insurance company.[226] This is a good example of the link between limited liability and public financial disclosure, i.e. the latter is dispensed with if the former is not present.[227] Of course, the unlimited liability company still has to produce and circulate accounts to the members, who have perhaps an even bigger interest in the proper running of the company if their liability is unlimited.

Small companies subject to the small company regime are not required to produce group accounts,[228] nor are they required to file a directors' report with their individual accounts.[229] In relation to their individual accounts, which they are required to produce, they are

---

[221] The company could, presumably, sue the directors to recover its loss resulting from their default. But unless the company goes into liquidation, administration or receivership this is unlikely to happen.

[222] *Companies in 2005–2006* (2006), Tables F3 and F4.

[223] ss.446 and 447.

[224] s.471.

[225] See above, para.21–28.

[226] s.448.

[227] The same distinction can be found between partnerships (accounts need not be made public) and limited liability partnerships (public disclosure required).

[228] Above, para.21–9.

[229] Small companies excluded from the small companies regime because a member of an ineligible group may also choose not to file a directors' report: s.444A, inserted by the 2008 Amending Regulations, reg.6.

required to file with the Registrar only the balance sheet (though they may file a profit and loss account if they wish).[230]

21–35   Further, the filed copy of the balance sheet is permitted to be less detailed than the balance sheet made available to the members, at least where the company produces Companies Act accounts. These are the so-called "abbreviated" accounts.[231] There may also be omitted from the notes to the abbreviated accounts the information which unquoted companies are required to produce about directors' remuneration. This applies to both Companies Act and IAS accounts of small companies.[232] The balance sheet must contain a statement that it has been prepared according to the special provisions for small company accounts.[233] The CLR took the view that the filed accounts of small companies were, in the result, "not meaningful", and proposed to remove the facility for filing abbreviated accounts.[234] Although the Government initially accepted this recommendation,[235] it did not make its way into the Act. The general conclusion is that little insight into the financial position of a company subject to the small company regime will normally be obtained from consulting its filed accounts.

A medium-sized company must file both the full annual accounts (individual and group, if necessary) and the directors' report, but may file the profit and loss account (but not the balance sheet) in abbreviated form.[236]

Information available from the Registrar

21–36   The annual accounts and reports are probably the most important documents filed with the Registrar[237] and thus made public, because they give reasonably current (though by no means completely up-to-

---

[230] s.444(1).

[231] s.444(3). The rules for small company abbreviated balance sheets are set out in the Small Companies and Groups (Accounts and Directors' Report) Regulations 2008/409, reg.6(1) and Sch.4. Where the small company produces IAS accounts (probably not a common choice), the option to file an abbreviated balance sheet is not available, because the requirements for small companies' balance sheets in such a case are set out in IAS and IFRS, not in the Act.

[232] Small Companies Regulations, reg.6(2).

[233] s.450(3) and the auditor's report, if there is one, must certify this as well and that the company is entitled to prepare abbreviated accounts: s.449(2). The auditor's report on the company's accounts, which is sent to the members, need not normally be filed as well, unless it is qualified or otherwise critical of the company: s.449(3).

[234] CLR, *Developing*, paras 8.32–8.34.

[235] *Modernising*, para.4.26.

[236] s.445(1),(3). The detail of what may be omitted is to be found in the Accounts Regulations 2008, reg.4(3). Again, the regulation applies only to Companies Act individual accounts. The omissions permitted are relatively slight, but include particulars of turnover. In this case the special auditor's report (see above) under s.449 may often be obligatory.

[237] Actually, there are three Registrars—one for each of the UK jurisdictions—though their functions are similar: s.1060.

date) information about the company's financial position.[238] However, the accounts and reports do not constitute the whole of the information about the company which is publicly available from the Registrar, as we see at various points in this work. The next most important document thus made available is probably the company's constitution, mainly its articles of association.[239] Perhaps after that in importance is the list of the company's directors, which must be updated as changes occur.[240] Amongst the other information available in this way are the address of its registered office,[241] the amount of its issued share capital[242] and details of charges on its property.[243]

"Any person" has the right to inspect the register maintained by the Registrar, subject to certain limited types of information not being publicly available.[244] There is also a right to obtain a copy of material on the register, subject to a fee,[245] and a copy duly certified by the Registrar is evidence in legal proceedings of equal validity to the original.[246] The applicant has the choice in relation to the most central items of information to make the request for inspection or copy electronically or in hard copy, and to receive the information in either way.[247]

Annual return

This is a document delivered annually to the Registrar by the company.[248] Unlike the accounts and reports considered above, it is not a document sent by the directors to the members, a copy of which is filed with the Registrar. The Registrar is the principal addressee of the annual return[249] (though, of course, any member may access it under the provisions discussed in the previous paragraph). Nevertheless it is convenient to consider it here. Moreover, it is a document

21–37

---

[238] Hence with companies whose securities are traded on a regulated market the obligation on the company (a) to produce reports more often than annually and (b) to report material changes as they occur. See Ch.26 below.

[239] See para.3–15.

[240] See para.14–10. Also to be disclosed is the identity of the company's secretary, if there is one: s.276.

[241] See ss.9(5)(a) and 86–87. This is important because it is there that legal process can be served on it.

[242] See para.11–3. The returns of allotments will show to whom the shares were initially issued but not who now owns them.

[243] See Ch.32. This is likely to be more up-to-date than the filed accounts and so a better indicator of creditworhiness.

[244] See ss.1085 and 1087, the latter excluding access, for example, to directors' residential addresses (see para.14–10).

[245] s.1086.

[246] s.1091(3).

[247] ss.1089 and 1090. The information in relation to which this right exists is set out in s.1078, which implements Art.3 of the First Company Law Directive (68/151/EEC) as amended by Directive 2003/58/EC, Art.1.

[248] s.854. The return date is normally the anniversary of the company's incorporation.

[249] Hence the provisions about the annual return are set out in a separate Part of the Act (Part 24).

required to be submitted by every company, whatever its obligations as to the accounts and reports.

To some significant extent the annual return simply makes the searcher's task easier: it collates much that should have been delivered for registration when the relevant transactions occurred, so that a searcher may find it unnecessary to search back beyond the latest annual return on the file. However, it also contains some information not otherwise required to be sent to the Registrar. This is particularly true of information about the members of the company,[250] in particular the number of shares in each class held by each member and the number of shares transferred by each member since the last return.[251] It is easy to see many situations in which information about members and their shareholdings may be of relevance. However, the annual return suffers from two defects in this respect. First, it reports the position only once a year and, in some companies, the shareholders may be a fluctuating body. Consequently, the share register maintained by the company is likely to be a better source of information than the annual return.[252] In fact, this is a point which is more generally true about information in the annual return. Much of it is also kept on registers required to be maintained by the company, and the company's registers will be more up-to-date and as equally available, at least to members of the company but not always to members of the public. Secondly, both the annual return and the company's share register contain information about only the shareholder who holds the legal title to the share (the "registered" member), who may be a mere nominee for someone else. Obtaining information easily about beneficial owners is provided for only in relation to companies whose securities are traded on regulated markets.[253]

Despite the criminal sanctions[254] for non-compliance with the obligation to make an annual return and facilitation by the Registrar of electronic means for submitting the annual return, companies are not always prompt in making their annual returns. In fact, failure to file the annual return alerts the Registrar and may lead to the taking

---

[250] ss.856A and 856B.

[251] In the case of a company whose securities are traded on a regulated market the particulars required to be given about a shareholder who holds 5 per cent or more of the company's shares include that person's address, as well as the name. The address to be given is that which appears on the company's share register, which need not be a residential address. See the draft Companies (Annual Return and Service Addresses) Regulations 2008, reg.12. Previously, an address had to be given for every member of every company: Companies Act 1985, s.364A.

[252] On the company's share register, see para.27–16.

[253] See para.26–12 below. The annual return must state where the company holds its share register and whether any shares of the company have been admitted to trading on a regulated market: s.855(1)(d), (f).

[254] s.858: offence by company, every director and secretary, and every other officer who is in default. The number of prosecutions for failure to file the annual return has been going up in recent years (reaching about 2,250 in 2005/6, with a conviction rate of just above one-half): *Companies in 2005–2006*, Table D3.

of steps which culminate in the company's removal from the register.[255]

Other publication of the accounts and reports

Although the Act requires only filing with the Registrar by way of **21–38** making the accounts and reports available to the public, in fact large companies often, and other companies sometimes, make their annual statements available more generally; and quoted companies are now required to provide website publication.[256] Where a company chooses to make its annual statements available in a way which is calculated to invite members of the public generally, or a class of them, to read it, then the Act requires the name of the person who signed the balance sheet or the DR or DRR on behalf of the company to be stated.[257] If a company publishes its accounts in this way, they must be accompanied by the auditor's report (if there is one) and a company preparing group accounts cannot publish only its individual accounts.[258] In short, a non-quoted company is not required to publish its annual accounts generally, but if it does so, it must do so in full.

The accounts described above are known as the company's "statutory accounts". A company is not prohibited from publishing other accounts dealing with the relevant financial year, thought this is in fact rare. If the company does so, it must include with them a statement that these accounts are not the statutory accounts and disclose whether the statutory accounts have been filed and whether the auditors have reported on them and, if so, whether the auditors' report was qualified. Nor may an auditors' report on the statutory accounts be published with the non-statutory accounts.[259] If the company is listed, it will be required under the Listing Rules to produce six-monthly accounts as well as annual ones, though such accounts do not fall into the category of "non-statutory accounts" because they do not cover an entire financial year.[260]

CONSIDERATION OF THE ACCOUNTS AND REPORTS BY THE MEMBERS

Circulation to the members

Since the accounts and reports are communications from the direc- **21–39** tors to the members, it is not surprising that the Act requires their

---

[255] See Appendix, para.A–12.
[256] s.430 and para.21–40.
[257] ss.433 and 436.
[258] s.434.
[259] s.435.
[260] See Ch.26 below.

circulation to the members.[261] However, not only the members but also the company's debenture-holders (i.e. its long-term lenders holding the company's debt securities)[262] must receive copies, since their chances of being repaid depend upon the financial health of the company. Thirdly, so must anyone who is entitled to receive notice of general meetings of the company be sent the accounts and reports, a category which includes the directors themselves (hardly a necessary requirement) and anyone else entitled to notice under the particular company's articles.[263] This obligation arises only if the company has a current address for the person in question.[264] Finally, those nominated to enjoy information rights will receive copies of the accounts and reports.[265] Just to make sure, the Act also provides that shareholders and debenture-holders can at any time demand copies of the most recent annual accounts and reports and the company must comply with the request within seven days.[266]

Summary financial statements

21–40 There are two linked problems with the circulation requirements. First, the full accounts and reports may be grist to the mills of the analysts, but lots of individual shareholders find the full set more daunting than useful. Secondly, the circulation requirement is an expensive one for the company to meet.[267] Both these concerns are addressed by the provisions as to summary financial statements, which replace the full accounts and reports otherwise required to be circulated.

This facility was previously available only to companies whose securities were traded on certain public markets, but now it is in principle open to all companies.[268] Moreover, the burden is on the recipient to ask to continue to receive the full accounts and report. If, after being sent an appropriate notice from the company, the recipient does not respond with a contrary statement within 28 days, he or she will be deemed to have opted for the summary, though that

---

[261] s.423(1). The content of the "annual accounts and reports" is specified in s.471(2) separately for unquoted and quoted companies.

[262] See Ch.31 below.

[263] s.307. In the case of companies without share capital only this third category need be circulated: s.423(4).

[264] s.423(2),(3).

[265] s.146. See para.15–21.

[266] ss.431 (unquoted companies) and 432 (quoted companies). This right is also extended to those nominated to enjoy information rights: s.146(3)(b).

[267] It is reported that in 2006 postmen in the UK were restricted as to the number of sets of the annual accounts and reports of HSBC bank they were permitted to carry at any one time, because of the weight of the document.

[268] s.426 and the Companies (Summary Financial Statements) Regulations 2008/374 (hereafter "Summary Statements Regulations").

"choice" can be reversed at any time.[269] The summary statement provisions are, however, default rules, in the sense that the company in its constitution or the instrument creating the debentures may deprive itself of this facility. The right to make use of the summary is also dependent on the company observing the relevant provisions of the Act relating to the audit, filing and approval of the full accounts and reports.[270]

The detailed rules for the format of the summary financial statements, as far as derived from the accounts, are set out in Schedules to the Regulations.[271] In addition, certain parts of the directors' reports are required to be included or summarised in the summary financial statement, in particular those parts dealing with the directors' remuneration.[272] Further, the summary must contain, or there must be sent separately, the information the Takeovers Directive requires to be provided annually about the company's control structures.[273] Finally, as far as content is concerned, the summary must contain statements warning the reader that it is only a summary and informing the reader how to obtain full copies.[274] The auditor is required to form a view whether the summary is consistent with the accounts and reports and complies with the provisions of the Act and the Regulations, and that view must be included in the summary.[275] The auditor must also state in the summary whether any of the reports required to be given by an auditor were adverse to the company and, if so, to include them.[276]

An alternative, or additional way, of addressing circulation costs is to encourage members to receive communications (whether full accounts and reports or a summary) from the company in electronic form or via the company's website. This has been discussed in Chapter 15.[277] A quoted company is in any event required to put its current annual accounts and reports on its website and to maintain it there throughout the following financial year.[278]

---

[269] s.426(2) and Summary Statements Regulations, regs.5–8. The consultation may take place as part of the circulation of the annual accounts and reports (and relate to future years) or be a free-standing consultation. Requesting to continue with the full set must be made easy, depending simply on ticking a box on a form, postage on which has been pre-paid by the company, at least if the recipient has an address in the EEA. Those who enjoy information rights are within this procedure as well: s.426(5).

[270] Summary Statements Regulations, reg.4.

[271] Summary Statements Regulations, reg.9.

[272] Summary Statements Regulations regs.9(6) and 10(4). A company could opt to provide summary accounts (and DRR, if applicable) but the directors' report in full. See s.427(1),(2) and 428(1),(2).

[273] See para.28–27.

[274] ss.427(4)(a)–(c), 428(4)(a)–(c).

[275] ss.427(4)(d), 428(4)(d).

[276] ss.427(e)–(g), 428(4)(e)–(g).

[277] At para.15–54.

[278] s.430.

Laying the accounts and reports before the members

21–41 Circulating the accounts and reports to the members and others allows them to consider them on an individual basis, but such consideration is not likely to lead to significant action in the case of companies with larger bodies of shareholders, unless there is some facility for collective consideration of the accounts and reports. As far as private companies are concerned, there is no longer any statutory requirement for such collective consideration, no matter how large a shareholding body that company may have. A private company is required by the statute to circulate its annual accounts and reports at the time it delivers them to the Registrar,[279] and any further action is a matter for the shareholders or the company's articles. The shareholders might seek to convene a meeting[280] or the articles might require annual consideration of the accounts and reports at a meeting, which the directors would be obliged to convene.

As far as public companies are concerned, the traditional obligation "to lay the accounts and reports before a general meeting" still applies.[281] This formulation implies that the shareholders are not required to consider a resolution to approve the accounts and reports (as is the case in many countries), but they must be afforded an opportunity to discuss them. Indeed, this item on the agenda is normally used to allow a wide-ranging discussion of the company's business.[282] The meeting at which the accounts and reports are considered is termed the "accounts meeting"[283] and it is in fact normally the company's annual general meeting. The accounts and reports must be circulated at least 21 days before the accounts meeting and the accounts meeting itself must be held not later than the end of the period for the filing of the accounts and reports with the Registrar, i.e. six months after the end of the financial year in the case of a public company. As we noted in Chapter 15,[284] the Government backed away from the CLR's proposal that, after circulation, there should be a pause of two weeks, during which shareholders could formulate, if they wished, resolutions on the accounts and reports to be considered at the meeting.

---

[279] s.424(2). For delivery to the Registrar, see above, para.21–32. Of course, the company cannot evade this obligation simply by not filing the accounts and report with the Registrar: s.424(2)(a).

[280] See para.15–29.

[281] ss.437–438.

[282] See para.15–24.

[283] s.437(3).

[284] At para.15–28.

CONCLUSION

Part 15 of the Act, dealing with the annual accounts and reports, **21–42** constitutes a substantial part of the Companies Act 2006, long though that Act is. Part 15 contains nearly one hundred sections, and this is an indication of the central role played by annual reporting in the structure of the companies legislation. Part 15 improves in a number of ways on the 1985 Act, though some of the significant changes, such as the requirement for a directors' remuneration report in the case of quoted companies,[285] were the result of reforms introduced before the 2006 Act and are simply consolidated in it in a more elegant way. Other changes have been driven by developments at Community level, such as the introduction and promotion of international accounting standards. Further, the drafters of Part 15 were ultimately reluctant to accept the (modest) proposals from the Company Law Review for tightening up the disclosure required of small and medium-sized companies. Most, though not all, of its proposals in this direction did not survive into the Act, whose approach in this area is heavily deregulatory, even though the Government had earlier indicated support for them. Thus, "abbreviated accounts" may still be filed by small companies.[286]

However, the "big issue" with Part 15 was whether it would be able to rescue the CLR's proposals for an Operating and Financial Review. On that matter, which has an importance going beyond reporting because of its links to the shareholder-centred formulation of directors' duties, the question remains an open one. The drafters of Part 15 strove valiantly to produce what one might view as an "OFR substitute", after the untimely demise of the real thing, but the quality of the reporting that will emerge from it in the light of the absence of relevant reporting standards remains to be seen.[287]

---

[285] Introduced in 2002: see para.14–16.
[286] See above, para.21–15. The earlier commitment to remove abbreviated accounts can be found in *Modernising*, para.4.26.
[287] See above, para.21–23.

CHAPTER 22

AUDITS AND AUDITORS

THE ROLE OF THE AUDITOR

The statutory reports and accounts discussed in the previous Chapter **22–1**
are the responsibility of the directors. However, all modern company
law systems have long accepted the principle that the reliability of the
accounts and reports will be increased if there is in place a system of
independent third-party verification of them. The temptation to
present the accounts in a light which is unduly favourable to the
management is one likely to afflict all boards of directors at one time

or another—and the temptation is likely to be at its strongest when the financial condition of the company is at its weakest and shareholders, creditors and investors are most in need of access to the truth. To provide such third-party verification is the traditional role of the audit.

To summarise briefly the role of the auditor, the core element of it is the production of a report to the members of the company which gives the auditor's opinion whether:

> (a) the annual accounts give a true and fair view of the financial position of the company (or the group in the case of group accounts);[1] have been properly prepared in accordance with the relevant financial reporting framework;[2] and have been prepared in accordance with the requirements of the Act or the IAS Regulation;[3]
>
> (b) the directors' report is consistent with the accounts;[4] and
>
> (c) the auditable part of the directors' remuneration report (DRR) has been properly prepared in accordance with the Act.[5]

The auditor's report must be either "qualified" or "unqualified".[6] An unqualified report is one where the auditor is able to give the opinions mentioned above; a qualified report (which is a serious thing for the company and its members) is one where one or more of the opinions mentioned above cannot be given.[7]

The auditor's report to the members must contain opinions on matters (a)–(c) above. According to the circumstances, it may also have to deal with further items. This arises out of the auditor's duty, in preparing the report, to carry out investigations so as to be able to form a view as to whether:

> (d) adequate accounting records have been kept by the company;
>
> (e) the company's individual accounts are in agreement with the accounting records; and

---

[1] For the distinction between individual and group accounts see para.21–7.
[2] On the meaning of this term see para.21–12.
[3] s.495(3). On the role of the IAS Regulation see para.21–12.
[4] s.496. On the directors' report see para.21–21.
[5] s.487. The auditable part of the DRR is that set out in Part 3 of Schedule 8 to the Large and Medium-sized Companies and Groups (Accounts and Reports) Regulations 2008/410 (see reg.11(3)). On the directors' remuneration report see para.14–16.
[6] s.495(4).
[7] The auditor may refer to matters to which attention needs to be drawn without necessarily qualifying the report: s.495(4)(b).

(f) the auditable part of the DRR is in agreement with the accounting records.[8]

If all is well in relation to the above three issues, the auditor need say nothing in the report. If it is not, the auditor must state this fact.

(g) In addition, if the auditor has failed to obtain all the information and explanations which he or she believes to be necessary for the purposes of the audit, that fact must be stated in the report.[9]

Finally, there are two specific provisions relating to the small company accounts and the DRR:

(h) where the directors have prepared the company's accounts in accordance with the small companies regime,[10] the auditor must likewise state in the report his opinion that they were not entitled to do so, if he forms such an opinion.[11]

(i) If the auditor finds that the statutory provisions on the disclosure of directors' remuneration have not been complied with, there is a duty upon the auditor, so far as he or she is reasonably able, to provide the particulars which should have been given in the directors' report or the DRR.[12] Apart from this, however, the auditor is not under an obligation the revise the accounts and reports so as to bring them into line with the applicable requirements: that is the task of their authors, the directors.

Undoubtedly, the most important and time-consuming of the auditor's tasks is that listed at (a) above, because it amounts to a general endorsement of the accuracy of the accounts. **22–2**

In some cases, the auditor may also be required to report facts uncovered to third parties, especially regulators, though this development has been controversial, as we shall see.[13]

There are three main issues of principle arising in debates on rules about auditors. First, is the benefit of the audit greater than its costs for all companies? If not, is there a case for exempting some classes of company from the requirement[14] to have an audit? Secondly, once an audit is required, the temptation on management to present the accounts in an unduly favourable light can be given effect only if they

---

[8] s.498(1),(2).
[9] s.498(3).
[10] See para.21–3.
[11] s.498(5).
[12] s.498(4).
[13] Below, para.22–33.
[14] The basic principle of a mandatory audit of the statutory accounts is laid down in s.475.

can persuade the auditors to accept such an unduly favourable presentation. What steps, then, can and should be taken to ensure the independence of the auditors from the management of the company? Thirdly, what role should be played by civil liability in damages on the part of the auditor towards those who relied on the reports in securing auditor independence and competence? We shall look at these issues in the remainder of this Chapter.

The auditor today, at least in large firms, is not an individual practitioner but a member of a firm, often of international scale, and the audit is carried out by a team of auditors under the leadership of one or more partners in the firm. Where necessary, the text below will refer to these realities. Otherwise, the word "auditor" is used, but to cover both firms and sole practitioners, individuals and teams of auditors.

AUDIT EXEMPTION

Small companies

22–3   Over a little more than a decade a very substantial set of audit exemptions has been introduced, to the point where more than ninety five per cent of registered companies are exempt from audit of their annual accounts (both individual and group). Of course, one must not exaggerate the economic significance of the companies so exempt, because the exemption is applied to small companies. Nevertheless, the definition of what counts as "small" for this purpose has been progressively enlarged over this relatively short period of time, and the CLR cautiously encouraged the Government to take the process further,[15] which it duly did.[16] This development also constitutes a significant change of policy on the part of Government, for previously it had been committed to a universal audit requirement.[17] What triggered the reversal seems to have been the additional costs generated by the implementation in the Companies Act 1989 of Council Directive 84/253 on auditors' qualifications,[18] which was alleged to have a disproportionate impact on the audit costs of very small firms. Once begun, the exemption process seems to have acquired a life of its own. Despite the opposition from some users of accounts, notably the Inland Revenue and some banks, the dereg-

---

[15] Completing, paras 2.32–2.33.
[16] The CLR's notion of an "independent professional review", falling short of an audit, for larger small companies was found not to be attractive: *Modernising*, paras 4.21–4.22.
[17] DTI, *Accounting and Audit Requirements for Small Firms: A Consultative Document* (1985) and *Consultative Document on Amending the Fourth Company Law Directive on Annual Accounts* (1989). The Fourth Directive, however, permits Member States to exempt small companies from the audit.
[18] Repealed and replaced by Directive 2006/43/EC as from June 2006.

ulatory pressure was successful and the current provisions are set out in sections 477 to 479 of the Act.

In order to qualify for the exemption from audit in a particular financial year, the company has to meet two conditions.[19] First it must meet the criteria for being classified as a "small" company for the purposes of the Act's accounting rules. As we have seen,[20] this means meeting two out of three criteria relating to the size of the company's balance sheet, turnover and workforce over a period of two years. These figures are not more than £6.5 million for turnover, £3.26 million for balance sheet total and 50 for employees.[21] Secondly, the company must meet the specified turnover and balance sheet tests in the financial year in which it claims audit exemption. Why this complex double requirement? Do the two conditions add anything to one another? It seems that they do.

A company which qualifies as small only through reliance on the employee numbers criterion will not be exempt from audit, since by definition it does not meet one or other of the turnover or balance sheet criteria in that year, and so it fails the second condition. In other words, the audit exemption rules require compliance with the turnover and balance sheet criteria.

But then, why not simply drop the employee numbers criterion and apply the small company condition for the purposes of the audit exemption on this reduced basis? The answer to that is that, as we have seen, a company which acquires small company status retains it for a year after it ceases to meet the criteria.[22] The effect of the second condition is that the audit exemption will be lost in that year, though the company may still prepare its accounts on a small company basis.

Why not then simply drop the first condition for being entitled to **22–4** the audit exemption and rely wholly on the second condition? As we have seen,[23] being a small company for accounts purposes requires the company to meet the relevant tests for two successive years. Retaining the first condition ensures that a company which cannot benefit from the small companies accounts regime cannot benefit from the audit exemption either.

Even if the company meets the two conditions noted above, it may be excluded from the audit exemption, on grounds which parallel the loss of small company status for accounts purposes.[24] In particular, the company must not be a public company or a banking, insurance

---

[19] s.477(2).

[20] s.382 and see para.21–3.

[21] s.382 as amended by SI 2008/393. In the case of the exemption from audit of group accounts, the turnover and balance sheet numbers are slightly larger if intra-group transactions are not eliminated. See s.479(2) and above at para.21–9.

[22] s.382(2)(c) and see above at para.21–3.

[23] Ch.21 at para.21–3.

[24] ss.478–479.

or fund management company.[25] In addition, if the company is a member of a group, it will qualify for the exemption only if the group qualifies as small and is not an ineligible group.[26]

An indication of the spread of the small company exemption from audit can be gained from looking at how the upper turnover figure for exemption has increased over the years. In 1994, this was set at £90,000;[27] it was raised to £300,000 in 1997;[28] and in 2000 to £1 million.[29] The CLR recommended a further increase, namely, to the level of the requirement for being a small company for accounts purposes, and that at the same time the UK's definition of a "small" company should be revised upwards to the level permitted by Community law.[30] This raised the turnover figure to £4.8 million. With a further raising of the EU limit, we reach the current number of £6.5 million. Thus, there has been a move from a very cautious approach to audit exemption, where the domestic rules remained well within the upper limit set by EU law, to one of taking full advantage of the exemption permitted at Community level.[31] In consequence, over a short period a very substantial process of removal of third party assurance in relation to the accounts of small companies has taken place.

22–5   Even if a company is exempt from audit on the ground of its size (or the ground of dormancy, discussed below) members representing at least 10 per cent of the nominal value of the company's issued share capital (or any class of it)[32] may demand an audit for a particular financial year, provided the notice is given after the financial year commences and within one year of its end.[33] Thus, notice must be given on a year-by-year basis and the members cannot make a demand relating to future financial years (when they might not meet the size threshold).

Where the exemption applies and is used, the directors must confirm in a statement attached to the balance sheet that the company was entitled to the exemption, that no effective notice has been delivered requiring an audit and that the directors acknowledge their responsibilities for ensuring that the company keeps accounting records and for preparing accounts which give a true and fair view of the state of the company's affairs.[34]

However, none of this means that small companies will not have

---

[25] ss.478(a),(b).
[26] s.479(2). The concept of an "ineligible group" we have analysed at para.21–9.
[27] Companies Act 1985 (Audit Exemption Regulations) 1994 (SI 1994/1935).
[28] Companies Act 1985 (Audit Exemption) (Amendment) Regulations 1997 (SI 1997/936).
[29] Companies Act 1985 (Audit Exemption) (Amendment) Regulations 2000 (SI 2000/1430).
[30] Final Report I, paras 4.29–4.31 and 4.43–4.45.
[31] Exemption from audit for small companies is permitted by Arts.51 and 11 of the Fourth Company Law Directive (78/660/EEC).
[32] Or 10 per cent in number of the members if there is no share capital.
[33] s.476.
[34] s.475(2)–(4). This provision applies to the exemption on grounds of dormancy as well.

their accounts audited in fact. If a company sees value in providing such assurance to members, creditors or investors, it may choose to have an audit. More likely, banks or other large creditors may insist on an audit as part of the process of considering whether to make a loan to the company.

Small charitable companies

22–6

From time to time it has been debated whether the upper ranges of the exempt small companies should be subject to some form of verification which falls short of a full audit. Thus, the CLR recommended trials of an "Independent Professional Review" for companies in the turnover range of £1 million to £4.8 million, in order to establish whether a cheaper but nevertheless worthwhile alternative to audit could be developed.[35] The Government later concluded that the trials had not been a success and did not take up this option.[36] However, between 1994 and 1997, a somewhat similar scheme operated for companies with turnovers in the range £90,000 to £350,000. Such companies were not "totally" exempt, but had to have their accounts "reported on" by an accountant, but were not required to have a full audit.

This restriction was removed in 1997 for most companies but it continues under the present law for charitable companies. Charitable companies with a gross income (the relevant test of charities, in place of turnover) of less than £90,000 are totally exempt.[37] However, if the company's gross income was between £90,000 and £500,000 and its balance sheet total was not more than £2.8 million, an accountant's report was required;[38] and above that level a full audit was required. Thus, in relation to both the requirement for a report and the lower level at which the full audit is required, charitable companies were less favourably treated than non-charities. The reason for this appears to be that the persons with the strongest financial interest in how well a charitable company uses its money are its donors, but they are not typically members of the company and so do not have access to the control rights over the management of the company which members have. For this reason, there is a stronger case for third-party verification than in the case of the accounts on non-charitable companies.[39]

No doubt for this reason as well one sees in the charities legislation full use made of the technique of requiring auditors or reporting

---

[35] Final Report I, paras 4.45–4.49.
[36] Modernising, paras 4.21–4.22.
[37] s.249A(3) and (3A) of CA 1985.
[38] s.249A(2) and (4) of CA 1985.
[39] And equally for the role of the Charities Commission in supervising charitable companies. See also, para.7–3 above for similarly less generous treatment of charitable companies in relation to board authority.

accountants to make reports to the regulator, the Charities Commission. If the auditor or reporting accountant becomes aware in the course of his or her duties of matters relating to the company's affairs which he or she has reasonable grounds for believing will be of material significance to the Commission in the exercise of its functions, those matters must be reported to the Commission. If they become aware of matters which are merely relevant to the exercise of the Commission's powers, a report may be made; and in either case the auditor or accountant will be protected from actions for breach of duty, most obviously by the company.[40]

In essence, the distinction between the accountant's report and the full audit was that in the former case the company's accounting records are taken on trust and are not independently verified. It must be doubted whether such a restriction of the accountant's functions will save more than half the cost of an audit, and some estimates put the cost saving even lower. However, as from April 2008 the special provisions relating to charitable companies were removed from the companies legislation (with regard to England and Wales) and regulation transferred to the charities legislation.[41]

Dormant companies

22–7 A further and less controversial type of company which is exempt from audit is the so-called "dormant" company.[42] A company is dormant during a period when there is "no significant accounting transaction" in relation to it, an accounting transaction being one which needs to be recorded in the company's accounting records.[43] Where the company has been dormant since its formation, no other conditions need be met before the exemption is granted.[44] The most obvious and common example of such a company is a "shelf company"[45] while it remains on the shelf (though there may be legitimate reasons for incorporating a company which is intended to remain dormant indefinitely). If the company has been dormant only since the end of the previous financial year, then its audit exemption is more circumscribed. It depends on the company not being a parent company required to produce group accounts and its being entitled to produce its individual accounts under the small companies regime[46] or being entitled to do so but for the fact that it is a public company

---

[40] Charities Act 1993, ss.44A and 68A, as inserted by the Charities Act 2006.
[41] See s.1175 and Sch.9 to CA 2006 and the Charities Act 2006 (Charitable Companies Audit and Group Accounts Provisions) Order 2008/527.
[42] s.480(1).
[43] s.1169.
[44] s.480(1)(a).
[45] See above, para.4–16.
[46] See above, para.21–3.

or a member of an ineligible group.[47] In practice, the most important extension which the dormant company exemption makes to that already provided for small companies is that it extends to include public companies.[48]

Non-profit public sector companies

This is a new exemption which, however, does not need detailed   **22–8** consideration because the companies entitled to it, although incorporated under the Companies Acts, are part of the public sector and are subject to public sector audit.[49] A company is non-profit making if it is so for the purpose of Article 48 of the European Community Treaty–though that article in fact contains no definition of "non-profit making". This is because such companies are excluded from the scope of Article 44(2)(g), under which the Fourth and Seventh Directives, requiring audit, were made.

AUDITOR INDEPENDENCE AND COMPETENCE

Although the issue of small company exemption from audit has been   **22–9** important over the past two decades, the most important policy issue relating to auditors concerns their independence. This was an issue brought to the fore in recent years by the collapse of the Enron Company and others in the United States in the early years of this century, which collapses were thought to reveal weaknesses in the provisions on auditor independence.[50] The essence of the independence issue is that the auditor is appointed and remunerated by the company whose accounts and reports are then audited. Although companies are required to have their accounts audited (unless exempted), they are not required to employ any particular auditor or to pay that auditor any particular level of remuneration. There thus develops the possibility that auditors will compete for mandates on the basis that they will engage in only a cursory scrutiny of the company's accounts or that they will act in this way in return for excessive remuneration (which might be disguised as remuneration for the provision of non-audit services to the company). The traditional response to this argument is that in the long- or even the medium-term such a business model is self-destructive. The auditor will obtain a reputation for laxness, which will, perversely, destroy its business. Whilst the company may want a lax audit, it is crucial that

---

[47] s.480(2).
[48] The dormant company exemption is not available to companies in the insurance, banking and fund management sectors: s.481.
[49] s.482(1).
[50] See John C. Coffee Jr, *Gatekeepers* (Oxford: OUP, 2006), especially Ch.5.

those who rely on the audit believe that the appropriate checks have been carried out. A lax audit by an auditor known to be lax is no good, even for the audited company, because it will not obtain the benefit it wants from the audit opinion. Whilst this argument may have much force, recent experience suggests that it does not operate at all times and in all circumstances so as to guarantee an appropriate audit. Individuals within the audit firm may have short-term incentives which outweigh the firm's longer term incentive to do a good job or the investors may move away from attaching much importance to the audited accounts in periods of market exuberance.

Consequently, there is a case for regulation to reinforce the market incentives supporting auditor independence. Much the same arguments can be made in relation to auditor competence. An audit firm has reputational reasons for providing a good service in general but in particular cases there may be incentives on individuals to operate inefficiently. Nor should the independence and competence issues be viewed as completely separate: a non-independent auditor displays dependence on management precisely by carrying out an inadequate audit.

There are six strategies which have been deployed by the law to address these problems.

(1) Laying down specific rules disqualifying persons from acting as auditor of a particular company on grounds of conflict of interest.

(2) On the basis that the board is the body within the company which has the greatest interest in a lax audit, increasing the role of the shareholders in relation to the auditors.

(3) On the basis that, within the board, it is the executive directors who have the greatest interest in a lax audit and that shareholders have serious collective action problems, increasing the role of the non-executive directors in relation to the auditors, notably via an audit committee consisting wholly of independent non-executive directors.

(4) Attacking the problem not from the side of the company but from the side of the auditor by subjecting auditors to greater regulatory control and more effective disciplinary mechanisms.

(5) Increasing the powers of the auditors as against the company.

(6) Imposing civil liability on auditors to those who rely on the audited accounts and reports where the auditors have been negligent and imposing criminal liability for false statements in audit reports.

We shall look at each in turn. Each has been deployed with greater vigour in recent years, except civil liability, where indeed the tendency has been to restrict liability.

Before we do so, however, a short word is necessary about the **22–10** structure of the regulation, which is far from straightforward. First, two widely separated Parts of the Act are relevant to this Chapter: Parts 16 and 42. Very broadly, Part 16 deals with the audit obligations of companies and the auditors' and companies' rights and duties to each other. Part 42 deals with the regulatory structure for the auditing profession. It applies to a person identified as the "statutory auditor", who is not simply someone who may carry out audits under the Companies Act but who may act also under legislation relating to similar bodies, such as building societies, friendly societies, or industrial and provident societies.[51] The purpose of Part 42 is to ensure that statutory auditors are properly supervised and qualified and that they carry out their duties properly.[52] It is not the aim of this book to provide a full guide to the professional regulation of auditors, but elements from Part 42 need to be considered.

The structure of Part 16 is not unusual: it generates rules, either contained in Part 16 itself or in some cases in statutory instruments made under it. Part 42, which has already been amended by statutory instrument to give effect to Community law,[53] is more complex. This is because the task of supervision of auditors is one which is, to a large extent, delegated under the Act to other bodies. Thus, the applicable substantive rule is often to be found in the rules made by the bodies to which there has been delegation rather than by Parliament, in either primary or secondary legislation. This is not unusual, of course, in this area. We saw in the previous Chapter the delegation of the setting of accounting standards to either the Accounting Standards Board or the International Accounting Standards Board and of the monitoring of the accuracy of accounts to the Financial Reporting Review Panel,[54] both the ASB and the FRRP being operating bodies of the Financial Reporting Council (FRC).[55] However, in Part 42 there are, in effect, two types of delegation. First, Part 42 confers certain functions on the Secretary of State but permits delegation of those functions to a designated body, either created by the act of delegation or already existing.[56] That delegation power has been used to confer powers on the Professional Oversight Board (POB), another subsidiary of the FRC.[57]

Secondly, those who act as statutory auditors must be members of

---

[51] s.1210. For a brief discussion of the nature of these bodies above at para.1–18.
[52] s.1209.
[53] The Statutory Auditors and Third Country Auditors Regulations 2007 (SI 2007/3494), as amended by SI 2008/499 (hereafter "Statutory Auditors Regulations").
[54] See paras 21–15 and 21–30, above.
[55] Above, para.3–7.
[56] ss.1252–1253.
[57] The Statutory Auditors (Delegation of Functions) Order 2008/496.

a "recognised supervisory body" and eligible to act as a statutory auditor under the rules of that body.[58] The Act then lays down in quite some detail the matters with which the rules of those recognised bodies must deal and even the results which must be achieved by them.[59] If the rules of the recognised body fall short of what is required, the body is in danger of having its recognition withdrawn by the Secretary of State and thus of losing its *raison d'être*.[60] Further, the rules must be binding on those who are or have been members of the body.[61] In this way the professional associations of accountants (notably the Institutes of Chartered Accountants for England and Wales, Scotland and Ireland, respectively) become part of the regulatory structure, but at the cost of having their rulebooks heavily controlled by the Act. A particular feature of this regulation of the professional rules, which we should notice, is that the professional institutes may be required to ensure that their members cooperate with and even comply with standards set by bodies other than the professional institutes themselves, such as the Auditing Practices Board (APB) or the Accountancy and Actuarial Discipline Board (AADB), both, yet again, subsidiaries of the FRC.[62] Through the rules of the professional bodies auditors thus become obliged to abide by rules laid down by quasi-public bodies.

22–11 Overall, through processes of delegation "from above" (by the Secretary of State) and through rules made "from below" (by the professional bodies) auditors are required to observe rules laid down by the relevant subsidiaries of the FRC. The advantages of this way of proceeding are that some degree of professional self-regulation is maintained (through the "recognised supervisory body" concept) whilst in areas of major concern the public interest is thought to be ensured through the role given to the various subsidiaries of the FRC. As to the FRC itself, it may be thought to have advantages over regulation by a governmental department through delegated legislation in that it probably is capable of reacting more quickly and more expertly than a governmental department would be, but the Government has ultimate control of the FRC through the appointment of its directors. As we shall see, this complex process of rule-making has been used to implement many of the requirements of the Audit Directive.[63] These requirements constitute obligations laid upon the

---

[58] s.1212.
[59] s.1217 and Sch.10, as amended.
[60] Sch.10, para.3. Alternatively, the Secretary of State (or POB) may apply to the court for an order that the recognised body comply with the obligation laid down in Sch.10—a less drastic and more useful way of proceeding, but even this is unlikely to be necessary in practice: s.1225.
[61] s.1217(1A).
[62] s.1217(3) makes it clear that the rules of the supervisory body include rules which the body has power to enforce "whether or not laid down by the body itself".
[63] Directive 2006/43/EC on statutory audits of annual accounts and consolidated accounts (OJ L157/87, 9.6.2006).

United Kingdom. In order to be sure that the United Kingdom is in compliance with its Treaty obligations at all times, the Secretary of State is given a general power to order recognised supervisory bodies and any body to which the Secretary of State's functions have been delegated (i.e. the POB) to take any action within their power required to implement the Community obligations of the United Kingdom (or any other international obligation) or to order those bodies to refrain from taking action which would contravene those obligations.[64]

DISQUALIFYING PERSONS FROM ACTING AS AUDITORS

Non-independent persons

A person may not act as an auditor on the ground of lack of independence if he is an officer or employee of the company to be audited or a partner or employee of such an officer or employee or, in the case of the appointment of a partnership, if any member of the partnership is ineligible on these grounds.[65] Nor may a person act if any of these grounds apply in relation to any associated undertaking[66] of the company. An auditor who comes within the section must immediately resign and give notice to the company of the reason for the resignation.[67] Failing to do so is a criminal offence. Further, the appointment or continuation in office of an auditor who is not independent within the statutory section triggers a power in the Secretary of State to require the company to appoint a proper person to conduct a second audit or to review the first audit, and the company may recover the costs of the additional audit work from the first person, provided that person knew he or she was not independent.[68]

22–12

---

[64] s.1254. In the case of the POB the direction is enforceable by injunction (s.1254(3)); in the case of a recognised supervisory body the provisions of s.1225 (above, fn.60) apply, to like effect: s.1225(1)(c).

[65] s.1214(1)–(3). S.1214(5) expressly states that, for this purpose, an auditor is not to be regarded as an "officer or employee". This hardly needs saying, for if he were, he would become ineligible immediately upon appointment! The definition of "officer" in the Act ("officer—includes a director, manager or secretary or, where the affairs of the company are managed by its members, a member": s.1261(1)) might seem in any event to exclude auditors. Nevertheless, they have been held to be "officers" in a number of corporate contexts: *Mutual Reinsurance Co Ltd v Peat Marwick Mitchell & Co* [1997] 1 B.C.L.C. 1, CA; *London & General Bank (No.1), Re* [1895] 2 Ch.166, CA; *Kingston Cotton Mills (No.1), Re* [1896] 1 Ch.6, CA.

[66] s.1214(6) i.e. a parent or subsidiary undertaking of the company or a subsidiary undertaking of any parent undertaking of the company.

[67] s.1215(1).

[68] ss.1248–1249. The provisions also apply—and in practice are probably more important—where the auditor is ineligible to be appointed (for example, because not qualified) rather than prohibited from acting on grounds of lack of independence: s.1248(3). The sections appear not to apply to lack of independence solely under the APB's rules discussed below.

Clearly, however, an employer-employee relationship with the audit company far is from being the only type of relationship which might impair the independence of the auditor, e.g. a debtor-creditor relationship or a substantial shareholding[69] in the company might do so. The prohibition is clearly not a sufficient compliance with the requirements of Article 22 of the Audit Directive[70] which imposes a general requirement upon Member States to ensure the independence of auditors and to exclude a person from acting as auditor "if there is any direct or indirect financial, business, employment or other relationship" between the auditor and audited company "from which an objective, reasonable and informed third party would conclude that the statutory auditor's . . . independence is compromised." That Article also requires the auditor to document significant threats to independence.

In fact, the Act empowers the Secretary of State to specify by regulations such further connections "between [the auditor] and any associate[71] of his and the company or any associated undertaking of it" which will also prevent him from acting as auditor.[72] No regulations have been made under this provision—or under its predecessor—and this appears to be an area which the Government prefers to see dealt with through the rules of recognised supervisory bodies and the subsidiaries of the FRC.[73] Thus, Schedule 10 requires, amongst many other things, that the supervisory body must have adequate rules and practices designed to ensure that a person is not appointed as auditor where they have an interest likely to conflict with the proper conduct of the audit, that auditors take steps to safeguard their independence from significant threats, record threats to independence and that the audit fee is not influenced by the provision of non-audit services nor provided on a contingent-fee basis.[74] The supervisory body must also "participate in arrangements" for laying down standards in the area of independence, but the laying down of standards must not be done by the supervisory body itself, whose rules nevertheless must require compliance with the standards so determined.[75] This otherwise impenetrable set of rules makes sense when put in the context of the regulatory institutions described above. In effect, the professional bodies' rules must require members to abide by the standards on independence laid down by the Auditing Practices Board. The APB has developed five Ethical Standards, of which the most relevant to the present discussion is number 2 (*Financial, Business, Employment and Personal Relationships*).

---

[69] Though the shareholding might make the auditor a more diligent watchdog over the members' interests—but members are not the only people whose interests he should protect.
[70] Above, fn.63.
[71] As defined in s.1260.
[72] s.1214(4).
[73] DTI, *Implementation of Directive 2006/43/EC: A Consultation Document*, March 2007, para.3.15 (URN 07/609).
[74] Para.9(1).
[75] Paras 9(2) and 21.

Auditors becoming non-independent

There is an argument to be made to the effect that, although the **22–13** auditor may have no other relationship with the company which generates a conflict of interest, over a period of time the auditor relationship itself becomes a threat to independence. The auditor may build up personal relationships with the management of the audited company which make him or her reluctant to challenge the management's picture of events. The watchdog may have become a lap dog. The Directive accepts this argument, at least in relation to "public interest entities", of which the most important example from our point of view is a company whose securities are traded on a regulated market.[76] The "key audit partners" are required to rotate every seven years and not to take up appointment again for two years.[77] The notion of a "key audit partner" is one derived from the Directive and it means the auditor designated by the audit firm as primarily responsible for carrying out the audit (normally referred to in the UK as the "engagement auditor") but also the auditor who signs the report, if different.[78] In fact, the ethical rule in the United Kingdom imposes a five-year rotation. As above, the Directive is implemented by making this ethical rule binding on auditors via the rules of their professional body.[79]

These provisions stop short of requiring the rotation of audit firms. The argument against mandatory rotation of firms is that it means the loss of the expertise of the whole of the existing audit team, which occurrence would be likely to reduce the quality of the audits immediately following a change of firm (unless, of course, the audit team simply changed firms, thus defeating the object of the exercise).

Auditors becoming prospectively non-independent

An auditor may have no current relationship with the company **22–14** which creates a conflict of interest (nor may he or she have a long association with the company as auditor) but there may be an understanding, falling short of a contract, that the auditor will resign in due course and take up a role in the management of the company. Since accountancy skills are much prized in some areas of management, movement from professional practice to management is quite common. Article 42 of the Directive, however, imposes a two-year "cooling off" period between ceasing to be the statutory auditor or key audit partner and the taking up of a "key" management position

---

[76] Audit Directive, Art.2(13). For the meaning of a "regulated market" see para.25–5. Also included in the term "public-interest entity" are banks and other deposit-taking institutions, which may not be publicly traded or even shareholder-owned, for example, mutual building societies, and insurance companies.

[77] Art.42(2).

[78] Art.2(16), apparently translated in the Act as "senior statutory auditor": s.504.

[79] Sch.10, paras 10C and 22B, and APB Ethical Standard 3 (*Long Association with the Audit Engagement*).

in the audited entity. This rule too is implemented via ethical standards in the United Kingdom.[80]

Auditors required to be appropriately qualified

22–15   A major concern of the Community law on auditors has been to require that they be appropriately trained and qualified.[81] We do not need to go into the details in this book. It is enough to note that the rules of the recognised supervisory bodies (i.e. normally the professional institutes)[82] must provide for appointment as statutory auditor to be confined to those who hold appropriate qualifications (or in the case of appointment of a firm that each individual responsible on behalf of the firm is so qualified and that the firm is controlled by such persons).[83] Schedule 11 then lays out in some detail the terms on which bodies may award professional qualifications. Following the Directive, the terms of the Schedule are quite detailed and include a power for the Secretary of State (or POB) to control the syllabus for the theoretical examination. Since a person who acts as an auditor without the appropriate qualifications is ineligible to do so,[84] the POB has the power to require a second audit in such cases and the ineligible auditor may be liable for its costs.[85] An auditor may also be appropriately qualified by virtue of a qualification granted in another European Community State and of having passed the conversion tests for practice in the United Kingdom.[86] The Secretary of State (POB) also has power to recognise qualifications obtained outside the European Community where it is thought that they are equivalent and where the country in question would provide reciprocal treatment of persons qualified in the United Kingdom.[87] The names of statutory auditors must be entered into a public register, which must include an indication of the other Member States (if any) in which the auditor is registered. It must also contain the names of third country auditors who sign the audit reports of third country companies whose securities are traded on a regulated market in the European Community.[88]

---

[80] Sch.10, paras 10C and 22B, and APB Ethical Standard 2 (above), para.43, which implements the provision by requiring the audit firm to resign the engagement immediately if the two-year rule is broken.

[81] Audit Directive (above, fn.63), Chapter 2.

[82] See above, para.22–12.

[83] Sch.10, para.6.

[84] s.1212(1)(b).

[85] See above, para.22–12.

[86] s.1219(1)(e).

[87] s.1221.

[88] ss.1239–1247 and the Statutory Auditors Regulations, Part 5.

The Role of Shareholders

The traditional regulatory strategy deployed by the domestic legis- **22–16** lation to reinforce auditor independence has been to enhance the role of the shareholders. In many ways this is an obvious strategy, since the accounts and reports are statements from the directors to the members and so putting control over those who verify those statements in the hands of the recipients rather than the originators of the statements is sensible. However, the shareholders have limited opportunities to exercise control, since they meet infrequently, and may face co-ordination problems over the exercise of the powers which are conferred on them.

Appointment and remuneration of auditors

Assuming a company is not covered by an audit exemption (or is not **22–17** thought by the directors to be on reasonable grounds) and is a public company, then the normal rule is that the appointment of the auditors must be done at each accounts meeting, normally the annual general meeting,[89] and the appointment is from the conclusion of that meeting until the conclusion of the next such meeting.[90] There are only exceptional circumstances in which the directors may appoint auditors.[91] However, the proposal to appoint the auditors, to re-appoint them or to appoint others in their place comes normally from the board (though it need not) and the meeting, almost invariably, will agree with the board's proposal. This is an example of a situation where the shareholders' co-ordination problems make it difficult, though not impossible, for them to generate a proposal of their own. They might do so if they had reason to believe that the auditor was in the board's pocket, but they rarely have grounds for so thinking, in which case accepting the board's proposal seems the rational course of action.

Where the auditors are appointed by the members in general meeting, their remuneration shall be fixed by the company in general meeting or in such manner as the general meeting shall determine.[92] This, too, is intended to emphasise that the auditors are the members' watchdogs rather than the directors' lapdogs. But in practice it serves little purpose since the members normally adopt a resolution proposed by the directors to the effect that the remuneration shall be agreed by the directors—as the provision permits them to do. Even if the shareholders actually fixed the auditor's remuneration, rather

---

[89] See para.21–41.
[90] ss.489(4) and 491(1)(b).
[91] s.489(3)—to fill a casual vacancy, after a period in which the company has not been required to have an audit, before its first accounts meeting.
[92] s.492(1).

than fixing the method for fixing it, they would invariably act on a recommendation from the board. A more effective protection, perhaps, is that the amount of the remuneration, which includes expenses and benefits in kind (the monetary value of which has to be estimated) has to be shown in a note to the annual accounts, thus enabling the members to criticise the directors if the amount seems to be out of line.[93]

For private companies shareholder meetings are not required to be held, but the principle of shareholder appointment and determination of remuneration still applies, except that the shareholders may act by written resolution and the rules are re-drafted so as to apply with reference to, not the accounts meeting, which will probably not be held, but the period of 28 days beginning with the day on which the accounts and reports were circulated to the members or, if later, the last day for circulating them.[94] However, the period of appointment may turn out to be much longer than a year. Assuming the auditor was not appointed by the directors under their exceptional powers,[95] failure to re-appoint or to appoint someone else the following year will mean the auditors in place are deemed to be re-appointed.[96] This process of deemed re-appointment in private companies, which may otherwise continue indefinitely, can be excluded by the company's articles,[97] or the auditor in post may be required to undergo re-election by a resolution of the members[98] or by notice received from members holding at least five per cent of the voting rights entitled to be cast on a resolution that the auditor should not be re-appointed,[99] the last of these being the least demanding method of bringing deemed re-appointments to an end.

Non-audit remuneration of auditors

22–18   The financial threat to auditor independence comes not only—or even principally—from the remuneration paid by the company to the auditor in that capacity. An auditor is normally a member of a firm of accountants which is capable of providing a wide range of services—well beyond accountancy services—to clients. These non-audit revenues from audit clients of accountancy firms have increased

[93] s.493 and the Companies (Disclosure of Auditor Remuneration and Liability Limitation Agreements) Regulations 2008/489, regs.4 and 5 (hereafter the "Remuneration and Liability Regulations"). Generally, they criticise only if the amount seems abnormally high; they should perhaps be more alarmed if it is abnormally low.
[94] ss.485, 487.
[95] s.485(3).
[96] s.487.
[97] s.487(2)(b).
[98] s.487(2)(d).
[99] ss.487(2)(c) and 488.

substantially in recent years.[100] There is a recognition of the importance of this issue in the provision authorising the Secretary of State to make regulations requiring the disclosure on a disaggregated basis of non-audit remuneration received by audit firms in notes to the accounts.[101] The Remuneration and Liability Regulations[102] divide the auditor's potential sources of remuneration into ten categories (including remuneration of the audit itself), require separate disclosure of remuneration earned from the company (and its subsidiaries) and from associated pension schemes,[103] and require disclosure of amounts paid to the auditor's "associates" as well as to the auditor.[104] However, these obligations are not imposed on small or medium-sized[105] companies, though they remain subject to the requirement to disclose audit remuneration, noted above.

Disclosure is no doubt a useful indicator, especially to audit committees, of potential problems, but it is doubtful whether it is a strong enough strategy to combat by itself the high-powered conflicts of interest which non-audit remuneration can generate. There is a case for simply prohibiting the provision of non-audit services to audit clients, as is done is some jurisdictions. In the United Kingdom the Final Report of the Co-ordinating Group on Audit and Accounting Issues[106] did not recommend a blanket ban on non-audit services, since sometimes the auditor is in the best position to deliver such services, because of the knowledge of the company obtained through the audit. However, the Group did propose that certain types of non-audit work should always or normally be avoided by the auditors. Examples were non-audit work which would involve the audit firm performing management functions for the audit client or being involved in the audit of its own work; the provisions of internal audit services; valuations involving a significant degree of subjectivity; likewise with tax advice. These recommendations substantially followed those contained in Commission Recommendation 2002/590/EC on statutory auditors' independence in the EU.[107]

The payment of non-audit remuneration to auditors is an example of the more general problem of the auditor having a relationship with the company which may jeopardize independence, discussed above.[108] Indeed, the payment of non-audit remuneration is specifically mentioned in Article 22 of the Audit Directive which deals with conflicts

---

[100] See David Kershaw, "Waiting for Enron: The Unstable Equilibrium of Auditor Independence Regulation" (2006) 33 *Journal of Law and Society* 388, 394. This is a valuable article on the whole issue of auditor independence.
[101] s.494.
[102] Above, fn.93, reg.5(3) and Sch.2.
[103] Remuneration and Liability Regulations, reg.5(4).
[104] Ibid., reg.5(1)(b)(ii) and Sch.1.
[105] Ibid., reg.4. For the definition of medium-sized, see para.21–4 above.
[106] DTI and Treasury, URN 03/567 (January 2003).
[107] [2002] OJ L191/22.
[108] Paras 22–12ff.

of interest in general. It is not surprising, therefore, that the United Kingdom has chosen to regulate non-audit remuneration in the same way as more general conflict situations. Thus, the provisions of Schedule 10 to the Act[109] dealing with professional rules on conflicts and the obligation to secure compliance with APB standards apply also to non-audit remuneration. The relevant standard from the APB is Ethical Standard 5 (*Non-Audit Services Provided to Audited Entities*) which adopts, but elaborates upon, the approach recommended by the Co-ordinating Group. The standard places the task of identifying and managing threats to independence arising out of non-audit work primarily on the auditor, but certain types of non-audit service are identified as particularly dangerous and "should not" be undertaken.

Removal of auditors
Requirement for shareholder resolution

22–19   As in the case of directors,[110] a company may by ordinary resolution passed at a meeting at any time remove an auditor from office.[111] However, the auditor, unlike a director, may not be removed prior to the expiration of the term of office other than by resolution of the shareholders.[112] In this way the auditor is given some protection against management pressure. If management wish to remove the auditor prematurely, they must do so by means of a proposal to the shareholders. If management goes down that route, further provisions of the Act come into play designed to permit or even require the auditor to put the contrary case to the shareholders. Hence, not only has special notice (28 days)[113] to be given to the company of a resolution to remove an auditor, but notice of the proposed resolution has to be given to the auditor.[114] The auditor is entitled to make written representations which, if received in time, have to be sent to the members with the notice of the meeting, and which, if not received in time, have to be read out at the meeting.[115] If the resolution is passed, the auditor still retains the right to attend the general meeting at which the term of office would otherwise have expired or at which the vacancy created by the removal is to be filled.[116] Nor does removal

---

[109]   Paras 9 and 21. See above, para.22–10.
[110]   See para.14–18.
[111]   s.510. A meeting is required, as for the removal of a director, even in the case of a private company: s.288(2).
[112]   s.510(4). The articles often provide other ways for directors to be removed than by resolution of the shareholders.
[113]   s.511.
[114]   s.511(2).
[115]   s.511(3)–(5). The auditor should ensure that it is received in time since otherwise members may return proxy forms before they see his representations. But see subs.(6) regarding restraint by the court if the section is being abused "to secure needless publicity for defamatory matter". The auditor also has a general right to attend and speak at shareholder meetings. See para.22–24 below.
[116]   ss.513 and 502(2).

deprive the auditor of any right to compensation or damages, arising, for example, under the contract between auditor and company, in respect of the termination of the appointment as auditor or any appointment terminating with that as auditor.[117]

A feature of the above rules is that, whilst protecting the auditor to some degree against management pressure, they give the shareholders a free hand over the removal of the auditor. If, for example, the shareholders of their own motion wish to remove an auditor they regard as too friendly with management, they are free to do so, provided the special notice and auditor statement provisions are complied with. However, the Audit Directive[118] caused a change to be made. Article 37 requires Member States to ensure that auditors may be removed only on "proper grounds" and says that "divergence of opinion on accounting treatments or audit procedures shall not be proper grounds for dismissal". The aim is clearly to give the auditor further protection against management pressure where the auditor has fallen out with the management, but it also makes it less easy for the shareholders to act where they think the auditor has become too cosy with the management, the latter being the more likely situation if the hold by the management over the auditor consists of the payment of non-audit remuneration.

In countries with controlling shareholders as the predominant form of shareholding even in large companies (common in continental Europe), it may have been thought unrealistic to regard the directors and the shareholders as two separate groups. However, it is not unrealistic in the United Kingdom, and the Government was clearly reluctant to implement the Directive in the obvious way, i.e. by building a "proper grounds" qualification into the shareholders' removal power in section 510.[119] Instead the Government opted to amend section 994 dealing with unfair prejudice.[120] Removal of an auditor on ground of divergence of opinion or any other improper ground is deemed to be conduct unfairly prejudicial to the interests of some part of the members.[121] This approach has the merit of addressing the policy issue probably underlying the Directive, i.e. unfair treatment of minority shareholders. However, it is difficult to see that it effects the Directive's formal requirement that the auditor "may be dismissed" only on proper grounds. The dismissal, even if challengeable under the unfair prejudice provisions by a shareholder, still seems to be effective as far as the auditor is concerned nor, whether the dismissal is effective or not, does the new provision give the auditor any rights as against the company. Further, there is no requirement that the court exercise its remedial powers under section

[117] s.510(3).
[118] Above, fn.63.
[119] DTI, above, fn.73, at paras 3.34ff.
[120] See Ch.20.
[121] s.994(1A).

996 to secure the reinstatement of the auditor. Whether this way of proceeding meets the Directive's requirements must be open to doubt.

Notifying the audit authorities

22–20　A new constraint on management, implementing Article 38(2) of the Audit Directive, is the requirement to notify the audit authorities if an auditor ceases to hold office before the end of the term of office, whether the cessation is brought about by dismissal or otherwise. Notification is required from both the auditor[122] and the company.[123] As far as notification by the auditor is concerned, it builds on the pre-existing obligation to make a statement *to the company* of the circumstances relating to the premature termination of office.[124] In the case of a dismissal this obligation to the company is likely to be overtaken in practice by the auditor's entitlement (discussed above) to circulate representations to the meeting at which the dismissal is to be considered (an opportunity which arises before the dismissal whilst the statement of circumstances is to be made only after dismissal). It is true that the statement of circumstances is obligatory, whilst making representations is a right rather than a duty, but it would be a rare auditor who refused to resign when pressurised by management but then failed to oppose his or her dismissal. For this reason the statement to the company is discussed more fully below in relation to resignations.

For dismissals, the crucial requirement is that an auditor who has been dismissed must notify the appropriate audit authority and the notification must be accompanied by the statement of circumstances.[125] Although this is formally a duty on the auditor, its effect is to increase the pressure on the company which has dismissed him, because the public authorities are involved in the event, at least *post hoc*. The appropriate authority varies according to whether the audit in question is a "major audit" or not. A major audit is one of a company whose securities have been admitted to the official list[126] or one of equivalent public interest.[127] For a major audit the appropriate authority is the Professional Oversight Board; otherwise it is the recognised supervisory authority.[128] The appropriate audit authority must then inform the accounting authorities, in practice the Financial Reporting Review Panel, responsible for dealing with defective accounts.[129] The notification required of the company goes to the

---

[122] s.522.
[123] s.523.
[124] s.519.
[125] s.522.
[126] On the meaning of which see para.25–8.
[127] s.525(2).
[128] s.525(1).
[129] s.524. On the work of the FRRP see above at para.21–30.

same bodies.[130] It must give the reasons for the auditor ceasing to hold office or attach the auditor's statement of circumstances (if such was made).

In short, the management cannot remove an auditor prematurely without facing a serious risk of a row at the general meeting (and, in the case of a listed company, adverse press publicity) and with the auditing and accounting authorities.

Resignation of the auditor

A breakdown in relations between auditor and management is more likely to reveal itself in the resignation, rather than the removal, of the auditor. Few auditors will want to retain office if relations with the management of the company have become seriously strained. In this case what is needed are provisions which make it difficult for the auditor to "go quietly" i.e. to resign office without ensuring that any matters which have caused concern will be ventilated. The Act contains two sets of notice provisions designed to achieve this objective, requiring notice to be given to the company, on the one hand, and the regulatory authorities on the other.

22–21

Although the Act provides that an auditor may resign by depositing a notice in writing to that effect at the company's registered office, the notice is not effective unless it is accompanied by the required statement.[131] In the case of an unquoted company, what is required is a statement of any circumstances connected with the resignation which the auditor considers should be brought to the attention of members or creditors or a statement that none exist, if that is what the auditor considers is the case.[132] In the case of a quoted company,[133] the statement is obligatory in all cases, i.e. a statement must be given of the circumstances connected with the resignation.[134]

If the statement does discuss the circumstances in which the auditor resigned (which it must do in the case of a quoted company and may do in other cases), the company must, within 14 days of its deposit, either send copies of it to any person who is entitled to be sent copies of the accounts (which will include the company's debenture-holders as well as its members)[135] or apply to the court and notify the auditor that it has done so.[136] If the company applies to the court, which is satisfied that the auditor is using the statement to secure needless publicity for defamatory matter, the court must direct that the statement need not be sent out and may order the company's

---

[130] s.523.
[131] s.516. The notice is effective on the date specified in it or, if none, the date of deposit.
[132] s.519(1),(2). This section applies if an auditor ceases to hold office "for any reason", including dismissal (above) or failure to be re-appointed (below).
[133] For the meaning of a quoted company, see para.14–16.
[134] s.519(3).
[135] See para.21–39, above.
[136] s.520(1)–(3).

costs to be paid, in whole or in part, by the auditors.[137] If the court is not so satisfied, the obligation to circulate the auditor's statement to those entitled to receive the accounts revives.

22–22 In addition, the auditor must send a copy of the statement to the Registrar, either shortly after it has been deposited with the company or, if there is an appeal to the court, after the appeal has been decided in the auditor's favour.[138] This makes the statement available publicly, especially to creditors, though debenture-holders will be sent it directly by the company. However, much more important are the notices required to be given to the audit authorities by the auditor and the company, which we have discussed above in relation to dismissals. In the case of the auditor, the effect of the notice provisions is to generate pressure not to go quietly. If the auditor does not disclose the true reasons for the resignation, the auditor, even if a victim of management pressure, will be committing a wrong. To strengthen this effect, the statute requires in the auditor's notice to the audit authority a statement of the reasons for the resignation, even if the auditor has said in the statement to the company that there are no circumstances which need to be brought to the attention of the members or creditors of the company.[139] The company's notification obligation operates to create an incentive for the company to be able to explain any pressure it has put on the auditor to resign.

Assuming the resigning auditor does not want to go quietly, but wishes to avoid the ignominy of being sacked, then the requirements to make a statement to the company for circulation and to notify the audit authority can be used to good effect by the departing auditor. The statute also gives the resigning auditor, who deposits a statement of circumstances with the company, the right to requisition a meeting of the shareholders for the purpose of receiving and considering the auditor's explanation of the circumstances connected with the resignation, and to have a statement of circumstances circulated to the members in advance of the meeting.[140] This applies to both public and private companies, but for those many private companies which are exempt from audit on grounds of being small, the rule is obviously inapplicable. If the auditor does not want to go that far, he or she may instead require circulation of a statement for the shareholder

---

[137] s.520(4). The company must then send to members or debenture-holders a statement setting out the effect of the order. There is a risk that a company will use the appeal procedure simply to delay circulation of the auditor's statement, discontinuing the application just before it is due to be heard. Such action places the company at risk of having to pay the auditor's costs on an indemnity basis: *Jarvis Plc v Pricewaterhouse Coopers* [2000] 2 B.C.L.C. 368.

[138] s.521(1), (2). Failure to do so constitutes a criminal offence, unless the auditor can show that all reasonable steps were taken and all due diligence was exercised.

[139] s.522(3).

[140] s.518.

meeting at which the term of office would otherwise have expired or at which the vacancy created by the resignation is to be filled.[141]

Thus, pressurised resignation is probably not a much more attractive way for the management to get rid of an auditor than an outright dismissal. It may be possible to avoid the shareholders' meeting (though the auditor may insist on one), but it will be difficult to hide the truth from the audit authorities—at least if the regulators do a good job.

Failure to re-appoint an auditor

Finally, a management which has fallen out with its auditors may simply wait until the end of the term of office and replace them. As we have seen, in the case of a public company this is an annual opportunity, since the term of office of the auditor runs, normally, from one accounts meeting to the next, and in the case of a private company the deemed re-appointment mechanism can be brought to an end by appointing substitute auditors during the annual period for appointing them.[142] Moreover, since a change of auditors, for good reasons, is not an uncommon event, failure to re-appoint may not be suspicious. However, the Act does take steps to flush out information about failures to re-appoint which are questionable. First, a resolution to appoint someone other than the existing auditors must be a resolution of which special notice (at least 28 days)[143] has been given to the company, and the company must make use of the advance notice to inform the outgoing auditor and the proposed replacement of the resolution.[144] The outgoing auditor then has the right to have representations circulated in advance of the meeting or read out at the meeting, similar to the rights arising on a resolution to dismiss.[145] If, in the case of a private company, the decision is to be taken by written resolution, the right is to have the representations circulated to the members of the company.[146] More important, because obligatory, the rules discussed above concerning the auditor's duty to deposit a statement of circumstances with the company apply to the outgoing auditor.[147]

However, in the case of failure to re-appoint, the duty on the auditor to notify the audit authority arises only in the case of a "major" audit.[148] Equally, the company's obligation to notify the

22–23

---

[141] s.518(3)(b).

[142] Above, para.22–17.

[143] s.312.

[144] s.515(2),(3). The provisions of the section apply also where the period for re-appointment has passed without an appointment being made and the company later decides to appoint someone other than the outgoing auditors. Otherwise the section's requirements could be easily avoided.

[145] ss.515(4)–(7).

[146] s.514.

[147] s.519, which applies where an auditor "ceases for any reason to hold office".

[148] s.522(1)(a). Otherwise the notification obligation applies only if the auditor ceases prematurely to hold office: s.522(1)(b). For the meaning of "major audit" see above, para.22–20.

audit authority does not arise at all in the case of failure to re-appoint.[149] Thus, a failure to re-appoint is treated largely as a matter of internal concern to the company rather than a matter for the external regulators, except in the case of "major" audits.

Information about resolutions and meetings

22–24 The auditor's relationship with the shareholders is underlined by the provision which requires him or her to be sent all notices and other communications relating to general meetings, to attend them and to be heard on any part of the business which affects or concerns the auditor.[150] In the case of a private company which takes its decision by written resolution, the right transmogrifies into a simple right to receive the communications relating to the written resolution, but there is no general right to make representations to the shareholders before they decide.[151] This is a pretty ineffective provision—though it needs to be recognised that many private companies will be exempt from audit on grounds of being "small".

The Role of the Audit Committee of the Board

Combined Code provisions

22–25 The argument in favour of a greater role for the board in relation to the company's audit is that it is able to give more continuous attention to the audit than are the shareholders, whose contribution is naturally episodic, normally at the annual general meeting when the auditors' report is considered and the auditors appointed or re-appointed. The conflict of interest which the board may have on audit matters can be dealt with, it is argued, by entrusting this supervisory role not to the board as a whole but to an appropriate committee of the board, relying on the modern reforms which have up-graded the role of independent non-executive directors (NEDs) on the board. Once such a committee is created, its role need by no means be confined to that of ensuring the auditor is independent of the management of the company, though that is an important part of its task. The Combined Code (discussed below) sees the audit committee as having six functions, only two of which are directly related to the issue of auditor independence. The audit committee is as much concerned with reviewing management in relation to the accounts as reviewing the auditors. Those functions are:[152]

---

[149] s.523(1).
[150] s.502(2).
[151] s.502(1).
[152] Combined Code, C.3.2.

(a) monitoring the integrity of the company's financial statements and, in particular, reviewing significant financial reporting judgments contained in them;[153]

(b) reviewing the company's internal financial controls and risk management systems (unless that is the responsibility of some other committee of the board);

(c) monitoring the effectiveness of the company's internal audit function;

(d) making recommendations to the shareholders about auditor appointment and remuneration;[154]

(e) reviewing the external auditor's independence and effectiveness;

(f) developing a policy on the supply of non-audit services to the company by the auditor.

The Combined Code applies to listed companies only and operates, as we have noted above,[155] on a "comply or explain" basis. This means that the rules of the FSA require listed companies to state each year the extent to which they have complied with the Combined Code and to explain areas of non-compliance, but non-compliance, if explained, is not improper.[156] From its inception the Combined Code and its predecessors attached great importance to the creation of an audit committee of the board which would be dominated by independent NEDs.

After a review of the audit committee provisions by a committee **22–26** chaired by Sir Robert Smith in 2002, the Combined Code was further strengthened. The audit committee should now consist of at least three independent NEDs and one of them should have "recent and relevant financial experience".[157] Further a more explicit statement of the role of the audit committee was included in the Code, which we have outlined above. Moreover, the committee devised extensive guidance for audit committees, which, whilst having no formal status, even on a "comply or explain" basis, probably does more than anything else to indicate the enhanced importance of the audit

---

[153] This moderates the pressure which the executive management might otherwise put on the auditors to accept reporting policies which distorted the company's true position by putting the ultimate decision with the audit committee.

[154] Thus recognising the reality that the shareholders themselves are unlikely to generate such proposals.

[155] See above, para.14–31.

[156] LR 9.8.6(5), (6).

[157] Combined Code C.3.1. Two independent NEDs are enough in smaller listed companies.

committee.[158] That guidance in places is noticeably adversarial in tone: "the audit committee has a particular role, acting independently from the executive, to ensure that the interests of shareholders are properly protected in relation to financial reporting and internal control."[159] For this reason, "a frank, open working relationship and a high level of mutual respect are essential, particularly between the audit committee chairman and the board chairman, the chief executive and the finance director. The audit committee must be prepared to take a robust stand …"[160] and "audit committees have wide-ranging, time consuming and sometimes intensive work to do."[161] Despite emphasis in the guidance on the unitary nature of the British board, such language is likely to underline further the division of function between executive and non-executive members of the board.[162]

The audit committee also has a particular, and even direct, relationship with the shareholders. The Combined Code recommends that a separate section of the annual report describe the work of the audit committee and that the chair of the audit committee (along with those of the remuneration and appointments committees) should be available at the AGM to answer shareholders' questions.[163] More ominously for the executive directors, the Code recommends that, if the audit committee's recommendations on the appointment and re-appointment of the auditors are not accepted by the full board, the existence of this disagreement and the reasons for it have to be explained in the papers for the shareholders' meeting.[164]

These provisions of the Combined Code are somewhat reinforced by sections 527 to 531 of the Act. We have seen above[165] that the Government did not take up the CLR's general proposal for a "pause" between the delivery of the annual accounts and reports to the members and the holding of the annual general meeting, during which period shareholders would have an opportunity, at no cost to themselves, to require the company to circulate resolutions for consideration at the AGM in relation to those documents. However, a weak form of that proposal is to be found in these sections. Shareholders of a quoted company[166] may require the company to post on its website a shareholder statement about the audit of the company's

---

[158] For the present version of that guidance see FRC, *Guidance on Audit Committees (the Smith Guidance)*, 2005.
[159] *Guidance on Audit Committees (the Smith Guidance)*, para.1.4.
[160] *Guidance on Audit Committees (the Smith Guidance)*, para.1.7.
[161] *Guidance on Audit Committees (the Smith Guidance)*, para.1.11.
[162] See para.14–33.
[163] Combined Code C.3.3 and D.2.3. The Smith guidance comments that: "This deliberately puts the spotlight on the audit committee and gives it an authority that it might otherwise lack." (para.1.6.)
[164] Combined Code, C.3.6.
[165] Ch.15 at para.15–34.
[166] One listed in the UK or any other EEA state or on the New York Stock Exchange or Nasdaq: ss.531 and 385.

accounts or about the circumstances in which an auditor has ceased to hold office, for consideration at the company's accounts meeting (normally its AGM). The tests for defining the members entitled to require website publication are the same as those for requiring circulation of a resolution to be considered at an AGM,[167] that is, members representing at least 5 per cent of the total voting rights of those entitled to vote at the accounts meeting or 100 voting members holding shares upon which an average of at least £100 has been paid up.[168] The company is required to post the statement on its website within three working days of its receipt and to keep it there until after the accounts meeting,[169] unless the company persuades a court that the shareholders are abusing their rights.[170] A copy of it must be sent to the auditor at the same time as it is posted.[171] The company may not charge the shareholders for the costs of website publication, which will normally be negligible.[172] Finally, when it gives notice of the accounts meeting, the company must draw attention to the existence of this facility and that it is without cost to the members, which may encourage them to take it up.

Mandatory provisions on audit committees

This picture of audit committee regulation via "comply or explain" provisions in the Combined Code was complicated by the adoption of the Audit Directive in 2006,[173] Articles 41 and 42 of which lay down mandatory provisions about audit committees of "public interest entities" (PIEs). The definition of a PIE substantially overlaps with the scope of the Combined Code, though it is not identical.[174] Some of the Directive's requirements do not require significant amendments to the current domestic rules. For example, Article 42 requires statutory auditors to confirm annually their independence to the audit committee of the PIE; to disclose to it any non-audit services provided to the PIE and to discuss with the audit committee threats to independence and the safeguards to be applied to mitigate them; and to provide a description of any material weaknesses in the company's internal control systems which the audit has revealed. Such interaction between the auditor and audit committee was already part of the ethical standards required by the APB,

22–27

---

[167] Above, para.15–33.
[168] s.527(2),(3). This is one of the sections where those to whom governance rights have been transferred may act: s.153(1)(d) and above, para.15–21.
[169] s.528(4). Failure to do so is a criminal offence on the part of every officer in default.
[170] s.527(5),(6).
[171] s.529(3).
[172] s.529(2).
[173] Above, fn.63.
[174] In particular, the CC applies to listed companies whereas a PIE is (subject to exceptions) a company whose securities are traded on a regulated market (potentially wider—see paras 25–5ff) plus banks and insurance companies (Directive, Art.2(13)).

so that all that was required was to make compliance with these standards an explicit legal requirement for statutory auditors.[175]

Somewhat more problematic were the Directive's requirement in Article 41 that PIEs have an audit committee and its prescription of that committee's functions. It is difficult to believe that this is a significant extra burden for the largest listed companies, which invariably have audit committees which fully follow the recommendations of the Combined Code, especially as the Directive's rules for audit committees are less demanding than those of the Code. Only one member of the audit committee is required by the Directive to be independent (though he or she must have competence in accounting or auditing)[176] and the list of the audit committee's functions does not exceed that of the Code.[177] However, the Directive's requirements are mandatory, not "comply or explain", and thus removed an element of flexibility in relation to audit committees which smaller listed companies may have found valuable. In the event the Government chose to implement the minimum requirements of the Directive via rules made by the Financial Services Authority.[178] The proposed new FSA rules make no reference to the Combined Code, so that the FSA and Combined Code rules exist in parallel.[179] The FSA's rules require PIEs to have audit committees which meet the minimum requirements of Article 41, whilst the CC still operates on a "comply or explain" basis in relation to a more demanding set of standards for most listed companies or will operate as the only set of rules for listed companies falling outside Article 41. The FSA's rules are enforced by that body and are subject to the sanctions available to it.[180]

AUDITOR REGULATION

22–28 As we have seen at various points above, regulation of the auditing profession and the auditing process can be used to address the issue of the independence of auditors by requiring of them compliance with ethical standards laid down by the Auditing Practices Board, which requirements are enforced through the rulebooks of the professional bodies of accountants (the recognised supervisory bodies). However,

[175] Sch.10, paras 10B and 22A and APB, *Ethical Standard 5: Non-audit Services Provided to Audited Entities* (Revised April 2008), especially paras 35–36.
[176] Art.41(1).
[177] Art.42(2), (3)—and Member States are permitted to allow these functions to be allocated to other bodies within the PIE.
[178] BERR, *Implementation of Directive 2006/43/EC: Policy Conclusions and Draft Regulations*, July 2007, pp.14–18 (URN 07/1239).
[179] FSA, *Implementation of the 8th Company Law Directive*, CP 07/24, December 2007, paras 2.10 and 2.11 and proposed new DTR 1B.
[180] On which see Ch.25.

the regulatory structure for auditors is more elaborate than just the APB and the supervisory bodies, and it has concerns which go beyond independence issues. As a result of the "post-Enron" initiative of the DTI[181] regulation in this area was substantially reformed at a domestic level and the necessary legislative changes to put the new scheme in place were made by the Companies (Audit, Investigation and Community Enterprise) Act 2004. In particular, the scope for professional self-regulation was substantially reduced. Some further, relatively minor, changes were required by the Audit Directive.

The umbrella body of the regulatory structure is the Financial Reporting Council, which, amongst other things, is responsible for keeping under review the Combined Code on Corporate Governance. As we have seen in the previous Chapter,[182] although a body incorporated under the Companies Act as a company limited by guarantee, its Chair and Deputy Chair are appointed by the Secretary of State and the organisation in the past was partly funded by the Government. It is, in fact, that common modern phenomenon, a body under ultimate governmental control but benefiting from higher levels of expertise and independence than would a governmental department or even agency.

The FRC operates through a number of operating bodies, as set out below.

FRC Organisation chart

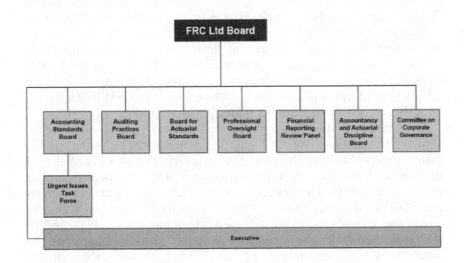

22–29 We have noted in the previous Chapter the role of the FRRP in relation to defective accounts and reports and the importance of the ASB in setting accounting standards. The Auditing Practices Board, as we have seen, sets Ethical Standards for auditors, but it also sets auditing standards of a more technical kind. The recognised supervisory bodies must have rules about the technical standards to be applied in statutory audits and those rules must also require compliance with the standards set by an independent body (in practice, the APB) in this area.[183] The auditing standards play a similar role in relation to the function of auditing as accounting standards play in relation to drawing up the accounts. An auditor is necessarily concerned with both sets of standards: the auditor must establish that the accounts have been drawn up properly (including in accordance with the relevant accounting standards) and he or she must carry out the job of checking the financial statements in a proper manner (in accordance with auditing standards). In the case of a negligence claim against the auditor, compliance with both accounting and auditing standards is likely to be a matter to which the courts attach great weight.[184] As with accounting standards, auditing standards are becoming internationalised. Article 26 of the Audit Directive requires Member States to secure compliance on the part of statutory auditors (in all cases, not just the audits of companies on regulated markets) with international auditing standards (ISAs), once these have been adopted by the Commission. Although not mentioned in the Article itself, the ISAs that the Commission has in mind are those produced by the International Auditing and Assurance Standards Board (IAASB), based in New York. However, the process of adoption of auditing standards for the Community lags behind that of adopting accounting standards, and, at the time of writing, none has been adopted, though the process of adoption is under way. In the United Kingdom, this delay is of little consequence since the approach of the APB to auditing standards has been to adopt those laid down by the IAASB, but with additional explanatory material.

The other two main functions of the regulators are to monitor the quality of audits undertaken by statutory auditors (including quality assurance reviews) and to investigate cases where auditors are alleged to have fallen below the required standards, and to impose discipline where appropriate. The first of these two functions is undertaken by the POB itself in relation to "major" audits,[185] (notably audits of companies whose securities are traded on a regulated markets) and by the recognised supervisory bodies otherwise, whose discharge of this function is itself monitored by the POB.[186] A somewhat similar

---

[183] Sch.10, paras 10 and 22.
[184] For accounting standards see above at para.21–15.
[185] See above, para.22–20.
[186] Sch.10, paras 12, 13 and 23.

division of functions between the professional bodies (as recognised supervisory bodies) and a subsidiary of the FRC (here the Accountancy and Actuarial Discipline Board—AADB) exists in relation to investigation and discipline. Investigation of complaints and the imposition of discipline is the task of the supervisory bodies, but they must participate in arrangements for investigations and discipline to be carried out by an "independent body" (i.e. the AADB) where the case raises questions affecting the public interest.[187]

EMPOWERING THE AUDITORS

Even if the statutory and professional rules produce loyal and competent auditors, they may fail to detect impropriety in the company if they are not given the co-operation of those who work for it. If an auditor does not receive the co-operation needed to assess the company's accounts, that fact can be reflected in the ultimate report to the shareholders,[188] but it is obviously more desirable that the auditor should be able obtain the necessary information. The issue of the auditor's powers as against the audited company and its management is one to which the legislature has given increasing attention in recent years.

22–30

Requesting information

Auditors have a right of access at all times to the company's books, accounts and vouchers.[189] They are entitled to require such information and explanations as they think necessary for the performance of their duties. Those under the obligation to provide the information and explanations now go beyond the company's officers and embrace (present or past): employees of the company; persons holding or accountable for the company's accounts (for example, where the company has outsourced this function); subsidiary companies incorporated in the United Kingdom; and persons falling within the above categories in relation to the subsidiary and the subsidiary's auditor (if different).[190] More problematic, though of great impor-

22–31

---

[187] Sch.10, paras 14–16 and 24. The AADB does not impose discipline itself but brings complaints before a Disciplinary Tribunal, at whose hands it suffered a major setback in relation to its first major complaint, arising out of the collapse of the Mayflower Company. See the Mayflower Judgments issued on January 22, 2007 (available on: http://www.frc.org.uk/aadb/tribunal/).

[188] As the Act requires: s.498(3).

[189] s.499(1).

[190] s.499(2). Statements so made may not be used in subsequent criminal proceedings against the maker (except in respect of offences connected with the making of the statement) and the requirement is subject to an exception for legal professional privilege: s.499(3), (4).

tance, is the position of subsidiaries incorporated outside the United Kingdom and the relevant persons connected with them. Here the problem of comity of legal systems is dealt with by putting an obligation on the parent, if required by its auditors to do so, to take such steps as are reasonably open to it to obtain such information and explanations from the subsidiary and the relevant persons.[191] A failure to respond "without delay" to a request for information is a criminal offence, unless compliance was not reasonably practicable. Also criminal is knowingly or recklessly making to the auditors a statement which conveys or purports to convey any information or explanation which is misleading, false or deceptive in any material particular.[192]

Volunteered information

22–32   The above rights for the auditor depend upon the auditor knowing which questions to ask. Since the auditor is by profession an investigator, it is reasonable to suppose that he or she will often be in a position to ask the right questions. However, the CLR[193] thought there was a good argument for requiring directors to "volunteer" information rather than leaving the auditor to find everything out. This reform was implemented in the 2004 Act via an addition to the matters required to be disclosed in the directors' report.[194] That report requires a statement on the part of each director to the effect that (a) so far as the director is aware, there is no information needed by the auditor of which the auditor is unaware and (b) the director has taken all steps he ought to have taken to make him- or herself aware of such information and to establish that the auditor is aware of it.[195] This may require the director to reveal his or her wrongdoing or that of fellow directors to the auditor.[196] The full extent of what is required of the director is to be assessed by reference to the director's objective duty of care,[197] but the Act specifically recognises that making enquiries of fellow directors and the auditor might be enough to discharge the duty (i.e. that the director can rely on satisfactory answers from such sources to appropriate questions).[198] A director is criminally liable if the statement is false but only if the director knew

---

[191] s.500.
[192] s.501. However, for the foreign subsidiary or those connected with it to make an inaccurate statement is not a criminal offence (s.501(1) applies only to s.499), probably an unavoidable loop-hole, since otherwise British law would be criminalising conduct committed abroad.
[193] CLR, Final 1, paras 8.119–8.122.
[194] See para.21–22.
[195] s.418(2) of the 2006 Act. Wilfully suppressing relevant information may be a ground for disqualification—potentially lengthy—of a director. See *TransTec Plc (No.2), Re* [2007] 2 B.C.L.C. 495 and Ch.10.
[196] A result which, as we have seen, the director's core duty of loyalty may also produce: above, para.16–31.
[197] See para.16–13.
[198] s.418(4).

of the falsity or was reckless as to whether the statement was true or false and if he or she failed to take reasonable steps to prevent the (inaccurate) directors' report from being approved.[199] However, as we shall see below, failure to comply with this provision may also limit the auditor's civil liability towards the company by virtue of the doctrine of contributory negligence.

Whistle blowing

Conversely, auditors who come into possession of information about **22–33** wrongdoing during the course of their audit may be obliged to report it to the relevant authorities. This may be helpful to the regulators, but it may cut down the flow of information to the auditor, despite the provisions considered above. There are no general "whistle blowing" obligations of this type in the legislation but auditing standards require auditors to consider whether the public interest requires such action,[200] and on the basis of this professional guidance it has been held that the auditor's duties to the company could embrace, as a last resort, a duty to inform relevant third parties of suspected wrongdoing.[201] A public interest defence is required in order to give auditors in such cases protection against an action at common law by the company for breach of confidence. The Financial Services and Markets Act 2000 puts this defence on a statutory basis where an auditor of a company authorised under that Act gives information to the FSA in good faith and in the reasonable belief that the information is relevant to the discharge of any of the Authority's functions.[202] More importantly, this Act gives the Treasury the power, which has been exercised, to require auditors to make such disclosures to the FSA.[203]

---

[199] s.418(5),(6). For the process of approving the directors' report, see para.21–28.

[200] APB, Statement of Auditing Standards No.110, *Fraud and Error* and No.120, *Consideration of Law and Regulations*, both 1995.

[201] *Sasea Finance Ltd v KPMG* [2000] 1 All E.R. 676, CA. For example, where the auditors discovered fraud on the part of those in control of the company so that simply warning the company was likely to be ineffective.

[202] s.342(3) of the FSMA 2000. In other cases the common law will provide the defence.

[203] FSMA 2000 (Communications by Auditors) Regulations 2001 (SI 2001/2587). The matters required to be disclosed are the fact that the auditor is unable to state that the accounts have been compiled in accordance with the Companies Act and his or her reasonable belief that the company is not or will cease to be a going concern, but they also extend to other matters which the auditor reasonably believes may be of material significance to the Authority in the exercise of various of its functions.

LIABILITY FOR NEGLIGENT AUDIT

The nature of the issue

22–34   If an auditor produces an audit report which is misleading and the inaccuracy can be traced to a lack of care, skill or diligence on the part of the auditor, then those to whom the auditor owed a duty to take care will be in a position to sue the auditor for damages, if they can show that the inaccurate report caused them loss. In the case of a single auditor, the liability will lie with that person; in the more common case of a firm being appointed auditor, then the individuals who were negligent will be liable but so also will the firm, either because the negligence of the individuals is regarded as the negligence of the firm or because the firm is vicariously liable for the negligence of the individuals.

The rules for determining the underlying liability of the auditor rests, even after the 2006 Act, with the common law,[204] though statute has played a role in fashioning the way that common law liability applies to auditors. It is important to distinguish among the potential claimants against the auditor between the audit client and everyone else. That the audit client in principle has a claim against the negligent auditor is well-established, that claim being based either on the contract between the auditor and the company or on the tort of negligence.[205] In relation to claims by persons other than the audit client, however, the question of how widely the duty of care in tort is owed has been, as we shall see, fiercely debated in the courts and the upshot of the litigation is a rather restricted duty of care. Of course, the matter might be decided even in relation to non-clients by contract, but there is less likely to be a contract between the auditor and the non-client upon which the claimant can rely. However, as we shall see, the thrust of the court decisions has been to accept liability in relation to non-clients only where a contract or a relationship akin to a contract has arisen.

The outcome of the litigation over the duty of care owed by auditors to non-client claimants is but one example of auditors' liability rules being restricted in recent years. One might have thought that increasing the civil liability of the auditor would be an effective

---

[204] In the case of the appointment of a firm as auditor, the senior statutory auditor must sign the report (s.503(3)), but s.504(3) provides that the person identified as the senior statutory auditor is not thereby subject to any civil liability to which he or she would not otherwise be subject. Nor would it seem that members of the audit team who would otherwise be liable are protected from liability by the signature of the senior statutory auditor.

[205] It makes little difference which way the claim is put, since the implied term in the contract to provide audit services will be, as in tort, only a duty to take reasonable care. In particular, the defence of contributory negligence is available whichever way the claim is put: *Forsikringsaktieselskapet Vesta v Butcher* [1989] A.C. 852 at 858–868, CA. Of course, the parties could by contract seek to increase the level of the duty (for example, to a warranty that the audit report was accurate), but their freedom to lower the duty is subject to the statutory provisions discussed below.

way of providing incentives to auditors to be both independent and competent. However, unlike all the legal strategies discussed above, which in one way or another have seen some expansion in recent years (most obviously in the expanded role of the audit committee), judicial decisions and legislative rules have ensured that there has been no such expansion in relation to civil liability; in fact, the tendency in recent years has been to rein in civil liability. Why should this be?

First, in relation to liability to non-clients, there is, as we shall see, **22–35** a particular problem that liability to third parties arises out of the fact that the accounts and reports and the auditor's report thereon are placed in the public domain.[206] It is therefore possible that a very large number of people will rely on them in order to carry out a very large range of transactions. Unrestricted liability on the part of auditors to third parties who rely on the accounts thus raises the prospect, as it was once famously described, of "liability in an indeterminate amount for an indeterminate time to an indeterminate class".[207] We discuss this problem further below in relation to the decision of the House of Lords in *Caparo Industries Plc v Dickman*.[208]

Even in relation to actions by audit clients, there are difficult issues about the proper scope of the liability rules. Thus, secondly, the general tort doctrine of joint and several liability may significantly increase the tort exposure of auditors. Under this doctrine, if two or more tortfeasors are liable in respect of the same loss, the injured party may recover from any one of them for the whole of the loss, leaving the defendant to seek contributions from the other tortfeasors. In the typical case where the misstatements in the company's accounts result from the fraud or negligence of someone within the company and the failure of the auditors to discover the wrongdoing, the claimant may recover the whole of the loss from the auditor, leaving the auditor to bear the risk that the original wrongdoers are judgment proof (as they likely will be). Thus, claimants are encouraged to sue the defendants with "deep pockets" for the recovery of the whole of their loss, even though the auditor may be only the minor party at fault. This problem is only partially addressed (and may even be exacerbated) by the professional indemnity insurance (or equivalent arrangements) which audit firms are obliged to carry.[209] That insurance may be very expensive and so increase the cost of audits; it may not be available for the full extent of the claim, so that the liability risk is only partially collectivised through the insurance mechanism; and the known availability of insurance may encourage litigation against auditors. There has been some movement in the common law world towards the substitution of "proportionate"

---

[206] See para.21–32.
[207] *Ultramares Corp v Touche* (1931) 174 N.E. 441 at 441, per Cardozo C.J.
[208] [1990] 2 A.C. 605, HL.
[209] Sch.10, para.17.

liability for joint and several liability for auditors (i.e. the auditor is liable only for the share of the loss which is fairly attributable to the auditor's negligence)[210] but in the United Kingdom, despite pressure from the accounting profession, there has been resistance to such a move on the grounds that it simply shifts the risk of insolvency from the auditor to the wholly innocent claimant.[211] However, a restriction of liability to the auditor's proportionate share of the loss would seem a permissible form of "liability limitation agreement" between auditor and audit client, as discussed below.

Where the auditor is an audit firm taking the form of a traditional partnership, further issues are raised. Thus, thirdly, the assets of the firm as a whole become available to satisfy the claimant in the case of loss caused to a third party by a partner (or employee) acting in the ordinary course of the business of the firm.[212] Fourthly, in the absence of limited liability in the traditional partnership, the personal assets of both the negligent partner and his or her fellow partners may be called on to meet the claim.[213]

Providing audit services through bodies with limited liability

22–36 Something has been done to address the fourth matter. It is now permitted that audit services be provided to a company by an accounting firm which is not a partnership. The Act provides that both individuals and firms are eligible to be appointed as auditors[214] and then defines a "firm" as "any entity, whether or not a legal person, that is not an individual".[215] Thus, the old idea that it was the hallmark of a professional that he or she provided services on the basis of personal liability for their quality has gone. Some accounting firms have set up their auditing arms as limited companies, but, by and large, the company form of internal organisation is not attractive to professional partnerships. The accounting firms therefore pressed for, and ultimately obtained in 2000, a new corporate vehicle, the limited liability partnership,[216] which has the internal structure of a partnership but provides a corporate body with limited liability. The origins of this new vehicle are demonstrated by the fact that, when

---

[210] See, for example, Australia: Austin and Ramsay, *Ford's Principles on Corporations Law* (12th ed, 2005) pp.609–610.
[211] DTI, *Feasibility Investigation of Joint and Several Liability by the Common Law Team of the Law Commission*, (1996); CLR, Final Report I, para.8.138. As to situations where the claimant is not wholly innocent, see below, para.22–39.
[212] Partnership Act 1890, s.10.
[213] Partnership act 1890, s.12. Joint and several liability operates again, this time among the partners.
[214] s.1212(1).
[215] s.1173(1).
[216] See above, para.1–2.

originally proposed, it was to be confined to professional businesses, but in the end it was made generally available.[217]

Conducting the audit through a vehicle with limited liability certainly protects the personal assets of the non-negligent partners from the tort claimant. Whether the personal assets of the negligent partner are so protected depends on whether the negligent misstatement in the audit report is analysed as having been made by the member, for whose tort the corporate body is vicariously liable (personal assets of the negligent member not protected), or whether the negligent misstatement is analysed as having been made by the corporate body through the auditor, in which case the personal assets of the negligent member are not at risk. The decision of the House of Lords in *Williams v Natural Life Health Foods*[218] suggests the latter analysis (personal assets not at risk) but it is unclear whether the *Williams* rationale extends to statements by professionals.[219]

Even if *Williams* does apply, the benefits of corporate personality are restricted to the personal assets of the members: the business of the corporate body itself could still be destroyed by a large claim which exceeded the insurance cover and pushed the body into insolvency. This is, indeed, the public policy crux. If there were many competing firms of auditors, the occasional insolvency of one of them might not matter in public policy terms. However, there are now only four international networks of firms capable of carrying out the audits of the largest multinational firms, and the collapse of Arthur Andersen in the aftermath of the Enron scandal in the United States is a reminder of how quickly such international firms can disintegrate.[220] The disappearance of another such firm would further reduce competition in the market for the audit of multinational companies from its already low level. However, this fear should not push legislators into hasty acceptance of arguments for the reduction of auditors' liability without rigorous scrutiny of the likely impact. For example, it was argued that a cap on auditors' liability would increase competition in the audit market, especially for large firm audits, on the grounds that a cap would encourage medium-sized audit firms to move up into the "big league". However, an analysis by the Office of Fair Trading concluded that such a result was not a likely impact of the reform.[221]

We will now turn to the ways in which the current liability rules

---

[217] For the origins of the LLP see Morse *et al.* (eds), *Palmer's Limited Liability Partnership Law* (Sweet & Maxwell, 2002), Ch.1.

[218] [1998] 1 W.L.R. 830, above, para.7–25.

[219] *Merrett v Babb* [2001] Q.B. 1171, CA; *Phelps v Hillingdon LBC* [2001] 2 A.C. 619, HL. For discussion see Whittaker [2002] J.B.L. 601.

[220] Arthur Andersen did not collapse because of a large liability claim but because of loss of reputation resulting from its being charged with and convicted of criminal offences (even though these convictions were overturned on appeal).

[221] OFT, *An Assessment of the Implications for Competition of a Cap on Auditors' Liability*, OFT 741, July 2004.

reflect the above concerns, looking separately at claims by the audit client and by others.

CLAIMS BY THE AUDIT CLIENT

Establishing liability

22–37 As we have already noted, the audit client's cause of action is normally quite clear. Thus, the litigation is likely to focus on the question of whether the auditor had in fact been negligent and, if so, whether and how much loss was caused to the claimant. As far as the standard of care is concerned, it is clear in law, though often not accepted in the commercial world, that the auditor is not a guarantor of the accuracy of the directors' accounts and reports. Indeed, in an old case the auditor was given a broad discretion to rely on information provided by management, so long as no suspicious circumstances arose which should put the auditor on inquiry.[222] However, the force of this proposition depends in considerable part on how willing the courts are to find that no circumstances had arisen which were suspicious, and there is some evidence that modern courts take a more demanding line than their predecessors.[223] Moreover, some dicta suggest that, even in the absence of suspicious circumstances, modern auditing standards might require auditors to do more of their own motion. As Lord Denning once put it, the auditor, in order to perform his task properly, "must come to it with an inquiring mind—not suspicious of dishonesty, I agree—but suspecting that someone may have made a mistake somewhere and that a check must be made to ensure that there has been none".[224] Given the extensive development by the Accounting Standards Board in recent years of Accounting Standards and by the Auditing Practices Board of Auditing Standards (and now by their international equivalents), it would be surprising if the courts were not guided to a very large degree by those standards in determining the standard of care at common law for auditors.[225] Thus, there is available to auditors much greater certainty about what the duty of care requires of them than is the case for some professionals.

As to the quantum of liability, that the published accounts do not

---

[222] *Kingston Cotton Mill (No.2), Re* [1896] 2 Ch. 279, CA, where the auditors relied on certificates as to levels of stock which were provided by the managing director who for years had grossly overstated the true position.

[223] See *Thomas Gerrard & Son Ltd, Re* [1967] 2 All E.R. 525, where the discovery of altered invoices, it was held, should have caused the auditors to carry out their own check on the stock.

[224] *Formento (Sterling Area) Ltd v Selsdon Fountain Pen Co Ltd* [1958] 1 W.L.R. 45, HL and see also the remarks of Pennycuick J. in *Thomas Gerrard, Re* (cited in previous note).

[225] As Woolf J. was in *Lloyd Cheyham & Co Ltd v Littlejohn & Co* [1987] B.C.L.C. 303.

show a true and fair view or are in some other way defective and that the auditor has not identified the defect does not cause the company any immediate pecuniary loss. What the auditors' failure does is to deprive the directors (or shareholders) of knowledge which might have afforded them an opportunity to take remedial action or to avoid incurring liability to third parties on the basis of the inaccurate accounts (for example, through representations and warranties in a contract for the scale of the company's business). That remedial action might take a number of forms, ranging from preventing a continuance of mismanagement or fraud to selling the company whose business model was under serious threat from changing economic circumstances whilst its undertaking still had substantial value. However, the auditor is not liable on a simple "but for" test for the company's failure through ignorance to take such action. The action which the company might have taken or avoided must be one that was within the scope of the auditor's duty of care. This principle will embrace the decisions that companies normally make on the basis of the accounts, such as declaring dividends or paying bonuses, whether to staff or policy-holders.[226] Thus, the auditor's liability will embrace losses caused to the company by decisions in these areas which the directors would have taken differently if they had known the full facts, even if the decision actually taken was perfectly lawful.

However, depending on the scope of the audit engagement, the auditor's liability may extend to other classes of decision, including strategic corporate decisions.[227] In many cases, for example where the remedial action was the sale of the company's undertaking, what the company will have lost is really the chance to take a particular step, i.e. to find a purchaser at an acceptable price—who might or might not have been forthcoming. The pecuniary value to be placed on that lost opportunity depends upon the degree of likelihood that action would have been taken and that it would have led to the outcome the company alleges would have been reached. The court will have to assess the value of that chance, awarding the chance no value if it thinks it purely speculative.[228] Even where there was a course of action the directors could have taken which was wholly within their own control, liability will depend on its being shown that the step would have been taken. Often this will be difficult, especially in the case of fraud or mismanagement, when those at fault include the directors. Then, it would seem, to establish any loss the claimant would have to show on the balance of probabilities that, had, say, the auditors' report been properly qualified, action would have been taken by the

---

[226] *Leeds Estate, Building and Investment Co v Shepherd* (1887) 36 Ch. D. 787; *Barings Plc v Coopers & Lybrand (No.1)* [2002] 2 B.C.L.C. 364; *Equitable Life Assurance Society v Ernst & Young* [2003] 2 B.C.L.C. 603, CA; *cf. MAN Nutzfahrzeuge AG v Freightliner Ltd* [2007] B.C.C. 986, CA.

[227] *Equitable Life Assurance Society v Ernst & Young* [2003] 2 B.C.L.C. 603, CA.

[228] *Equitable Life Assurance Society v Ernst & Young* [2003] 2 B.C.L.C. 603, CA.

shareholders which would have led to the removal of the directors. And to recover any substantial damages, the claimant would further have to establish a probability that the ill-consequences of the former directors' negligent or fraudulent reign would have been effectively remedied. The difficulties of establishing all this are obvious.

Limiting liability

22–38 Even if the claimant can establish liability and substantial loss, there are two arguments available to the auditors to reduce their liability for the whole of that loss, one based on the partial defence of contributory negligence and the other on contract.

Contributory negligence

22–39 Under the doctrine of contributory negligence, a claimant who suffers loss as a result partly of his or her own fault and partly of the defendant's fault will have the damages payable by the latter reduced by such amount as the court thinks just and equitable, having regard to the claimant's share of the responsibility for the damage.[229] Thus, where harm has been inflicted on the company by fraud of its employees which the directors failed to discover because they had inadequate internal controls in place, and which the auditors failed to discover because they did not realise the internal controls were inadequate, the failures of the directors are the failures of the company which the auditors can pray in aid to reduce their damages. The disclosure statement now required of directors in the directors' report is likely to increase the incidence of this defence being run by the auditors.[230]

In fact, a somewhat similar result seems to have been obtained before this reform through the use by auditors of "representation letters", which companies are required to sign before the auditors will certify the accounts. In these letters the company typicallsy promises "to the best of its knowledge and belief" that certain important matters concerning the company's financial situation are in a particular state. If such a representation letter is signed negligently on behalf of the company, the auditors would have the partial defence of contributory negligence if subsequently sued by the company and it can be shown that the auditors would not have certified the accounts, or not certified them without further investigation, had they known the true facts. If the representation letter is signed fraudulently, it appears that the auditors have a complete defence.[231]

---

[229] Law Reform (Contributory Negligence) Act 1945, s.1(1).
[230] Above, para.22–32. Although misleading disclosure is not a civil wrong under the Act, it can still constitute "fault" on the part of the company for the purposes of the contributory negligence rule.
[231] *Barings Plc v Coopers & Lybrand (No.2)* [2002] 2 B.C.L.C. 410, where an example of a representation letter can be found.

Limitation by contract

It was formerly impossible for auditors to limit their liability to the **22–40** company by means of a contract with it or by provision in the company's articles, and one of the main changes in the 2006 Act was to permit such contracts, subject to safeguards. The prohibition on directors' limiting their duties to the company[232] by contract applied originally to auditors as well (as officers of the company), and the Act sets out that prohibition in relation to auditors, and the linked one concerning indemnities provided by the company, as its starting point.[233] The indemnity prohibition does not apply if it relates to an agreement or provision to indemnify the auditor against a liability incurred in defending proceedings, criminal or civil, in which the auditor is successful or in making a successful application for relief under section 1157 of the Act.[234] This does no more than track the provisions relating to directors.

The innovation is the permission for the auditor and company to contract to limit the amount of a liability the auditor owes to the company arising out of a breach of duty in the conduct of the audit. The section is widely enough drafted to permit the parties to introduce proportionate liability by agreement. This reform was recommended by the CLR but it is subject to reasonably strict safeguards. The principal ones are as follows:

(a) The agreement is effective to limit the auditor's liability only to the amount that is fair and reasonable in the circumstances, having regard, amongst other things, to the auditor's responsibilities under the Act and the professional standards expected of the auditor.[235] If the agreement goes further than is permitted by this provision, then it operates so as to limit liability to the permitted level, i.e. the agreement does not fail altogether.[236] In exchange the agreement is exempted from the control provisions of the Unfair Contract Terms Act.[237]

(b) The agreement may relate to only a single financial year, i.e. a new agreement is needed for each set of annual reports and accounts.[238]

(c) The agreement must be approved by the members, though in the case of a private company the members, before the

---

[232] See above at para.16–88.
[233] s.532.
[234] See para.16–93.
[235] s.537(1). In determining what is fair and reasonable the court must ignore matters occurring after the loss or damage has been incurred (an attempt to restrain hindsight) and the possibility of recovering compensation from other persons.
[236] s.537(2).
[237] s.534(3).
[238] s.535(1).

company enters into the agreement, may pass a resolution waiving the need for approval.[239]

To provide a check that these requirements have been met, a note to the companies accounts must set out the principal terms of the liability limitation agreement and the date on which it was approved by the members (or approval was waived).[240]

Criminal liability

22–41   In policy terms, the permission for agreements by auditors with their clients to limit liability in damages to the company was accompanied by an increase of criminal liability for an auditor who knowingly or recklessly makes a statement in the audit report which is misleading, false or deceptive. In other words, the deterrent effect of unlimited liability in damages for negligence was to some extent replaced by a narrower criminal liability for intentional or reckless misstatements.[241] Curiously, however, this sanction applies only to that part of the auditor's report which deals strictly with the accounts. Thus, it does apply to the statement that the accounts give a true and fair view[242] and to statements in the audit report about the compliance of the company's accounts with its accounting records, about whether the necessary information and explanations were forthcoming from management and others, and about whether the company was entitled to prepare accounts under the small companies regime.[243] However, it does not apply to the auditor's report on either the directors' report or the auditable part of the directors' remuneration report. In this respect, the criminal liability of auditors is narrower than that of directors, which extends to knowing or reckless authorisation of publication of non-compliant directors' reports as well as of accounts.[244] There was much pressure in Parliament from the auditing profession to remove the liability for recklessness, but the Government stoutly resisted it.[245]

---

[239] s.536. Approval may be given before or after the company enters into the agreement; in the former case only the "principal terms" of the agreement need to be approved.

[240] The Companies (Disclosure of Auditor Remuneration and Liability Limitation Agreements) Regulations 2008/489, reg.8.

[241] HL Debs, Grand Committee, Eighth Day, col. 407, March 14, 2006 (Lord Sainsbury of Turville).

[242] And the other matters listed at point (a) on para.22–1.

[243] s.507(1)–(3). The auditor might also be liable under s.397 of FSMA 2000 in the case of publicly-traded companies: see para.26–8.

[244] See ss.414(4) (accounts), 419(3) (directors' report), 422(2) (directors' remuneration report).

[245] ss.508–509 provide for the Secretary of State or, in Scotland, the Lord Advocate to give guidance to the regulatory and prosecuting authorities about how misconduct should be handled which appears to fall both within the criminal prohibition and the regulatory provisions discussed above.

CLAIMS BY THIRD PARTIES

The duty of care in principle
The issues discussed above relating to breach of duty and loss arise in   **22–42**
relation to third-party claims (i.e. claims by anyone other than the
audit client), but the prior and most controversial issue has been to
define the circumstances in which a duty of care will be owed at all by
the auditors to third parties. Here the courts have applied in the
auditing context the general common law rules governing a duty of
care in relation to economic loss caused by negligent misstatement.
Until less than fifty years ago, this was an issue which was not a live
one, because until the decision in *Hedley Byrne & Co Ltd v Heller &
Partners Ltd*[246] the law of negligence did not recognise a general duty
to take care to avoid negligent misstatements causing economic loss.
Liability in damages could, and still can, be based on the tort of
deceit, as had been recognised in the nineteenth century, but that
liability is subject to two major restrictions. First, liability arises only
if the maker of the statement knows that it is false or makes it not
caring whether it is true of false, so that an honest, even if unreasonable, belief in the truth of the statement protects its maker from
liability in deceit (or fraud).[247] Secondly, the maker of the statement
must intend the claimant (or a class of persons of whom the claimant
is one) to rely on the statement.[248] The effect of the first limitation is
to restrict the circumstances in which liability will arise and the effect
of the second is to restrict the range of potential claimants if it does
arise. The impact of the decision in *Hedley Byrne* was to side-step
both these limitations, which are not part of the tort of negligence.
However, it was not at all clear from *Hedley Byrne* (which was not a
case concerning the audit) when the new duty of care to avoid misstatements causing economic loss would be imposed on auditors.

The answer to these questions, at least in broad outline, was provided by what is undoubtedly the leading case on the application of
these rules to auditors, the decision of the House of Lords in *Caparo
Industries Plc v Dickman*,[249] and was provided in a way which gave
greater comfort to auditors than to investors. The facts of the case are
worth recounting briefly. Like many of the cases decided around this
period, the factual background of *Caparo* involved the purchase of a
company whose economic prospects were discovered after the purchase to be less promising than the purchaser had thought before-

---

[246] [1964] A.C. 465, HL.
[247] *Derry v Peek* (1889) 14 App. Cas. 337, HL. The terms "deceit" and "fraud" (in the civil
sense) seem to be used interchangeably.
[248] *Bradford Equitable BS v Borders* [1941] 2 All E.R. 205, HL.
[249] [1990] 2 A.C. 605, HL. The litigation concerned the preliminary issue whether on the facts
pleaded a claim against the auditors could succeed. What the facts of the case actually were
was never decided.

hand. Such purchasers then looked around for someone to sue in respect of what was alleged to be the misleading information about the company which had been made available. In *Caparo* the purchase was of a target company listed on the London Stock Exchange by another such company through a takeover offer preceded by share purchases in the market. The target company had issued a profit-warning in March 1984, which caused its share price to halve. In May 1984 the directors of the target made a preliminary announcement of its annual results for the year to March 1984, which confirmed that profits were well short of expectations. This caused a further, though less dramatic, fall in the share price. In June the annual accounts were issued to the shareholders. Shortly before that, Caparo, which had previously owned no shares in the target, began acquiring shares in tranches until it reached a shareholding of 29.9%, at which point it made a general offer for the remaining shares, as the City Code required it to do if it was to acquire any more of the target's shares.[250] Caparo asserted that the 1984 accounts, although gloomy, in fact overvalued the company and that the auditors had been negligent in not detecting the irregularities or fraud which had led to the over-statements in the accounts and in certifying the accounts as repre-senting a true and fair view of the company's financial position.

22–43   The House of Lords' examination of the statutory framework for company accounts and audits led them to the following conclusions. The statutory provisions establish a relationship between those responsible for the accounts (the directors) or for the report (the auditors) and some other class or classes of persons, and this rela-tionship imposes a duty of care owed to those persons. Among these "persons" is the company itself, to which, apart altogether from the statutory provisions, the directors are in a fiduciary relationship and the auditors in a contractual relationship by virtue of their employ-ment by the company as its auditors. However, the statutory provi-sions do not establish such a relationship with everybody who has a right to be furnished with copies of the accounts or report or, a fortiori, with everybody who has a right to inspect, or obtain, copies of them from the Registrar of companies.[251] If a relationship other than with the company is to be established under the statutory pro-visions, it can be only with members (and perhaps debenture-holders) and, even in their case, the scope of the resulting duty of care extends only to the protection of what may be described as those persons' corporate governance powers to safeguard their interests in the company. That does not include their decisions to buy further shares

---

[250] See below at para.28–40.
[251] On the circulation and filing of the company's annual reports and accounts see paras 21–32ff.

in the company even if it is a perusal of the annual accounts and reports that led them to do so.[252]

To establish a duty of care to members which is greater in scope than this, or to establish any duty of care to other persons, there must be an additional "special" relationship with the person who suffered loss as a result of relying on the accounts or report. To succeed in establishing that, the claimant must show that the defendant contemplated that the accounts and report:

> "would be communicated to the plaintiff either as an individual or as a member of an identifiable class, specifically in connection with a particular transaction or transactions of a particular kind (*e.g.* in a prospectus inviting investment)[253] and that the plaintiff would be very likely to rely on it for the purpose of deciding whether or not to enter upon that transaction or upon a transaction of that kind."[254]

Caparo thus represented a firm rejection by the House of Lords of the proposition that negligent auditors were liable to those who it was reasonable to foresee would rely on the audited accounts and who suffered loss as a result of such reliance.[255] Instead, the House confined the common law duty of care within the statutory framework set by the Companies Act for company accounts and their audit, which by itself is a policy which has much to commend it.[256] What

---

[252] This was the specific point that had to be determined in *Caparo*. The Court of Appeal had held unanimously that auditors owed no duty of care to members of the public who, in reliance on the accounts and reports, bought shares (in the absence of a special relationship—see below) but, by a majority, that they did owe such a duty to existing shareholders who, in such reliance, bought more shares. The House of Lords thought the distinction between liability for investment decisions made by shareholders and investment decisions made by non-shareholders unsustainable.

[253] As pointed out below at para.25–31 the statute law on prospectus liability has gone beyond the common law which will normally be irrelevant. But it remains highly relevant where the statute does not apply. See *Al-Nakib Investments Ltd v Longcroft* [1990] 1 W.L.R. 1390, and the comment thereon at para.25–37, below.

[254] Per Lord Bridge at 621E–F. This was clearly the unanimous view, adopting the dissenting judgment of Denning L.J. in *Candler v Crane Christmas & Co* [1951] 2 K.B. 164, CA and affirming the decision of Millett J. in *Al Saudi Banque v Clark Pixley* [1990] Ch. 313, but rejecting the wider views expressed in *JEB Fasteners Ltd v Marks Bloom & Co* [1981] 3 All E.R. 289 and in *Twomax Ltd v Dickson, McFarlane & Robinson*, 1982 S.C. 113, and by the majority of the New Zealand Court of Appeal in *Scott Group Ltd v McFarlane* [1978] N.Z.L.R. 553.

[255] The case concerned only the purchase of shares and the court left open the question of whether sales of shares (for example, where the accounts negligently undervalued the company) were within the scope of the duty, on the grounds that only shareholders could sell shares so that sales were necessarily a shareholder activity. However, the judges showed little enthusiasm for this argument; and a thorough-going governance analysis would seem to exclude sales as well as purchases on the grounds that both are investment, not governance, decisions.

[256] For a similar refusal to use the common law to supplement the statutory framework but within an analysis of the statutory purposes which seems more faithful to the legislative intent (in this case the New Zealand Securities Act 1978) see *Deloitte Haskins & Sells v National Mutual Life Nominees* [1993] A.C. 774, PC.

was surprising to a company lawyer about *Caparo* was the narrow view taken by the court of the purposes Parliament had in mind when steadily expanding over the century the disclosure provisions of the Act and especially when requiring ever greater levels of public disclosure of financial reports rather than just their circulation to members and other current investors in the company.

Special circumstances

22–44 Not surprisingly, the case-law after *Caparo* has concentrated on seeking to determine the basis or bases upon which it will be possible for claimants to establish a "special relationship" or, as it is now often called in the light of subsequent general developments in the law of negligence, an "assumption of responsibility" on the part of the auditors towards the claimant. A crucial initial issue is that the special relationship does not require that the auditor should consciously have assumed responsibility. The test is an objective one and the question for the court is whether, in all the circumstances, it is appropriate for the auditors to be treated as having assumed responsibility.[257] A number of different situations have been considered in this light in the case law.

First, within groups of companies, the courts have accepted that it is arguable that the auditors of a subsidiary company owe a duty of care to the parent company, since the auditors will be aware that the parent will rely on the audit of the subsidiary to produce accounts which reflect a true and fair view of the parent and the group as a whole.[258] However, the losses for which the auditors are potentially liable in such a case will be restricted by the uses to which it can be contemplated the accounts will be put by the parent. Thus, in the standard case it may be correct to say that the subsidiary's auditors should have contemplated that the parent would use the group or parent's accounts for the purposes to which parent companies normally put them (payment of dividends to shareholders or bonuses to senior staff) but not to hold them liable for losses arising simply from the fact that the parent continued to fund the subsidiary on the assumption that it was in good financial health.[259] However, there may be special situations in which, by virtue of the way the group is run in practice and of the way the auditors of its various components have co-operated, the subsidiary's auditors owe greater duties in tort to the parent than those indicated above.[260] Underlying this approach is a recognition that, whilst the subsidiary and the parent have a

---

[257] *Electra Private Equity Partners v KPMG Peat Marwick* [2001] 1 B.C.L.C. 589, CA; *Caparo*, above, fn.249 at 638, per Lord Oliver.

[258] *Barings Plc v Coopers & Lybrand* [1997] 2 B.C.L.C. 427, CA.

[259] *Barings Plc v Coopers & Lybrand (No.1)* [2002] 2 B.C.L.C. 364.

[260] *Bank of Credit & Commerce International (Overseas) Ltd v Price Waterhouse* [1998] B.C.C. 617, CA.

separate legal personality, it may be easier within a corporate group to recognise duties owed by auditors to a person other than the client, where that person is the client's parent company because of the practice within the group of which the auditor is or ought to be aware.

A second area of tortious duty to "third" parties involves the directors of the company by which the auditors have been engaged. Although the Act presents the compilation of the accounts by the directors and their audit as consecutive and separate events, in practice the two overlap, with the directors finalising the accounts at the same time as the audit is in progress on the basis of draft accounts. On this basis, it has been held to be arguable that the auditors are under a duty to alert the directors immediately if the auditors form the view that the directors' approach to the accounts is misconceived in some respect. The directors are not obliged to accept the auditors' views but are entitled to be informed before they commit themselves, with the risk that their approach may lead to the accounts being qualified by the auditors.[261]

However, the most obvious strategy suggested by the *Caparo* **22–45** decision for investors in or lenders to the company (or, sometimes, its regulator), who do in fact propose to rely on the company's accounts, is to seek to make the auditors aware in advance of the transaction of their intentions and to secure from the auditors an ad hoc assumption of responsibility for the accounts in relation to the contemplated transaction. Where such an approach is made explicitly and openly and the auditors accept responsibility, there is little to be said against holding the auditors liable for negligently prepared accounts. The auditors have the opportunity not to accept wider responsibility or to do so on explicit terms, which either limit their liability or involve compensation being paid to them for assuming the additional risk. The question is whether the auditors can or should be made liable on the basis of anything less than a near-explicit bargain with the lender or investor. It has been held that it is not enough to attract liability to the third party that the auditor repeated its conclusions to that person. The crucial question is whether the terms of the request from the third party can be said to have made it clear to an auditor in the defendant's position the purpose for which the repetition was required and the fact that the auditor's skill and judgment were being relied upon.[262] Although this approach falls short of an explicit bargain, it does require that the auditor be made aware of the nature of

---

[261] *Coulthard v Neville Russell* [1988] 1 B.C.L.C. 143, CA. The claimant directors, who were subsequently disqualified, sought compensation from the auditors for the losses caused by the disqualification. The court refused to strike out the claim.

[262] *Andrew v Kounnis Freeman* [1999] 2 B.C.L.C. 641, CA (where the tests were held to have been satisfied); *James McNaughton Papers Group Ltd v Hicks Anderson & Co* [1991] 2 Q.B. 113, CA (where they were not); *Galoo Ltd v Bright, Grahame Murray* [1994] 1 W.L.R. 1360, CA (claims partly struck out and partly allowed to proceed). For the application of this approach to circulars issued in the course of takeover bids see para.28–56.

its commitment before liability in tort is imposed for the benefit of the third party.

Although the *Caparo* decision was controversial amongst those interested in the general theory of the law of tort (because of its rejection of the foreseeability test in the area of negligent misstatements) and although the court's reliance on the statutory structure for the accounts seems overblown, the line drawn in that case has been followed by other top-level courts in the common law world, notably Australia and Canada.[263] Its effect, in the core case where no duty arises, is to insulate the audit transaction (and thus the fee charged by auditors to companies for carrying it out) from having to bear the investigation costs of other transactions which third parties may wish to carry out (whether by way of loan or equity purchase) with the company. Since the auditors are in a very poor position to estimate the risks associated with those transactions, about which it will have little, if any, information, their exclusion is probably necessary for the maintenance of the market in audit services. The burden thrown on third parties by this ruling is, by contrast, relatively slight. If the state of the company's finances is important to the transaction, as it often will be, they can either pay someone else to replicate the due diligence which the auditors have carried out or, more likely, seek through the special circumstances exception to persuade the auditors to accept responsibility for their report in the context of the third party's transaction. This gives the auditors the opportunity to assess the risks of the particular transaction and to respond appropriately.[264]

Other issues

22–46 Even if duty is established, the claimant will still have to satisfy the other ingredients for tortious liability which have been discussed above in relation to claims by the audit client. Thus in *JEB Fasteners Ltd v Marks Bloom & Co*,[265] which would today be regarded as a "special circumstances" case, Woolf J. held that, although all the conditions necessary for success other than causation had been established, the claimant failed on that since it would have entered into the transaction (a takeover) even if the accounts on which it had relied had presented a wholly true and fair view of the company's

---

[263] *Essanda Finance Corp Ltd v Peat Marwick Hungerford* (1997) 188 C.L.R. 241 (High Court of Australia) and *Hercules Management Ltd v Ernst & Young* (1997) 146 D.L.R. (4th) 577 (Supreme Court of Canada).

[264] This analysis depends, of course, on the courts not expanding the special circumstances exception so as to swallow up the *Caparo* rule. Contrast the sophisticated approach in *Peach Publishing Ltd v Slater & Co* [1998] B.C.C. 139, CA with the rather easy way in which assumption of responsibility was found in *ADT Ltd v BDO Binder Hamlyn* [1996] B.C.C. 808.

[265] [1981] 3 All E.R. 289; affirmed on other grounds [1983] 1 All E.R. 583, CA.

financial position, its main object having been to secure the managerial skills of two executive directors.[266]

Further reform?

With the introduction in the Companies Act 2006 of the permission **22–47** for limitation of liability agreements with the audit client and the apparent continuing robustness of the *Caparo* principle in relation to third-party claims, the impetus for reform of the rules on auditors' civil liability at domestic level seems to have exhausted itself. However, Article 31 of the Audit Directive required the Commission to present a report on the impact of the national liability rules on the European capital markets and, if appropriate, to make recommendations to the Member States. Auditor liability rules vary greatly among the Member States, for example, some States recognising a duty of care to third-party investors quite easily, but capping liability at a multiple of the audit fee. The Commission's consultation paper explored two main options for reform: a cap on liability (of various types) and the introduction of proportionate liability.[267] Neither of these possible reforms sits well with what has occurred recently in the United Kingdom: mandatory proportionate liability has been consistently rejected as a solution domestically; it is not clear whether a limitation of liability agreement falls within the Commission's notion of a cap;[268] and the *Caparo* solution of restricting the duty of care fails to be noted in the consultation paper because the paper focuses solely on the quantum of liability and does not deal with the situations in which liability arises. It is in fact very odd to make recommendations on quantum and to leave duty on one side.

It might be thought that this does not matter very much since Article 31 contemplates only a Recommendation to Member States, which a particular Member State might not respond to because it had achieved the same functional result in another way. However, Recommendations do produce their own political pressures and are sometimes the precursor to more intrusive forms of Community intervention, for example, through Directives. It is suggested that, were that contemplated, duty and quantum would have to be considered together if a rational system were to result.[269] A combination of a low monetary cap or even proportionate liability and a *Caparo* duty rule, for example, might be well be too favourable to auditors.

---

[266] Who, in fact, resigned!

[267] Directorate General for Internal Market and Services, *Consultation Paper on Auditors' Liability and its Impact on the European Capital Markets*, January 2007. A summary of the responses was later published.

[268] The document seems to envisage a limit set by legislation rather than one set by the parties.

[269] The Commission in fact carried out a broader study some years ago (*A study on systems of civil liability of statutory auditors in the context of a Single Market for auditing services in the European Union*, January 2001) but then dropped this "hot potato" until the issue emerged in a weaker form in Article 31 of the Directive.

CONCLUSIONS

22–48   The audit has been subject to two very different legislative policy influences in recent years: on the one hand, a desire to relieve small companies of the need to have one and, on the other, a desire to make the audit of large, especially listed, companies a more effective check on the financial probity of management. The former is easy to effect as a matter of legal technique, though conclusive cost/benefit analysis of the audit of small companies is not available to demonstrate where the line should be drawn and the audit remains mandatory. The latter policy drive has had a positive consequence so that the status of company auditors has, in the course of the past century, been transformed from that of somewhat toothless strays given temporary house-room once a year, to that of trained rottweilers, entitled to sniff around at any time and, if need be, to bite the hands that feed them. However, even rottweilers may learn that biting the hand that feeds you is not a policy conducive to happiness for the biter. Through a combination of domestic and Community initiatives a substantial structure has been put in place aimed at addressing issues of independence and competence, using a wide range of legal techniques, some more firmly located in company law than others.

PART SIX

EQUITY FINANCE

In the course of the book we have referred frequently to the rights of shareholders but less often to the function which they perform in the company. In Part Four, for example, we discussed the accountability of management to the shareholders, but did not investigate in any detail what the shareholders contribute in return for that ultimate control over the company. In very small companies, the purpose of issuing shares may indeed be simply to give the shareholders control over the company. In a two-person quasi-partnership, for example, the founders of the company may take one low-value share each, and no other shares may be issued by the company. The issue of shares in such a case operates to give the partners complete control over the running of the company, for, in all likelihood, they will use their voting rights as shareholders to appoint themselves as directors of the company. Financing for the company will come from elsewhere, probably in the form of a bank loan secured on the partners' personal assets.

However, in larger companies the purpose of share issues is not simply, or even primarily, to allocate control over the company but also to raise finance for it, and it is on that function of the share issue that we concentrate in this part. As we have seen,[1] ordinary shares constitute a particularly flexible form of finance for companies, because, so long as the company is a going concern, the shareholders are entitled to no particular level of return by way of dividend and cannot withdraw the contribution made in exchange for their shares without the company's consent, given either at the time of issue of the shares (e.g. where they are issued as redeemable at the option of the shareholder) or later (e.g. where the company offers to re-purchase

---

[1] Chs. 12 and 13.

some of its shares). During periods of economic strain the company can hang on to the shares but pay low or no dividends, whilst the shareholders hope that things will turn around eventually and they will be well rewarded for their patience. Even where the company is wound up and the shareholders obtain rights to repayment of their shares, they stand at the end of the queue after the creditors and so may find that their rights are in fact worthless.[2] The economic exposure of the shareholders goes a long way to explain the traditional stance of the law that control rights over the management should be invested in those shareholders.

However, not all shares are "ordinary" or "equity" shares, though it is rare for a company not to issue some shares of this type. The economic and control rights of shareholders are a matter largely of contract between company and investor, rather than of statutory stipulation, so that a company may issue several classes of share, with differing rights attached to them. As we have already seen,[3] this can create risks of oppression of one class of shareholder by another, to combat which the statute has developed special protective mechanisms. More important for this Part, the rights conferred upon "preference" shares may make it difficult to distinguish in practice between share-based finance of companies and debt-based finance, considered in the final Part of this book. Typically, a lender to a company does not become a member of it and obtain control rights over it but is entitled to a fixed return on the loan, which must be paid whatever the economic circumstances of the company. Since, however, the terms of loans can be structured so as to give the lenders considerable control over what the management of the company does, whilst preference shareholders may be entitled to a fixed return and have limited control rights, the line between debt and equity is sometimes difficult to identify.

For many years the raising of "risk" finance for large companies has itself been a large-scale activity. Since the investor's contribution to the company is "locked in", the investor is likely to look more favourably on a public offer of shares which is linked to the introduction of those shares to trading on a public securities market. This will restore liquidity to the investor by enabling him or her to dispose of the shares to another investor at any time through the "stock exchange" (if not necessarily at an attractive price). The United Kingdom has long had institutional arrangements to facilitate the raising of equity finance (notably the London Stock Exchange) but in recent years, with deregulation, the number of markets has increased (some are run by the LSE and some are not) and international competition among exchanges has grown. This has led to (and partly resulted from) a very rapid growth in the rules relating to the public

---

[2] IA 1986; ss.107 and 143.
[3] See above, paras 19–11ff.

offerings of shares and the disclosure obligations placed upon publicly traded companies, as well as to a strong interest in the proper regulation of the "market for corporate control", whereby control of companies passes into new hands through the acquisition of shares traded on public exchanges. At the same time, with the goal of creating a single market, much of the regulatory initiative has passed from domestic bodies to the European Community. As a result of both domestic and Community initiatives there has been not insignificant revolution in the structure and content of the relevant rules.

THE NATURE AND CLASSIFICATION OF SHARES

Frequent references have been made to the shares which a company **23–1** can issue. It is now necessary to look a little more closely at the exact nature of these shares and to indicate the various forms they may take.

LEGAL NATURE OF SHARES

What, then, is the exact juridical nature of a share? At the present day **23–2** this is a question more easily asked than answered. In the old deed of settlement company, which was merely an enlarged partnership with the partnership property vested in trustees, it was clear that the members' "shares" entitled them to an equitable interest in the assets of the company. It is true that the exact nature of this equitable interest was not crystal clear, for the members could not, while the firm was a going concern, lay claim to any particular asset or prevent the directors from disposing of it. Even with the modern partnership, no very satisfactory solution to this problem has been found, and the most one can say is that the partners have an equitable interest, often described as a lien, which floats over the partnership assets throughout the duration of the firm, although it crystallises only on dissolution. Still, there is admittedly some sort of proprietary nexus (however vague and ill-defined) between the partnership assets and the partners.

At one time it was thought that the same applied to an incorporated company, except that the company itself held its assets as trustee for its members.[1] But this idea has long since been rejected. Shareholders have ceased to be regarded as having equitable interests in the company's assets; "shareholders are not, in the eyes of the law, part owners of the undertaking".[2] As a result, the word "share" has become something of a misnomer, for shareholders no longer share any property in common; at the most they share certain rights in respect of dividends, return of capital on a winding up, voting, and the like.

Today it is generally stated that a share is a chose in action.[3] This, however, is not helpful, for "chose in action" is a notoriously vague term used to describe a mass of interests which have little or nothing in common except that they confer no right to possession of a physical thing, and which range from purely personal rights under a contract to patents, copyrights and trade marks.

It is tempting to equate shares with rights under a contract, for as we have seen[4] the articles of association constitute a contract of some sort between the company and its members and it is this document which directly or indirectly defines the rights conferred by the shares. But a share is something far more than a mere contractual right *in personam*. This is sufficiently clear from the rules relating to infant shareholders, who are liable for calls on the shares unless they repudiate the allotment during infancy or on attaining majority,[5] and who cannot recover any money which they have paid unless the shares have been completely valueless.[6] As Parke B. said[7]:

> "They have been treated, therefore, as persons in a different situation from mere contractors for then they would have been exempt, but in truth they are purchasers who have acquired an interest not in a mere chattel, but in a subject of a permanent nature ...."[8]

---

[1] *Child v Hudson's Bay Co* (1723) 2 P. Wms. 207. As in the case of partnerships it was clear long before the express statutory provisions to this effect (see now s.541) that shares were personalty and not realty even if the company owned freehold land.

[2] Per Evershed L.J. in *Short v Treasury Commissioners* [1948] 1 K.B. 122, CA.

[3] See, per Greene M.R. in [1942] Ch. 241, and *Colonial Bank v Whinney* (1886) 11 App.-Cas.426, HL.

[4] See above, at paras 3–13 *et seq.*

[5] *Cork & Brandon Railway v Cazenove* (1847) 10 Q.B. 935; *N.W. Railway v M'Michael* (1851) 5 Exch. 114. If they repudiate during infancy it is not clear whether they can be made liable to pay calls due prior thereto: the majority in *Cazenove*'s case thought they could, but Parke B. in the later case (at 125) stated the contrary.

[6] *Steinberg v Scala (Leeds) Ltd* [1923] 2 Ch. 452, CA.

[7] (1851) 5 Exch. at 123.

[8] Later he suggested that the shareholder had "a vested interest of a permanent character in all the profits arising from the land and other effects of the company" (at 125). This can hardly be supported in view of later cases.

The definition of a share which is, perhaps, the most widely quoted is **23–3**
that of Farwell J. in *Borland's Trustee v Steel*[9]:

> "A share is the interest of a shareholder in the company mea-
> sured by a sum of money, for the purpose of liability in the first
> place, and of interest in the second, but also consisting of a series
> of mutual covenants entered into by all the shareholders *inter se*
> in accordance with [s. 33]. The contract contained in the articles
> of association is one of the original incidents of the share. A
> share is not a sum of money ... but is an interest measured by a
> sum of money and made up of various rights contained in the
> contract, including the right to a sum of money of a more or less
> amount."

It will be observed that this definition, though it lays considerable and
perhaps disproportionate stress on the contractual nature of the
shareholder's rights, also emphasises the fact that he has an interest *in*
the company. The theory seems to be that the contract constituted by
the articles of association defines the nature of the rights, which,
however, are not purely personal rights but instead confer some sort
of proprietary interest in the company though not in its property. The
company itself is treated not merely as a person, the subject of rights
and duties, but also as a *res*, the object of rights and duties.[10] It is the
fact that the shareholder has rights in the company as well as against
it, which, in legal theory, distinguishes the member from the debenture-holder whose rights are also defined by contract (this time the
debenture itself and not the articles) but are rights against the company and, if the debenture is secured, in its property, but never in the
company itself. Farwell J.'s definition mentions that the interest of a
shareholder is measured by a sum of money. Reference has already
been made to this[11] and it has been emphasised that the requirement
of a nominal monetary value is an arbitrary and illogical one which
has been rejected in certain other common law jurisdictions. The
nominal value is meaningless and may be misleading, except in so far
as it determines the minimum liability. Even as a measure of liability,
it is of less importance now that shares are almost invariably issued
on terms that they are to be fully paid-up on or shortly after allotment and are frequently issued at a price exceeding their nominal
value. But reference to liability is valuable in that it emphasises that

---

[9] [1901] 1 Ch. 279 at 288. Approved by the Court of Appeal in *Paulin, Re* [1935] 1 K.B. 26,
and by the House of Lords *ibid.*, sub nom. *IRC v Crossman* [1937] A.C. 26. See also the other
definitions canvassed in that case.

[10] "A whole system ... has been built up on the unconscious assumption that organisations,
which from one point of view are considered individuals, from another are storehouses of
tangible property": Arnold, *The Folklore of Capitalism* (New Haven, Conn., 1959) p.353.

[11] See above, para.11–6.

shareholders *qua* members may be under obligations to the company as well as having rights against it.

23–4   This analysis may seem academic and barren, and to some extent it is, for a closer examination of the rights conferred by shares and debentures will show the impossibility of preserving any hard and fast distinction between them which bears any relation to practical reality. Nevertheless, the matter is not entirely theoretical, for in a number of cases the courts have been faced with the need to analyse the juridical nature of a shareholder's interest in order to determine the principles on which it should be valued. The most interesting of these cases is *Short v Treasury Commissioners*[12] where the whole of the shares of Short Bros were being acquired by the Treasury under a Defence Regulation which provided for payment of their value "as between a willing buyer and a willing seller".[13] They were valued on the basis of the quoted share price, but the shareholders argued that, since all the shares were being acquired, stock exchange prices were not a true criterion and that either the whole undertaking should be valued and the price thus determined apportioned among the shareholders, or the value should be the price which one buyer would give for the whole block, which price should then be similarly apportioned. The courts upheld the method adopted and rejected both the alternatives suggested, the first because the shareholders were not "part owners of the undertaking" and the second because the regulation implied that each holding was to be separately valued. It was conceded that had any individual shareholder held a sufficient block to give him "control" of the company then he might have been entitled to a higher price than the total market value of his shares,[14] since he would then have been selling an item of property—control—additional to his shares. But as no one shareholder had control to sell, the Government was able to acquire control of the company's assets for a fraction of their true value (and for a fraction of what it would have had to pay on a takeover bid).[15]

One thing at least is clear: shares are recognised in law, as well as in fact, as objects of property which are bought, sold, mortgaged and bequeathed. They are indeed the typical items of property of the modern commercial era and particularly suited to its demands because of their exceptional liquidity. To deny that they are "owned" would be as unreal as to deny, on the basis of feudal theory, that land is owned—far more unreal because the owner's freedom to do what he likes with his shares in public companies is likely to be con-

---

[12] [1948] 1 K.B. 116, CA, affirmed [1948] A.C. 534, HL.

[13] This popular formula is much criticised by economists who argue with some force that the willingness of the buyer and seller depends on the price and not vice versa.

[14] Hence in *Dean v Prince* [1953] Ch. 590 (reversed on the facts [1954] Ch. 409, CA) Harman J. held that the "fair value" of a block of shares conferring control must include something above the "break-up" value of the assets, in respect of this control.

[15] On which, see Ch.28, below.

siderably less fettered. Nor, today, is the bundle of rights making up the share regarded as equitable only. On the contrary, as Chapter 27 will show, legal ownership of shares is recognised and distinguished from equitable ownership in much the same way as a legal estate in land is distinguished from equitable interests therein. Nor must this emphasis on the proprietary and financial aspects of a shareholder's rights obscure the important fact that shares cause their holder to become a member of an association, with rights, at least in relation to ordinary shares, to take part in its deliberations by attending and voting at its general meetings.

THE PRESUMPTION OF EQUALITY BETWEEN SHAREHOLDERS

The typical company—one limited by shares—must issue some **23–5** shares, and the initial presumption of the law is that all shares confer the same rights and impose the same liabilities. As in partnership[16] equality prevails in the absence of agreement to the contrary. Normally the shareholders' rights will fall under three heads: (i) dividends, (ii) return of capital and participation in surplus assets on a winding up (or authorised reduction of capital) and (iii) attendance at meetings and voting. Unless there is some indication to the contrary, all the shares will confer the like rights to all three. So far as voting is concerned this is a comparatively recent development, for, on the analogy of the partnership rule, it was long felt that members' voting rights should be divorced from their purely financial interests in respect of dividend and capital, so that the equality in voting should be between members rather than between shares. A stage intermediate between these two ideas was reflected in the Companies Clauses Act 1845[17] which provided that in the absence of contrary provision in the special statute every shareholder had one vote for every share up to ten, one for every additional five up to a hundred and one for every ten thereafter, thus weighting the voting in favour of the smaller holders. However, attempts to reduce the proportion of voting rights as the size of holdings increased were doomed to failure since the requirement could be easily evaded by splitting holdings and vesting them in nominees. It is now recognised that if voting rights are to vary, separate classes of shares should be created so that the different number of votes can be attached to the shares themselves and not to the holder. Even today, however, the older idea still prevails on a vote by a show of hands, when the common law rule is that each member has one vote irrespective of the number of shares

[16] Partnership Act 1890, s.24(1).
[17] s.75.

held; a rule which, although it can be altered by the constitution, is normally maintained,[18] if only because the number of a human being's hands cannot be more than two.

For many years it was thought that, in the absence of express provision in the original constitution, the continued equality of all shares was a fundamental condition which could not be abrogated by an alteration of the articles so as to allow the issue of shares preferential to those already issued.[19] This idea was, however, finally destroyed in *Andrews v Gas Meter Co*[20] which established that the articles could be altered so as to authorise such an issue.

There is a similar presumption of equality in relation to shareholders' liabilities but it too can be altered by provisions in the articles. In the case of a company limited by shares, normally the only liability imposed on a shareholder as such will be to pay up the nominal value of the shares and any premium in so far as payment has not already been made by a previous holder. This, however, does not mean that all the shares, even if of the same nominal value and of the same class, will necessarily be issued at the same price, or that, even if they are, all shareholders will necessarily be treated alike as regards calls for the unpaid part. Section 581 provides that a company, if so authorised by its articles, may: (a) make arrangements on an issue of shares for a difference between shareholders in the amounts or times of payments of calls; (b) accept from any member the whole or part of the amount remaining unpaid although it has not been called up; or (c) pay a dividend in proportion to the amount paid up on each share where a larger amount is paid up on some shares than on others.[21] Subject to that, however, calls must be made *pari passu*.[22]

CLASSES OF SHARES

23–6   As will have been apparent, the prima facie equality of shares can be modified by dividing the share capital into different classes with different rights as to dividends, capital or voting or with different nominal values. By permutations of these various incidents the number of possible classes is limited only by the total number of shares. On the whole it is not the present fashion for public companies to complicate their capital structures by having a large number of

---

[18]   For the law and practice regarding voting at meetings, see Ch.15, above.
[19]   *Hutton v Scarborough Cliff Hotel Co* (1865) 2 Dr. & Sim. 521.
[20]   [1897] 1 Ch. 361, CA.
[21]   Table A 1985 appeared to authorise (a) only (see Art.17) probably rightly in view of the complications which (b) and (c) would cause a public company.
[22]   *Galloway v Halle Concerts Society* [1915] 2 Ch. 233.

share classes—though much ingenuity is displayed in devising the most attractive methods of marketing issues and in creating types of company securities other than shares, but with rights to convert into shares.[23] But, both in the case of public and private companies, there may well be two or three different classes and sometimes more. The division of shares into classes and the rights attached to each class will normally be set out in the company's articles but, in contrast with the Companies Acts of some other common law countries, that is not compulsory.[24] Instead, steps have been taken to ensure that the classes and their rights can be ascertained from the company's public documents. For this purpose the "return of allotments" (i.e. the information which the company has to provide to the Registrar of companies within one month of the allotment of shares)[25] is used. This must give the "prescribed particulars" of the rights attached to the shares in relation to each class of shares.[26] If the company assigns a class a name or other designation or changes an existing one, that too must be notified.[27] The same applies if and when there is any variation of the class rights.[28]

Preference shares

Where the differences between the classes relates to financial entitle-   **23–7**
ment, i.e. to dividends and return of capital, the likelihood is that they will be given distinguishing names, though these may be no more informative than "preference" and "ordinary" (perhaps, in the case of the former, preceded by "first" or "second" where there are two classes of preference shares). If a potential investor should assume that "preference" means that he should prefer them to the ordinary shares he would be sorely in need of professional advice. The advice received would probably not be couched in terms of relative merits and de-merits of preference and ordinary shares but of security and levels of risk. And if the client's needs suggested the former, the

---

[23] It is beyond the scope of this book to do more than draw attention to a further recent development, namely the extent to which investors are being beguiled into including in their investment portfolios "futures", options, and contracts for differences whereby they speculate in, or bet on, fluctuations in the price of shares or indices of such prices.

[24] This is now true even in relation to redeemable shares, provided the articles or a resolution of the company authorises the directors to determine the terms of redemption: s.685. See para.13–10. Shareholders' rights are sometimes set out on the back of the share certificate (where such is issued) but a misstatement of the rights on the certificate will not override the statement in the articles or in the offer document: *Hunting Plc, Re* [2005] 2 B.C.L.C. 211.

[25] On allotment see the following Chapter at para.24–15.

[26] ss.555(4)(c) and 556(3), applying to limited and unlimited companies respectively. In the latter case there will be no question of differences in respect of rights to dividends or return of capital but the members may nevertheless be of different classes in respect of voting rights.

[27] s.636.

[28] s.637. The question of how class rights may be varied is discussed in Ch.19, above.

investor would probably be advised to invest not in shares but in debentures. For preference shares may often be virtually indistinguishable from debentures except that they afford less assurance of getting one's money back or a return on it until one does. On the other hand, if in addition to being "preferential" they are also "participating" (i.e. have a right to share in the profits of the company after the ordinary shareholders have received a specified return), they may be a form of equity shares with preferential rights over the ordinary shares (and in consequence should be, and often are, designated "preferred ordinary"). Section 548 defines the company's equity share capital as all its issued share capital except that part which "neither as respects dividends nor as respects capital, carries any right to participate beyond a specified amount in a distribution".[29] Participating preference shares will thus normally fall within the definition of equity capital, even if the right to participation is confined to surplus assets when the company is wound up and the shareholders' dividend right is limited to a fixed (and perhaps not very generous) amount.

The truth of the matter is that an enormous variety of different rights, relating to dividends, return of capital, voting, conversion into ordinary shares,[30] redemption and other matters, may be attached to classes of shares, all of which are conventionally described as "preference" shares. What these rights are in any particular case and whether any particular issue of preference shares is located more at the debenture end or the ordinary share end of the spectrum will depend on the construction of the articles or other instrument creating them. Unfortunately, in the past the drafting of these documents has often been deplorably lax.[31] Hence the courts have had to evolve various "canons of construction" of the documents which, even more unfortunately, have themselves fluctuated from time to time, thus overruling earlier decisions and defeating the legitimate expectations of investors who purchased preference shares in reliance on the construction adopted earlier.[32] In former editions of

[29] This definition seems to be of equivalent effect to the differently phrased definition of "relevant shares" for the purpose of the pre-emption rules (below, para.24–6), which excludes "shares which as respects dividends and capital carry a right to participate only up to a specified amount in a distribution": s.94(5)(a).

[30] The apparently simple matter of converting preference shares into ordinary shares can become one of considerable complexity, at least where the nominal value and number of the ordinary shares into which the preference shares are to be converted differ from those of the preference shares to be converted, so that there is a danger that the transaction will involve an unauthorised return of capital, on the one hand, or the issue of shares at a discount, on the other. For a clear explanation of the ways of avoiding this result, see (1995) VI *Practical Law for Companies* (No.10) at p.43.

[31] Even to the extent of simply providing that the share capital is divided into so many X per cent Preference Shares and so many Ordinary Shares and issuing them without further clarification.

[32] The classic illustration is the overruling, by the House of Lords in *Scottish Insurance v Wilsons & Clyde Coal Co* [1949] A.C. 462, of the Court of Appeal decision in *William Metcalfe Ltd, Re* [1933] Ch. 142.

this book the story of these vacillations was traced, in some detail,[33] starting with the virtually irreconcilable decisions of the House of Lords[34] and the Court of Appeal[35] relating to the winding-up of the Bridgewater Navigation Company in 1889–91. Since, at long last, a reasonably clear finale now appears to have been reached, there is no longer a justification for that indulgence, especially in view of the present unpopularity of preference shares. It suffices to summarise what the present canons of construction appear to be.

Canons of construction

1. Prima facie all shares rank equally. If, therefore, some are to have priority over others there must be provisions to this effect in the terms of issue. **23–8**

2. If, however, the shares are expressly divided into separate classes (thus necessarily contradicting the presumed equality) it is a question of construction in each case what the rights of each class are.[36]

3. If nothing is expressly said about the rights of one class in respect of (a) dividends, (b) return of capital, or (c) attendance at meetings or voting, then, prima facie, that class has the same rights in that respect as the residuary ordinary shares. Hence, a preference as to dividend will not imply a preference as to capital (or vice versa).[37] Nor will an exclusion of participation in dividends beyond a fixed preferential rate necessarily imply an exclusion of participation in capital (or vice versa) although it will apparently be some indication of it.[38]

4. Where shares are entitled to participate in surplus capital on a winding-up, prima facie they participate in all surplus assets and not merely in that part which does not represent undistributed profits that might have been distributed as dividend to another class.[39]

---

[33] 4th ed. (1979), pp.414–421.

[34] *Birch v Cropper* (1889) 14 App.Cas. 525, HL.

[35] *Bridgewater Navigation Co, Re* [1891] 2 Ch. 317, CA.

[36] *Scottish Insurance v Wilsons & Clyde Coal Co*, above, fn.32; *Isle of Thanet Electric Co, Re* [1950] Ch. 161, CA.

[37] *London India Rubber Co, Re* (1868) L.R. 5 Eq. 519; *Accrington Corp Steam Tramways, Re* [1909] 2 Ch. 40.

[38] This is implied in the speeches in the *Scottish Insurance* case, above, and in *Dimbula Valley (Ceylon) Tea Co Ltd v Laurie* [1961] Ch. 353.

[39] *Dimbula Valley (Ceylon) Tea Co Ltd v Laurie*, above: *Saltdean Estate Co Ltd, Re* [1968] 1 W.L.R. 1844. These cases "distinguished" *Bridgewater Navigation Co, Re*, above (on the basis that the contrary decision of the Court of Appeal depended on the peculiar wording of the company articles) but it is thought that *Bridgewater* can now be ignored; in *Wilsons & Clyde Coal Co* Lord Simonds pointed out the absurdity of supposing that "parties intended a bargain which would involve an investigation of an artificial and elaborate character into the nature and origin of surplus assets": [1949] A.C. at 482.

5. If, however, any rights in respect of any of these matters are expressly stated, that statement is presumed to be exhaustive so far as that matter is concerned. Hence if shares are given a preferential dividend they are presumed to be non-participating as regards further dividends,[40] and if they are given a preferential right to a return of capital they are presumed to be non-participating in surplus assets.[41] The same clearly applies to attendance and voting;[42] if they are given a vote in certain circumstances (e.g. if their dividends are in arrears), it is implied that they have no vote in other circumstances. It is in fact common to displace the preference shareholder's presumed equality in relation to voting by expressly restricting their voting rights to situations in which their dividends have not been paid for a period of time, on the basis that only in such cases will the preference shareholders need to assert their voice in the management of the company.[43]

6. The onus of rebutting the presumption in 5 is not lightly discharged and the fact that shares are expressly made participating as regards either dividends or capital is no indication that they are participating as regards the other—indeed it has been taken as evidence to the contrary.[44]

7. If a preferential dividend is provided for, it is presumed to be cumulative (in the sense that, if passed in one year, it must nevertheless be paid in a later one before any subordinate class receives a dividend).[45] This presumption can be rebutted by any words indicating that the preferential dividend for a year is to be payable only out of the profits of that year.[46]

---

[40] *Will v United Lankat Plantations Co* [1914] A.C. 11, HL.

[41] *Scottish Insurance v Wilsons & Clyde Coal Co,* above; *Isle of Thanet Electric Co, Re* above.

[42] *Quaere* whether attendance at meetings and voting should not really be treated as two separate rights. It seems, however, that express exclusion of a right to vote will take away the right to be summoned to (or presumably to attend) meetings: *MacKenzie & Co Ltd, Re* [1916] 2 Ch. 450. If, under this canon they have votes but the articles do not say how many, the effect of s.284 appears to be that they have one vote per share or, if their shares have been converted to stock (on which see para.23–11, below) per each £10 of stock and that if the company has no share capital each member has one vote.

[43] See, for example, *Bradford Investment Ltd, Re* [1991] B.C.L.C. 224.

[44] *National Telephone Co, Re* [1914] 1 Ch. 755; *Isle of Thanet Electric Co, Re,* above and *Saltdean Estate Co Ltd, Re,* above. This produces strange results. If, as the House of Lords suggested in the *Scottish Insurance* case, the fact that shares are non-participating as regards dividends is some indication that they are intended to be non-participating as regards capital (on the ground that the surplus profits have been appropriated to the ordinary shareholders), where the surplus profits belong to both classes while the company is a going concern, both should participate in a winding-up in order to preserve the *status quo*.

[45] *Webb v Earle* (1875) L.R. 20 Eq. 556.

[46] *Staples v Eastman Photographic Materials Co* [1896] 2 Ch. 303, CA.

8. It is presumed that even preferential dividends are payable only if declared.[47] Hence arrears even of cumulative dividend are prima facie not payable in a winding-up unless previously declared.[48] But this presumption may be rebutted by the slightest indication to the contrary.[49] It may thus be advantageous to specify that the dividend is automatically payable on certain dates (assuming profits are available) rather than upon a resolution of the directors or shareholders. When the arrears are payable, the presumption is that they are to be paid provided there are surplus assets available, whether or not these represent accumulated profits which might have been distributed by way of dividend,[50] but that they are payable only to the date of the commencement of the winding-up.[51]

The effect of applying these canons of construction has been, as Evershed M.R. pointed out,[52] that over the past 100 years:

"the view of the courts may have undergone some change in regard to the relative rights of preference and ordinary shareholders ... and to the disadvantage of the preference shareholders whose position has ... become somewhat more approximated to [that] of debenture holders."

Unless preference shareholders are expressly granted participating rights they are unlikely to be entitled to share in any way in the "equity" or to have voting rights except in narrowly prescribed circumstances. Yet they enjoy none of the advantages of debenture-holders; they receive a return on their money only if profits are earned[53] (and not necessarily even then), they rank after creditors on a winding-up and they have less effective remedies against the com-

---

[47] *Burland v Earle* [1902] A.C. 83, PC; *Buenos Ayres Gt Southern Railway, Re* [1947] Ch. 384; *Godfrey Phillips Ltd v Investment Trust Ltd* [1953] 1 W.L.R. 41. *Semble*, therefore, non-cumulative shares lose their preferential dividend for the year in which liquidation commences: *Foster & Son, Re* [1942] 1 All E.R. 314; *Catalina's Warehouses, Re* [1947] 1 All E.R. 51. But, if the terms clearly so provide, a prescribed preferential dividend may be payable so long as there are adequate distributable profits in accordance with Ch.12, above: *Evling v Israel & Oppenheimer* [1918] 1 Ch. 101.

[48] *Crichton's Oil Co, Re* [1902] 2 Ch. 86, CA; *Roberts & Cooper, Re* [1929] 2 Ch. 383; *Wood, Skinner & Co Ltd, Re* [1944] Ch. 323.

[49] *Walter Symons Ltd, Re* [1934] Ch. 308; *F de Jong & Co Ltd, Re* [1946] Ch. 211, CA; *E.W. Savory Ltd, Re* [1951] 2 All E.R. 1036; *Wharfedale Brewery Co, Re* [1952] Ch. 913.

[50] *New Chinese Antimony Co Ltd, Re* [1916] 2 Ch. 115; *Springbok Agricultural Estates Ltd, Re* [1920] 1 Ch. 563; *Wharfedale Brewery Co, Re*, above, not following *W.J. Hall & Co Ltd, Re* [1909] 1 Ch. 521.

[51] *E.W. Savory Ltd, Re* above.

[52] *Isle of Thanet Electric Co, Re* [1950] Ch. at 175.

[53] This necessarily follows from the principle laid down in s.830(1) that "a company shall not make a distribution except out of profit available for the purpose". See above, para.12–2.

pany. Suspended midway between true creditors and true members they may get the worst of both worlds, unless the instrument creating the preference shares is carefully drafted.

Ordinary shares

23–9   Ordinary shares (as the name implies) constitute the residuary class in which is vested everything after the special rights of preference classes, if any, have been satisfied. They confer a right to the "equity" in the company and, in so far as members can be said to own the company, the ordinary shareholders are its proprietors. It is they who bear the lion's share of the risk and they who in good years take the lion's share of the profits (after the directors and managers have been remunerated). If, as is often the case, the company's shares are all of one class, then these are necessarily ordinary shares, and if a company has a share capital it must perforce have at least one ordinary share whether or not it also has preference shares. It is this class alone which is unmistakably distinguished from debentures both in law and fact.

But as we have seen, the ordinary shares may shade off imperceptibly into preference, for, when the latter confer a substantial right of participation in income or capital, or a fortiori both, it is largely a matter of taste whether they are designated "preference" or "preferred ordinary" shares. Moreover, distinctions may be drawn among ordinary shares, ranking equally as regards financial participation, by dividing them nevertheless into separate classes with different voting rights. In this event they will probably be distinguished as "A" "B" "C" (etc.) ordinary shares. Some public companies have issued non-voting A ordinary shares. Alternatively, both classes of ordinary share may have voting rights but the votes of a share of one class may be a high multiple of the votes attached to a share of another. In either case, control may be retained by a small proportion of the equity leading to a further rift between ownership and control. This disturbing development (a response to the threat of takeover bids[54]) gave rise to demands that the Stock Exchange should refuse to list such shares, or, failing that, that the legislature should intervene. The Jenkins Committee in the early 1960s was divided on this issue. The majority took the view that the case for banning non-voting ordinary shares had not been made out but that such shares should be clearly

---

[54] See Ch.28, below. After the initial battle in the 1950s for control of Savoy Hotel Ltd the capital of the company was reorganised so that £21,198 B ordinary stock could outvote £847,912 A ordinary stock. There the A stock had voting rights but the votes were so weighted in favour of the B class that over 97 per cent of the equity could be outvoted by the remainder! Over 40 years later, despite changes in the share capital, the balance of power remained much the same and the continued efforts of the holders of a large majority of the equity to wrest control from the minority did not succeed. For an attempt to overcome the problem through a scheme of arrangement see para.29–5. However, at the end of 1989 a truce was declared when the majority was allowed representation on the board.

labelled and that their holders should be entitled to receive notices of all meetings so as to be kept informed.[55] A minority of three recommended that all equity shareholders should have a right to attend and speak at meetings and that there should be a prohibition on the listing of non-voting or restricted-voting equity shares.[56] No legislative action was taken on either recommendation. However, opposition from institutional investors has caused issues of non-voting shares to be less frequent and many companies have enfranchised their non-voting shares. The solution to this problem, incomplete though it is, thus turned out to be a market, rather than a legal, one in the United Kingdom. More recently, the European Commission again took up the question, in a somewhat broader framework, of whether there should be legal regulation of disproportionate voting structures, but in the end decided not to proceed, despite strong arguments from the European Corporate Governance Forum that at least much greater disclosure of such structures was desirable.[57]

Special classes

Although in most cases the shares of a company will fall into one or other of the primary classes of preference or ordinary, it is, of course, possible for the company to create shares for particular purposes and containing terms which cut across the normal classifications. An example of this is afforded by employees' shares. Frequent references have already been made to "employees share schemes". Under the present definition of such schemes,[58] the beneficiaries of them may include not only present employees of the company concerned, but also employees, or former employees, of it or any company in the same group, and the spouses, civil partners, children or stepchildren under the age of 18, of any such employees. When employees' share schemes first came to be introduced here, the normal practice was to create a special class of shares with restricted rights regarding, in particular, votes and transferability; only in relation to share option schemes, designed as incentives to top management, were ordinary

23–10

---

[55] Report of the Company Law Committee, 1962, Cmnd. 1749, paras 123–140.
[56] Report of the Company Law Committee, pp.207–210.
[57] The basic study carried out for the Commission was Shearman & Sterling, ISS and ECGI, *Report on the Proportionality Principle in the European Union* (undated but available on *http://ec.europa.eu/internal_market/company/shareholders/indexb_en.htm*, together with two academic analyses by Burkart and Lee and Adams and Ferreira). The Commission's decision not to proceed was announced by Commissioner McCreevy in a speech to Legal Affairs Committee of the European Parliament on October 3, 2007. The views of the ECGF are to be found in Statement of the European Corporate Governance Forum on Proportionality, August 2007 (available on *http://ec.europa.eu/internal_market/company/ecgforum/index_en.htm*, together with a paper from the Forum's working group).
[58] s.1166.

voting equity shares on offer. Now, however, that is usual in all cases[59] in order that employees' share schemes may enjoy the special tax concessions conferred on "approved profit-sharing schemes" or "approved savings-related share option schemes". Hence today such schemes will rarely lead to the creation of a special class of share; it is only in relation to their allotment, financing, and provision for re-purchase by the company or the trustees of the scheme that there will be special arrangements which the Act facilitates by exclusions from the normal restrictions on purchase of own shares and on the pro-vision of finance by a company for the acquisition of its shares.[60]

Conversion of shares into stock

23–11 Shares may no longer be converted into stock.[61] This is a change made by the 2006 Act, though one of minor, almost undetectable, significance, since companies had abandoned the practice for the reason that, today, stock has no advantage over shares. Some com-panies which date back to before the 1948 Act still have stock, which removed the practical advantages of converting shares into stock.[62] For this reason, the 2006 Act still permits stock to be re-converted to shares by ordinary resolution of the shareholders, but this is now an irreversible decision.[63] Thus, the phrase "stock exchange" becomes even more of a misnomer than it was previously. However, turning debentures into debenture stock does retain some advantages and may still be done.[64]

---

[59] But it would be rare indeed for this to have led to employees controlling a large public company—as has occurred in the USA.

[60] See paras 13–8 and 13–8. And note also the special treatment in relation to pre-emptive rights: below, para.24–7.

[61] s.540(2). See also the prohibition in s.617 on a company altering its share capital, except as permitted by that section, which permissions no longer include conversion into stock.

[62] This was the requirement that, throughout its life, each share had to have a distinctive number, thus creating some bureaucratic work for the company, whilst stock did not.

[63] s.620.

[64] See para.31–4. The prohibition in s.617 refers only to share capital.

CHAPTER 24

SHARE ISSUES: GENERAL RULES

In the previous Chapter we examined how the company attaches **24–1** rights to shares. We now need to look at the process by which a company issues shares to those who wish to invest in it. The crucial regulatory divide is between offers to the public to acquire the company's shares and offers which are non-public. The regulatory regime is much more elaborate in the former case. In addition, since a public offer is often combined with the provision of a trading facility for the shares on a stock exchange (though it need not be), the rules governing that process become of crucial importance as well. Where there is no public offer, by contrast, the relevant rules are still to be found mainly in the Companies Act and the common law of companies, rather than in the Financial Services and Markets Act 2000 and in rules made by the FSA. In this Chapter we deal with the rules that apply to offers of securities, whether the offer is a public one or not. The additional requirements applying to public offers are treated in the following Chapter. The domestic law considered in this Chapter has been substantially influenced by the Second Company Law Directive of the Community,[1] but, in contrast with its provisions on legal capital, its rules on share issuance have generally been welcomed by shareholders as strengthening their position, though, often, not as strongly as they would wish.

---

[1] Directive 77/91/EEC [1997] OJ L26/1.

Public and Non-public Offers

24–2 A public company has a choice whether to make a public offer of its shares. It is not obliged to do so and if it refrains from making a public offer, it will escape the regulation analysed in the following Chapter, though, equally, it will find that its fundraising possibilities are much constrained. Hence the ambiguity of the term "public company". By those concerned with capital markets the term is used to refer to companies which have indeed made a public offering of their securities, which are probably traded on a public exchange. However, in order to meet the requirements for a public company under the Companies Act, there is no need to for a company to have made a public offer. In fact, the chain of argument is rather the other way: one of the consequences of being a public company under the Act is that the company may lawfully make a public offering of its securities. By contrast, the Companies Act prohibits a private company limited by shares from offering securities[2] to the public, either directly or via an offer for sale via an intermediary,[3] though the validity of any agreement to sell or allot securities or of any sale or allotment is not affected by breach of the section.[4] Thus, a private company may make only a non-public offer of its shares, and, indeed, this is the defining characteristic of a private company; but a public company (under the Companies Act) may or may not have done so.

The definition of what is a public offer for the purpose of the Act is in section 756. This section makes it clear that "public" includes a section of the public ("however selected").[5] On the other hand, the definition excludes an offer which "can properly be regarded, in all the circumstances, as not being calculated to result, directly or indirectly, in the shares or debentures becoming available for subscription or purchase by persons other than those receiving the offer or invitation".[6] Also excluded are offers which are of "domestic concern" to the company, into which category fall, presumptively, offers to the company's existing members or employees, their families, debenture-holders of the company or a trustee for any of the above.[7]

The main issue with this definition is that it does not fit exactly with

---

[2] Thus, the prohibition applies to both shares and debentures: s.755(5).
[3] See para.25–10 for a discussion of direct and indirect share offerings.
[4] ss.755(1) and 760. Nor may a private company secure admission of existing securities to the official list without making a public offer: FSMA 2000, s.74 and the Financial Services and Markets Act 2000 (Official Listing of Securities) Regulations 2005 (SI 2005/2956), reg.3. On the "official list" see the following Chapter at para.25–8.
[5] s.756(2).
[6] s.756(3)(a). If the securities do in fact end up in public hands within six months of their initial allotment or before the company has received the whole of the consideration for the shares, the company is presumed to have allotted them with a view to their being offered to the public: s.755(3).
[7] s.756(3)(b)–(6). Such offers may be renounceable in favour of other persons, provided such persons also fall within the "domestic" category.

the definition of a "public offer" used for the purposes of determining the applicability of the additional regulation discussed in the next Chapter. In particular, it does not fit with the definition of a public offer in the Prospectus Directive,[8] which determines whether a prospectus is required (and regulates its contents, if it is). On the one hand, some offers regarded as private under the Act might be public under the Directive. This is because the "offerees only" exemption of the Act has no exact equivalent in the Directive, and appears to require no limit to be set on the number of people who receive the offer nor to impose any qualification as to their experience or qualifications. In other words, a private company might make what is a public offer for the purposes of the Directive without contravening the prohibition in the Act. In such a case, of course, it will have to comply with the requirements of the Directive, as transposed into domestic law.[9]

On the other hand, a private company may be prevented by the Act **24–3** from making an offer in respect of which, if it were a public company, it would not need to produce a prospectus, because the offer fell within one of the exemptions contained in the Directive. The Company Law Review, whilst recommending that some alignment of the definition of "public offer" in the Act with that in the Directive, did not think that the lack of fit was in principle objectionable, because different policies were being pursued by the two sets of rules. Further, since the Directive is part of Community law, it is not possible to exempt offers which are private under the Act from the need to comply with the Directive where the Directive applies. Without contravening Community law, however, it would be possible to permit a private company to make an offer whenever that offer fell within the exemptions provided by the Directive, but the CLR's view was that some of these exemptions were "wholly inappropriate" for a private company, because they might allow the private company to reach "very large economic scale". This should be permitted only if the company were prepared to undertake the burdens of a public company.[10] Of course, most share issues by private companies come nowhere near being classified as public for the purposes of either the Act or the Directive.

Under the previous legislation, the prohibition was backed by criminal sanctions. The approach in the current Act is to require a private company which is proposing to make a public offer to convert to public company status. If it does not do so, any member or creditor or the Secretary of State may apply to the court for an order

---

[8] Discussed at paras 25–7ff.

[9] Unless it can fit itself with the numerous exemptions contained in the Directive, which are discussed at para.25–22.

[10] Completing, paras 2.77–2.82; Final Report I, paras 4.57–4.58. Examples of exemptions under the Directive which might be thought inappropriate for private companies were offers to professional investors, as part of takeovers, and of large denomination shares.

restraining the company from making the public offer, and such an order may also be made in unfair prejudice proceedings.[11] The company can clearly escape the effect of this order by converting to public status. Even if the contravention is not picked up until after the offer has been made, the primary order which the court is to make is an order that the company re-register as a public company.[12] Only if the company does not meet the criteria for being a public company, which are not demanding,[13] or if the court thinks it is impractical or undesirable for the company to re-register, does it make another order: either a "remedial order" or an order winding up the company (which is a drastic remedy).[14] A remedial order is aimed at putting the person affected by the contravention of the prohibition in the position he or she would have been in, had there been no contravention.[15] This is a general power, but the Act gives the court, after allotment, a specific power to require a person knowingly concerned in the contravention to purchase the securities at such a price and on such terms as the court may direct.[16] That power may be exercised in favour of a holder of shares who is not the allottee (but a subsequent holder) and against a person knowingly concerned, whether he or she is an officer of the company or not (for example, a third-party adviser, such as an investment bank).[17] The category of subjects of the order includes, of course, the company itself, in which case the court may provide for a reduction in the company's capital.[18] Finally, a private company escapes the prohibition altogether if undertakes in the terms of the offer to re-register as a public company within six months of the date of the offer or if it acts in good faith in pursuance of arrangements under which it is to re-register before the securities are allotted (but, presumably, after they have been offered).[19]

Directors' Authority to Allot Shares[20]

24–4   Issuance of shares by a company involves essentially three steps. First, the company must decide to make an offer of shares, public or non-public, and set the terms of the offer. Secondly, some person or

---

[11] s.757. On unfair prejudice proceedings see Ch.20.
[12] s.758(2).
[13] The main requirement relates to minimum capital: para.11–4.
[14] s.758(2),(3). In this case the member who can apply is one who was a member at the time of the offer or became one as a result of the offer.
[15] s.759.
[16] s.759(3).
[17] s.759(4). Any contrary provision in the company's constitution is also overridden.
[18] s.759(5).
[19] s.755(3),(4). On the meaning of "allotment" see below.
[20] Most of the provisions of the Companies Act 2006 discussed in the rest of this Chapter are scheduled to come into force on October 1, 2009.

persons must agree with the company to take the shares (at which point the shares can be said to have been "allotted"). Thirdly, in implementation of that contract, those persons must take the shares and be made members of the company, thus completing the process of issuance. We shall look at each stage in turn

The first question is whether the decision to allot shares[21] is one for the board alone or whether the shareholders' concurrence is required. We have seen that the company's decision to allot shares ranking along with or even ahead of the company's existing shares does not normally amount to a variation of the rights of the existing share-holders, so that their consent will not be required under the variation of class-rights procedure,[22] even though the practical value of those rights may well be affected by such an issue. Even if the new shares are to rank behind the existing shares, the shareholders may still have doubts about the directors' plans for the use of the finance which will be raised. Thus, it is a matter of some importance whether the Act requires the shareholders' consent to a share issue or whether the matter is left entirely to the company's articles of association. In the latter case it is likely that the board will have the power to issue shares as part of its general management power, and the articles may or may not give the shareholders a role in the decision-making process. Thus, the question becomes whether the Act should make shareholder consent mandatory.

The Second Company Law Directive[23] contains the principle that consent of the shareholders is required, though that principle is quite heavily qualified, notably by the facility for giving permission in advance of the allotment. The Second Directive applies only to public companies, although the Government, when transposing it into domestic law, chose to apply the principle to private companies as well, albeit in a more flexible way. However, the CLR proposed[24] to remove the requirement of shareholder authorisation for the issuance of shares by private companies, except where the company had or the directors' proposal would create more than one class of shares. This would be a default rule, for private companies' articles might restore the requirement of shareholder approval. This reform has been implemented in the Act.[25] The requirement for shareholder consent was thought to be an unnecessary formality in private companies, with their greater overlap of directors and members. However, such overlap would not necessarily obtain, and there would be the risk of greater opportunism, if the company had, or was about to create, more than one class of share.

---

[21] The rules discussed in this section, unlike those relating to public offers, do not apply to debt securities which have no equity element.

[22] See para.19–16.

[23] Council Directive 77/91/EEC, Art.25.

[24] Developing, paras 7.28–7.33.

[25] s.550.

24–5   Except in relation to the private company with only one class of share, however, shareholder consent, in one form or another, is still required for the allotment of shares. Not to obtain it is a criminal offence on the part of the directors knowingly involved,[26] although such failure does not affect the validity of the allotment.[27] The requirement is applied not only to the allotment of shares but also to the grant of rights to subscribe for or to convert a security into shares in the company, for example, a convertible bond.[28] In the latter case, however, the requirement for shareholder approval does not apply at the conversion stage.[29] Two types of allotment or grant are excluded from the requirement for shareholder approval: allotments pursuant to an employees' share scheme and the right to subscribe for or to convert a security into shares already allotted. The latter is presumably because the consent requirement was satisfied on the initial allotment of the share. Thus, if, unusually, a convertible bond is convertible into existing, rather than new, shares of the company, then shareholder consent would not be needed at the allotment stage either.

Such authorisation may take the form of the directors putting before the shareholders a proposal for the issuance of a particular amount of shares to fund a specific project, with full details of how the finance raised will be used. This is authorisation for "a particular use of the power".[30] However, authorisation can be given in advance (i.e. "generally"), either in the articles or by (ordinary) resolution, for (renewable) periods of up to five years.[31] With general authorisation, where no specific use of the power may be under contemplation at the time, information about how the funds raised will be used will necessarily be very general and will be phrased so as to give management maximum freedom of action. However, the authority, whether general or particular, must state the maximum number of securities which can be allotted under it and the date at which the

---

[26] s.549(3)–(4).

[27] s.549(6).

[28] s.549(1). This may help to explain in part why the "shareholder rights plan" or "poison pill" against takeovers is uncommon in the United Kingdom, for the effectiveness of the plan depends heavily upon the directors being able to adopt it without shareholder approval.

[29] s.549(3).

[30] s.551(2). The section does not in terms require details of the use to which the funds will be put to be given to the shareholders. However, if the directors are also seeking authority in relation to the allotment to remove pre-emption rights, they are obliged to put forward a justification: see s.571(6) and fn.61 below. Moreover, the general rules on resolutions at meetings of shareholders may require it. See para.15–39. The resolution need only be an ordinary resolution, even if it amends the company's articles (s.551(8)), but the resolutions must be notified to the Registrar (s.551(9)). Authorisation can be given in the articles, but this is unlikely in the case of "particular" authorisation.

[31] s.551(2), (3), (4). Renewals of authority are to be given by resolution, even if the original authority was contained in the articles: s.551(4)(a). As s.551(7) makes clear, the time limit relates to the directors' authorisation of the share offer, not to the allotment of the shares (which might occur after the time limit had expired). A time limit is required even for particular exercises of the power.

authority will expire.[32] Moreover, the authorisation may be made conditional,[33] and it may be revoked or varied at any time by resolution of the company, even if the original authority was contained in the articles.[34] Little use, however, seems to be made of either of these expressions of shareholder control.

PRE-EMPTIVE RIGHTS

The statutory policy

Whether or not collective shareholder consent is required for allotment of shares, there is an argument that the allotment should not take place in a manner which undermines the position of the existing shareholders, considered individually. This is what the doctrine of pre-emption seeks to achieve. The basic principle underlying the pre-emption rules is that a shareholder should be able to protect his or her proportion of the total equity by having the opportunity to subscribe for any new issue for cash of equity capital or securities having an equity element.[35] In short, the Act requires companies, which wish to raise new capital, in certain circumstances to do so by giving the existing shareholders a "right of first refusal" over the shares on offer. There are two main reasons why a shareholder might wish to exercise this right and thus to prevent the "dilution" of his or her holding of equity shares. First, if new voting shares are issued and a shareholder does not acquire that amount of the new issue which is proportionate to his or her existing holding, that person's influence in the company may be reduced because he or she now has control over a smaller percentage of the votes. In listed companies this is likely to be of concern only to large, often institutional, shareholders. Here, pre-emptive rights operate as a potential limit on the freedom of the directors to effect a shift in the balance of control in the company by issuing new equity shares carrying voting rights.[36]

Secondly, large issues of new shares by a company are likely to be at a discount to the existing market price of the securities, in order to encourage their sale. Once the new shares are allocated, all the shares of the relevant class, new and old, will trade on the market at a price somewhere between the issue price and the previous market price, the

24–6

---

[32] s.551(3). In relation to allotments of rights to subscribe or to convert, what has to be stated is the maximum number of shares that can be allotted pursuant to the rights: s.551(6).

[33] s.551(2).

[34] s.551(4)(b). This will be a case of an ordinary resolution amending the articles. See fn.30 above.

[35] This principle is also to be found in the Second Directive (Art.29) but has again been applied in the UK to some extent to private as well as public companies.

[36] See also para.16–21 on the collateral purposes doctrine which has a similar effect but operates only when the directors' predominant purpose is an improper one.

new market price depending upon the size of the discount and the market's view of the company's plans for its new resources. If an existing shareholder does not acquire the relevant proportion of the new shares, the loss of market value of the existing holding, attributable to the discount, will not be compensated for by the increase in the value of the new shares above the offer price. The new shareholders, in effect, will have been let into the company too cheaply, and the existing shareholders will have paid the price for that decision.[37]

The protection against voting dilution afforded by the pre-emption rules is only partial. The shareholder must also be in a position financially to take up the shares on offer.[38] Full protection against financial dilution can be achieved, however, if the shareholder is able to sell his or her pre-emption rights in the market, where the shareholder does not desire to acquire any new shares. The rights will have a value equal to the difference between the issue price of the new shares and the (higher) price at which the whole class will trade after the issue, which will compensate the shareholder for loss caused to him or her by the difference between the pre-issue market price of the old shares and the (lower) price at which the enlarged class will trade after the new issue.[39] However, for the rights to be marketable they must be transferable to third parties. There is an established way of providing this facility. The company issues a "renounceable" letter of allotment, which enables the shareholder to transfer the right to subscribe for the new shares to a third party, the overall process being known as a "rights issue".[40] The shareholder accepts the right to acquire the new shares and then, at least in a public company, assigns (or "renounces") the right, for payment, to someone who wishes to buy the new shares. In this way, an existing shareholder may compensate himself for the loss in value of his existing shareholding, even if he or she is not in a position to maintain its proportionate size.[41] However, although the Act recognises that the pre-emption right may be effected by means of a rights issue,[42] it does not seem to require it, i.e. the company may simply make what is usually termed an "open"

---

[37] See the distinction drawn between the loss suffered by the company and that by the shareholders when shares are issued for an inadequate consideration in *Pilmer v Duke Group Ltd* [2001] 2 B.C.L.C. 773, Aus. HC.

[38] In the case of small companies, the shareholder may be able to challenge the decision to issue new shares under the unfair prejudice procedure. See *A Company, Re* [1986] B.C.L.C. 362 and *Sam Weller Ltd, Re* [1990] Ch. 682.

[39] For a worked example of this analysis see Bank of England, *Guidance on Share Issuing*, 1999, Technical Annex.

[40] See para.25–14.

[41] A third course of action is for the shareholder to sell part of the rights so as to maintain the value of his or her shareholding in the company (but not the proportion of the shares held), i.e. to compensate for the drop in market value caused by the issue at a discount. This action is called, obscurely, "tail-swallowing". The "discount" referred to in this discussion is, of course, a discount to the prevailing market price of the shares, not to their par value, which is not permitted (see para.11–10, above).

[42] See the reference to renouncement of rights to allotment in s.561(2).

offer to its existing shareholders. It is, however, common practice in listed companies for pre-emption offers to be made on a renounceable basis.[43]

The scope of the right

The ambit of the pre-emptive provisions extends only to issues for cash of "equity securities". These are defined as ordinary shares (and rights to subscribe for or convert securities into ordinary shares); and an ordinary share is any share other than one where the holder's right to participate in a distribution (whether by way of dividend or return of capital) is limited by reference to a fixed amount.[44] It does not matter whether the shares carry votes or not, and in fact it can be argued that pre-emption rights are particularly important for the holders of non-voting shares, who will obtain no protection from the rules on shareholder authorisation discussed in the previous section. Certain types of share issue are excluded from the pre-emption rules, even if they arguably involve the issue of equity shares for cash: bonus shares (where the pre-emption problem does not arise)[45] or shares to be held under an employees' share scheme.[46] Nor do the rules apply to shares taken by subscribers on the formation of a company.[47]

However, pre-emption rights will be triggered only if the proposed issue is exclusively for cash;[48] when it is proposed to allot ordinary shares as consideration payable to the vendor on the acquisition of a business or real property, it would be impossible to make an offer to the existing shareholders on the same terms. Nevertheless, the restriction of the statutory pre-emption provisions to cash issues, even if compelled by necessity, does make a severe hole in the principle of protecting shareholders against dilution, especially dilution of their voting position. In relation to financial dilution some alternative

24-7

---

[43] For further discussion see E. Ferran, "Legal Capital Rules and Modern Securities Markets" in Hopt and Wymeersch (eds), *Capital Markets and Company Law* (Oxford: OUP, 2003).

[44] s.560(1). There is no upper limit to this amount (and it would be impracticable to set one) with the result that it is possible to prescribe amounts so high that the holders would in fact be entitled to the whole or the lion's share of the equity (unless subsequent issues were made) without affording them pre-emptive rights.

[45] s.564. See para.11–18. Since issuance of a bonus share involves the capitalisation of the company's reserves, no payment by shareholders is involved and the shares must be allotted pro-rata to those entitled to the reserve, were it distributed, or, in the case of an undistributable reserve, whose contributions constituted the reserve (as in the case of the share premium account).

[46] s.566. Even if those scheme members may be entitled to renounce or assign their rights so that, if they do, the shares when allotted will not be "held in pursuance of the scheme". Employees' share schemes would be unworkable if every time a further allotment was to be made pursuant to them all equity shareholders had to be offered pre-emptive rights. If, however, equity shares have been allotted under the scheme, the employee holders should have the same rights to protect their proportion of equity as any other shareholder.

[47] s.577. Indeed, it is difficult to see how the rules could be so applied.

[48] s.565.

protection is provided by Chapter 6 of Part 17, requiring an independent valuation report in the case of share issues by public companies for a non-cash consideration,[49] but, even so, that section does not confer individual rights upon shareholders in the way that the pre-emption rules do.

24–8 Moreover, the exclusion of issues which are wholly or partly other than for cash gives rise to possibilities of manipulation so as to avoid the pre-emption rules. For example, if any part of the consideration, even a minor part, is not cash, then it appears that the pre-emption rules are excluded. This may be of particular interest to private companies. In other cases it may well be possible to restructure the transaction so that the cash is provided otherwise than to the issuer in exchange for its shares. Thus, where company A wishes to acquire part of the business of company B, the latter wishing to receive cash, the obvious way to proceed would be for company A to issue new shares to raise the necessary money, if it does not have sufficient available cash, thus attracting the pre-emption provisions. Instead, however, company A may issue its shares to company B, in exchange for the latter's assets and thus without attracting the pre-emption provisions, company A having previously arranged for an investment bank to offer to buy the shares from company B at a fixed price and to place them with interested investors. Such a "vendor placing" gives company B the cash it wanted, whilst relieving company A of the need to abide by the pre-emption rules.[50]

The pre-emption obligation on the company is that it may not allot equity securities to any person unless it has first offered, on the same or more favourable terms, to each person who holds shares covered by the right a proportion of those equity securities which is as nearly as practicable equal to the shareholder's existing proportion in nominal value of the existing shares. Only if the period for the existing shareholders to accept the offer has expired (at least 21 days)[51] without the offer being accepted (or if it was positively rejected within this period) may an offer be made to outsiders.[52] If the

---

[49] See above, para.11–15. But the Chapter does not apply to private companies or to share issues even by public companies in connection with takeover offers or mergers, where there is in fact a considerable risk of financial dilution. Listed companies are somewhat more tightly regulated. Where a listed company proposes to enter into a transaction involving the issue of equity shares for a consideration (whether in cash or otherwise) equivalent to 25 per cent or more of the existing market value of its equity shares, that will be a "Class 1" transaction and the prior approval of the shareholders will be required: Listing Rules 9.5.

[50] It is difficult to regard this scheme with great disapprobation, since, if company B had been prepared to take the shares of company A in exchange for its assets, no question of pre-emption would have arisen. A legitimate concern of the existing shareholders in such a case arises if the shares are placed with their new holders at a discount to the market price. For listed companies, the Listing Rules restrict the discount to 10 percent, unless the shareholders have approved something larger: LR 9.5.10.

[51] s.562(5). Nor can the offer be withdrawn, once made: s.562(4).

[52] s.561(1). Treasury shares are excluded from the calculations required by this section: s.561(4). The details of how communication is to be made with the shareholders are set out in s.562.

pre-emptive offer is not accepted in full, shares not taken up may be allotted to anyone; accepting existing shareholders do not have to be given further pre-emptive rights in respect of those unaccepted shares

Waiver

However, despite the above, the statutory pre-emptive rights are far from being entrenched; in certain circumstances they can be excluded or disapplied. As far as exclusion is concerned, under section 567 the need to offer pre-emptive rights (or a provision relating to the method of offering, most likely the time during which the offer must be open) may be excluded by a provision in the articles of a private company— either generally or in relation to allotments of a particular description.[53] In relation to public companies exclusion is available only where the articles provide a pre-emption alternative to the statutory scheme. This provision is designed to deal with situations where the company has more than one class of ordinary share.[54] The statutory pre-emption obligation[55] is drafted in such a way as not to differentiate among different classes of ordinary shares, so that an offer of ordinary shares of one class would have to be made pre-emptively to all classes of ordinary shareholder. Section 568 permits a company to substitute an alternative pre-emption right in its articles which operates on a class basis. Non-compliance with the procedure in the articles carries the same consequences as non-compliance with the statutory procedure.[56]

24–9

More significant are the disapplication provisions. Disapplication differs slightly from exclusion in that disapplication gives the directors a discretion whether to use the statutory pre-emption procedure, to modify it, or not to use it at all. By section 569 the articles or a special resolution of a private company with only one class of shares may give the directors power to issue shares as if the pre-emption right (or some aspect of it) did not apply.[57] This complements the provision, discussed above, permitting the authorisation of the directors to issue shares without collective shareholder consent. In the case of public companies (or private companies with more than one class of share) the disapplication provisions are more restricted but still much more generous than the exclusion provisions relating to public companies. As we shall see below, it has been the unwillingness of the institutional shareholders to give management the freedom which full use of the disapplication provisions for public companies

---

[53] A provision in the memorandum or articles which is inconsistent with ss.561 or 562 has effect as an exclusion of that subsection: s.567(3).

[54] s.568. The problem does not arise if the other classes of share are not ordinary but preference shares, because they will not benefit from a pre-emption right.

[55] s.561.

[56] ss.568(4),(5), on which see below.

[57] Note that, where there is another class of share, the facility is not available, whether the other class of share is ordinary or preferred.

would entail, that has been a subject of considerable controversy and a public investigation in recent years.

24–10   The position for public companies differs according to the extent of the authority which has been conferred on the directors to allot shares under the provisions discussed above. If the directors are authorised generally, they may also be given power, by the articles or by a special resolution, to allot equity securities as if the statutory pre-emption right did not apply or applied with such modifications as the directors determine.[58] When they are authorised, whether generally or in relation to a particular allotment, the company may resolve by special resolution that the statutory pre-emption right shall not apply to a specified allotment under that authority or shall apply with such modifications as are specified in the resolution.[59] In either event, the power to disapply pre-emption rights ceases with the expiration or revocation of the authority conferred under the above provisions,[60] though it can be renewed by special resolution when, and to the extent that, the authority is renewed. This means that pre-emption rights may be disapplied for periods up to five years—the maximum period for which directors may be given sole authority to allot shares. However, a special resolution in relation to a specified allotment may not be proposed unless it has been recommended by the directors, and there is circulated a written statement by the directors of their reasons for making the recommendation, the amount to be paid to the company in respect of the proposed issue, and the directors' justification of that amount.[61] A person, director or otherwise, who knowingly or recklessly authorises or permits the inclusion in the statement of information which is misleading, false or deceptive commits a criminal offence.[62]

Finally, there may be disapplication in relation to treasury shares.[63] The sale of treasury shares is caught in principle by the statutory pre-emption right.[64] However, the directors may be given power to allot free of that right, either generally (by the articles or by special resolution) or in relation to a specified allotment (by special resolution).[65] The point about this provision is that it allows disapplication of pre-emption rights, even though the directors have not been authorised

---

[58] s.570(1)—whereupon "the provisions of this Chapter have effect accordingly", i.e. only to the extent that they are consistent with the disapplication in the articles or resolution.

[59] s.571.

[60] ss.570(3) and 571(3).

[61] ss.571(5)–(7). The Listing Rules also require a resolution effecting a general disapplication of pre-emption rights to be accompanied by a circular stating the maximum amount of equity securities the disapplication will cover and the percentage of the ordinary share capital that represents: LR 13.8.2. The Act has no specific disclosure requirements for general dis-applications, the only limit being the amount the directors are authorised to issue without shareholder approval.

[62] s.572.

[63] On which see above at para.13–17.

[64] s.560(2)(b).

[65] s.573.

under the above provisions to issue shares without shareholder consent. This provision is necessary technically, because shareholder consent to issuance is not required in principle for the sale of treasury shares, so that, without it, the company would always have to apply pre-emption to sales of treasury shares. Moreover, one of the arguments for permitting treasury shares was that it gave companies freedom to raise relatively small amounts of capital quickly, which a pre-emption right would hinder, so that it seems correct policy to facilitate the disapplication of the pre-emption right.[66]

Sanctions

A civil (but not a criminal) sanction is provided by the Act. When there has been a contravention of the pre-emption right (either by not providing it all or by not providing it in the way required by the Act), the company and every officer of it who knowingly authorised or permitted the contravention are jointly and severally liable to compensate any person to whom an offer should have been made for any loss, damage, costs or expenses.[67] Where under the provisions discussed immediately above, the statutory provisions are applied in a modified way, these sanctions will equally apply to a contravention of the modified provisions.[68] The Act does not invalidate an allotment of shares made in breach of the pre-emption provisions, no doubt in order to protect the legitimate interests of third parties. However, in *Thundercrest Ltd, Re*[69] the judge was prepared to rectify the register[70] as against the directors of a small company, with only three shareholders, where the directors responsible for the breach of the pre-emption provisions had allotted the shares in dispute to themselves.

24–11

Listed companies

Where the company is listed on the Stock Exchange the protection afforded shareholders is greater than under the Act. First, the Listing Rules require a listed company to obtain the consent of its shareholders if any of its major subsidiaries makes an issue for cash of securities having an equity element which would dilute the percentage equity interest of the company and its shareholders in that subsidiary in a major way, i.e. would be equivalent to a disposal of one-quarter

24–12

---

[66] However, existing shareholders in listed companies are protected against dilution by the imposition of a limit of 10 percent to any discount applied on the sale of the treasury shares: LR 9.5.10.

[67] s.562. Proceedings must be commenced within two years of the filing of the relevant return of allotments or, where rights to subscribe or convert are granted, within two years from the grant: s.563(3). As noted, the same applies to contraventions of the substitute right in the company's articles relating to classes of ordinary shares: s.568(4), (5).

[68] ss.569(2), 570(2), 571(2), 573(3),(5).

[69] [1995] 1 B.C.L.C. 117.

[70] See para.27–19.

or more of the assets of the group.[71] This is really an expression of the policy, considered elsewhere, that major transactions require the company's consent.[72] Secondly, and rather at the other end of the scale, while both the Act and the Listing Rules allow fractional entitlements to be ignored,[73] they differ as regards the treatment of rights that are not taken up. The effect of the Act is that the shares concerned may then be offered to anybody. Under the Listing Rules regarding rights issues, the rights must normally be sold for the benefit of the non-accepting shareholders.[74] However, where the amount to which the shareholders will be entitled is small, they may be sold for the benefit of the company or, if no premium exists, allotted to the underwriters.[75]

A final difference between the Act and the Listing Rules is that the latter specifically permit pre-emptive offers to exclude holders whom the company considers "necessary or expedient to exclude from the offer on account of the laws or regulatory requirements of another territory".[76] The nearest approach to this in the Act is the provision to the effect that the statutory pre-emption obligation on the company is "without prejudice" to any enactment by virtue of which the company is prohibited (either generally or in specified circumstances) from offering or allotting equity securities to any person.[77] This, however, is designed to make it clear that an offer must not be made to those whose shares are subject to a restriction order under the Act;[78] for the situation at which the Listing Rule is directed, companies have to rely on the "as nearly as practicable" in section 561 and the decision in *Mutual Life Insurance of N.Y. v Rank Organisation*.[79]

Pre-emption guidelines

24–13   The overall picture which emerges of the above analysis is that the individual rights to participate in share issues, which the Act apparently creates, may be quite easily removed by collective decision

---

[71] LR 10.2.8.

[72] See para.14–8.

[73] s.561(1) (which only requires the offer to be "*as nearly as practicable*" equal to his proportion). Hence, if there is a one-for-ten rights issue, a shareholder with, say, 475 shares will be offered only 47 new shares.

[74] Listing Rule 9.5.4.

[75] LR 9.5.4.

[76] LR 9.3.12. This is primarily designed to deal with the situation where a company has shareholders resident in the USA. Under the Federal securities legislation it may have to register with the SEC if it extends the offer to such shareholders. Hence the present practice is to exclude such shareholders and to preclude those to whom the offer is made from renouncing in favour of a US resident. This practice was upheld in *Mutual Life Insurance of N.Y. v Rank Organisation* [1985] B.C.L.C. 11, but a fairer arrangement would surely be for the rights of the American shareholders to be sold for their benefit?

[77] s.574.

[78] On which see paras 28–49ff, above.

[79] See fn.76. Nor is it clear that the Second Directive permits this exception unless Art.42 can be construed as qualifying the obligation laid down in Art.29.

of the shareholders, and this remains true of listed companies, even though the Listing Rules are more alert to possible opportunism in relation to the removal of the pre-emption requirement. So the matter becomes one of collective shareholder decision whether to displace the prima facie rule in favour of pre-emption which the Act creates. This is an area in which the growth of institutional shareholding[80] has made itself felt. Institutional shareholders are strongly opposed to dilution of their position, both in relation to voting and the value of the shares held, without their individual consent. In addition to influencing the Listing Rules on this matter, they have agreed, as members of the Pre-emption Group, informal guidelines, originally under the auspices of the Stock Exchange but now under those of the Financial Reporting Council. These guidelines express institutional shareholder unwillingness to vote for disapplication of pre-emption rights in companies quoted on the Main Market of the London Stock Exchange to the full extent permitted by the Act. The guidelines have no legal status but they articulate a strongly held and practically significant attitude about the value of pre-emption rights. This policy of the institutional investors has turned the pre-emption requirement in the Act into a good example of a "strong" default rule whose alteration creates a significant hurdle for the management of the company. The default (pre-emption) is removable only with share-holder consent (and within the rather lax confines set by the Act) but that consent is difficult to obtain for extensive disapplications of the default. Thus, the statutory provisions have much more bite because of the difficulty of securing shareholder consent to their disapplica-tion. On the other hand, the statutory rules remain important because they impose the default rule and thus make available to the institu-tional shareholders the opportunity to vote for or against particular disapplication proposals. If there were no statutory default, the institutional shareholders would face the more demanding task of securing an amendment to a company's articles of association, introducing a pre-emption right.[81]

The guidelines were adopted initially in 1987, and so they are by no means a novelty.[82] They have always been unpopular with some types of company and, especially, among the investment banks, on the grounds that they hinder access to cheaper sources of equity finance than the existing shareholder body. Eventually, the Government asked Paul Myners to review them and his report in 2005 sub-stantially supported them.[83] He was particularly impressed by the

---

[80] See further above, paras 15–10ff.

[81] Hence the reported opposition of the institutional investors to the removal of the pre-emption requirement from the Second Directive: *Financial Times*, UK edition, October 22, 2007, p.18 and *ibid.* October 23, 2007, p.23. Of course, the removal of the right from the Second Directive would not prevent the UK from maintaining the statutory default.

[82] The original pre-emption guidelines are set out in Monopolies and Mergers Commission, *Underwriting services for share offers*, Cm. 4168 (1999), App.3.1.

[83] DTI, *Pre-Emption Rights: Final Report*, February 2005 (URN 05/679).

corporate governance argument in favour of pre-emption. This is that this doctrine makes it difficult for a management, which has failed its existing shareholders, to obtain finance from a new group of investors, letting them into the company cheaply (and at the expense of the existing investors) as part of an implicit bargain to back the existing management against the complaints of the first group of investors. By contrast, pre-emption makes management seeking further equity finance sensitive to the views of the existing investors from whom it must be raised. However, he did criticise the guidelines for having become too rigid, i.e. as being in danger of being regarded by all concerned as rules rather than guidance which might be set aside if a company had a good case for disapplication, even though that case did not fit within the guidelines.

The 1987 guidelines were replaced in consequence by new guidelines in 2006, now called a Statement of Principles.[84] The Principles do indeed put much more emphasis on the factors which might be relevant to a decision on the part of institutional shareholders[85] to vote in favour of a disapplication not falling within the type of disapplication regarded as routine—although they make almost no commitments as to outcome in any particular non-standard case. Thus, companies know that obtaining institutional shareholder support for disapplication in non-routine cases will still be hard work. Companies will therefore often seek to remain within the routine classification, where the institutional investors will normally support management's proposals without extensive scrutiny of the reasoning behind them. A routine disapplication is one where the company is seeking to raise on a non-pre-emptive basis no more 5 per cent of the ordinary share capital of the company in any one year and no more than 7.5 per cent in any rolling period of three years, and restricts the discount to 5 per cent of the market price.[86] It is notable that the 2006 Principles do not repeat in terms a provision from the original guidelines to the effect that, in strong contrast with what is permitted by the Act, institutional investors will support disapplication resolutions, even of a routine nature, only if they run from one AGM to the next (and certainly not for a period of five years). Perhaps, this practice has become so ingrained among listed companies that the point did not need emphasising in 2006. What is abundantly clear from the Principles is that, where the institutional shareholders hold sway, the company will have no chance of securing a general, large-scale disapplication of the pre-emption requirement. The Principles envisage non-routine resolutions being supported only in the context

---

[84] Available on: http://www.pre-emptiongroup.org.uk/principles/index.htm.
[85] The Principles are supported by the Association of British Insurers, the National Association of Pension Funds and the Investment Management Association.
[86] Principles, paras 8–11. These were the figures set in 1987 and they still obtain.

of a specific project, where the need for non-pre-emptive finance can be demonstrated and justified.[87]

THE TERMS OF ISSUE

As noted in the previous Chapter,[88] the rights attached to the shares to be issued are likely to be set out in the company's constitution. What will not be set out there is the price or other consideration to be asked in exchange for the shares. Here the directors have a free hand, subject to the rules on capital maintenance discussed in Chapter 11.[89] As far as private companies are concerned, these rules are not demanding, consisting mainly of the rules on commissions and requiring shares not to be issued at a discount to their nominal value (not to be confused with a discount to the market price, against which the pre-emption right, as we have just seen, aims to provide protection). With regard to public companies, the rules, implementing the Second Directive, are more constraining, though they have recently been relaxed somewhat.

24–14

ALLOTMENT

The process by which the company finds someone who is willing to become a shareholder of the company is not something about which the law says very much if there is no offer to the public of the company's shares[90]—although, as we shall see in the next Chapter, this is in fact now a very heavily regulated area, if there is a public offer. What the Act does assume is that the process of becoming a shareholder is a two-step one, involving first a contract of allotment and then registration of the member. As Lord Templeman said in 1995:

24–15

> "The Act of 1985 preserves the distinction in English law between an enforceable contract for the issue of shares (which contract is constituted by an allotment) and the issue of shares which is completed by registration. Allotment confers a right to be registered. Registration confers [legal] title."[91]

---

[87] Principles, para.17.
[88] See above, para.23–6.
[89] See above, paras 11–10ff.
[90] The general common law rules on fraud, misrepresentation and negligence will provide some protection to investors: see paras 25–35ff, below.
[91] *National Westminster Bank Plc v IRC* [1995] 1 A.C. 111 at 126, HL. From this, Lord Templeman reasoned that shares were not "issued" (the Companies Act does not define the term) for the purposes of a taxing statute until the applicants for the shares were registered as members of the company.

This is consistent with the Act which defines the point at which shares are allotted as the time when a person acquires the unconditional right to be included in the register of members, but does not require actual entry in the register to meet the definition.[92] In the case of a private company the processes of agreement and registration will be achieved with little formality and without the issue of allotment letters. If someone wants to become a shareholder and the company wants him to, he will be entered on the register and issued with a share certificate without more ado.

However, the advantage of constituting the agreement to become a member in a formal letter of allotment is that it facilitates the process we described above in relation to pre-emption rights[93] of "renouncing" the entitlement to be registered as a member in favour of someone else, though the technique is not confined to rights issues. Printed on the back of the letter there will be forms enabling, for the duration of a short specified period, the allottee to renounce the right to be registered as a member and the person to whom they are ultimately renounced to confirm that he or she accepts the renunciation and agrees to be entered on the register. Normally the original allottee will not insert the name of the person to whom they are to be renounced and the effect is then to produce something similar to a short-term share-warrant to bearer.[94] It is not a negotiable instrument but once the renunciation is signed by the original allottee, the rights can be assigned by manual delivery of the allotment letter without a formal transfer. Before the stated period ends, however, it will be necessary for the name of the ultimate holder to be inserted, a signature obtained, and the allotment letter lodged with the company or its Registrars.

Implementing Article 28 of the Second Directive, the Act lays down a default rule for public companies that no allotment of shares shall be made pursuant to an offer to subscribe[95] for shares (whether the offer is to the public or not) unless the shares on offer are taken up in full.[96] This rule is designed to prevent an investor ending up holding shares in a company which is less fully capitalised than was expected when the offer was accepted. If a full take-up of the shares is not achieved within 40 days of making the offer, the money[97] received from the offerees becomes repayable in full, though without interest,[98] and must actually be repaid within a further eight days. The sanction

---

[92] s.558.

[93] See above, para.24–6. Of course, a private company may not want to grant this facility, which might be inconsistent with its articles (see para.27–7 below). The statutory scheme of pre-emption rights does not *require* renouncing to be made available.

[94] See below.

[95] The section thus does not apply to offers for sale of shares (see para.25–11) and does not need to because the issue has been in effect underwritten.

[96] s.578(1). In fact, however, the rule has a much longer pedigree: CA1948, s.47.

[97] The rule applies, *mutatis mutandis*, where the consideration for the offer is wholly or partly otherwise than in cash: s.578(4),(5).

[98] s.578(2).

for this latter requirement is that the directors then become jointly and severally liable to repay the money, with interest.[99] If the company actually proceeds with an allotment in breach of the Act then the allotment is voidable by the offeree within one month of the allotment (even if the company is in course of winding up),[100] and any director who knowingly contravenes or permits the contravention on the prohibition on allotment becomes liable to compensate the allottee and the company for any loss, damages, costs or expenses.[101] Despite these fearsome sanctions, the rule is not enormously important in practice, for two reasons. First, if the offer in terms says that the allotment will proceed, even if not fully subscribed, or will proceed if conditions falling short of full subscription are met, the prohibition on allotment does not apply.[102] So, the rule is really one which requires only that the investors be told what risk they run in relation to the take-up of the offer. Secondly, in relation to offers to the public, failure to achieve a full take-up of the offer is a serious matter, not only for the investors, but also for the issuer, so that companies will arrange for the offer to be "underwritten" in some way (i.e. normally that an investment bank agrees to take up the shares which are not bought by the public).[103]

Once the shares have been allotted, the company must make a return of allotment to the Registrar of companies, as discussed in the previous Chapter.[104]

REGISTRATION

As Lord Templeman indicated, allotment does not make a person a member of the company. Entry in the register of members is also needed to give the allottee legal title to the shares. Section 112(2) says explicitly that a person "who agrees to become a member of the company and whose name is entered on the register of members is a member of the company".[105] The Act now requires registration "as

24–16

---

[99] s.578(3). A director can escape liability if it can be shown that the failure was not due to misconduct or negligence on the director's part.

[100] s.579(1),(2). This means the assets contributed by the allottee are taken out of the insolvent company's estate, but only if the allotee acts within the one-month period.

[101] s.579(3), subject to a two-year limitation period: s.579(4).

[102] s.578(1)(b)—or if the offer is stated to be subject only to certain conditions (such as a 75 per cent acceptance) and those conditions are met.

[103] See para.25–11.

[104] At para.23–6.

[105] On which, see *Nuneaton Football Club, Re* [1989] B.C.L.C. 454, CA, holding that "agreement" requires only assent to become a member. The subscribers to the memorandum of association (above, para.4–15) are the first members of the company and should be entered on its register of members, but in their case it appears that they become members, whether this is done or not: *Evans' Case* (1867) L.R. 2 Ch.App. 247; *Baytrust Holdings Ltd v IRC* [1971] 1 W.L.R. 1333 at 1355–1356.

soon as practicable" and in any event within two months of the date of allotment, except in the case of share warrants (see below).[106] Even when registered, the shareholder will find difficulty in selling the shares, if they are to be held in certificated form, until a share certificate is received from the company. If the shares are to be held in uncertificated form,[107] then by definition no share certificate will be issued. Instead, the company, by computer instruction, will inform the operator of the electronic transfer system of the identity of those to whom the shares have been allotted and of the number of shares issued to each person.[108] The lapse of time between allotment and registration in the share register by informing the operator of the electronic transfer system of what the company has done should be very much shorter than the gap between allotment and the issue of share certificates, where the Act gives the company up to two months to complete the process.[109]

Bearer shares

24–17   A major exception in principle, though much less so in practice, to the requirement of entry on the register in order to become a member of the company is created by share-warrants to bearer. Section 779 provides that a company, if so authorised by its articles, may issue with respect to any fully paid shares a warrant stating that the bearer of the warrant is entitled to the shares specified in it. If similarly authorised, it may provide, by coupons attached to the warrant or otherwise, for the payment of future dividends.[110] Title to the shares specified then passes by manual delivery of the warrant,[111] which is a negotiable instrument.[112] On their issue, the company removes from its register of members the name of the former registered holder and merely states the fact and date of the issue of the warrant and the number of shares to which it relates.[113] The bearer of the warrant from time to time is unquestionably a shareholder but to what extent, if at all, he is a member of the company depends on a provision to

---

[106] s.554. Failure to register is a criminal offence on the part of the company and every officer in default.
[107] See Ch.27.
[108] Uncertificated Securities Regulations 2001 (SI 2001/3755), reg.34.
[109] s.769.
[110] s.779(3). Share-warrants to bearer must be distinguished from what is perhaps the more common type of warrant, which gives the holder the right to subscribe for shares in the company at a specific price on a particular date or within a particular period. Such warrants are a form of long-term call option over the company's shares. They may be traded, but their transfer simply gives the transferee the option and does not make him or her a member until the option is exercised.
[111] s.779(2).
[112] *Webb, Hale & Co v Alexandria Water Co* (1905) 21 T.L.R. 572.
[113] s.122(1). However, as recommended by the CLR, it is no longer necessary that the share be issued in nominal form and then converted into a warrant. Share warrants may be issued directly.

that effect in the articles.[114] Hence shareholding and membership are not necessarily coterminous if share warrants are issued. However, again subject to the articles, the bearer of the warrant is entitled, on surrendering it for cancellation, to have his name and shareholding re-entered on the register.[115] In practice this exception is unimportant because bearer securities have never been popular with British investors or British companies and are rarely issued and hardly ever in respect of shares, as opposed to bearer bonds (i.e. debentures) which are sometimes issued to attract continental investors who have a traditional liking for securities in bearer form. It is fortunate that bearer shares are such a rarity for, if they became common, it would play havoc with many provisions of the Act.[116]

CONCLUSION

Where a company makes a non-public offer of shares, a situation which will necessarily include most share offers by private companies, the rules discussed above are all that the company will need to concern itself with. Where, however, a public offer of shares is to be made, the extensive regulation considered in the next Chapter will come into play. Even then, the relevant regulation is additional to the rules considered in this Chapter and, though it may supplement, does not replace them. In fact, rules discussed in this Chapter, for example those relating to pre-emption rights, can be very important in public offers, but the point is that such rules are not confined to public offers but apply to share issues of a non-public type as well. Protection of the position of existing shareholders through pre-emption is as important in a private as in a public company, indeed arguably more so in the absence of a market upon which the shares of a disgruntled shareholder can be disposed of. **24–18**

---

[114] s.122(3).
[115] s.122(4).
[116] e.g. those relating to purchase of own shares (see Ch.12, above) and especially, those relating to disclosure of share-ownership and dealings: see Ch.26, below).

CHAPTER 25

PUBLIC OFFERS OF SHARES

INTRODUCTION

This Chapter is concerned with a subject which takes us into the area **25–1**
of securities regulation or capital markets law. Nevertheless, it is not
a subject which books on company law can ignore; students of that
subject need to have some understanding of how public companies go
about raising their share capital from the investing public and of the
legal regulations that have to be complied with when they do. An
elaborate discussion of this specialised branch of legal practice is
inappropriate in a book of this sort but an outline is essential.

Public offers and introductions to public markets
There are two distinct, though usually combined, operations which **25–2**
may take place when a large company seeks to raise finance from the

investing public. In the first place, it needs to make its case to those people who may be interested in investing in it by purchasing its shares. As we shall see below, the company may choose among a number of different ways of putting itself before investors. The most heavily regulated of these methods is the public offer of securities, simply because the company addresses its publicity to a wide range of persons and thus may include the ill-informed and the gullible among the addressees as well as the experienced and well-informed. As we shall see, the law regulates heavily the document (the "prospectus") by which such a public offer is made. From this perspective, the law relating to prospectuses can be viewed as a branch of consumer protection legislation, but one in which the product on offer is very difficult to evaluate, because the value of shares depends heavily upon the future performance of the company and cannot be identified, as with a motor car, for example, by visual inspection and a test drive.

It will normally be the case that a company seeking to raise substantial funds from investors will also secure that the shares to be issued will be admitted to trading on a public securities market, such as one of the markets operated by the London Stock Exchange or perhaps an exchange elsewhere. The reason the company will normally take this extra step is that the willingness of investors to buy its shares will be increased if there is a liquid market upon which those shares can be traded after they have been issued. As we have seen, a shareholder is normally "locked into" the company after the shares have been purchased, in the sense that the investor, short of winding up, cannot require the company to buy back the shares, even at the later prevailing market price, except in the case of some types of redeemable share. Therefore, a shareholder who wishes to liquidate his or her investment will normally be constrained to find another investor who would like to purchase the shares. A liquid securities market upon which the shares are traded will facilitate this operation, to the benefit of both investors and the company, which is likely to be able to sell its securities at a higher price if they are admitted to trading on a public exchange.

The admission of shares to trading on a public market is thus a matter in which both companies and investors have a strong interest, and some of the rules in this area are designed to ensure that that interest is not arbitrarily denied by those who operate the relevant public market. However, the admission of shares to trading on an exchange also involves putting those shares before the investing public, since it is now open to the public to acquire the company's securities, this time not directly from the company but from those who already hold the shares. Hence, there is a strong argument for having the same information disclosure upon admission of securities to a public market as when the company offers its securities directly to the public. In fact, for the reasons given, when a company engages in a public offer it normally ensures that the securities on offer will immediately be tradeable on a public exchange, so one set of documentation may do, more or less, for both purposes. However, there is no legal requirement that these two operations occur at the same time or that both take place. A company may offer its shares to the public without securing their admission to public market (for example, where it does not expect or want the securities to be traded to any significant degree and so is content to rely on sellers seeking out potential purchasers privately). Or the driving force[1] behind the admission of the securities to the market may be an existing large shareholder (for example, the Government in a de-nationalisation issue) which wishes to liquidate or reduce its holding, but the company does not intend at that time to make a public offer of further shares in the company.

Our main concern in this Chapter is with the financing of the company and the public offer of securities as a form of corporate finance. Consequently, the core transaction which we examine is one in which the company both makes a public offer of its shares and, at the same time, secures the admission of the securities to trading on a public market.

Types of regulation

We have referred above to the law relating to public offers as con-   **25–3**
sumer law and that is a very strong strand in the thinking of those responsible for the rules in this area. However, it would be wrong to see the regulation as nothing but a form of consumer protection. In fact, scholarship today stresses the function of regulation in this area as a way of promoting "allocative efficiency", that is, of promoting the direction by investors of their funds on the basis of an accurate understanding of the risk and reward profile of particular projects which the issuance of the shares will finance. This object is not only in the interests of investors but of companies and of the economy generally, for effective regulation promotes the allocation of scarce investment resources to the projects with the highest returns. But what sort of regulation will best achieve that objective?

It is conventional in this branch of law to make a distinction between "merit" regulation and disclosure of information. Under the former approach, a regulator permits an offer to be made to the public only if the securities on offer or the issuer pass certain quality tests, whereas the latter simply puts information in the hands of investors and leaves it up to them to make up their own minds. Although the initial regulation of public offers (at State level in the

---

[1] Securities cannot be admitted to the official list (see below) without the consent of the issuer (FSMA 2000, s.75(2)), but the impetus for the listing may come from the shareholder.

United States) adopted the merit regulation approach,[2] the disclosure approach has been the predominant one in all jurisdictions since its adoption by federal US law in the great reforms of 1933 and 1934.[3] However, disclosure has never driven out all elements of merit regulation. Although what is required varies as from market to market, disclosure is never all that is required. As a Canadian committee once remarked, with heavy irony, "it would be improbable that a securities commission in a disclosure regime would approve a prospectus that said, truthfully, that the promoters of the company intended to abscond with the proceeds of the public offering, or that the company's business enterprise had no hope of success."[4] Thus, elements of merit regulation, sometimes referred to in the UK as "eligibility requirements", survive in even the most disclosure-oriented regime.

The reason for the triumph of disclosure as the predominant regulatory philosophy in this area is probably a consequence of the decision the investor has to make. A prospective subscriber to the ordinary shares to be issued by a company is essentially making a judgment about the company's prospects in the future in relation to the price asked for the shares. This involves, among other things, taking a view about how the industry in which the company is active will evolve and about the qualities of the company's management. Nobody can be sure about the future and those responsible for merit regulation are likely to shy away from any appearance that they are giving a guarantee about the company's future success. Merit regulation thus tends to focus on past facts (for example, the company's recent trading history) which, whilst relevant, is not necessarily the most relevant information for the decision the investor has to take. Moreover, merit regulation may exclude from making an offer a company whose track record is not good but which has a perfectly decent story to tell about its future. Even disclosure of information does not make the investor's task easy, because the one piece of hard information the investor requires—what will be the issuer's financial results in the future?—is by definition not available. However, information about the company's present and recent activities and about the terms of the securities on offer, together with some judicious forward-looking information, can help to guide the investment decision, even if it cannot take all risk out of the process. Indeed, if all risk could be eliminated, there would be no need for equity finance in the first place.

25–4 A further question, which has been hotly debated, about the disclosure regime is whether production of the requisite level of infor-

---

[2] Often referred to as "blue sky laws" because the securities on offer were backed, it was said, only by the blue sky. The first significant State law in the US seems to have been that of Kansas in 1911.

[3] The Securities Act 1933 and the Securities Exchange Act 1934.

[4] Toronto Stock Exchange, *Toward Improved Disclosure*, Interim Report of the Committee on Corporate Disclosure, 1995, para.3.9.

mation requires mandatory disclosure rules. It can be argued that, a prospectus being a selling document, those companies with good stories to tell would make full disclosure of information and use private "bonding" mechanisms (such as certification by independent third parties) to convince investors of the truth of what they say. Companies with less good stories would follow suit, for fear that investors would deduce from inadequate disclosure that the prospects for the company were dire. Only companies with truly dire prospects would make inadequate disclosure and investors would draw the correct conclusions from such inadequate prospectuses. Whether this theory works in practice seems never to have been tested satisfactorily, but even if self-interest would generate extensive disclosure, mandatory disclosure rules have certain advantages over leaving it to the issuers to decide for themselves. First, the sanctions available for breaches of the mandatory rules (criminal, civil and administrative sanctions) may be more credible to investors than the private bonding mechanisms companies themselves could produce. Secondly, mandatory rules may produce more uniformity in disclosure (thus helping investors to compare different public offerings). Thirdly, mandatory rules may overcome forces acting against full disclosure even when, from one point of view, disclosure is in the company's interest, for example, the disclosure of information which, whilst it would make the company attractive to investors, would also help the company's competitors.[5] In any event, the detail required by the disclosure rules applicable on public offerings is now staggering, as we shall see.

Finally, regulation of the investor's decision whether to purchase the securities on offer is not the only decision which needs to be regulated. Given the importance to companies of access to public securities markets, there is a question whether the decision of the market operator to deny admission or subsequently to suspend or de-list the shares should be regulated. Traditionally, exchanges have been seen by legislators (or, at least, by the European Community legislator) as monopolies and thus at risk of abusing their position. This may seem an odd view in the light of the current intense competition among exchanges on a global basis, but, even so, a particular issuer in a particular case may find the exchange on which its securities are traded has acted unfairly towards it, and the prospect of simply de-camping to another exchange may not be a real one. Regulation of exchange decisions necessarily does not focus on disclosure of information but is more in the nature of a court review of a decision by a public body.

---

[5] J. Coffee, "Market Failure and the Economic Case for a Mandatory Disclosure System" (1984) 70 *Virginia L R* 717.

Types of public market

25–5   Most people, if asked, would probably say that there is one stock market in the United Kingdom and that is the London Stock Exchange (LSE). However, this is not the case. The LSE itself runs two separate markets, namely the "Main Market" and the "Alternative Investment Market" (AIM)[6] for well-established and less well-established companies respectively.[7] However, the LSE has no monopoly on the operation of public markets in securities, even in the United Kingdom, and there exist a number of smaller markets, of which the best known are probably those operated by PLUS Markets Plc, which operates partly in competition with those run by the LSE and partly to provide a market for companies needing to raise smaller sums of money than is usual on AIM.[8] However, there is no legal reason why a British registered company should not have its securities traded on a public market in another country. A number of large British companies have primary listings in London and secondary listings elsewhere, usually in continental Europe or the United States, and some non-British companies equally have secondary listings in London. More interestingly, a small number of British companies have their primary listings outside the United Kingdom and a somewhat larger number of foreign companies have their primary listings in London. Indeed, there has been a certain international competition in recent years among the exchanges to secure such listings, notably from Chinese and Russian companies, which have become a feature of the AIM market.

Carrying on the business of operating a stock market is, not surprisingly, one of the activities regulated under the Financial Services and Markets Act 2000 (FSMA), which is the primary piece of domestic legislation which will be considered in this Chapter. Those who operate the exchange must either be persons authorised to carry on financial business in the United Kingdom or the investment exchange must be a "recognised" investment exchange (RIE).[9] Applications for recognition can be made under Part XVIII of FSMA to the Financial Services Authority (FSA), which is the primary regulator in the area covered by this Chapter. The requirements[10] which have to be met relate to both the initial setting up of the exchange and its continued operation. Thus, any public market in

---

[6] AIM replaced the previous and more usefully entitled Unlisted Securities Market (USM) in 1995.

[7] There are also a number of other markets or segments of markets run by the LSE which, however, need not concern us here.

[8] Also quite well-known, though a very different exchange, is virt-x, a subsidiary of the Swiss stock exchange, which is used to trade Swiss stocks in London and also other liquid European stocks.

[9] Otherwise they will fall foul of the "general prohibition" in section 19 of FSMA 2000 on carrying on regulated financial activities in the United Kingdom.

[10] Set out in more detail in the Financial Services and Markets Act 2000 (Recognition Requirements for Investment Exchanges and Clearing Houses) Regulations 2001 (SI 2001/995).

securities operating in the United Kingdom will be subject to the regulation of the FSA.

The purpose of the above regulation of investment exchanges is to ensure the security of their operation. Thus, the recognition requirements deal with matters such as the suitability of the persons running the exchange and the level of financial resources available to them. However, when we come to look at the public offering rules we shall see that a distinction is drawn between "regulated" and "non-regulated" markets. This is a distinction drawn by European Community law, which, as we shall also see, is now the primary source of the disclosure rules applicable on a public offer. The EU distinction thus relates to markets, whereas the RIE rules refer to market operators. How does this distinction between regulated and non-regulated markets map onto the pattern of investment exchanges found in the United Kingdom?

The Community requirements for a regulated market are now set **25–6** out in Title III of Directive 2004/39/EC on markets in financial instruments (MIFID),[11] Article 36 of which states that "Member States shall reserve authorisation as a regulated market to those systems which comply with the provisions of this Title". The Title then sets out a number of requirements for the status as a regulated market, many of which cover the same ground as is to be found in the domestic rules governing the award of recognised investment exchange status. It might therefore be thought that RIEs would seek to have all the markets they run characterised as regulated markets.[12] However, there is no obligation on an RIE to apply for regulated status for all or any of its markets and not having regulated status does not prevent that market from continuing to operate in the United Kingdom, provided it continues to meet the domestic law requirements. In the language of MIFID a market which is not a regulated market is a "multilateral trading facility" (MTF),[13] though in this Chapter we shall refer to such markets as non-regulated or exchange-regulated. On the other hand, a market which does not obtain regulated status under MIFID loses the benefits and the burdens placed by Community law on regulated markets, those benefits and burdens being found across the Community law governing securities. For RIEs, therefore, the question was whether the benefits Community law attached to a regulated market outweighed the burdens. Centrally for our purposes, the LSE decided not to seek regulated status for AIM.[14] This needs to be borne firmly in mind

---

[11] OJ L145/1, 30.4.2004.

[12] Especially as the requirements for recognition were upgraded in response to Title III of MIFID: see subs (4A) to (4E) inserted into FSMA 2000, s.286 by SI 2006/2975.

[13] See MIFID, Title II. Where trading takes place outside both a regulated market and a MTF, it is generally called "over the counter" trading (OTC).

[14] This decision was taken in 2004 under the then applicable Directive concerning regulated markets, i.e. Directive 93/22/EEC, the investment services Directive, which was repealed by MIFID.

when analysing the impact of the Community rules on prospectuses in the United Kingdom. The Main Market of the LSE is a regulated market.

The regulatory structure

25–7 Domestic statutory law regulating prospectuses has a long history: the Directors' Liability Act 1890,[15] imposing liability for negligent misstatements in prospectuses, was an advanced piece of legislation for its time and significantly influenced the US Securities Act 1933. However, over the past thirty years Community law has gradually occupied the legislative space in relation to public offers and admission of securities to public markets, as part of a broader strategy to create a single European financial market.[16] The result of Community occupation of the field plus the legislative strategies adopted at national level has been a multi-layered rule-making process, where five distinct layers can be identified: primary community law; secondary community law; primary or secondary domestic legislation; FSA rules; and rules generated by stock exchanges.

The modern Community legislative instruments aimed at achieving this goal were proposed in the Financial Services Action Plan (FSAP),[17] adopted in 1999 for the period up to 2005 and substantially achieved in that period. We shall look at some of the FSAP instruments in this and the following Chapter. As far as disclosure of information is concerned the central piece of Community law is now Directive 2003/71/EC on prospectuses (the Prospectus Directive or PD).[18] However, some other aspects of the process of making a public offer and securing admission of securities to a public market are regulated by Directive 2001/34/EC[19] on the admission of securities to official stock exchange listing, a consolidating Directive sometimes referred to as the "Consolidated Admissions Requirements Directive" (or CARD).

As far as the PD is concerned, it has two features which need to be noted. First, it is what is inelegantly referred to as a "maximum harmonisation" Directive. This means that it sets out not only standards below which the Member States may not fall but also standards above which they may not rise. Since it is also a very

---

[15] The modern version of that law can be found in FSMA 2000, s.90.
[16] For an excellent general analysis of this process see E. Ferran, *Building an EU Securities Market* (Cambridge: CUP, 2004).
[17] COM(1999)232, 11.05.99. It was succeeded by a less ambitious White Paper on Financial Services Policy 2005–2010, which is also less relevant to the concerns of this book than its predecessor.
[18] OJ L345/64, 31.12.2003.
[19] OJ L184/1, 6.7.2001. This Directive consolidated Directives going back to 1979, when the Community first became interested in regulating the admission of securities to public markets. Substantial parts of the 2001 Directive have now been themselves replaced by Directives adopted under the FSAP.

detailed Directive, especially when taken with the subordinate Community legislation—see below—the Member States have rather little discretion over its implementation in domestic law and it functions more like a Regulation than a Directive.[20] The reason for this approach was the Community's desire to produce a prospectus which, without changes other than translation, could be used simultaneously in more than one Member State in a cross-border offer. We shall look at this "EU passport" concept in more detail below.[21]

The second notable feature of the PD results from an adaptation of the Community legislative process introduced for FSAP instruments and known as the "Lamfalussy process", after the name of the chairman of the committee which put forward this proposal. An important part of this process is that the European Commission obtained the power to make what we would call subordinate legislation (through *Commission* Directives or Regulations), without going through the full Community legislative process but after consulting the Member States,[22] where the parent Directive provides for such "second-tier" legislation. In fact, in the case of disclosure of information in public offers the detailed information required is to be found in Commission Regulation (EC) No.809/2004,[23] a document of some one hundred pages and being, as a Regulation, directly applicable[24] in the Member States and so not requiring transposition by them. The purpose of this shift of legislative power to the Commission was said to be to enable the details of the FSAP legislation to be adapted more quickly to changing market practices than would be the case if the full Community legislative process had to be used. Law-making by the Commission thus constitutes the second layer of rules in this area, after the adoption of the parent legal instrument by the Community.

However, the PD, the parent Community instrument in our area, **25–8** and Commission instruments taking the form of a Directive do require transposition into national law. This gives rise to the third level of law-making, i.e. by the British legislature (which itself may take the form of primary or secondary legislation). The most obvious expression of the domestic law-making process is FSMA 2000, as subsequently amended. This replaced an earlier piece of domestic law, the Financial Services Act 1986, whose date indicates that it preceded the FSAP. FSMA 2000, therefore, may contain three broad types of rules: those simply transposing the Community law, those

---

[20] The PD is thus some distance from the description of a Directive in Art.249EC as an instrument "which is binding as to the result to be achieved ... but shall leave to the national authorities the choice of form and methods."

[21] Para.25–41.

[22] This consultation takes place through the Committee of European Securities Regulators (CESR).

[23] OJ L215/3, 16.6.2004 (the corrected version).

[24] Art.249EC.

both transposing and adding to the Community requirements (where Community law permits this) and those dealing with matters not subject to Community regulation. However, from the outset of domestic financial services regulation, the policy of embodying all the relevant rules in a statute or even in statutory instruments was rejected in favour of conferring broad rule-making and enforcement powers on a regulator, the Financial Services Authority (FSA). This is a statutory body[25] but funded by market participants and designed to be more attuned to the needs of the markets than would be a Governmental Department. It has a very wide remit in the financial services area but for the purposes of this Chapter we concentrate on its role in public offerings. Rules made by the FSA thus constitute the fourth level of rule-making. For the purposes of this Chapter particularly important are its Prospectus Rules (PR), though on some matters its Listing Rules (LR) are relevant as well.

The role of the PR is perhaps obvious but what are Listing Rules? Under Article 5 of CARD Member States are required to "ensure [that] securities may not be admitted to official listing" on a stock exchange operating in their territory "unless the conditions laid down by this Directive are satisfied" and it is from this Directive that certain "merit" requirements flow, as we shall see below. Article 105 requires that Member States appoint a "competent authority" for the purposes of the Directive, and in the United Kingdom that authority is the FSA, acting as the United Kingdom Listing Authority (UKLA). Section 74 requires the FSA to maintain the "official list" and to include securities in it only in accordance with the provisions of the Act. But what is the "official list"? In a somewhat circular fashion, the "official list" is simply the list of those securities which have applied for inclusion in it and have satisfied the relevant requirements. But why should a company wish its securities to be included in the "official list"? The answer to that is that admission to the official list constitutes a quality mark, which companies may be anxious to have. In particular, it is only companies whose securities are in the official list which will be admitted by the LSE to its Main Market,[26] whilst, equally, the FSA will not include securities in the official list if they have not been admitted to trading on a RIE's market for officially listed securities.[27] Thus, admission of securities to trading on the Main Market of the LSE is a twin-track process: the FSA (or the competent authority in some other EEA State in the case of companies incorporated there) controls inclusion in the official list and the RIE controls admission of the securities to trading on the market. Traditionally, the Main Market of the LSE has been the market on which listed securities are traded, though PLUS Markets

---

[25] Established under FSMA 2000, Part I.
[26] LSE, *Admission and Disclosure Standards*, July 2005, para. 1.1.
[27] LR 2.2.3.

now offers as well the "PLUS-listed" market for such securities.[28] The company has to satisfy both sets of requirements in order to give its securities the status of being on the official list and its shareholders the facility to trade in those securities. As a consequence of these rules and procedures, it is probably better to confine the term "listed security" to securities admitted to trading on the Main Market of the LSE (or any other market for listed securities in the EEA) and to use a different word for securities admitted to trading on any public market (for example, AIM), such as publicly traded.[29]

However, it would be wrong to think that the FSA's Listing Rules **25–9** exist only for the purpose of implementing the CARD Directive in the UK. Listing Rules are of some antiquity in the United Kingdom and deal with many matters falling outside the scope of CARD or any other EU Directive or add to the requirements of those Directives.[30] For example, the LR contain corporate governance rules and rules on related-party transactions which, as we have seen, substantially add to the Companies Act requirements in the case of listed companies.[31] In effect, the LR identify a group of large and economically important companies and apply to them a set of requirements which could as well have been incorporated in the Companies Act, but which are more palatable to those concerned when embodied in rules made by the FSA.

This twin-track approach to listing, involving both the FSA and the LSE, may seem over-elaborate. Indeed, until 2000 the process was in the hands wholly of the LSE, which was the originally designated "competent authority" under the EU legislation. This made sense because the LSE had for a long time produced Listing Rules for its own purposes and implementing the EU requirements via an expansion of the LSE's role was attractive. However, with the demutualisation of the LSE the Exchange no longer wished to carry out this regulatory function, which was transferred, in consequence, to the FSA.[32] However, if inclusion in the official list is now a matter for the FSA, admission of securities to the Main Market is still a matter for the LSE. Consequently, we have the fifth layer of rule-making, that by the exchanges themselves. In the case of the Main

---

[28] This is also a "regulated" market in Community terms. By contrast, "PLUS-quoted", the older of the PLUS markets, is an exchange-regulated market and operates in competition with the AIM market of the LSE.

[29] "Quoted" might have been another possible term but the word has been appropriated by the Companies Act 2006 to mean only companies whose securities are included in the official list of any EEA State or admitted to dealing on the New York Stock Exchange or Nasdaq (CA 2006, s.385).

[30] Art.8 of CARD makes it clear it is a "minimum harmonisation" Directive, to whose requirements the Member States may add.

[31] Above, paras 14–31, 16–55 and 19–2.

[32] By the Official Listing of Securities (Change of Competent Authority) Regulations 2000 (SI 2000/968). In other European countries the exchange typically still acts as the competent authority.

Market this takes the form of *Admission and Disclosure Standards*,[33] which are only a shadow of the LR as they were when the Exchange was in charge of them. In the case of unlisted securities, especially if they are traded on an exchange-regulated market, however, the exchange's rules will be much more substantial, because the role of Community law and of the FSA is much less in such a case.[34]

Thus, we have identified a distinction between securities which are on the official list of securities and traded on a market for listed securities, and securities which are not and are traded on a different market. We have also identified a distinction between regulated and non-regulated (or exchange-regulated) markets. These two distinctions are not congruent. Whereas traditionally the market for listed securities has been a regulated market, markets for unlisted securities may or may not be regulated, according to how they view the benefits and costs of such a status. Today, even regulated markets for listed securities face serious challenges from electronic trading platforms operating as MTFs and supported by the international banks. However, the actual situation in relation to the LSE does produce greater parallelism between the two distinctions: the Main Market for listed securities is a regulated market and AIM for unlisted securities is an exchange-regulated market.[35]

Types of public offer

25–10   On an initial public offering, a company's choice of method will be severely restricted. If the issue is large it will have to proceed by way of an offer for sale or subscription coupled with an introduction to listing (or admission to the AIM), whilst smaller amounts may be raised via a placing plus an introduction. In some cases a third way of proceeding may be available. Where the company's securities have somehow become sufficiently widely held (which is unlikely but conceivable) it may be possible to raise the new money needed by a rights or open offer to its existing shareholders, but this course of action is normally available only on subsequent offers, not on an initial public offering (IPO). We shall look briefly at each type of offer.

Offers for sale or subscription

25–11   A full-blown public offer will prove to be an expensive and time-consuming operation. The company's finance director (and probably

---

[33] See above, fn.26.

[34] See, for example, LSE, *Aim Rules for Companies*, February 2007 (hereafter "AIM Rules").

[35] This is something of a simplification but will do for our purposes. For example, the LSE's Professional Securities Market for wholesale corporate debt is exchange-regulated as well. For the full picture see: http://www.londonstockexchange.com/en-gb/products/member-shiptrading/rulesreg/regmkts.htm. Equally, virt-x Exchange Ltd, a subsidiary of the Swiss exchange but based in London, operates a regulated market in the top European securities, including the FTSE 100 shares.

other executives) and representatives of the advising investment bank and their respective solicitors will for weeks or months devote most of their time to working as a planning team. At a later stage the services of a specialist share registrar will generally be needed to handle applications and the preparation and dispatch of allotment letters. The offer will have to be made by a lengthy prospectus which will have to be published. To ensure that the issue is fully subscribed, arrangements will have to be made for it to be underwritten. Today this is normally achieved by the sponsoring investment bank agreeing to subscribe for the whole issue and for it, rather than the company, to make the offer. Thus, large public offers are normally in the form of offers for sale not offers for subscription, the investment bank having already subscribed for all the shares on offer.[36] In major offerings, such as the Government's privatisation issues,[37] a syndicate of issuing houses may be employed. The issuing house or houses will endeavour to persuade other financial institutions to sub-underwrite. Ultimately the cost of all this, including the commissions payable to underwriters and sub-underwriters,[38] will have to be borne by the company.

The most ticklish decision that will have to be made is the price at which the securities should be issued and, for obvious reasons, this is normally left to the last possible moment. If it proves to have been set too low, so that the issue is heavily over-subscribed, the company will be unhappy, while, if it is set too high so that much of the issue is left with the underwriters, it is they who will be unhappy since their commission rates will have assumed that they will end up with a handsome profit and not be left with securities that, initially, they cannot sell except at a loss. Nor, probably, will the company be best pleased since it is generally believed that an under-subscribed issue will reduce the company's prospects of raising further capital in the future. The nightmare of all concerned is that there will be an unforeseen stockmarket collapse between the date of publication of the prospectus and the opening of the subscription list.[39] The sweet dream is that the issue will be modestly over-subscribed and that trading will open at a small premium.

If the issue is over-subscribed it will obviously be impossible for all **25–12**

---

[36] In an offer for subscription the underwriters simply take up the shares for which the public have not subscribed.

[37] Most of the privatisation offers were not primary distributions (i.e. offers of securities by the company) but secondary distributions (i.e. offers by a large or sole shareholder of its shares to the public). This Chapter is concerned mainly with the raising of capital by a public offer by the company.

[38] On which see para.11–13, above.

[39] Which came true in the case of one of the privatisation issues in the "Crash of 1987". Yet thousands of small investors continued to put in applications notwithstanding that the media were warning them that trading would open at a massive discount.

applications to be accepted[40] in full. Hence, the prospectus will need to say how that situation will be dealt with. Normally this will be by accepting in full offers for small numbers of shares and scaling down large applications, balloting sometimes being resorted to. The company will probably wish to achieve a balance between private and institutional investors. To succeed in that aim multiple applications by the same person will probably be expressly prohibited.[41] An abuse which also needs to be guarded against is that "stags" will apply but seek to withdraw and stop their cheques if it seems likely that dealings will not open at a worthwhile premium to the offer price. However, offer documents will require applications to be accompanied by cheques for the full amount of the securities applied for, the cheques being cleared immediately on receipt and any refund sent later. This means that an applicant may not only fail to get all or any of the shares he hoped for but may, for a period, lose the interest that he was earning on his money.[42]

The offer price is normally stated as a fixed and pre-determined amount per share. It can however, be determined under a formula stated in the offer, though this is uncommon except in offers addressed to professional investors. Alternatively applicants can be invited to tender on the basis that the shares will be allocated to the highest bidders. This, however, is rarely used in relation to issues of company securities. Nevertheless, a variation of it became popular in the early 1980s. Under this, a minimum price will be stated and applicants invited to tender at or above that price, an issue price then being struck at the highest price which will enable the issue to be subscribed in full, all successful applicants paying the same price, and those applicants who tendered below the striking price being eliminated. This, however, did not prove to have the advantages expected of it and is now seldom used though it still has its advocates.[43]

Placings

25-13 Obviously, the expense of an offer for sale plus introduction to listing is prohibitive unless a very large sum of money is to be raised. For lesser amounts the placing may be more attractive. Under this method the investment bank or other adviser to the issue obtains firm commitments, mainly from its institutional investor clients (instead of advertising an offer to the general public), coupling this with an

---

[40] The so-called "offer" is normally not an offer (as understood in the law of contract) which on acceptance becomes binding on the offeror. It may be in the case of a rights issue (see below) but on an offer for sale or subscription it is an invitation to make an offer which the company may or may not accept.

[41] Breaches are difficult but not impossible to detect where applications are made in different names.

[42] This causes bona fide applicants who are unsuccessful understandable resentment.

[43] See the Stock Exchange Report, *Initial Public Offers* (1990), pp.17 and 18, where the pros and cons are summarised.

introduction to trading. The absence of the need for newspaper advertisements, "road-shows" and the like makes this a much less expensive procedure. On the other hand, it prevents the general public from acquiring shares at the issue price. For this reason, the LSE, the then regulatory body, used to look upon placings with some disfavour, but since the middle of the 1990s this has no longer been the case.

Another way of proceeding is the "intermediaries offer", whereby financial intermediaries take up the offer for the purpose of allocating the securities to their own clients. This way of proceeding should be only marginally more expensive than a straightforward placing, but has the advantage that it is more likely to result in a wide spread of shareholders and a more active and competitive subsequent market.

Rights offers

Once a company has made an initial public offering it will have additional methods whereby it can raise further capital and, even if it proceeds by an offer for sale, this will be less expensive if the securities issued are of the same class as those already admitted to listing or to the AIM. More often, however, it will make what is called a "rights issue" and, if it is an offering of equity shares for cash, it will generally have to do this unless the company in general meeting otherwise agrees. This is because of the pre-emption provisions discussed in the previous Chapter.[44] As we saw, the semi-mandatory nature of pre-emption rights, and in particular the unwillingness of institutional shareholders to disapply them except within certain strict limits, had been criticised by some companies and investment banks for restricting access to low-cost capital, but after a governmental enquiry the existing practice was largely endorsed.

25–14

In one sense a rights issue is considerably less expensive than an offer for sale: circulating the shareholders is cheap in comparison with publishing a lengthy prospectus in national newspapers and mounting a sales pitch to attract the public. But in another sense it may be dearer: if the issue price is deeply discounted the company will have to issue far more shares (on which it will be expected to pay dividends) in order to raise the same amount of money as on an offer.

Analogous to, but distinguishable from, rights issues are Open Offers. Under these an offer is made to the company's existing security holders, *pro rata* to their existing holdings, but not affording them rights to renounce. Such offers are less common than rights issues. Other methods of issue, which can be used in appropriate circumstances, include exchanges or conversions of one class of securities into another, issues resulting from the exercise of options or warrants, and issues under employee share-ownership schemes—

---

[44] Discussed at paras 24–6ff, above.

though these will not necessarily raise new money for the company. Nor, of course, will capitalisation issues, dealt with in Chapter 13, above.

We now turn to an examination of the legal rules governing public offers and the admission of securities to trading on a public market.

ADMISSION TO TRADING ON A PUBLIC MARKET

25–15 We have already noted that admission to trading on a public market is a normally a concomitant feature of a public offer—though admission may be sought independently of an offer of shares by the company to the public—and that it is important for both companies and investors that this facility be made available. Direct legal regulation of the admission process is to be found only in relation to certain types of securities market, namely those where officially listed securities are traded.[45] CARD and the relevant domestic rules focus on the process of obtaining and retaining listed status and engage in two types of regulation. One is a limited form of merit regulation, referred to as "eligibility criteria", relating either to the offering company or the nature of its offer. The second is regulation of action which the listing authority may take which is adverse to the company or its shareholders.

Eligibility criteria for the official list
25–16 Chapter II of Title III of CARD lays down certain conditions for the admissibility of shares to the official list, and Chapter III lays down a lesser set of requirements for debt securities.[46] The conditions may be divided into those related to the company and those related to the securities on offer. These requirements of CARD are transposed into domestic law by the Listing Rules under powers conferred on the FSA by section 73A of FSMA 2000. To some extent, the LR extend the requirements of CARD, as that Directive permits.[47]

In relation to both equity and debt securities one of two major policy concerns of CARD is to ensure that there should be a liquid

---

[45] AIM relies mainly on certification from the "nominated adviser" that the issuer is appropriate for that market.

[46] The merit requirements are less for debt securities presumably because the security itself will normally give the investor greater contractual protections than in the case of an equity security.

[47] CARD Art.8. The FSA contemplated removing all the "super-equivalent" eligibility requirements when implementing the PD, but in the end retained most of them (discussed below) whilst removing some. For a discussion of the policy balance here see FSA, *The Listing Review and the implementation of the Prospectus Directive*, CP 04/16, October 2004, paras 3.22–3.37.

market in the securities in question after listing, so that the buying and selling of the securities at a price which is reliable can be facilitated.[48] To this end certain conditions on admission to the official list are laid down.

(i) The expected market value of the securities to be admitted must be at least £700,000 for shares and £200,000 for debt securities.[49]

(ii) All the securities on offer must be admitted to listing.[50]

(iii) The securities must be freely transferable.[51] Without this requirement the development of a market in the shares would clearly be inhibited.

(iv) In the case of shares a "sufficient number" of the class of shares in question must be distributed to the public (as opposed to being held in non-trading blocks by insiders), which is translated as a rule of thumb into 25 per cent of the shares for which admission is sought.[52]

The other main driver of the CARD rules, beyond certain formal requirements, is that the issuer should have a certain quality. These requirements apply to the issue of shares rather than debt securities.

(v) The company must produce audited accounts for a period of three years, ending not earlier than six months before the application for admission.[53]

(vi) Going beyond CARD, the company must show that "at least 75% of the applicant's business is supported by a historic revenue earning record" for the three years in question; that it controls the majority of its assets and has done so for the three years in question; and that it will be

---

[48] Where there is only a thin market in a security, the prices at which those securities can be traded may be volatile.

[49] CARD Arts 43 and 58; LR 2.2.7. This rule does not apply if the shares on offer are of a class already listed; and, in any event, the FSA may grant a derogation if satisfied that nevertheless there will be "an adequate market for the securities concerned".

[50] CARD Arts 49, 56, 62; LR 2.2.9. The LR do not avail themselves of the exemption in Art.49(2) for the non-admission to listing for "blocks serving to maintain control of the company".

[51] CARD Arts 46, 54, 60; LR 2.2.4. The FSA may make arrangements to accommodate the transfer of partly paid shares or shares whose transfer needs the consent of the applicant (rare in listed companies but found in some denationalised companies in order to subject control transfers to scrutiny).

[52] CARD Art.48; LR 6.1.19. In the case of the admission of further shares of a class already admitted the sufficiency test may be applied so as to take account of the shares already in issue.

[53] CARD Art.44; LR 6.1.3. The accounts must have an unqualified audit certificate (not a requirement of CARD).

carrying on an independent business as its main activity.[54] The aim of these requirements is not that the applicant show that it has been profitable over the three years (though it may not find takers for its shares if it has not been) but to enable investors to evaluate the significance of the historical information in the accounts for the future operation of the company. The three years of accounts may not be a good guide if, for example, the company has only recently acquired the business which now constitutes its main activity or if the continuity of its business is subject to the consent of a third person.[55]

(vii) Again going beyond CARD, the applicant must show, subject to exceptions, that it will have sufficient working capital to meet its requirements for the twelve months after listing.[56] This is some protection against the company suffering a "cash crunch" in the short-term after listing. Of course, where the admission is coupled with a public offer, the working capital is likely to be raised in that offer. The purpose of this requirement is that the applicant show it has made a realistic forecast of what its cash needs will be in the near term.

In addition to these specific requirements in relation to the company and its securities, there is a general power in Article 11 of CARD for Member States to reject an application for listing "if, in their opinion, the issuer's situation is such that admission would be detrimental to investors' interests". This is transposed into domestic law by FSMA 2000, section 75(5), which gives the power of rejection to the FSA as the competent authority. It is unclear in what circumstances this power might be used, though no doubt it is a useful back-stop to deal with the unexpected.

Rights of appeal

25–17 The procedure for dealing with applications for listing and subsequent discontinuance or suspension of listing is set out, at least in broad outline, in the statute rather than the Listing Rules. This is hardly surprising since the purpose of these rules is in part to supervise the decisions of the FSA. The overall picture is that the FSA is given a broad statutory discretion over these matters, but subject to a right to challenge the Authority's decision before the

---

[54] LR 6.1.4.
[55] LR 6.1.7 identifies a further set of specific cases where the accounts may not be enough to secure admission. The FSA may dispense with the requirements of LR 6.1.3 and 6.1.4 where it thinks this desirable in the interests of investors and that investors have the necessary information to arrive at an informed judgment: CARD Art.44 and LR 6.1.13.
[56] LR 6.1.16.

Financial Services and Markets Tribunal (FSMT), set up under Part IX of and Schedule 13 to the Act. Subject to the power of the Treasury to exclude certain types of security from listing,[57] the FSA has a broad power to refuse listing, not only where the applicant has not complied with the Listing Rules' requirements for admission, set out above, but also where it has not satisfied other requirements laid down by the FSA or in any case where, as indicated above, the Authority "considers that granting it would be detrimental to the interests of investors".[58] The decision must be taken by the Authority normally within six months of the application and failure to do so may be treated by the applicant as a refusal to admit. The application is normally made by the issuer in question. Moreover, the consent of the issuer to the application is a pre-condition for admission,[59] so that, for example, a large shareholder cannot make an application for listing if the company does not wish it. If the FSA proposes not to accept an application for listing, it must give the applicant a "warning notice", giving the applicant a reasonable period within which to make representations, and if the proposal is confirmed, the matter may be referred to the Tribunal.[60]

The Authority may cancel listing "if it is satisfied that there are special circumstances which preclude normal regular dealings in them".[61] It may also suspend the listing of securities, without limitation of grounds, though it must do so in accordance with the provisions of the Listing Rules, which confer a power of suspension "if the smooth operation of the market is, or may be, temporarily jeopardised or it is necessary to protect investors".[62] In either case, written notice must be given in advance to the issuer and the Authority must take into account representations the issuer may wish to make.[63]

Given these broad powers, in relation to both the initial application to list and subsequently, it is perhaps surprising that before the

---

[57] s.74(3)(b), a power which has been exercised to exclude the shares of private companies: above, at para.24–2.

[58] s.75(4) and (5). A further ground for refusal arises in relation to shares already listed in another EEA State, where the applicant is in breach of the requirements arising from such listing: s.75(6).

[59] s.75(2).

[60] The warning notice procedure is laid down in s.387 of FSMA 2000 and fleshed out in the FSA's Decision Procedure and Penalties Manual (DEPP 2.2).

[61] s.77(1), for example, where the "free float" has fallen below 25 per cent, above, para.25–17, and is not likely to return to that level in the near future. See further, LR 5.2.2.

[62] s.77(2) and LR 5.1.1. LR 5.1.2 gives examples of situations where a company's listing may be suspended, including failure to meet its continuing obligations (see Ch.26); failure to publish the required financial information about itself; the issuer's inability to assess its financial position; or there is insufficient information in the market about a proposed transaction. The provisions of s.77 on both suspension and cancellation follow the requirements of Art.18 of CARD.

[63] s.77(2)–(8). Although giving those concerned the right to make representations, the written notice procedure is less formal than the warning notice to be given in the case of refusal of admission to listing (above).

enactment of the FSMA, control over their exercise was effected only by means of judicial review. Now the Act establishes an independent Tribunal, with a legally qualified chairperson and practitioner lay members, which determines appeals from the FSA by way of rehearing, with appeal on a point of law to the Court of Appeal (or Court of Session). Appeals against a refusal of listing may be made by the applicant[64] and against discontinuance or suspension by the issuer.[65] The shareholder has no right of appeal, or even to be consulted by the Authority before the decision is taken, even though in the case of discontinuance or suspension his or her financial position is crucially affected.[66] An additional role for the Tribunal is hearing appeals from a new power conferred by the FSMA upon the FSA, i.e. the power to impose civil penalties on issuers and, more importantly, their directors and shadow directors[67] for non-compliance with the FSA's Rules.[68] The exercise of this power, in many cases, will constitute a more appropriate response to managerial misconduct in the shape of breaches of the Listing Rules than suspension of listing.

Disclosure of information

25–18 We noted above that the introduction of securities onto a public market is a method of making them available to the public, so that disclosure of information about the issuer and the securities is appropriate, even if the introduction is not accompanied by a public offer of new securities by or on behalf of the company. In consequence, it is no surprise to discover that section 85(2) of FSMA requires the production of a prospectus, not only when securities are included on the official list, but whenever admission of securities to trading on a regulated market is sought. However, section 85(1) equally requires the production of a prospectus when a company offers its securities to the public. Since the normal course of events is that the public offer and the admission of securities to trading on a public market occur as part of a single process, we will discuss below the disclosure of information requirements through the prospectus together with our analysis of the public offer.

However, there is reference in FSMA to something called "listing particulars" which constitute an information disclosure document and which adopt some of the requirements for prospectuses.[69] However, although more significant in the past, the listing particulars

---

[64] s.76(6), normally but, not necessarily, the issuer (see above).
[65] s.77(5).
[66] In *R. v International Stock Exchange Ex p. Else (1982) Ltd* [1993] Q.B. 534, CA—a cancellation case—it was held that the Community Directives did not require that access to the courts be granted to the shareholders. The Court was influenced by the argument that to decide otherwise would enormously slow down decision-taking by the competent authority.
[67] s.417(1).
[68] s.91. It may instead issue a public censure: s.91(3).
[69] See LR 4.2 ff.

now constitute a residual category of document. The LR may not require listing particulars for any category of security for which a prospectus is required.[70] The effect of this is that listing particulars have little importance for most companies[71] and will not be considered further in this book.[72]

Other markets
The above rules on eligibility apply only to admission to the official   **25–19** list and to trading in listed securities. Where admission to trading is sought for securities not on the official list, whether (in EU terms) the market on which the securities are to be traded is a regulated market or not, the provisions of CARD do not apply. CARD is concerned, as its title indicates, only with "the admission of securities to official stock exchange listing". Outside listing, eligibility requirements are a matter for the exchange. For example, the LSE lays down no general eligibility requirements for admission to AIM (other than the appointment of a "nominate adviser").[73] However, eligibility requirements are laid down in certain specific cases. For example, paragraph 7 of the AIM Rules stipulates:

> "Where an applicant's or quoted applicant's main activity is a business which has not been independent and earning revenue for at least two years, it must ensure that all related parties and applicable employees as at the date of admission agree not to dispose of any interest in its securities for one year from the admission of its securities."

This rule obviously reflects in a muted way the independence requirements of the LR.[74] The Exchange has also reserved to itself the power to subject any applicant for admission to a special condition.[75]

The Exchange has also taken power to cancel the admission of the securities of a company which has contravened its rules (along with the power to fine or censure) and has provided a procedure through which such action must be taken, including provision of an appeal. The appeal procedure also applies in relation to a refusal of admission.[76] These rules apply as a matter of contract between the company

---

[70] s.79(3A).
[71] See s.85(5),(6) and Sch.11A of FSMA 2000 and LR 4.1.1. The securities, where listing particulars are required, which come nearest to the concerns of this book are certain debt instruments issued by banks and certain securities issued by charities, housing associations and industrial and provident societies (Sch.11A, paras 5, 7 and 8).
[72] Confusingly, the civil liability provisions in s.90 of the Act are still drafted primarily in terms of the listing particulars. However, subs (11) makes it clear that the section applies also to prospectuses, in practice the principal type of document with which it is concerned.
[73] LSE, *AIM Rules for Companies*, February 2007, Rule 1.
[74] Above, para.25–16.
[75] Above, fn.73 Rule 9.
[76] Above, fn.73 Rules 42 and 44–45.

and the LSE. How far the courts would be prepared to review the decisions of the Exchange beyond its contractual arrangements is unclear.

THE PROSPECTUS

25–20 The core mechanism by which the law achieves its disclosure objectives is the prospectus, to which we now turn. The relevant Community rules are in the PD, a maximum harmonisation Directive,[77] and in subordinate Community law made by the Commission. They are transposed, as necessary, into domestic law by amendments to FSMA and through rules made by the FSA—the Prospectus Rules (PR). We have noted already that there are two triggers for the requirement to produce a prospectus: a public offer and the admission of securities to trading on a regulated market.[78] Where securities are both offered to the public and admitted to trading on a regulated market, both triggers will be pulled, but either will do. We have also noted that AIM is not now a regulated market and so simple admission to trading on AIM will not trigger the prospectus requirement. That will be irrelevant if the admission is accompanied by a public offer, but an AIM company will be able to escape the prospectus requirements of FSMA if it makes an offer which falls outside the concept of a public offer, as certain types of placing, for example, will. Thus, a non-public offer plus admission to trading on AIM will enable the company to avoid the statutory prospectus rules. This does not mean the company can make its offer without meeting any disclosure requirements. This is because the Exchange's own rules for AIM have disclosure obligations built into them. Those rules require an applicant for admission to AIM to produce a publicly available "admission document". This document is a slimmed down version of what is required under the PD: in fact the information required for the admission document is defined by express reference to the annexes of Commission Regulation (EC) No.809/2004.[79] Where the securities are to be traded on a regulated market, refraining from making a public offer will not avoid the statutory requirements for a prospectus, but in some cases, the statute itself does not require securities admitted to trading to be accompanied by a prospectus (where there is no public offer).

We shall look in turn at each of the triggers.

---

[77] See above, para.25–7.
[78] s.85(1),(2). The meaning of a regulated market is discussed above at para.25–6.
[79] Above, fn.73, Rule 3, Schedule 2 and Glossary. The function of the Commission Regulation is mentioned above at para.25–7. Sch.2 makes it clear that, where a prospectus is required, that requirement overrides the AIM Rules.

The public offer trigger

Producing an acceptable definition of a public offer has long proved a **25–21** difficult exercise. The predecessor of the current PD[80] did not even attempt the exercise, noting rather disarmingly in its preamble that "so far, it has proved impossible to furnish a common definition of the term 'public offer' and all its constituent parts." It was lauded as one of the achievements of the current PD that it does contain such a definition. That definition is as follows:

> " 'offer of securities to the public' means a communication to persons in any form and by any means, presenting sufficient information on the terms of the offer and the securities to be offered, so as to enable an investor to decide to purchase or subscribe to these securities."

This, it will be observed, is not a great example of the drafter's art, for it is hardly helpful to define the trigger for a disclosure obligation in terms of the information which has to be disclosed if there is a triggering event. Thus, as before, one has to proceed by taking an essentially broad and imprecise concept ("communication to persons in any form and by any means") and then seeking to give meaning to it by examining the specific provisions in the Directive which state when something is not a public offer, even though on the general approach it might otherwise be.

More important than the legal technique, however, are the reasons for excluding some types of offer. Producing and verifying the information required for a prospectus is a costly business. There is therefore a strong argument for not requiring a prospectus if its recipients do not need the information it contains. This could be for a number of reasons. Again, even if the information would be of benefit to the recipients, the costs of providing it may outweigh the benefits of having it provided. This is likely to be true of small offers. The provisions of the PD can be seen to reflect these concerns.

The exemptions which seek to identify the investors who can look **25–22** after themselves and so do not need the prospectus information are the following.

- Offers addressed to "qualified investors" only.[81] These are defined in Article 2(1)(e) so as to include legal entities authorised to operate in the financial markets (for example, fund managers or investment banks); governmental bodies at both national and international level; and, the widest category, other legal entities which do not fall within the small or

---

[80] Directive 89/228/EEC.
[81] PD Art.3(1)(a); FSMA s.86(1)(a). Even though no prospectus is required, information given to some qualified investors must be given to them all: PD Art.15(5).

medium category.[82] In relation to authorised persons the British legislation makes an important clarification that included in the category of qualified investor is the offeree who is not qualified but whose agent is, provided the agent has authority to accept the offer without reference to the client.[83] Member States are also given the power to include in the category of qualified investors individuals who satisfy two of the following criteria and who ask to be considered as qualified investors. The criteria are: having carried out at least ten transactions of significant size per quarter over the previous four quarters; having a securities portfolio of at least half a million euros; working or having worked for a year in the financial sector in a position requiring knowledge of securities investment.[84] Member States may also apply the exemption to SMEs which asked to be so considered. A register of these last two categories of qualified investor has to be kept by the competent authority. The United Kingdom has taken up both these options.[85]

To avoid a rather obvious way around the prospectus requirements, it is provided that, if there is a subsequent resale of the securities by a qualified investor, the question of whether that resale counts as a public offer is to be tested afresh.[86]

- Offers of securities where each investor is to pay at least 50,000 euros in response to the offer.[87] The idea is that such a large consideration will deter all but investors who can look after themselves.

- Offers of securities in denominations of at least 50,000 euros—another way of expressing the same point.[88]

A second category of those who, it can be said, do not need the prospectus information, are those who will receive the relevant information through some other mechanism. The PD identifies in this way[89] the target's shareholders in a share-exchange takeover bid[90] and the shareholders of companies involved in a merger.[91]

The third category where a prospectus is not regarded as useful is

---

[82] The Community definition of SME is discussed at paras 21–3ff.
[83] s.86(2).
[84] Art.2(2).
[85] FSMA s.87R and PR 5.4.
[86] PD Art.2(2).
[87] PD Art.3(2)(b); FSMA s.86(1)(c).
[88] PD Art.3(2)(d); FSMA s.86(d).
[89] PD Art.4(1)(b),(c); FSMA s.85(5)(b); PR 1.2.2.
[90] See below at para.28–55. Where, as is common, the offer is in cash, the issue does not arise, because the target's shareholders are not acquiring any securities.
[91] See below at para.29–7.

where those who receive the offer do so other than as part of a fund-raising exercise by the company. The PD identifies in this way[92] those receiving new shares in substitution for their existing shares, if there is no increase in the issued share capital; bonus shares and script dividends;[93] and shares issued under employee or directors' share schemes.

As for the more contentious case where the information is admittedly useful but the cost of providing it is out of proportion to the benefits flowing from it, the PD excludes a number of small offers. The Directive as a whole does not apply where the total amount to be raised in the offer is no more than 2,500,000 euros over a period of twelve months.[94] Somewhat oddly, there is then a separate exemption from the definition of a public offer for "an offer of securities with a total consideration of less than EUR 100,000" over a period of twelve months.[95] The policy seems to be to leave the Member States free to impose or not their domestic prospectus rules on offers below the 2,500,000 euro limit, but to prohibit them from so doing in the case of offers below 100,000 euros.[96] In addition, offers addressed to fewer than 100 persons (natural or legal) per EEA State are exempted, and qualified investors do not count against this number.[97]

Probably the most practically significant of these exemptions are those for offers to qualified investors and to small numbers of investors. An offer made by a company to institutional investors and brokers operating discretionary portfolios for clients, followed by admission to trading on AIM, can escape the statutory prospectus requirements, though not the Exchange's own disclosure rules.

The admission to trading trigger

The second trigger for the prospectus is a request for admission of **25–23** securities to a regulated market.[98] Thus, if shares are to be introduced onto the Main Market of the LSE, even though there is no offer to the public by the company, a prospectus will normally be required. A placing which manages to fall within one of the exceptions to the definition of a public offer, discussed above, will not normally avoid the need to produce a prospectus if the shares are to be admitted to the Main Market of the LSE. However, there are certain exceptions

---

[92] PD Art.4(1)(a), (d), (e); FSMA s.85(5)(b); PR 1.2.2.

[93] See para.11–18.

[94] PD Art.1(2)(h); FSMA s.85(5)(a), Sch.11A, para.9.

[95] PD Art.3(2)(e); FSMA s.86(1)(e),(4).

[96] I am grateful to Eilis Ferran for discussion of this point. If offers below the upper limit are outside the scope of the Directive, it is unclear how the Directive can say anything binding on the Member States about offers below the lower limit. The UK position appears to be that a prospectus is not required for offers beneath the upper limit: see fn.94.

[97] PD Art.3(2)(b); FSMA s.86(1)(b). Section 86(3) treats as an offer to a single person as an offer made to the trustees of a trust, the members of a partnership as such and two or more persons jointly. Under the earlier PD the number was 50.

[98] s.85(2).

to the rule which requires a prospectus upon admission to a regulated market. It is thus conceivable that the company's offer could fall within both sets of exceptions and thus not require a prospectus even though the shares are to be admitted to trading on a regulated market.

The exceptions to the admissions trigger are to be found in Article 4(2) of the PD and in the PR.[99] In large part they repeat some of the categories of exception to the public offer trigger. Thus, the second category of situations where there is an exception to the public offer trigger on the grounds that a prospectus is unnecessary (takeovers and mergers) appears again in relation to the admission trigger. Otherwise, in the case of share-exchange takeover, a prospectus would often have to be produced, not because the offeror was making a public offer, but because the securities on offer were to be admitted to trading on a regulated market.

The third category exception on the unnecessary ground (non-fundraising offers) is also repeated, provided the securities in question are already admitted to trading on the same regulated market. Again, given the two triggers, these exceptions need to be repeated in order to effect the policy underlying them that no prospectus needs to be produced.

25–24   The interesting exceptions are, thus, those which do not reflect the public offer exceptions. The most important of these, however, reflects the same policy as that underlying some of the public offer exceptions: a prospectus should not be required if the costs of so doing are likely to outweigh its advantages. Thus, Article 4(2)(a) exempts from the prospectus requirement requests to admit shares representing less than ten per cent of the number of shares of the same class already admitted to trading on that regulated market (measured over a twelve-month period). Combined with the qualified investor exception for public offers, this enables companies to raise relatively small amounts of new capital via a carefully structured placing, even if the shares in question are admitted to trading on a regulated market.[100] The "qualified investor" exception to the public offer trigger cannot, of course, be used in terms in the case of admission of securities to trading, because there is no mechanism to control the ownership of the shares once they have been admitted to the market. The argument instead is that, if the class of share is already traded on the market, there will be a lot of information about them and the issuer in the market[101] and a relatively small offering of

---

[99] Made under s.85(6)(b). See in particular PR 1.2.3. S.85(6)(a) excludes the securities identified in Part I of Sch.11A, but these are of little concern to the ordinary company.

[100] The LSE does not normally require an admission document for a further issue of shares of any size on AIM (above, fn.73 at Rule 26) and so in the case of an AIM company only the exceptions to the public offer trigger are relevant in the standard case.

[101] See in particular the following Chapter on continuing disclosure.

additional shares will not mark a dramatic change of direction for the company.

In order to encourage a single financial market in the EU, Article 4(2)(h) permits securities already admitted to trading on another regulated market to be admitted to trading without the production of a prospectus. This facility is subject to conditions, notably that securities of the same class shall have been traded on the other market for at least eighteen months[102] and that the ongoing obligations for trading on that other market have been complied with.

The form and content of prospectuses

Before an offer is made to the public or a request is made for admission of securities to trading on a regulated market a prospectus must be made available to the public.[103] The prospectus is a disclosure document and the overriding rule to which it is subject is that it "shall contain all information which ... is necessary to enable investors to make an informed assessment of the assets and liabilities, financial position, profit and losses, and prospects of the issuer and of any guarantor, and of the rights attaching to [the] securities."[104] This comes close to making contracts resulting from public offers into contracts of the utmost good faith demanding disclosure by the offerors of all material facts. However, the PD does not content itself with this important general rule: far from it. This is an area where the Commission is given law-making powers in relation to the format of the prospectus and in pursuance of this power has produced Commission Regulation (EC) No.809/2004,[105] containing some 36 Articles (more than the PD itself) and, remarkably, some 19 annexes. The Regulation is directly applicable in Member States (and so does not need transposition).[106] The purpose of the "sweeping up" rule in the Directive is thus to require those drawing up a prospectus, after they have complied with the detailed rules in the Regulation, to ask themselves, as a final check, whether overall it gives the investors all the information they require. Thus, whereas the PD is, as against the Member States, a maximum harmonisation Directive, the Commission Regulation is, as against those who draw up prospectuses, a

25–25

---

[102] Reflecting the Community's traditional fear that otherwise there would be a regulatory "race to the bottom" with a companies securing admittance to the laxest market and then immediately moving to the market of choice. Given that the PD is a maximum harmonisation Directive, this may be thought an over-blown worry.

[103] PD Art.3; FSMA s.85(1),(2).

[104] PD Art.5(1); FSMA s.87A(2). The previous qualification to this obligation that it applied only to information within the knowledge of those responsible or that it would be reasonable to obtain by making enquiries is retained only for the minority cases where listing particulars are required rather than a prospectus: FSMA s.80(1),(3).

[105] Above, fn.23.

[106] In a number of places the PR (made under powers conferred by FSMA s.84) repeat rules from the Commission Regulation but do not seek to transpose it into domestic law.

minimum requirement.[107] The Member States may not add to the minimum required but those responsible for a prospectus may put in more than the Regulation requires and, indeed, may be obliged to do so under the "sweeping up" rule of the Directive.

In a work of this nature the Commission Regulation does not need to be analysed in detail. Despite its formidable size it is not quite as fearsome as it seems. First, it contains rules which to some extent were previously to be found in Directives[108] and so it is not as big a regulatory extension as it seems. Indeed, one of the purposes of giving the Commission law-making powers in this area was to remove a lot of the detail from Community Directive to Commission subordinate law, which could more easily be adjusted to changing needs. Secondly, the annexes contain "building blocks" to be used in the construction of the prospectus, but only some, often a small number, of those building blocks will be relevant to any one prospectus.[109]

Nevertheless, a prospectus is likely to be a forbiddingly long and detailed document, a tendency to which the civil liability rules, discussed below, only contribute. It is doubtful whether many retail investors read it in full or at all before deciding whether to invest. Professional investors and analysts may pore over it, but most retail investors will not find it a user-friendly document, despite the PD's requirement that the information in it "shall be presented in an easily analysable and comprehensible form"[110] It is therefore sensible that the PD requires a summary to be part of the prospectus, conveying "the essential characteristics and risks associated with the issuer ... and the securities" but with a warning that it should be read only as an introduction to the prospectus.[111] The summary in effect replaces the "mini prospectus", a document separate from the prospectus, which was a common feature of large British public offers in the past.

25–26   Despite these disclosure requirements, there is likely to be one crucial piece of information which it may not be possible to insert into it, namely, the price of the security. For the reasons given above,[112] those involved will want to leave this to the last possible

---

[107] PD Art.7.

[108] Most recently in Directive 2001/34/EC, above, fn.19, Annex 1 (now repealed).

[109] Commission Regulation Art.3. For example, the Regulation not only distinguishes between offers of equity and debt securities but has special provisions for asset-backed securities, depository receipts, derivative securities, closed-end collective investment schemes and public authority offerors, some or all of which may be irrelevant in many cases.

[110] PD Art.5(1); FSMA s.87A(3). This is not to say that the prospectus may not influence retail investors' decisions, for example, through the comments of financial journalists who, one hopes, have read it.

[111] PD Art.5(2); FSMA s.87A(5),(6). The Directive does not require the production of a summary in the case of "heavy weight" debt securities (denominations of 50,000 euros or above) on the grounds, presumably, that these securities are likely to be bought only by professional investors who can be expected to read the whole prospectus. Although offers of such securities do not count as public offers (see above, para.25–21), a prospectus is required if they are to be admitted to trading on a regulated market.

[112] At para.25–11.

moment, in order to be able to react to late changes in the market. Connected with the price uncertainty, it may not be possible to say how many securities will be on offer. Article 8 of the PD permits these omissions, provided either the prospectus contains the criteria by which these matters will be determined or anyone who has accepted the offer before the final price and amount of securities on offer have been published is allowed to withdraw their acceptance during the following two working days.[113]

It is also not a rare event that information becomes available after the prospectus has been published which requires the published information to be qualified. Article 16 of the PD requires "every significant new factor, material mistake or inaccuracy" relating to the information contained in the prospectus which "arises or is noted" after its issuance and before the closing of the offer to be the subject of a supplementary prospectus, if the new information is capable of affecting the investors' evaluation of the offer; and for investors to have a right of withdrawal during the two working days after the supplementary prospectus is published. The transposing British legislation puts any person responsible for the prospectus who knows of the change under a duty to notify it to the company or the applicant for admission, if different.[114] It is unclear whether this duty arises if the issuer is unaware of the event and it cannot be said that it should have been.[115]

The traditional British prospectus has been a single document containing all the relevant information. Under the Directive it may consist of two documents and incorporate some information by reference. Where there are two documents, the prospectus will consist of a "registration statement" and a "securities note".[116] The registration statement, containing information about the issuer, can be filed with the relevant authority and, if approved, be valid for twelve months. The securities note can then be produced later and contain the information about the securities on offer plus updated information, if any is needed, about the issuer. When the securities note and the summary (see above) are produced they can be put together with the registration statement to form a valid prospectus (which will in turn be valid for twelve months).[117] The purpose of this facility is to cut down the time needed between the decision to raise capital and

---

[113] FSMA s.87Q. In practice, companies will structure matters so that acceptances are received only after the final price has been announced. However, they will probably have given an indicative price range to investors whilst drumming up support for the offer. Somewhat similar reasoning underlies the notion of a "base prospectus" which, however, is confined to the issuance of debt securities on "a continuous and repeated manner": Art.5(4).

[114] FSMA s.87G.

[115] The phrase "is noted" might suggest knowledge is required but "arises" does not. S.81(3), applying only to listing particulars, makes it clear that for supplementary listing particulars to be required knowledge of the new event is required.

[116] PD Art.5(3).

[117] PD Arts 12 and 9(3); PR 2.2–6.

the making of the public offer by obtaining approval in advance for part of the required information.

Incorporation of information by reference was not previously permitted in the United Kingdom, on the grounds that it makes the information less accessible to the reader of the prospectus. Article 11 of the PD now requires Member States to allow certain information to be incorporated in this way (other than in the summary) and Article 28 of the Commission Regulation spells out which information may be incorporated by reference. The list is reasonably long, though most of it ought to be available electronically, for example, the company's audit reports and financial statements and earlier approved prospectuses.

Verifying the prospectuses

25–27   As we shall see below, the law provides *ex post* remedies for those who suffer loss as a result of omissions or inaccuracies in a prospectus or supplementary prospectus. However, it is obviously more desirable if the law or regulation can provide *ex ante* mechanisms designed to ensure that the information as provided is complete and accurate. A number of such mechanisms are to be found in the FSA Rules or FSMA.

A first mechanism, long relied on in the United Kingdom, not mandated by the PD but evidently not regarded as regulated by it, is the use of a reputational intermediary, who guides the applicant for admission to trading through the applicable rules and certifies to the Exchange that there has been compliance. Certification of compliance with the requirements by the intermediary may be more reliable than that by the company alone because of the intermediary's greater experience in the field and because the intermediary's business model depends on its certifications being accurate, for otherwise future issuers will not have an incentive to use that intermediary as opposed to one of its competitors. Use of an intermediary in this way involves in effect a partial delegation by the FSA or the Exchange of its supervisory powers to an adviser to the company, who is of course paid for by the company. In any event, a company applying for a primary listing of its equity securities on the Main Market must appoint a sponsor[118] whose role is defined in general as being to "(1) provide assurance to the FSA when required that the responsibilities

---

[118]   LR 8.2.1, made under FSMA s.88. The "nominated adviser" (or "nomad") plays a similar role in relation to the admission document (see above, para.25–20) required for admission to AIM. A sponsor is also required on certain other occasions, for example, when the company issues a "Class 1" circular (see para.14–8), but a listed company is not required to have a sponsor at all times, unlike a company admitted to AIM where a condition for continued admission of the company is that it always has a nomad: AIM Rules for Companies, Rule 34. The nomad has similar responsibilities to the sponsor at admission stage and must give the Exchange the same assurance: *AIM Rules for Nominated Advisers*, February 2007, Sch.2.

of the listed company or applicant under the listing rules have been met; and (2) guide the listed company or applicant in understanding and meeting its responsibilities under the listing rules ..."[119] The sponsor thus owes duties to both its client (to use reasonable care in guiding it through the application process) and to the FSA by providing assurance to the regulatory body that those requirements have been met. It is the sponsor (normally an investment bank) which submits the application for listing to the FSA and accompanies it with a "sponsor's declaration" that it has fulfilled its two duties.[120] In the case of an application for listing of equity securities where the production of a prospectus is required, the sponsor must not submit such an application "unless it has come to a reasonable opinion, after having made due and careful enquiry, that (1) the applicant has satisfied all the requirements of the Listing Rules relevant to the admission of securities to listing and (2) the applicant has satisfied all the requirements set out in the prospectus rules".[121]

Secondly, certain specific items of information in the prospectus may be subject to third-party verification. We have already noted the requirement on applicants for admission to the official list to produce three years' of accounts which have been audited.[122] However, backward-looking information is less useful to—or at least less likely to impress itself upon—investors than future-regarding statements, which directly addresses their concerns, i.e. how well is the company likely to do in the future. On the other hand, a requirement to state the company's prospects gives the directors a golden opportunity to present the company in a rosy light for the future, without the check which historical data provides on their descriptions of the past. Accordingly, the Commission Regulation is keen to expose to public light and professional scrutiny the assumptions upon which statements about the future are based. This is especially true of profit forecasts, which are likely to be especially influential with unsophisticated investors. The assumptions underlying profit forecasts contained in prospectuses must be stated and a distinction made between assumptions directors can influence and those outside their control. The assumptions must be specific and precise and readily understandable by investors. The company's auditors or reporting accountants must confirm that the forecast has been properly compiled on the basis stated in the forecast; that the basis of the accounting used in the forecast is compatible with the issuer's general

---

[119] LR 8.3.1.
[120] LR 8.4.3. The sponsor declaration can be found on: http://www.fsa.gov.uk/pubs/forms/ LR_listing_application.pdf. Given the importance of sponsors provisions have to be made for their independence, qualifications and supervision. See, for example, LR 8.3.6, 8.6 and 8.7, but those matters do not need to be considered further in this book.
[121] LR 8.4.2 and 8.4.8. There are other requirements relating to the ongoing obligations of companies, which are discussed in the next Chapter.
[122] Above, para.25–16.

accounting policies; and that the forecast is compatible with the company's historical accounts.[123]

25–28   Finally, the prospectus must be vetted by the FSA.[124] Following the requirements of the PD, FSMA requires the submission of a draft prospectus, and indeed various other documents, to the FSA at least 10 business days prior to the intended publication date.[125] The purpose of the vetting is to put the FSA in a position to assure itself that the information is complete before it is published.[126] Inevitably, given the time and resources available, the FSA can concern itself only to a limited extent with the accuracy of the information put forward by the company, for example, it should spot glaring inaccuracies appearing on the face of the document. Nor can the FSA guarantee even completeness, except to the extent of seeing that something is said on all the matters upon which the Commission Regulation requires information and that, once again, the information is not obviously inadequate. Nevertheless, the obligation to obtain the prior approval of the FSA is, no doubt, a valuable discipline upon the issuer and its professional advisers, especially the sponsor. It should also be noted in this regard that the FSA and its officers are protected from liability in damages for acts and omissions in the discharge of the functions conferred upon them, unless bad faith is shown or there has been a breach of the Human Rights Act 1998, s.6 (unlawful for a public authority to act in a way incompatible with a convention right), so that it will be rare for the FSA to be worth suing if the prospectus turns out to be incomplete or inaccurate.[127] A refusal of approval on the part of the FSA must be accompanied by reasons and the applicant may appeal to the Tribunal (see above) against the decision.[128] The regulator is more likely simply to require that information be corrected or provided and to refuse approval only if it is not forthcoming.[129]

A particularly important part of the approval role of the FSA is the power given it by section 87B of FSMA, following Article 8(2) of the PD, to authorise omissions from the prospectus of information which would normally be required to be included. Given the range of information which the Commission Regulation requires to be included, it is likely that the applicant will regard some disclosure to be commercially harmful, because, for example, it will aid competitors. Apart from omission of information "in the public interest" on a

---

[123] Commission Regulation (EC) No.809/2004, Annex 1, para.13.
[124] PD Art.13; FSMA s.87A.
[125] FSMA s.87C: twenty days if the issuer has no securities traded on a regulated market and has never previously made a public offer. The submitted information must include the documents which the prospectus incorporates by reference: PR 3.1.1.
[126] PD Art.13(4).
[127] PD Art.13(6); FSMA s.102.
[128] FSMA s.87D.
[129] FSMA s.87J, following Art.21(3)(a)–(c) of the PD.

certificate from the Treasury,[130] however, the grounds for omission are limited, in the sense that the interests of investors are given predominant weight in the balance over the interests of the issuer and its current shareholders. Omissions may be authorised only if (a) the disclosure would be "seriously detrimental" to the issuer *and* the omission would be unlikely to mislead the public over matters "essential" for an informed assessment of the offer or (b) if the information is only of minor importance for the offer and unlikely to influence an informed assessment of the offer.[131] One might summarise the policy underlying these rules as being that, where the information is important to investors, they should be provided with it, despite the harm to the company.

Publication of prospectuses and other material

All the effort involved in drawing up a prospectus and having it approved by the FSA is, of course, simply a prelude to its publication when the securities are offered to the public. This matter is regulated by Article 14 of the PD and the PR. The issuer is given a choice of methods of publication to the public: insertion in a widely circulating newspaper; in hard copy available free of charge to the public from the issuer, its financial advisers or the regulated market in question; in electronic form on the website of the issuer, financial adviser or regulated market. Where publication is in electronic form, any member of the public is entitled to a hard copy upon request.[132] **25–29**

Despite the requirement that the prospectus include a summary, designed to be more easily accessible to unsophisticated investors, it is likely that an issuer will want to publish documentation other than the prospectus, designed to generate interest in the offer. Such "advertisements", as Article 15 of the PD terms them, run the risk of subverting all the careful regulation of the prospectus, if unsophisticated investors read only the advertisements and those documents are carelessly constructed. Consequently, any advertisement[133] must be clearly recognisable as such; must state that a prospectus is or will be available and how it may be obtained; must not contain inaccurate or misleading information; and the information in it must be consistent with the prospectus.[134] However, unlike previously,[135] advertisements do not need to be submitted to the FSA in advance or to be

---

[130] FSMA s.87B(1)(a),(2).

[131] FSMA s.87B(1)(b),(c). The same two exemptions are found for AIM admissions documents: *AIM Rules for Companies*, Rule 4.

[132] PR 3.2.4–5. There is further detail in Arts 29, 30 and 33 of the Commission Regulation.

[133] Widely defined in Art.34 of the Commission Regulation.

[134] PR 3.3.2–3. The FSA's guidance is that the advertisement should state that it is not a prospectus and contain the warning that investors should not subscribe for securities without reading the prospectus.

[135] FSMA s.98 (now repealed). The wide definition of "advertisement" (above, fn.133) would probably make such a requirement impractical.

approved by it. On the other hand, section 85 makes it unlawful to offer securities to the public before the time of publication of the prospectus required by FSMA, so any "warm-up" material will have to stop short of actually offering the securities to the public, "offer" being defined for these purposes as including the communication of sufficient information to a person to enable him or her to decide whether to invest, even if it is not an offer in contractual terms, and to embrace an offer to even a single investor.[136]

SANCTIONS

25–30   The rules examined above aim to put at the disposal of investors a considerable amount of information about companies and their shares when the latter are offered to the public and to keep that information updated thereafter. Although there may be adverse market consequences for companies which issue misleading prospectuses (their future fundraising efforts are likely to be greeted with scepticism), nevertheless an effective prospectus regime is likely to require legal sanctions as well. There are three categories of sanctions in principle available for breach of the disclosure regime: criminal, civil and administrative. However, the criminal and administrative sanctions are today effectively in the hands of the FSA and so can be looked at together. We start with an analysis of the civil sanctions.

Compensation under the Act

25–31   Before turning to the statutory provisions which create a compensation remedy for those who have suffered loss as a result of misstatements in or omissions from prospectuses, we should note that the Act provides a civil remedy also for a person who has suffered loss as a result of a breach of the prohibition on offering shares to the public before a prospectus is published. The contravention is treated as a breach of statutory duty.[137] As far as misstatements and omissions are concerned, Article 6 of the PD requires Member States to apply "their laws, regulations and administrative provisions on civil liability" to those responsible for the information contained in the prospectus, but it does not seek to stipulate what that liability regime shall be. Consequently, despite the maximum harmonisation characteristic of the PD, the impact in practice of the rules may vary from Member State to Member State, because of differences in their

---

[136] FSMA s.102B. This is not necessarily straightforward, since the commission does not accept that merely refraining from inviting offers removes the advertisement from the category of prospectus. See Financial Markets Law Committee, *Prospectus Directive "Offer to the Public"*, FMLC Issue 103.

[137] FSMA s.85(4).

enforcement regimes. The same point can be made in relation to enforcement by the "competent authority": Article 21(3) of the PD stipulates the powers each regulator must have but not the sanctions available to enforce them.

In relation to compensation the United Kingdom has long had a strong regime in place, basing liability on negligence and, indeed, reversing the burden of proof on this matter. That regime dates back to the Directors' Liability Act 1890, passed in reaction to the decision of the House of Lords in *Derry v Peak*[138] which, by insisting upon at least recklessness, exposed the inadequacy of the common law tort of deceit as a remedy for investors who suffered loss as a result of misleading prospectuses. The modern version of that liability can be found in section 90 of FSMA and it still constitutes, as we shall see in the following Chapter, a strong contrast with the liability rules for misstatements in continuing disclosures.

(a) Liability to compensate

Subject to the exemptions in (b), below, those responsible for the prospectus (or supplementary prospectus) are liable to pay compensation to any person who has acquired any of the securities to which it relates and suffered loss as a result of any untrue or misleading statement in it or of the omission of any matter required to be included under the Act.[139] This is a considerable improvement on the former provisions of the Companies Act 1985, which applied only to those who subscribed for shares and therefore excluded from protection those who bought on the market when dealings commenced. Now anyone who has acquired[140] the securities whether for cash or otherwise and whether directly from the company or by purchase on the market and who can show that he or she suffered loss as a result of the misstatement or omission will have a prima facie case for compensation.[141] This may seem at first sight an unreasonable extension of liability from the company's point of view, but in fact the prospectus is normally intended to influence not only applications to the company for shares but also the initial dealings in them in the market.[142] In addition, whereas the former version applied only to

25–32

---

[138] (1889) 14 App.Cas.337, HL. At this time, of course, liability in the tort of negligence for purely economic loss caused by misstatements was not accepted either (and that remained in effect the case until the House of Lords' decision in *Hedley Byrne & Co Ltd v Heller & Partners Ltd* [1964] A.C. 465), so that the tort of negligence could not be used to circumvent the restrictions on liability under the tort of deceit.

[139] s.90(1). Where the rules require information regarding a particular matter or a statement that there is no such matter, an omission to do either is to be treated as a statement that there is no such matter: s.90(3).

[140] "Acquire" includes contracting to acquire the securities or an interest in them: s.90(7).

[141] To be assessed presumably on the tort measure, i.e. to restore the claimant to his or her former position: *Clark v Urquart* [1930] A.C. 28, HL, i.e. normally the difference between the price paid and the value of the securities received.

[142] For the difficulties the common law has had with this point, see below, para.25–37.

misleading "statements", the new provisions specifically include omissions. The provisions do not require the claimant to show that he or she relied on the misstatement in order to establish a cause of action: it is enough that the error affected the market price, even if the claimant never read the prospectus. Obviously, however, a causal connection between the misstatement or omission and the loss will have to be proven. So, for example, market purchasers who buy after such a lapse of time that the prospectus would no longer have any influence on the price of the securities will not be able to satisfy this causal test. Finally, the statute does not require the maker of the statement to have "assumed responsibility" towards the claimant, a requirement that limits the operation of the common law of negligent misstatement.[143]

On the other hand, as far as public offers are concerned, the statutory provisions under discussion apply only to misstatements in prospectuses. This will now include the summary, which is part of the prospectus, but here liability is restricted to situations where the summary is misleading when read together with the rest of the prospectus, thus reinforcing the warning in the summary that investment decisions should not be taken on the basis of it alone.[144] However, the section does not apply to advertisements issued in connection with a public offer but separately from the prospectus. Nor, it seems, does the section apply to the Admission Document required for an AIM admission (assuming no public offer triggering the requirement for a prospectus, even for admission to AIM). In such cases compensation might be available at common law or under the Misrepresentation Act but, as the origins of the current legislation suggest, investors in that situation will in all likelihood benefit from a lower level of protection than if they could invoke the civil liability provisions of FSMA.[145]

(b) Defences

25–33   Schedule 10 provides persons responsible for the misstatement or omissions with what the headings to the sections describe as "exemptions", but which are really defences that may be available if a claim for compensation is made. The purpose of Schedule 10 is to implement the policy of imposing liability on the basis of negligence but with a reversed burden of proof. The overall effect[146] of these

---

[143]   See above, para.22–44 in relation to auditors, and below, para.25–37.

[144]   s.90(12).

[145]   The common law rules are discussed briefly below. It is not entirely unarguable that s.90 applies to an AIM admission document, which is a cut-down version of the PD prospectus. The section does not in terms say that it applies only to prospectuses required by the PD. Nor is it clear that a "prospectus" (not defined for the purposes of s.90) is confined to the documentation accompanying a public offer of shares. Nevertheless, s.90 is probably understood by most people to be limited in the way stated in the text.

[146]   This sentence merely summarises the very complex drafting of Sch.10.

defences is that the defendant escapes liability under s.90, but only if he can satisfy the court (a) that he reasonably believed that there were no misstatements or omissions and that he had done all that could reasonably be expected to ensure that there were not any, and that, if any came to his knowledge, they were corrected in time or (b) that the claimant acquired the securities with knowledge of the falsity of the statement or of the matter omitted. Where the statement in question is made by an expert and is stated to be included with the expert's consent, these rules mean that a non-expert escapes liability on the basis of a reasonable belief that the expert was competent and had consented to the inclusion of the statement.

(c) Persons responsible

The sensitive question of who are "persons responsible" and thus liable to pay the compensation is now dealt with by the PR.[147] In the case of an offer of equity shares, they are:[148]   **25–34**

    (a) the issuer (i.e. normally the company, provided the company is making the offer or seeks admission or has authorised these steps)—a further improvement on earlier versions which did not afford a remedy against the company itself;

    (b) the directors of the issuer, unless the prospectus was published without the director's knowledge or consent;

    (c) each person who has authorised himself to be named, and is named, as having agreed to become a director, whether immediately or at a future time;

    (d) each person who accepts, and is stated as accepting, responsibility for, or for any part of, the prospectus, but only in relation to the part to which the acceptance relates;[149]

    (e) each other person who has authorised the contents of the prospectus or any part of it, but again only in relation to the part authorised; and

    (f) the offeror of the securities or the company seeking admission and its directors where it is not the issuer.[150]

---

[147] PR 5.5. S.90 and Sch.10 apply also to misstatements in listing particulars but in that case the persons responsible are set out in FSMA 2000 (Official Listing of Securities) Regulations 2001 (SI 2001/2956), reg.6.

[148] PR 5.5.3.

[149] For example, the reporting accountant and any other "experts".

[150] This takes account expressly of secondary offers (above, fn.37), but the offeror will not be liable if it is a joint offer with the issuer and the issuer has taken the lead in drawing up the prospectus.

In the case of offers of other types of security,[151] directors of the issuer or offeror are excluded, unless they fall within one of the other categories (stated as accepting responsibility for the prospectus, for example), whilst the guarantor (if there is one, as there might be for offers of debt securities) is made liable for information relating to the guarantor.

PR 5.5.9 provides that nothing in the rules shall be construed as making a person responsible by reason only of his giving advice in a professional capacity. This is generally regarded as excluding the lawyers involved, though confidence in this belief may be misplaced: the leading firms of solicitors admittedly carry on investment business, "arrange" as well as "advise" and are authorised persons under the Act. It clearly does not exclude the sponsor required by the Listing Rules.[152]

A crucial problem facing misled investors is to identify all the "persons responsible" so as to be in a position to decide whether any of them is worth powder-and-shot. Article 6 of the PD requires those responsible to be identified in the prospectus and it must also contain a declaration by them that, to the best of their knowledge, the prospectus is not misleading. Somewhat stealthily, the Commission Regulation requires the declaration to state that it is made after "having taken all reasonable care to ensure that such is the case".[153] In some Member States this by itself might be used to ground liability, but in the United Kingdom section 90 of FSMA would seem to be a more secure basis for liability.

Attention should also be drawn to s.90(6) and (8). Section 90(6) says that the section "does not affect any liability which any person may incur apart from this section", but s.90(8) limits the effect of that by providing that no person, by reason of being a promoter or otherwise, shall incur any liability for failing to disclose in a prospectus information which he would not have had to disclose if he had been a person responsible for the prospectus or, if he was a person responsible, which he would have been entitled to omit by virtue of s.87B. Hence, it seems, s.90 pre-empts and overrules any duty, which a promoter or other fiduciary might be under, to disclose in the prospectus particulars of matters additional to those required under the statutory prospectus regime.

Civil remedies available elsewhere

25–35 As explained above, the damages remedy available under the Act is superior to that available under the general law. However, there may be cases where the legislation does not apply. The most obvious

---

[151] PR 5.5.4.
[152] See above, para.25–27.
[153] Commission Regulation, Annex I, para.1.

examples are non-prospectus material issued in connection with public offers or, where there is no public offer, an Admission Document issued in connection with an application for admission to AIM, which does require, as we have seen,[154] significant disclosure by applicants, even if less than under the PD. Alternatively, the claimant may want a remedy other than damages, such as rescission. Thus, a brief examination of the law relating to misrepresentation as it applies to issue documents is in order, but only a sketch of the relevant principles will be provided.

(a) Damages

The common law provides civil remedies for misrepresentations which have caused loss to those who have relied upon them. A misrepresentation is understood at common law as being a misstatement of fact rather than an expression of opinion or a promise or forecast. There must be a positive misstatement rather than an omission to state a material fact. However, this rule is heavily qualified by a further rule that an omission which causes a document as a whole to give a misleading impression or falsifies a statement made in it is actionable.[155]

25–36

Historically, the common law has provided a damages remedy only for fraudulent misstatements through the tort of deceit. This requires the maker of the statement to know that it is false or at least to be reckless as to its truth. In any event, an honest, even if wholly unreasonable, belief in the truth of the statement will not amount to deceit. As we have seen, it was the decision of the House of Lords to this effect in *Derry v Peek*[156] which led to the introduction of the predecessor of the statutory provisions relating to misstatements in prospectuses which we discussed above. In addition, the tort of deceit requires reliance by the recipient on the statement and, further, that the maker of the statement should have intended the recipient to rely on it. These are formidable hurdles to liability.

Since then, however, there have been two significant developments. Section 2(1) of the Misrepresentation Act 1967 introduced a statutory remedy for negligent misstatement, which also reverses the burden of proof. The 1967 Act was in effect a generalisation of the principle contained in the statutory provisions relating to prospectus liability, and will therefore be of use where the misstatement was not contained in a prospectus but in some other document issued in connection with the offer. However, the generalisation in s.2(1) extends only to misstatements made by a party to the subsequent contract[157]

---

[154] Above, para.25–20.
[155] *R. v Kylsant* [1932] 1 K.B. 442, CCA.
[156] (1889) 14 App.Cas.337.
[157] Or his agent, but even then not so as to make the agent liable but only the principal: *The Skopas* [1983] 1 W.L.R. 857.

and the section gives a cause of action only to the other party to it, so that it would seem impossible to use it to sue directors or other experts or advisers who are involved in public offers of shares by the company. The company itself may be sued, certainly in an offer for subscription or a rights issue or an open offer and perhaps even on an offer for sale, since a new contractual relation between a purchaser and the company comes into existence when the purchaser is registered as the holder of the securities. Where the subsection applies, it makes the misrepresentor liable as if he had been fraudulent. This had led the Court of Appeal to conclude that the measure of damages under s.2(1) is a tortious, rather than a contractual, one, but that the rules of remoteness are those applicable to actions in deceit, so that the person misled can recover for all losses flowing from the misstatement.[158]

25–37   Because of these limitations on the new statutory cause of action, it can be said that the more significant development in recent times has been the acceptance of liability for negligent misstatement at common law following the decision of the House of Lords in *Hedley Byrne & Co Ltd v Heller & Partners Ltd*.[159] This is a general principle of liability, not confined within the precise words of a statutory formulation, and so capable of being used against directors and advisers as well as the company itself in the case of negligent misstatements in prospectuses and other documents associated with public offers. However, the common law liability does require a finding by the courts that the defendants owed a duty of care to those wishing to invoke the principle, and this is a matter towards which the courts have taken a restrictive attitude in recent years.

It was established in the nineteenth century that in an action for deceit the prima facie rule is that, where the false statement is contained in a prospectus, only those who rely upon it to subscribe for shares in the company have a cause of action, and subsequent purchasers in the market do not, even though they may have relied upon the prospectus.[160] The purpose for which the prospectus was issued was to induce subscriptions of shares and that purpose circumscribed the range of plaintiffs who could sue in respect of false statements contained in it. That this is only the prima facie position is demonstrated by the subsequent decision of the Court of Appeal in *Andrews*

---

[158] *Royscot Trust v Rogerson* [1991] 2 Q.B. 297, CA. However, in *Smith New Court Securities Ltd v Scrimgeour Vickers (Asset Management) Ltd* [1996] 4 All E.R. 769 the House of Lords refused to commit themselves to acceptance of the proposition laid down in the *Royscot Trust* case. That decision of the House of Lords also held that it was no longer an inflexible rule that in deceit the shares acquired had to be valued on the basis of the market price at the time of the transaction. In that case the shares acquired as a result of the deceit of the defendants were in fact worth much less than the market thought at the time of acquisition because of an independent and unconnected fraud which had been committed against the company, and the misrepresentee was able to have damages assessed on the basis of the share price at the later time when the unconnected fraud became known to the market.

[159] [1964] A.C. 465.

[160] *Peek v Gurney* (1873) L.R. 6 H.L. 377, HL.

v Mockford[161] where the jury were held to be entitled to conclude that the false prospectus was only one of a series of false statements made by the defendants, whose purpose was not simply to induce subscriptions but also to encourage purchases in the market when dealings began. There, the subsequent market purchasers could maintain their claims.

This emphasis upon the purpose of the statement and the nature of the transaction in issue has now entered the law of negligent misstatement following the decision of the House of Lords in *Caparo Plc v Dickman*[162] and is illustrated by the subsequent holding in *Al-Nakib Investments Ltd v Longcroft*[163] that allegedly misleading statements in a prospectus issued in connection with a rights issue could form the basis of a claim by a shareholder who took up his rights in reliance upon the prospectus but not when the (same) shareholder purchased further shares on the market. Although this too is presumably a prima facie rule, it seems that the presumption will be hard to rebut if all that can be pointed to is the false statement in the prospectus. While *Caparo* is part of a more general move in the law of tort to restrict liability for negligent statements causing purely economic loss, it has to be said that the consequence in this area of drawing a distinction between subscribers and market purchasers in the immediate period after dealings commence is, in commercial terms, highly artificial. Companies have an interest not only in the issue being fully subscribed but also in a healthy aftermarket developing so that subscribers can easily dispose of their shares, if they so wish.[164] The statutory provisions on liability for misstatements recognise the force of this argument.[165] Perhaps the way forward in the common law would be for the courts to take a more inclusive view of the issuer's purposes.[166]

(b) Rescission

The common law has traditionally permitted rescission (i.e. reversal) of contracts entered into as a result of a misrepresentation, whether that misrepresentation be fraudulent, negligent or wholly innocent.

25–38

---

[161] [1892] 2 Q.B. 372.

[162] [1990] 2 A.C. 605. See above, para.22–44.

[163] [1990] 1 W.L.R. 1390.

[164] "The issue of a prospectus establishes a basis for valuation of the securities and underpins the development of a market in them, irrespective of the precise circumstances of the initial offer": DTI, *Listing Particulars and Public Offer Prospectuses: Consultative Document* (July 1990), para.10.

[165] Above, para.25–36.

[166] An indication of judicial willingness to take this view is the decision of Lightman J. in *Possfund Custodian Trustees Ltd v Diamond* [1996] 1 W.L.R. 1351, refusing to strike out a claim that an additional and intended purpose of a prospectus issued in connection with a placing of securities was to inform and encourage purchasers in the aftermarket, in this case the USM. At the time the relevant provisions of the Companies Act 1985 conferred a statutory entitlement to compensation only upon subscribers.

This remedy is a useful supplement to the right to claim damages, even when an extensive damages remedy is provided through the special statutory provisions relating to prospectuses. In many cases, all the investor may wish or need to do is to return the securities and recover his or her money. The value of this remedy has been somewhat reduced by section 2(2) of the Misrepresentation Act 1967, giving the court a discretion in appropriate cases to substitute damages for the rescission, a provision included largely for the benefit of misrepresentors.[167] This subsection might be invoked, for example, where the court thought that the rescission was motivated by subsequent adverse movements in the stock market as a whole rather than the impact of the misrepresentation as such. However, it is still an important weapon in the investor's armoury.

The right will be exercisable against the company, if the contract for the securities is with the company, or against the transferor if the acquisition is from a previous holder. In the case of rescission against the company, it will be necessary to show, of course, that the misrepresentation was in fact made by the company, but in the case of statements included in the prospectus, even those made by experts, it seems that the company will be prima facie liable for them and that it carries a heavy burden to disassociate itself from them.[168]

The most important limitations on the right to rescind arise out of the various "bars" on its exercise. Although s.1(b) of the 1967 Act has removed the bar, which was once thought to exist, that an executed contract could not be rescinded, nevertheless the investor is still well-advised to act quickly once the truth is discovered. If he or she accepts dividends, attends and votes at meetings or sells or attempts to sell the securities after the truth has been discovered, the contract will be taken to have been affirmed,[169] and even mere delay may defeat the right to rescind. The reason for this strictness is that the company may well have raised credit from third parties who have acted on the basis of the capital apparently raised by the company, which appearance the rescission of the shareholder's contract would undermine. A rescission claim is also defeated by the liquidation of the company (at which point the creditors' rights crystallise), or even perhaps by its becoming insolvent but before winding up commences,[170] so that the shareholder must have issued a writ or actually

---

[167] However, in *Thomas Witter Ltd v TBP Industries Ltd* [1996] 2 All E.R. 573 there is a dictum of Jacob J. to the effect that the court's power to award damages under s.2(2) is not limited to situations where the misrepresentee still has the right to rescind, thus opening up the possibility of damages under the statute for non-negligent misstatements, a development which would benefit misrepresentees. This dictum was not followed in *Government of Zanzibar v British Aerospace (Lancaster House) Ltd* [2000] 1 W.L.R. 2333.

[168] *Mair v Rio Grande Rubber Estates Ltd* [1913] A.C. 853, HL; *Pacaya Rubber Co, Re* [1914] 1 Ch. 542, CA.

[169] *Sharpley v Louth and East Coast Railway Company* (1876) 2 Ch.D. 663; *Scholey v Central Railway of Venezuela* (1869) L.R. 9 Eq. 266n; *Crawley's case* (1869) L.R. 4 Ch.App. 322.

[170] *Tennent v The City of Glasgow Bank* (1879) 4 App.Cas.615.

had his name removed from the register before that event occurs.[171] Finally, inability to make *restitutio in integrum* will bar rescission, though in the case of shares that principle would seem to be relevant mainly where the shareholder has disposed of the securities before discovering that a misrepresentation has been made.[172]

(c) Breach of contract

Finally, in the general law of contract it not uncommonly occurs that the courts treat a misrepresentation as having been incorporated in the subsequent contract concluded between the parties. The advantage of establishing this would be that the misrepresentee would have a claim to damages to be assessed on the contractual basis, rather than on a tortious basis as is the position with claims based on the statutory prospectus provisions, the Misrepresentation Act or, of course, the *Hedley Byrne* principle. In particular, the shareholder might be able to claim for the loss of the expected profit on the shares. However, a difficulty facing such claims against the company is that the processes of allotment of shares and entry in the register are to be regarded as a complete novation, i.e. the substitution of a new contract for the old contract based on the prospectus.[173] It has to be said, too, that prospectuses normally stop short of making explicit promises about future value or performance, so that the basis for finding a promise to be enforced may not be available.

25–39

Criminal and administrative sanctions

Criminal sanctions play a rather limited role in the area of public offers, but it is to be noted that the central obligation in this area— not to make a public offer of securities or to request admission of securities to a regulated market unless an approved prospectus has

25–40

---

[171] *Oakes v Turquand* (1867) L.R. 2 H.L. 325; *Scottish Petroleum Company, Re* (1882) 23 Ch.D. 413. Whether this would apply in the case of rescission as against a transferor (rather than the company) is less clear, but the liquidator's consent would be needed for the re-transfer: Insolvency Act 1986, s.88.

[172] Even in this context one should note the dictum of Lord Browne-Wilkinson in *Smith New Court Securities Ltd v Scrimgeour Vickers (Asset Management) Ltd* [1996] 4 All E.R. 769 at 774: "... if the current law in fact provides ... that there is no right to rescind the contract for the sale of quoted shares once the specific shares purchased have been sold, the law will need to be carefully looked at hereafter. Since in such a case other, identical shares can be purchased on the market, the defrauded purchaser can offer substantial *restitutio in integrum* which is normally sufficient." However, this comment was made in the context of a purchase from a shareholder, not a subscription to shares issued by the company.

[173] The possibilities and problems arising out of breach of contract claims against the company are illustrated by *Addlestone Linoleum Co, Re* (1887) 37 Ch.D. 191, CA, which, however, must now be read in the light of the abolition of the rule that a shareholder cannot recover damages against the company unless the allotment of shares is also rescinded. See CA 2006, s.655.

been made publicly available—is supported not only by civil but also criminal sanctions.[174] The principal non-civil sanctions, however, are administrative ones in the hands of the FSA, which also has power to invoke the criminal law just mentioned.[175] We have mentioned above the most central of the FSA's administrative powers, namely a refusal to approve the prospectus, thus preventing the public offer or admission to a regulated market from proceeding.[176] If approval has been given and the offer launched or admission process begun, the FSA has power to suspend further action for a period of up to ten days, if it has reasonable grounds for suspecting that a provision of Part VI of FSMA or of the PR or any other provision required by the PD has been infringed. If it finds that such a provision has been infringed, it may require the offer to be withdrawn or the market operator to prohibit trading in the securities.[177] The issuer or other person offering the securities or seeking admission is also liable to public censure by the FSA for failure to comply with the requirements mentioned above.[178] The suspension or prohibition decision of the FSA may take effect immediately, without the issuer or other involved person having the opportunity to make representations, for such action may be urgent, but that person must be given a notice, stating the reasons for the action and giving the person the possibility of making representations (which may cause the FSA to vary or revoke its decision) and notifying it of its right to refer the FSA's decision to the Tribunal.[179]

The administrative sanctions considered in the previous paragraph, other than public censure, encourage compliance with the relevant rules essentially by preventing the issuer, permanently or temporarily, from achieving its business goal i.e. making a public offer and/or securing admission to trading on a regulated market. This is a very powerful set of sanctions and a strong inducement to compliance, for, otherwise, all the considerable preparation costs risk being thrown away. However, those sanctions can be applied effectively only to breaches of the rules which the FSA picks up in advance of the offer or admission to trading. The FSA will obviously be reluctant to use its power to prohibit trading once admission has been secured, and cannot do anything about a public offer which has been carried

---

[174] FSMA s.85(3): on indictment the maximum penalty is a prison term of not more than two years or a fine or both.

[175] FSMA s.401.

[176] See above, para.25–28.

[177] FSMA ss.87K and 87L. In the case of an offer, the FSA may require it to be withdrawn also where it has reasonable grounds for suspecting that it is likely a requirement will be infringed (s.87K(4)), but no such power exists in the case of securities admitted to trading. This is presumably because of the adverse impact of ending trading on the company's shareholders, whereas an offer, if subsequently cleared, can be resuscitated. These provisions follow those of Art.21(3)(d)–(h) of the PD.

[178] s.87M.

[179] s.87Q. On the Tribunal see above, para.25–17. A censure decision may also be referred to the Tribunal: s.87N.

through to the point of the allotment of securities. Furthermore, it can be said that the administrative sanctions considered so far impose costs on the issuer (i.e. the shareholders) rather than on the officers of the company who may be those responsible for the non-compliance.[180] It is therefore of some significance that the FSA has the power to impose monetary penalties where there has been a breach of the rules mentioned in the previous paragraph. The FSA may impose a penalty of such amount as it considers appropriate on the issuer, any other person offering shares to the public, seeking approval of a prospectus or requesting their admission to trading on a regulated market, and any other person to whom a requirement of the PD applies.[181] This penalty-imposing power extends to any person who was a director of a company involved where the director was "knowingly concerned" in the contravention.[182] The FSA may engage in public censure in lieu of imposing a penalty.[183] The power to impose a monetary penalty is a general power of the FSA under Part VI, not confined to the PD and PR, as we shall see in the following Chapter. Even in the context of public offers this is an important point because we have seen that the provisions of CARD on admission to the Official List are implemented in the LR, not the PR, and, further, that the LR include some requirements which extend beyond those of CARD.[184] A similar penalty-imposing power exists in relation to breaches of the LR.[185] In the case of suspected breaches of Part VI of FSMA or of the PR or LR the FSA also has formal investigatory powers which may help it to uncover the truth.[186]

This penalty-imposing power is naturally surrounded by some safeguards. The FSA is required to develop outside the context of a particular case a policy about the circumstances in which it will exercise its powers and the amount of the penalty it will impose.[187] A proposal to impose a penalty must be communicated to the person in question by means of a "warning notice", giving at least 28 days for representations to be made, and a decision to impose a penalty may be appealed to the Tribunal.[188]

---

[180] Even if those officers of the company are also shareholders, they will be able to share the costs with the non-officer shareholders. It will be recalled that an FSA penalty is one of the matters against which a company may not agree in advance to indemnify the director: above, Ch.16 at para.16–93.

[181] s.91(1A). This implements Art.25 of the PD.

[182] s.91(2).

[183] s.91(3).

[184] Above, para.25–16.

[185] s.91(1) and (2) for "knowingly concerned" directors.

[186] FSMA s.97 and Part XI (but the investigatory powers are not confined to authorised persons, as they normally are under Part XI).

[187] s.93. See FSA, DEPP, Ch.6.

[188] s.92 and s.387 on warning notices.

CROSS-BORDER OFFERS AND ADMISSIONS

25–41 We have noted above that the Community's strong drive to remove obstacles to cross-border offers and admissions to regulated markets led to the maximum harmonisation character of the PD. The notion is that an issuer should be able to use the same documentation (subject in some cases to translation requirements) when it makes offers or seeks admission to trading in more than one Member State. Since there is not currently a single Community regulator, an immediate question which arises is where regulatory responsibility should be allocated in cross-border offers. The basic choice in the PD is to allocate responsibility to the state in which the company is incorporated (has its registered office) in the case of companies incorporated within the Community (the "home state"). The competent authorities of "host states", i.e. states in which an offer to the public is made or admission to trading is sought, "shall not undertake any approval or administrative procedures relating to prospectuses".[189]

This choice, which applies even if there is to be no public offer or admission in the home state, is controversial. It potentially puts regulatory responsibility in the hands of inexperienced regulators in countries with undeveloped markets and prohibits the authority in the jurisdiction where the offer or trading will occur from taking action, even though the latter has the stronger incentive to discharge its regulatory functions effectively. If the host state regulator finds that breaches of the relevant rules have occurred or are taking place, it is obliged to refer the matter to the home state authorities, and, only if this is ineffective, may the host state regulator act, informing the Commission at the same time.[190] Equally, if the host state authority forms the view that a supplementary prospectus is needed, it is the home state authority which must require it and the host state authority is permitted simply to draw the home state authority's attention to the need.[191] Consequently, FSMA is drafted so that the obligation to seek FSA approval of a prospectus is applied only to issuers whose home state is the United Kingdom,[192] and most of the PR apply only to offers and admissions involving issuers whose home state is the United Kingdom.[193] It follows as well that the administrative sanctions for breach of the PR do not apply to issuers not incorporated in the United Kingdom (the home state authority has

---

[189] PD Arts. 17(1) and 2(1)(m), (n). There are procedures to be followed by the home State to certify to the FSA its approval of the prospectus: PD Art.18; FSMA s.87H.
[190] PD Art.23.
[191] PD Art.17(2).
[192] s.87A(1)(a).
[193] PR 1.1.1. However, the FSA does have the task of applying the eligibility requirements (above, para.25–16) to all applicants, for CARD does not insist on home state regulation.

responsibility) but the statutory and common law compensation regimes will (subject to the relevant conflicts of law rules).

There are two exceptions to the rule of home state regulation. First, for companies incorporated outside the EEA a home state has to be attributed, and this is the state in which securities are first offered to the public or where the first admission to trading on a regulated market is made, at the issuer's choice.[194] For non-EEA issuers, therefore, the home state is what would be the host state for an EEA issuer. However, third-country issuers may also benefit from a further relaxation. The relevant EU regulator may permit the third-country issuer to draw up a prospectus under the third country's laws if the information is equivalent to that required by the PD and the third country rules meet international standards.[195] No doubt this is done in the expectation that EEA issuers will be treated similarly, so that international offerings will be promoted. Secondly, even for EU-incorporated issuers, issuers of debt securities denominated in amounts of at least EUR 1,000 may choose as regulator the state of incorporation, the state of offer or the state of admission to trading.[196]

The second contentious issue with cross-border offerings is that of language. If a translation is required in all the official languages of the states in which the offering is to take place and where the securities are to be admitted to trading and in the language of the state of incorporation, then the additional costs of the cross-border offer are likely to be substantial. On the other hand, the Member States can hardly be expected to agree a single language in which alone pro-spectuses need be circulated. The result, however, is a complex set of rules. The language issue is solved in the following way in Article 19. Where the offer or admission takes place in the home state only, then the competent authority of the home state determines the appropriate language. Where the offer or admission takes place in one or more Member States *not including the home state*, then the offeror or person seeking admission has a choice between a language acceptable to the competent authorities in those Member States or "a language cus-tomary in the sphere of international finance" (though the competent authorities of the host states can require the summary to be translated into its official language). How far this Delphic phrase goes to embrace languages other than English is anyone's guess—and,

---

[194] PD Art.2(1)(m)(iii).

[195] PD Art.20; PR 4.2.

[196] PD Art.2(1)(m)(ii). This rule applies to non-EU incorporated issuers as well, who, however, cannot choose the State of incorporation because they are not within the EU. The advantage for them of being within (ii) rather than (iii) appears to be that the choice arises each time a relevant issue of debt securities is made, whereas for non-EU issuers the choice is otherwise a once-and-for-all one.

indeed, that was probably the primary virtue of the phrase in the Community legislator's mind. The offeror or person seeking admission has a similar choice of language in respect of the home state authority (for prospectus approval purposes) except that here the alternative is a language acceptable to the home state authority. Where the offer is not made in the home state, the incentive created by these rules is clearly for the offeror etc. to use "a language customary in the sphere of international finance", since that language can be used for both home and host state purposes (the incentive would not arise if the home and host states shared a particular language).

Where the offer or admission to listing is to take place in two or more Member States, *including* the home state, then the prospectus must be produced in a language acceptable to the home state competent authority and, in addition, in either a language acceptable to each host state or a language customary in the sphere of international finance.

However, in the case of admission to trading of heavy-weight debt securities (i.e. those denominated in amounts of 50,000 euros or more), the offeror etc. always has the choice of using a customary language only, even where admission will occur in the home state, or it may instead choose a language acceptable to both home and host state competent authorities.

De-listing

25–42   This Chapter has focussed on the processes by which the securities of a company become publicly held and traded on a public market. This is a reversible process. Companies may seek voluntarily to retire from a market upon which their securities were traded, notably after a successful takeover bid (discussed in Chapter 28), whether that takeover be by another company operating in the same field or by a financial buyer, such as a private equity house. If the securities of the company are all held by one person as a result of the bid, this is a straightforward exercise. If, however, there are some outside shareholders, they may oppose the proposal to de-list because it will reduce the liquidity of the securities even further. Indeed, the proposal to de-list may be part of an attempt by the controllers of the company to squeeze out the minority in a situation where the statutory squeeze-out provisions (also discussed in Chapter 28) would not operate. The requirement previously was that companies simply inform their shareholders of the decision to de-list, but the LR now require requests from companies for the cancellation of a primary listing of equity shares to be approved by a three-quarters majority at a meeting of the class of shareholders in question, after the circulation to them of a statement, approved by the FSA, of the reasons for this step.[197]

---

[197] LR 5.2.5. For the policy behind the change see FSA, *Review of the Listing Regime*, CP 203, October 2003, paras 9.21–9.27. There are certain exceptions to the requirement for shareholder approval, for example, where the shares are already traded on a regulated market in another EEA State (so that what is being effected is a shift in primary listing); if the company is in severe financial difficulties; the securities in question are debt securities; the controller has reached a 75 percent holding as a result of a takeover bid in which the offer document made clear the offeror's intention to de-list.

CHAPTER 26

CONTINUING OBLIGATIONS AND DISCLOSURE OF INFORMATION TO THE MARKET

INTRODUCTION

It would be a mistake to think that, once a company has been **26–1** admitted to a public market, in accordance with the rules discussed in the previous Chapter, the rules of the FSA or of the London Stock Exchange (or other market operators) cease to be relevant. Both sets of rules impose obligations on publicly traded companies, upon compliance with which their continued admission to the public market ultimately depends. But what is the content of these continuing obligations?

It might be though that regulation specific to companies whose securities have been admitted to the Official List or are traded on a regulated or other public market,[1] would be concerned solely with

---

[1] For definitions of the "Official List" and "regulated markets" see the previous Chapter at paras 25–5ff.

relations between the company and its investors, whether or not those investors are shareholders in the company at the relevant time.[2] In fact, however, the publicly traded company, and especially the listed company, is a category which attracts additional regulation of corporate law type, i.e. the regulation is directed at relations between the company and its shareholders as such. Such rules could appropriately have been included in the Companies Act. However, they are to be found in fact in rules made by the FSA under powers conferred by FSMA 2000[3] or in contractual obligations imposed by the London Stock Exchange (or other market operator) on issuers which choose to obtain admission to exchange-regulated markets, notably the Alternative Investment Market (AIM). This form of rule-making has the advantage of making the rules more easily changeable and of involving market participants more closely in their formulation, and the disadvantage of reducing the level of Parliamentary scrutiny to which they are subject.[4] Whatever the source of the rules, the thinking behind them is that it is appropriate to apply to companies with the largest shareholder base additional corporate law requirements which reflect that fact. The Companies Act already distinguishes between private companies and public companies, the latter being companies which are permitted by the Act to offer their shares to the public,[5] and applies additional rules to companies which are public in the Companies Act sense. The special company law rules for listed companies take that process a stage further, by imposing a further additional layer of rules on companies which not only are permitted to offer their shares to the public but have in fact done so and have had those securities admitted to the Official List.[6] These might be regarded as companies which are public in the stock exchange sense of the term.

We have already noted the main additional corporate law rules applying to listed companies at various points in this book. We need only recapitulate them briefly here.

- The obligation to observe, on a comply or explain basis, the provisions of the Combined Code on Corporate Governance, dealing crucially with the composition of the board and the role of independent non-executive directors and of committees of the board.[7]

---

[2] When considering whether to buy or subscribe for shares in the company, they may or may not be existing shareholders, depending on their previous decisions; when considering whether to sell, they necessarily will be.

[3] s.73A.

[4] In its recent review of the Listing Rules the FSA decided to keep the "corporate law" features of the Rules: FSA, *Review of the Listing Regime*, CP 203, October 2003, Ch.9.

[5] CA 2006, s.755. See above at para.24–2.

[6] In the case of AIM companies somewhat less demanding versions of the requirements for listed companies apply by virtue of the AIM Rules, which apply as a matter of contract between the company and the London Stock Exchange. See para.25–9.

[7] Listing Rule (LR) 9.8.6(5); above, para.14–31.

- The rules on "related-party" transactions, especially the requirement of shareholder approval (from which voting interested shareholders are excluded), which rules supplement both the Companies Act provisions on directors' duties and the common law controls over voting by controlling shareholders.[8]

- The rules on "significant" transactions requiring shareholder approval of large transactions, whether or not there is an element of self-dealing. These provisions supplement the Companies Act provisions which require shareholder approval for certain types of transaction and they thus affect the distribution of power as between shareholders and the board.[9]

The rules of exchange regulated markets impose similar, but less developed, obligations on the issuers whose securities are traded on those markets.[10] **26–2**

Further, and consistently with the disclosure philosophy which dominates the rules on public offerings and admission to trading,[11] many of the continuing obligations are based on that philosophy. Three points can be made about these disclosure rules. First, they are no longer driven by purely domestic requirements. Disclosure obligations of a continuing nature are now increasingly governed by Community instruments made as part of the Financial Services Action Plan—with a concomitant multiplicity of layers of law-making.[12] Secondly, those disclosure obligations hover uncertainly between disclosure for the benefit of shareholders and disclosure for the benefit of investors. Probably the latter is the dominant objective of the Community instruments, but there is no doubt that shareholders benefit from this process to some extent as well. As the European Commission's High Level Group of Company Law Experts remarked:

> "Information and disclosure is an area where company law and securities regulation come together. It is a key objective of securities regulation in general to ensure that market participants have sufficient information in order to participate in the market on an informed basis. Where the relevant security is a share in a company, the information required from a securities regulation

---

[8] LR 11; above, Ch.16 at para.16–55 and Ch.19 at para.19–2.
[9] LR10. See above, para.14–8.
[10] See, for example, LSE, *AIM Rules for Companies*, rules 12–13.
[11] See para.25–18.
[12] See para.25–7.

point of view overlaps with the information to be provided from a company law perspective."[13]

Thirdly, the disclosures required are not only disclosures by the company but also disclosures to the company by corporate insiders or major shareholders (usually coupled with a further disclosure obligation on the company). The purpose of this Chapter is to discuss these continuing disclosure obligations, except in so far as they have not already been discussed. For the purposes of brevity we will take as our core case a UK incorporated company whose securities are traded on one of the London markets.[14]

PERIODIC REPORTING OBLIGATIONS

26–3 We saw in Chapter 21 that all companies must report on an annual basis to their shareholders and that such reporting is now extensive, especially for "quoted" companies.[15] However, for a long time companies with securities traded on public markets have been subject to more frequent periodic reporting requirements, for the market's appetite is not satisfied by yearly reporting. Such companies may be required to report half-yearly and even quarterly. As far as companies are concerned whose securities are traded on a regulated market,[16] these obligations currently stem from Directive 2004/109/EC on the harmonisation of transparency requirements (hereafter the "Transparency Directive" or "TD").[17] Such reports may help shareholders in the exercise of their governance powers, though only the annual report is tied to a shareholder meeting, but they will also, since they are public, inform investors' trading decisions. In the eyes of the drafters of the Community instrument, the latter was probably the predominant purpose of the Directive.

Article 4 of the TD requires the publication of audited annual accounts and reports. By and large, the requirements of this article

---

[13] *Report of the High Level Group of Company Law Experts on a Modern Regulatory Framework for Company Law in Europe* (Brussels, November 4, 2002), Ch. II.3.

[14] Thus, we shall not deal in any detail with companies incorporated in other EEA States or outside the EU whose securities are traded on a London market or with UK-incorporated companies whose sole or primary listing is outside the UK.

[15] "Quoted companies" are those officially listed in any EEA State or admitted to trading on the New York Stock Exchange or Nasdaq: CA 2006, s.385.

[16] For the meaning of a "regulated market" see para.25–5. It can be equated in the UK, with some degree of inaccuracy, with the Main Market of the London Stock Exchange. The Alternative Investment Market (AIM) is not a regulated market, but the LSE's own rules for that market require half-yearly statements (but not quarterly reports): LSE, *AIM Rules for Companies*, February 2007, rule 18.

[17] OJ L390/38, 31.12.2004. Implemented by the FSA's Disclosure and Transparency Rules (DTR).

are met by the rules contained in the Companies Act 2006 and considered in Chapters 21 and 22.[18] However, the requirement for speedier publication than the 2006 Act requires (four, rather than six, months from the end of the financial year) is implemented domestically in rules (Disclosure and Transparency Rules or "DTR") made by the FSA.[19] Further, Article 4 requires a more explicit "responsibility statement" than is to be found in the case of accounts approved by the directors and signed by a director on behalf of the board under the Act.[20] The article requires the names of all those responsible within the issuer for the accounts and reports to be stated and the responsibility statement must certify that, to the best of their knowledge, the accounts have been prepared in accordance with the relevant standards and give a true and fair view of the company's financial position, and the management report includes a fair review of the company's business. This is implemented domestically in the DTR.[21]

More significant is the requirement of the Directive for half-yearly reports, to be published within two months of the end of the half year. The half-yearly reports are required to be less detailed than the annual ones and are not required to be audited (though if they are audited or reviewed, the audit report or review must be published).[22] The accounts required to be produced are a condensed set of financial statements, the directors' report is an "interim review" and the responsibility statement is adjusted accordingly.[23]

The issue of quarterly reporting has been contentious. Some argue **26-4** that it adds to the efficiency of securities markets; others than it encourages management to focus on the short-term. In the end, Article 6 of the Directive does not require a set of quarterly accounts but only an "interim management statement", which must give an explanation of material events and transactions which have taken place and their impact on the issuer and a general description of the company's financial position and performance.[24] The interim management statement is required for the quarters where no yearly or half-yearly report is required and must be produced in the period

---

[18] The CA contains some rules specific to quoted companies, for example, the requirement for website publication: s.430.
[19] DTR 4.1.3. However, some of the statutory material is repeated in the DTR in order to make it applicable to companies not incorporated in the United Kingdom but which have their securities traded on a regulated market in the United Kingdom.
[20] See para.21–28.
[21] DTR 4.1.12. On the sanctions available to the FSA see para.25–40.
[22] Art.5(4). The Auditing Practices Board has produced guidance on the review of interim statements.
[23] Art.5(2). Some detail about what is required in the half-yearly accounts and reports is set out in Commission Directive 2007/14/EC (OJ L69/27, 9.3.2007) Art.3. The transposing domestic legislation is in DTR 4.2.
[24] Implemented in DTR 4.3. A company which does produce quarterly financial reports under a Member State's domestic rules is exempt from this requirement: Art.6(2).

between the three weeks before the end of the quarter and seven weeks after its end.[25]

Failure to comply with the rules contained in the DTR will attract the sanctions of the FSA, as well as any sanctions available under the 2006 Act, if a breach of the latter's requirements has occurred. As we have noted in Chapter 21, the power to review the accounts and reports of companies for compliance with the relevant requirements is one which has been delegated by the Government to the Financial Reporting Review Panel; and that body's powers extend to all the periodic reports required to be produced by listed companies, whether annual or otherwise.[26] Civil liability for inaccuracies in the periodic reports is discussed below.

EPISODIC OR AD HOC REPORTING REQUIREMENTS

The substantive requirements

26–5 In addition to the requirement to make reports every three months, publicly quoted companies are required to report events as they occur. There seem to be two main arguments behind this requirement. First, it can be seen as a way of keeping shareholders and investors up-to-date about developments in the business of the company or about other factors which affect its business, because they may wish to take investment or governance decisions on the basis of it. This view was reflected in the now-repealed Article 68(1) of the Directive on the admission of securities to the Official List ("CARD").[27] The information should be disclosed because it is relevant to investors and shareholders. The second argument, reflected in Article 7 of the first and now-repealed Community Directive on insider dealing,[28] applying to all regulated markets, is that the information should be disclosed publicly in order that it shall no longer be known only to a small group of persons who may be tempted to trade on the basis of the information to their profit precisely because it is not known to the market in general. On this rationale disclosure is a way of reducing opportunities of "insider trading" i.e. trading in securities on the basis of price-sensitive information which is not generally available. Insider dealing is both a criminal offence[29] and a breach of the FSMA 2000 provisions on

---

[25] Art.6(1)—so that it is not necessarily a quarterly statement if it is produced before the quarter's end.
[26] See para.21–31.
[27] On which see the previous Chapter at para.25–15.
[28] Council Directive 89/592/EEC.
[29] Criminal Justice Act 1993, Part V.

market abuse.[30] On both arguments, the purpose of the rules is to have the information disclosed to the market, but, in the first argument because market participants and shareholders need the information to inform action they might take and, on the second argument, because disclosure is the way of depriving the information of its "inside" character.

The current version of these Community requirements is to be found in Article 6 of Directive 2003/6/EC on insider trading and market manipulation (market abuse) (hereafter "Market Abuse Directive"(MAD)), applying to companies whose securities are traded on a regulated market. The disclosure provisions of MAD are implemented in the United Kingdom via FSA rules, the Disclosure and Transparency Rules ("DTR").[31] Although MAD is the modern version of the original insider dealing Directive, it is doubtful whether the episodic disclosure requirements should be viewed solely as an anti-insider trading mechanism, since the current Directive aims at controlling market abuse, which includes market manipulation as well as insider trading within its scope. In addition, investors will in practice react to disclosures of significant information by companies by taking investment decisions, so that ad hoc disclosures inform the market at the same time as they deprive the inside information of its non-public character.

The emphasis in Article 6 is on disclosure by the company of inside information "as soon as possible". The essence of inside information is that it is information which is not known to the market but, if it were known, would have a significant effect on the price of the company's securities because it is "precise" information relating either to the company or to its securities.[32] Companies naturally generate such information in the normal course of their business and the purpose of the Directive is to secure the speedy release of such information to shareholders and the market. Common examples of such information would be the discovery of a fraud committed in one of the group's subsidiaries; or of a gas or oil find by one of its exploration teams; that its well-respected CEO was about to retire unexpectedly; or that the company was in discussions about a takeover bid. Clearly, not all inside information about the company is generated by the company itself. It may result from the activities of a competitor (whose new invention may cast doubt on the viability of

---

[30] ss.118ff. See further Ch.30.
[31] In particular DTR 2. Although these rules apply only to issuers whose securities are (or are to be) admitted to a regulated market (see para.25–5), ad hoc disclosure rules are imposed on AIM companies under the AIM Rules (see LSE, *Aim Rules for Companies*, February 2007, Rule 11) but, of course, in this case as a matter of contract between AIM and the company, which gives the FSA no enforcement role. But see below the discussion of market abuse and the FSA.
[32] MAD, Art.1.

the company's business)[33] or from government whose policies (for example to encourage renewable forms of energy or to tax certain sorts of vehicle more heavily) may encourage or discourage a particular company's business. In such a case no disclosure obligation seems to fall upon the company, but in the case of information generated by the company or otherwise in its possession the obligation will arise.[34]

26–6   In the design of any rules relating to the disclosure of events "as soon as possible", there are two problems which have to be faced. One is to define the point at which the event has crystallised and so triggers the disclosure obligation. If impending developments or matters under negotiation are disclosed too soon, their completion may be jeopardized and the market possibly be given information whose value is difficult to assess because it relates to inchoate matters. The Directive permits issuers "under their own responsibility" (i.e. they cannot require the national regulatory authority to give advance clearance of non-disclosure, though the regulator must be informed of the decision not to disclose)[35] to delay disclosure to protect their "legitimate interests", but subject to the rider that the non-disclosure must not be likely to mislead the public and provided the company can ensure the confidentiality of the information on the part of those to whom it will have to be disclosed.[36] The implementing Commission Directive recognises that matters in the course of negotiation may fall within this definition where the outcome of the negotiations would be likely to be affected by disclosure.[37]

The second problem is that public disclosure of adverse developments may make it more difficult for the issuer to handle them. The FSA's interpretation of Community law here is rather strict, perhaps stricter than what is required. For example, whilst accepting that a company in serious financial difficulty may delay disclosure of detailed information about negotiations to secure the company's future, if those negotiations are still on foot, the FSA requires the fact that the company is in financial difficulty and is in negotiation to be disclosed at once.[38] Indeed, the Authority commits itself to the gen-

---

[33] In that case the competitor may be required to make disclosure, but not if its securities are not traded publicly.

[34] Remarkably Art.6 of MAD does not in terms confine the company's disclosure obligation to information which it possesses, but such a limitation may be thought to be inherent in a disclosure obligation, and it is so interpreted in the FSA's rules: DTR 2.2.9. There may still be a question of when a company "possesses" information: is any piece of inside information held by an employee of the company information the company possesses?

[35] Previously the FSA was empowered to grant dispensations from the disclosure obligations in certain cases.

[36] Art.6(2). The recipients of confidential information may include employee representatives and trade unions: DTR 2.5.7. Article 3(2) of the Commission Directive (see next note) lays down what the company must do to ensure confidentiality, including arrangements for immediate public disclosure if confidentiality is breached.

[37] Commission Directive 2003/124/EC, OJ L339/70, 24.12.2003, Art.3(1)(a). On the place of Commission law-making in the scheme of things see previous Chapter at para.25–7.

[38] DTR 2.5.4.

eral propositions that "an issuer cannot delay disclosure of inside information on the basis that its position in subsequent negotiations to deal with the situation will be jeopardised by the disclosure of its financial condition";[39] and that other than in relation to impending events and negotiations on foot "there are unlikely to be other circumstances where delay would be justified."[40] The balance is clearly weighted in favour of disclosure and away from protection of "legitimate interests" except in very narrow circumstances.

The Directive requires the information disclosed to be displayed on the company's website for an appropriate period,[41] but this is not in fact a very good way of disclosing information simultaneously to all market participants. Rather, the FSA requires release via a "Regulated Information Service" (RIS) i.e. one, approved by the FSA, which carries news about all companies in the market and so does not favour those who happened to be logged onto a particular company's website at the time the information was posted.[42] Further, information required to be disclosed under Article 6 of MAD constitutes "regulated information" which, by virtue of Article 21 of TD, is subject to additional requirements, notably that it be disseminated to the public simultaneously, as nearly as possible, in all EEA Member States.[43] It must also be communicated at the same time to the FSA.[44]

Over a period of time a company could release a number of statements to the market about developments affecting its business. Article 10 of the Prospectus Directive (PD)[45] requires companies on regulated markets to publish and file with the competent authority (i.e. the FSA in the case of the United Kingdom) an annual statement containing or referring to all the information made public over the previous year, including information made available in other countries.[46]   **26–7**

We noted above that an issuer which decides it has grounds not to disclose inside information must ensure that this information is not

---

[39] DTR 2.5.4.
[40] DTR 2.5.5. The issue of delayed disclosure emerged as a major issue in the Emergency Liquidity Assistance given to Northern Rock Plc in 2007. The government subsequently proposed that the FSA should "clarify" the scope of the delay power and itself proposed to examine whether the obligation to register a charge (see Ch.32) should be removed from the CA 2006 for banks in receipt of ELA: HM Treasury, *Financial Stability and Depositor Protection*, Cm 7308, January 2008, paras 3.41 and 3.43.
[41] Art.6(1). The information must remain on the website for a year: DTR 2.3.5.
[42] DTR 2.2.1; 6.3.3. In this vein, the FSA requires that website publication must not precede disclosure via the RIS: DTR 2.3.3.
[43] DTR 6.3.4. "Regulated information" is any information required to be disclosed under Art.6 of MAD, the TD, the LR or the DTR (FSA Handbook, *Glossary*).
[44] DTR 6.2.2.
[45] The Commission's Regulation on Prospectuses (see para.25–7) Art.27 contains some further detail on what is required, in particular that the annual statement should "include a statement indicating that some information may be out of date, if such is the case." Unless the particular information which is out of date is identified and the identification is constantly updated, one wonders how much use the annual statement will be to investors.
[46] In domestic law this is implemented by PR 5.2. Publication will probably take the form of companies putting the list on their websites. The annual statement may well contain information beyond the episodic disclosures discussed here: PR 5.2.3.

partially disclosed, except to those under a confidentiality obligation. The rules thus accept that, at any one time, there is likely to be price-sensitive information to which company insiders are privy but which is not known more widely. Article 6(3) of MAD requires the company to issue the information publicly if it is deliberately or accidentally disclosed to a third party not subject to a confidentiality obligation. Somewhat bureaucratically, Article 6(3) also requires issuers to draw up, and keep updated, lists of those working for them (whether as employees or self-employed persons) who have access to inside information; and to send the lists to the FSA, if the FSA so requests. Each list must be kept for five years. Those acting on behalf of the issuer (for example, an investment bank or law firm) must also draw up such a list.[47] The list must give the reason why a particular person is on the list. All those on the list must be made aware of the insider dealing rules and of the sanctions for breaking them.[48]

Penalties for breaches of the FSA's rules

26–8 Failure to disclose information when it should be disclosed is a breach of the rules made by the FSA implementing the disclosure requirements of MAD and opens up the company and any of its directors knowingly concerned in the contravention to the imposition of penalties or to public censure by the FSA.[49] The rules and procedures governing the imposition of penalties and the FSA's investigatory powers[50] are as described in the previous Chapter in relation to breaches of LR and PR.[51] Breach of the rules might involve the company not disclosing on time or disclosing on time but inaccurately or incompletely (or, of course, both). Whereas non-disclosure seems to be subject to strict liability under the FSA's rules, in relation to inaccurate or partial disclosure the standard is one of negligence:

> "An issuer must take all reasonable care to ensure that any information it notifies to a RIS is not misleading, false or deceptive and does not omit anything likely to affect the import of the information."[52]

The FSA makes relatively light use of its penalty-imposing powers and seems to concentrate on cases of late disclosure.[53] Thus, in the case of Marconi in 2003 the company was censured for a delay of a

---

[47] DTR 2.8.
[48] Much of the exotic detail of what is required derives, not from the Directive itself, but from the second-level Commission Directive 2004/72/EC, Art.5.
[49] FSMA 2000, s.91(1ZA),(2),(3).
[50] Under s.97.
[51] See above, para.25–40.
[52] DTR 1.3.4.
[53] See HM Treasury, *Davies Review of Issuer Liability: Discussion Paper*, March 2007, Table 1: nine cases over four years, including the cases on breach of s.397, discussed below.

mere 24 hours, at a time when its securities were already suspended from trading, though admittedly in respect of a statement concerning the company's expectations about its performance which had a major impact on the price of its shares. The FSA remarked that "save in exceptional circumstances, a listed company must prioritise its disclosure obligations under the Listing Rules."[54]

In extreme cases non-disclosure or inaccurate disclosure might also constitute the offence created by section 397(1) and (2) of FSMA 2000, for breaches of which the FSA may prosecute.[55] This offence can be traced back to s.12 of the Prevention of Fraud (Investments) Act 1939 and consists of making a statement, promise or forecast knowing it to be misleading or reckless whether it is so, for the purpose of inducing someone (or reckless whether it may induce someone) to enter into or to refrain from entering into an investment agreement or to exercise or refrain from exercising a right conferred by an investment. The section also catches the dishonest concealment of material facts done for the like purpose.[56] The range of investments covered by the prohibition is widely drawn.[57] The section is thus broadly drawn and is certainly broad enough to cover the standard case with which we are concerned, i.e. misleading statements made for the purpose of inducing someone to buy or sell shares in a publicly traded company. The section is a useful weapon in the prosecutor's armoury since only recklessness (not intent) needs to be established, and promises and forecasts (not just statements or omissions of facts) are covered. However, the misleading disclosure must be for the required purpose: the fact that a recipient of the statement in fact makes an investment decision on the basis of a statement which its maker knows to be false would not be enough to secure a conviction. Conviction on indictment may lead to a sentence of imprisonment of up to seven years.[58] All the ingredients for criminal liability were found in *R. v Bailey and Rigby*,[59] where the chief executive and chief financial officers of a company were convicted of issuing a misleading trading statement[60] which caused its share price to rise and investors to purchase its shares when the contracts on which the trading statement had been based had not been concluded and in fact never were. The basis of the conviction was recklessness, both as to the truth of the statement and as to

---

[54] FSA, Final Notice, *Marconi Plc*, April 11, 2003, para.43.
[55] s.401 (except in Scotland).
[56] The person thus persuaded to act need not be the same person as the one to whom the statement is made: s.397(2).
[57] s.397(9)–(14) and the FSMA 2000 (Misleading Statements and Practices) Order 2001 (SI 2001/3645), as amended.
[58] s.397(8).
[59] [2006] 2 Cr.App.R.(S.) 36. Although custodial sentences were upheld, the CA reduced them from three-and-a-half years to eighteen months and from two-and-a-half years to nine months.
[60] A statement updating the market on the company's trading performance.

whether investors would rely on it. When the truth emerged the share price fell to one-fifth and then one-tenth of its pre-correction level.

Episodic disclosure and market abuse

26–9 The DTR apply only to companies with securities admitted to trading on a regulated market, for example, the Main Market of the LSE.[61] They do not apply to exchange-regulated markets. However, the AIM rules impose a similar obligation on companies traded on that market, but enforcement of compliance with that obligation is a matter for the LSE, as the market operator, rather than the FSA.[62] However, even in relation to exchange-regulated markets, the FSA may have a role by virtue of the FSMA 2000 provisions on market abuse. The market abuse provisions apply to "prescribed markets". This term includes all markets established by a UK-recognised investment exchange, including therefore all markets run by the LSE.[63] Thus, AIM securities will be included under the market abuse rules but will not be covered by the DTR.[64] This aspect of the FSMA's rules on market abuse thus merit discussion here.[65]

As far as domestic law is concerned, the definition of market abuse is to be found in s.118 of FSMA 2000. Following Article 1 of MAD, that section divides market abuse into two main categories: insider trading (mentioned above) and market manipulation. It is the second category which is relevant to misleading or delayed corporate disclosures. In particular, the relevant sub-category is the form of market manipulation which is constituted by "behaviour [which]

---

[61] DTR 1.1.1.

[62] *AIM Rules for Companies*, February 2007 Rules 11 and 42 and *AIM Rules for Nominated Advisers*, February 2007, Rule 17.

[63] FSMA 2000, s.118(1); Financial Services and Markets Act 2000 (Prescribed Markets and Qualifying Investments) Order 2001 (SI 2001/996), reg.4. Although both the episodic disclosure requirements and the prohibition on market abuse are derived from MAD, which applies only to regulated markets, the Government decided to maintain the wider scope of the market abuse prohibition as it had existed in British law before the adoption of the Community Directive. See HM Treasury and FSA, *UK Implementation of the EU Market Abuse Directive*, June 2004, paras 3.7–3.8. It should be noted that, if a security is traded on a regulated market, MAD will apply even if the infringing act took the form of a trade on a non-regulated market.

[64] On the status of AIM as a non-regulated market see previous Chapter at para.25–5.

[65] In the Shell case, that company was fined £17 million for misleading disclosures to the market on the basis that its actions constituted market abuse. See FSA, Final Notice, August 24, 2004, *The "Shell" Transport and Trading Company Plc and The Royal Dutch Petroleum Company N V*. Clearly Shell is a listed company but the analysis would seem equally applicable to an AIM company. The case was also decided on an earlier version of s.118 of FSMA 2000, but the same conclusion seems available under the current wording of the law.

consists of the dissemination of information by any means which gives, or is likely to give, a false or misleading impression as to a qualifying investment[66] by a person who knew, or could reasonably be expected to have known that the information was false or misleading."[67] The standard of liability is thus a negligence standard.

In the case of a company the question arises as to whether a person making a statement on behalf of a company should be treated as knowing information of which he or she was in fact unaware but which was known to someone else in the organisation. The FSA's Code of Market Conduct, which the FSA is required to produce to give guidance on its approach to the determination of market abuse,[68] states that its opinion is that this attribution will not be made if the information known to the other person is held behind a "Chinese wall" or other effective arrangement for keeping information known in a particular segment of a business from those working in other segments.[69] The effect of such a statement of opinion on the part of the FSA is to provide a "safe harbour" from liability,[70] but the implication is that, where no such arrangement is in place, attribution could be made.

However, it appears that this part of section 118 does not catch non-disclosure of information, though it doubtless catches partial disclosure. Although the domestic transposition of this provision of the Directive refers to "behaviour consist[ing] of the dissemination of information" and the Act defines "behaviour" so as to include "inaction",[71] it is difficult to see how "dissemination" can embrace simple non-disclosure. In this respect, the provisions of the DTR go further, even if they apply only to regulated markets.[72] On the other hand, simple non-disclosure might constitute the form of market abuse which consists of "behaviour" (thus including inaction) "likely to give a regular user of the market a false or misleading impression

---

[66] The relevant subordinate legislation (SI 2001/996, art.5) defining a "qualifying investment" simply refers back to the definition of "financial instruments" in MAD, Art.1(3), which in turn refers (now) to the definition in Section C of Annex 1 to MIFID (see para.25–7). For the company lawyer the intricacies of this definition do not need to be explored, for it covers, as its first item, "transferable securities".

[67] FSMA 2000, s.118(7). The word "dissemination" is clearly wide enough to cover any form of release of information by the company, whether required by the DTR and whether disseminated through a RIS or not.

[68] FSMA 2000, s.119(1).

[69] MAR 1.8.3.

[70] s.122. See further on market abuse in Ch.30.

[71] s.130A(3).

[72] See above, fn.61.

as to the ... value of qualifying investments."[73] However, it is unclear whether this further provision will survive beyond June 2008.[74]

Penalties for market abuse

26–10 The FSA may impose penalties on those who engage in market abuse.[75] A striking example of the operation of the above provisions can be seen in the fine of £17 million imposed on Shell in August 2004 in relation to misstatements made to the market over a number of years about the extent of its oil and gas reserves.[76]

Compensation for misleading episodic statements

26–11 It is a controversial issue what civil sanctions are, or ought to be, available to investors in relation to misleading periodic or episodic statements put out by companies. If the negligence rules applied by the law of tort to auditors apply here also,[77] as seems likely, then neither the company nor its directors will normally owe a duty of care to investors, whether existing shareholders or not, who buy or sell shares in response to a misleading statement put out by the company and then suffer a loss when the truth emerges. In fact, the exclusion of negligence liability has been confirmed in relation to periodic disclosures required by the TD by section 90A of FSMA 2000.[78] On the other hand, that section also confirms the availability of liability for fraudulent misstatements and, in fact, makes such liability somewhat more likely under the statute than at common law. This is because the common law requires for liability in deceit that the maker of the statement intends the recipient (or a class of persons of whom the recipient is one) to rely on the misstatement, whereas section 90A merely requires that such reliance be reasonable on the part of the recipient. However, section 90A confines liability to the issuer, thus

---

[73] s.118(8)—and the behaviour of the person in question must be likely to be regarded by a regular user of the market as a failure to observe the standard of behaviour reasonably to be expected of that person.

[74] s.118(8) is not required by MAD, though it was part of the previous domestic regime. Its retention under the current regime was controversial and the compromise was that it should be subject to a "sunset" provision, i.e. it will expire on June 30, 2008, unless Parliament decides to re-enact it. See HM Treasury, *Feedback Statement following June 2004 Consultation on UK implementation of EU Market Abuse Directive (2003/6/EC)*, February 2005, paras 4–10.

[75] s.123. Defendants are protected against penalties if they can prove an absence of negligence (s.123(2)), so that the burden of disproving negligence under section 118(7) appears to be on the defendant. The same rules about policy, procedure and appeal to the Financial Services and Markets Tribunal apply as in the case of FSA penalties imposed for breaches of the LR or PR: see ss.123–127 and para.30–40.

[76] See fn.65 above.

[77] See para.22–42.

[78] The liability of the director in negligence to the company is preserved (s.90A(6)(b)), but subject to s.463 of CA 2006 (above para.21–26).

excluding directors and advisers to the company, whereas the common law does not.

However, section 90A does not apply to episodic disclosures, so that the common law still applies.[79] That would seem to mean that liability in negligence would be rare. As for deceit it is difficult to measure how much of a barrier the requirement that the maker of the statement intends the recipient to rely on it will be in the case of an episodic disclosure. It could be argued that disclosure is required only in the case of information likely to have an impact on the price of the securities, so that intention that there should be reliance could be found fairly readily by a sympathetic court. The Government established a review to examine the question of whether the statutory regime for liability for TD disclosures should be extended more widely, so as to include MAD disclosures. That review suggested that the principles of section 90A should apply to MAD disclosures as well and, indeed, to periodic and episodic disclosures made by companies whose securities are publicly traded but not on a regulated market.[80]

Irrespective of whether private litigation to enforce investors' rights is feasible, a further question is whether the FSA can seek compensation on their behalf. FSMA 2000 appears to confer this power. Under sections 382 and 383 the FSA has the power to apply to the court, in cases of market abuse or contravention of its rules,[81] where profits have accrued to the person in breach, or loss or other adverse effect was suffered by other persons.[82] The court may order the person in breach to pay to the FSA such amount as it thinks just, having regard to the profits made or loss suffered. That amount is to be paid out by the FSA to such persons as the court may direct who fall within the categories of those who have suffered loss or are the persons to whom the profit is "attributable".[83] This provision is potentially important. It constitutes a form of class action for investors, with the costs paid by the FSA, but how willing will the FSA be to invoke its powers? The FSA's Enforcement Guide suggests that it will not use its powers to seek restitution whenever they are available but

---

[79] Equally, the statutory negligence-based liability for prospectuses (see previous Chapter at paras 25–31ff) will not apply to episodic disclosures made by companies after the public offer or admission to trading.

[80] See Davies Review of Issuer Liability, *Discussion Paper* (March 2007) and *Final Report* (June 2007), available on: www.hm-treasury.gov.uk/independent_reviews/davies_review/davies_review_index.cfm.

[81] s.382 applies to breaches of the FSA's rules (see the definition of "relevant requirement" in s.382(9)(a)) and s.383 to market abuse. The powers conferred are similar as far as the company's liability for non-disclosure is concerned. For directors, liability for breach of the FSA's rules is imposed on a person "knowingly concerned" in the company's contravention (s.382(1)), whereas for market abuse the liability is on the basis that a person [the director] "has required or encouraged" another person [the company] to engage in behaviour which, if engaged in by the director would amount to market abuse by the director (s.383(1)(b)).

[82] s.384 empowers the FSA to make a restitution order under its own authority, but only in relation to persons authorised by it to carry on financial business, a category into which neither issuer nor director is likely to fall.

[83] ss.382(3),(8), 383(5),(10).

only when it regards their use as more effective than alternative courses of action. In particular, is not likely to use them to obtain compensation for market counterparties where compensation can be obtained at reasonable cost by the counterparties themselves.[84]

26–12   Were the FSA to use its restitution powers in this area, the court would be faced by the sections with two difficult questions: how much should be paid and to whom should it go? Depriving the issuer of the profit made may be uncontroversial, but losses may have been suffered on a wide scale in the market which go far beyond the profit made. For example, where a company makes an inaccurate statement to the market which moves the market price upwards, but the price later falls when the truth emerges, losses may well have been suffered by all those who bought shares in the market after the statement and still held them at its correction. Making the issuer compensate for all those losses might be disproportionate to the wrong involved. As to who should share in the restitution, here the difficulties are the other way around. Those who have suffered loss should presumably share in the pay-out, but where there are no losses but only profits made by the company, to whom are those profits "attributable"? If it is all those who traded in the market at the relevant time, whether with the defendant or not, then the defendant's profit may not go very far when split among all the traders.

The above powers to seek restitution embrace the situation where the defendant has committed the criminal offence of making an intentionally or recklessly misleading statement under section 397.[85] If such conduct leads to an actual conviction, a further avenue to compensation may be opened up, namely compensation orders made under the general criminal law provisions.[86]

The Act also gives the FSA power to seek injunctions from the courts in respect of apprehended or repeated violation of its requirements.[87]

DISCLOSURE OF DIRECTORS' SHAREHOLDINGS

26–13   For a long time the Companies Acts have required directors to disclose to their companies their interests in the securities of the companies of which they are directors, an obligation which was extended so as to impose upon the director the duty to disclose the interests of

---

[84] EG 11.3.
[85] See above, para.26–8.
[86] See *Rigby and Bailey v R.* [2006] 1 W.L.R. 3067 (though the FSA's attempted use of general confiscation powers was unsuccessful). Some £200,000 was paid to Morley Fund Management and £120,000 to Standard Life.
[87] ss.380 and 381.

spouses, civil partners and children.[88] In the case of a company with securities listed on a recognised investment exchange[89] the company was then under an obligation to notify the exchange, which was permitted to publish the information to the market.[90]

The principal, though not the exclusive, rationale behind this disclosure requirement was to combat insider trading. Although directors are not the only people under a temptation to engage in insider dealing, they are particularly at risk because their relationship with the company will routinely generate inside information, i.e. information which, at least for a short while, is known to them but not outside the company. The original provisions requiring disclosure of directors' securities dealings were introduced following a recommendation from the Cohen Committee, just after the Second World War, which identified the insider dealing rationale for requiring the disclosure.

> "The best safeguard against improper transactions by directors and against unfounded suspicions of such transactions is to ensure that disclosure is made of all their transactions in the shares or debentures of their companies."[91]

Insider dealing is now a matter which is prohibited by the criminal law, at least as far as trading on a regulated market or through a professional intermediary, is concerned,[92] but the disclosure provisions still operate to supplement the operation of the prohibition, by making detection of improper transactions easier. However, these disclosure rules should not be regarded as aimed solely at insider trading. As the Law Commissions put it:

> "the interests which a director has in his company and his acquisitions and disposals of such interests convey information about the financial incentives that a director has to improve his company's performance and accordingly these provisions form part of the system put in place by the Companies Acts to enable shareholders to monitor the directors' stewardship of the company".[93]

The insider dealing rationale for disclosure by directors is to be found again at Community level in MAD, Article 6(4) of which

---

[88] The provisions of the Companies Act 1985 were ss.324–326 and 328.
[89] For the meaning of this term see para.25–5.
[90] s.329.
[91] Board of Trade, *Report of the Committee on Company Law Amendment*, Cmd. 6659, June 1945, para.87.
[92] Criminal Justice Act 1993, Part V. See Ch.30 below.
[93] Law Commission and Scottish Law Commission, *Company Directors: Regulating Conflicts of Interest and Formulating a Statement of Duties: A Joint Consultation Paper* (1998), para.5.2.

requires those "discharging managerial responsibilities within an issuer" and persons "closely associated" with them to notify the competent authority (not the company) of their dealings in the shares of the issuer (or derivatives linked to them) and for that information to be made publicly available "as soon as possible". MAD, as we have seen, applies only to regulated markets and so, despite being wider in some respects than the Companies Act provisions, the Directive was, on balance, considerably narrower. For this reason, and because Article 14 of MAD requires administrative sanctions to be available against those who contravene the domestic laws transposing the Directive, a disclosure obligation on directors was inserted into the rules made by the FSA.[94] For a while, the Companies Act and the FSA regimes proceeded in parallel, but after the enactment of the 2006 Act the Companies Act rules were removed, leaving only the FSA regime in place.[95] The paradoxical result of MAD was thus to trigger a domestic reassessment of the disclosure rules relating to directors' transactions in the securities of their companies which led to a narrowing of the disclosure regime.

Which companies?

26–14   Under the current regime, the FSA's rules on disclosure by directors apply only in respect of companies incorporated in the United Kingdom whose securities are admitted to trading on a regulated market (or where an application for admission has been made).[96] This is a considerably narrower set of companies than under the 1985 Act, which applied to the directors of all companies, public or private, which was probably too wide a set of companies. However, in so far as insider trading is a phenomenon of public markets, the restriction of the rules to regulated markets can be argued to be too narrow.[97]

Who has to disclose?

26–15   In terms of who has to disclose, the phrase now used is "a person discharging managerial responsibilities",[98] defined so as to go some-

---

[94] DTR 3, made under powers conferred by s.73A of FSMA 2000. DTR 3 contains in fact Disclosure rather than Transparency Rules, a distinction which is important in relation to the FSA's penalty imposing powers.

[95] ss.324–329 of the CA 1985 were repealed by the Companies Act 2006 (Commencement No.1, Transitional Provisions and Savings) Order 2006 (SI 2006/3428), Schedule 4 as from April 6, 2007.

[96] DTR 1.1.1(2), though the DTR will apply even if the regulated market is outside the UK.

[97] The AIM Rules require companies to disclose transactions by directors and require the company to have in place rules and procedures under which the director is to provide the necessary information to the company, but do not directly impose obligations on the directors: see *AIM Rules for Companies*, Rules 17 and 31 and Schedule 5. The AIM Rules require disclosure of only directors' deals and are drafted in a less detailed manner than the FSA's rules.

[98] As laid down in Commission Directive 2004/72/EC, Art.1(1).

what wider than just directors to include senior (but non-directorial) executives who (i) have regular access to inside information relating to the issuer and (ii) have power to make managerial decisions affecting the future development and business prospects of the issuer.[99] This is a welcome recognition of the importance of senior executives, though condition (ii) will bring only a small number of non-directorial executives within the definition. In this respect the current definition goes beyond the scope of the 1985 Act. On the other hand, the 1985 Act applied to shadow directors,[100] who would not seem to fall within the current definition, since they will not typically be executives of the company. For example, a large shareholder will not fall within this definition, though its transactions may be caught by the less demanding rules on "vote holder" disclosure, discussed below.

The disclosure obligation falls, however, not only on those discharging managerial responsibilities but also on those connected with them. The interests required to be notified to the company under the 1985 Act extended to those of spouses, civil partners and children, but the disclosure obligation remained that of the director. Now a disclosure obligation is imposed directly on the connected person. Moreover, the range of persons who are treated as connected is now much broader than spouses, civil partners and children.[101] The definition of "connected person" for these purposes is set out in section 96B of FSMA 2000 and has three elements. (a) At its core is the definition of a person "connected with a director" in section 346 of the Companies Act 1985.[102] The decision to keep the old definition and not to adopt the definition in the current Companies Act[103] seems to have been driven by a desire not to again amend the scope of the disclosure regime. (b) In addition, the definition brings in any relative of the person discharging managerial responsibilities who has shared the same household for at least twelve months, though many members of the director's family and living with him are brought into the "connected person" definition by section 253. (c) Also added is a body corporate where there is a person discharging managerial responsibilities who is also a person exercising managerial responsibilities within the issuer or a person connected to such a person by

[99] FSMA 2000, s.96B(1).

[100] CA 1985, s.324(6).

[101] Both points result from Community law: MAD Art.6(4) imposes the reporting obligation on "persons closely associated", for which the domestic law retains the more familiar term "connected person", and Commission Directive 2004/72/EC, Art.1(2) lays down a definition of a "person closely associated", though the latter definition is not simply copied out in FSMA 2000.

[102] FSMA 2000, s.96B(2). Section 346 of CA 1985 is preserved in relation to s.96B(2) of FSMA by the Companies Act (Commencement No.3, Consequential Amendments, Transitional Provisions and Savings) Order 2007/2194, Sch.3, para.50.

[103] ss.252–254.

virtue of (a) or (b). The effect of (c) is to extend the disclosure net widely to companies with which the person exercising managerial responsibilities in the issuer is connected,[104] but what has to be disclosed are only transactions in the shares of the issuer by the connected company.

What has to be disclosed, to whom and when?

26–16   Article 6(4) of MAD requires the disclosure of "transactions on their own account relating to the shares" of the issuer or "derivatives or other financial instruments linked to them". This again is both narrower and wider than the former 1985 Act requirement. First, transactions in debentures are excluded, the new provisions applying only to equities, presumably because debt instruments normally give their holders neither voting rights in the company nor a strong interest in maximising its profits. However, the inclusion of "derivatives or any other financial instruments linked to" the shares seems to bring in transactions which give the director a purely economic interest in the share (but no ownership interest), which probably fell outside the 1985 Act.[105] Secondly, whereas the 1985 Act required disclosure of interests in the securities of other companies in the same corporate group by a person who was a director of any one group company,[106] the DTR applies only to shares in the company in respect of which the person exercises managerial responsibilities.[107] Thirdly, the disclosure is triggered by "transactions" conducted on their own account by those discharging managerial responsibilities within the issuer. The 1985 Act required the disclosure of "interests" in securities, which, as Schedule 13 of that Act demonstrated, included many things which would seem not to fall within "transactions on their own account", for example, transactions in the shares by the trustees whose beneficiaries include the director. Under the new scheme the disclosure obligation will fall on the trustees.[108]

The DTR[109] require information about the transaction to be disclosed to the company (issuer), as did the former Companies Act, but

---

[104]   The FSMA definition is much wider than that in s.254 of the CA, since the latter section makes a director connected with a company only on the basis of a substantial share- or vote-holding in that company.

[105]   An example would be "a contract for differences" where the contracting party becomes entitled to the difference between the price of the share at two different times without ever obtaining a property interest in the share itself. In such a case the party to the CfD clearly has a strong interest in the price of the company's shares.

[106]   CA 1985, s.324(1).

[107]   The somewhat wider definition of who has to disclose will not make up for the much narrower application of the disclosure requirements in relation to groups, though of course a person who is a director of group company A may fall within the second limb of the definition of a person discharging managerial responsibilities (see above) in relation to some other group company B without being a director of B and thus come under an independent disclosure requirement in relation to B.

[108]   See CA 2006, s.252(2)(c).

[109]   DTR 3.1.

then require the issuer to give the information to the market (as again did the Companies Act 1985) and, since it is regulated information, to the FSA.[110] The information to be given to the issuer includes "the price and volume of the transaction" (so that the director cannot simply say that he or she has bought some shares in the company).[111] Given the complexity of the connected persons definition the information is wisely required to specify "the reason for responsibility to notify", which both requires the notifying person to work out how the definition applies to them and enables the company to check the reasoning. The financial instrument and the nature of the transaction must also be described. The transaction must be notified to the issuer within four business days of the transaction occurring,[112] and the issuer must release the information to the market within a further business day, thus meeting the Community requirement of notification to the competent authority within five working days.[113]

This way of making notification, besides reflecting the prior British law, underlines the company's interest in knowing about the transactions of its directors in the company. However, the company no longer has to keep a register of the transactions disclosed to it under the DTR, as it had to do with the Companies Act 1985 disclosures,[114] nor, in consequence, report the position on directors' interests at the end of the financial year in the directors' report.[115] However, as we have seen, companies are required to file an annual statement with the FSA referring to all the information made public over the previous twelve months.[116] The dissemination of the notified information to interested persons outside the company is thus to be in future solely via disclosure to the market. However, some, but not complete, information about directors' shareholdings will appear from the directors' remuneration report, which the company has to prepare,[117] where grants of shares or of options to purchase shares in the company are part of the director's remuneration package.

Sanctions for non- or inaccurate disclosure

Under the prior law a failure by a director to disclose to the company   **26–17** or making an inaccurate disclosure where the maker was aware of its falsity or was reckless as to its accuracy was a criminal offence,

---

[110] DTR 6.2.2.
[111] DTR 3.1.3, transposing Article 6(3) of Commission Directive 2004/72/EC.
[112] DTR 3.1.2.
[113] DTR 3.1.2 and 3.1.4 and Commission Directive 2004/72/EC, Art.6(1). The information is to be disclosed through a Regulated Information Service (RIS), which ensures simultaneous release to all market participants and to the FSA. The five day timetable is a day quicker than under the previous law, which gave the director five days to notify the company (CA 1985, Sch.13, paras 14 and 15) and the company a further day to tell the market (s.329).
[114] CA 1985, s.325.
[115] CA 1985, Sch.7, paras 2–2B.
[116] Above, para.26–7.
[117] Above, para.14–16.

punishable by a fine or imprisonment or both; and failure by the company to disclose to the stock exchange was also a criminal offence on the part of the company and any officer in default.[118] The criminal sanctions have necessarily disappeared under the current regime, to be replaced by the power of the FSA to impose penalties on those discharging managerial responsibilities within an issuer, a person connected with such a person, and the issuer itself; and, where any of these is a company, on a director knowingly concerned in the contravention.[119]

DISCLOSURE OF MAJOR SHAREHOLDINGS

Rationale and history

26–18   This is a further area where British law has long required disclosure but where Community legislation has now become dominant, leading to a transfer of a substantial part of the disclosure requirements from the Companies Acts to FSMA. There is an initial puzzle about why these provisions are necessary at all. It is rare for companies in the United Kingdom to issue "bearer" shares,[120] so that shares are issued instead in the name of a person (natural or corporate) and are referred to as "registered" shares. The names of the holders of such shares, as we have seen,[121] must be entered in a register, which is kept by the company, and reported to Companies House in the annual return, so that the names of the shareholders are public knowledge. It may be wondered why further provision is required. However, the requirement that the shareholder's name be registered in the company's share register does not mean that the name of the beneficial owner needs to be registered. The use of nominee names has long been popular among big investors and now the dematerialisation of shares[122] has put some pressure upon even small investors to use nominees. Thus, inspection of the share register will not necessarily, perhaps not even typically, reveal who has the beneficial interest in the share.[123] Finally, the list of shareholders in the annual return may not be up-to-date.

Granted this, it is still necessary to say why holders of large shareholdings should be required to reveal their interests publicly. In

---

[118] ss.324(7) and 329(3).
[119] FSMA 2000, s.91(1ZA),(2). For the constraints on the FSA's penalty imposing powers see para.25–40. The issue, rather remote in this case, of civil liability for inaccurate RIS announcements has been touched on above at para.26–11.
[120] See para.24–17.
[121] See above, at paras 21–37ff.
[122] See Ch.27 below.
[123] We have discussed in Ch.15 above the problems which this causes in relation to shareholders' governance rights.

part, but only in small part, these provisions aim to deter insider dealing, as with those discussed in the previous section. However, the main purpose of these provisions is better put as follows:

> "A company, its members and the public at large should be entitled to be informed promptly of the acquisition of a significant holding in its voting shares ... in order that existing members and those dealing with the company may protect their interests and that the conduct of the affairs of the company is not prejudiced by uncertainty over those who may be in a position to influence or control the company."[124]

This statement explains the concentration in the successive legal regimes on disclosure of holdings of voting shares, because it is disclosure of actual or potential control of the company that is aimed at, rather than interests in its securities in general.

However, the above statement might be thought to run together two rationales for the provisions. One is protection of the management of the company and, to some extent, its members, by making them aware of who is building up a stake in the company. Disclosure here operates as an early-warning device about potential takeover bids in particular. But the statement refers also to the protection of "the public". Public disclosure may be said to be promoting the conceptually separate goal of "market transparency". Obviously, a single set of disclosure rules might aim to promote both policies. This would seem to be true of the rules, discussed below, requiring the disclosure of shareholdings once a certain size threshold has been crossed. This is an obligation generated automatically by the law once the appropriate threshold has been reached. However, there is also an additional disclosure obligation, still contained in the Companies Act, that is triggered by the company asking any person to reveal the extent of their interest in the company's voting shares. This latter set of disclosure rules we discuss not in this Chapter but in Chapter 28 dealing with takeovers, because their rationale is the solely the first one identified above.

The British rules requiring disclosure of interests in shares once **26–19** certain size thresholds have been exceeded are of long standing. The principle of disclosure was introduced as a result of the recommendations of the Cohen Committee[125] in 1945 that the beneficial ownership of shares be publicly disclosed, and, over time, the starting threshold has been lowered, the speed of the required disclosure increased and the range of interests to be disclosed made more sophisticated. Community law also showed an interest in this topic at

---

[124] Department of Trade, *Disclosure of Interests in Shares* (1980), p.2.
[125] Report of the Committee on Company Law Amendment, Cmd. 6659 (1945), pp.39–45. It is to be noted that the domestic legislation has still not been lowered to the one per cent threshold recommended by that Committee.

an early stage.[126] The current Community principles are laid down in the Transparency Directive (TD) not, it should be noted, in the Market Abuse Directive.[127] The main impact of Community law was, once again, to spark off a fundamental review of the purposes of these disclosure rules. In particular, the emphasis in the Directive upon disclosure as an instrument to improve the functioning of the securities markets[128] led the DTI to propose[129] that the "market transparency" rationale be given pre-eminence over the others. This policy was implemented by the removal of the automatic disclosure requirements from the companies legislation whilst at the same time the 2006 Act amended FSMA so as to permit the area to be regulated by FSA rules, thus giving rise to the current regulatory structure.[130] However, the disclosure obligation triggered by the company remains part of the companies legislation.[131] As far as the automatic disclosure obligation is concerned, the result, as with directors' disclosures, was an overall narrowing of the regime, despite the fact that on a number of important points the domestic rules still go beyond the minimum requirements of the TD.[132]

The scope of the disclosure obligation
Which companies are subject to the regime?

26–20 The 1985 Act regime applied to all public companies (in the company law sense of that term).[133] The Directive applies only to companies (issuers) whose securities are admitted to trading on a regulated market.[134] The domestic regime implementing the Directive applies to all companies with securities traded on a prescribed market, which includes any market operated by a Recognised Investment Exchange, on the grounds that transparency of shareholding is as important on exchange-regulated as on regulated markets.[135] Thus, both the Main Market of the LSE and AIM are covered by the current domestic

---

[126] Its first Directive on disclosure of major shareholdings was Directive 88/627/EEC, [1988] OJ L348/62 (December 17, 1988), later consolidated into Directive 2001/34/EC, Arts 89–97.
[127] Directive 2004/109/EC, Chapter III.
[128] See especially the preamble to the TD.
[129] DTI, *Proposals for Reform of Part VI of the Companies Act 1985* (April 1995). The CLR touched only lightly on this topic, largely endorsing the 1995 proposals: Completing, para.7.32.
[130] CA 2006, s.1266, introducing new FSMA 2000, s.89A–G. The relevant provisions of the CA 1985 were repealed as from January 20, 2007 by the Companies Act 2006 (Commencement No.1, Transitional Provisions and Savings) Order 2006/3428, Schedule 3.
[131] CA 2006, Part 22.
[132] The policy underlying the FSA's regime is laid out in two FSA documents: *Implementation of the Transparency Directive and Investment Entities Listing Review*, CP06/4, March 2006, Ch.3 and *Implementation of the Transparency Directive*, PS06/11, October 2006, Ch.3.
[133] CA 1985, s.198.
[134] TD Art.9(1).
[135] FSMA 2000, s.89A(1),(3)(a); DTR 5.1.1(3); Glossary, *Issuer* (2B); Financial Services and Markets Act 2000 (Prescribed Markets and Qualifying Investments) Order 2001 (SI 2001/996), art.4. For the distinction between "regulated" and "prescribed" markets see para.26–9.

disclosure obligation, as is Plus Markets. In this respect, the FSA's rules on shareholder disclosure have a wider range than those on directors' disclosure, which are confined to regulated markets.

When does the disclosure obligation arise?
What the rules are concerned with is disclosure of the percentage of **26–21** voting rights held in a company, as certain thresholds are passed, rather than just holdings of shares. For that reason DTR 5 is entitled "Vote Holder Notification". Holdings of non-voting shares do not have to be disclosed, because they do not contribute to the ability to exercise control over the company. Nor do holdings of shares which are entitled to vote only in particular circumstances have to be disclosed, for example, normally non-voting preference shares whose class rights are being varied under the statutory procedure[136] or which are entitled to vote only if their preference dividend has not been paid, provided, of course, that the event has not occurred which gives the class of shares general voting rights.[137] By contrast, those exercising managerial responsibilities do have to disclose holdings in non-voting shares under the rules discussed in the previous section, because opportunities to engage in insider dealing can easily arise in relation to such shares, and holdings of non-voting equity shares may provide economic incentives for directors to act in particular ways, despite the absence of a vote.

The disclosure thresholds are three percent of the total voting rights in the company and every one percent increase thereafter. Decreases must also be notified on the same scale, though once the holding has been notified as below three per cent no further disclosure is required.[138] These disclosure triggers are those of the previous companies legislation regime, but are more demanding than those in the TD.[139] Almost as important as the definition of the threshold is the question of how soon after the threshold has been crossed does the notification obligation have to be discharged. A notification obligation which did not have to be discharged until, for example, a month after the threshold had been crossed would be of very little use to the company, its shareholders or the market in general. In fact, the current regime, following the 1985 Act, imposes a "two-day" rule, i.e. disclosure as soon as possible but in any event by the end of the second trading day following the day on which the obligation to disclose arose.[140]

---

[136] See para.19–12.
[137] DTR 5.1.1(3).
[138] DTR 5.1.2.
[139] TD Art.9(1), which has triggers only at 5, 10, 15, 20, 25, 30, 50 and 75 per cent. Only these triggers are used by the British law in relation to non-UK incorporated companies on a regulated market for which the UK is nevertheless the Home State.
[140] DTR 5.8.3. This applies to UK incorporated companies only; for non-UK companies the rule is the Directive minimum "four-day" rule (i.e. the end of the fourth trading day following).

In the simple case, the event giving rise to the obligation to disclose will be the purchase or sale of the voting shares by the shareholder who is then obliged to make the notification. However, in the light of the discussion immediately below, it will be seen that the event might be something else. For example, Company A, holding two per cent of the voting shares of Company X, acquires control of Company B, which also holds two per cent of the shares. Neither company had a notifiable interest in Company X beforehand, but after the acquisition Company A will have a notifiable interest. The notification obligation in relation to X's shares is thus triggered by the acquisition of B's shares by A, not the acquisition of X's shares by A or B, which could have occurred much earlier. Much more complex cases are possible to imagine, which is why, no doubt, the obligation to disclose is imposed on a person who "learns of the acquisition or disposal or the possibility of exercising voting rights" or "having regard to the circumstances, should have learned of it", rather than the date on which the acquisition, disposal or possibility actually occurred or arose.[141]

The obligation to disclose might even arise as a result of events with which the person upon whom it falls is wholly unconnected. For example, a company engages in a share buy-back programme in relation a class of voting shares. The shareholder does not participate in the buy-back, but as a result of other shareholders' decisions the shareholder finds that his or her holding now exceeds one of the notification thresholds. The opposite development could occur if the company issued new voting shares other than to the existing shareholders. The scheme of the FSA rules on this point is that the company is required at the end of the month in which there has been an increase or decrease in the number of its voting shares to give details of the resulting voting structure; and that is the event which causes the disclosure obligation to arise.[142]

Indirect holdings of voting rights

26–22 Clearly, the acquisition (or disposal) of shares carrying voting rights has to be disclosed if a relevant threshold is crossed. However, if the rules stopped there, the disclosure obligation would be easy to avoid; and it would fail to require disclosure in all cases by the person in fact in a position to influence the exercise of voting rights. The rules thus go further and require disclosure of voting rights arising out of a person's "direct or indirect holding of financial instruments".[143] So, there may be liability to disclose as a result of an indirect as well as a direct holding of shares or as a result of a holding (again direct or

---

[141] DTR 5.8.3, following Art.12(2) of the TD.
[142] DTR 5.8.3, 5.1.2(2), 5.6, following TD Arts 12(2), 9(2) and 15.
[143] DTR 5.1.2.

indirect) of certain other types of financial instrument. The financial instruments to which the TD potentially applies are those set out in Section C of Annex 1 to the Markets in Financial Instruments Directive,[144] including instruments such as options, swaps and other derivative contracts relating to securities. However, these rather esoteric instruments will be of relevance for present purposes only to the extent that they give the holder an unconditional right to acquire a share carrying voting rights.[145] A clear example would be the purchase by someone of an option to acquire a voting share at some point in the future. The purchase of the option may thus give rise to an obligation to disclose, either by itself or together with other voting rights which that person holds.

A much-debated current issue is the proper treatment of "contracts for differences" (CfDs), which are at the moment normally excluded from the disclosure obligation. In these contracts, as more fully explained in Chapter 28,[146] the subject-matter of the contract is the difference in the price of a security at two points in time, rather than the actual security itself. As such, it would seem to give rise to no disclosable issue at all. However, in relation to "long" CfDs the counterparty to the contract (usually an investment bank) will often hedge its position under the contract by buying the underlying security. In some cases this will enable the other person entering into the CfD contract to influence the way the votes attached to those shares are exercised by the bank or to acquire the shares from the bank when the CfD is settled. If that person has a contractual right to either of these things under the CfD, then there is no doubt that the present rules give that person a potentially disclosable interest, assuming the CfD relates to voting shares. What, however, if no contractual right exists, but in practice the CfD holder can either acquire the shares or influence the exercise of voting rights?

In a recent Consultation Paper[147] the FSA, noting that today some 30 per cent of equity trades are by way of CfDs, usually in order to increase leverage or to avoid stamp duty, concluded that investment banks normally require the CfDs to be "closed out" with cash (rather than the delivery of the underlying shares) and are resistant to CfD holders seeking to influence voting rights attached to the shares bought as a hedge. Nevertheless:

[144] See para.25–7.
[145] Commission Directive 2007/14/EC, Art.11(1), containing "second level" implementing rules (hereafter "TD implementing Directive"); DTR 5.3.
[146] At para.28–43.
[147] FSA, *Disclosure of Contracts for Difference*, CP 07/20, November 2007.

"There are some instances of CfDs being used in ways which the intention of the current regulatory regime is designed to catch, and that while this only happens occasionally, it is not fully caught by the requirements of the Takeover Panel regime.[148] Specifically, we conclude that CfDs are sometimes being used, firstly, to seek to influence votes and other corporate governance matters on an undisclosed basis and, secondly, to build up stakes in companies, again without disclosure. We have therefore decided that we should take action now to address these failures."[149]

26–23   Its (slightly) preferred policy response was to extend the current DTR disclosure rules so as to apply them to CfDs, unless the terms of the CfD contract explicitly excluded the CfD holder from exercising voting rights and excluded any understanding or arrangement as to the acquisition of the shares by that person, and the CfD holder explicitly stated that it did not intend to use the CfD to acquire voting rights.[150] In the absence of such provisions, the CfD would have to be aggregated with the holder's other interests for the purposes of the DTR.[151]

However, indirect interests in shares can arise other than through holdings of financial instruments. There is no need to explore in this book the full details of these situations, but some of them are significant. Among them are:[152]

> (i) Voting rights held by an undertaking controlled by a person are to be treated as voting rights of that person.[153] The FSA rules suggest the use of the definition of parent and subsidiary in the 1985 Companies Act to identify a controlled undertaking, with the extension that the controller can include a natural person and not be confined to a controlling company.[154] The controlled undertaking would also have to notify its holding, if one of the triggering events applied.

---

[148]   The Takeover Panel introduced disclosure of CfDs under its rules in November 2005. See para.28–43.
[149]   Para.1.24.
[150]   Para.1.28.
[151]   Paras 5.32–5.34.
[152]   The governing Community law is set out in Article 10 of the TD. This article is "copied out" in DTR 5.2.1.
[153]   TD Art.10(e).
[154]   FSA, *Handbook, Glossary*; FSMA 2000, s.420.

(ii) Voting rights attached to shares held by a nominee on behalf of another will constitute an indirect holding of voting rights by that other person.[155] The nominee will be a direct holder of the voting rights unless, as will often be the case, the nominee may exercise those rights only on the instructions of the beneficial owner.[156]

(iii) Voting rights attached to shares deposited with someone are to be treated as voting rights of the depositee, if the depositee has the right to exercise the votes at its discretion in the absence of instructions from the shareholder.[157] In the same way, a person engaged in investment management is to be treated as the holder of voting rights if it can effectively determine the manner in which voting rights attached to shares under its control are exercised, in the absence of specific instructions from the shareholders.[158] One or other of these provisions is likely to be applicable in the common situation in the United Kingdom where an institutional shareholder has outsourced the management of its investment portfolio to a fund manager, though the shares themselves may be vested in a custodian.[159] The fund manager will be an indirect holder of voting shares, assuming, as will usually be the case, the relevant discretion. Again, the institutional shareholder may well have to make disclosure as well, the disclosure being in this case of a disposal of voting rights upon the giving of the mandate to the fund manager.[160] The custodian will not have to disclose if, as is usual, it can vote only upon instruction (see (ii) above).

A further issue arises where, as is common, the investment management company is part of a larger financial conglomerate. The rules on controlled undertakings ((i) above) would suggest the parent of the group must aggregate the fund-management subsidiary's indirect holdings with its own. However, Article 12(5) of the TD provides an exemption from this further aggregation, subject to certain

---

[155] Art.10(g).
[156] DTR 5.1.3(3).
[157] Art.10(f).
[158] Art.10(h).
[159] See above at para.15–12.
[160] However, one notification may serve both purposes: DTR 5.8.5.

conditions, notably that the fund management subsidiary exercises its voting rights independently of the parent.[161] This seems correct in principle, since the fund manager will be required to exercise the voting rights attached to the shares it controls in the interests of the beneficial owner (the institutional shareholder) and not those of its parent.

(iv) Where there is an agreement between two or more people under which they are obliged to implement "a lasting common policy" towards a company through a concerted exercise of voting rights, then each of the parties to the agreement will have the voting rights of the other parties attributed to it.[162] Such "concert parties" are a common feature of the long-term governance of companies in some continental European jurisdictions. Although they are less popular in the United Kingdom, they do arise, for example in connection with takeover bids, where the Takeover Panel has developed its own sophisticated and more far-reaching definition of "acting in concert".[163] The Companies Act provisions on company-initiated disclosure requirements also aggregate the interests of those acting in concert, but that definition requires simply an agreement to acquire shares in a particular company, whether or not the adoption of a lasting common policy towards the company by the parties to the agreement can be identified.[164] It is likely to be very difficult to judge whether investors who buy stakes in a company at around the same time are simply reacting to market assessment of the company's prospects or are doing so in order to implement a common policy towards it.

(v) A person will be regarded as an indirect holder of voting rights if he or she has concluded an agreement with the shareholder for the temporary transfer of voting rights.[165] The most common example of this situation arising is in relation to stock lending.[166] The borrower will be treated as acquiring voting rights if such are attached to the stock borrowed. However, will the lender of the stock be regarded as disposing of voting rights, thus potentially triggering a

---

[161] TD implementing Directive Art.10. Both Art.12 of TD and Art.10 of the implementing Directive are transposed in DTR 5.4.

[162] Art.10(a) of the Directive.

[163] See para.28–42. "Acting in concert" is defined in the Code so as to include "understandings" as well as agreements and the Code contains an extensive list of "presumed" cases of acting in concert (see *The Takeover Code*, C1). On the other hand, the Code only applies where the common policy towards the company is to obtain or consolidate control of it.

[164] CA 2006, s.824. See below at para.28–49.

[165] Art.10(b).

[166] See above at para.15–50.

disclosure obligation? The FSA was anxious to continue the prior rules which relieved the lender of the duty to notify on the grounds that its right to call for the re-delivery of the stock was an acquisition of voting rights and so the acquisition could be netted off against the loss of voting rights arising out of the stock-lending agreement, thus producing no overall change in its position.[167]

Exemptions

Given the range of notifiable interests, some exemptions needed to be **26–24** provided. We have already noted that relating to custodians.[168] Another is the acquisition of shares for the purposes of clearing and settlement, i.e. of completing a bargain to buy and sell shares.[169] Probably the most significant is that relating to "market makers", i.e. those who hold shares (usually in a particular range of companies) on their own account in order to be able to offer continuous trading opportunities to those who want to buy or sell those shares.[170] Market makers enhance the liquidity of public securities markets but they do not provide this service for altruistic reasons but in the hope of making a profit overall out of the difference between the price at which they acquire and dispose of the securities. If they were obliged to disclose the details of their purchases and sales, their ability to make this profit and so their willingness to offer their services as market makers would be reduced. Even this exemption is limited: it does not apply when the market maker's holding in a particular company reaches ten per cent and it is conditional upon the market maker not intervening in the management of the company or exerting any influence over the company to acquire its shares. There is a similar exemption for financial instruments held in the trading books of banks and related institutions, but in this case the disclosure obligation bites at the five per cent level.[171]

---

[167] See DTR 5.1.1(5) and the FSA's documents referred to at fn.132 above (CP 06/04, paras 3.17–3.21; PS 06/11, paras 3.21–3.25).

[168] See para.26–23 above.

[169] DTR 5.1.3(1). On clearing and settlement see para.27–2. This is a limited exemption since it applies only to acquisitions made for the sole purpose of settlement and is limited to acquisitions made during the three trading days following the striking of the bargain to which it relates. The FSA considers the exemption applies only to a central clearing house which interposes itself between buyer and seller, assuming the obligations of each to the other: FSA, CP 06/04, above, fn.132 at para.3.15.

[170] DTR 5.1.3(3) and 5.1.4.

[171] DTR 5.1.3(4). Either this or the previous exemption normally permit the bank party to the CfD (see above, para.26–22) which buys the underlying shares as a hedge not to disclose its holding of the shares.

The disclosure process

26–25   Assuming a disclosure obligation has arisen, the person upon whom it falls must act within the time limits discussed above and give the required information. In the case of a direct acquisition or disposal of voting shares the required information is straightforward: simply the "resulting situation in terms of voting rights" i.e. the percentage of shares now held and the date upon which the threshold was crossed. Unlike in the case of disclosure by directors there is no obligation to disclose information about the terms upon which the shares were acquired or disposed of. In the case of indirect holdings of shares, some further information is required. For holdings via controlled companies the chain of control must be identified, partly, no doubt, to encourage disclosers to give their mind to this issue. The identity of the shareholder must be given (even if that shareholder has no notification obligation, for example a custodian voting only under instructions) and that of the person entitled to exercise the voting rights, if not the shareholder.[172] For voting rights exercisable through financial instruments, some basic information about those instruments must also be given, notably, the name of the underlying issuer and details about the exercise period (if any) and the date of maturity or expiry of the instrument.[173]

This information must be given to the company. However, the purposes of the disclosure rules can be met only if the information given to the issuer is publicised further. The DTR require issuers on a regulated market to make public the information received as soon as possible and, in any event, by the end of the following trading day, as is the rule for directors' notifications. In the case of issuers whose securities are traded on a prescribed (but not a regulated) market the maximum period for the further disclosure is the end of the third trading day following.[174]

Sanctions for non-disclosure

26–26   The FSA's powers to fine and censure[175] apply to persons who fail to make disclosure as required by the DTR, whether the disclosure is to or by an issuer.[176] Where the obligation falls upon a company, any director "knowingly concerned" in the contravention can be penalised or censured.

---

[172] DTR 5.8.1.
[173] DTR 5.8.2.
[174] DTR 5.8.12 (the period for prescribed markets is that required by the TD, Art.12(6)).
[175] Discussed above at para.26–8.
[176] FSMA 2000, s.91(1B),(2),(3).

CONCLUSION

In this Chapter we have looked at the additional periodic reporting **26–27**
requirements of publicly traded companies and at three types of
continuous disclosure required by companies whose securities are
traded on public markets. Companies must disclose on a continuing
basis price-sensitive information which concerns the company or its
business; directors must disclose information about their shareholdings in the company to the company which in turn must disclose
that information to the market; and major shareholders must disclose
vote-holder information to the company which again must disclose it
to the market. The movement of the second and third of these
requirements from the companies legislation to the financial services
rules has underlined the function of all three sets of provisions as
being the disclosure of information to the market. However, rules
made by or, mostly, under FSMA display some hesitation about
regulating all public markets on which securities are traded. Traditionally, the rules made by the FSA have focused on companies
which have sought admission to the Official List[177] and hence the
name give to the primary set of rules made by the FSA, the Listing
Rules. However, the Directives made under the Community's
Financial Services Action Plan generally apply to "regulated markets", of which the Main Market of the LSE is just one example.
Consequently, the FSA's rules implementing the Community disclosure obligations are now contained in a separate set of rules, the
DTR, with a wider scope. However, not all securities markets are
regulated: AIM, in particular, is not, but rather is an "exchange-
regulated" market or, in the new terminology, a "multilateral trading
facility". Some of the DTR apply across markets, notably the vote-
holding rules and the rules on market abuse, whilst others, those
requiring periodic disclosure and disclosure of directors' transactions,
apply only to regulated markets. This does not necessarily mean that
there are no such rules applying to exchange-regulated markets but
rather that decisions about the adoption and enforcement of such
rules are left to the market operator.

One may speculate that, if there were no provisions on periodic and
directors' disclosure in the AIM Rules, there would be pressure to
extend the FSA's rules. No doubt it is part of the self-image of the
AIM that it, rather than the FSA, whether acting on its own
authority or as transposer of EU Directives, should control the primary disclosure obligations of issuers and their directors. But why
have the rules applying to shareholder disclosure (and the market
abuse rules) been taken up by the FSA? This may be because

---

[177] See paras 25–5ff and 26–20 for a discussion of the terms "official list", "regulated market"
and "prescribed market".

shareholders and many of those who may engage in market abuse lie outside the reach of the LSE, whose powers rest essentially on the contract entered into by the company and the Exchange when a company seeks to have its securities admitted to that market.

There is more than one way in which the efficient functioning of the market is promoted by the requirements discussed in this Chapter. The reduction of insider trading opportunities is promoted by rules requiring price-sensitive information about the company to be made public or revealing directors' trading in the shares of their companies. However, continuous disclosure of information about companies also helps the accuracy of the price-formation process in securities markets, whilst information about directors' holdings helps shareholders assess the financial incentives to which the management is subject. Thus, both market efficiency and corporate governance objectives are promoted by the disclosure requirements. The vote-holder disclosure rules address a different need of investors: to know who is in a position to control the company or, perhaps more importantly, who may be building up a stake in the company as a prelude to effecting a change in the current control position. As so often in company law, the substance of the legal requirement may be the modest one of disclosure, but the underlying objectives, which the disclosure requirements are aimed to promote—it is unclear how effectively—are fundamental.

Chapter 27

TRANSFERS OF SHARES

Once shares have been issued by the company, it is only infrequently **27–1** that the company will buy them back. Moreover, this cannot happen without the company's consent, either at the time the shares were issued (as with shares which are issued as redeemable at the option of the shareholder)[1] or at the time of re-acquisition (as in the case of shares redeemable at the option of the company or a re-purchase of shares).[2] In any event, the re-acquisition cannot occur unless the rules on capital maintenance, imposed for the benefit of creditors, are observed.[3] Although companies do occasionally use surplus cash to re-purchase shares rather than to pay a dividend, a shareholder who wishes to realise his or her investment in the company will normally have to find, or wait for, another investor who will purchase the shares and take the shareholder's place in the company. This is precisely the reason why a company which secures the admission of its shares to a public market is likely to find it easier to persuade investors to buy the shares in the first place.

Although the above principle is true of all types of company, there is, as always, a major difference between companies with large and fluctuating bodies of shareholders whose shares are traded on a

---

[1] See above, para.13–9.
[2] Para.13–9.
[3] Para.13–11.

public exchange ("listed" companies) and companies with small bodies of shareholders whose composition is expected to be stable and where the allocation of shares is as much about the allocation of control in the company as it is about its financing ("non-listed" companies). In the former case, the law or the rules of the Exchange will require the shares to be freely tradable as far as the issuer is concerned,[4] so that except in a few cases the transfer of the shares will be simply a matter between the existing shareholder and the potential investor. Free transferability tends to be taken for granted in listed companies, but it does become controversial when what is proposed is the wholesale transfer of the shares to a single person, in the shape of a takeover bidder, because in that situation, even in an open company, the transfer of the shares has clear implications for the control of the company. We shall examine takeovers in the following Chapter.

In non-listed companies, by contrast, even the transfer of shares by a single shareholder may have implications for the control of the company and often also for its management, since a shareholding in such a company may be perceived as giving rise to a formal or informal entitlement to membership of the board of directors and participation in the management of the company.[5] In those companies, therefore, it is common for the articles of association to contain some restrictions on the transferability of the shares, perhaps by making transfers subject to the permission of the board or requiring the shares to be offered initially to the other shareholders before they can be sold outside the existing shareholder body. The latter obligation is normally referred to as giving the other shareholders pre-emption rights, but these are pre-emption rights arising on transfer and are to be distinguished from pre-emption rights arising on issuance, which are discussed in Chapter 25. The latter bind the company; the former the selling shareholder.

27–2   Share transfers involve a two-step process. In the first step the buyer and the seller conclude a sales contract where they agree on the price which the shares are sold for and on other terms of the transaction. Bankers sometimes refer to this first step as "trading". In the second step the transfer is carried out. At the end of the second step the buyer becomes the owner of the shares that formed part of the sales transaction. This second step is sometimes referred to as "settlement". Settlement is a process which in itself consists of two or more stages depending on whether certificated or uncertificated shares are sold.

When shares in private companies and non-listed public companies are sold the buyer and the seller frequently know each other's identity

---

[4] Rule 2.2.4 Listing Rules as of April 2008.
[5] In the case of an informal entitlement, it may be protected by the unfair prejudice remedy: above, Ch.20.

and are often personally involved in negotiating the terms of the transaction. Sales transactions are completed by way of delivery of certain transfer documents from the seller to the buyer and by way of registering the buyer's name on the shareholder register.

When listed shares are sold, the transaction is frequently more standardised. In most cases, the seller does not go out to find a buyer him- or herself, but enlists the services of a broker who sells the shares for him or her. The broker does this either through the electronic trading system operated by the London Stock Exchange or by making a contract with another financial services provider over the telephone. In both cases buyer and seller rarely know each other's identity. After the contract has been concluded, the buyer's name is also entered on the shareholder register, but this settlement process is carried out electronically through a settlement system known as CREST.

In this Chapter we will focus on the second step of the transfer process, the completion of the sales transaction. We shall examine the difference between certificated and uncertificated shares, transfers of certificated and transfers of uncertificated shares as well as the rules governing the shareholder register and transmission of shares by operation of law. We shall first address the difference between uncertificated and certificated shares.

CERTIFICATED AND UNCERTIFICATED SHARES

In British companies shares are predominantly issued in registered   **27–3** form. Companies issuing registered shares keep a register of the names of their shareholders. Until 1996 all registered shares were issued in what is now called the "certificated form". This means that, in addition to having his or her name noted on the shareholder register, every shareholder receives a paper certificate evidencing his or her shareholding. When shares are transferred the seller completes and signs a transfer form and delivers this together with the share certificate to the buyer. The buyer then lodges the certificate with the company to have his or her name entered on its shareholder register.

This paper-based transfer process still applies to non-listed shares. These are shares in private companies and shares in public companies which are not listed on the London Stock Exchange.

Until 1996 listed shares were also transferred by means of paper documents. The London Stock Exchange operated a transfer system entitled TALISMAN. Under the TALISMAN regime, the Stock Exchange received transfer forms and share certificates from buyers and ensured that the sellers' names would be registered on the shareholder register. There was a gap of two to three weeks between trading and settlement. If shares were sold in the meantime, TALISMAN would keep track of that transaction and arrange for the name of the ultimate buyer to be registered.

In the years leading up to the introduction of CREST in 1996, the UK privatised a large number of previously state-owned enterprises. The number of listed shares and with that the number of share transactions increased significantly. When share prices fell sharply on October 19, 1987, trading volumes soared and substantial delays in settlement occurred. Delays in settlement pose a significant risk to a share market. The longer the delay between trading and settlement the greater the risk that parties suffer loss by transactions not completing successfully. In many cases, the law will provide remedies if the transaction comes to a halt part way through, but the enforcement of those rights will be expensive and in some cases, for example, in the insolvency of an involved party, the rights may not have any value.

27–4   In the discussion following the 1987 market crash, it became apparent that the paper-based transfer process was unable to cope with large volumes of share transactions. It was decided that paper transfers should be phased out for listed shares and that a new electronic share transfer system should be introduced. This process of replacing paper with electronic shares transfers is referred to as dematerialisation. Listed shares were dematerialised in the UK in 1996 when the CREST system went live. Since then, all UK shares listed on the London Stock Exchange must be issued in the uncertificated form.[6] CREST operates on the basis of sections 784–790 of the 2006 Act and of the Uncertificated Securities Regulations 2001 (USR 2001).[7] These Regulations have termed electronic shares as uncertificated shares and paper shares as certificated shares.

The introduction of uncertificated shares requires the consent of a number of parties. CRESTCo, as the operator of the electronic system, must agree to admit the securities of the company in question to the system, though it clearly has a strong commercial incentive to do so, if the shares are heavily traded. Moreover, since an operator of an electronic system of share holding and transfer requires the approval of the Treasury and that approval requires the operator's rules not to distort competition,[8] it will not be in a position to set rules which discriminate improperly among companies.

In addition, the company itself must agree to permit its securities to be held in uncertificated form. Shares or individual classes of shares are in principle admissible to the electronic system only where the holding of shares in uncertificated form and their transfer electronically is permitted by the company's constitution.[9] The standard constitution requires the company to issue shareholders with a cer-

---

[6] Rule 6.1.23–6.1.24, Listing Rules as of April 2008.
[7] SI 2001/3755.
[8] USR 2001, Sch.1.
[9] Reg.15.

tificate of their holding.[10] To facilitate the change-over to uncertificated shares, USR 2001 reg.16 permits such provisions in the articles to be disapplied by resolution of the directors, rather than by the normal route for altering the articles by resolution of the shareholders,[11] provided the shareholders are given prior or subsequent notice of the directors' resolution. The Regulations then provide that the shareholders by ordinary resolution may vote to overturn the directors' resolution, but, unless they do so, the articles will be modified *pro tanto* without the shareholders' positive approval. Thus, the Regulations encourage uncertificated shares by putting the burden of objection on the shareholders.

Having briefly looked at the characteristics of certificated and uncertificated shares in this section, we shall examine transfers of certificated shares in the following section. After that transfers of uncertificated shares will be addressed.

TRANSFERS OF CERTIFICATED SHARES

To transfer certificated shares, the seller needs to complete a transfer form and deliver that form together with the share certificate to the buyer. The transfer form needs to comply either with the requirements contained in the company's constitution or with the simplified requirements put in place by the Stock Transfer Act.[12] This, however, is not enough to make the transferee a member of the company. Neither the agreement to transfer nor the delivery of the signed transfer form and share certificate will pass legal title to the transferee (though it may pass an equitable interest in the shares to the transferee).[13] The normal rule is that a person becomes a member of a company when they have agreed to this and their name has been entered into the company's register of members. For the transferee to become the legal owner of the shares, the company must discharge a function. It must enter his or her name on the register of members in place of the transferor's name.[14] It is precisely this requirement which

27–5

---

[10] The (draft) Companies (Model Articles) Regulations 2007, reg.24.
[11] See above, para.3–20.
[12] s.770(1).
[13] See below, para.27–8.
[14] And, it seems, what then occurs is a novation (i.e. the relationship between the company and the transferor is ended and is replaced by a new relationship between the company and the transferee) rather than an assignment of the transferor's rights to the transferee (*Ashby v Blackwell* (1765) 2 Eden 299 at 302–303; 28 E.R. 913 at 914; *Simm v Anglo-American Telegraph Company* (1879) 5 Q.B.D. 188 at 204; R.R. Pennington, *Company Law* (8th ed, 2001) 398–399; J. Benjamin, *Interests in Securities* (2001) 3.05; E. Micheler, "Legal Title and the Transfer of Shares in a Paperless World—Farewell Quasi-Negotiability", [2002] J.B.L 358). If this is the rule, it is favourable to transferees, for in general on assignment the assignee is in no better position than was the assignor.

gives a closed company the opportunity to control the process of transfer of shares to new holders.

It also follows from this analysis that a share certificate (unlike a share warrant to bearer)[15] is not a negotiable instrument. Legal title does not pass by mere delivery of the certificate to the transferee but upon registration of the transferee by the company. In fact, even registration is not conclusive of the transferee's legal title. Section 127 provides that the register of members is only "prima facie evidence" of matters directed or authorised to be inserted in it and section 768 correspondingly says that a share certificate issued by the company (for example, to the transferee) is "prima facie evidence" of the transferee's title to the shares.[16] Where there is a conflict between the register and the certificate, the former is stronger prima facie evidence than the latter but neither is decisive. Ownership of the shares depends on who is entitled to be registered. Suppose, say, that A, who is registered and is entitled to be registered, loses his certificate, obtains a duplicate from the company[17] and transfers to B who is registered by the company. Subsequently A finds the original certificate and, either because he has forgotten about the sale to B or because he is a rogue, then purports to sell the shares to C. The company will rightly refuse to register C whose only remedy will be against A (who may by this time be a man-of-straw).

More importantly, suppose D loses the certificate to E, a rogue, who forges D's signature and secures entry on the register in place of D. D will nevertheless be entitled to have the register rectified[18] so as to restore D's name, because D is still the holder of the legal title to the shares and so is entitled to be entered on the register. This appears to be so, even if D's conduct has been such as to provide the opportunity for E to commit the fraud, for example because D had deposited the certificate with E.[19] Furthermore, D will be entitled to insist on rectification if, as is all too likely, E has made a further transfer of the shares to a wholly innocent third party, F, who is registered before D learns of the fraud. D may still rectify the register against F. This system of rules provides a high level of protection of D's legal rights, but is hardly conducive to the free circulation of shares.

---

[15] See above, para.24–17.

[16] Or in Scotland "sufficient evidence unless the contrary is shown". It is not thought that the reference in s.768 to a certificate "under the common seal of the company" requires the use of the common seal, if it instead uses an official seal which is a facsimile of its common seal (see s.50) or has the certificate signed by two directors or one director and the secretary (see s.44). S.768 (2) makes the position clear for Scotland.

[17] Companies do this readily enough so long as the registered holder makes a statutory declaration regarding the loss and supplies the company with a bank indemnity against any liability it may incur. Since the risk is negligible (see below, fn.52) and what banks charge for this is not, this must be a profitable business for the banks.

[18] On rectification, see below, para.27–19.

[19] *Welch v Bank of England* [1955] Ch. 508; *Simm v Anglo-American Telegraph Co* (1879) 5 Q.B.D. 188.

However, the position of people such as F is ameliorated by the **27–6** doctrine of estoppel by share certificate, which may give F a right to an indemnity against the company, if D insists on rectification of the register. In other words, the risk of fraud (or other unauthorised transfer) falls on the company, which is perhaps defensible on the grounds that it is the company which benefits from legal rules which encourage the free circulation of shares.[20] The doctrine of estoppel by share certificate produces what has been termed "quasi-negotiability".[21]

A share certificate contains two statements on which the company knows that reliance may be placed. The first is the extent to which the shares to which it relates are paid up. The second is that the person named in it was registered as the holder of the stated number of shares. The company may be estopped from denying either statement if someone in reliance upon it has changed his position to his detriment. This may afford a transferee who, in reliance on the transferor's share certificate, has bought what he believed, wrongly, to be fully paid shares a defence if the company makes a call upon him.[22] The company will also be estopped if the transferee has relied on a false statement in his transferor's certificate that the transferor was the registered holder of the shares on the date stated in the certificate.[23] Thus, F, the transferee from the rogue, will be entitled to an indemnity from the company if the company rectifies the register in favour of D, the legal owner, because F will have relied upon the certificate issued by the company to the rogue.

---

[20] The company may in turn be entitled to an indemnity from the person who asked it to register the transfer which led to the issuance by the company of the misleading certificate. An indemnity against the fraudster is likely to be worthless, but the entitlement embraces also the broker who acted on behalf of the fraudster, who may well be worth suing. See *Royal Bank of Scotland Plc v Sandstone Properties Plc* [1998] 2 B.C.L.C. 429, where the earlier cases are reviewed. Presumably, the rationale for the company's entitlement is that the broker is in a better position to detect unauthorised transfers than is the company. No liability arises, however, if the broker who instructed the issuer to amend the register did so in reliance on genuine but inaccurate share certificates issued by the issuer or its registrar (*Cadbury Schweppes Plc v Halifax Share Dealing Ltd* [2007] 1 B.C.L.C 497).

[21] E. Micheler, "Farewell to Quasi-negotiability? Legal Title and Transfer of Shares in a Paperless World" [2002] J.B.L. 358.

[22] *Burkinshaw v Nicholls* (1878) 3 App.Cas.1004, HL; *Bloomenthal v Ford* [1897] A.C. 156, HL. If the reason why the shares were not fully paid up is because of a contravention of the provisions regarding payment in ss.97 *et seq.* of the Act (see Ch.11, above, at para.234) a bona fide purchaser and those securing title from him will be exempted from liability to pay calls by virtue of s.112(3) and will not have to rely on estoppel.

[23] *Dixon v Kennaway & Co* [1900] 1 Ch. 833; *Bahia and San Francisco Railway Company, Re* (1868) L.R. 3 Q.B. 584. This, in contrast with resisting a call, may seem to be committing the heresy of using estoppel as a sword rather than a shield. The justification is that a purchaser who has bought from the registered owner has a prima facie right to be registered in his place and that the company is estopped from denying that the transferor was the registered owner.

However, this argument will rarely[24] benefit an original recipient of
the incorrect certificate because receipt of the certificate normally
marks the conclusion of the transaction and is not something which
was relied on in deciding to enter into it. In the example above, E, the
rogue, is the original recipient of the incorrect certificate and we need
have no regrets about the weakness of E's legal position. However,
suppose E, instead of transferring the shares fraudulently into his
own name and then disposing of them to F, in fact, as is all too likely,
short-circuited this procedure by transferring them directly to F, and
the company then issued a new certificate to F. F could not claim to
have relied on the new certificate when entering into the transaction
which pre-dated its issue. F did rely on the certificate issued to D but
E's fraud did not turn on a denial of D's ownership of the shares but
rather upon E pretending to be D. In this situation, only a transferee
from F would be able to rely on the doctrine of estoppel by share
certificate. Perhaps this result may be justified on the basis that D is in
a better position to detect E's fraud than is the company.

Restrictions on transferability

27–7   The directors of non-listed companies are frequently empowered by
the articles to refuse to register transfers or there will be provisions
affording the other members or the company[25] rights of pre-emption,
first refusal or even compulsory acquisition. This does not apply to
listed shares because the Listing Rules require there to be no
restrictions of the transfer of shares.[26]
Provisions restricting share transfers require the most careful
drafting if they are to achieve their purpose; and have not always
received it, thereby facing the courts with difficult questions of
interpretation. The following propositions can, it is thought, be
extracted from the voluminous case-law.

(a) The extent of the restriction is solely a matter of construction
of the company's constitution. But, since shareholders have a
prima facie right to transfer to whomsoever they please, this
right is not to be cut down by uncertain language or doubtful
implications.[27] If, therefore, it is not clear whether a restriction applies to any transfer or only to a transfer to, say, a

---

[24] But in exceptional circumstances it may do so: *Balkis Consolidated Co v Tomlinson* [1893]
A.C. 396, HL; *Alipour v UOC Corp* [2002] 2 B.C.L.C. 770 (where the holder was even held
entitled to be registered as a member, since no innocent party was thereby preduiced).

[25] Acquisition by the company itself will, of course, be lawful only if it is able to comply with
the conditions enabling a company to buy its own shares: see above, at para.13–7. Less
usually, the provision may impose an obligation on other members to buy.

[26] Rule 2.2.4, Listing Rules as of April 2008.

[27] Per Greene M.R. in *Smith & Fawcett Ltd, Re* [1942] Ch. 304 at 306, CA. See also *New Cedos
Engineering Co Ltd, Re* [1994] 1 B.C.L.C. 797 (a case decided in 1975); *Stothers v William
Steward (Holdings) Ltd* [1994] 2 B.C.L.C. 266.

non-member,[28] or to any type of disposition or only to a sale[29] the narrower construction will be adopted.

(b) However, this does not help the courts much when faced with a common provision in the articles that a shareholder "desirous" or "intending" or "proposing" to transfer his or her shares to another must give notice to the company to trigger pre-emption procedures. On the one hand, the provision would be unworkable if the courts had held that as soon as a shareholder formed the relevant intention, the provision in the articles was triggered, especially as the shareholder is normally permitted to withdraw the notice, if he or she does not wish to sell to the person who comes forward to buy the shares. There must be something in addition to the required intention. On the other hand, a shareholder who enters into an agreement with an outsider to sell the shares to that person or to give that person an option to buy them will fall within the provision in the articles, even if the outsider has not completed the agreement (and so has only an equitable interest in the shares) or has not taken up the option to purchase.[30] Drafters have spent much ingenuity on producing agreements which do not fall within the second category and have been rewarded. The courts have held that agreements do not trigger the notice provision if they transfer only the beneficial interest in the shares and entitle the transferee to be registered as the legal owner of the shares only once the pre-emption right has been removed from the articles.[31] The execution of a transfer form and its deposit with the company's auditor, however, can amount to a transfer which triggers pre-emption rights contained in the company's constitution.[32]

(c) Where the regulations confer a discretion on directors with regard to the acceptance of transfers, this discretion, like all the directors' powers, is a fiduciary one[33] to be exercised bona fide in what they consider—not what the court considers—to be in the interest of the company, and not for any

---

[28] *Greenhalgh v Mallard* [1943] 2 All E.R. 234, CA; *Roberts v Letter "T" Estates Ltd* [1961] A.C. 795, PC; see also *Rose v Lynx Express Ltd and another* [2004] 1 B.C.L.C. 455.

[29] *Moodie v Shepherd (Bookbinders) Ltd* [1949] 2 All E. R. 1044, HL.

[30] *Lyle & Scott Ltd v Scott's Trustees* [1959] A.C. 763, HL; *Owens v GRA Property Trust Ltd* (July 10, 1978, unreported).

[31] *Sedgefield Steeplechase Co (1927) Ltd, Scotto v Petch and others, Re* [2000] All E.R. (D) 2442 (CA) (Lord Hoffmann sat as an additional judge of the Chancery Division, where the previous cases are reviewed); *Theakston v London Trust Plc* [1984] B.C.L.C. 390; see also *Safeguard Industrial Investments Ltd v National and Westminster Bank Ltd* [1980] 3 All E.R. 849.

[32] *Hurst v Crampton Bros (Coopers) Ltd and others* [2003] 1 B.C.L.C. 304.

[33] For the application of the fiduciary principle to the transfer of shares in the context of takeover bids, see para.28–34, below.

collateral purpose. But the court will presume that they have acted bona fide, and the onus of proof of the contrary is on those alleging it and is not easily discharged.[34]

(d) Prior to the Companies Act 2006 it was possible for the articles of association to stipulate that the directors shall not be bound to state their reasons for not registering a transfer.[35] The Companies Act 2006 now states in section 771 that the company must provide the transferee with such further information about the reasons for the refusal as the transferee may reasonable request. This, however, does not include minutes of the meetings of directors. The CLR hopes that this will make it possible to apply the fiduciary tests and section 994 on unfair prejudice in a transparent way to such refusals.[36]

(e) If, on the true construction of the articles, the directors are entitled to reject only on certain prescribed grounds and it is proven that they have rejected on others, the court will intervene.[37] If the directors state their reasons (as they are now obliged to do) the court will investigate them to the extent of seeing whether they have acted on the right principles and would overrule their decision if they have acted on considerations which should not have weighed with them, but not merely because the court would have come to a different conclusion.[38] If the regulations are so framed as to give the directors an unfettered discretion the court will interfere with it only on proof of bad faith.[39]

(f) If, as is normal, the regulations merely give the directors power to refuse to register, as opposed to making their passing of transfers a condition precedent to registration,[40]

---

[34] In *Smith & Fawcett Ltd, Re* above, fn.58, the directors refused to register but agreed that they would register a transfer of part of the shareholding if the transferor agreed to sell the balance to one of the directors at a stated price. It was held that this was insufficient evidence of bad faith but it might today be "unfairly prejudicial" under s.994; see Ch.20. See also *Village Cay Marina Ltd v Acland* [1998] 2 B.C.L.C. 327, PC.

[35] *Berry & Stewart v Tottenham Hotspur Football Co* [1935] Ch. 718; see also *Sutherland v British Dominions Corp* [1926] Ch. 746.

[36] Final Report I, paras 7.42–7.45.

[37] *Bede Steam Shipping Co, Re* [1917] 1 Ch. 123, CA; see also *Sutherland v British Dominions Corp* [1926] Ch. 746.

[38] *Bede Steam Shipping Co, Re* above; *Smith & Fawcett Ltd, Re* above. Indeed, if there are rights of pre-emption at a fair price to be determined by the auditors the court can investigate the adequacy of this price only if the auditors give a "speaking valuation" stating their reasons: *Dean v Prince* [1954] Ch. 409, CA; *Burgess v Purchase & Sons Ltd* [1983] Ch. 216.

[39] *Smith & Fawcett Ltd, Re* above; *Charles Forte Investments Ltd v Amanda* [1964] Ch. 240, *Village Cay Marina Ltd v Acland and others (Barclays Bank Plc third party)* [1998] 2 B.C.L.C 327, PC.

[40] It is common to state that transfers have to be passed by the directors but under normal articles that is not so (The Companies (Model Articles) Regulation 2007, reg.26; and in the light of s.771 it is doubtful if the articles could make the directors' approval a condition precedent.

the transferee is entitled to be registered unless the directors resolve as a board to reject. Hence in *Moodie v Shepherd (Bookbinders) Ltd*[41] where the two directors disagreed and neither had a casting vote, the House of Lords held that registration must proceed. The directors have a reasonable time in which to come to a decision,[42] but since section 771(1) imposes an obligation on them to give to the transferee notice of rejection within two months of the lodging of the transfer, the maximum reasonable period is two months.[43]

The positions of transferor and transferee prior to registration

It may be of importance to determine the precise legal position of the transferor and transferee pending registration of the transfer which, if there are restrictions on transferability, may never occur. As we have seen, only if and when the transfer is registered will the transferor cease to be a member and shareholder and the transferee will become a member and shareholder. However, notwithstanding that registration has not occurred, the beneficial interest in the shares may have passed from the transferor to the transferee. In the case of a sale of certificated shares the transaction will normally go through three stages:—(1) an agreement (which, particularly if a block of shares conferring de facto or de jure control is being sold, may be a complicated one); (2) delivery of the signed transfer form and the certificate by the seller and payment of the price by the buyer and; (3) registration of the buyer's name on the shareholder register.

27–8

Notwithstanding that the transfer is not lodged for registration or registration is refused, the beneficial interest in the shares will, it seems, pass from the seller to the buyer at the latest at stage (2) and, indeed will do so at stage (1) if the agreement is one which the courts would order to be specifically enforced.[44] The seller then becomes a trustee for the buyer and must account to him for any dividends he

---

[41] [1949] 2 All E.R. 1044, HLSc.

[42] *Shepherd's* case (1866) L.R. 2 Ch. App. 16.

[43] *Swaledale Cleaners Ltd, Re* [1968] 1 W.L.R. 1710, CA; *Tett v Phoenix Property and Investment Co Ltd and others* [1986] B.C.L.C. 149; *Inverdeck Ltd, Re* [1998] 2 B.C.L.C. 242. And normally it seems that they will not be treated as acting unreasonably if they take the full two months: *Zinotty Properties Ltd, Re* [1984] 1 W.L.R. 1249 at 1260.

[44] The fact that the agreement is subject to fulfilment of a condition beyond the control of the parties will not prevent it from being specifically enforceable, notwithstanding that the condition has not been fulfilled, if the party for whose benefit the condition was inserted is prepared to waive it. In *Wood Preservation Ltd v Prior* [1969] 1 W.L.R. 1077, CA, where the condition was for the benefit of the buyer, the court was prepared to hold that the seller ceased to be "the beneficial owner" on the date of the contract notwithstanding that the buyer did not become the beneficial owner until he later waived the condition. In the interim, beneficial ownership was, apparently, in limbo! See also *Michaels and another v Harley House (Marylebone)* [1997] 2 B.C.L.C. 166; *Philip Morris Products Inc and another v Rothmans International Enterprises Ltd and another* [2001] All E.R. (D) 48 (Jul); *Kilnoore Ltd (in liquidation) Unidare Plc v Cohen and another, Re* [2006] 1 Ch.489.

receives and vote in accordance with his instructions (or appoint him as his proxy).[45] This, however, begs several questions. The first arises because at stage (2) delivery of the documents may not necessarily be matched by payment of the full price; the agreement may have provided for payment by instalments[46] and the seller will then retain a lien on the shares as an unpaid seller. This will not prevent an equitable interest passing to the buyer but the court will not grant specific performance unless the seller's lien can be fully protected,[47] and until paid in full he is entitled to vote the shares as he thinks will best protect his interest.[48] Instead of being a bare trustee his position is analogous to that of a trustee of a settlement of which he is one of the beneficiaries.

The second begged question is whether the foregoing can apply when the articles provide for rights of pre-emption or first refusal when a shareholder wishes to dispose of his shares. In such a case the transferor (perhaps with the full knowledge of the transferee[49]) has breached the deemed contract under s.14 between him and the company and his fellow shareholders. There are observations of the House of Lords in *Hunter v Hunter*[50] to the effect that accordingly the transfer is wholly void, even as between the transferor and transferee. However, in later cases[51] courts have refused to follow this and, it must surely be right (at any rate if the price has been paid) that the buyer obtains such rights as the transferor had. This will not benefit the buyer if all the shares are taken up when the transferor is compelled to make a pre-emptive offer, but it does not follow that all of them will be taken up and, if not, the transferee has a better claim to those shares not taken up than has the transferor.

27–9   When the transaction is not a sale but a gift, there need be no agreement. Even if there is, it will not be legally enforceable under English law because there will be no valuable consideration and because, under the so-called rule in *Milroy v Lord*,[52] "there is no equity to perfect an imperfect gift". One might have supposed, therefore, that if the donor has chosen to make the gift by handing to the donee a signed transfer and the share certificate, rather than by a

---

[45] *Hardoon v Belilios* [1901] A.C. 118, PC.
[46] The normal practice then is to provide that the transfer and share certificate shall be held by a stakeholder and not lodged for registration until released to the buyer on payment of the final instalment.
[47] *Langen & Wind Ltd v Bell* [1972] Ch. 685; *Prince v Strange* [1977] 3 All E.R. 371.
[48] *Musselwhite v Musselwhite & Son Ltd* [1962] Ch. 964; *JRRT (Investments) Ltd v Haycraft* [1993] B.C.L.C. 401; *Michaels and another v Harley House (Marylebone)* [1997] 2 B.C.L.C. 166.
[49] As in *Lyle & Scott Ltd v Scott's Trustees* [1959] A.C. 763, HLSc.
[50] [1936] A.C. 222, HL.
[51] *Hawks v McArthur* [1951] 1 All E.R. 22; *Tett v Phoenix Property Co* [1986] B.C.L.C. 149, where the Court of Appeal was not required to rule on this point because the appellants did not argue that the decision on it at first instance was wrong. *Cottrell v King and another* [2004] 2 B.C.L.C. 413; but see *Claygreen Ltd; Romer-Ormiston v Claygreen Ltd and others, Re* [2006] 1 B.C.L.C. 715.
[52] (1862) 4 De G., F. and J. 264.

formal declaration of trust in favour of the donee, the gift would not be effective unless and until the transfer was registered. In modern cases,[53] however, it has been held that so long as the donor has done all he needs to do, the beneficial interest passes from him to the donee.[54]

Priorities between competing transferees

Questions may also arise in determining the priority of purported **27–10** transfers of the same shares to different people. In answering these questions the courts[55] have relied on two traditional principles of English property law: i.e. (1) that as between two competing holders of equitable interests, if their equities are equal the first in time prevails and (2) that a bona fide purchaser for value of a legal interest takes free of earlier equitable interests of which he has no notice at the time of purchase.

In applying these principles to competing share transfers, a transferee prior to registration is treated as having an equitable interest only but registration converts his interest into a legal one.[56] Hence if a registered shareholder, A, first executes a transfer to a purchaser, B, and later to another, C, while both remain unregistered B will have priority over C. If, however, C succeeds in obtaining registration before B, he will have priority over B so long as he had no notice, at the time of purchase, of the transfer to B. If C did have notice, although he has been registered, his prima facie title will not prevail over that of B, who will be entitled to have the register rectified (assuming that there are no grounds on which the company could refuse to register B) and in the meantime C's legal interest will be subject to the equitable interest of B.[57] If both transfers were gifts, the position would presumably be different; the gift to B[58] would leave A without any beneficial interest that he could give to C and, not being a "purchaser", C could not obtain priority by registration; his legal

---

[53] *Rose, Re* [1949] Ch. 78; *Rose, Re* [1952] Ch. 499, CA; *Pennington and another v Waine and others* [2002] 2 B.C.L.C 448, CA.

[54] Thus, until the transfer is registered, placing the donee in the same position as if the donor had instead made a declaration of trust.

[55] The leading cases are *Shropshire Union Railway v R.* (1875) L.R. 7 H.L. 496; *Société Générale v Walker* (1885) 11 App.Cas.20, HL; *Colonial Bank v Cady* (1890) 15 App.Cas.267, HL. Among more recent decisions, see *Hawks v McArthur* [1951] 1 All E.R. 22; *Champagne Perrier-Jouet v Finch & Co* [1982] 1 W.L.R. 1359; *Macmillan Inc v Bishopsgate Investment Trust Plc and others (No.3)* [1995] 3 All E.R. 747.

[56] Notwithstanding a suggestion by Lord Selbourne (in *Société Générale v Walker* (1885) 11 App.Cas.20, HL) that "a present absolute right to have the transfer registered" might suffice, it seems that nothing less than actual registration will do. In *Ireland v Hart* [1902] 1 Ch. 521 the transfer had been lodged for registration and the directors had no power to refuse but it was held that the legal interest had not passed.

[57] *France v Clark* (1884) 26 Ch.D. 257, CA; *Earl of Sheffield v London Joint Stock Bank* (1888) 13 App.Cas. 332, HL; *Rainford v James Keith & Blackman* [1905] 2 Ch. 147, CA.

[58] So long as it has been "perfected"—as interpreted in *Rose, Re* [1949] Ch. 78; *Rose, Re* [1952] Ch. 499, CA.

interest, on his becoming the registered holder, would be subject to the prior equity of B.

It should perhaps be pointed out once again that even registration affords only prima facie evidence of title. If the registered transferor, A, was not entitled to the shares, what will pass when he transfers to B or C is not, strictly speaking, either a legal or equitable interest but only his imperfect title to it, which will not prevail against the true owner. If, for example, the transfer to A was a forgery the true owner will be entitled to be restored to the register.[59] Hence a transferee can never be certain of obtaining an absolute title in the case of an off-market transaction. But his risk is slight so long as he promptly obtains registration of the transfer. And this he can do unless there are restrictions on the transferability of the shares or unless there are good reasons for failing to apply for registration.

The principal example for the latter occurs when the shareholder wants to borrow on the security of his shares. This can be done by a legal mortgage, under which the shareholder transfers the shares to the lender (who registers the transfer) subject to an agreement to retransfer them when the loan is repaid. Generally, however, this suits neither party; the lender normally has no wish to become a member and shareholder of the company and the borrower does not want to cease to be one. Hence a more usual arrangement is one whereby the shareholder deposits with the lender his share certificate and, often, a signed blank transfer, this usually being accompanied by a written memorandum setting out the terms of the loan. The result is to confer an equitable charge which the lender can enforce by selling the shares if he needs to realise his security. Custody of the share certificate is regarded as the essential protection of the lender.[60] In the case of shares, dealt with through CREST,[61] its rules provided for uncertificated shares to be held in "escrow" balances, which provision appears to give the bank an equivalent security.[62]

The company's lien

27–11 As we have seen,[63] a public company is not permitted to have a charge or lien on its shares except (a) when the shares are not fully paid and

---

[59] The transferee will have no remedy against the company based on estoppel by share certificate: it made no false statement: see para.689 above. The Forged Transfers Acts 1891 and 1892 enabled companies to adopt fee-financed arrangements for compensating innocent victims of forged transfers but this is purely voluntary and seems to have been virtually a dead-letter since its inception.

[60] Banks usually grant their clients overdrafts on the security of an equitable charge by a deposit of share certificates without requiring signed blank transfers.

[61] Shares not listed or dealt with on the AIM are rarely accepted as security for loans because of their illiquidity and, usually, restrictions on their transferability. Banks will instead want a charge on the undertaking and assets of the company itself plus, probably, personal guarantees of the members or directors.

[62] See Evans (1996) 11 B.J.I.B.F.L. 259.

[63] Para.13–7, above.

the charge or lien is for the amount payable on the shares, or (b) the ordinary business of the company includes the lending of money or consists of the provision of hire-purchase finance and the charge arises in the course of a transaction in the ordinary course of its business.[64] Neither exception is of much importance in the present context.

Hence it is only in respect of private companies that problems are still likely to arise when their articles provide, as they frequently do, that "the company shall have a first and paramount lien on shares, whether or not fully-paid, registered in the name of a person indebted or under any liability to the company". Since the decision of the House of Lords in *Bradford Banking Co v Briggs, Son and Co*[65] it appears to be accepted that the effect of such a provision is that:

(a) once a shareholder has incurred a debt or liability to the company, it has an equitable charge on the shares of that shareholder to secure payment which ranks in priority to later equitable interests and, it seems, to earlier ones of which the company had no notice when its lien became effective; and

(b) in determining whether the company had notice,[66] s.360 has no application; if the company knows of the earlier equitable interest (because, for example, a transfer of the shares has been lodged for registration even if that is refused) it cannot improve its own position to the detriment of the holder of that known equitable interest.

An interesting modern illustration is afforded by *Champagne Perrier-Jouet v Finch & Co*.[67] There the company's articles provided for a lien in the above terms. One of its shareholders[68] had been allowed to run up substantial debts to the company resulting from trading between him and the company and it had been agreed that he could repay by instalments. Another creditor of the shareholder subsequently obtained judgment against him and a charging order on the shares by way of equitable execution. It was held that the company's

---

[64] s.670; for listed companies see also rule 2.2.4, Listing Rules as of April 2008.

[65] (1886) 12 App.Cas.29, HL.

[66] It is not altogether clear why notice should be relevant. Since the company's lien is merely an equitable interest, its priority vis-à-vis another equitable interest should depend on the respective dates of their creation. But the decisions seem to assume that the company's lien will have priority over an equitable interest if the company has not received notice of the latter.

[67] [1982] 1 W.L.R. 1359.

[68] He had also been a director and it was argued that the debt he incurred to the company was a loan unlawful under what is now s.197 so that the company could not have a valid lien. It was held that it was not a loan; it would, however, today be "a quasi-loan" as defined in s.198 and as such unlawful if the company was a "relevant company" (e.g. a subsidiary of a public company) as defined in s.198.

lien had become effective when the debts to it were incurred (even though they were not then due for repayment) and as this occurred before the company had notice of the charging order,[69] the company's lien had priority.[70]

As this case shows, an equitable charge on shares in a private company with articles conferring a lien on the company is likely to be an even more undesirable form of security than shares in private companies always are. It may, however, be the only security obtainable, for an attempt to obtain a legal charge will almost certainly be frustrated by the refusal of the directors to register the transfer. If, *faute de mieux*, it has to be accepted, notice should immediately be given to the company, making it clear that this is a notice which it cannot disregard in relation to any lien it may claim, and an attempt should be made to obtain information about the amount, if any, then owed to the company.

Transfers of Uncertificated Shares

27–12 We have seen in the previous section that certificated shares are transferred by way of delivery of certain transfer documents to the company. The company being so notified of a transfer then registers the transferee's name on the shareholder register. When uncertificated shares are sold, the register is updated through electronic instructions.

For a transfer of uncertificated shares to be possible, both the seller and the buyer need to have access to the CREST system. There are three ways in which investors can access CREST. They can either hold an account with CREST themselves and acquire the hard- and software necessary to establish a safe connection with CREST. The cost involved in doing this makes this option unappealing to small scale private investors. An investor can also have his or her account with CREST operated by a broker who accesses the system or his or her behalf. This option is referred to as private membership in the CREST documentation. With both options, the account is operated in the name of the investor who holds legal title to the shares. The third option for an investor is not to hold an account with CREST but to instruct a broker to act as a nominee on his or her behalf. In that case, the investor's name does not appear on the company's

---

[69] It also ante-dated the charging order but the court seems to have regarded the date of notice as decisive: see at 1367B–E.
[70] It was also held that if the company enforced its lien by selling the shares it would have to comply with provisions in the articles conferring pre-emptive rights on the other members of the company.

register. The nominee rather than the investor has an account with CREST and holds legal title to the shares.

When uncertificated shares are transferred, both the selling and the buying account holder need to instruct the system to carry out the transfer. When shares are sold through the Stock Exchange's electronic trading system, the sales information is transferred into the CREST system automatically and the selling and the buying account holder have an opportunity to verify the data before the transfer is effected.

Upon receiving transfer instructions, CREST verifies them, matches them and carries them out on the day specified by the parties. On that day CREST transfers the shares from the seller to the buyer and causes the purchase price to be paid over to the seller. The buyer becomes the legal owner of the shares when they are credited to his or her account. This is because, since 2001, CREST not only operates an electronic transfer system, but also keeps the shareholder register for all UK uncertificated shares.[71] Having updated the register, CREST needs to immediately inform the issuing company which keeps records of all transfers relating to uncertificated shares.

In order to preserve the integrity of the shareholder register, the **27–13** USR 2001 stipulates that CRESTCo must not amend the shareholder register, except on completion of a trade in uncertificated units, unless ordered to do so by a court[72] or unless shares have been transferred by operation of law.[73] Equally, there are only limited circumstances in which CRESTCo may or must refuse to alter the operator register if it has received appropriate instructions from system members. Of course, the Regulations recognise that, in rare cases, events outside the system may impinge on the Operator's freedom of action in relation to the Operator register, just as they do on the issuer register kept by the company (for the uncertificated shares) or the share register, also kept by the company, for companies which have not entered the electronic transfer system. Thus, unless it is impracticable to stop it, CREST must not make a change in the Operator register which it actually knows is prohibited by an order of a court or by or under an enactment or involves a transfer to a deceased person.[74] There are further cases where CREST may refuse to make a change, for example, where the transfer is not to a legal or natural person or is

---

[71] USR 2001 reg.27(1) obliges the Operator upon settlement of the transfer to amend the operator register (unless the shares thereafter are to be held in certificated form). The Operator must also, immediately after making the change, notify the company: reg.27(7).

[72] USR 2001 reg.27(5)—for example, upon rectification of the register. Or unless it receives an issuer instruction to the effect that the shares have been converted into uncertificated form or there has been a compulsory acquisition of shares after a takeover (see para.28–61): reg.27(1).

[73] USR 2001 reg.27(6). On transfer by operation of law, see below, para.696.

[74] USR 2001 reg.27(2) and (3).

to a minor.[75] Section 771(1)[76] applies in cases where CREST refuses to register a transfer,[77] but a two-month limit for notifying transferees of a failure to register hardly seems an appropriate one for an electronic system.

Title to uncertificated shares and the protection of transferees

27–14 The CREST system has reduced the time that lapses between trade and settlement. It has also caused transfers of uncertificated shares to be carried out almost simultaneously with payment of the purchase price. This has significantly reduced the transactional risk investors in shares are exposed to. The risk involved in shares transaction has, however, not been eliminated completely. In particular, the Regulations do not introduce a rule to the effect that entry on the Operator register confers title to the shares on the person registered. On the contrary, reg.24(1) provides, in the same way as the Act,[78] that "a register of members" is simply prima facie evidence of the matters directed or authorised to be stated in it, and "register of members" is defined to include both the issuer and Operator register of members.[79] In principle, therefore, a legal owner of shares may seek rectification of the Operator register if CREST removes his or her name from it without cause, and a court order restoring the legal owner to the register would be, as we have seen, something to which the Operator is obliged to respond.[80] In fact, it is doubtful whether the statutory provision under which the Regulations were made is wide enough to effect a general change in the rules as to the status of the register.

This is not to say, however, that the protection of transferees is provided in the same way or to the same extent under the Regulations in relation to uncertificated shares as it is in relation to certificated shares. As we have seen, that protection in relation to the latter class of shares depends heavily upon the doctrine of estoppel by share certificate. Since, by definition, there is no share certificate in relation to uncertificated shares, the immediate position seems to be that the third party cannot be protected by this doctrine. Is this in principle a problem for the transferee of shares? The answer is that, if the matter were not dealt with in the Regulations, it would be. There are obvious risks that either an unauthorised person obtains access to the system or a person with authorised access uses the system in an unauthorised way, in both cases sending an instruction to transfer shares not belonging to him or her to an innocent third party. Can the former

---

[75] USR 2001 reg.27(4).
[76] See above at para.27–7.
[77] USR 2001 reg.27(8) and (9).
[78] s.127; below, para.27–16. Naturally, s.768 (certificate to be evidence of title) has no application to uncertificated shares, though the section seems still to apply to certificated shares of participating companies.
[79] USR 2001 reg.3(1).
[80] USR 2001 reg.27(5).

holder of the shares secure the restoration of his or her name to the Operator register to the detriment of the third party?

One technique for protecting the third party might be to transfer the doctrine of estoppel by share certificate to the entry on the register, but it is no accident that, in relation to certificated shares, the doctrine is based on the certificate, not on the register entry, even though both are available. This is because it is rare for a transferee to rely on the register entry before committing him- or herself to the transaction. This is true of both the Operator register and the issuer register, and so estoppel does not seem an effective protective device as against either the company or CREST.

In fact, the Regulations take an entirely different approach to the protection of transferees. If the unauthorised instruction in the situations above is sent in accordance with the rules of the Operator, the recipient of the instruction is entitled, subject to very few exceptions, to act on it and the person by whom or on whose behalf it was purportedly sent may not deny that it was sent with proper authority and contained accurate information.[81] Unlike at common law, where even careless conduct does not prevent the legal owner from asserting his or her title to the shares,[82] even a legal owner who was in no way to blame for the fraud may find that title to the shares has been lost. The transferor may have a remedy in such a case against the system participant whose equipment was used to send the unauthorised instructions.[83] There may also be a liability of the Operator in such a case, but only if the instruction was not sent from a system computer or the system computer it purported to be sent from. Thus, purely unauthorised activity by a broker's employee is not caught.[84] In any event, the liability is capped at £50,000 in respect of each instruction[85] and falls away entirely if the Operator identifies the person responsible, even if the transferor is not able to recover any compensation from that person.[86]

Thus, it seems right to conclude that transferees are somewhat better protected under the Regulations than under the common law doctrine of estoppel, since even first transferees from the rogue are protected. However, that protection is provided at the expense of the transferor, rather than of the company, as at common law, and it is

27–15

---

[81] USR 2001 reg.35.

[82] See above, para.27–5.

[83] The Regulations do not create such a liability but do preserve it if it exists under the general law (USR reg.35(7)), for example, as between the transferor and his or her broker.

[84] See the definition of "forged dematerialised instruction" in USR reg.36(1). In effect, the Operator is liable for security defects in its system but not for unauthorised use of the system.

[85] USR reg.36(6).

[86] USR reg.36(4), unless the Operator has been guilty of wilful neglect or negligence (USR reg.36(9)).

certainly arguable that company liability is the better principle because of the benefit companies obtain from effective markets.[87]

The Register

27–16 We have already seen that companies issuing registered shares must keep a register containing the names of their members.[88] We shall now examine the rules governing the shareholder register more closely. The register of companies which issue only certificated shares is subject to the 2006 Act. Companies which issue only uncertificated shares or both certificated and uncertificated shares are subject to the Uncertificated Securities Regulation 2001 (USR 2001).[89]

Under both regimes, the register contains the name and address of each member and the date on which each person was registered as a member and the date on which any person ceased to be a member.[90] It also states the number and class[91] of shares held by each member and the amount paid up on each share.[92] In the case of a private company there must also be noted on the register the fact and the date of the company becoming, or ceasing to be a single member company.[93]

The register of members of both certificated and uncertificated shares constitutes prima facie evidence of any matters which are by the respective regulatory regime directed or authorised to be inserted in it.[94]

In order to become a member or shareholder of a company an investor has to have his or her name entered on that shareholder register. A buyer normally acquires legal title to shares at the point in

---

[87] Micheler, fn.14, above.

[88] s.113. The majority of the provisions of the 2006 Act relating to the share register (including overseas branch registers) are scheduled to come into effect on October 1, 2009.

[89] The USR 2001 (SI 2001/3755) was introduced to bring forward the point in time at which an investor acquires legal title to uncertificated shares from the moment at which the company amends the shareholder register to the moment at which the Operator of the uncertificated transfer system credits the shares to the buyer's securities account (HM Treasury, *Modernising Securities Settlement*, 2001; Bank of England, *Securities Settlement Priorities Review*, September 1998 and March 1998). This was done by entrusting the Operator of the uncertificated transfer system with the maintenance of the shareholder register for uncertificated shares.

[90] s.113; USR 2001 Sch.3, paras 2(1), (2) and 4(1).

[91] In the case of a company without a share capital but with different classes of membership the register has to state the class to which each member belongs (s.113(3); USR 2001 Sch.3, para.2(2)). This fills the lacuna revealed in *Performing Right Society Ltd, Re* [1978] 1 W.L.R. 1197.

[92] s.113(3); USR 2001 Sch.3, paras 2(2), (3), 4(1) and 5(1). In the case of the amount paid up, this appears only on the issuer's record.

[93] s.123(2); USR 2001 Sch.3, para.3. It is rather unlikely that a company issuing uncertificated shares would fall into the state of having only one member, but it might do if it became part of a group of companies.

[94] s.127; USR 2001 reg.24(1).

time at which his or her name is entered on the shareholder register.[95] This rule applies irrespective of whether shares are held in the certificated or in the uncertificated form.

Certificated and uncertificated shares differ in terms of who **27–17** maintains the shareholder register. The register for certificated shares is maintained by the company itself or by a registrar on behalf of the company. The register for uncertificated shares is maintained by the Operator of the uncertificated transfer system, CREST. The register of companies which issue certificated shares and uncertificated shares consists of two parts. Entries relating to certificated shares are maintained by the company. They are referred to as the "issuer register of members". Entries relating to uncertificated shares are maintained by the Operator of the uncertificated transfer system, and are referred to as "Operator register of members". The company maintains a "record" relating to uncertificated shares. This record does not constitute a shareholder register. It must be regularly reconciled with the Operator register of members.[96] In relation to uncertificated shares, the Operator register prevails over the record kept by the company.[97] The record does not provide for prima facie evidence. It enables the company to inform those inspecting the register about entries that have been made on the register maintained by CREST.

The issuer register may be kept at the company's registered office or at a place specified in regulations under section 1136.[98] If kept otherwise than at the company's registered office, notice must be given to Companies House (and thus to the public) of the place where it is kept and of any change of that place.[99]

If a company has more than 50 members then, unless the register is kept in such a form as to constitute an index of names of members, such an index must be kept at the same place as the register.[100]

The shareholder register and the index are available for public **27–18** inspection. Any member of the company may inspect the register free of charge.[101] Any other person may inspect the register on payment of such fee as may be prescribed.[102] In the case of uncertificated shares,

---

[95] s.112; *J Sainsbury Plc v O'Connor (Inspector of Taxes)* [1991] 1 W.L.R. 963 at 977 (CA); *Rose, Rose v Inland Revenue Commissioners, Re* [1952] Ch.499, at 518–519 (CA).

[96] USR 2001 reg.23 and Sch.3, para.5(2).

[97] USR 2001 reg.24(2).

[98] The (draft) Companies (Company Records) Regulations 2008.

[99] s.114(2); USR 2001 Sch.3 para.6(3) and (4). The place must be in England or Wales if the company is registered in England and Wales or in Scotland if it is registered in Scotland. But if the company carries on business in one of the countries specified in s.129(2) it may cause to be kept an "overseas branch register" in that country (s.129(2)). This, in effect, is a register of shareholders resident in that country, a duplicate of which will also be maintained with the principal register (s.132). This provision is not affected by the Uncertificated Securities Regulations (USR 2001, Sch.4, paras 2(7) and 4(4)).

[100] s.115.

[101] s.116. This provision (and sections 117–119) are already in force.

[102] s.116.

the inspection right is granted against the record held by the company rather than against the Operator register itself.[103] This exposes the searcher to the risk that the company's record will not accurately reflect the Operator register. Provided the company regularly reconciles its record with the Operator register, except in so far as matters outside its control prevent such reconciliation, the company is not liable for discrepancies between the record and the register.[104]

The right to inspect the register is a legitimate help to a takeover bidder and makes it possible for members to communicate with each other. It also has, in the past, been abused by traders who advertised their wares by unsolicited mail or telephone calls and who were able to obtain more cheaply than in any other way a list of potential victims by buying a copy of the shareholder register of, say, British Telecom or British Gas. With a view to putting an end to this illegitimate use of the shareholder register, the 2006 Act revised the right to inspect the register. The right to inspect the register may now be denied by the Court if it is satisfied that the request was not sought for a proper purpose.[105]

Under section 358 of the 1985 Act a company had the power to close the shareholder register for any time or times not exceeding in total 30 days in any year. The provision enabled companies to draw up a list of those who are entitled to attend the annual general meeting or to receive dividends. The 2006 Act does not contain a power to that effect.

Under the USR 2001, companies participating in CREST are entitled to specify a time not more than 48 hours before a general meeting by which a person must have been entered on the register in order to have the right to attend and vote at the meeting and may similarly choose a day not more than 21 days before notices of a meeting are sent out for the purposes of determining who is entitled to receive the notice.[106] This way of proceeding enables transfers to continue in the period before the meeting (thus reducing the risk to transferees) without landing the company in the position of having to deal with a constantly changing body of shareholders.

---

[103] USR 2001, Sch.3, para.9.

[104] USR 2001, Sch.3, para.5(3).

[105] s.117; under the CA 1985 there was no explicit provision enabling the court to deny access to the register. The Court of Appeal held nevertheless that it had discretion not to order compliance with a request to inspect the register, which it should exercise against the applicant only on narrow grounds and in such a way as not to defeat the legitimate aim of members to communicate with each other (*Pelling v Families Need Fathers Ltd* [2002] 1 B.C.L.C. 645, CA, following *O'Brien v Sporting Shooters Association of Australia (Victoria)* [1999] 3 V.R. 251, VicSC. In *Pelling* the company in question was a charitable company limited by guarantee, the effectiveness of whose work depended upon the identity of its members being undisclosed. The application by a member was refused on the company's undertaking to circulate the applicant's statement to the other members.)

[106] USR 2001, reg.40.

Rectification

The register is "prima facie evidence of any matters which are by this **27–19** Act directed or authorised to be inserted in it".[107] It is not, however, conclusive evidence for, as we have seen, membership is dependent both on agreement to become a member and entry in the register, and it may be that other requirements in the company's articles have to be met. If they are not, it seems that the registered person does not become a member.[108] In any event, if the entry does not truly reflect the agreement or other requirements, the register ought to be rectified. Hence section 125 provides a summary remedy whereby:

> "(a) the name of any person is without sufficient cause entered in or omitted from a company's register of members, or
>
> (b) default is made or unnecessary delay takes place in entering on the register the fact of any person having ceased to be a member, the person aggrieved or any member of the company, or the company may apply to the court for rectification of the register."[109]

This wording is defective because it ignores the fact that the register is not just a register of members but also a register of shareholdings and that a likely error is in the amount of a member's shareholding. However, common sense has prevailed and in *Transatlantic Life Assurance, Re*[110] Slade J. felt able to hold that "the wording is wide enough in its terms to empower the court to order the deletion of some only of a registered shareholder's shares".[111] It must follow that it is similarly empowered to order an addition to the registered holding.

On an application the court may decide any question relating to the title of any person who is a party to the application whether the question arises between members or alleged members,[112] or between members or alleged members on the one hand and the company on the other hand,[113] and may decide "any question necessary or expe-

---

[107] s.127; USR 2001 reg.24. In case of conflict between the issuer and Operator registers, the latter prevails (USR reg.24(2)). The rule applies to the Operator register provided the transfer has occurred in accordance with the Regulations.

[108] *POW Services Ltd v Clare* [1995] 2 B.C.L.C. 435; *Domoney v Godinho and another* [2004] 2 B.C.L.C. 15. The issue of restrictions in the articles is not one which arises in relation to listed companies or companies whose shares are held in uncertificated form, since the Listing Rules and the rules of CREST require such shares to be freely transferable.

[109] s.125(1). This power operates equally in relation to shares held in uncertificated form (USR 2001 reg.25(2)(b)).

[110] [1980] 1 W.L.R. 79. The case arose because the allotment of some shares was void because Exchange Control permission had not been obtained as at that time was necessary. See also *Cleveland Trust Plc, Re* [1991] B.C.L.C. 424.

[111] *Transatlantic Life Assurance, Re* [1980] 1 W.L.R. 79 at 84F–G.

[112] e.g. when A and B are disputing which of them should be the registered holder.

[113] e.g. when there is a dispute between the company and A or B on whether either should be.

dient to be decided for rectification ...".[114] Moreover, the court may order payment by the company of "damages sustained by any party aggrieved".[115]

27–20   There is some uncertainty as to the extent to which the company can rectify the register without an application to the court. But in practice here again commonsense prevails. Sections 113, 115, and 122 envisage, and indeed demand, alterations without which the register could not be kept up-to-date and fulfil its purpose, and although there is no express provision for alterations of members' addresses that takes place all the time. Indeed it would be quite absurd if companies could not correct any mistake if all interested parties agree.

The USR 2001 also contemplate that a company may rectify the issuer register other than by order of a court, but, in order to preserve the integrity of the electronic transfer system, require the company in such a case to have the consent of the Operator of the system if the change would involve rectification of the Operator register. Equally, the Operator may rectify the Operator register, but must inform the issuer and the system-members concerned immediately when the change is made.[116]

It must be emphasised, however, that although the register provides prima facie evidence of who its members are and what their shareholdings are, it provides no evidence at all, either to the company or anyone else, of who the beneficial owners of the shares are.[117]

TRANSMISSION OF SHARES BY OPERATION OF LAW

27–21   The Act[118] recognises that shares may be transmitted by operation of law and that, when this occurs, the prohibition on registering unless a proper instrument of transfer has been delivered does not apply.[119] The principal examples of this are when a registered shareholder dies or becomes bankrupt. As regards the death of a shareholder, the Act further provides that a transfer by the deceased's personal representative, even if he is not a member of the company, is as valid as if

---

[114] s.125(3). Despite this wide wording, it has been held the summary procedure of CA 1985 s.359 should not be used when substantial factual issues have to be investigated (*Hoicrest Ltd, Keene v Martin and another, Re* [2001] 1 B.C.L.C. 194, CA).

[115] s.125(2). "Compensation" would be a better word than "damages" and "party aggrieved" is an expression which courts have constantly criticised, but apparently without convincing Parliamentary Counsel responsible for drafting Government Bills.

[116] USR 2001, reg.25.

[117] For the rules dealing with the disclosure of beneficial interests see paras 26–18 to 26–23, above.

[118] And see The Companies (Model Articles) Regulations 2007, reg.27.

[119] s.773; for uncertificated shares see USR reg.27(6).

he had been.[120] The company is bound to accept probate or letters of administration granted in any part of the United Kingdom as sufficient evidence of the personal representative's entitlement.[121] However, he or she does not become a member unless he or she elects to apply to be registered and is registered as a member. In the meantime, the effect is that he has the "same rights as the holder had".[122]

> "But transmittees do not have the right to attend or vote at a general meeting, or agree to a proposed written resolution, in respect of shares to which they are entitled by reason of the holder's death or bankruptcy or otherwise unless they become the holders of those shares."[123]

If the shares are those of a listed company, this anomalous position can be ended rapidly because, unless the shares are not fully paid, there will not be any restrictions on transferability and the personal representative will either obtain registration of him- or herself or execute a transfer to a purchaser or to the beneficiaries. In relation to a private company, however, it may continue indefinitely and prove detrimental to the personal representative, the deceased's estate and, sometimes, the company. The personal representative may suffer because it may not be possible for him fully to wind up the estate and to obtain a discharge from his fiduciary responsibilities. The estate may suffer because it may be impossible for the personal representative to sell the shares at their true value, especially if any attempt to dispose of them would trigger rights of pre-emption or first refusal.[124] The company may suffer because, as we have seen,[125] unless such rights have been most carefully drafted, they will not come into operation so long as no action regarding registration is taken by the personal representative. In order to assist personal representatives, the statute has extended the remedies afforded to members so that

---

[120] s.773.
[121] s.774. If it does so without such production of the grant it may become liable for any tax payable as a result of the transmission (*NY Breweries Co v Attorney-General* [1899] A.C. 62, HL) but in the case of small estates, companies may be prepared to dispense with production of a grant if the Revenue confirms that nothing is payable. If the deceased was one of a number of jointly registered members, the company, on production of a death certificate, will have to recognise that he has ceased to be a member and shareholder and that the others remain such. But the whole beneficial interest in the shares will not pass to them unless they and the deceased were beneficial owners entitled jointly rather than in common.
[122] The Companies (Model Articles) Regulations 2007, reg.27(2).
[123] The Companies (Model Articles) Regulations 2007, reg.27(3).
[124] If there are any restrictions on transfers all the articles relating to restriction on transfers apply both to a notice that the personal representative wishes to be registered and to a transfer from him (The Companies (Model Articles) Regulations 2007, reg.28.
[125] See above, para.27–7.

they can be invoked by personal representatives of members.[126] It is also now obligatory for the company to give reasons explaining the refusal to register a transferee.[127]

The position on bankruptcy of an individual shareholder[128] is broadly similar. His rights to the shares automatically vest in the trustee in bankruptcy as part of his estate.[129] But, as in the case of a personal representative, until he elects to become registered and is so registered, he will not become a member of the company entitled to attend meetings and to vote. In contrast, however, with the position on the death of a member, the bankrupt will remain a member and be entitled to attend and vote—though he will have to do so in accordance with the directions of the trustee. As in the case of personal representatives, the company's articles will probably provide that any restrictions on transferability apply on any application to be registered and to any transfer by him or her[130] and these restrictions may handicap the trustee in obtaining the best price on a sale of the shares, particularly if the articles confer pre-emption rights.[131] If a personal representative or trustee in bankruptcy elects to be registered, and is, he becomes personally liable for any amounts unpaid on the shares and not merely representationally liable to the extent of the estate. Trustees in bankruptcy, but not personal representatives, may disclaim onerous property,[132] which the shares might be if they were partly paid or subject to an effective company lien.

---

[126] See, in particular, s.994(2) which makes it possible for personal representatives to invoke the "unfairly prejudicial" remedy which might well be effective if it could be shown that the directors were exercising their powers to refuse transfers in order to enable themselves or the company to acquire the shares of deceased members at an unfair price: see Ch.20, above.

[127] s.771.

[128] On winding up of a corporate shareholder there is no transmission of the company's property; it remains vested in the company but most of the directors' powers to manage it pass to the liquidator.

[129] Insolvency Act 1986, ss.283(1) and 306. But not if the shareholder held his shares as a trustee for another person: *ibid.*, s.283(3)(a).

[130] The (draft) Companies (Model Articles) Regulations 2007, reg.28.

[131] In *Borland's Trustee v Steel Bros* [1901] 1 Ch.279, a provision in the articles that in the event of a shareholder's bankruptcy (or death) his shares should be offered to a named person at a particular price was held to be effective and not obnoxious to the bankruptcy laws.

[132] Insolvency Act 1986, s.315. Disclaimer puts an end to the interest of the bankrupt and his estate and discharges the trustee from any liability: *ibid.*, s.315(3).

CHAPTER 28

TAKEOVERS

INTRODUCTION

A takeover bid consists of an offer from A (usually another company) **28–1**
to the shareholders of B Co to acquire their shares for a consideration
which may be cash or securities of the offeror or a mixture of both.

The legal mechanism at the heart of the bid is thus a transfer of shares, but the rules discussed in the previous Chapter, although relevant, do not capture the significance of the takeover bid. A takeover involves—indeed, this is normally its aim—not simply a transfer of shares but a shift in the control of the target company. Previously, B Co may in effect have been under the control of its board (for example, where its shareholdings were widely dispersed) or of one or a few shareholders with a controlling block of shares. After a successful bid B Co will be controlled by A and, depending upon who previously had control of the company, that change of control will therefore be a matter of some moment to the board of B Co (who will have lost control) or the minority shareholders of B Co (who will be faced with a new controller, unless they themselves have accepted a cash offer). The change of control may also affect other stake-holders in the company (for example, employees) because bidders do not normally obtain control of companies simply to run them in the same way as previously. The change of control of B Co may thus have wide ramifications for those who have interests in the businesses run by B Co.

This little description reveals the two main issues which takeover regulation has to address. First, should it seek to prevent the management of the target company from taking any steps to discourage a potential bidder from putting an offer to its shareholders or from discouraging those shareholders from accepting it? In other words, is the takeover bid to be analysed as a transaction purely between bidder and target company shareholders or as one in the outcome of which the management of the target company also has a legitimate self-interest which it may take steps to defend? As we shall see, the rules in the UK have traditionally been based on the former view (no frustration of the bid by the target management). This rule is expressed in a strong form once a bid is imminent, and somewhat less strongly and more diffusely in relation to defensive action taken by target management in advance of any specific offer. This policy gives the offeror company a free run at the target shareholders and prevents the board from using its management powers so as to frustrate the bid. It is a policy which can be justified on the grounds that it supports the principle of free transferability of the shares of listed companies and, more importantly, on the grounds that it is a significant element in the British system of corporate governance. A board, it is argued, which is at risk of an unwelcome takeover bid will be sure to promote the interests of its shareholders, in order to decrease the chances of a bid being made (because the share price will be high) and increase the chances that those shareholders will reject an offer if one is made (because they think they will be at least as well off with the current management). In this way, the accountability of the board to the shareholders is promoted by takeovers, especially "hostile" ones, i.e. offers not recommended by the target board to its shareholders but rather made over the heads of the incumbent management to the shareholders.[1]

The second major issue for takeover regulation is the steps to be taken to protect non-controlling shareholders if a bid is launched. Obviously, the transfer of shares could be left, like any other commercial transaction, to be regulated by the ordinary law of contract. In the case of controlling shareholders, who are well-placed to take care of themselves, this is probably sensible policy. However, in the typical case in the UK, where the shareholdings in the target are dispersed, the shareholders may lack up-to-date information upon which to evaluate the offer which has been made to them. Moreover, if left to its own devices, the offeror may be able to put pressure in various ways on the shareholders of the target company to accept the bid, often by proposing to treat some groups of target shareholders more favourably than others. To counter these risks we shall see that takeover regulation puts considerable emphasis on two policies: disclosure of information (by both bidder and target) to the shareholders of the target, and equality of treatment of the target shareholders. Equality means that some shareholders of the target cannot be offered a better deal than is available generally. As we shall see below,[2] this second policy is taken even to the point of requiring a bid to be launched where an offeror company has acquired in the market or by private treaty a sufficient shareholding in the target to give it control. The "mandatory bid" permits non-controlling shareholders to exit the company at a fair price upon a change of control.

Thus, the two central tenets of the British regulation of takeovers **28–2** are that the shareholders alone decide on the fate of the offer and equality of treatment of shareholders. The regulation is both orthodox and rigorous in putting the target shareholders centre stage, and in this respect it differs from takeover regulation in both the United States and some, though not all, continental European countries (for example, Germany). However, these are not the only objectives of take-over regulation. A takeover offer is disruptive of the normal running of the target company's business and it is therefore in the interests of all those involved in it that this period of disruption should be minimised by the setting of a firm timetable for the bid. Thus, a bidder which has indicated it might make a bid should be required to do so or to withdraw within a relatively short period ("put up or shut up"); the offer, if made, should remain open only for as long as is necessary for the shareholders to make up their minds about it; and a bidder whose offer fails should not be able immedi-

---

[1] This is a crucial and highly controversial proposition. For a balanced assessment see J. Coffee, "Regulating the Market for Corporate Control" (1984) 84 *Columbia Law Review* 1145. See also Paul Davies and Klaus Hopt "Control Transactions" in Reinier R Kraakman et al (eds), *The Anatomy of Corporate Law* (Oxford: OUP, 2004).

[2] Below, para.28–40.

ately to come back with another bid. Thus, the bid should be a relatively quick event and not partake of the nature of a siege of the target company by the offeror.

We shall look at these and other aspects of the substantive rules for the regulation of take-over bids below, but we begin by examining the rather special machinery which exists in the United Kingdom for the creation and application of those rules.

THE TAKEOVER CODE AND PANEL

28–3 So far, we have referred rather coyly to the "UK regulation" and it is time to say a bit more about that. Since the takeover does not require a corporate decision on the part of the target company,[3] there is no obvious act of the target upon which company law can fasten. For this reason, most European countries treat takeover regulation as part of their securities laws, i.e. they rightly take the transfer of the shares as the central act. The United Kingdom follows this pattern, but it developed takeover regulation long before statutory regulation of the securities markets was established, and so the regulation of takeovers took a quasi self-regulatory approach. In the 1950s and 1960s, bidders took full advantage of the absence of regulation.[4] Alarmed by what was happening,[5] a City working party published in 1959 a modest set of "Queensberry Rules" entitled *Notes on Amalgamation of British Businesses*, which was followed in 1968 by a more elaborate *City Code on Takeovers and Mergers* and the establishment of a Panel to administer and enforce it. It is this Code, in its various editions, which has since constituted the main body of rules relating to takeovers, with the Companies Act and the Financial Services and Markets Act, and rules and regulations made thereunder, performing an accessory role. However, the element of self-regulation in this

---

[3] Though sometimes the approval of the offeror company's shareholders will be required under the Listing Rules if the proposed transaction is a very large one: above, at para.14–8. This is an aspect of a major issue which arises as between the offeror directors and its shareholders, especially as many takeovers enhance the wealth of the target shareholders but not that of the bidder's. However, this relationship is not dealt with by specific takeover regulation, which concentrates on relationships with and within the target company. Other than the Listing Rules, the general company law will apply to offeror directors, notably the rules on directors' duties, though its controls are rather weak: it would be a bold court which concluded that an offeror board's decision to launch a takeover offer constituted a breach of duty. See A. Kouloridas, *The Law and Economics of Takeovers: An Acquirer's Perspective* (Oxford: Hart, 2008).

[4] A. Johnston, *The City Take-over Code* (OUP, 1980), Chs 1–4.

[5] Which, in some cases, was horrendous, with rival bidders badgering each of the target's shareholders by night and day telephone calls offering him a special price because, so it was falsely alleged, only his holding was needed to bring that bidder's acceptances to over 50 per cent. In one case the result was that the bidder who eventually succeeded paid prices ranging from £2 to £15 per share.

arrangement can easily be overestimated. The Panel had no statutory authority but its success as a regulator depended largely on the recognition on the part of those routinely involved in advising on takeovers (mainly investment banks and large law firms) that to flout its authority would probably induce Parliament to replace the Code and Panel with something they liked even less.

The Panel and its methods of operation
The status and composition of the Panel
In any event, discussion of the self-regulatory status of the Panel is now rather beside the point. The regulation of takeovers is a further area where Community Law has come to be a significant source of the relevant rules. After a very long gestation period the Community eventually adopted Directive of the European Parliament and the Council 2004/25/EC on takeover bids (hereafter the "takeover directive").[6] One of the requirements of the Directive is that Member States should "designate the authority or authorities competent to supervise bids" (Article 4(1)), so that the United Kingdom was required to place the takeover rules on some sort of a statutory footing. In fact, the proposed change in the legal status of the Panel was the basis for the UK Government's initial opposition to the Directive, despite the fact that the Directive's substantive content was heavily influenced by the City Code, since the UK had the greatest experience among the Member States with takeovers, especially hostile ones, and had a long history of regulation in this area. During the Community legislative process changes were made in the draft Directive so as to allay, as far as possible, the Government's fears that the Panel's way of working would be undermined by the Directive. The Government's goal was to produce a situation in which the Panel could carry on in practice much as before, even though now with its powers derived from statute. Article 4 of the Directive makes it clear, which might otherwise be in doubt, that the

28–4

---

[6] For an excellent early analysis of the impact of the Directive on the UK see J. Rickford, "The Emerging European Takeover Law from a British Perspective" [2004] EBLR 1379. The Directive was required to be implemented by May 2006. This was effected in the UK initially by the Takeovers Directive (Interim Implementation) Regulations 2006 (SI 2006/1183), replaced by Part 28 of the Companies Act 2006 as from April 6, 2007 (SI 2007/1093, art.2). The Interim Regulations were necessary because the 2006 Act was still in the Parliamentary process in May 2006. The Interim Regulations, made under the European Communities Act 1972, could be used to implement only the Community obligations of the UK. This meant in particular that they applied, as does the Directive, only to takeovers of companies whose securities were traded on a regulated market whereas Part 28 of the Act applies to all takeovers within the scope of the Code.

designated authorities may be "private bodies recognised by national law".[7] Thus, section 942 of the Companies Act 2006 simply confers certain statutory powers upon the Panel but does not seek to regulate the constitution of the Panel, in contrast to the way in which, for example, the constitution of the FSA is regulated by Schedule 1 of FSMA 2000. The composition of the Panel is to be found, not in legislation, but in the Code itself.[8] It consists of a Chairman and up to two Deputy Chairmen appointed by the Panel itself, up to a further 20 members appointed by the Panel and individuals appointed by representative bodies of those involved in takeovers, such as the Association of British Insurers, the National Association of Pension Funds, the Association of Investment Companies and other investor groups, the British Bankers' Association and the London Investment Banking Association, the Institute of Chartered Accountants and the Confederation of British Industry. The Panel appointees come from similar backgrounds as those of the representative appointees, though they include a former general secretary of a large trade union.

Tactical litigation and appeals

28–5   However, the Panel's and the Government's central concern was not with the formal status of the Panel but with preserving in the statutory framework its way of working, in particular its freedom to give flexible and speedy binding rulings in the course of the bid, which could not be easily challenged in litigation before the ordinary courts. A particular concern was to discourage "tactical litigation", i.e. litigation designed to disrupt the bid timetable or to delay the operation of a decision of the Panel which is against the interests of a particular party, whilst providing a method of appeal for those with a genuine grievance. Before the implementation of the Directive, this result was achieved though a system of speedy appeal within the Panel itself,

---

[7] The competent authority may be, of course, a public body of a more traditional kind. The Government did toy, probably not very seriously, with the idea of giving takeover regulation to the FSA, or alternatively keeping the Panel on a non-statutory basis but treating breaches of the Code as breaches of the FSA's rules, but rejected both ideas. See DTI, *Company Law Implementation of the European Directive on Takeover Bids: A Consultation Document* (January 2005, URN 05/11) paras 2.7 and 2.17—hereafter "DTI Consultation Document". That idea does demonstrate, however, that the Government was not obliged to give these functions to the Panel nor is it obliged to leave them there, should the Panel act in a way the Government finds unacceptable.

[8] See The Takeover Code, 8th edition, 2006 (as amended), *Introduction*, p.8 (hereafter the "Code"). This perhaps illustrates better than anything the status of the Panel, since it is circular for the Code, which is the responsibility of the Panel, to determine the composition of the body which creates the Code. Under earlier editions of the Code the chair and two deputies of the Panel were appointed by the Governor of the Bank of England, which reflects the historical reality of how the self-regulatory process was initiated, but he no longer has a formal role in the Panel's composition. Ss.957–959 also maintain the Panel's present funding arrangements. It is not supported out of taxation, but by fees for its services and a levy on share transactions, but of course a statutory body could be funded in a similar manner, as the FSA is.

coupled with the courts' adoption of a limited and after-the-event approach to judicial review of the Panel's decisions. Article 4(6) of the Directive does its best to preserve the viability of this system by providing that:

> "this Directive shall not affect the power of the Member States to designate judicial or other authorities responsible for dealing with disputes and for deciding on irregularities committed in the course of bids or the power of Member States to regulate whether and under which circumstances parties to a bid are entitled to bring administrative or judicial proceedings. In particular, this Directive shall not affect the power which courts may have in a Member State to decline to hear legal proceedings and to decide whether or not such proceedings affect the outcome of a bid."

Thus fortified, the DTI decided to maintain the intra-Panel appeal system rather than seek to devise a new system.[9] The Panel Executive (i.e. its full-time employees, some of whom are seconded from investment banks, law firms, accountancy firms and similar bodies) gives rulings on the Code in the course of a bid, either on its own initiative or at the request of one or more parties to the bid.[10] Rulings of the Executive may be referred to the Panel's Hearing Committee (or the Executive may refer a matter to the Hearing Committee itself), and disciplinary proceedings for breach of the Code or a ruling may be initiated before the Hearing Committee by the Executive. The Hearing Committee was formerly known as the "Full Panel". The Executive may require any appeal to the Hearing Committee to be lodged within a specific period, possibly a period as short as a few hours. The Hearing Committee normally sits in private and operates informally, but does issue public statements of its rulings.

A party to the hearing before the Hearing Committee may appeal to the Takeover Appeal Board (formerly known as the "Appeal Committee"), normally within two business days of receipt in writing of the ruling of the Hearing Committee. This is a rather wider right of appeal than existed previously when many appeals required leave of the Appeal Board. The Appeal Board is an independent body, whose chairman and deputy chairman, appointed by the Master of the Rolls, will usually have held high judicial office[11] and whose other members (normally four) are experienced in takeovers. The Appeal Board operates in a similar way to the Hearing Committee, including

---

[9] DTI Consultation Document, paras 2.35–36. The system is set out in the Code, *Introduction*, 5–8.

[10] If a complaint of a breach of the Code is not made promptly, the Executive may decline to deal with it: Code, *Introduction*, 10(a). Delegation by the Panel of functions to officers or members of staff is specifically provided for by s.942(3)(b).

[11] Currently Lord Steyn as chairman and Sir Martin Nourse as deputy chairman.

the publication of its decision. It may confirm, vary, set aside or replace the ruling of the Hearing Committee. This was, broadly, the system in operation before the Act came into force and section 951 requires that system to be maintained. The section requires, as was the previous practice, that a Panel member who is or has been a member of its Code Committee (responsible for drawing up the Code) may not be a member of the Hearing Committee or Appeal Board. The separation of the Code Committee from the committees involved in administering the Code was a response to the Human Rights Act 1998.[12]

28–6   The second limb of the pre-Directive system for dealing with tactical litigation consisted of restraint by the courts in exercising their powers of judicial review. Article 4(6) (above) of the Directive permits the British courts to maintain their restraint, but, of course, does not require it. The Act does not seek explicitly to regulate the process of judicial review of the Panel by the courts, probably wisely, and so the matter is left to the domestic courts themselves. It was perhaps surprising that the pre-Directive Panel, as a body which, as it was put in *R. v Panel on Take-overs and Mergers, ex p. Datafin Ltd*,[13] performed its functions "without visible means of legal support", was made subject to judicial review at all. However, that was the step taken in the *Datafin* case, seemingly on the grounds that the Panel, although then a private body, was performing a public function. Its susceptibility to judicial review is now beyond doubt. Having taken that decision of principle, the then Master of the Rolls set out his "expectations" as to how judicial review of the Panel would operate, emphasising its limitations.

First, it was expected that the Panel would require obedience to its rulings and the parties would abide by them, even if one of them had signalled it was intended to seek judicial review. Secondly, the grounds for review would be limited: an argument that the Panel had propounded rules which were ultra vires was "a somewhat unlikely eventuality"; the Panel in its interpretation of its rules must be given "considerable latitude"; attacks on the Panel's dispensing powers would be successful only in "wholly exceptional circumstances"; and the Panel's exercise of its disciplinary powers would be open to attack only "in the absence of any credible allegation of lack of bona fides". Thirdly, and most importantly, the expectation was that the courts would only intervene only after the bid was concluded ("the relationship between the panel and the court [would] be historic rather than contemporaneous"), perhaps to relieve individuals of disciplinary sanctions, perhaps to deliver a declaratory judgment to guide the Panel in the future. Thus, a party involved in a bid (most

---

[12] The Takeover Panel, *Report on the Year Ended March 31, 2001*, pp.8–9.
[13] [1987] Q.B. 815, CA. See Cane, "Self Regulation and Judicial Review" [1987] C.J.Q. 324. See also *R. v Takeover Panel, ex p. Guinness Plc* [1990] 1 Q.B. 146, CA.

obviously the board of the target company) was given little incentive to seek judicial review during the offer in order to secure a tactical advantage (most obviously delay, during which the target's defences can be better organised), but the Panel was not given an entirely free hand in interpreting the Code or its own jurisdiction.

It seems likely that this attitude of deference on the part of the courts to the Panel (and especially the Takeover Appeal Board) will continue, despite the statutory framework within which the Panel is now placed. The statute does one or two things to encourage the courts in that direction. The Panel is given power to "do anything that it considers necessary or expedient for the purpose of, or in connection with, its functions", thus protecting the Panel's vires in its new statutory guise; it is given a wide rule-making power; it is explicitly given a dispensing power; and it is explicitly given the power to making rulings and give directions.[14] Overall, the Government's policy seems to have been to fit the requirements of the Directive to the existing practice of the Panel, rather than vice versa.[15]

Nevertheless, the fact of putting the Panel on a statutory footing potentially opens up avenues of civil litigation not previously available. The Act seeks to block off these paths to the courts. This seems to be permitted by the further sentence in Article 4(6) of the Directive that "this Directive shall not affect the power of the Member States to determine the legal position concerning the liability of supervisory authorities or concerning litigation between the parties to a bid". Consequently, no action for breach of statutory duty lies in respect of contravention of a requirement imposed by or under the Panel's rules or a requirement imposed by the Panel to produce information or documents.[16] Contravention of a rule-based requirement does not render the transaction in which it occurs void or unenforceable or affect the validity "of any other thing" (unless the Rules so provide).[17] However, civil litigation between the parties is not entirely excluded by these provisions. A claim based on fraudulent or negligent misstatement, for example, arising out of the documentation put out by bidder or target, is not excluded, but, as we shall see below, such claims were previously possible, though they are not without their difficulties. Finally, and following the scheme applied to the FSA, the Panel itself is not liable in damages in connection with the discharge of its functions, unless it was acting in bad faith or there is a claim against it for breach of section 6(1) of the Human Rights Act 1998 (which in the circumstances laid down in section 8 of that Act could

[14] See ss.942(2), 943, 944(1) and 945.
[15] "It is intended that the implementing legislation should neither undermine nor be inconsistent with the principles established in the Datafin case." (DTI Consultation Document, para.2.38.)
[16] s.956(1). The definitions of "rule-based requirement" and "disclosure requirement" are given in s.955(4), the latter referring to the Panel's disclosure powers in s.947, which are discussed below.
[17] s.956(2).

lead a court to award damages for breach by a public authority of the rights guaranteed by the European Convention on Human Rights).[18] This protection extends to members, officers and employees of the Panel and any person authorised by the Panel to act under its information disclosure powers. Thus, the risk of tactical litigation is minimised, but cannot be entirely eliminated (see below).

Powers of the Panel

28–7 This and the following section deal with the areas where there has been the biggest formal change in the Panel's position as a result of its being put on a statutory basis. At least the basic elements of the Panel's powers and the sanctions to support them had to be set out in, or provided for by, the legislation, since Article 4(5) of the Directive requires that "supervisory authorities shall be vested with all the powers necessary for the purpose of carrying out their duties, including that of ensuring that the parties to a bid comply with the rules made or introduced pursuant to this Directive." Again, however, the aim of the legislation was to reflect, rather than substantially to alter, the Panel's existing methods of working. The main powers of the Panel are as follows.

First, the Panel is given both an obligation and a power to make rules to govern the conduct of bids.[19] Thus, the legislation does not purport to discharge that rule-making function itself but requires or empowers the Panel to do so. The Panel is required to make rules in those areas where the Directive requires Member States to introduce rules, thus ensuring that the United Kingdom is not in breach of its obligations under the Directive, but the Panel is empowered to make rules more generally, a power which is very widely formulated.[20] In consequence, the whole of the Panel's regulatory activity is placed on a statutory basis. It would have been possible to confine the statutory structure to the bids and topics covered by the Directive, leaving the remainder of the Panel's activities to continue on a non-statutory basis, but that was thought likely to cause confusion.[21] The Panel is permitted to arrange for its rule-making power (and, indeed, any of its functions) to be discharged by a committee of the Panel, so that

---

[18] s.961. The provisions of the Convention most likely to affect that Panel are those of a procedural nature, for example, Article 6 relating to the fair trials in civil law. The liability of the Panel under the Human Rights Act 1998 is not new.

[19] s.943. It is not absolutely clear that Article 4 of the Directive contemplates that the supervisory authority shall make the rules, but the Directive does not explicitly forbid it, which one would have expected it to do if its authors had wanted to bring about such a major change in British practice, which was very much to the forefront in the formulation of Article 4.

[20] s.943(2),(3). S.944(1) permits the Panel to make rules in a flexible form.

[21] DTI Consultation Document, para.2.10. The Directive applies only to bids for companies whose shares are traded on a regulated market, whilst the Code applied more broadly (see below), and even in relation to regulated markets the Code covers a number of topics not touched on by the Directive.

there can be a further stage of delegation before the power to make rules is actually exercised.[22] This reflects the fact that, since the enactment of the Human Rights Act 1998, responsibility for the rules has been assigned to a Code Committee of the Panel and that membership of the Hearing Committee (see above) and of the Code Committee does not overlap. Thus, the "legislative" and "judicial" functions of the Panel have been separated.

Secondly, the Panel "may give rulings on the interpretation, application or effect of rules", in the way described in above, such rulings having binding effect.[23] This is the Panel's "judicial" function. Giving the Panel's rulings legal effect is, of course, new, and the sanctions available to support this provision are discussed below. Further, Article 4(5) of the Directive permits Member States to give supervisory authorities powers to waive national rules, either to "take account of circumstances determined at national level" or "in other specific circumstances, in which case a reasoned decision must be required", provided in either case that the derogation does not contravene the general principles laid down in Article 3(1) of the Directive (see below). Section 944(1)(b) takes up the former option by authorising the Panel to make rules which are "subject to exceptions or exemptions" in the rules themselves. Section 944(1)(d) takes up this latter option by authorising the Panel "to dispense with or modify the application of rules in particular cases and by reference to any circumstances", subject to the requirement to give reasons. This reflects the Panel's traditional practice to use its dispensing power where a rule "would operate unduly harshly or in an unnecessarily restrictive or burdensome, or otherwise inappropriate, manner".[24]

28–8 The rules may, and do, also confer upon the Panel the power to make directions to secure compliance with the rules. In practice, this is a very important power for the Panel. Having identified a breach of the rules, its focus in practice is on requiring remedial action which will enable the bid to continue in the normal way.[25] This is the great virtue of having a regulator which can give rulings during the course of a bid, as contrasted with a body which comes to the matter only after the bid has succeeded or failed and so no longer has the possibility of getting the transaction back on track.

Thirdly, the Panel may require a person by notice in writing to produce to it specified documents or to provide specified information, where such disclosure is "reasonably required in connection with the

---

[22] s.942(3)(a).
[23] s.945, but binding effect only "to the extent and in the circumstances specified in the rules".
[24] City Code, *Introduction*, p.3.
[25] s.946 and City Code, *ibid.*, pp.18–19.

exercise by the Panel of its functions".[26] This again is a new legal power for the Panel, which in the past has been able to survive without it. There is the usual protection for legal professional privilege (or confidentiality of communications in Scotland).[27] There is also the usual requirement that the Panel keep confidential information disclosed to it (whether under the compulsory disclosure power or not) which relates to the private affairs of an individual or to any particular business. A person who breaches this requirement is guilty of a criminal offence unless that person had no reason to suspect that the information had been provided to the Panel in connection with its functions or that the person took all reasonable steps and exercised all due diligence to avoid disclosure in breach of the statute. However, this confidentiality provision is subject to the usual long list of permitted "gateways" for disclosure of the information to other official bodies, and to disclosure by the Panel itself for the purpose of facilitating the carrying out of any of its functions (so that some such information may be found in the public rulings of the Hearing Committee or Takeover Appeal Board).[28]

Sanctions

28–9   Thus, the Act confers upon the Panel three basic legal powers: to make rules for takeover bids, to interpret those rules and to require the disclosure of information. None of these functions is new for the Panel: all were previously carried on, though without legislative support. Having put those powers in place, the statute was required by the Directive to go on and provide sanctions for non-compliance with them on the part of bid participants. As a self-regulatory body and, in particular, as a body with not even a contractual relationship with those involved in takeovers, whether as participants or advisers, the Panel's formal sanctions were previously extremely limited. The Panel itself could administer only a private reprimand or public censure if there was non-compliance with the Code. For more pressing measures it was dependent on the action of other regulatory authorities, such as the Department of Trade and Industry, the FSA or the Stock Exchange. However, these bodies, even if willing to act,

---

[26] s.947(1)–(3). This section can also be seen as implementing Article 6(5) of the Directive. The Code itself requires those dealing with it to disclose any known and relevant information (Code, *Introduction*, p.17) and the Panel expects this to be the power it normally relies on rather than the statutory one. Those firms subject to the jurisdiction of the FSA are required under its rules to provide information and documents to the Panel and to provide such other assistance which the Panel requests in the performance of its functions and the firm is reasonably able to provide: see MAR 4.3.5 and below, fn.37. This disclosure obligation is also subject to an exemption relating to legal professional privilege: see s.413 of FSMA.

[27] s.947(10).

[28] ss.948 and 949 and Sch.2. In the Parliamentary debates it was controversial that the Panel has no responsibility for the further disclosure of the information by a body which receives it through one of the gateways, though it is difficult to see how in practice the Panel could have exercised such supervision.

might not have appropriate sanctions at their disposal.[29] In the early days of the Panel such problems threatened the Panel's credibility and even its future, but gradually the Panel gained acceptance for its rulings, partly because of a realisation among advisers in particular that an ineffective Panel was likely to lead to the transfer of its functions to a statutory regulator.[30] Further, the Panel's relationship with the FSA in particular was placed on a more explicit footing when FSMA was enacted in 2000.[31]

Perhaps the strongest expression of the new policy of giving the Panel statutory sanctions is to be found in section 955 which confers upon the Panel a power to apply to the court (High Court or Court of Session) where a person has contravened or is likely to contravene a requirement imposed by or under a Code rule or has failed to comply with a disclosure requirement under the statutory provisions just discussed. The court may then make such order as it thinks fit to secure compliance with the requirement, which order will be backed by the sanctions for contempt of court. The Panel, no doubt, expects not to have to make use of this new power, just as it has operated effectively in the past without it. One important question which arises is whether this section will provide an avenue whereby a party can obtain judicial scrutiny of the Panel's or Appeal Board's rulings during the course of the bid. Of course, the decision to apply to the court for an enforcement order is in the hands of the Panel, so that a party cannot trigger the procedure.[32] However, if the Panel does so apply, the question will be whether the courts in this new context will maintain the after-the-event approach which has been adopted for judicial review and simply enforce the Panel's ruling without scrutinising its legality or without scrutinising it rigorously. This may be a more difficult line for the court to take where the court's order is backed by the sanctions for contempt of court than when the Panel's rulings lacked extensive formal sanctions. Further, if the question is raised whether the Panel's ruling is compatible with the Directive, the court would have to consider making a preliminary reference to the European Court of Justice (with all the delay that implies).

The statute places at the disposal of the Panel a number of other sanctions, but they all require adoption by the rules in order to be brought into force. Thus, section 954 says that the rules may confer

---

[29] In one notorious case, concerning St Piran Ltd, such action by the Exchange proved singularly ineffective, despite belated undertakings by the guilty party to behave in future. See the Annual Reports of the Panel for 1981 and 1984. See also *St Piran Ltd, Re* [1981] 1 W.L.R. 1300, CA, where intervention by the Secretary of State was saved from futility only because a shareholder in the company was prepared to bring a petition for the winding-up of the company on the just and equitable ground.

[30] Thus, in the Guinness case, above, fn.13, the bidder agreed to pay £85 million to the shareholders of the target company in order to comply with a ruling of the Panel.

[31] See in particular ss.138 and 143 of FSMA 2000. The current provisions are discussed further below.

[32] s.955(2) makes it clear that only the Panel can so apply and not, for example, the party to the bid which stands to benefit from the Panel's ruling.

power on the Panel to order a person to pay such compensation as it thinks just and reasonable if that person is in breach of a rule "the effect of which is to require the payment of money". This power thus falls short of a general remit to require compensation for breaches of the rules, but it covers the situations where in the past the Panel has required monetary payments.[33] The Code now applies this section to those rules which determine the price at which an offer has to be made or the form of the consideration (for example, where cash or a cash alternative is required).[34]

Finally, there is a general provision in section 952 that the rules may give the Panel the power to impose sanctions on a person who has acted in breach of the rules or of a direction given by the Panel to secure compliance with the rules (see above). This is the section under which the Panel now bases its disciplinary powers, which are exercised, except in case of agreement with the offender, by the Hearings Committee (with Appeal to the Takeover Appeal Board). The Code sets out the Panel's disciplinary powers and they are the established ones of private or public censure, reporting the offender's conduct to another body for that body to take action against the offender if thought appropriate, and triggering the "cold shouldering" of the offender.[35] It is clear that section 952 permits the rules to adopt a wider range of penalties, notably financial penalties of the type available to the FSA. However, where the Panel adopts a sanction of a kind not previously provided for by the Code, it must produce, again following the FSA model, a policy statement with respect to the imposition of that sanction and, in the case of a financial penalty, the amount of the penalty.[36] So far, the Panel has not ventured into this territory.

28–10 Where the Panel reports conduct to a third party, it is up to the regulator (domestic or overseas) or a professional body to decide whether it is appropriate to take further action. The most likely recipient of such a report from the Panel is the FSA. The FSA could conclude that a person who has broken the City Code is also in breach of its obligations under the FSA's rules and impose sanctions upon that person. The persons most obviously within the FSA's scope are those who need its authorisation to carry on their professional activities within the financial services sector. This will cover the principal advisers to bidders and target companies (notably investment banks) but not bidder and target companies themselves or their directors. To deal with this lacuna, a system of FSA-required "cold

---

[33] See fn.30 above, where the company had been in breach of a Code rule requiring the bidder to increase the price offered to the target shareholders because shares had been purchased in the market at that higher price. For the current version of that requirement see below at para.28–39.

[34] Code, *Introduction*, p.19.

[35] Code, *ibid.*, pp.20–21. The Panel may also withdraw or qualify any special status or exemption it has granted the offender, for example, as an "exempt principal trader".

[36] s.952(2)–(8). For a discussion of the FSA's penalty powers see above at para.25–40.

shouldering" was introduced in FSMA 2000 and is carried forward under the new arrangements. Cold shouldering involves advisers within the scope of the FSA's powers being required not to deal with those who are likely not to observe the Code. In this situation, there is no suggestion that the adviser is in breach of the Code. Indeed, the "cold shoulder" operates generally and covers all those who might act for persons likely not to observe the Code, whether they have acted for that person in the past or not. In this way, the range of the FSA's sanctions is extended to companies and their directors: if they act, or are likely to act, in breach of the Code, they may find that they are denied the facilities of the City of London in relation to takeover bids. The FSA's rules, as contained in its Code of Market Conduct (MAR), require firms not to act in connection with transactions to which the Takeover Code applies if they have reasonable grounds to believe that the person in question is not likely to act in accordance with the Takeover Code.[37] The Hearing Committee has the power, as a disciplinary sanction under the Code, to make a public statement that a person is, in its view, not likely to comply with the Code. In such a case the FSA "expects" that the above rule will require the firm not to act for the person in question.

Apart from these sanctions, which the Act places in the hands of the Panel, the legislation creates a criminal offence in addition to the one we have already discussed in relation to the disclosure of confidential information. This applies to non-compliance with the Code's rules on bid documentation. As we shall see below, much of the Code is concerned with specifying the information a bidder or target must provide, and failure to comply with these rules will clearly fall within the powers and sanctions of the Panel, discussed above. It is also the case that there might be civil litigation between those involved in the bid in the case of misstatements in the bid documentation. Despite this, the Government was convinced that the Directive's (standard) requirement that the sanctions provided for breaches of the transposing national rules should be "effective, proportionate and dissuasive" (Article 17) required an additional criminal sanction to be provided in domestic law. The Government feared that inadequacies in the bid documentation might emerge only after the bid had been completed (and when the Panel might be reluctant to involve itself again) so that the Panel's sanctions could not be relied upon, whilst the possibilities of civil litigation were uncertain. Consequently, section 953 creates a narrow criminal offence. It applies only to offers for companies whose voting securities are quoted on a regulated market (which is the scope of the Directive) and it imposes liability on a

---

[37] The FSA rules discussed in this paragraph are set out in MAR 4.3. These rules are made by the FSA under FSMA 2000, s.138. The range of services in connection with a bid which must not be undertaken in such a case is widely defined (MAR 4.3.3–4), though it does not extend to the giving of legal advice. S.143, dealing with formal endorsement of the City Code by the FSA, has been repealed in the light of the statutory sanctions given to the Panel.

person only if he knew the offer documentation did not comply with the Code's requirements (or was reckless as to that) and failed to take all reasonable steps to secure compliance. In the case of a response document, the liability falls on any director or officer of the target company; in the case of an offer, which need not be made by a company, on the person making the bid and, in the case of a bid by "a body of persons", any director, officer or member of the body who caused the document to be published. Typically, this will be the directors and officers of the bidder company.[38]

Overall, the policy of the Act in relation to the Panel and the Code can be said to have been that of "replicating, to the greatest extent possible, the Panel's current jurisdiction, practices and procedures within a statutory framework."[39]

THE SCOPE OF THE CITY CODE

28–11 The scope of application of the City Code (i.e. the types of companies and types of transactions to which it applies) is wider than that of the Directive. The latter applies to public offers to the holders of securities in the target company, where those securities are traded on a regulated market in the EEA and where the objective of the offer is to secure control of the target company.[40] For present purposes it is enough to equate a "regulated market" in the UK with the Main Market of the London Stock Exchange. The Code is not confined to companies whose securities are traded on a regulated market (and thus covers companies whose securities are traded on AIM) and it takes in certain transactions which are analogous to public offers. The expanded scope of the Code (or, alternatively put, the narrow scope of the Directive) would raise no particular problems in the light of the decision (discussed above) to put the whole of the Panel's operations on a statutory footing, were it not for the fact that the two take a different approach to the regulation of takeovers which have a cross-border element. The approach of the Directive, as laid down in

---

[38] s.953(2),(4). In the Parliamentary debates the Solicitor-General gave an assurance that the provision was not intended to reach investment banks when they make offers as agents of bidders—though it must be said that it would be a pretty poor investment bank which knew of the defect in the documentation and did not take reasonable steps to correct it. See HC Debs, Standing Committee D, Nineteenth Sitting, July 18, 2006, cols 804–806.

[39] DTI Consultation Document para.2.18. See also Panel on Takeovers and Mergers, *Implementation of the Takeover Directive, Consultation Paper*, PCP 2005/5, November 2005, (hereafter "Panel Consultation Document") para.2.4: "Overall, the Panel remains confident that while its status and the status of the Code will be different under the new statutory regime, there will be little material substantive change either to its procedures or to the Rules of the Code."

[40] Directive, Arts.1(1) and 2(1)(a). On the definition of a "regulated market" see above at para.25–5.

Article 4, is to divide jurisdiction in such cases among the relevant regulators. By contrast, the Panel's approach, as a national body, is either to accept jurisdiction over all aspects of the offer or not to accept it at all. Consequently, it is necessary to identify not only the offers to which the Code applies (anything outside this set is not regulated at all by the Code) but also the narrower set of offers to which the Directive applies, at least in cross-border takeovers, in order to establish the precise jurisdiction of the Panel (is it all or only some aspects of the bid process?).[41]

Transactions in scope

Let us turn first to the range of transactions covered. The crucial **28–12** point here is that the Directive applies only to the core method of implementing a takeover, namely an offer by the bidder to the holders of the securities of the target, which offer is accepted, if so desired, by the shareholders of the target, thus creating a contract for the transfer of the shares from offeree to offeror. Thus, a mechanism of private law is used to implement the takeover. The Code traditionally has applied more widely, i.e. beyond takeover offers, though obviously it includes them. It is, in fact, not uncommon for non-hostile takeovers to be implemented in the United Kingdom, not in this way, but via a scheme of arrangement, to which the Code in principle applies.[42] The scheme of arrangement, which is not confined to control-shift transactions, is discussed in Chapter 29, but the essence of the scheme, when used as a substitute for a takeover offer, is that the company, through a decision of its shareholders, adopts a plan, the end result of which is that achieved by the contract mechanism (the shares in the target company end up with the bidder and the shareholders receive a consideration in exchange). The scheme has certain advantages in the case of a non-hostile offer (notably that all the shareholders are bound once the scheme is adopted and approved by the court), so that the squeeze-out mechanism referred to later in this Chapter does not have to be used. However, technically the offer is implemented not through each individual shareholder's decision to accept an offer made for the transfer of their shares but by the shareholders collectively, acting as the company, voting to adopt a

---

[41] We have also noted above that the criminal sanctions for inaccuracies in the bid documentation apply only to offers within the scope of the Directive. See para.28–10.

[42] The Code's provisions, discussed in this and the following paragraph, are set out in its *Introduction*, para.3(b). Although a control shift by means of a scheme of arrangement does fall within the Panel's jurisdiction, the Code has hitherto been drafted almost wholly with reference to contractual offers. In the light of the "significant increase in recent years in the use of schemes of arrangement in order to implement transactions which are regulated by the Code" the Code Committee proposed to introduce a "Schemes Appendix" into the Code, which would set out in detail the variations of the Rules in their application to schemes: PCP 2007/1, *Schemes of Arrangement*. These changes were implemented in January 2008 by Code Committee Instruments 2007/1 and 1A.

scheme of arrangement. In this case, a mechanism of corporate law is used to effect the takeover. For this reason, a takeover effected by a scheme of arrangement appears not to fall within the Directive's definition of a takeover,[43] so that a scheme is outside the scope of the Directive, even if it involves companies whose securities are traded on a regulated market. For this reason, the jurisdiction splitting provisions of the Directive will not apply to a takeover effected by a scheme of arrangement which has a cross-border element, which may itself be regarded as an advantage by the parties involved.

The Code also applies to offers by a parent company to acquire outside shares in its subsidiary, a transaction not normally within the Directive because it does not have as its objective the acquisition of control. The Code applies as well to other mechanisms which have "as their objective or potential effect (directly or indirectly) obtaining or consolidating control". This covers a wide range of possible methods, not involving a general offer to acquire securities, such as the issue of new shares and share capital reorganisations, which, if structured appropriately, could shift control of the company into new hands. Although not much invoked in practice, the inclusion of these analogous control-shift mechanisms removes any temptation for the parties to seek to avoid the Code's provisions by adopting one or other of them.

Companies in scope: full jurisdiction to the Panel

28–13　　The scope of the Directive and of the Code, as far as companies are concerned, is defined by focussing on the status of the target company. Let us look first at the cases where the Panel will be the sole regulator, i.e. where the target is what might be called a purely UK company. The Code divides the companies to which it applies in full into two categories: those with securities traded on a regulated market and those not.[44] This may seem unnecessarily refined, since the substantive provisions of the Code apply equally in the two cases. However, what this division reveals is another distinction between the approach of the Directive and the traditional approach of the Code to the determination of what is a "UK company". The Directive takes incorporation as the touchstone for this (together with the securities being traded on a regulated market in the UK), whereas the Code has traditionally focussed on the "residence" of the company, which is interpreted to require both incorporation (i.e. its registered

---

[43] A takeover bid is defined in Art.2(1)(a) as "a public offer (other than by the offeree company itself) made to the holders of the securities of a company to acquire all or some of those securities, whether mandatory or voluntary, which follows or has as its objective the acquisition of control of the offeree company in accordance with national law."

[44] *Introduction*, 3(a) and (b). The note on p.A3 makes it clear that company for the purposes of the Code includes UK unregistered companies, to which, in addition, the statutory provisions of Chapters 2 and 3 of Part 28 are applied by regulation. See para.1–17.

office to be) in the United Kingdom and that the place of its central management should be in the United Kingdom. Consequently, where the Directive applies, i.e. where the company is traded on a regulated market in the United Kingdom, it is enough for the Panel to have (sole) jurisdiction that the target is incorporated in some part of the United Kingdom. That the target's central management is located outside the United Kingdom will make no difference. To this extent, the Directive expands the jurisdiction of the Panel compared to the pre-Directive position.[45]

However, the Code also applies to companies whose securities are not traded on a regulated market. To determine whether such companies are within the scope of the Code, the requirement that the "place of central management and control" be in the United Kingdom is retained so that mere incorporation in the United Kingdom is not enough in these cases. The extent to which the Code applies, and always has applied, beyond regulated markets is in fact quite significant. It covers companies with securities traded on exchange-regulated markets, such as AIM.[46] It brings into its coverage in fact all public companies (in the Companies Act sense of the term), whether they have securities traded on a public market or not. It even brings in private companies, but only where in the previous decade their securities have been traded in a public or semi-public way or a prospectus has been issued in relation to them. In quantitative terms, probably only AIM companies are frequently subject to takeover offers, but the inclusion of the other categories at least means the Code's provisions cannot be evaded by first de-listing the company from a public market. The Code applies to UK incorporated companies, whether they are registered companies or, statutory or chartered companies.[47] To meet the Community obligations of the UK the Code also applies to companies incorporated in the Channel Islands and the Isle of Man (though this was the case previously), but it does not apply to offers for open-ended investment companies (again as previously).[48]

---

[45] For an application of the former rule see Xstrata Plc, Panel Statement 2002/7: company incorporated in the United Kingdom and to be listed on the Main Market of the LSE not within the jurisdiction of the Panel because the place of its central management was Switzerland. The Panel's insistence on the central place of management being in the UK seems to have been linked to the question of whether that management would be amenable to its authority. With the Panel being put on a statutory basis, it is not clear that the Panel's jurisdiction should depend so heavily on the location of the central management of the company, as it will continue to do in cases falling outside the scope of the Directive. See immediately below.

[46] Code, *Introduction*, 3(a)(ii) sets out the rules discussed in this paragraph. On the distinction between regulated and exchange-regulated markets see para.25–5.

[47] For these distinctions see para.1–16. Statutory and chartered companies, of course, have no registered office and so the reference in these cases is to the principal office, i.e. the distinction drawn in the text between registered office and main place of management rather collapses.

[48] This is an exemption permitted by Art.1(2) of the Directive.

Divided jurisdiction

28–14   In the above cases, if the Panel has jurisdiction at all, it has jurisdiction over all aspects of the bid. In the cases now to be examined
the Panel's jurisdiction will be shared with another regulator. This
division results from the approach adopted by Article 4 of the
Directive. Because division of competence is a Directive concept, it
applies only to bids for target companies whose securities are traded
on a regulated market. In any other case, the Panel will either have
full jurisdiction or no jurisdiction.

The problem arises where the two factors the Directive uses to
identify its scope are satisfied in different jurisdictions, for example, a
company incorporated in one Member State but having its securities
traded on a regulated market in another Member State. The Directive
could have allocated jurisdiction wholly to the State of incorporation,
as is done with the Prospectus Directive,[49] but this is hardly feasible
with takeover regulation, which involves much more than information disclosure and is in parts intimately related to the operation of
the market on which the target's securities trade. Alternatively, jurisdiction could have been allocated wholly to the State where the
target's securities trade. In fact, Article 4 of the Directive appears
initially to proceed in this way by identifying the competent authority
to supervise the bid as the one in the Member State where the
company's securities are admitted to trading on a regulated market
(even if the company is incorporated elsewhere). If the securities are
admitted to trading on a regulated market in more than one Member
State, the competent authority is the State where the securities were
first admitted. If the securities are admitted to markets in more than
one Member State (other than the State of incorporation) simultaneously, the company makes the choice of competent authority from
among the various Member States, but must do so in advance, that is,
the choice must be made on the first day of trading, and the choice
seems subsequently to be unalterable.[50]

However, Article 4(2)(e) then proceeds to say, not simply that the
takeover rules of the Member State of incorporation shall be the
operative ones for certain matters, but also that in respect of those
matters the competent authority shall be that of the State of incorporation. In this way, the Directive does end up with a divided jurisdiction. In particular, what the Directive refers to as "company
law" matters are allocated to the competent authority of the State of
incorporation. These include the definition of the threshold at which
a mandatory bid shall be launched and any derogations from the
obligation to launch such a bid, the rules governing frustrating action

---

[49] See para.25–41.
[50] Art.4(2)(b) and (c). If the simultaneous listing had occurred before the Directive came into
force, the relevant competent authorities must agree within four weeks of that date which of
them is to be the competent authority for that company or, in default of agreement, the
company chooses on the first day of trading after that four-week period.

by the directors of the target company and the provision of information to employees. By contrast, the competent authority of the Member State where the securities are traded will deal with the rules relating to the price to be offered, bid procedure, disclosure and the contents of the offer document. For the Panel this means that: (a) where a company is incorporated in the United Kingdom but traded on a regulated market in another EEA Member State, the Panel will deal with the "company law" aspects of the bid; (b) where the company is incorporated in an EEA Member State (other than the United Kingdom) but traded only on a regulated market in the United Kingdom, the Panel will deal with the "bid procedure" aspects of the offer; and (c) where the company is incorporated as in (b) but traded on regulated markets in more than one Member State of the EEA, including the United Kingdom, the Panel may or may not be the competent authority to deal with the "bid procedure" aspects of the offer.

Presumably, the drafters of the Directive regarded these two lists as **28–15** exhaustively allocating to one competent authority or the other all the matters which might arise during the course of a bid. Not surprisingly, the Directive and the Act require competent national authorities to cooperate with one another and with the relevant national authorities under the Prospectus Directive (in the case of the United Kingdom, the FSA).[51] The division of applicable rules and competent authorities is very important, both because the Directive itself gives the Member States significant choices about how they implement the Directive's provisions and because Member States are free to add to them.[52] Thus, the relevant takeover rules are likely to be significantly different from one Member State to another.

Finally, it should be noted that the Directive does not apply at all if the target company is not incorporated in Member State of the EEA or does not have its securities traded on a regulated market in the EEA.[53] However, the Code, as we have seen, does apply to public companies incorporated and having their central management and control in the United Kingdom, no matter where, or indeed whether, their securities are publicly traded. Thus, a bid for a company incorporated outside the EEA will escape British regulation even if its securities are listed on a public market in the United Kingdom; whilst a bid for one which is incorporated in and has its central management in the United Kingdom will be regulated by the Panel, even if its securities are traded on a public market outside the EEA or, even, on

---

[51] Art.4(4) and s.950.

[52] Articles 9–12 on pre- and post-bid frustrating action are notorious for the range of options provided to Member States (see below, paras 28–17ff), whilst Art.13 requires Member States to have rules on certain matters, without specifying what those rules should be, and Art.3(2) permits Member States to add to the Directive's minimum rules provisions which are "more stringent".

[53] Art.1(1).

a non-regulated market within the EEA (but outside the UK). For this reason, no doubt, section 950 requires the Panel to co-operate not only with foreign national authorities designated for the purposes of the Directive but also with any foreign regulator that appears to exercise functions similar to those of the Panel.

THE STRUCTURE OF THE CODE

28–16   The Code consists, in its eighth edition of 2006, and always has consisted of a small number of General Principles and a larger number of Rules. Currently, there are six General Principles (GPs) and thirty-eight Rules. Before the amendments made in 2006 to accommodate the Directive, there were ten General Principles and the same number of Rules as currently. The current six GPs are simply a copy out of the general principles laid down in Article 3 of the Directive. The decision simply to substitute the Directive's GPs for those previously in place seems to have been driven in part by the consideration that the Panel's derogation power must be exercised in such a way as not to contravene the Directive's GPs. It was thought that the cleanest way of implementing this requirement was to simply adopt the Directive's list of GPs.[54] The original notion behind the GPs was that they constituted high-level standards, compliance with which was required even though no specific Rule of the Code had been broken. This was thought to be a desirable regulatory technique because, as it was put in the seventh edition of the Code, "it is impracticable to devise rules in sufficient detail to cover all the circumstances which can arise in offers."[55] However, the reduction in the number of GPs in the current Code has somewhat reduced the force of this regulatory argument, not simply because the current GPs cover less ground than those previously in place and because, where they cover the same ground, the Directive's GPs are in general more weakly expressed, but also because the Rules have been amended to take account of the loss of coverage at GP level.[56] This movement of material between GPs and Rules casts some doubt on the significance of the distinction between those two types of norm.

In any event, it is also the case that, over successive editions of the Code, the Rules had become more detailed and elaborate, so that the

---

[54] Panel Consultation Document, para.2.1. On the Panel's derogation and waiver powers see above at para.28–7. Of course, the Directive restricts the Panel's derogation powers only by reference to its GPs and not by reference to any additional GPs which a Member State chooses to adopt, but copying out the Directive's GPs at least removes a source of possible confusion about which of the domestic GPs simply implement the Directive's GPs and which add something beyond the Directive's requirements.

[55] City Code, 7th ed., 2002, B1.

[56] Panel Consultation Document, para.2.1.

gap-filling rationale given for the GPs had become less convincing. The Rules acquired sub-rules and both acquired "notes", some of which are prescriptive and not just explanatory. It is perhaps not surprising that the view just quoted about the role of GPs is not repeated in the current version of the Code. The best view is probably now that the GPs are there because the Directive requires them to be and that they serve to highlight some, but not all, of the fundamental principles underlying the Code. It seems likely in the future that the Rules will continue to grow in importance in comparison with the GPs. Both Rules and GPs are interpreted by the Panel purposively,[57] so that no penalty in terms of rigidity of interpretation is paid by dealing with a matter in the Rules. Further, if the content of the GPs is effectively controlled by the Directive, the response to domestic pressures for change or elaboration of takeover regulation will have to be revealed in changes to the Rules. Such changes in the Rules can be readily made through the Code Committee of the Panel, whose task it is to keep the Code under review and to propose changes, after public consultation,[58] whereas, on the Panel's current approach, changes to the GPs would require legislation at Community level.

The current General Principles are as follows:

1. All holders of securities in the offeree company of the same class must be afforded equivalent treatment. Where a person acquires control of a company, the other holders of securities must be protected. These are the two limbs of GP 1 and they constitute a partial expression of a more elaborate notion of equality which underlies the Code and which is discussed below.

2. Holders of securities in the offeree company must have sufficient time and information to enable them to reach a properly informed decision on the bid. If it advises the shareholders, the board of the offeree company must give its views on the effects of the implementation of the bid on employment, conditions of employment and the location of the company's place of business. The first part of GP 2 is clearly central to any takeover regulation; the second part, specifically requiring the provision of employee-related information, constitutes a relatively minor protection of the interests of the employees. They or their representatives are given no formal role in the takeover decision, but the provision of the required information may enable them to apply pressure outside the formal requirements of the Code. Although the second part of the GP is conditional upon the board of the offeree company giving advice to the share-

[57] City Code, *Introduction*, 2(b).
[58] City Code, *Introduction*, 4(b).

holders of the target company, in fact, as we shall see, the
Code requires such advice to be given.

3.   "The board of an offeree company must act in the interests
     of the company as a whole and must not deny the holders of
     securities the opportunity to decide on the merits of the bid."
     The phrase "the company as a whole" is, as ever, ambiguous
     as to whether it means only the shareholders as a whole or
     includes stakeholder interests.[59] The answer to that question
     may not be very significant since the second part of the
     principle puts the decision on the bid in the hands of the
     shareholders, to whom the "company as a whole" duty does
     not apply. As already noted, the allocation of the decision on
     the bid as between target board and target shareholders is a
     crucial question for takeover regulation. The City Code has
     always allocated that decision to the shareholders, though,
     somewhat oddly, the Directive permits Member States to opt
     out of Article 9 of the Directive, which gives effect to GP 3
     (see below).

4.   False markets should not be created, whether in the secu-
     rities of the offeror, offeree or any other company concerned
     in the bid.

5.   An offeror may announce an bid only if has ensured that it
     can meet in full any cash consideration payable and after
     taking "all reasonable steps" to secure the implementation of
     any other type of consideration.

6.   The offeree company should not be hindered in the conduct
     of its affairs by the bid for longer than is reasonable. This is a
     GP not previously expressed in the Code, though the policy
     underlying it was certainly implemented in the Code, and it is
     rather odd that it was not there. The point is that a bid is
     likely to cause the senior management of the target to divert
     their attention wholly to the bid from the moment it is
     imminent to the point where it succeeds or fails, so that there
     is a strong argument that this distraction from the other
     aspects of company's activities should be subject to limits.

THE ALLOCATION OF THE ACCEPTANCE DECISION

28–17   As already indicated at the beginning of this Chapter, a, perhaps the,
crucial question for takeover regulation is whether the decision on the

---

[59] See para.16–24.

bid should be that of the shareholders alone or one to which both shareholders and the target board must consent. Allocating the decision to the shareholders alone allows the creation of a market in the control of companies, which acts as a powerful incentive for the managements of companies, at all times and not just when a bid is imminent, to act in the interests of the shareholders. Bidders are able to make "hostile" takeover offers, i.e. offers which the board of the target opposes but which it is not able to prevent being put to their shareholders. The market in corporate control is probably a much more powerful mechanism for the promotion of the interests of shareholders than all the corporate governance techniques discussed in Part Three of this book, including the law of directors' duties. On the other hand, some have argued that the threat of a takeover makes management too responsive to shareholder needs, in particular by inducing management to take a short-term view of the company's success, which may be detrimental to the longer term development of its business and thus to the long-term interests of the shareholders themselves. Those taking this latter view would wish to permit management to have some say in whether the bid is successful and would not allocate the decision wholly to the shareholders. Those concerned about the impact of takeovers on non-shareholder groups, notably employees, tend to support this managerialist stance, as being the best protection they can secure in the absence of a stakeholder input into the acceptance decision.[60]

Since the standard takeover transaction is one between the bidder and the shareholders of the target company, the question of whether the board of the target company is to have a say on the transfer of shares comes to focus on the question of whether the board of a target or potential target company shall be permitted to exercise their general powers of management so as to discourage an offeror from making or continuing with a bid. This is usually referred to as the issue of whether takeover regulation should adopt a "no frustration" rule, i.e. whether the board of a target is to be prohibited from taking action which constrains the freedom of the shareholders as a whole to decide to accept an offer, even though such action would normally be within the scope of the board's powers of management. This issue needs to be addressed at two different points of time: when a bid is imminent and when no bid is in prospect. The reason for this distinction is that the imposition of a strict no frustration rule is feasible once a bid is imminent, because it will operate only so long as the bid is in issue. The imposition of a strict "no frustration" rule where no bid is imminent (i.e. at all times) would constitute an infringement of the board's powers of management which was undesirable even from the shareholders' point of view (because it reduce the benefits

---

[60] For an analysis of the competing views see R. Kraakman *et al* (eds), *The Anatomy of Corporate Law* (Oxford: OUP, 2004) Ch.7.

shareholders obtain from centralised management), whilst the risk of self-serving decisions by management is less severe when a bid is not imminent. Thus, even those in favour of the "no frustration" principle would not necessarily want the same rules to apply both pre- and post-bid. In the United Kingdom this distinction in point of time is reinforced by a division in terms of regulatory responsibility, for the City Code applies only once a bid is imminent.

Post-bid defensive measures

28–18 The Code has always adopted a strong "no frustration" rule, thus helping to make the United Kingdom a very active takeover market. The principle used be expressed in GP 7, which said that after a bona fide offer had been communicated to the board of the target or the board had reason to believe that such an offer was imminent, no action might be taken by the board without the approval of the shareholders in general meeting which could result in the offer being frustrated or to shareholders being denied an opportunity to decide on its merits.[61] This language no longer appears in the GPs, though there is a paler version of it in the current GP 3. In a strong example of the GP to Rule transfer brought about by the Directive, however, this exact formulation can be found in Rule 21.1(a) of the current Code. This Rule makes it difficult for the existing controllers to erect any of the defences against being ousted from control by an unwelcome takeover unless they have succeeded in doing so in advance of a threatened takeover. It is a particularly strict rule. Unlike the common law relating to improper purposes,[62] Rule 21 requires shareholder approval for any action proposed by the directors of the target company which could have the result of preventing the shareholders of the target company from deciding on the merits of the bid. Whether the directors of the target had this purpose in mind or whether it was their predominant purpose in proposing the action in question is beside the point under the Rule. The Rule looks to consequences, not to purposes. Equally important, the Rule requires shareholder approval to be given for the specific defensive measure proposed by the target board and thus to be given in the context of the bid; it cannot be given in general and in advance of the bid.

Rule 21.1(b), together with Rule 37.3, spells out some common situations where the approval of the shareholders will be required, for example, in relation to share issues; acquisition or, more likely, disposals of target company assets of a "material amount";[63] entering

---

[61] This prohibition, however, seems to be restricted to internal corporate action of the sort specified in r.21 and it is not regarded as breached by lobbying the competition authorities seeking to persuade them to take action to prohibit the bid or subject it to conditions unacceptable to the offeror

[62] See paras 16–21ff, above.

[63] On which see Note 2 to r.21.1.

into contracts other than in the ordinary course of business (which may include the declaration and payment of interim dividends); and the redemption or purchase of shares.[64] But Rule 21.1(a) covers any frustrating action, whether specifically mentioned in the Rules or not, and it has been held by the Panel to cover even the initiation of litigation on behalf of the target once an offer is imminent.[65] The overall effect of the Rule is to reduce the defensive tactics available to the management of the target company to three general categories: convincing the shareholders that their future is better assured with the incumbent management than with the bidder; persuading the competition authorities, at national or Community level, that the bid ought to be referred on public interest grounds; and encouraging another bidder to come forward as a "white knight" and make an alternative offer to the shareholders. In all three situations the directors of the target are thrown back on their powers of persuasion: in all three cases the final decision on the success of these defensive moves rests with others. However, the board of the target company is not required as a general rule to co-operate with the bidder and to smooth its path. Rule 21 is framed by way of stipulations about what the board must not do, not about how it should act positively. Thus, the board may find itself in a stronger negotiating position than Rule 21 might suggest if either (a) a recommendation in favour of the offer from the target board is, for one reason or another, important to the bidder or (b) the bidder needs the target board's cooperation to launch the bid. We discuss such situations below under "bid procedure".

The requirement for shareholder approval for frustrating action is reflected in Article 9 of the Directive, but this is one of the articles of which Member States are permitted to opt out. Not surprisingly, the United Kingdom chose not to do so, since Article 9 reflects the established policy of the Code. Hence Rule 21 of the Code. However, there is a further issue about company opt outs from the no-frustration rule. Although not completely clear on the point, Article 12(3) can be interpreted so as to permit Member States to permit companies to opt out of the no-frustration rule of Article 9 in limited circumstances, namely, when faced with a bid from a company to which Article 9 does not apply (for example, because the bidder is from a Member State which has opted out of Article 9). This is the so-called "reciprocity" principle, i.e. a target should be subject to the ban of frustrating action only where the bidder is subject to it. However, the

---

[64] Of course, the management of the target company may, and often do, promise as part of their defence to the bid to carry out one or more of these actions after their shareholders have rejected the offer.

[65] See Panel Statement 1989/7, *Consolidated Gold Fields* and Panel Statement 1989/20, *BAT Industries*, which explore the complications which arise when the litigation is initiated in a foreign jurisdiction by a partially owned subsidiary or when the "litigation" takes the form of enthusiastic participation in regulatory hearings.

United Kingdom chose not to adopt this more limited form of opt-ing-out either, on the grounds that it was not part of the existing Code structure and that the benefits to the United Kingdom of an open market for corporate control obtained even if the bidder is not an available target.[66] In short, Rule 21 is a mandatory rule out of which companies may not opt.

Defensive measures in advance of the bid

28–19 This is an area where the Code does not operate. Rule 21 applies only where the "board has reason to believe that a bona fide offer might be imminent". Before that point regulation is left to general company law,[67] which, however, has not developed a single rule to deal with pre-bid defensive tactics. Rather, a number of rules may be relevant, depending upon the precise action the directors of a potential target company wish to take. The most general of these company law rules is section 171 of the Companies Act requiring the directors to exercise their powers for a proper purpose or to obtain shareholder approval of action not proposed for a proper purpose. As we have noted in relation to post-bid defences, however, because that section focuses on the directors' purpose, rather than on the effects of their acts, and indeed on their predominant purpose, where there is more than one, the section is a weaker control than Rule 21. Provided there is a commercial justification which the directors can plausibly put for-ward as the predominant purpose of their action, it will be difficult for a shareholder to challenge it on the grounds that an effect of the decision will be to make the company less attractive to a bidder or less easy to take over. In the absence of a current bid, there is also less incentive for a shareholder to seek to challenge the directors' action through a derivative action. An example of a board decision, having the effect of making the company less easy to take over but having also a plausible commercial justification, might be the creation of a joint venture with another company, to which each commits part of its existing assets, on terms that a change of control in either partner

---

[66] DTI Consultation Document, para.3.12. The most prominent country which does not apply the board neutrality rule in takeovers is Germany, though even there defensive measures need (a) the approval of the shareholders which can be given in general and for periods of up to eighteen months and need not be given in the face of the bid, as the Code demands, or (b) the approval of the supervisory board. See William Underhill and Andreas Austmann, "Defensive Tactics" in J. Payne (ed.), *Takeovers in English and German Law* (Oxford: Hart Publishing, 2002) pp.95–98.

[67] These rules apply to post-bid defensive tactics as well, but there their impact is normally hidden beneath that of Rule 21 of the Code. They might be important, even post-bid, in the exceptional case where the Code did not apply to the target company, for example, where it was a private company or a public company whose securities were traded on AIM and whose central management was outside the UK. See fn.45 above.

permits the other partner to buy the first partner out.[68] Alternatively, the board of a company might seek to make it less attractive to a bidder by gearing up its balance sheet (i.e. altering the ratio of debt to equity in the company's financial structure) and distributing the immediate gains of that exercise to the shareholders, on the basis that the opportunity of carrying out this exercise is what makes the company attractive to a private equity bidder. It is not surprising that section 171 is less stringent than Rule 21. Rule 21 is very restrictive of managerial initiative, because of its requirement for shareholder consent. This is a policy which may be sustainable for the short period after a bid has been launched and before its fate is decided, but applied to corporate decision-making across the board it would subvert the delegation in the articles of managerial powers to the board whenever a decision might have the effect of making the company a less attractive bid target.[69]

Other rules can be pointed to which require shareholder consent in specific circumstances. Thus, section 551 requires shareholder authorisation for decisions by the directors of public companies to issue shares or to grant rights to subscribe for or convert any security into shares.[70] This section, together with the improper purposes doctrine, makes it much more difficult for a British company to adopt a US-style "poison pill" or "shareholder rights plan". In the United States the efficacy of that device depends crucially on the board being able to adopt the plan without the consent of the shareholders and upon the courts not regarding the adoption of such a plan as a breach of fiduciary duty on the part of the directors. Section 551 lays down the principle of shareholder consent for the conferment of such rights, and a poison pill might well be regarded by British courts as falling foul of the proper purposes doctrine, since the pill has no commercial rationale except in the context of the bid and its role then is simply to make it very unattractive for a bidder to put an offer to the shareholders of which the target board does not approve.[71] However, section 551 is again a less rigorous provision than Rule 21 of the Code, because it allows shareholders to approve the issuance of shares by directors up to five years in advance, though institutional shareholders are in fact reluctant to give a blank cheque to the directors for such a long period. Asking shareholders to approve share issues in advance, for which permission there may well be good commercial reasons, does not focus shareholders' attention as sharply

[68] For an example of the legal pitfalls which can be created if the drafters of the joint venture agreement are overly ambitious see *Criterion Properties Plc v Stratford UK Properties LLC* [2004] 1 W.L.R. 1846, HL and see generally above at paras 16–21ff.
[69] On the division of powers between shareholders and the board see para.14–2.
[70] See para.24–4.
[71] The shareholder rights plan, which comes in many varieties, in its core version gives shareholders other than the bidder the right to subscribe for shares in the target company at a very attractive price. Given the discrimination between the bidder and non-bidder shareholders a rights plan would also cause difficulties for the target board under s.172(1)(f).

on the potential costs to them as does the approval required, as under Rule 21, in the course of a bid, where the shareholders know the terms of the offer they will be rejecting if they adopt the defensive measures.[72]

The drafters of the Takeover Directive, however, were concerned with a different form of pre-bid defensive measure. This was the creation by companies of capital structures in which the voting rights attached to equity shares are not proportionate to the economic interests held by the equity shareholders, or where there were restrictions on the transferability of the shares. Both arrangements make the bid less likely to succeed, in the former case because the voting shares may be concentrated in the hands of those, for example members of the founding family, who oppose a change of control in principle; and in the latter because it may simply not be possible for shareholders to accept the bidder's offer. A disjunction between voting and economic rights can be achieved in a number of different ways, of which the most obvious are the creation of a class of non-voting equity shares or a class of shares with multiple voting rights. Let us assume that in each case there is also a class of equity share-holder having one vote per share, but with rights and obligations otherwise the same as those of the other class of equity shareholder. In the former case, the class with one vote per share will control the company, even though they have contributed only a part of the company's equity share capital. In the latter, this class will have its voting power diluted by the multiple-vote shares, even though the holders of the shares with multiple votes have not contributed a proportion of the company's equity capital that is equivalent to their votes.

28–20   As we have seen in Chapter 23 there is nothing in British law that prohibits or regulates such capital structures, though the European Commission at one stage seemed keen to introduce a "one share, one vote" principle at Community level. In the discussions on the drafts of the Takeover Directive the concern was with deviations from the proportionality principle in the specific context of takeovers. The "Winter group",[73] to whom the issue was referred by the European Commission, wished, putting the matter broadly, to assert the mandatory operation of a "one share, one vote" rule in two bid situations. These were: (a) any vote by shareholders called to approve or not post-bid defensive measures; (b) at a general meeting called after the bidder has acquired a specified proportion of the company's equity for the purpose of installing its own nominees as directors of the target or changing the target's articles of association. This so-called "break through" rule would also apply to restrictions on the

---

[72] Pre-emption rights, which might also stand in the way of rights plans, suffer from the same weakness of disapplication in advance. See s.570 and above at para.24–6.

[73] Report of the High Level Group of Company Law Experts on Issues Related to Takeover Bids, Brussels, January 10, 2002, Ch.1, especially pp.28–36.

transferability of shares, whether to be found in the company's articles or in contracts with or among shareholders. The aim of the break-through rule was to render nugatory the defensive qualities of the capital structures or of the transfer restrictions once a bid emerges. This was a controversial proposal, which was rendered more, rather than less, controversial by the watered-down way in which it was ultimately implemented in Article 11 of the Directive.

There is no doubt that the issue identified in Article 11 of the Takeover Directive is an important one. To take an extreme example, Rule 21 of the Code, requiring shareholder approval of post-bid defensive measures, would be of little value if the company's articles allocated the voting rights on such a question entirely to the board of the target company. However, this theoretical problem has never loomed large in British policy-making, mainly because of the opposition of institutional shareholders to acquiring non- or limited-voting equity shares. This is not to say that such capital structures do not exist in British companies, but that, broadly, where they continue, institutional shareholders have been convinced that there is a good reason for that situation. In other words, the solution to the problem in the United Kingdom has traditionally been market-led rather than to be found in the law, and British law, in consequence, has not previously contained a break-through rule. In those Member States which make extensive use of disproportionate capital structures or restrictions on transfer, there was strong opposition to a Community rule which would set them aside, even in the limited, if important, context of a takeover bid. The result was that Article 11 of the Directive, like Article 9, was made optional for the Member States at the final point in the Community's legislative process.

The British Government decided to opt out of Article 11, contrary to its decision in relation to Article 9, for the reasons indicated above, i.e. the problem was not a significant one in the United Kingdom and the flexibility to retain disproportionate capital structures was valuable where these were justified.[74] One might think, therefore, that the break-through rule needs no further attention in this book. Unfortunately, Article 12, which provides for the opt-out, also stipulates that where a Member State has opted out, it must permit opting back in on a company-by-company basis.[75] In short, a company may override the decision of the Member State to opt out of Article 12, so far as that particular company is concerned. Article 12 also provides

28–21

---

[74] DTI Consultation Document, para.3.9. In this respect the UK followed the "vast majority" of the Member States: see Commission of the European Communities, *Report on the implementation of the Directive on Takeover Bids*, SEC (2007) 268, February 2007, para.2.1.4 (hereafter "Commission Report").

[75] Article 12(2). This provision applies to opt-outs from both Articles 9 and 11, though only the latter is relevant in the United Kingdom. Article 12(3) provides for the reciprocity exception.

that Member States may permit companies, which have opted back in, to opt out again on the reciprocity principle, i.e. when faced with a bid from a company that is not subject to Article 11. Here, as with Article 9, the British Government decided not to permit opting out on the basis of the reciprocity principle, though, as we shall see, the decision on the part of a company to opt into the break-through rule is reversible under certain conditions. Thus, the choice for a company incorporated in the United Kingdom and having its securities traded on a regulated market is, during any single period of time, to be wholly within or wholly outside the break-through rule.

Why should a United Kingdom company wish to opt back into Article 11? There might be two reasons. One might be where the company has a disproportionate share structure and its investors pressurise it to take this action. Certainly, in the past companies coming to the market for further equity capital have been able to obtain it only on the basis of agreeing to enfranchise existing classes of non-voting shares. Opting into Article 11 might be seen as a mechanism for achieving this result, though in fact the restricted scope of the break-through rule, as finally adopted in the Directive, makes it probably an unattractive way of proceeding for this purpose. Secondly, a company whose capital structure complies with the break-through rule and which intends to maintain that position might want to opt into Article 11 in order to prevent a target in another Member State of the Community, which is permitted to take reciprocal action, from taking defensive measures against it.[76]

Whether opting back into Article 11 is likely or not on the part of United Kingdom companies, the Directive requires the Act to provide a set of provisions on break-through, in order to make that option available. This is what Chapter 2 of Part 28 of the Act aims to achieve. The freedom for companies to opt into the break-through rule is subject to three pre-conditions set out in section 966. The first is that the company has voting shares admitted to trading on a regulated market.[77] This means that the opt-in is available only to companies within the scope of the Directive, in which case the United Kingdom is required to provide it. This strongly suggests that the Government did not view the opt-in as a valuable tool for companies, for it might then have been expected to make it available to com-

---

[76] The extent to which such defensive measures on the part of the target are permitted and the extent to which opting back into Article 11 by the UK company would be effective against such defensive measures depends upon some difficult issues in the interpretation of the singularly ill-drafted Article 12(3) of the Directive. First, it is not clear whether reciprocity is permitted to companies to which either Article 9 or 11 applies on a mandatory basis. The strict wording of the Directive suggests not, but this seems an odd result and the Commission seems to take a different view. See Commission Report para.2.1.3. Secondly, it is not clear on what precise basis the equivalence of the positions of the bidder and target companies is to be assessed, so as to exclude retaliatory measures. See Rickford, above, fn.6 at pp.1406–1408.

[77] s.966(2). On the meaning of a regulated market see para.25–5.

panies with voting shares traded on exchange-regulated markets, such as AIM. The third condition set out in the section is that the Government holds no "golden share" in the company or that no other similar situation exists in relation to that company.[78] The Directive deals with two further, and more important sources of restriction: those found in the articles and those in contracts. The Act deals with the break-through of restrictions contained in these two sources in different ways. The second condition set out in the section is that the company has no restrictions in its articles which would be broken through by Article 11. However, the absence of contractual restrictions is not a pre-condition for a company to opt into the break-through rule. We will look at the regulation of these two types of restriction in turn.

Restrictions in the articles
The legislative technique adopted in the Act for dealing with restrictions in the articles, to which the break-through rule applies, is one of elegant simplicity—albeit that its effect is to transfer all the legal risks to the company which wishes to opt-in. This technique shows itself in the second condition, which simply says that a company must not have in its articles any provision that offends Article 11 of the Directive. The company may achieve this result either by not having the objectionable restrictions in its articles at all or by ensuring that the restrictions do not operate in any situation to which Article 11 of the Directive is applicable.[79] Thus, the burden is transferred entirely to the company wishing to opt in to determine what the requirements of Article 11 of the Directive may be and to bring its articles into compliance with them. The Act provides no help or guidance on this matter: it simply makes the bringing of the articles into compliance with Article 11 of the Directive a condition for opting into the break-through rule. This means that, if a company's articles are not in compliance with the Directive, its decision to opt into the break-through rule will have been ineffective; it does not mean that those aspects of its articles which contravene Article 11 will be broken through by the opting-in decision. The burden is wholly on the company to put its house in order, as far as its articles are concerned, before it opts into the break-through rule, which, as formulated in the statute, applies only to contractual restrictions.

What, however, will a company have to do in order to meet in its articles the requirements of the Directive? To answer that question its

28–22

[78] s.966(4). Article 12(7) permits this restriction, provided the rights of the Member State are compatible with the Treaty.
[79] s.996(3).

legal advisers will have to examine the Directive. Article 11 deals with two types of restrictions in the articles: restrictions on the transfer of shares and restrictions on voting rights. The typical transfer restrictions, often found in private companies, requiring those who wish to transfer their shares to offer them first to existing shareholders, are not likely to be found in the articles of shares traded on a regulated market because of the requirement, to be found elsewhere in Community law and reflected in the Listing Rules, that such shares be freely transferable.[80] On the other hand, restrictions in the form of a cap on the percentage of the share capital any one person may hold in a company are sometimes found in companies' articles, and this would be effective to stymie a general offer for the shares. Assuming the existence of such restrictions, Article 11(2) says that they are not to apply "vis-à-vis the offeror" during the offer period; and Article 11(4) appears to remove the restrictions on transfer (to anyone) in perpetuity once the offeror has received acceptances from the holders of 75 per cent of the capital "carrying voting rights". Thus, a company thinking of opting in under the Act will need to make sure its articles contain no restrictions on transfer which operate during the offer period or at all if the bid is successful to the extent indicated.

Restrictions on voting rights, if they exist at all, are likely to be found in the articles. However, the notion of a "restriction" on voting rights is given a narrow meaning in the Directive. In particular, it appears that the classic British mechanism, the non-voting share, for creating a disjunction between economic interests and voting rights is *not* caught by the Directive. First, it is not clear that the phrase "restrictions on voting rights" is apt to catch a situation where a class of shareholders simply has no voting rights. Secondly, Article 11 applies to restrictions on the voting rights of "securities" and Article 2(1)(e) defines the latter term as "securities carrying voting rights in the company". In other words, Article 11 appears to catch only restrictions on the voting rights of a class of shares that in principle has been allocated voting rights.

28–23   It might be thought that shares carrying multiple voting rights are not caught by the Directive either, since a multiple voting share is arguably not a restriction on the voting rights of those shareholders who have only one vote per share. However, Article 11(3) makes it clear that the effect of the break-through rule is that multiple voting

---

[80] See Ch.25 above at fn.51. Such restrictions are perhaps more likely to be found in agreements (dealt with below). It should be noted that Art.11 in fact applies to restrictions on the transfer of "securities" (not just of shares) and Art.2(1)(e) defines "securities" as "transferable securities carrying voting rights in a company".

shares carry only one vote per share on the appropriate occasions.[81] The logic of applying the break-through rule to multiple voting shares but not to non-voting shares is far from clear.[82] In so far as the rule has any constraining effects in its optional form, the effect of formulating it in this limited way is likely to be that companies which feel deeply about retaining non-proportionate voting structures will shift into one of the types of capital structure not caught by the Directive. This curious outcome of the Community's legislative process probably reflects the profound disagreements among the Member States about the desirability of insisting upon proportionality between economic interests and voting rights.

With rather greater logic, Article 11(6) of the Directive provides that the break-through rule does not apply to restrictions on voting rights of securities where those restrictions are "compensated for by specific pecuniary advantages". This compendious phrase would seem to embrace preference shares that are often given voting rights only in restricted circumstances (if they are given them at all), for example, where the company is in arrears with the payment of the preferred dividend.[83] It is unclear whether the Directive requires that the company, when issuing the preference shares, should have contemplated that there was to be a trade-off between the preference and the restrictions on voting rights and, still less, whether the value of the preference needs to correspond roughly to the value of the lost voting rights. It is thought that neither is required, though this does mean that a company has a further way of evading the break-through rule, that is, by attaching only a minor preference to the class of shares with restricted voting rights. Article 11(6) does not apply to restrictions on transfer, so that a company opting in will have to remove any such restrictions on preference shares.

Assuming the existence of restrictions on voting which offend the Directive, the company contemplating opting in under the Act will need to ensure that any restrictions on voting rights, as defined above, are either removed entirely or do not apply in the two situations broadly corresponding to the two we have discussed above in relation to restrictions on transferability. First, those restrictions must not apply to voting by shareholders on defensive measures in the

---

[81] Even here, the concept of multiple voting rights seems not to capture the arrangement found in some Member States whereby shares held for a period (for example, a year) attract double the votes of those of the same class held for shorter periods. This is because Article 2(1)(g) defines multiple voting securities as "securities included in a distinct and separate class and carrying more than one vote each", which seems to exclude differences in voting rights among members of the same class of shares. Such an arrangement is a distinct impediment to a bid because it means the share has a greater voting weight in the hands of a long-term shareholder who does not accept the bid than in the hands of the bidder, which is necessarily a new holder of the share.

[82] See generally John C. Coates IV, "The Proposed Break-Through Rule" in Ferrarini *et al* (eds), *Reforming Company and Takeover Law in Europe* (Oxford: OUP, 2004).

[83] See above at para.23–7.

immediate post-bid situation.[84] The second situation where the voting right restrictions must be removed arises where the bidder holds seventy-five per cent of the shares carrying voting rights "following the bid".[85] This way of formulating the reference to the relevant shares means that the shares so acquired need not themselves carry 75 per cent of the votes. If they do, the break-through rule is probably unnecessary. All the bidder need achieve is the acquisition of 75 per cent of the shares to which voting rights have been attributed, even if the acquired shares carry less than 75 per cent of the votes, for example, because the holders of the multiple-voting shares have opposed the offer. Once this situation has been achieved, the articles may not impose restrictions on voting rights (including the allocation of multiple votes to shares), at the first general meeting called after the bid to amend the articles of association or to appoint members of the board,[86] if the company is to opt into the break-through rule. Nor may the articles contain any special rights for particular shareholders to appoint or remove members of the board at this meeting, though creditors' rights in this regard are unaffected. In other words, the bidder must be given one opportunity post-bid to install its nominees on the board and to remove from the articles restrictions on voting rights (including the removal of multiple voting rights), by voting its shares on a mandatory "one share, one vote" basis. However, if it is not successful at this meeting, the voting restrictions will continue to operate. Normally, a person holding 75 per cent of the voting rights may change the articles, but subject, of course, to the requirement for the consent of any class of shares whose rights are varied.[87] The bidder may thus find it easier to secure amendments to the articles which confer extra voting rights on classes of shareholder whose voting rights were previously restricted than to take away multiple voting rights from classes of shareholder who currently enjoy them.

28–24   However, the need for class consent will arise at a much earlier and more important stage than that of a successful bidder seeking to rely on the break-through rule. It will arise when a company is seeking to put its articles into compliance with Article 11 of the Directive in order to opt into the break-through rule in the first place. Those classes of shareholders who will see their rights reduced under the amended articles may simply not be willing to agree to the proposed changes in the articles. If they do not consent, there is no statutory mechanism for overriding their refusal. The company's articles will

---

[84] Art.11(3).

[85] Art.11(4). This wording shows that shares held by the bidder pre-bid count towards the 75 per cent figure.

[86] Art.11(4) is not clearly drafted, but recital 19 of the Directive indicates that the break-through of voting restrictions operates only at the first general meeting called for the relevant purposes by the successful bidder, and s.968, dealing with contractual restrictions and discussed below, applies only to the first general meeting.

[87] On the variation of class rights see Ch.19 above.

remain out of compliance with Article 11 and the company will not be able to opt into the break-through rule, because it will not be in a position to satisfy the "second condition" laid down in section 966 for opting in. Does the second condition constitute an infringement of the UK's obligation under Article 12 of the Directive "to grant companies . . . the option . . . of applying . . . Article 11"? It seems not, for Article 12(2) provides that the opting in decision shall be taken in accordance with the Member State's rules "applicable to amendment of the articles of association", which, in the case of the United Kingdom, includes the rules on variation of class rights.

Nevertheless, it cannot be said that, overall, the drafters of the Act set out to facilitate the process of opting into the break-through rule. However, shifting the burden onto the company to adopt appropriate amendments to its articles as a condition for opting in had one further benefit in terms of saving legislative effort. Article 11(5) provides that, "where rights are removed" under Article 11, "equitable compensation" shall be provided to those who lose rights. The Act, however, provides no compensation for changes brought about through amendments to the articles to prepare for or to implement the opt-in. This appears to be on the ground that the use of the normal mechanism for changing the articles, including variation of class rights protections, involves no removal of rights, since rights conferred by the articles are always granted subject to defeasance through the statutory procedure for amending the articles.

Restrictions in contracts

Article 11 also breaks through restrictions contained in contracts **28–25** between members and the company or among members alone, and so the company's option to adopt a break-through rule must cover such restrictions as well. The simple method adopted in the Act to deal with restrictions contained in the articles cannot be applied to contractual restrictions, since the articles cannot override contractual rights existing independently of them. Those rights have to be overridden by the statute itself. Indeed, the whole purpose of the statutory provisions on opting in is to do precisely that. Assuming that the three conditions for opting in have been complied with (in particular, the requirement that the company's articles comply with Article 11 of the Directive) and that the company has taken the decision to opt in, sections 968 and 969 override contractual rights to the extent required by Article 11 of the Directive. Thus, in relation to restrictions contained in contracts, the statute does the legal work for the company, once it has opted in.

In broad terms, contractual restrictions on the transfer of shares and on the voting rights of shares are overridden to the same extent and in the same circumstances as the similar restrictions in the articles need to be amended to bring them into line with Article 11. This is achieved by section 968(2).[88] Contractual restrictions may be found in agreements to which the company is party or to which only share-holders are party. The latter fall within the section only if the agreement was entered into on or after April 21, 2004, i.e. the date upon which the Directive was adopted. Thus, purely private agree-ments between shareholders are not subject to break-through, if entered into before the law which potentially sets them aside was adopted.[89] The issue of compensation for loss of rights needs to be squarely faced in relation to contractual rights, which the statute overrides without any justification for so doing which is derivable from the contract itself. Section 968(6) deals with this issue by pro-viding a right to compensation for loss (of such amount as the court thinks just and equitable) from those persons who, but for the stat-utory break-through, would be liable to the claimant in contract for breach of contract or in tort for inducing breach of contract. In practice, the compensation may be offered by the bidder, but the bidder is not formally liable to pay compensation unless it is a party to the contract or has committed the tort of inducing breach of contract (as it may well do by taking a transfer of the shares with knowlede of the restrictions). For the purposes of compensation, therefore, the contractual provisions are not broken through but the value of those rights is rendered uncertain by the "just and equitable" formula for the assessment of the compensation. The significance of the break-through rule is thus that it excludes the possibility of a contracting party seeking an injunction to prevent the transfer of shares or the argument that a shareholder decision is void because not taken in accordance with the agreed arrangements for voting.

Finally, the break-through of contractual restrictions on voting at the first general meeting after the bidder has acquired 75 per cent in value of the voting shares (and indeed removal of such restrictions from the articles before the opt-in) would be of little use to the bidder if it could not convene a meeting of the shareholders. Article 11(4) requires that the bidder be given the right to convene such a meeting at short notice (provided this is not less than two weeks). Section 969 transposes this obligation by entitling the bidder to trigger the pro-visions of sections 303 to 305 in such a case (which apply generally to

---

[88] The restrictions on transfer are removed from "shares" (see s.968(2)(a),(b)). This seems at first sight too narrow because Art.11 refers to securities (see fn.80 above), but s.971(2) gives "shares" an extended meaning so as to embrace securities which are convertible into shares of the company or entitle the holder to subscribe for such shares, and debentures which (as will be unusual) carry voting rights in the company. On the other hand, the term "shares" seems broader than Art.11 because that term embraces non-voting shares. However, s.968 applies only where there is a "takeover bid" and "takeover bid" is defined in s.974(1) so as to adopt the Directive's definition of that term, and Art.1(a) and (e) make it clear that a takeover bid under the Directive is an offer for voting shares.

[89] s.968(3). That subsection also makes it clear that, provided the agreement relates to a company covered by the Act, the break-through rule will apply to contractual restrictions, even if the contract is not governed by the law of any jurisdiction of the United Kingdom.

the summoning of meetings by shareholders).[90] Since section 303 in its general form permits a shareholder with 10 per cent of the shares carrying voting rights (not 10 per cent of the voting rights) to require directors to convene a meeting, it is very doubtful whether a bidder will need to rely on section 303, as modified by section 969, as against relying on section 303 in its general form.

Procedure for opting in and out

Opting into the break-through rule is a decision the company must take by special resolution of the shareholders.[91] The resolution may set an "effective" date for its operation which is later than the date on which the resolution is passed, in which case the first condition for opting in (having voting shares traded on a regulated market) need not be met until the effective date and the effective date may be specified as the date upon which the securities are admitted to trading.[92] This facilitates the setting up of opting-in arrangements which will apply as soon as the securities are admitted to trading. The other two conditions, however, must be satisfied at the time the resolution is passed. Having opted in to the break-through rule, the company may later opt out of it, also by special resolution, and again, if it wishes, with an effective date for opting out which is later than the date the resolution was passed. However, a company may not opt out until a year has passed from the date upon which the opting-in resolution was forwarded to the registrar.[93] Thus, opportunistic use of the opting-in and opting-out procedure will not be easy, in fact probably impossible, though it should be noted that there appears to be no restriction on how quickly a company, which has opted out, may opt back in again. Until an opted-in company has opted out again, any purported change of its articles which would mean that they contravened the requirements of Article 11 of the Directive will be ineffective. However, it appears that any such change will automatically become effective on the effective date of the opting-out resolution, without the need for the shareholders to re-pass the resolution altering the articles.[94] Both opting-in and opting-out resolutions must be notified to the Panel and the relevant supervisory body if its voting shares have been admitted to trading on a regulated market in an EEA State other than the United Kingdom.[95]

28–26

---

[90] See para.15–29.
[91] s.966(1).
[92] s.967(1),(2) and (4).
[93] s.967(6). Copies of all special resolutions are required to be forwarded to the registrar within 15 days of being passed (s.30). If the effective date of the resolution is much later than the date the resolution was passed, it is conceivable that the resolution will never have been in effect, or in effect for only a short time, before it is reversed.
[94] s.967(7).
[95] s.970.

Disclosure of control structures

28–27 Given the optional nature of the break-through rule, it may well be in practice that Article 10 of the Directive turns out to be more important. The purpose of this Article, as Recital 18 of the Directive recounts, is to make "defensive structures and mechanisms" more transparent. Consequently, companies within the scope of the Directive (i.e. with securities admitted to trading on a regulated market) are required to give information on them as part of their annual report and the board must give an "explanatory report" on them, though it is rather unclear what sort of explanation is called for and how far it should include elements of justification. In the United Kingdom the mechanism used for this disclosure is the directors' report.[96] The domestic rules, following the Directive, require a wide range of information to be given, though some of it will either not be relevant to British companies or is already required to be disclosed. The main items to be covered are:

(a) the structure of the company's capital, notably the rights and obligations of each class of share, whether all those classes of capital are traded on a regulated market or not;

(b) restrictions on the transfer of securities (i.e. both shares and debentures);

(c) the identity of persons with significant direct or indirect holdings of securities in the company and the size and nature of that holding, so far as known to the company;[97]

(d) similar information about a person with "special rights" with regard to the control of the company;

(e) how control rights are exercised under employee share schemes, where the rights are not exercisable by the employees directly;

(f) restrictions on voting rights, notably voting caps (restricting the percentage of total votes a shareholder has, no matter that the shareholding exceeds that percentage) or arrangements for splitting the financial and control rights of securities and placing them in different hands, where the company cooperates in making these arrangements;

(g) agreements between holders of securities, if known to the

---

[96] The Large and Medium-sized Companies and Groups (Accounts and Reports) Regulations 2008/410, Sch.7, Part 6.

[97] In the case of "vote-holding" such disclosure by the vote-holder to the company and then by the company is required by the Transparency Directive (see para.26–18), but this disclosure obligation goes wider to embrace not just voting shares, though it is not accompanied by any obligation of disclosure on the security-holder.

company, which contain restrictions on transfer or the exercise of voting rights;[98]

(h) powers of the board to issue or buy back shares in the company;[99]

(i) significant agreements to which the company is party which will operate differently if there is a change of control (such as loans containing repayment covenants upon a change of control—sometimes referred to as "poisoned debt"), but subject to the exception that disclosure is not required if that would be "seriously prejudicial" to the company;

(j) agreements between the company and its directors or employees for compensation payments to be made upon a change of control.[100]

TARGET MANAGEMENT PROMOTION OF AN OFFER

In the previous section we have proceeded on the assumption that the **28–28** target board's conflict of interest in relation to a bid leads them to seek to maintain the independence of the target company and thus of their positions within it, and hence the "no frustration" rule. This does indeed constitute the most obvious expression of the target board's conflict of interest, but it is not the only one. The board might perceive its future interests as being best served by the company coming under a new controller, especially, for example, where the bidder is a private equity group which wishes to retain the existing senior management of the target and give them a much larger financial stake in the company than they had when it was in public ownership and traded on a stock market.[101] It is thus incorrect to think that the conflict of interest of the target board will always take the form of resisting the bid, to the detriment of the interests of the shareholders. The board may promote the bid—or, if there are competing bids, one of the bids—to the shareholders, again possibly

---

[98] Shareholder pacts are particularly important in some continental European countries in giving groups of investors holding a substantial, but nevertheless minority, stake in the company complete control of it. See *Financial Times*, March 28, 2007, UK edition, p.15 (discussing Italy).

[99] These are likely to be the subject of annual shareholder resolutions in any event: see para.13–6 and para.24–13.

[100] Which in the UK will often be required as part of the directors' remuneration report: see para.14–16.

[101] It does not necessarily follow that a private equity group will want to keep the existing management of the target in place. Conversely, a public bidder may be happy to keep the existing management, where it is buying the target for synergy reasons rather than because it thinks the target badly run.

to their detriment. We shall now look at the Code rules and more general provisions designed to deal with this issue, first where there is only one bid and, secondly, where there are competing bids.

Promoting the only bid

28–29   The Code and the general law use a number of different techniques for addressing the problem of conflicted promotion of a bid by target management.

Disclosure and independent advice

28–30   One technique used by the Code is to inject an element of independence into the advice which the board is required to give to the shareholders on any offer made to the shareholders by a bidder. Under Rule 3.1 the board is required to obtain competent independent advice[102] on any offer and the substance of that advice must be made known to the shareholders.[103] Independent advice is regarded as of particular importance on a management buyout or an offer by controlling shareholders.[104] However, Rule 25 requires the board to circulate its own opinion on the offer to the shareholders (that is, they cannot simply hide behind the independent advice). If the board of the target "is split in its views of an offer, the directors who are in a minority should also publish their views" and "the Panel will normally require that they be circulated by the [target] company".[105]

Where directors have a conflict of interest, they should not normally join with the other members of the board in expressing a view on the offer. In the case of a management buy-out, the director will normally be regarded as having a conflict of interest if he or she is to have a continuing role in either offeror or offeree company.[106] Thus, where the whole of the executive director team of the target is to be taken on by the bidder, the conduct of the target company's response falls on the non-executive directors and if, as happened in a recent case, the non-executives are conflicted because they are involved with the bidder as well, the chair of the board may become largely responsible for the target board's response to the bid. Some help is provided to the independent directors by Rule 20.3, which requires the offeror to provide to the independent directors, on request, all the information which the offeror has furnished to the potential external providers of finance in relation to the buy-out. This does something

---

[102] Normally from an investment bank not disqualified under r.3.3.

[103] A similar obligation applies to the board of the offeror when the offer is made in a "reverse takeover" (i.e. one in which the offeror may need to increase its issued voting equity share capital by more than 100 per cent: see n.2 to r.3.2) or when the directors are faced with a conflict of interests: r.3.2.

[104] r.3.1, Note 1.

[105] Note 2 to r.25.1.

[106] Note 4 to r.25.1.

to equalise the information available to the independent directors and the executive directors who are part of the bidding team. Overall, the formalisation of the distinction between executive and non-executive directors, which has come about in recent decades, is used by the Code to handle the most pressing examples of conflict of interest which might lead the board to promote a bid, though at the cost of the non-executive directors suddenly finding themselves more heavily involved in the affairs of the company than they probably contemplated when taking on that role.

Looking at these matters from the bidder's point of view, Rule 24.5 requires the bidder to disclose in its offer document "any agreement, arrangement or understanding" between it (or any person acting in concert with it) and any of the target's directors or recent directors which are connected with or dependent on the offer, giving full particulars of them. This would clearly include the details of any proposed arrangement concerning employment of the directors of the target in either the target or the offeror after the bid. Rule 16 requires Panel consent for special deals offered by the bidder to some shareholders where that deal is not being extended to all shareholders. This rule creates a potential problem for management buy-outs, where, as will be usual, the target management holds shares in the target company but is also part of the bidding entity and is being offered the special deal that it will continue to be involved in the running of the target if the bid is successful. In practice, the Panel does not apply Rule 16 to management buy-outs where the management of the target can be regarded as a joint bidder with the other bodies which are financing the bid. For this reason "joint offerors may make arrangements between themselves regarding the future membership, control and management of the business being acquired."[107]

Shareholder consent

A much cruder form of conflict of interest which gives rise to managerial promotion of a bid arises out of the compensation which a director expects to receive if the bid is successful and he or she is removed from office. The anticipation of a large windfall may shape the directors' response to the bid, consciously or unconsciously, and, moreover, a part of the consideration which the bidder is willing to pay for the target may be diverted to the directors. In those jurisdictions which allocate to the target board a major role in the determination of the fate of an offer, such monetary incentives to accept the bid may well be viewed with favour, as providing a counterweight to the alternative course of action of simply sitting tight. However, in the United Kingdom, where the decision on the

28–31

---

[107] Panel Statement 2003/25, *Canary Wharf Ltd*, para.12. But see n.4 to r.16 on incentive schemes.

fate of the bid is allocated primarily to the shareholders, such financial incentives for target directors have been viewed as distorting the direction of the consideration the bidder is willing to pay. The amount of compensation a director is entitled to if dismissed from office depends upon the terms of his or her contract, the regulation of which we discussed in Chapter 14 above. Moreover, Rule 25.4 requires the target's first circular to the shareholders to contain particulars of the directors' service contracts and of any earlier contract which has been replaced in the six months preceding the circulation. However, the statute goes further in relation to the making of gratuitous payments to directors upon loss of office after a takeover, over and above their contractual entitlements. These payments are in effect made by the bidder, even if the formal payer may be the target company after the bidder has acquired control of it. The regulatory technique here deployed is that of shareholder approval, a requirement the Companies Act have long contained.

Section 219(1) lays down the core requirement of shareholder consent for payments for loss of office to a director where such payments are made in connection with a takeover bid for the shares of the company or of a subsidiary. The inclusion of a takeover bid for the shares of a subsidiary might be important where there are outside minority shareholders in the subsidiary.[108] "Takeover bid" is not defined for the purpose of this section, and so it is unclear whether the section embraces a takeover effected by means of a scheme of arrangement or whether payments made in that context fall only within section 217, discussed below. However, "payment for loss of office" is defined. Section 215(1) includes payments for loss of any other office or employment in connection with the management of the company or of its subsidiaries, and payments made in connection with retirement from such offices or employment, paid to the director whilst he is director of the company or in connection with his ceasing to be director of it. This is a very important provision, since compensation payments are often made to executive directors in connection with the loss of their management positions in the company, rather than in connection with the loss of the directorship itself. For this reason, it is also sensible to bring shadow directors within the scope of section 219. Although loss of the status of shadow director itself is not within it, compensation payments for the loss of other offices or employment within the company will be caught.[109]

---

[108] s.219(6) makes it clear that approval is not required where compensation is paid in relation to the takeover of a wholly-owned subsidiary. The requirement for shareholder approval also applies only to payments by UK-registered companies.

[109] s.223. This might seem to mean that a company could escape the statutory controls by paying a shadow director compensation for loss of the shadow directorship. However, since the shadow directorship is not a formal position, payment for loss of it is likely to be a breach of duty on the part of the non-shadow directors and recoverable from the shadow director who has received it, knowing of the facts which make its payment improper.

On the other hand, payments made to the director "in discharge of an existing legal obligation"[110] are excluded from the approval requirement. This confirms the prior law which had taken the unsatisfactory view that expressly negotiated payments which were triggered upon a change of control in the company were not caught by the equivalent provisions in earlier companies legislation.[111] The payment of such sums (sometimes referred to as "covenanted payments") is now, however, subject to the qualification that the obligation "was not entered into for the purpose of, in connection with or in consequence of" the takeover".[112] Thus, covenanted payments entered into in the face of a bid (even, in appropriate circumstances, before the bid is formally announced) will need shareholder approval. Otherwise, they are to be regulated by the general provisions on directors remuneration, as discussed in Chapter 14. Also excepted from the need for shareholder approval are payments to the director by way of damages for breach of such an obligation or by way of settlement of a claim arising in connection with the termination of a director's office or employment. Thus, payments to directors, especially executive directors, by way of compensation for breach of contract (for example, dismissal without proper notice) or which are due to directors under statutory employment law (for example, the law of unfair dismissal) or settlements of claims for such payments will not need shareholder approval.[113] Again, the contractual entitlements of directors upon termination are determined mainly by the notice or term provisions in their contracts, which are regulated by the general provisions on directors' remuneration. Thus, the overall purpose of the provisions is to subject to shareholder approval gratuitous payments made to directors for loss of office upon a takeover, but also to include within that category contractual entitlements generated in order to facilitate the particular offer in question. Finally, payments "by way of pension in respect of past services" are exempted from the need for shareholder approval,[114] apparently even if they are gratuitous. This is a potentially large loop-hole, since directors towards the end of their careers may positively welcome compensation payments which take the form of a pension.

As is inevitable with statutory provisions of this kind, the drafters **28–32** need to anticipate avoiding action which may be taken by those to

---

[110] s.220(1)(a).

[111] *Taupo Totara Timber Co v Rowe* [1978] A.C. 537, PC; *Lander v Premier Pict Petroleum* 1997 S.L.T. 1361. In the former case the director's service contract provided that, if the company were taken over, he could within twelve months resign from the company and become entitled to a lump-sum payment of five times his annual salary.

[112] s.220(3).

[113] s.220(1)(b), (c). Such payments must be made "in good faith" and so the parties to the transaction run a legal risk if they use a damages claim to inflate the compensation payable to the director beyond his or her contractual or statutory entitlements.

[114] s.220(1)(d). Again the payment must be made "in good faith", which may constrain egregious use of this provision.

whom the provisions are intended to apply. Thus, although the payer is typically the target company after the takeover has succeeded, the requirement for shareholder approval applies to payments for loss of office made by "any person".[115] This will clearly include payments by a parent company (i.e. the successful bidder) or a subsidiary of the target. Payments to a director include payments to a person connected with a director and payments to any person at the direction or on behalf of the director or connected person.[116] Payments are rebuttably presumed to be payments for loss of office if made in pursuance of an arrangement (not necessarily a contract) made within the period extending from one year before to two years after the transfer of the shares and either bidder or target is privy to the arrangement.[117] If the price paid to the director for his or her shares is in excess of that available to other shareholders or if, in connection with the transfer of the shares, any valuable consideration is given to the director by any person, the excess is irrebuttably treated as a payment for loss of office.[118] Finally, compensation is treated as including benefits otherwise than in cash, though cash is in fact the typical form of compensation provided.[119] On the other hand, there is a *de minimis* exception for payments by the company or its subsidiaries where the amount or value of the payment does not exceed £200, a very small amount.[120]

The shareholders whose consent is required are those to whom the bid relates, since they are the persons whose consideration is potentially reduced by the payment to the directors.[121] Obtaining such consent may be problematic indeed in the case of payments made under an arrangement entered into after the transfer of the shares (which, as noted, are rebuttably presumed to be payments for loss of office) and in such cases the requirement for shareholder consent may operate in practice as a prohibition on such payments.[122] Even in the course of the bid the bidder and target management may regard holding a meeting to obtain shareholder approval as a very unwelcome distraction, although it is possible for the approval to be sought by way of a written resolution in the case where the target company is

---

[115] s.219(1).
[116] s.215(3). The definition of a connected person is given in s.252 and discussed above at para.16–51.
[117] s.219(7). The date of the transfer of the shares is presumably the date upon which the bid became unconditional as to acceptances.
[118] s.216.
[119] s.215(2).
[120] s.221. The Secretary of State has power to raise the figure: s.258.
[121] s.219(2). Holders of shares of the same class also participate in the vote, even if not included in the offer, a very rare situation. The bidder itself will be excluded from voting shares held by it before the bid was launched: see below.
[122] Unlike s.315(1) of the CA 1985, s.219 does not require shareholder approval before the transfer of shares under the offer but only before the payment is made. However, failure to achieve a quorum at two successive meetings triggers the rule that the payment is deemed to have been approved: s.219(5).

a private company. Information about the proposed payment, notably its amount, must be made available to the shareholders in advance of the vote.[123] Neither bidder nor any associate may vote on the resolution, though they may attend and speak at a meeting of the shareholders.[124] Where a payment is made without shareholder approval, then it is treated as held on trust by the recipient for those who have sold their shares as a result of the offer and the expenses of making the distribution to those entitled to it are to be borne by the recipient.[125] Here, therefore, the legislation has avoided the absurdity illustrated in *Regal (Hastings) Ltd v Gulliver*,[126] by providing restitution to those truly damnified, rather than to the company when, in effect, that would result in an undeserved reduction of the price that the successful offeror has paid.

For the sake of completeness, it should be mentioned that section 217 applies similar provisions for shareholder consent in relation to payments for loss of office by a company to a director or a director of its holding company, unless the payment has been approved by the shareholders of the company and, if appropriate, its holding company, whether that payment is made in connection with a takeover or not. Clearly, a payment for loss of office in a takeover context could contravene this section as well, and so it is made clear that the specific takeover provision takes precedence where both apply.[127] This is important because a payment made in breach of the general requirement is held on trust for the company, not the selling shareholders.[128] Finally, shareholder approval is required for loss-of-office payments made on the transfer of the whole or a part of the company's undertaking.[129] Although economically similar, a transfer of control of assets by transferring the assets themselves rather than control of the company which owns the assets is legally a very different thing, and need not be further considered here.

Competing bids

One post-bid defensive measure which the Code does permit is the search by the target board for an alternative bidder. Such action is **28-33**

---

[123] s.219(3). The director is no longer under a statutory obligation, as was the case with the 1985 Act, to take all reasonable steps to secure that details of the proposed payment are included in the offer document, though r.24.5 (above) of the Code requires the offeror to include such information.

[124] s.219(4). The definition of "associate" is given in s.988 and is discussed below. The bidder's shares will not normally be a shares "to which the bid relates" though that is not necessarily true of associates' shares.

[125] s.222(3).

[126] See para.16–65 above.

[127] s.222(5).

[128] s.222(1). For this reason, it would seem that a takeover effected by way of a scheme of arrangement should be within s.219, for otherwise the payments will not be held on behalf of the selling shareholders, who have suffered the loss, at least potentially.

[129] s.218.

not held to breach the non-frustration rule, because the decision on the bids still rests with the shareholders of the target company, whose choices have in fact been widened by the presence of the so-called "white knight". The Directive makes it clear that "seeking alternative bids" is not caught by the prohibition on post-bid defensive action.[130] However, conflicts of interest on the part of the target board may arise here also, either because the board wishes to discourage a competitor because its interests will be better served by the initial bidder or, vice versa, where the target board seeks a competitor because it does not favour the initial bidder. Of course, in either case the board's decisions may be driven by a desire to promote the interests of the shareholders of the target, rather than the directors' interests, and so the Code and other rules need to focus on this problem with some degree of sophistication. Another troublesome question is whether it is, in fact, in the interests of the shareholders to encourage competing bids. In the context of a particular offer, that is clearly so, since the competitor drives up the price on offer and may even trigger an auction. However, the initial bidder often loses out in the auction, thus throwing away the costs it has incurred in identifying a target and mounting a bid. Knowing of this risk, companies may be less willing to bid initially than if they could be sure that there would be no competitor, thus reducing the incidence of bids, arguably to the detriment of shareholders. It is thus conceivable that the encouragement of competing bids would mean fewer bids overall. In this situation, devising an appropriate policy for competing bids is not easy.

A duty to auction or a duty to be even-handed?

28–34 One policy, at one end of the spectrum, would be to require the target board to seek out any available competing offers. In bid situations there will often be pressure from investors on the board of the target to do this. However, the Code itself contains no such obligation. In the case-law on fiduciary duties the question has sometimes arisen, but the upshot of that limited case-law seems to amount to no more than the proposition that, if a competing bid does in fact emerge, the directors may not obstruct the shareholders from accepting the bid they prefer, but the directors are not obliged to further that offer by, for example, assenting their own shares to it. In *Heron International Ltd v Lord Grade*[131] there were two competing bids for a company whose directors held over 50 percent of the shares and where, unusually for a public company, the consent of the directors was required for the transfer of shares. The directors had given irrevocable undertakings to accept what turned out to be the lower bid and stood

---

[130] Art.9(2).
[131] [1983] B.C.L.C. 244, CA.

by those undertakings, so that the higher bidder was defeated. The Court of Appeal declared that:

> "Where directors have decided that it is in the best interests of a company that the company should be taken over and there are two or more bidders the only duty of the directors, who have powers such as those in [the company's articles], is to obtain the best price. The directors should not commit themselves to transfer their own voting shares to a bidder unless they are satisfied that he is offering the best price reasonably available."[132]

This dictum clearly suggests that the directors' freedom to assent their own shares to the bidder favoured by them is restricted by their duty as directors to the other shareholders. In *A Company, Re*,[133] where a similar issue arose in the context of a s.459 petition but involving this time a small private company, Hoffmann J., however, refused to accept "the proposition that the board must inevitably be under a positive duty to recommend and take all steps within their power to facilitate whichever is the highest offer", especially where that alleged duty restricted the directors' freedom of action in relation to their own shares. Their duty went no further than requiring them not to exercise their powers under the articles so as to prevent those other shareholders, who wished to do so, from accepting the higher offer, and requiring them, if they gave advice to the shareholders, to do so in the interests of those shareholders and not in order to further the bid preferred by the directors.

The view of Hoffmann J. seems more in accord with generally accepted principles of fiduciary law and with the Code which, as we have seen above, requires the directors to give advice to the shareholders in order to promote the interests of the latter, but stops short of requiring directors to take decisions in relation to their shares other than in their own interests. More generally, in relation to the exercise of directorial discretion the Code can be said to adopt the policy of requiring the directors to be even-handed as between competing bids: they are not required to seek out alternative offers but, if such emerge, the choice between them should be one for the shareholders. This can be seen as an application or, perhaps, extension of the "no frustration" principle in the context of competing bids. The central provision here is Rule 20.2 which requires the target board to provide information to an offeror or potential offeror which it has made available to another offeror or potential offeror "even if that other offeror is less welcome". This is an important provision, because, as we shall see below, the target board is not normally under an obligation to provide information to a potential bidder to help it

---

[132] [1983] B.C.L.C. 244, at 265.
[133] [1986] B.C.L.C. 382.

decide whether to make an offer or on what terms. However, if the board decides to do so for one offeror or potential offeror, it cannot refuse this facility to a competitor. This principle is applied not only to the information itself but also to the terms on which it is made available (for example, confidentiality requirements). However, the rule does not permit the competitor to ask simply for all the information given to the initial offeror: the competitor has to specify the questions to which it wants answers, and the target company must answer them if it has done so for the other bidder.[134] There is an obvious difficulty in applying this rule in relation to a management buy-out, because the existing management element of the bidder will have comprehensive knowledge of the target company. Note 3 to Rule 20.2 confines the disclosure obligation in such a case to the information provided to the external providers of finance for the buy-out bid.

28–35   Quite apart from regulation of the conduct of the target board towards competing bidders, the question can be asked whether the design of the takeover Code facilitates the emergence of competitors. In many ways it does, though mainly as a side-wind from the implementation of policies designed to further other goals. Thus, as we shall see below, the timetable for the offer (the gap between the initial approach and the formal offer, the need for the formal offer to be open for a minimum period of time) does create a space in which competing bidders have the opportunity to put together an alternative offer. The offeror may seek to dilute this risk by buying shares in the target on the market in advance of the public announcement of the approach or offer. The insider dealing legislation is so drafted as not to catch a bidder who buys shares in the market knowing that it intends to make a bid at a higher price in the near future.[135] Nevertheless, market purchases on any scale are likely to drive up the price of the potential target's shares very rapidly. Alternatively, the bidder may deal privately with the larger shareholders in the target (if there are any) and seek their agreement, in advance of the bid, to accept an offer if one is made (i.e. to give what are known as "irrevocable commitments"). However, those who give such commitments normally in fact reserve the right to withdraw the acceptance if a competitor emerges. More simply, the bidder might simply seek to buy the shares of any large shareholders in advance of the bid, but their willingness to sell might be forthcoming only in situations where they

---

[134] Note 1 to r.20.2.
[135] See paras 30–25 and 30–39.

think the company is unlikely to attract rival bids.[136] Moreover, as we shall see below, pre-bid purchases may restrict the freedom of the bidder to determine the level of its offer. Overall, the Code does expose a bidder to a significant risk that a rival bid will emerge.[137]

Binding the target board by contract

In this situation, the initial bidder may seek, by contract, to enlist the   **28–36** directors of the target on its side in dealing with any future competitor. There are two contractual techniques which have been used to this end, though obviously they are potentially available only where the target board approves of the proposed bid. First, the initial bidder may wish to secure from the directors of the target company a legally binding undertaking to recommend the bid to the shareholders of the target in any event and not to seek, encourage or co-operate with any "white knight". Such an agreement with the directors is not necessarily against the interests of the target's shareholders, for the initial bidder may not be willing to make a bid at all for the target unless such undertakings are forthcoming. The courts, however, have been unwilling to give full effect to such agreements, especially the commitment always to recommend the initial offer, even if a better one emerges, whilst offering a variety of rationales for their reluctance.

In one case, the Outer House of the Court of Session held that an agreement not to seek, co-operate with or recommend a competing bid, in the context of the (then) self-regulatory code, was not to be construed as an agreement which the parties intended to be legally binding.[138] This, however, is a relatively weak regulatory tool, since it can be overridden if the parties make it clear they do intend to create a legally binding agreement. A stronger argument is that such an agreement contravenes the rule that the directors must not fetter the

---

[136] R.5 of the Code forbids pre-bid purchases (at least once a bid is in contemplation) which would take the bidder over the 30 per cent threshold, which triggers a mandatory bid (see below), or over the 50 per cent threshold, giving de jure control of the company, except purchases from a single shareholder (and in certain other cases). The purpose of r.5 is to ensure that "the board of the company has a sufficient opportunity to make the company's shareholders aware of all relevant matters before control of the company passes." See Panel Consultation Paper 2005/5, para.6.1. (However, the rules on Substantial Acquisitions of Shares, which previously formed an addendum to the Code and prevented, or at least slowed down, market raids, were repealed in 2006.)

[137] However, the Code does not encourage competing bids, as some systems do, by automatically releasing those who have accepted the offer if a competing bidder emerges, but only if the offer has not become unconditional as to acceptances within 21 days of the first closing date of the initial offer (r.34). For this reason, experienced investors do not accept an offer until the final moment, so as to be able freely to consider competing offers, whilst those who find the terms of the offer attractive may simply sell their shares in the market. On the other hand, once a competing bidder emerges, the bid timetable is re-set for both offerors according to that appropriate for the competitor (see n.4 to r.31.6) so that the offer period is extended to give target company shareholders adequate time to consider both offers.

[138] *Dawson International Plc v Coats Paton Plc* [1991] B.C.C. 278.

exercise of their discretion. However, as we have seen, the proposition that "the directors can never bind themselves as to the future exercise of their fiduciary powers" has been rejected by the Court of Appeal in *Fulham Football Club Ltd v Cabra Estates Plc*[139] and section 173(2) now provides that the duty to exercise independent judgment is not infringed by a director "acting in accordance with an agreement duly entered into by the company that restricts the future exercise of discretion by its directors". However, in the *Fulham* case, the Court of Appeal stopped short of overruling earlier cases in which directors' undertakings to secure necessary shareholder approval of corporate decisions were regarded as subject to the limitation that the directors were obliged to abide by their undertakings only so long as they continued to hold the genuine belief that the transaction was in the interests of the shareholders.[140] Moreover, section 173(2) does not in terms apply to section 172, laying down the directors' core duty of loyalty, thus leaving open the argument that the director can bind him- or herself to act in the future only in a way which is consistent with the core duty. However this conflict is ultimately resolved, there is a lot to be said for not permitting directors to bind themselves to give advice of a particular kind on a bid to the shareholders in the future, if the directors no longer believe that advice to be consistent with their core duty of loyalty when they come to give it. To hold otherwise is to undermine both the basic allocation of decision-making power on the fate of the bid to the shareholders and General Principle 2 of the Code that the shareholders must be given the information necessary to enable them to reach a properly informed decision on the bid.

Given the uncertainties surrounding agreements which seek to control the target board's actions towards competing bidders, it is not surprising that alternative contractual arrangements have been developed. A common form of agreement is the "break fee" or "inducement fee", i.e. an agreement between the target company (through its directors) and the initial bidder that, if the bidder's offer is not accepted for one of a number of reasons, which might include the shareholders' acceptance of an alternative offer, the target company becomes liable to pay a sum of money to the disappointed bidder. In this way, the initial bidder seeks to protect itself against the

---

[139] [1994] 1 B.C.L.C. 363, CA. The case concerned an agreement made for a substantial consideration by the football company with a property developer whereby the former undertook to maintain a particular attitude towards planning proposals in relation to land owned by the development company but leased to the football company, from which agreement the football company subsequently wished to resile. However, in this case, unlike in the shareholder approval cases, the decision which the contract sought to regulate was a decision of the directors, not of the shareholders. See above at para.16–38.

[140] *Rackham v Peek Foods Ltd* [1990] B.C.L.C. 895; *John Crowther Group Ltd v Carpets International Plc* [1990] B.C.L.C. 460. See also the decision of the Inner House in the interlocutory proceedings in the *Dawson* case: (1989) 5 B.C.C. 405. It is to some degree unclear in these cases whether the result was arrived at as a matter of interpretation of the contract in question or of the application of a mandatory rule of the law of directors' duties.

financial costs of its failed bid. However, the effect of a large break fee may be to discourage a competing bidder, since it effectively reduces the value of the target in the hands of the competitor, but not in the hands of the bidder which has negotiated the break fee. Consequently, the negotiation of a break fee can operate as frustrating action in relation to a potential competing bid, and so Rule 21.2 of the Code puts a cap on the level of the fee (or similar inducement) at one per cent of the offer price.[141] The board and its financial adviser must also confirm in writing to the Panel that they believe the fee arrangement to be in the best interests of the target's shareholders, and, of course, it must be publicly disclosed. It is unclear how the statutory rules on financial assistance apply to such fees. Although the fee is payable only if the bidder's acquisition of the target's shares fails, the agreement for the fee could nevertheless be regarded as entered into for the purpose of the acquisition (as section 678 requires).[142]

EQUALITY OF TREATMENT OF TARGET SHAREHOLDERS

Once an offeror makes an offer to the target's shareholders, whether **28–37** with the support of or against the indifference or hostility of the target company's management, a further set of regulatory concerns arises which the Code must address. In essence, the bidder will want to acquire the shares as cheaply as possible and the target shareholders to sell them as dearly as possible. To a large extent, the decision on the price to be offered, and whether it should subsequently be revised upwards, can be left to the judgment of the bidder and to the play of market forces. Certainly, "the Code is not concerned with the financial or commercial advantages or disadvantages of a takeover".[143] However, the bidder's freedom to structure the bid as it pleases might result in shareholders of the target being pressurised into accepting an offer they do not think is optimal. For this reason the Code puts some limits on the terms the bidder may offer to the shareholders, and, since its early days, has had resort to the notion of equal treatment of target shareholders to express its policy in this regard, a notion which has now been developed to a considerable degree of sophistication. Reflecting the Directive, GP 1 of

---

[141] See also Panel Practice Statement No.4 of 2004.
[142] Financial assistance is considered at paras 13–26ff. On the application of the prohibition in this particular context see H. Tarbert, "Merger Breakup Fees: A Critical Challenge to Anglo-American Corporate Law" (2003) 34 *Law and Policy in International Business* 627. It is arguable that financial assistance given in this way falls only within the catch-all provision of "any other financial assistance" which is unlawful only if the net assets of the company giving it are reduced "to a material extent" (s.677(1)(d)), which a 1% commitment does not generate.
[143] Code, *Introduction*, A1.

the Code stipulates that "all holders of the securities of an offeree company of the same class must be afforded equivalent treatment" but the Rules in fact go beyond this. The equality principle, in all its manifestations, is another demonstration that, whilst the Code facilitates takeovers, it does not make the maximisation of the number of bids its goal, for otherwise it would permit offerors to pay more to those who agree early in the process to accept the offer made to them.

Voluntary offers

28–38   Under Rule 14, when the target company has more than one class of equity share capital a "comparable" offer[144] must be made for each, whether it carries voting rights or not. Thus, an offeror company may not bid only for equity shares carrying voting rights but must bid for all classes of equity share. This reflects the policy that a change of control in a company is a significant event for equity shareholders (whose returns depend on the discretion and success of the controllers) and so all such shareholders should be given the opportunity to exit the company on fair terms when a change of control is in prospect.[145] When such an offer is made for more than one class of shares, separate offers must be made for each class. The offer for the non-voting equity must not be made conditional upon any particular level of acceptances by that class, unless the offer for the voting shares is conditional upon that same level of acceptances by the non-voting equity shareholders. In other words, the non-voting equity shareholders may not be left locked into the target if the offeror company obtains control by acquiring a sufficient proportion of the voting equity. However, the offeror can protect itself against ending up with a majority of the non-voting equity but too little of the voting equity by inserting identical conditions, relating to the non-voting equity, into both (or all) offers.

In a voluntary bid, classes of non-equity shares need not be the subject of an offer, even if they carry voting rights. Of course, an offeror company may wish to make an offer for non-equity shares carrying voting rights, but an offer is not required, presumably on the theory that the non-equity shareholders are normally protected by their contractual entitlements.[146] However, Rule 15 requires that, on an offer for voting equity share capital, an appropriate offer or proposal must be made to holders of securities convertible into equity shares (who clearly are potentially affected by the change of control).

---

[144] Notes to r.14 make it clear that comparable is not the same as identical and that normally the difference between the offers should reflect the differences in market prices over the previous six months. "Equity share capital" seems to be as defined in CA 2006, s.548. See para.23–7.

[145] See further in relation to mandatory bids, below.

[146] See Ch.24, above.

Further, in some circumstances the Code determines the level of consideration which is required to be offered for the shares, if an offer is made. The purpose of these equality rules is to prevent the offeror from distorting the decision of the target's shareholders by offering an attractive price to some shareholders to gain control whilst offering an inadequate price to the remainder, who have the choice of accepting the low offer or being locked into the company under a new controller. The first and most obvious expression of the equality principle is to be found in the requirement that, if the offer is revised upwards after an initial offer at a lower level, the original acceptors are entitled to the higher consideration.[147] This rule probably does more to protect inexperienced shareholders than to prevent opportunistic behaviour on the part of offeror companies. More important in this regard is the rule requiring the initial offer to be open for acceptance for at least 21 days[148] and revised offers to be open for at least 14 days.[149] Both rules prevent an offeror from putting undue pressure on the target shareholders by making an attractive offer which is to be open for only a very short time and which will close before the shareholders have had a chance to assess its merits. Finally, on this aspect, we should note again Rule 16, whereby, except with the consent of the Panel, the offeror may not make any special arrangements, either during an offer or when one is reasonably in contemplation, whereby favourable conditions are offered to some shareholders which are not extended to all of them.[150]

A more significant expression of the equality principle is between **28–39** those who accept the offer and those who sell their shares to the offeror outside the offer, either before the offer is made or during it. Again, Rule 6 of the Code seeks to prevent private and favourable deals being done with a few selected shareholders. An offeror (or person acting in concert) which purchases shares of a class in the three months before the offer period[151] or during that period[152] must either make or raise the level of the offer for that class to that paid outside it, if it is higher.[153] However, Rule 6 distinguishes between purchases made before the offer period begins and those made after a firm intention to make an offer has been announced. In relation to

---

[147] r.32.3.
[148] r.31.1.
[149] r.32.1.
[150] Note 1 makes it clear that this bans the not-unknown practice of buying a shareholding coupled with an undertaking to make good to the seller any difference between the sale price and the higher price of any successful subsequent bid. It also covers (Note 3) cases where a shareholder of the target company is to be remunerated for the part he has played in promoting the offer ("a finder's fee").
[151] r.6.1 Or even earlier if the Panel thinks this is necessary to give effect to General Principle 1: r.6.1(c).
[152] r.6.2.
[153] Before an announcement is made of a firm intention to make an offer the Panel has a discretion to relax the rule, though it will do so only rarely, but not thereafter. Compare rr.6.1 and 6.2.

purchases made beforehand, it is clear that the rule does not necessarily require that the offer be in cash even if the prior acquisitions
have been for cash. To that extent, Rule 6 permits inequality: the
offer later made may be on a share-exchange basis but the securities
offered by the bidder must have the value equal to the highest consideration paid outside the offer. However, if the post-announcement
acquisitions at above the offer price are for cash, the offer will have to
be (or become) a cash offer or be accompanied by a cash
alternative.[154]

However, even in respect of acquisitions made before the offer
period, the subsequent offer will have to be in cash (or accompanied
by an alternative cash offer, probably provided by the offeror's
investment bank rather than the offeror itself), if the conditions of
Rule 11.1 are met. Where the offeror and persons acting in concert
acquire "for cash" shares of a class in the target company, which
carry at least 10 per cent of the voting rights of the class, in the 12
months prior to the offer, the subsequent offer must be in cash or be
accompanied by a cash alternative at the highest level of the prices
paid outside the offer.[155] In this rule "cash" has an extended meaning
in its application to acquisitions "for cash", though it bears its
ordinary meaning in relation to the requirement that the offer be "in
cash". It includes acquisitions by the offeror company in exchange for
securities, unless the vendor to the acquirer is not free to dispose of
the securities until the offerees in the general bid receive their consideration (or the offer lapses).[156] The thinking is that, since securities
are saleable, they are the equivalent of cash. The overall effect of Rule
11.1 is that the offer must be in cash or accompanied by a cash
alternative because the sellers prior to the bid have received cash (or
its equivalent). The rule is triggered only at the 10 per cent level and
so it can be argued that r.11.1 is not a full implementation of the
equality principle. Beneath the 10 per cent threshold, Rule 6.1
applies, not normally requiring a cash offer. The contrary argument is
that a stronger rule would discourage bids because bidders would
either have to forgo pre-bid acquisitions or always launch cash bids
where they had made previous acquisitions for cash. Building up a
pre-bid stake is a way of obtaining some degree of protection against
a competing offer, either because the stake will deter a competitor or
because, if the initial bidder fails, it can recoup some of its costs by
selling its stake at a profit to the successful bidder.

What Rule 11.1 does not deal with is the converse case, i.e. where
the prior acquisitions were in exchange for securities but the bid is in

---

[154] Note 3 to r.6. For this reason some systems prohibit post-offer purchases outside the bid if
the offer is on a share-exchange basis.
[155] The Panel has a discretion to apply the cash rule even if fewer than 10 per cent of the voting
rights have been acquired (see r.11.1(c)), something Note 4 to r.11.1 suggests it might do,
and at a considerably lower level than 10 per cent, if the vendors were directors of the target.
[156] See Note 5 to r.11.1.

cash and the target shareholders claim they should be offered the securities provided in the prior acquisitions. This is a rarer situation than the one where the general offerees claim cash, because cash is in general more attractive than securities, but there might be exceptional circumstances where the securities were attractive but not readily available on the market. In the light of this, a new rule was introduced in 2002, similar, but not identical, to Rule 11.1, but requiring securities to be offered in the general bid. Under Rule 11.2, if, during the three months prior to the commencement of the offer and during the offer period, the offeror has acquired shares of a class in the target which carry 10 per cent of the voting rights of the class in exchange for securities, then the general bid must offer the same number[157] of securities to the target shareholders. However, this will not displace the obligation to offer cash or a cash alternative under Rule 11.1, if the securities accepted outside the bid have triggered Rule 11.1.[158] Rule 11.2 is less far-reaching than the combined effect of Rules 6.2 and 11.1 because it is triggered only by the 10 per cent threshold (even if the securities have been offered during the bid) and because it reaches back only to the three months before the bid.

Mandatory offers

The strongest expression of the equality rule, however, is to be found **28–40** in the mandatory bid rule. Here, a bidder is obliged to make an offer in a situation where it has already obtained de facto control of the company and might not therefore wish to make a general offer to the shareholders of a company it already controls. However, because the sellers to the new controller were able to exit the company upon a change of control, the Code requires the remaining shareholders to be given the same opportunity. A mandatory bid rule is now required of Member States by Article 5 of the Takeover Directive. This led to some minor changes to the Code rules, though in general the mandatory bid rule contained in the Code is tougher than that required by the Directive. Under Rule 9.1 when:

(a) any person acquires an interest in shares which (with any shares held or acquired by any persons acting in concert) carry 30 per cent or more of the voting rights of a company; or

(b) any person who, with persons acting in concert, already holds not less than 30 per cent but not more than 50 per cent of the voting rights and who, alone or with persons acting in concert, acquires an interest in additional shares which increase the percentage of the voting rights held; then,

---

[157] Which may not now have the same value as when offered prior to the offer: see Note 1 to r.11.2.

[158] See fn.156, above.

unless the Panel otherwise consents, such a person must extend offers, on the basis set out in subsequent provisions of Rule 9, to the holders of any class of equity share capital, whether voting or non-voting, and also to the holders of any other class of transferable securities carrying voting rights (though the non-equity security carrying voting rights is not often found in practice) Offers for the different classes of equity share capital must be comparable and the Panel should be consulted in advance.

The effect of this is that, once acquisitions have secured "control" (circumstance (a)) or acquisitions have been made to consolidate control[159] (circumstance (b)) a general offer must be made, thus giving shareholders an opportunity of quitting the company and sharing in the price paid for the control or its consolidation. However, the force of the requirement lies not in the obligation to make an offer by itself, but in the supplementary rules which determine the nature of the offer which has to be made. After all, an obligation to make an offer which none of the offerees would find attractive would be a futile gesture on the part of the rule-maker. Crucial here are the requirements that a mandatory offer must be a cash offer, or with a cash alternative, in respect of each class of shares and at the highest price paid by the offeror or a member of his concert party within the past 12 months prior to the commencement of the offer.[160] On a voluntary offer this is so only if shares were purchased for cash and carried 10 per cent or more of the voting rights of that class, or if the Panel considers that it is necessary in order to give effect to General Principle 1.[161] In addition, a mandatory bid must not contain any conditions other than that it is dependent on acceptances being such as to result in the bidder holding 50 per cent of the voting rights;[162] on a voluntary offer, there may well be further conditions.[163]

---

[159] In the case of consolidation, the holder will necessarily have been able to cross the 30 per cent threshold without triggering the mandatory bid, notably where it falls into one of the exceptions discussed below. The Code used to allow consolidation of control at the rate of 1 per cent a year without imposing a mandatory bid requirement. However, this facility was removed, seemingly in response to the decision in *Astec (BSR) Plc, Re* [1998] 2 B.C.L.C. 556, in which the court took a narrow view of the application of the unfair prejudice remedy in relation to future actions of a shareholder which had obtained "creeping control" of a company under this facility. In this case the target company was non-resident in the UK, and so not subject to the Code when it acquired 45 per cent of the target, but it then entered into an agreement with the other investors under which it made itself subject to the Code. Today, the company's initial purchase would be subject to the Code since the company was incorporated in the UK and its shares were traded on the Main Market of the LSE, and the fact that its headquarters were in Hong Kong would not put it outside the Code. See above, para.28–13.

[160] r.9.5. Unless the Panel agrees to an adjusted price in a particular case: see r.9.5, Note 3, r.9.3.

[161] r.11.1. Then, too, the Panel has a discretion to agree an adjusted price: r.11.3.

[162] r.9.3. But, when the mandatory offer comes within the provisions for a possible reference to the competition authorities, it must be a condition of the offer that it will lapse if that occurs. But, in contrast with voluntary offers (r.12), it *must* be revived if the merger is allowed and, if it is prohibited, the Panel may require the offeror to reduce its holdings to below 30 per cent: r.9.4, Note 1.

[163] e.g. on a share for share offer that it is conditional on the passing of a resolution by members of the offeror to increase its issued capital.

Furthermore, where directors of the target company (or their close relatives and family trusts) sell shares to a purchaser as a result of which the purchaser is required by Rule 9 to make a mandatory offer, the directors must ensure that, as a condition of the sale, the purchaser undertakes to fulfil its obligations under the rule and, except with the consent of the Panel, the directors must not resign from the board until the closing date of the offer or the date when it becomes wholly unconditional, whichever is the later. Further, whether the directors have been involved on the sell side of the acquisition or not, a nominee of the new controller may not be appointed to the board of the target company nor may it exercise the votes attached to any shares it holds in the target company until the formal offer document has been posted.[164]

The mandatory bid requirement of the Code is one of its out- **28–41** standing features. It could clearly have a major financial impact upon a company or concert party which exceeds the 30 per cent threshold and finds itself subject to an obligation to make a general offer. Especially this is so because there is no element in the rule that the obligation bites only if the acquirer has been in some sense "at fault": an accidental exceeding of the threshold is in principle enough to trigger the obligation.[165] Moreover, the level at which the bid has to be pitched (the highest level of the pre-bid acquisitions) also applies in principle[166] even if the market subsequently declines before the general offer is made. In this situation, a great deal of attention comes to be focused on the Panel's discretion to exempt acquirers, wholly or partly, from the mandatory bid obligation, which the notes to Rule 9 indicate it is prepared to do in certain circumstances, sometimes on its own decision and sometimes only if a majority of the shareholders of the potential target company agree, though these notes do not constrain the Panel's discretion to grant exemptions in other cases.

For example, if an acquirer envisages that a particular financial operation, such as a placing, will take it over the 30 per cent limit, it may escape the obligation to bid if it puts in place in advance firm arrangements to place the shares with non-connected parties within a very short period after their acquisition.[167] Again, a redemption or repurchase by a company of its shares may take a shareholder over

---

[164] r.9.6 and 9.7.

[165] But see text below.

[166] See Note 3 to r.9.5 for the factors the Panel will take into account in considering whether to grant a dispensation from the highest price rule. For a strong example of the application of the "highest price" rule, even in the face of a serious market decline triggered by the terrorist bombings in New York, see Panel Statement 2001/15 (WPP Group Plc).

[167] Note 7 to r.9.1. Notes 8 to 15 deal with a number of other cases where dispensation may be granted, for example, indirect acquisitions of controlling interests, convertible securities, further acquisitions after a reduction of the holding below 30 per cent; share lending arrangements.

the 30 per cent mark without the shareholder having taken any action at all. This situation is given a Rule of its own (Rule 37), in which the Panel states that it will normally[168] waive the bid obligation, provided the Panel is consulted in advance and the independent shareholders of the target agree and the stringenxst "whitewash" procedure (set out in Appendix 1 to the Code) is followed. Finally, a Note on Dispensations from Rule 9, appended to the Rule, lists six situations where a mandatory bid is not normally required, either because the policy behind the Rule has not in truth been infringed or because it is subordinated to other policies regarded as of greater value to the company and its shareholders. Into the first category fall (a) inadvertent mistakes, provided the holding is brought below the threshold within a limited period; and (b) situations where, in addition to the person who would otherwise be required to launch a mandatory bid, another single person holds 50 per cent of the voting rights (so that the acquisition of the 30 per cent or more did not in fact confer control on the acquirer).[169]

Into the second category fall situations where the 30 per cent threshold is breached as a result of (c) a rescue operation of a company in a serious financial position, even if the independent shareholders of the target have not approved the acquisitions, since insolvency is a more serious threat to shareholder wellbeing than a new controller; (d) where a lender enforces its rights and acquires shares given as security (for otherwise the value of shares as collateral would be undermined); (e) where a holding of more than 30 per cent of the voting rights results from an enfranchisement of previously non-voting shares (showing that enfranchisement is to be encouraged); and (f) where a company issues new shares either for cash or in exchange for an acquisition, provided a majority of the independent shareholders agree to removal of the bid obligation, through what is known as the "whitewash" procedure.[170] This last covers a variety of situations, including that where an offeror company makes a share exchange offer as a result of which a large shareholder in the target, who is perhaps already a significant shareholder in the offeror, ends up with more than 30 per cent of the combined entity.[171] Thus, the

---

[168] But not if the person seeking the waiver bought shares in the target company after the point at which it had reason to believe that a redemption or repurchase would take place: Note 2 to r.37.1.

[169] Dispensation Notes 4 and 5. Note 5 also waives the bid where the holders of 50 per cent of the voting rights indicate they would not accept the bid, no matter by how many people those rights are held.

[170] Dispensation Notes 3, 2, 6 and 1 respectively. In the case of (d) the security must not have been taken at a time when the lender had reason to believe that enforcement was likely, and of (e) the shares must not have been purchased at a time when the purchaser had reason to believe that enfranchisement was likely. The "whitewash" procedure is set out in Appendix 1 of the Code, which involves tight Panel control over the procedure.

[171] In the case of entities of equal size, this could occur if a person held 15 per cent of the voting rights of both offeror and target companies.

mandatory bid rule, although strictly formulated in Rule 9, is applied with some flexibility by the Panel.

Acting in concert and interests in shares

Although the definition of "acting in concert" is relevant to the **28–42** percentage tests used in all the rules which implement the equality principle, the consequences of the mandatory bid rule focus particular attention on the concept in this context. Indeed, in its introduction to the notes on Rule 9.1 the Code states that "the majority of questions which arise in the context of Rule 9 relate to persons acting in concert", and the notes then provide five pages of guidance on the concept in the context of Rule 9, in addition to what is said in the "Definitions" section of the Code about the concept in general. When a group of persons act in concert to acquire control of a company, Rule 9.2 and the note thereto impose the obligation to make general offer on the person whose acquisition takes the group's holding over the relevant threshold, but also extend the obligation to each of the "principal members" of the group, if the triggering acquirer is not such a member. It appears that the offer need not be made to the other members of the concert party, but only to the outside shareholders.

Turning to the detail of the concept of acting in concert and starting with the "Definitions" section, one finds the following general statement:

> "Persons acting in concert comprise persons who, pursuant to an agreement or understanding (whether formal or informal) co-operate to obtain or consolidate control of a company or to frustrate the successful outcome of an offer for a company."

The "Definitions" section then goes on to provide that six categories of persons are presumed to be acting in concert unless the contrary is proved.[172] In the context of Rule 9, a troublesome question has been the relationship between shareholder activism, which the Government encourages,[173] and acting in concert and the mandatory bid obligation. Are shareholders likely to be deterred from coming together to influence the board for fear that they will be required by

---

[172] This definition reflects Art.2(1)(d) of the Directive and omits the requirement in the previous version of the Code that the co-operation should express itself "through the acquisition by any of them of shares in a company". The presumed categories of acting in concert are: (i) a company with any others in the group and associated companies (widely defined, so as to make a company an associated company if another company controls 20 per cent of its equity share capital); (ii) a company with any of its directors and their close relatives and related trusts; (iii) a company with any of its pension funds or the pension funds of other group or associated companies; (iv) a fund manager with any of its discretionary managed clients. (v) a connected adviser with its client; (vi) the directors of the target company.

[173] See above, paras 15–12ff.

the Code to make a general offer for the company's shares? The notes to Rule 9.1 give some assurance to shareholders on this point, but it is limited, because in principle Rule 9 does apply to shareholders who obtain control of a company by pooling their existing holdings as well as those who obtain control by acquiring additional shares. In applying the mandatory bid rule in this situation, the Code focuses on what the shareholders do, rather than simply on their shareholdings. Thus, Note 1 makes it clear that shareholders are not caught by the mandatory bid obligation at the moment they come together in order to obtain control of a company, even if at that point their prior and independently acquired shareholdings together exceed the 30 per cent threshold. What will trigger the mandatory bid is their subsequent acquisition of interests in shares. However, one or other member of a group of institutional shareholders, who come together to exercise their rights as shareholders, is quite likely in the ordinary course of its affairs to acquire shares in the company. Will this automatically trigger a bid requirement? This issue has received explicit attention from the Code Committee[174] and the results of its deliberations are now reflected in Note 2 to Rule 9.1. The Panel's prior position was that shareholders who come together to seek control of a company's board are to be presumed to be acting in concert in respect of their subsequent actions. The Panel was clearly under some pressure not to place obstacles in the way of an important government policy and the new Note means that "the Panel will be less likely than it has been in the past to rule that activist shareholders are acting in concert".[175] Although not altering its fundamental approach in this area, the Panel through the new Note makes the crucial clarification that, even where the shareholder coalition seeks to change the whole of a company's board, their efforts will not be classified as "board control seeking" if there is no "relationship" between the activist shareholders and the proposed directors. Thus, voting a new management team into place, or even finding it as well, will not trigger a finding of acting in concert if the new directors' relationship with the activists does not go beyond the normal board/shareholder relationship.

28–43   A second notable feature of the percentage tests to be found in the equality rules of the Code is that they apply, not just to the acquisition of shares, but to the acquisition of "interests in shares". A definition of "interests in shares" was introduced as part of a major reform of the Code in 2005. The "Definitions" section of the Code sets out a list of situations which will be regarded as involving the acquisition of an interest in a share. Some of them are quite obvious, such as the acquisition of the right to control the exercise of voting rights attached to shares, without actually owning them, as where a

---

[174] *Shareholder Activism and Acting in Concert*, Consultation Paper 10, issued by the Code Committee of the Panel (2002).

[175] *Shareholder Activism and Acting in Concert*, para.1.6.

shareholder agrees, as is permissible, to vote in the way the other party to a contract directs.[176] However, the main impetus for the 2005 changes was to deal with the issue of derivatives, and, in particular, with the form of derivative known as a "contract for differences" (CfD), the only form of derivative which will be discussed here. The essence of the problem of the CfD is that it is a contract which, on its face, gives the holder of it only an economic interest in the movement of the market price of the security over a period of time and not an entitlement to exercise any of the rights attached to the share. On this basis, a CfD is irrelevant to control of a company. In practice, however, the holder of a CfD is often able to control the exercise of voting rights attached to the shares in question and sometimes even to acquire them at the end of the contract. In brief, the holder of a "long" CfD contracts to receive from the counterparty any upward difference between the market prices of the security at two points in time or to pay to the counterparty any downward difference (or the contract may be based on a starting "reference" price, which is something other than the then current market price). The counterparty, usually an investment bank or securities house, will normally hedge its position, but is not obliged to do so, by acquiring a corresponding number of underlying securities at around the "start" price of the CfD. It is this action on the part of the counterparty, usually found but not legally required, that generates the problem for control rights. The counterparty, conversely to the holder of the CfD, has no economic interest in the shares, which are held only for hedging, and will normally be prepared to exercise its voting rights as the holder of the CfD requires (if only to obtain repeat CfD business from the holder) and at the end of the contract may well be happy to close out its position by transferring the shares to the holder of the CfD, if the holder so requires.[177]

Thus, a person seeking to exercise control over a company, but being aware of the restrictions in the Code, could have sought to circumvent its restrictions by exercising some or all of its control rights via CfDs. The changes made prevent that step. The definition of "interests in securities" now provides, generally, that "a person who has long economic exposure, whether absolute or conditional, to changes in the price of securities will be treated as interested in those securities", and, in particular, that a person will be regarded as having an interest in securities if "he is party to any derivative: (a) whose value is determined by reference to their price; and (b) which results, or may result, in his having a long position in them." It

---

[176] *Puddephat v Leith* [1916] 1 Ch. 200.
[177] Panel Consultation Papers 2005/1–3, *Dealings in Derivatives and Options*, set out the nature of the problem (see in particular PCP 2005/1, section A) and the Panel's proposals for reform of the Code. The CfD may work in the opposite way (i.e. the holder obtains the downward difference in the market prices) but then the counterparty will protect itself by selling "short", which does not create the control problems noted in the text.

should be noted that, unlike the FSA's proposals for CfDs under its general disclosure powers,[178] the Panel's rules contain no "safe harbour" for purely economic interests in shares arising out of CfDs. A person might trigger the mandatory bid rule purely on the basis of such interests, and would be reliant on the consent of the Panel to escape the consequences of that rule.

Conclusion

28–44   The mandatory bid rule is a very strong expression of the Code's principle that all shareholders in the target company must be treated equally upon a change of control. Underlying the principle is the view that the prospects of minority shareholders in a company depend crucially upon how the controllers of the company exercise their powers and that the provisions of company law proper, even after the enactment of the new "unfair prejudice" provisions of the Companies Act (discussed in Chapter 20), are not capable of protecting minority shareholders against unfair treatment, at least not in all cases. Consequently, when there is a change of control of a company, all the shareholders should be given an opportunity to leave the company and to do so on the same terms as have been obtained by those who have sold the shares which constitute the new controlling block. The availability of this opportunity should not be dependent on the new controller wishing to make a general offer for the shares of the target, but is to be made available by the Code on a compulsory basis in all cases of change of control by acquisition of shares.[179]

It should be noted that there are two aspects of the policy underlying Rule 9. The first is the opportunity for all shareholders to exit the company upon a change of control by selling their shares to the new controller, and the second is the opportunity to do so on the same terms as have been obtained by those who sold to the holder of the 30 per cent block. Of these two aspects it is the second which is the more controversial. In particular, the latter aspect of the Rule makes it impossible for the holder of an existing controlling block of shares to obtain any premium for control upon the sale of the shares. Since the purchaser of the block will know that the Code requires it to offer the same price to all shareholders, the purchaser is forced to divide the consideration for the company's securities rateably among all the shareholders. In the United Kingdom, where shareholdings in listed companies are widely dispersed, this is probably not an

---

[178] See para.26–22.
[179] Of course, 30 per cent is only a rough approximation of the point at which a change of de facto control of a company occurs. In the early versions of the Code the figure was set at 40 per cent, but it was reduced to 30 per cent in 1974. However, a precise percentage makes the Rule easier to operate than would a case-by-case examination of whether a particular shareholder had acquired sufficient shares in a particular company to enable it to control that company.

important issue, but in countries where family shareholdings in even listed companies are of significant size, the Rule might operate as a disincentive to transfers of control.

Partial offers

Given the Code's general insistence upon equality and its particular requirements for mandatory bids it is not surprising that, by Rule 36, the Panel's consent is needed for partial offers.[180] Consent will normally be given if the offer could not result in the offeror being interested in shares carrying 30 per cent or more of the voting rights of the target company.[181] If it could result in the offeror holding more than 30 per cent but less than 100 per cent, consent will not normally be granted if the offeror or its concert party has acquired, selectively or in significant numbers, interests in shares in the target company during the previous 12 months or if any shares were acquired after the partial offer was reasonably in contemplation.[182] Nor, without consent, may any member of the concert party purchase any further interests in shares within 12 months after a successful partial bid.[183] Both rules promote equality of treatment, since the sellers outside the offer may have been able to dispose of the entirety of their shareholdings.

28–45

If the offer is one which could result in the offeror being interested in not less than 30 per cent and not more than 50 per cent of the voting rights, the offer must state the precise number of shares bid for and the offer must not be declared unconditional unless acceptances are received for not less than that number.[184] And, most importantly, any offer, which could result in the offeror being interested in more than 30 per cent, must not merely be conditional on the specified number of acceptances but also on approval of the offer by shareholders holding over 50 per cent of the voting rights not held by the offeror and persons acting in concert with it.[185] This consent need not be given at a meeting[186] and is normally secured, as permitted by the Rule, by means of a separate box on the form of acceptance. Finally, an offer which could result in the offeror holding shares carrying over 50 per cent of the votes must contain a prominent warning that, if the offer succeeds, the offeror will be free, subject to Rule 36.3, to acquire

---

[180] i.e. those in which the offeror bids for a proportion only of the shares or a class of shares.
[181] r.36.1, so that the mandatory bid principle is not in issue.
[182] r.36.2.
[183] r.36.3.
[184] r.36.4.
[185] r.36.5. This may occasionally be waived if 50 per cent of the rights are held by a single shareholder: *ibid.*
[186] It might be difficult to achieve the 50 per cent plus at a meeting, even though proxy voting is permitted. Nor will it always be easy to obtain by the "box" method because those who are not going to accept will probably not return the acceptance forms and the majority needed is a majority of the whole and not, as in the case of most resolutions, of those voting.

further shares without incurring an obligation to make a mandatory offer.[187] Each shareholder must be able to accept the offer in full for the relevant proportion of his holding and if shares are tendered in excess of this proportion they must be scaled down rateably.[188] When an offer is made for a company with more than one class of equity capital which could result in the offeror acquiring 30 per cent or more of the votes, a "comparable" offer must be made for each class.[189]

These Rules of the Code display an obvious antipathy to partial offers, even though equality of treatment is apparently maintained by the Rule that all shareholders who accept the offer must have the same proportion of their holdings acquired by the bidder. In consequence, partial bids are infrequent, though not unknown. There seem to be two reasons for the Panel's dislike of partial bids. First, if they could be made without restriction, they would constitute an obvious way around the policy underlying the mandatory bid requirement.[190] In giving consent to a partial bid the Panel is, in effect, waiving the mandatory bid requirement. Secondly, the partial bid for control, when allowed, is thought to put undue pressure on shareholders to accept the offer. There will be a change of control if the bid is successful, but the existing shareholders will remain members of the target company, at least as to part of their shareholdings. They may well regard this as unsatisfactory: hence the requirement that shareholders should have the double opportunity to vote outlined above. Shareholders may vote to accept the offer in relation to the relevant proportion of their shares, thus preserving their position as far as possible if the bid does go through, whilst voting against the bid as a matter of principle. The partial bid will be successful only if the bidder obtains at least 50 per cent approval in relation to each question.[191]

At a more general level, the Rules on partial bids do something to counteract the ease with which hostile bids may be mounted in the United Kingdom.[192] Although the Code makes it difficult for the management of the target to block a bid addressed to their shareholders, the disfavouring of partial bids means that normally the bidder must offer to acquire the whole of the equity share capital of a company if it wishes to obtain control through a takeover.[193] The

---

[187] r.36.6.

[188] r.36.7.

[189] r.36.8.

[190] The mandatory bid rule does not apply to control positions acquired as a result of a voluntary offer made in accordance with the Code (r.9.1). Conversely, as r.36.1 suggests, where the partial bid would result in the offeror holding less than 30 per cent of the target's shares, this objection to the partial bid falls away.

[191] See r.36.5, discussed above. For discussion of how this issue in handled in relation to general bids, see r.31.4 and para.28–66, below.

[192] See para.28–17, above.

[193] The fact that all classes of equity capital must be bid for, whether or not the shares carry voting rights (see r.14.1), again suggests that the Code is solicitous of the interests of shareholders whose prospects may be adversely affected by a change of control.

Code frowns upon the acquisition of control "on the cheap" through an offer to purchase only a part of the target's equity capital.

THE PROCEDURE FOR MAKING A BID

Having dealt with the two central features of the Code, the allocation of decision-making on the bid to the shareholders of the target company and equal treatment of target shareholders, we now turn briefly to the procedure for making the offer. Much of this is concerned with putting the shareholders of the target in a position in which they can effectively take the decision which has been allocated to them, but other policy goals are also evident, such as that the company should not be subject to a bid or bid speculation for an excessive period of time or that false markets in the securities involved should not be created.

28–46

Before a formal offer is made to the target shareholders

Rule 1(a) prohibits an offeror from simply putting its offer directly to the shareholders of the target: it must be "put forward in the first instance to the board of the offeree company or its advisers". This is to enable the board of the target to form a view on the merits of the offer and to advise the shareholders accordingly. As we have seen above, the Code requires the board to give such advice to the shareholders and, indeed, to obtain independent advice on the bid and make it known to the shareholders. Rule 1 facilitates this process: without it, the board of the target might be left scrambling around trying to fulfil its duties under Rule 3. In fact, as Rule 1(b) recognises, what the board of the target often first receives is not so much the details of an offer proposed to be made to the shareholders as "an approach with a view to an offer being made". There are a number of good reasons why this should be. First, the offeror may wish to obtain the target board's recommendation of the offer and so wishes to indicate that there is some flexibility in the terms of its offer and that it is prepared to negotiate with the board for its support. Secondly, the offeror may genuinely be in doubt about the value of the target and may wish to secure access to the target's books in order to be able to formulate a precise offer to be put to the shareholders. Especially in the case of highly leveraged bids, it is crucial for the offeror not to find any unpleasant surprises after it has obtained control which would jeopardize its ability to pay the interest on or repay the often very large loans it has taken out to finance the bid. Offers by private equity bidders, accordingly, are rarely hostile. This puts the target board in a negotiating position, because there is

28–47

nothing in the Code or the general law which requires the board to give the potential bidder such access. Thirdly, the bidder may wish to make an informal approach, but also let it be known publicly that such an approach has been made, in order to induce the larger shareholders to put pressure on their board to co-operate with the bid, notably by granting access to the company's books.

What are the regulatory concerns at the pre-offer stage? First, an informal approach, made public, puts the company "in play" and certainly leads senior management of the potential target to concentrate on little else than the possible bid. However, no formal intention to make an offer having yet been announced, the time limits contained in the Code are not triggered. To meet this concern, the Code now contains a "put up or shut up" provision (Rule 2.4), enabling the potential target to request the Panel to set a time limit within which the bidder has either to make an announcement of a firm intention to make an offer or to state that it does not intend to make a bid, and in the latter case the bidder (and a person acting in concert) will not normally be able to bid until six months have passed.[194] Such applications to the Panel by potential targets are not infrequent. This rule clearly promotes the policy underlying GP 6 that "an offeree company must not be hindered in the conduct of its affairs for longer than is reasonable by a bid for its securities."

Faced with this requirement, a potential bidder may seek to make an announcement of an intention to make an offer, but so hedge it about with conditions, that it is doubtful that it is of value to the target company's shareholders. Where a bidder seeks to make an actual offer subject to conditions, its freedom to do so is severely constrained by the provisions of Rule 13, but previously that rule did not apply to announcements of a firm intention to make an offer, where, in consequence, the bidder had a freer hand. However, in 2004 the Panel decided to apply the provisions of Rule 13 (discussed below) to "firm intention" statements as well.[195] This Rule promotes certainty, for both the shareholders and the board of the target company. A target can use the "put up or shut up" rule to force the potential bidder to clarify its intentions and Rule 13 constrains the bidder's freedom to qualify the statement which it is forced to make, at least if it decides not to "shut up".

28–48   A second major concern of the Code at this early stage is that either the approach to the target board should remain secret or its fact should be publicly announced. A possible bid offers tempting opportunities for insider trading on the part of those privy to the bid preparations, not only those within the bidder itself but those

---

[194] r.2.8. Irrespective of a "put up or shut up" application by the target, an announcement of a firm intention to make an offer is required when the board receives one, whether it welcomes it or not.

[195] PCP 2004/4, *Conditions and Pre-Conditions*, especially section 7. The "pre-conditions" to an offer are the conditions attached in the "firm intention" statement. See now r.2.7.

involved as financial or legal advisers. We have seen that the acquisition of shares in the target by or on behalf of the bidder itself does not normally amount to insider trading, but acquisitions by or on behalf of other persons would.[196] Insider dealing also constitutes market abuse under section 118 of the Financial Services and Markets Act 2000, in respect of which the FSA can impose civil penalties, including, in this case, on corporate bodies involved. In spite of the frequent and unexplained rises in the share prices of target companies in the period before takeover announcements are made, the FSA has not had great success in identifying the culprits.[197]

The Code approaches this problem by, first, insisting on the "vital importance of absolute secrecy before an announcement of a bid" (Rule 2.1) and, secondly and probably more effectively, by requiring an announcement if that secrecy is not or is not likely to be maintainable, for example, where the target is subject to "rumour and speculation" or where the bidder is taking its discussions about a possible bid beyond "a very restricted number of people" (Rule 2.2). Once an approach has been made to the board of the offeree company, the primary responsibility for making an announcement rests with that board, but what is announced will depend upon how far matters have progressed when an announcement has to be made. It may be no more than a statement that an offer may possibly be forthcoming (but with no guarantee that it will), and Rule 13 about conditions does not apply to such announcements.[198]

Once a "firm intention" announcement is made, whether because the target board has received one or one is required because of leakages of inside information or because of a "put up or shut up" order from the Panel, the offeror becomes obliged in the normal case to proceed with its bid and to post the formal offer document to the shareholders within 28 days of the announcement.[199] Moreover, at the firm announcement stage a good deal of information about the forthcoming bid must be provided, including the terms of the offer and the identity of the offeror, the conditions to which it is subject (so far as Rule 13 permits conditions) and any inducement fee payable.

---

[196] Above, para.28–35. Even those acting on behalf of the bidder may find themselves caught by the insider trading prohibition, if as a result of being granted access to the target's books, they obtain, as is likely, price-sensitive but non-public information. This is because the exemption in Sch.1 to the CJA 1993 is confined to "market information" which is information about the acquisition or disposal of securities. Thus, to take an extreme example, if the bidder's due diligence reveals the company has just made a potentially very lucrative discovery, the fact that the bidder is now prepared to pay more for the target's shares is market information, but the fact of the discovery would appear not to be.

[197] FSA, *Market Watch*, No.21, July 2007.

[198] Rules 2.3 and 2.4 and n.1 to r.2.4, though the Panel must be consulted in advance if it is proposed to include conditions and there are some requirements in the note designed to make the potential bidder's intentions clear. The Panel (above, fn.195) took the view that, since a "possible bid" announcement was not binding on the bidder in any event, more information was preferable to less.

[199] rr.2.7 and 30.1.

Before the approach to the target board

28–49   We noted above that Rule 1 of the Code, requiring an approach on
the part of the bidder initially to the board of the target company, is
designed to give the board an opportunity to put its view to the
shareholders as soon as the approach becomes public. Nevertheless,
the rule does not give the board much time to react, and the approach
may come out of the blue, as far as the board is concerned. Thus, a
board fearing a takeover will want to try and ascertain before the
bidder's approach whether one is likely. To that end, it will want to
keep a close eye on its share register, both in order to see if a potential
bidder is building up a stake in the company and to see if shareholders are appearing who are likely to be susceptible to an offer, if
one is made (for example, certain types of hedge fund). Of course, the
shareholder may hide behind a nominee name. The rules on vote-
holding disclosure, discussed in Chapter 26, will help considerably in
getting behind the nominee names, though they apply only to holdings at or above the three per cent level. Below that, however, there
are provisions which, unlike the vote-holding rules, are still contained
in the companies legislation. Further, unlike the vote-holding rules,
the provisions of Part 22 of the Act do not impose an automatic
disclosure obligation on shareholders but rather permit the company
to trigger the disclosure obligation. Part 22 may be particularly useful
if the company has reason to believe that a beneficial shareholder,
perhaps one resident abroad, is not complying with the automatic
disclosure rules.

   Section 793 provides that a public company (whether its shares are
traded on a public market or not) may serve notice on a person whom
it knows to be, or has reasonable cause to believe to be, or to have
been at any time during the three years immediately preceding the
date of the notice, interested in voting shares of the company. The
notice may require that person to confirm that fact and, if so, (a) to
give particulars of his own past or present interest; (b) where the
interest is a present interest and any other interest subsists or sub-
sisted during the three-year period at a time when his own interest
did, to give particulars known to him of that other interest; or (c)
where his interest is a past interest, to give particulars of the identity
of the person to whom that interest was transferred.[200] In cases (a)
and (b) the particulars to be given include the identity of persons
interested and whether they were members of a concert party or there
were any other arrangements regarding the exercise of any rights

[200]   s.793(2) and (6).

conferred by the shares.[201] The notice must require a response to be given in writing within such reasonable time as may be specified in the notice.[202]

The initial notice will normally be sent to the person named on the membership register and, if he is the sole beneficial owner of the shares, he will normally say so (at any rate once the likely consequences of refusing to respond are explained to him). But in other cases the notice may merely be the beginning of a long and often abortive paper-chase. If the recipient of the notice is a nominee he may well decline to say more than that, claiming that his duty of confidentiality forbids disclosure or, if the nominee is, say, a foreign bank, that the foreign law makes it unlawful to disclose. In principle, this is a breach of the duty under section 793 (since the nominee is bound to give details of the "other interests" known to him, i.e. that of the person upon whose behalf the nominee holds the shares). Alternatively, the nominee may disclose the nominator's identity, but the latter, if resident abroad, may refuse to provide any further information. Ultimately, as a result of the possibility of the freezing and disenfranchisement of the shares (see below), the true ownership may be disclosed—but not always.[203] Such information regarding interests in the shares as may be elicited as a result of the notice (or a succession of notices as the company follows the trail) must be entered on a public register, with the information being entered against the name of the present holder of the shares.[204] The rules applying to this register, including court control of public access for a non-proper purpose, are the same as those applying to the company's register of members, and most companies will use the share register for this purpose as well.[205]

The Act recognises that members of the company may have a **28-50** legitimate interest in securing that the company exercises its powers under section 793, even if the board does not want it to (perhaps because the directors or some of them may fear that it may bring to light breaches by them of their obligations to notify their dealings under the rules discussed in Chapter 26). Hence, under section 803, members holding not less than one-tenth of the paid-up voting capital may serve a requisition stating that the requisitionists require the company to exercise its powers under section 793, specifying the

---

[201] s.793(5). In the light of the complications of the statutory provisions defining "interests" and "concert party agreements" (see below) a lengthy explanation accompanying the notice may be needed if the recipient (particularly if a foreigner) is to understand precisely what is being asked.

[202] If the time allowed is unreasonably short, the notice will be invalid: *Lonrho Plc (No.2), Re* [1989] B.C.L.C. 309.

[203] In some cases the information sought has never been obtained and the shares have remained frozen.

[204] s.808. Assuming there is a present holder and assuming the holder's identity is known. If not, the information must be entered against the name of the holder of the interest. The entry must state the fact that, and the date when, the requirement was imposed.

[205] ss.808–819. For discussion of the share register see para.27–16.

manner in which those powers are to be exercised[206] and giving reasonable grounds for requiring the powers to be exercised in the manner specified.[207] It is then the company's duty to comply.[208] If it does not, every officer of the company who is in default is liable to a fine.[209] On the conclusion of a shareholder-initiated investigation, the company, under section 805, has to prepare a report of the information received which has to be made available at the company's registered office within a reasonable time[210] after the conclusion of the investigation.[211] If it is not concluded within three months beginning on the day after the deposit of the requisition, an interim report on the information already obtained has to be prepared in respect of that and each succeeding three months.[212] Any report has to be made available for inspection by any person at a place notified to the registrar, unless the company chooses to make it available at its registered office[213] and the requisitionists must be informed within three days of the report becoming available.[214]

A person who fails to comply with a section 793 notice, whether initiated by board or shareholders, or, in purported compliance with the notice, knowingly or recklessly makes a false or misleading statement commits an offence, which can be sanctioned by imprisonment, unless the defendant shows the requirement was frivolous or vexatious.[215] What, however, makes the foregoing sections more effective than they would otherwise be is that, if a notice is served on a person who is or was interested in shares of the company and he fails to give any information required by the notice, the company may apply to the court for an order directing that the shares in question be subject to restrictions.[216] However, it should be noted that the information a company may require under the notice is, perhaps not surprisingly, limited by what the person asked knows. If the company obtains no useful information, because the person asked does not

---

[206] In particular, of course, in respect of which persons they require notices to be served.
[207] s.803(2) and (3).
[208] s.804.
[209] s.804(2).
[210] Not exceeding 15 days: s.805(1).
[211] s.805(1). On the meaning of "concluded" see s.805(7).
[212] s.805(2).
[213] ss.805(5) and 807. Not to give notice to the registrar is an offence on the part of the company and any officer in default, as is a failure to make the report available for inspection: ss.806 and 807. There is no "proper purpose" control over public access to the report.
[214] s.805(6) and it must remain available for inspection at the registered office for at least six years: s.805(4).
[215] s.795. After consulting the Governor of the Bank of England, the Secretary of State may exempt persons from compliance with a s.793 notice where for "special reasons" an undertaking is substituted for the obligation to comply with the section: s.796.
[216] s.794.

have it, there is no breach of section 793 and restrictions cannot be imposed on the shares.[217]

The restrictions are that:

    (a) any transfer of the shares is void;

    (b) no voting rights are exercisable in respect of them;

    (c) no further shares may be issued in right of them or in pursuance of an offer made to their holder; and

    (d) except in a liquidation, no payment by the company, whether as a return of capital or a dividend, may be made in respect of them.[218]

Thus, although the company may never track down the ultimate beneficial owner of the shares, it can take them out of consideration with regard to a takeover bid through the restrictions imposed by the court. Nevertheless, the restrictions constitute a draconian penalty,[219] which may be detrimental to wholly innocent parties, for example bona fide purchasers of, or lenders on the security of, the shares. Although the court has a discretion whether to make the order imposing the restrictions, an order should normally be made if that knowledge has not been obtained, since "the clear purpose [of Part 22 of the Act] is to give public companies, and ultimately the public at large, a prima facie unqualified right to know who are the real owners of its voting shares". If an order is made, it has to impose all four restrictions without any qualifications designed to protect innocent parties.[220] However, as a result of reforms dating from 1991, an application can be made to the court by the company or any aggrieved person for the restrictions to be relaxed on the grounds that they "unfairly affect" the rights of third parties, and the court is given a broad power to do so.[221] The court also has the power to remove the restrictions altogether,[222] but this normally can be done only if the court is "satisfied that the relevant facts about the shares have been disclosed to the company and no unfair advantage has accrued to any person as a result of the earlier failure to make that disclosure".[223] To this there are two exceptions. If the shares are to be transferred for valuable consideration and the court approves the transfer,[224] an

---

[217] It appears to be open to companies—and some have taken this step—to make provisions in their articles entitling the board to impose restrictions in a wider range of circumstances, including where information is not forthcoming following a request, even if the person asked does not have the information.

[218] s.797(1).

[219] Made the more so since any attempt to evade the restrictions may lead to a heavy fine: s.798.

[220] *Lonrho Plc (No.2), Re* [1990] Ch. 695.

[221] s.799.

[222] s.800: on the application by the company or any person aggrieved.

[223] s.800(3)(a).

[224] s.800(3)(b).

order can be made that the shares should cease to be subject to the restrictions.[225] Further, the court, on application by the company, may order the shares to be sold,[226] subject to the court's approval as to the terms of the sale,[227] and might then also direct that the shares should cease to be subject to the restrictions.[228]

28–51   It will be noted that the information which a person can be required to disclose relates not just to shares, but to "interests in shares". However, the legislation does not use the Code's definition of "interests in shares" but has its own, set out in sections 820 to 823. It is widely formulated so as to include an interest in shares "of any kind whatsoever", but it is not so wide as to include interests in shares of a purely economic character, such as CfDs.[229] A person has an interest in shares when he enters into a contract to acquire them or if, without being the registered holder of the shares, he is entitled to exercise any right conferred by the shares.[230] Equally, a person is interested who has a right to call for delivery of shares or a right to subscribe for shares.[231] A person is interested in shares in which a spouse, civil partner or infant child or step-child is interested.[232] Finally, a person is interested if a body corporate is interested of which that person is a shadow director or is entitled to exercise or control the exercise of one-third or more of the voting power at general meetings.[233]

Part 22 also contains a "concert party" provision, again not that of the Code, but set out in sections 824 and 825, under which the interests of one concert party can be attributed to all members. Section 824(1) provides that an obligation of disclosure may arise

---

[225] But the court has a discretion whether to allow the transfer and whether or not also to remove the restrictions; in particular it may continue restrictions (c) and (d) either in whole or in part so far as they relate to rights acquired or offered prior to the transfer: see s.800(4).

[226] s.801. The only transaction that can be *ordered* is a sale. The word is used in conscious contradistinction to "transferred for valuable consideration" in s.800(3), which would include a share exchange takeover offer: *cf. Westminster Group Plc, Re* [1985] 1 W.L.R. 676, CA.

[227] s.801(1). The court may then make further orders relating to the conduct of the sale: s.800(3). The proceeds of sale have to be paid into court for the benefit of the persons who are beneficially interested in the shares who may apply for the payment out of their proportionate entitlement: s.802.

[228] Though it appears that it does not have to remove them.

[229] s.820(1). For a discussion of CfDs see above, para.28–43. The FSA has proposed to extend the right of a company whose securities are traded on a regulated market or on AIM to seek disclosure on reasonable grounds of economic interests in shares arising by way of a CfD. However, such issuer-triggered disclosure would not apply to CfDs falling within the FSA's proposed safe harbour (see para.26–22) and would apply to other types of CfDs only if the person's holding exceeded a 5 per cent threshold. This extended right for issuers would arise under the DTR, not the Act, and so the sanctions would be presumably those of the FSA, not the imposition of restrictions on shares. See FSA, *Disclosure of Contracts for Difference*, CP 07/20, November 2007, Ch.5.

[230] s.820(3),(4),(5).

[231] ss.820(6), 821.

[232] s.822.

[233] s.823. And any beneficiary of a trust whose assets include shares is interested in them: s.820(3).

from an agreement, between two or more persons, which includes provision for the acquisition by any one or more of them of interests in voting shares of a particular public company (referred to as the "target company").[234] Thus, the agreement must relate to the acquisition of interests in shares and indeed the agreement is not caught by the section until an interest in securities is in fact acquired by one of the parties to it in pursuance of the agreement.[235] Thus, the section does not apply to a voting or other agreement between existing shareholders unless that also requires at least one of them to acquire more shares. Further, the agreement must include provisions imposing restrictions on their dealing with the interests so acquired:[236] an agreement to acquire shares which the acquirer is then free immediately to dispose of is not caught by the section. Section 824(5) provides that "agreement" includes "any agreement or arrangement" and that "provisions of an agreement" include "undertakings, expectations or understandings" whether "express or implied and whether absolute or not". Hence the "agreement" need not be an enforceable contract. But subsection (6) introduces a further refinement by providing that the section does not apply to an agreement which is not legally binding "unless it involves mutuality in the undertakings, expectations or understandings of the parties to it".[237]

Each member of the concert party is taken for the purposes of the disclosure notice to be interested in all shares in which any member of the concert party has an interest, whether or not those interests were acquired in pursuance of the agreement.[238] This will included interests which a member of the concert party has by virtue of family or corporate connections. Any notification which a party makes with respect to his interest must state that he is a party to a concert party agreement, must include the names and (so far as known to him) the addresses of the other parties and must state whether or not any of the shares to which the notification relates are shares in which he is interested by virtue of the concert party provision and, if so, how many of them.[239]

---

[234] A potentially misleading phrase since the company requiring notification may not be, or ever become, a target in a takeover bid, even if it is potentially so.

[235] s.824(2)(b). Though, see below, once an agreement is triggered by an acquisition, the notification requirements extend beyond interests acquired in pursuance of it.

[236] s.824(2)(a).

[237] Of course, the presence of mutuality will normally make the agreement legally binding, but the subsection deals with the doctrine of intention to create legal relations, which the parties might use to declare an agreement not binding at law. The subsection also excludes an underwriting or sub-underwriting agreement provided that that "is confined to that purpose and any matters incidental to it".

[238] s.825(1)–(3).

[239] s.825(4).

The formal offer

Conditions

28–52   Once a company posts its formal offer documents to the shareholders of the target, the bid is open to acceptance by the shareholders to whom it is addressed. One aim of the Code in this situation is that the shareholders should have a clear proposition to accept or reject. As we have noted already, Rule 13 of the Code imposes restrictions on the conditions which the bidder can attach to its offer. An offer must not be subject to conditions which depend solely on subjective judgments by the directors of the offeror or the fulfilment of which is in their hands. Otherwise, offerors would be free to decide at any time to withdraw an offer, whereas one purpose of the Code is to ensure that only serious offers are put forward for consideration. The note to Rules 13.1 to 13.3 makes it clear that this means that normally the bidder cannot make its offer subject to satisfactory financing being available for the offer: the bidder must not make an offer, or even announce a firm intention to make an offer, if the financing is not already in place.[240] This implements GP 5. The main exception to this principle arises where the bidder intends to raise the cash for the bid through a new issue of shares and its shareholders' approval is required for the share issue, either by the Act or under the Rules of the FSA or a public market. In this case, the offer must be made conditional on the necessary consent and the condition is not waivable by the bidder.[241] Even if the inclusion of the condition does not fall foul of the above restriction, the condition must not actually be invoked by the bidder unless the circumstances which have arisen are of "material significance" to the offeror in the context of the bid.[242]

However, some conditions are common in offers, and are even required by the Code. The offeror is required by Rule 10 to make its offer for voting securities conditional on acceptances of a sufficient level to give it, together with securities already held, 50 per cent of the voting rights in the offeree company. Thus, the bidder must either end up with legal control of the target company or the bid must lapse. This is regarded by the Panel as a very important provision, as the

---

[240] In the case of pre-conditions the Code shows a little more flexibility, notably where a regulatory condition must be satisfied for the bid to proceed and that is likely to take a long time, and it would thus not be "reasonable" for the potential offeror to have to maintain, and pay for, committed financing throughout this period.

[241] In fact, this concession may enable the company to escape having to proceed with the bid. The shareholders (including the directors in their capacity as shareholders) will not be obliged to approve the share issue (especially if they think conditions have changed since the offer was first announced): *Northern Counties Securities Ltd v Jackson & Steeple Ltd* [1974] 1 W.L.R. 1133. And it is not even clear that the Code can require the directors to recommend approval to the shareholders if the directors think it would be a breach of their core fiduciary duty to do so: see above, para.28–36. (In the *Jackson & Steeple* case the contrary was held, but on the basis that the directors had already given an undertaking to the court to recommend positively.) Perhaps for this reason, the Code attempts to prevent this situation arising in the case of a mandatory bid: r.9.3(b).

[242] r.13.4 and see the WPP case, above, fn.166.

extensive notes to Rule 10 make clear, dealing with the operation of the Rule in a variety of circumstances likely to arise in practice. As Rule 9.3 makes clear, it also applies to mandatory bids. In practice, the offeror may choose to make the offer conditional upon a higher level of acceptances, though it will normally also reserve to itself the right to waive the condition. The offer may be conditional upon the offeror achieving 75 per cent of the voting rights, so as to be able to pass a special resolution; or even on achieving 90 per cent of the shares bid for (so as to be able to avail itself of the statutory squeeze-out procedure discussed below). Hence, an important stage in the progress of a bid is when it becomes or is declared "unconditional as to acceptances".

Rule 12 requires a condition to be inserted in the offer to deal with the fact that a competition authority consent may be needed for the offer to be consummated. The condition is to the effect that the bid will lapse if there is a reference to the competition authorities before the offer becomes unconditional as to acceptances. Again except for a mandatory bid, the offeror has a choice to resuscitate its bid or not, if the competition authorities ultimately clear it.[243]

Timetable

We have already seen that Rule 30.1 imposes a 28 day limit for the posting of the offer document after a firm intention to bid has been announced. That is a maximum limit in order not to leave the target board and shareholders in a state of uncertainty. Once the offer is posted, the Code is still concerned with the overall length of the process and Rule 31.6 stipulates that the offer may not remain open for acceptances once the 60th day after the offer was posted has passed. There are some exceptions, in particular that the "60th day" is set by reference to the competing bidder's timetable if there is a competing offer or where the board of the target company agrees to a longer period.

However, within the offer period, the Code is also concerned with setting minimum time periods, in order that the shareholders have an opportunity to properly consider the offer and are not pushed into a "snap" decision on it. An offer must initially be open for acceptance for at least 21 days, as required by Rule 31.1. This date is referred to as the "first closing date" of the offer. If this is later extended, as it normally may be, a new date must be specified, but there is no obligation to extend an offer which has not become unconditional as to acceptances (Rules 31.2 and 31.3). However, if it is stated that the offer will not be further extended, only in exceptional cases will the

28–53

---

[243] Normally a lapsed bid cannot be revived within twelve months: see r.35 below. However, the bidder must decide whether to re-offer within 21 days of the clearance: note on r.35.1 and 35.2. The new offer need not be on the same terms as the lapsed one. For a mandatory bid, revival is required and the new offer must be on the same terms: note on r.9.4.

Panel allow it to be extended. This is laid down in Rule 31.5, not merely because the offeror should not break its promises but in order to prevent shareholders being pressurised into accepting before the current closing date by false statements that they will lose all chance of availing themselves of the offer unless they accept before that date.

In some cases the offer may be revised (i.e. improved), sometimes more than once. This is particularly likely to occur if there is a contested takeover between two or more bidders. In such circumstances each rival bidder, having already incurred considerable expense, is likely to go on raising its bid and trying to get its new one recommended by the board of the target. Even if it loses the battle, it will at least be able to recover part of the expenses out of the profit it will make by accepting the winner's bid in respect of its own holdings.[244] Moreover, even if there is no contest, an offeror may be forced to increase its bid if proves unattractive to the target shareholders or if the bidder or its associates or members of its concert party have acquired shares at above the price of its offer, as we have seen above. If an offer is revised, it must be kept open for at least 14 days after the revised offer document is posted (Rule 32.1). All shareholders who have accepted the original offer are entitled to the revised consideration (Rule 32.3) and new conditions must not be introduced except to the extent necessary to implement an increased or improved offer and with the prior consent of the Panel (Rule 32.4). "No increase" statements are treated by Rule 32.2 in essentially the same way, and for the same reasons, as "no extension" statements, i.e. the bidder is allowed to go back on them only in "wholly exceptional" circumstances, unless the bidder has specifically reserved its freedom in the "no increase" statement to increase the offer in the circumstances which have arisen.

28–54   In general, as Rule 33.1 makes clear, the foregoing rules apply equally to alternative offers in which the target's shareholders are given the option of accepting various types of consideration (e.g. shares, convertible debentures, non-convertible debentures, cash or combinations or different proportions of these). In other words, the shareholders retain their options so long as the offer remains open. But where the value of a cash alternative provided by a third party is more than half the maximum value of the primary share option, the offeror is not obliged to keep that offer open, or to extend it, if not less than 14 days' written notice to shareholders is given reserving the right to close it on a stated date.[245] This "shutting off" of the cash alternative provided by a third party is permitted because underwriters will be reluctant to agree to remain at risk for an indeterminate period. However, the bidder's freedom to "shut off" a cash

---

[244] By contrast, the successful bidder may suffer from the "winner's curse" of having overpaid for the target.

[245] r.33.2. But such a notice must not be given if a competing offer has been announced until the competitive situation ends. For the exclusion of mandatory offers see n.2 to r.33.2.

alternative does detract from the offeree's freedom to wait and see what the other shareholders do before accepting the offer. It is significant that it is not permitted in mandatory bids, where a cash offer or a cash alternative is required, and there is no danger of bidders responding to the lack of a "shut off" opportunity by simply not arranging for a cash alternative to be available.

The combination of the maximum period for the bid (60 days) and the minimum period for revised offers to remain open (14 days) means that an offer cannot normally be revised after the 46th day. However, where there are competing bidders still in the field at this point, the Panel has come to the conclusion that this freezing of the offers on the 46th day is an unacceptably inflexible rule. It will therefore conduct an auction, with revisions being announced into the final period, according to a procedure determined ad hoc for the particular bid (Rule 32.5).

Bid documentation

The offer will, of course, be a longer and more detailed document **28–55** than the announcement of the firm intention to make a bid. After a general statement in Rule 23 that shareholders must be given sufficient information and advice to enable them to reach a properly informed decision as to the merits or demerits of an offer and early enough to decide in good time, Rule 24 (divided into 13 sub-rules) states what financial and other information the offer document must contain and Rule 25 (divided into six sub-rules) what information must be contained in circulars giving advice by the target company's board. The information required is extensive but need not be considered in detail here, beyond saying that it is very much what one would expect in the light of the nature of the documents. It is worth noting that the documentation issued by a bidder on a share-exchange offer need no longer comply with the FSA's rules, since it does not constitute a prospectus.[246]

Following the adoption of the Directive, the interests of employees receive slightly more explicit consideration in the Code than before, mainly at the level of information provision. Rule 24.1, as it did previously, requires the bidder to state in its offer document "its intentions with regard to the continued employment of the employees and management of the offeree company" and, it now adds, "including any material change in the conditions of employment". However, intentions formed at the time of the offer may change once the bidder has obtained control. Rule 25.1(b) requires the board of the target, when giving its opinion on the offer, to include its views, and the reasons for those views, on the implications of the bid for the employees—an obligation now stated slightly more fully than pre-

---

[246] PR 1.2.2(2) and 1.2.3(3).

viously. These documents, and any revised offer and a target board opinion thereon, must be made "readily and promptly available" to the representatives of the employees or, in their absence, to the employees themselves.[247] None of this gives the employees any formal say in the bid decision, though it may give them information upon which to organise political or social pressure in relation to the offer. For a more formal input to the bid decision, the employees or their representatives must look elsewhere. Thus, where a statutory information and consultation arrangement is in place, both bidder and target may need to consult employee representatives on the employment consequences of the bid or of defensive measures.[248]

Curiously, however, the strongest mechanism for the protection of employee interests may found in the pensions legislation. Where a highly leveraged bid for a target company is successful, the level of risk in the target company increases, including the risk that the company will default on its obligations under an occupational pension scheme. In that situation, the Pensions Regulator has a, still somewhat ill-defined, power to require the bidder to make extraordinary payments into the fund, which the bidder may either do, and so give the pensioners greater financial protection, or refuse to do and decide not to make an offer. The potential power of the Regulator puts the pension scheme trustees in a position to negotiate with the bidder as to the terms upon which they will regard it proper not to seek the Regulator's intervention.[249]

In the case of an agreed recommended takeover with no rival bidders, no more may need stating than the Code requires. But, in the case of a hostile bid or where there are two or more rival bids, each of the companies involved will probably want to make optimistic profit forecasts about itself[250] and to rubbish those of the others. All profit forecasts are unreliable and those made in a takeover battle more unreliable than usual. Hence Rule 28 (with eight sub-Rules) lays

---

[247] rr.26 and 32.7. The same obligation is imposed in relation to bid announcements: r.2.6.

[248] Information and Consultation of Employees Regulations 2004 (SI 2004/3426), reg.20. The FSA's rules indicate that it will not be market abuse for a company involved in a bid to disclose information to an employee representative in fulfillment of an obligation imposed by the Regulations, provided the information is subject to a confidentiality requirement: MAR 1.4.5(2)(e). Equally, disclosure of inside information to an employee representative will not be a criminal offence on the part of a manager under section 52 of CJA 1993 if the disclosure is "in the proper performance of the functions of his employment", though it might be for the representative to trade on the information or to further disclose it. See Case C-384/02, *Criminal Proceedings against Grøngaard* [2006] IRLR 214, ECJ.

[249] Pensions Act 2004, ss.43–51 ("financial support directions"). The point is that the pension deficit revealed in the accounts may no longer be an accurate indication of the amount of money needed to secure the pension obligations, if the bidder's risk profile changes significantly. A better test might be the amount an insurance company would require to transfer to itself the company's pension obligations. In the case of the takeover of Boots by a private equity bidder in 2007 the trustees negotiated additional payments of £418m over 10 years into the pension fund: *Financial Times fm*, June 25, 2007, p.6. In the earlier case of WH Smith it appears that a potential bidder decided not to make a bid because of the target's pension fund deficit.

[250] The offeror will not need to do so on a pure cash offer for all the shares; but the target will.

down stringent conditions about them. In particular, the forecast "must be compiled with due care and consideration by the directors whose sole responsibility it is" but "the financial advisers must satisfy themselves" that it has been so compiled.[251] The assumptions on which the forecast is based must be stated both in the document and in any press release.[252] Except on a pure cash offer, the forecast must be reported on by the auditors or consultant accountants (and sometimes by an independent valuer[253]) and the report sent to the shareholders[254] and, if any subsequent document is sent out, the continued accuracy of the forecast must be confirmed.[255] All this is wholly admirable but the evidence does not suggest that it has made such forecasts significantly more reliable.

Somewhat similar requirements apply when a valuation of assets is given in connection with an offer.[256] These valuations tend to vary according to whether it is in the interests of the company which engages the "independent" valuer that the value should be high or low; but at least the valuer of real property is likely to have more objective evidence to guide him in the form of prices recently paid for comparable properties. Rule 19.1 lays down a general principle that all documents, advertisements and statements made during the course of an offer "must be presented with the highest standards of care and accuracy and the information given must be adequately and fairly presented." Note 8 makes it clear that statements about the expected financial benefits of a takeover to the bidder (often referred to as "synergies"), which fall short of constituting profit forecasts, are nevertheless regulated in a similar manner, with assumptions stated and reports from financial advisers.

Although there has not been space here to discuss the details, it is **28–56** clear that the Code attaches the highest importance to the provision to shareholders of complete and accurate information about the bid and any defence to it. Without such guarantees, the Code's purpose of placing the decision on the commercial acceptability of the offer in the hands of the shareholders of the target company might seem unrealistic, as might the Panel's own refusal to make any assessment of the commercial merits of the bid.[257]

Suppose, however, an inaccuracy is present in the information put out by the bidder or target companies and a person later wishes to claim compensation for the loss said to have been suffered thereby. The Panel now has the power to award compensation but this is not one of the areas in which it has sought to apply it, nor will com-

---

[251] r.28.1.
[252] r.28.2 (and see the Notes thereto).
[253] r.28.3.
[254] r.28.4.
[255] r.28.5.
[256] r.29.
[257] Code, Introduction, 2(a).

pensation under FSMA normally be available.[258] However, this is an area in which the Code intersects with the general law, in the sense that there may well be legal remedies available to shareholders who have suffered loss as a result of inaccurate or incomplete information provided in the course of a takeover bid.[259] Applying generally, that is, to both bidder and target documentation, is the common law liability for negligent misstatement, which, even after the decision of the House of Lords in *Caparo Industries Plc v Dickman*,[260] would seem capable of imposing liability upon the issuers of documentation in the course of takeover bids towards the shareholders of the target company, to whom it is clearly addressed, where such shareholders act in reliance upon the information to either reject or accept the offer made.[261] Indeed, in the post-*Caparo* case of *Morgan Crucible & Co v Hill Samuel & Co*[262] the Court of Appeal refused to strike out a claim by the bidding company against the directors of the target that inaccurate statements made by the target company in the course of a bid had been intended to cause the bidder to raise its bid, which it had done to its detriment.

Dealings in shares

28–57 GP 4 states that "false markets must not be created in the securities" of the offeror or offeree company. The Code has always sought, however, to permit dealings in the securities of companies involved in a bid to continue during the bid period. Apart from the insider dealing laws, already discussed, the main restrictions are these. Once the "offer period" starts (triggered by the first public announcement about the bid, even if it is only about a possible offer) and has not ended (with the first closing date or, if later, the offer becoming or

---

[258] On the Panel's powers to award compensation, see above, para.28–9 and on the PR see fn.246 above. We have also seen that in some limited cases there are criminal sanctions for misstatements (above, para.28–10).

[259] In addition to the liabilities discussed in the text, the bidder might also be liable in damages under s.2(1) of the Misrepresentation Act 1967 (unless it could disprove negligence) or to have its contract with the accepting shareholders rescinded in equity, though in both cases this could apply only between the bidder and the target company shareholders and where the shareholders had accepted the bidder's offer.

[260] [1990] 2 A.C. 605. See paras 22–42 *et seq.*, above.

[261] Proving that the negligent misstatement caused the plaintiff the loss in question may be, of course, a very difficult matter. See *JEB Fasteners Ltd v Marks Bloom & Co* [1981] 3 All E.R. 289 (above, para.22–46).

[262] [1991] Ch. 295, CA. However, this decision has to be read in the light of subsequent developments on assumption of responsibility. See *Partco Group Ltd v Wragg* [2002] 2 B.C.L.C. 323, CA, where a successful bidder sued the directors of the target on the basis of statements made to the bidder in the course of due diligence carried out by the bidder prior to making a recommended offer. The CA refused to strike out the claim but were clearly sceptical as to whether it would ultimately succeed, because the directors could be said to have assumed responsibility for the accuracy of the statements only on behalf of the target (now owned by the bidder) and not personally. See also above, at para.22–44. See further the refusal to strike out in a claim by the bidder against the target's auditors on special facts in *Galoo Ltd v Bright Grahame Murray* [1994] 1 W.L.R. 1360, CA.

being declared unconditional as to acceptances),[263] the offeror and persons acting in concert with it must not sell any securities in the target company without the consent of the Panel.[264] Moreover, during that period disclosure of dealings, additional to and stricter than that required by the Act, comes into operation.[265]

Solicitation

There is an obvious temptation for both bidder and target to engage   **28–58** in high-pressure salesmanship in the case of a hostile or, especially, a contested takeover. There are firms specialising in the art of persuading reluctant shareholders. It is increasingly common for the services of such firms to be recruited by the parties or their financial advisers. Rule 19 of the Code is designed to curb the excesses which may result (and sometimes have done). The sub-rules of particular interest include Rule 19.4 which prohibits the publication of an advertisement connected with an offer unless it falls within one of nine categories, and, with two exceptions,[266] it is cleared with the Panel in advance. The Panel does not attempt to verify the accuracy of statements,[267] but if it subsequently appears that any statement was inaccurate the Panel may, at least, require an immediate correction.[268] This pre-vetting, however superficial, is a powerful disincentive to window-dressing and to "argument or invective".[269] The rule applies not only to press advertisements (which must not include acceptance or other forms[270]) but also to television, radio, video, audio-tapes and posters[271] and in each case the advertisement must "clearly and

---

[263] See Code, "Definitions".

[264] r.4.2. Such action is likely to cause great confusion in the market. If the Panel does consent, it will require 24 hours' notice to be given to the market and will require the sale to be at above the offer price. Not abiding by the Code's provisions on sales might well be a criminal offence under s.397 of FSMA 2000, if the object was to rig the market by causing a fall in the quoted price of the target's shares, thus making the offer more attractive; or under the insider dealing legislation if information available to the offeror suggested that its offer would not succeed and it wanted to "make a profit or avoid a loss" by selling before the quoted market price fell back when the offer lapsed. See Ch.30 below.

[265] In particular 1 per cent shareholdings (instead of 3 per cent) must be disclosed (r.8.3) and all dealings by the parties or their "associates" (as defined in "Definitions") must be disclosed to the Panel and the markets no later than noon on the business day following the transaction. Dealings in derivatives must also be disclosed. See notes 3–5 to r.8. However, in the case of cash offers, dealings in the shares of the offeror do not have to be disclosed under the Code's provisions. There are extensive notes to r.8 about the implementation of its disclosure obligations.

[266] A product advertisement, not bearing on the offer (which is not really an exception), and advertisements in relation to schemes of arrangement (when the relevant regulator is the court): see Ch.29, below.

[267] Time constraints do not permit this to be done; the Panel requires only 24 hours to consider the proof of the advertisement which must have been approved by the company's financial adviser: r.19.4, Note 1.

[268] r.19.4, Note 2.

[269] Specifically excluded from exceptions (iii) and (iv) to r.19.4.

[270] r.19.4, Note 5.

[271] r.19.4, Note 4.

prominently" identify the party on whose behalf it is being published.[272]

The Rule, however, covers only advertising material of which there will be a record. The greater danger arises from unrecorded oral communications, which cannot be vetted in advance or scrutinised afterwards. However, an attempt is made to control these. Rule 19.5 provides that, without the consent of the Panel, campaigns in which shareholders are contacted by telephone may be conducted only by "staff of the financial advisers who are fully conversant with the requirements of, and their responsibilities under, the Code", and it adds that only previously published information which remains accurate and not misleading may be used, and that "shareholders must not be put under pressure and must be encouraged to consult their financial advisers". However, in recognition, no doubt, that the parties will have selected their financial advisers on the basis of their financial expertise and reputation rather than their ability to woo, the Panel may consent to the use of other people, subject to the Panel's approval of an appropriate script which must not be departed from, even if those rung up ask questions which cannot be answered without doing so, and to the operation being supervised by the financial adviser.[273]

28–59 Rule 4.3 provides that any person proposing to contact a private individual or small corporate shareholder with a view to seeking an irrevocable commitment consult the Panel in advance. A Note to Rule 4.3 states that the Panel will need to be satisfied that the proposed arrangements will provide adequate information as to the nature of the commitment sought and a realistic opportunity to consider whether or not it should be given and with time to take independent advice. It adds that the financial adviser will be responsible "for ensuring compliance with all relevant legislation and other regulatory requirements".[274] Furthermore, Note 3 to Rule 19.5 stipulates that the Panel must be consulted before a telephone campaign is conducted with a view to gathering irrevocable commitments in connection with an offer. Short of a total ban on cold-calling this seems to regulate it in this context as satisfactorily as is reasonably possible—assuming that financial advisers can be relied on to observe the Rules.

Rule 19.6 says that parties, if interviewed on radio or television, should seek to ensure that the interview, when broadcast, is not interspersed with comments or observations made by others. It also provides that joint interviews or public confrontations between representatives of the contesting parties should be avoided.

---

[272] r.19.4, Note 3.

[273] r.19.5, Note 1. It is difficult to see how the financial adviser can supervise effectively unless it insists upon all calls made being recorded; but the rules and notes do not require or suggest that.

[274] This warning ought to frighten the financial adviser!

The more serious problem, arising from meetings with share-holders or those who are likely to advise them, is dealt with in Rule 20.1 which provides that "information about companies involved in an offer must be made equally available to all offeree company shareholders as nearly as possible at the same time and in the same manner".[275] Despite this, meetings with institutional shareholders, individually or through their professional bodies, are likely to be held, as, often, are meetings with financial journalists and investment analysts and advisers. Note 3 to the Rule permits this, "provided that no material new information is forthcoming and no significant new opinions are expressed". If that really is strictly observed, one wonders why anybody bothers to attend such meetings.[276] But many do, and when a representative of the financial adviser or corporate broker of the party convening the meeting is present (as must be the case unless the Panel otherwise consents), the representative generally seems able to confirm in writing to the Panel (as the Note requires) that this Rule was observed. If such confirmation is not given, a circular to shareholders (and, in the later stages, a newspaper advertisement also) must be published giving the new information or opinions supported by a directors' responsibility statement.

The post-offer period
Bidding again
Rule 35.1 provides that, except with the consent of the Panel, when an offer[277] has not become wholly unconditional within the bid timetable or has been withdrawn or has lapsed, neither the offeror nor any person who has acted or now is acting in concert with it, may, within the next 12 months: (a) make or announce another offer for the target company; (b) acquire any shares of the target company which would require a mandatory bid on the part of the acquirer; (c) be a member of a concert party which acquires 30 per cent or more of the voting rights in the offeree company;[278] (d) make any statement which raises the possibility that an offer might be made for the offeree company; (e) take any preliminary steps in connection with an offer (for example, one to be made after the end of the twelve months) which might become known outside the immediate circle of the

28–60

---

[275] This does not preclude the issue of circulars to their own investment clients by brokers or advisers provided that the circulars are approved by the Panel.

[276] The risk of new information being given out on a partial basis in such cases materialised in the Kvaerner bid for AMEC, where a financial public relations company employed by the target made statements in closed meetings about the target's future profits which had not been contained in the defence document: Panel statement 1995/9. The PR company was censured by the Panel and dismissed by the target.

[277] Or even if no offer has been made but a firm announcement of an intention to bid has been made. A bidder is not normally free simply to withdraw a bid, but may do in some limited circumstances.

[278] As we have seen above (para.28–42), the obligation to bid might not fall to the particular member of the concert party who is the former bidder.

company's top management and its advisers. Similar restrictions apply following a partial offer, where, as is unusual, one is permitted. Interestingly, the restrictions apply to a partial bid for between 30 and 50 per cent of the target, even if that bid is successful. In other words, having had one bite at the cherry, the bidder cannot come back for a second within 12 months: if the bidder wants to obtain a legally controlling interest through a partial bid, it must try for this the first time around.[279] Furthermore, if a person or concert party following a takeover offer holds 50 per cent or more of the voting rights it must not, within six months of the closure of the offer, make a second offer, or acquire any shares from the shareholders on better terms than those under the previous offer.[280] Overall, these provisions prevent the offeror from continuously harassing the target and, while the maximum waiting period is only 12 months, that may be long enough to enable the target's board to strengthen its defences against further hostile bids by the offeror.

The bidder's right to squeeze out the minority

28–61   As we have seen above, a bidder is permitted to make its offer conditional upon a certain level of acceptances on the part of the target's shareholders. Where it is important to the bidder to obtain complete control of the target (for example, where it wishes to conduct its business in a way which will not necessarily be in the interests of the minority shareholders of the target), it will seek to get to a position where it can squeeze out any dissenting (or simply non-responsive) minority shareholders. This may be particularly true of private equity bidders, which will want to use the target's assets to secure the loans made to the bidder to finance the bid. Since 1929, the Companies Act has contained a provision enabling the bidder to squeeze out a minority after a successful bid. Given the expropriatory nature of the squeeze-out, it would obviously have been ineffective to include those provisions in the self-regulatory Code, and so they have remained in the legislation. Article 15 of the Takeover Directive now requires Member States to provide a squeeze-out right, and the Directive's provisions led to some amendments in the 2006 Act to the previous legislation, though the report of the Company Law Review was a more significant source of reforms.[281] As we have noted, one attraction of the scheme of arrangement mechanism for effecting a takeover

---

[279] r.35.2.
[280] r.35.3.
[281] Final Report 1, pp.282–300. However, that report rejected the argument that a squeeze-out right should be extended so as to operate whether the 90 per cent holding results from a takeover or not, largely on the grounds that valuation in such a case would be difficult. Nevertheless, the functional arguments for the squeeze-out from the 90 per cent holder's point of view are just as strong in such a case. The European Commission included such a proposal in its draft Directive amending the Second Directive (see COM(2004) final, 21.9.2004, proposed new article 39a) but it was later dropped.

is that once the scheme has been approved by a resolution of the shareholders and approved by the court, dissenting minorities (or those who simply do not accept the offer as a result of inertia) will be bound to transfer their shares, though a scheme is not attractive in a competitive situation.[282] More importantly, the majority required for a scheme is 75 per cent of those voting on the resolution, rather than the 90 per cent figure required (see below) for a post-bid squeeze-out.

The current rules on squeeze-outs are set out in Chapter 3 of Part 28 of the Act. The basic principle is quite straightforward, though its implementation gives rise to some complicated provisions. Assuming a single class of shares has been bid for, the offeror is entitled to acquire compulsorily the shares of the non-acceptors if the offer has been accepted by at least 90 per cent in value of the shares "to which the offer relates" and, if the shares are voting shares, those shares represent at least 90 per cent of the voting rights carried by those shares.[283] Note that the 90 per cent figure relates to the shares bid for, not to the total number of shares of the class, some of which may be held by the offeror before the bid is launched and which, therefore, are to be excluded from both the numerator and the denominator when working out whether the appropriate fraction of the shares has been acquired as a result of the bid.[284] Where there is more than one class of shares bid for, the 90 per cent test is to be applied to each class separately, so that a bidder could end up in a position to squeeze out the minority of one class but not that of another.[285]

In contrast to the Code, Chapter 3 applies to takeovers of any type of company within the meaning of the Act whether it is public or private.[286] The offeror need not be a company though in practice it will usually be a body corporate[287] (or in some cases two or more such bodies).[288] The definition of "takeover offer" is one (a) to acquire all[289] the shares of the company (or all the shares of a class) which on the date of the offer the offeror does not already hold[290] and (b) to do

---

[282] Above, para.28–12.
[283] s.979(2). If, as is usual, the voting rights are on a one vote per share basis, the two requirements amount to the same thing.
[284] See further below.
[285] s.979(4). In the case of a company with voting shares or debentures admitted to trading on a regulated market, debentures carrying voting rights are treated as shares of the company: s.990. This provision is necessary because Art.15 of the Directive refers to "securities" (not just to shares), though Art.2(1)(e) makes it clear that the Directive includes only securities carrying voting rights. Voting debentures are uncommon in the UK.
[286] s.974(1) and see *Fiske Nominees Ltd v Dwyka Diamond Ltd* [2002] 2 B.C.L.C. 123.
[287] But it could be an unincorporated body, e.g. the trustees of a pension fund.
[288] See s.987 on joint offers, which deals with the problem identified in *Blue Metal Industries v Dilley* [1970] A.C. 827, PC, that the legislation at the time of that case was not well-adapted to deal with joint offers.
[289] Hence it does not apply to "partial offers": but, where the Code applies, the Panel would not be likely to allow a partial offer which might lead to the acquisition of 90 per cent.
[290] "Shares" here means shares allotted at the date of the offer and excludes treasury shares (s.974(4)) but see below for the handling of these shares.

so on the same terms for all the shares (or all the shares of a particular class).[291]

28–62   All the apparently simple terms used above are capable of raising questions of interpretation, most, though not all, of which are expressly addressed now in the legislation. What, for example, is an "offer"? In *Chez Nico (Restaurants) Ltd, Re*,[292] Browne-Wilkinson V.-C. held that this definition had to be construed strictly, since the provisions enabled a bidder who had acquired 90 per cent of the shares to expropriate the remaining shares, and that accordingly they operated only if the bidder had made an "offer" in the contractual sense of the word. In the instant case two directors of the company who were its major shareholders had circulated the other shareholders inviting them to offer to sell their shares to them and indicating the price that those directors would be prepared to pay if they accepted the offers. As a result, the directors succeeded in acquiring over 90 per cent and then sought to acquire the remainder. On an application by one of the remaining shareholders, the court declared that the directors were not entitled to do so, since they had not made any "offer" but instead had invited the shareholders to do so. While this produced the right result in the instant case,[293] the importation into company law of the subtle distinctions drawn by the law of contract seems regrettable; in company law many transactions are described as "offers" or "offerings" when strictly they are invitations to make offers.[294] Moreover, the decision has adverse consequences for a minority shareholder who, instead of wanting to remain a shareholder in the taken-over company, wishes to exercise his rights to be bought out (see below); the effect of the decision is that he will not be entitled to do so if the bidder has proceeded as the directors did in this case.

The requirement that the offer be on the same terms is relaxed in two minor respects by section 976. If the difference simply reflects differences in the dividend entitlements (for example, because later allotted shares carry a lower dividend entitlement in that particular financial year as contrasted with shares allotted earlier), the offer is nevertheless on the same terms. This is deemed to be the case also where an offer is made of "substantially equivalent" consideration to

---

[291] s.974(2) and (3). "Shares" here means shares allotted at the date of the offer but the offer may include shares to be allotted before a specified date: s.428(2).

[292] [1992] B.C.L.C. 192.

[293] Since the directors had failed to make proper disclosure to the other shareholders.

[294] Browne-Wilkinson V.-C. emphasised that his decision was only on the meaning of "takeover offer" for the purposes of the squeeze-out and sell-out provisions and that he had no doubt that what had occurred would be a takeover offer for the purposes of many statutory or non-statutory provisions. This is certainly true of the non-statutory Code. Indeed, the Panel had treated the *Chez Nico* takeover as subject to the Code (the company had been a Plc at the time of the circularisation and remained subject to the Code after its conversion to a private company since, while a public company, it had made a public offering) but the only penalty that the Panel had imposed was to criticise the two directors for their ignorance of, and failure to observe, the Code: see at p.200.

those outside the UK whose law either prohibits or subjects to unduly onerous conditions the consideration offered to the main body of the shareholders.[295]

A similar problem to this second one arises with the requirement that the offer be made to all the shareholders (of the relevant class) where the target has a few shareholders resident in countries with elaborate securities laws and where the inclusion within the offer of such shareholders is likely to trigger the need to comply with those laws. An established technique for dealing with this situation is to make the offer capable of acceptance by the foreign shareholders but to take elaborate steps to ensure that the formal offer documentation is not addressed to them. When challenged in court, this practice was upheld with some unease by the Court of Appeal on the specific facts of the case.[296] To make it secure, the CLR recommended that the technique be given specific statutory cover and that, in order to deal with the difficulty that the foreign resident might never know of the offer until it received the compulsory acquisition notice from the offeror, that the offer be communicated in the same way as for pre-emption offers.[297] By this, if a foreign resident has given an EEA address for service, that is used; otherwise notice is to be given in the *Gazette*.[298] This recommendation is implemented in section 978, but only where the offer was not communicated in order not to contravene the local law. Section 978(2) also saves from failure under the squeeze-out provisions an offer which is communicated but whose acceptance is made impossible or difficult as a result of local law. Finally, section 978(3) makes it clear the courts should not deduce from the section that, in all other cases, a failure to communicate the offer to each holder or an offer which it is impossible or more difficult for some shareholders to accept fails to be a "takeover offer" within the meaning of the Act: the courts will decide on a case-by-case basis.

Further, there is the question of which are the shares "already held by the offeror" at the date of the offer.[299] In general, the larger the stake held by the offeror before the bid, the more difficult it is for it to achieve the 90 per cent, since the smaller becomes the proportion of the class as a whole which is needed to stop it reaching the **28–63**

---

[295] For example, local securities laws might make a share-exchange offer in a particular jurisdiction "unduly onerous". The requirement for "equivalent consideration" is a better solution than that adopted by the directors in *Mutual Life Insurance Co of New York v The Rank Organisation Ltd* [1985] B.C.L.C. 11, in order to avoid US securities laws, which was simply to exclude the US shareholders from any pre-emption entitlements in a public offering.

[296] *Joseph Holt Plc, Re* [2001] 2 B.C.L.C. 604, CA.

[297] s.562(3).

[298] Final Report I, paras 13.24 and 13.43–13.45.

[299] s.974(2).

threshold.[300] In consequence, it becomes important to know how one determines whether a share is acquired before or after the offer is made. The CLR recommended that the present understanding should be clarified in the legislation, which is that shares conditionally acquired before the offer do not count towards the 90 per cent except where the promise by the existing holder is to accept the offer when and if it is made ("irrevocable undertakings") and the undertaking is given for no significant consideration beyond, if this is the case, a promise to make the offer.[301]

Finally, the bidder's ability to reach the 90 per cent threshold will be enhanced if it can count shares acquired after the date of the offer but outside the bid. Section 977(1) excludes such acquisitions in principle from the definition of "shares to which the offer relates" i.e. they count towards neither the numerator nor the denominator. However, there is a major qualification to this principle, i.e. the shares will be regarded as shares to which the offer relates if the price paid does not at that time exceed the value of the consideration specified in the offer or the offer is subsequently revised so that it no longer does so.[302] In other words, the offeror cannot count towards the 90 per cent shares which it acquires outside the bid by offering more than the final offer price but can count those which it was able to buy at or at less than that price.

There are also potentially tricky issues about shares which are allotted after the bid is made (for example, as a result of a conversion of another security into shares of the class in question) and about treasury shares, which may be held in treasury throughout the bid or become or cease to be treasury shares during the bid period. The statute handles this point by giving the bidder a choice whether it includes in the shares to which the offer relates after-allotted shares or

---

[300] This is not compensated for by the fact that the number of shares which the bidder has to acquire to reach 90% acceptances is also reduced. Thus, if there are 200 allotted shares and the bidder holds none of them at the outset, it takes a holding of 21 shares to block the squeeze-out, but if the bidder holds 100 at the outset, 11 objectors are enough to block it, i.e. the blocking percentage falls from just over 10% of the class to just over 5%. This would not matter if the bidder could rely on having acquired shares pre-bid rateably from acceptors and non-acceptors, but, in the nature of things, the non-acceptors are likely to be under-represented among those who have sold out voluntarily to the bidder.

[301] Final Report I, paras 13.26–13.42. Implemented in s.975(2). The reason for insisting on no significant consideration is to maintain the rule that the offer must be on the same terms to all the shareholders. In general, shares conditionally acquired ahead of the bid do count as shares already held: s.975(1).

[302] s.979(8)–(10). This rule is also applied to acquisitions by associates.

treasury shares of different categories.[303] If it decides to include them in the offer, a cut-off date must be specified in the offer beyond which such shares will not be regarded as being within the offer. If any of those categories of shares are included within the offer, then the question of whether the 90 per cent threshold has been met is calculated by taking into the account the shares allotted or which have ceased to be treasury shares on the date on which the bidder triggers the compulsory acquisition procedure (section 979(5)). Subsequently allotted shares or shares subsequently ceasing to be treasury shares do not affect that determination, once made, though if the offeror gives a subsequent notice (for example, because the first is defective in some way) the 90 per cent figure will have to be calculated on that second date. If the offeror chose not to make an offer for after-allotted or treasury shares, then, naturally, the compulsory transfer provisions will not apply to them.

Challenging the squeeze-out

Given the demanding nature of the 90 per cent threshold, the above **28–64** detailed provisions may well be of practical importance in particular cases in establishing whether the threshold has been exceeded. Assuming it has, the successful bidder triggers the compulsory acquisition process by giving notice to the non-accepting shareholders, with a copy to the target company, accompanied by a statutory declaration of its entitlement to serve the notice.[304] That notice must normally be given within three months of the last day on which the offer could be accepted.[305] The effect of the notice is, under section 981(2), that the offeror becomes entitled and bound to acquire the shares on the final terms of the offer. If the offer gave shareholders alternative choices of consideration (e.g. shares or a cash alternative), the notice must offer a similar choice and state that the shareholder

---

[303] s.974(4)–(7). A decision to exclude all or any such shares from the offer does not cause it to fail to meet the requirement that the offer be for all the shares or all the shares of a class: s.974(4), which excludes such shares from the universal obligation. Convertible securities, so long as they remain unconverted into shares, are treated as shares of the company but as a class of shares separate from the class into which they can be converted: s.989. R.15 of the Code normally requires the bidder to bid for convertible shares. For the problems caused by convertible shares before the introduction of these statutory reforms see *Simo Securities Trust, Re* [1971] 1 W.L.R. 1455. R.4.5 prohibits an offeree company from accepting an offer in respect of shares still held in treasury until after the offer is unconditional as to acceptances. On treasury shares see above at para.13–17.

[304] ss.979(4)–(8), 980(4)–(8). This requirement is buttressed by criminal sanctions for failing to send a notice to the company or for intentionally or negligently making a false statement in the declaration. S.986(9),(10) provide a limited exemption from the 90% threshold: if the failure to reach it is due entirely to the non-response of untraceable shareholders, the court may permit the bidder to serve a compulsory acquisition notice, provided it is satisfied (a) the consideration is fair and reasonable and (b) it is just and equitable to do so (taking into account in particular the number of untraceable shareholders).

[305] s.980(2),(3). Where the offer is not governed by the Code, so that there is no fixed closing date for the offer, the period is six months from the date of the offer.

may, within six weeks from the date of the notice, indicate the choice by a written communication to the offeror and must also state which consideration will apply in default of a choice. This applies whether or not any time limit or other conditions relating to choice in the offer can still be complied with and even if the consideration was to have been provided by a third party who is no longer bound or able to provide it.[306] The remainder of sections 981 and 982 prescribes in detail the procedures that have to be adopted to ensure that the shares which the offeror is bound to acquire are transferred to it and that the consideration that it is bound to pay reaches the shareholders concerned.[307]

The dissenting shareholder does not have to take the notice lying down. He or she can appeal to the court under section 986(1) for an order either (a) that the offeror shall not be entitled to acquire the shares or (b) that the terms of the acquisition shall be amended "as the court thinks fit".[308] The shareholder must act within six weeks of the date on which the acquisition notice was given by the bidder, but the application has the effect of suspending the bidder's rights until the appeal is disposed of. Section 986(4) provides that, where the petitioner seeks relief of type (b), the court may not increase the level of consideration to be provided by the bidder beyond that available in the offer, unless "the holder of the shares shows that the offer value would be unfair" (but it cannot in any event require a consideration of lower value). Thus, the burden of showing unfairness is on the challenger.

What are the petitioner's chances of success? They will be excellent if the petitioner can show that the statutory requirements for a "takeover offer" have not been met or that the 90 per cent threshold has not been reached, under the provisions discussed above, because then the court will have no jurisdiction to make an order for the compulsory acquisition of the shares. However, it should not be thought that the merits are always on the side of the non-accepting minority. They may simply be interested in exploiting to the full the position of power which the bidder's desire for complete control has

---

[306] s.981(4),(5). Normally the alternative which was to have been provided by a third party will have been cash, in which case the bidder now has to supply it. If the consideration which cannot now be provided, whether by bidder or third party, was a non-cash one, a requirement for equivalent cash applies. This adopts and codifies the effect of the decision of Brightman J. in *Carlton Holdings Ltd, Re* [1971] 1 W.L.R. 918.

[307] The main problem that has had to be solved is that many of the non-acceptors of the offer will probably be untraceable. The solution adopted causes the offeror little trouble (see s.982(4) ff), but the target company, now a subsidiary of the offeror, may have to maintain trust accounts for 12 years or earlier winding-up and then pay into court.

[308] It seems that the offeror cannot deprive the court of its jurisdiction to amend the terms of the squeeze-out by accepting the petitioner's right not to be squeezed out, at least where the petitioner has not indicated he or she seeks only the right not to be compulsorily acquired: *Greythorn, Re* [2002] 1 B.C.L.C. 437. In this case the petitioner had reasons for thinking that the closely-held target company had been taken over at a gross undervalue, and the bidder evidently preferred to allow the petitioner to remain in the company than to have that issue examined in court.

given them. If the court cannot order a compulsory acquisition because the statutory requirements have not been met, the bidder may think of other devices to achieve the same result.

In *Rock Nominees Ltd v RCO (Holdings) Plc*[309] the bidder, faced **28–65** with highly opportunistic conduct of this sort on the part of a shareholder which narrowly blocked achievement of the 90 per cent threshold, caused the newly acquired subsidiary to sell its business to another company in the same group (at a fair price) and then put the seller into voluntary liquidation, for which only a special resolution is required, distributing the price received on the sale to the shareholders (including the minority) and thus achieving the same result as a compulsory acquisition. The Court of Appeal refused to hold that this was unfairly prejudicial conduct on the part of the majority.[310]

Where the court has jurisdiction to prevent the compulsory purchase or amend its terms, the petitioner will have a more uphill struggle. Section 986(4) indicates the nature of the difficulty: if 90 per cent of the shareholders have accepted the offer, that is normally strong evidence that it is a fair one. Indeed, that subsection, introduced as a result of the Directive, appears to put a very high burden on the petitioner seeking to amend the bid terms: the petitioner must show, not simply that the offer value is unreliable, but that it was too low and, by implication, what the right price should be.[311] Consequently, the petitioner may have a better chance of success if he or she simply seeks an order that there should be no compulsory acquisition, for there the requirement to show that the offer value is unfair does not apply. Even in relation to simple denial of the compulsory purchase request, however, the British courts have traditionally relied on the high level of acceptances achieved to conclude that they should exercise their discretion in favour of the compulsory acquisition.[312] However, in more recent times the courts have been prepared to refuse compulsory acquisition where, unusually, the acceptances are an unreliable indicator of fairness, without requiring the petitioner to establish what the correct level of consideration should have been. Two such indicators of unreliability have emerged in particular in the cases. If the acceptors of the offer are not independent of the bidder or if the acceptors were not given adequate information upon which to take their decision, the court will not necessarily draw the conclusion that a 90 per cent acceptance indicates a fair offer.[313] In

---

[309] [2004] 1 B.C.L.C. 439, CA.

[310] This way of proceeding was undoubtedly more expensive for the bidder than a compulsory acquisition. On unfair prejudice see Ch.20 above and on voluntary winding up, para.A–6 below.

[311] For the courts' traditional reluctance to fix a price (as opposed to simply ratifying or not the bid price) see *Grierson, Oldham & Adams Ltd, Re* [1967] 1 W.L.R. 385.

[312] *Hoare & Co Ltd, Re* (1933) 150 L.T. 374; *Press Caps Ltd, Re* [1940] Ch. 434.

[313] *Bugle Press Ltd, Re* [1961] Ch. 270, CA; *Chez Nico (Restaurants) Ltd, Re* [1992] B.C.L.C. 192; *Lifecare International Plc, Re* [1990] B.C.L.C. 222; *Fiske Nominees Ltd v Dwyka Diamond Ltd* [2002] 2 B.C.L.C. 123.

practice, this means the petitioner's chances of success are much greater if the bid was not governed by the Code than if it was.

The sell-out right of non-accepting shareholders

28–66 The squeeze-out provisions introduced in 1929 were not originally accompanied by a right on the part of the non-accepting minority to have their shares bought by the bidder. This right was added only in 1948. Although similar formally, in fact the two rights perform very different functions. The sell-out right permits the shareholder, who does not wish to accept the bid, but who, if the majority do accept, would rather leave the company as well, to give effect to that set of preferences. He or she can refuse to accept the offer, but then change his or her mind, once the results of the other shareholders' decisions have become clear. This analysis reflects the fact that there are three, not two, possible outcomes of the bid for any one shareholder: the bid fails, the bid succeeds and the shareholder exits the company, and the bid succeeds but the shareholder remains in the company. The shareholder's preferences may run in the same order as that list of possible outcomes, and the ability to change one's mind after the outcome of the offer is known enables the preferences to be ranked fully.

However, the Code already provides a more effective mechanism for giving the shareholder that facility. Rule 31.4[314] requires the offeror to keep the offer open for a further 14 days after it has become unconditional as to acceptances. Since the Code rule is not dependent upon the 90 per cent threshold and it operates without a court order, it is a much more attractive mechanism for those who are quick enough to use it. This perhaps explains why there has been little litigation on the sell-out right provided by the statute.

The sell-out right, like the squeeze-out right, depends upon there having been a takeover offer which relates to all the shares in the company, as those terms are defined for a squeeze-out.[315] However, the 90 per cent threshold is calculated in relation to a different set of shares. The question is whether the shares which the offeror has acquired or unconditionally contracted to acquire as a result of acceptances of the offer *together with* other shares which the offeror (or an associate of the offeror) has acquired (or conditionally or unconditionally contracted to acquire) constitute 90 per cent of the voting shares in the company (and, where relevant, 90 per cent of the votes). If there is more than one class of share, this rule is applied

---

[314] Subject to the shut-off of cash alternatives: see above, para.28–54.
[315] s.983(1).

class by class.[316] In other words, unlike in the squeeze-out, the question is not whether there has been a 90 per cent level of acceptance of the offer, but rather whether the bid has left the offeror holding 90 per cent of the shares. This seems the correct test: the mischief which is sought to be remedied is the minority position into which the bid has put the shareholder and the precise degree of enthusiasm displayed by the shareholders for the offer is of secondary importance.[317] Thus, it is probably rather easier for the sell-out threshold to be attained than the squeeze-out threshold, because, in a sell-out, a lower level of acceptances might be compensated for by a higher level of pre-bid holdings on the part of the bidder or its associate.

The offeror must give each of the non-accepting shareholders notice of their entitlement to be bought out within one month of the end of the offer period. The shareholder wishing to take up this right must give notice to the offeror, either within three months of the end of the offer period or, if later, as it usually will be, of the notice given by the offeror.[318] Provisions apply as to the consideration to be provided which are equivalent to those for a squeeze-out.[319] It is in this case, rather than in relation to a squeeze-out, that the need to provide a choice of all the original alternatives (including a cash underwritten alternative) is so unpopular with offerors and their advisers. And it is, perhaps, rather remarkable and not altogether easy to reconcile with the provisions of the Code. As we have seen, under the Code an offer has to remain open for at least 14 days after it becomes unconditional as to acceptances. However, an offeror is not obliged to keep most types of cash underwritten alternatives open if it has given notice to shareholders that it reserves the right to close them on a stated date being not less than 14 days after the date on which the written notice is given.[320] The effect of the Act is virtually to keep the offer open for considerably longer than is required under the Code in all cases where the offer has been 90 per cent successful. And clearly the parties cannot contract out of the statutory provisions. Nor can the Panel or the Code waive them. The CLR endorsed this position.[321]

However, it is sometimes argued that what is now section 985 does **28–67** not apply if the cash alternative is described in the offeror's offer

---

[316] s.983(2)–(4), (8). "Associate" is broadly defined in s.988. If conditionally acquired shares are not in fact ultimately acquired and that would mean the threshold would not be met if they were excluded, there is a standstill procedure which may result in the shareholder losing the right to be bought out: s.983(6),(7).

[317] As with the squeeze-out right, however, this is not a general right for a minority to be bought out: if the final step in the process whereby the majority acquires 90% of the shares is not a takeover bid, the right to be bought out does not arise.

[318] s.984(1)–(4). The offeror's obligation is supported by criminal sanctions on the bidder and any officer in default: s.984(5)–(7).

[319] s.985.

[320] Above, para.28–54.

[321] Final Report I, para.13.61.

document as a separate offer by the underwriting investment bank. In the light of the section that argument seems unsustainable. The fact is that, as the section and the Code clearly recognise, the offeror's "offer" may and probably will contain a number of separate offers and that some of those offers may be made by third parties. All fall within the phrase "the terms of the offer". The only way, it is submitted, in which offerors and their investment banks might be able to achieve their aim is by making no mention at all of a cash underwritten alternative hoping that an independent investment bank, not acting on behalf of, or paid for its services by, the offeror will come forward and make an offer on its own account to the target's shareholders to buy the shares of the offeror received on the takeover. That is a somewhat unlikely scenario.

Under section 986(3), when a shareholder exercises his sell-out rights by notice to the offeror, an application may be made either by the shareholder or the offeror and the court may order that the terms on which the offeror shall acquire the shares shall be such as the court thinks fit. The parties may be in disagreement about whether there is an obligation on the offeror to acquire the shares at all or they may be in disagreement about the terms. The same provisions about raising or lowering the consideration in relation to the bid value apply as in a squeeze-out, since Article 16 of the Directive requires Member States to provide a sell-out right; and the shareholder will be in the same difficulty when arguing that the sell-out should be at a higher level than was provided for in the bid.

CONCLUSION

28–68 This Chapter has not attempted to answer the hotly disputed question of whether, on balance, takeovers are a "good thing" or a "bad thing". However, it is clear that the form of regulation of takeovers adopted in the United Kingdom does facilitate shifts in control achieved in this way. Especially important in this regard are the restrictions imposed by the Code on the defensive steps which are open to the management of the target company and its insistence that the shareholders of the target should not be denied the opportunity to decide on the merits of the bid.[322] In other countries, it is easier for the

---

[322] See Paul, "Corporate Governance in the Context of Takeovers of UK Public Companies" in Prentice and Holland (eds), *Contemporary Issues in Corporate Governance* (Oxford, OUP 1993), especially at pp.139–143.

incumbent management to take steps to defend itself against unwelcome bids, though not necessarily to the point of preventing them entirely.[323] The argument in favour of the regime adopted by the Code is that it provides a cheap and effective method of keeping management on their toes and protects shareholders from management slackness or self-dealing—or, in any event, provides a method for the shareholders to exit the company on acceptable terms if such managerial misbehaviour produces a takeover bid. Moreover, the Code seems to reflect in this respect the dominance of the institutional shareholders in the United Kingdom, which, even in pre-bid situations, where the Code does not apply, have set their faces against the adoption of defensive devices by the management of potential takeover targets.[324] However, it is perhaps easy to overestimate the beneficial effect upon management performance of the threat of the takeover bid,[325] which is not to say that the takeover bid has no role to play in the British system of corporate governance. Moreover, it might be very unwise to put the decision on the fate of the takeover bid entirely in the hands of the management of the target company when it is their discharge of their managerial functions which may be the main issue of contention in the bid. Going beyond these considerations of shareholder and management relations, however, is the broader question of the impact of takeovers on the public interest and on the interests of those other than the current shareholders whom company law now recognises as having an interest in the company, notably the employees.[326] This leads into the much wider subject of whether the current pattern of regulation of takeovers is part of a broader institutional structure which encourages "short-termism" on the part of the management of British companies, to the detriment of all those with a stake in the efficient running of the British economy. That, however, is a debate which cannot be embarked upon here.

---

[323] See Davies, "Defensive Measures: The Anglo-American Approach" (now somewhat dated on the US side) and Schaafsma, "Defensive Measures: The Continental Approach" in Hopt and Wymeersch (eds), *European Takeovers: Law and Practice* (London, Butterworths, 1992).

[324] See Davies, "Institutional Investors in the United Kingdom" in Prentice and Holland (eds), *Contemporary Issues in Corporate Governance*, especially at pp.85–87.

[325] See Coffee, "Regulating the Market for Corporate Control" (1984) *Columbia Law Review* 1145.

[326] See para.28–55, above.

ARRANGEMENTS AND RECONSTRUCTIONS

In most countries' companies legislation there is to be found a section **29–1** headed "Mergers" which will contain language somewhat along the following lines:

> "Any two or more corporations existing under the laws of this State may merge into a single corporation, which may be any one of the constituent corporations, or may consolidate into a new corporation formed by the consolidation, pursuant to an agreement of merger or consolidation, as the case may be, complying and approved in accordance with this section."[1]

The shareholders of the merging companies will end up as shareholders in the "resulting company" (which may be a new company formed for the purpose of the merger or one of the merging companies), each of the previously separate bodies of shareholders holding, more or less, the proportion of shares in the resulting company which reflects the respective valuations of the companies

---

[1] Delaware General Corporation Law §251.

which came together to form that company. The implementation of a merger normally requires the consent by resolution of the share-holders of the companies involved and of their boards of directors. Thus a merger involves a corporate decision taken on behalf of each of the companies adopting the merger plan. In this respect it is very different from a takeover (discussed in the previous Chapter) where the legal mechanism of assimilation is a transaction between the bidder company and the shareholders of the target and where the bidder and the target become parent and subsidiary companies, if the takeover is successful, rather than a single company (though they may seek to merge later). Once the directors have proposed and the requisite majority of the shareholders have approved the merger plan, thought needs to be given to protection of the shareholders who do not favour the merger. There are three main protective techniques which may be used, alone or in combination: verification by an independent expert of the valuations put on the merging companies (i.e. of the exchange ratio between shares in the resulting company and shares in the merging company), but otherwise the dissenting shareholders are bound to the merger; giving the shareholder a right of appeal to the court, either to prevent the merger occurring or to adjust some element of it; or giving the dissentient an appraisal right, i.e. a right to exit the merging company at a price which is fixed by some mechanism, rather than being bound into the resulting company.

No such clear-cut merger provision is to be found in the British statute, even after the reforms of 2006. Instead, there are two sets of provisions to be found in legislation which can be used to achieve a merger, one in the Companies Act and one in the Insolvency Act. Besides their different legislative homes, the two procedures are different in other ways as well. The one to be found in Part 26 of the 2006 Act is capable of being used for a wide range of purposes other than a merger, whilst sections 110 and 111 of the Insolvency Act can be used to achieve only certain types of merger. They differ as well in the third-party protections they use, Part 26 relying on court super-vision and sections 110–111 on appraisal, though Community law has had some impact on the protection provided by Part 26. Neither mechanism at first sight constitutes an obvious way of effecting a merger, amalgamation or fusion (none of these terms has a precise technical meaning) of companies, but they do in fact function as such. We shall look at each mechanism in turn.

SCHEMES OF ARRANGEMENT

The uses of a scheme

Part 26 applies "where a compromise or arrangement is proposed **29–2** between a company and its creditors or any class of them or its members or any class of them."[2] This immediately shows how this part of the Act extends well beyond mergers. The arrangement may not be with the company's members at all but with its creditors. In fact, when these provisions were introduced by the Joint Stock Companies Arrangement Act 1870, they applied only to arrangements with creditors (and indeed only to arrangements proposed by companies in the course of being wound up). The members were added in 1900 but not until the Companies (Consolidation) Act 1908 was the winding-up requirement dropped and the forerunner of the modern provision emerged. In practice, a very common use of the provisions today is to secure compromises with creditors of a company in financial trouble. In some cases the getting in and distribution of the company's assets can be effected more quickly and expeditiously through a scheme than a winding-up, in which case the scheme will operate alongside the winding-up, but in effect be determinative of most of the substantive issues; or the company may be able better to continue as a going concern under an arrangement than any of the procedures contained in the insolvency legislation for handling insolvent companies.[3] It has even been held that the courts have jurisdiction, though they should be slow to exercise it, to make a scheme which is binding on the liquidator and which would give the company's creditors different entitlements than those they would obtain in a winding-up.[4] However, the focus of this Chapter is on arrangements with members rather than with creditors.

Even where the "scheme of arrangement" (as it is invariably called) involves the company's members, it can be used for many purposes other than effecting a merger. In fact, the wording appears to encompass any restructuring of the mutual rights and obligations of the members and the company. Such restructuring may be confined to the affairs of a single company (so that no question of a merger arises). This is indicated by the definition of "arrangement", which is expressly stated to include a reorganisation of the company's share

---

[2] s.895.
[3] For a modern example see *T&N Ltd (No.3), Re* [2007] 1 B.C.L.C. 563.
[4] *Anglo American Insurance Ltd, Re* [2001] 1 B.C.L.C. 755. The scheme may even be sanctioned before the provisional liquidator is appointed. For a similarly broad view of what can be achieved through a scheme involving creditors see *Cape Plc, Re* [2007] 2 B.C.L.C. 546.

capital by the consolidation of shares of different classes or by the division of shares into shares of different classes or by both.[5]

However, that the procedure can be used for the amalgamation of two or more companies is made clear by section 900 which deals specifically with compromises or arrangements under section 895 "proposed for the purpose of or in connection with a scheme for ... the amalgamation of two or more companies" and involving the transfer of the undertaking or property of one company involved in the scheme to another.[6] In particular, the court is given the power to make ancillary orders when sanctioning a scheme or after sanctioning it so as to transfer the undertaking from transferor to transferee company and to dissolve the transferor company without winding it up.[7]

29–3   Rather than producing a merger, a scheme may be used as an alternative to a takeover offer. An example is a scheme under which the shareholders of the target agree to the cancellation of their shares in the target company; the reserve so created in the target is used by the target to pay up new shares which are issued to the offeror; and the shareholders of the target receive in exchange for their cancelled shares cash or shares in the offeror company.[8] The result in this case is the same as a successful takeover bid. As we have seen above, effecting an agreed takeover through a scheme is an increasingly popular move, so that the Takeover Panel, which has always applied its rules to takeovers through schemes (where its rules are not displaced by statutory rules specific to schemes), has recently sought to set that practice on a more systematic basis.[9]

An advantage of the scheme is that it becomes binding on all the shareholders in question if approved by three-quarters of the shares (and a majority in number of them),[10] whereas, as we have seen,[11] a takeover offer becomes binding on all shareholders only if accepted by 90 per cent of the shares offered for and the company then suc-

---

[5] s.895(2)(a). In so far as the rights of shareholders are contained in the articles, they can be altered by the simpler procedure for altering the articles, subject in appropriate cases to the separate consent of the class of shareholders whose rights are being affected: see paras 19–11ff, above.

[6] s.900(1). The section also applies to the "reconstruction" of a company by way of the transfer of its undertaking or property to another company, but in the case of a reconstruction it has been held that the shareholders of the transferor company must be substantially the shareholders of the transferee company (but liabilities may be left with the transferor): *South African Supply and Cold Storage Co, Re* [1904] 2 Ch.268, 281–2; *MyTravel Group Plc, Re* [2005] 2 B.C.L.C. 123 (Mann J.).

[7] s.900(2)(a),(d).

[8] This way of proceeding under what is now Part 26 was sanctioned nearly a century ago: *Guardian Assurance Co Ltd, Re* [1917] 1 Ch.431 (though in that case the shareholders of the target company were compensated, unusually, by a transfer to them of part of the existing shareholdings of the acquirer's shareholders rather than by the issue of new shares in the acquirer).

[9] Above, at para.28–12. On the complications which can arise when competing bids are put through the scheme mechanism see *Allied Domecq Plc, Re* [2000] 1 B.C.L.C. 134.

[10] s.899(1).

[11] See above at paras 28–61 *et seq.*

cessfully "squeezes out" the non-accepting shareholders. For this reason, it was argued that, if the scheme procedure was used where a takeover offer could be made, the court should insist on 90 per cent approval of the scheme by the shareholders. However, the argument was rejected on the grounds that in the scheme procedure the shareholders had the protection of the requirement of prior court sanction, even if the level of approval required of them was lower than for a compulsory buy-out.[12] A crucial step in this reasoning is that the court must form its own judgment on the merits of the scheme when it comes to consider its approval and not grant approval simply because the appropriate proportion of the members have approved it.

In the case of a hostile offer, the disadvantages of the scheme normally outweigh its advantages as against the takeover offer. The main disadvantage is that the shareholders are not bound until they have voted in favour of the scheme or, even, until the court has sanctioned it, and the necessary delays involved in calling a shareholder meeting give rival bidders the time to organise a competing bid. By contrast, in a takeover offer the bidder can start soliciting "irrevocable commitments"[13] even before the formal offer is made, and those who accept the offer, whether before or after it is formally launched, are not released from their acceptances simply because a rival offer has appeared.[14] Therefore, a scheme is likely to prove attractive only where the takeover is agreed with the board of the target and is not likely to precipitate a rival offer and the offeror is keen to achieve complete ownership of the target.

Overall, whether the scheme involves just a single company or more than one company, the courts have construed "arrangement" as a word of very wide import and as not to be read down by its association with the word "compromise" in the section, so that an arrangement involving members need not, and usually does not, involve an element of compromise.[15] The term covers almost every type of legal transaction,[16] and, as the takeover example shows, in substance the transaction may be between the shareholders and a third party, though a scheme will only be available if the company is formally a necessary party to the transaction.[17] Only the case of

---

[12] *National Bank, Re* [1966] 1 W.L.R. 819; *BTR Plc, Re* [2000] 1 B.C.L.C. 740, CA.
[13] See above, at para.28–63.
[14] Ch.28, at para.28–35.
[15] *National Bank Ltd, Re* [1966] 1 W.L.R. 819 at 829; *Calgary and Edmonton Land Co, Re* [1975] 1 W.L.R. 355 at 363; *Savoy Hotel Ltd, Re* [1981] Ch.351 at 359D–F; *T&N Ltd (No.3), Re* [2007] 1 B.C.L.C. 563 at [46]–[50].
[16] If it involves a reduction of capital, as it often will, this can be sanctioned without the need for separate proceedings under the procedure analysed in Ch.13, above.
[17] In the example given above the company was a necessary party because of the need to cancel the members' existing shares and to issue new shares to the bidder.

simple expropriation of the shareholders has so far been excluded by the courts from the scope of the term.[18]

The mechanics of the scheme of arrangement

29-4   There are three main steps in a scheme of arrangement:

(a) A compromise or arrangement must be proposed between the company and its members or creditors.[19]

(b) Meetings of the members or creditors must be held to seek approval of the scheme by the appropriate majorities. These meetings are convened by the court on application to it.[20]

(c) The scheme is sanctioned by the court.[21]

Proposing a scheme

29-5   This first stage, which is often overlooked, is important because, in practice, it is difficult to use the scheme procedure unless the scheme is approved by the board, which then proposes it on behalf of the company. Formally, it would seem that the general meeting could propose a scheme on behalf of the company,[22] but the shareholders' co-ordination problems make this course of action often difficult. The point is illustrated by the decision in *Savoy Hotel Ltd, Re*,[23] which is instructive in a number of ways. The company, which had survived a hostile takeover bid in the early 1950s,[24] introduced a dual-class share structure, consisting, at the time of the litigation, of some 28 million A shares and some 1.3 million B shares, with identical financial entitlements, but with the B shares having (in effect) 20 times the number of votes attached to the A shares. The board held directly or indirectly some two-thirds of the B shares. Such a degree of voting leverage may have been thought to have rendered the company impregnable to a takeover. However, this distribution of voting rights did mean that the A shareholders held just over half the votes in the company. This did not create the risk of an ordinary takeover offer succeeding, because it was reasonable to assume that enough holders of the A shares would oppose a bid to prevent the bidder obtaining 50

---

[18] *NFU Development Trust Ltd, Re* [1972] 1 W.L.R. 1548: held that the court had no jurisdiction to sanction a scheme whereby all the members were required to relinquish their financial rights without any quid pro quo.

[19] s.895(1). The term "creditor" is a wide one and includes contingent creditors, who would not have a provable debt in a liquidation: *T&N Ltd (No.2), Re* [2006] 2 B.C.L.C. 374.

[20] ss.896–899(1).

[21] s.896.

[22] The possibility of shareholder proposal was recognised in *Savoy Hotel Ltd, Re* [1981] Ch.351.

[23] See previous note.

[24] See para.16–33 at n.126.

per cent of the total votes, as required by the Takeover Code,[25] given that the B shareholders would be solidly against an offer.

Instead the bidder (THF) sought to put forward a scheme for the transfer to it of the A and B shares in exchange for cash, the scheme providing that if one class of shareholders did not approve of it (the B shareholders), the scheme could proceed in favour of the other class alone (the A shareholders). It was reasonable to suppose that three-quarters in value and a majority in number of the A class share-holders[26] might approve the scheme. The dissentient A class share-holders would then be bound by it (subject to court sanction) and the bidder would end up with just over half the voting shares in the company, even if the scheme were rejected by the B class share-holders. THF, which held a few A class shares, applied to the court as a member[27] under step (b) above for an order for separate meetings of the A and B shareholders to be held to consider the scheme. Nourse J. held that he had power to order such meetings but declined to do so, on the grounds that they would be futile. This was because the scheme had not been proposed by the company but by a third party (THF). Thus, step (a) was not satisfied and so the court would not have jurisdiction to sanction it at stage (c).[28]

Convening and conducting meetings

When the proposed scheme has been formulated, the first step is an application (normally *ex parte*) to the court by or on behalf of the company (or companies) to which the compromise or arrangement relates for the court to order meetings of the creditors or classes of creditors or members or classes of members to be summoned.[29] This the court will generally do and will give directions about the length of notice, the method of giving it and the forms of proxy. The major difficulty has proved to be decisions about whether the members or creditors should be split into separate classes for the purpose of voting on the scheme. The fact that the members or creditors in question have the same rights as against the company does not necessarily mean that they are part of the same class for scheme purposes, because the scheme may propose to treat different groups of those members or creditors differently. Indeed, the proposed different treatment may be a good argument for separate meetings.[30]

29–6

---

[25] See para.28–52.
[26] The level of approval of a scheme required. See below.
[27] s.896(2) contemplates applications under step (b) by a creditor or member as well as by the company or its liquidator or administrator.
[28] THF would not be able to get around this problem by seeking to convene a general meeting to propose the scheme, because at a general meeting both A and B shareholders would vote together and the reasons given in the text why a bid would fail would apply also to a shareholder resolution to adopt a scheme.
[29] s.896(1).
[30] See *Anglo American Insurance Ltd, Re* [2001] 1 B.C.L.C. 755.

The issue was rendered particularly acute by the former practice of the courts of leaving the decision about class meetings at stage (b) almost wholly to the company (i.e. of simply accepting what the company proposed) and taking a view whether that decision was correct only at stage (c), by which time it was too late to do anything about it and the court could only refuse to sanction the scheme on the grounds it had no jurisdiction to do so, since the proper meetings had not been held!

This approach was roundly criticised by Chadwick L.J. in *Hawk Insurance Co Ltd, Re*[31] and, as far as creditors are concerned, where identifying the correct classes is often particularly difficult, a Practice Direction was subsequently issued designed to produce substantive consideration of the classes issue at stage (b). Although a creditor may still challenge the way the meetings were convened at stage (c), the court "will expect them to show good reason why they did not raise a creditor issue at an earlier stage."[32] The CLR proposed that the court should have the general discretion to determine the appropriate classes at stage (b), when asked to do so by the company, and that, if it exercised its discretion at this stage, it should be bound by it when it came to consider sanctioning the scheme after member or creditor approval (stage (c)).[33] It further proposed that the court should have a discretion to sanction the scheme even if the appropriate class meetings had not been held, provided the court was satisfied that the incorrect composition of the meetings had not had any substantive effect on the outcome, i.e. it would no longer be a matter going to the jurisdiction of the court.[34] However, these proposed reforms were not taken up in the Act and so the procedure in relation to classes of members remains somewhat obscure. It seems likely that the courts will adapt the creditor procedure where difficult issues as to the composition of classes of member arise.

As far as the general test is concerned for determining whether the members or creditors should meet as a whole or in one or more separate classes, it has long been clear that it is whether the rights of those concerned "are not so dissimilar as to make it impossible for them to consult together with a view to their common interest".[35] However, the application of this general test in practice is far from easy, even in the case of members. In general, it can be said that, the

[31] [2002] B.C.C. 300, CA. He thought it particularly unfortunate that the court should feel obliged to raise the issue of its own motion at stage (c), even though no member or creditor sought to argue that class meetings should have been held.

[32] Practice Direction [2002] 1 W.L.R. 1345. See for an account of modern practice *T&N Ltd (No.3), Re*, above, fn.3, at [18]–[20]

[33] The court does already decide at stage (b) issues relating to the jurisdiction of the court to sanction a scheme at stage (c), though not issues going to the fairness of the scheme: *Savoy Hotel, Re*, above, fn.22; *Telewest Communications Plc (No.1), Re* [2005] 1 B.C.L.C. 752 at [14]–[15]; *My Travel Group Plc, Re* [2005] 2 B.C.L.C. 123.

[34] Final Report I, paras 13.6–13.7. This would not otherwise affect the tasks to be performed by the court at the sanctioning stage, on which see below.

[35] *Sovereign Life Assurance Co v Dodd* [1892] 2 Q.B. 573 at 583, per Bowen L.J.

greater the number of classes, the greater the chances the scheme will fail to obtain the consent of one or more of those classes.[36] Further, the tests for determining classes should be reasonably simple and applicable by the company without extensive investigation into the position of particular members or creditors. For this reason, the courts have used the rights of shareholders as the touchstone for determining the class issue, rather than their interests, the latter being a test which it is both difficult for the company to apply and likely to lead to a large number of classes being constituted. Thus, in *BTR Plc, Re*,[37] a case of a takeover being effected through a scheme, the judge sanctioned the scheme which had been approved in a single meeting of the target's shareholders and rejected the argument that those shareholders of the target company who already held shares in the bidder should have been put in a separate class. The judge distinguished the earlier case of *Hellenic and General Trust, Re*,[38] where the judge had refused sanction because the shares already held by a subsidiary of the bidder in the target had been voted in favour of the scheme. The explanation of *Hellenic, Re* was that the subsidiary's shares had been excluded because the scheme did not concern them: in effect, they were already held by the bidder.

On the other hand, the fact that the members or, more likely, creditors—where this issue is often acute—have different rights or claims against the company does not necessarily mean that they cannot be put together for scheme purposes. The issue has proved controversial in recent years in relation to the distinction between vested and contingent creditors, as the Court of Appeal has sought to make more flexible the traditional practice of treating these two groups separately.[39] The newer approach does not mean, it is thought, that the obvious distinctions between secured debenture-holders, unsecured lenders and trade creditors should be ignored.

29–7

Section 897 requires any notice sent out summoning the meetings to be accompanied by a statement explaining the effect of the compromise or arrangement and in particular stating any material interests of the directors (whether in their capacity of directors or otherwise) and the effect on those interests of the scheme in so far as

---

[36] *Equitable Life Assurance Society, Re* [2002] 2 B.C.L.C. 510.

[37] [1999] 2 B.C.L.C. 675. The decision and reasoning were upheld on appeal: [2000] 1 B.C.L.C. 740, CA. See also *Industrial Equity (Pacific) Ltd, Re* [1991] 2 HKLR 614.

[38] [1976] 1 W.L.R. 123.

[39] See *Hawk Insurance Co Ltd, Re* above, fn.31. However, it is important to see that the *Hawk* case involved an insolvent company; putting vested and contingent creditors of a solvent company together might well not be appropriate: *British Aviation Insurance Co Ltd, Re* [2006] 1 B.C.L.C. 665.

that differs from the effect on the interests of others.[40] Where the scheme affects the rights of debenture-holders, the statement must give the like statement regarding the interests of any trustees for the debenture-holders.[41] If the notice is given by advertisement,[42] the advertisement must include the foregoing statements or a notification of where and how copies of the circular can be obtained, and on making application a member or creditor is entitled to be furnished with a copy free of charge.[43]

The level of approval required at the meeting is a majority in number,[44] representing three-fourths in value,[45] of its creditors or members present and voting in person or by proxy.[46] The question of whether the approval of both creditors and members or of a particular class of member or creditor is required in any case is to be answered by determining with whom the company proposes to effect a compromise or arrangement. If members or creditors or any class of them are not included within the scheme, their consent is not required, but the company runs the risk that the implementation of the scheme may later be held to infringe the rights of those left out of it.[47]

The sanction of the court

29–8 The application for the court's approval is made by petition of the applicants and may be opposed by members and creditors who object to the scheme. In the oft-quoted words of Maugham J.,[48] the duties of the court are twofold:

---

[40] s.897(1),(2).

[41] s.897(3). If the interests of the directors or the trustees change before the meetings are held, the court will not sanction the scheme unless satisfied that no reasonable shareholder or debenture-holder would have altered his decision on how to vote if the changed position had been disclosed: *Jessel Trust Ltd, Re* [1985] B.C.L.C. 119; *Minster Assets, Re* [1985] B.C.L.C. 200.

[42] Which will be the only way of notifying holders of share warrants to bearer or of bearer bonds. It may also be necessary to advertise in this way to creditors.

[43] s.897(1)(b),(4). A default in complying with any requirement of the section renders the company and every officer, liquidator, administrator, or trustee for debenture-holders liable to a fine unless he shows that the default was due to the refusal of another director or trustee for debenture-holders to supply the necessary particulars of his interest: s.897(5)–(8). In that case the criminal offence is committed by that director or trustee: s.898.

[44] The CLR recommended the removal of the number requirement, which does indeed appear anomalous in the context of the Companies Act approach to shareholder approval: Final Report I, para.13.10.

[45] In relation to creditors further difficulties may arise in valuing their claims and thus determining whether the majority does represent three-fourths in value. See the discussion of the "IBNR claims" in *British Aviation Insurance Co Ltd, Re* [2006] 1 B.C.L.C. 665.This is a problem met whenever this formula is employed in respect of creditors—as it is throughout the Insolvency Act.

[46] s.899(1).

[47] *MyTravel Group Plc, Re*, above, fn.33, CA.

[48] In *Dorman Long & Co, Re* [1934] Ch.635, 655 and 657. See also *National Bank Ltd, Re* [1966] 1 W.L.R. 819, 829.

"The first is to see that the resolutions are passed by the statutory majority in value and number ... at a meeting or meetings duly convened and held. The other duty is in the nature of a discretionary power ... [W]hat I have to see is whether the proposal is such that an intelligent and honest man, a member of the class concerned and acting in respect of his interest, might reasonably approve."

The first of these duties involves not only ensuring that the meeting was given the information the statute requires and that the requisite majority was obtained, but also that the class was fairly represented at the meeting. Thus, the sanction of the court can be refused if the meeting were unrepresentative of the class as a whole or if those whose votes were necessary to secure the required level of approval did so in order to promote some special interest which they did not share with the ordinary members of the class.[49] This latter test seems to involved something akin to the "bona fides" test applied to majority decisions to change the articles.[50] However, the court's second duty takes it beyond a bona fides test and opens up the way to a more rigorous judicial scrutiny of the scheme, though the weight of majority approval will be heavy if the meetings have been properly called and conducted.

The scheme becomes binding on the company and all members and creditors (or all members of the class concerned) and, if the company is in liquidation, on the liquidator, so long as it is sanctioned by the court.[51] Indeed, the binding effect of schemes on minorities is one of its attractions over a takeover bid.[52] But its order sanctioning the scheme does not take effect until a copy is delivered to the Registrar and, where relevant, a copy of it has to be attached to every copy of the company's articles of association issued by the company thereafter.[53]

Additional requirements for mergers and divisions of public companies
Under British practice, mergers of companies are rarely carried out by means of transfers of undertakings (as opposed to shares) using a scheme of arrangement. For this, there are said to be two reasons. **29–9**

---

[49] *BTR Plc, Re* above, fn.12, at 747.
[50] Above, at para.19–3.
[51] s.899(3). This will be so even if the scheme involves the commission of acts which would be unlawful on the company's part without the sanction of the court: *British and Commonwealth Holdings Plc v Barclays Bank Plc* [1996] 1 W.L.R. 1, CA.
[52] The courts have rejected arguments that a scheme which satisfies the requirements of the Act might nevertheless amount to deprivation of possessions contrary to Article 1 of the First Protocol of the European Convention on Human Rights: *Equitable Life Assurance Society, Re* [2002] 2 B.C.L.C. 510; *Waste Recycling Group Plc, Re* [2004] 1 B.C.L.C. 352.
[53] ss.899(4) and 901.

First, such transactions necessarily raise issues of third party rights and creditor protection. By the former is meant that, by virtue of the contracts which the transferring company has entered into with third parties, those third parties may have the right to terminate their relationship with the transferor or to insist on different terms of business if the transferor is replaced by the transferee as the contracting party. Any court order under section 900[54] (transferring property) will not override these third-party rights and so transferor and transferee will have to negotiate an acceptable set of arrangements with the third party. However, it should be noted that contractual restrictions can easily be drafted so as to apply where control of the company changes without there being any transfer of assets (as in a takeover, whether effected by a scheme or not), so that in this respect a merger may put the company in no worse a position. By the latter is meant that creditors of the transferor may see their position as being weakened by the proposed amalgamation (because they will now be in competition with the transferee's creditors who may have proportionately greater claims) and they may be able to persuade the court to impose various safeguards in their favour. This will not arise in the case of a takeover, since the court is not involved in approving it, but this will not avail the bidder company if the creditors have used the contractual route to protection.

A second part of the explanation may be that a merger effected by a scheme is very likely to trigger Part 27 of the Act, which imposes extra requirements and costs on the implementation of schemes for reconstruction[55] or amalgamation involving a public company, in order to meet the requirements of the Third and Sixth Company Law Directives on mergers and divisions of public companies.[56] Part 27 does not apply where a scheme is used to effect a takeover, because bidder and target remain separate companies after the scheme has been effected. There are three major additional requirements,[57] of which the most important is the third, which deploys the protective device, not otherwise found in the domestic rules on schemes of arrangement, of an independent expert's report. However, although no formal independent expert's report may be required of the bidder in the case of a proposed takeover, any prospective bidder will in fact do due diligence, possibly of a very extensive sort, before launching a bid.[58] Thus, Part 27 may not add much in substance to the bidder's costs. Perhaps the truth is that tax rules make amalgamations through schemes unattractive or that British practitioners have

---

[54] See above, para.29–2.

[55] See fn.6 above.

[56] Directives 78/855/EEC and 82/891/EEC, respectively.

[57] The details differ somewhat according to the "Case" (see below) within which the scheme falls, the main differences being between those within Case 1 or 2 (mergers) and Case 3 (divisions).

[58] See para.28–47.

become so familiar with the takeover that alternative means of amalgamation are not seriously explored. In any event, the scheme-based merger seems to be a dead letter in British practice.

The additional requirements of Part 27 are: **29–10**

1. Normally, a draft scheme has to be drawn up by the boards of all[59] the companies concerned, a copy delivered to the Registrar and the latter has to publish a notice of its receipt in the *Gazette*. All this must be done at least one month before the meetings are held.[60]

2. What has to be stated in the board's circulars is considerably amplified.[61]

3. In addition, there generally[62] have to be separate written reports on the scheme to the members of each company by an independent expert appointed by that company or, if the court approves, a single joint report to all companies by an independent expert appointed by all of them.[63]

However, the Directives, although widely framed, do not apply to all forms of merger (or division), and Part 27 goes no wider. Hence, there is some considerable scope for framing a merger scheme which avoids the additional requirements. In particular, Part 27 applies only where the consideration for the transfer is or includes shares in the transferee, so that a merger for a purely cash consideration is excluded.[64] Secondly, where in the case of a merger "by absorption" (see below) the transferee company already holds all, or in some cases 90 per cent, of the securities carrying voting rights in the transferor, the requirements mentioned above are substantially reduced.[65] This facilitates mergers within corporate groups and, in particular, a merger of parent and new subsidiary following a successful takeover

---

[59] This includes the transferee company, whose consent is not required under a scheme governed purely by Part 26, unless the rights of the shareholders or creditors of the transferee are proposed to be changed. However, it is enough that the members of the transferee are given the option to call a meeting (on the basis of a 5% threshold: ss.918 and 932) so that the burden of action falls on the shareholders rather than the company in such a case. Of course, if the transferee is a UK listed company, the "Class 1" transaction rules might require it to obtain shareholder approval. See para.14–8.

[60] ss.905–6, 920–921.

[61] ss.908, 910, 923, 925.

[62] As a result of amendments to the Directives introduced by Directive 2007/63/EC the requirement for an independent report can be dispensed with if all the shareholders agree. See the Companies (Mergers and Divisions of Public Companies (Amendment) Regulations 2008/690, introducing a new s.918A into the Act.

[63] ss.909, 924 and 935–937. The matters to be dealt with in the report are specified in some detail. In some respects it resembles the report required (also as a result of an EC Directive) when a public company makes an issue of shares paid-up otherwise than in cash: see paras 11–15ff, above.

[64] s.902(1)(c).

[65] s.915. In these cases, as well, the requirement for a meeting of members is relaxed: ss.916–917 and 931.

bid. Thirdly, Part 27 does not apply if the transferor company is being wound up,[66] rather than being dissolved without winding-up after the merger. Thus, the requirements of Part 27 can be avoided by incurring the expense of putting the transferor into liquidation—probably not an attractive course of action.

Finally, the merger or division must fall within one of the three "Cases" specified in the Directives. The three "Cases" are:

1. Where the undertaking, property and liabilities of the public company are to be transferred to another public company, other than one formed for the purpose of, or in connection with, the scheme ("merger by absorption").[67]

2. Where the undertakings, property and liabilities of each of two or more public companies, including the one in respect of which the arrangement is proposed, are to be transferred to a new company, whether or not a public company, formed for the purpose of, or in connection with, the scheme ("merger by formation of new company").[68] Thus, a transfer to a new company, public or private, by a single public company escapes from both 1 and 2, and equally a reconstruction of a single company can be carried out purely under Part 26.[69]

3. Where, under the scheme, the undertaking, property and liabilities of the public company are to be divided among, or transferred to, two or more companies each of which is either a public company or a company formed for the purposes of, or in connection with, the scheme ("division by acquisition" or "division by formation of new company").[70]

29–11   Despite the discouraging history of the use of schemes to effect mergers, the CLR consulted on the issue of whether there should be introduced into the Act a statutory merger procedure, as in many other jurisdictions.[71] For the CLR the crucial element of a statutory merger procedure was that the merger should not require approval by the court, though in appropriate cases those adversely affected by the proposal should have a right of appeal to the court. Its goal of providing a "court free" merger procedure was thus in line with what it recommended in the case of reductions of capital.[72] However, it also took the view that, where the Third and Sixth Directives applied, it would be impractical to implement a proposal except under the

---

[66] s.902(3).
[67] ss.904(1)(a) and 902(2)(b).
[68] ss.904(1)(b) and 902(2)(a).
[69] See the scheme proposed in *MyTravel Group Plc, Re*, above, fn.33.
[70] ss.919 and 902(2).
[71] *Completing*, paras 11.40–11.53.
[72] See paras 13–5ff.

supervision of the court.[73] The result of the restrictions in effect imposed by the Directives was that the statutory merger procedure seemed to the CLR to be feasible only in two cases. The first was the merger of wholly-owned subsidiaries of a parent company. The CLR thought this a useful reform, and it was supported on consultation, because "many groups of companies include subsidiaries which are kept alive for no good reason other than to avoid the expense and problems associated with getting rid of them".[74] The second and somewhat more general area for the operation of a statutory merger procedure was where a company formed a new wholly-owned subsidiary, into which the assets and liabilities of an existing company were transferred, the transferor being dissolved. On consultation a majority thought the new procedure should be made available in this situation as well.[75] However, neither of these proposals was taken up in the Act.

Cross-border mergers

With the reduction in barriers to trade on a global basis, cross-border amalgamations of companies are ever more common, both within the European Community and more widely. Such amalgamations can be carried out relatively easily by means of a takeover (if the participants are willing), for the transfer of shares in a company incorporated in one jurisdiction to a shareholder located in another presents no particular difficulties, at least in developed countries. An amalgamation across border achieved by means of a merger is more problematic, because it requires the law of one State to recognise the existence of a new or enlarged company (created by the merger) and the law of another State to recognise the dissolution of a company merging into the resulting company. At the very least, the laws of the States involved need to be closely co-ordinated. Despite this difficulty, the European Court of Justice has held it to be an infringement of a company's freedom of establishment under the Treaty[76] for companies from one Member State to be excluded in principle from another Member State's merger law. In *SEVIC*[77] a German company purported to carry out a merger with a Luxembourg company which took the form of a dissolution without liquidation of the latter and the transfer of its assets to the German company, but the relevant German authority refused to register the merger because the German merger law was open only to German companies.

29–12

---

[73] Completing, para.11.46.
[74] Completing, para.11.50. A potential use for the SE (above, para.1–21) is to achieve a similar result within multinational groups.
[75] Final Report I, paras 13.14–13.15.
[76] Art.43EC.
[77] Case C-411/03, [2005] E.C.R. I-10805. It was not entirely clear whether it was the freedom of establishment of the German or the Luxembourg company or both which the Court regarded as having been infringed.

Part 26 of the 2006 Act is not as tightly circumscribed as the German provisions were. The companies whose compromises or arrangements fall within it include a company liable to be wound up under the Insolvency Act 1986.[78] That Act applies to "unregistered" companies, which term is wide enough to include companies incorporated in a foreign State.[79] It has been held that both insolvent and solvent companies incorporated elsewhere fall within the jurisdiction of the English courts for the purposes of schemes of arrangement, though the English courts would not exercise that jurisdiction unless there was a sufficiently close connection with England on the part of the company in question.[80] These cases were not, however, cases of schemes to achieve cross-border mergers and the difficulty of using the British legislation to that end is perhaps indicated by the fact that a British court's powers to make ancillary orders to effect an amalgamation, through, for example, an order for the transfer of assets and a dissolution of the transferor company, is restricted to companies within the meaning of the Companies Act 2006.[81] Germany's justification for its exclusionary rule, that the German courts could not on their own afford appropriate protection to shareholders, creditors and employees of foreign companies, will in most cases be decisive, even if the ECJ found a blanket exclusion of companies from other Member States from the German procedure disproportionate.

However, the issue of co-ordination among the laws of the Member States of the European Community has now been addressed by the Cross-Border Mergers Directive,[82] implemented in the United Kingdom by the Companies (Cross-Border Merger) Regulations 2007.[83] Subject to the always thorny issue of employee representation on the board of the resulting company (see below), the scheme of the Directive is simple and relatively elegant. Each company in the cross-border merger is subject to its national merger procedure,[84] on the basis of a common merger plan.[85] However, that national merger

---

[78] s.895(2)(b).
[79] s.220 of the Insolvency Act 1986.
[80] *Drax Holdings Ltd, Re* [2004] 1 B.C.L.C. 10; *Sovereign Marine and General Insurance Co Ltd, Re* [2007] 1 B.C.L.C. 228.
[81] s.895(2)(a).
[82] Directive 2005/56/EC on cross-border mergers of limited liability companies (OJ L310/10, 24.11.2005).
[83] SI 2974, a self-standing set of regulations made under the European Communities Act 1972 and constituting a major piece of corporate law which is not located in the 2006 Act at all.
[84] Art.4. Where the resulting company in a merger by absorption is a private company, Art.9 requires approval at a general meeting of the shareholders, but that article does not specify a qualified majority. Since Part 27 does not apply (it covers only public companies), it appears in this case an ordinary majority will do.
[85] Art.5.

procedure, not surprisingly, is required to comply with the standards set out in the Third Directive and noted above, in particular the requirement for a report by an independent expert.[86] Each national authority (the court in the UK) has to certify compliance with its procedures (the "pre-merger certificate").[87] The appropriate authority in the State where the resulting company is to be registered completes the merger process (notably by ensuring that the participating companies have operated on the basis of a common plan and that the requirements for employee participation have been met).[88] On registration of the resulting company, all the assets and liabilities of the merging companies are transferred to it,[89] the members of the merging companies receiving securities becoming members[90] of the resulting company and the merging companies cease to exist.[91] Parts 2 and 3 of the Regulations transpose the above provisions into domestic law in such a way as to provide a virtually free-standing code for cross-border mergers. An expert is one who is eligible to be appointed as a statutory auditor and is independent if he meets the statutory tests for independence as an auditor.[92] The approval level required, following the Directive, is 75 per cent in value of each class of members or creditors whose consent is required, without any requirement for a majority in number.[93]

The cross-border merger Directive appears to give the merging companies a free choice as to the Member State jurisdiction which will govern the resulting company. If a jurisdiction is desired which is not one in which any of the merging companies is currently incorporated, then a new resulting company can be incorporated in the desired jurisdiction and the existing companies merged into it. However, if the desired jurisdiction is a "real seat" State, then the Directive appears to permit the authorities of that State not to register the resulting entity, if the company's "central administration" is not also in that State.[94] This would be a significant obstacle to the

29–13

---

[86] Arts. 6–8. A simplified procedure can be followed where the merger is between a wholly-owned subsidiary and its parent and the expert's report may be dispensed with where the transferee holds 90% of the securities of the transferor carrying voting rights: Art.15. The UK has taken up this latter option: reg.9(1).

[87] Art.10.

[88] Arts.11–12.

[89] Including the rights and obligations of the merging companies under contracts of employment: Art.14(4).

[90] The members of the transferring companies may also receive part of their consideration in cash, unlimited provided that at least one of the Member States involved permits this, which the UK does; otherwise the cash is limited to 10% of the nominal value of the newly issued shares: Arts. 2(2) and 3(1). However, there may be tax disadvantages if the 10% figure is exceeded.

[91] Art.14.

[92] Reg.9(7)–(8), invoking ss.1212 and 1214 of the Act, on which see Ch.22 at para.22–10.

[93] Regs. 12 and 13.

[94] Art.4(1)(b). For discussion of this issue, and a number of other pertinent observations on the Directive, see J. Rickford, "The Proposed Tenth Company Law Directive on Cross Border Mergers and its Impact in the UK" [2005] E.B.L.R. 1393.

merging companies' choice of jurisdiction and may well not be compatible with those companies' freedom of establishment rights under the EC Treaty.

The Directive and domestic Regulations become complicated over the issue of whether the resulting company is required to have in place a system of worker participation in relation to its board (either a one-tier board or the supervisory board in a two-tier system). Participation includes not only the right to elect or appoint members of the board but also rights to recommend or oppose board members.[95] No more than a sketch of the provisions can be offered here, but in general the rules follow those for the SE (European Company).[96] The following points can be made, looking at the matter from the point of view of a UK resulting company.

(1) The general rule (though it has significant exceptions) is that the resulting company is subject to the participation rules applying in its State of registration.[97] On this basis a resulting company registered in the United Kingdom would not be subject to participation rules.

(2) However, participation is required in principle in UK transferee companies in three situations.[98] It is required (a) where any merging company in the six months prior to the publication of the draft terms of the merger had an average number of employees exceeding 500 and operated a system of employee participation. Further, it is required when (b) a UK merging company has a proportion of employee representatives amongst the directors. Finally, it is required when (c) a merging company has employee representatives on the board or their committees or on "the management group which covers the profit units of the company." These often overlapping definitions can be understood only in the light of the variety of employee participation arrangements existing in other Member States. Situation (b) is likely to be of the least significance for UK transferee companies since UK companies are not required to have employee representatives on the board. Situations (a) and (c) are likely to be the most important. Situation (a) covers any merging company (not just a UK one) and any system of employee participation,

---

[95] Art.16, referring to Art.2(k) of Directive 2001/86/EC on involvement of employees in the SE. The consultation provisions of the latter Directive are irrelevant to the Cross-Border Mergers Directive: the resulting company will always be governed by the national consultation provisions of its State of registration.

[96] See para.14–28.

[97] Art.16(1) and reg.22.

[98] The general rule does not apply either if the national system gives participation rights only to employees of the resulting company employed in the State of registration, an important point, but clearly of no application in the UK.

whether based on board level representation or some other form of influence over the composition of the board. It is, however, limited to companies with an average of 500 employees in the six months prior to the publication of the draft merger agreement. Situation (c) is not limited by this requirement as to employee numbers, but embraces only employee influence via board membership or membership of board committees or other "management groups".

(3) If the general rule does not apply, the merging companies may choose unilaterally to opt for the "standard rules" on participation to apply to the resulting company.[99] This means that the employees have participation rights in relation to that number of board members which is equal to the highest proportion to be found in the merging companies in which participation applied. There might be two systems with equal proportions, but operating in different ways, for example, one system on an appointment basis, another on an opposition basis. The merging companies choose which system to adopt. Thus, a resulting company registered in the United Kingdom might in this way become subject to mandatory participation rules. The advantage of this way of proceeding from the point of view of the merging companies is that the merger may be completed more quickly.[100]

(4) Alternatively, the merging companies may choose to negotiate with representatives of the employees of the merging companies with the aim of agreeing on some alternative to the standard rules. This involves the creation of a "Special Negotiating Body" (SNB) of employee representatives to negotiate on behalf of the employees of all the merging companies.[101] The parties have six months (extendable by agreement once to twelve months) to reach a participation agreement, which agreement will then determine the participation arrangements in the company.[102] That agreement may increase or reduce the participation rights of the employees.[103] The SNB can even decide not to have a participation agreement, in which case the employees of the merged entity are subject to the rules on participation of the

---

[99] Art.16(3)(h), (4)(a) and reg.38.
[100] Completion of the employee participation arrangements is a condition for the registration of the resulting company: Art.11(1).
[101] Chapter 2 of Part 4 of the Regulations.
[102] Regs. 28 and 29.
[103] But if at least one-quarter of the employees of the merging companies had participation rights, any decision by the SNB on an agreement which reduces participation rights below the highest proportion previously operating requires a two-thirds majority of the members of the SNB: reg.30.

Member State in which the employees of the resulting company are employed.[104]

(5) If the parties either do not reach agreement within the specified period or agree that the standard rules shall apply, then the resulting company will be subject to those rules.[105] In this case, however, the standard rules cap the proportion of board members subject to employee influence at one-third in the case where the resulting company has a one-tier board, even if in fact one of the merging companies was subject to higher requirements under its national law.[106] In effect, the Directive recognises that parity participation on a supervisory board of a two-tier system is a different thing from parity participation on a single board. However, the cap applies only if the merging companies end up with the standard rules after negotiation rather than by way of unilateral choice.

(6) The employee participation system applied by the Directive to the first resulting company must be applied to a subsequent merger by that company for a period of three years, so that the second resulting company cannot escape the participation rules imposed on the first resulting company.[107] However, after three years it would appear to be open to the first resulting company, in a jurisdiction which does not require employee participation, to merge with a domestic company under the domestic merger procedure and thus escape from the Directive's participation requirements.

29–14 As with the European Company, which has been little used by United Kingdom companies, the main question is whether the cross-border merger procedure will be much used in practice. One impact it might have is to reduce what little demand there is for the SE to be used to effect a cross-border merger, since the purely corporate rules which apply to the resulting company (i.e. the national rules of the jurisdiction where that company is registered) are probably better known and clearer than the mixture of Community level and

---

[104] Reg.31. This requires not only a two-thirds vote of the SNB, but also that those voting in favour should represent two-thirds of the employees of the merging companies.

[105] Reg.36. However, failure to agree will trigger the standard rules where fewer than one-third of the employees of merging companies were subject to participation only where the SNB has positively opted (by a majority of its members) for them. Thus, a majority of representatives, perhaps from countries not having a participation system, could block its imposition on the resulting company, perhaps in exchange for some different type of concession from the companies.

[106] Reg.39, whether those higher prior requirements applied to a one-tier or the upper tier of a two-tier system. The best example is a large German company which would be subject to "parity" co-determination on the supervisory board under its national rules, though for most Member States one-third or less is the limit under national law.

[107] Reg.40.

domestic rules which apply to the SE, and the SE provisions lack the facility for the management unilaterally to adopt the standard rules.[108] Further, the cross-border merger procedure is available on a broader basis than the SE, since it can be used by private companies,[109] whereas only public companies may form an SE by merger.[110] The main question, however, is whether the cross-border merger will displace the takeover as a way of effecting a cross-border amalgamation. The takeover has a major advantage in terms of speed (at least where the target is in the United Kingdom), for the documents relevant to a merger must be made public at least two months before the national meetings to approve the merger,[111] whereas a bidder can begin acquiring irrevocable commitments before it makes a public announcement of the bid and can receive acceptances of its offer as soon as that is put out. The takeover also avoids all questions of employee participation: the bidder and target remain subject to whatever, if anything, their national laws provide in this regard.[112]

Finally, it is worth noting that it is possible to produce a cross-border merger through a "dual-listed structure". In this arrangement the companies remain formally independent (i.e. they do not merge) nor does the one become a subsidiary of the other, as in a takeover. Instead, by contract, including provisions in their respective constitutions, the companies produce a unified management (i.e., the same people sitting on the boards of directors of the two companies or, normally, top companies of the two groups of companies which are coming together). The shareholder bodies remain separate but each body is given voting rights in the meetings of the other, so as to produce a single decision from the two votes; and the profits of the two companies are equalised. Such structures are complex to create (and to understand) but may have advantages over a merger, for example, where national susceptibilities are involved. There are not many such companies but a number of well-known multinational companies take this form (Unilever, BHP Billiton, Reed Elsevier) and others did so for a substantial period of time before moving to a more conventional single company (or group) structure (Shell, ABB).

---

[108] On the other hand, some merging companies may see positive value in the "SE" brand.

[109] Directive Art.1 and reg.3 ("UK company").

[110] Regulation (EC) No.2157/2001 on the Statute for a European Company, Art.2(1). Presumably an SE may count as a merging or resulting company for the purposes of the cross-border merger rules, since it is to be treated in the same way as a public company of its State of registration. See para.1–21.

[111] Reg.11

[112] This is in fact highly unsatisfactory in one respect. Where a German company, subject to co-determination, takes over a British company, the British workers will have no right to participate in board level representation arrangements of the German parent, even though the strategy of both companies is probably determined at that level, unless, as sometimes happens, voluntary arrangements are made to accommodate the interests of the non-German workers.

REORGANISATION UNDER SECTIONS 110 AND 111 OF THE INSOLVENCY
ACT 1986

29–15   Under this type of reorganisation the company concerned resolves
first to go into voluntary liquidation[113] and secondly to authorise by a
special resolution the liquidator to transfer the whole or any part of
the company's business or property to another company[114] or a
limited liability partnership in consideration of shares or like interests
in that company (or membership in the LLP) for distribution among
the members of the liquidating company. This procedure affords a
relatively simple method of reconstructing a single company or of
effecting a merger of its undertaking into that of another. In the
former case, the transferee company will be incorporated with a
capital structure different from that of the liquidating or transferor
company and the liquidator will transfer its undertaking to the new
company in consideration of an issue of its securities which will be
distributed to the members of the liquidating company. A new
company may also be formed when the procedure is adopted for the
purposes of a merger of two or more existing companies. Alternatively, when the arrangement is essentially an agreed merger that
existing company may buy the transferors's undertaking from its
liquidator, paying for it by securities of the transferee which will be
distributed *in specie* to the liquidating company's members.

Use of this method has the advantage that confirmation by the
court is not required.[115] But what it can achieve is somewhat limited.
Creditors of the transferor will be entitled to prove in its liquidation
and the liquidator must ensure that their proved claims are met and
cannot rely upon an indemnity given by the acquiring company.[116]
Although members' rights will be varied, since it is unlikely that their
rights under the securities of the transferee company will be identical
with the members' former holdings, it is unsafe to make them seriously less attractive. This is because s.111 provides that, in the case
of a members' voluntary winding-up, any member of the company
who did not vote in favour of the special resolution may, within seven
days of its passing, serve a notice on the liquidator requiring him

---

[113] Under former versions of these provisions it had to be a *members'* voluntary liquidation, i.e.
one in which the directors have made a "declaration of solvency" declaring that all the
company's debts will be paid in full within 12 months. It can now be employed also in a
creditors' voluntary liquidation so long as it is sanctioned by the court or the liquidation
committee (Insolvency Act, s.110(3)) but that sanction is unlikely to be given unless all
creditors are paid in full.

[114] Whether or not the latter is a company within the meaning of the Companies Act (Insolvency Act, s.110(1)) so that it could be a company registered in another jurisdiction.

[115] Though the court's sanction may be needed if the company is to be wound up in a creditors'
winding-up.

[116] *Pulsford v Devenish* [1903] 2 Ch. 625. But the sale of the undertaking will be binding on the
creditors who will not be able to follow the assets transferred to the transferee company:
City & County Investment Co, Re (1879) 13 Ch.D. 475, CA.

either to refrain from carrying the resolution into effect or to purchase his shares at a price to be determined either by agreement or by arbitration.[117] It is normally essential if advantage is to be taken of stamp duty concessions that the membership of the old company and the new should be very largely the same. If a number of the members elect to be bought out, there is a grave risk that the reorganisation will have to be abandoned as prohibitively expensive.

The CLR found the Insolvency Act procedure to be a popular method for reconstructing private or family-controlled companies or groups and also for reconstructing investment trust companies.[118] It therefore recommended its retention with, however, the modernisation of the arbitration procedure which operates when a member exercises the appraisal right and a valuation of the member's interest cannot be agreed. The procedure under the current law is antiquated, invoking as it does the arbitration provisions of the Companies Clauses Consolidation Act 1845 or its Scottish equivalent,[119] doubtfully in compliance with the Human Rights Act and unclear about the basis upon which the member's interest should be valued. The CLR proposed that the valuation should be based on the dissentient's proportionate share of the consideration offered by the transferee for the transferor's business.[120] However, these provisions being in the Insolvency Act 1986, they were not touched by the Companies Act 2006.

CONCLUSION

We remarked at the beginning of this Chapter that the Companies Act does not contain a statutory merger procedure of the type typically found in other jurisdictions. Instead, the scheme of arrangement is available for this purpose, but that procedure is available also to achieve a number of other objectives which have nothing to do with mergers of two or more companies. Indeed, since the scheme procedure, although available, is rarely used to achieve a merger, it would be odd to use the term statutory merger procedure to refer to the scheme of arrangement. Just to confuse things further, the alternative to the merger—the takeover bid—can be, and increasingly is, effected

29–16

---

[117] This is an example, rare under UK law (but more widely used in some other common law jurisdictions) of protecting dissenting members by granting them "appraisal rights". The courts will not permit the company to deprive members of their appraisal rights under the section by purporting to act under powers in its articles to sell its undertaking in consideration of securities of another company to be distributed *in specie*: *Bisgood v Henderson's Transvaal Estates* [1908] 1 Ch. 743, CA.

[118] Completing, para.11.13.

[119] s.111(4).

[120] Final Report I, para.13.13.

by means of a scheme. The scheme of arrangement is thus an immensely flexible instrument. However, because it is as much an instrument of insolvency law as of corporate law and because it elides what is regarded in other jurisdictions as the fundamental difference between a takeover bid and a merger, the scheme of arrangement has a rather uncertain image. There can be almost as many types of schemes of arrangement as there are inventive corporate and insolvency lawyers, which indicates both the significance of the scheme procedure and the impossibility of identifying such a thing as a typical scheme of arrangement.

CHAPTER 30

INSIDER DEALING AND MARKET MANIPULATION

With these topics we reach the margins of company law. As we have **30–1** had occasion to notice already, insider dealing (or trading)[1] occurs when a person in possession of price-sensitive information about a company buys or sells securities in that company and so obtains better terms in the contract of sale than would have been the case had the counterparty been aware of the information in question. In that way, the insider can either make a profit or avoid a loss, depending on

---

[1] The Criminal Justice Act 1993, Pt V, uses the word "dealing".

whether the information, once public, will drive the share price up or down.[2] The issue is at the margins of company law because the insider trader does not have to be an insider of the company (though he or she very often is)—take, for example, a governmental official who knows that the agency for which he or she works is about to issue an adverse report on a particular company which will affect the price of its shares. Equally, insider dealing is not confined to securities issued by companies, but can equally occur in the market for government bonds.[3] Thus, insider trading can be regarded as properly a matter for securities markets law. Nevertheless, the company does have a vital interest in the effective control of insider dealing. This arises in the following way.

Anyone buying or selling shares in the market knows that he or she runs a risk of doing so just before some good or bad news is announced about the company. Sometimes this will benefit the trader; sometimes not. It will depend on whether the news is good or bad and whether the investor has bought or sold. In the long run, however, and in the absence of insider dealing, the investor can expect that these pieces of good or bad fortune will average out. If, however, insider dealing is rife in the market, the non-insider will know that the market prices will systematically fail to reflect the true worth of the company and will do so in a way which is unfavourable to the outsiders. In the absence of regulation, this will be an inherent risk of holding shares in companies and outsiders will build this risk into their investment decisions, by lowering the price they are prepared to pay for companies' shares. This in turn will increase companies' cost of capital because they will be able to issues shares on less favourable terms than if investors could be assured that there was no or little[4] insider trading in the market. Thus, companies have an interest in effective insider dealing legislation or regulation.[5]

The same general argument can be made in relation to the wider notion of market manipulation, which can be regarded as any

---

[2] Clearly, the insider buys in the former case and sells in the latter.

[3] One of the earliest cases on market manipulation occurred in the market for government bonds. In *R. v De Berenger* (1814) 3 M. & S. 68 the fraudsters pretended to be soldiers returning from France with news of the defeat of Napoleon (before this event actually came to pass). The false rumours which they spread caused the price of British government bonds to rise, thus enabling the accused to dispose of their holdings at a profit.

[4] If there is minimal insider dealing the price of the shares will not be distorted and the flow of information into the market will not be slowed down. In this way, insider dealing legislation does not have to be fully effective in order to achieve its goal. It may also be that, in the case of minimal levels of insider dealing, but only in this case, nobody suffers from the activity and that insider dealing in this situation is indeed a "victimless crime". However, it is very difficult to design legislation so that an act is prohibited only so long as not too many other people are doing it as well. This factor can be taken into account when deciding whether to legislate, but hardly in the legislation itself.

[5] See H. Schmidt, "Insider Dealing and Economic Theory" in K. Hopt and E. Wymeersch (eds), *European Insider Dealing* (Butterworths, 1991).

behaviour which distorts the operation of the markets in securities.[6] If extensive, such behaviour may systematically produce prices which are unfavourable to outsiders, thus again causing them to re-assess the riskiness of corporate securities as a class. Indeed, it is becoming common these days to treat insider dealing and market manipulation under the umbrella heading of market abuse. Nevertheless, since insider dealing has a longer history of legislative attention in the United Kingdom than market manipulation, we shall begin with the former and widen out our focus so as to include the latter only when we get to the more recent rules which treat the two together. Again, market manipulation is not an activity which is confined to corporate insiders or to markets in corporate securities so that, like insider dealing, market manipulation is on the edge of company law. In the discussion which follows we concentrate on those aspects of insider dealing and market manipulation which concern either corporate insiders or the activities of companies (and thus ignore behaviour by market participants which may be reprehensible but which is remote from the concerns of company law, such as cornering the market in a particular commodity).

APPROACHES TO INSIDER DEALING

Disclosure

A number of approaches to the regulation of insider dealing are to be found in our current law. Mandatory disclosure has long been used, but disclosure may be used to control insider dealing in a number of different ways. For example, directors, as potential insider dealers, may be required to disclose dealings in their company's shares on the theory that if they know that the fact of their dealings will be public knowledge, they will be less likely to trade on the basis of inside information.[7] Indeed, this is the oldest anti-insider dealing technique, having been introduced upon the recommendation of the Cohen Committee of 1945.[8]

30–2

Alternatively, or in addition, the disclosure rules may aim at those who have the inside information and require them to disclose it, whether or not they are likely to trade on the basis of it. The point here is that putting the information into the public domain reduces the opportunities of others to engage in insider dealing. This, too, we have discussed above in the shape of the obligation laid upon issuers

---

[6] For an example see the *De Berenger* case, above, fn.3. For the specific statutory definition of market abuse in the FSMA, see para.30–28, below.

[7] See above, paras 26–13ff.

[8] *Report of the Company Law Committee*, Cmnd. 6659 (1945), paras 86–87.

to disclose inside information promptly to the market.[9] Even the obligation to disclose the beneficial ownership of shares at the three per cent level and above[10] may constitute a disclosure obligation of this type, for it shows who is accumulating a stake in a company, perhaps preparatory to a bid.[11]

Prohibiting trading
Section 323 of the Companies Act 1985

30–3   At the other end of the spectrum, the law could ban trading by potential insiders, irrespective of whether they are in possession of inside information or not. Given the wide range of potential insiders, such an approach, if used generally, would be likely to bring the markets to a halt. However, this approach could be found in section 323 of the Companies Act 1985, introduced in 1967 on the recommendation of the Jenkins Committee[12] and creating a criminal offence. The section was narrowly confined to directors and shadow directors (and their spouses and infant children)[13] and applied only to the taking of options to buy or sell shares or debentures in the company or other companies in the group[14] to which it belonged, provided the company in question is a listed company. Moreover, the options prohibited were those to acquire from or sell to other market participants, not to subscribe for shares (or debentures) from the company itself,[15] the latter type of option constituting, as we have seen, a significant part of the remuneration of directors of listed companies.[16] Even as confined, the section still needed some explanation. It seemed to be based on the theory that there is a high risk of insider dealing by directors in relation to such options (because of their speculative nature),[17] whilst they have little positive value, since a director who wishes to become a member of the company can buy shares outright, whilst appropriate incentives can be given by means of options to subscribe, which are to some degree under the control of the shareholders.[18] Nevertheless, the Law Commissions recom-

---

[9] See above, paras 26–5ff.
[10] Paras 26–18 *et seq.*
[11] Though note that for the prospective bidder itself to buy shares on the basis of its knowledge that it is going to launch a bid is not regarded as insider trading (see below, para.30–25), but it would be for a person in the know to do so for his or her own account.
[12] See fn.18, below.
[13] s.327. In this case, unlike in relation to the disclosure obligation, the substantive rule applied to the relatives, but they had a defence that they had no reason to believe that the spouse or parent was a director of the company in question: s.327(1).
[14] Specifically, the company's subsidiary, holding company or subsidiary of the holding company: s.323(5).
[15] s.323(5).
[16] See above, paras 14–15ff.
[17] If the market moves against the option-holder, the option will not be exercised, but the holder's loss is relatively limited because he or she has paid for only the option, not the full price of the underlying securities. An option is, in effect, a form of leverage.
[18] *Report of the Company Law Committee*, Cmnd. 1749 (1962), para.90.

mended the repeal of the section on the grounds that there was not anything "intrinsically objectionable to directors' dealings in options if there is full disclosure" and that dealing, including the taking of options,[19] when in possession of inside information was now covered by later legislation.[20] Consequently, the prohibition was not carried forward into the 2006 Act.

The FSA's model code

Despite the Law Commissions' disapproval of pure trading prohibitions, the same idea is to be found in the *Model Code*,[21] developed originally by the Stock Exchange but now part of the Listing Rules applied by the FSA in its capacity as UK Listing Authority. Listed companies are required to ensure that those discharging managerial responsibilities comply with the Code or such stronger requirements as the company may impose. Thus, the Code is not directly binding on directors but is a model which listed companies are required to adopt with such refinements as are thought desirable. In practice it is normally adopted virtually verbatim. The listed company is required to take "all proper and reasonable" steps to secure compliance with the Code by those discharging managerial responsibilities within it.[22] However, if there is a breach of the code adopted by any particular company, the duty which is breached is one owed by the director to the company, not to the FSA. The duty owed to the FSA is simply to adopt and enforce the code and that is a duty owed by the listed company. For this reason, in *Chase Manhattan Equities Ltd v Goodman*[23] Knox J. refused to hold that the director who sold shares in breach of his company's code incurred for that reason any liability towards the market maker which purchased the shares. The importance of the Code is that, in addition to emphasising that in no circumstance should directors deal when they are forbidden from doing so under the insider dealing legislation, it prescribes that, subject to exceptions, they should not do so within a period of two months preceding the preliminary announcement of the company's annual results and similar limitations are imposed in relation to the announcement of the half-yearly and quarterly reports. In addition, clearance to deal has to be obtained in advance from the chairman of

30–4

---

[19] See Criminal Justice Act 1993, Sch.2, para.5.

[20] *Company Directors: Regulating Conflicts of Interests and Formulating a Statement of Duties*, Cm. 4436 (1999), para.11.46. The CLR agreed: Developing, para.3.87. The argument is perhaps less strong than it seems in view of the difficulties arising out of attempts to enforce the general legislation against insider dealing: below, para.30–27.

[21] Appended to Ch.9 of the Listing Rules.

[22] LR 9.2.8. On the meaning of those "discharging managerial responsibilities", which term includes both directors and senior executives, see para.26–15.

[23] [1991] B.C.L.C. 897. The force of the learned judge's argument seems not to be diminished by the fact that the obligation to comply with the Model Code is no longer required to be imposed on directors by board resolution, for it is still an obligation owed by the director to the company.

the board, the CEO or the company secretary, as appropriate.[24] Thus, the prohibition relates to dealing during certain periods of time rather than, as under the 1985 Act, in certain types of security interest, but it is equally based on the theory that there is a high risk of improper trading in the specified period so that a blanket ban is justified.[25]

Relying on the general law

30–5   A third approach is to not to legislate specifically for insider dealing but to rely on established doctrines of the common law to deal with it. Company law offers its fiduciary duties for this purpose, and more general doctrines of the common law may also have a role. For one reason or another, however, these doctrines fail to capture the problem of insider dealing comprehensively. Yet they need to be borne in mind because they offer civil remedies under the control of private parties, whereas, as we shall see, the specific insider dealing legislation relies wholly on criminal sanctions or regulatory sanctions which are, in effect, under the control of the FSA.

Directors' fiduciary duties

30–6   As pointed out in Chapter 16,[26] if directors make use of information acquired as director for their personal advantage they may breach their fiduciary duties to the company and be liable to account to it for any profits they have made. A great advantage of the civil suit brought by the company for breach of fiduciary duty is that it does not have to show that it has suffered loss as a result of the insider dealing, simply that the insider fiduciaries have made an undisclosed profit.[27] In practice, however, it is unlikely that the company will call them to account unless and until there is a change of control. If only one director has committed the breach, the others may cause the company to take action against him but most public companies are likely to avoid damaging publicity by persuading the errant director to resign "for personal reasons" and to go quietly.

It is also possible that, for example, in relation to a takeover of a small company,[28] the directors may place themselves in the position

---

[24] Nor may the company or any other company in the group trade in its securities at a time when the director is prohibited from trading, unless this is done in the ordinary course of securities dealing or at the behest of a third party: LR 9.2.7.

[25] Like the Law Commissions, however, the FSA raised the question of whether the Model Code was needed any longer in the light of developments reflected in the FSMA 2000 (see below, para.30–27) and the Community's Market Abuse Directive. See FSA, *Review of the Listing Regime*, Discussion Paper 14 (July 2002), para.4.14. However, it was decided to retain the Code, with amendments.

[26] See paras 16–63ff, above.

[27] The leading case is the decision of the New York Court of Appeals in *Diamond v Oreamuno* (1969) 248 N.E. 2d 910. The precise situation has not yet arisen in an English court.

[28] For an early example of the directors constituting themselves agents in this way, see *Allen v Hyatt* (1914) 30 T.L.R. 444, PC.

of acting as agents negotiating on behalf of the individual share-holders and thereby, despite *Percival v Wright*,[29] owe fiduciary duties to the shareholders. If so, they would breach those duties if they persuaded any shareholder to sell to them at a price which they knew (and the shareholders did not) was materially lower than that which a bidder or any other purchaser was likely to offer. It is, however, highly unlikely that the directors of a listed company would create such a relationship. If they did engage in insider dealing, it would be by dealing anonymously on a stock exchange so that no fiduciary relationship was created.

Hence, the general equitable principle is, on its own, rarely an effective deterrent. Moreover, the law relating to directors' fiduciary duties is simply incapable of applying to the full range of insiders and, except in the rare case where the decision in *Percival v Wright* can be overcome, it has the demerit of concentrating on the relationship between the director and the company rather than on the relationship between the director and other traders in the market.

Breach of confidence

Somewhat similar criticisms can be made of the second source of **30–7** equitable obligation which is relevant here, namely that imposed by the receipt of information from another person where the recipient knows or ought to have known that the information was imparted in confidence. However, the range of persons potentially covered by this obligation is much wider that those covered by the fiduciary duties applying to directors and officers of companies. It will extend to the professional advisers of companies who, say, are involved in preparing a takeover bid which the company is contemplating, and to the employees of such advisers, since no contractual link between the confider and the confidant is necessary to support this fiduciary obligation. Indeed, the obligation extends to anyone who receives information knowing that they are receiving it in breach of a duty of confidentiality imposed upon the person communicating the information.[30]

If the duty attaches, the holder of the information may not use it (for example, by trading in securities) or disclose it (for example, to another person so that that person may trade)[31] without the permission of the confider. Breach of the duty gives rise to a liability to account for the profits made, potentially the most useful civil sanction in the case of insider dealing on securities markets, and, though much less certainly in this situation, to an action for damages (because it is

---

[29] [1902] 2 Ch. 421: see para.16–5, above.
[30] For both these propositions see *Schering Chemicals Ltd v Falkman Ltd* [1982] Q.B. 1, CA.
[31] And by virtue of the *Schering Chemicals* case (see previous note) the recipient of the information (the "tippee") would also be in breach of duty by using or disclosing the information if aware that it had been communicated in breach of the duty of confidence imposed on the tipper.

far from clear that the confider actually suffers any loss if the confidant uses the information for the purposes of insider dealing and does not, in so doing, communicate the information to other persons). However, the cause of action again lies in the hands of the person to whom the fiduciary obligation is owed (i.e. the confider), not in the hands of the person with whom the confidant has dealt in the securities transaction or other participants in the market at the time. This might not matter if in fact the duty of confidence was routinely used to deprive insiders of their profits,[32] but, although much inside information must also be received in confidence and although the law in this area has achieved much greater prominence in recent years than it had previously, there are no reported cases of its use against insider dealers. This may be because the difficulties of detection and proof, which abound in this area, operate so as to deprive confiders of the incentive to use their private law rights to secure the transfer of insider dealing profits from the insiders to themselves.

Misrepresentation

30–8   When in 1989 the Government was considering its response to the Community's first Directive on insider dealing, it decided to continue its policy of not providing civil sanctions under the insider dealing legislation partly on the grounds that these worked satisfactorily only in face-to-face transactions and that the general law already provided remedies in that situation.[33] Apart from the insider's liability to the company, discussed above, the Government referred to liability for fraudulent misrepresentation. Misrepresentation-based liability, however, whether for fraudulent, negligent or innocent misrepresentation, faces a formidable obstacle in relation to insider trading. This is the need to demonstrate either that a false statement has been made or that there was a duty to disclose the inside information to the other party to the transaction. As to the former, the insider can avoid liability by not making any statements to the other party relating to the area of knowledge in which he holds the inside information, so that the liability of the insider comes to depend upon the other party having the good luck or the right instinct to extract a false statement from the insider by probing questions. Liability in such cases seems likely to be quite haphazard.

As to non-disclosure, the current legislation does not adopt the technique contained in some earlier proposals for insider dealing legislation: requiring insiders in face-to-face transactions to disclose the information before dealing.[34] Consequently, the potential plaintiff

---

[32] That is, one might be more concerned with depriving the insiders of their profits than with working out who precisely are the best persons to receive them.

[33] DTI, *The Law on Insider Dealing: A Consultative Document* (1989), paras 2.11–2.12.

[34] Companies Bill, Session 1978/79, H.C. Bill 2, cl. 59.

has to fall back on the common law, which imposes a duty of disclosure in only limited circumstances. The most relevant situation would be where the insider was in a fiduciary or other special relationship with the other party, but, as we have seen above, even as between directors and shareholders, the current law recognises such a relationship only exceptionally, whilst many insiders and their counterparties are simply not in the relationship of director and shareholder at all.[35] There is also little evidence at present of a willingness on the part of the courts to expand the categories of fiduciary or other special relationships in this area[36] or to bring securities contracts within the category of contracts *uberrimae fidei*.

Other approaches

The above analysis leaves two approaches to the regulation of insider **30–9** dealing which have been extensively used in the United Kingdom and which can be said to constitute the core of the current law. The first involves the criminalisation of insider dealing and certain associated acts and that is the basis of the general anti-insider legislation in Great Britain. The original general legislation on insider dealing was contained in Pt V of the Companies Act 1980 and was later consolidated in the Company Securities (Insider Dealing) Act 1985. However, as a result of the adoption by the European Community of Directive 89/592/EEC co-ordinating regulations on insider dealing,[37] some amendment of the British law became necessary, and the Department of Trade and Industry also took the opportunity to simplify the 1985 Act in some respects. However, Part V of the Criminal Justice Act 1993, the current law, is still recognisably in the mould established by the 1980 Act, though it contains some interesting new features and has abandoned some old obfuscations.[38] Experience showed, however, that it was difficult to secure convictions for this offence, partly because of difficulties of detection but partly also because of the standards of evidence and proof required in criminal trials. The legislature responded in the market abuse provisions of the FSMA 2000, which allow the FSA to impose penalties upon those who engage in such activity, which is defined so as to include insider dealing. Thus, the second main feature of the current law is the deployment of regulatory sanctions against insider dealing,

---

[35] For example, where the director is selling shares in the company to a person who is not presently a shareholder or where the insider is not a corporate fiduciary at all.

[36] See *Chase Manhattan Equities v Goodman* [1991] B.C.L.C. 897, discussed above, para.30–4, where the judge passed up the opportunity to use the FSA's *Model Code* as the basis of an extended duty of disclosure.

[37] [1989] OJ L334/30. This Directive was replaced by Directive 2003/6/EC (the Market Abuse Directive) in 2003, but the Government took the view that the criminal law provisions of domestic law did not require amendment as a result, though the 2006 Directive had a substantial impact on the administrative sanction regime.

[38] For an analysis of the changes see Davies (1991) 11 O.J.L.S. 92.

an approach which was enormously controversial on human rights grounds, when proposed, and whose effectiveness still has to be shown.

THE CRIMINAL JUSTICE ACT 1993, PART V

Regulating markets

30–10   Section 52(1) of the 1993 Act defines the central offence which it creates in the following terms: "An individual who has information as an insider is guilty of insider dealing if, in the circumstances mentioned in subs. (3), he deals in securities that are price-affected securities in relation to the information." This definition, however, conceals as much as it reveals, for it is much elaborated and qualified in the remaining sections of the Part. It is proposed in the following sections to try to elucidate the central elements of the offences created and of the defences available.

Pursuing the reference to s.52(3), contained in the above definition, reveals at once that the Act does not aim to control all dealings in shares where one of the parties has price-sensitive, non-public information in his or her possession. On the contrary, it is only when the dealing takes place "on a regulated market" and in certain analogous situations does the Act bite. If, say, the transaction occurs face-to-face between private persons, then the situation is outside the control of this particular legislation. The Act leaves regulated markets to be identified by statutory instrument and the Insider Dealing (Securities and Regulated Markets) Order 1994[39] stipulates that in the United Kingdom these include any markets established under the rules of the London Stock Exchange (thus including AIM) and Plus Markets.

However, the legislation has always applied to certain "off-market" deals and these are now defined as those where the person dealing "relies on a professional intermediary or is himself acting as a professional intermediary".[40] Section 59 makes it clear that the profession in question must be that of acquiring or disposing of securities (for example, as a market maker[41]) or acting as an intermediary

---

[39] SI 1994/187, art.10, as amended. Confusingly, the term "regulated market" in the 1993 Act does not have the meaning attached to the term in the Prospectus, Market Abuse and Transparency Directives: see para.25–5. In particular, trading on AIM does fall within the CJA (AIM being a market established under the rules of the LSE), even though AIM is not a regulated market for Community law purposes.

[40] s.52(3).

[41] A firm which has undertaken to make a continuous two-way market in certain securities, so that, in relation to those securities, it will always be possible to buy from or sell to the market maker, though, of course, at a price established by the market maker.

between persons who wish to deal (for example, as a stockbroker[42]), and that a person does not fall within the definition if the activities of this type are merely incidental to some other activity or are merely occasional. This approach to off-market dealing is rather broader (and simpler) than that adopted under the previous legislation, which confined liability to those situations where there was trading on an informal or inchoate market. Under the current legislation, reliance on a professional intermediary (as defined) or trading by a professional intermediary acting as such brings the trading within the Act, even though no element of an organised market can be shown to exist.

Despite this extension, which was in any event required by the 1989 Directive,[43] the main thrust of the legislation is the regulation of dealings on formalised markets, and the extension was designed to prevent the evasion of such regulation, which might occur if trading were driven off formalised markets into less efficient, but, without the extension, unregulated forms. What does emerge clearly from this analysis is that the 1993 Act is at least as much a part of the law of securities regulation as it is of company law. As the preamble to the Directive put it, it is the public interest in securing the confidence of investors in the operation of the securities markets which provides the rationale for the legislation on insider dealing.[44] The 1993 Act recognises[45] the logic of this view by extending its regulation to debt securities issued by public authorities[46] as well as to corporate securities.[47] This was a welcome extension, and, although required by the Directive, was one to which the Government in any event had committed itself in 1985.[48] The 1993 Act also brings expressly within its scope futures contracts[49] and contracts for differences,[50] both of

30–11

---

[42] Following the "Big Bang" on the Stock Exchange in 1986 it is no longer required that market makers and brokers be entirely distinct functions, though equally it is not required that brokers make a continuous two-way market in any particular securities. Some broking firms act as market makers as well; others do not.

[43] Art.2(3).

[44] "Whereas the secondary market in transferable securities plays an important role in the financing of economic agents ... whereas the smooth operation of that market depends to a large extent on the confidence it inspires in investors..."

[45] The securities to which the Act applies are those which are identified in its Sch.2 and which satisfy the conditions set out in the 1994 Order. See s.54, and for the 1994 Order fn.39 above.

[46] Thus "gilts", i.e. debt instruments issued by the Government, and local authority bonds are included.

[47] Thus, the *name* of the 1985 Act—the Company Securities (Insider Dealing) Act—if nothing else, would have had to be changed.

[48] *Financial Services in the United Kingdom*, Cmnd. 9472 (1985).

[49] A contract of the sale or purchase of securities at a future date.

[50] A contract not involving an agreement to transfer an interest in the underlying securities but simply to pay the difference between the price of the securities on a particular date and their price on a future date. For discussion of the problems which CfDs have created in relation to disclosure obligations see above at para.26–22 and at para.28–43.

which may be the subject of trading which is distinct from the trading in the securities to which these contracts relate.[51]

The concentration of the prohibition on dealing on regulated markets also makes it much easier to justify the restriction of the sanctions for breaches of the Act to the criminal law.[52] In addition to the other difficulties which surround the creation of a coherent civil remedy in this area, the fact that the trading has occurred on a public exchange means that the identity of the counterparty in the transaction with the insider is a matter of chance. In any liquid stock many thousands of persons may be trading in the market at the same time as the insider. To give a civil remedy to the person who happened to end up with the insider's shares and not to the others who dealt in the market at the same time in the security in question would be arbitrary, whilst to give a civil remedy to all relevant market participants might well be oppressive of the insider.[53] By confining the sanction to the criminal law, Parliament avoided the need to address these difficulties. Moreover, if the main argument against insider trading is that it undermines public confidence in the securities markets, the criminal law is capable of expressing the community's view of that public interest, provided it can be effectively enforced.[54]

Finally, in this section on the definition of markets a few words should be said about the international dimension of insider dealing. It is now extremely easy, technically, for a person in one country to deal in the shares of a company which are listed or otherwise open to trading in another country; or for a person to deal in shares of a company quoted on an exchange in his or her own country via instructions placed with a foreign intermediary. For the domestic legislator not to deal with this situation runs the risk that the domestic legislation will be circumvented wholesale. To apply the domestic sanctions irrespective of the foreign element, on the other hand, is to run the risk of creating criminal law with an unacceptable extra-territorial reach. The latter risk is enlarged by the 1989 Directive's requirement that the Member States must prohibit insider dealing in transferable securities "admitted to a market of a Member State"[55] and not just those admitted to its own markets. In line with this requirement, the 1994 Order extends the application of the Act to securities which are officially listed in or are admitted to dealing

---

[51] Certain types of security are omitted, perhaps most obviously the purchase or sale of units in unit trusts, though shares in companies which operate investment trusts are within the scope of the Act. Presumably, the former were excluded on the pragmatic grounds that it was unlikely that a person would have inside information which would significantly affect the price of the units, which normally reflect widely diversified underlying investments, though query whether this is always the case with more focused unit trusts; whereas the latter were swept in under the general prohibition on insider dealing in shares. In any event, the Treasury has power to amend the list of securities contained in Sch.2 (see s.54(2)).

[52] See further below, para.30–41.

[53] In some cases it might not even be possible to identify the counterparty.

[54] See further below, para.30–27.

[55] Art.5.

under the rules of any investment exchange established within any of the States of the European Economic Area.[56]

This clearly should not mean, however, that a French citizen dealing on the basis of inside information on the Paris *Bourse* or even on the Milan Exchange in the shares of a British company (or a company of any other nationality) is guilty of an offence under domestic law. Consequently, s.62(1)[57] of the Act lays down the requirement of a territorial connection with the United Kingdom before a criminal offence can be said to have been committed in the United Kingdom. This requires the dealer or the professional intermediary to have been within the United Kingdom at the time any act was done which forms part of the offence or the dealing to have taken place on a market regulated in the United Kingdom.[58] Consequently, our French citizen will commit a criminal offence in the United Kingdom only if the deal is transacted on a market regulated in the United Kingdom,[59] unless he or the professional intermediary through whom the deal is transacted is in the United Kingdom at the time of the dealing.[60] This approach does not eliminate all potential of the insider dealing legislation for extra-territorial effect, but it does limit it to situations where there is some substantial connection between the offence and the United Kingdom.

Regulating individuals

A striking feature of the 1993 Act, like its predecessor, is that it **30–12** regulates insider dealing only by individuals. The Act does not use the more usual term "person" to express the scope of its prohibition, so that bodies corporate are not liable to prosecution under the Act. Corporate bodies were excluded, not because it was thought unde-

---

[56] Insider Dealing (Securities and Regulated Markets) Order 1994, Arts 4 and 9 and Sch.
[57] s.62(2) provides that in the case of the offences of encouraging dealing or disclosing inside information (see para.30–22, below) either the encourager or discloser must be in the United Kingdom when he did the relevant act or the recipient of the encouragement or information must be.
[58] See above, para.30–10.
[59] If French law adopts the same territorial rules as the United Kingdom, the citizen would also commit a criminal offence under French law if he gave the instructions to deal from France. His liability in the United Kingdom would not depend, of course, upon the nationality of the company in whose shares on a United Kingdom regulated market the trading occurred.
[60] If the French citizen is in the United Kingdom at the relevant time, he will commit a criminal offence in the United Kingdom even if the trading occurs on a regulated market outside the United Kingdom but within the EEA. However, if the market is outside the EEA (say, New York or Tokyo) and involves no professional intermediary who is within the United Kingdom it would seem that the offence of dealing is not committed in the United Kingdom even if the instruction to deal is given by a person in the United Kingdom. This is because the dealing will not have taken place on a regulated market within s.52(3) and the 1994 Order and will not have involved a professional intermediary who is within the scope of s.62. However, the offence of encouraging dealing may have been committed, the encourager being in the United Kingdom even if the person encouraged is not. See fn.57, above.

sirable to make them criminally liable but because of the difficulties it was thought would be faced by investment banks when one department of the bank had unpublished price-sensitive information about the securities of a client company and the dealing departments had successfully been kept in ignorance of that information by a "Chinese Wall"[61] or otherwise. If someone in the dealing department entered into a trade, it was thought to be arguable that the bank as a single corporate body would have committed an offence, had the Act applied to corporate bodies, the act of one employee and the knowledge of the other being attributed to the bank. However, it should be noted that these arguments were not regarded as decisive by those who drafted the regulatory regime under the Financial Services and Markets Act 2000. Their policy was to bring insider dealing, even by corporate bodies, within the scope of the regulatory prohibitions but then to deal expressly with the problem of attributed knowledge.[62]

Finally, it should be noted that the Criminal Justice Act does not have the effect that no individual can be liable under it if the dealing in question is done by a company. Companies can act only through human agents, and, as we shall see below,[63] the Act's prohibition on dealing extends to procuring or encouraging dealing in securities. Thus, if the individuals who move the company to deal do so on the basis of unpublished price-sensitive information, they may well have committed the criminal offence of procuring or encouraging the company to deal, even if the company itself commits no offence in dealing.

Inside information

30–13   Issues surrounding the definition of inside information have always been controversial, and rightly so, for the essence of the offence is trading on the basis of information which is known to the trader but is not available to the market generally. The general principle stated in the preamble to the 1989 Directive was: investor confidence in security markets depends inter alia on "the assurance afforded to investors that they are placed on an equal footing and that they will be protected against the improper use of inside information". However, it is much easier to state this general principle than to cast it into precise legal restrictions. Placing investors "on an equal footing" cannot mean that all those who deal on a market should have the same information. Otherwise, there would be no incentive for investors and their advisers to spend time and resources investigating

---

[61] An arrangement designed to prevent information in one part of a firm from being available to individuals working elsewhere in the firm.

[62] See FSA, *Code of Market Conduct*, para.1.1.1 and Glossary Definition "person". "Chinese Walls" are then referred to at appropriate points in the Code.

[63] See below, para.30–22. Otherwise a person could avoid the prohibition on insider dealing simply by setting up a company to do the trading.

the prospects of particular companies or sectors of the economy, so as to make better informed investment decisions; and if this incentive were removed, investment decisions, and the market as a whole, would simply become less efficient. The aim of the legislation, therefore, should not be to eliminate all informational advantages, but to proscribe those advantages whose use would be improper, often because their acquisition is not the result of skill or effort but of the mere fact of holding a particular position. This general issue will be seen to recur in relation to all four of the limbs of the statutory definition of "inside information".

Section 56 defines inside information as information which:

(a) relates to particular securities or to a particular issuer of securities and not to securities generally or to issues of securities generally,

(b) is specific or precise,

(c) has not been made public,

(d) if it were made public would be likely to have a significant effect on the price of any securities.

Particular securities or issuers

The first limb of the definition is the subject of a crucial clarification **30–14** in s.60(4) that information shall be treated as relating to an issuer of securities "not only where it is about the company but also where it may affect the company's business prospects". This makes it clear that the definition of inside information includes information coming from outside the company, for example, that the Government intends to liberalise the industry in which the company previously had a monopoly, as well as information coming from within the company, say, that the company is about to declare a substantially increased or decreased dividend or has won or lost a significant contract. This casts the net very widely, but it is difficult to see that any narrower formulation would have been effective. The information must relate to particular securities or a particular issuer[64] or particular issuers of securities and not to securities or issuers generally. So information relating to a particular company or sector of the economy is covered, but not information which applies in an undifferentiated way to the economy in general. This is not an entirely easy distinction; nor is its policy rationale self-evident. It would seem to mean that knowledge that the Government is, unexpectedly, to increase or decrease interest rates would fall within the definition because it has specific relevance

---

[64] The Act uses the term "issuer" rather than "company" because, as we have seen (above, para.30–11), the Act applies not only to securities issued by companies but also to government securities or even, though this is unlikely, securities issued by an individual: s.60(2).

to the price of gilts (government stocks) by indicating the rate at which the Government is prepared to borrow money. On the other hand, possession of government information, good or bad, about the recent performance of the economy might not, even though its release will cause the price of shares in general to rise or fall.

Specific or precise

30–15 The second limb of the definition restricts the scope of inside information further. The information, in addition to what has been discussed in the previous paragraph, must be specific or precise.[65] The 1989 Directive required simply that the information be "precise",[66] but this was thought by Parliament to be possibly too restrictive, so the alternative of "specific" was added. The example was given of knowledge that a takeover bid was going to be made for a company, which would be specific information, but might not be regarded as precise if there was no knowledge of the price to be offered or the exact date on which the announcement of the bid would be made.[67] However, the crucial effect of this restriction is that it should relieve directors and senior managers of the company and analysts who have made a special study of the company from falling foul of the legislation simply because they have generalised informational advantages over other investors, arising from their position in the one case and the effort they have exerted in the other. Having a better sense of how well or badly the company is likely to respond to a particular publicly known development does not amount to the possession of precise or specific information.

Made public

30–16 The tension between the policy of encouraging communication between companies and the investment community and of stimulating analysts and other professionals to play an appropriate role in that process, on the one hand, and that of preventing selective disclosure of significant information to the detriment of shareholders who are not close to the market, on the other, is further revealed in section 58 of the Act, which deals with the problem of when information can be said to have been "made public". The Government initially proposed to leave the problem to be solved by the courts on a case-by-case basis, but came under pressure in Parliament to deal with the issue expressly. The pressure probably reflected the accurate perception that, with the broadening of the definition of "insider",[68]

---

[65] s.56(1)(b).
[66] Art.1.
[67] HC Debs, Session 1992–93, Standing Committee B, col. 174 (June 10, 1993). It seems that, on this argument, precise information will always be specific.
[68] See para.30–19, below.

more weight would fall on the definition of "inside information" and especially this limb of the definition. Section 58 is not, however, a comprehensive attempt to deal with the issue. It stipulates four situations where the information shall be regarded as having been made public and five situations where the court may so regard it; otherwise, the court is free to arrive at its own judgment.[69]

The most helpful statement in section 58 from the point of view of analysts is that "information is public if ... it is derived from information which has been made public".[70] It is clear that this provision was intended to protect analysts who derive insights into a company's prospects which are not shared by the market generally (so that the analyst is able to out-guess his or her competitors) where those insights are derived from the intensive and intelligent study of information which has been made public. An analyst in this position can deal on the basis of the insights so derived without first disclosing to the market the process of reasoning which has led to the conclusions, even where the disclosure of the reasoning would have a significant impact on the price of the securities dealt in. This seems to be the case even where the analyst intends to and does publish the recommendations after the dealing, i.e. there is what is called "front running" of the research.[71]

The utility of this subsection to the analyst and others is enhanced **30–17** by the other provisions of section 58(2). Section 58(2)(c) comes close to providing an overarching test for whether information is "made public" by stating that this is so if the information "can readily be acquired" by those likely to deal in the relevant securities. In other words, the public here is not the public in general but the dealing public in relation to the securities concerned (which is obviously sensible) and, more controversially, the issue is not whether the information is known to that public but whether it is readily available to them. This is a more relaxed test than that applied under the previous legislation, which required knowledge of the information on the part of the public.[72] The former test required those close to the market to wait before trading until the information had been assimilated by the investment community. Now it appears that trading is permitted as soon as the information can be readily acquired by investors, even though it has not in fact been acquired. In

---

[69] In the permissive cases the situation is, presumably, that the facts described in the subsections do not prevent the court from holding the information to have been made public, but whether the court in a particular prosecution will so hold will depend on the circumstances of the case as a whole.

[70] s.58(2)(d).

[71] Query whether front-running a recommendation, not based upon any research but where its publication will have an impact on the price of the securities because of the reputation of the recommender, would be protected by s.58(2)(d). *cf. US v Carpenter* (1986) 791 F. 2d 1024. The trader might have a defence under para.2(1) of Sch.1 to the Act, but that would depend upon his having acted "reasonably": see para.30–25, below. Such conduct might in extreme cases even be a breach of section 397 of the FSMA. See para.30–26 below.

[72] Company Securities (Insider Dealing) Act 1985, s.10(b).

other words, a person who has advance knowledge of the information can react as soon as it can be "readily acquired" and reap a benefit in the period before the information is in fact fully absorbed by the market. This consequence of section 58(2)(c) is strengthened by the express provisions that publication in accordance with the rules of a regulated market or publication in records which by statute are available for public inspection mean that the information has been made public.[73]

However, the extent of the move away from actual public knowledge in the current legislation should not be exaggerated. The test laid down in section 58(2)(c) is not that information is public if it is available to the relevant segment of investors but whether it "can readily be acquired" by them. That information could be acquired by investors, if they took certain steps, is surely not enough in every case to meet the test of ready availability. One can foresee much dispute over what in addition is required to make information readily available. Section 58(3) helps with this issue to the extent of stating that certain features of the information do not necessarily prevent it from being brought within the category of information which "can be readily acquired". Thus, information is not to be excluded solely because it is published outside the United Kingdom, is communicated only on payment of a fee, can be acquired only by observation or the exercise of diligence or expertise, or is communicated only to a section of the public. However, in the overall context of particular cases, information falling within these categories may be excluded from the scope of "public information", for instance because the information supplied for a fee is supplied to a very restricted number of persons. To this extent, the legislation has necessarily ended up adopting the Government's initial standpoint that much would have to depend upon case-by-case evaluation by the courts in the context of particular prosecutions.

Impact on price

30–18   The final limb of the definition of inside information is the requirement that it should be likely to have "a significant effect" on the price of the securities, if it were made public.[74] The law has chosen not to pursue those who will reap only trivial advantages from trading on inside information. At first sight, the test would seem to present the court (or jury) with an impossibly hypothetical test to apply. In fact, in most cases, by the time any prosecution is brought, the information in question will have become public,[75] and so the question will

---

[73] s.58(2)(a) and (b) respectively. The former would cover publication on a Regulatory News Service and the latter documents field at Companies House or the Patents Registry.

[74] s.56(1)(d).

[75] Insiders have little incentive to trade on the basis of inside information which will never become public or will do so only far into the future.

probably be answered by looking at what impact the information did in fact have on the market when it was published. However, it would seem permissible for an insider to argue in an appropriate case that the likely effect of the information being made public at the time of the trading was not significant, even if its actual disclosure had a bigger effect, because the surrounding circumstances had changed in the meantime.

Insiders

We have already noted[76] the important restriction in the legislation   **30–19** that insiders must be individuals. Beyond that, it might be thought that nothing more needs to be said other than that an insider is a person in possession of inside information. In other words, the definitional burden in the legislation should fall on deciding what is inside information and the definition of insider should follow as a secondary consequence of this primary definition. The Government's consultative document on the proposed legislation[77] rejected this approach as likely to cause "damaging uncertainty in the markets, as individuals attempted to identify whether or not they were covered". This is not convincing. Either the definition of inside information is adequate or it ought to be reformed. If it is adequate, so that it can be applied effectively to those who are insiders under the Act, then it is not clear why it cannot be applied to all individuals, whether they meet the separate criteria for being insiders or not. If the definition of inside information is not adequate, it is not proper to apply it even to those who clearly are insiders under the legislation and it should be changed. In fact, the proposal that insiders should be defined as those in possession of inside information would to some extent reduce uncertainty, because the only question which would have to be asked is whether the individual was in possession of inside information and the additional question of whether the individual met the separate criteria for being classed as an insider would be irrelevant.

However, the Government stuck to its guns whilst simplifying the criteria which had been used in the earlier legislation and, following the Directive, expanding the category of insiders quite considerably.[78] By virtue of section 57(2)(a) two categories of insider are defined. The first are those who obtain inside information "through being" a director, employee or shareholder of an issuer of securities.[79] Although it is not entirely clear, it seems that the "through being"

---

[76] See above, para.30–12.
[77] DTI, *The Law on Insider Dealing* (1989), para.2.24.
[78] In particular, the requirement of "being connected with the company" was removed. See the Company Securities (Insider Dealing) Act, s.9.
[79] The relationship does not have to exist with the issuer of the securities which are dealt in. So a director of company A who is privy to his or her company's plans to launch a bid for company B is an insider in relation to the securities of company B (as well as those of A).

test is simply a "but for" test. If a junior employee happens to see inside information in the non-public part of the employer's premises, he or she would be within the category of insider, even if the duties of the employment do not involve acquisition of that information. On the other hand, coming across such information in a social context would not make the employee an insider, even though the information related to the worker's employer. In other words, there must be a causal link between the employment and the acquisition of the information, but not in the sense that the information must be acquired in the course of the employee's employment (though the latter remains a possible interpretation of the subsection). It may be thought that shareholders, who were excluded from the definition of insider in the previous legislation, are unlikely to obtain access to inside information "though being" shareholders, but this is in fact a likely situation in relation to large institutional shareholders, which may, either as a general practice or in specific circumstances, keep in close touch with at least the largest companies in their portfolios.

The second category of insider identified by section 57(2)(a) is the individual with inside information "through having access to the information by virtue of his employment, office or profession", whether or not the employment, etc., relationship is with an issuer. Thus, an insider in this second category may be, or be employed by, a professional adviser to the company;[80] an investment analyst, who has no business link with an issuer; a civil servant or an employee of one of the burgeoning regulatory bodies; or a journalist or other employee of a newspaper or printing company.[81] Again, the question arises about the exact meaning of the phrase "by virtue of": is it again a simple "but for" test or does it mean "in the course of" (perhaps a slightly stronger suggestion in this second situation)? Even if the latter interpretation is ultimately adopted, this second category would be wide enough to embrace partners and employees of an investment bank or solicitors' firm retained to advise an issuer on a particular matter, employees of regulatory bodies who are concerned with the issuer's affairs, journalists researching an issuer for a story and even employees of a printing firm involved in the production of documents for a planned but unannounced takeover bid.[82] If the broader "but

---

[80] Again one must remember that in the course of their professional duties such individuals may well obtain inside information in relation to a company other than the instructing company. Thus, employees of an investment bank preparing a takeover bid would become insiders in relation to both the proposed bidder (i.e. the bank's client) and in relation to the target company.

[81] Of course, the journalist's employer may be a listed company, in which case he would seem to fall within the first category as well.

[82] cf. *US v Chiarella* (1980) 445 U.S. 222.

for" test is adopted, then employees of these organisations, not employed on the tasks mentioned, but who serendipitously come across the information in the workplace, would be covered too.[83]

Recipients from insiders

In practice, the need to define the exact scope of the second category of insider is reduced by the third category, created in this country by section 57(2)(b). In the United States persons in this third category are distinguished from primary insiders by the use of the graphic expression "tippee",[84] but the British legislation lumps them in with primary insiders. This third category consists of those who have inside information "the direct or indirect source of" which is a person falling within either of the first two categories. Thus, subject to the point about *mens rea* made in the next paragraph, the employee of an investment bank who overhears a colleague talking about a takeover bid on which the latter is engaged would be in all probability an insider in the third category if he or she does not fall within the second category.[85] This example also makes it clear that the more striking American terminology might be somewhat misleading. It does not matter whether the primary insider has consciously communicated the information to the secondary insider (i.e. "tipped the latter off"). Provided the latter has acquired the information from an inside source, even indirectly, he or she will fall within the scope of the Act; indeed, as in the example, the "tipper" may be entirely unaware that inside information has been communicated to anyone else.[86] Furthermore, a certain type of tipping will not in fact make the tippee liable for dealing. If the insider within the first two categories encourages another person to deal without communicating to that other person any inside information, the latter can deal without being exposed to liability under the Act.[87] In short, the focus of the legislation is on the holding of inside information which has come from an

30–20

---

[83] An even more restrictive test would be in the course of an employment which is likely to provide access to inside information. Such a test would exclude the famous, if unlikely, example of the cleaner who finds inside information in a waste-paper basket. However, there seems to be no warrant in the Act or the Directive for such a restrictive test, which would come close to reinstating the clearly discarded test of s.9(b) of the 1985 Act.

[84] The guru of securities regulation, Professor Louis Loss of Harvard Law School, first used this expression and the Oxford English Dictionary has credited him with this fact.

[85] The third category is also apt to cover shadow directors, who were not brought within the first category and might not fall within the second category either: an independent businessman or woman, who was a shadow director, might have neither employment, office nor profession.

[86] Moreover, since it is enough that the individual in the third category "has" the information from a source falling within the first or second categories, it does not matter either whether the "tippee" has solicited the information. Inadvertent acquisition of inside information is covered. This was a point of controversy under the previous legislation until cleared up by the House of Lords, in favour of liability. See *Attorney-General's Reference (No.1 of 1988)* [1989] A.C. 971.

[87] The tipper would be liable for encouraging the dealing. See below, para.30–22.

inside source; how that information came to be transmitted to the present holder did not concern the drafters of the Act but the fact of its transmission did.

Mens rea

30–21   Finally, the requirement of having information "as an insider" in section 57 was used by the drafters to put a crucial limitation on the scope of the offence created by the Act. This is the requirement of *mens rea*, a not surprising precondition for criminal liability, but nevertheless one which has made enforcement of the legislation often difficult.[88] The requirement in this regard is a two-fold one: the accused must be proved to have known that the information in question was inside information and that the information came from "an inside source", i.e. that he or she fell within one or other of the three categories discussed above. The requirement of knowledge is likely to be difficult to meet in the case of persons falling within the third category,[89] especially if the argument is that the information came indirectly from the primary insider to the suspect via a chain of communications. Proving that a "sub-tippee" or even a "sub-sub-tippee" knew that the ultimate source of the information was a primary insider could be fraught with problems.

Prohibited acts

30–22   What is an individual who has knowledge as an insider prohibited from doing? There are four prohibitions and, before describing them, it should be pointed out that it is not necessary that the accused should be an insider at the time he or she does the prohibited act. Once inside information has been acquired by an insider, the prohibitions apply even though the accused, say, resigns the directorship or employment through which he obtained the information.[90] On the other hand, if the information acquired ceases to be inside information, because it enters the public domain, the prohibitions of the Act will equally cease to apply. This demonstrates again that the focus of the Act is on the information inequality between the insider or former insider and the rest of the market.

First and most obviously, there must be no *dealing* in the relevant securities.[91] The relevant securities are those which are "price-affec-

---

[88] See para.30–27, below.
[89] The fact that someone is a director will presumably raise a pretty strong prima facie case that he or she knew that fact, and so move the evidential burden to the director to disprove knowledge.
[90] This is the significance of prohibiting acts by a person who has information "as an insider", which s.57 makes clear refers to the situation at the time of the acquisition of the information, rather than the simpler formulation of prohibiting acts *by* an insider, which might well refer to the accused's status at the time of the prohibited acts.
[91] s.52(1).

ted", i.e. those upon the price of which the inside information would be likely to have a significant effect, if made public.[92] Dealing is defined as acquiring or disposing of securities.[93] Thus, a person who refrains from dealing on the basis of inside information is not covered by the legislation.[94] In principle, it is difficult to defend this exclusion since the loss of public confidence in the market will be as strong as in a case of dealing, if news of the non-dealing emerges. The exclusion was presumably a pragmatic decision based on the severe evidential problems which would face the prosecution in such a case. The dealing prohibition is broken quite simply by dealing; the Act does not require the prosecution to go further and prove that the dealing was motivated by the inside information, though the accused may be able to put forward the defence that he would have done what he did even if he had not had the information.[95] The Act covers dealing as an agent (not only as a principal) even if the profit from the dealing is thereby made by someone else, for one can never be sure that the profit made by the third party will not filter back to the trader in some form or other. And it covers agreeing to acquire or dispose of securities as well as their actual acquisition or disposal, and entering into or ending a contract which creates the security[96] as well as contracting to acquire or dispose of a pre-existing security.

Secondly, the insider is prohibited from *procuring*, directly or indirectly, the acquisition or disposal of securities by any other person. This is done by bringing this situation within the definition of dealing.[97] Procurement will have taken place if the acquisition is done by the insider's agent or nominee or a person acting at his or her direction, but this does not exhaust the range of situations in which procurement can be found.[98] Since the person procured to deal may well not be in possession of any inside information and the procurer has not in fact dealt, without this extension of the statutory meaning of "dealing" there would be a lacuna in the law.

Thirdly, there is a prohibition on the individual *encouraging* another person to deal in price-affected securities, knowing or having reasonable cause to believe that dealing would take place on a regulated market or through a professional intermediary.[99] Again, it does not matter for the purposes of the liability of the person who does the encouraging that the person encouraged commits no offence, because, say, no inside information is imparted by the accused. Indeed, it does not matter for these purposes that no dealing at all in

[92] See s.56(2) and para.30–18, above.
[93] s.55.
[94] So a person who acquires bad news about a company and so decides not to buy its shares or discovers good news and decides not to dispose of its shares is not caught.
[95] See below, para.30–24.
[96] As is the case with derivatives.
[97] s.55(1)(b).
[98] s.55(4) and (5).
[99] s.52(2)(a).

the end takes place, though the accused must at least have reasonable cause to believe that it would. The existence of this offence is likely to discourage over-enthusiastic presentations by company representatives to meetings of large shareholders or analysts.

Finally, the individual must not *disclose* the information "otherwise than in the proper performance of the functions of his employment, office or profession to another person".[100] Unlike in the previous two cases, the communication of inside information is a necessary ingredient of this offence, but no response on the part of the person to whom the information is communicated need occur nor be expected by the accused. However, in effect, this element is built into the liability, for the accused has a defence that "he did not at the time expect any person, because of the disclosure, to deal in securities" on a regulated market or through a professional intermediary.[101] So, even if it occurs outside the proper performance of duties, disclosure which is not expected to lead to dealing will not result in liability, but the burden of proving the absence of the expectation falls on the accused.

Defences[102]

30–23   The Act provides a wide range of defences, which fall within two broad categories. First, there are two general defences which carry on the task of defining the mischief at which the Act is aimed.[103] Secondly, there are the special defences, set out mainly but not entirely, in Schedule 1 to the Act, which frankly accept that in certain circumstances the policy of prohibiting insider trading should be overborne by the values underlying the exempted practices. These special defences, which were foreshadowed in the recitals to the 1989 Directive, will be dealt with only briefly here.[104]

General defences

30–24   The more important of the general defences is that the accused "would have done what he did even if he had not had the information".[105] This defence replaces with a general formulation the specific defences which had existed in the former legislation in respect of

---

[100] s.52(2)(b).

[101] s.53(3)(a).

[102] We have already dealt, in the previous paragraph, with one of the defences relevant to the disclosure offence.

[103] Though s.53 makes it clear that the burden of proof falls on the accused, thus obviating a possible ambiguity which was found by some in the previous legislation. See *R. v Cross* [1991] B.C.L.C. 125.

[104] Sch.1 may be amended by the Treasury by order (s.53(5)), presumably so that it may be kept current with developments in financing techniques.

[105] s.53(1)(c) and (2)(c). This defence does not apply to the disclosure offence, though it is an essential ingredient of that offence that the disclosure should not have occurred in the proper performance of the accused's functions.

liquidators, receivers, trustees, trustees in bankruptcy and personal representatives,[106] who, for example, may find themselves in the course of their offices advised to trade when in fact themselves in possession of inside information. Thus, a trustee, who is advised by an investment adviser to deal for the trust in a security in relation to which the trustee has inside information, will be able to do so, relying on this defence. But the defence applies more generally than that and would embrace, for example, an insider who dealt when he did in order to meet a pressing financial need or legal obligation. However, the accused will carry the burden of showing that his or her decision to deal at that particular time in that particular security was not influenced by the possibility of exploiting the inside information which was held.

The other general defence is that the accused did not expect the dealing to result in a profit attributable to the inside information.[107] This is considerably narrower than the defence in the 1985 Act which applied when the individual traded "otherwise than with a view to the making of a profit"[108] and many of the situations covered by this provision of the old law—for example, trading to meet a pressing financial need—will now fall under the first general defence discussed above. Although the defence is general in the sense that it is not confined to particular business or financial transactions, the range of situations falling within it is probably quite narrow. The Government's attempts in the Parliamentary debates to produce examples of situations for which this defence was needed and which were at all realistic were not entirely convincing.[109]

Special defences

The Act provides six special defences, two in the body of the Act and four in Schedule 1. One of those provided in the body of the Act appears to be a general defence and is to the effect that dealing is not unlawful if the individual "believed on reasonable grounds that the information had been disclosed widely enough to ensure that none of those taking part in the dealing would be prejudiced by not having the information".[110] In short, the defence is that, although the information had not been made public, it was widely enough disclosed to avoid harm to the others involved. In fact, however, this defence is aimed particularly at underwriting arrangements,[111] where

30–25

---

[106] 1985 Act, ss.3(1)(b) and 7.
[107] s.53(1)(a). The same defence is provided, *mutatis mutandis*, in relation to the other offences by s.53(2)(a) and (3)(b). Making a profit is defined so as to include avoiding a loss: s.53(6).
[108] 1985 Act, s.3(1)(a).
[109] HC Debs, Session 1992–93, Standing Committee B (June 10, 1993). A suggestion was where the insider sold at a price which took into account the impact the (bad) information would have on the market when released.
[110] s.53(1)(b),(2)(b) provide a similar defence in relation to the encouraging offence.
[111] On underwriting see above, para.25–11.

those involved in the underwriting may trade amongst themselves on the basis of shared knowledge about the underwriting proposal but which information is not known to the market generally. The other defence provided in the body of the Act[112] concerns things done "on behalf of a public sector body in pursuit of monetary policies or policies with respect to exchange rates or the management of public debt or foreign exchange reserves". So reasons of state, relating to financial policy, trump market integrity.[113]

The four special defences provided in the Schedule do not extend to the disclosure of inside information. Where the defences apply, those concerned may trade or encourage others to do so but may not enlarge the pool of persons privy to the inside information. In all four cases, what are judged to be valuable market activities would be impossible without the relaxation of the insider dealing prohibitions. Thus, market makers[114] may often be in possession of inside information but would not be able to discharge their undertaking to maintain a continuous two-way market in particular securities if they were always subject to the Act. So paragraph 1 of Schedule 1 exempts acts done by a market maker in good faith in the course of the market-making business. More controversially, paragraph 5 does the same thing in relation to price stabilisation of new issues.[115]

The final two special defences relate to trading whilst in possession of "market information", which is, in essence, information about transactions in securities being contemplated or no longer contemplated or having or not having taken place. First, an individual may act in connection with the acquisition or disposal of securities and with a view to facilitating their acquisition or disposal where the information held is market information arising directly out of the individual's involvement in the acquisition or disposal.[116] An example is where the employees of an investment bank advising a bidder on a proposed takeover procure the acquisition of the target's shares on behalf of the bidder but before the bid is publicly announced, in order to give the bidder a good platform from which to launch the bid. This defence would not permit the employees to purchase shares for their own account, because they would not then be acting to facilitate the proposed transaction out of which the inside information arose. Even so, permitting a bidder to act in this way is somewhat controversial for those who procure the purchase of the shares know that a bid at a price in excess of the current market price is about to be launched and those who sell out to the bidder just before the public announcement

---

[112] s.63, applying to all offences under the Act. Technically, s.63 does not provide a defence but rather describes a situation where the Act "does not apply".
[113] As Art.2(4) of the Directive permits.
[114] See above, para.26–24.
[115] This is discussed further below at para.30–37.
[116] See para.3.

may feel that they have been badly treated.[117] Another situation covered by the provision is that of a fund manager who decides to take a large stake in a particular company. The manager can go into the market on behalf of the funds under management and acquire the stake at the best prices possible, without announcing in advance the intention to build up a large stake, which would immediately drive up the price of the chosen company's shares.

Under the second and more general "market information" defence the individual may act if "it was reasonable for an individual in his position to have acted as he did" despite having the market information.[118] This is so broadly phrased that it would seem wide enough to cover the situations discussed in the previous paragraph. The more specific provisions were included as well presumably in order to give comfort to those who would otherwise have had to rely on the general reasonableness provision and who might have wondered whether the courts would interpret it in their favour.

CRIMINAL PROHIBITIONS ON MARKET MANIPULATION

The criminal prohibition on market abuse is to be found in section   **30–26** 397 of FSMA 2000. This section creates two distinct offences. The first, which can be traced back to s.12 of the Prevention of Fraud (Investments) Act 1939, consists of making a statement, promise or forecast knowing it to be misleading or reckless whether it is so, for the purpose of inducing someone (or reckless whether it may induce someone) to enter into or to refrain from entering into an investment agreement or to exercise or refrain from exercising a right conferred by an investment. The section also catches the dishonest concealment of material facts done for the like purpose. We have discussed this aspect of section 397 in Chapter 26.[119] It can clearly be used to catch egregious cases of market abuse.[120]

The second offence is more interesting and was introduced by s.47(2) of the Financial Services Act 1986 (now repealed). This

---

[117] Nevertheless, the City Code on Takeovers and Mergers adopts the same approach as the Act. See r.4.1. However the potential bidder would have to comply with the statutory provisions on the disclosure of shareholdings. See paras 26–18 *et seq.*, and Davies, "The Takeover Bidder Exemption and the Policy of Disclosure" in Hopt and Wymeersch (eds), *European Insider Dealing* (London, 1991). Even so, the bid facilitation argument ought not to be employed to justify the purchase of derivatives where the aim of the purchase is simply to give the bidder a cash benefit rather than to take a step towards the acquisition of voting control.

[118] See para.2(1). Some guidance on what is reasonable is given in para.2(2).

[119] Above at para.26–8.

[120] As in the *De Berenger* case, above, fn.3.

criminalises an act or course of conduct[121] which creates a false or misleading impression as to the market in or price or value of any investment (as widely defined), if done for the purpose of creating that impression and thereby inducing a person to acquire or dispose of investments or to refrain from doing so or to exercise or not to exercise rights attached to investments.[122] It is to be noted that the offence is complete whether or not the accused knew that, or was reckless whether, the impression created was misleading: all that has to be shown is that he acted for the purpose of creating an impression which was in fact misleading. However, a defence is provided where the accused can show that he reasonably believed that the impression was not misleading.[123] In effect, negligence as to the misleading nature of the impression is made a crime and the burden of disproving negligence is placed upon the maker of the impression. This second offence is aimed particularly at market manipulation. Some basic forms of this activity are offences at common law,[124] but the statute extends and makes clearer the reach of the criminal law in this area. This offence is rarely prosecuted, but the following examples of contraventions can be given. The promoters of a company fund the underwriters of a share issue to buy shares in the market when dealings begin in order to give the impression that there is a greater market interest in the shares than is in fact the case;[125] or the directors of a company, believing the market price of its shares not to reflect the net tangible asset value of the company, persuade its brokers to buy shares in the market at some four times the previous market price, in order to move the market price closer to what the directors believe to be the "true" value of the shares.[126]

PROHIBITION OF MARKET ABUSE IN PART VIII OF FSMA

30–27   With the enactment of the Financial Services and Markets Act 2000, the main thrust of the legal rules controlling market abuse, in which term is to be included both insider dealing and market manipulation, shifted from the criminal law to administrative sanctions which have been placed in the hands of the FSA. The main source of the rules is Part VIII of FSMA, though certain important additional sanctions,

---

[121] The act or course of conduct must occur in the United Kingdom or the misleading impression must be created in the United Kingdom: s.397(7).
[122] s.397(3).
[123] s.397(5)(a).
[124] *Scott v Brown Doering & Co* [1892] 2 Q.B. 724.
[125] As in *Scott v Brown Doering & Co* (previous note).
[126] *North v Marra Developments* (1981) CLR 42, HCA. Both this and the case mentioned in the previous note were civil actions in which the criminal nature of the activity was used to defeat a contractual claim on grounds of the illegality of the contract.

where the courts have a role, are to be found in Pt XXV. It is important to note that Part VIII of FSMA applies to all those whose actions have an effect on the market, whether they are persons authorised to carry on financial activities under that Act or not. It thus applies as much to industrial companies and their directors, for example, as it does to investment banks and their directors and employees.

Successful deployment of the criminal law on a wide scale against insider dealing and market manipulation proved impossible, and the move towards a regime based on administrative penalties was driven by the desire to address two of those obstacles, namely the need to show intention or *mens rea*, at least in relation to insider dealing,[127] and the high evidential requirements of the criminal law. However, this proposal proved highly controversial during the Parliamentary debates on the Bill, those opposing it claiming that it would infringe rights conferred by Article 6 of the European Convention on Human Rights (right to a fair trial).[128] The central claim of the opponents was that the penalty regime proposed by the Government, although clearly not part of the domestic criminal law, would be classified as criminal by the European Court of Human Rights, whose classification criteria are independent of those used by the laws of the Member States. Without ever conceding the correctness of this claim, the Government nevertheless did make substantial amendments to its proposals in order to promote the fairness of the new regime, the regime being subject in any event to a general fairness test under the European Convention, even if regarded as civil rather than criminal in nature. These amendments related in particular to the elaboration of a Code on market abuse, to be produced by the FSA in order to give guidance on the scope of the prohibitions, and the creation of rights of appeal to an independent tribunal (the Financial Services and Markets Tribunal) to be granted to persons penalised by the FSA.[129]

Shortly after the re-casting of the domestic law, the Community in 2003 replaced the 1989 Directive with Directive 2003/6/EC on insider dealing and market manipulation (market abuse).[130] Although the

---

[127] As we have seen, in relation to misleading impressions, *mens rea* is required only in an attenuated form under s.397.

[128] See Joint Committee on Financial Services and Markets, First Report, *Draft Financial Services and Markets Bill*, Vol. I, Session 1998/99, HL 50-I/HC 328-I, pp.61–67 and Annexes C and D; Second Report, HL 66/HC 465, pp.5–10 and Minutes of Evidence, pp.1–27.

[129] The FSMT has tended to view the penalty proceedings as being criminal in nature for the purposes of the Convention. However, the standard of proof required by the Convention is not necessarily that of "beyond reasonable doubt". The standard will depend, as is the case with the civil burden in domestic law, on the seriousness of the allegation which has to be proved. See *Davidson & Tatham v FSA*, FSM Case No. 31 and *Parker v FSA*, FSM Case No. 37, available on: http://www.financeandtaxtribunals.gov.uk/decisions/FinancialServices MarketsTribunal.htm.

[130] OJ L96/16, 12.4.2003.

principles underlying the Directive were the same as those animating the earlier domestic reforms—extension of the prohibition beyond insider dealing to cover market manipulation and the emphasis on civil penalties as the leading sanction[131]—the Directive required some re-casting of the civil penalty regime for market abuse just adopted.[132] Moreover, in some respects the Directive was narrower in scope than the 2000 Act, which raised the question of whether the newly-adopted domestic provisions should be slimmed back to the minimum required by the Directive.[133] First, the Directive applies, as far as financial instruments are concerned, only to those traded on a regulated market (in the EU sense of that term),[134] whereas the domestic provisions applied more broadly to "prescribed" markets, so as to include, for example, any market operated by a body recognised by the FSA.[135] This broader market coverage was maintained after the reforms to transpose the Directive, so that, in particular, the AIM and Plus markets are covered.[136]

Secondly, in certain respects the prior domestic definitions of both insider dealing and market manipulation were wider than those contained in the Directive. It was decided to maintain these wider provisions, but, after pressure, subject to a "sunset clause", by which the broader provisions[137] would cease to have effect on June 30, 2008, unless renewed. The Treasury proposed in 2008 that the provisions should be extended until the end of January 2010, in part because the Community was itself engaged in a review of the scope of the Directive.[138] These "super-equivalent" provisions of the domestic law are discussed below together with the other elements of the current definition of market abuse.

---

[131] Art.14.

[132] The necessary amendments to FSMA 2000 were effected by the Financial Services and Markets Act 2000 (Market Abuse) Regulations 2005 (SI 2005/381). As we have noted, the Government's view was that no changes were required in the criminal provisions dealing with insider dealing and market abuse. This was presumably because, whilst Art.14 of the Directive requires Member States to deploy administrative measures against market abuse, it does not require (though it permits) the use of the criminal law.

[133] Treasury and FSA, *UK Implementation of the EU Market Abuse Directive: A Consultation Document*, June 2004.

[134] Art.1.3. For the meaning of a "regulated market" see para.25–5.

[135] That, is a "recognised investment exchange" (RIE). See para.30–10.

[136] s.118(1) and the Financial Services and Markets Act 2000 (Prescribed Markets and Qualifying Investments) Order 2001 (2001/996), art.4, as amended. Provided the proscribed conduct occurs in the UK and provided the conduct is required to be prohibited by the Directive (see the second point discussed in the text), prescribed markets also include any regulated market in the EEA (s.118A(1)).

[137] Contained in s.118(4) and (8). In certain other respects the Directive's provisions were wider than those of the prior domestic law, which was why the domestic law could not simply be left unamended.

[138] HM Treasury, *FSMA Market Abuse Regime: A Review of the Sunset Clauses*, February 2008.

Inside information

The definition of market abuse is to be found in section 118 of the   **30–28**
Act. It is divided into seven types of behaviour, of which the first
three relate to the use of inside information or of information which
is not generally available and the second four are various types of
market manipulation. Further guidance about the proscribed behaviour is then given in the FSA's Code of Market Conduct, which was
also revised as a result of the transposition of the Directive. In respect
of both types of behaviour, it must occur in relation to "qualifying
investments" admitted to a "prescribed market" or where a request
for such admission has been made. We have noted the meaning of a
"prescribed market" above. "Qualifying investments" are defined[139]
by reference to Article 1.3 of the Directive which, for our purposes,
includes transferable securities and any other instrument admitted to
trading on a regulated market.

Dealing on the basis of inside information

The first type of prohibited behaviour is familiar from the Criminal   **30–29**
Justice Act 1993: "where an insider deals, or attempts to deal, in
qualifying investments or related investments on the basis of inside
information relating to the investment in question." Liability thus
depends upon the trader being an insider and having inside information: simply holding inside information does not make one an
insider. The definition of "insider" in section 118B shows a good deal
of similarity with that to be found in section 57 of the CJA, and it
raises some of the same problems.[140] To be an insider the person must
have inside information "as a result of" being a director or shareholder of the issuer, "having access to the information through the
exercise of his employment, profession or duties", or, which is new, as
a result of criminal activities.[141] However, the final category is a significant extension: information is inside information if its holder "has
obtained it by other means and which he knows, or could reasonably
be expected to know, is inside information."[142] This bring us very
close to the position that an insider is one who has inside information, but subject to the qualification that its holder ought to know
that the information has this character.

The definition of "inside information" is also similar to that in the
CJA:[143] this is information which is precise, not generally available,
relates directly to one or more issuers or qualifying investments, and
would, if generally available, be likely to have a significant effect on

[139] In art.5 of the 2001 Regulations (above, fn.136).
[140] See above, para.30–19.
[141] Thus, a burglar who finds inside information during the course of a break-in will be within
the definition.
[142] s.118B(e).
[143] s.56: above, para.30–13.

the price of the securities.[144] It is slightly broader than its CJA equivalent in that it does not have to relate to particular securities or particular issuers of securities, so that information which has an impact on the securities markets generally could be inside information for the purposes of FSMA.

The crucial difference between the FSMA approach to insider dealing and that of the CJA is that there is no requirement of *mens rea*, i.e. no equivalent to the requirement in section 57(1) of the CJA that the person know the information is inside information and know that he or she has it through being an insider.[145] As far as section 118 goes, it appears that a person is open to liability under the FSA penalty regime if he or she deals on the basis of inside information, even if totally unaware that the information is inside information or that he or she is an insider. Of course, it was one of the main objectives of introducing the civil penalty regime that the *mens rea* requirements of the criminal law should be circumvented. However, the Act does not go quite so far as to impose strict liability for insider dealing. It provides that a penalty may not be imposed on someone if there "are reasonable grounds to be satisfied" that either (a) that person believed, on reasonable grounds, that he or she was not acting in breach of the insider trading prohibition or (b) that he or she had taken all reasonable precautions and "exercised all due diligence" to avoid the prohibition.[146] These may be referred to as the "reasonable belief" and "reasonable care" defences. Thus, the basis for liability is in fact negligence, which means that the assessment of the facts, initially by the FSA, will be crucial.

It should also be noted that liability under FSMA arises only if the person deals "on the basis of" inside information, whilst, provided the *mens rea* requirement is satisfied, the CJA criminalises dealing by an insider who "has" inside information. However, it is likely that the two sets of provisions are not far apart since the CJA provides a defence to a person who shows that he or she would have done what he did even if not in possession of the information.[147]

Disclosure of inside information

30–30 Following the CJA, FSMA also penalises disclosing inside information otherwise than in the "proper course of the exercise of [a person's] employment, profession or duties".[148] However, section 118 contains no equivalent to criminal prohibition on encouraging

[144] s.118C(2). However, s.118C(5) brings specificity back into the definition of precision, as in the CJA (see above, para.30–15). Further, information is likely to have a significant effect on price only if a reasonable investor would be likely to use the information as part of an investment decision: s.118C(6).

[145] See above, para.30–21.

[146] s.123(2).

[147] CJA s.53(1)(c), (2)(c), and see above, para.30–24.

[148] s.118(3), *cf*. s.52(2)(b) of CJA.

another to trade, but such action is in fact caught by section 123. This authorises the FSA to impose penalties on those who engage in market abuse or who have "required or encouraged" a person to act in a way which would constitute market abuse, if done by the person sought to be penalised.[149] However, section 123 is not wide enough to catch mere disclosure of inside information, which is, no doubt, why it is subject to a separate provision in section 118.

Both the dealing and the disclosure prohibitions apply to "related investments" as well as to qualifying investments.[150] A "related investment" is one whose price or value depends on the price or value of the qualifying investment.[151] This means that these prohibitions cannot be avoided by, for example, dealing not in the company's shares but in a derivative based on those shares, including, it would seem, a contract for differences.[152]

Relevant information not generally available (RINGA)
We now come to the first of the "super-equivalent" provisions **30–31** maintained in the domestic legislation, even after the transposition of MAD. Its supplementary nature is indicated by the fact that it applies only when the behaviour is not caught by the first two prohibitions mentioned above. Despite its supplementary nature, however, it achieves a potentially significant extension of the insider trading prohibition. It adds to it in four ways.[153]

> 1. The prohibition applies to "information which is not gen-
>   erally available" and not just to "inside information",[154]
>   provided a "regular user of the market"[155] would regard the
>   information as relevant to the transaction in question. Hence
>   the acronym RINGA. The effect is to extend the prohibition
>   to information which would not meet the definition of inside
>   information, because it is not specific or precise, but which
>   market users would regard as an illegitimate basis for trad-
>   ing. The FSA's Code of Market Conduct gives the following
>   example:
>
>   > An employee of B Plc is aware of contractual negotiations
>   > between B Plc and a customer. Transactions with that

---

[149] s.123(1)(b). This provision seems wide enough to embrace the extension of the term "dealing" to "procuring" a dealing in CJA s.55.

[150] s.118A(1)(b)(iii). For "qualifying investments" see above, fn.136.

[151] s.130A(4).

[152] See fn.50.

[153] Though being a provision of purely domestic origin it does not apply to a regulated market outside the UK: see Financial Services and Markets Act 2000 (Prescribed Markets and Qualifying Investments) Order 2001 (SI 2001/996), art.4(2).

[154] On the definition of which see above, para.30–28.

[155] Defined in s.130A(3) as "a reasonable person who regularly deals on [a particular] market in investments of the kind in question."

customer have generated over 10 percent of B Plc's turnover in each of the last five financial years. The employee knows that the customer has threatened to take its business elsewhere, and that the negotiations, while ongoing, are not proceeding well. The employee, whilst being under no obligation to do so, sells his shares in B Plc based on his assessment that it is reasonably likely that the customer will take his business elsewhere.[156]

2. The prohibition extends to behaviour, not just to dealing. Thus, it is capable of capturing a decision not to deal taken on the basis of inside information (though the evidentiary problems facing the FSA in such a case might be formidable).

3. The prohibition extends to a wider range of actions than dealing in qualifying instruments or related investments. Again, the FSA Code gives a helpful example.

X, a director at B Plc, has lunch with a friend, Y. X tells Y that his company has received a takeover offer. Y places a fixed odds bet with a bookmaker that B Plc will be the subject of a bid within a week, based on his expectation that the takeover offer will be announced over the next few days.[157]

Placing a bet would not seem to constitute trading in a qualifying investment or even a related investment, but seems to be capable of constituting behaviour covered by the section.[158]

4. The prohibition is not limited to insiders: any person whose behaviour falls within the sub-section is caught. Thus, in this case a holder of relevant information is a person to whom the prohibition applies, whether he or she is an insider or not, subject, of course, to the reasonable belief and reasonable care defences.

Market manipulation
Transactions and orders to trade
30–32 We turn now to market manipulation and the fourth and fifth types of market abuse can be considered together.[159] They both arise out of effecting transactions or orders to trade (for example, in securities).

---

[156] MAR 1.5.10. And see *Parker v FSA*, above, fn.129.
[157] MAR 1.5.10.
[158] See the expanded meaning given to "behaviour" for the purposes of s.118(4) by s.118A(3)(a), which includes "behaviour which occurs in relation to anything that is the subject matter ... of the qualifying investments."
[159] s.118(5) and (6).

The fourth covers trades which give or are likely to give a false impression as to the market supply or demand or price of a qualifying security or secure the price of the investment at an artificial level. As we have seen above, such behaviour constitutes a criminal offence if done for the purpose of inducing investment decisions,[160] but section 118 applies if the behaviour is likely to give a false impression (though again subject to the reasonable belief and reasonable care defences).[161] The fifth covers transactions or orders which employ some form of deception. The market itself has developed graphic terms to apply to some of the forms of behaviour falling within these prohibitions. Examples are "wash trades", (where a person trades with himself or two persons acting together trade between themselves, but so that there is no real transfer of beneficial ownership or market risk) and "painting the tape" (entering into a series of transactions that are publicly reported for the purpose of suggesting a level of activity or price movement which do not genuinely exist) fall within the fourth type of behaviour.[162] "Pump and dump" (taking a long position in an investment, disseminating misleading positive information about it, and then selling out) and its opposite, "trash and cash" (taking a short position in a security and disseminating misleading negative information before closing out the short position) fall within the fifth type of market manipulation.[163]

Dissemination of information

Given the reliance of markets on information, it is not surprising that a common form of market manipulation consists of supplying mis-leadingly good or bad information to the market (as the examples given in the previous paragraph show). The sixth type of behaviour prohibited by section 118 consists of disseminating information which is likely to give a false or misleading impression as to a qualifying investment by a person who could reasonably have been expected to have known that the information was false or misleading. In this case, a negligence standard is built into the definition of the prohibited conduct.[164] In effect, a person who makes a negligent misstatement to the market about a qualifying investment is exposed to the FSA's penalties, but without it being a requirement for liability that the maker of the statement should have intended or expected that any particular person or class of person should rely on it, still less

30–33

---

[160] FSMA s.397. Above, para.30–26.
[161] s.123(2).
[162] MAR 1.6.2.
[163] MAR 1.7.2.
[164] Though the defences in s.123(2) are still available.

that any such reliance should have occurred.[165] As we have seen,[166] there is liability under section 91 of the Act to the FSA's penalties on the part of an issuer (and its directors) which negligently makes a misleading disclosure required by the Disclosure and Transparency Rules. However, liability under the market abuse provisions (which was invoked in the *Shell* case)[167] is a useful supplement because the market abuse provisions are not confined to regulated markets.[168]

Misleading behaviour and market distortion

30–34 The seventh and final form of market abuse constitutes the second example of a super-equivalent provision in section 118. It may be considered more briefly since its main importance seems to be in relation to markets in commodities.[169] Like the super-equivalent provision dealing with information, it applies only where the behaviour does not fall within one of the forms of market manipulation described above.[170] In its misleading behaviour form it consists of behaviour likely to give a regular user of the market a false or misleading impression as to the supply or demand or price of a qualifying investment and the behaviour is likely to be regarded by a regular user of the market as a failure to observe standards of behaviour reasonably expected of a person in the defendant's position.[171] Unlike the fourth and fifth forms of behaviour, this one is not limited to effecting transactions or orders and unlike the sixth is not limited to the dissemination of information. On the other hand, it is subject to the reasonable user qualification, both as to what constitutes a misleading impression and what constitutes the failure to observe appropriate standards of behaviour. The Code gives the example of moving an empty cargo ship around and thus giving a false impression as to the demand for a particular commodity.[172] In its market distortion form it consists of behaviour that would be likely to be regarded by the regular user as behaviour likely to distort the market in an investment, again provided the behaviour falls below the standard expected by that user.[173]

---

[165] The breadth of the prohibition was thought to put financial journalists at particular risk and so s.118A(4) provides that liability of journalists is to be assessed on the basis that the FSA takes into account codes of conduct governing that profession, provided the journalist derives no direct or indirect benefit from the dissemination of the information.
[166] Ch.26 at para.26–8.
[167] Ch.26 at para.26–9.
[168] See above para.30–27.
[169] See MAR 1.9.2.
[170] s.118(8).
[171] s.118(8)(a).
[172] MAR 1.9.2.
[173] s.118(8)(b).

Safe harbours
Share buy-backs

Article 8 of the Directive, implemented by a Commission "second-level" Regulation,[174] provides that its prohibitions are not to apply to two types of activity.[175] These are share buy-backs and stabilisation occurring in the period after a public offer of securities. In both cases, the exemptions are available only where the provisions of the Commission Regulation are complied with.

30–35

The creditor and shareholder protection aspects of share buy-backs have been considered in Chapter 13.[176] It is by no means impossible for a company to effect a buy-back programme for its shares without falling foul of the market abuse prohibition. However, it seems to have been thought that buy-backs were an important corporate tool, so that companies should be given, in effect, a "safe harbour" for their implementation. The Government decided to provide that compliance with the Commission Regulation would give protection against criminal liability under section 397[177] and the CJA[178] as well as against civil penalties.

The conditions laid down in the Regulation for access to the safe harbour are four. None of this is particularly novel in the UK, where the Listing Rules contained such provisions before the adoption of the 2003 Directive.[179]

(a) The purpose of the buy-back programme must be to reduce the company's capital or to meet its obligations under a debt instrument convertible into equity or an employee share scheme.[180] This appears to mean that the shares bought back will normally be required to be cancelled (rather than held in treasury). And the safe harbour applies only to behaviour directly related to the purpose of the buy-back programme.

30–36

(b) Apart from meeting the requirements of Article 19 of the Second Directive, as transposed into domestic law,[181] details of the buy-back programme must be disclosed to the market in advance of any purchases and the issuer must report purchases actually made within seven working days, giving amounts acquired and prices.[182] Thus, the acquisitions cannot occur clandestinely and the market will know what may happen and what has happened.

---

[174] Commission Regulation (EC) No.2273/2003.
[175] The Regulation applies directly in the UK, but Article 8 needs transposition into domestic law and this is effected by s.118A(5)(b).
[176] At paras 13–13ff.
[177] s.397(4)(c) and (5)(d).
[178] CJA 1993, Sch.1, para.5.
[179] See, for example, FSA, *The Listing Rules*, May 2000 edition, Ch.15.
[180] Regulation, Art.3.
[181] See above, para.13–13.
[182] Art.4. The details of the programme include the maximum consideration, maximum number of shares to be bought and duration of the authority. In fact, this information in any event will be contained in the resolution of the shareholders approving the on-market acquisition and that resolution must be filed with the registrar: s.701 of the CA 2006 (above, para.13–16).

(c) The acquisitions must not be at a price higher than the pre-vailing market price (even if the authorisation from the shareholders permits a higher price) and, normally, not more than one quarter of the average daily volume of the shares may be bought in any one day.[183] This rule reduces the impact of the acquisitions on the trading price of the share.

(d) The issuer may not sell its own shares (presumably those held in treasury) during the programme, thus removing an incentive to pay an above-market price.[184] Nor may it effect acquisitions under its programme at a time when it is making use of the permission not to disclose otherwise disclosable inside information.[185] Finally, it may not make purchases under the programme during a "closed period", i.e. in the case of the UK those laid down in the Model Code.[186] However, the issuer can avoid all three restrictions by either adopting a programme under which the amounts and times of the acquisitions are set out in the public disclosure required above (a "time-sched-uled" programme) or by outsourcing the programme to an invest-ment bank which makes the trading decisions independently of the issuer.[187]

Price stabilisation

30–37   Share or price stabilisation is, as its name suggests, a somewhat more questionable procedure from the point of view of market abuse than share repurchases, since the very purpose of the behaviour is to set the price of the security at a different level from that which would otherwise prevail. However, it is permitted in connection with new shares issues, for reasons which the FSA has explained as follows.

> "Because new securities are usually issued at irregular intervals, they may result in a temporary oversupply of those securities leading to an artificially low market price during and immedi-ately after issue. Such short-term price fluctuations may be to the detriment of both issuers and investors. Price stabilising activity involves the lead managers of a new issue of securities sup-porting the price of those securities for a limited period, thereby reducing the risk of price falls."[188]

Article 8 of the Directive and the Chapter III of the Commission Regulation provide a safe harbour for price stabilisation and, again,

---

[183] Art.5. In cases of low liquidity the figure may rise to one-half.
[184] Art.6. There are exceptions for investment firms and banks which have effective Chinese walls in place.
[185] See para.26–6.
[186] See above, para.30–4 and MAR 1.1.13, LR 12.2.1 and LR 9 Annex 1.
[187] Art.6.3.
[188] FSA, *The Price Stabilising Rules*, CP 40, January 2000.

the domestic rules extend that safe harbour to criminal liability under the CJA and section 397 of FSMA.[189] As is in the nature of a safe harbour, its extent is rather narrowly defined, but it does not necessarily follow that price stabilisation activity which occurs outside it amounts to market abuse[190] (though it must run a not inconsiderable risk of being so characterised); and the right of civil action by private persons against persons authorised under the Act for failure to follow the stabilisation rules is specifically excluded.[191]

The conditions to be met for the price stabilisation safe harbour are, briefly, as follows.

(a) The stabilisation may be carried out only within a limited period   **30–38** of time, for example, in the case of shares, within 30 calendar days of the date on which shares offered in an initial offer commence trading.[192]

(b) The market must be informed before the shares are offered to the public that stabilisation may be undertaken (but that there is no guarantee that it will or that it will be at any particular level) and of the period during which it may be undertaken and who will be undertaking it.[193] Stabilisation activity must be reported to the FSA within seven working days of its taking place and within one week of the end of the stabilisation period the market must be informed of what stabilisation activity occurred, including the dates and prices.[194]

(c) The price at which the stabilisation activity took place must not be above the offer price.[195]

Other cases

FSMA provides that if a person acts in such a way as is described in   **30–39** the Code as not amounting to market abuse in the FSA's opinion, that behaviour is to be taken as not amounting to market abuse.[196] This was part of the response to the concerns, noted above,[197] which were expressed when the civil penalty regime was adopted in 2000. The FSA was in effect given power to give binding interpretations of

---

[189] See CJA Sch.1, para.5 and FSMA s.397(4)(a),(c) and (5)(b),(d). Since the Commission Regulation, like the Directive itself, applies only to regulated markets, whilst the domestic civil penalty rules extend to prescribed markets (see above, para.30–27), it was necessary to authorise the FSA to make rules to extend the safe harbour even in relation to civil penalties to this wider range of markets, as was done by FSMA s.144.

[190] MAR 2.2.5. Some hints of what the FSA requires in such a case are given in MAR 2.4. The same is true of buy-back regimes not within the safe harbour (MAR 1.10.1).

[191] MAR 2.2.9, invoking FSMA s.150(2). The person conducting the stabilisation will normally be an authorised person (the lead investment bank) and s.150 gives private persons a right of action against authorised persons to recover loss, unless that right of action is excluded in relation to specific parts of the FSA's rules.

[192] Commission Regulation, Art.8.

[193] This matter is now covered in the Commission Regulation (EC) No.809/2004, Annex III, para.6.5, implementing the Prospectus Directive.

[194] Commission Regulation implementing the Market Abuse Directive, Art.9.

[195] Commission Regulation implementing the Market Abuse Directive, Art.10.

[196] s.122(1).

[197] At para.30–27.

the legislative provisions, at least in the negative sense of being empowered to take certain behaviour out of the legislative scope. With the adoption of the Market Abuse Directive, however, such a power became legally questionable, since competent authorities are not given such powers in the Directive. However, the recitals to the Directive do give an indication that the Community legislator did not intend to bring certain sorts of conduct within the scope of the prohibition, and the FSA's dispensing power has been used to give effect to the recitals in domestic law. Thus, in relation to insider dealing the FSA has stipulated that the following types of behaviour will not amount to contraventions.

(a) Carrying out one's own intention to buy securities without first announcing it to the market.[198] Thus, a person intending to build up a position in a company does not have to move the market against it by announcing its intentions in advance of the purchases—though as we saw in Chapter 26[199] at the 3 per cent level holdings of voting shares become disclosable.

(b) Market makers may deal in pursuit of their legitimate business interests without falling foul of the prohibition.[200]

(c) Executing a client's orders in a proper manner, even if the person executing the order possesses inside information in relation to the security.[201]

(d) Trading on the basis of inside information in the shares of a target company on the part of a bidder in a takeover offer.[202] The protected information here is of two (rather different) types: that a potential offeror is actually going to make an offer (i.e. information about the bidder's intentions) and information about the target which the offer has obtained by examining the target's books. This rule facilitates the execution of takeover offers.

Where the Code does not go so far as to say that a particular behaviour does not amount to market abuse, nevertheless it "may be relied upon so far as it indicates whether or not that behaviour should be taken to amount to market abuse."[203] This somewhat unobvious provision seems to mean that, where the FSA indicates in the Code, as it often does, the factors which should be taken into account in assessing whether a particular provision of the Commission Regulation has been broken, it is bound to follow that approach (and not, for example, add new factors or take away existing ones) when making its assessment, unless it has gone through the procedures for altering the Code and, even then, only in relation to conduct occurring after the amendment.

---

[198] Recital 30 and MAR 1.3.6.
[199] At para.26–18.
[200] Recital 18 and MAR 1.3.7. For the CJA equivalent provision see para.30–25 above.
[201] Recital 18 and MAR 1.3.12.
[202] Recital 29 and MAR 1.3.17.
[203] s.122(2).

SANCTIONS AND ENFORCEMENT

Sanctions for breaches of Part VIII of FSMA
Penalties
The central sanction for market abuse under Part VIII of FSMA is   **30–40**
the imposition of a penalty by the FSA. In fact, apart from the power
given to the FSA to substitute a public censure for the penalty,[204] Part
VIII envisages only the penalty as a sanction for market abuse,
though, as we see below, elsewhere in the Act other sanctions can be
found. The penalty provisions were another of the human rights
battle grounds in the Parliamentary debates and a number of
restrictions on the FSA's powers are the result. First, although there
is no statutory restriction on the size of penalty the FSA may impose,
the FSA is required to produce a statement of policy on the factors
which will determine its approach to penalties.[205] That policy now
appears in the Decision Procedure and Penalties Manual (DEPP)
which contains a list of the factors the FSA considers relevant to the
decisions whether to seek a financial penalty, whether to substitute
public censure for a monetary penalty and to determining the level of
penalty. It is also in DEPP that one finds the FSA's views on the
factors relevant to determining whether a person has the benefit of
the reasonable belief and reasonable care defences.[206]

Secondly, the FSA may not impose a penalty upon a person
without sending him first a "warning notice" stating the level of
penalty proposed or the terms of the proposed public statement.[207]
Among other things, this gives the person in question the opportunity
to raise matters which may be relevant to the defences of reasonable
care and reasonable belief.[208]

Thirdly, if the FSA does impose a penalty or make a public
statement, it must issue the person concerned with a decision notice
to that effect,[209] which triggers the person's right to appeal to the
Financial Services and Markets Tribunal, set up under Pt IX and
Schedule 13 of the Act.[210] That right must normally be exercised
within 28 days.[211] The Tribunal, consisting of a legally qualified chair
and one or more experienced lay persons, operates by way of a rehearing of the case, and so can consider evidence not brought before
the FSA, whether it was available at that time or not,[212] and must

---

[204] s.123(3).
[205] ss.124 and 125.
[206] DEPP 6.
[207] s.126.
[208] s.123(2).
[209] s.127.
[210] And under the Financial Services and Markets Tribunal Rules 2001 (SI 2001/2476) as amended.
[211] s.133(1).
[212] s.133(3).

arrive at its own determination of the appropriate action to be taken in the case,[213] which, presumably, could be a tougher penalty than the one the FSA had proposed. There is a legal assistance scheme in operation for proceedings before the Tribunal, funded by the FSA, which recoups the cost from a levy on authorised persons.[214] Appeals lie on a point of law from the Tribunal to the Court of Appeal or Court of Session.[215]

Fourthly, the prohibition on the use of compelled testimony[216] applies not only to subsequent criminal charges but also to proceedings for the imposition of a penalty, whether before the FSA or the Tribunal.[217]

Restitution

30–41   The statutory penalty regime may have a significant deterrent effect, though that remains to be seen, but in any event it will not provide compensation for those who have suffered loss as a result of behaviour amounting to market abuse. However, the statute creates no private right of action in the civil courts in cases of market abuse.[218] What the statute does instead by s.383 is to confer upon the FSA the right to apply to the High Court or Court of Session in cases of market abuse (including encouraging or requiring action by others) for a restitution order.[219] The FSA has the power to apply to the court where profits have accrued to the person who engaged in the market abuse as a result of his or her activity or loss or other adverse effect was suffered by other persons.[220] The court may order the person who engaged in the market abuse to pay to the FSA such amount as it thinks just, having regard to the profits made or loss suffered.[221] That amount is to be paid out by the FSA to such persons as the court may

---

[213] s.133(4). The action must be one the FSA could have taken.
[214] ss.134 and 135, even though in the case of market abuse appeals, the appellant may not be an authorised person. The details of the assistance scheme are set out in Financial Services and Markets Tribunal (Legal Assistance) Regulations 2001 (SI 2001/3632) and the Financial Services and Markets Tribunal (Legal Assistance—Costs) Regulations 2001 (SI 2001/3633).
[215] s.137.
[216] See below, para.30–46.
[217] s.174(2).
[218] s.150 creates a limited right of action for damages by private persons against authorised persons who have acted in breach of the FSA's rules. However, in the case of the Pt VIII prohibition on market abuse the breach seems to be of a statutory requirement set out in s.118, rather than of FSA rules, which simply give guidance on the meaning of the statutory prohibition. An authorised person will be subject, in addition to Pt VIII, to Principles for Businesses, of which Principle 5 (market conduct) is wide enough to encompass market abuse. However, the FSA has taken its high-level Principles out of the damages regime of s.150.
[219] This is subject to the reasonable belief and reasonable care defences: see para.30–29, above. Where the FSA does apply to the court under this section, it may take the view that the court should also deal with the issue of the imposition of a penalty as well, in which case it may ask the court to take this decision rather than deal with it itself: s.129.
[220] s.383(2).
[221] s.383(4).

direct who fall within the categories of those who have suffered loss or are the persons to whom the profit is "attributable".[222] This provision obviously raises a number of important questions, which have been considered in Chapter 26 in relation to misleading statements to the market.[223]

Furthermore, in the case of market abuse, the FSA is not bound to seek a restitution order from the court. It may impose one itself, subject to a right of appeal to the Tribunal.[224] The two powers are drawn in parallel terms (except, of course, that where the FSA makes the restitution order, it has to take the decisions allocated to the court in the court procedure) and therefore the crucial question is whether the FSA will prefer the court route or the exercise of its own powers. It has to be said that the Enforcement Guide is not forthcoming on the point,[225] though it does perhaps suggest that, where the abuser is an authorised person it will prefer its own administrative powers.[226]

Injunctions
Finally, the FSA may apply to the court under s.381 for an injunction **30–42** to restrain future market abuse, whether such abuse has taken place already or not, and the court may grant an injunction where there is a "reasonable likelihood" that the abuse will occur or be repeated.[227] Not surprisingly, the defences of reasonable belief and reasonable care do not operate where a court is asked to impose an injunction restraining future market abuse. The injunctive power is confined to the court. The court has two further and independent powers. If, on the application of the Authority, the court is satisfied that a person may be, or may have been, engaged in market abuse, it may order a freeze on all or any of that person's assets. This helps to ensure that any later restitution order has something to bite on. Secondly, if the court is satisfied that the person is or has been engaged in market abuse, it may, on the application of the Authority, order the person to take such steps to remedy the situation as the court may direct.[228]

---

[222] s.383(5) and (10).
[223] Paras 26–11 to 26–12.
[224] s.384(2).
[225] Enforcement Guide Ch.11.4ff.
[226] EG 11.4. Where the abuser is an unauthorised person, the Handbook simply does not offer a view, even as to the relevant factors.
[227] s.381(1).
[228] This probably does not go so far as to permit the court to require the person to pay compensation: *SIB v Pantell (No.2)* [1993] Ch.256, CA.

Sanctions for breach of the criminal law

30–43   The Criminal Justice Act places exclusive reliance upon criminal sanctions for its enforcement. Section 63(2) states that no contract shall be "void or unenforceable" by reason only of an offence committed under the Act, a provision which was redrafted in 1993, it would seem, in order to close the loophole, as the Government saw it, identified in *Chase Manhattan Equities v Goodman*.[229] Although the Act does not deal expressly with the question of whether a civil action for breach of statutory duty could be built on its provisions, it seems unlikely that the Act would be held to fall within either of the categories identified for this purpose in the case-law.[230]

The criminal sanctions imposed by the Act are, on summary conviction, a fine not exceeding the statutory maximum and/or a term of imprisonment not exceeding six months, and on conviction on indictment an unlimited fine and/or imprisonment for not more than seven years.[231] The power of the judge on conviction on indictment to impose an unlimited fine means that, in theory at least, the court could ensure that the insider made no profit out of the dealing.[232] Prosecutions in England and Wales may be brought only by or with the consent of the Secretary of State or the Director of Public Prosecutions. In England and Wales prosecutions may be brought by the FSA as well as by the usual prosecution bodies, the Crown Prosecution Service, the Serious Fraud Office and the DTI.[233] Indeed, the FSA has the prime responsibility for bringing criminal prosecutions for breach of the criminal laws in the area of market abuse.

It is difficult to make a wholly accurate assessment of the extent of the use of the criminal process in this area but the figures for the numbers of prosecutions and convictions initiated by the DTI are not encouraging.

Restitution orders and injunctions

30–44   On the application of the FSA or the Secretary of State, the court may impose a restitution order or an injunction where a breach has

---

[229] [1991] B.C.L.C. 897 at 930–935, where the judge held that the previous legislative formulation did not prevent the court from holding a contract unenforceable when it had been concluded in breach of the 1985 Act's provisions.

[230] See especially *Lonrho Ltd v Shell Petroleum Co Ltd (No.2)* [1982] A.C. 173, HL.

[231] s.61.

[232] The Crown Court has power under the Criminal Justice Act 1988, as amended by the Proceeds of Crime Act 1995, to make an order confiscating the proceeds of crime, which could also be used to this end.

[233] FSMA, s.402(1)(a).

occurred or is threatened of section 397 or the CJA.[234] In practice, it is unlikely this adds anything significant to the court's and FSA's powers to seek restitution or an injunction on grounds of a breach of Part VIII of the Act, since the criminal law is narrower than the civil penalty regime.

Disqualification

In addition to the traditional criminal penalties which may be visited upon insiders, it seems that the disqualification sanction is available against some insiders in some cases, the effect of which is to disable the person disqualified from being involved in the running of companies in the future.[235] In *R. v Goodman*[236] the Court of Appeal upheld the Crown Court's decision to disqualify, for a period of 10 years, a managing director convicted of insider dealing. The Crown Court had invoked section 2 of the Company Directors Disqualification Act 1986 which enables a court to disqualify a person who has been convicted of an indictable offence in connection with the management of a company. The Court of Appeal took a liberal view of what could be said to be "in connection with the management of the company", so as to bring within the phrase the managing director's disposal of his shares in the company in advance of publication of bad news about its prospects. It would seem, too, that a disqualification order could be made on grounds of unfitness under section 8 of the 1986 Act upon an application by the Secretary of State, following an investigation into insider dealing under s.168 of the Financial Services and Markets Act (see below). In this case, conviction by a court of an indictable offence would not be a pre-condition to a disqualification order, but the court would have to be satisfied that the person's conduct in relation to the company made him unfit to be concerned in the management of a company and this section, unlike section 2, is capable of applying to insider dealing only by directors and shadow directors.

30–45

Investigation in cases of market abuse

It was, or should have been, apparent to everyone that a regime of criminal sanctions for insider trading would operate effectively only if there was an efficient system of investigating cases of suspected insider dealing. In this context, it is odd that when the criminal law

30–46

---

[234] FSMA ss.382(9) and 380(6).
[235] See Ch.10, above.
[236] [1993] 2 All E.R. 789, CA.

was first deployed against insider dealing in 1980, the well-established technique of appointing persons to investigate aspects of companies' affairs was not extended to this new area of regulation. The defect was remedied only with the enactment of the Financial Services Act 1986. Under section 168 of FSMA the FSA or the Secretary of State may appoint an investigator if it appears to them that an offence may have been committed under section 397 or the CJA or that market abuse may have taken place (whether involving a criminal offence or not). However, the FSA is now the primary enforcer, with BERR expected to take action only where investigation by the FSA would be inappropriate for some reason.[237] The Secretary of State Department did not usually announce the appointment of investigators under the old provisions, and it is expected that the FSA will follow the same practice. The DTI, however, did report annually on the number of investigations started, which averaged about 15 over the five years up to and including the year 2001–2002, though with quite considerable fluctuations around the average.[238] There is no provision for the publication of the reports of investigators appointed under FSMA. The information obtained by investigators under the Act is in principle confidential,[239] but may be disclosed for a variety of enforcement purposes, including for the purposes of criminal proceedings and disqualification applications.[240]

The general considerations relating to the conduct of investigations were considered in Chapter 18. The provisions of FSMA 2000 track those of the CA 1985 (as amended) dealing with company investigators appointed by the Secretary of State and so do not need to be considered again here. However, it should be noted that there appears to be no equivalent to the CA provisions for the protection of voluntary disclosures against actions for breach of confidence (though the common law provides a defence in many cases) nor powers for a FSA investigator to require entry to premises other than via a warrant issued by a Justice of the Peace.[241] On the other hand,

---

[237] DTI, *Companies in 2001–2002* (London, 2002), p.13.

[238] DTI, *Companies in 2001–2002*, Table 7.

[239] s.348—note that the definition of "expert" in s.348(6)(b) is wide enough to include investigators appointed under the investigatory powers.

[240] s.349 and the FSMA 2000 (Disclosure of Confidential Information) Regulations 2001 (SI 2001/2188), especially regs 4 and 5.

[241] See paras 18–2 and 18–3 above. The Bill which later become the FSMA did originally include powers of entry without warrant but these were removed after Parliamentary opposition.

the FSA does have the additional power, in relation to those authorised under FSMA and "connected persons", to require the production of specified information or documents where this is reasonably required for the exercise of the FSA's statutory functions, and even to require a report on such a matter, without the appointment of an investigator.[242]

International co-operation

Sophisticated insider dealing rings are likely to involve the use of financial intermediaries based abroad. For this reason, the Market Abuse Directive requires Member States to designate administrative authorities with supervisory and investigatory powers and then requires those administrative authorities to co-operate with one another.[243] Equally, Memoranda of Understanding relating to co-operation between regulators in the field of insider dealing, amongst other areas, have been agreed between the United Kingdom and other leading countries in the financial services field, such as the United States, Japan, Hong Kong, Switzerland and Australia. These international agreements and the EU obligations show themselves in s.169 of FSMA, which authorises or, in the case of the EU obligation, requires the FSA to appoint investigators at the behest of a non-British regulator to investigate "any matter". The FSA may permit a representative of the overseas regulator to be present and ask questions, provided the information obtained is subject to the same confidentiality requirements in the hands of the overseas regulator as it would be under the FSMA.[244] Where assistance is not obligatory, the overseas regulator may be required to contribute to the costs of the investigation and the FSA should consider, before granting the request, whether similar assistance would be forthcoming from the overseas regulator if it were requested by a British regulator, whether the breach of the law to be investigated has no close parallel in the United Kingdom, whether the matter is of importance to people in the United Kingdom and whether the public interest requires that the assistance be given.[245] In the case of insider dealing, it seems likely that these criteria could easily be satisfied, so that assistance should normally be given, even where there is no EU obligation to provide it, subject to the matter of cost.

30–47

It is to be noted that s.169, unlike the other sections of the FSMA 2000 discussed above, empowers only the FSA to take action in aid of overseas regulators. This is because similar powers are conferred

---

[242] ss.165 and 166.
[243] Arts 12 and 16.
[244] s.169(7) and (8).
[245] s.169(4).

upon the DTI and (now) the Treasury[246] by the Companies Act 1989, sections 82–89, which are not repealed by the Companies Act 2006. However, just as the FSA has become the primary enforcer of the insider dealing laws in a purely domestic context, presumably requests for assistance from overseas regulators in this area will be directed at it in the future rather than at the DTI or the Treasury.[247] Certainly, the obligation to co-operate imposed by Art.10 of the Directive[248] would seem to fall on the FSA as the competent administrative authority, and this presumably is why s.169 contemplates the FSA being under an obligation to investigate on behalf of an overseas regulator, whilst the provisions of the Companies Act 1989 are wholly in discretionary form.[249]

CONCLUSION

30–48   Market abuse has been an area of regulation of enormously rapid growth in recent years. Only just over a quarter of a century ago, insider dealing was tackled mainly through statutory disclosure requirements, whilst broader forms of market abuse received at best a shadowy control in the common law of crimes. Today, both insider dealing in particular and market abuse in general are the subject of detailed criminal and regulatory rules. Why should this have happened? Though it may be tempting to say so, it is doubtful whether this is the result of a deterioration in standards of market conduct. More likely, it constitutes another example of the growth of shareholder (or, in this case, investor) power as financial markets have come to play a more important role in national and international business.[250] In general, the regulation discussed in this Chapter aims to protect investors, individual and collective, against opportunistic behaviour by corporate and market insiders and thus makes markets more attractive places to carry on business.

Of course, it is another question whether the law is as effective in practice as it could be. Research published by the FSA itself suggests there is still a high level of abnormal price movements ahead of takeover announcements, though in recent years there has been a

---

[246] See the Transfer of Functions (Financial Services) Order 1992 (SI 1992/1315), Art.5, Sch.3, para.3.

[247] Overseas regulators make their requests for assistance to the Treasury in the first place, but this does not mean that the Treasury necessarily carries out the investigation.

[248] See above, fn.254.

[249] CA 1989, s.82(4). The relevant criteria are the same as those specified in s.169 of FSMA 2000.

[250] *cf.* the increased importance of shareholder interests in corporate governance, above, Part Three.

decline in such movements ahead of trading statements.[251] We have noted above that criminal prosecutions for insider dealing have been few and not very successful. On the other hand, we saw in Chapter 26[252] that the FSA has devoted some enforcement effort to combating delay in issuers' required episodic disclosures, which may go some way to explain the second empirical finding just noted. Overall, however, whilst the FSA's budget is not out of line with that of its US equivalent, the Securities Exchange Commission, when adjusted for market capitalisation, it seems to devote a lower proportion of its budget to enforcement and to impose lower penalties when it does take action.[253]

---

[251] FSA, *Updated Measurement of Market Cleanliness*, Occasional Paper 25, March 2007.

[252] At para.26–8.

[253] John C. Coffee, "Law and the Market: The Impact of Enforcement", March 2007, Columbia Law and Economics Working Paper No.304. Available on www.ssrn.com/ abstract = 967482.

PART SEVEN

DEBT FINANCE

At various points in this book we have referred to the comparative advantages of equity and debt finance for companies. Even more so than with the rights of shareholders, the rights of lenders to the company depend heavily on the terms upon which they contract with the company. Nevertheless, one can say that, in general, debt is a cheaper but less flexible form of finance than equity shares. It is cheaper because lenders are entitled to only a fixed rate of interest (or one which fluctuates within narrow limits), but it is less flexible because they are normally entitled to that interest, whether the company is doing well or badly, whereas the declaration of a dividend on ordinary shares is usually a matter for the discretion of the directors.

Clearly, the rate of interest a company has to pay for its debt depends to some considerable extent on whether it can offer a lender security for its loan and the quality of the security offered. Much of the law applicable here is the general law relating to lenders and borrowers, and does not have to be analysed in a book on company law. However, three aspects of the relevant law do deserve discussion in a company law text. First, as part of its debt-raising activities, a company may issue securities and those securities may be traded on a public market, in the same way as equity securities are.[1] We thus need to say something about the nature of a company's debt securities. Secondly, although the issue of how to assign priorities to charges held by different persons is a general problem in the law of secured lending, for reasons which are not entirely easy to understand the rules governing the registration of charges by companies have not developed in a satisfactory way and have recently been the subject of

---

[1] Thus, some reference to such securities has already been made in Ch.25 (public offers).

attention from the Law Commission. Thus, we need to examine the rules of registration of company charges. Thirdly, in the creation of one form of security company lawyers took the lead in the nineteenth century. This was the floating charge, still a controversial mechanism because of the way it can operate to crowd out the interests of unsecured creditors, in terms both of the scope of the charge and the mechanisms for enforcing it. Thus, the floating charge is the third topic we need to look at in some detail.

CHAPTER 31

DEBENTURES

INTRODUCTION

A company may finance itself not only through the issuance of shares **31–1** (of various classes) but also by taking loans, i.e. by incurring debt. As with shares, the rights of the debtors against the company are essentially a matter of contract between the company and the lender; and the agreements struck between debtors and the company can be as varied as those between shareholders and the company.[1] Large-scale debt financing for companies comes in two main forms: from banks and from the public securities markets. Big transactions may involve both types of debt. Take the example of an acquisition of a company whose securities are traded on a public market by a private equity fund. Here the private equity bidder makes an offer to the shareholders of the publicly traded company to acquire their shares (to "take the target private").[2] Private equity funds have traditionally financed bids largely through debt, using relatively small amounts of equity, even though they are purchasing equity securities from the

---

[1] See Ch.23 above.

[2] The target is thus "taken private" in two senses: first, its shares will no longer be traded on a public market if the bid is successful but, secondly and perhaps more importantly, the acquirer, the private equity fund, is not normally traded on the public markets either, though there is no reason in principle why it should not be and one important private equity fund has recently gone public on the New York Stock Exchange.

existing shareholders of the target. Since the debt is repayable out of the income generated by the target's business (and to some extent may be secured on the assets of the target company after the take-over), the private equity acquisition significantly alters the financial structure of the target company's business by shifting it in favour of debt finance (a process known as leverage or gearing). The initial debt finance for the acquisition is likely to be provided wholly by banks, and to come in a variety of types of senior and junior (or "mezzanine") debt, the terms "senior" and "junior" referring to the order in which the debt falls to be repaid (the ranking of their claims on the assets of the debtor).[3] However, some of this bank debt is intended to be only short-term and is provided on such financially unattractive terms that the acquirer has a strong incentive to re-finance it as soon as possible, for example, by causing the target to make an offer of debt securities on the public markets. In this way, both bank debt and debt raised in the public markets contribute to the financing of the acquisition.

One advantage to a lender of advancing money to the company through a debt security, especially if it is traded on a public market, rather than through a direct loan, may be a higher level of liquidity for the lender. Although the rules on legal capital do not stand in the way of re-purchases of its debt securities by a company, unlike in the case of shares,[4] it may well be financially extremely inconvenient for the company to do so. Thus, as with shares, the company has an incentive to arrange for its debt securities to be traded on a public market, which provides an alternative route by which a lender to the company can liquidate its investment, i.e. by selling it to a third party. However, in the case of large banks, it is normally possible for the lender to find liquidity in other ways. There may be a market in the loans which the banks have provided to the acquirer, at least in good times, so that the bank can assign its loans to third parties (for example, hedge funds). Some banks lending to private equity funds aim to have only a small, if any, proportion of the loans made on their books six months after the transaction completes.[5] Alternatively, the bank itself may make an offering of debt securities in which the securities are supported by the loans made by the bank, though this is normally possible only where the loans in question are secured on the assets of the borrower from the bank.[6]

This Chapter is mainly concerned with the "money" side of debt securities. However, one word on the governance aspects of debt finance is in order. As noted in Chapter 8, holders of debt, whether in

---

[3] For a description of typical funding arrangements see FSA, *Private Equity: a discussion of risk and regulatory engagement*, DP 06/6, November 2006, paras 3.52ff.

[4] See paras 13–7 *et seq.* The capital maintenance rules do not apply to debt because debt is not legal capital: above, para.11–1.

[5] FSA, above, fn.3, paras 3.67ff.

[6] See the discussion of "covered bonds" below, para.31–9.

the form of debt securities or not, may seek to protect their position by inserting "covenants" in the loan agreements. Such covenants (or contractual provisions) seek to restrict the discretion of the borrower company, lest it take action which reduces the likelihood of the debtor being re-paid, such as distributing large (but legal) dividends to the shareholders or entering into more risky areas of business activity. The covenants usually make the loan repayable if such steps are taken without the consent of the lender—a very powerful sanction.[7] Through such covenants, lenders become part of the corporate governance structure of the company, and have a more significant impact on the management than the shareholders if the company is near to breaching its "banking covenants". Of course, the extent to which banks and other lenders are able to insert such covenants in their loans depends upon the level of competition in the market for such loans. For a period up until the middle of 2007 competition among banks for the opportunity to fund private equity buy-outs was so great that "covenant-light" loans became common, i.e. bank loans with little in the way of restrictive covenants inserted. In more normal circumstances, however, significant loans by banks and other substantial lenders will be subject to important constraints on management.[8]

Debt securities

A debt security issued by a company is, as noted, largely a matter of contract between lender and company. The legislature does not specify one, or even a number, of forms that a debt security must take, any more than it does so with shares. It is thus difficult to describe a "typical" debt security. However, the security will normally have, unlike a share, an end-date, i.e. a point at which the amount still outstanding has to be repaid (its "maturity date")—though it is possible to make the loan totally irredeemable. That maturity date can be set as the parties wish, but is often quite long, for example, forty years. Normally, however, the instrument requires the amount lent to be repaid in regular instalments over the life of the loan (in which case it is called "amortising" debt). However, the parties may provide that nothing needs to be repaid either until maturity (which is unlikely in the case of long maturities, unless the loan is backed by very high quality assets) or only after a considerable period of time has passed (say, eight to ten years), at which point the

31–2

---

[7] However, since these are contractual restrictions, they will not bind third parties (in whose favour, for example, assets have been pledged in breach of covenant), unless the ingredients of the tort of inducing breach of contract have been established, notably knowledge on the part of the third party of the contractual restrictions: *Swiss Bank Corp v Lloyds Bank Ltd* [1979] Ch. 548.

[8] W.W. Bratton, "Bond Covenants and Creditor Protection" (2006) 7 *European Business Organization Review* 39.

amount becomes repayable which would have been paid over this period through a normal amortisation arrangement. Such debt is sometimes called "bullet" debt, perhaps because of its likely impact on the borrower.[9] The lender may have the right to recall or the borrower to repay the loan ahead of the repayment schedule or they may be specifically prohibited from so doing. Section 739[10] recognises that the security may be made irredeemable by the borrower or redeemable only in certain circumstances "any rule of equity to the contrary notwithstanding". This removes any doubt about the validity of such a restriction which might arise in the case of a debt instrument secured by way of a mortgage on the company's property, to which the equitable doctrine might otherwise apply that a "clog" on the equity of redemption is not permitted.

The instrument will normally provide for the periodic payment of a fixed rate of interest at fixed points in time, but there is no reason why the interest rate should not vary (provided there is a clear mechanism for working out what it is at any one time) nor why interest should not be "rolled up" and be payable at a later date (sometimes on the maturity of the loan). In such a case the lender earns a return by buying the security at a discount to its face (or nominal or principal) value (i.e. the amount the company promises to repay) and takes the return as a capital gain rather than income, but only at maturity or, if the price of security in the market rises, upon sale to a third party. Finally, a debt instrument may be convertible into equity securities in certain circumstances, in which case they are a type of "hybrid" instrument.[11]

In contrast with a shareholder, the holder of a debt instrument is in law not a member of the company having rights in it, but a creditor having rights against it. In reality, however, the difference between the debt- and the shareholder may not be anything like as clear-cut, for the debt instrument may give the holder contractual rights akin to those of a shareholder, e.g. to appoint a director; to a share of profits

---

[9] Where such debt is part of a private equity transaction, it is a strong candidate for early re-financing.

[10] A provision first introduced by the Companies Act 1907.

[11] This may seem to provide a way around the prohibition on issuing shares at a discount to their nominal value. To issue at a discount debt instruments which can be immediately converted into shares of the full par value would be a colourable device to evade the prohibition on issuing shares at a discount (*Moseley v Koffyfontein Mines* [1904] 2 Ch. 108, CA) but appears to be unobjectionable if the instrument is convertible only when the debentures are due for repayment at par since the shares will then be paid up in cash "through the release of a liability of the company for a liquidated sum": s.583(3)(c). See also, above at para.11–14 on debt/equity swaps.

(whether or not available for dividend);[12] to repayment at a premium; to attend and vote at general meetings.[13] Covenants in the loan instrument may also give the debenture-holders considerable influence over the way in which the company is managed. Moreover, where the debt instrument is secured by a floating charge on all the undertaking and assets of the company, the holder will have a legal or equitable interest in the company's business, albeit of a different kind from that of its shareholders. The line between the holder of a debt instrument and a share is particularly narrow if the contrast is made with a preference shareholder, who is a member of the company, but the terms of issue of whose share may limit the shareholder's dividend to a fixed percentage of the nominal value of the share and give that shareholder no right to participate in surplus assets in a winding-up. The main difference between the two in such a case may then be that the dividend on a preference share is not payable unless profits are available for distribution,[14] whereas the debt-holder's interest entitlement is not subject to this constraint; and that the debt-holder will rank before the preference holder in a winding-up. Thus, the accounting rules operate with a binary divide between debt and equity, but practice leads to the creation of securities whose classification in accordance with this divide is problematic. These difficulties of classification are explicitly recognised in the terminology used in relation to certain securities as being "hybrid" in character, for example, a bond convertible into equity at a later date and on fixed terms. A simple way of looking at such securities is to say that they are debt until conversion, at which point they become equity. However, where the bond is required to be converted into equity at a certain future date, it may be possible to classify it as equity in the company's accounts from the beginning, whilst treating the tax payable on the debt before conversion as deductible for tax purposes, so that the same security is equity for one purpose and debt for another.[15]

---

[12] *Lemon v Austin Friars Investment Trust Ltd* [1926] Ch. 1 (instrument not prevented from being a debenture because interest payable only out of profit, which might or might not be earned in any particular year).

[13] But the debt-holder's vote should not be counted if the Act requires the resolution to be passed by "members".

[14] See para.12–1. Whether the preference shareholder is entitled by contract to the dividend, even if the company cannot lawfully pay it, is a separate question. And a potentially important one, because non-payment of the contractually due dividend may trigger voting rights for the preference shareholders or affect the amount due to the preference shareholders when the company returns to profit or is wound up: *Bradford Investments Ltd, Re* [1991] B.C.L.C. 224.

[15] See generally Pope and Puxty, "What is Equity? New Financial Instruments in the Interstices between Law, Accounting and Economics" (1991) 54 M.L.R. 889.

Difficulty of defining a debenture

31–3   Perhaps because the debt instrument is simply a creature of contract
and perhaps also because the relationship between debt-holder and
company creates no particular conceptual puzzles—the relationship
is simply the contractual relationship of debtor and creditor, coupled,
if the debt is secured on some or all of the company's assets, with that
of mortgagor and mortgagee—the terminology used in this area to
refer to debt securities issued by a company is not settled, either in the
Act or in commercial practice, but is rather variable. The terms
debentures, bonds and notes, in particular, are common in this area.
Of these, the rather old-fashioned term "debenture" is the only one
noticed in the Act. It would be wrong to say that the term is defined
in the Act, for section 738 merely says that the term includes
"debenture stock, bonds and any other securities of a company,
whether or not constituting a charge on the assets of the company."
This is helpful in indicating that a debenture need not be secured on
the company's assets, but for not much else. This is despite the fact
that the Act contains a (short) Part 19, headed "Debentures", as well
as frequent references throughout the Act to debentures and debenture-holders. In commercial practice, when referring to debt securities
which can be traded, it is more common to use the term "bonds" or
"notes", the difference between the two being that bonds have longer
maturities than notes, though it is not clear where the line is precisely
to be drawn.[16] However, since "debenture" is the traditional legal
term for a company's debt securities and is the term used in the
legislation, that will be the focus of this Chapter.

If the legislature has baulked at the task of defining a debenture,
the courts have not done much better. As Chitty J. lamented over a
century ago:

> "I cannot find any precise definition of the term, it is not either in
> law or commerce a strictly technical term, or what is called a
> term of art."[17]

There is no doubt that where a company creates a series of securities,
acknowledging the indebtedness of the company, offers them to the
public and introduces them to trading on a public market, then there
exists a debenture. However, it seems that something a good deal less
than this can suffice for the creation of a debenture and, in particular,
that loan agreements which companies enter into with banks to raise
debt finance may also constitute "debentures" in some cases. So

---

[16] Perhaps it is fair to say that debt securities with a maturity of less than a decade are normally
called "notes".

[17] *Levy v Abercorris Slate & Slab Co* (1887) 37 Ch. 260 at 264. See also Lindley J. in *British
India Steam Navigation Co v IRC* (1881) 7 Q.B.D. at 172 and Warrington L.J. in *Lemon v
Austin Friars Trust* [1926] Ch. 1 at 17, CA and the House of Lords in *Knightsbridge Estates
Co v Byrne* [1940] A.C. 613.

much seems to be clear from the decision in *Knightsbridge Estates Ltd v Byrne*,[18] which concerned an ordinary mortgage on houses, shops and a block of flats by a company to secure a loan of £310,000 from an insurance company. The loan was to be repayable by 80 half-yearly instalments spread over 40 years but became immediately repayable if the mortgagor should sell the equity of redemption. The company was forbidden from selling any of the properties free from the mortgage or from granting leases for more than three years without the consent of the mortgagee. Five years later the company wished to pay off the mortgage in full and argued that the term making the mortgage irre-deemable for 40 years was void as a clog on the equity of redemption. The question was whether the mortgage was a debenture for the purposes of what is now section 739 (above), saving irredeemable debentures from this equitable doctrine. The House of Lords held that it was, whilst accepting that the mortgage would not be a "debenture", for the purposes of some of the other sections of the Act.[19]

However, it is still not clear when the line between a debenture and a straightforward bank loan (for most purposes not a debenture) is crossed. In principle, the question has been made more pressing by recent developments in banking and commercial circles which have led to the invention of a remarkable array of new and highly sophisticated types of "securitised" loan investments. As a result, finance, which would formerly have been raised by a straightforward bank loan, may be obtained through the issue of instruments, some of which for most purposes unquestionably are debentures and others of which may or may not be. In practice, the absence of a precise definition has given rise to surprisingly few problems and to even fewer reported cases. This may well be because Part 19 of the Act does not engage in significant regulation of debentures, beyond lar-gely administrative requirements (the registration of allotments and a register of debenture-holders) and some provisions about debenture trustees (see below). In other words, except in very unusual cases, commercial life can continue without it being necessary to determine whether a particular contract has created a debenture or not.

Debenture stock

The definition of debenture in section 738 includes debenture stock. **31–4** Unlike the largely meaningless distinction between "shares" and "stock"[20] the similar distinction between "debentures" and "deben-

---

[18] [1940] A.C. 613.

[19] Per Viscount Maugham at 624. Clearly such a mortgage does not have to be registered in the company's register of debenture-holders under s.743 in addition to registration of the mortgage under Part 25.

[20] See above, para.23–11 where it is noted that conversion of shares into stock is no longer permitted. In practice, trust deeds contain "no action" clauses constraining enforcement action by individual holders.

ture stock" is far from meaningless and debenture stock has considerable practical advantages. The difference between debentures
and debenture stock is that the former can be transferred only in
complete units, whereas stock is expressed in terms of an amount of
money and may be transferred in any fraction of that amount. Thus,
if a public company wishes to raise £1 million it could seek to do so
by an issue of a series of, say £1, £10, £100, or £1,000 debentures, each
representing a separate debt totalling in aggregate £1 million. This
would result in an enormous bundle of paper for the company to
process and subscribers to handle. And, if a subscriber for a single
debenture wanted to sell half of it, he would not be able to make a
legal transfer of that half. If, however, the company creates £1 million
of debenture stock it can issue it[21] to subscribers in such amounts as
each wants,[22] giving each a single certificate[23] and each subscriber can
sell and transfer any fraction of it. A further advantage is that,
whereas with a series of debentures with a charge on the company's
assets it will be necessary to say expressly in each debenture that it is
one of a series each ranking *pari passu* in respect of the charge,[24]
debenture stock achieves that result without express provision.

Trustees for debenture-holders

31–5   The deed required on the creation of debenture stock may be a deed
poll executed by the company alone, but it is now invariable practice[25]
for the deed to be made with trustees. This, too, is normally done
when there is an issue of a series of debentures. In other words,
trustees, normally a trust corporation,[26] are interposed between the
company and the debenture-holders. Any charge can then be in
favour of the trustees who hold it on trust for the debenture-holders.
Such an arrangement has many advantages.

In the first place it will enable the security to be by way of specific
legal mortgage or charge on the company's land as well as by way of
equitable floating charge on the rest of the assets. Clearly, the ideal

---

[21] Debenture stock can be created *de novo*; there is no need to create debentures and then to
convert them to debenture stock as there is in relation to shares and stock.

[22] In practice there is likely to be a prescribed minimum amount which can be subscribed for or
transferred. If this minimum amount is equal to the nominal value of the debentures which
the company might otherwise issue, then, of course, the advantage of debenture stock
disappears.

[23] A simple document of one sheet, similar to a share certificate, in contrast with a debenture
which will, unless there is a trust deed (see below), have to set out all the terms.

[24] Without this their respective priorities might depend on the dates when each debenture was
issued.

[25] Except with unsecured loan stock.

[26] Formerly it was common for banks to undertake this work but they have tended to fight shy
of it since *Dorman Long & Co, Re* [1934] Ch. 635 drew attention to the conflict of interest
and duty which might arise when the bank was both a creditor in its own right and a trustee.
Today, therefore, the duties are generally undertaken by other trust corporations, such as
insurance companies, though sometimes by the separate trustee companies formed by certain banks. Very occasionally individual trustees are still employed.

security is one so constituted, but a legal interest cannot be vested in thousands of debenture-holders,[27] nor can the deeds be split up amongst them. If, however, there are trustees, the legal mortgage can be vested in them, on trust for the beneficiary debenture-holders, and the trustees retain custody of the title deeds.[28] Again, if there is to be a specific charge on shares in subsidiary companies (which may be a necessary precaution) trustees are needed in order that someone independent of the holding company shall be able to exercise the voting rights attached to the shares.

Secondly, it will provide a single corporation or a small body of persons charged with the duty of watching the debenture-holders' interests and of intervening if they are in jeopardy. This is obviously far more satisfactory than leaving it to a widely dispersed class of persons each of whom may lack the skill, interest and financial resources required if he is to take action on his own.[29] It will also be possible, by the trust deed, to impose on the company or its directors additional obligations, regarding the submission of information and the like, which might not otherwise be practicable.[30] Similarly, the trustees can be empowered to convene meetings of the holders in order to acquaint them with the position and to obtain their instructions.

In consequence of the above developments, the debenture-stock-holders remedies are primarily against the trustees, rather than the company, and debenture-holders as well are dependent on the trustees for the proper protection of their interests. Complaints have been made in the past that the trustees are all too often content to act as passive recipients of their remuneration rather than as active watchdogs. The Cohen Committee admitted that these complaints were not altogether unfounded,[31] but all that resulted, as far as the Act is concerned, is what is now section 750 which invalidates provisions in trust deeds (or elsewhere) which purport to exempt a trustee from, or to indemnify him against, "liability for breach of trust where he fails to show the degree of care and diligence required of him as a trustee having regard to the provisions of the trust deed

[27] Since 1925, a legal estate in land cannot be vested in more than four persons.
[28] However, it is in fact uncommon for major publicly traded companies today to give security over their assets in public issues of debentures.
[29] Although there are trustees, an individual stockholder can take steps to enforce the security but he is not regarded as a creditor with the latter's personal remedies against the company: *Dunderland Iron Ore Co, Re* [1909] 1 Ch. 446.
[30] See the facts which gave rise to the litigation in *New Zealand Guardian Trust Co Ltd v Brooks* [1995] 1 W.L.R. 96. PC.
[31] Cmnd. 6659 (1945), paras 61–64.

conferring on him any powers, authorities or discretions".[32] Today, the powers and obligations of the trustee are likely to be set out fairly fully in the trust deed. Even so, the caution of trustees in fulfilling their obligations are well illustrated by the recent decision in *Concord Trust v Law Debenture Trust Corporation Plc*,[33] where the House of Lords found that the company had "terrified the trustee" into declining to implement a valid instruction given to it by the requisite majority of the bond-holders, unless the trustee was given by the bond-holders an indemnity against what the court thought was a fanciful liability to the company on the part of the trustee, should the trustee's action of declaring a default and accelerating the bond (i.e. requiring it to be repaid) turn out to be ill-founded.

THE ISSUANCE AND TRANSFER OF DEBENTURES

31–6 The act of issuing debentures (assuming no public offer) is not much regulated by the Act. The one significant provision is to the effect that a contract with a company to take up and pay for debentures is specifically enforceable,[34] thus overriding the normal contractual rule that the lender is liable only in damages. This seems to reflect an analysis to the effect that, in the case of a public offer of debentures (see below), a change in market conditions would deprive the company of the alternative upon which the general contractual rule is based, i.e. that the company could raise the money from another borrower. However, the rule applies to any contract to take up a debenture, whether in a public offer or not.[35] Otherwise, in the absence of a public offer, the Act is notable for the absence of regulation of the issuing process. Unlike with shares,[36] there is no rule in the Act that, even for public companies, the authorisation of the shareholders or the existing debenture-holders is required for an issue

---

[32] But note the exceptions and qualifications in subss.(2)–(4) permitting 75% in value of the debenture-holders present and voting to give a release from liability to the trustee in respect of prior specific acts or omissions of the trustee (or on the latter's death or ceasing to act). In addition, reg.40(2) of the Uncertificated Securities Regulations 2001 (above, Ch.27) exempts the trustees from liability simply for assenting to amendments of the trust deed to enable title to debentures to be held and transferred under the electronic system and for rights attached to debentures to be exercised in that way.

[33] [2006] 1 B.C.L.C. 616, HL. The event of default was a failure to maintain on the board of the borrowing company a nominee of the lenders, who had been placed there to protect the bond-holders' interests. Having accelerated the bond, as a consequence of the HL judgment, and secured substantial payments from the company, the trustee then took an overly cautious line about how much of the monies recovered it could distribute to the bond-holders: *Law Debenture Trust Corporation Plc v Concord Trust* [2007] EWHC 1380 (Ch).

[34] s.740.

[35] And so might be available in the case of a bank loan taking the form of a debenture: see *Knightsbridge Estates Ltd v Byrne*, above, fn.18.

[36] See para.24–4.

of debentures, though this matter may well be one of the matters regulated in the trust deed of the existing debenture-holders. In some ways this is surprising, since a large increase in the company's debt could have a significant impact—positive or negative depending on whether the venture in which the new funds are embarked is successful—on the prospects of the shareholders.[37] Nor does the Act create pre-emption rights[38] on an issue of debentures, probably because the rights of the existing debenture-holders are not affected by a new issue, though their value might be, since a company seen to be overburdening itself with debt would cause the market value of its existing debt instruments to fall. Again, however, this matter can be dealt with in the trust deed governing the existing debentures. Finally, since debt does not count as legal capital, the rules relating to issuance at a discount and governing the quality of the consideration received, which apply to shares,[39] are not extended to debentures. For the same reason, the distribution and capital maintenance rules[40] do not apply to debentures, so that interest may (normally must) be paid on debentures, even though no profits have been earned, and debentures may be freely repurchased by the company, assuming in both cases it has the cash to do so. The only specific statutory provision in this area in fact facilitates repurchases of debt by providing that redeemed debentures may be reissued with their original priority, rather than cancelled, unless the company's articles contain provisions to the contrary or the company in some other way resolved to cancel them.[41] Of course, the general duties of directors will still apply to their decisions relating to the issuance of debentures, even, perhaps especially, in the absence of specific statutory regulation in the area.

The Act does contain certain, largely administrative, provisions relating to the issuance of debentures. Section 741, a new section in the 2006 Act, requires companies to register an allotment of debentures with the Registrar of companies, as is required for shares, so that the existence of the debentures is public knowledge. However, a company is not obliged itself to keep a register of debenture-holders, but, if it does, it must locate it and make it available for inspection by debenture-holders and members of the public in the same way as the register of shareholders.[42] This includes the new power, applicable also to the share register, to apply to the court for an order not to

---

[37] Even the "Class 1 transaction" rule, requiring shareholder consent, of the Listing Rules does not apply to an issue of securities, unless the transaction involves the acquisition of a fixed asset of the company or a subsidiary: LR 10.1.3.

[38] On pre-emption rights for shareholders see para.24–6.

[39] See Ch.11.

[40] See Chs 12 and 13.

[41] s.752. On treasury shares see para.13–17. Note also s.753 which is designed to remove the technical difficulties revealed in *Russian Petroleum Co, Re* [1907] 2 Ch. 540, CA when a company secures its overdraft on current account by depositing with the bank a debenture for a fixed amount.

[42] ss.743–748. Less detail is required in the register of debentures, if there is one, than in the share register. On the share register see para.21–37 above.

comply with the request for inspection.[43] Probably more important in practice is the provision which entitles a debenture-holder to be provided at any time (on payment of the appropriate fee) with a copy of the trust deed on which the debentures are secured, if, as is normal, there is such a trust.[44] This provision is perhaps the functional equivalent of the public availability of the articles in the case of shareholders.

However, matters change radically if there is a public offer of debt securities. In that case, much of the law discussed in Chapter 25 will be applicable, since, in general, that applies to public offers of all types of security, not just of shares. However, in this context the term securities will normally embrace "debentures" only in its narrow sense of debenture stock or a series of identical debentures and not in its wider meaning of a single mortgage, charge or bond.[45] The prohibition on private companies offering their shares to the public extends to a public offer of any securities.[46] The prospectus rules apply equally to securities (not just shares), though with some modifications, notably by giving issuers of debt alone more flexibility in the area of the home/host State distinction and in the choice of language.[47] What is required of a debt issuer by way of disclosure under the Prospectus Regulation is necessarily not the same as that required of an equity issuer,[48] and, again, the issuer of "heavy weight" debt securities is treated somewhat more lightly than other debt issuers.[49]

31–7   The legislation also assumes that debentures or debenture stock will be transferred in much the same way as shares. Hence, subss. (1), (2), (5) and (6)[50] of s.183 (relating to the need for written transfers, except when the transmission is by operation of law, and to the recognition of personal representatives) expressly apply. So do ss.184 (certification of transfers) and 185 (duty to issue certificates). And estoppel, similar to estoppel by share certificate, clearly could arise from statements in certificates of debenture stock or in debentures. Equally, the Uncertificated Securities Regulations, as the use of the word "securities" rather than the word "shares" suggests, permit the transfer of title to debentures held in uncertificated form.[51]

One could also be faced with problems, similar to those in relation to shares, regarding equitable and legal ownership of debentures and

---

[43] s.745.
[44] s.749. Non-compliance is a criminal offence on the part of any officer of the company in default.
[45] See above, para.31–3.
[46] s.755. See para.24–2.
[47] See above at para.25–41.
[48] Compare Commission Regulation (EC) No.809/2004, Annexes I and IV.
[49] Compare Comission Regulation (EC) No.809/2004 Annex V.
[50] But not subss.(3) and (4) which relate only to "members", which debenture-holders are not.
[51] Reg.19 and the definition of "security" in reg.3(1). See generally above Ch.27.

the priority of competing transferees. But the great difference here is the lesser role played by registration. Unlike with members, a company is not compelled to maintain a register of debenture-holders. At least this is the traditional rule. In relation, however, to debentures held in uncertificated form the operator is now required to maintain in the United Kingdom a register of the names and addresses of those holding debentures in this way, together with a statement of the size of the individual holdings.[52] Even in relation to certificated debentures, the Act assumes that a company probably will maintain a register if it issues debenture stock or a series of debentures and the Act contains provisions similar to, but not identical with, those relating to the membership register, concerning where the register shall be kept[53] and who shall be entitled to inspect and obtain copies of it.[54] But it says nothing about the register being evidence of ownership, and it is not clear what role, if any, it plays in converting an equitable interest to a legal one. On general principles relating to assignments of choses-in-action, a transfer of a debenture should be an equitable assignment only, until it becomes a legal assignment when the company receives notice of it. In principle, therefore, the legal interest should pass from transferor to transferee when the company is given notice of it, and that date, rather than the later date of actual registration, should be the relevant one in determining its priority over earlier unnotified transfers.

Other differences flow from the fact that, whereas the rights of shareholders depend mainly on the provision of the company's articles, which will have been drafted in the interests of the company, those of debenture-holders depend upon the terms of a contract between lender and borrower and its terms will have to be acceptable to the lender. Hence, in practice, there will be no problems arising from restrictions on transferability or from a company's lien; debentures will invariably provide that the money expressed to be secured will be paid, and that the debentures are transferable, free from any equities or claims between the company and the original or any intermediate holder.[55] It is possible that the terms of issue of the

---

[52] Uncertificated Securities Regulations 2001, reg.22(3). If the terms of issue of the debentures require the company to maintain a register of holders in the UK, then this rule still applies but the company's register reflects that of the Operator: reg.22(1) and (2). S.113 (above, para.27–16) is applied to the Operator.

[53] s.743.

[54] s.744.

[55] Without this, debenture-holders and their transferees would be in grave danger, for a debenture, unless in bearer form and thus a negotiable instrument, would, as a chose-in-action, be transferable only subject to the state of the account between the company and the transferor. As stressed in Ch.27, neither shares (unless in the form of share warrants to bearer) nor debentures (unless bearer bonds) are negotiable instruments like bills of exchange. Although CARD (above, para.25–16) requires listed shares and debt securities to be "freely negotiable" (Arts 46 and 60) this is interpreted as "freely transferable" and not as prescribing that they must be "negotiable instruments" in full sense.

debentures will be inconsistent with their being held in uncertificated form, in which case they will need to be altered if the company wishes to make this form of holding debentures available.[56] The Regulations do not provide a simple shortcut to the necessary amendments, as they do in the case of shares, but they do something to encourage trustees to agree to such amendments without holding a meeting of the debenture-holders. A trustee for debenture-holders is not to be chargeable with breach of trust by reason only of his assenting to changes in the trust deed necessary to enable the debenture-holders to hold the debentures in uncertificated form or to transfer them or exercise any rights attached to them electronically.[57] The great contrast, however, is that debentures secured by charges on the company's property throw up problems regarding the priority between conflicting charges. These problems are dealt with in the next Chapter.

PROTECTION OF DEBENTURE-HOLDERS' RIGHTS

31–8 The rights of the debenture-holder are to be found in the debenture which confers contractual rights independent of the company's articles. It is, nonetheless, possible that those contractual rights might be affected as a result of the exercise by the company or the general meeting of its statutory powers. If, for example, the debenture provided that the holder should be entitled to appoint a director of the company and if a provision to that effect was inserted in the company's articles, a question similar to that discussed in relation to shareholders might arise on whether an attempt to delete that provision could be restrained by injunction.[58] But this would rarely be a live question for the breach would normally entitle the debenture-holder to require the debt to be repaid and, if it was secured by a charge on the company's property, to enforce the security. This the debenture-holder would do rather than sue for damages for the breach. Thus, while the value of the rights may depend on the continued prosperity of the company, particularly if the debenture is unsecured loan stock, the debenture-holder is normally not subject, as is a shareholder, to any serious possibility that his rights will be varied by the company by corporate action without the lender's consent.

To this, however, there is one exception. If the debenture is one of a

---

[56] See Ch.27 above.
[57] Reg.40(2), provided notice is given to the holders at least 30 days before the changes become effective.
[58] See above, para.19–25. Even if it could, it seems clear that an injunction could not be granted to restrain the general meeting from removing his nominated director under s.303.

series or is debenture stock, its terms may, and normally will, provide for the variation of the holders' rights with the consent of a prescribed majority of the holders or an extraordinary resolution of the holders. In such a case, while the debenture-holder will not be vulnerable to action by the company or its members as such, he or she will be vulnerable to that of the requisite majority of fellow debenture-holders who may have interests conflicting with him or her because they are also shareholders or directors. In such circumstances the holder will not have the protection of the unfair prejudice provisions which apply only to "members".[59] However, where there is a series of debentures or debenture stock there will almost invariably be independent trustees who should ensure that any proposed variations are fair and are fully and fairly explained in the circulars seeking the needed consents.[60] Further, the courts have applied to decisions of a majority of the debenture-holders, binding on the minority, to change the terms of the debenture deed the common law doctrine applied to decisions by shareholders to alter the articles, i.e. the decision must be made bona fide in the interests of the debenture-holders. This is a limited protection, though not nugatory.[61]

Thus, in *British America Nickel Corp Ltd v O'Brien*[62] a decision of the majority of the bond-holders, modifying their rights, was invalidated on the grounds that one of the bond-holders, whose support was necessary for the passing of the resolution, was to receive under the scheme a block of ordinary shares, which opportunity was not available to the other bond-holders. However, as with the application of this principle to decisions of shareholders, the courts have found it difficult to define when this principle is infringed, at least in less egregious cases. Provided a reasonable debenture-holder could think the alteration in the interests of the class, it is unlikely the courts will intervene, in the absence of proof of bad faith, which proof will normally not be available. In the *O'Brien* case Viscount Haldane said that the power of alteration "must be exercised for the purpose of benefiting the class as a whole". However, the courts have found it difficult to apply this test in anything like its literal sense, as requiring no discrimination against any members of the class. Since the doctrine applies to debenture variations apparently by virtue of being an implied term in the contract of loan, it has been held that the strong rule laid down by Viscount Haldane should not apply where the debenture-holders fall into two or more classes and commercial

---

[59] See para.20–1. Nor, of course, will the class rights provisions afford protection as they too apply only to members. See para.19–12.
[60] The Listing Rules require that any circular must include an explanation of the effect of proposed amendments: LR 17.3.10.
[61] See para.19–4.
[62] [1927] A.C. 369, PC.

context from which the agreement emerged was one which contemplated one of the classes being outvoted.[63]

COVERED BONDS

31–9   From the above analysis it will be clear that the terms and structure of debt which companies take on are left very much to be bargained out between lenders and borrowers. Consequently, most of the law in this area consists of the principles of the law of contract and the law of property, with relatively little in the way of special company law regulation, except where the company gives a charge over its property to secure the loan, which is the topic for the following Chapter. However, there has recently emerged an exception to this pattern, in the form of the Recognised Covered Bonds Regulations 2008. A "covered" bond (sometimes called a "structured covered bond" is a particular form of bond which is backed by a specific pool of high quality assets. Such bonds were not brought into existence by the Regulations, though they are a relatively recent development in the United Kingdom.[64] The essence of them is that they are backed by high-quality assets as collateral, that the collateral is always sufficient to meet the entitlements of the lenders and associated costs and that on the insolvency of the issuer the collateral does not fall into the estate of the company for insolvency purposes. A simple example is as follows.

1. The company (invariably a bank or similar body) issues a bond or note (usually the latter) to investors.

2. The monies received by the issuer in exchange for the notes are lent to a "Special Purpose Vehicle" (usually a limited liability partnership), controlled by the company,[65] which uses the loan to purchase mortgages from the company, thus creating an "asset pool". The SPV is thus usually referred to in this context as "the owner" i.e. of the assets.

3. The SPV gives a charge over its assets (now the mortgages) to a trustee who holds the security on behalf of the noteholders.

4. The value of the mortgages transferred to the SPV by the company is greater than the value of the loan and this

---

[63]   *Redwood Master Fund Ltd v TD Bank Europe* [2006] 1 B.C.L.C. 149—a decision relating to a decision by lenders under a syndicated bank loan facility, but applicable to debentures.

[64]   They have a very much longer history in Germany where they are known as *Pfandbriefe*.

[65]   Since the loan is made by the issuing company and the SPV is, normally, a wholly-owned subsidiary of the issuer, the transaction remains on the balance sheet of the issuer, and so the covered bond is *not* an example of "off-balance sheet" financing.

situation will be maintained through the life of the loan. This produces "over-collateralisation" which ensures that the note-holders will be repaid in full, even taking into account the expenses of realising the collateral.

What has this structure achieved? From the company's point of view, it has turned (illiquid) mortgages into cash through the a loan from the investors. This is an example of a process known as "securitisation". Thus, the bank has raised further finance which it can use to expand its business, probably at a low rate of interest because of the collateralisation of the notes. Conversely, from the investors' point of view, they have made a loan to the company but of a highly secure type. Provided the SPV has been set up in such a way that the assets purchased by the SPV cannot be clawed back by the issuer in the latter's liquidation and provided the issuer is obliged to maintain the quality and value of the mortgages held by the SPV, the note-holders can remain unconcerned about such an event because their security will remain intact. This is why the bond is "covered".[66] Overall, the issuer is incurring debt through the covered bond in order to further the business of itself making secured loans to others, its business model turning on its ability to borrow money through the bond at a lower rate of interest than it itself charges when lending to others.

It will be apparent that the above structure can be created by contract and so it may be wondered how the need for the Regulations arises. In fact, the purpose of the Regulations is to create a more ready market for covered bonds rather than to bring them into existence. The market for them is restricted, in the absence of the Regulations, by provisions in Community law and, equally, Community law indicates the way forward to the expansion of that market. In particular, the UCITS Directive (undertakings for collective investment in transferable securities), which governs what are or used to be referred to in the UK as unit and investment trusts, contains the prudential rule that such a body may invest no more than five per cent of its assets in the securities issued by the same body.[67] However, this limit may be raised to 25 per cent in the case of bonds meeting certain quality standards, set out in the Directive.[68] A similar restriction on investment by insurance companies and relaxation of that restriction in the case of UCITS-compliant bonds are also to be found in Community law. Finally, UCITS-compliant

31–10

---

[66] The structure would be even simpler if the notes were issued by the SPV and the investors' money paid directly to it. However, investors may have good reasons for preferring the loans to be made to the issuer, so that the investors have both the benefit of both the issuer's promise to repay and the claim on the asset pool held by the SPV. Where the note or bond is issued by the SPV itself, the arrangement is referred to as an "asset-backed" or "mortgage-backed" security, but does not count as a covered bond.

[67] Directive 85/611/EEC, as amended, Art.22(1).

[68] Art.22(4).

bonds are less heavily weighted in banks' risk profiles than non-compliant bonds.[69]

However, producing a UCITS-compliant covered bond requires the use of legislation. Article 22(4) of the UCITS Directive requires (a) that the issuer (which may only be a "credit institution" i.e. a bank or similar deposit-taking body) be "subject by law to special public supervision designed to protect bond-holders"—presumably additional to the supervision to which it is already subject by virtue of being a bank—and (b) that the law control the assets in which the proceeds of the bond may be invested and ensure the priority of the investors' claims in the event of the insolvency of the issuer. It is perfectly lawful to continue to issue covered bonds which do not comply with the new regulations, but in this case they will not benefit from the additional market possibilities, noted above. The Regulations implement the above principles by creating registers of "recognised" issuers and issues of covered bonds, access to which is controlled by the Financial Services Authority.[70] An applicant must have its registered office in the UK and be a body already authorised under the Financial Services and Markets Act to carry on activities as a deposit-taker and the FSA must also be satisfied that the applicant issuer and the owner of the asset pool (i.e. the SPV), will comply with the requirements imposed on them by the Regulations.[71] To claim to issue recognised covered bonds without issuer and issue being on the registers is a breach of the Regulations and makes the issuer liable at a minimum to monetary penalties imposed by the FSA.[72]

The proceeds of the issue may be used only to acquire "eligible assets" which term goes beyond mortgages on residential or commercial real property to include public sector loans, loans to a registered social landlord which may be secured on the income arising from letting of the properties as well as loans secured on the properties themselves, and loans to project companies under certain types of public-private partnerships. The property must be situated in any EEA State or in one of a limited number of other designated States.[73] Those assets must be transferred to an asset pool which must be

---

[69] HM Treasury and FSA, *Proposals for a UK Recognised Covered Bonds regulatory framework*, July 2007, para.1.7. The third advantage, as with the other two, accrues, of course, to a bank which purchases the bonds, not to the issuer bank.

[70] The Regulated Covered Bonds Regulations 2008/346, Parts 2 and 3.

[71] Reg.9. The owner is not an applicant for registration, though various obligations are laid on it by the Regulations. The proposals (above fn.69) did not envisage a requirement for UK registration, but in this, and a number of other, respects the "credit crunch" of 2007 caused the Regulations to be more tightly drawn.

[72] The enforcement powers of the FSA are set out in Part 7 of the Regulations and follow those normally available to it. See para.25–40.

[73] Reg.2. Partly, this definition is achieved by cross-reference to para.68 of Annex VI to Directive 2006/48/EC (the consolidated banking directive), which determines which assets may be used to collateralise a covered bond, if a bank investing in such bonds is to benefit from a lower risk rating. However, a recognised covered bond is not limited to such collateral, though an issuer which uses the wider type of collateral will not be able to confer the benefit of the lower risk rating on banks which purchase the bonds.

capable throughout the life of the bond of covering the bond-holders' claims and the costs of administering the pool.[74] Priority is given to the claims of bond-holders in insolvency of the owner.[75]

[74] Reg.17(2), imposing the obligation on the issuer; reg.23(1) imposing it on the owner of the asset pool.
[75] Reg.27. The proposals (above fn.69) envisaged an alternative model (the "integrated" model) in which the assets remained with the issuer but were ring-fenced. Insisting on a SPV made the priority issue somewhat simpler to deal with.

CHAPTER 32

COMPANY CHARGES

Borrowers are often obliged to provide security for the repayment of **32–1** their debts. In this respect a company is no different from any other borrower. Almost invariably, debentures (debt instruments) issued by a company will be protected by some form of security over the company's assets. However, there are sufficiently unique features associated with the granting of security by a company to justify it being treated as a separate topic. In particular, one type of security (the floating charge) is practicable only if created by a body corporate,[1] there is a separate system for the registration of company charges,[2] there are distinct statutory procedures for the enforcement

---

[1] See above at para.2–11.

[2] See paras 32–22 et seq., below.

of the floating charge,[3] and certain provisions of the Insolvency Act 1986 affecting company charges are unique to corporate insolvency.[4] Coupled with these, the granting of security by a company is subject to the law relating to corporate capacity and directors' duties.[5] As regards these latter matters, it will be assumed for the remainder of the Chapter, unless the contrary is stated, that a company has capacity to grant the security and that the directors were not acting in breach of their duty to the company or exceeding their authority.

SECURITY INTERESTS

The legal nature of security interests

32–2   Some knowledge of this general topic is essential in order to understand the particular nature of the rights conferred on a secured charge holder, the priorities of charges, and the system for the registration of company charges.[6] Some comment is also needed on nomenclature. Various forms of security are possible, as described below, but the most common form granted by a company is a charge. "Charge" has a restricted technical meaning in equity. However, technical distinctions in nomenclature are not always drawn in the literature, and, unless the context indicates otherwise, the terms "charge", "security" or "security interest" are often used interchangeably to indicate any form of security, including by way of fixed or floating charge, over a company's property present or future.

Browne-Wilkinson V.-C., without claiming that it was comprehensive, accepted the following as a description of a security interest:

> "Security is created where a person ('the creditor') to whom an obligation is owed by another ('the debtor') by statute or contract, in addition to the personal promise of the debtor to discharge the obligation, obtains rights exercisable against some

---

[3] See paras 32–35 *et seq.*, below.
[4] In certain situations there are analogues in the case of personal bankruptcy.
[5] See Chs 7 and 16.
[6] There is a considerable volume of literature on this vast and vexed topic. See Beale, Bridge, Gullifer and Lomnicka, *The Law of Personal Property Security* (Oxford, 2007); Goode, *Commercial Law* (3rd ed., London, 2004), Part 4, especially Ch.25; P. Ali, *The Law of Secured Finance* (Oxford, 2002); Oditah, *Legal Aspects of Receivables Financing* (London, 1991), Ch.1; and Worthington, *Personal Property Law: Text and Materials* (Oxford, 2000) Ch.3, for helpful analyses.

property in which the debtor has an interest in order to enforce the discharge of the debtor's obligation to the creditor."[7]

More recently in *Smith (Administrator of Cosslett (Contractors) Ltd) v Bridgend County Borough Council*, Lord Scott remarked that:[8]

"a contractual right enabling a creditor to sell his debtor's goods and apply the proceeds in or towards satisfaction of the debt is a right of a security character. [It is important to note that] the conclusion does not depend on the parties' intention to create a security. Their intention, objectively ascertained, is relevant to the construction of their contract. But once contractual rights have, by the process of construction, been ascertained, the question whether they constitute security rights is a question of law that is not dependent on their intentions."

These two statements highlight the essential features of a security interest. First, the classification of security interests is a matter of law, and depends upon the rights agreed between the parties, not on their intention to create one form of security rather than another, nor on the economic effect of their agreement. Secondly, every security interest ultimately gives the holder of the security a proprietary claim over assets,[9] normally the debtor's, to secure payment of the debt. The position of a secured creditor is to be contrasted with that of an unsecured creditor who merely has a personal claim to sue for the payment of his debt and to invoke the available legal processes for the enforcement of any judgment that he may obtain.[10]

Security interests can be divided broadly into consensual and non-consensual securities. As the name implies, consensual security **32–3**

---

[7] *Bristol Airport Plc v Powdrill* [1990] Ch. 744 at 760. The only significant refinement that one might want to add to this description is that the property of a third party can also be made available by way of security, without any associated personal promise by the third party to meet the secured obligation: *Bank of Credit and Commerce International SA (No.8), Re* [1998] A.C. 214. See also *Curtain Dream Plc, Re* [1990] B.C.L.C. 925 at 935–937; *Welsh Development Agency v Export Finance Co Ltd* [1992] B.C.L.C. 148; Insolvency Act 1986, s.248. A charge can be created not only to secure the payment of a monetary obligation but also to secure other types of obligations: *Cosslett (Contractors) Ltd, Re* [1998] Ch.495.

[8] [2002] 1 A.C. 336, para.[53].

[9] That being said, there is disagreement between scholars as to the sort of property interests that are held, especially those held by the floating chargee in the charged assets prior to crystallisation. At one extreme it is claimed that the floating chargee has no proprietary interest at all in the charged asset. At the other, the floating chargee may be seen to have the same quality of proprietary interest as is recognised in the context of a fixed charge, albeit a far more precarious one. This is discussed in more detail later.

[10] See Goode, *op. cit.*, at pp.582–583. An unsecured creditor may be able to invoke certain types of court procedures which make a party's assets security for his claim: for the nature of these procedural securities see Goode, *op. cit.*, at pp.622–623.

interests arise by way of agreement of the parties. As regards consensual security, English law only recognises the following: the mortgage, the charge, the pledge and the lien.[11] In contrast to consensual security interests are those security interests that arise by operation of law. The classification of this category is not free from difficulty but it includes at least the common law lien and the equitable lien arising by operation of law.[12] Many commentators also include statutory charges, equitable rights to set-off, equitable rights to trace and procedural securities.[13]

It is not possible in a text of this nature to describe security interests in any great detail, but a number of questions typically arise with respect to the creation of such interests by a company:

    (i) First, is the interest created by the security equitable or legal? This has a bearing on the priorities of different charges and of course an equitable charge holder can be defeated by a bona fide purchaser for value.[14]

    (ii) Secondly, is the security interest possessory in the sense that possession, either actual or constructive, of the property subject to the security is necessary in order to confer a security interest on the security holder? Obviously, if all security interests had to be possessory it would make secured borrowing virtually impossible as the debtor would be unable to use the secured assets in the course of business. The classic example of a possessory security is the pledge, which involves the pledgee (the security holder) taking possession of the goods of the debtor (the pledgor) until the debt is paid or the pledgee takes steps to enforce the pledge. The common law lien is also possessory. In the interests of commercial vitality, English law has thankfully long recog-

---

[11] *Cosslett (Contractors) Ltd, Re* [1998] Ch. 495 at p.508 (Millett L.J.). Also see Bell, *Modern Law of Personal Property in England and Ireland* (London, 1989), Ch.6; Oditah, *op. cit.*, at pp.85–88; Goode, *Legal Problems of Credit and Security* (3rd ed., London, 2003) Ch.1, pp.31–38.

[12] Bell, *op. cit.*, at pp.138–141. Note that s.246 of the Insolvency Act 1986 deprives certain types of merely possessory liens of effect against an administrator or liquidator: *Aveling Barford Ltd, Re* [1989] 1 W.L.R. 360 at 364–365.

[13] Goode, *Commercial Law, op. cit.*, pp.619–623; Finch, *Corporate Insolvency Law—Perspectives and Principles*, (Cambridge, 2002) pp.75–6.

[14] Most securities created by companies are charges (using that term in its technical sense), and most charges are equitable. A *legal mortgage* is created if the borrower transfers legal title to the property to the lender on the condition that it will be given back when the obligation is met. An *equitable mortgage* is created in the same way, but where the transfer is of equitable title rather than legal title; an equitable mortgage is also created by a specifically enforceable contract to create a legal mortgage. Note that a legal mortgage of land is no longer possible: these arrangements are now deemed by statute to create a *legal charge* (LPA 1925 ss.85(1) and 86(1)). All other charges, using "charge" in its technical sense, are *equitable charges*. These arise where, by contract, a specific item of property is appropriated to, or made answerable for, meeting the debtor's obligation.

nised non-possessory security interests, such as mortgages, charges and equitable liens.[15]

(iii) Thirdly, what type of "proprietary" interest is vested in the chargee by the charge? This has a direct bearing on remedies. The remedies of charge holders will be dealt with in greater detail later. But some brief comment is needed as to the remedies available to the holders of other types of security interests. First is to be contrasted the mortgage and the charge. Although the words are often used interchangeably, there is technically an essential difference between them: "a mortgage involves a conveyance of property subject to a right of redemption, whereas a charge conveys nothing and merely gives the chargee certain rights over the property as security for the loan."[16] This essential difference has an impact on remedies: unless the charge document expressly provides otherwise (which it usually does[17]), the remedy of a chargee is to apply to the court for an order for sale or for the appointment of a receiver; this is because a charge, unlike the mortgage, does not involve a conveyance of a proprietary interest, so a chargee cannot automatically foreclose or take possession.[18] By contrast, the principal remedy of a pledgee is that of sale of the pledged goods; he can also sub-pledge the goods.[19] A common law lien holder merely has the right to detain the goods subject to the lien until the debt has been paid.[20]

(iv) Fourthly, is the security interest one that is created by the act of the parties or is it one created by operation of law?

---

[15] Note that equitable liens are not at all like common law liens, despite their similar names: an *equitable lien* carries with it the same rights as a charge, the difference being simply that the first arises by operation of law, the second consensually. A *common law lien*, by contrast, arises when possession of goods is given to a creditor otherwise than for security—for example, so that the goods can be stored, repaired or transported—and the creditor is given, by custom, statute or contract, a right to retain the goods if the debt is not satisfied.

[16] See *Bond Worth Ltd, Re* [1980] Ch. 228 at 250. Such a charge is, however, a present existing charge. For some of the difficulties in distinguishing an equitable charge from a mortgage in terms of the quality of the security granted, see Oditah, *op. cit.*, at pp.94–96. Also see *Leyland Daf Ltd; Buchler v Talbot, Re* [2004] 2 A.C. 298, where Lords Hoffmann (at para.[29]) and Millett (at para.[51]) used the language of mortgages, not charges, in describing the chargor of a crystallised charge as having only an equity of redemption.

[17] The usual provision is that, in the event of specified types of default by the chargor, the chargee is entitled to appoint a receiver to act as the agent of the chargor to sell the charged assets and use the proceeds to repay the outstanding debt to the chargee, after first paying those with statutory priorities, as discussed later.

[18] The point is that the chargee does not have an estate.

[19] See Bell, *op. cit.*, at pp.136–137.

[20] The lienee will normally have the right to sell by contract and where this is the case some argue that it is tantamount to a pledge. Other charge holders may of course take subject to the lien: *George Barker (Transport) Ltd v Eynon* [1974] 1 W.L.R. 462.

This point has already been referred to above. It is of critical importance with respect to the registration of company charges, since charges created by a company over its assets are treated differently from charges (or, more correctly, equitable liens) over a company's assets arising other than by the creation of the company. Registration is dealt with in greater detail later.

(v) Fifthly, if the charge has been created by the company, is it of a type that is registrable under the provisions for the registration of company charges? Again this will be dealt with in greater detail later.

(vi) Finally, is the charge created by the company fixed or floating? This will have a profound impact on the rights and remedies available to the chargee, and to other third parties associated with the failing company, and will be dealt with in greater detail later.

The above is a very compressed survey of the issues that are material in considering corporate security interests. To complicate the picture further, there are a number of other devices which, although not strictly security interests in the sense of vesting some type of proprietary interest in the creditor or giving the creditor possessory control over assets of the debtor company, nevertheless function as security. These devices often put a creditor in a position superior to that of other unsecured creditors in the event of a company's insolvent liquidation and are therefore referred to as quasi-security devices. Two illustrative examples of such devices are (i) the negative pledge clause in unsecured lending, and (ii) retention of the title by a seller of goods. The first of these is an agreement by a debtor company and its unsecured creditor that the company will not create any securities which have priority to the claim of the creditor. Although this does not vest a security interest in the creditor, it has been claimed (rightly) that it "behaves"[21] like a security interest since it is an attempt to preclude the debtor from freely using its assets and thus, as with a security interest, it provides the creditor with a measure of protection. The retention of title is an arrangement whereby the seller of goods retains title to the goods until at least the buyer of

---

[21] See Oditah, *op. cit.*, at p.11. For a list of other types of quasi-security interests see Oditah, *ibid.*, at p.11. See also Goode, *Commercial Law*, *op. cit.*, Ch.22.

the goods pays for them.[22] Some of the problems raised by this type of security will be dealt with later in the discussion on registration.[23]

The benefits of taking security

There are a number of compelling reasons for a creditor to obtain a **32–4** charge and not rely solely on a personal action against a debtor company. First, in the event of the insolvency of a company a secured creditor will have priority over unsecured creditors (at least to the extent that the secured assets are of sufficient value to fund repayment of the secured debt), and will also, according to the seniority of his claim, have priority over any less senior security holders. This is a direct consequence of the fact that a security interest confers some type of proprietary interest on its holder. Priority-gaining in the event of a company's liquidation is one of the principal reasons for taking security.[24]

Secondly, the secured creditor has the right of pursuit. This arises where a company wrongfully and in violation of the rights of a chargee disposes of the property subject to the charge. The chargee is then entitled to enforce the security against any identifiable proceeds of the disposition.[25]

Thirdly, a security interest gives its holder the right of enforcement. Once a charge becomes enforceable, in circumstances determined by the agreement itself, the chargee may take steps to enforce the charge. English law has traditionally placed few impediments in the way of enforcement of a charge: liberal rights are given by statute[26] and can be enhanced by contract. These rights of enforcement allow a chargee to remain largely outside any concurrent insolvency proceedings and to enforce the charge independently of such proceedings,[27] although, as discussed later, this principle is substantially modified in the case of floating charges by various statutory rules that give priority to pre-ferential debts and to liquidation expenses,[28] and by the rules that

---

[22] See generally, McCormack, *Reservation of Title* (2nd ed., London, 1995). As a matter of economic substance, but not legal substance, these arrangements operate much like a chattel mortgage securing a loan: Diamond, *A Review of Security Interests in Property* (DTI, 1989), at para.3.6; *Welsh Development Agency v Export Finance Co Ltd* [1991] B.C.L.C. 936 at 950; [1992] B.C.L.C. 148. As a result, there have been several attempts to align their treatment at law with the treatment of other security interests, but so far unsuccessfully. Also see below, paras 32–31—32–33.

[23] There are also self-help remedies such as set-off, abatement, rejection of goods and forfeiture of deposit, all of which firm up the position of a creditor: see Harris *et al*, *Remedies in Contract and Tort* (2nd ed., London, 2006), Ch.2.

[24] See Report of the Review Committee on Insolvency Law and Practice, Cmnd. 8558 (Cork Report), Ch.35.

[25] He may also be able to assert a claim against the property subject to the security unless it is acquired by a bona fide purchaser for value without notice of the earlier equitable interest.

[26] IA 1986 s.42(1) and Sch.1, for example.

[27] *Sowman v Samuel (David) Trust Ltd* [1978] 1 W.L.R. 22; *Potters Oils Ltd, Re* [1986] 1 W.L.R. 201.

[28] See paras 32–12 *et seq.*, below.

operate in relation to the administration procedure (and its accompanying moratorium) as extended by the Enterprise Act 2002.[29]

Lastly, a charge affords a chargee a measure of control over the business of the debtor company. The terms of the security agreement may require the debtor company to report regularly to the chargee and, if the company gets into financial difficulties, the chargee may be made privy to management decisions.[30] In addition, the charge may be so all-embracing that it confers on the chargee as a matter of fact the exclusive right to supply the debtor company with secured credit.[31] A charge will obviously deter a second financier from providing the company with funds where its charge would rank after a charge that the company has already created over its assets. Also, unsecured creditors are often deterred from seeking a winding-up where it appears that the secured creditors are entitled to all the company's assets.[32]

THE FLOATING CHARGE

The practical differences between fixed and floating charges

32–5 Subject to the issue of registration, discussed in the next section, the creation of a charge by a company is no different from the creation of a charge by any other debtor. And the creation of a floating charge, although devised for companies and still confined to them and to analogous vehicles, is no more difficult than the creation of a fixed charge.

A charge is an equitable proprietary security interest. It is created whenever parties agree that certain property belonging to the debtor (or some third-party guarantor) will be appropriated to the discharge of the debt or other obligation (e.g. the machinery in a factory may be charged in favour of repayment of the loan that funded its purchase, or, alternatively, a loan granted for an entirely separate purpose). The agreement is by contract, without any transfer of title. The proprietary interest created in this way is less than an ownership interest

---

[29] See paras 32–36 *et seq.*, below.

[30] Although the chargee has to be careful not to become a shadow director and thus, e.g. potentially liable under the Insolvency Act 1986, s.214. The chances of this are, on the whole, minimal: see *Hydrodam (Corby) Ltd, Re* [1994] 2 B.C.L.C. 180.

[31] For an unsuccessful attempt to challenge a charge precluding the creation of charges in favour of third parties as being in violation of Arts 85 and 86 of the EC Treaty, see *Oakdale Richmond Ltd v National Westminster Bank Plc* [1996] B.C.C. 919.

[32] Although see below, paras 32–13—32–15, for the rules on preferred creditors and on the prescribed fund to be dedicated to unsecured creditors from floating charge realisations. Also see generally Wood, *Law and Practice of International Finance 2007 Series* (7 volume set, 2nd ed. volumes, London, 2007), which sets out in great detail the law in this area; see especially *International Term Loans, Bonds, Guarantees and Legal Opinions*, which sets out the reasons for the various types of bond covenants that can be taken by a creditor.

(either legal or equitable), but it allows the secured property to be appropriated and sold, with the proceeds of sale dedicated to the repayment of the outstanding secured obligation.[33] On the debtor's insolvency, this arrangement removes the secured property from any insolvency proceedings,[34] and so the secured creditor is more likely to be repaid in full when compared with the unsecured creditors who have to share *pari passu* in the proceeds derived from sale of the remaining unsecured assets.

All charges created in this way are either fixed or floating. A fixed (or "specific") charge expressly or impliedly restricts the debtor's power to dispose of, or otherwise deal with, the property without the creditor's consent. By contrast, a floating charge leaves the chargor free to deal with the charged property in the ordinary course of business without reference to the chargee. A floating charge thus has the very practical advantage that it allows a company to give security over assets which are continually turned over or used up and replaced as a matter of routine trading; a business can thus raise money on secured loans without removing any of its property from routine business activities.[35] The charge remains floating and the company is free to use the assets subject to the charge until the charge is converted into a fixed charge. This is referred to as "crystallisation" of the charge. The normal crystallising event is the taking of steps to enforce the charge, but there are others and these are dealt with later.[36]

No particular form of words is necessary to create a floating **32–6** charge. From the earliest cases, it was recognised as sufficient if (a) the intention is shown to impose a charge on assets both present and future, (b) the assets are of such a nature that they would be changing in the ordinary course of the company's business, and (c) the company is free to continue to deal with the assets for its own benefit in the ordinary course of its business.[37] Recent authorities make it clear that only the last of these three attributes is crucial.[38]

Interestingly, at the same time that courts in the UK were confirming the legitimacy of floating charges, courts in the United States

---

[33] And if the proceeds are more than sufficient to repay all the secured debts (and other claims on the secured assets—see below, paras 32–13—32–15 [preferred creditors, etc.]), then the excess is returned to the debtor/chargor.

[34] Although see below, paras 32–16—32–17, for particular rules relating to floating charges.

[35] See para.2–11, above. For valuable analyses of the floating charge see Getzler and Payne, *Company Charges: Spectrum and Beyond* (Oxford, 2006); Goode, *Commercial Law* (3rd ed.), Ch.25; Gough, *Company Charges* (2nd ed., London, 1996), Ch.5. Floating charges and receivers in Scotland are dealt with by CA 2006, Pt.25 Ch.2, and IA 1986, Pt.III, Ch.II.

[36] See paras 32–8—32–9 *et seq.*

[37] *Yorkshire Woolcombers' Association Ltd, Re* [1903] 2 Ch. 284, at p.295 (Romer L.J.); *Illingworth v Houldsworth* [1904] A.C. 355, HL. In practice, it is usual to state specifically that the charge is "by way of floating charge" but it suffices if it is expressed to be on the "undertaking" or the like: *Panama Royal Mail Co, Re* (1870) L.R. 5 Ch.App. 318; *Florence Land and Public Works Co, Re* (1879) 10 Ch.D. 530. CA; *Colonial Trusts Corp, Re* (1880) 15 Ch.D. 465.

[38] *Spectrum Plus Ltd, Re* [2005] 2 A.C. 680.

were moving in the opposite direction. According to US courts, allowing such freedom to the debtor/chargor was incompatible with the creation of a genuine security interest and was a fraud on the creditors; if the creditor did not exercise reasonable dominion over the secured asset, then the security was illusory and void,[39] and any rights created could only be contractual, not proprietary.[40]

Despite this early judicial acceptance in the UK, the floating charge has always been treated by the legislature with something approaching suspicion, and successive Companies Acts and Insolvency Acts have adopted a variety of rules designed to restrict its full impact, which is potentially to sweep up *all* the company's resources (by securing "the undertaking" or "all the assets and undertaking" of the company) and dedicate them to securing the debt of *one* of the company's creditors,[41] leaving all the other creditors unprotected, unable even to share *pari passu* in the company's remaining unsecured resources on a winding-up.

32–7   Because of these various statutory incursions, floating charges (i.e. all charges *created* as floating charges[42]) are now subjected to more, and more onerous, invalidating provisions (including general registration requirements as well as specific invalidity rules), and are also subjected to compulsory distributions to prior-ranking claims from preferential creditors, and administrator's and liquidator's costs and expenses. This differential treatment, discussed in more detail below,[43] gives creditors an incentive to ensure their charges are classified as fixed, not floating.[44]

Given the vulnerability of floating charges, the question arises as to why a creditor should bother to obtain one. While obviously the fixed charge accords superior protection, there are sound reasons for taking a floating charge. First, where a subsequent holder of a registrable charge is deemed to have notice of a negative pledge clause, then this accords priority to the floating charge holder. Secondly, the charge provides security against unsecured creditors. Thirdly, the floating charge holder will be able to take steps to enforce the charge and, as will be seen, this accords him considerable control over the company's affairs. Fourthly, the holder of a floating charge will have some measure of control over the company, even without taking any steps to enforce it.[45] Lastly, the holder of a floating charge may be

---

[39] *Geilfuss v Corrigan* 95 Wis. 651, 70 N.W. 306 (1897); *Benedict v Ratner* 268 U.S. 354, 45 S.Ct. 566, 69 L.Ed. 991 (1925).

[40] The commercial inconvenience of this judicial approach probably contributed to the early adoption of an alternative mechanism to achieve similar ends by way of the Uniform Commercial Code, Article 9.

[41] *Panama, New Zealand and Australian Royal Mail Co, Re* (1870) 5 Ch.App.318, CA, provided early confirmation that this is possible.

[42] IA 1986, s.251 provides that "floating charge" means "a charge which, *as created*, was a floating charge". See below, para.32–20.

[43] See paras 32–12—32–19.

[44] See paras 32–20—32–21 for the way the courts classify charges as fixed or floating.

[45] See para.32–4, above.

able to block the appointment of an administrator, although now only in a limited range of cases.[46]

Crystallisation

As indicated above, a floating charge (unlike a fixed charge) leaves **32–8** the debtor company free to use the secured assets in the ordinary course of its business until the charge is converted into a fixed charge. Crystallisation is the term used to describe the process by which this happens.[47] Crystallisation is an important event, since it enables definition of the pool of assets available to the chargee as security for the obligation: a crystallised charge bites on all the assets that are presently in, or in the future come into, the hands of the chargor and are properly within the description of the charged assets.[48]

The effect of crystallisation is to deprive the company of the autonomy to deal with the assets subject to the charge in the normal course of business.[49] The events of crystallisation, on which there is general agreement, are:[50] (i) the making of a winding-up order;[51] (ii) the appointment of an administrative receiver;[52] (iii) the company's

---

[46] See below, para.32–36. Generally, see Goode, *Legal Problems of Credit and Security* (3rd ed., London, 2003), pp.151–153 where these points are developed.

[47] The language is often muddled: crystallisation is described as operating as an equitable assignment (by way of charge): *George Barker (Transport) Ltd v Enyon* [1974] 1 W.L.R. 462, at 467, 471, 475; or as conversion to a specific (fixed) charge: *Griffin Hotel Co Ltd, Re* [1941] Ch. 129. And see the assertion that the company has an equity of redemption: *Ultraframe (UK) Ltd v Fielding* [2005] EWHC 1638 (Ch.), LTL 11/8/2005 at [1401].

[48] A floating charge agreement does not usually provide for crystallisation over part only of the assets to which it relates. There is no doctrinal reason for this. Partial crystallisation could, theoretically, be provided for by agreement, so long as the class of assets to be affected could be specified with certainty so as to define those which the chargor can and cannot deal with. This practicality creates the problem. It is submitted that *Robson v Smith* [1895] 2 Ch. 118 is not authority against partial crystallisation since the floating charge in that case did not confer any such right. In any event, such a provision is unlikely to be attractive in practice: it confers no significant benefit on the chargor, since the essence of security is that it only secures the outstanding debt, and any surplus (in cash or kind) is returned to the chargor; and it reduces the rights of the chargee in ways that may turn out to be unnecessarily detrimental when the event occurs.

[49] At the time the event of crystallisation occurs, there must be: (a) an outstanding obligation which the charge secures; (b) a valid and subsisting charge agreement; (c) identifiable charged assets in which the chargor has an interest or rights.

[50] See Goode, *Legal Problems of Credit and Security* (3rd ed., London, 2003) at pp.133–151.

[51] *Wallace v Universal Automatic Machines* [1894] 2 Ch. 547, CA; *Victoria Steamboats Ltd, Re* [1897] 1 Ch. 158. Even if the winding-up is for purposes of reconstruction: *Crompton & Co, Re* [1914] 1 Ch. 954. It is the making of the order and not, for example, the presentation of the petition since there is always the chance that the court will decline to make the winding-up order. In Scotland the charge crystallises on the commencement of the winding-up of the company: Destination in Bankruptcy and Diligence (Scotland) Act 2007, s.45.

[52] *Evans v Rival Granite Quarries Ltd* [1910] 2 K.B. 979. The same applies to the appointment of a receiver by the court. See para.32–39 on administrative receivership.

ceasing to carry on business;[53] (iv) the taking of possession by the debenture-holder;[54] and (v) the happening of an event expressly provided for in the debenture, often referred to as "automatic crystallisation". Events (i)–(iii) are implied as crystallising events in every floating charge agreement unless explicitly excluded.

Automatic crystallisation is not a term of art. It covers at least two situations which at first blush appear dissimilar. One is where the charge is made to crystallise on the happening of an event provided for in the charge agreement without there being any need for a further act by the chargee,[55] and the other is where the charge is made to crystallise on the serving of a notice of crystallisation on the company. However, these events have one important common feature and that is they will normally not be known to a person dealing with the company and therefore it seems appropriate to treat them together.

32–9   Initially there was some doubt about both the validity and the desirability of automatic crystallisation provisions. On validity, the matter is now settled beyond dispute, following acceptance of the judgment of Hoffmann J. in *Brightlife Ltd, Re*[56] upholding the validity of a provision enabling the floating charge holder to serve a notice of crystallisation on the company. Hoffmann J. saw crystallisation as being a matter of agreement between the parties. On this reasoning there can be no objection to a charge being made to crystallise on the happening of a specified event. On the desirability of automatic crystallisation clauses, their acceptance as a matter of law indicates at least tacit approval that the benefits outweigh the detriments. The earlier arguments against such clauses focused on the disadvantages suffered by third parties. For example, insofar as insolvency law is committed to the principle that property within the apparent ownership of the company should be treated as the company's in the event of its insolvent liquidation, permitting party autonomy to effect automatic crystallisation clearly undermines this policy, but then English insolvency law is littered with similar exceptions.[57] Similarly, it has been argued that automatic crystallisation may prejudice subsequent purchasers and chargees who do

---

[53] This occurs because the cessation removes the raison d'etre of the floating charge, which is to permit the company to carry on business in the ordinary way insofar as the class of assets charged is concerned. *Woodroffes (Musical Instruments) Ltd, Re* [1986] Ch. 366 (it is the cessation of business and not ceasing to be a going concern assuming the latter is different). Express provisions for crystallisation will only exclude this implied provision for crystallisation if they expressly do so: *The Real Meat Co Ltd, Re* [1996] B.C.C. 254.

[54] *Evans v Rival Granite Quarries Ltd* [1910] K.B. 979 at 997.

[55] The crystallising event could, for example, be the failure by the debtor to pay any monies due or to insure the charged property.

[56] [1987] Ch. 200.

[57] English insolvency law achieves this policy to some extent by requiring registration of non-possessory securities. It does not, however, require registration of title retention clauses or trusts, and any assets in the possession (and apparent ownership) of the company but which are subject to these arrangements do not form part of the company's assets in a winding-up.

not know, and indeed who may have no way of knowing, that the charge has crystallised.[58] Whether this is indeed the case is not clear cut. The matter is usually resolved as one of priorities,[59] and subsequent purchasers or chargees will not necessarily be defeated by the earlier equitable charge.[60] In addition, Professor Goode has pointed out that the fact that the charge has crystallised will affect the relationship between the chargee and the company, but it does not necessarily affect a third party since, if the company is left free to deal with the assets in the normal course of its business, then the chargee (under the prior, now crystallised, floating charge) should be estopped from denying the company's authority to do so.[61]

The events implied as crystallising events in every floating charge agreement have already been mentioned. For the avoidance of doubt, there are no further implied terms defining events that cause crystallisation. In particular, default in the payment of interest or capital are not crystallising events,[62] nor (more controversially[63]) is the crystallisation of another floating charge, whether created earlier or later than the charge in question.[64] Of course, given the validity of automatic crystallisation clauses, these events could be nominated as crystallising events.

Note that even where default does not result in crystallisation, the company will be in breach of contract and the chargee will have appropriate contractual remedies. For example, the holder of an uncrystallised charge may apply for an injunction to prevent the

---

[58] It is common when taking a fixed charge or purchasing a substantial asset of the company to serve on it inquiries as to whether any floating charge has crystallised. This provides limited protection since the company can lie or, more likely, it may not appreciate that the charge has crystallised. In an early effort to overcome this problem, provisions were inserted into CA 1989, s.102, that empowered the Secretary of State to pass regulations whereby events of crystallisation would have no effect until notified to the Registrar; however, these provisions were never brought into effect and have not been included in CA 2006.

[59] Where the subsequent interest-holder (purchaser or chargee) may have no actual or constructive notice that the earlier floating charge has crystallised. See Goode, *Commercial Law, op. cit.*, at pp.662–666.

[60] The interests that lose out to the crystallised floating charge are the subsequent equitable charge (provided the equities are equal), the common law lien over chattels and the interests of execution creditors: see Gough, "The Floating Charge: Traditional Themes and New Directions" in Finn (ed.), *Equity and Commercial Relationships* (Sydney, 1977), at p.262.

[61] Goode, *Commercial Law, op. cit.*, at pp.687–688; Goode, *Legal Problems of Credit and Security, op. cit.*, at pp.181–182; a similar point is made by Gough, *op. cit.*, at pp.255–256.

[62] *Government Stock and Other Securities Investment Co Ltd v Manila Railway Co Ltd* [1897] A.C. 81.

[63] See Beale *et al*, *The Law of Personal property Security, op. cit.*, para.4.56, indicating that where crystallisation of one of the floating charges effectively causes the company's business to cease, the other charge must necessarily crystallise. But *cp.* Goode, *Legal Problems of Credit and Security, op. cit.*, p.140.

[64] *Woodroffes (Musical Instruments) Ltd, Re* [1986] Ch. 366.

company dealing with its assets otherwise than in the ordinary course of its business.[65]

Priority accorded to floating charges

32–10   Since a floating charge gives the debtor company management autonomy over the secured assets, the most serious risk facing the charge holder is that the assets will be dissipated, without replacement, leaving no security to support the outstanding obligation. Subject to any specific restrictions in the charge agreement, the debtor company is free to deal with the charged assets in the ordinary course of business. Of course this means that the chargor may sell the assets in the ordinary course of business, and purchasers take free of the security.

In addition, the company may grant subsequent security interests, and the earlier floating charge will be deferred to any subsequent fixed legal or equitable charge created by the company over its assets,[66] or any subsequent floating charges provided they are not over precisely the same assets,[67] but are over only part of the pool of assets[68] where the first charge contemplates the creation of the later charge.[69] In Scotland, however, where the same property (or any part of the same property) is subject to two floating charges they rank according to the time of registration unless the instruments creating the charges otherwise provide.[70]

Similarly, if debts due to the company are subject to a floating charge, the interest of the floating charge holder will be subject to any lien or set off that the company creates with respect to the charged

---

[65] *Woodroffes (Musical Instruments) Ltd, Re* [1986] Ch. 366 at p.378: "it is a mistake to think that the chargee has no remedy while the charge is still floating. He can always intervene and obtain an injunction to prevent the company from dealing with its assets otherwise than in the ordinary course of its business. That no doubt is one reason why it is preferable to describe the charge as 'hovering,' a word which can bear an undertone of menace, rather than as 'dormant.'"

[66] *Wheatley v Silkstone and Haigh Moor Coal Co* (1885) 29 Ch.D. 715; *Robson v Smith* [1895] 2 Ch. 118 at 124 (any dealing with the property subject to a floating charge "will be binding on the debentureholders, provided that the dealing be completed before the debentures cease to be merely a floating security"); *Castell and Brown Ltd, Re* [1898] 1 Ch. 315. Although note that if B has *actual* notice that A's charge prohibits the creation of a later charge having priority, then A's charge will prevail: *Siebe Gorman & Co Ltd v Barclays Bank Ltd* [1979] 2 Lloyd's Rep. 142 (overruled by *Spectrum Plus Ltd, Re* [2005] 2 A.C. 680, but not on this point): see below, para.32–11, on negative pledges.

[67] If the subsequent floating charge is over the same assets, then, the equities being equal, the first in time prevails: *Benjamin Cope & Sons Ltd, Re* [1914] 1 Ch. 800.

[68] *Automatic Bottle Makers Ltd, Re* [1926] Ch. 412, CA.

[69] *Automatic Bottle Makers Ltd, Re*, above, implies that this depends on the wording of the charge and of the express provision, if any, relating to the creation of further charges.

[70] Bankruptcy and Diligence (Scotland) Act 2007 ss.40, 41. But when the first chargee receives written notice of the registration of the later charge his priority is restricted to present advances and future advances which he is legally required to make plus interest and expenses: s.40(5) and (6).

assets prior to crystallisation,[71] since a floating charge is not regarded for this purpose as an immediate assignment of the *chose in action*,[72] but becomes such only on crystallisation.[73] In the same vein, if a creditor has levied and completed execution,[74] the debenture-holders cannot compel him to restore the money, nor, unless the charge has crystallised, can he be restrained from levying execution.[75] The floating charge holder will take the company's property subject to the rights of anyone claiming by title paramount. However, once the floating charge crystallises,[76] this ability to deal with the charged assets in the ordinary course of business ceases, and the usual priority rules apply to determine whether the (now fixed) equitable charge has priority over any subsequently created legal or equitable interests.[77]

In an effort to enhance the security offered by a still floating charge **32–11** as against subsequent security interests that would otherwise have priority, floating charge agreements almost invariably contain a provision that restricts the right of the company to create charges that have priority to or rank equally with the floating charge (called a negative pledge clause). Such restrictions are strictly construed,[78] but because they limit the company's actual authority to deal with its assets in the ordinary course of business, they remove the basis described above on which floating charges are automatically postponed to later charges. Instead, orthodox priority rules must be applied (e.g. an earlier equitable (floating charge) interest is deferred to a subsequent legal interest obtained bona fide and without notice of the earlier interest). It follows that, despite the negative pledge, a floating charge may still be postponed to later mortgages. If the later mortgage is legal, for example, the mortgagee will obtain priority by virtue of his legal interest unless he has notice not only of the floating charge but also of the restriction on dealing contained in it.[79] And if the subsequent interest is equitable, the later chargee may be preferred on the ground that the company has been allowed to represent that it is free to deal with the assets in the normal course of business

---

[71] Even though, if *George Barker (Transport) Ltd v Eynon* [1974] 1 W.L.R. 462, CA is rightly decided, the lien or set off has not actually accrued.

[72] *Biggerstaff v Rowatt's Wharf* [1896] 2 Ch. 93, CA; *Rother Iron Works Ltd v Canterbury Precision Engineers Ltd* [1974] Q.B. 1, CA; *George Barker (Transport) Ltd v Eynon* [1974] 1 W.L.R. 462, CA.

[73] See *Cretanor Maritime Co Ltd v Irish Marine Management Ltd* [1978] 1 W.L.R. 966, CA, where the company's assets were subject to an injunction against their removal from the jurisdiction, obtained by an unsecured creditor. On the application of the holder of the debenture whose charge had crystallised, the court discharged the injunction. See also *Capital Cameras Ltd v Harold Lines Ltd* [1991] 1 W.L.R. 54 (successful application of a receiver to dismiss a *Mareva* injunction).

[74] Seizure alone does not suffice: *Norton v Yates* [1906] 1 K.B. 112, CA.

[75] *Evans v Rival Granite Quarries* [1910] 2 K.B. 979, CA.

[76] On crystallisation, see paras 32–8 *et seq.*

[77] *ELS Ltd, Re* [1994] 1 B.C.L.C. 743.

[78] *Brunton v Electrical Engineering Corp* [1892] 1 Ch. 434; *Robson v Smith* [1895] 2 Ch. 118.

[79] *English & Scottish Mercantile Investment Co Ltd v Brunton* [1892] 2 Q.B. 700, CA; *Valletort Sanitary Steam Laundry Co Ltd, Re* [1903] 2 Ch. 654.

as though they were unencumbered. For example, if the title deeds are left with the company, an equitable mortgagee by deposit will take priority.[80]

Notice (actual or constructive) of the terms of the floating charge (and any negative pledge) is thus crucial in determining priority disputes.[81] Mere knowledge of the existence of a floating charge,[82] or of its registration at the Companies' Registry, is not sufficient to give constructive notice of any restriction on the creation of other charges.[83] It is normal practice for the debenture-holders (or their trustees) to ensure that the registered particulars also include a note of the negative pledge restriction. The efficacy of this practice has been questioned,[84] however, on the ground that constructive notice cannot extend to matters beyond those which are required to be inserted in the registered particulars, and in particular does not include all matters that would in fact have been discovered if a search had been made. On this basis, there must be actual knowledge of the restriction before the priority of a subsequent charge holder is adversely affected.[85] Because of the ineffectiveness of negative pledge clauses, practical measures are often adopted to inhibit the creation of subsequent interests: e.g. it is a wise precaution to deprive the company of the title deeds of its secured properties. Finally, despite the foregoing, subsequent interests that can be classed as purchase money security interests may have priority: where a company grants a floating charge containing a negative pledge provision and then later purchases a property leaving part of the purchase secured by a mortgage, the mortgagee will take priority, even if the mortgagee has actual notice,

---

[80] *Castell & Brown Ltd, Re* [1898] 1 Ch. 315; *Valletort Sanitary Steam Laundry, Re* [1903] 2 Ch. 654.

[81] *Portbase Clothing Ltd, Re* [1993] Ch. 388, at p.401. Contrast *Griffiths v Yorkshire Bank* [1994] 1 W.L.R. 1427, which must be doubted: see Beale *et al, op. cit.,* para.13.44.

[82] *cf. Ian Chisholm Textiles Ltd v Griffiths* [1994] 2 B.C.L.C. 291, at pp.303–304.

[83] *Wilson v Kelland* [1910] 2 Ch. 306: this case held that registration of a charge in the register of charges constitutes notice to the whole world that a charge of a particular type exists, but does not constitute notice of the terms and conditions of the charge. In other words, he cannot be deemed to have notice of the existence of the negative pledge clause in the charge contract. See also the decision of the Hong Kong High Court in *ABN AMRO Bank NV v Chiyu Banking Corp Ltd* [2000] 3 HKC 381, which held that the registration of a floating charge constitutes constructive notice of the charge but not of any restrictive provision contained therein, since particulars of such a provision are not required to be registered. *cf. Mechanisations (Eaglescliffe) Ltd, Re* [1966] Ch.20 and *Eric Holmes (Property) Ltd, Re* [1965] Ch. 1052. LCA 1972, s.10(4), and LPA 1925, s.198 do not appear to affect this.

[84] See Gough, *op. cit.,* Ch.10. de Lacy goes even further in "Constructive Notice and Company Charge Registration" [2001] *Conv* 122, by arguing that registration does not give notice of the existence of a charge at all.

[85] It is submitted that the dictum of Morritt J. that such restrictions do not affect priorities as a matter of property law is wrong: see *Griffiths v Yorkshire Bank Plc* [1964] 1 W.L.R. 1427, at p.1435. See also *Ian Chisholm Textiles Ltd v Griffiths* [1994] 2 B.C.L.C. 291, at pp.303–304.

so long as what the company acquired by purchase was merely the equity of redemption subject to the mortgage.[86]

Most of the problems in this area would be resolved by a requirement that undertakings by a company not to create subsequent charges having priority to an existing charge be registered in the company's register of charges and that this will constitute notice to any person who is taking a charge which also has to be registered. A reform to enable this to be done was introduced by the Companies Act 1989,[87] but never implemented, and now CA 2006 s.1180 repeals Part IV of the Companies Act 1989.

Finally, in *Cheah v Equiticorp Finance Group Ltd*,[88] Lord Browne-Wilkinson made it clear that where there were two charges over the same property, the chargees could agree to alter the priority of their security interests without the consent of the debtor. These types of subordination agreements are recognised in other jurisdictions too. For example, UCC Article 9 allows a secured party to give up its priority voluntarily, or by way of a contractual arrangement. Indeed Art.9–339 expressly validates subordination agreements.

Statutory limitations on the floating charge

Certain statutory provisions add further to the vulnerability of the floating charge. These provisions relate to (i) preferential creditors—which affects the priority of the charge; (ii) defective floating charges—which affects the validity of the charge; (iii) the right of an administrator to override a floating charge—which affects the enforcement rights of the charge; (iv) costs of the liquidation—which diminishes the assets available for the floating charge holders. These matters are dealt with in turn.

32–12

(i) Preferential creditors

The general rule on insolvency is that pre-insolvency rights are respected, and the company's unsecured creditors share the losses *pari passu*. However, this general rule has been varied by statute, giving certain classes of creditors added protection[89] by according them a statutory preference over some or all of the company's

32–13

---

[86] *Connolly Bros Ltd (No.2), Re* [1912] 2 Ch.25, CA; *Abbey National Building Society v Cann* [1991] 1 A.C. 56, HL. This directly addresses the issue of priority but does not, however, deal with the separate issue of registration and hence voidness. It is submitted that there is a sufficient degree of involvement by the company so as to make the charge one "created" by it and thus void for non-registration if not registered within 21 days of its creation: see *Tatung (UK) Ltd v Galex Telesure Ltd* (1989) 5 B.C.C. 325, at p.327 *et seq.*; *Stroud Architectural Systems Ltd v John Laing Constructions Ltd* [1994] 2 B.C.L.C. 276.

[87] CA 1989 s.103 inserting s.415(2)(a) into the Companies Act 1985.

[88] [1992] 1 A.C. 472.

[89] The same policy decisions have to be made with respect to bankruptcy: see, e.g. Insolvency Act 1986, s.336 dealing with the matrimonial home.

creditors. Perhaps surprisingly, the enforcement of a floating charge is to some extent treated as an insolvency proceeding whether or not the company is in the course of being wound up,[90] and these preferential creditors are given a similar priority out of the pool of floating charge assets (although only to the extent that the general assets of the company are insufficient to meet their claims).[91] To this extent, floating charge holders are treated a little like unsecured creditors (whose repayments are deferred in this way on the company's insolvency) rather than like other secured creditors with mortgages or fixed charges (who are entitled to realise the secured assets outside this insolvency regime).

There are various reasons supporting the adoption of this policy. It had been a strong criticism of the Cork Committee that banks, through a combination of fixed and floating charges, could scoop the asset pool and, in many cases, leave unsecured creditors with nothing in an insolvency. In addition, as already pointed out, some large-scale debt-financing arrangements are structured so that the ranks of debenture-holders (with floating charge security) closely resemble shareholders, forming a class that is interested in the company rather than merely one with claims against it. Consequently, it has been thought unjust that they should obtain priority over employees (one of the categories of preferential creditor) who have priority over the shareholders in the event of the company's liquidation.[92]

The preferential debts of the employees are set out in Sch.6 to the Insolvency Act 1986 and include four months' wages up to £800 per employee and accrued holiday remuneration.[93] In the case of a floating charge, the relevant date for quantifying the preferential debts is the date of the appointment of the receiver by the debenture-holders.[94] Anyone who has advanced money for the payment of the

---

[90] e.g. the enforcement of the floating charge is dealt with in Pt III of the Insolvency Act 1986; administrative receivers have to be qualified insolvency practitioners (s.230(2)); and s.247(1) defines insolvency as including the appointment of an administrative receiver. IA 1986, ss.40, 175, 386–387 and Sch.6, and CA 2006, s.754 are the most relevant for the subordination of the floating charge. For the ability of these provisions to reach through earlier contractual engagements, see *Oval 1742 Ltd (in CVA) v Royal Bank of Scotland Plc, Re* [2007] EWCA Civ 1262. Of course, if realisation of the security and application of the priority rules leaves the chargee carrying a loss, the floating chargee then ranks with the other unsecured creditors to the extent of any outstanding debts.

[91] IA 1986, s.175(2)(b).

[92] Another argument made in favour of employees is that they have no way of obtaining security for the payment of their salary which is normally made after the provision of the services. This is not strictly correct since money to pay employees could be placed in a trust account to be paid on the appropriate date. But this would be cumbersome and as a matter of practice does not happen.

[93] See IA 1986, Sch.6, paras 9 and 10. Para.8 brings in contributions to occupational pension schemes.

[94] IA 1986, s.387(4)(a). For the date of the appointment see IA 1986, s.33.

employee debts which would have been preferential is subrogated to the rights of the employee.[95] It is important to note that the preferential creditors are given priority where a receiver is appointed with respect to a charge "which, as created, was a floating charge";[96] thus the fact that the charge has crystallised at the time a receiver is appointed does not result in preferential debts being denied their statutory priority.[97]

Employees have other protections. Where the company becomes **32-14** insolvent, an alternative and speedier route for the employee to recover monies due is by way of application to the Secretary of State. Under Pt XII of the Employment Rights Act 1996, the Secretary of State is obliged to pay certain amounts due and then is subrogated to the employee's position in the employer's insolvency, including the employee's preferential rights, in so far as the debts discharged would have preferential status against the company.[98] This provision and its associated priority have remained, despite the more recent abolition of Crown priorities in the Enterprise Act 2002 (see below). In practice, the National Insurance Fund is probably the main beneficiary from this preference.

Prior to 2002, there were other preferential creditors on the statutory list, but these have now been all but eliminated by the Enterprise Act 2002. This Act went even further than the Cork Committee's recommendations for abolition of Crown preferences in respect of taxes owed by the company other than those where the company merely acted as a tax collector (such as PAYE income tax and social security contributions due from employees, and VAT), on the grounds that creditors had no right to expect that companies would be financed by such sources.[99] This policy was implemented by the IA 1986, but the Enterprise Act 2002 s.251 now abolishes Crown preferences entirely, leaving only employee remuneration and contributions to pension schemes with a preference in insolvency, together with the narrow case of levies on coal and steel production, derived from EU law, which the United Kingdom is not free to repeal.

---

[95] IA 1986, Sch.6, para.11. This enables the company to be kept going where it is in financial difficulties but there is some chance that it can trade out of its difficulties. For case law on the previous statutory provisions see *Primrose (Builders) Ltd, Re* [1950] Ch. 561; *Rutherford (James R) & Sons Ltd, Re* [1964] 1 W.L.R. 1211; *Rampgill Mill Ltd, Re* [1967] Ch. 1138.

[96] IA 1986, s.40(1).

[97] Under the old law the crystallisation of the charge prior to the appointment of a receiver resulted in the preferential creditors being denied their priority: see *Brightlife Ltd, Re* [1987] Ch. 200. This alteration of the old law has made automatic crystallisation clauses less attractive.

[98] Employment Rights Act 1996, s.189. The Pt XII rights of the employee as against the Secretary of State are in some respects wider and some respects narrower than the preferences accorded by the Insolvency Act against the company. Theoretically, the employee might want to pursue the preferential claim against the company in so far as it does not fall within Pt XII.

[99] See above, fn.91.

Employees are not the only preferential creditors to eat into the assets available to the floating chargee, however. There is now provision for limited priority to general unsecured creditors. The Cork Committee had proposed the introduction of a "Ten Per Cent Fund", whereby that percentage of the funds which would otherwise be paid to the floating charge holder should be set aside to meet the claims of the unsecured creditors.[100] This idea was not taken up at the time, but the Enterprise Act 2002 s.252 has now adopted another version of it. It amended IA 1986, inserting s.176A, which came into force on September 15, 2003, and which requires that when the assets of a company subject to a floating charge are realised, a certain proportion must be set aside for the unsecured creditors.[101] The percentage is defined as follows:[102] (i) 50 percent of the first £10,000; plus (ii) 20 percent of the remainder; up to a maximum of £600,000.[103] The rule does not apply where (i) the company's net property is less than £10,000;[104] or (ii) the costs of distribution to unsecured creditors would be disproportionate and the court makes an order accordingly.[105] These provisions are now collectively referred to as the ring-fencing provisions of the IA 1986.

32–15   These rules may affect companies other than those registered under the Act if, but only if, they are being wound up under it.[106]

None of these statutory incursions alter the fact that the first payments to come out of the floating charge realisations are the costs and expenses of liquidation (if the company goes into liquidation),[107] then the costs and expenses of receivership,[108] and only then the preferential creditors, finally leaving a pool (if the parties are lucky) that is split between the floating chargee and the unsecured creditors according to the formula outlined above.

The position of fixed charge holders is quite different. Their asset pool is not subjected to claims from liquidators to fund liquidation expenses, nor from preferential or unsecured creditors. Any change to these rules would obviously affect both the terms of credit and the amount of credit available to chargors, but it is not clear that this adequately or rationally justifies the present position.

---

[100] See above, fn.24, paras 1538–1549.
[101] Which category does not include the charge holder in relation to that part of the debt which has not been satisfied by the security, unless the unsecured debts have been fully met: IA 1986, s.176A(2).
[102] Insolvency (Prescribed Part) Order 2003 (SI 2003/2097).
[103] It is possible to vary this rule by means of a voluntary arrangement: IA 1986, s.176A(4).
[104] IA 1986, s.176A(3)(a), SI 2003/2097, art.2.
[105] IA 1986, s.176A(3)(b) and (5).
[106] i.e. a floating chargee who appoints a receiver of a statutory or chartered company will not be subject to the claims of preferential creditors unless the company goes into compulsory liquidation under Pt V of the 1986 Act.
[107] See below, para.32–19.
[108] See below, para.32–19.

(ii) Defective floating charges

An unsecured creditor with advance notice that insolvent liquidation **32–16**
is imminent may well be tempted to seek security to cover the outstanding obligation, thereby obtaining priority over the other unsecured creditors. Directors, perhaps more than most, are likely to have
early warning of such danger in repayment of their own unsecured
loans.[109] And the only security likely to be available when the company is distressed is a floating charge security—the company's fixed
assets will usually have been secured much earlier.

To prevent this, s.245 of the Insolvency Act 1986[110] provides that a
floating charge created in favour of an unconnected person within 12
months[111] of the commencement of the winding-up or the making of
an administration order[112] shall be invalid (except to a prescribed
extent) unless it is proved that the company was solvent immediately
after the creation of the charge.[113] If these conditions are not satisfied
the charge is valid only to the extent of any new value in the form of
cash, goods or services supplied to the company,[114] or the discharge of
any liability of the company, where these take place "at the same time
as, or after, the creation of the charge".[115] It has been held that the
phrase in quotations requires the new value to be provided con-
temporaneously with the creation of the charge.[116] Any delay, no
matter how short, in the execution of the debenture after the advance
has been made will result in the new value falling outside s.245.[117]
Hence those who take a floating charge from a company which
cannot be proved to be solvent,[118] and which does not survive for a
further year, cannot thereby obtain protection in respect to their

---

[109] In some cases the company has been deliberately floated with the intention of defrauding
creditors by granting floating charges to the promoters and then winding up, the charge
attaching to goods which the company has purchased on credit: see Cohen Report, Cmnd.
6659, para.148.
[110] This applies to Scotland: IA 1986, s.245(1).
[111] The period was three months in the 1908 Act and six months in the 1929 Act: each was
found to be inadequate in view of the ingenuity displayed in staving off liquidation.
[112] IA 1986, s.245(3)(b) and (5).
[113] The test of solvency is that laid down in s.123 of the 1986 Act: IA 1986, s.245(4).
[114] The value of the goods or services is their market value: IA 1986, s.245(6).
[115] IA 1986, s.245(2)(a) and (b).
[116] *Power v Sharpe Investments Ltd* [1994] 1 B.C.L.C. 111.
[117] *Power v Sharpe Investments Ltd*, at p.123a–b. If the delay is *de minimis*, for example, a
coffee-break, it can be ignored: *ibid*. The inconvenience of this can be avoided by the parties
creating a present equitable right to security rather than a promise to create security in the
future: see *Jackson & Bassford, Re* [1906] 2 Ch. 467.
[118] There is nothing in the section to displace the normal rule that he who asserts must prove
and thus the burden of proof would be on the liquidator or administrator. This should cause
no great hardship as they will normally have sufficient information to found their action.

existing debts, but only to the extent that they provide the company with new value[119] and thus potentially increase the assets available for other creditors.

Where the floating charge is in favour of a "connected person", the rules are even more restrictive: the charge is vulnerable for two years after its creation,[120] and there is no need to show that at the time the charge was created the company was insolvent. The definition of connected person is complex, but includes a director, the director's relatives, and companies within a group.[121]

32–17   These provisions cannot be avoided by sleight of hand, for example by advancing further money on a floating charge on the under-standing that this is to be used to repay existing loans specifically to the connected or unconnected person: a creditor cannot by use of the floating charge transmute an unsecured debt into a secured debt by manipulating the saving provisions of s.245.[122] In addition, it is important to note that not all value is "new value" for the purpose of s.245 as the latter is confined to money, goods or services and excluded are, for example, intellectual property rights and rights under a contract.[123]

These rules apply to floating charges and not to fixed charges. The policy justification for this has been questioned. The Cork Committee considered that these rules should not be extended to fixed charges since such charges would relate to the company's existing assets, whereas the floating charge could cover future assets.[124] This dis-tinction is not in fact true,[125] but why it should make a critical dif-ference in any event is far from clear. The exclusion of fixed charges from IA 1986 s.245 arguably reflects the favouritism shown to secured creditors in English company law. A fixed charge may of

---

[119] For interesting illustrations of the way in which the rule in *Clayton*'s case ((1816) 1 Mer. 572) may protect a bank when the charge secures a current account, see *Thomas Mortimer Ltd, Re* (1925) now reported at [1965] Ch. 186n; *Yeovil Glove Co Ltd, Re* [1965] Ch. 148, CA. The Cork Committee recommended that *Yeovil Glove Co Ltd, Re* be reversed by statute (paras 1561–1562) but why this should be so is far from clear since the bank by permitting the company to continue to draw on its overdrawn account is providing it with new value: see Goode (1983) 4 Co.L. 81.

[120] s.245(3)(a).

[121] See ss.249 and 435 of the 1986 Act.

[122] *Destone Fabrics Ltd, Re* [1941] Ch. 319 (this would now be a transaction with a connected person, on which see below); *GT Whyte & Co Ltd, Re* [1983] B.C.L.C. 311. It is submitted that the transactions in these cases would not fall within s.245(2)(b) as there would be no discharge as a matter of substance of the debts at the time of the creation of the charge. Contrast *Mathew Ellis Ltd, Re* [1933] Ch. 458, CA. The test seems to be whether the company receives what is genuinely new value.

[123] See Goode, *Principles of Corporate Insolvency Law* (3rd ed., London) at p.181.

[124] Cmnd. 8558 at paras 1494 and 1553. The other reason given was that the extension of IA 1986, s.245 to fixed charges would compel creditors to seek repayment if fixed security could not be granted. This argument could also be applied to obtaining a floating charge.

[125] A company can create a fixed charge of accounts receivables, or a mortgage of future property, for example. The critical distinction between a fixed and a floating charge is that assets can be removed from the latter, and not from the former, without the specific consent of the chargee. Whether assets can be added (or not) is immaterial to the characterisation of the charge, and possible with both forms of charge: see below, paras 32–20—32–21.

course be attacked as a preference where it is given to secure past value,[126] although not as a transaction at an undervalue since the assets of the company are not diminished by the creation of the charge.[127]

(iii) Powers of administrator

The third statutory limitation on the right of a floating charge holder is para.70 of Sch.B1 to the Insolvency Act 1986 which empowers an administrator to sell property subject to a charge which as created was a floating charge without the need to obtain a court order.[128] As protection, the floating charge holder is given the same priority with respect to any property representing directly or indirectly the property disposed of as he would have had with respect to the property subject to the floating charge.[129]

32–18

(iv) Costs of liquidation

Chargees expect the expenses of their own receivership proceedings to be paid in priority to their secured debt, on the basis that the person "who has actually produced the fund for distribution is to have his costs of producing it paid in priority."[130] Indeed, on the same rationale, these receivership expenses also rank ahead of the debts due to preferential creditors (see (i) above).[131] But floating charge realisations are also subject to an unexpected additional claim: if the company goes into liquidation, the total costs of the liquidation (to the extent that they cannot be paid out of the company's general assets) constitute a claim on floating charge receipts in priority even to the receivership expenses.[132] This can be a substantial drain on the funds eventually available to the floating chargee.

32–19

This decision that liquidation expenses constitute a prior claim on floating charge receipts (but not on fixed charge receipts) was first reached by the Court of Appeal in *Barleycorn Enterprises Ltd, Re*[133]

---

[126] One important difference between the rules relating to preferences and to defective floating charges is that the time within which a preference in favour of an unconnected person can be challenged is six months (not 12 months). Also note that a preference will involve a diminution in the company's assets (giving one creditor a preference in repayment), whereas a floating charge constitutes a preferential claim on them.

[127] *MC Bacon Ltd, Re* [1990] B.C.L.C. 324.

[128] IA 1986, s.15(1) and (3).

[129] Where the charge has crystallised, the priority will be that of a fixed equitable charge.

[130] *Batten v Wedgwood Coal and Iron Co* (1884) 28 Ch.D. 317.

[131] A receiver has a duty not to incur expenses if to do so would lessen the amount otherwise available to pay the preferential creditors: *Woods v Winskill* [1913] 2 Ch. 303; *Westminster Corp v Haste* [1950] Ch. 442, both cases concerning the expenses in carrying on the company's business.

[132] And to the extent that the floating chargee is unable to recoup the outstanding debt from the floating charge proceeds, that shortfall becomes an unsecured debt, repayable *pari passu* with all the other unsecured debts owed by the company.

[133] [1970] Ch. 465.

on the basis that such receipts were assets *of the company*, and it is a principle of insolvency law that the expenses of a company's liquidation are payable out of the assets of the company[134] in priority to all other claims.[135] This decision was overruled 35 years later by the House of Lords in *Buchler v Talbot* (also known as *Leyland Daf, Re*),[136] which held that liquidation expenses are not payable out of floating charge assets, those being the property of the chargee and not the chargor. The Government has, however, legislatively reversed this decision in CA 2006: CA 2006 s.1282 inserts s.176ZA into the Insolvency Act 1986, which reads:

> "the expenses of winding up in England and Wales, so far as the assets of the company available for payment of general creditors are insufficient to meet them, have priority over any claims to property comprised in or subject to any floating charge created by the company and shall be paid out of any such property accordingly."[137]

So the current position, now determined by statute, is that assets subject to a floating charge (i.e. assets subject to a charge that was created as a floating charge, even though it will have crystallised on liquidation) are available for payment of liquidation expenses.[138] Where several charges have been granted over the same asset, this rule can lead to nice questions about the priority as between the various charges: if the charge with first priority is a floating charge, then the proceeds are subject to claims for liquidation expenses, but if the first charge (or equal ranking charge) is a fixed charge, the fixed chargee can realise the charged assets without making any such provision (either for the liquidation expenses or for the preferential creditors). This outcome advantages those many creditors who typically take a "fixed and floating charge" over all the company's assets: to the extent that a fixed charge is possible, it ranks equally

---

[134] The assets must, however, be the assets of the company and not, for example, assets held on trust. In certain limited circumstances, however, the court may order liquidation expenses to be paid out of assets the beneficial interest in which is not vested in the company: e.g. *Berkeley Applegate (Investment Consultants) Ltd (No.3), Re* [1989] 5 B.C.C. 803, where the activities and efforts of the liquidator were essential in establishing and preserving the rights of the trust beneficiaries, and to that extent (only) his fees were payable out of the trust assets.

[135] For voluntary winding up see IA 1986, s.115; this section has been held to be a priority section and does not deal with the question of what constitute properly incurred expenses in a liquidation: see *MC Bacon Ltd, Re* [1991] Ch. 127. The position as regards court-ordered winding up is not so explicit but a combination of s.156 and Insolvency Rules 1986, rr.4.218 and 4.220 produces this effect.

[136] [2004] 2 A.C. 298.

[137] See Look Chan Ho, "Reversing *Buchler v Talbot*—The Doctrinal Dimension of Liquidation Expenses Priority" (2006) 3 JIBFL 104. Note that IA 1986, s.176ZA(3) may allow these expenses to be restricted to expenses either approved by the chargee and preferential creditors, or by the court.

[138] It remains to be seen how these rules on expenses are translated into regulations.

with the floating charge and is protected from these expenses.[139] On the other hand, if the charge with priority is a floating charge, even if priority was gained by crystallisation, then the assets are subject to these rules relating to liquidation expenses and preferential debts.[140] These costs, combined with the claims of the preferential creditors, entail a substantial erosion of the entitlement of the floating charge holder.[141]

Distinguishing between fixed and floating charges

The previous sections (on priority, preference and invalidity rules) **32–20** demonstrate why chargees prefer to have fixed rather than floating security over the assets of a corporate debtor. Prior to 1986, it was possible to achieve this status simply by showing that the charge had crystallised (and thereby become a *fixed* charge) before the commencement of the liquidation or other relevant statutory date.[142] This loophole was eliminated by IA 1986, s.251, which provides that "floating charge" means "a charge which, *as created*, was a floating charge". This means that lenders must now ensure that their security, as created, is categorised as a fixed charge, not a floating charge, if they are to avoid the disadvantages outlined earlier.

Given the consequences that follow the categorisation of a charge as fixed or floating, the courts do not simply accept the labels attached by the parties. The fact that a charge is called a "fixed" charge by the parties does not necessarily make it so. As Lord Millet indicated in the Privy Council decision, *Agnew v Commissioner for Inland Revenue* (also known as *Brumark, Re*):[143]

> "in deciding whether a charge is a fixed charge or a floating charge, the court is engaged in a two-stage process. At the first

---

[139] *Lewis Merthyr Consolidated Collieries Ltd, Re* [1929] 1 Ch. 498; *GL Saunders Ltd, Re* [1986] 1 W.L.R. 215.

[140] *Portbase Clothing Ltd, Re* [1993] Ch. 388 at 407–409. A more difficult problem arises where the two successive charges are floating charges, the second one crystallises first and so has priority over the first, but the receiver is not appointed under the second charge but under the first one. *Griffiths v Yorkshire Bank Plc* [1994] 1 W.L.R. 1427 may be technically correct in deciding that since no receiver is appointed under the second charge, the assets are not subject to the claims of preferential creditors. But this leaves the way open for floating chargees to avoid the operation of these provisions, and so the more strained analysis in *H and K (Medway) Ltd, Re* [1997] 2 All E.R. 321, which concluded that the preferential debts had priority over both charges, may be preferable.

[141] Attempts to extend the *Portbase* principle decision have not been successful. In *MC Bacon Ltd, Re* [1991] Ch. 127 the court held that the costs of the liquidator in bringing an action under s.214 of the 1986 Act and to challenge a transaction as a preference were not costs of realising the company's assets and thus did not enjoy the priority accorded to such expenses in a winding-up.

[142] This was the case in *Brightlife Ltd, Re* [1987] Ch. 200, where the debenture-holder had given the company a notice converting the floating charge into a fixed charge a week before a resolution for voluntary winding up was passed. The court held that the preferential creditors no longer had any right to be paid in priority to the charge.

[143] [2001] 2 A.C. 710 (PC), para.[32].

stage it must construe the instrument of charge and seek to gather the intentions of the parties from the language they have used ... The object of this stage of the process ... is to ascertain the nature of the rights and obligations which the parties intended to grant to each other in respect of the charged assets. Once these have been ascertained, the court can then embark on the second stage of the process, which is one of categorization, [which] is a matter of law."

In *Spectrum Plus Ltd, Re*,[144] the House of Lords approved this approach and held that in characterising a charge as fixed or floating, the crucial element is the freedom of the company to use the assets in the ordinary course of its business, not the nature of the assets charged.[145] The House of Lords had to consider a charge over book debts expressed in the same terms as that in *Siebe Gorman*[146] (which had been accepted as a fixed charge: see below). In a decision that overruled *Siebe Gorman* and reversed the Court of Appeal below, the House of Lords held that the charge was floating. This was so, despite the fact that the debenture prohibited the chargor from charging or assigning the debts, and required it to pay the proceeds of collection of the debts into an account with the lending bank (i.e. despite following the recipe prescribed in *Siebe Gorman*), because the debenture did not go on to specify any restrictions on the chargor's operation of the account. This very restrictive definition of a fixed charge removes the element of judgment permitted by earlier cases: a charge is fixed if and only if the chargor is legally obliged to preserve the charged assets, or their permitted substitutes, for the benefit of the chargee. In all other cases, the charge is floating and therefore subject to the disadvantageous statutory regime already described.[147]

32–21 The change effected by this approach can be seen most clearly by comparing earlier decisions. The easy cases remain easy. Suppose the charge holder is a bank with a charge over a company's book debts: if use of the proceeds of the book debts is not controlled at all, then the charge is floating;[148] and if use of the proceeds is completely restricted, then the charge is fixed.[149] But if neither the freedom nor the control is absolute, then a judgment used to be required. In *Siebe*

---

[144] [2005] 2 A.C. 680. Also see *Armagh Shoes Ltd, Re* [1984] B.C.L.C. 405, Ch.D. (NI).
[145] Thus clarifying the relevance of the description of a floating charge advanced by Romer L.J. in *Yorkshire Woolcombers Association Ltd, Re* [1903] 2 Ch. 284, at p.295 (see above, para.32–5).
[146] *Siebe Gorman & Co Ltd v Barclays Bank Ltd* [1979] 2 Lloyd's Rep.142.
[147] Worthington, "An 'Unsatisfactory Area of the Law'—Fixed and Floating Charges Yet Again" (2004) 1 *International Corporate Rescue* 175–184 (adopted by the House of Lords in *Spectrum*), and "Floating Charges: Use and Abuse of Doctrinal Analysis", in Getzler and Payne, *op. cit.* p.28.
[148] *Brightlife Ltd, Re* [1987] Ch. 200, although in this case the chargee was not itself a bank.
[149] *Keenan Bros Ltd, Re* [1986] B.C.L.C. 242, where the chargee bank stipulated that the account could not be drawn against without the counter-signature of one of its officers.

Gorman & Co Ltd v Barclays Bank Ltd,[150] Slade J. (as he then was) held that a debenture over the borrower's book debts and its proceeds was correctly classified by the parties as a fixed charge. The charge agreement provided that the company could not assign or charge the secured book debts, and that the proceeds of the debts had to be paid into a designated bank account with the lending bank, although the chargor was then free to use the funds in the account.[151] On the basis of Slade J.'s decision, this form of debenture became a precedent and was widely used by most banks. The mere fact that the assets sought to be charged were a fluctuating class of present and future assets was not by itself a fatal objection to the creation of a fixed charge.[152] This decision has now been overruled by *Spectrum*.

In *New Bullas Trading Ltd, Re*,[153] the agreement provided for a fixed charge over the book debts while they remained uncollected, but, when collected and paid into a designated account (unless written instructions to the contrary were given by the chargee), the monies so received were released from the fixed charge and became subject to a floating charge. No directions were ever given. The Court of Appeal, reversing Knox J., held that the parties were contractually able to reach such an agreement, and the arrangement constituted a fixed charge over the (uncollected) book debts, and a floating charge over their (collected) proceeds in the bank account. This case, too, was overruled by the House of Lords in *Spectrum* on the basis that, since the chargor was free to deal with the charged assets (the book debts), *or their proceeds*, for its own benefit and without the consent or interference of the chargee, the charge over the book debts was therefore floating.

The restriction on the chargor's ability to deal with the assets must be legally binding. In *Royal Trust Bank v National Westminster Bank Plc*,[154] for example, an instrument creating a charge over book debts gave the chargee bank the *right* to demand that the company should open a dedicated account and pay all monies received on the collection of the debts into that account, but the bank never exercised this right, and in practice monies collected went into the company's ordinary trading account. The charge was held by Millett L.J. to be floating.[155] Similarly, in *Double S Printers Ltd, Re*,[156] the chargee, as a director of the company, had de facto control over the proceeds of

---

[150] [1979] 2 Lloyd's Rep.142.

[151] On this last point, Slade J. may have interpreted the arrangement otherwise, assuming the bank was required to give permission for each release of funds; on that basis the decision was accepted in *Agnew*, but, on the contrary interpretation, was overruled in *Spectrum*.

[152] Of course, in many cases, the fluctuating nature of the assets, especially of physical assets, means that managerial control of them can be given to the company only in a way which is inconsistent with a fixed charge: *Smith v Bridgend CBC* [2002] 1 A.C. 336.

[153] [1994] 1 B.C.L.C. 485, CA.

[154] [1996] 2 B.C.L.C. 699, CA.

[155] All three members of the court concurred in the result; Nourse L.J. on other grounds, and Swinford Thomas L.J. without giving reasons.

[156] [1999] 1 B.C.L.C. 220.

the charged book debts since he had actual control of the bank account, but this was not backed by any contractual restraint on their disposal in the instrument itself. As in the *Royal Trust Bank* case, it was held that the company's freedom (at least in law) to deal led to the conclusion that the charge was floating. And a legally binding arrangement to create a fixed charge that is in fact ignored by the parties, who operate as if the charge is floating, will be treated by the courts as a sham.[157]

REGISTRATION OF CHARGES

The purpose of a registration system

32–22 Part 25 of the Companies Act 2006 contains provisions requiring a company to register particular details in relation to certain charges with the Registrar of Companies.[158] These provisions are not confined to floating charges, although those charges are included.[159] This requirement has been a feature of the Companies Acts since 1900. What are the possible purposes of such a registration requirement?

First, and most obvious, the aim might be to give potential lenders to the company more accurate information about the company's apparent wealth by revealing the true extent of any earlier secured lending[160] that may rank ahead of their own contemplated advances. Such information may also be of interest to credit analysts, insolvency practitioners appointed upon the company's insolvency, shareholders and investors. Secondly (and for reasons aligned with the first objective), registration might be treated as an essential part of the process whereby a person obtains a security interest against the company. Without registration, the security interest would be void, and could not be relied upon as against the unsecured creditors of the company in the latter's insolvency.[161] The usual terminology is that registration is necessary for the "perfection" of the security. Thirdly, registration might determine priority among secured creditors. For

---

[157] *Agnew v CIR* [2001] 2 A.C. 710.

[158] The provisions of the 2006 Act relating to company charges are scheduled to come into force on October 1, 2009. In addition to the registration of charges at Companies House, CA 2006 s.876(1)(b) requires the company itself to keep a register of the charges on its undertaking and property: see below, para.32–24.

[159] CA 2006, s.860(7)(g).

[160] Registration for this purpose is confined to registration of non-possessory securities. An obligation secured by a possessory security necessarily entails transfer of the secured asset into the possession of the security-holder, so that it does not remain on site as part of the "apparent wealth" of the borrowing company.

[161] This rule does not avoid the underlying obligation, and if the loan fell for repayment whilst the company was a going concern, for example, then it could simply be repaid by the company without any question of enforcement of a security arising. The problem arises on insolvency, when the protection of a security interest is most needed.

example, priorities among secured creditors could be determined simply by the date of the registration of the security (and not, for example, by reference to the date of creation of the security, or by whether the later taker of a security knew of the earlier one): such a system is generally referred to as a system of "notice filing".

As the law currently stands (with CA 2006 introducing few significant changes to Pt XII of CA 1985), none of these objectives is delivered. The first fails, since not all security interests need to be registered: CA 2006 s.860(7) provides a list of the types of charges[162] that must be registered, but any others, including all quasi-securities,[163] need not be registered. The second fails for the same reason of limited application, although within that limited range any charges that ought to be registered, but are not, are void as against the liquidator, administrator and any creditor.[164] And the third fails, as this is simply not part of the rules of the current system: instead, if the security is valid (including properly registered, if it needs to be), then priority is judged according to the usual common law rules, generally based on the time of creation, the type of interest created, and the notice to subsequent security holders.

What is remarkable about this area of law is that proposals for radical change have been made by highly respected official bodies for over 35 years, but no change, of either a radical or a tinkering kind, has been put in place.[165] Radical change was proposed by the Crowther Committee[166] in 1971, endorsed by the Cork Committee[167] in 1983 and re-proposed by Professor Diamond in 1989.[168] The CLR began in tinkering mood,[169] partly because consultation on the previous radical proposals had not produced an enthusiastic response, but concluded by advocating radical reform.[170] In this positive spirit, the issue was handed over to the Law Commission,[171] which produced a consultation paper and a "consultative report", both favouring radical change, proposing a comprehensive scheme of notice-filing and associated priority rules that would extend to all securities and quasi-securities, whether granted by companies, unincorporated businesses or individuals.[172] Despite the early support, further con-

32–23

---

[162] Where "charge" includes "mortgage": CA 2006 s.861(5).

[163] For example, retention of title agreements or *Quistclose* trusts, both of which leave the debtor company with the appearance of greater unencumbered wealth than is the reality.

[164] CA 2006, s.874, and see the discussion below at paras 32–27.

[165] Some tinkering reform was included in the Companies Act 1989, but never brought into force. These provisions have been repealed by CA 2006, Schedule 16.

[166] *The Report of the Committee on Consumer Credit*, Cmnd. 5427 (1971).

[167] Insolvency Law and Practice, Cmnd. 8558 (1982).

[168] *A Review of Security Interests in Property*, HMSO (1989).

[169] CLR, *Registration of Company Charges*, (October 2000) URN 00/1213.

[170] Final Report I, Ch.12.

[171] Reference was also made to the Scottish Law Commission, but in narrower terms: now see *Report on Registration of Rights in Security by Companies* (Scot Law Com No 197, 2004).

[172] Law Commission, *Registration of Security Interests: Company Charges and Property other than Land*, Consultation Paper 164 (2002); *Company Security Interests: A Consultative Report* (Law Com Consultation Paper No 176, August 2004).

sultation on this detailed proposal produced a more cautious response, and the Law Commission's final Report on Company Security Interests in 2005 recommended a less radical scheme, preserving its recommended notice-filing and priority rules for charges and outright sales of receivables, but not including quasi-securities nor, yet, unincorporated debtors.[173]

Even this scaled-down proposal seems unlikely to see the light of day, although no decision to that effect has been announced. New legislation must now be preceded by a Regulatory Impact Assessment. In July 2005, the Department of Trade and Industry (the predecessor to the Department of Business, Enterprise and Regulatory Reform) considered the recommendations of both Law Commissions (England and Wales, and Scotland), and published a consultation document.[174] It set out three options for England and Wales: no change to the current regime; implementation of the Law Commission's recommendations; or implementation of the CLR's alternative, more limited, proposals[175] supplemented by some of the Law Commission's proposals.[176]

The end result is to leave the UK with a system that is quite unlike those now operating in other Anglo-American legal systems. No major or minor changes were implemented in CA 2006, which merely renumbers and changes the order of the provisions that appeared in CA 1985. The Secretary of State is also given new special powers to make orders for three defined purposes,[177] but these would not cover radical reform in this area. The alternatives that had been proposed are considered in a little more detail below,[178] but first the existing rules are outlined.

The current system
The mechanics of registration

32–24 CA 2006 requires certain types of corporate security interests to be registered at Companies House, and also to be registered on a register maintained by the company itself. The first of these requirements is the more significant one. CA 2006 s.860(1)[179] requires prescribed

---

[173] Law Commission, *Company Security Interests* (Law Com No 296, Cm 6654, August 2005), especially paras 1.31, 1.46–1.57, and 1.60–1.66.
[174] DTI, *The Registration of Companies' Security Interests (Company Charges): The Economic Impact of the Law Commissions' Proposals* ("DTI, RIA") (July 2005), *http://www.dti.gov.uk/ files/file13994.pdf*.
[175] CLR, Final Report I, Ch.12, paras 12.70–12.83.
[176] DTI, RIA, *op. cit.*, paras 3.1–3.3.4.
[177] CA 2006, ss.893 and 894. Also see Hansard HL, vol. 686, col. 480–481 (November 2, 2006), on the limited use expected to be made of the power in s.894.
[178] See below, paras 32–31—32–34.
[179] CA 2006 ss.878ff make separate provisions in substantially the same terms for companies registered in Scotland.

particulars of registrable[180] charges to be delivered to Companies House, together with the instrument (if any) by which the charge is created or evidenced, within 21 days.[181] Failure to comply with this requirement is an offence,[182] and also renders the security void against the liquidator, administrator and other creditors.[183] CA 2006 s.862 also requires a company to register charges already existing over property that it subsequently acquires; failure to do this is an offence, but does not render the security invalid.[184]

It is the debtor company's duty to submit these particulars to the Registrar,[185] although registration may be effected by any person interested in the charge,[186] and is normally effected by the chargee. Failure to register as required is an offence committed by the debtor company and every officer in default.[187] The Registrar is in turn under a statutory obligation to maintain a register setting out certain prescribed particulars, and to provide a certificate of registration.[188] The register of charges is open for public inspection, for a fee.[189] Once it is proved that the secured obligation has been satisfied in whole or in part, the Registrar can enter a memorandum of satisfaction to that effect on the register.[190]

In addition to this registration at Companies House, the company itself must keep a register of *all* charges created by the company[191] on its undertaking and property.[192] This register is thus more comprehensive than the register at Companies House. This register must contain an entry for each charge giving a short description of the property charged, the amount of the charge and the name of the persons entitled to it.[193] Failure to comply with these provisions may lead to the imposition of a fine,[194] but the omission does not affect the validity of the charge in any way.[195]

---

[180] See below, para.32–25. The list of registrable charges appears in CA 2006 s.860(7); also see ss.861–865.
[181] CA 2006 s.870 allows 21 days, subject to extension under *ibid.* s.873. See below, para.32–28.
[182] CA 2006 s.860.
[183] CA 2006 s.874.
[184] CA 2006 ss.862, 874.
[185] CA 2006 s.860.
[186] CA 2006 s.860(2).
[187] CA 2006 s.860(4) and (5).
[188] CA 2006 s.869.
[189] CA 2006 s.869(7). Note that inspection of the register will not necessarily reveal all valid charges existing at the time of inspection, because of the 21 days allowed for registration. This is often called the "21-day invisibility problem".
[190] CA 2006 s.872.
[191] So excluding charges described in CA 2006 s.862.
[192] CA 2006 s.876(1)(b).
[193] CA 2006 s.876(2).
[194] CA 2006 s.876(3) and (4).
[195] *Wright v Horton* (1887) 12 App.Cas.371.

What has to be registered

32–25 CA 2006 s.860(7) sets out the charges which, if created by a company, must be registered. Since failure to register such charges means they will be void against the liquidator, administrator and other creditors,[196] there are frequent arguments after the event about whether the charge was one that required registration.[197]

First, a charge that is not created by the company is valid even if not registered (unless it is an existing charge on property acquired by the company[198]). This means that proprietary interests that arise by operation of law (e.g. solicitor's liens, or vendor's liens), rather than consensually, do not need to be registered.[199]

Secondly, an interest that is not an interest by way of charge (which includes a mortgage[200]) need not be registered. This means that interests such as contractual liens,[201] and, at least arguably, liens on sub-freights,[202] do not need to be registered. The position with charge-backs[203] remains unclear, but it seems these should be registered.[204] The more difficult cases are those where the agreement itself does not clearly distinguish between an unregistrable outright sale of property and a registrable mortgage of the same property,[205] or between an unregistrable assignment of the proceeds of a book debt and a registrable charge over them.[206]

Finally, even if the interest is created by the company, and is a

---

[196] CA 2006 s.874.
[197] Recall that CA 2006 s.862 also requires a company to register charges already existing over property that it subsequently acquires; failure to do this is an offence, but does not render the security invalid.
[198] CA 2006 s.862.
[199] *London and Cheshire Insurance Co Ltd v Laplagrene Property Co Ltd* [1971] Ch. 499.
[200] CA 2006 s.861(5).
[201] *Hamlet International Plc, Re* [1998] 2 B.C.L.C. 164.
[202] *Agnew v CIR* [2001] 2 A.C. 710, PC, *obiter*, disapproving Nourse J. in *Welsh Irish Ferries Ltd* [1986] Ch. 721, who had held the interest to be a registrable charge on book debts.
[203] A "charge-back" is an arrangement between a lending bank and its borrowing customer whereby the customer agrees that if a specific obligation is not met, then the bank can use the positive balance in the customer's account to meet the obligation and is relieved from its contractual obligation to repay the credit balance to the customer.
[204] The legal categorisation of these agreements is controversial. In *Charge Card Services Ltd, Re* [1987] Ch. 150, at p.175, Millett J. expressed the view that a charge in favour of X over X's own indebtedness to the chargor is conceptually impossible (so no registration is required). To the same effect, see Goode, (1998) 114 LQR 178. By contrast, in *BCCI SA (No.8), Re* [1998] A.C. 214, HL, Lord Hoffmann (*obiter*) thought these arrangements created a charge, but thought it unlikely that such a charge was registrable as charge over a "book debt". But see *Permanent Houses (Holdings) Ltd, Re* [1988] B.C.L.C. 563. The Registrar considers that a charge over a credit balance is registrable: (1985) 82 LS Gaz 2868. Lord Hoffmann did not consider whether the charge might in any event be registrable as a floating charge: see below.
[205] *Bond Worth Ltd, Re* [1980] Ch. 228, at p.248 (Slade J.); *Welsh Development Agency v Export Finance Co Ltd* [1992] B.C.L.C. 148, at p.161 (Dillon L.J.).
[206] *Siebe Gorman and Co Ltd v Barclays Bank Ltd* [1979] 2 Lloyd's Rep. 142 (example of irrevocable assignment by RH McDonald Ltd, rather than a charge). Also see all the retention of title cases where the seller of goods has attempted to create by contract an interest in the proceeds of the sale of those goods or their products; these have invariably been held to create registrable charges, not outright assignments: *Borden (UK) Ltd v Scottish Timber Products Ltd* [1981] Ch. 25.

charge or mortgage, it need not be registered unless it is one of the charges listed in CA 2006 s.860(7), as amplified by the succeeding sections. Clearly a charge on land,[207] a charge which if created by a person would need registration as a bill of sale,[208] a floating charge on the company's undertaking or property[209] and a charge on goodwill or intellectual property,[210] all have to be registered. So do charges over the company's "book debts",[211] although this is a term without any precise definition.[212] Registration is also required of charges over any property acquired by a company which, when acquired, is already subject to a charge of a class requiring registration.[213] On the other hand, charges over other *choses in action*, such as company shares, government stock, options, insurance contracts, and so on, are not registrable.

Geographical reach of these registration provisions
The provisions discussed here apply to charges created by companies **32–26** registered in England and Wales (Part 25, Chapter 1) or in Scotland (Part 25, Chapter 2), whether or not the charge is created in the UK, and whether or not the property being charged is located in the UK, although the particulars to be filed are fewer if the property is outside the UK, and the time limit for registration is extended if the charge is created outside the UK.[214]

Despite these requirements, if the secured property is located outside the UK, then the effectiveness of any security is likely to depend upon the property law rules applying within that jurisdiction, and not on whether the charge should have been registered in the UK.[215]

If the debtor company is not one that is registered in England, Wales or Scotland, then special rules apply. CA 2006 s.1052(1) gives the Secretary of State power to make regulations requiring registered overseas companies[216] (not unregistered ones) to register specified charges granted over any property in the UK. Draft regulations have

---

[207] CA 2006 s.860(7)(a) (excluded is a charge for rent or for the payment of some other periodical sum).
[208] CA 2006 s.860(7)(b).
[209] CA 2006 s.860(7)(g).
[210] CA 2006 s.860(7)(i).
[211] CA 2006 s.860(7)(f).
[212] A contingent debt is not a "book debt" until the contingency occurs. So a charge on a contingent debt before the contingency arises is not registrable (*Paul and Frank Ltd v Discount Bank (Overseas) Ltd* [1967] Ch. 348), although a charge on the proceeds payable under such a contingent contract *is* registrable as a charge on a future book debt (*Brush Aggregates Ltd, Re* [1983] B.C.L.C. 320).
[213] CA 2006 s.862(2).
[214] CA 2006 ss.866, 867, 870, 884, 886.
[215] Beale *et al*, *op. cit.*, paras 8.43–8.48.
[216] CA 2006 s.1046(1).

now been published.[217] These regulations effectively impose the same registration requirements on registered overseas companies, with the same invalidity consequences,[218] to the extent that the charged property is located in the UK[219] at the time the charge is created,[220] and provided it is still in the UK at the end of the 21-day registration period.[221] As the draft regulations currently stand, there is no requirement on an overseas company to register a charge created over property that is not in the UK at the time the charge is created, but is subsequently brought into the UK. Such an unregistered charge would therefore not fall foul of the invalidity provisions,[222] although nice priority problems might arise if the overseas company subsequently created additional securities over the property. These regulations clarify and simplify the rules that operated under the 1985 Act,[223] which applied to any overseas company with "an established place of business" in the UK, whether or not registered there, did not define the location of the property, and, as already noted, left unresolved the problems that arise when property is relocated.[224]

The effect of failure to register

32–27 Failure to comply with any of the various registration requirements mentioned above is an offence that attracts a fine.[225] More importantly, failure to register at Companies House any registrable charges *created* by the company (as opposed to existing charges on property acquired by the company) destroys the validity of the charge:[226] unless the prescribed particulars of the charge are delivered to the Registrar

---

[217] The Overseas Companies Regulations 2008 (Draft), Part 7 (see *http://www.berr.gov.uk/files/ file42859.doc*).

[218] The Overseas Companies Regulations 2008 (Draft), reg.62.

[219] The Overseas Companies Regulations 2008 (Draft), reg.59 defines where property is located.

[220] The Overseas Companies Regulations 2008 (Draft), reg.56(c).

[221] The Overseas Companies Regulations 2008 (Draft), regs 56, 57(4).

[222] Contrast this with the outcome under CA 1985, where the requirement to register was not limited to charges over property in the UK *at the time the charge was created*, so when charged property was subsequently brought into the UK, the charge was viewed as one that ought to have been registered within time, but was not, and was therefore invalid: see *NV Slavenburg's Bank v Intercontinental Natural Resources Ltd* [1980] 1 W.L.R. 1076, at p.1078–9 (Lloyd J.).

[223] CA 1985 s.409(1).

[224] *NV Slavenburg's Bank v Intercontinental Natural Resources Ltd* [1980] 1 W.L.R. 1076. This decision gave rise to the "Slavenburg register", which is a register of securities that would need to be registered if the overseas company were found to have a place of business in the UK. Companies House would record certain details on a separate register that could not be searched, and return the documentation to the company with a letter confirming that registration requirements had been complied with, and advising the company to keep the letter as evidence.

[225] CA 2006 ss.860, 862, 876, 878, 880, 891; The Overseas Companies Regulations 2008 (Draft), reg.57.

[226] CA 2006 ss.874, 889; The Overseas Companies Regulations 2008 (Draft), reg.62. More accurately, it is the failure to deliver particulars of the charge to the Registrar that results in the charge being rendered void but this will be referred to as non-registration. Non-registration in the company's own register has no such sanction.

within 21 days of the creation of the charge, it will be void against the administrator, liquidator or any creditor of the company.[227] The person disadvantaged is the chargee, not the company; hence the provision previously mentioned allowing any person having an interest in the charge to register it. If the company or the chargee fails to do so,[228] the consequences are grave: the chargee effectively loses the security. To reduce this hardship, the Act provides that if the charge is void to any extent for non-registration the whole of the sum thereby secured becomes immediately repayable on demand.[229] This, of course, also provides the company with an incentive to register. In addition, the unregistered charge is not void against the company (if still solvent), and there is nothing to prevent the chargee enforcing it (although often little advantage if the company is solvent).[230] An unsecured creditor has no standing to prevent the holder of an unregistered but registrable charge from enforcing it.[231]

Late registration

CA 2006 s.873(2) enables the holder of a registrable charge that has **32–28** not been registered within 21 days of its creation to apply to the court for an order extending the time for registration. This can be done if the court is satisfied that the failure to register was accidental or inadvertent and not likely to prejudice creditors or shareholders, or is satisfied on other grounds that such relief is just and equitable.[232] The jurisdiction of the court is very wide,[233] but the court will not normally make an order under s.873 once a winding-up has commenced.[234] This is because winding up is a procedure for the benefit of unsecured creditors, and registering a charge after the commencement of winding up would defeat their interests. The court may also refuse to exercise its discretion if the company is insolvent,[235] or if the

---

[227] CA 2006 s.874(1)(c). It is the security which is void, not the underlying obligation (CA 2006 s.874(3)), and so for this purpose, creditor means secured creditor: *Teleomatic Ltd, Re* [1994] 1 B.C.L.C. 90 at 95. Of course, if the company goes into liquidation or administration and the charge is unenforceable, this *pro tanto* protects the interests of the unsecured creditors: see *R. v Registrar of Companies, ex p. Central Bank of India* [1986] Q.B. 1114 at 1161–1162.

[228] This happens surprisingly often; e.g. because of failure to realise that the charge is of the registrable class, or because both the company and the lender assume that the other will register.

[229] CA 2006 s.874(3).

[230] If the chargee does so then the charge is spent and a liquidator or administrator cannot retrospectively challenge the enforcement of the charge.

[231] *Ehrmann Bros Ltd, Re* [1906] 2 Ch. 697, CA.

[232] CA 2006 s.873(1).

[233] CA 2006 s.873(2). However, the chargee, once the failure to register is discovered, must act expeditiously: the court will not exercise its discretion favourably where the chargee hangs back to see which way the wind blows: *Teleomatic Ltd, Re* [1994] 1 B.C.L.C. 30.

[234] *S Abrahams and Sons, Re* [1902] 1 Ch. 695. In exceptional circumstances, however, the court may make such an order: *RM Arnold & Co Ltd, Re* [1984] B.C.L.C. 535. See *Barclays Bank Plc v Stuart London Ltd* [2001] 2 B.C.L.C. 316, CA, for conditions imposed where liquidation was imminent.

[235] See *Ashpurton Estates Ltd, Re* [1983] Ch. 110.

company is in administration and it is inevitable that this will proceed to insolvent liquidation.[236]

If the court does exercise its discretion, the charge is normally registered on terms that it does not prejudice the secured rights acquired by third parties prior to the actual date of registration.[237] Since a charge does not become ineffective until the normal time limit has expired, this standard proviso only protects third parties acting between the date when the charge ought to have been registered and its actual registration.[238] Unsecured creditors are not protected by such a proviso, and are not part of the court's considerations.[239]

Defective registration

32–29 CA 2006 s.873(2), which allows applications in relation to late registration, also allows applications for rectification of omissions or misstatements in the registered particulars. The jurisdiction is defined in the same way (see above). The particulars may, for example, fail to state accurately the property subject to the charge or the amount secured by the charge.[240] Note that the court's power is limited to correcting omissions or misstatements within an entry. The court cannot order the removal of an entry,[241] nor can it order the removal of information that the company would prefer not to be there,[242] and nor does the court's jurisdiction extend to particulars which are not required to be registered.[243]

Effect of registration

32–30 Where a charge is registered, the Registrar has to issue a certificate of registration and this is made conclusive evidence that the requirements of CA 2006, Part 25, Chapter 1 have been complied with.[244] This provides assurance to any transferees of the security that the validity of its registration cannot be challenged. The conclusiveness of

---

[236] *Barrow Borough Transport Ltd, Re* [1990] Ch. 227.
[237] *IC Johnson and Co Ltd, Re* [1902] 2 Ch. 101. The proviso will also preserve any agreements about priorities already made by the late-registering chargee with other creditors: *ibid.*
[238] *Watson v Duff Morgan and Vermont (Holdings) Ltd* [1974] 1 W.L.R. 450.
[239] *MIG Trust Ltd, Re* [1933] Ch. 524, at pp.569–572 (Romer L.J.).
[240] See generally, Prentice, "Defectively Registered Charges" (1970) 34 Conv. (N.S.) 410. The company's registered number is a detail required to be supplied but not a particular of the charge, so that an error in that regard cannot invalidate the charge: *Grove v Advantage Healthcare (TIO) Ltd* [2000] 1 B.C.L.C. 611.
[241] *Exeter Trust Ltd v Screenways Ltd* [1991] B.C.L.C. 888.
[242] *Igroup Ltd v Ocwen* [2004] 1 W.L.R. 451.
[243] *Igroup Ltd v Ocwen ibid.*
[244] CA 2006 s.869(5) and (6).

the certificate means that the charge will be treated as validly registered even if it was not, but was registered by mistake;[245] and even if the registered particulars are inaccurate.[246] Note, however, that where there is such inaccuracy, registration validates the charge, but the operative terms are those agreed between the parties notwithstanding that third parties may have been misled[247] by incorrect particulars.[248] Because the certificate is conclusive evidence of registration, there can be no judicial review of the Registrar's decision to register.[249]

On the other hand, registration does not cure any flaw in the charge itself as between the parties, so the validity of the charge remains challengeable by the company.[250] In addition, registration does not determine priority as between competing security interests (although failure to register renders the charge void, and therefore registration is a necessary, although not sufficient, condition to obtain priority). Priority is determined by the usual common law and equitable rules of property. Indeed, the register does not even provide accurate information to chargees about earlier charges that may rank ahead of any charge currently being negotiated. This is because of the "21 day invisibility problem", whereby if A registers a charge on January 21, for example, there is no guarantee that the company has not created a charge prior to this which may be registered within 21 days[251] and thus have priority. In applying the normal priority rules as between competing interests, any person taking a registrable charge over the company's property (and only such persons) will have constructive notice of any matter that requires registration and has been disclosed. To take an example, a person taking a contractual lien is not affected by the register since this is not a registrable charge, but a person taking a floating charge would be.

Reform proposals and registration systems elsewhere
The fate of recent and not so recent proposals for reform of the **32–31** registration system for company charges in England and Wales has already been described.[252] Although some commentators doubt the

---

[245] *Ali v Top Marques Car Rental Ltd* [2006] EWHC 109 (Ch.).
[246] *National Provincial and Union Bank v Charnley* [1924] 1 K.B. 431, CA (where the property charged was incorrectly stated); *Mechanisations (Eaglescliffe) Ltd, Re* [1966] Ch. 20 (amount secured misstated); *Eric Holmes (Property) Ltd, Re* [1965] Ch. 1052; *CL Nye Ltd, Re* [1971] Ch. 442 (date of creation misstated).
[247] On those rare occasions where the mistake is that of the Registrar, it is unlikely the Registrar would be liable to anyone suffering damages, despite *Ministry of Housing and Local Government v Sharp* [1970] 2 Q.B. 223: see *Davis v Radcliffe* [1990] 1 W.L.R. 821, HL and the cases cited therein; *Banque Keyser Ullmann SA v Skandia (UK) Insurance Co Ltd* [1990] 1 Q.B. 665 at 796–798 (on appeal [1991] 2 A.C. 449).
[248] *Ibid.*
[249] *R. v Registrar of Companies, ex p. Central Bank of India* [1986] Q.B. 1114.
[250] Most usually on the grounds of capacity or authority, especially in dealings between the company and its directors.
[251] CA 2006 s.870(1)(a).
[252] See above, para.32–23.

need for a registration system at all,[253] most developed countries have one. Indeed, the proposals most recently rejected in England and Wales had strong parallels with the systems already operating in the US (Uniform Commercial Code, Article 9),[254] Canada[255] and New Zealand, and under consideration in Australia and Singapore.[256] The most disappointing feature of the current position in England and Wales is not simply that the UK has been left with an outdated regime, but that it missed an opportunity to provide the first draft for a model European scheme. The work being done by the EBRD, UNCITRAL and UNIDROIT indicates the demand for sophisticated input on this front.[257]

Given that the Law Commission's proposals have not quite been laid to rest,[258] and that they mirror in important respects the systems operating in some other major financial centres, a little more detail on their approach is warranted.[259] Recall the three principal objectives of most registration systems: i.e. the provision of information, perfection rules and priority rules.[260] The Law Commission proposed a system that affected all of these features when compared with the current system.

32–32   First, the Law Commission proposed a system of "notice filing" to replace the current system, which is a "transaction filing" system.[261] Under notice filing, it is not the transaction creating the registrable charge which is filed at Companies House, but rather notice that a person has taken or intends to take security over designated assets of the company. This may seem a small change, but it facilitates a number of further features seen as advantageous.

Crucially, notice filing works on the basis that the register simply provides an alert to subsequent lenders and other third parties; it does not provide full details of the earlier securities. Those details must be

---

[253] U Drobnig, "Present and Future of Real and Personal Property" (2003) *European Review of Private Law* 623, at p.660: "If all the information it [the register] offers is a notice that there may exist a security interest, so that intending creditors are put on notice but have to turn to the debtor in order to verify the true state of affairs . . . is not nearly the same effect achieved in countries without a registration system where the courts proceed from a general presumption that business people must know that any major piece of equipment is bought on credit?"

[254] This has been adopted by all the States and the District of Columbia.

[255] Nine of the ten Canadian Provinces and three territories have a Personal Property Security Act modelled on UCC Art.9.

[256] Beale *et al*, *op. cit.*, Ch.21, paras 21.17–21.21.

[257] Beale *et al*, *op. cit.*, Ch.21, paras 21.22–21.24.

[258] See above, para.32–23.

[259] References here are to the consultation paper and the consultative report, rather than the less radical final report: see above, para.32–23.

[260] See above, para.32–22.

[261] See above, fn.172, Consultation Paper 164, Pt IV.

acquired from the relevant parties themselves (although even under the current system, this is often the case, as information is rarely complete[262] and may sometimes be inaccurate[263]). The information required for an effective notice filing is therefore less than for transaction filing.[264] This makes it possible to use shorter, more standardised details of charges, which in turn facilitates online electronic filing. It also makes it feasible to expand the range of charges to be notified (including quasi-securities), and reduces the workload of Companies House (since its staff no longer need to examine documents creating the charge, and the Registrar no longer issues a certificate, the effect of which is in any event irrelevant under a priority system based on filing[265]).[266]

In addition, the register performs a "perfection" function, perfecting the charge as against unsecured creditors:[267] if notice is not filed, then in principle the charge would not be perfected, and would not operate as a security, although, as now, the underlying obligation would persist as an unsecured obligation.

Finally, the register permits a simple system of priority, determined by the date of filing (see below). Under such a scheme, failure to file and late filing are problems only for the intending chargee, who will either lose the benefit of any security, or lose priority. However, there is still the problem of erroneous filing. Here the Law Commission proposed that "seriously misleading" filing[268] should invalidate the charge, although perhaps only against the person who has been misled, coupled with the rule that a chargee could not claim a greater interest than was revealed in the notice actually filed.[269]

A little more should be said about the range of securities that the Law Commission initially proposed to be registered.[270] It proposed

32–33

---

[262] For example, it is not possible to register any changes in registered particulars, other than satisfaction in whole or in part of the secured obligation, and this is not obligatory: CA 2006 s.872. In many cases, therefore, a person searching the register will not know how much is currently secured, or may be advanced in the future under the existing security, and will be obliged to seek that information from the debtor or from the relevant chargee.

[263] See above, para.32–29.

[264] Some commentators see this reduction in available information as a serious problem: see R. Calnan, "The Reform of the Law of Security" [2004] Butterworths Journal of International Banking and Financial Law 88, at pp.89–90.

[265] See below, para.32–34.

[266] Law Commission, above fn.261, paras 4.19–4.38.

[267] Law Commission, above, fn.261, paras 4.55–4.58. Since only the chargee seems to lose if the notice is not filed, the Law Commission thought that filing should be voluntary (i.e. no criminal sanctions for not filing) and that filing could take place at any time, subject possibly to controls over filing by corporate insiders in the period immediately preceding insolvency (*cf.* above, at para.32–28): *ibid.*, paras 4.74–4.80.

[268] In an electronic system, this would mean filing errors that made an effective search impossible.

[269] Law Commission, above, fn.261, paras 4.39–4.50. Thus, if the charge was in fact taken over premises A and B, but the filed particulars referred only to A, the charge could not be asserted in respect of B.

[270] See para.32–23.

making certain "quasi-securities" subject to notice filing.[271] A "quasi-security" is not a true security (it does not involve allocation by the debtor of an interest in the debtor's property as surety for an obligation), but it performs the same function. The quasi-securities put forward for inclusion were retention of title clauses, conditional sale agreements, hire-purchase agreements, finance leases, factoring and block discounting agreements and securitisations, and consignments having a security purpose. The list can prove controversial, with different commentators thinking it over- or under-inclusive.[272] Assessment perhaps depends upon whether the aim of a registration system is seen as the provision of information on the debtor's apparent wealth, or the ordering of priorities. In this vein, and arguably justified on either view, the Law Commission also excluded certain securities from filing, with the excluded list including: possessory securities (such as pledges[273] where registration is not needed to give information to the inquirer because the assets will be in the possession of the creditor, not the debtor); charges over shares and investment securities where the chargee has perfected the security by taking control of it or being registered as the owner (for similar reasons); contractual liens over sub-freights (on the grounds that they are not charges);[274] charges over bank balances (on the grounds that information is easily discoverable by the inquirer);[275] and a number of other specialised cases.[276]

In addition, notice filing allows a notice to be filed of an intention to create a charge, i.e. in advance of its actual creation. Coupled with the rule for establishing priority by reference to the date of filing (see below), this enables the potential chargee (A) to be sure that when the charge is created, it will obtain priority over any other charge not registered at the time that A files his or her notice. In short, it avoids the current "21 day invisibility problem".[277] The priority of A's charge, when created, will date back to the date of the notice. This will be the case even if the other charge existed (but had not been notified) at the time of the filing of A's notice and even if the other charge was notified before the creation of A's charge (but after the notification of A's charge). This enables a potential lender to conclude discussions with the company knowing that, once notice is filed, his or her priority position is ensured. It is necessary, of course, to

---

[271] See Part VII of the consultative report, above, fn.172.

[272] I. Davies, "The Reform of English Personal Property Security Law" [2004] LS 295, at p.321.

[273] Including the deposit of a negotiable instrument to secure payment of a book debt, which was already specifically excluded by CA 1985 s.396(2) (and now by CA 2006 s.861(3)).

[274] This has been a subject of great controversy. See *Welsh Irish Ferries Ltd, Re* [1986] Ch. 471; *Agnew v Commissioner for Inland Revenue* [2001] 2 A.C. 710 at 727–728; Oditah [1989] L.M.C.L.Q. 191.

[275] Whether it is possible for a bank to take a charge over a bank account in favour of itself has been long disputed, but the question seems to have been decided in favour of a positive answer: *Bank of Credit and Commerce International SA (No.8), Re* [1998] A.C. 214, HL.

[276] Law Commission, above, fn.261, Pt V.

[277] See above, para.32–24.

have rules to deal with the situation which arises if notice of an intention to take a charge is filed, but the charge is never in fact created.[278]

On priorities, the Law Commission proposed a simple system of **32–34** priority based on the date of filing. Even actual knowledge of an earlier charge would not defeat the priority of the person who filed first. However, this simple system is necessarily subject to some complexities. Three issues deserve special mention. First, filing cannot give priority over charges which are not registrable, and there would be a number of these.[279] Priority as between registrable and non-registrable charges (and among non-registrable charges), it was proposed, should be by the date of perfection (which would be the date of filing for registrable charges and some other event for non-registrable charges). Indeed, the proposal included a major addition to the list of unregistrable charges, namely charges over land, on the grounds that their validity and priority should depend solely upon the rules relating to the registration of charges over land, whether those charges are created by a company or not.[280]

Secondly, the Law Commission proposed[281] the continuation of the current rule whereby later "purchase-money" security interests have priority over earlier charges.[282] Suppose a company grants a fixed charge over present and future property and a later creditor advances money to buy a specific piece of property, taking a security interest over that property. The proposed exception would give the financer of the purchase of the specific property priority over the earlier general charge. Without this exception, the company might find it difficult to raise finance to purchase the later property; and the holder of the earlier general charge is not prejudiced, since the net assets of the company are not reduced by the later loan, purchase, and grant of security, taken together.

Thirdly, and more controversially, certain commentators thought a system of priority by date of filing would fundamentally affect the floating charge, and indeed at first sight would seem enormously to improve the position of the floating charge holder, since one of the vulnerabilities of the floating charge is that the company remains free to create subsequent fixed charges which will have priority over it, until such time as the floating charge crystallises.[283] A simple notice system, by contrast, would give the floating charge automatic priority over any subsequent charges, even before crystallisation. But that situation is often achieved (or sought to be achieved) today by virtue

---

[278] Law Commission, above, fn.261, paras 4.109–4.115.
[279] See above, para.32–33. Moreover, no charges created by operation of law would be registrable.
[280] To be found in the Land Registration Act 2002 or the Land Charges Act 1972, for registered and unregistered land respectively.
[281] Law Commission, above, fn.261, paras 4.155–4.162.
[282] *Abbey National Building Society v Cann* [1991] 1 A.C. 56, HL.
[283] See above, para.32–10.

of the inclusion of a negative pledge clause[284] in the floating charge, coupled with registration of the details of the negative pledge clause. The Law Commission proposed to bite the bullet and simply to repeal the rule whereby the floating charge permits the company to grant later charges having priority over it, thus in effect endorsing policy underlying the negative pledge clause.[285]

Finally, for completeness, if this proposal were implemented, the Law Commission would be content to see the company's own register of charges dispensed with.[286]

ENFORCEMENT OF FLOATING CHARGES

Receivers and administrators

32–35 The methods of enforcing a security interest depend upon the nature of the rights which it confers and are often in no way peculiar to company law. However, company law has traditionally provided a distinct proceeding for the enforcement of a floating charge by the appointment of a receiver—termed, since the insolvency reforms of the 1980s, an "administrative receiver".[287] In this section, therefore, we return to our preoccupation with the floating charge. A major reform brought about by the Enterprise Act 2002 was substantially to restrict use of receivership in the future and to channel the enforcement of floating charges into the administration procedure, which is a general procedure for the handling of insolvent companies and thus not specific to the enforcement of the floating charge.

The main driver behind this reform was the desire to produce an enforcement mechanism for the floating charge in which the relevant insolvency practitioner owed duties to all the creditors of the company and not primarily to the floating charge holder.[288] Consistently with the case-law origins of the floating charge in the nineteenth century, the receiver is a person appointed out of court by the charge holder under the provisions of the instrument creating the charge, who takes management control of the company in order to realise sufficient assets to repay the appointor (the charge holder) and then

---

[284] See above, para.32–11.
[285] Law Commission, above, fn.261, paras 4.125–4.138.
[286] CA 2006 s.876. See Law Commission, above, fn.261, paras 4.68–4.71.
[287] The distinction is typically made between a person who has control of all, or substantially all, the assets of a company (an administrative receiver: IA 1986 s.29(2)) and a person who simply has control of a single asset or limited class of secured assets (a receiver). The former is in a position to manage the company as a going concern; the latter is not. Both hold their positions in order to realise the rights of the secured creditor (and other creditors, if the charge is floating—see above, para.32–14).
[288] Insolvency Service, White Paper, *Productivity and Enterprise: Insolvency—A Second Chance*, Cm. 5234 (July 2001), para.2.2.

hands the company back to its directors or to a liquidator,[289] depending on the financial state of the company at the end of the receivership.

Compared with receivership, administration is a much more recent mechanism, introduced as a result of the recommendations of the Cork Committee.[290] Ironically, the statutory administration procedure was based on the common law receivership. Although the Cork Committee had criticisms to make of receivership, it took the view that it had one inestimable advantage over the then principal alternative way of dealing with an insolvent company, namely winding up. This was because the receivership was structured on the basis that the receiver would normally continue to run the company and in the process save the viable parts of its business (though often by selling them off to others). Such a "rescue culture" was thought to be more protective of the interests of all stakeholders in the business than a winding-up, and so the Committee recommended that the benefits of receivership be made available where there was no floating charge, so that the rescue culture could be extended to such cases.

Of course, the receivership rules could not simply be applied in total to a situation where there was no floating charge. In the absence of a charge holder to appoint the insolvency practitioner, that task was given to the court, on application by the company or its creditors. Further, the opportunity was taken of giving the statutory administrator the benefit of an institution which the receiver, as a product essentially of private law, had not had, namely, a moratorium during the administration on the enforcement of creditors' rights against the company. Finally, and in line with the notion of the administration as an extension of the receivership, the floating charge holder, if such had been created, was initially given, in effect, a veto over the appointment of an administrator.[291] This last feature was subsequently removed by the Enterprise Act 2002 and, going in the opposite direction, is supplanted by a prohibition in the normal case on the appointment by the floating charge holder of an administrative receiver.[292] Thus under the Enterprise Act 2002, it is not possible to appoint an administrative receiver under a floating charge created on or after September 15, 2003, except as in the cases specified in IA 1986 ss.72B–72H. Instead, the chargee is given the right to appoint an administrator: see IA 1986, Schedule B1, para.14(1). Chargees of charges created prior to this date may appoint an administrator, but retain the right to appoint an administrative receiver. The aim, stated

32–36

---

[289] On winding up and liquidation, see the Appendix to this book.

[290] See above, fn.167, Ch.9. The Committee's proposals were not implemented precisely in the way the Committee had envisaged. See Finch, *Corporate Insolvency Law* (Cambridge, 2002), pp.273–275.

[291] IA 1986, s.9(2) and (3), repealed by the Enterprise Act 2002.

[292] IA 1986, s.72A, introduced by the 2002 Act, s.250. The prohibition does not apply to appointments under floating charges in existence before the date on which the new rules are brought into operation: s.72A(4).

in the White Paper preceding the Enterprise Act 2002, was that
"administrative receivership should cease to be a major insolvency
procedure."[293] The administrative receiver would instead be replaced
by an administrator, who is an officer of the court, and must "perform his functions in the interests of the company's creditors as a
whole."[294] Note that a chargee whose charge does not cover the whole
or substantially the whole of the assets of the company can still
appoint a receiver (who will not be an administrative receiver), and
cannot appoint an administrator.

This policy of statutory patricide was subject, however, to two
qualifications which concern us. First, the White Paper recognised
that the procedure for appointing a receiver had the advantages for
the floating charge holder of being quick, cheap and entirely under
the charge holder's control. It was further recognised that the earlier
administration procedure would need to be reformed so as to
reproduce those advantages, as far as possible, within the new
structure. "Secured creditors," said the White Paper, "should not feel
at any risk from our proposals."[295] Accordingly, the current administration procedure is not simply one that applies more generally, but
is itself reformed, a new Pt II being inserted into the IA 1986 by the
Enterprise Act 2002.[296]

Secondly, the common law administrative receivership system is
retained in certain exceptional cases as mentioned above.[297] Most of
these do not need to be discussed in a work of this nature, but one is
of crucial importance to us. Under the new IA 1986 s.72B, as interpreted in the new Sch.2A,[298] a receiver may still be appointed where a
company issues secured debentures[299] and where (a) the security is
held by trustees on behalf of the debenture-holders;[300] (b) the amount
to be raised is at least £50 million;[301] and (c) the debentures are to be
listed or traded on a regulated market.[302] In terms of enforcement,
therefore, an important distinction is drawn between two common
forms of corporate finance. Where the debt is raised from the public
by way of a large-scale offering of securities, the administrative
receivership procedure will continue to be available. Where the debt
is raised from a bank (or syndicate of banks), administration will be
the enforcement procedure, unless one of the other exceptions con-

---

[293] See above, fn.288, para.2.5.
[294] IA 1986, Sch.B1, para.3(2).
[295] See above, fn.288, para.2.6.
[296] Enterprise Act 2002, s.248. The operative provisions are contained mainly in a new Sch.B1
    to the IA 1986, set out in Sch.16 to the 2002 Act.
[297] IA 1986, ss.72A–H.
[298] Set out in Sch.18 to the 2002 Act.
[299] IA 1986, s.72B(1)(b) and Sch.2A, para.2(1)(a)—which makes a further reference to art.77 of
    the FSMA 2000 (Regulated Activities) Order 2001 (SI 2001/544), where the inclusion of
    debentures and debenture stock can be found.
[300] IA 1986, s.72B(1) and Sch.2A, para.1(1)(a).
[301] IA 1986, s.72B(1)(a).
[302] IA 1986, Sch.2A, para.2.

tained in IA 1986 ss.72C–72G applies.[303] For this reason it is necessary to discuss briefly both the receivership and administration
methods of enforcing the floating charge.[304] We begin with the older
procedure.

Receivership
Appointment of an administrative receiver
Where an appointment of an administrative receiver remains possi- **32–37**
ble, because the case falls within one of the exceptions noted above
and the power is contained in an existing debenture, almost invariably the first step in the enforcement of a charge is for the debenture-
holders or their trustee to obtain the appointment of a receiver.[305]
This appointment will normally be made by the debenture-holder
under an express or implied[306] power in the debenture, or by the
court. Where the appointment is pursuant to a provision in the
debenture then it must be clear that the conditions justifying the
appointment have arisen, otherwise the receiver will be a trespasser
and also liable for conversion.[307]

Once the conditions for the enforcement of a charge have arisen,
English law places few constraints on the rights of the security holder
to enforce the charge, and in this respect the regime is pro-security
holder. For example, if the chargee is entitled to payment on demand,
it is only necessary to give the company reasonable time to put into
effect the mechanics of payment, not reasonable time in which to raise
the funds to make payment.[308] Indeed, if the debtor makes it clear
that funds are not available, this constitutes a sufficient act of default
and there is no need to allow the debtor any time before treating it as

---

[303] Note *Feetum v Levy* [2006] Ch.585: a right to appoint an administrative receiver does not
amount to step-in rights.

[304] The use of administration generally is not discussed in this book.

[305] If the state of the company is so parlous that it is doubtful whether there will be enough to
cover the receiver's remuneration it may be necessary for the trustees to take possession. If
the "debenture" is just an ordinary mortgage of particular property the debenture-holder
may, of course, exercise its power of sale without the preliminary step of appointing a
receiver.

[306] i.e. under LPA 1925, s.101 when applicable.

[307] Where the appointment is defective, the court can order the person making the appointment
to indemnify the receiver: IA 1986, s.34. See also IA 1986, s.232, which deals with the
validity of acts of a defectively appointed administrative receiver, and IA 1986, s.234 dealing
with the seizure or disposal by an administrative receiver of property that does not belong to
the company, and generally see *London Iron and Steel Co Ltd, Re* [1990] B.C.L.C. 372;
Welsh Development Agency v Export Finance Co Ltd [1992] B.C.L.C. 148.

[308] *Bank of Baroda v Panessar* [1987] Ch. 335; this is normally a matter of hours during normal
banking hours. In addition, the company may be estopped by its conduct from challenging
the validity of the appointment of a receiver, and the appointment of a receiver on invalid
grounds may be subsequently cured if grounds justifying the appointment are subsequently
discovered: *Bank of Baroda* at 352–353 and *Byblos Bank SAL v Al-Khudairy* [1987] B.C.L.C.
232 respectively. There is no need for the debenture-holder to specify the exact sum due in
any demand: see *NRG Vision Ltd v Churchfield Leasing Ltd* [1988] B.C.L.C. 624.

being in default.[309] In addition, the chargee is not under any duty to the debtor company to refrain from exercising its rights merely because by doing so it could avoid loss to the company,[310] nor to exercise its rights promptly because the security is declining in value.[311]

32–38   If the security is not yet enforceable, but the debenture-holder's position is in jeopardy, the court may exercise its inherent discretion to appoint a receiver.[312] This is now very rare, but can be done by a debenture-holder's action, taken by one of the debenture-holders, on behalf of himself and all other holders. "Jeopardy" is established when, for example, execution is about to be levied against the company,[313] or when the company proposes to distribute to its members its one remaining asset.[314] "Jeopardy" is not assumed whenever the circumstances make it unreasonable, in the interests of the debenture-holder, that the company should retain power to dispose of the property subject to the charge. This is the statutory definition under Scottish law,[315] but the English decisions hardly go so far, and the fact that the assets on realisation would not repay the debentures in full has been held insufficient.[316]

Despite this option, appointment out of court is certainly preferable. The procedure in a debenture-holders' action is lamentably expensive and dilatory, since the receiver, as an officer of the court, will have to work under its closest supervision and constant applications will have to be made in chambers throughout the duration of the receivership, which may last years if a complicated realisation is involved. Since the 1986 Act allows a receiver, even though appointed out of court, to obtain the court's directions,[317] it is difficult to envisage circumstances in which an application to the court can be justified if the cheaper alternative is available, and the professional adviser who recommended it would be laying himself open to grave risk of criticism. In the discussion which follows, it will be assumed that what is being referred to is a receiver appointed out of court.

---

[309] *Sheppard & Cooper Ltd v TSB Bank Plc* [1996] 2 All E.R. 654.
[310] *Potters Oils Ltd, Re* [1986] 1 W.L.R. 201; *Standard Chartered Bank Ltd v Walker* [1982] 1 W.L.R. 1410.
[311] *China and South Sea Bank Ltd v Tan* [1990] 1 A.C. 536, PC; of course it will always be in the commercial interests of the chargee to exercise his rights if the security is declining in value. On other aspects of the receiver's duties to the company and others, see para.845, below.
[312] But the court will not normally have any power to appoint a receiver unless the debentures are secured by a charge: *Harris v Beauchamp Bros* [1894] 1 Q.B. 801, CA; *Swallow Footwear Ltd, Re The Times*, October 23, 1956. Also the court will not imply a term into a debenture empowering a chargee to appoint a receiver where his security is in jeopardy: see *Cryne v Barclays Bank Plc* [1987] B.C.L.C. 548, CA.
[313] *McMahon v North Kent Co* [1891] 2 Ch.148; *Edwards v Standard Rolling Stock* [1893] 1 Ch.574; and see *Victoria Steamboats Co, Re* [1897] 1 Ch.158.
[314] *Tilt Cove Copper Co, Re* [1913] 2 Ch.588.
[315] IA 1986, s.52(2) (for the purpose of appointing a receiver), s.122(2) (for the purpose of making a winding-up order).
[316] *New York Taxicab Co, Re* [1913] 1 Ch.1.
[317] IA 1986, s.35.

Function and status of the receiver and administrative receiver

The 1986 Insolvency Act views the appointment of an administrative   **32–39**
receiver as being in some respects similar to insolvency proceedings
and regulates it accordingly.[318] Thus administrative receivers must be
qualified to act as insolvency practitioners[319] and can only be removed
from office by the court.[320] Also, like the liquidator, the administrative receiver can compel those involved in the affairs of the company to provide him with information relating to the company's
affairs[321] and is also obliged to report to the Secretary of State if he
forms the opinion that the conduct of a director makes him unfit to
act as a director of a company.[322] The effect of the appointment of a
receiver upon the company directors is that they no longer have any
authority to deal with the company property. They do however
officially remain in office and continue to be liable for the submission
of documents to Companies House, and may still institute proceedings in the company's name. In other ways, too, the appointment of a
receiver must not be equated with that of a liquidator: (i) where a
receiver is appointed the company need not go into liquidation[323] and
if it does, the same person who acted as receiver will normally not be
appointed liquidator; (ii) liquidation is a class action designed to
protect the interests of the unsecured creditors whereas, as we shall
see, receivership is designed to protect the interests of the security
holders who appointed the receiver and it is for this reason that a
receiver can be appointed even where the company is in liquidation;[324]
(iii) liquidation terminates the trading power of the company,[325]
whereas this is not the case with receivership; (iv) a liquidator has
power to disclaim onerous property,[326] something not possible in the
case of receivership; (v) a liquidator in a compulsory winding-up is an
officer of the court,[327] whereas this is not the case with a receiver
unless appointed by the court;[328] (vi) lastly, it is easier to obtain
recognition of liquidation as opposed to receivership in proceedings

---

[318] See IA 1986, s.247(1) for the definition of "insolvency".

[319] IA 1986, s.388(1). A body corporate, an undischarged bankrupt, or a person disqualified to
act as a director may not act as an insolvency practitioner: see IA 1986, s.390(1) and (4).

[320] IA 1986, s.45(1); they can resign, *ibid.*

[321] IA 1986, ss.47 and 236; *Aveling Barford Ltd, Re* [1989] 1 W.L.R. 360; *Cloverbay Ltd (Joint
Administrators) v BCCI SA* [1991] Ch.90.

[322] Companies Directors Disqualification Act 1986, s.7(3)(d).

[323] See IA 1986, s.247(2). Although generally a receiver should not be seen as a doctor but
rather as an undertaker.

[324] *Potters Oils Ltd, Re* [1986] 1 W.L.R. 201.

[325] Also without the leave of the court legal proceedings cannot be brought against the company: see IA 1986, s.130.

[326] See IA 1986, s.178.

[327] *Parsons v Sovereign Bank of Canada* [1913] A.C. 160.

[328] It is contempt of court to interfere with the exercise of power by a court-appointed receiver
without the leave of the court.

in foreign courts.[329] These are the most important differences but there are others, particularly with respect to liability on contracts.[330]

An administrative receiver might be assumed to be the agent of those who appointed him but this is not the case; IA 1986 s.44 makes him the agent of the company.[331] The reason for this is to avoid those who appointed the administrative receiver being treated as mortgagees in possession[332] or being held liable for the receiver's acts, which would be the case were the receiver to be treated as their agent.[333] As many have pointed out, the receiver's agency is a peculiar form of agency. This is because the primary responsibility of the receiver is to protect the interests of the security holders and to realise the charged assets for their benefit.[334]

The powers of the administrative receiver are extensive and he will have complete control over the assets subject to the charge under which he was appointed.[335] In addition he can apply to the court for an order empowering him to dispose of property subject to a prior charge.[336] In the exercise of his powers, a receiver is under a duty to the debtor company to take reasonable care to obtain the best price reasonably possible at the time of sale;[337] this duty is also owed to a guarantor of the company's debts.[338] However, as the receiver in exercising his power of sale is in a position analogous to that of the mortgagee, he is not obliged to postpone sale in order to obtain a better price or to adopt a piecemeal method of sale.[339] He is also under a duty, while he manages the property, to manage it with

---

[329] IA 1986, s.72 permits an English or Scottish receiver to act throughout Great Britain provided local law permits this. The White Paper (above, fn.288 at para.23) suggested that an advantage of greater use of administration was that it would receive easier international recognition.

[330] See paras 32–41 *et seq.*

[331] Also the debenture will invariably provide that irrespective of the type of receiver appointed by the charge holder he is to be the agent of the company. A receiver appointed by the court is not an agent of anyone but an officer of the court: see *Moss SS Co v Whinney* [1912] A.C. 254, HL.

[332] The duties of a mortgage in possession are onerous: see Beale *et al, op. cit.*, para.17.39.

[333] If the chargee interferes with the receiver's discharge of his duties this could, provided the interference is sufficiently pervasive, result in the receiver being treated as the agent of the chargee: see *American Express International Banking Corp v Hurley* [1985] 3 All E.R. 564.

[334] The receiver would not, for example, be considered to be participating in the management of the company since he is not managing the company but the assets of the company: *B Johnson & Co (Builders) Ltd, Re* [1955] Ch. 634; *North Development Pty Ltd, Re* (1990) 8 A.C.L.C. 1004. Although contrast the analysis in *Buchler v Talbot* [2004] 2 A.C. 298, above, para.32–19.

[335] IA 1986 s.42 confers on an administrative receiver the powers set out in Sch.1 to the Act in so far as they are not inconsistent with the terms of the debenture. There are 23 powers enumerated and they are very wide; for example, number 14 confers on an administrative receiver "Power to carry on the business of the company".

[336] IA 1986 s.43. The rights of the security holder are protected in the same way as they are in the case of administration: see para.32–18, above.

[337] *Cuckmere Brick Co Ltd v Mutual Finance Ltd* [1971] Ch.949; *Bishop v Bonham* [1988] 1 W.L.R. 742.

[338] *Standard Chartered Bank Ltd v Walker* [1982] 1 W.L.R. 1410; *American Express International Banking Corp v Hurley* [1985] 3 All E.R. 564.

[339] *Tse Kwong Lam v Wong Chit Sen* [1983] 1 W.L.R. 1349.

reasonable care and due diligence.[340] The basis of the receiver's duty set out above was initially considered to involve the extension of the common law of negligence to supplement equity,[341] but the courts now treat it as something which flows from the nature in equity of the relationship between the mortgagee and mortgagor.[342] This reflects a reluctance to impose common law liability in negligence, or to impose a duty owed to multiple stakeholders (although a duty is conceded as owed to the company and to all parties interested in the company's equity of redemption). But the equitable version of this duty goes further than a duty to act bona fide and for proper purposes, and requires the receiver to have regard to the chargor's interests while at the same time allowing that the chargee's interests are paramount.

Indeed, the most recent significant English authority, *Medforth v Blake*,[343] treated the standard of care required in equity as the same as that required at common law and held receivers, who negligently conducted the business of which they had taken control, liable to the mortgagor, who suffered loss when the business was handed back to him after the secured debt had been discharged in a less good state than if it had been properly run by the receivers. Although this decision goes some way towards protecting debtor companies (and, by extension, their unsecured creditors) from the incompetence of receivers, the Court of Appeal made it clear that it was not purporting to overturn the principle that the primary duty of the receiver is to bring about the repayment of the debt owed to the secured creditor. In this particular case, there was no conflict of interest between the mortgagor and mortgagee, since both potentially suffered harm as a result of the receivers' incompetence.[344] The case, thus, is not authority for the proposition that it is negligent for the receivers to give primacy to the appointor's interests as against those of the mortgagor (or the company and its unsecured creditors).

A person dealing with an administrative receiver in good faith and **32–40** for value is not bound to enquire if the receiver is acting within his or her powers.[345] Unlike a winding-up, the board of directors is not discharged on the appointment of a receiver, but the directors' powers are substantially superseded since they cannot act so as to

---

[340] *Medforth v Blake* [2000] Ch.86.

[341] See Lightman and Moss, *The Law of Administrators and Receivers of Companies* (4th ed., London, 2007) Ch.7.

[342] *Parker-Tweedale v Dunbar Bank Plc* [1991] Ch.12, CA (mortgagee owes no duty to beneficiary of mortgaged property); *Downsview Nominees Ltd v First City Corp* [1993] A.C. 295, PC.

[343] [2000] Ch.86, CA, thus somewhat back-tracking on the decision of the Privy Council in *Downsview Nominees Ltd v First City Corp* [1993] A.C. 295. See also *Knight v Lawrence* [1993] B.C.L.C. 215.

[344] On the facts, the appointor suffered no loss because the business, even in its damaged state, generated enough profit to satisfy the appointor's claims.

[345] IA 1986 s.42(3). If an administrative receiver is seen as being an organ of the company, then this provision is arguably not in compliance with Art.9(2) of the First Directive. See Ch.7, above.

interfere with the discharge by the receiver of his responsibilities and accordingly their powers are suspended "so far as is requisite to enable a receiver to discharge his functions".[346] Given the extent of the powers of the administrative receiver, the directors will have a miniscule aperture within which they are free to exercise their powers. However, they do possess certain residual powers and, for example, it has been held that they can bring proceedings in the company's name.[347] This authority has been doubted because of the conflict that would arise were the receiver and the directors to have different views on whether an action should be brought, and also on the handling of any counterclaim.[348] Whatever the status of the *Newhart* decision,[349] it is clear that it will be confined to very narrow limits, since to allow every such action would interfere with the primary duties of the receiver to protect the interests of the security holder.[350] On the other hand, the directors can certainly take proceedings to challenge the validity of the receiver's appointment,[351] or sue the receiver for breach of duty,[352] or oppose a petition to wind up the company.[353]

Finally, as the directors remain in office, the receiver is under an obligation to provide the directors with the information that they request to enable them to comply with their reporting obligations under the Companies Act.[354] The receiver is also obliged at the end of his receivership to hand over to the company any documents belonging to the company other than those brought into existence for

---

[346] *Emmadart Ltd, Re* [1979] Ch.540 at 544; see also *Gomba Holdings UK Ltd v Homan* [1986] 1 W.L.R. 1301.

[347] *Newhart Developments Ltd v Co-operative Commercial Bank Ltd* [1978] Q.B. 814, CA (it is important to note that in that case the company was indemnified for any costs that it might incur and the receiver had decided not to bring any action against his appointor).

[348] *Tudor Grange Holdings Ltd v Citibank NA* [1992] Ch. 53. As Browne-Wilkinson V.-C. pointed out in that case, it would be more appropriate for receivers or their appointor to use IA 1986 s.35. *Tudor Grange* has itself come in for criticism: see *Geneva Finance Ltd, Re* (1992) 7 A.C.S.L.R. 415, at pp.426–432.

[349] It could be argued that the right to bring an action against the debenture-holder could not be an asset covered by the charge. This, however, proves too much since it would mean that the directors would always be in a position to bring an action against the debenture-holder even when the special factors in *Newhart* were not present. And while this argument rightly emphasises the scope of the receiver's authority it fails to give effect to his functions. Also the agency of the receiver may have sufficient content to impose on him a duty to seek redress against a debenture-holder in appropriate cases.

[350] See also *Gomba Holdings UK Ltd v Homan* [1986] 1 W.L.R. 1301; *Watts v Midland Bank Plc* [1986] B.C.L.C. 15 (a case which illustrates that since the power to use the corporate name in litigation is normally vested in the directors a shareholder will normally be precluded from bringing a derivative action against a receiver).

[351] *Hawkesbury Development Co Ltd v Landmark Finance Pty Ltd* (1969) 92 WN (NSW) 199.

[352] *Watts v Midland Bank Plc* [1986] B.C.L.C. 15.

[353] *Reprographic Exports (Euromat) Ltd, Re* (1978) 122 SJ 400.

[354] *Gomba Holdings UK Ltd v Homan*, fn.350, above; see also at 1305–1306 where Hoffmann J. points out that equity may impose on a receiver a duty to account which is wider than his statutory obligations.

the discharge of his own professional duties or his duties to the chargee.[355]

The receiver's liability with respect to contracts

An administrative receiver taking over the management of a company will need to manage the company's existing (partly performed) contracts, and will need to enter into new contracts on behalf of the company. These raise separate issues.

32–41

Consider first the contracts already in existence when the receiver is appointed. As an administrative receiver is the agent of the company, his appointment does not of itself affect existing contracts. If, in the interests of the chargee, the receiver causes the company to repudiate these contracts, the injured parties will be left to their normal contractual remedies in damages, and with the company unlikely to be left with the funds to pay such claims.[356] In doing this, the receiver acts as an agent of the company, and so cannot be liable for the tort of inducing a breach of contract.[357] The only exceptions to this general rule are the normal exceptions applying with contracts that are specifically enforceable[358] or subject to injunctions: the appointment of an administrative receiver makes no difference to the court's response in these cases. On the other hand, if the receiver does not repudiate the contract, he is said to "adopt" it.[359] This is rather misleading terminology: the contract is not a new contract at all; it remains the contract entered into by the company on the terms agreed by the company. Indeed, this itself can cause problems for receivers where adoption brings into play contractual liens[360] or set-offs.[361]

As a matter of policy, it seems desirable to impose a limited duty on the receiver to continue to trade or otherwise act positively where this would not jeopardize the chargee's interests and a failure to do so would impose gratuitous damage on the company.[362] Not to extend his duty in this way would stretch the pro-creditor bias of receivership

---

[355] *Gomba Holdings UK Ltd v Minories Finance Ltd* [1988] 1 W.L.R. 1231, CA. Once a receiver has sufficient funds to pay off the debt and his own expenses he should cease managing the company's assets: *Rottenberg v Monjack* [1993] B.C.L.C. 374.

[356] *Airline Airspares Ltd v Handley Page Ltd* [1970] Ch.193.

[357] *Said v Butt* [1920] 3 K.B. 497; *Welsh Development Agency v Export Finance Co Ltd* [1992] B.C.L.C. 148.

[358] *Freevale Ltd v Metrostore (Holdings) Ltd* [1984] Ch.199; *AMEC Properties Ltd v Planning Research and Systems Plc* [1992] B.C.L.C. 1149; and cf. *Ash & Newman Ltd v Creative Devices Research Ltd* [1991] B.C.L.C. 403.

[359] *Powdrill v Watson* [1995] 2 A.C. 394.

[360] *George Barker (Transport) Ltd v Eynon* [1974] 1 W.L.R. 462, CA.

[361] *Rother Iron Works Ltd v Canterbury Precision Engineers Ltd* [1974] Q.B. 1.

[362] See Lightman and Moss, *op. cit.*, at pp.112–118; *Knight v Lawrence* [1991] B.C.C. 411; *Medforth v Blake* [2000] Ch.86. See below, para.32–48. Contrast the two *obiter* comments that a receiver does (*R. v Board of Trade, ex p. St Martins Preserving Co Ltd* [1965] 1 Q.B. 603) and does not (*B Johnson and Co (Builders) Ltd, Re* [1955] Ch.364) have a duty to preserve the goodwill of the company.

to ridiculous lengths. But, as described below, this obligation is limited: the primary purpose of receivership is to realise the assets for the benefit of the secured creditor.

32–42   Special mention should be made of contracts of employment. These contracts are not automatically terminated by the receiver's appointment unless the receiver does something which is inconsistent with the continuation of the contract,[363] for example a sale of the company's business.[364] If the receiver sees no hope of selling the business as a going concern, then he is likely to dismiss the employees forthwith. Such dismissal will likely be because of redundancy, and will almost certainly not be unfair dismissal (provided there is no unfair selection of the persons to be dismissed). The receiver may take some time to decide what to do. Nothing that is done or omitted to be done in the first 14 days of the receiver's appointment is taken as showing that the receiver has adopted a contract of employment.[365] After that, if nothing is done, the receiver will be taken to have impliedly adopted these contracts.[366] Once adopted, the administrative receiver is, by statute, personally liable for the company's liability for wages or salary, contributions to an occupational pension scheme, holiday and sick pay, and deductions for income tax and national insurance,[367] from the date of adoption of the contract.[368] The administrative receiver cannot contract out of this liability for adopted employment contracts,[369] but is entitled to an indemnity out of the assets of the company.[370]

Where the receiver enters into new contracts, this is done as agent for the company, and the contracts will therefore be binding on the company. More importantly, however, the receiver is also personally liable by statute on any contract entered into on behalf of the company unless the contract provides otherwise.[371] Exclusion of liability may be express or implied. Administrative receivers will invariably try to contract out of liability. They will in any event have a statutory indemnity out of the company's assets[372] and will usually also have an indemnity from the chargee.

---

[363] *Griffiths v Secretary of State for Social Services* [1974] Q.B. 468. The appointment of the receiver by the court does terminate contracts of service: *Reid v Explosives Co Ltd* (1887) 19 Q.B.D. 264; *cf. Sipad Holding v Popovic* (1995) 19 A.C.S.R. 108.

[364] *Foster Clark's Ltd's Indenture Trusts, Re* [1966] 1 W.L.R. 125.

[365] IA 1986 s.44(2).

[366] *Powdrill v Watson* [1995] 2 A.C. 394.

[367] *FJL Realisations Ltd, Re* [2001] ICR 424.

[368] IA 1986 s.44.

[369] But contrast newly negotiated contracts, below.

[370] IA 1986 s.44(1)(c).

[371] s.44(1)(b) of the 1986 Act as amended by the Insolvency Act 1994, s.2. He is entitled to indemnification out of the assets of the company (s.44(1)(c)), and can also contract for indemnification by those who appointed him (s.44(3)).

[372] IA 1986 s.44(1)(c).

Publicity of appointment and reports

Where a receiver or manager is appointed then this must be stated in **32–43** various business documents relating to the company.[373] All receivers also have to make prescribed returns to the Registrar,[374] and the administrative receiver has to report to creditors, including unsecured creditors.[375] A receiver who fails to comply with his reporting obligations can be ordered to do so[376] and, more importantly, can be disqualified from acting as a receiver or manager.[377] There is no similar obligation to report where a debenture-holder enters into possession and it has been recommended that this omission be corrected.[378]

Administration[379]

Function

The "rescue" goals of the revised administration procedure are **32–44** clearly displayed in the current definition of the objectives of administration, set out in Sch.B1 to the IA 1986. Three objectives are listed but are put into a clear hierarchy. Priority is given to "rescuing the company as a going concern",[380] which is the objective which the administrator must pursue unless he or she thinks it is not practicable to achieve it or that the second objective would better serve the creditors' needs.[381] That second objective is "achieving a better result for the company's creditors as a whole than would be likely if the company were wound up".[382] Thus, preservation of the company as a going concern, to the benefit, for example, of employees, is not essential if the creditors would be worse off as a result. The third objective is "realising property in order to make a distribution to one or more secured or preferential creditors".[383] The administrator may pursue this objective only if it is not reasonably practicable to achieve the other two objectives, and it must be pursued in such a way that it will "not unnecessarily harm the interests of the other creditors of the company as a whole".[384] Subject to the qualification implied where the administrator legitimately pursues the third objective, the

---

[373] IA 1986 s.39.
[374] IA 1986 s.38 (receivers) and s.48 (administrative receivers).
[375] IA 1986 s.48.
[376] IA 1986 s.41. Also of relevance are the Insolvency Rules 1986, Pt 3.
[377] Company Directors Disqualification Act 1986, ss.1(1)(c), 3 and 22(7); see *Artic Engineering Ltd (No.2), Re* [1986] 1 W.L.R. 686.
[378] Jenkins Committee, para.306(k).
[379] This discussion will concentrate on the appointment of an administrator where the company has granted a floating charge, though, as we have seen (above, para.32–35) administration is not confined to such situations.
[380] Sch.B1, para.3(1)(a).
[381] para.3(3).
[382] para.3(1)(b).
[383] para.3(1)(c).
[384] para.3(4).

administrator must act "in the interests of the company's creditors as a whole".[385]

Although on an application to the court, the purpose of the proposed administration has to be stated, that purpose does not have to be confined to a single goal. It is more likely, therefore, that the statutory purposes will simply control the way in which the administrator, after appointment, exercises his or her powers. The floating charge holder may read these provisions with some gloom, for the priority given to the second objective over the third appears to mean that if the creditors as a whole would be better off than in a winding-up, the administrator should pursue that course of action, even if the charge holder will be worse off.[386]

Appointment

32–45   As is now generally required in the insolvency area, only a qualified insolvency practitioner may be appointed as an administrator.[387] An administrator may be appointed by the court, on application by the company, its directors or one or more creditors,[388] where the company is or is likely to become unable to pay its debts[389] and the appointment is "reasonably likely" to achieve one of the specified purposes.[390] This seems to put into statutory form the position at which the courts had arrived under the old law, which used a different form of wording, namely, that there must be a "real prospect" that the purpose or purposes will be achieved.[391] The change is important, for a higher hurdle materially increases the costs (as well as decreasing the chances) of securing an administration order, especially by encouraging applicants to commission an extensive report by an independent person in support of the application.[392]

An administrator may also be appointed out of court, and this now is the preferred route in the interest of saving costs. The ability to do

---

[385] para.3(2).

[386] This is subject to the "unfair harm" protection discussed below.

[387] IA 1986, Sch.B1, para.5.

[388] para.12 (or by the chief executive of a magistrates court in the case of fines imposed on companies).

[389] In one case (see para.35) this is not a requirement: this is where the application is made to the court by a floating charge holder who has the power to make an appointment out of court (see below). As we have seen above (para.824), the terms of debentures may give charge holders the power to appoint even though the company is able to pay its debts.

[390] para.11.

[391] *Harris Simmons Ltd, Re* [1989] 1 W.L.R. 368; *Primlaks (UK) Ltd, Re* [1989] B.C.L.C. 734; *cf. Consumer & Industrial Press Ltd, Re* [1988] B.C.L.C. 177.

[392] Provision is made for such reports by r.2.2 but they are not mandatory and the Chancery Division judges have sought to encourage concise reports not based on protracted and expensive investigation: Practice Note [1994] 1 W.L.R. 160.

this[393] was one of the important changes introduced by the Enterprise Act 2002, to reduce opposition to the proposals from banks.[394] The holder of a "qualifying floating charge",[395] being a charge or charges which relate to the whole or substantially the whole of the company's property, may appoint an administrator out of court where the instrument creating the charge gives the holder the power to do so.[396] Such an administrator will still be an officer of the court,[397] and what has been said above about the objectives of the administration still applies. Notice and other documents have to be filed with the court after the appointment.[398] If it turns out that the appointment was invalid (for example, because the appointor did not hold a valid floating charge),[399] the court may order the appointor to indemnify the person appointed against liability arising (for example, to the company in trespass or conversion).[400]

The company or the directors may also appoint an administrator out of court,[401] but not if a receiver is in office[402] and five days' notice of the intention to appoint has to be given to any floating charge holder, whose consent to the appointment is required.[403] This has two consequences. First, it gives the floating charge holder the opportunity to act first and appoint an administrator of its own choosing.[404] Secondly, in those cases where the charge holder still has the right to appoint an administrative receiver,[405] such an appointment may be made instead. Alternatively, the floating charge holder could simply block the appointment proposed by the company or its directors by not giving consent. In such a case the company or its directors would presumably apply to the court for an appointment. Indeed, it appears

---

[393] Though, as we have seen (above, para.32–45), the floating charge holder is not excluded from applying to the court for an appointment.

[394] Banks feared not only the cost of court applications, but, more so, the delay involved, during which desperate directors might spirit assets out of the company, once they knew of the petition.

[395] A floating charge over a company's property is a qualifying floating charge if it alone, or in conjunction with other floating or fixed charges, covers the whole, or substantially the whole of the company's property and the contract creating the floating charge states that the chargee may so appoint an administrator (IA 1986 s.72A and Sch.B1, para.14).

[396] para.14. He or she must give two days' notice of the intention to appoint to the holder of any prior floating charge (so that that person may take action, if desired), but the intention does not have to be advertised generally, which would defeat one of the objectives of this power.

[397] para.5.

[398] para.46.

[399] This means that the charge must be enforceable when the notice of appointment is filed under para.18, as that is when the appointment is made: *Fliptex Ltd v Hogg* [2004] EWHC 1280 (Ch); [2004] B.C.C. 870.

[400] para.21.

[401] para.22.

[402] para.25(c).

[403] para.28.

[404] In addition, on an application to the court by a non-floating charge holder, the charge holder has a presumptive right to have its nominee for administrator appointed in place of the applicant's: para.36.

[405] See above, para.32–36.

that the court can appoint an administrator even though a receiver has already been appointed,[406] but the situations in which the court may exercise this power are limited.[407] Thus, where the appointment of an administrative receiver is still allowed under the new regime, it is logically given priority over the appointment of an administrator.

Powers and duties

32–46   The first task of the administrator is to produce a set of proposals for the future of the company's business which are put before its creditors for their approval. This must be done within eight weeks of appointment, and sooner if possible.[408] The time limit may be extended by the court on application by the administrator.[409] Notice of the proposals has to be given to members as well as creditors,[410] since in some cases the members may have a financial interest in the success of the rescue. A wide range of outcomes is possible in the case of an administration. They do not need to be examined in detail here. They may be successful, as in acceptance by the creditors of proposals for a restructuring of their rights under a scheme of arrangement[411] that enables the company to come out of administration and be returned to its previous management, although perhaps with the former creditors now owning a majority of the shares. They may be unsuccessful, as in rejection of the administrator's plans by the creditors and the company being put into liquidation. And there are many variations in between. Whatever the decision reached, the administrator must report the outcome to the court and to the Registrar. Failure to do so attracts a fine.[412]

Between appointment and approval of the proposals, the administrator may exercise all the powers conferred by IA 1986 Sch.B1, para.59, and Sch.1, and this includes the power to dispose of the company's property if an attractive offer is made.[413]

During the administration process, the company benefits from a moratorium on both winding up[414] and legal proceedings for the enforcement of claims against it, except, in the latter case, with the

---

[406]   para.12(1)(a) clearly contemplates that a receiver may be in place when the application to the court for an administrator is made, as does para.41, which provides for an administrative receiver to vacate office when an administrator is appointed.

[407]   para.39—essentially where the charge holder consents or the charge is thought to be subject to challenge, for example under s.245 (above, para.32–16).

[408]   para.49(5).

[409]   paras 49(8) and 107.

[410]   para.49(4).

[411]   See above, Ch.29.

[412]   Para.53(2) and (3).

[413]   *Transbus International Ltd, Re* [2004] 1 W.L.R. 2654, at paras [12]–[14].

[414]   But not winding up under IA 1986 s.124A on public interest grounds: see Ch.18, para.18–10. See para.42(4)(a).

consent of the administrator or the court.[415] A somewhat more limited moratorium also applies from the moment any formal step is
taken to seek an administration order.[416] The administrator has
general authority to manage the company's business, acting as its
agent,[417] as well as the powers specified in Sch.1 to the Act;[418] may
appoint and remove directors;[419] and, as we have noted,[420] may dispose of property subject to the floating charge[421] and, with the consent of the court, even property subject to a fixed charge.[422] However,
the court may so order only if the court thinks the disposal would be
likely to promote the purposes of the administration and there is
applied to discharging the security the net proceeds of the disposal
and any additional amount needed to bring that amount up to the
market value of the asset. Since the moratorium will prevent the
charge holders (fixed or floating) from enforcing their security, the
position may be that charge holders not only cannot repossess their
property but that the administrator has disposed of it. However, the
floating charge holder will have his or her security transferred to the
proceeds of the sale,[423] whilst the conditions attached to the court's
power to sanction a sale over property in relation to which a fixed
charge obtains mean the only detriment to the fixed charge holder is
that he cannot control the timing of the realisation of his security,
which will be undertaken by the administrator, probably as part of a
larger disposal, instead of by the security holder as a single
transaction.

Overall, the administrator has all the powers normally vested in the
board of directors.[424] In contrast with an administrative receiver,[425] he
is not personally liable on contracts which he enters into on the
company's behalf. However, the Act contains an alternative
mechanism for ensuring that the administrator secures the discharge
of the obligations he causes the company to incur. When the
administrator relinquishes office, undischarged liabilities are charged

---

[415] paras 42 and 43. Para.43(4) includes the landlord's right of forfeiture by peaceable re-entry,
which had been an issue disputed in the pre-2002 case-law. This extension was made initially
by the Insolvency Act 2000, s.9. However, intervention by regulators appears to remain
outside the moratorium. See *Air Ecosse Ltd v Civil Aviation Authority* (1987) 3 B.C.C. 492;
Railtrack Plc, Re [2002] 2 B.C.L.C. 755.

[416] para.44.

[417] para.69, so that the company, not the appointor, is liable for unlawful acts of the
administrator.

[418] para.59.

[419] para.61.

[420] See above, para.32–18.

[421] para.70.

[422] para.71.

[423] para.70(2), thus in effect putting the charge holder in the position which obtained before the
charge crystallised.

[424] The directors, although still in place, may not exercise management power without the
consent of the administrator: para.64.

[425] Who, despite the fact that he too acts as an agent is personally liable on contracts he enters
into unless they provide to the contrary. See above, para.32–41.

on the company's assets and rank ahead of any floating charge or the administrator's own remuneration.[426]

32–47   The moratorium which, as we have noted, was not available to the administrative receiver, may prove an important means of reconciling the banks to the use of the administration. Although it prevents them from enforcing their security, it also keeps unsecured creditors at bay and may promote the sale of the company's business at a higher price, from which those with security will be the first to benefit financially. However, the impact of the moratorium depends in part on how willing the courts are to grant leave. Some guidance on this was given by the Court of Appeal in *Atlantic Computer Systems (No.1), Re*[427] of which the following is a summary. Since the prohibitions in section 11 are intended to assist the administrator to achieve the purpose of the administration, it is for the person who seeks leave (or consent) to make out a case for being granted it. If leave is unlikely to impede the achievement of that purpose, leave should normally be given. In other cases it is necessary to carry out a balancing exercise, weighing the legitimate interests of the applicant and those of the other creditors of the company. In carrying out that exercise the underlying principle is that an administration should not be conducted at the expense of those who have proprietary rights which they are seeking to exercise, except to the extent that this may be inevitable if the purpose of the administration is to succeed and even then only to a limited extent. Thus, it will normally be a sufficient ground for granting leave if significant loss would otherwise be suffered by the applicant, unless the loss to others would be significantly greater. In assessing the respective losses all the circumstances relating to the administration should be taken into account and regard paid to how probable they are likely to be. The conduct of the respective parties may sometimes also be relevant. Similar considerations apply to decisions regarding imposing terms.

Of course, an unpaid creditor of a company in administration does not have an obligation to continue with supplies or to make further advances unless contractually or statutorily required to do so.[428] Thus, the moratorium may protect the company in administration from pressure from its existing creditors, but it falls far short of guaranteeing that the administrator will be able to carry on the business effectively during the administration. That is likely to require fresh funding and the availability (or not) of such funding is one of the matters the court needs to consider when deciding whether to appoint an administrator.

---

[426] para.99(4). For the application of this rule in relation to adopted employment contracts, see *Powdrill v Watson* [1995] 2 A.C. 394, HL, partially reversed by the Insolvency Act 1994, and Pollard (1995) 24 I.L.J. 141.

[427] [1992] Ch. 505. See also *Bristol Airport Plc v Powdrill* [1990] Ch. 744, CA.

[428] *Leyland DAF Ltd v Automotive Products Plc* [1994] 1 B.C.L.C. 245, CA.

Protections for creditors and members as against the administrator

It is clear that an administration may give rise to many of the same **32–48** agency problems which we have examined in previous Chapters in relation to companies that are going concerns. There may be conflicts between majority and minority creditors, and administrators may exercise their wide powers unfairly or incompetently. The Schedule provides some remedies aimed at such conduct. First, administrator proposals to the creditors may not involve downgrading the rights of secured or preferential creditors, without their consent or use of a scheme of arrangement or a company voluntary arrangement (which contain mechanisms for the protection of minorities).[429] Thus, although the secured creditor is put into a collective insolvency procedure, it is given specific protection that the administrator may not propose action which "affects the right of a secured creditor to enforce his security".[430] Secondly, and more generally, protection against unfair prejudice[431] is extended to actions of the administrator, so that any member or creditor of the company can apply to the court for relief[432] on the grounds that the administrator is acting, has acted or proposes to act in a way which is "unfairly harms" the interests of the applicant.[433] It is not clear whether the substitution of the phrase "unfairly harms" for the phrase "unfairly prejudicial", which is used in the equivalent CA provision[434] and was used in the original version of the IA 1986[435] is intended to produce a substantive change. Thirdly, an application can also be made on the grounds that the administrator "is not performing his functions as quickly or efficiently as is reasonably practicable",[436] thus giving members and creditors an uncomplicated route to complain about negligence on the part of the administrator.[437] Fourthly, the misfeasance provisions from IA 1986 s.212[438] are elaborated in their application to administrators.[439] Together, these last three provisions lay down standards

[429] para.73. Thus, in creditor meetings to approve a scheme secured and unsecured creditors would be put in separate classes: above, Ch.29 at paras 29–6—29–7.

[430] It is important not to overestimate the extent of this specific protection. It applies only to the right to enforce the security; it would not apply to action which fails to maximise the value of the assets to which the security attaches.

[431] See above, Ch.20.

[432] The court has broad relief powers (para.74(3) and (4)), but there is no specific mention of a power to order litigation in the name of the company (though presumably the court could do so under its general authority to "grant relief") or the compulsory purchase of shares (hardly likely to be an appropriate order in an administration).

[433] para.74. This applies whilst the company is "in administration". If it is not, the creditor may no longer petition; if it is, this paragraph effectively replaces CA 2006 s.994 as far as members are concerned, for the administrator's or court's consent would be needed under the moratorium provisions for a s.994 petition to be launched.

[434] Now CA 2006 s.994.

[435] IA 1986 s.27, now repealed.

[436] para.74(2).

[437] *cf.* the uncertainties surrounding the use of CA 2006 s.994 (previously CA 1985 s.459) against negligence, above, Ch.20 at paras 20–3 *et seq.* and fn.51.

[438] See above, Ch.17.

[439] para.75.

by which the creditors and members can challenge conduct of the administrator which either falls below the standard of competence they are entitled to expect or which does not give appropriate weight to their interests.[440]

Publication of appointment

32–49 A newly appointed administrator must notify the company, the Registrar, and the company's creditors of the appointment.[441] While the company is in administration, every business document must state that fact and name the administrator.[442]

Administration expenses

32–50 Debts or liabilities arising out of contracts entered into by the administrator have priority (often called "super-priority") over the administrator's own remuneration and expenses.[443] This can amount to a hefty liability. The expenses of administration, including the administrator's remuneration, then have priority over a debt secured by a floating charge.[444] After this, the normal priority rules apply.[445]

End of administration

32–51 Under IA 1986 s.76, the appointment of an administrator ceases to have effect at the end of the period of one year beginning with the date on which the appointment took effect, unless the term of office is extended by the court or with the consent of the creditors. The term may be extended by consent only once[446] and by no more than six months.[447]

Alternatively, on the application of the administrator, the court may provide for the appointment of the administrator to cease to have effect, if the purpose of the administration has been sufficiently

---

[440] The risk that these provisions will be used by particular creditors or members opportunistically to block a resolution of the company's problems is somewhat reduced by para.74(6) which says that no order by way of relief may be made by the court if it would "impede or prevent the implementation of a scheme agreed under the CA or a company voluntary arrangement agreed under Pt I of the IA or administrator proposals approved by creditors, unless, in the last case, the application is made within 28 days. However, a fixed charge holder can use this procedure even when the court has authorised the administrator to dispose of the property (see para.74(5)(b)), presumably lest the administrator carry out the disposal in an unfair or negligent way.

[441] IA 1986, Sch.B1, para.46.

[442] para.45.

[443] para.99. But the provisions are strictly construed, and damages for wrongful dismissal or other payments in lieu are not entitled to super-priority: *Leeds United Association Football Club Ltd (in admin.), Re* [2007] I.C.R. 1688 at 1761 (Ch).

[444] para.99.

[445] See above, para.32–13.

[446] para.78(4).

[447] para.76(2)(b).

achieved in relation to the company.[448] Administrators are often keen for these provisions to be interpreted pragmatically in order to enable them to escape accruing business liabilities; the courts have generally complied.[449]

CONCLUSION

A company must be able to raise debt finance, and so it must be able **32–52** to grant effective security to lenders. It is possible to conceive of a legal regime in which the position of companies giving security is in essence no different from that of any other borrower. There would inevitably be some company law aspects to security transactions—for example, are the directors authorised to enter into the particular transaction contemplated?—but those company law aspects would not be unique to security transactions. As we saw in Chapter 7, the issue of directors' authority can easily arise in relation to transactions that do not involve a grant of security.

In fact, however, as this Chapter has shown, the current law on the granting of security does have two features that are specific to the corporate nature of the debtor. These are the availability of the floating charge and the system of registration of charges granted by companies. We have also seen, however, that the modern tendency is to whittle away these uniquely corporate features. Thus, the unique enforcement mechanism for the floating charge by means of the appointment of an administrative receiver has been substantially replaced by the general insolvency mechanism of the appointment of an administrator, as introduced by the Enterprise Act 2002. Going further, the Law Commission has queried the justification for retaining the provisions in the Bills of Sales Acts which prevent non-corporate businesses granting floating charges (as have other bodies before them).[450] Equally, in its proposals for radical reform of the companies charges system, the Law Commission clearly regards the optimal solution as being a registration system applying to charges (and quasi-securities) granted by all debtors,[451] although its proposals were not adopted. Could it be that, like corporate insolvency and public offers of corporate securities before them, security interests granted by companies is a topic which is on its way out of core company law, in order to join up with the rules that apply where a company is not involved?

---

[448] para.79(3)(b).
[449] *TM Kingdom Ltd, Re* [2007] B.C.C. 480; *GHE Realisations Ltd, Re* [2006] B.C.C. 139.
[450] See above, fn.168, Pt IX. In one limited area, that of farmers, the problem was addressed as long ago as 1928 in the Agricultural Credits Act of that year.
[451] Para.32–23, fn.261, Pt X and paras 1.17–1.18.

A NOTE ON WINDING-UP, DISSOLUTION AND RESTORATION

The provisions relating to winding-up and dissolution are now to be **A–1** found almost exclusively[1] in the Insolvency Act 1986 and Pt IV of the Insolvency Rules,[2] and not in the Companies Act: and rightly so where the company is insolvent. But, although insolvency is the most common reason for winding up, it is far from being the only one and, when the company is fully solvent, it seems, on the face of it, somewhat illogical to treat the process as part of insolvency law rather than company law. The reason why the legislation relating to liquidation of solvent companies is in the Insolvency Act is probably to avoid duplicating those many provisions that apply whether or not the company is insolvent—to repeat them in the Companies Act would have added substantially to the length of the combined legislation. But it can also be justified as realistic. Once a company goes into liquidation, the distinction between shareholders and creditors becomes more than usually difficult to draw: the members' interests

---

[1] But see Part 31 of the Companies Act 2006, below, para.A–12.
[2] Both eschew the use of the word "members" and substitute "contributories", thus giving the misleading impression that it means only members who are called upon to contribute because their shares are partly paid (or in the case of guarantee companies because of the minimal amounts that they have agreed to contribute on a winding-up). To avoid this impression, here "members" has been substituted; but readers should be warned that that too is not wholly accurate for "contributories" also includes past members unless they ceased to be members more than 12 months before the commencement of the winding-up: see IA ss.74 and 76 and *Anglesea Collieries, Re* (1866) L.R. 1 Ch. 555, CA and *Consolidated Goldfields of New Zealand, Re* [1953] Ch. 689.

will, in effect, have become purely financial interests deferred to those of the creditors.

TYPES OF WINDING-UP

A–2 The basic distinction is between voluntary winding-up and compulsory winding-up by the court.[3] But voluntary winding-up is subdivided into two types—members' voluntary winding-up and creditors' voluntary winding-up. In relation to companies registered under the Companies Acts which are dealt with in Part IV of the Insolvency Act, Chapters I and VII–X of that Part relate to all three types, except where it is otherwise stated; Chapters II and V relate to both types of voluntary winding-up; Chapter III relates only to members' voluntary winding-up; Chapter IV only to creditors' voluntary winding-up; and Chapter VI only to winding-up by the court. This arrangement of the sections is not exactly "user friendly" for it means that, to grasp which sections apply to the type of winding-up with which one is concerned, it is necessary to refer to various chapters of Part IV. Nor is life made easier because other Parts of the Act may also be relevant: for example Part VI on "miscellaneous provisions" and Part VII on "interpretation for first group of Parts".

As their names imply, an essential difference between compulsory winding-up by the court and voluntary winding-up is that the former does not necessarily involve action taken by any organ of the company itself, whereas voluntary winding-up does. The essential difference between members' and creditors' winding-up is that the former is possible only if the company is solvent, in which event the company's members appoint the liquidator, whereas, if it is not, its creditors have the whip hand in deciding who the liquidator shall be. In all three cases, the winding-up process is not exclusively directed towards realising the assets and distributing the net proceeds to the creditors and, if anything is left, to the members, according to their respective priorities: it also enables an examination of the conduct of the company's management to be undertaken. This may result in civil and criminal proceedings being taken against those who have

---

[3] In relation to the winding-up of "unregistered companies" (on which see para.6–7, above) winding-up by the court is the only method allowed: see Pt V of the Act. A company incorporated outside Great Britain which has been carrying on business in Britain may be wound up as an unregistered company notwithstanding that it has ceased to exist under the law of the country of incorporation: s.225. There used to be a further (hybrid) type of voluntary winding-up subject to the supervision of the court, but this had ceased to be used and was abolished by the reforms of 1985/1986.

engaged in any malpractices thus revealed[4] and in the adjustment or avoidance of various transactions.[5]

Winding-up by the court

Under s.122 of the Insolvency Act a company may be wound up by the court[6] on one or more of seven specified grounds. Of these grounds, by far the most important is ground (f), that the company is unable to pay its debts, and the next most important is ground (g), that the court is of the opinion that it is just and equitable that the company should be wound up. The latter has been dealt with in Chapter 20 (where we saw that it may be used as a remedy in cases where members are being unfairly prejudiced or there is a deadlocked management) and in Chapter 18 (where we saw that it may be invoked by the Secretary of State following the exercise by him of his investigatory powers). The presence of a minority protection remedy in the Insolvency Act is, in fact, something of an anomaly. It should be noted that the company itself can opt for winding-up by the court, since ground (a) is that the company has by special resolution resolved that the company be so wound up. But normally that is the last thing that those controlling the company will want: it is the most expensive type of winding-up and the one in which their conduct is likely to be investigated most thoroughly.[7]

Section 123 affords creditors owed more than £750 a simple means of establishing ground (f), that the company is unable to pay its debts.[8] Creditors are among those who may petition for a winding-up[9] and this they are likely to do once it becomes widely known that the company is in financial difficulties;[10] like a petition for the bankruptcy of an individual, a petition for winding-up is the creditors' ultimate remedy. The company itself or its directors[11] or

A–3

---

[4] See Pt IV, Ch.X of the Act.
[5] See Pt VI, ss.238–246.
[6] Normally the High Court, but the county court of the district in which the company has its registered office has concurrent jurisdiction if the company's paid-up capital is small and if that county court has jurisdiction in relation to bankruptcy of individuals: s.117.
[7] But it might be used if the court is already involved because the liquidation of the company is part of a scheme requiring its sanction in accordance with the provisions discussed in Ch.29, above.
[8] By serving a "statutory notice" in accordance with s.123(1)(a).
[9] s.124. As may the chief executive of a magistrates' Court.
[10] Until then each may try to obtain judgment and levy execution thus getting ahead of the pack.
[11] Prior to the 1985/86 statutory reforms, it was held, somewhat surprisingly, that directors could not apply: *Emmerdart Ltd, Re* [1979] Ch. 540. Now they can. For the interpretation of "the directors" see *Equiticorp International Plc, Re* [1989] 1 W.L.R. 1010.

members[12] may petition but the court will be reluctant to grant it on ground (f) if it is opposed by a majority of the creditors.

If a winding-up order is made, the first step needing to be taken will be to appoint a liquidator to whom, as in all types of winding-up, the administration of the company's affairs and property will pass. In contrast with an individual's trustee-in-bankruptcy the company's property does not vest in the liquidator;[13] but the control and management of it and of the company's affairs do and the board of directors, in effect, becomes *functus officio*. A liquidator may, indeed, be appointed before a final order is made, for at any time after the presentation of a winding-up petition the court may appoint a provisional liquidator, normally the official receiver attached to the court.[14]

The important role played by official receivers in compulsory liquidations in England and Wales[15] is perhaps the major difference between compulsory and voluntary liquidations.[16] Official receivers are officers of the Insolvency Service, an Executive Agency of BERR, attached to courts having bankruptcy jurisdiction.[17] Not only will an OR normally be the provisional liquidator (if one is appointed) but he will generally be the initial liquidator and often will remain the liquidator throughout. On the making of a winding-up order[18] the OR automatically becomes liquidator by virtue of his office and will remain so unless and until another liquidator is appointed.[19] The OR may succeed in getting rid of the office by summoning separate meetings of the creditors and of the members for the purpose of appointing another liquidator.[20] And if that does not succeed,[21] the

---

[12] But unless the membership has been reduced below two, a member cannot apply unless his shares were originally allotted to him or have been held and registered in his name for at least 6 months during the 18 months prior to the commencement of the winding-up (on which see below) or have devolved on him through the death of a former holder: s.124(2). This is designed to prevent a disgruntled person (e.g. an ex-employee) from buying a share and then bringing a winding-up petition (or threatening to do so).

[13] Unless the court so orders, as it may: s.145(1).

[14] s.135.

[15] Scotland manages without them but when the Government, in a desire to reduce civil service manpower and public expenditure, proposed to remove their role in individual bankruptcy there was bitter opposition (not least from the Cork Committee: see Cmnd. 8558, Ch.14) and the proposal was dropped.

[16] In the latter, their role is principally in relation to disqualification of directors under the Directors Disqualification Act (on which see Ch.10 at para.000, above).

[17] Official receivers have the unique distinction of being entitled to act as liquidators notwithstanding that they are not licensed insolvency practitioners under Pt XIII of the Act: ss.388(5) and 389(2).

[18] Except when it is made immediately upon the discharge of an administration order or when there is a supervisor of a voluntary arrangement under Pt I of the Act when the former administrator or the supervisor of the arrangement may be appointed by the court as liquidator: s.140.

[19] s.136(1) and (2).

[20] See s.136(4) and (5). The nominee of the creditors prevails unless, on application to the court, it otherwise orders (s.139) which it is unlikely to do if the company is insolvent.

[21] Which it may not since both creditors and members may be happy to leave the liquidation to the official receiver since that may prove less expensive.

OR may decide to refer the need to appoint another liquidator to the Secretary of State who may appoint.[22] But, whenever any vacancy occurs, the OR again becomes the liquidator until another is appointed.[23]

Whether or not the official receiver becomes the liquidator the OR **A–4** has important investigatory powers and duties. When the court has made a winding-up order the OR may require officers, employees and those who have taken part in the formation of the company to submit a statement as to the affairs of the company verified by affidavit.[24] It is the duty of the OR to investigate the causes of the failure, and to make such report, if any, to the court as he thinks fit.[25] The OR may apply to the court for the public examination of anyone who is or has been an officer, liquidator, administrator, receiver or manager of the company or anyone else who has taken part in its promotion, formation or management and must do so, unless the court otherwise orders, if requested by one-half in value of the creditors or three-quarters in value of the members.[26] And if the OR is not the liquidator, the person who is must give the OR all the information and assistance reasonably required for the exercise of these functions.[27]

On the making of a winding-up order the winding-up is deemed to have commenced as from the date of the presentation of the petition (or, indeed, if the order is made in respect of a company already in voluntary winding-up, as from the date of the resolution to wind up voluntarily).[28] This dating back is important since it can have the effect of invalidating property dispositions[29] and executions of judgments[30] lawfully undertaken during the period between the presentation of the petition and the order,[31] and of affecting the duration of the periods prior to "the onset of insolvency" in which, if certain transactions are undertaken, they are liable to adjustment or avoidance in the event of winding-up or administration.[32]

Once a liquidator is appointed, the process of the winding-up proceeds very much as it would in the case of a voluntary liquidation since the objective is identical and his functions are the same as those in voluntary windings up, namely "to secure that the assets of the company are got in, realised, and distributed to the company's

---

[22] s.137.
[23] s.136(3).
[24] s.131. See also ss.235 and 236.
[25] s.132.
[26] ss.133 and 134. It is this public examination that is the most dreaded ordeal, particularly if the company is sufficiently well known to attract the attention of the general public and the Press.
[27] s.143.
[28] s.129.
[29] s.127.
[30] s.128.
[31] Which may be considerable if hearings are adjourned, as is not infrequent.
[32] See ss.238–245.

creditors[33] and, if there is a surplus, to the persons entitled to it".[34] The main difference is that, in a winding-up by the court, the liquidator in the exercise of powers given under Schedule 4 to the Act will more often be required to obtain the sanction of the court before entering into transactions and that throughout the liquidator will be subject to the surveillance of the OR acting, in effect, as an officer of the court.

Voluntary winding-up

A–5   In contrast with winding-up by the court, voluntary winding-up always starts with a resolution of the company. In the unlikely event of the articles fixing a period for the duration of the company[35] or specifying an event on the occurrence of which it is to be dissolved,[36] all that is required is an ordinary resolution in general meeting.[37] Otherwise, what is required is a special resolution that the company be wound up voluntarily.[38] In either case the resolution is subject to the requirement that a copy of it has to be sent to the Registrar within 15 days[39] and the company must give notice of the resolution by advertisement in the *Gazette* within 14 days of its passing.[40] A voluntary winding-up is deemed to commence on the passing of the resolution;[41] there is no "relating back" as there is in the case of winding-up by the court. As from the commencement of the winding-up, the company must cease to carry on its business, except so far as may be required for its beneficial winding-up,[42] and any transfer of shares, unless made with the sanction of the liquidator, is void, as is any alteration in the status of the members.[43]

---

[33] Giving priority, of course, to preferred creditors as set out in Sch.6 to the Act.
[34] s.143(1). Normally the members (except in the case of non-profit-making or charitable companies) in accordance with their class rights on a winding-up.
[35] This is rare but charters of incorporation of limited duration are not uncommon.
[36] It is possible to conceive of circumstances in which this might be done: e.g. when a partnership converts to an incorporated company because its solicitors and accountants advise that this would be advantageous tax-wise, the partners might wish to ensure that it could be dissolved by a simple majority if they were later advised that it would be better to revert to a partnership.
[37] s.84(1)(a).
[38] s.84(1)(b). The former provision for the passing of an extraordinary resolution (s.84(1)(c)) was repealed by the Companies Act 2006 (Commencement No.3, Consequential Amendments, Transitional Provisions and Savings) Order 2007 (SI 2007/2194), art.10(3) and Sch.5, on the grounds that a meeting at which a special resolution is to be proposed can now be convened on 14 days' notice (s.307 of the CA 2006), in contrast to the 21 days previously required, speed being of the essence where the company is insolvent.
[39] s.84(3).
[40] s.85(1).
[41] s.86.
[42] s.87(1).
[43] s.88. Contrast the wording of the comparable s.127, above, in relation to winding-up by the court: that avoids also any disposition of the company's property (unless the court otherwise orders) which s.88 does not.

Members' winding-up

The most important question which the directors of the company will **A–6** have had to consider prior to the passing of the resolution is whether they can, in good conscience and without dire consequences to themselves, allow the voluntary winding-up to proceed as a members', as opposed to a creditors', winding-up. In order for that to occur they, or if there are more than two of them, the majority of them, must, in accordance with s.89, make at a directors' meeting[44] a statutory declaration (the "declaration of solvency") to the effect that they have made a full inquiry into the company's affairs and that, having done so, they have formed the opinion that the company will be able to pay its debts in full, together with interest at the "official rate",[45] within such period, not exceeding 12 months from the commencement of the winding-up, as may be specified in the declaration.[46] This was the origin of the declaration of solvency now used in the out-of-court procedure for a reduction of capital[47] and in respect of an acquisition of shares out of capital.[48]

The declaration is ineffective unless:

(a) it is made within five weeks preceding the date of the passing of the resolution; and

(b) it embodies a statement of the company's assets and liabilities as at the latest practicable date before the making of the declaration.[49]

If a director makes the declaration without having reasonable grounds for believing that the company will be able to pay its debts with interest within the period specified in the declaration he or she is liable to a fine and imprisonment,[50] and if the debts are not so paid it is presumed, unless the contrary is shown, that the director did not have reasonable grounds for that opinion.[51] It therefore behoves the directors to take the utmost care and to seek professional advice before they make the declaration. Especially is this so because, even if the winding-up is a members' one, a licensed insolvency practitioner will have to be appointed as liquidator and the liquidator is likely to detect whether the declaration was over-optimistic long before the

[44] This, on the face of it rather curious, use of a board meeting as a venue for the making of statutory declarations ensures that all the directors know what is going on.
[45] i.e. whichever is the greater of the interest payable on judgment debts or that applicable to the particular debt apart from the winding-up: ss.189(4) and 251.
[46] s.89(1). In practice the declaration will play safe and not specify a shorter period than 12 months even if the directors expect that it will be shorter.
[47] See para.13–5.
[48] See para.13–19.
[49] s.89(2). The declaration must be delivered to the Registrar within 15 days immediately following the passing of the resolution: s.89(3) and (4).
[50] s.89(4).
[51] s.89(5).

expiration of the 12 months. Formerly, small private companies could, and often did, appoint as liquidator one of the directors and, in effect, continued to proceed much as they would have when a partnership was being dissolved. This is no longer possible:[52] despite the efforts begun by the 1989 Act to reduce the burdens on private companies, the Insolvency Act has increased their burdens as regards winding-up even if they are quasi-partnerships.

A–7   If the professional liquidator forms the opinion that the company will not be able to pay its debts within the stated period, he or she must summon a meeting of the creditors and supply them with full information in accordance with section 95 and, as from the date when the meeting is held, the winding-up is converted under section 96 from a members' to a (insolvent) creditors' voluntary winding-up.[53] So long, however, as the liquidator shares the view of the directors (and if they are wise they will have consulted him, as their proposed nominee, before they made the declaration) all should proceed smoothly as a members' winding-up. The company in general meeting will appoint one or more liquidators for the purpose of winding up the company's affairs and distributing its assets[54] whereupon "all the powers of the directors cease except so far as a general meeting or the liquidator sanctions their continuance."[55] If a vacancy in the office of liquidator "occurs by death, resignation or otherwise" the company in general meeting may fill the vacancy,[56] subject to any arrangement with the creditors.[57] If the winding-up continues for more than a year,[58] the liquidator must summon a general meeting at the end of the first and any subsequent year or at the first convenient date within three months from the end of the year or such longer period as the Secretary of State may allow.[59] The liquidator must lay before the meeting an account of his acts and dealings, and of the conduct of the winding-up during the year.[60]

When the company's affairs are fully wound up the liquidator must draw up an account of the winding-up, showing how it has been

---

[52] But see below at paras A–13 *et seq.* for the possible resort to s.1003 of the Companies Act.
[53] Indeed, it may become a winding-up by the court, for a winding-up order may be made notwithstanding that the company is already in voluntary winding-up and an official receiver, as well as the other persons entitled under s.124, may present a petition: s.124(5). But unless the court, on proof of fraud or mistake, directs otherwise, all proceedings already taken in the voluntary winding-up are deemed to have been validly taken: s.129(1).
[54] s.91(1).
[55] s.91(2).
[56] s.92(1). The meeting to do so may be convened by any continuing liquidators if there was more than one or by a member: s.92(2).
[57] This reference to "creditors" is presumably to cover the case where the members' voluntary winding-up forms part of a reorganisation of one of the types dealt with in Ch.29 above, in which creditors are involved.
[58] Which it may, because although the creditors should be paid within 12 months the subsequent distribution of the remaining assets or their proceeds does not have to be completed within any prescribed time.
[59] s.93(1).
[60] s.93(2).

conducted and the company's property disposed of, and must call a final meeting of the company for the purpose of laying before it the account and giving an explanation of it.[61] The fact that this meeting is being called is something which is of wider interest than to members alone for, as we shall see,[62] it will lead to the final dissolution of the company. The Act provides that it shall be called by advertisement in the *Gazette*, specifying its time, place and object and published at least one month before the meeting.[63] Within one week after the meeting he must also send the Registrar a copy of the account and make a return to him of the holding of the meeting.[64]

Creditors' winding-up

Here, in contrast with members' winding-up, the company is assumed   **A–8** to be insolvent and it is the creditors in whose interests the winding-up is undertaken and they who have the whip hand. If no declaration of solvency has been made, the company must cause a meeting of its creditors to be summoned for a day not later than the 14th day after the resolution for voluntary winding-up is to be proposed. It must cause notices to be sent by post to the creditors not less than seven days before the date of the meeting and must advertise it once in the *Gazette* and once at least in two newspapers circulating in the locality in which the company's principal place of business in Great Britain was situated during the previous six months.[65] This must state either (a) the name of a qualified insolvency practitioner[66] who, before the meeting, will furnish creditors with such information as they may reasonably require or (b) a place where, on the two business days before the meeting, a list of the company's creditors will be available for inspection free of charge.[67] Further, the directors must prepare a statement of the company's affairs verified by affidavit and cause it to be laid before the creditors' meeting. The directors must also nominate one of their number to preside at the creditors' meeting—an unenviable task which it is the nominee's duty to perform.[68]

At the respective meetings the creditors and the company may nominate a liquidator and if the creditors do so their nominee becomes the liquidator, unless, on application to the court by a director, creditor or member, it directs that the nominee of the

---

[61] s.94(1).

[62] Paras A–10ff below.

[63] What is surprising is that neither the Act nor the Rules seem to require the liquidator to give written notice to the members. If he does not, it is not surprising that the final meeting is frequently inquorate.

[64] s.94(3) and (4). If a quorum is not present the liquidator must send instead a return that the meeting was duly summoned and that no quorum was present.

[65] s.98(1).

[66] In practice he will probably be the person that the directors intend to propose to the company meeting for appointment as liquidator.

[67] s.98(2).

[68] s.99.

company shall be liquidator instead of, or jointly with, the creditors' nominee, or it appoints some other person instead of the creditors' nominee.[69] Provisions, similar in effect, apply when a members' winding-up is converted to a creditors' winding-up because the liquidator concludes that the company's debts will not be paid in full within the 12 months, except that the obligations of the directors have to be undertaken by the incumbent liquidator.[70]

In a creditors' voluntary winding-up,[71] or in a winding-up by the court,[72] the creditors may decide at their initial or a subsequent meeting to establish what used to be called a "committee of inspection" but which the Act now calls a "liquidation committee", and, in the case of a creditors' winding-up, may appoint not more than five members of it.[73] If they do so, the company in general meeting may also appoint members not exceeding five in number.[74] However, if the creditors resolve that all or any of those appointed by the general meeting ought not to be members of the committee, the persons concerned will not be qualified to act unless the court otherwise directs.[75]

The functions of a liquidation committee are to be found in the Rules rather than the Act and for present purposes can be summarised by saying that they give the liquidator the opportunity of consulting the creditors and the members without having to convene formal creditors' and company meetings and also provide additional means whereby the creditors and members can keep an eye on the liquidator. In the latter respect, liquidation committees are, perhaps, likely to be more valuable in creditors' voluntary windings-up (rather than in windings-up by the court) owing to the lesser role played by official receivers.

It may be thought somewhat anomalous that, when the company is insolvent, the members should have equal (or any) representation on the liquidation committee. But the Cork Committee rejected the argument that they should not, because "it is rarely possible to assess the interest of shareholders at the outset of proceedings."[76] This is certainly true. What at the commencement of the winding-up would seem to be a clear case of the company's liabilities greatly exceeding its assets (so that the shareholders have no prospective stake in the

---

[69] s.100.

[70] ss.95 and 96.

[71] s.101, and, when a members' is converted to a creditors' winding-up, s.102.

[72] s.141.

[73] s.101(1). In the case of windings-up by the court the position under s.141 and Ch.12 of Pt IV of the Rules is somewhat different and is designed to ensure that, when the official receiver is the liquidator, the committee's functions are performed instead by the Insolvency Service and that, if the liquidator is some other person, it is left to that person to decide whether to convene a meeting of creditors to establish a liquidation committee (unless one-tenth in value of the creditors require him to do so).

[74] s.101(2).

[75] s.101(3).

[76] Cmnd. 8558, para.939.

outcome of the winding-up) may turn out otherwise if the winding-up is prolonged.[77]

In other respects a creditors' winding-up proceeds up to and including the final meeting in much the same way as in a members' winding-up.

Conclusion

No attempt has been made here to deal with the many important **A–9** matters which may arise in the course of winding-up, whether by the court or voluntarily; for example how creditors "prove" their debts (dealt with in detail by the Rules rather than by the Act). However, a word ought to be said about the position of secured creditors in order to draw attention to the difference between their position on a winding-up compared with that during an administration. As we saw, in the latter, unless they have taken steps to enforce their security prior to the administration, they may be in difficulties in doing so while it lasts.[78] In contrast, on a winding-up, a secured creditor is in the enviable position of having the choice of realising his security and, if this does not raise sufficient to pay what is due in full, to prove for the balance, or to surrender his security for the benefit of the general body of creditors and prove for the whole debt.[79] Normally, of course, the former option will be adopted.[80]

DISSOLUTION

After winding-up

In contrast with the formalities attendant on the birth of a com- **A–10** pany,[81] its death takes place with a singular absence of ceremony. In the case of voluntary liquidations, once the liquidator has sent to the Registrar his final account and return,[82] on the expiration of three months from their registration the company is deemed to be dissolved,[83] unless the court, on the application of the liquidator or any

---

[77] But, unless it is, the reverse is at present likely to be the case, resulting in members' windings-up having to be converted into creditors' (or to winding-up by the court).

[78] See paras 32–44ff, above.

[79] Rule 4.88. If the winding-up follows an administration in which the administrator has exercised his powers under Sch.B1, paras 70 and 71 (para.32–46, above) it would seem that the effect of paras 70(2) and 71(3) will be to preserve the security holder's rights by treating the sums mentioned in those subsections as the security in the winding-up.

[80] Unless the secured creditor is unusually altruistic or wants to maximise his or her votes at a creditors' meeting.

[81] See Ch.4.

[82] In accordance with s.94 (members' voluntary) or s.106 (creditors' voluntary).

[83] s.201(1) and (2).

other person who appears to the court to be interested, makes an order deferring the date of dissolution.[84]

Normally, the position is much the same where the winding-up is by the court. Once it appears that the winding-up is for all practical purposes complete, the liquidator must summon a final meeting of creditors[85] which receives the liquidator's report on the winding-up and determines whether the liquidator shall be released.[86] The liquidator then gives notice to the court and to the Registrar that the meeting has been held and of the decisions (if any) of the meeting. When the Registrar receives the notice, it is registered and, unless the Secretary of State, on the application of the official receiver or anyone else who appears to be interested, directs a deferment,[87] the company is dissolved at the end of three months from that registration.[88]

If the official receiver is the liquidator the procedure is the same except that registration is of a notice from the official receiver that the winding-up is complete.[89] However, there is a sensible procedure whereby the OR may bring about an early dissolution if it appears that the realisable assets are insufficient to cover the costs of the winding-up[90] and that the affairs of the company do not require any further investigation.[91] Before doing so, the OR must give at least 28 days' notice of the proposal to the company's creditors and members and to an administrative receiver if there is one,[92] and, with the giving of that notice, the OR ceases to be required to undertake any duties other than to apply to the Registrar for the early dissolution of the company.[93] On the registration of that application the company becomes dissolved at the end of three months[94] unless the Secretary of State, on the application of the official receiver or any creditor,

---

[84] s.201(3). It is then the duty of the applicant to deliver a copy of the order to the Registrar for registration: s.201(4).

[85] The relevant statutory provisions appear to apply to windings-up by the court on any ground and whether or not the company is insolvent and not to require any final meeting of the company (as in a voluntary liquidation). If this is correct, it is very curious. In a winding-up on the petition of a member on the ground that it is just and equitable, if the company's creditors have been fully paid it is only the members who will have any interest in the result of the winding-up.

[86] ss.146 and 172(8).

[87] s.205(3). An appeal to the court lies from any such decision of the Secretary of State: s.205(4).

[88] s.205(1) and (2).

[89] s.205(1)(b).

[90] In Scotland (lacking official receivers) there is a procedure for early dissolution on this ground alone but it involves an application to the court: s.204.

[91] s.202(1) and (2).

[92] s.202(3).

[93] s.202(4).

[94] s.202(5).

member or administrative receiver,[95] gives directions to the contrary before the end of that period.

The grounds upon which the application to the Secretary of State **A–11** may be made are (a) that the realisable assets are in fact sufficient to cover the expenses of the winding-up or (b) that the affairs of the company do require further investigation,[96] or (c) that for any other reason the early dissolution of the company is inappropriate.[97] And the directions that may be given may make provision for enabling the winding-up to proceed as if the official receiver had not invoked the procedure or may include a deferment of the date of dissolution.[98]

There are no similar provisions for early dissolution on a voluntary winding-up; once the company has resolved on voluntary winding-up it is expected to go through with it. But if there is a vacancy in the liquidatorship and no one can be found who is willing to accept the office because there is clearly not enough left to pay the expenses of continuing it (no insolvency practitioner will accept office in such circumstances unless someone is prepared to pay the costs), it is difficult to see how the Registrar could do other than to strike the company off the register as a defunct company (see below)—as, indeed, that section specifically recognises. To the striking off of defunct companies we now turn because it affords a method whereby a small company can, in practice, often be inexpensively dissolved without any formal winding-up. Although the rules are contained in Part 31 of the Companies Act, rather than the Insolvency Act, they are an integral part of the machinery by which companies cease to exist.

Defunct companies[99]

Under section 1000 of the Companies Act 2006, if the Registrar has **A–12** reasonable cause to believe that a company is not carrying on business or is not in operation, the Registrar may send to the company a letter inquiring whether that is so. If within a month of sending the letter a reply is not received, the Registrar shall, within 14 days thereafter, send a registered letter referring to the first letter and stating that no answer to it has been received and that, if an answer to the second letter is not received within one month from its date, a

---

[95] There is an apparent inconsistency between s.202(5) which says that the application can be made by the official receiver "or any other person who appears to the Secretary of State to be interested" and s.203(1) which says that it must be by one of the persons mentioned in the text above. Presumably the Secretary of State will not regard any other person as "interested".

[96] Neither of which is likely to be accepted by the Secretary of State if the official receiver has concluded the contrary.

[97] s.203(2).

[98] s.203(3). There can be an appeal to the court against the Secretary of State's decision: s.203(4).

[99] Part 31 of the Act is scheduled to come into force on October 1, 2009.

notice will be published in the *Gazette* with a view to striking the company's name off the register.[100] If the Registrar receives a reply to the effect that the company is not carrying on business or is not in operation, or if, within one month of sending the second letter, no reply is received, the Registrar may publish in the *Gazette* and send to the company by post a notice that at the expiration of three months from the date of the notice the name of the company will, unless cause to the contrary is shown, be struck off the register and the company will be dissolved.[101] At the expiration of the time mentioned in the notice, the Registrar may, unless cause to the contrary is shown, strike the company off the register and publish notice of this in the *Gazette*, whereupon the company is dissolved.[102]

This section is most commonly used when what has afforded the Registrar reasonable cause to believe that the company is not carrying on business or in operation is the fact that it is in arrears with the lodging of its annual returns and accounts.[103] When so used by the Registrar, it is both a method of inducing those companies that are operating in breach of their filing obligations to mend their ways as well as a method of clearing the register of companies which are indeed defunct. A problem discovered by the CLR arises out of the fact that the section requires the Registrar to communicate with the company at its registered address[104] which, for a variety of good and not-so-good reasons, might be an ineffective form of communication. The CLR encouraged the Registrar to experiment with writing also to the directors of the company at their last known residential address, where correspondence to the company's address was returned, before striking the company off, and it appears that this measure has had some success and is now part of the Registrar's administrative practice.[105] The advantage is that it may avoid striking off companies which are in fact in operation and thus avoid the expense of seeking to restore them to the register when they discover they have been struck off (see below).

However, the above procedure can also be used to deal with the situation referred to above when winding-up proceedings have been started but insufficient resources are available to complete them.[106] If the Registrar has reasonable cause to believe either that no liquidator is acting or that the affairs of the company are fully wound up and, in either case, that the returns required to be made by the liquidator have not been made for a period of six consecutive months, the Registrar shall publish in the *Gazette* and send to the company or the

---

[100] CA, s.1000(2). From hereon references to "the Act" are to the Companies Act 2006 unless the context otherwise requires.
[101] s.1000(3).
[102] s.1000(4)–(6).
[103] See para.21–33.
[104] See s.1002 for the methods of communication with the company.
[105] Final Report I, para.11.20.
[106] s.1001.

liquidator (if any) a like notice which causes the company to be dissolved.[107]

Voluntary striking off

Further, the predecessor to the above sections used to provide   **A–13**
companies with a method of dissolving without the expense of a
formal winding-up and especially without the appointment of an
insolvency practitioner to oversee the process: the directors of a
company which had ceased trading would simply write to the
Registrar inviting that person to exercise the statutory power to strike
it off. Under the Deregulation and Contracting Out Act 1994,[108]
perhaps somewhat ironically, this practice was formalised in the
statute and it is understood that the Registrar discontinued the old
practice and will now entertain only formal applications for striking
off under the new procedure. The new sections in large part replicated
the old practice, so the change helped to make this course of action
more transparent.

The procedure enables a company,[109] which has not traded or
carried on business[110] during the previous three months, to apply by
its directors (or a majority of them)[111] to the Registrar for the company to be struck off. The directors must ensure that notice of the
application is given to a list of persons, who include, notably, its
creditors (contingent and prospective creditors being embraced
within the term),[112] its employees, the managers and trustees of any
pension fund and its members.[113] On receipt of the application the
Registrar publishes a notice in the *Gazette* stating that the company
may be struck off and inviting any person to show cause why it
should not be.[114] Not less than three months later the Registrar may
strike the company off and, on publication of a notice to this effect in
the *Gazette*, the company is dissolved.[115] The purpose of requiring
notice to be given by the directors is obviously to see if the people
most likely to object to the striking-off in fact oppose this course of
action, but the legislation lays down no particular procedure which
the Registrar must follow in dealing with objections. The fact that the
company has creditors clearly does not debar it from using this
procedure (otherwise the Act would not require notice to be given to

---

[107] s.1001(1)–(4).
[108] s.13 and Sch.5.
[109] Under s.652A of the 1985 Act the provision applied only to private companies, but s.1003 of
the 2006 Act applies to public companies as well.
[110] What this involves (or rather does not involve) is set out in some detail in s.1004. A change
of name during the period will bar an application even if there has been no trading:
s.1004(1)(a).
[111] s.1003(2).
[112] s.1011.
[113] s.1006(1).
[114] s.1003(3).
[115] s.1003(4),(5).

creditors) but it is not intended to be used in place of liquidation where the company has substantial assets or liabilities outstanding at the time of application.[116] Nor may an application be made for striking off where the company is currently the subject of an application to the court for consent to a compromise or arrangement under the Companies Act[117] or other procedures for handling insolvent companies contained in the Insolvency Act 1986.[118]

The range of matters which the Registrar must keep in mind upon an application under section 1003 is much reduced by the provision that dissolution under the procedure does not inhibit the enforcement of any liability of the erstwhile company's directors, managing officers or members, so that these people cannot escape their common law or statutory duties by causing their company to be dissolved.[119] Moreover, a company dissolved under the new procedure, like companies dissolved in other ways, may be restored to the register in certain circumstances, a topic to which we now turn.

Resurrection of dissolved companies

A–14   A contrast between the death of an individual and that of a company is that, without divine intervention, a dissolved company can be resurrected. Following the CLR,[120] the Act made two innovations in this area. First, it introduced a limited form of administrative restoration to the register, a result which had previously required a court order. Secondly, a single method of court restoration replaced the formerly existing two methods, which the courts had found some difficulty in making sense of and which overlapped to a considerable extent.

Administrative restoration

A–15   The new form of administrative restoration applies only where the company was dissolved by the Registrar under the provisions relating to defunct companies.[121] Thus, it does not apply to either voluntary striking off or to dissolution after winding up. The conditions for administrative restoration to the register confine it to situations where

---

[116] If the company has assets and the application is successful, these will become *bona vacantia* upon the dissolution of the company and so pass to the Crown or one of its emanations: s.1012. Ch.2 of Pt.31 contains provisions dealing with the methods and consequences of disclaimer by the Crown of *bona vacantia*, which are not dealt with here.

[117] See Ch.29 above.

[118] s.1005—or the Insolvency (Northern Ireland) Order 1989. If an application for striking off has been made and any of these events occurs or the company does any of the acts mentioned in s.1004 (see fn.110 above), the then directors of the company are under a duty to withdraw the application: s.1009.

[119] s.1003(6)(a). The same provision applies to a striking off under the Registrar's own motion: s.1000(7)(a).

[120] Final Report I, paras 11.17–11.19.

[121] s.1024(1).

the company was carrying on business or in operation at the time it was struck off.[122] Thus, the main purpose of administrative restoration is to deal more cheaply with reversing a striking off which, ideally, should not have occurred in the first place. For probably the same reason, the application for restoration may be made only by a former director or former member of the company,[123] but no application for restoration may be made more than six years after its dissolution.[124] If any of the company's property is vested in the Crown as *bona vacantia*,[125] the Crown's representative must consent and the applicant must offer to pay any costs of the Crown in relation to the application and, more importantly, dealing with the property during the period of dissolution.[126] Finally, the applicant must deliver to the Registrar such documents as are necessary to bring the company's public records up-to-date and to pay any penalties outstanding at the time the company was dissolved.[127]

If these conditions are met, the Registrar is under a duty to restore the company to the register.[128] Notice of the decision must be given to the applicant and the restoration takes effect when that notice is sent.[129] Public notice must be given of the restoration.[130] The effect of restoration is that the company is deemed to have continued in existence as if it had not been struck off.[131] However, any consequential directions, if necessary, for placing the company and all other persons in the position (as nearly as possible) as they would have been in, had the company not been struck off, are to be given, not by the Registrar, but by a court, to which application may be made within three years of the restoration.[132]

---

[122] s.1025(2). See *Priceland Ltd, Re* [1997] 1 B.C.L.C. 467.

[123] s.1024(3)—who must provide a certificate that he or she has the necessary standing: s.1026.

[124] s.1024(4). By that time, it may be thought, those involved with running the former company will have accepted its striking off.

[125] See fn.116 above.

[126] s.1025(3),(4).

[127] s.1025(5).

[128] s.1025(1). There is no formal right of appeal if the Registrar refuses to restore, but (a) presumably judicial review is available and (b) the disappointed applicant could re-apply under the court-based procedure (see below) and is given 28 days to do so, even if the six-year time limit for that procedure has expired: s.1030(5).

[129] s.1027(2).

[130] s.1027(3),(4).

[131] s.1028(1)—but not so as to make the company liable for failing to file reports and accounts during the period of dissolution (s.1028(2))! S.1033 deals with the situation where the company cannot be restored under its former name without a breach of s.66 because another company now has that name. See Ch.4.

[132] s.1028(3),(4). The statute appears not to undermine the distinction drawn by the courts between dissolution after winding up and administrative striking off (of either type) in terms of the impact of restoration on action purportedly taken by the company in litigation during the period of dissolution. In the latter case subsequent restoration automatically validates action during the period of dissolution: *Top Creative Ltd v St Albans D C* [2000] 2 B.C.L.C. 379, CA.

Restoration by the court

A–16   The two court-based restoration methods previously provided were contained in sections 651 and 653 of the 1985 Act. The current provisions are based on those of section 653, the somewhat simpler procedure. The court-based procedure applies to all forms of dissolution[133] and a much wider range of persons may apply for restoration. These include not just former directors or members but any creditor of the company at the time of its dissolution, anyone who but for the dissolution would have been in a contractual relationship with it, any person with a potential legal claim against the company, any manager or trustee of an employee pension fund, any person interested in land in which the company had an interest, and the Secretary of State.[134] This caters for a much wider range of reasons for wanting to have the company restored to the register, a common one being in order to sue or assert a right against it. Normally, such persons must act within six years of the date of dissolution,[135] but a claim for restoration in order to bring a claim for damages for personal injury against the company may be made at any time.[136]

The court has power to order restoration if (a) in the case of striking off of a defunct company, it was carrying on business or in operation at the time; (b) in the case of voluntary striking off, the conditions for such a striking off were not complied with; and (c) in any other case the court thinks it just to do so.[137] Restoration, if ordered, takes effect from the time the court's order is delivered to the Registrar and the Registrar must give publicity to the order in the usual way.[138] The effect of restoration by the court is the same as with administrative restoration,[139] and the court may give the necessary directions to effect the principle that the company should be treated as if never dissolved.[140]

---

[133]   s.1029(1).

[134]   s.1029(2).

[135]   s.1030(4). Under the 1985 Act the limitation period for s.651 claims was two years and for s.653 claims twenty years. Six years is the period in England and Wales after which many claims against the company will be time-barred.

[136]   s.1030(1)—though if the claim against the company appears to the court to be time-barred, it may not order the restoration of the company: s.1030(2),(3). However, the court may order under s.1032(3) that the period of dissolution should not count for limitation purposes in respect of the personal injury claim. See *Smith v White Knight Laundry Ltd* [2002] 1 W.L.R. 616, CA.

[137]   s.1031(1). The wording of the section suggests that the third ground applies as well to a defunct company and voluntary striking off where the particular ground set out in (a) or (b) is not available. On the exercise of the court's discretion see *Priceland Ltd, Re* (above, fn.122); *Blenheim Leisure (Restaurants) Ltd (No.2), Re* [2000] B.C.C. 821; *Blue Note Enterprises Ltd, Re* [2001] 2 B.C.L.C. 427.

[138]   s.1031(2),(3).

[139]   s.1032(1),(2).

[140]   s.1032(3).

INDEX

1235